ULTIMATE AFRICA ATLAS

Published in 2007 by MapStudio™

John Loubser Production Manager
Elaine Fick Project Manager
Ryan Africa Designer
Ryan Africa Senior Project Cartographer
Christine Flemington Main Map Cartographer
Steven Felmore Regional Map Illustrations
Sean Fraser Regional & Adventure text
Denielle Lategan Researcher
Myrna Collins Production Manager
John Loubser Cover Design

Printed in Singapore by Tien Wah Press (Pte) Ltd
ISBN 978-1-86809-924-5

Forward any comments on this product to
research@mapstudio.co.za

Cover Ariadne Van Zandbergen
5a   Jason Laure
5b   Mary Duncan
5c   Rudolf Pigneter - Tony
      Stone - Gallo
29a   Gable - Sylvia Cordaiy
29b   Pictor - Photo Access
29c   National Geographic Image
      Collection
35   Peter & Jeanetta Baker
37a   David Rogers
37b   Justine Fox
37c   Jack Jackson
45a   Ariadne Van Zandbergen
45b   Gable - Sylvia Cordaiy
45c   Ariadne Van Zandbergen
51a   Pierre Hinch - Gallo Images
51b   Chanan Weiss
51c   Gable - Sylvia Cordaiy
61   Ariadne Van Zandbergen
63a   Kerstein Geier - Gallo
      Images
63b   Marco Turco - Gallo Images
63c   Jason Laure
71a   Ariadne Van Zandbergen
71b   Andrea Booher, Tony
      Stone - Gallo
71c   Ariadne Van Zandbergen
79a   Gerald Cubitt
79b   Martin Harvey
79c   Martin Harvey
87   Ariadne Van Zandbergen

89a   Ariadne Van Zandbergen
89b   Chanan Weiss
89c   Jacques Marais
95   IOA - Andrew Bannister
97a   Chanan Weiss
97b   IOA - Peter Ribton
97c   David Rogers
113   IOA - Peter Blackwell
115a Martin Harvey
115b Gerald Cubitt
115c Ariadne Van Zandbergen
129a P Wagner - Getaway -
      Photo Access
129b Daryl & Sharna Balfour
129c David Rogers
139   IOA - Nigel Dennis
141a Gerald Cubitt
141b David Steele - Getaway -
      Photo Access
141c Gerald Cubitt
153   IOA - Nigel Dennis
155a Jean Du Plessis
155b Claudio Velasquez
155c Roger De La Harpe -
      Africa Imagery
171a Walter Knirr
171b Roger De La Harpe -
      Africa Imagery
171c Roger De La Harpe -
      Africa Imagery
205   IOA - Colour Library
(Images are numbered clockwise)

Contents

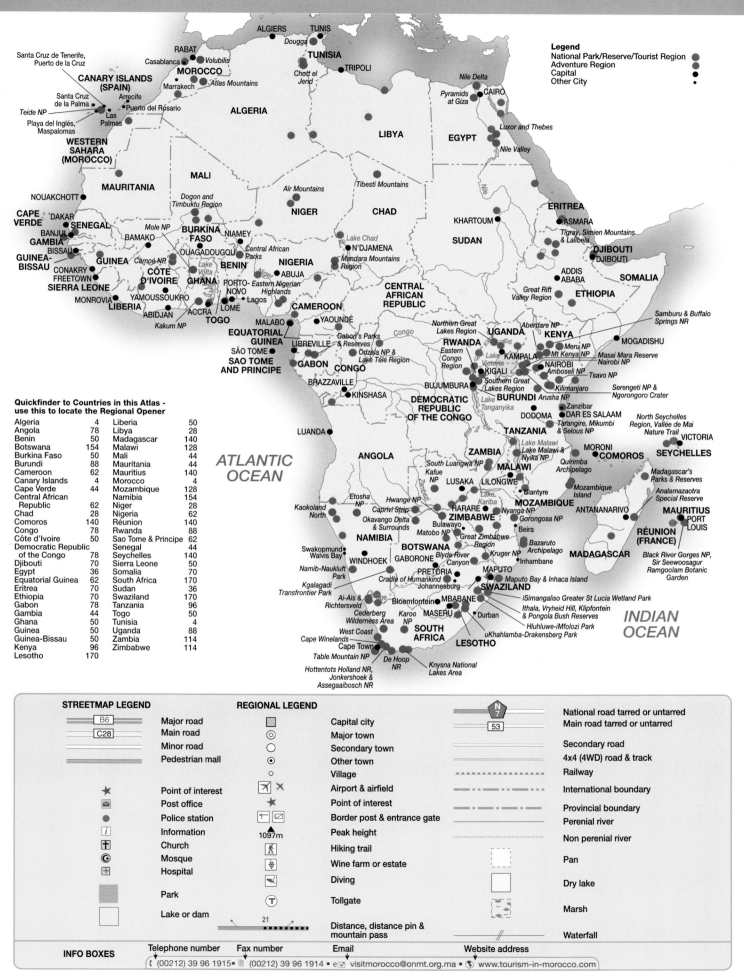

Legend
National Park/Reserve/Tourist Region
Adventure Region
Capital
Other City

Quickfinder to Countries in this Atlas - use this to locate the Regional Opener

Country	Page	Country	Page
Algeria	4	Liberia	50
Angola	78	Libya	28
Benin	50	Madagascar	140
Botswana	154	Malawi	128
Burkina Faso	50	Mali	44
Burundi	88	Mauritania	44
Cameroon	62	Mauritius	140
Canary Islands	4	Morocco	4
Cape Verde	44	Mozambique	128
Central African Republic	62	Namibia	154
Chad	28	Niger	28
Comoros	140	Nigeria	62
Congo	78	Réunion	140
Côte d'Ivoire	50	Rwanda	88
Democratic Republic of the Congo	78	Sao Tome & Principe	62
		Senegal	44
Djibouti	70	Seychelles	140
Egypt	36	Sierra Leone	50
Equatorial Guinea	62	Somalia	70
Eritrea	70	South Africa	170
Ethiopia	70	Sudan	36
Gabon	78	Swaziland	170
Gambia	44	Tanzania	96
Ghana	50	Togo	50
Guinea	50	Tunisia	4
Guinea-Bissau	50	Uganda	88
Kenya	96	Zambia	114
Lesotho	170	Zimbabwe	114

STREETMAP LEGEND

- B6 Major road
- C28 Main road
- Minor road
- Pedestrian mall
- ★ Point of interest
- ✉ Post office
- ● Police station
- *i* Information
- ✝ Church
- Ⓖ Mosque
- ✚ Hospital
- Park
- Lake or dam

REGIONAL LEGEND

- ◻ Capital city
- ⊙ Major town
- ○ Secondary town
- ⊙ Other town
- ∘ Village
- ✈ ✕ Airport & airfield
- ★ Point of interest
- Border post & entrance gate
- ▲ 1097m Peak height
- Hiking trail
- Wine farm or estate
- Diving
- Ⓣ Tollgate
- 21 Distance, distance pin & mountain pass

- N7 / 53 National road tarred or untarred
- Main road tarred or untarred
- Secondary road
- 4x4 (4WD) road & track
- Railway
- International boundary
- Provincial boundary
- Perenial river
- Non perenial river
- Pan
- Dry lake
- Marsh
- Waterfall

INFO BOXES
Telephone number Fax number Email Website address
☏ (00212) 39 96 1915 • ▤ (00212) 39 96 1914 • e✉ visitmorocco@onmt.org.ma • ⊕ www.tourism-in-morocco.com

3

The Maghreb

The Maghreb is an area of fertile coastal plains, olive groves, towering mountain ranges and baking desert sands, and the latter-day politics of the region remains as varied as its landscape. Morocco, which includes the Western Sahara (its occupied territory since 1975), is a constitutional monarchy, while Tunisia is a multiparty republic and Algeria is governed by a military regime. The people of the region are predominantly of Arabic and Berber descent, with a scattering of Europeans, largely because of the area's proximity to Europe and colonial ties with France. These ties were only fairly recently severed, with Morocco gaining independence in 1956 and Algeria in 1962. Off the coast of Western Sahara lie the Canary Islands, a self-governing protectorate of Spain. Despite these close associations with the West, the Maghreb remains distinctly African, bustling with markets and punctuated with palm-fringed oases linked by nomadic desert caravans.

MOROCCO

RABAT
Steeped in a long and colourful history, the modern city of Rabat is every inch the nation's capital. Unmistakably influenced by the distinct flavours of Phoenicia and Carthage, the cosmopolitan centre is the country's administrative hub and, as such, lacks the same exotic appeal as enticing Marrakech and Casablanca. The contrasting faces of the old and the new in Rabat, however, remain a fascinating tribute to the history of the nation, and it continues to play a significant role in latter-day Morocco.

MARRAKECH
Framed by the snow-covered peaks of the High Atlas Mountains, ancient Marrakech is virtually surrounded by some 13,000 hectares of palm and olive groves. In the heart of the city is the market square of Djemaa el Fna, a heady mix of bustling stalls selling everything from dates and oranges to carpets and traditional aphrodisiacs. A parade of snake charmers and belly dancers, monkey trainers and henna artists weaves through the haphazard tent-like booths. Winding alleys lead off the market into a maze of cubicles and shopfronts, while above looms the towering 70-metre minaret of Koutoubia, its magnificent proportions and elaborate design a breathtaking monument to Islam that has influenced many of Morocco's architectural masterpieces.

CASABLANCA
Considered to be the nation's unofficial capital, Casablanca is a thriving modern city far removed from the exotic literature emanating from the West. Scattered along its panoramic shore are beach clubs and nightclubs, fashionable cafés and exclusive boutiques. Many public buildings were built in authentic Art Deco style, and there are a number of monuments and mosques, cathedrals and theatres. Casablanca is permeated throughout with the rich and distinct flavour of its colourful past, but nowhere is this more evident than in the Old Medina. This provides a fascinating insight into the history of the old city with its eclectic mix of opulent and dilapidated markets and malls.

WESTERN SAHARA
The expansive stretch that is the Western Sahara is officially considered by Morocco as its 'Saharan provinces', but the sparsely populated region has been disputed territory since Spain withdrew from the area in 1975. Although an uneasy ceasefire prevails between the Moroccan government and resident rebels, the status of the Western Sahara remains undecided. Morocco retains a firm hold over the extensive lands, having erected a 1,600-kilometre sand wall to curb militant activity. The Moroccans have also injected considerable capital into the development projects that will help uplift both the desert infrastructure and the city of Laayoune. There are roadblocks and police cordons, yet traffic between the Western Sahara and Morocco remains relatively unimpeded.

HIGH ATLAS
The Atlas is the highest mountain range in North Africa, its forests, crests, peaks and valleys a climber's dream and an adventure paradise. Long, winding rivers carve their way through deep granite gorges, while a series of watercourses, terraced fields and almond groves lies scattered around tiny Berber villages constructed almost entirely of local stone and timber. The jagged peaks, smattering of sacred shrines and derelict palaces lure adventurers and sightseers to the zigzagging tracks and trails towered over by the impressive Jebel Toubkal. At a height of 4,167 metres, the looming massif is the highest in the Atlas range and provides some of the world's greatest treks. Both challenging and inspiring, the steep valleys and sheer rock faces attract ardent climbers, while a number of lesser walks and hikes cater for the casual hiker. Interspersed along this network of mule trails are numerous Berber settlements, isolated pockets of an age-old culture that has seen little change over the centuries. The emphasis here is on the warmth and hospitality for which the deeply spiritual Berbers are renowned. Visitors should adhere to the rather strict local code of conduct.

ALGERIA

HAIDRA
Although very little of the original Roman town remains, a number of small sites hint at Haidra's affiliation with the old Empire: an ancient forum, citadel, Roman baths and fluted columns, and an enormous Byzantine fort.

KABYLIA
Like much of the country, Algeria's Kabylia region has been ravaged by the continuing civil war. It is perhaps best renowned for its traditional Berber communities and for the riding skills of the Berber horsemen. By far the majority of Algeria's population is of Arab-Berber origin, and the locals still speak an area-specific dialect, with only a smattering of French. Custom plays a fundamental role in the daily lives of these people, who are relatively isolated from 'civilization'. They place much importance on their means of transport – camels and horses – and have developed remarkable skills as riders.

ALGIERS
Algiers is the capital of war-torn Algeria, Africa's second-largest country, where Islamic fundamentalists are intent on bringing the national economy and the government to its knees in their quest for an Islamic state. Travel in and around the capital is ill-advised, in particular for casual sightseers and tourists with little comprehension of the political complexities that continue to ravage Algeria.

TUNISIA

MONASTIR
Tracing its history to Punic and Roman times, Monastir is a popular resort destination and vital centre of tertiary education. It boasts all the amenities of prominent tourist stopovers, including an airport, a variety of watersports and night-time entertainment for the throngs of holiday-makers.

TUNIS
Once little more than a small fishing village, Tunisia's capital is the most cosmopolitan of all North African cities. Within its ancient walls are the souks and minarets of old, but the expanding city includes a sophisticated network of wide boulevards, busy streets, chic pavement cafés and lush parks well accustomed to the tourist traffic.

CHOTT EL JERID
As flat as glass, the crystalline Chott el Jerid is the most expansive of the salt lakes characteristic of central Tunisia and spans some 250 kilometres by 20 kilometres. These pans form soggy marshes in winter, attracting an array of water birds to the wetlands. In summer, the salt crystallizes to form a gleaming crust.

SIDI BOU SAID
Picturesque Sidi Bou Said is blessed with uninterrupted views dotted with whitewashed cottages cascading with pink bougainvillea, and the landscape is straight from a picture postcard. High up on the hill overlooking the quaint little village stands the old Arab fort around which the settlement developed in the 13th century. Famed as a popular modern-day retreat for acclaimed artists rather than for its unique beauty, the art galleries of Sidi Bou Said remain the village's top attractions.

GABES
The Gulf of Gabes sweeps down from Sfax to the isle of Jerba in a deep crescent and offers a welcome respite from the more frenetic tourist spots. The settlement here comprises a thriving little town that reached its peak in the Middle Ages, but today its principal functions include heavy industry and commerce rather than the tourism market. Gabes has nevertheless retained much of its charm and remains unspoilt, long sandy beaches baking under the North African sun.

The Maghreb has been embroiled in conflict between the various powers seeking control of the region during its long and often turbulent history, yet the territory is one of the most stable on the continent. Tunisia, Morocco and the Canary Islands are relatively prosperous and cater well for tourist travel, while Algeria is a notable exception.

Sidi Bou Said, Tunisia

Marrakech market, Morocco

Tangier (Tanger)
Mediterranean Sea
ALGIERS (ALGER)
Bejaia
Sidi Bou Said
Ruins at Carthage
TUNIS
Sousse
Tlemcen
Qairouan
Monastir
Fez
Haidra
TUNISIA
RABAT
Meknes
Casablanca
MOROCCO
Chott el Jerid
Gabes
HIGH ATLAS
Marrakech
ATLAS MOUNTAINS
ATLANTIC OCEAN
Agadir
GRAND ERG OCCIDENTAL (Great Western Dunes)
GRAND ERG ORIENTAL (Grand Eastern Dunes)
La Palma
Santa Cruz de Tenerife
Timanfaya National Park
Lanzarote
Las Palmas
Tenerife
CANARY ISLANDS (SPAIN)
Laayoune
A L G E R I A
TASSILI MOUNTAINS
WESTERN SAHARA (MOROCCO)
S A H A R A
AHAGGAR MOUNTAINS
N

Km 250 500
Some water features have been exaggerated for detail

High Atlas mountains, Morocco

CANARY ISLANDS (Spain)

TENERIFE

As the largest island in the Canary archipelago, Tenerife is also the capital of the Western Islands, a striking conglomeration of 13 islands set in the sparkling waters of the Atlantic. The rocky ridge that forms Tenerife's spine is covered in the most part with lush banana plantations, orchards and fields of green, and culminates in the 3,718-metre Mount Teide – still heralded as the highest point 'in Spain'. The islands are administered as part of Spain, yet lie just 96 kilometres off the African coast and some 1,120 kilometres from the European mainland. The island of Tenerife, with its own capital at Santa Cruz de Tenerife on the northeast coast, is quite spectacular, lined with holiday resorts, pristine beaches and leafy old villages. Each of the hamlets has its own town square that hints at its connection to colonial Spain, and sprinkled across the island are historic sites and places of interest for holiday-makers.

ATLAS MOUNTAINS

TO MARRAKECH · TO ARHBALOU · TO ARHBALOU

Asni · Tassaft n Tizi · Agourii 2011m · Akerker · Setti Fatma
Tansghart · Iguenane · Teourit n Ikis · 2577m
Imsker · Ait el Qaq 3195m · Tiourdiou · Tadrart
Arg · Oukaimeden · Timichi · Arjout 3741m
Ouaussaf · Jebel Oukaimeden 3273m · l'bbassene · 3010m · Borj n Oufraou 3868m
Matat · Ikis · Jebel Angour 3616m
Irkoubeline · Imlil · Tamatert · Bou Iguenouane 3615m
Tizi Oussem 2664m · Aroumd · Aksoual 3842m · Azib Likemt
Sidi · Azib Chamharouch · Azib Tifni · Toubkal National Park
Tamsoult · Tichki 3753m · Adrar Tinilim 3670m · 3674m
Aguelzim 3547m · Jebel Toubkal 4167m · Tissaldai 3853m
Tazaghart 3843m · Amrourough 3280m
4015m · Tizi Melloul
Ouanoukrim 4088m · Ifni · Issoual · Tizgui

AZ IZOUGGAGHENE

Km 4 8

ASLOUN · ADRAR N TIZRAG · JEBEL TASGHIMOUT · ADRAR N INEGHMAR · ADRAR MIGHIAN · ADRAR N DERN

TOUBKAL CIRCUIT HIKING TRAIL

SPAIN

Gibraltar(UK)
Tangier (Tanger) · Strait of Gibraltar · Ceuta (SPAIN)
Cap Spartel · Ksar es Seghir · Restinga · Mediterranean Sea
Smir
Asilah · Tetouan · Oued Laou · Targa · Bou Hamed
Arba des Beni Hassan · El Jebha · Torres de Alcala
Larache · Chechaouene · 2159m · Cheferat
Réserve de Merdja Zerga · Ksar el Kebir · Bab Taza · Ketama · Targuist
Moulay Bousselham · Souk el Arba du Rharb · Ouezzane · Lalla Outka 1600m · 2448m · Taharsouk
Allal Tazi · Barrage al Wahda · Rafsai · Taounate · RIF
Mehdiya Plage · Mechra Bel Ksiri · Oued Querrha · Mjara · S302
Kenitra · Sidi Kacem · Oued Sebou · Fez · Abjelil · 1980m
Sale · Sidi Slimane · Moulay Idriss
RABAT · Sidi Allal el Babraoui · Meknes · Bir Tam Tam
Skhirat · Tiflet · Sefrou · El Menzel
Mohammedia · Khemisset · El Hajeb · Imouzzer du Kandar
Ben Slimane · Azrou · Ifrane · Boulemane
Casablanca · Bettache · Rommani · Oulmes · Timahdite · Enjil
Mediouna · Sidi Hajjaj · Ez Zhiliga · Mrirt · Itzer · Ksabi
Bir Jhid · Aguelmouss · Khenifra · Bouma · Midelt · Amersid
Azemmour · Berrechid · Benahmed · Oued Zem · Boujad · Ayachi 3737m
El Jadida · Settat · Khouribga · Kasba Tadla · El Ksiba · Rich
Sidi Moussa · Guisser · Fkih Ben Salah · Beni Mellal · Oued Ziz
Boulaouane · Mechra Bnabbou · El Borouj · Oued el Abid
Sidi Smail · Skhour des Rehamna · MOYEN ATLAS
Oualidia · Khemis des Zemamra · Sidi Bennour
Cap Beddouza · Tiettai Sidi Bouguedra · Youssoufia · El Kelaa Srarhna · Cascades d'Ouzoud · Azilal · Er Rachidia
Safi · Chemaia · Bin el Ouidane · Tabant · Goulmima · Aoufous
Sept des Gzoula · Benguerir · Tamelelt · M'goun 4071m · Tinerhin · Erfoud
Talmest · Demnate · HAUT ATLAS · Rissani
Taftecht · Sidi Mokhtar · Chichaoua · Tahanaoute · Taddert · Kasbah Telouet · Ait Moudzit · Boumalne du Dades 2064m · Alnif
Ounara · Dar Caid Khoubbane · Arbalou · Tizi n'Tiga Pass · Skoura · JEBEL SARHRO
Imi n Tanoute · Asni · Setti Fatma · Agoulm · Ouarzazate · Nkob · Ait Saadaut
Amizmiz · Jebel Toubkal NP 4167m · Tachakoucht · Agdz · Tazzarine
Imouzzer des Ida Ou Tanane · Ijoukak · Askaoun · Sirwa 3305m · Tazenakht · Drâa Valley
Agadir · Argana 3555m · Aoulouz · Talioune · Zagora
Inezgane · Taroudant · Foum Zguid · Tagounit
Oulad Teima · Irherm · MOROCCO · Mhamid
Biougra · Ait Baha · 2320m · ANTI ATLAS · ALGERIA · Hassi Bou Laadam eau bonne
Ait Mellou · 1723m
Tafraoute · Tata · JEBEL BANI · HAMADA DU DRÂA
Akka · Hassi el Khebi · Trans-Sahara "Route De La Mauritanie"

ATLANTIC OCEAN

N

Km 30 60

Rabat: (00212) 37 67 4013/37 29 4913 • Casablanca: (00212) 22 27 9533 • e⊠ visitmorocco@onmt.org.ma • 🌐 www.tourism-in-morocco.com

6

Volubilis — Morocco

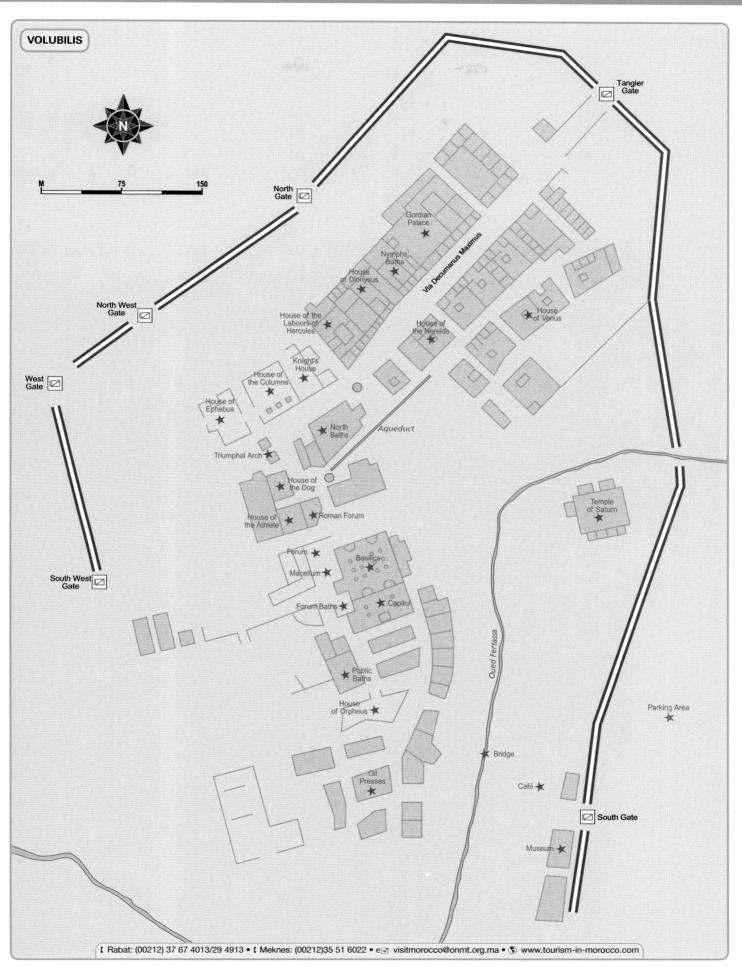

VOLUBILIS

N

M   75   150

- Tangier Gate
- North Gate
- North West Gate
- West Gate
- South West Gate
- Gordian Palace
- Nymphs' Baths
- House of Dionysus
- Via Decumanus Maximus
- House of Venus
- House of the Labours of Hercules
- House of the Nereids
- Knight's House
- House of the Columns
- House of Ephebus
- North Baths
- Aqueduct
- Triumphal Arch
- House of the Dog
- House of the Athlete
- Roman Forum
- Forum
- Basilica
- Macellum
- Temple of Saturn
- Forum Baths
- Capitol
- Oued Fertassa
- Public Baths
- House of Orpheus
- Parking Area
- Bridge
- Café
- Oil Presses
- South Gate
- Museum

☏ Rabat: (00212) 37 67 4013/29 4913 • ☏ Meknes: (00212)35 51 6022 • e✉ visitmorocco@onmt.org.ma • 🖰 www.tourism-in-morocco.com

Teide National Park   Canary Islands

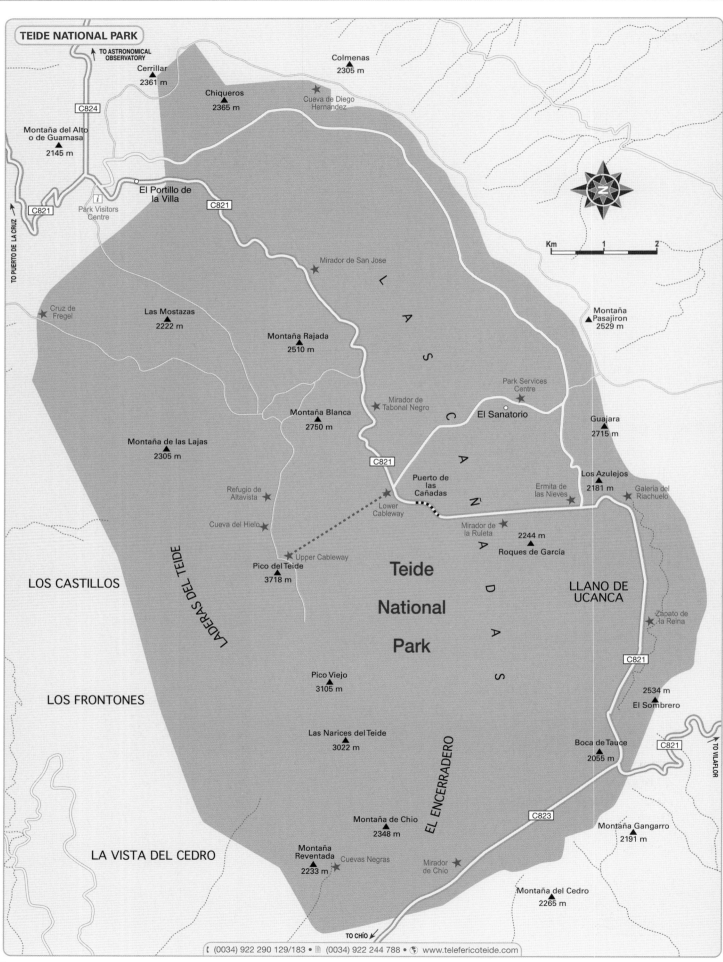

TEIDE NATIONAL PARK

TO ASTRONOMICAL OBSERVATORY

Cerrillar
2361 m

Colmenas
2305 m

Chiqueros
2365 m

Cueva de Diego Hernandez

C824

Montaña del Alto o de Guamasa
2145 m

El Portillo de la Villa

C821

Park Visitors Centre

C821

TO PUERTO DE LA CRUZ

Mirador de San Jose

L
A
S

Cruz de Fregel

Las Mostazas
2222 m

Montaña Pasajiron
2529 m

Montaña Rajada
2510 m

Park Services Centre

Montaña Blanca
2750 m

Mirador de Tabonal Negro

C
A
Ñ

El Sanatorio

Guajara
2715 m

Montaña de las Lajas
2305 m

C821

Puerto de las Cañadas

A

Ermita de las Nieves

Los Azulejos
2181 m

Galeria del Riachuelo

Refugio de Altavista

Lower Cableway

D

Mirador de la Ruleta

Cueva del Hielo

Ñ'

2244 m

Roques de García

Upper Cableway

Pico del Teide
3718 m

Teide

LOS CASTILLOS

National

A

Zapato de la Reina

LADERAS DEL TEIDE

Park

LLANO DE UCANCA

D

C821

LOS FRONTONES

Pico Viejo
3105 m

A

S

2534 m

El Sombrero

Las Narices del Teide
3022 m

EL ENCERRADERO

Boca de Tauce
2055 m

C821

TO VILAFLOR

C823

Montaña Gangarro
2191 m

Montaña de Chio
2348 m

LA VISTA DEL CEDRO

Montaña Reventada
2233 m

Cuevas Negras

Mirador de Chio

Montaña del Cedro
2265 m

TO CHÍO

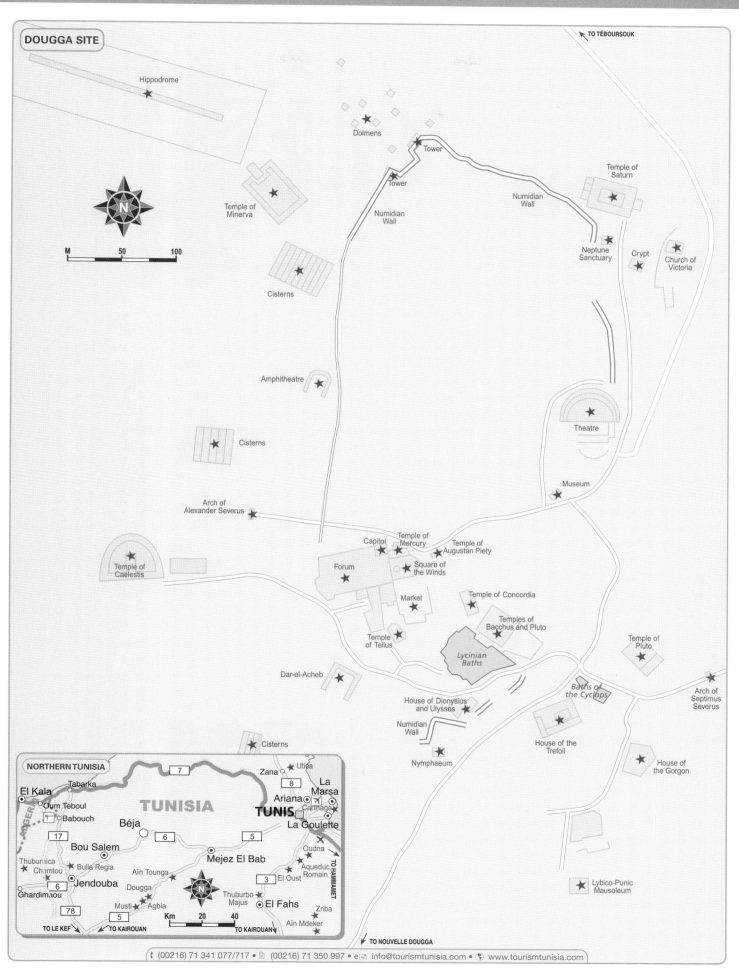

DOUGGA SITE

TO TÉBOURSOUK

Hippodrome

Dolmens

Tower

Temple of Saturn

Tower

Numidian Wall

Numidian Wall

Temple of Minerva

Neptune Sanctuary

Crypt

Church of Victoria

M   50   100

Cisterns

Amphitheatre

Theatre

Cisterns

Museum

Arch of Alexander Severus

Capitol

Temple of Mercury

Temple of Augustan Piety

Temple of Caelestis

Forum

Square of the Winds

Temple of Concordia

Temple of Pluto

Market

Temples of Bacchus and Pluto

Temple of Tellus

Lycinian Baths

Dar-el-Acheb

Baths of the Cyclops

Arch of Septimus Severus

House of Dionysius and Ulysses

House of the Trefoil

House of the Gorgon

Numidian Wall

Nymphaeum

NORTHERN TUNISIA

7

Zana   Utica

El Kala   Tabarka

8   La Marsa

Oum Teboul   Ariana   Carthage

TUNISIA

Babouch   TUNIS

17   Béja   6   La Goulette

Bou Salem   5

Thuburnica   Bulla Regia   Mejez El Bab   Oudna

Chemtou   Aïn Tounga   Aqueduc Romain

6   Jendouba   Dougga   3   El Oust

Ghardimaou   Musti   Agbia   Thuburbo Majus   El Fahs

78   N   Zriba

5   Km   20   40   Aïn Mdeker

TO LE KEF   TO KAIROUAN   TO KAIROUAN

Lybico-Punic Mausoleum

TO NOUVELLE DOUGGA

☏ (00216) 71 341 077/717 • 🖷 (00216) 71 350 997 • e✉ info@tourismtunisia.com • 🌐 www.tourismtunisia.com

9

Casablanca Morocco

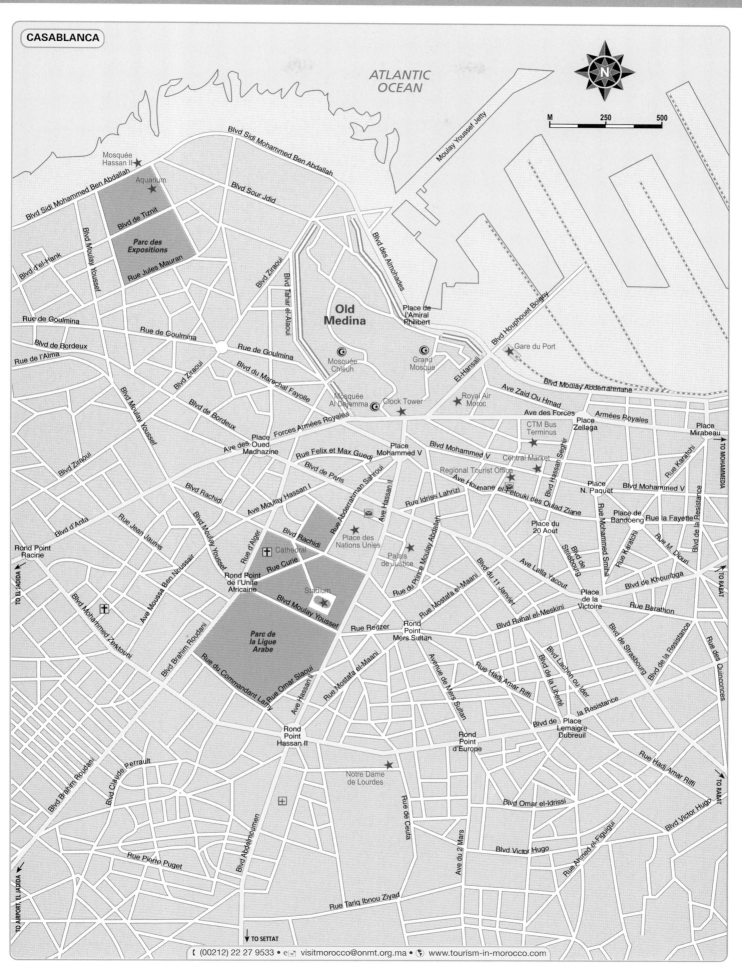

CASABLANCA

ATLANTIC OCEAN

N

M   250   500

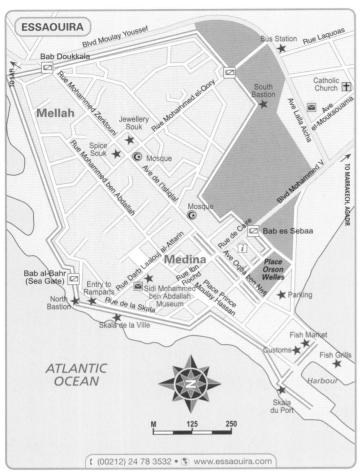

Essaouira map. Labels include: Blvd Moulay Youssef, Bab Doukkala, Mellah, TO SAFI, Rue Mohammed Zerktouni, Rue Mohammed ben Abdallah, Jewellery Souk, Spice Souk, Mosque, Ave de l'Istiqlal, Mosque, Bab al-Bahr (Sea Gate), Entry to Ramparts, North Bastion, Rue de la Skala, Skala de la Ville, Rue Darb Laalouj al-Attarin, Rue Ibn Rochd, Sidi Mohammed ben Abdallah Museum, Medina, Place Prince Moulay Hassan, Rue de Caire, Rue Mohammed el-Qory, South Bastion, Bus Station, Rue Laquoas, Catholic Church, Ave Lalla Aïcha, Ave el-Moukaouama, Bab es Sebaa, Place Orson Welles, TO MARRAKECH, AGADIR, Blvd Mohammed V, Ave Oqba ben Nafi, Parking, Fish Market, Customs, Fish Grills, Harbour, ATLANTIC OCEAN, Skala du Port. Scale: M 125 250. (00212) 24 78 3532 • www.essaouira.com

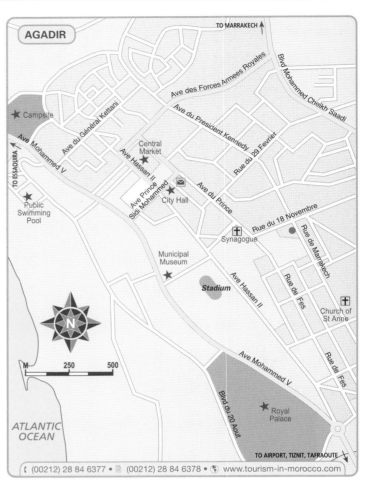

Agadir map. Labels include: TO MARRAKECH, Campsite, Ave des Forces Armees Royales, Blvd Mohammed Cheikh Saadi, Ave du Général Kettani, Ave du President Kennedy, Ave Mohammed V, Central Market, Ave Hassan II, Ave du 29 Fevrier, TO ESSAOUIRA, Public Swimming Pool, Ave Prince Sidi Mohammed, City Hall, Ave du Prince, Rue du 18 Novembre, Rue de Marrakech, Synagogue, Municipal Museum, Ave Hassan II, Stadium, Rue de Fes, Church of St Anne, Rue de Fes, Ave Mohammed V, Blvd du 20 Aout, Royal Palace, ATLANTIC OCEAN, TO AIRPORT, TIZNIT, TAFRAOUTE. Scale: M 250 500. (00212) 28 84 6377 • (00212) 28 84 6378 • www.tourism-in-morocco.com

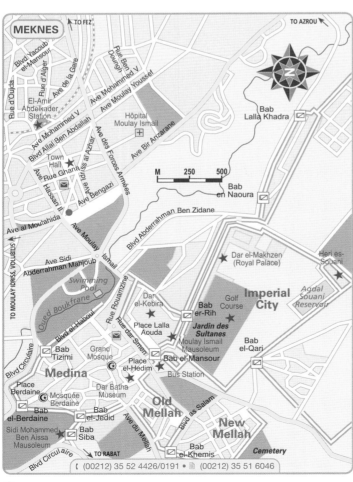

Meknes map. Labels include: TO FEZ, TO AZROU, Blvd Yacoub el-Mansour, Rue d'Alger, Rue de la Gare, Rue Ben Dourgh, Ave Mohammed V, Ave Moulay Youssef, Rue d'Oujda, El-Amir Abdelkader Station, Ave Mohammed V, Blvd Allal Ben Abdallah, Rue Rais al Azhar, Hôpital Moulay Ismail, Ave Bir Anzarane, Bab Lalla Khadra, Town Hall, Rue Ghana, Ave Hassan II, Ave Bengazi, Ave des Forces Armées, Ave al Moutahida, Ave Moulay Ismail, Blvd Abderrahman Ben Zidane, Bab en Naoura, Ave Sidi Abderrahman Mahjoub, TO MOULAY IDRISS, VOLUBILIS, Swimming Pool, Oued Boukfrane, Dar el-Kebira, Rue Rouamzine, Rue dar Smen, Dar el-Makhzen (Royal Palace), Heri es-Souani, Golf Course, Imperial City, Agdal Souani Reservoir, Bab er-Rih, Blvd el-Haboul, Place Lalla Aouda, Jardin des Sultanes, Moulay Ismail Mausoleum, Bab el-Qari, Bab Tizimi, Grand Mosque, Bab el-Hedim, Bab el-Mansour, Blvd Circulaire, Medina, Dar Batha Museum, Bus Station, Place Berdaine, Mosquée Berdaine, Bab el-Berdaine, Bab el-Jedid, Old Mellah, Sidi Mohammed Ben Aissa Mausoleum, Bab Siba, Ave du Mellah, Blvd as Salam, New Mellah, Bab el-Khemis, Cemetery, Blvd Circulaire, TO RABAT. Scale: M 250 500. (00212) 35 52 4426/0191 • (00212) 35 51 6046

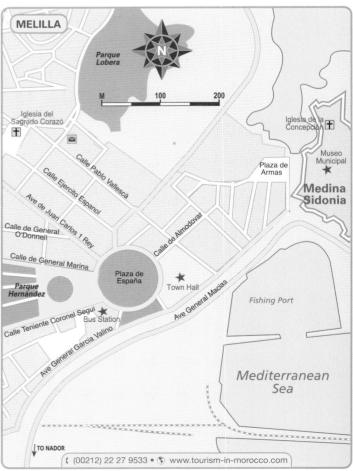

Melilla map. Labels include: Parque Lobera, Iglesia del Sagrado Corazó, Iglesia de la Concepción, Calle Pablo Vallescá, Museo Municipal, Calle Ejército Espanol, Plaza de Armas, Medina Sidonia, Ave de Juan Carlos 1 Rey, Calle de General O'Donnell, Calle de Almodovar, Calle de General Marina, Plaza de España, Parque Hernández, Town Hall, Calle Teniente Coronel Segui, Bus Station, Ave General Macias, Fishing Port, Calle General García Valino, Mediterranean Sea, TO NADOR. Scale: M 100 200. (00212) 22 27 9533 • www.tourism-in-morocco.com

12

Marrakech Morocco
Rabat Morocco

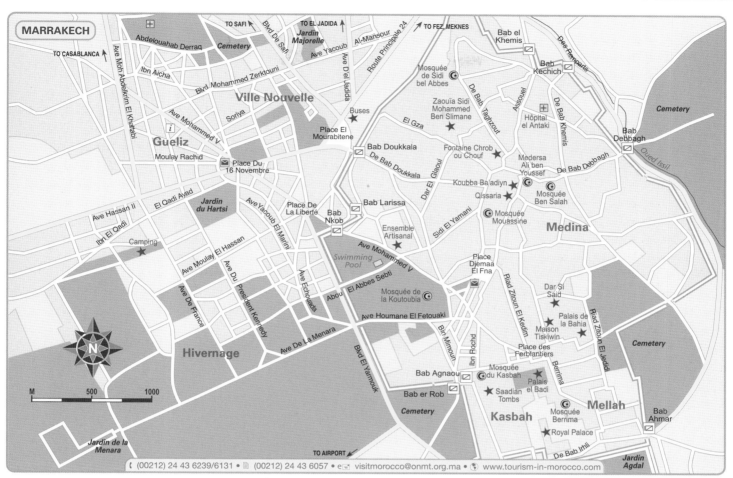

MARRAKECH

TO CASABLANCA
TO SAFI
TO EL JADIDA
TO FEZ, MEKNES

Abdelouahab Derraq
Cemetery
Jardin Majorelle
Al-Mansour
Route Principale 24
Bab el Khemis
Des Remparts
Bab Kechich
Cemetery

Ibn Aicha
Blvd De Safi
Ave Yacoub
Ave D'el Jadida
Mosquée de Sidi bel Abbes
De Bab Taghzout
Hôpital el Antaki
Bab Debbagh
Oued Issil

Ave Moh Abdelkrim El Khattabi
Blvd Mohammed Zerktouni
Ville Nouvelle
Zaouïa Sidi Mohammed Ben Slimane
De Bab Khemis

Ave Mohammed V
Soriya
El Gza
Bab Doukkala
Fontaine Chrob ou Chouf
Medersa Ali ben Youssef
De Bab Debbagh

Gueliz
Buses
De Bab Doukkala
Dar El Glaoui
Koubba Ba'adiyn
Qissaria
Mosquée Ben Salah

Moulay Rachid
Place El Mourabitene
Bab Larissa
Sidi El Yamani
Mosquée Mouassine

Place Du 16 Novembre
Bab Nkob
Ensemble Artisanal
Medina

Ave Hassan II
El Qadi Ayad
Jardin du Hartsi
Place De La Liberté
Ave Mohammed V

Ibn El Qadi
Ave Yacoub El Manni
Swimming Pool
Place Djemaa El Fna

Camping
Ave Moulay El Hassan
Abou El Abbes Sebti
Mosquée de la Koutoubia
Dar Si Said

Ave Du President Kennedy
Ave Echouada
Ave Houmane El Fetouaki
Palais de la Bahia
Riad Zitoun El Kedim

Ave De France
Maison Tiskiwin
Riad Zitoun El Jedid

N
Hivernage
Bin Mimoun
Ibn Rochd
Place des Ferblantiers
Cemetery

M 500 1000
Ave De La Menara
Blvd El Yarmouk
Bab Agnaou
Mosquée du Kasbah
Palais el Badi
Mellah

Bab er Rob
Saadian Tombs
Mosquée Berrima
Bab Ahmar

Jardin de la Menara
Cemetery
Kasbah
Royal Palace

TO AIRPORT
De Bab Ihril
Jardin Agdal

(00212) 24 43 6239/6131 • (00212) 24 43 6057 • e visitmorocco@onmt.org.ma • www.tourism-in-morocco.com

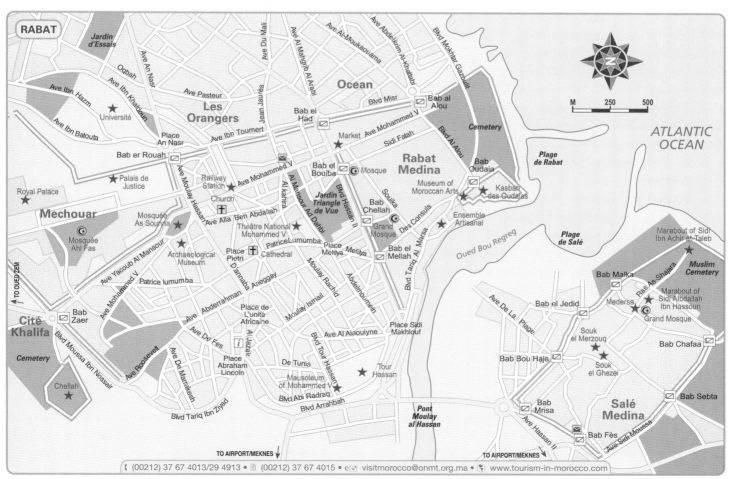

RABAT

Jardin d'Essais
Ave Du Mali
Ave Al-Moukaouama
Ave Abdelkrim Al-Khattabi
Blvd Mokhtar Gazouli

Ogbah
Ave An Nasr
Ave Al Mahgrib Al Arabi
Ocean
Z

Ave Ibn Hazm
Ave Ibn Khatdoun
Ave Pasteur
Blvd Misr
Bab al Alou
M 250 500

Université
Les Orangers
Bab el Had
Cemetery
ATLANTIC OCEAN

Ave Ibn Batouta
Place An Nasr
Ave Ibn Toumert
Market Ave Mohammed V
Sidi Fatah
Plage de Rabat

Bab er Rouah
Ave Mohammed V
Bab el Bouiba
Mosque
Rabat Medina
Bab Oudaia

Palais de Justice
Railway Station
Ave Mohammed V
Museum of Moroccan Arts
Kasbah des Oudaias

Royal Palace
Church
Al Mansour Ad Dahbi
Jardin Triangle de Vue
Bab Chellah
Souika
Des Consuls
Ensemble Artisanal
Plage de Salé

Mechouar
Mosquée As Sounna
Théâtre National Mohammed V
Grand Mosque
Oued Bou Regreg
Marabout of Sidi Ibn Achir at-Taleb

Mosquée Ahl Fas
Archaeological Museum
Place Pietri
Patrice Lumumba
Place Meliliya
Bab el Mellah
Muslim Cemetery

TO OUED ZEM
Ave Yacoub Al Mansour
Cathedral
Anegaay
Moulay Rachid
Bab Malka
Medersa
Marabout of Sidi Albdallah Ibn Hassoun

Ave Mohammed V
Patrice lumumba
Ave Abderrahman
Abdelmoumen
Grand Mosque

Cité Khalifa
Bab Zaer
Place de L'unité Africaine
Ave Al Alaouiyne
Place Sidi Makhlouf
Bab el Jedid
Souk el Merzouq
Bab Chafaa

Ave De Fes
Al Jazair
Blvd Moussa Ibn Nossair
Blvd Tour Hassan
Bab Bou Haja
Souk el Ghezel

Cemetery
Ave Roosevelt
Place Abraham Lincoln
De Tunis
Tour Hassan
Bab Mrisa
Salé Medina

Chellah
Ave De Marrakesh
Mausoleum of Mohammed V
Pont Moulay al Hassan
Bab Sebta

Blvd Tariq Ibn Zyad
Blvd Abi Radraq
Blvd Arrahbah
Bab Fès
Ave Hassan II
Ave Sidi Moussa

TO AIRPORT/MEKNES
TO AIRPORT/MEKNES

(00212) 37 67 4013/29 4913 • (00212) 37 67 4015 • e visitmorocco@onmt.org.ma • www.tourism-in-morocco.com

13

Tangier Morocco

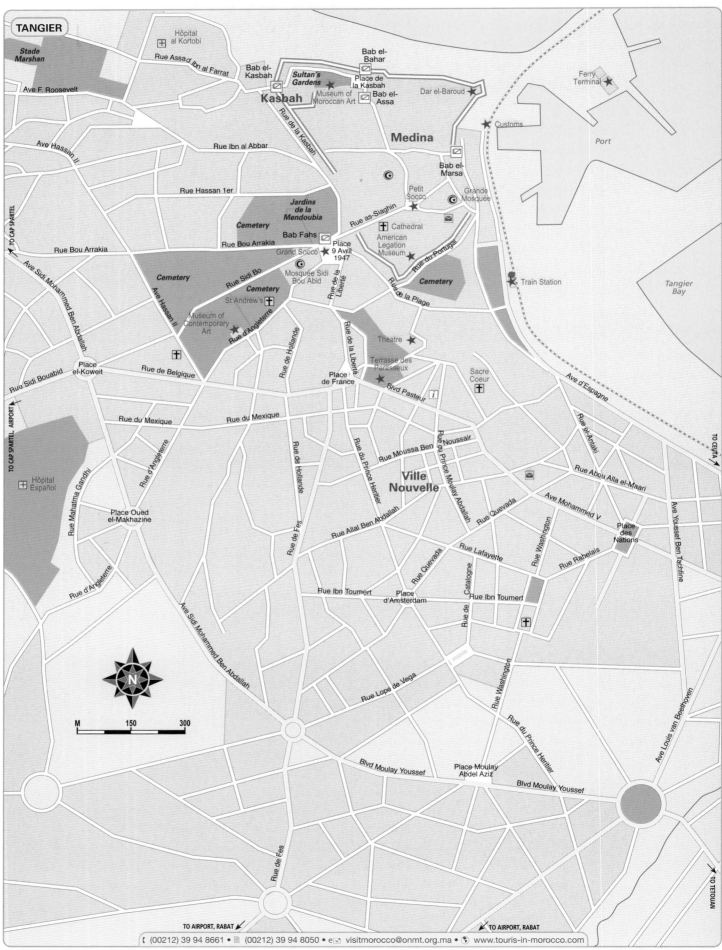

TO AIRPORT, RABAT

TO AIRPORT, RABAT

(00212) 39 94 8661 • (00212) 39 94 8050 • e visitmorocco@onmt.org.ma • www.touris-in-morocco.com

Tetouan Morocco
Fez Morocco

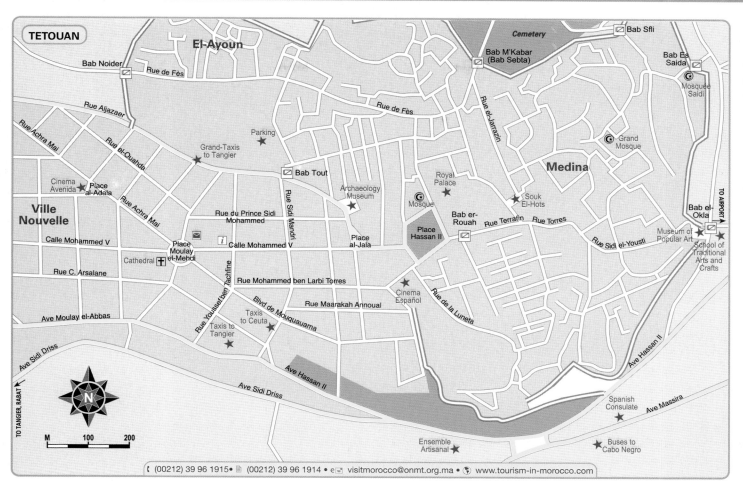

TETOUAN

El-Ayoun

Cemetery

Bab Sfli

Bab M'Kabar
(Bab Sebta)

Bab Noider

Bab Es
Saida

Rue de Fès

Mosquée
Saidi

Rue Aljazaer

Rue el-Ouahda

Rue Achra Mai

Grand Mosque

Medina

Rue de Fès

Rue el-Jarrazin

Parking

Grand-Taxis
to Tangier

Rue Achra Mai

Bab Tout

Royal
Palace

Souk
El-Hots

Cinema
Avenida

Place
al-Adala

Rue Sidi Mandri

Archaeology
Museum

Mosque

Bab el-
Okla

Ville
Nouvelle

Rue du Prince Sidi
Mohammed

Place
Hassan II

Bab er-
Rouah

Rue Terrafin

Rue Torres

Museum of
Popular Art

Calle Mohammed V

Calle Mohammed V

Place
al-Jala

Rue Sidi el-Yousti

School of
Traditional
Arts and
Crafts

Place
Moulay
el-Mehdi

Cathedral

Rue C. Arsalane

Rue Youssef ben Tachfine

Rue Mohammed ben Larbi Torres

Ave Moulay el-Abbas

Blvd de Mouquauama

Rue Maarakah Annoual

Cinema
Español

Taxis
to Ceuta

Taxis to
Tangier

Rue de la Luneta

Ave Sidi Driss

Ave Hassan II

Ave Hassan II

Ave Sidi Driss

Spanish
Consulate

Ave Massira

TO TANGIER, RABAT

N

M 100 200

Ensemble
Artisanal

Buses to
Cabo Negro

TO AIRPORT

✆ (00212) 39 96 1915 • 🖷 (00212) 39 96 1914 • e🖂 visitmorocco@onmt.org.ma • 🌐 www.tourism-in-morocco.com

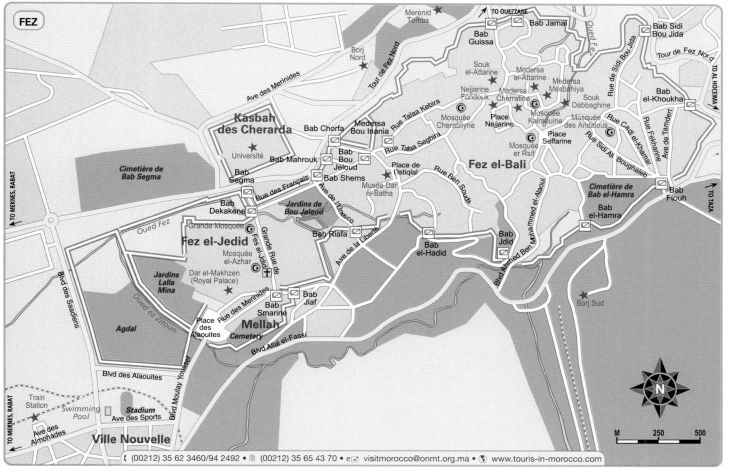

FEZ

Merenid
Tombs

TO OUEZZANE

Bab Jamai

Bab Sidi
Bou Jida

Borj
Nord

Bab
Guissa

TO AL HOCIMA

Tour de Fez Nord

Souk
el-Attarine

Medersa
el-Attarine

Medersa
Mesbahiya

Tour de Fez Nord

Bab
el-Khoukha

Ave des Merinides

Nejjarine
Fondouk

Medersa
Cherratine

Souk
Dabbaghine

Rue de Sidi Bou Jida

Kasbah
des Cherarda

Bab Chorfa

Medersa
Bou Inania

Rue Talaa Kebira

Mosquée
Cherabliyne

Place
Nejjarine

Mosquée
Kairaouine

Mosquée
des Andalous

Rue Cadi el-Khamar

Bab
el-Khoukha

Université

Rue Talaa Seghira

Place
Seffarine

Rue Sidi Ali Boughaleb

Ave de Tamdert

Bab
Mahrouk

Bab
Bou
Jeloud

Mosquée
er Rsif

Fez el-Bali

Rue Fekharine

Cimetière de
Bab Segma

Bab
Segma

Bab Shems

Place de
l'Istiqlal

Rue Ben Souda

Cimetière de
Bab el-Hamra

Rue des Français

Musée Dar
él-Batha

Bab Flouh

Bab
Dekakene

Jardins de
Bou Jeloud

Ave de l'Unesco

Bab
el-Hamra

TO TAZA

Oued Fez

Bab Riafa

Ave de la Liberté

TO MEKNES, RABAT

Grande Mosquée

Fez el-Jedid

Bab
Jdid

Mosquée
el-Azhar

Blvd Ahmed Ben Mohammed el-Alaoui

Jardins
Lalla
Mina

Dar el-Makhzen
(Royal Palace)

Bab
el-Hadid

Blvd des Saadiens

Agdal

Oued ez Zitoun

Rue des Merinides

Bab
Smarine

Bab
Jiaf

Borj Sud

Place
des
Alaouites

Mellah

Cemetery

Blvd Allal el-Fassi

Blvd Moulay Youssef

TO MEKNES, RABAT

Train
Station

Swimming
Pool

Stadium
Ave des Sports

N

M 250 500

Ave des
Almohades

Ville Nouvelle

✆ (00212) 35 62 3460/94 2492 • 🖷 (00212) 35 65 43 70 • e🖂 visitmorocco@onmt.org.ma • 🌐 www.touris-in-morocco.com

15

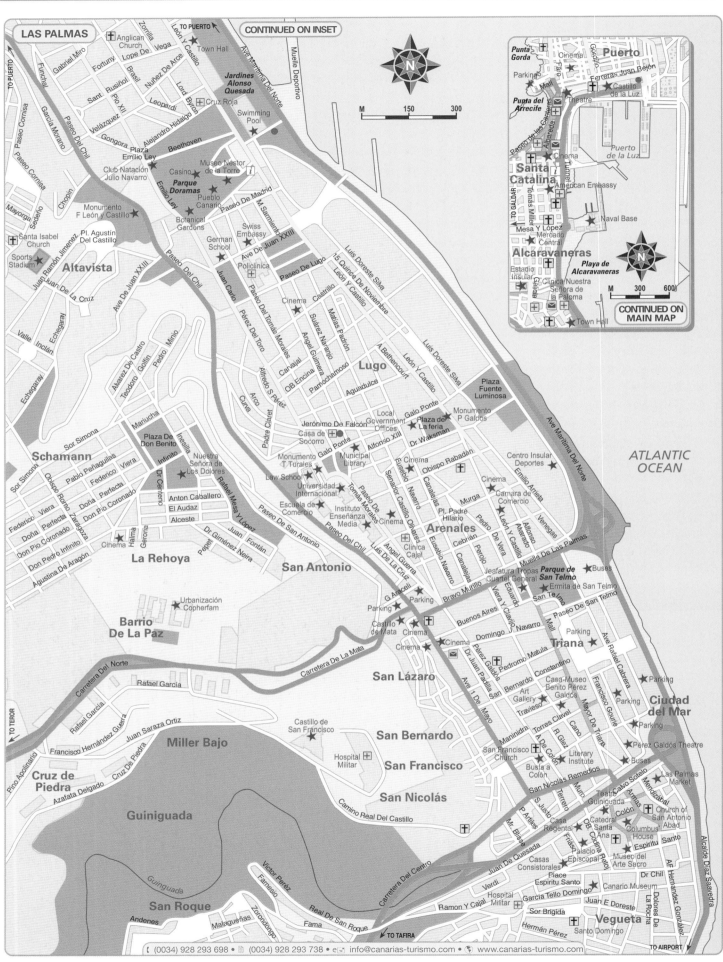

Las Palmas   Gran Canaria

TO PUERTO

TO PUERTO

Anglican Church

TO PUERTO

Town Hall

CONTINUED ON INSET

Jardines Alonso Quesada

Cruz Roja

Swimming Pool

Muelle Deportivo

Ave Marítima Del Norte

N

M   150   300

Plaza Emilio Ley

Museo Néstor de la Torre

Club Natación Julio Navarro

Casino

Parque Doramas

Pueblo Canario

Botanical Gardens

Monumento F León y Castillo

Santa Isabel Church

Pl. Agustín Del Castillo

Sports Stadium

Altavista

German School

Swiss Embassy

Ave De Juan XXIII

Policlínica

Paseo De Lugo

Paseo De Madrid

M. Sarmiento

Paseo Del Tomás Morales

Cinema

Castillo

Suárez Naranjo

Matías Padrón

15 Quince De Noviembre

León Y Castillo

Luis Doreste Silva

León Y Castillo

Luis Doreste Silva

Lugo

A Bethencourt

Angel Guimerá

Carvajal

OB Encina

Parrochámoso

Aguadulce

Plaza Fuente Luminosa

Schamann

Sor Simona

Mariucha

Insellsa

Plaza De Don Benito

Nuestra Señora de Los Dolores

Infinito

Galo Ponte

Local Government Offices

Plaza del La feria

Monumento P Galdos

Centro Insular Deportes

Emilio Arrieta

ATLANTIC OCEAN

Jerónimo De Falcón

Casa de Socorro

Alfonso XIII

Dr Waksman

Cinema

Obispo Rabadán

Cinema

Cámara de Comercio

Anton Caballero

El Audaz

Alceste

Rafael Mesa Y López

Dr Centeno

Monumento T Turales

Galo Ponta

Municipal Library

Paseo De Tomás Morales

Eusebio Navarro

Senador Castillo Olivares

Cinema

Pl. Padre Hilario

Murga

Arenales

León Y Castillo

Alonso Alvarado

Venegas

Law School

Universidad Internacional

Escuela de Comercio

Instituto Enseñanza Media

Cinema

Angel Guerra

Clínica Cajal

Eusebio Navarro

Cebrián

Pedro De Vera

Perojo

La Rehoya

Cinema

Halma

Gerona

Pepet

Juan Fontán

Dr. Giménez Neira

Paseo De San Antonio

Paseo Del Chil

Luis De La Cruz

Canalejas

San Antonio

Urbanización Copherfam

Barrio De La Paz

G Araceli

Parking

Parking

Castillo de Mata

Cinema

Cinema

Buenos Aires

Domingo

Navarro

Jefatura Tropas Cuartel General

Viera Y Clavijo

Parque de San Telmo

Buses

Ermita de San Telmo

San Telmo

Paseo De San Telmo

Carretera De La Mata

Carretera Del Norte

Rafael García

Rafael García

Juan Saraza Ortiz

Francisco Hernández Guerra

Miller Bajo

Castillo de San Francisco

San Lázaro

San Bernardo

Hospital Militar

San Francisco

Pérez Galdós

Dr. Juan Padilla

Pedromo Matula

Art Gallery

San Bernardo

Constantino

Casa-Museo Benito Pérez Galdós

Travieso

Parking

Parking

Triana

Parking

Ciudad del Mar

Parking

Pérez Galdós Theatre

Cruz de Piedra

Pino Apolinario

Azafata Delgado

Cruz De Piedra

Francisco Hernández Guerra

Guiniguada

Camino Real Del Castillo

San Nicolás

Mayor De Triana

Torres Clavel

Cano

R Glez

San Francisco Church

Maninidra

Av 1 De Mayo

A De Colón

Busta a Colón

Literary Institute

Buses

San Nicolás Remedios

S. Justo

Terrero

Muro

P Artiles

Teatro Guiniguada

Colón

Calvo Sotelo

Casa Regental

Arriba

Las Palmas Market

Mendizábal

Church of San Antonio Abad

Columbus House

Cocina

Francia

Espíritu Santo

Catedral Santa Ana

Palacio Episcopal

Museo del Arte Sacro

Santo

Dr Chil

Canario Museum

Place Espíritu Santo

Casas Consistoriales

Juan De Quesada

Verdi

Hospital Militar

Ramón Y Cajal

García Tello Domingo

Sor Brígida

Juan E Doreste

Santo Domingo

Dolores De La Rocha

Af Hernández González

Alcalde Diaz Saavedra

Vegueta

San Roque

Andenes

Malagueñas

Zorondongo

Víctor Peréz

Fanesio

Real De San Roque

Fama

Guinguada

Carretera Del Centro

TO TAFIRA

TO TERON

TO AIRPORT

Ave Marítima Del Norte

Punta Gorda

Cinema

Parking

Mall

Puerto

Godolio

Ferreras Juan Rejón

Castillo de la Luz

Theatre

Punta del Arrecife

Paseo de los Canteros

Albareda

Cinema

Santa Catalina

American Embassy

Naval Base

Tomás Miller

Mesa Y López

Mercado Central

Puerto de la Luz

Alcaravaneras

Estadio Insular

Galicia

Clínica Nuestra Señora de la Paloma

Playa de Alcaravaneras

TO GALDAR

M   300   600

Town Hall

CONTINUED ON MAIN MAP

☎ (0034) 928 293 698 • 📠 (0034) 928 293 738 • e📧 info@canarias-turismo.com • 🌐 www.canarias-turismo.com

Santa Cruz de Tenerife Tenerife

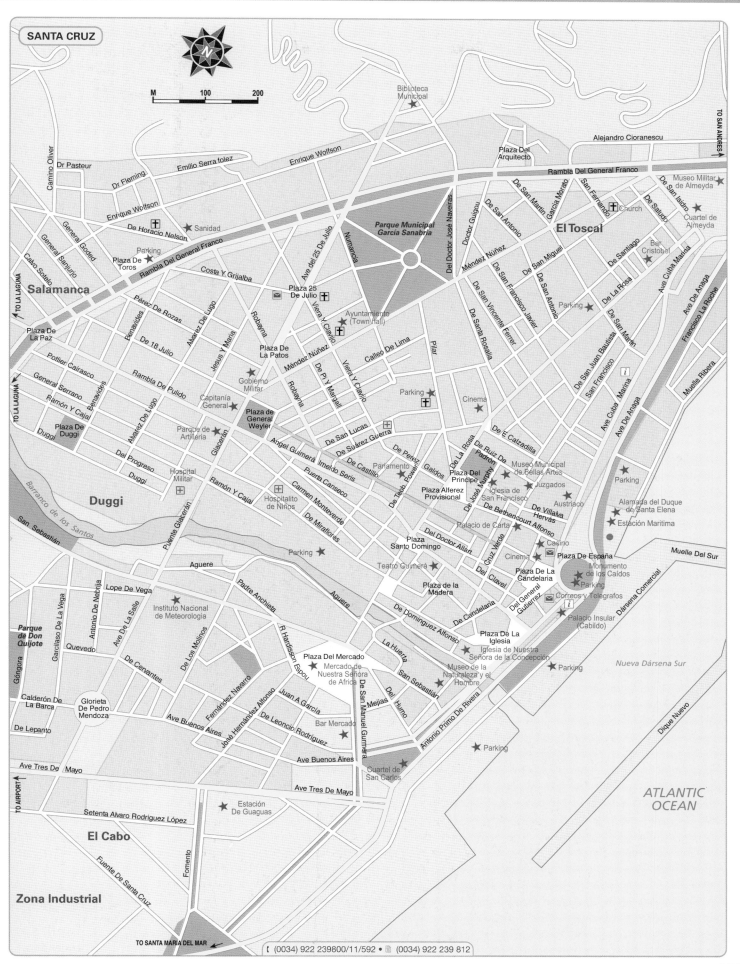

SANTA CRUZ

M   100   200

TO SAN ANDRES

Dr Pasteur
Camino Oliver
Dr Fleming
Emilio Serra folez
Enrique Wolfson
Biblioteca Municipal
Plaza Del Arquitecto
Alejandro Cioranescu
Rambla Del General Franco
Museo Militar de Almeyda

Enrique Wolfson
De Horacio Nelson
Sanidad
Parking
De San Martín
Garcia Morato
San Fernando
De Saludo
Church
Cuartel de Almeyda

General Goded
General Santjurio
Plaza De Toros
Rambla Del General Franco
Costa Y Grijalba
De San Antonio
El Toscal
Bar Cristobel

Calvo Sotelo
Salamanca
Plaza 25 De Julio
Parque Municipal García Sanabria
De San Miguel
De San Antonio
Méndez Núñez
De Santiago
Ave Cuba Marina
De Anaga

TO LA LAGUNA
Plaza De La Paz
Pérez De Rozas
Robayna
Plaza 25 De Julio
Numancia
Del Doctor José Naveiras
De San Francisco Javier
Parking
De La Rosa
De San Martín
Francisco La Roche

Benavides
De 18 Julio
Alvarez De Lugo
Jesus Y Maria
Ayuntamiento (Town hall)
Calleo De Lima
Pilar
De Santa Rosalia
De San Vicente Ferrer
De San Juan Bautista
Muelle Ribera

Potlier Cairasco
Rambla De Pulido
Plaza De La Patos
Méndez Núñez
Viera Y Clavijo
San Francisco

General Serrano
Ramón Y Cajal
Benavides
Alvarez De Lugo
Gobierno Militar
Robayna
Parking
Cinema
De San Francisco
De Anaga
Ave Cuba Marina

TO LA LAGUNA
Plaza De Duggi
Duggi
Capitania General
Plaza de General Weyler
De San Lucas
De E Calzadilla
Parking

Del Progreso
Duggi
Parque de Artillería
Glaceran
Ángel Guimerá Imeldo Seris
De Suárez Guerra
De Perez Galdos
De La Rosa De Ruiz De Padron
Museo Municipal de Bellas Artes
Alamada del Duque de Santa Elena

Duggi
Hospital Militar
Ramón Y Cajal
Carmen Monteverde
Parlamento
De Castillo
Plaza Del Príncipe
Iglesia de San Francisco
Juzgados
Austriaco
Estación Maritima

Hospitalito de Niños
Puerta Canseco
De Miraflores
De Tebb Power
Plaza Alferez Provisional
De Villalva Hervás
De Bethencourt Alfonso
Parking

Barranco de los Santos
San Sebastián
Parking
Aguere
Plaza Santo Domingo
Palacio de Carta
Cruz Verde
Casino
Plaza De España
Muelle Del Sur

Aguere
Teatro Guimerá
Del Doctor Allart
Cinema
Plaza De La Candelaria
Monumento de los Caídos
Dársena Comercial

Parque de Don Quijote
Lope De Vega
Padre Anchieta
Plaza de la Madera
Del Clavel
Plaza De La Candelaria
Parking

Antonio De Nebija
Ave De La Salle
Instituto Nacional de Meteorologia
Aguere
De Candelaria
Del General Guterez
Correos y Telegrafos

Garcilaso De La Vega
Quevedo
De Dominguez Alfonso
Palacio Insular (Cabildo)
Nueva Dársena Sur

Góngora
De Cenantes
De Los Molinos
R Hardisson Espou
La Huerta
Plaza De La Iglesia
Iglesia de Nuestra Señora de la Concepción

Parque de Don Quijote
Calderón De La Barca
Glorieta De Pedro Mendoza
Fernández Navarro
Plaza Del Mercado
Mercado de Nuestra Señora de Africa
De San Manuel Guimera
San Sebastián
Museo de la Naturaleza y el Hombre
Parking

De Lepanto
José Hernández Alfonso
De Leoncio Rodríguez
Juan A Garcia
Mejias
Del Humo
Ave Buenos Aires
Bar Mercado

TO AIRPORT
Ave Tres De Mayo
Ave Buenos Aires
Antonio Primo De Rivera
Parking
Dique Nuevo

Setenta Alvaro Rodriguez López
Estación De Guaguas
Cuartel de San Carlos
ATLANTIC OCEAN

El Cabo
Ave Tres De Mayo

Fuente De Santa Cruz
Fomento

Zona Industrial

TO SANTA MARIA DEL MAR

((0034) 922 239800/11/592 • (0034) 922 239 812

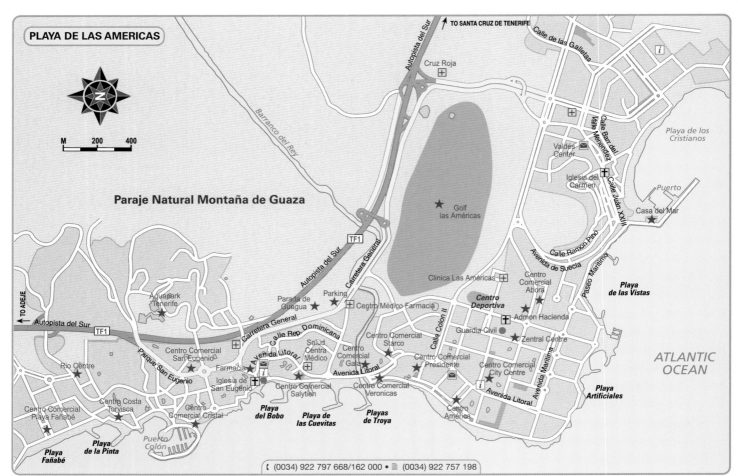

PLAYA DE LAS AMERICAS

TO SANTA CRUZ DE TENERIFE

Autopista del Sur

Calle de las Galletas

Cruz Roja

Barranco del Rey

N

M 200 400

Paraje Natural Montaña de Guaza

Playa de los Cristianos

Valdés Center

Iglesia del Carmen

Calle Juan XXIII

Calle Barr. del Valle Menéndez

Puerto

Casa del Mar

Golf las Américas

Calle Ramon Pino

Avenida de Suecia

Paseo Marítimo

Playa de las Vistas

TO ADEJE

Autopista del Sur TF1

Aquapark Tenerife

Parada de Guagua

Parking

Carretera General

Calle Rep. Dominicana

TF1

Autopista del Sur Carretera General

Centro Médico Farmacia

Clinica Las Américas

Centro Comercial Abora

Centro Deportiva

Admon Hacienda

ATLANTIC OCEAN

Rio Centre

Parque San Eugenio

Centro Comercial San Eugenio

Farmacia

Avenida Litoral

Salud Centra Médico

Centro Comercial G Gala

Centro Comercial Starco

Calle Colón II

Guardia Civil

Centro Comercial Presidente

Zentral Centre

Centro Comercial City Centre

Avenida Martima

Playa Artificiales

Centro Costa Toryisca

Iglesia de San Eugenio

Centro Comercial Cristal

Avenida Litoral

Centro Comercial Salytien

Centro Comercial Veronicas

Avenida Litoral

Centro América

Centro Comercial Playa Fañabé

Playa del Bobo

Playa de las Cuevitas

Playas de Troya

Playa Fañabé

Playa de la Pinta

Puerto Colón

(0034) 922 797 668/162 000 • (0034) 922 757 198

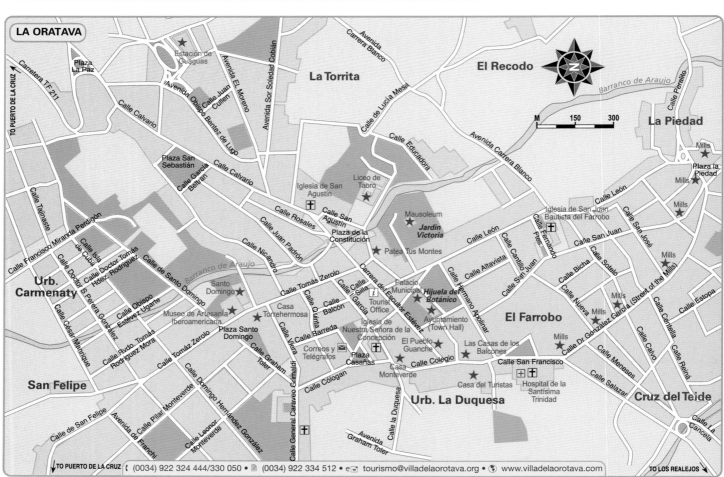

LA ORATAVA

Carretera TF 211

TO PUERTO DE LA CRUZ

Plaza La Paz

Estación de Guaguas

Avenida Carrera Blanco

Avenida Sor Soledad Cobián

La Torrita

Calle de Lucía Mesa

El Recodo

N

M 150 300

Barranco de Araujo

La Piedad

Calle Peraltho

Calle Calvario

Avenida Obispo Calle Juan Benítez de Lugo Cullen

Avenida EL Moreno

Calle Educadora

Avenida Carrera Blanco

Mills

Plaza la Piedad

Plaza San Sebastián

Calle García Beltrán

Calle Calvario

Iglesia de San Agustín

Liceo de Taoro

Calle León

Iglesia de San Juan Bautista del Farrobo

Calle San Juan

Calle León

Mills

Mills

Calle Taimaste

Calle Francisco Miranda Perdigón

Calle Isla de Cuba

Calle Rosales

Calle San Agustín

Mausoleum

Jardin Victoria

Calle Fernando Fies

Calle San Juan

Calle San José

Mills

Urb. Carmenaty

Calle Doctor Tomás Hdez. Rodríguez

Calle de Santo Domingo

Calle Juan Padrón

Plaza de la Constitución

Patea Tus Montes

Calle León

Calle Altavista

Calle Cantillo

Calle Bicha

Calle Sotelo

Mills

Calle Doctor S Perera González

Barranco de Araujo

Calle Nicandro

Carrera del Escultor Estévez

Palacio Municipal

Calle Hermano Apolinar

Calle Nueva

Mills

Santo Domingo

Calle Tomás Zerolo

Tourist Office

Hijuela del Botánico

El Farrobo

Calle Estopa

Museo de Artesanía Iberoamericana

Casa Torrehermosa

Calle Quinta

Calle Silla

Iglesia de Nuestra Señora de la Concepción

Ayuntamiento (Town Hall)

Mills

Calle Dr González García (Street of the Mills)

Calle Centella

Calle Reina

Calle César Manrique

Calle Rvdo. Tomás Rodríguez Mora

Plaza Santo Domingo

Calle Barreda

Calle Balcón

El Pueblo Guanche

Las Casas de los Balcones

Calle Calvo

Calle Meneses

San Felipe

Calle Tomaz Zerolo

Calle Vieta

Correos y Telégrafos

Plaza Casañas

Calle Colegio

Calle San Francisco

Calle Domingo Hernández González

Calle Graham Toler

Casa Monteverde

Casa del Turistas

Hospital de la Santísima Trinidad

Cruz del Teide

Calle de San Felipe

Avenida de Franchi

Calle Pilar Monteverde

Calle General Caraveo Grimaldi

Calle Cólogan

Calle la Duquesa

Urb. La Duquesa

Calle Salazar

Calle La Cancela

Calle Leonor Monteverde

Avenida Graham Toler

TO PUERTO DE LA CRUZ (0034) 922 324 444/330 050 • (0034) 922 334 512 • e tourismo@villadelaorotava.org • www.villadelaorotava.com TO LOS REALEJOS

18

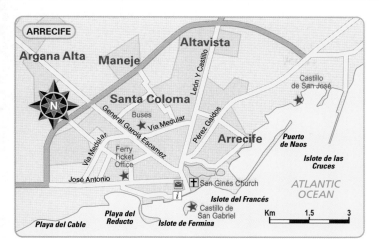

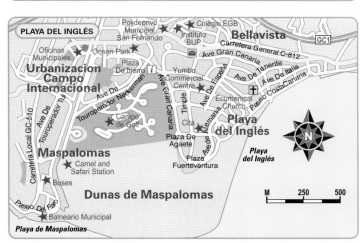

Arrecife: ((0034) 928 811 762 • ◻ (0034) 928 800 080 • 🌐 www.lanzarote.com

La Laguna: ((0034) 922 239 800/601 100 • ◻ (0034) 922 608 830

Los Cristianos: ((0034) 922 752 492/757 137 • ◻ (0034) 922 757 138

Puerto del Rosario: ((0034) 928 866 235/862 359 • 🌐 www.fuerteventuraturismo.com

Playa del Inglés: (/ ◻ (0034) 928 767 848

Puerto del la Cruz: ((0034) 922 386 000/605 590 • ◻ (0034) 922 38 47 69

Santa Cruz de la Palma: ((0034) 922 239 800/811/ 928 239 592 • ◻ (0034) 922 239 812

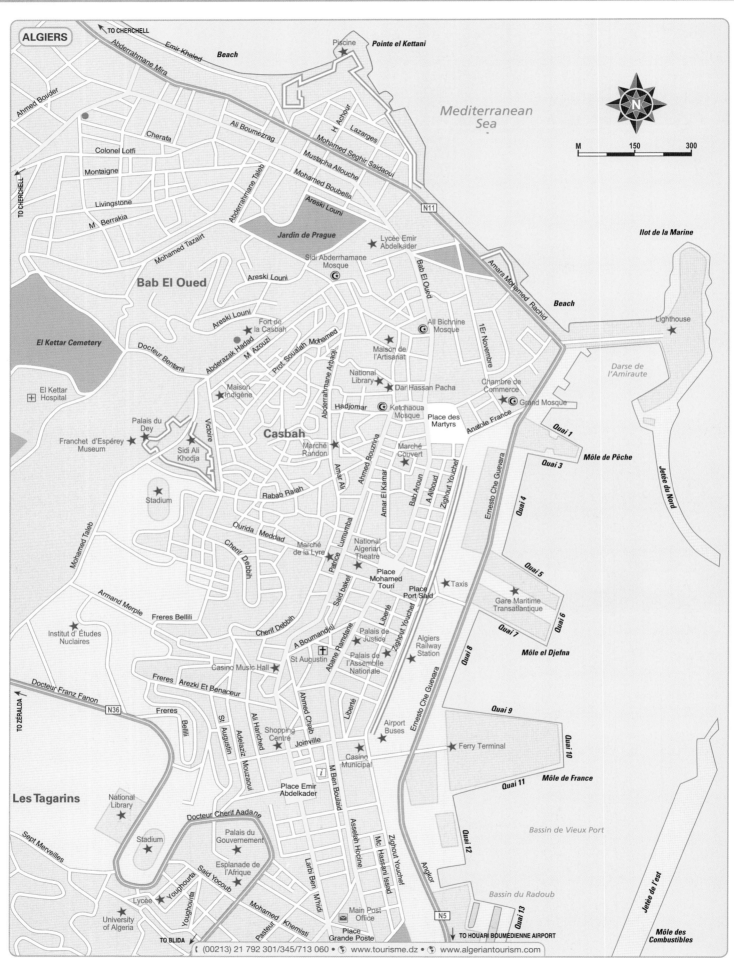

Algiers
Algeria

Mediterranean Sea

M   150   300

TO CHERCHELL

Abderrahmane Mira

Emir Khaled

Beach

Piscine

Pointe el Kettani

Ahmed Bouder

Cherafa

Colonel Lotfi

Montaigne

Livingstone

M. Berrakia

Ali Boumezrag

H. Achour

Lazarges

Mohamed Seghir Saidaoui

Mustapha Allouche

Mohamed Boubella

Areski Louni

Jardin de Prague

Lycée Emir Abdelkader

N11

Mohamed Tazairt

Abderrahmane Taleb

Sidi Abderrahamane Mosque

Bab El Oued

Areski Louni

Areski Louni

Fort de la Casbah

Ali Bichnine Mosque

Bab El Oued

1Er Novembre

Amara Mohamed Rachid

Beach

Ilot de la Marine

Lighthouse

El Kettar Cemetery

Docteur Bentami

Abderazak Hadad

M. Azouzi

Prof. Soualah Mohamed

Abderrhamane Arbadji

Maison de l'Artisanat

National Library

Maison Indigène

Dar Hassan Pacha

Chambre de Commerce

Grand Mosque

Darse de l'Amiraute

El Kettar Hospital

Hadjomar

Ketchaoua Mosque

Place des Martyrs

Anatole France

Quai 1

Palais du Dey

Victoire

Casbah

Marché Randon

Marché Couvert

Bab Aroun

A. Alloud

Zighout Youchef

Môle de Pêche

Quai 3

Franchet d'Espérey Museum

Sidi Ali Khodja

Amar Ali

Ahmed Bouzrina

Amar El Kamar

Ernesto Che Guevara

Quai 4

Stadium

Rabab Ralah

Ourida Meddad

Patrice Lumumba

Quai 5

Mohamed Taleb

Cherif Debbih

Marché de la Lyre

National Algerian Theatre

Said bakel

Quai 6

Gare Maritime Transatlantique

Quai 7

Armand Merple

Freres Bellili

Place Mohamed Touri

Place Port Said

Taxis

Môle el Djefna

Institut d'Études Nuclaires

Cherif Debbih

A Boumandjel

Abane Ramdane

Liberte

Palais de Justice

Algiers Railway Station

Quai 8

St Augustin

Palais de l'Assemblée Nationale

Casino Music Hall

Freres

Arezki Et Benaceur

Ahmed Chaib

Liberte

Docteur Franz Fanon

TO ZÉRALDA

N36

Freres

Belili

St. Augustin

Adelaziz Mouzaoui

Ali Hanched

Shopping Centre

Joinville

Airport Buses

Ernesto Che Guevara

Quai 9

Quai 10

Ferry Terminal

Môle de France

Casino Municipal

Quai 11

Les Tagarins

National Library

Place Emir Abdelkader

Asselah Hocine

Mc Hassani Issad

Zighout Youchef

Quai 12

Bassin de Vieux Port

Sept Merveilles

Stadium

Docteur Cherif Aadane

Palais du Gouvernement

Larbi Ben M'hidi

Angkor

Esplanade de l'Afrique

Said Yocoub

Youghourta

Mohamed

Main Post Office

N5

Bassin du Radoub

Jetée de l'est

Lycée

University of Algeria

Youghourta

Pasteur

Mohamed Khemisti

Place Grande Poste

Quai 13

TO BLIDA

TO HOUARI BOUMEDIENNE AIRPORT

Jetée du Nord

Môle des Combustibles

((00213) 21 792 301/345/713 060 • www.tourisme.dz • www.algeriantourism.com

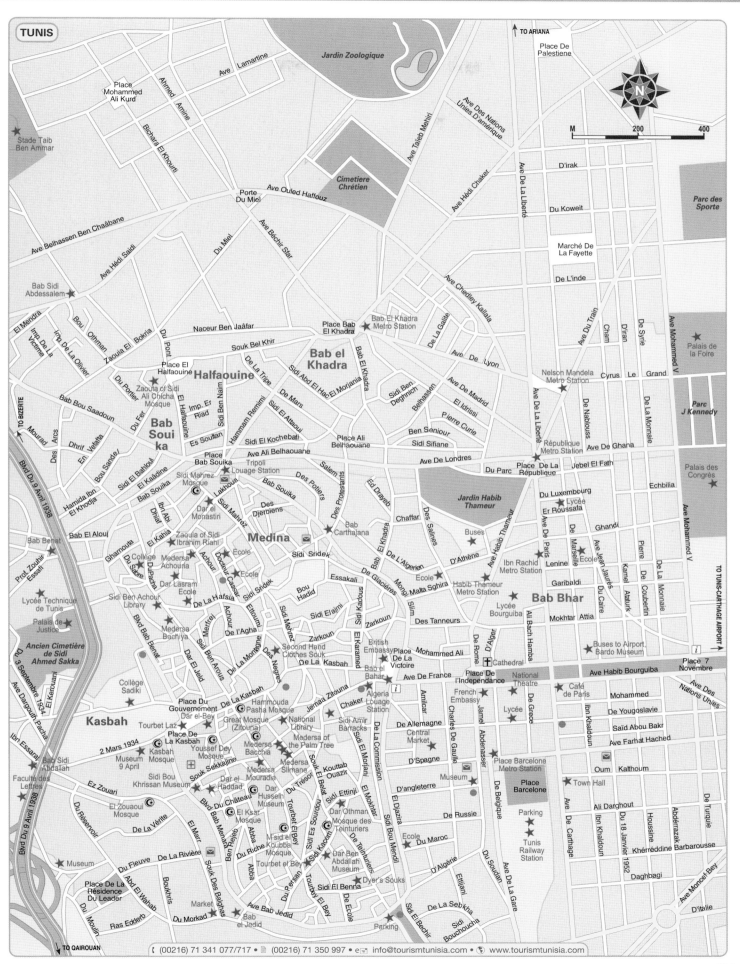

☏ (00216) 71 341 077/717 • 🖨 (00216) 71 350 997 • e✉ info@tourismtunisia.com • 🌐 www.tourismtunisia.com

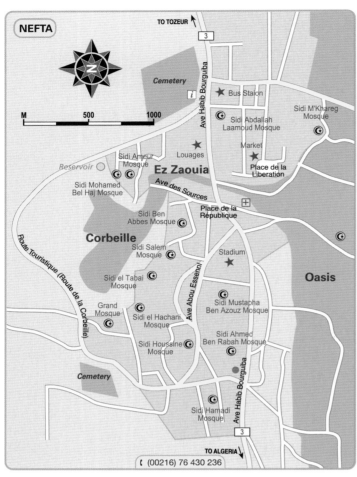

NEFTA

TO TOZEUR
3

N

M 500 1000

Cemetery

Ave Habib Bourguiba
Bus Station
Sidi M'Khareg Mosque
Sidi Abdallah Laamoud Mosque
Market
Sidi Ameur Mosque
Louages
Place de la Liberation
Ez Zaouia
Reservoir
Sidi Mohamed Bel Haj Mosque
Ave des Sources
Place de la République
Sidi Ben Abbes Mosque
Corbeille
Sidi Salem Mosque
Stadium
Oasis
Route Touristique (Route de la Corbeille)
Sidi el Tabai Mosque
Ave Abou Essenni
Sidi Mustapha Ben Azouz Mosque
Grand Mosque
Sidi el Hachani Mosque
Sidi Ahmed Ben Rabah Mosque
Sidi Houssine Mosque
Cemetery
Ave Habib Bourguiba
Sidi Hamadi Mosque
3
TO ALGERIA

((00216) 76 430 236

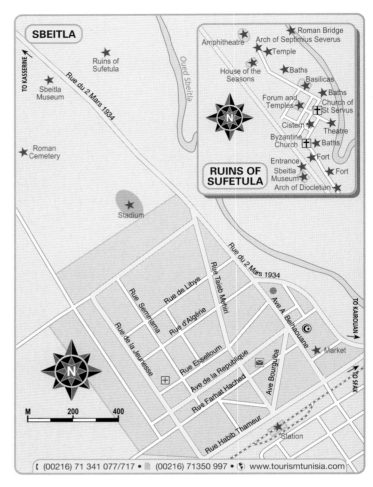

SBEITLA

Roman Bridge
Arch of Septimius Severus
Amphitheatre
Temple
Ruins of Sufetula
House of the Seasons
Baths
Basilicas
Sbeitla Museum
Forum and Temples
Baths
Church of St Servus
N
Cistern
Theatre
Byzantine Church
Baths
RUINS OF SUFETULA
Entrance
Fort
Sbeitla Museum
Fort
Arch of Diocletian

TO KASSERINE
Oued Sbeitla
Rue du 2 Mars 1934
Roman Cemetery
Stadium
Rue du 2 Mars 1934
Ave A. Belhaouane
TO KAIROUAN
Rue Taieb Mehiri
Rue de Libye
Rue Semmama
Rue d'Algérie
Market
Rue de la Jeunesse
Rue Esselloum
Rue de la République
Ave Bourguiba
TO SFAX
N
Rue Farhat Hached
M 200 400
Rue Habib Thameur
Station

((00216) 71 341 077/717 • 🖨 (00216) 71350 997 • 🌐 www.tourismtunisia.com

KAIROUAN

TO TUNIS
Ave Ibn Jazzar
Ouled Farhane Cemetery
Blvd Est
Rue Sidi Abd
El Kader
N
TO SOUSSE
Great Mosque
Rue Ibrahim Ibn El Aghlab
Zaouia Sidi El Kader Abd
Rue de la Kasbah
M 125 250
Ave El Moizz. Ibn Badiss
Kasbah
Rue El Kadraoui
Route du Bathen
Rue Kchelfa
Rue Dar El Bey Koud
Rue Kenansa
Place de Tunis
Rue Salah Soussi
TO GAFSA
Market
Rue du Haut Marche
Rue Sidi Gaid
Zaouia Sidi Amor Abbada
Ave Habib Bourguiba
Rue des Arceaux
Rue de Sousse
Rue El Gacraoui
Bab Chellah
Mosque of the Three Doors
Rue Zuoagha
Zitouna Mosque
Rue Homet El Bey
Bir Barouta
TO SOUSSE
Rue Ibn Nached
Bab Djedid
Zaouia of Sidi el Ghariani
Ave Ali Zouaoui
Rue des Arceaux
Place du Commandant M. El Bejaoui
De la Rose Mosque
Rue du Gabsi
Rue Moncet Bey
Ave de la République
Blvd Hedi Chaker
Rue de Garsa
Rue el Moriz
Rue du 20 Mars
Museum
Ave Farhat Hached
Ave de Fes
TO YOUTH HOSTEL
TO SFAX, GABES

((00216) 77 231 897

TABARKA

TO EL KALA
7
Borj Messaoud
El Kraymia
Basilica
Old Harbour
Ile de Tabarka
Rue E. Hached
Rue du Peuple
Rue de la Constitution
Bus Station
Rue Hedi Chaker
Genoese Fort
Ave Habib Bourguiba
17
Station
Rue du Slade
Fishing Port
TO JENDOUBA
Ave 7 Novembre
Marina
O. El Kebir
7
Route Touristique
Mediterranean Sea
TO TUNIS
N
M 250 500
Golf Course

((00216) 78 671 491/673 496 • 🖨 (00216) 673 428

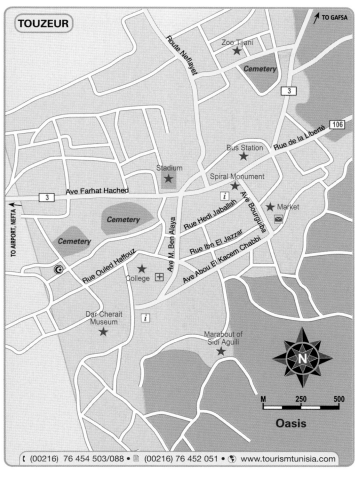

TOUZEUR

TO GAFSA

Route Nefflayet

Zoo Tijani

Cemetery

3

106

Bus Station

Stadium

Spiral Monument

Rue de la Liberté

Ave Farhat Hached

Market

3

Ave Bourguiba

Rue Hedi Jaballah

Rue M. Ben Alaya

Rue Ibn El Jazzar

Rue Abou El Kacem Chabbi

Cemetery

Cemetery

TO AIRPORT, NEFTA

Rue Ouled Haffouz

College

Dar Cherait Museum

Marabout of Sidi Aguili

Oasis

N

M   250   500

((00216) 76 454 503/088 • (00216) 76 452 051 • www.tourismtunisia.com

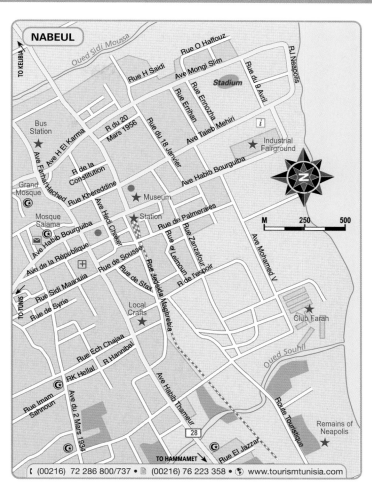

NABEUL

Oued Sidi Moussa

TO KELIBIA

Rue O Haffouz

Rue H Saidi

Ave Mongi Slim

Rue Ennozha

RJ Neapolis

Rue du 9 Avril

Stadium

Bus Station

Ave H El Karma

R du 20 Mars 1956

Rue du 18 Janvier

Rue Ertihan

Ave Taieb Mehiri

i

Industrial Fairground

Ave Farhat Hached

R de la Constitution

Ave Habib Bourguiba

N

Grand Mosque

Rue Khereddine

Museum

Station

Mosque Salama

Ave Hedi Chaker

Rue de Palmeraies

M   250   500

Ave Habib Bourguiba

Rue Zanzafour

Rue el Lamoun

Ave de la République

Rue de Sousse

R de l'espoir

Club Farah

Rue de Sfax

Rue Jedeida Maghrabia

Rue Sidi Maaouia

Local Crafts

TO TUNIS

Rue de Syrie

Rue Ech Chajaa

R Hannibal

Oued Souhil

RK Hellal

R Hannibal

Route Touristique

Rue Imam Sahnoun

Ave du 2 Mars 1934

Ave Habib Thameur

Remains of Neapolis

28

Rue El Jazzar

TO HAMMAMET

((00216) 72 286 800/737 • (00216) 76 223 358 • www.tourismtunisia.com

HAMMAMET

TO NABEUL

Market Place

Rue A Zayane

Baie du Soleil Vacation Village

28

Ave Assad Ibn El Fourat

Rue Mohammed Ali

Ave de la Liberation

Rue Sidi Bou Ali

Ave Hedi Ouali

Ave Tahar Sfar

Rue Taieb

Rue El Azzabi

Rue du Stade

College

Ave Habib Thameur

Ave de la République

Rue de Jasmins

Ave Mongi

Rue Salsaf

Rue des Pins

Ideal Camping

Bus Station

Cemetery

Oued El Gaid

Ave Hedi Chaker

Rue Ibn Khaldoun

Rue du 20 Mars 1956

Rue Ali Belhouane

Station

Medina

i

Museum

Ave du President Habib Bourguiba

Kasbah

Ave du Roi Faycal Ibn Abdelaziz

Rue A Chaouki

Rue el Jahedh

Rue Tahar Khmiri

Rue de la Corniche

Ave des Nations Unies

Rue El Kharrouba

Rue des Fontaines

Mediterranean Sea

N

28

M   200   400

TO CULTURAL CENTRE

((00216) 72 280 423 • www.tourismtunisia.com

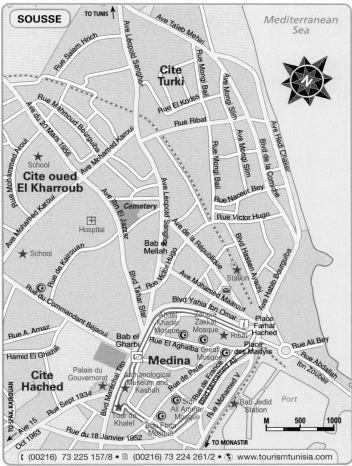

SOUSSE

TO TUNIS

Mediterranean Sea

Ave Taieb Mehiri

Rue Salem Hrich

Ave Léopold Sanghor

Rue Mongi Bali

Cite Turki

Rue El Kodss

Ave Mongi Slim

Rue Mahmoud Bourguiba

Rue Ribat

Ave Hedi Chaker

Ave du 20 Mars 1956

Rue Mongi Bali

Blvd de la Corniche

School

Rue Mohamed Karoui

Rue Mongi Bali

Cite oued El Kharroub

Ave Léopold Sanghor

Rue Naceur Bey

Ave Mohamed Karoui

Cemetery

Ave Ibn El Jazzar

Rue Victor Hugo

Hospital

Ave de la République

School

Bab el Mellah

Blvd Hassen Ayachi

Rue de Kairouan

Blvd Tahar Sfar

Rue Victor Hugo

Ave Mohamed Maarouf

Station

Rue du Commandant Béjaoui

Blvd Yahia Ibn Omar

Ave Habib Bourguiba

Abdel Khader Mosque

Zaouia Zakkat Mosque

Place Farhat Hached

i

Rue A. Arnaz

Bab el Gharbi

Rue El Aghalba

Ribat

Rue Ali Bey

Hamid El Ghazali

Great Mosque

Place des Martyrs

Ibn Zoubeir

Rue Mohamed Ali

Cite Hached

Palais du Gouvernorat

Archaeological Museum and Kasbah

Medina

Rue de Paris

Rue de France

Port

TO SFAX, KAIROUAN

Blvd Marechal Tito

Sidi Ali Ammar Mosque

Bou Ftata Mosque

Bab Jedid Station

Ave 15 Oct 1963

Rue Sept 1934

Tour de Khalef

Rue du 18 Janvier 1952

TO MONASTIR

N

M   500   1000

((00216) 73 225 157/8 • (00216) 73 224 261/2 • www.tourismtunisia.com

23

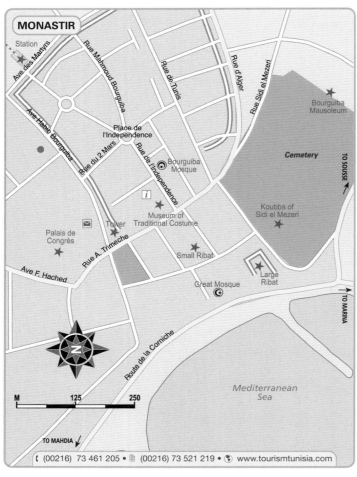

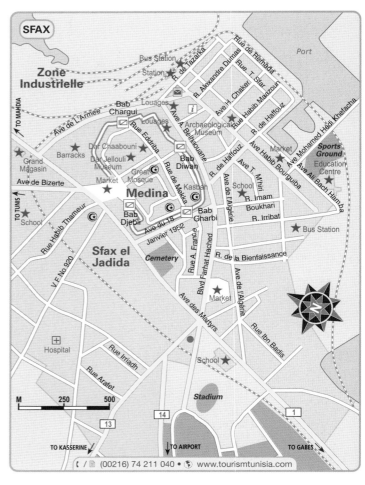

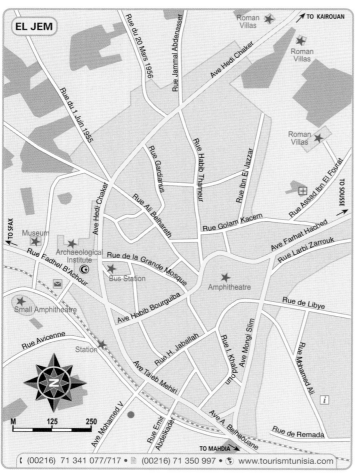

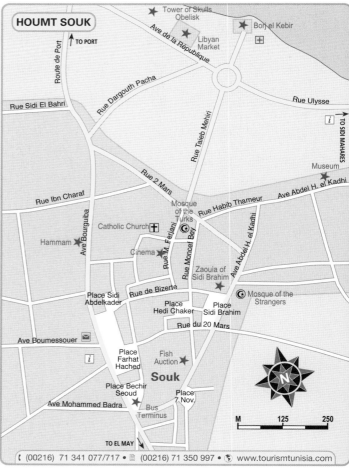

Adventures

Adventure	Country	Duration
Trekking the High Atlas Mountains	Morocco	2 days +
Surfing the West Coast	Morocco	3 hours +
Camel Trekking the Drâa Valley	Morocco	1 - 14 days
Sailing Chott El Jerid	Tunisia	1 - 4 days
Exploring Tassili	Algeria	1 - 4 days
Driving the Dunes of Laayoune	Western Sahara	1 - 6 days

Trekking the High Atlas Mountains

Requirements:
Valid passports (6 months); citizens of EU countries, USA, Australia, Canada and New Zealand do not need visas for stays of less than 90 days. Consult your local embassy. No hiking permits are required.

Climate:
Best time to trek is summer (May-October), when nights are cool and days warm to hot, with seasonal storms.

Risk factor:
Although the Atlas does not offer easy walking, it is neither too technical nor too inaccessible for the determined hiker.

Health:
No immunizations are required, unless visitors are travelling through or from countries with a recent history of yellow fever. There is a moderate AIDS risk in the area.

Pack:
Sturdy but comfortable walking boots, a sleeping bag and tent are essential, as are sunscreen and bottled water. Shorts are not recommended.

Facilities:
Apart from a tent and sleeping bag, most other requirements for the trek are usually provided by the operators' guides. Overnight accommodation, although simple, is comfortable.

Contact:
Club Alpin Francais, B.P. 6178, Casablanca.
Tel: 00212-2-270090

Surfing Morocco's West Coast

Requirements:
Valid passports (6 months); citizens of EU countries, USA, Australia, Canada and New Zealand do not need visas for stays of less than 90 days. Consult your local embassy.

Climate:
Balmy and sunny with good surfing conditions virtually year-round.

Risk factor:
Fun far surpasses risk.

Health:
No immunizations are required, unless visitors are travelling through or from countries with yellow fever. There is a moderate AIDS risk in the area.

Pack:
Sunscreen and surfboards and/or windsurfers, but local surfing schools may offer equipment to hire. Women should cover legs and arms as beachwear may be frowned upon in public places.

Facilities:
Main holiday towns have plenty of accommodation, ranging from the basic to the plush, while more out-of-the-way destinations have simple overnight hostels for backpackers. Ablution facilities are virtually nonexistent along undeveloped coastal areas.

Contact:
Royal Moroccan Surfing Federation.
Tel: 00212-2-259530

Camel Trekking the Drâa Valley

Requirements:
Valid passports (6 months); citizens of EU countries, USA, Australia, Canada and New Zealand do not need visas for stays of less than 90 days. Consult your local embassy.

Climate:
Valleys are cooler and more hospitable to visitors than the often oppressive heat beyond the Oued Drâa. Best times are September-February.

Risk factor:
Minimal, but riding and negotiating skills are an advantage; 4x4 vehicles are recommended for travel beyond camel routes.

Health:
No immunizations are required, unless visitors are travelling through or from countries with yellow fever. There is a moderate AIDS risk in the area.

Pack:
Cool, comfortable and light clothes for the day, and warm gear for nights. If hiring camels from private individuals, take water, bedding and sunscreen.

Facilities:
Even small towns and villages have simple but adequate overnight facilities, but few beyond the larger centres have anything remotely luxurious.

Contact:
Best of Morocco (UK-based).
Tel: 0044-1380-828533
www.realmorocco.com

Sailing Tunisia's Chott El Jerid

Requirements:
Valid passports should be sufficient for short stays, but visas may be required for travellers from certain countries for visits of longer than a few weeks. Consult your local embassy. No sand yachting permits are required.

Climate:
Generally hot and windy on the exposed chott and dunes. Best from November, but March-May are idyllic.

Risk factor:
No risks, other than a few bumps and bruises, but be sensible – emergency help can be problematic – and beware of sunburn and dehydration.

Health:
No immunizations are required, but hygiene levels are generally poor and waterborne disease is not uncommon. There is a moderate AIDS risk in the area.

Pack:
Sunscreen, hardwearing clothing, protective gear, and bottled water.

Facilities:
Adequate introduction by operators connected to upmarket hotels in nearby towns, such as Tozeur, Gabès, Douz, Degache and Kebili.

Contact:
Palm Beach Palace, Tozeur
Tel: 00216-76-453111 / 211
* Note: Most hotels around the principal towns offer sand yachting expeditions.

Exploring Tassili, Algeria

Requirements:
Given the political instability, travel may be perilous or even restricted. Consult your local embassy.

Climate:
Day temperatures are searing, while nights can be icy. Rain is scarce.

Risk factor:
Risks are very high indeed, and private travel to and through Algeria is tenuous at best and extremely dangerous at worst, exacerbated by inaccessibility and harsh desert conditions virtually throughout the country.

Health:
No immunizations are required, unless visitors are travelling through or from countries with a recent history of yellow fever. The risk of AIDS is uncertain.

Pack:
Take with you virtually every day-to-day necessity, from drinking water to vehicle parts and spares.

Facilities:
Overnight and visitor facilities are improving, but continued internal strife means that existing amenities may be lacking. Camping and hiking in small, unprotected private parties is ill-advised.

Contact:
US Embassy, B.P. 408,
Algiers, 16000.
Tel: 00213-21-691425 / 255 / 186

Driving the Dunes of Laayoune

Requirements:
Valid passports (6 months); citizens of EU countries, USA, Australia, Canada and New Zealand do not need visas for stays of less than 90 days. Consult your local embassy. No driving permits are required.

Climate:
Best time to visit is April/May, but days can become very hot.

Risk factor:
There should be few risks around Laayoune, but deal only with reputable operators affiliated with upmarket hotels.

Health:
No immunizations are required, unless visitors are travelling through or from countries with a recent history of yellow fever. Moderate AIDS risk.

Pack:
Cool, lightweight clothing is essential. The harsh desert demands the use of a hat and sunscreen, while bottled water is a good idea. Don't wear shorts.

Facilities:
Private excursions are not recommended. Operators provide vehicles. Basic but comfortable accommodation is available in and around Laayoune.

Contact:
Delegation Regionale du Tourisme, B.P. 471,
Morocco, Laayoune.
Tel: 00212-28-891694 / 5

Canary Islands

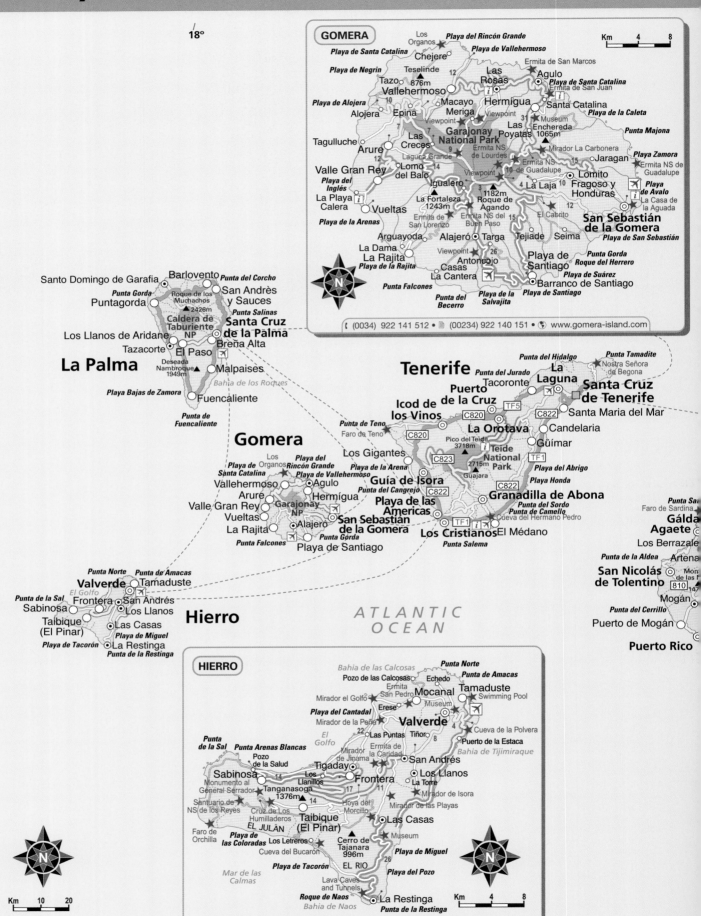

GOMERA

Km 4 8

Los Organos
Playa del Rincón Grande
Playa de Santa Catalina
Playa de Vallehermoso
Chejere
Playa de Negrin
Teselinde
Las Rosas
Ermita de San Marcos
Agulo
Playa de Santa Catalina
Tazo
876m
Ermita de San Juan
Vallehermoso
Macayo
Hermígua
Santa Catalina
Playa de Alojera
Meriga
Viewpoint
Museum
Playa de la Caleta
Alojera
Epina
Viewpoint
31
Enchereda
7
Las
1065m
Punta Majona
Tagulluche
7
Garajonay
Poyatas
Arure
National Park
Playa Zamora
Las
Ermita NS
Mirador La Carbonera
12
Creces
de Lourdes
Jaragan
Laguna Grande
Ermita NS
15
Valle Gran Rey
Lomo
14
de Guadalupe
Lomito
Playa del
del Balo
Viewpoint
10
La Laja
10
Fragoso y
Inglés
Igualero
3
4
Honduras
La Playa
La Fortaleza
1182m
El Cabrito
Playa
Calera
1243m
Roque de
12
de Avalo
Vueltas
Agando
La Casa de
Playa de la Arenas
Ermita de
Ermita NS del
15
la Aguada
San Lorenzo
Buen Paso
San Sebastián
Arguayoda
Alajeró Targa
Tejiade
Seima
de la Gomera
La Dama
Viewpoint
26
Punta Gorda
Playa de San Sebastián
La Rajita
Antoncojo
Roque del Herrero
Playa de la Rajita
Casas
Playa de
Punta de Suárez
La Cantera
Santiago
Playa de Santiago
Punta del
Becerro
Playa de la
Barranco de Santiago
Salvajita
Punta Falcones
Playa de Santiago

N

((0034) 922 141 512 • 🖷 (00234) 922 140 151 • 🌐 www.gomera-island.com

18°

Santo Domingo de Garafia
Barlovento
Punta del Corcho
Punta Gorda
Roque de los
San Andrès
Puntagorda
Muchachos
y Sauces
▲2426m
Punta Salinas
Caldera de
Taburiente
Santa Cruz
Los Llanos de Aridane
NP
de la Palma
Tazacorte
Breña Alta
El Paso
La Palma
Deseada
Nambroque▲
Malpaises
1949m
Bahia de los Roques
Playa Bajas de Zamora
Fuencaliente
Punta de
Fuencaliente

Gomera
Los
Playa del
Playa de
Organos
Rincón Grande
Santa Catalina
Playa de Vallehermoso
Vallehermoso
Agulo
Arure
Hermígua
Valle Gran Rey
Garajonay
Vueltas
NP
La Rajita
Alajeró
San Sebastian
de la Gomera
Punta Gorda
Punta Falcones
Playa de Santiago

Tenerife
Punta del Hidalgo
Punta Tamadite
Nostra Señora
de Begona
Punta del Jurado
La
Puerto
Tacoronte
Laguna
Santa Cruz
de la Cruz
de Tenerife
Icod de
Santa Maria del Mar
los Vinos
C820
TF5
C822
Punta de Teno
La Orotava
Candelaria
Faro de Teno
C820
Güímar
Pico del Teide
Teide
3718m
National
Los Gigantes
C823
Park
Playa del Abrigo
Playa de la Arena
2715m
Playa Honda
Guía de Isora
Guajara
Punta del Cangrejo
C822
Playa de las
Granadilla de Abona
Americas
Punta del Sordo
Punta de Camello
Punta Sal
Los Cristianos
TF1
Cueva del Hermano Pedro
Faro de Sardina
El Médano
Gálda
Punta Salema
Agaete
Los Berrazale
Punta de la Aldea
Artena
San Nicolás
Mon
de Tolentino
de las
810
Mogán
Punta del Cerrillo
Puerto de Mogán
Puerto Rico

ATLANTIC OCEAN

Punta Norte
Punta de Amacas
Valverde
Tamaduste
Punta de la Sal
El Golfo
Sabinosa
Frontera
San Andrés
Los Llanos
Taibique
Hierro
(El Pinar)
Las Casas
Playa de Tacorón
Playa de Miguel
La Restinga
Punta de la Restinga

HIERRO

Bahia de las Calcosas
Punta Norte
Pozo de las Calcosas
Echedo
Punta de Amacas
Ermita
Mocanal
Tamaduste
Mirador el Golfo
San Pedro
Swimming Pool
Erese
Museum
Playa del Cantadal
Mirador de la Peña
Valverde
El
22
Cueva de la Polvera
Golfo
Las Puntas
Tiñor
Puerto de la Estaca
Punta
8
Bahia de Tijimiraque
de la Sal
Punta Arenas Blancas
Mirador
Pozo
de Jinama
San Andrés
de la Salud
Ermita de
Sabinosa
14
Tigaday
la Caridad
Los Llanos
Los
Monumento al
Llanillos
Frontera
La Torre
General Serrador
Tanganasoga
17
11
Mirador de Isora
Santuario de
1376m
14
Mirador de las Playas
NS de los Reyes
Hoya del
Cruz de Los
Morcillo
Humilladeros
Taibique
EL JULÁN
(El Pinar)
Las Casas
Faro de
Museum
Orchilla
Playa de
Cerro de
las Coloradas
Los Letreros
Tajanara
Playa de Miguel
Cueva del Bucarón
996m
26
EL RIO
Playa del Pozo
Playa de Tacorón
Lava Caves
and Tunnels
Mar de las
Roque de Naos
La Restinga
Calmas
Bahia de Naos
Punta de la Restinga

N

Km 4 8

N

Km 10 20

((0034) 922 550 302 • 🖷 (0034) 922 551 052 • 🌐 www.elhierro.es

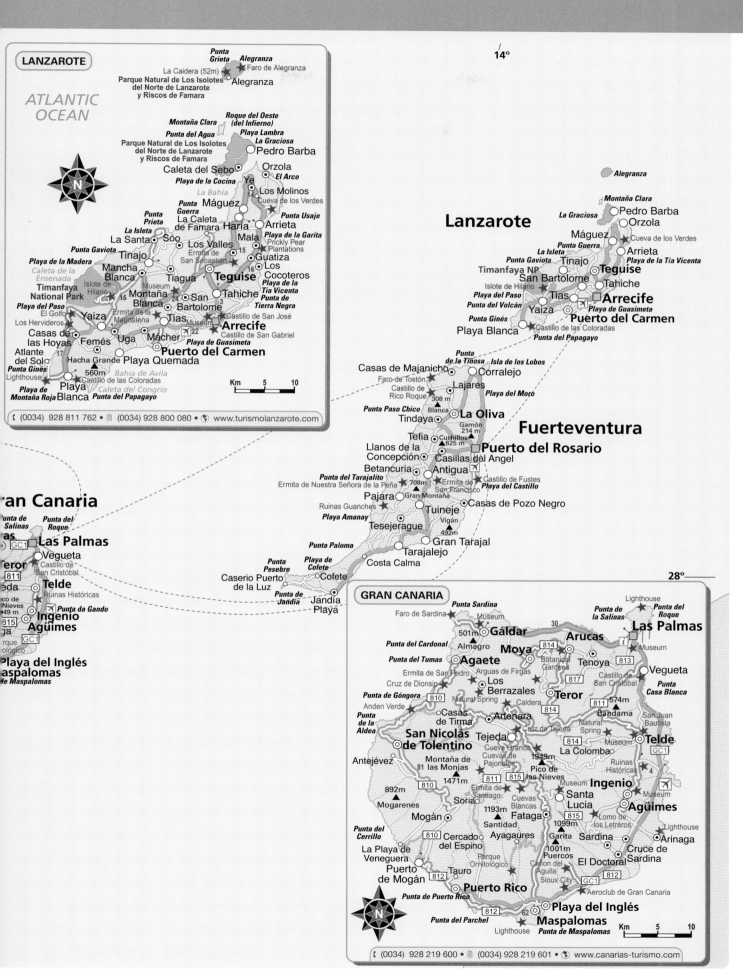

LANZAROTE

ATLANTIC OCEAN

Punta Grieta
Alegranza
La Caidera (52m)
Faro de Alegranza
Parque Natural de Los Isolotes del Norte de Lanzarote y Riscos de Famara
Alegranza

Roque del Oeste (del Infierno)
Montaña Clara
Punta del Agua
Playa Lambra
La Graciosa
Parque Natural de Los Isolotes del Norte de Lanzarote y Riscos de Famara
Pedro Barba
Caleta del Sebo
Orzola
El Arco
Playa de la Cocina
Ye
Los Molinos
La Bahía
Cueva de los Verdes
Punta Guerra
Punta Prieta
Máguez
La Caleta de Famara
Harla
Punta Usaje
La Isleta
Arrieta
La Santa
Sóo
Los Valles
Mala
Playa de la Garita
Punta Gaviota
Tinajo
Ermita de San Sebastián
Guatiza
Prickly Pear Plantations
Playa de la Madera
Mancha Blanca
Tiagua
Museum
Los Cocoteros
Caleta de la Ensenada
Teguise
Playa de la Tia Vicenta
Timanfaya National Park
Islote de Hilario
Montaña Blanca
San Bartolome
Tahiche
Punta de Tierra Negra
Playa del Paso
El Golfo
Ermita de la Magdalena
Tias
Castillo de San José
Los Hervideros
Yaiza
Mácher
Museum
Arrecife
Casas de las Hoyas
Femés
Uga
Playa de Guasimeta
Atlante del Sol
Hacha Grande
Puerto del Carmen
Punta Ginés
Playa Quemada
Castillo de San Gabriel
Lighthouse
560m
Bahía de Avila
Castillo de las Coloradas
Playa de Montaña Roja
Playa Blanca
Caleta del Congrio
Punta del Papagayo

Km 5 10

(0034) 928 811 762 • (0034) 928 800 080 • www.turismolanzarote.com

14°

Alegranza

Montaña Clara
La Graciosa
Pedro Barba
Orzola
Lanzarote
Máguez
Cueva de los Verdes
Punta Guerra
Arrieta
La Isleta
Punta Gaviota
Tinajo
Teguise
Playa de la Tia Vicenta
Timanfaya NP
San Bartolome
Tahiche
Islote de Hilario
Tias
Arrecife
Playa del Paso
Yaiza
Playa de Guasimeta
Punta del Volcán
Puerto del Carmen
Punta Ginés
Castillo de las Coloradas
Playa Blanca
Punta del Papagayo

Punta de la Tiñosa
Isla de los Lobos
Casas de Majanicho
Corralejo
Faro de Tostón
Lajares
Castillo de Rico Roque
Playa del Moró
308 m
Punta Paso Chico
Blanca
Tindaya
La Oliva
Gamón 214 m
Fuerteventura
Tefia
Cuchillos 625 m
Llanos de la Concepción
Puerto del Rosario
Casillas del Angel
Betancuria
Antigua
Punta del Tarajalito
Castillo de Fustes
Ermita de Nuestra Señora de la Peña
708m
Ermita de San Francisco
Playa del Castillo
Pajara
Gran Montaña
Casas de Pozo Negro
Ruinas Guanches
Tuineje
Playa Amanay
Vigán 492m
Tesejerague
Punta Paloma
Gran Tarajal
Tarajalejo
Costa Calma
Punta Pesebre
Playa de Cofete
Caserio Puerto de la Luz
Cofete
Punta de Jandía
Jandía Playa

ran Canaria
unta de Salinas
Punta del Roque
as
GC1
Las Palmas
Vegueta
eror
Castillo de San Cristóbal
eda
Telde
811
co de Nieves 49 m
Ruinas Históricas
Punta da Gando
Ingenio
ja
815
Agüimes
GC1
rque ológico
laya del Inglés
aspalomas
e Maspalomas

28°

GRAN CANARIA

Punta Sardina
Lighthouse
Punta del Roque
Faro de Sardina
Museum
Punta de la Salinas
Las Palmas
501m
Gáldar
Arucas
i
Punta del Cardonal
Almagro
Moya
814
Museum
Punta del Tumas
Agaete
Tenoya
813
Botanical Gardens
Vegueta
Ermita de San Pedro
Arguas de Firgas
Castillo de San Cristóbal
Cruz de Dionsip
Los Berrazales
817
Punta Casa Blanca
Punta de Góngora
810
Natural Spring
814
Teror
Caldera
811
574m
Anden Verde
Bandama
Punta de la Aldea
Casas de Tirma
Artenara
Cruz de Tejeda
San Juan Bautista
San Nicolás de Tolentino
Tejeda
Natural Spring
814
Museum
Telde
Cueva Grande
La Colomba
GC1
Antejévez
Cuevas de Pajonales
1949m
Ruinas Históricas
Montaña de las Monjas
Pico de las Nieves
4
1471m
811
815
Museum
Ingenio
Ermita de Santiago
892m
Cuevas Blancas
Santa Lucia
Museum
Mogarenes
Soria
1193m
Fataga
Agüimes
Mogán
Santidad
1099m
Lomo de los Letreros
Punta del Cerrillo
810
Ayagaures
Garita
Sardina
Cercado del Espino
Parque Ornitológico
1001m
Puercos
El Doctoral
Lighthouse
La Playa de Veneguera
Tauro
Cañon del Aguila
Cruce de Sardina
Puerto de Mogán
812
Sioux City
GC1
Arinaga
812
Aeroclub de Gran Canaria
Puerto Rico
Punta de Puerto Rico
62
Playa del Inglés
812
Maspalomas
Punta del Parchel
Lighthouse
Punta de Maspalomas
Km 5 10

(0034) 928 219 600 • (0034) 928 219 601 • www.canarias-turismo.com

27

The Sahara

The central corridor extending from the Mediterranean south to the heart of Africa offers some of Africa's finest desert panoramas, covering as it does so much of the great Sahara, which reaches across North Africa to create the world's most extensive desert. The proximity to Europe and the cultural diversity of nations that occupy this stark but beautiful space have meant that the sands of Libya, Chad and Niger have seen an endless stream of hard-fought battles and fruitless wars, the remnants of which still plague parts of the region today. The long-standing disputes that have arisen as a result of Chad's long civil war, Libya's dubious foreign policy and Niger's Tuareg uprising have meant that security is at times precarious, causing concern for the safety of Western travellers. Because of the volatility of the political situation, Libya is, perhaps not altogether fairly, considered a rather risky travel destination.

NIGER

NIAMEY
Nestled on the edge of the Sahara and enclosed by the stark beauty of the desert, Niamey is a delightful blend of the old and new. With a population of over half a million, the city was declared the nation's capital in the 1920s and boasts adequate visitor's facilities, while retaining much of its desert character and African charm. The second-largest country in West Africa, and Africa's main producer of uranium, Niger plays an important role in the regional economy. It is a pretty enough place with great markets, such as the Grand and Petit Marchés, and a few surprising highlights, most notably the National Museum complex.

TÉNÉRÉ DESERT
The rolling dunes of this remote region – dotted with small herds of gazelle, occasional oases and small fields of vegetables and wheat – hide centuries-old tracks of camel caravans. The panorama of massive dunes is ever changing, and all life is susceptible to the whims of a sandstorm and the rare downpour of seasonal rains. The winds that whip across the vast emptiness produce a strange hum or whistle, almost unnoticed by the groups of nomadic Tuareg (a proud race of the Sahara's Berber people). Dressed in flowing robes like Lawrence of Arabia, Berbers live a Spartan life, constantly on the move across the searing sands. Great stretches are rarely broken by a single bush, shrub or tree, and pivotal to existence here is the hardy camel, bought, sold and milked at every oasis or village. Vast tracts of sand alternate with rock-strewn piste, many decorated with rock paintings illustrating cattle, giraffe, and even ostrich.

DJADO
Well off the beaten tourist track is one of the country's most intriguing, yet least visited, cultural attractions. This is the village of mud huts erected some 700 years ago by the Toubou people. Set against a backdrop of rugged mountainscape and barricaded from civilization by an expanse of wild and windy wasteland, the sense of isolation here is bewildering, the long-abandoned homes of crumbling mud and primitive bricks haunted by an eerie silence. Virtually unchanged since the convoluted labyrinth of cave-like dwellings were deserted by their occupants more than two centuries ago, the wind and elements have taken their toll on the walls and foundations of the huts that still stand atop the hill. The mystical aura that pervades the mud homes of Djado is one that can only be found on the desert dunes of Africa at its emptiest.

AGADEZ
In a region of desolate plains circled by imposing volcanic peaks, framed by the Aïr mountains, ancient Agadez was one of the most vibrant centres in the southern desert. For centuries, the booming town was the congregation point for travellers and traders, and an important centre for desert wanderers and merchants. The bustling town is as picturesque as any cinematographer would have us believe, while centuries of trade and travel have created a latter-day population that is a mix of people and languages. The desert architecture is typical of the Sahel, and the 500-year-old minarets of the Grand Mosque were revered as one of the finest Muslim places of worship on the continent.

NIGER RIVER
One of Niger's few reliable water sources, the Niger River is the lifeblood of a nation plagued by drought and uncertain rainfall. It passes through Mali into the southwest corner of Niger and on to Nigeria, its waters integral to the survival of fishing villages, farming communities and settlements on its banks. The river's course remains one of the least explored in modern history, despite the many camel caravans, intrepid explorers and modern-day adventurers that ply its waters. The river's waters irrigate the lands alongside, helping to balance the erratic rains, leaving the rice paddies lush and verdant. The health of the river is preserved largely by the bourgou grass that covers sections of its flood plains, providing the staple fish diet of locals, fodder for cattle and a breeding ground for aquatic life.

CHAD

N'DJAMENA
The principal city of one of the most impoverished nations in Africa, N'Djamena has few natural resources, endures a punishing climate and has suffered enormously through a 25-year civil war – yet it is one of the most gratifying destinations on the outskirts of the Sahara. Its buildings are scarred by bullets and shrapnel, and many are dilapidated and run down. The central urban district still struggles with substandard accommodation, petty crime, prostitution, and soldiers who will not hesitate to draw their weapons for the slightest transgression. Nonetheless, a renewed life pervades the city streets, and the severely pillaged National Museum is taking on a more alluring look, boasting some fine exhibits and displays.

LAKE CHAD
Although scenically splendid and uniquely picturesque, in stark contrast to the natural splendour of the magnificent Tibesti mountain range in the country's northern reaches, Lake Chad is a popular getaway for locals in southern Libya. For foreigners, getting to and from the lake is an arduous task, caught up in red tape and bureaucratic authorities' suspicions

ABÉCHÉ
Surrounded by the desert sands of Libya and some 800km east of N'Djamena, Abéché's stone inlaid walkways and shaded alleys are a long way from its bustling days as a devoutly Muslim settlement (capital of the Ouadaï sultanate and its vital slave trade, and a critical stop on the merchant route that crossed the country en route to the shipping ports along the Indian Ocean). An important Islamic centre, Abéché offers a fascinating insight into the history of both the immediate precinct and the broader region, but is not particularly accommodating to visitors.

LIBYA

TRIPOLI
With a population of just over 1.5 million, Tripoli – with Banghazi, the joint capital of Libya – is one of the most alluring of Africa's great capitals. A thoroughly modern city, with tall contemporary structures, a well-planned infrastructure and latter-day tourist traps, the old section was built on the original site of ancient Oea. The grand old medina is a maze of side streets, darkened doorways and haphazard souks. With a staunchly Muslim community, alcohol is hard to come by, a strict dress code is rigidly adhered to and the rowdy thoroughfares are dotted with a series of charming old mosques that date from the heyday of the Ottomans. The most impressive is the Karamanli Mosque off Green Square which, in turn, is guarded over by the most recognized landmark in Tripoli: the Old Castle – known locally as Assai al Hamra – overlooking both the harbour front and the ancient medina. The city itself is perhaps the region's safest stopover, with a friendly and generally hospitable community who welcome visitors to their almost forgotten home ground. The city and the country can be frustrating to navigate, especially if you are unfamiliar with the language, culture and geography, but as long as you observe the traditions and customs of the locals and reserve judgment on the political situation, it may prove to be one of the safest and most enjoyable destinations in North Africa.

LEPTIS MAGNA
Widely acknowledged as one of the very best surviving Roman ruins in the region – if not the world – and, along with the ancient Greek metropolis of Cyrene, offering some of the finest historical experiences in Africa, the crumbling city of Leptis Magna is undoubtedly one of the highlights on the country's tour route. Situated not far from the town of Al Khums and no more than 120km to the east of the capital, it is a masterpiece of ancient architecture that covers a relatively large stretch of the Libyan interior. Originally erected by the Carthaginian invaders, the Roman town at the mouth of the Wadi Lebda – conveniently positioned into a burgeoning merchant town, dealing in olive oil and grain supplies. Circled by a forest of stately pine trees and stands of olive trees – and within easy access to some of Libya's finest beaches – the ancient archaeological site was well preserved by the encroaching sands and was only discovered in the 20th century.

ACACUS MOUNTAINS
Although the political instability of the broader region hinders access to the Acacus Mountains, the hilly landscape in the far south remains one of Libya's most enduring natural heritage sites, boasting a remarkable array of outstanding prehistoric rock art. The principal human settlement in this desolate wilderness is the small, historic town of Ghat, a dull place aside from the extraordinary desert architecture and some of the Sahara's most spectacularly scenic vistas. The town and the surrounding hillsides are populated by the nomadic Tuareg, many of whom now act as travel guides.

The desert landscape, harsh climate and troubled histories of Libya, Niger and Chad have prevented them from becoming booming tourist destinations, but although there are indeed very real dangers, in many cases these may not be life-threatening, especially as each nation emerges to take advantage of the potential offered by a growing tourism industry.

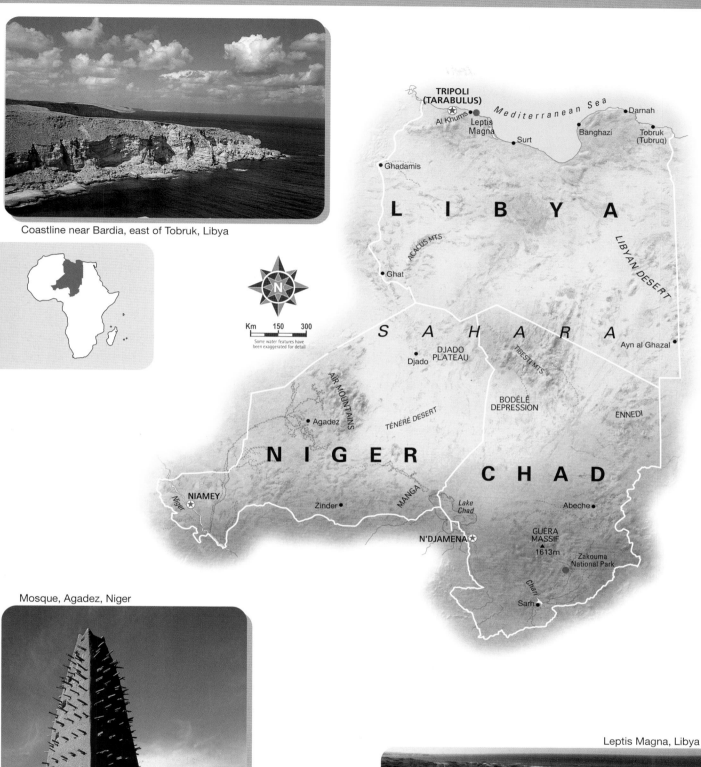

Coastline near Bardia, east of Tobruk, Libya

LIBYA

TRIPOLI (TARABULUS)
Mediterranean Sea
Al Khums
Leptis Magna
Surt
Banghazi
Darnah
Tobruk (Tubruq)
Ghadamis
ACACUS MTS
LIBYAN DESERT
Ghat

Km   150   300
Some water features have been exaggerated for detail

S A H A R A

DJADO PLATEAU
Djado
TIBESTI MTS
Ayn al Ghazal
AÏR MOUNTAINS
BODÉLÉ DEPRESSION
ENNEDI
Agadez
TÉNÉRÉ DESERT

NIGER
CHAD

NIAMEY
Niger
Zinder
MANGA
Lake Chad
Abeche
GUÉRA MASSIF
1613m
Zakouma National Park
N'DJAMENA
Chari
Sarh

Mosque, Agadez, Niger

Leptis Magna, Libya

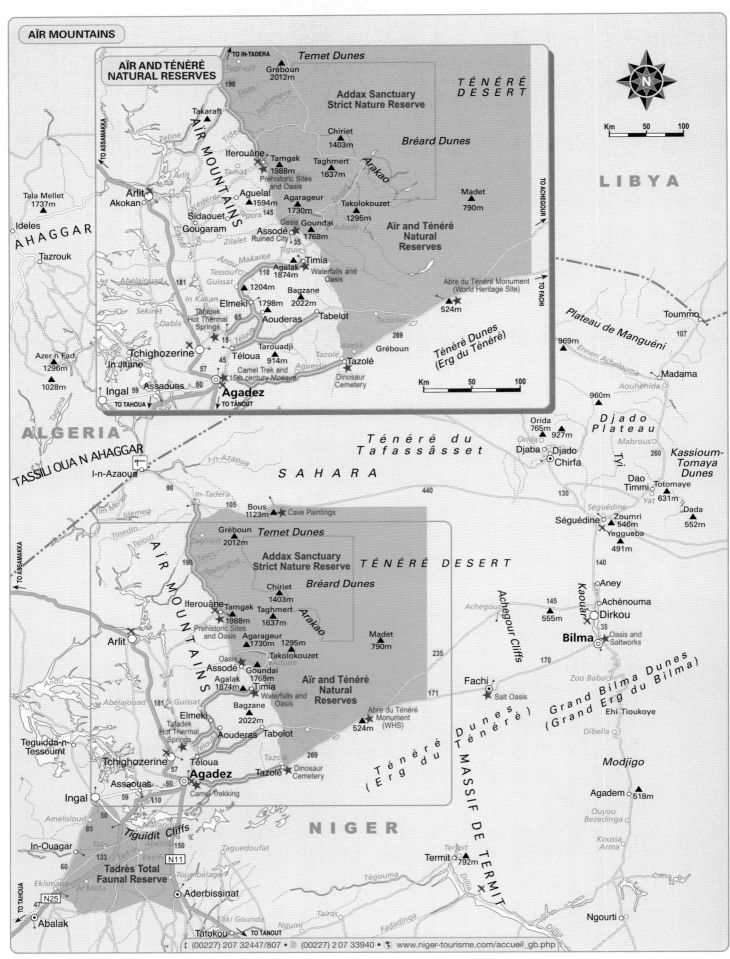

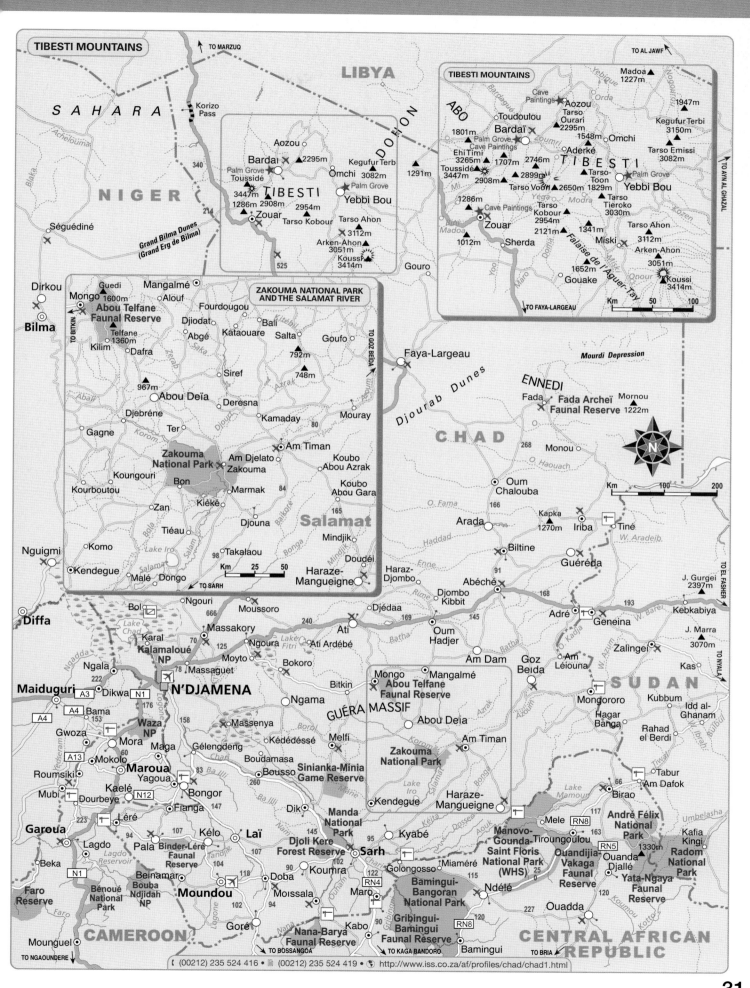

Tripoli Libya

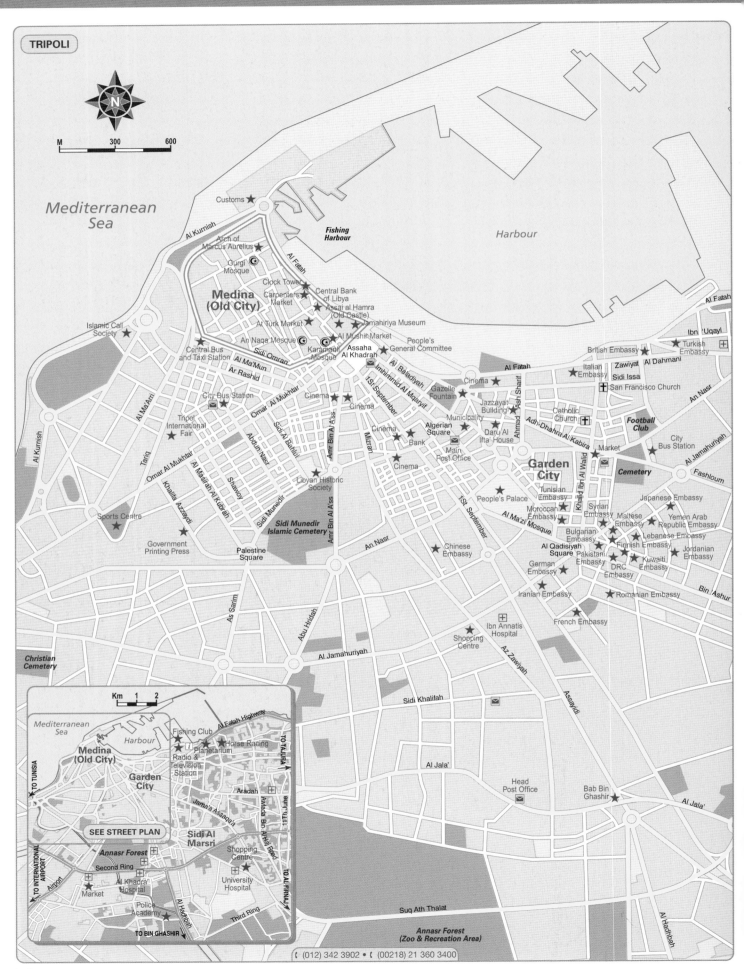

TRIPOLI

M   300   600

Mediterranean
Sea

Customs ★

Fishing
Harbour

Harbour

Al Kurnish

Arch of
Marcus Aurelius ★

Al Fatah

Gurgi
Mosque ©

Clock Tower ©
Carpenters
Market ★

Central Bank
of Libya

Medina
(Old City)

At Turk Market ★

Assai al Hamra
(Old Castle)

Jamahiriya Museum

Al Mushir Market

Al Fatah

Islamic Call
Society ★

An Naga Mosque ©

Karamanli ©
Mosque

Assaha
Al Khadrah

People's
General Committee

Ibn 'Uqayl

Turkish
Embassy

British Embassy ★

Central Bus
and Taxi Station ★

Sidi Omran

Al Ma'Mun

Al Khadrah

Al Baladiyah

Al Fatah

Italian
Embassy ★

Zawiyat Al Dahmani

Sidi Issa

An Nasr

Ar Rashid

Imhimmid Al Mqariyit

Cinema ★

Asr Sharif

San Francisco Church ✝

City Bus Station ✉ ★

Omar Al Mukhtar

Cinema ★

1 St. September

Gazelle
Fountain

Jazzayat
Building

Ahmad

Catholic
Church ✝

Football
Club

Tripol
International
Fair

Sidi Al Bahlul

Cinema ★

Mizran

Cinema ★

Algerian
Square ★

Municipality

Adh-Dhahra Al Kabira

Daru Al
Ifta' House

Khalid Ibn Al Walid

Market

City
Bus Station

Al Jamahuriyah

Abdun Nasr

Shawqy

Bank ★

Main
Post Office ✉

Garden
City

Fashloum

Khalifa Azzaydi

Libyan Historic
Society

Cinema ★

1 St. September

People's Palace ★

Tunisian
Embassy ★

Syrian
Embassy

Japanese Embassy ★

Sports Centre ★

Al Masirah Al Kubrah

Sidi Munedir

Sidi Munedir
Islamic Cemetery

Amr Bin Al A'ss

Moroccan
Embassy ★

Al Ma'zi Mosque

Maltese
Embassy ★

Yemen Arab
Republic Embassy ★

Government
Printing Press ★

Palestine
Square

An Nasr

Bulgarian
Embassy ★

Finnish Embassy ★

Lebanese Embassy ★

Al Qadisiyah
Square

Pakistani
Embassy ★

Jordanian
Embassy ★

Chinese
Embassy ★

German
Embassy ★

DRC
Embassy ★

Kuwaiti
Embassy ★

Bin 'Ashur

Iranian Embassy ★

Romanian Embassy ★

As Sarim

Abu Hiddah

1 St. September

French Embassy ★

Ibn Annatis
Hospital ✚

Shopping
Centre

Az Zawiyah

Al Jamahuriyah

Assaydi

Sidi Khalifah

Sidi Khalifah ✉

Al Jala'

Head
Post Office
✉

Bab Bin
Ghashir ★

Al Jala'

Christian
Cemetery

Inset map

Km 1 2

Mediterranean
Sea

Harbour

Medina
(Old City)

Garden
City

TO TUNISIA

Fishing Club ★

Horse Racing ★

Planetarium ★

Radio &
Television
Station

Aradah ✚

Al Fatah Highway

TO TAJURA

1 St. June

Awlada Bin Awjaj Raed

Jama'a Assaqa'a

TO AL FIRNAJ

SEE STREET PLAN

Sidi Al
Marsri

Shopping
Centre ✚

Al Jala'

Suq Ath Thalat

Annasr Forest ✚

Second Ring

Al Khadra'
Hospital ✚

TO INTERNATIONAL
AIRPORT

Airport

Market ★

University
Hospital ✚

Police
Academy ★

Al Hadhbah

Third Ring

TO BIN GHASHIR

Annasr Forest
(Zoo & Recreation Area)

Al Hadhbah

☎ (012) 342 3902 • ☎ (00218) 21 360 3400

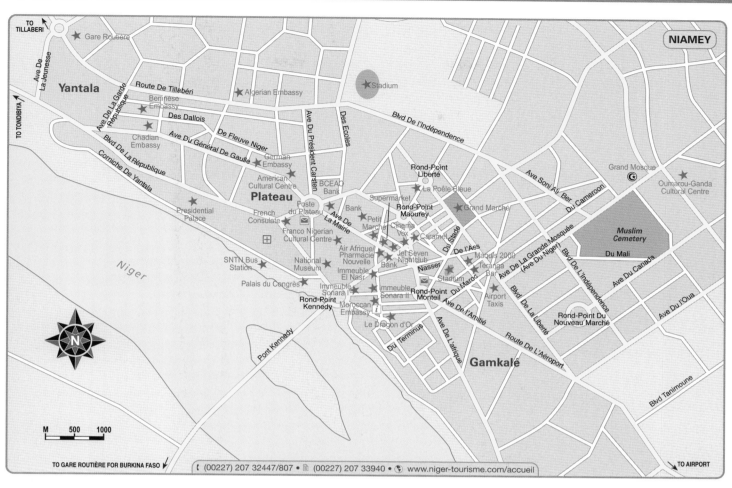

NIAMEY

TO TILLABÉRI

TO TONDIBIYA

Yantala

Gare Routière

Route De Tillabéri

Algerian Embassy

Stadium

Blvd De l'Indépendance

Ave Soni Ali Ber

Grand Mosque

Oumarou-Ganda Cultural Centre

Ave De La Garde République

Béninese Embassy

Des Dallois

Ave Du Général De Gaulle

De Fleuve Niger

Des Écoles

Ave Du Président Carsten

German Embassy

Rond-Point Liberté

Du Cameroon

Chadian Embassy

Blvd De La République

American Cultural Centre

Plateau

BCEAO Bank

La Poêle Bleue

Ave De La Grande Mosquée (Ave Du Niger)

Muslim Cemetery

Du Mali

Corniche De Yantala

Poste du Plateau

French Consulate

Bank

Supermarket

Rond-Point Maourey

Grand Marché

Blvd De l'Indépendance

Ave Du Canada

Presidential Palace

Franco Nigerian Cultural Centre

Ave De La Maire

Petit Marché

Cinéma Vox

Caramel

Du Stade

De l'Ass

Maquis 2000

Ave Du l'Oua

Niger

SNTN Bus Station

National Museum

Air Afrique/Pharmacie Nouvelle

Jet Seven Nightclub

Nasser

Teranga Bar

Blvd De La Liberté

Rond-Point Du Nouveau Marché

Palais du Congrès

Immeuble El Nasr

Bank

Stadium

Du Maroc

Airport Taxis

Rond-Point Kennedy

Immeuble Sonara I

Immeuble Sonara II

Rond-Point Monteil

Ave De l'Amitié

Route De L'Aéroport

Moroccan Embassy

Le Dragon d'Or

Ave De l'afrique

Gamkalé

Pont Kennedy

Du Terminus

Blvd Tanimoune

N

M   500   1000

TO GARE ROUTIÈRE FOR BURKINA FASO

TO AIRPORT

(00227) 207 32447/807 • (00227) 207 33940 • www.niger-tourisme.com/accueil

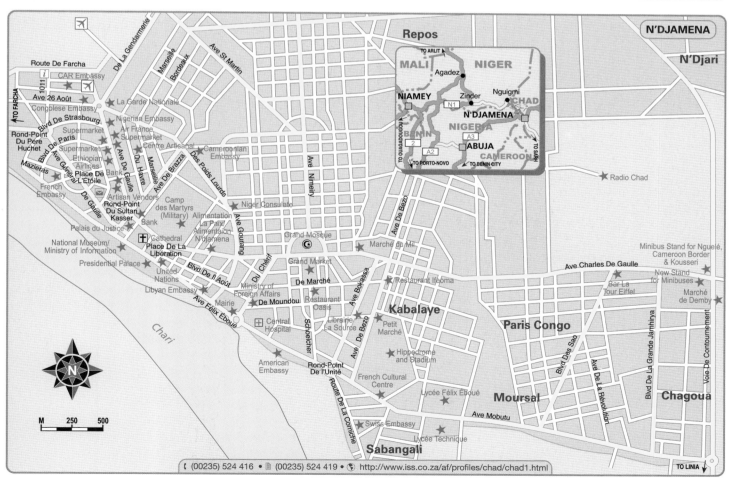

N'DJAMENA

Repos

N'Djari

Route De Farcha

CAR Embassy

TO FARCHA

Ave 26 Août

De La Gendarmerie

Marseille

Bordeaux

Ave St Martin

MALI   NIGER

TO ARLIT

Agadez

Congolese Embassy

La Garde Nationale

NIAMEY

Zinder

Nguigmi

CHAD

Blvd De Strasbourg

Nigerian Embassy

Air France

Supermarket

N1

Rond-Point Du Père Huchet

Supermarket

Paris

Centre Artisanal

Camerounian Embassy

NIGERIA

Ave Niméiry

N'DJAMENA

A3

ABUJA

CAMEROON

TO SARH

Ethiopian Airlines

Bank

Mazieras

Place De L'Étoile

Des Poids Lourds

BENIN

2

A2

TO OUAGADOUGOU

TO PORTO-NOVO

TO BENIN CITY

Radio Chad

French Embassy

Rond-Point Du Sultan Kasser

Du Havre

Marseille

Ave De Brazza

Niger Consulate

De Gaulle

Artisan Vendors

Bank

Camp des Martyrs (Military)

Alimentation La Paix

Alimentation N'djamena

Ave Goutang

Ave De Bezo

Minibus Stand for Nguelé, Cameroon Border & Kousséri

Palais du Justice

National Museum/Ministry of Information

Cathedral

Place De La Libération

Grand Mosque

Marché du Mil

Ave Charles De Gaulle

New Stand for Minibuses

Presidential Palace

United Nations

Blvd De Il Août

Grand Market

Restaurant Ifeoma

Bar La Tour Eiffel

Marché de Demby

Libyan Embassy

Ministry of Foreign Affairs

De Marché

Restaurant Oasis

Ave Bokassa

Kabalaye

Paris Congo

Chari

Mairie

De Moundou

Ave Félix Éboué

Central Hospital

Librarie La Source

Petit Marché

Blvd Des Sao

Blvd De La Grande Jamhirya

Chagoua

American Embassy

Rond-Point De l'Unité

Hippodrome and Stadium

Ave De la Révolution

Voie De Contournement

Schoelcher

Ave Bezo

French Cultural Centre

Lycée Félix Éboué

Moursal

Swiss Embassy

Ave Mobutu

Route De La Corniche

Lycée Technique

N

M   250   500

Sabangali

TO LINIA

(00235) 524 416 • (00235) 524 419 • http://www.iss.co.za/af/profiles/chad/chad1.html

Adventures

Adventure	Country	Duration
Discovering the Niger River from Niamey	Niger & Nigeria	1 - 14 days
Camel Trekking the Ténéré Desert	Niger	3 - 7 days
Driving Libya's Mediterranean Coast	Libya	3 - 5 days
Exploring Libya's Desert Towns from Birak	Libya	1 day +
Crossing Libya's Acacus Mountains	Libya	3 days +
Discovering Lake Chad	Chad	4 hours +

Discovering the Niger River from Niamey

Requirements:
Passports, visas and yellow-fever certificates are essential – officials may want to see a return ticket. Although the capital is relatively safe, take no chances with bureaucracy.

Climate:
Days can be warm, but being on the water means that temperatures are moderate, particularly during the rains. Best time to canoe is October–May, when the water levels have risen.

Risk factor:
Although large tracts wind through open savanna, certain sections cut through forested banks and there may be several rapids. Most are simple to navigate, but a few may be challenging, especially after good rains.

Health:
The Niger is relatively clean with no real health hazards for swimmers. Hippos should be avoided, although they tend to stay well clear of boats.

Pack:
You will need your own tent, camping equipment and food rations, with a set of waterproof clothing for canoeing and a set of warm clothing.

Facilities:
Facilities are generally basic but adequate, with no five-star treatment. Aim to be entirely self-sufficient.

Contact:
Niger Car Voyages, Avenue de l'Afrique.
Tel: 00227-732-331

Camel Trekking the Ténéré Desert

Requirements:
Passports, visas and yellow-fever certificates are essential – officials may want to see a return ticket. To cross the Ténéré you need a local guide, and police insist you travel in convoy. Take no chances.

Climate:
Conditions are unbelievably hot and dry. Best times to visit are the coolest months: November–January.

Risk factor:
At certain points you will have to report to the Gard Nomadique, the Niger desert police, but this is simply a formality and there should be no complications, especially if travelling with a local guide. Extreme caution is advised in the desert, with careful planning.

Health:
Drink lots of fluids. Respect the environment and the military.

Pack:
Pack clothes to cater for extreme temperatures, plus sunscreen, protective headgear, water and a first-aid kit.

Facilities:
A number of international agencies offer carefully planned and well-executed tours into desert regions. Niamey and other large settlements offer alternatives, but are not always reliable.

Contact:
Nigercar-Voyages, Avenue de l'Afrique.
Tel: 00227-732-331

Driving Libya's Mediterranean Coast

Requirements:
Visitors will need a letter of invitation from a Libyan citizen and a visa – neither are easy to obtain. Extreme caution should be taken when travelling and all necessary documentation must be verified and approved prior to departure. You need a permit to drive on Libya's roads, plus a desert permit and a local guide to ride off-road.

Climate:
Best time to drive the coast is November–January.

Risk factor:
Libya is difficult to travel in, so visitors are urged to use an operator with reliable links to a Libyan agency. Off-road driving is controlled and fuel stops congregate on main routes only.

Health:
There are few health risks, but confirm with your operator in advance.

Pack:
The coast is well developed, so items should be available in big towns.

Facilities:
English is rarely spoken, so independent travel is near impossible. Without a knowledgeable guide, even basic requirements are hard to obtain.

Contact:
Libyan Tourism Treasures,
25 Shari'a, Istanbul, Tripoli.
P.O. Box 5144, Tripoli.
Tel: 00218-21-444-9199

Exploring Libya's Desert Towns from Birak

Requirements:
Visitors will need a letter of invitation from a Libyan citizen and a visa – neither are easy to obtain. Caution should be taken when travelling and all necessary documentation must be verified and approved prior to departure. You need a desert permit and a local guide to ride off-road.

Climate:
Best time to enter the Libyan desert is in winter, when conditions are cooler. Nights and early mornings are generally cold throughout the year.

Risk factor:
Libya is difficult to travel in, so visitors are urged to use an operator with reliable links to a Libyan agency. Off-road driving is controlled and fuel stops congregate on main routes only.

Health:
Other than standard precautions, there should be few health risks when crossing the desert. Confirm the status of the area as conflicts tend to erupt.

Pack:
Be as self-reliant as possible, even when travelling with an operator.

Facilities:
English is rarely spoken, so independent travel is near impossible.

Contact:
Coast and Desert Travel,
P.O. Box 3139, Tripoli.
Tel: 00218-21-444-0029

Crossing Libya's Acacus Mountains

Requirements:
Visitors will need a letter of invitation from a Libyan citizen and a visa – neither are easy to obtain. Caution should be taken when travelling and all necessary documentation must be verified and approved prior to departure. You need a desert permit and a local guide to ride off-road.

Climate:
The Acacus Mountains and the Fezzan are hot, dry and windswept.

Risk factor:
Desert winds can play havoc with vehicles and movement may be severely restricted. Civilization is sporadic, and any supplies or spare parts take some time to reach these outposts – if at all. Off-road driving is controlled, and fuel stops tend to congregate only around principal towns.

Health:
Other than standard precautions, there should be few health risks when crossing the desert. Confirm the status of the area as conflicts tend to erupt.

Pack:
Be as self-reliant as possible, even when travelling with an operator – an option that is highly recommended.

Facilities:
English is rarely spoken, so independent travel is near impossible.

Contact:
Akakus Tours, Tripoli, Libya.
Tel: 00218-274-2813 / 04

Discovering Lake Chad

Requirements:
A yellow-fever certificate is essential and you may be required to produce proof of a cholera inoculation. All visitors – except French and German citizens – need a visa. Travellers need to register immediately with N'Djamena's immigration office.

Climate:
Days can be uncomfortably hot, but time on the water allows for cooler conditions. October–April are best.

Risk factor:
Although much of Chad is volatile, N'Djamena and its surrounds are relatively trouble-free. Confirm status with your agent and relevant authorities.

Health:
Malaria remains a problem. Cholera is a hazard, but it is unlikely to affect fleeting visitors aware of the dangers. Take water purification tablets.

Pack:
Take anything you think you may need as the region is virtually devoid of infrastructure. Sunscreen and protective clothing are advisable.

Facilities:
Western-style facilities are virtually non-existent, and what is available is basic and best avoided. Try to be as self-sufficient as possible.

Contact:
Department of Tourism and Parks, B.P. 86, N'Djamena, Chad.
Tel: 00235-512303 / 5 / 524470 / 416

The Nile Valley

Nestled in the bowl of the great Nile Basin, Egypt and Sudan are both hot and, at times, stifling. Both nations have as many differences as similarities and, although they may be neighbours, the topography of the land and the political landscape are quite disparate. Although rain is scarce throughout much of Egypt and northern Sudan, the southern reaches of Sudan – covered by grassland, savanna, forest and marsh – may experience rainfall for as much as eight months of the year. Their governments are equally diverse – Egypt is a relatively stable republic, largely pro-West and with a history of ethnic tolerance, while military Islamic fundamentalists have governed Sudan since 1989. Sudan has also been plagued by civil unrest between Arab Muslims in the north and African Christians in the south since 1983. Although travel to Egypt remains an important earner of foreign income, security fears have had some effect in recent years, and travel in Sudan may still be risky.

EGYPT

CAIRO

The largest city in Africa as well as the Middle East, Cairo is a delightful clamour of taxis and traffic, sights, sounds and smells, and is home to 16 million Egyptians. Its shimmering skyline is a rich amalgamation of modern highrises and rickety flat-topped dwellings, many of which trace their origins back centuries and even tens of centuries. Cairo is a traveller's delight, providing a fascinating look into the age-old empire of the pharaohs, with markets, museums and music conjuring up the spirits of the ancients. Among Cairo's great treasures is the mosque of El Azhar, founded more than 1,000 years ago and still the religious centre of Islamic Cairo. Another is the bustling Khan el Khalili bazaar, the commercial heart of the city.

PYRAMIDS AT GIZA

Approximately 17km to the west of Cairo's famed university, and accessible from the capital by either bus or taxi, stand the Great Pyramids at Giza, acclaimed by the ancients as one of the Seven Wonders of the World. The entire conurbation of antediluvian tombs, seemingly swathed in mystery, is spellbinding in its stature. The monumental Sphinx, along with the conical mausoleums of Cheops and Chephren that pierce the desert sky, form El Giza's imposing centre. So ancient are these magnificent structures that, though they were built adjacent to the Nile, over the centuries the river has meandered over 5km away. Greek myth has it that the Sphinx (meaning 'to hold fast') guarded ancient Thebes, killing any traveller unable to answer her puzzling riddle – until the mythological Oedipus correctly answered the riddle. The Sphinx then killed herself.

VALLEY OF THE KINGS

Although the valley on the west bank of Luxor is barren and apparently lifeless, it is home to one of the most unashamed treasures of the ancient world: a series of long-forgotten crypts crowned by the breathtaking tomb of Tutankhamun, the boy-god-king who died at the tender age of 19. This most spectacular of all the ancient tombs was first discovered and opened in 1922 by Howard Carter. The four diminutive rooms within the tomb revealed an unparalleled hoard of astounding artefacts and magnificent jewels that had been buried with the young pharaoh who lived during one of the most splendid periods of ancient Egypt.

SINAI

The rocky, undulating landscape of this mountainous peninsula in northeastern Egypt is situated at the northern end of the Red Sea, flanked by the gulfs of Suez and Aqaba. The imposing edifice of Jebel Musa stands 2,285m high, making it one of Egypt's highest mountains and the spiritual heart of the rugged peninsula. It was immortalized in scripture as Mount Sinai, where God gave the Judaic leader Moses the stone tablets that bore the Ten Commandments.

RED SEA

The blue water of the Red Sea – a long, narrow stretch of water separating Arabia from northeast Africa – is an underwater wonderland of marine gardens, mesmerizing schools of fish, spectacular dive sites and some of the finest coral reefs in the world. Fringing the bewitching desert and the jagged horizon of the highlands, the 438,000km² of the Red Sea is said to be anything from 20 to 40 million years old. It links with the Mediterranean in the north via the Suez Canal and spills out into the Indian Ocean in the south. It takes its name from its occasional red appearance as algae congregate in surface waters. The reefs here are festooned with magnificent corals and bursts of colour that originate from the amazing aquatic life. The sandy depths of the great sea are hunted by lionfish and spotted stingray, and the region is so abundant in wildlife that some of the most respected marine scientists of modern time have spent lifetimes studying the enormous biodiversity of this bowl of water.

ASWAN

Situated just below the Nile's First Cataract, Aswan remains a relatively small town, with a population of about 200,000, yet it plays a vital role in the lives of millions of Egyptians, most of whom draw their power from the Aswan High Dam. Officially opened in 1971, the huge dam forms a reservoir on Lake Nasser and stretches some 480km from the First to the Third Cataract. It was constructed just 6km upstream from the old 1902 dam, and the water remains the centre of life here, with domestic cattle and water buffalo grazing on its endless banks. Mystery writer Dame Agatha Christie penned a portion of Murder on the Nile from her suite in the Cataract Hotel overlooking the First Cataract.

NILE RIVER

In the west lies the great Qattara Depression, a remarkable 133m below sea level, and to the east stretches the Red Sea. While the upper reaches of the river are often very narrow and lined by precipices, the lower valley emerges into the expansive and heavily populated Nile Delta. In contrast to the dry and dusty sands beyond the relatively lush course of the river, no less than 95 per cent of Egypt's population have made their home in the Nile Valley from what comprises only three per cent of the country's landmass.

ELEPHANTINE ISLAND

In the middle of the mighty Nile, opposite the Aswan High Dam – the latter-day successor to the original dam built in 1902, and twice raised during the course of the 20th century – is the ancient settlement of Elephantine Island, whose island fortress of Yebu acted as the border post between Egypt and Nubia.

SUDAN

KHARTOUM

Virtually decimated by the warring Mahdists in 1885, the old city of Khartoum acted as the seat of the Anglo-Egyptian government that ruled Sudan until independence in January 1956, when it became the capital of the largest country in Africa. Nestled into the corner formed by the junction of the Blue and White Nile, Khartoum's population is less than one million, yet it remains the economic hub of the Sudan. Battered by dust storms and suffering precariously low water supplies, the city is picturesque in its own distinct way. Some 80 per cent of the workforce is occupied in farming on just five per cent of the land, growing cotton, peanuts, gum arabic, sugar and the like. Weak global agricultural prices, a limited infrastructure and ruthless climatic conditions have taken their toll on the capital, but an increase in oil production, regular rainfall and foreign investment in local irrigation projects have brought some respite.

MOUNT KINYETI

Standing proudly on Sudan's border with Uganda, Mount Kinyeti is perhaps Sudan's most significant natural landmark, and the 3,187m peak is the nation's tallest. It covers much of the flat countryside to the south of the rather featureless plain, and is bound in the east and west by separate mountain ranges. Surrounded by the tropical landscape of the southern reaches, its relatively lush slopes are sheltered from the harshness that pervades the aridity of the northern plains and stand in stark contrast to the inhospitable terrain that stretches north. Mount Kinyeti is a remarkable unspoiled wilderness but is virtually inaccessible to all but the bravest and most determined traveller.

NUBIAN DESERT

Commonly considered a desert, the Nubian is little more than a vast, virtually horizonless sandstone plateau that stretches across northeastern Africa from the cliffs of the Nile Valley to the shores of the Red Sea. The people here have always been an amalgamation of nomadic groups and subsistence farmers. In recent times the lives of many Nubians were adversely affected by the construction of the reservoir projects at Aswan, when the waters were dammed and thus flooded their traditional farmlands. Fortunately, commerce and the tourist trade now provide the bulk of employment.

OMDURMAN

Situated on the banks of the Nile just north of the capital in central Sudan, this centre of industry and finance is the largest town in the country. Omdurman was the setting for the great Battle of Omdurman in 1898, in which the Mahdi was expelled by the armed forces of Lord Horatio Herbert Kitchener (the 1st Earl of Khartoum and, the head of the Egyptian army). Enjoying a stark yet surprisingly beautiful setting, Omdurman is a significant contributor to the national economy – largely thanks to its proximity to Khartoum and its location on the course of the Nile.

'There was no answer, save the incessant angry murmer of the Nile as it raced around a basalt-walled bend and foamed across a rock ridge half a mile upstream. It was as though the brown weight of the river would drive the white men back to their own country.' Sir Rudyard Kipling, 1890.

Pyramids of Meroe, Sudan

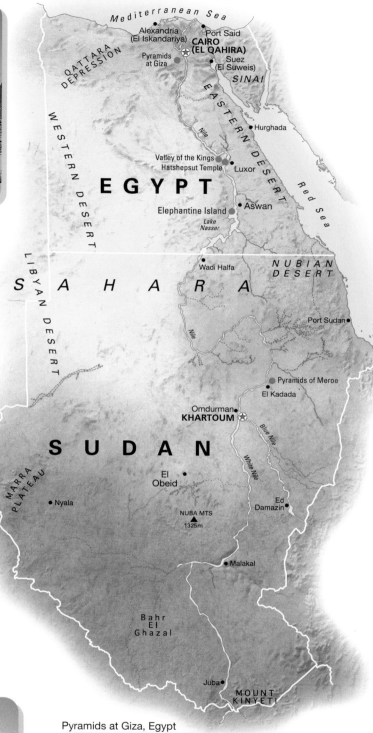

Mediterranean Sea

Alexandria (El Iskandariya)
Port Said
CAIRO (EL QAHIRA)
Pyramids at Giza
Suez (El Suweis)
QATTARA DEPRESSION
SINAI

Hurghada

WESTERN DESERT

Nile

EASTERN DESERT

Valley of the Kings
Hatshepsut Temple
Luxor

E G Y P T

Elephantine Island
Aswan
Lake Nasser

Red Sea

LIBYAN DESERT

Wadi Halfa

NUBIAN DESERT

S A H A R A

Nile

Port Sudan

Pyramids of Meroe
El Kadada

Omdurman
KHARTOUM

Blue Nile

S U D A N

White Nile

El Obeid

Nyala

NUBA MTS
1325m

Ed Damazin

MARRA PLATEAU

Malakal

Bahr El Ghazal

Juba
MOUNT KINYETI

Km   150   300

Some water features have
been exaggerated for detail

Feluccas, Nile River, Egypt

Pyramids at Giza, Egypt

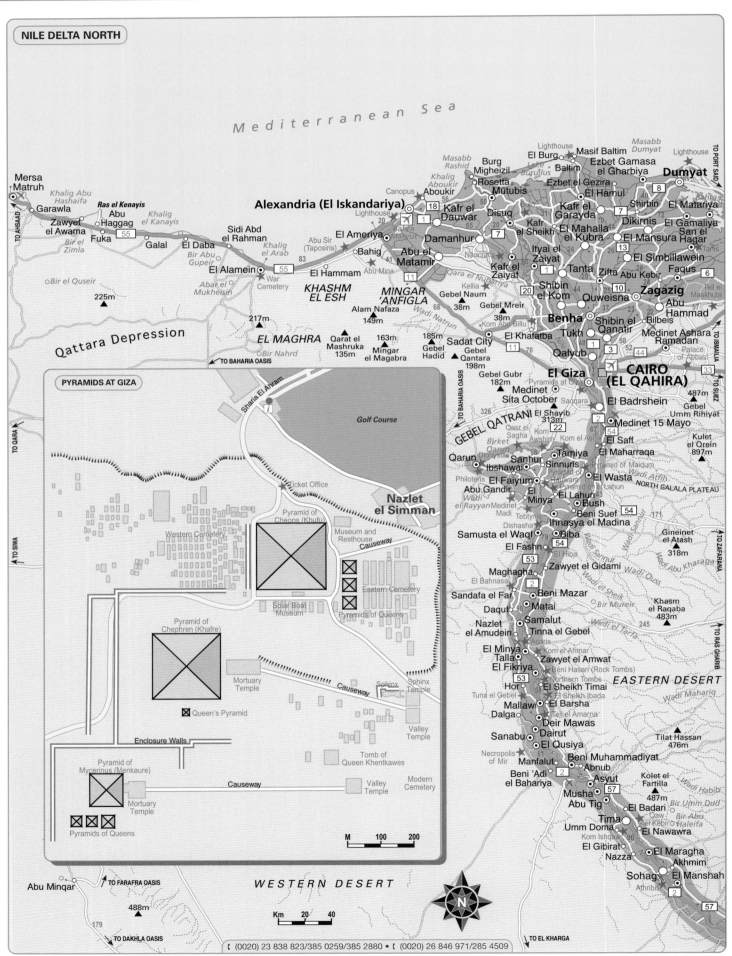

NILE DELTA NORTH

PYRAMIDS AT GIZA

Mediterranean Sea

Golf Course

Western Cemetery

Pyramid of Cheops (Khufu)

Museum and Resthouse

Causeway

Eastern Cemetery

Solar Boat Museum

Pyramids of Queens

Pyramid of Chephren (Khafre)

Mortuary Temple

Causeway

Sphinx

Sphinx Temple

Queen's Pyramid

Enclosure Walls

Valley Temple

Pyramid of Mycerinus (Menkaure)

Mortuary Temple

Causeway

Tomb of Queen Khentkawes

Valley Temple

Modern Cemetery

Pyramids of Queens

Ticket Office

Sharia El Ahram

Nazlet el Simman

M 100 200

Mersa Matruh

Khalig Abu Hashaifa

Garawla

Ras el Kenayis

Abu Haggag

Zawyet el Awama

Khalig el Kanayis

Fuka

El Daba

Galal

Bir el Zimla

El Abu Gupeir

Bir el Quseir

225m

Qattara Depression

217m

EL MAGHRA

Bir Nahrd

Qarat el Mashruka 135m

163m

Mingar el Magabra

TO BAHARIA OASIS

Sidi Abd el Rahman

El Alamein

War Cemetery

55

83

El Hammam

Abu Mina

KHASHM EL ESH

Abu Sir (Taposiris)

Bahig

El Ameriya

MINGAR 'ANFIGLA

Alam Nafaza 149m

185m

Gebel Hadid

Sadat City

Gebel Qantara 198m

Alexandria (El Iskandariya)

Lighthouse

Canopus

Aboukir

20

18

Kafr el Dauwar

Damanhur

7

Kafr el Zaiyat

Naucratis

Qara el Nubariya

Kom Abu Billu

Kom

El Khatatba

Gebel Naum 38m

Gebel Mreir 38m

Masabb Rashid

Khalig Aboukir

Burg Migheizil

Rosetta

Mutubis

Disuq

Lake Burullus

El Burg

Baltim

Masif Baltim

Ezbet el Geziza

El Hamul

Kafr el Sheikh

Kafr el Zaiyat

Ityai el Zaiyat

Shibin el Kom

Quweisna

Benha

24

Tanta

Zifta

Shibin el Qanatir

Tukh

Qalyub

1

Masabb Dumyat

Lighthouse

Ezbet Gamasa el Gharbiya

Dumyat

8

Shirbin

El Mataria

Dikirnis

El Gamaliya

San el Hagar

El Mahalla el Kubra

El Mansura

13

El Simbillawein

Abu Kebir

Faqus

6

Zagazig

Tanis

Tell el Maskhuta

Abu Hammad

Bilbeis

Medinet Ashara Ramadan

TO ISMAILIA

Palace of Abbasi

Gebel Gubr 182m

El Giza

Pyramids at Giza

Saqqara

CAIRO (EL QAHIRA)

33

TO SUEZ

Medinet Sita October

El Badrshein

487m

Gebel Umm Rihiyat

GEBEL QATRANI

Qasr el Sagha

Birket Qarun

Kom Aushim

22

El Shayib 313m

2

Medinet 15 Mayo

54

67

Kulet el Qrein 897m

TO BAHARIA OASIS

Qarun

Dionysias

Ibshawai

Sanhur

Tamiya

Sinnuris

Kom el Asl

El Saff

El Maharraqa

Pyramid of Maidum

El Faiyum

Abu Gandir

Philoteris

Hawara

Pyramid of Lahun

El Wasta

Wadi Atfih

NORTH GALALA PLATEAU

El Minya

Wadi el Rayyan

Medinet Madi

Tebtynis

El Lahun

Bush

Beni Suef

54

Dishasha

Ihnasya el Madina

Gineinet el Atash 318m

TO ZAFARANA

Samusta el Waqf

Biba

El Fashn

54

El Hiba

53

Maghagha

El Bahnasa

2

Zawyet el Gidami

Wadi el Sheikh

Wadi Abu Kharaga

Wadi Quss

Sandafa el Far

Daqut

Samalut

Beni Mazar

Matai

Bir Mureir

Khasm el Raqaba 483m

Nazlet el Amudein

Tinna el Gebel

Acoris

Wadi el Tarfa

245

El Minya

Talla

El Fikriya

Zawyet el Amwat

Beni Hasan (Rock Tombs)

Northern Tombs

EASTERN DESERT

Hor

53

El Sheikh Timai

Tuna el Gebel

El Sheikh Ibada

Wadi Mahariq

Mallawi

Dalga

El Barsha

Tell el Amarna

Deir Mawas

Tilat Hassan 476m

Sanabu

Dairut

El Qusiya

Necropolis of Mir

Manfalut

81

Beni Muhammadiyat

Abnub

2

Beni 'Adi el Bahariya

Asyut

Kolet el Fartilla 487m

Bir Umm Dud

Musha

57

Abu Tig

El Badari

Bir Abu Haleifa

Qaw el Kebir

Tima

Umm Doma

El Nawawra

Kom Ishqaw

96

El Gibirat

El Maragha

Nazza

Akhmim

Sohag

El Manshah

Athribis

2

57

Abu Minqar

TO FARAFRA OASIS

488m

179

TO DAKHLA OASIS

WESTERN DESERT

N

Km 20 40

TO OARA

TO SIWA

TO EL KHARGA

TO RAS GHARIB

TO PORT SAID

TO AHSAAD

(0020) 23 838 823/385 0259/385 2880 • (0020) 26 846 971/285 4509

Nile Valley, Luxor & Thebes   Egypt

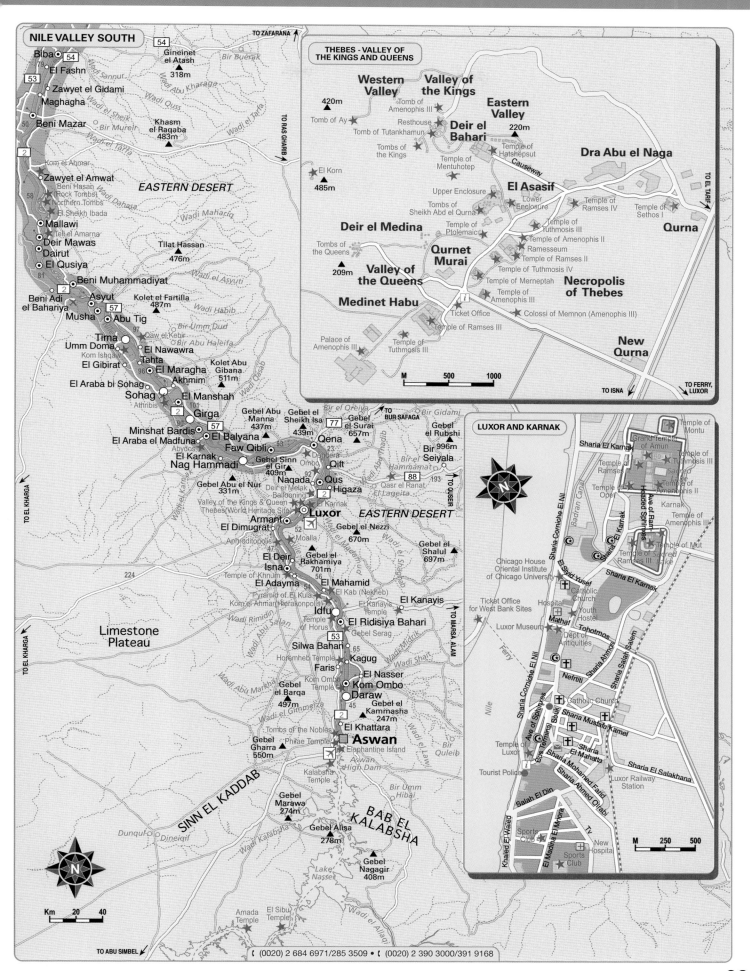

Cairo Egypt

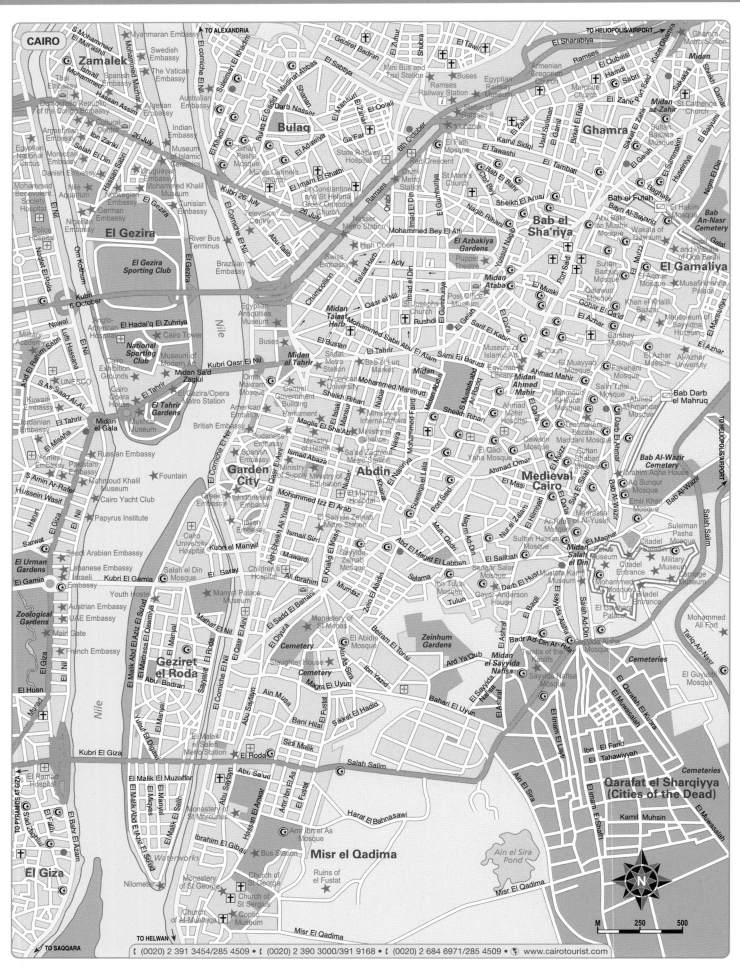

☎ (0020) 2 391 3454/285 4509 • ☎ (0020) 2 390 3000/391 9168 • ☎ (0020) 2 684 6971/285 4509 • 🌐 www.cairotourist.com

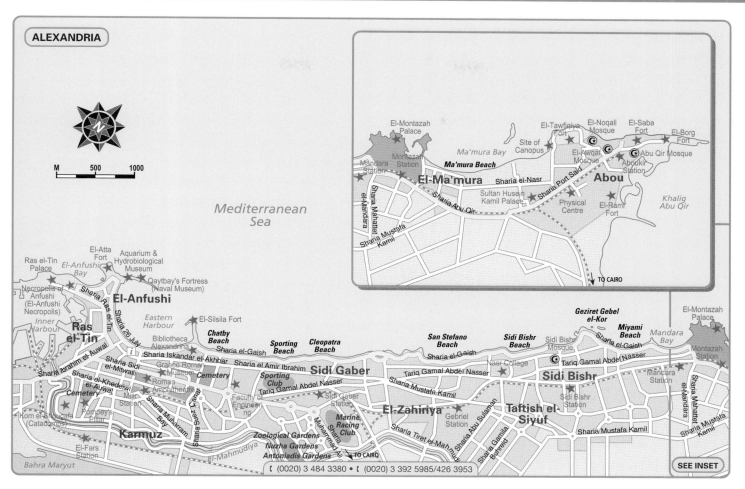

ALEXANDRIA

M 500 1000

Mediterranean Sea

El-Montazah Palace
Montazah Station
Mandara Station
El-Tawfiqiya Fort
El-Noqali Mosque
El-Saba Fort
El-Borg Fort
Ma'mura Bay
Site of Canopus
El-Awqaf Mosque
Abu Qir Mosque
Aboukir Station
El-Ma'mura
Sharia el-Nasr
Sharia Port Said
Abou
Khalig Abu Qir
Ma'mura Beach
Sultan Husein Kamil Palace
Physical Centre
El-Raml Fort
Sharia Mahhatet el-Mandara
Sharia Abu Qir
Sharia Mustafa Kamil
TO CAIRO

Ras el-Tin Palace
El-Atta Fort
El-Anfushi Bay
Aquarium & Hydrobiological Museum
Qaytbay's Fortress (Naval Museum)
Necropolis of Anfushi (El-Anfushi Necropolis)
Sharia Ras el-Tin
El-Anfushi
Inner Harbour
Eastern Harbour
El-Silsila Fort
Ras el-Tin
Sharia 26 July
Bibliotheca Alexandrina
Sharia Ibrahim el-Auwal
Sharia Sidi el-Mitwalli
Sharia Iskander el-Akhbar
Graeco Roman Museum
Sharia el-Gaish
Chatby Beach
Sharia el-Amir Ibrahim
Sporting Beach
Cleopatra Beach
San Stefano Beach
Sidi Bishr Beach
Sidi Bishr Mosque
Geziret Gebel el-Kor
Miyami Beach
Sharia el-Gaish
Mandara Bay
El-Montazah Palace
Montazah Station
Sharia el-Gaish
Sharia el-Khedeiwi el-Auwal
Roman Amphitheatre
Cemetery
Sidi Gaber
Tariq Gamal Abdel Nasser
Nasr College
Tariq Gamal Abdel Nasser
Sidi Bishr
Sidi Bishr Station
Mandara Station
Sharia Mahhatet el-Mandara
Sharia Mustafa Kamil
Kom el-Shoqafa (Catacombs)
Pompey's Pillar
Misr Station
Cemetery
Sharia Muharram
Karmuz
Sporting Club
Tariq Gamal Abdel Nasser
Faculty of Engineering
Sidi Gaber Station
Marine Racing Club
El-Zahiriya
Gebriel Station
Sharia Mustafa Kamil
Taftish el-Siyuf
Sharia Gamila Buhreid
Sharia Mustafa Kamil
El-Fars Station
Sharia Suez Canal
Zoological Gardens
Nuzha Gardens
Antoniadis Gardens
Sharia Muhammad Ali
Sharia Tiret el-Mahmudi
Sharia Abu Sulaman
Bahra Maryut
Sharia el-Mahmudiya
TO CAIRO

SEE INSET

☎ (0020) 3 484 3380 • (0020) 3 392 5985/426 3953

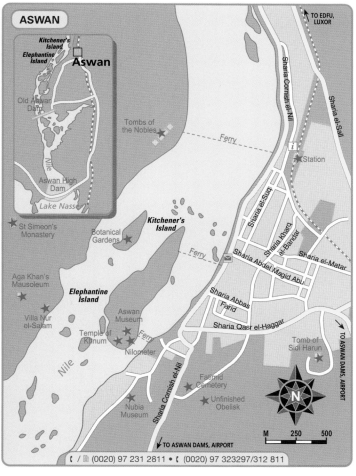

ASWAN

Kitchener's Island
Elephantine Island
Aswan
Old Aswan Dam
Aswan High Dam
Lake Nasser
Nile
TO EDFU, LUXOR
Sharia Cornish el-Nil
Sharia el-Sali
Tombs of the Nobles
Ferry
ℹ Station
St Simeon's Monastery
Botanical Gardens
Kitchener's Island
Ferry
Sharia el-Suq
Sharia Khariq el-Bandar
Sharia el-Matar
Sharia Abdel Magid Abu
Aga Khan's Mausoleum
Elephantine Island
Villa Nur el-Salam
Aswan Museum
Temple of Khnum
Nilometer
Ferry
Sharia Abbas Farid
Sharia Qasr el-Haggar
Tomb of Sidi Harun
TO ASWAN DAMS, AIRPORT
Nile
Nubia Museum
Fatimid Cemetery
Unfinished Obelisk
M 250 500
TO ASWAN DAMS, AIRPORT

☎ / 🖷 (0020) 97 231 2811 • (0020) 97 323297/312 811

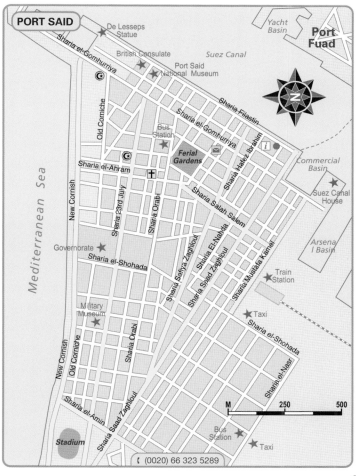

PORT SAID

De Lesseps Statue
Sharia el-Gomhurriya
British Consulate
Port Said National Museum
Suez Canal
Yacht Basin
Port Fuad
Sharia Filastin
Old Corniche
Bus Station
Sharia el-Gomhurriya
Ferial Gardens
Sharia Hafez Ibrahim
ℹ
Commercial Basin
Sharia el-Ahram
Mediterranean Sea
New Cornish
Sharia 23rd July
Sharia Orabi
Sharia Safiya Zaghloul
Sharia Salah Salem
Sharia El-Nahda
Sharia Saad Zaghloul
Sharia Mustafa Kamel
Suez Canal House
Governorate
Sharia el-Shohada
Arsenal Basin
Train Station
Military Museum
Sharia Orabi
Sharia el-Shohada
Taxi
New Cornish
Old Corniche
Sharia el-Amin
Sharia el-Nasr
M 250 500
Stadium
Sharia Saad Zaghloul
Bus Station
Taxi

☎ (0020) 66 323 5289

41

Khartoum Sudan

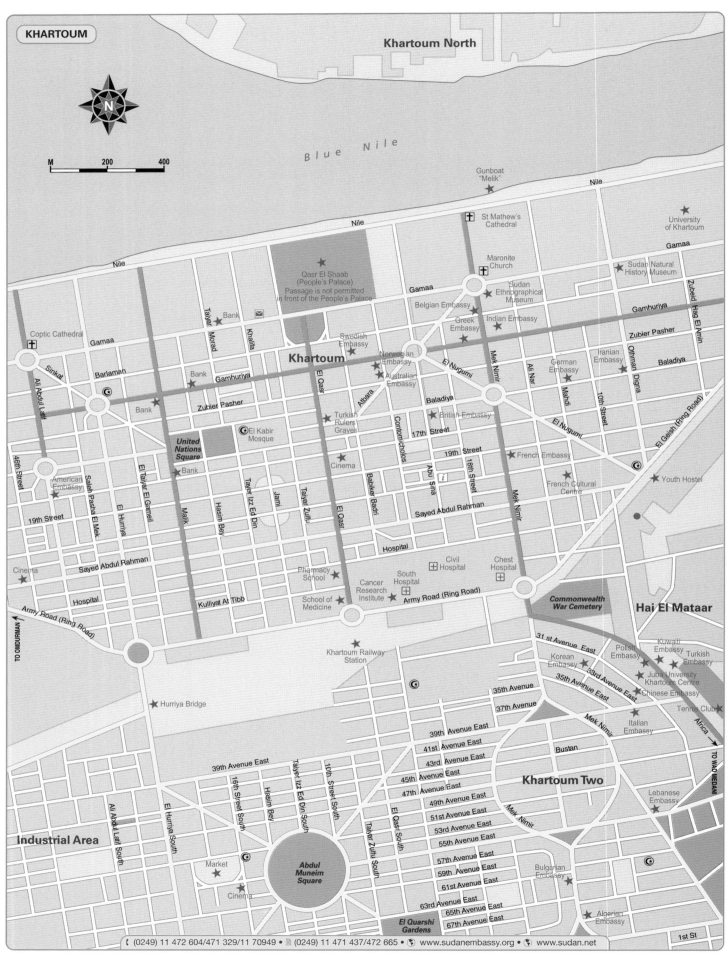

KHARTOUM

Khartoum North

Blue Nile

Nile

Nile

Nile

Gunboat "Melik"

Nile

St Mathew's Cathedral

University of Khartoum

Gamaa

Maronite Church

Sudan Natural History Museum

Qasr El Shaab (People's Palace) Passage is not permitted in front of the People's Palace

Gamaa

Sudan Ethnographical Museum

Belgian Embassy

Zubier Pasher

Zubeid Hag El Amin

Coptic Cathedral

Gamaa

Bank

Taiyar Morad

Khalifa

Swedish Embassy

Khartoum

Greek Embassy

Indian Embassy

Gamhuriya

Sinkat

Barlaman

Bank

Gamhuriya

El Qasr

Norwegian Embassy

El Nugumi

German Embassy

Iranian Embassy

Othman Digna

Baladiya

Ali Abdul Latif

Australian Embassy

Mek Nimir

Ali Nar

10th Street

Bank

Zubier Pasher

Atbara

Baladiya

Mahdi

El Nugumi

El Geish (Ring Road)

Turkish Rulers Graves

El Kabir Mosque

British Embassy

17th Street

Contomicholos

United Nations Square

Cinema

19th Street

18th Street

French Embassy

Youth Hostel

46th Street

Bank

Abu Sina

i

French Cultural Centre

American Embassy

Saleh Pasha El Mek

El Taiyar El Gameli

Malik

Hasim Bey

Tayer Izz Ed Din

Jami

Taiyar Zulfu

El Qasr

Babiker Badri

Sayed Abdul Rahman

Mek Nimir

19th Street

El Huriya

Sayed Abdul Rahman

Hospital

Cinema

Hospital

Kulliyat At Tibb

Pharmacy School

School of Medicine

Cancer Research Institute

South Hospital

Civil Hospital

Chest Hospital

Army Road (Ring Road)

Commonwealth War Cemetery

Hai El Mataar

TO OMDURMAN

Army Road (Ring Road)

Khartoum Railway Station

31st Avenue East

Polish Embassy

Kuwaiti Embassy

Turkish Embassy

Korean Embassy

33rd Avenue East

Juba University Khartoum Centre

Chinese Embassy

Hurriya Bridge

35th Avenue East

35th Avenue

Tennis Club

37th Avenue

Mek Nimir

Italian Embassy

Africa

TO WAD MEDANI

39th Avenue East

39th Avenue East

41st Avenue East

43rd Avenue East

Bustan

16th Street South

Hasim Bey

Taiyar Izz Ed Din South

10th Street South

El Qasr South

Taiyar Zulfu South

45th Avenue East

47th Avenue East

49th Avenue East

Khartoum Two

51st Avenue East

Mek Nimir

53rd Avenue East

Lebanese Embassy

Industrial Area

Ali Abdul Latif South

El Hurriya South

55th Avenue East

57th Avenue East

Market

59th Avenue East

Bulgarian Embassy

Cinema

Abdul Muneim Square

61st Avenue East

63rd Avenue East

65th Avenue East

Algerian Embassy

El Quarshi Gardens

67th Avenue East

1st St

(0249) 11 472 604/471 329/11 70949 • (0249) 11 471 437/472 665 • www.sudanembassy.org • www.sudan.net

42

Adventures

Adventure	Country	Duration
Diving the Red Sea	Egypt	1 day +
Sailing down the Nile Valley	Egypt	2 - 3 days
Crossing the Sinai Desert	Egypt	1 - 2 days
Wreck Diving off the Sudanese Coast	Sudan	1 day
Train Journey from Khartoum to Wadi Halfa	Sudan	7 days +
Ballooning over the Nile's West Bank	Egypt	1 - 3 hours

Diving the Red Sea

Requirements:
Most visitors will need a passport and an easy-to-obtain visa.

Climate:
The climate is dry and hot all year, with temperatures reaching 40ºC in summer and seldom falling below 15ºC in winter.

Risk factor:
The inadequacies of divers pose the most danger. Know your own limits and level of expertise and never dive alone in unknown waters.

Health:
Wash all raw fruit and vegetables and drink only bottled water. Pollution is present but should pose little danger to divers using common sense.

Pack:
Dive operators are generally well equipped and knowledgeable about what is required on diving expeditions. Be sure to use only reputable operators who are well established. Equipment may be hired, often at an additional charge.

Facilities:
Diving facilities range from adequate to impressive. Most dive schools or centres offer courses of various durations and degrees of skill. Accommodation and other amenities are more limited but are also generally more comfortable the further south you dive.

Contact:
Red Sea Diving Club.
Tel: 0020-65-3401551

Sailing down the Nile Valley

Requirements:
Almost all foreign visitors will require a valid passport and a relatively easy-to-obtain visa.

Climate:
The air is hot and humid, so the cooler climes of the Nile Valley have attracted the most attention from visiting adventurers. It can get a little windy, but not enough to cause discomfort.

Risk factor:
Risks are few, but bilharzia is a scourge of the Nile. Both the river and its delta are infested with the disease-carrying mollusc, so swimming is not advised; any protracted contact with the water may be risky.

Health:
Wash all the raw fruit and vegetables you eat and drink only bottled water. Do not swim in the Nile.

Pack:
Take lightweight travelling clothes, and your own bottled water.

Facilities:
Other than the boat ride, few amenities are offered by felucca operators, and you will generally be expected to be self-sufficient. Areas such as Aswan are fairly well geared towards the foreign traveller.

Contact:
Egyptian Tourist Authority,
5 Sharia Adly St, Cairo.
Tel: 0020-2-3913454 / 6846971

Crossing the Sinai Desert

Requirements:
Almost all visitors need a passport and an easy-to-obtain visa.

Climate:
The climate is dry and hot all year, with temperatures reaching 40ºC in summer and seldom falling below 15ºC in winter. Nights on the peninsula can be extremely cold.

Risk factor:
Land mines and bandits are present, so travel in groups or hire an overland operator who knows the area.

Health:
Wash fruit and vegetables and drink bottled water. To avoid heat exhaustion, cover up and drink plenty of fluids.

Pack:
Lightweight (days) and warm (nights) clothing – temperatures drop rapidly. Take sturdy hiking boots and essentials to walk Mount Sinai; a torch and warm clothing for the 'sunrise hike'.

Facilities:
Accommodation is not varied but is adequate – book through a reputable operator. Entry to certain areas, such as Ras Mohammed, will not automatically form part of your Sinai trip – separate arrangements must be made. Special permits are required for camping.

Contact:
Egyptian Tourist Authority,
5 Sharia Adly St, Cairo.
Tel: 0020-2-3913454 / 6846971

Wreck Diving (from Port Sudan) off the Sudanese Coast

Requirements:
All travellers need a visa, and obtaining one can be a lengthy and frustrating process. Travel permits (available in Khartoum) are required for trips beyond the capital. Never rely on flight schedules, and be aware that customs are very strict with even everyday items.

Climate:
Temperatures are warm to hot, with the best months to dive June–July. Water temperatures, partly because of underground volcanic activity, are very warm, peaking at about 30ºC.

Risk factor:
Sharks, lionfish and stinging corals are present, so never take chances.

Health:
Take standard precautions such as drinking only bottled water. Divers may be susceptible to ear infections and the usual risks of diving and snorkelling.

Pack:
Facilities are limited, and divers are advised to take their own equipment and accessories to be self-sufficient.

Facilities:
There are few diving operators, and equipment is non-existent. Bring your own! The best way to dive is from live-aboard boats in Port Sudan.

Contact:
First Class Travel Agency,
P.O. Box 2068, Khartoum, Sudan.
Tel: 00249-1-837-71414

Train Journey from Khartoum to Wadi Halfa

Requirements:
All travellers need a visa, and obtaining one can be a lengthy and frustrating process. Travel permits (available in Khartoum) are required for trips beyond the capital.

Climate:
Dry and inhospitable, with little rain or relief from the harsh sun.

Risk factor:
With some common sense and a sensible itinerary, travellers should face few risks and the train trip is relatively hassle-free. There may be other dangers in Sudan (check with authorities and/or travel agents prior to departure).

Health:
Health risks are few, apart from the standard precautions such as drinking only bottled drinking water.

Pack:
Days can be sweltering even on board the train, but nights are icy. Take your own bedding and food if travelling in 'economy class', although the latter is readily available at the stopover towns.

Facilities:
Amenities are adequate, albeit basic, with a few more comforts enjoyed in the 'luxury class' compartments.

Contact:
First Class Travel Agency,
P.O. Box 2068, Khartoum, Sudan.
Tel: 00249-1-837-71414

Ballooning over the Nile's West Bank (Luxor to Qena)

Requirements:
Most visitors will need a passport and an easy-to-obtain visa.

Climate:
Dry and hot all year, with temperatures reaching 40ºC in summer and seldom falling below 15ºC in winter.

Risk factor:
Risks are few, especially as most balloon trips are short. Pilots are experts who have flown for years, and crews do this every day of their lives.

Health:
Ballooning over Egypt provides no health hazards, as long as passengers have a head for heights. Early-morning air is crisp and generally clean.

Pack:
Dress warmly on departure, but garments should be easily removable as the temperature rises. Binoculars and cameras are invaluable.

Facilities:
These excursions are popular with established package-tour companies, and over the peak tourist seasons (Egypt seems eternally popular with visitors) balloon enthusiasts should make reservations well in advance. Most operators are well organized and hospitable.

Contact:
Balloons Over Egypt,
P.O. Box 52, Sharia Khaled Ibn el-Walid.
Tel: 0020-95-376515 / 0638

The Taoudenni Basin

From the Fulani to the Wolof people, the sands of the Sahara to the Caribbean-like beaches of the Cape Verde Islands, the ancient mosques to the towering office blocks, the vast lands covered by the western Sahara are as diverse as anywhere on the continent. It is a lively mix of vibrant markets, skyscraper-like minarets and charming little museums all clustered together in surprisingly modern cities. Although plagued with political instability in parts, and ravaged by drought and poverty in others, the western Sahara is, in its own way, gentle and unassuming, its rugged landscape crisscrossed by age-old caravan routes and modern highways characteristically lined with stands of palm trees and dusty little villages.

GAMBIA

BANJUL

Dry, dusty and far from beautiful in the conventional sense, the Gambian capital can hardly be considered the tourist hot spot it purports to be, yet it offers a relaxing holiday and UK tourists inject vital foreign currency into Gambia annually. The flooding of the river means that Banjul's urban centre is small and compact, with a distinctly colonial feel, despite the change in street names that now claim to be more representative of the heritage of Gambia's indigenous people. The buildings may be dilapidated and the rains may bring an uncomfortable humidity, but there are interesting excursions into the interior. Banjul is often overlooked by the more worldly traveller, despite its attractive beaches lined with fields of peanut plantations.

GAMBIA RIVER

In an otherwise empty countryside, the Gambia River is undoubtedly the most prominent feature of the landscape and is virtually the only worthwhile attraction. Its modest origins are to be found in the Fouta Djallon highlands of Guinea, more than 500km from its exit into the Atlantic Ocean. The life of virtually every Gambian revolves around the movements of the river, from its tides to its floods. The majority of the nation's people eke out their meagre living in attractive little villages, characteristically rural in nature, on the banks of the river. The shanty towns, rice paddies, water pumps and occasional colonial ruins give some indication of the pivotal role played by the river in the day-to-day lives of Gambians. Mangrove swamps are alive with mud-skippers and crabs, and the towering tree-tops are inhabited by small primates, best seen further inland on the Kombo Peninsula in the Abuko Nature Reserve. The surrounding wildlife sanctuaries comprise either mud flats or dusty savanna, but prove to be gems of indigenous fauna.

MALI

BAMAKO

The principal city of the largest country in West Africa and a converging point of some of the oldest caravan routes across the great Sahara, Bamako is still very locked in its past. Bamako is dirty and shabby, agriculturally completely at the mercy of the elements and riddled with poverty. Wracked by drought and other natural plagues, it is hot and oppressive, crowded and uninviting, with its modernisation process lamentably slow. In the same breath, Bamako is slowly emerging from the dust and sand to take its rightful place as a promising indication of what can transpire in even the most desolate of African destinations. The oases of the desert fringes occur naturally where underground watercourses break through the ground surface, and it is here that palm trees flourish, providing shade and shelter for orchards and vegetable patches that help sustain the local people. Large areas are given over to the commercial cultivation of date palms, which plays a crucial role in the latter-day economy.

SENEGAL

DAKAR

In parts colonial and in others distinctly African, Dakar is possibly the finest capital in West Africa. Still suffering the effects of a troubled history of slavery and human misery, the functional city is a frenzy of energetic crowds and lively banter. High-rise buildings stand proudly alongside charming little homes circled by ramshackle vehicles weaving in and out of traffic that shows no signs of order. As the world slave capital, ancient Dakar is very French and very Muslim, with the distinctive influences of both cultures emerging in the architecture and the cultural heritage of the million-plus population (the majority are made up of the tall and dignified Senegalese). There is a series of small but picturesque beaches and a number of parks, along with museums and places of worship – most notably the Grand Mosque in the old city, or medina. Many of the typical tourist sites are the most impressive in all of West Africa, but it is the life of the city and the ambience lent to it by its people that remain the main attraction. Busy markets, such as at Kermel and Sandaga, remain the lifeblood of the capital.

ÎLE DE GORÉE

The tiny stretch of volcanic rock – no more than 800m long and 300m wide – that emerges from the ocean a few kilometres offshore from Dakar Peninsula is the World Heritage Site known as the Island of Tears, Île de Gorée. As the centre of the highly lucrative slave trade that once ravaged much of Africa, the island remains soaked in the tears of human pain and suffering, and the House of Slaves forms the focal point of this living museum. There are no vehicles on the island, which is punctuated with slave museums, the architecture of the colonial occupants and the much publicized Guns of Navarone. Despite this tormented heritage, there is a passion among the people seldom seen anywhere else in Africa. It is from Gorée that West Africans were shipped off to the cotton plantations of the USA, forever separated from their families, and where over the following centuries they would help to establish one of the world's most diverse cultures.

DOGON COUNTRY

The landscape of Mali's southern reaches is a vast, empty country most noted for the unusual mud configurations that are the dwellings of the Dogon people, constructed along the forms of a female body and steeped in centuries of mystery and wonder. This is Dogon Country, or Pays Dogon, where every Dogon family fashions their collection of mud huts and animal pens according to the structure and scheme of the village. These fascinating remnants of an ancient culture, with their numerous granaries and outbuildings, bear testimony to a rich cultural heritage that remains relatively intact. High above the Seno Plain is a series of cave homes meticulously carved into the towering rock face of the escarpment.

MAURITANIA

NOUAKCHOTT

The capital city of Nouakchott ('place of the wind') is truly unremarkable and is laid-back in every sense, although it is perhaps one of the richest cultural centres in West Africa. Occupied largely by nomadic Moors the itinerant lifestyle of the nation's people means that there are few tangible examples of artistic expression. It is the day-to-day customs and traditions of the locals that make it such a fascinating stopover, particularly for those who are still amazed by the intricacies of African culture and the latter-day adaptions that have ensured the survival of near-forgotten civilizations. Nouakchott today is home to some 30 per cent of the country's population, and the urban development forms the eye of the dust storm and endless sands that surround the biggest city in the Sahara. Slums and unremarkable buildings are counteracted by well-to-do commercial and suburban districts that are home to dignitaries and government officials. There is none of the frenetic activity of other capitals, and the wide streets offer very little interesting activity for tourists or locals. Quiet and even lonely, the only real life focuses on the busy markets that remind you that you are indeed in the heart of Africa. The favourite drawcard is the expansive beach, enclosed by dunes separating the city from the cold waters of the ocean.

ADRAR PLATEAU

Although never extending higher than 1,000m the Adrar Plateau must be Mauritania's most promising wilderness attraction. Blessed with exceptional vistas and panoramas of sweeping dunes and rough-hewn escarpments, the vast flatlands are wild and isolated, dotted with oases and groves of date palms that indicate the existence of some sort of urban settlement. Some of the lonely little towns are dour and uninviting, many no more than ghost towns. The surrounding landscape, punctuated with the odd attraction – such as the ancient Berber ruins at Azougui – is best traversed by 4x4 vehicle, donkey or camel, and features some fine examples of indigenous rock art. Atar provides a pleasant diversion, covering a wide-open space and acting as the centre of life in the country's northern reaches. The prominent tourist stop is the town of Chinguetti, graced with an extraordinary backdrop and once considered one of Islam's most venerated cities, preceded only by Jerusalem, Mecca and Medina.

Although the region covered by the western sands of the great Sahara is a wide-open expanse of desert landscape – fringed in parts by rocky outcrops and isolated stands of scrappy vegetation – it remains one of the most culturally diverse areas on the continent.

Slave House, Île de Gorée, Senegal

Sahara Desert, Mauritania

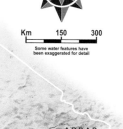

Djin Mosque, Timbuktu, Mali

CAPE VERDE

PRAIA

With a name that means 'beach', it is little wonder that Praia is the pride of Cape Verde, a conglomeration of nine main islands, separated into the Barlaventos (Windwards) and Sotaventos (Leewards). São Tiago is the largest of the islands and, like the others in the group, has only been occupied for the last 500 years. The approximately 4,000km² of land covered by the islands is populated largely by the decendants of emancipated slaves who settled during the reign of Portuguese explorers, and the islands have only recently emerged as a modern democracy. The coastline of São Tiago, on which Praia is situated, is untainted by modern development and offers a number of swimming beaches, with some of the most picturesque coastal landscape of Africa's offshore islands. Boa Vista's beaches are spectacular, and the main attractions are the island's rugged east coast and mountainous interior. Hopping from island to island is also a relatively hassle-free process.

Dogon & Timbuktu Region Mali

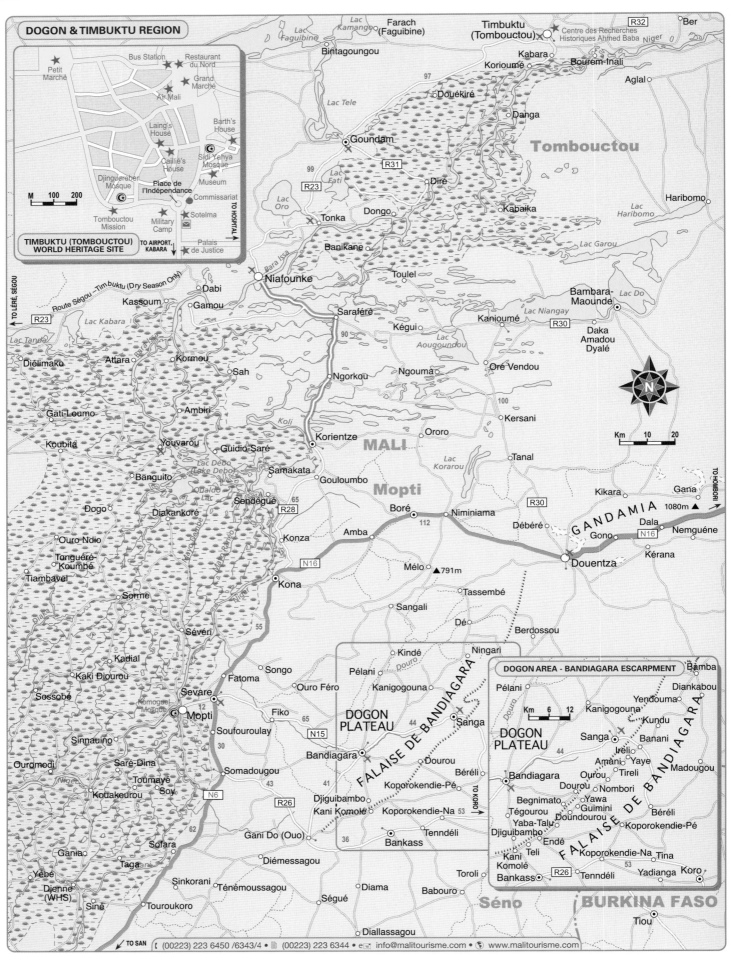

DOGON & TIMBUKTU REGION

Petit Marché
Bus Station
Restaurant du Nord
Grand Marché
Air Mali
Laing's House
Barth's House
Caillié's House
Sidi Yahya Mosque
Djingueréber Mosque
Museum
Place de l'Indépendance
Commissariat
Tombouctou Mission
Military Camp
Sotelma
Palais de Justice
TO HOSPITAL
TO AIRPORT, KABARA

M 100 200

TIMBUKTU (TOMBOUCTOU) WORLD HERITAGE SITE

Farach (Faguibine)
Lac Kamango
Lac Faguibine
Bintagoungou
Timbuktu (Tombouctou)
Centre des Recherches Historiques Ahmed Baba
R32
Ber
Niger
Kabara
Korioumé
Bourem-Inali
Aglal
97
Douékiré
Lac Tele
Danga
Tombouctou
Goundam
R31
Diré
Kabaika
99
Lac Fati
R23
Dongo
Lac Haribomo
Haribomo
Lac Oro
Tonka
Lac Garou
Banikane
Toulel
Bambara-Maounde
Lac Do
Niafounke
Bara Issa
Saraféré
Lac Niangay
Kanioumé
R30
Daka Amadou Dyalé
Dabi
Route Ségou – Timbuktu (Dry Season Only)
Kassoum
Gamou
Kégui
90
Lac Aougoundou
Ngouma
Oré Vendou
R23
Lac Kabara
Diélimako
Attara
Kormou
Sah
Ngorkou
Lac Tanda
100
Kersani
Ambiri
Koli
Gati-Loumo
MALI
Ororo
Tanal
Koubita
Youvarou
Korientze
Lac Debo (Lake Debo)
Guidio-Saré
Lac Korarou
Km 10 20
Banguito
Samakata
Gouloumbo
Mopti
Kikara
Gana
TO HOMBORI
Dogo
Sendégué
65
R28
Boré
Niminiama
R30
1080m
GANDAMIA
Diakankoré
Konza
112
Débéré
Dala
N16
Nemguéne
Ouro Ndio
Amba
Gono
Tonguéré Koumbé
N16
Mélo
791m
Kérana
Tiambavel
Kona
Tassembé
Douentza
Sorme
Sangali
55
Dé
Berdossou
Séveri
Kadial
Kindé
Ningari
DOGON AREA - BANDIAGARA ESCARPMENT
Bamba
Kaki Diourou
Songo
Pélani
Douro
Pélani
Diankabou
Sossobé
Fatoma
Ouro Féro
Kanigogouna
Yendouma
Kanigogouna
Sevare
Km 6 12
Kundu
Sinnauino
Fiko
65
DOGON PLATEAU
44
Sanga
Sanga
Banani
Saré-Dina
Mopti
Komoguel Mosque
Soufouroulay
N15
DOGON PLATEAU
Iréli
Ouromodi
30
Bandiagara
Dourou
Amani
Yaye
Tireli
Madougou
Toumayé
Soy
N6
Somadougou
43
Béréli
Bandiagara
Ourou
Nombori
Kouakourou
Djiguibambo
41
Koporokendie-Pé
Dourou
Yawa
Guimini
Béréli
Gani Do (Ouo)
Kani Komolé
Koporokendie-Na
53
Begnimato
Tégourou
Doundourou
Koporokendie-Pé
Gania
36
Tenndéli
Yaba-Talu
Djiguibambo
Endé
Koporokendie-Na
Tina
Sofara
Bankass
Kani Komolé
Teli
53
Yadianga
Koro
Taga
Diémessagou
Séno
Bankass
R26
Tenndéli
Yébé
Sinkorani
Diama
Babouro
BURKINA FASO
Djenne (WHS)
Ténémoussagou
Ségué
Toroli
Sine
Touroukoro
Tiou
Diallassagou

TO LÉRE, SÉGOU
Niger
Diaka
Niani Bango
Ouaido Lac
Niani Bango
Niger
TO SAN
TO KORO
FALAISE DE BANDIAGARA
FALAISE DE BANDIAGARA

((00223) 223 6450 /6343/4 • ▤ (00223) 223 6344 • e info@malitourisme.com • 🌐 www.malitourisme.com

Banjul
Gambia
Bamako
Mali

Nouakchott
Mauritania

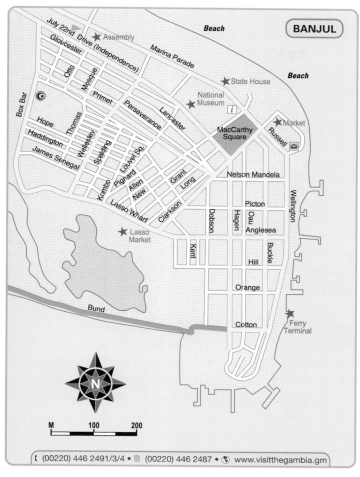

BANJUL

July 22nd Drive (Independence)
Assembly
Beach
Marina Parade
Beach
Gloucester
Otto
Mosque
Primet
State House
Box Bar
Perseverance
Lancaster
National Museum
Thomas
Hope
Haddington
Wellesley
Spalding
Pignard
Allen
New
Grant
Long
MacCarthy Square
Market
James Senegal
Kombo
Lasso Wharf
Clarkson
Nelson Mandela
Russell
Kent
Dobson
Hagen
Oau
Anglesea
Picton
Wellington
Lasso Market
Buckle
Hill
Orange
Bund
Cotton
Ferry Terminal

M   100   200

☎ (00220) 446 2491/3/4 • 🖨 (00220) 446 2487 • 🌐 www.visitthegambia.gm

NOUAKCHOTT

Olympic Stadium
Oiseau de Paradis Restaurant
Senegalese Embassy
Pizza Lena
L'Ambassade Du Sénégal
TO AIRPORT
Route Des Ambassades
Ave Du Général De Gaulle
Restaurant Guervoum
L'Hôtel Halima
Monotel
Moroccan Embassy
Arguin Tours
German Embassy
French Embassy
Malian Embassy
Abdallaye
Spanish Embassy
Alliance Française
St Joseph Cathedral
Mamadou Konaté
American Embassy
Le Bambou Restaurant
National Archives and Direction Artisanat et Tourisme
Restaurant la Dune
Abou Baker
Librairie Vents du Sud
L'Independance
Restaurant le Palmier
AVT/ Soreci Voyages
Grande Mosquée
Mohamed Lemine Sakho
Ali Baba Restaurant
Restaurant Alioune Phenica
La Nouvelle Boucherie
Snack Al Moulouk
Air Algérie
Restaurant Rimal
Air Afrique
TO THE BEACH
Taxis
Beach Taxis
Restaurant-Pâtisserie Andalous
Ave Abdel Nasser
Grand Marché
Bank
GCAL Voyages (Europcar)
Commissariat Central
L'Artisanal Féminin
Museum
Baker Ahmed
Hennoune Ould Bouccif
Wrestling Arena
Restaurant Talba
Racing Club
Ely Ould Mohamed
Restaurant Zoubeida
Ave Kennedy
Bakary Hakna
Mohamed El Habib
L'Independance
Mohamed Lemine Sakho
Stadium
TO BOUTILIMIT
L'Espoir
Moroccan Mosque
Mosquée Marocaine
L'Espoir

M   200   400

☎ (00222) 525 3572 • 🖨 (00222) 525 7671 • 🌐 www.mauritania.mr

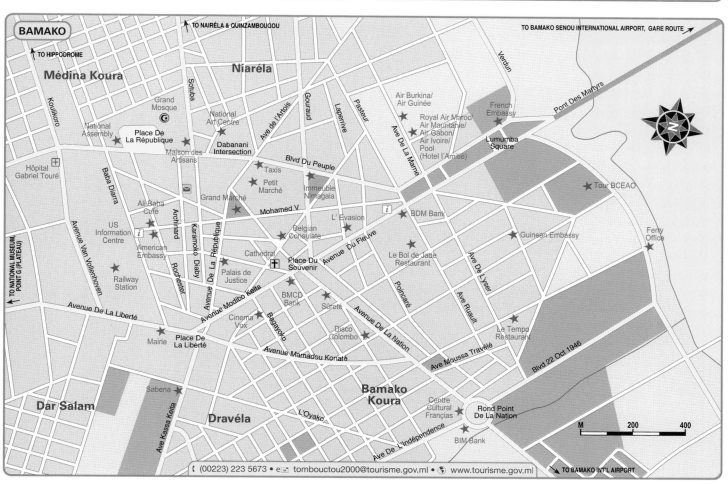

BAMAKO

TO NAIRÉLA & QUINZAMBOUGOU
TO BAMAKO SENOU INTERNATIONAL AIRPORT, GARE ROUTE
TO HIPPODROME
Médina Koura
Niaréla
Verdun
Koulikoro
Grand Mosque
Sotuba
National Art Centre
Ave de l'Artois
Gouraud
Laperrine
Pasteur
Air Burkina/ Air Guinée
Pont Des Martyrs
National Assembly
Place De La République
Dabanani Intersection
Royal Air Maroc/ Air Mauritanie/ Air Gabon/ Air Ivoire/ Pool (Hotel l'Amitié)
French Embassy
Maison des Artisans
Blvd Du Peuple
Ave De La Marne
Lumumba Square
Hôpital Gabriel Touré
Taxis
Petit Marché
Immeuble Nimagala
Baba Diarra
Grand Marché
Ali Baba Café
Archihard
Mohamed V
Tour BCEAO
US Information Centre
Karamoko Diaby
Avenue De La République
L' Evasion
BDM Bank
American Embassy
Cathédral
Rochester
Avenue Van Vollenhoven
Railway Station
Palais de Justice
Place Du Souvenir
Avenue Du Fleuve
Le Bol de Jade Restaurant
Guinean Embassy
Ferry Office
TO NATIONAL MUSEUM, POINT G (PLATEAU)
Avenue Modibo Keita
BMCD Bank
Sûreté
Avenue De La Nation
Poincaré
Ave De L'yser
Avenue De La Liberté
Cinema Vox
Bagayoko
Disco Colombo
Ave Ruault
Le Tempo Restaurant
Mairie
Place De La Liberté
Avenue Mamadou Konaté
Ave Moussa Travélé
Blvd 22 Oct 1946
Sabena
Dar Salam
Dravéla
L'Oyako
Bamako Koura
Centre Cultural Français
Rond Point De La Nation
Ave De L'Indépendance
BIM Bank
TO BAMAKO INT'L AIRPORT

☎ (00223) 223 5673 • 📧 tombouctou2000@tourisme.gov.ml • 🌐 www.tourisme.gov.ml

47

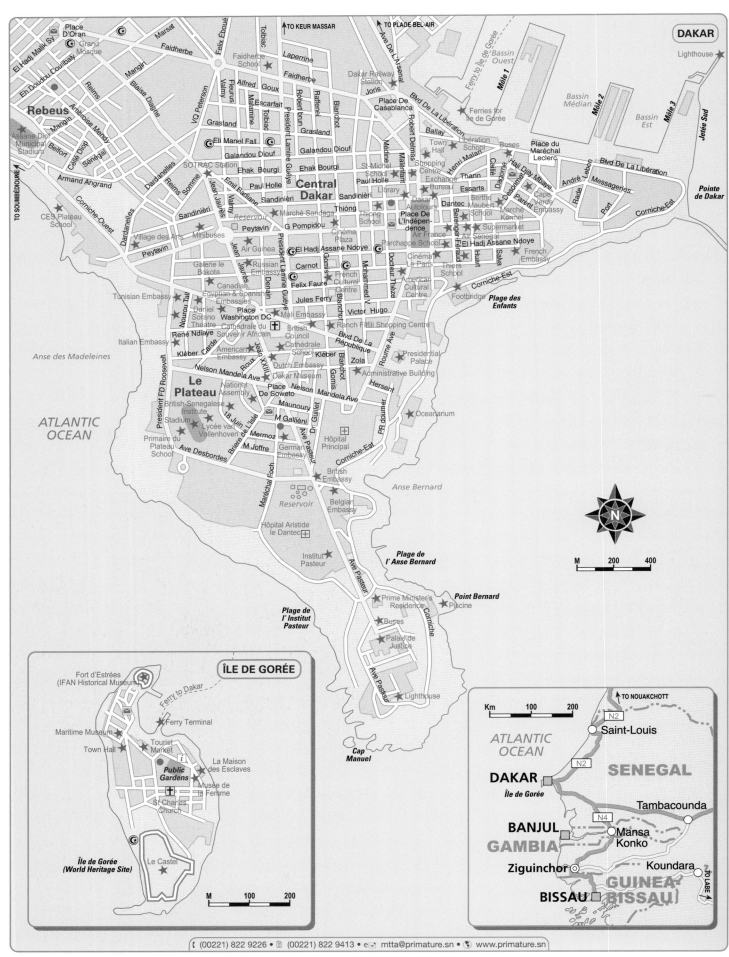

Dakar Senegal

DAKAR

TO KEUR MASSAR
TO PLAGE BEL-AIR

Place D'Oran
Grand Mosque
Marsat
Faidherbe

Rebeus

El Hadj Malik Sy
En Doudou Coulibaly
Mangin
Blaise Diagne
Reims
Ambroise Mendy

Assane Diof Municipal Stadium
Belfort
Celie Diop
Sénégal
Armand Angrand

TO SOUMBÉDIOUNE

CES Plateau School
Corniche-Ouest
Dardanelles
Reims
Somme

Village des Arts
Minibuses

Peytavin

Tunisian Embassy
Galerie le Bokota
Jean Jaurès
Air Guinea
Russian Embassy
Canadian, Egyptian & Spanish Embassies
Nourou Tall
Denain
Daniel Sorano Theatre
Place Washington DC
Carde
Italian Embassy
René Ndiaye
Kléber
Roux
American Embassy

Nelson Mandela Ave
Jean XXIII

Le Plateau
National Assembly
President FD Roosevelt
Primaire du Plateau School

Place De Soweto
Maunoury
18 Juin

ATLANTIC OCEAN

Anse des Madeleines

British-Senegalese Institute Stadium
Lycée van Vollenhoven
Briere de l'Isle
Mermoz
M Joffre
Ave Desbordes

Faidherbe School
Laperrine
Faidherbe
Felix Éboué
Tolbiac

Alfred
Goux
Escarfait
Madaline
Fleurus
Vairny
Grasland
Raffenel
Robert brun
Blandhot
Président Lamine Guèye
VO Peterson

Eli Manel Fall
Galandou Diouf
Ehak Bourgi
Paul Holle
SOTRAC Station
Emil Badiane
Sandinièri
Vairny
Jean Jaurès
Marché Sandaga
Peytavin
G Pompidou

Reservoir

El Hadj Assane Ndoye
Carnot
Gomis
Felix Faure
Jules Ferry
Mali Embassy
Cathédrale du Souvenir Africain
British Council
Dakar Museum
Jeliny

Place Nelson Mandela Ave
M Gallièni

Dakar Railway Station
Joris
Place De Casablanca
Ballay
Town Hall
Libération School
Buses
Place du Maréchal Leclerc

Henri Malan
Médine
St-Michel School
Shopping Centre
Thann
Essarts
Calle
Hadj Dlly Mbaye

Blvd De La Libération

Robert Delmas

Place De L'Indépen-dence
Dantec
Berenger-Féraud

Cinéma Le Paris
Thiers School
Victor Hugo
Ranch Fitfili Shopping Centre

Blvd De La République

Kléber
Zola
Administrative Building
Hersent

Oceanarium

Hôpital Principal
German Embassy
British Embassy
Reservoir
Belgian Embassy

Hôpital Aristide le Dantec

Institut Pasteur

Plage de l'Institut Pasteur

Corniche-Est
Plage des Enfants
French Embassy
American Cultural Centre
Footbridge

Presidential Palace
Roume Ave
PR doumer
Ave Pasteur

Anse Bernard

Plage de l'Anse Bernard

Point Bernard
Prime Minister's Residence
Piscine
Buses
Palais de Justice

Ave Pasteur
Corniche
Lighthouse

Cap Manuel

Blvd De La Libération
Bassin Ouest
Môle 1
Bassin Médian
Môle 2
Bassin Est
Môle 3
Jetée Sud
Lighthouse
Pointe de Dakar
Corniche-Est

Ferry to Île de Gorée
Ferries for Île de Gorée
Libération

Central Dakar

M 200 400

N

ÎLE DE GORÉE

Fort d'Estrées (IFAN Historical Museum)
Ferry to Dakar
Ferry Terminal
Maritime Museum
Town Hall
Tourist Market
Public Gardens
St Charles Church
La Maison des Esclaves
Musée de la Femme

Île de Gorée (World Heritage Site)
Le Castel

M 100 200

Km 100 200

TO NOUAKCHOTT
N2
Saint-Louis
ATLANTIC OCEAN
DAKAR
Île de Gorée
SENEGAL
N2
Tambacounda
BANJUL
N4
Mansa Konko
GAMBIA
Ziguinchor
Koundara
BISSAU
GUINEA BISSAU
TO LABE

☎ (00221) 822 9226 • 🖨 (00221) 822 9413 • e mtta@primature.sn • 🌐 www.primature.sn

Adventures

Adventure	Country	Duration
Cycling in Basse-Casamance	Senegal	4 hours +
Navigating Senegal's Waterways	Senegal	6 hours +
Sailing the Gambia River	Gambia	1 day +
Driving the Adrar Region (Atar)	Mauritania	2 days +
Trekking the Dogon Plateau	Mali	1 day +
Rock Climbing at Hombori	Mali	1 day +

Cycling in Basse-Casamance

Requirements:
A valid passport, visa and yellow fever vaccination are all essential. Keep your travel documents with you at all times, especially when travelling in areas considered unsafe.
Climate:
The heat and humidity can be rather uncomfortable. The best times to travel are between October and May.
Risk factor:
Malaria is a constant problem throughout the region, and tap water is not safe to drink. Independent travel beyond Dakar is generally considered risky, so make the necessary enquiries before departure.
Health:
Malaria-carrying mosquitoes are a constant irritation. Drink only bottled water, and eat no raw foodstuffs. Carry a personal first-aid kit for emergencies.
Pack:
Lightweight clothing should be sufficient for the first six months of the year, but be sure to pack sunscreen, a sun hat and a first-aid kit.
Facilities:
Food and accommodation are both inexpensive and good, but expect few additional facilities beyond the larger, established towns.
Contact:
Ministry of Tourism,
B.P. 4049, Ave Peytavin, Dakar.
Tel: 00221-821-1126 / 822-9226
info@senegal-online.com
www.senegal-tourism.com

Navigating Senegal's Waterways

Requirements:
A valid passport, visa and yellow fever vaccination are essential. Keep travel documents with you at all times, especially when in 'unsafe' areas.
Climate:
Heat and humidity can be oppressive, and is only slightly less uncomfortable on the Casamance and its tributaries. Best times are October–May.
Risk factor:
Malaria is a constant threat; tap water is undrinkable. Parts of the river are polluted. Independent travel beyond Dakar is considered risky; make relevant enquiries before departure.
Health:
Malaria-carrying mosquitoes are a constant irritation. Drink only bottled water, and eat no raw foodstuffs. Carry a personal first-aid kit for emergencies.
Pack:
Lightweight clothing should do for the first six months of the year, but pack sunscreen, a sun hat and a first-aid kit.
Facilities:
Food and accommodation are both inexpensive and good, but one can expect few additional facilities beyond the confines of Cap Skiring.
Contact:
Ministry of Tourism,
B.P. 4049, Ave Peytavin, Senegal.
Tel: 00221-821-1126 / 822-9226
info@senegal-online.com

www.senegal-tourism.com

Sailing the Gambia River

Requirements:
A passport and visa and/or visitor's pass are required, but no vaccinations are necessary.
Climate:
Tropical, with oppressive heat and high humidity levels.
Risk factor:
Travelling on the Gambia River offers few risks, other than those usually associated with water adventures. Take precautions against malaria and drink bottled water.
Health:
Malaria is present and parts of the river may be polluted, but the most serious concern is the heat and humidity, especially when travelling on the water.
Pack:
A high-factor sunscreen and personal water supply is essential and, although it can be uncomfortably hot on the water, night temperatures have been known to drop sharply.
Facilities:
In the more tourist-oriented centres – such as Cap Skiring – there are many good operators from which choose, although some may be rather pricey. Locals also offer a more informal service, but are not as well organized.
Contact:
Ministry of Tourism, New Administrative Bldg, State House, Banjul, Gambia.
Tel: 00220-446-2491 / 3 / 4
www.gambiatourism.info

Driving the Adrar Region (Atar)

Requirements:
Most visitors need a passport and visa, which is not difficult to come by. No vaccinations are required, but check prior to departure.
Climate:
Oppressively hot April–September, with days peaking at about 50°C. Best November–January.
Risk factor:
Risks are few, but the poverty means that some vehicles may not be entirely safe. Unscrupulous operators may offer unreliable vehicles.
Health:
Heat and humidity are more of a discomfort than a risk, but drink plenty of fluids. Local water may not be palatable for Westerners. Malaria is present but slight. Emergency medical facilities are limited – so don't take chances.
Pack:
Light clothing for steamy days and a warm cover-up for evenings. If you plan to do serious walking, take boots, a sun hat, sunscreen and your own water.
Facilities:
Atar will probably cater to most needs – from car and camel hire to overnight stays – but beyond there is very little. Fuel stations are very rare.
Contact:
Adrar Voyages, P.O. Box 926, Nouakchott.
Tel: 00222-5251717
adrarvoyages@toptechnology.mr

Trekking the Dogon Plateau

Requirements:
All visitors, except citizens of France, need standard travel documents, including a visa and a yellow fever vaccination. Overland drivers need a special tourist visa for vehicles.
Climate:
Dogon Country is usually very hot and uncomfortably so, with little offer of shade beyond local settlements.
Risk factor:
Trekking the Dogon is relatively safe for level-headed and discreet travellers. Some sort of formal tour package is advised as the police and military are best handled by those in the know.
Health:
The water at the villages is relatively safe, but it is best to use purification tablets or to boil drinking water.
Pack:
Water, light clothing and good walking shoes, not special hiking boots.
Facilities:
Apart from the overland tour operators, who are generally well organized, there are few options through which to visit the Dogon, and the alternatives seldom meet Western standards.
Contact:
Wilderness Travel (California-based).
Tel: 001-510-558-2488 or 001-800-368-2794
info@wildernesstravel.com
www.wildernesstravel.com

Rock Climbing at Hombori

Requirements:
All visitors, except citizens of France, will need standard travel documents, including a visa and a yellow-fever vaccination. Overland drivers need a special tourist visa for vehicles.
Climate:
Northeastern Mali is extremely inhospitable, with conditions often oppressively hot and dry.
Risk factor:
The climb up Le Main de Fatma is for skilled climbers. Beyond the main Mopti to Gao route, travel (relatively secure) can be confusing and is best tackled with a local guide. There is a strong police and military presence.
Health:
Apart from physical dangers of the climb, dehydration is a threat. Water at the villages is relatively safe, but it is best to stick to bottled water.
Pack:
Take all your equipment and gear and make sure they are in good order.
Facilities:
Apart from a handful of generally well-organized local operators, there are few options. Do not rely on local shops to stock any equipment.
Contact:
Wilderness Travel (California-based).
Tel: 001-510-558-2488 or 001-800-368-2794
info@wildernesstravel.com
www.wildernesstravel.com

The Ivory Coast

The Gulf of Guinea was the centre of the world's most notorious slave trade for centuries, during which the vast majority of its population lived in terror. The modern countries that exist here have survived years of repressive colonialism, and – despite the considerable political turmoil and extreme poverty that continue to pervade many of these nations – are slowly re-establishing their own identities and emerging as popular, if not entirely sophisticated, travel destinations. The cities may be small, the architecture unremarkable, the industries economically vulnerable and the societies still struggling to throw off the shackles of their past, but even the capitals are rich in a cultural diversity found in few other places in Africa. Traditional beliefs have survived centuries of colonialism along with the imposed structures of Christianity and Islam, and indigenous cultures and customs remain the dominant feature on the social landscape of the far western reaches of West Africa.

GUINEA-BISSAU

BISSAU

One of the smallest countries in Africa, Guinea-Bissau has emerged as a nation that continues to balance the atrocities of a colonial past with the latter-day uncertainties that plague so much of undeveloped Africa. Home to a relatively small population, the port city is still under strict military control. The waterfront boasts some architectural gems, yet cosmopolitan Bissau is not a pretty city. One of the last of the West African states to achieve independence from Portugal, it is run-down and lacks the glamour of other great capitals, and is a dangerous place to visit. On the outskirts of the city are some picturesque beaches and impressive scenery, but the inner city has a distinct lack of cultural attractions. Bissau's annual carnival in February sees the city spring to life as citizens parade their floats and lavish costumes down the city streets.

GUINEA

CONAKRY

Despite a rich history, the capital offers only an inkling of what lies beyond the urban settlement. The first of France's colonies in Africa to become independent, Guinea was closed to foreign travel for many years. Situated on a promontory 20km offshore and with a population of about one million – 10 per cent of the country's total – the capital's cultural diversity is vast, with many of its people well versed in the politics of the day. A good base from which to explore the surrounding hills and countryside, the city is a dirty and muggy settlement riddled with corruption and violence. Conakry is far more inviting now than a few decades ago, and attractions such as the Grand Mosque offer respite from the littered streets. The offshore islands of Îles de Los, Île de Kassa, Île Tamara and, most notably, Île Roume offer a great diversion from one of the least exciting of Africa's capital cities.

SIERRA LEONE

FREETOWN

Freetown's very name is symbolic of its history, its present and, quite possibly, its future. Established in the 18th century, the capital of Sierra Leone is peopled largely by the half a million citizens descended from the emancipated slaves returning from the USA and Britain, who founded the settlement. Sierra Leone remains unsafe for travellers in the aftermath of the civil war of the 1990s and it is one of the poorest nations in the world. The dominant Creole culture is influenced by its Anglo-American heritage, yet modern-day Sierra Leone remains rich in tradition and staunch in its authenticity. It has always been at the centre of a majestic countryside with an abundance of wildlife and within easy access of some outstanding beaches, most notably Lumley. Freetown is surprisingly clean and efficient, with plenty of restaurants and fast-food outlets in addition to nightclubs of every description.

LIBERIA

MONROVIA

Founded in 1847, Monrovia is the capital of the oldest republic in Africa and promises to become one of the continent's most desirable destinations. Having survived the misery imposed by the slave trade, the half a million Americo-Liberian citizens continue to struggle with sociopolitical issues. As the country's principal port and the seat of the 150-year-old University of Liberia, Monrovia should be a lively centre, with an abundance of offerings for tourists. Unfortunately, little of the old city remains intact and the infrastructure is a shadow of its former self. Blessed with extraordinary scenery and surrounded by some of the continent's last remaining rainforests, Monrovia is still not safe, and independent travel is riddled with dangers.

CÔTE D'IVOIRE

YAMOUSSOUKRO

Hailed as one of the largest of the continent's western countries, with a relatively stable economy and a good reputation as one of Africa's most hospitable, Côte d'Ivoire has essentially two separate – and very different – capitals. Although Abidjan is the biggest city, the most glamorous and more inviting, Yamoussoukro is today the official principal city, having usurped Abidjan as the capital in 1983. Yamoussoukro is a conglomeration of uninspiring government buildings with aspirations of grandeur and, although it is dotted with some grand hotels, accommodation standards vary from poor to fair, with only a handful of the luxury variety. Perhaps the only really successful attempt at splendid architecture during its years of transformation is the massive Basilique de Notre Dame de la Paix, paid for by the late President – Félix Houphouët-Boigny – and consecrated, albeit somewhat reluctantly, by the Pope.

GHANA

ACCRA

The diamond on the Gold Coast is historic Accra, capital of one of Africa's most prosperous nations in former times. It was founded on a site on the Gulf of Guinea that was the original location of three fortresses erected by English, Dutch and Danish colonists in the 1600s. Accra's population, numbering about one million, originated from 74 ethnic groups, resulting in a varied cultural mix. The buildings are dull, but a committed attempt at rehabilitation has seen a number of development programmes that have reintroduced some of its glamour. Alive with energy, the city is remarkably green and has few of the big-city problems of other capitals.

TOGO

LOMÉ

Once considered the financial powerhouse of the western region, the port of Togo is the capital of what was one of Africa's most politically constant countries. Togo is a tiny nation and saw its fair share of suffering towards the end of the 20th century. Despite a moderate climate and pretty beaches along its 56km coast – the beach at Lomé still has the air of a sleepy seaside town – the settlement that once served as a crossroads for travellers began to crumble after conflict set in. Slowly rebuilding, there is still a long way to go to restore its reputation as a travellers' haven. The old French quarter remains the heart of Lomé and, apart from a handful of bars, clubs and discos, there is little to lure visitors beyond the bustling marketplaces that sell anything from fresh produce and handicrafts to traditional medicines and handmade clothing. Despite a certain charm, Lomé – as with most politically volatile cities – is increasingly dangerous for the naïve.

BURKINA FASO

OUAGADOUGOU

Previously known as the Upper Volta (up until 1984), Burkina Faso epitomizes the very worst of Africa's most destitute. The capital, Ouagadougou may be hot and dirty, poor and ramshackle, dusty and crowded, yet its half a million citizens have made it surprisingly inviting and welcoming to the visitor. Living up to the virtues extolled by the very name of the country – honour, dignity, nobility and integrity – the people of Ouagadougou have energetically set about transforming their city. As the traditional seat of the nation's Mossi emperors, Ouagadougou is a rich tapestry of cultures and customs, reflecting most of the country's population groups, while welcoming newcomers and sightseers to a growing collection of hotels, museums and restaurants, with clubs and bars catering for the intrepid traveller.

BENIN

PORTO-NOVO

Benin can be justifiably proud that, after a long and bitter struggle against oppression by Portuguese colonists, it was one of the first of the West African countries to embrace democracy. As a port city situated on a coastal lagoon, Porto-Novo also served as an important centre of West Africa's slave trade. Porto-Novo has a post office and hospital and is delightfully unaffected by bustling tourist traffic. Spread out along the banks of a lagoon and the surrounding foothills, Porto-Novo was the ancestral seat of the Gun kingdom and boasts an extraordinarily rich cultural legacy, most clearly discerned in traditional craft work such as wood carvings, musical instruments, traditional weapons and even the architecture of its simple homes and luxurious palaces.

With few natural resources and economies that are struggling to shed the bleak image that blanketed West Africa over the last 100 years of revolutions and civil wars, the development of the hospitality industry may provide a valuable source of foreign income for the impoverished countries of the Ivory Coast.

Abidjan, Côte d'Ivoire

Local fishermen, Winneba, Ghana

Sindou mountain range, Burkina Faso

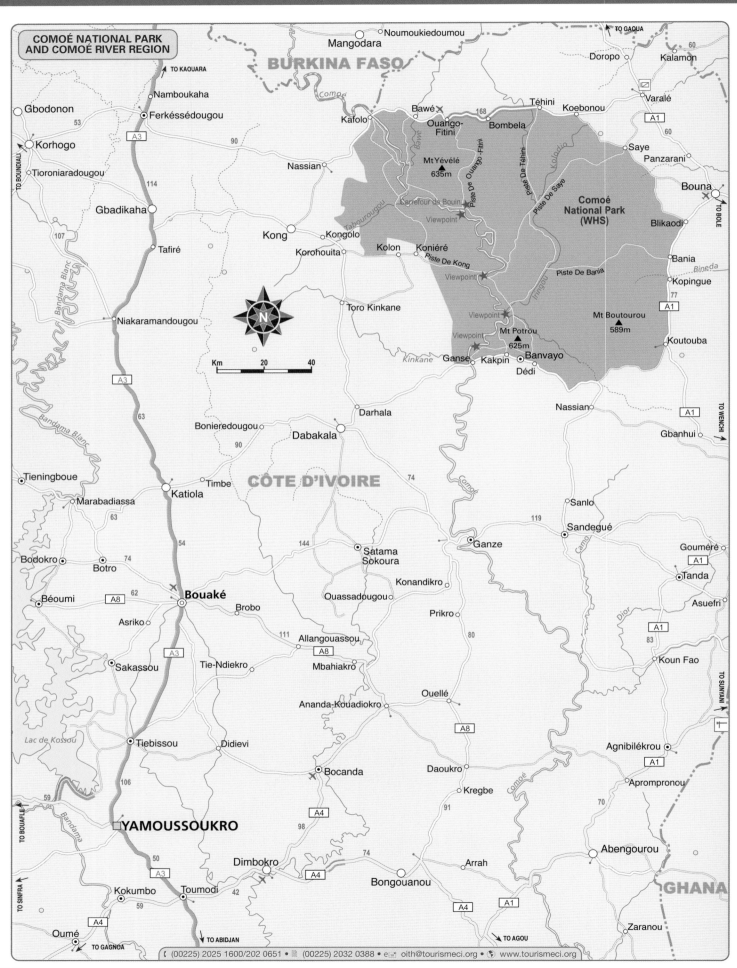

COMOÉ NATIONAL PARK
AND COMOÉ RIVER REGION

((00225) 2025 1600/202 0651 • (00225) 2032 0388 • e oith@tourismeci.org • www.tourismeci.org

Central African Parks Niger, Benin, Burkina Faso

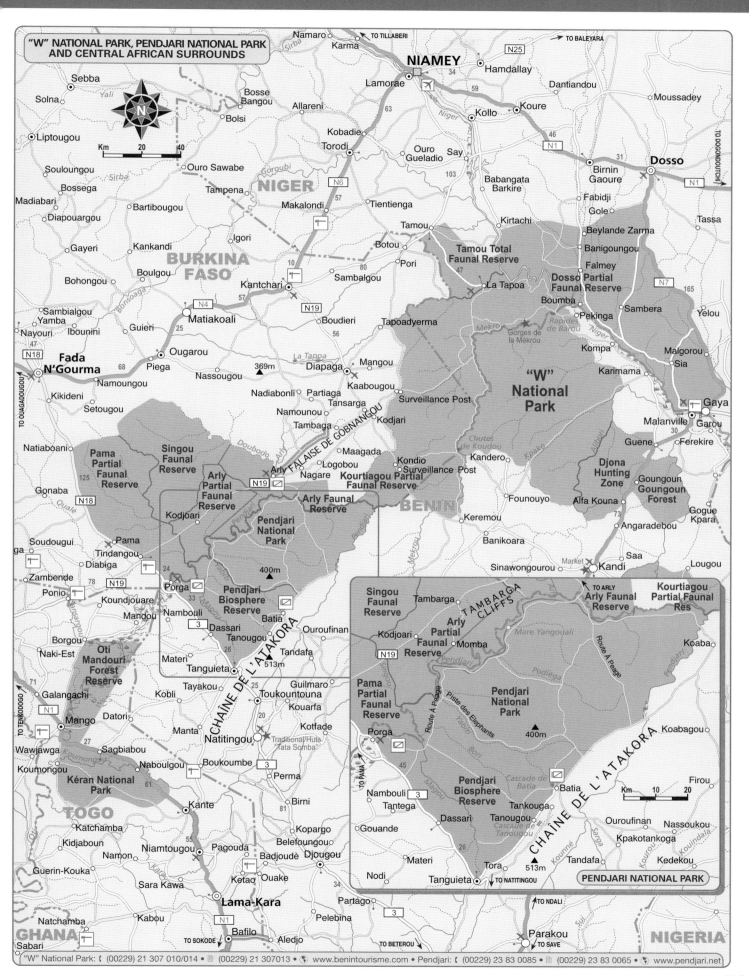

"W" NATIONAL PARK, PENDJARI NATIONAL PARK
AND CENTRAL AFRICAN SURROUNDS

Km 20 40

NIGER

BURKINA
FASO

Sebba
Solna
Liptougou
Souloungou
Bossega
Madiabari
Diapouargou
Gayeri
Bohongou
Sambialgou
Yamba
Nayouri
Ibounini
Fada
N'Gourma
Kikideni
Setougou
Natiaboani
Gonaba
Soudougui
Pama
Tindangou
Diabiga
Zambende
Ponio
Koundjouare
Mandou
Borgou
Naki-Est
Galangachi
Mango
Datori
Wawjawga
Koumongou
Sagbiabou
Naboulgou

Namaro TO TILLABERI TO BALEYARA
Karma NIAMEY N25 Hamdallay
Bosse Lamorae Kollo Koure Dantiandou Moussadey
Bangou Allareni 63 Kollo Say 46 N1 Dosso
Bolsi Torodi Ouro Birnin 31 N1
Ouro Sawabe Kobadie Gueladio Gaoure
Tampena N6 Tientienga Babangata Fabidji Gole
Makalondi 57 Tamou Barkire Falmey Tassa
Igori Botou 80 Pori Kirtachi Beylande Zarma N7 165
Kantchari 10 Sambalgou Tamou Total Banigoungou
N4 57 N19 Boudieri Faunal Reserve Dosso Partial Sambera
Matiakoali 25 Tapoadyerma La Tapoa Faunal Reserve Pekinga Yelou
Ougarou 56 Boumba Karimama
Piega Nassougou Diapaga Mangou "W" Malgorou
Namoungou 369m La Tappa Kaabougou National Sia
Nadiabonli Partiaga Surveillance Post Park Gaya
Namounou Tansarga Malanville
Tambaga Kodjari Garou
Maagada Chutes Guene Ferekire
Pama Logobou Kondio de Koudou Djona
Partial Nagare Surveillance Post Hunting Goungoun
Faunal 125 Arly Kourtiagou Partial Kandero Zone Goungoun
Reserve N19 Faunal Reserve Forest
Singou Arly BENIN Founouyo Alfa Kouna Gogue
Faunal Partial Kpara
Reserve Faunal Keremou 73 Angaradebou
Kodjoari Reserve Arly Faunal
Reserve Banikoara
Pendjari Market Saa
National Sinawongourou Kandi Lougou
Park 400m Porga Pendjari
Biosphere Batia
Nambouli Reserve Ouroufinan
Dassari Tanougou
Materi Tandafa
Tanguieta 513m

Tayakou Guilmaro
Kobli Toukountouna
Manta Kouarfa
Natitingou Kotfade
Traditional Huts
"Tata Somba"
Perma
Boukoumbe 3 Birni
Keran National 81
Park Kante Kopargo
Belefoungou Djougou
Katchamba Kidjaboun Pagouda
Namon Niamtougou Badjoude
Guerin-Kouka Sara Kawa Ketao Ouake
Sabari Lama-Kara Partago
Natchamba Kabou Pelebina
Bafilo Aledjo 3 TO NDALI
TO SOKODE TO BETEROU Parakou
GHANA N1 TO SAVE NIGERIA

Inset: PENDJARI NATIONAL PARK

Km 10 20

Singou Faunal Reserve
Tambarga TAMBARGA CLIFFS
Kodjoari Arly TO ARLY Arly Faunal Kourtiagou
Partial Momba Reserve Partial Faunal
Faunal N19 Mare Yangouali Res
Reserve Koaba
Pama Route A Peage
Partial Porga Piste des Elephants
Faunal Pendjari Podiega
Reserve National Koabagou
Route A Peage Park
Nambouli 45 400m Cascade de
Tantega 3 Batia Batia
Gouande Pendjari Tankouga Firou
Biosphere Ouroufinan
Materi Reserve Nassoukou
Dassari Tanougou Kpakotankoga
Cascade de 26 Kedekou
Tanougou
Tora 513m Tandafa
Nodi Tanguieta TO NATITINGOU Kounne
CHAINE DE L'ATAKORA
PENDJARI NATIONAL PARK

53

"W" National Park: ☎ (00229) 21 307 010/014 • 🖷 (00229) 21 307013 • 🖰 www.benintourisme.com • Pendjari: ☎ (00229) 23 83 0085 • 🖷 (00229) 23 83 0065 • 🖰 www.pendjari.net

Mole National Park Ghana
Kakum National Park Ghana

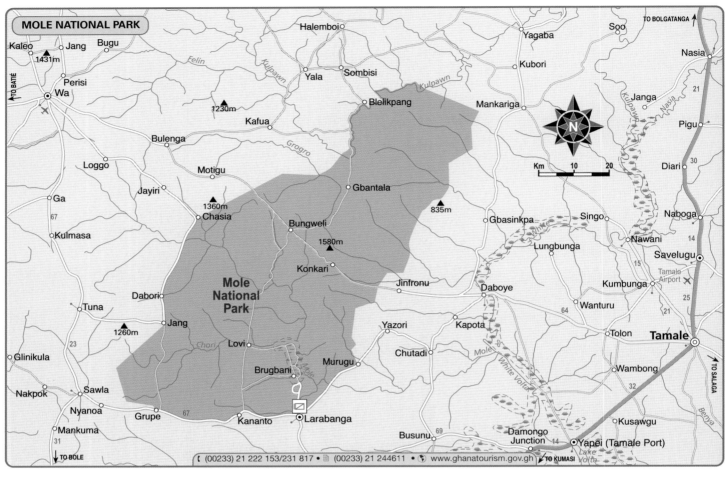

MOLE NATIONAL PARK

TO BOLGATANGA
TO BATIÉ
Kaleo
Jang
Bugu
1431m
Perisi
Wa
Halemboi
Yagaba
Soo
Nasia
Kubori
Janga
21
Felin
Kulpawn
Yala
Sombisi
Mankariga
Pigu
1230m
Blelikpang
Kulpawn
Diari
30
Bulenga
Kafua
Grogro
Loggo
Motigu
Gbantala
Naboga
14
Ga
Jayiri
1360m
Chasia
Bungweli
835m
Gbasinkpa
Singo
Nawani
Savelugu
Kulmasa
67
1580m
Lungbunga
Tamale
Airport
15
Konkari
Daboye
Kumbunga
25
Daboro
Mole
National
Park
Jinfronu
64
Wanturu
21
Tuna
Jang
1260m
Yazori
Kapota
Tolon
Tamale
23
Lovi
Chutadi
Mole
White Volta
TO SALAGA
Glinikula
Brugbani
Murugu
Wambong
32
Nakpok
Sawla
Mankuma
Grupe
Kananto
Larabanga
Busunu
69
Damongo
Junction
14
Kusawgu
Benya
31
TO BOLE
Lake
Volta
Yapei (Tamale Port)
TO KUMASI
☎ (00233) 21 222 153/231 817 • 🖥 (00233) 21 244611 • 🌐 www.ghanatourism.gov.gh

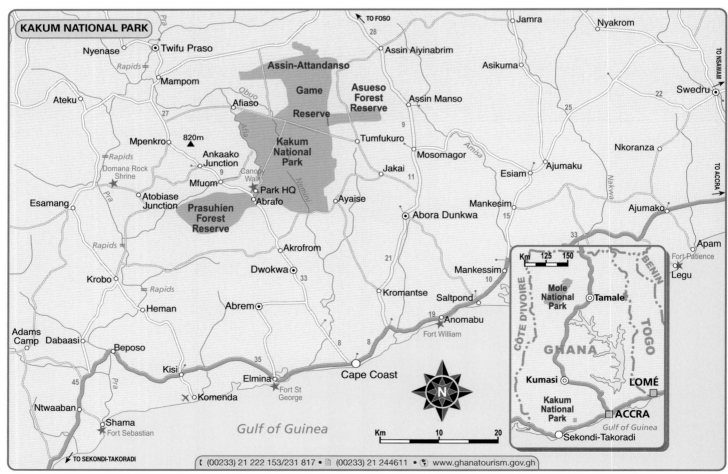

KAKUM NATIONAL PARK

TO FOSO
Pra
Jamra
Nyakrom
TO NSAWAM
Nyenase
Twifu Praso
28
Assin Aiyinabrim
Asikuma
Swedru
Rapids
Mampom
Assin-Attandanso
22
Ateku
Obuo
Afiaso
Game
Asueso
Forest
Reserve
25
27
Reserve
Assin Manso
Mpenkro
820m
Afia
Kakum
National
Park
Tumfukuro
9
Nkoranza
Ankaako
Junction
Mosomagor
Amisa
Ajumaku
TO ACCRA
Domana Rock
Shrine
Mfuom
9
Canopy
Walk
Nemini
Jakai
11
Esiam
Rapids
Atobiase
Junction
Park HQ
Abrafo
Ayaise
Mankesim
Ajumako
Esamang
Prasuhien
Forest
Reserve
Abora Dunkwa
15
Rapids
Akrofrom
Apam
Fort Patience
Krobo
Dwokwa
33
21
Mankessim
Legu
Heman
Kromantse
10
Adams
Camp
Dabaasi
Abrem
Saltpond
Beposo
35
19
Anomabu
Kisi
8
Fort William
45
Pra
Elmina
8
Cape Coast
Ntwaaban
Komenda
Fort St
George
Shama
Fort Sebastian
Gulf of Guinea
TO SEKONDI-TAKORADI
☎ (00233) 21 222 153/231 817 • 🖥 (00233) 21 244611 • 🌐 www.ghanatourism.gov.gh

Inset map
CÔTE D'IVOIRE
BENIN
Mole
National
Park
Tamale
GHANA
TOGO
Kumasi
LOMÉ
Kakum
National
Park
ACCRA
Gulf of Guinea
Sekondi-Takoradi

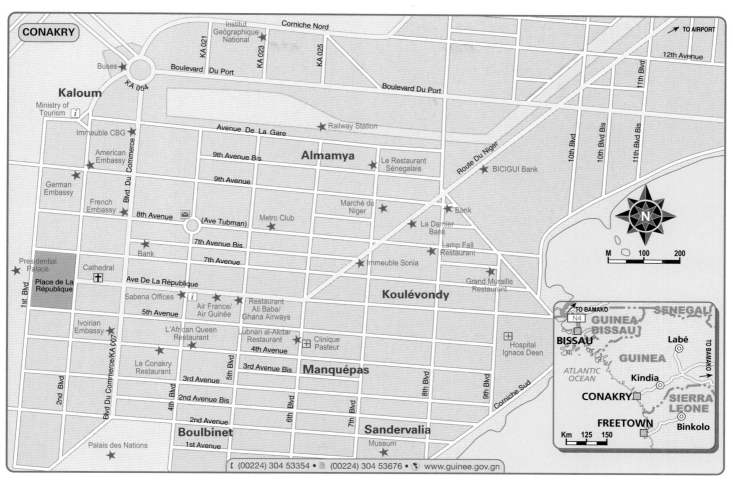

CONAKRY

Corniche Nord

TO AIRPORT

Institut
Geógraphique
National

KA 021   KA 023   KA 025

12th Avenue

Buses

Boulevard Du Port

11th Blvd

KA 05A

Boulevard Du Port

Kaloum

Ministry of
Tourism *i*

Avenue De La Gare   Railway Station

10th Blvd

10th Blvd Bis   11th Blvd Bis

Immeuble CBG

9th Avenue Bis

Almamya

Le Restaurant
Sénégalais

Route Du Niger   BICIGUI Bank

American
Embassy

9th Avenue

German
Embassy

Blvd Du Commerce

French
Embassy

8th Avenue

(Ave Tubman)

Metro Club

Marché du
Niger

Bank

La Damier
Bank

7th Avenue Bis

Bank

7th Avenue

Lamp Fall
Restaurant

Presidential
Palace

Cathedral

Ave De La République

Immeuble Sonia

Koulévondy

Grand Muraille
Restaurant

1st Blvd

Place de La
République

Sabena Offices *i*

Air France/
Air Guinée

Restaurant
Ali Baba/
Ghana Airways

5th Avenue

Hospital
Ignace Deen

Ivoirian
Embassy

Blvd Du Commerce/KA 007

L'African Queen
Restaurant

Lubnan al-Akdar
Restaurant

Clinique
Pasteur

4th Avenue

2nd Blvd

Le Conakry
Restaurant

3rd Avenue

5th Blvd

3rd Avenue Bis

Manquépas

8th Blvd

9th Blvd

Corniche Sud

4th Blvd   2nd Avenue Bis   6th Blvd   7th Blvd

2nd Avenue

Boulbinet

1st Avenue

Sandervalia

Palais des Nations

Museum

M 100 200

TO BAMAKO

N4 **SENEGAL**

**GUINEA
BISSAU**

BISSAU   Labé

GUINEA

ATLANTIC
OCEAN   Kindia

CONAKRY   **SIERRA
LEONE**

FREETOWN   Binkolo

Km 125 150

(00224) 304 53354 • (00224) 304 53676 • www.guinee.gov.gn

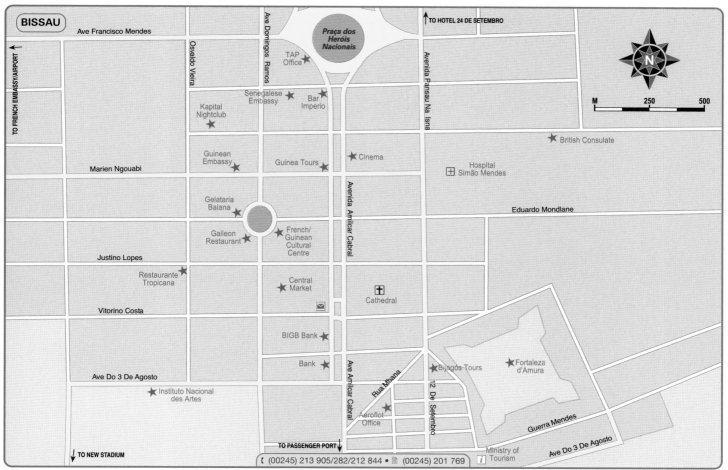

BISSAU

Ave Francisco Mendes

Ave Domingos Ramos

**Praça dos
Heróis
Nacionais**

TO HOTEL 24 DE SETEMBRO

TAP
Office

Osvaldo Vieira

TO FRENCH EMBASSY/AIRPORT

Senegalese
Embassy

Bar
Imperio

Avenida Pansau Na Isna

British Consulate

Kapital
Nightclub

Guinean
Embassy

Guinea Tours

Cinema

Hospital
Simão Mendes

Marien Ngouabi

Gelataria
Baiana

Avenida Amílcar Cabral

Eduardo Mondlane

Galleon
Restaurant

French/
Guinean
Cultural
Centre

Justino Lopes

Restaurante
Tropicana

Central
Market

Vitorino Costa

Cathedral

BIGB Bank

Bank

Fortaleza
d'Amura

Ave Do 3 De Agosto

Instituto Nacional
des Artes

Ave Amílcar Cabral

Rua Mbana

Bijagós Tours

12 De Setembro

Guerra Mendes

Aeroflot
Office

Ministry of
Tourism *i*

Ave Do 3 De Agosto

TO NEW STADIUM

TO PASSENGER PORT

M 250 500

(00245) 213 905/282/212 844 • (00245) 201 769

55

Freetown Sierra Leone
Abidjan Côte d'Ivoire

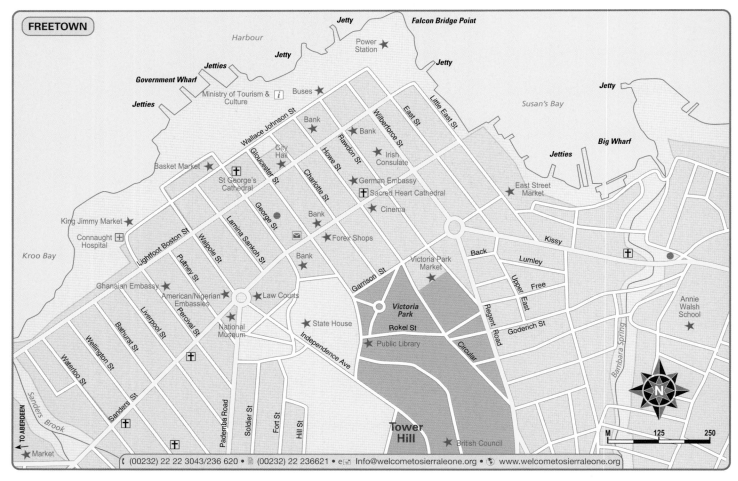

FREETOWN

Harbour · Jetty · Falcon Bridge Point · Jetty · Jetties · Jetty

Power Station

Government Wharf · Jetties

Ministry of Tourism & Culture · Buses · Susan's Bay

Wallace Johnson St · Bank · East St · Wilberforce St · Little East St · Jetty · Big Wharf · Jetties

City Hall · Bank · Rawdon St · Irish Consulate · East Street Market

Basket Market · Gloucester St · Howe St · German Embassy

St George's Cathedral · Charlotte St · Sacred Heart Cathedral

George St · Cinema

King Jimmy Market · Lamina Sankoh St · Bank · Forex Shops · Kissy

Connaught Hospital · Back · Lumley

Kroo Bay · Lightfoot Boston St · Walpole St · Bank · Garrison St · Victoria Park Market · Upper East · Free

Ghanaian Embassy · Pultney St · American/Nigerian Embassies · Law Courts · Victoria Park · Regent Road · Goderich St · Annie Walsh School

Liverpool St · Percival St · National Museum · State House · Rokel St · Circular

Bathurst St · Public Library · Bambara Spring

Wellington St · Independence Ave

Waterloo St · Sanders St · Pademba Road · Soldier St · Fort St · Hill St · Tower Hill · British Council

TO ABERDEEN · Sanders Brook · Market

((00232) 22 22 3043/236 620 • ▤ (00232) 22 236621 • e✉ Info@welcometosierraleone.org • 🌐 www.welcometosierraleone.org

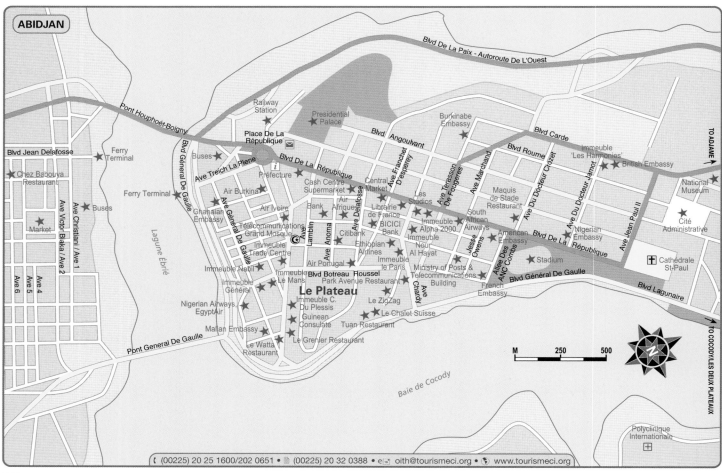

ABIDJAN

Blvd De La Paix - Autoroute De L'Ouest

Pont Houphoét-Boigny · Railway Station · Presidential Palace · Burkinabe Embassy · Blvd Carde · TO ADJAME

Place De La République · Blvd Angoulvant · Immeuble 'Les Harmonies' · British Embassy

Blvd Jean Delafosse · Ferry Terminal · Blvd Général De Gaulle · Buses · Ave Treich La Plene · Blvd De La République · Blvd Roume · National Museum

Chez Babouya Restaurant · Préfecture · Cash Centre Supermarket · Central Market · Ave Franchet D'esperey · Ave Marchand · Ave Du Docteur Crozet · Ave Du Docteur Jamot

Ferry Terminal · Air Burkina · Bank · Air Afrique · Les Studios · Ave Terrasson De Fougeres · Maquis de Stade Restaurant · Cité Administrative

Buses · Ave Christian / Ave 2 · Air Ivoire · Librairie de France · South African Airways · American Embassy · Ave Jean Paul II

Market · Ave Victor Biaka / Ave 1 · Télécommunications · Ghanaian Embassy · BICICI Bank · Immeuble Alpha 2000 · Nigerian Embassy

Ave 6 · Ave 5 · Ave 4 · Grand Mosque · Citibank · Ave Anoma · Immeuble Noir Al Hayat · Jesse Owens · Blvd De La République

Lagune Ébrié · Immeuble Trade Centre · Ave Lamblin · Ethiopian Airlines · Immeuble le Paris · Allée Des ANC Combs · Stadium

Immeuble Nabil · Air Portugal · Ministry of Posts & Telecommunications Building · Cathédrale St-Paul

Immeuble Général · Immeuble Le Mans · Blvd Botreau Roussel · Park Avenue Restaurant · Ave Chardy · French Embassy · Blvd Lagunaire

Nigerian Airways / EgyptAir · Le Plateau · Immeuble C. Du Plessis · Le ZigZag · Blvd Général De Gaulle

Malian Embassy · Guinean Consulate · Tuan Restaurant · Le Chalet Suisse · TO COCODY/LES DEUX PLATEAUX

Le Watta Restaurant · Le Grenier Restaurant · Pont General De Gaulle

Baie de Cocody · Polyclinique Internationale

((00225) 20 25 1600/202 0651 • ▤ (00225) 20 32 0388 • e✉ oith@tourismeci.org • 🌐 www.tourismeci.org

Ouagadougou Burkina Faso

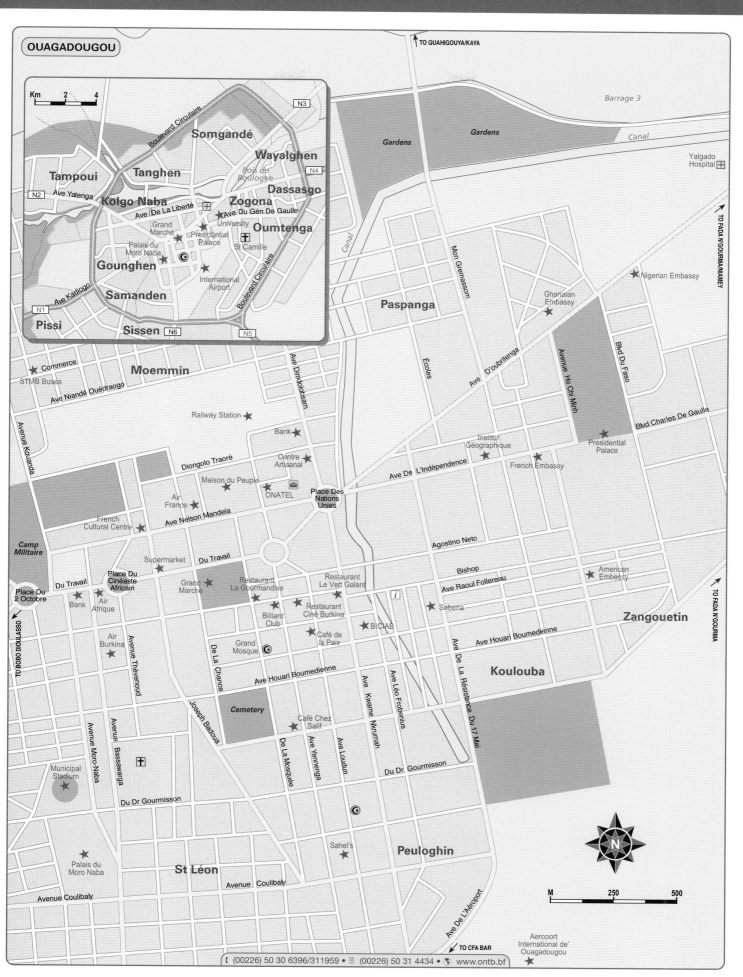

OUAGADOUGOU

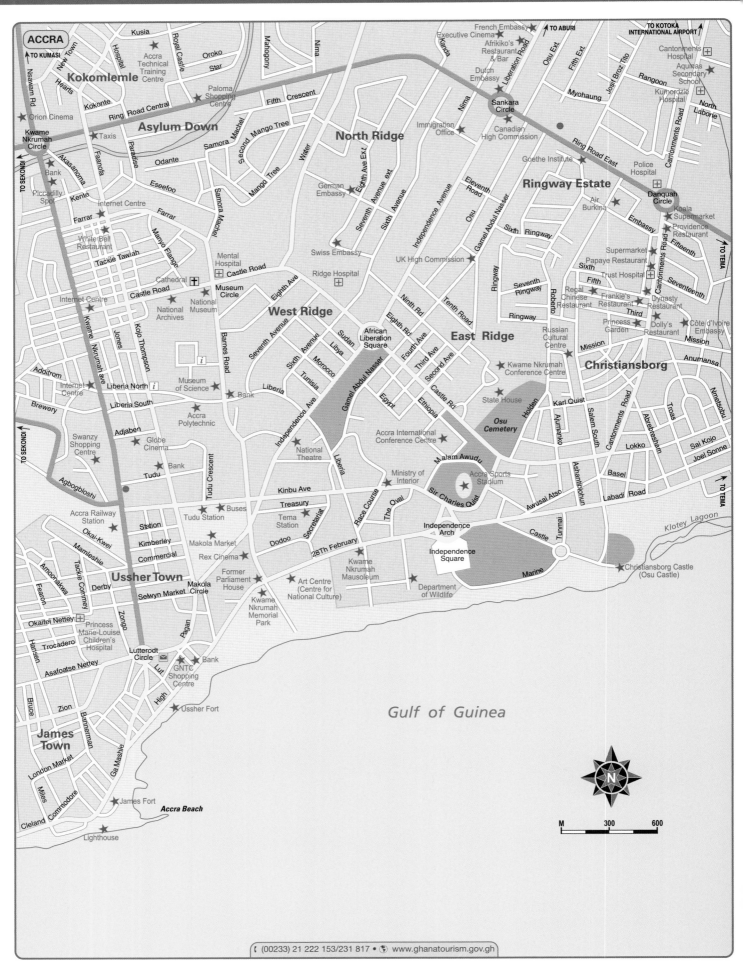

ACCRA
TO KUMASI

Kusia
Kokomlemle
Royal Castle
Oroko
Star
Accra Technical Training Centre
Paloma Shopping Centre
Fifth Crescent
French Embassy
TO ABURI
TO KOTOKA INTERNATIONAL AIRPORT
Executive Cinema
Afrikiko's Restaurant & Bar
Cantonments Hospital
Aquinas Secondary School
Kumordzie Hospital
Rangoon
North Labone

Nsawam Rd
New Town
Hospital
Kokonte
Ring Road Central
Asylum Down
Second Mango Tree
Fifth Crescent
Water
North Ridge
Dutch Embassy
Kanda
Liberation Road
Osu Ext
Fifth Ext
Josif Broz Tito
Myohaung
Cantonments Road

Orion Cinema
Hearts
Kwame Nkrumah Circle
Akasanoma
Bank
Piccadilly Spot
Kente
Internet Centre
Farrar
Faanofa
Paradise
Odante
Eseefoo
Samora Machel
Samora Machel
Mango Tree
Mahogony
Nima
Nima
German Embassy
Eighth Ave Ext.
Seventh Avenue
Immigration Office
Sankara Circle
Canadian High Commission
Goethe Institute
Ring Road East
Ringway Estate
Police Hospital
Danquah Circle
Koala Supermarket

White Bell Restaurant
Tackie Tawiah
Manyo Flange
Mental Hospital
Castle Road
Ridge Hospital
Swiss Embassy
Sixth Avenue
UK High Commission
Eleventh Road
Osu
Gamel Abdul Nasser
Air Burkina
Ringway
Sixth Ringway
Supermarket
Papaye Restaurant
Trust Hospital
Embassy
Providence Restaurant
Fifteenth
Seventeenth

Internet Centre
Cathedral
Museum Circle
National Museum
National Archives
West Ridge
Eighth Ave
Seventh Avenue
Sixth Avenue
Sudan
Libya
African Liberation Square
Ninth Rd
Eighth Rd
Tenth Road
East Ridge
Kwame Nkrumah Conference Centre
State House
Russian Cultural Centre
Regal Chinese Restaurant
Seventh Ringway
Sixth
Fifth
Third
Dynasty Restaurant
Christiansborg
Princess Garden
Dolly's Restaurant
Mission
Côte d'Ivoire Embassy
Mission
Anumansa

Kojo Thompson
Jones
Additrom
Internet Centre
Liberia North
Museum of Science
Barnes Road
Seventh Avenue
Sixth Avenue
Morocco
Tunisia
Liberia
Gamel Abdul Nasser
Fourth Ave
Third Ave
Second Ave
Castle Rd
Egypt
Ethiopia
Holden
Karl Quist
Alumanko
Salem South
Cantonments Road
Abrebesham
Troaas
Sai Kojo
Joel Sonne

Brewery
Liberia South
Accra Polytechnic
Adjaben
Globe Cinema
Bank
Tudu
Swanzy Shopping Centre
Agbogbloshi
TO SEKONDI
Independence Ave
Liberia
National Theatre
Accra International Conference Centre
Ministry of Interior
Osu Cemetery
Malam Awudu
Accra Sports Stadium
Sir Charles Quist
Lokko
Basel
Labadi Road
TO TEMA

Accra Railway Station
Okai-Kwei
Mamleshie
Station
Kimberley
Commercial
Buses
Tudu Station
Makola Market
Rex Cinema
Former Parliament House
Tudu Crescent
Kinbu Ave
Treasury
secretariat
Tema Station
Dodoo
28Th February
Kwame Nkrumah Mausoleum
Race Course
The Oval
Awusal Atso
Tunmai
Independence Arch
Independence Square
Castle
Marine
Klotey Lagoon
Christiansborg Castle (Osu Castle)

Ussher Town
Amoonakwa
Tackie Commey
Derby
Fearon
Okaitei Nettey
Princess Marie-Louise Children's Hospital
Trocadero
Asafoatse Nettey
Hansen
Zongo
Lutterodt Circle
Makola Circle
Selwyn Market
Lut
High
GNTC Shopping Centre
Bank
Art Centre (Centre for National Culture)
Kwame Nkrumah Memorial Park
Department of Wildlife

James Town
Bruce
Zion
Bannerman
Commodore
Cleland
Miles
Ga Mashie
London Market
Ussher Fort
James Fort
Accra Beach
Lighthouse

Gulf of Guinea

N

M   300   600

℡ (00233) 21 222 153/231 817 • 🌐 www.ghanatourism.gov.gh

Lomé Togo
Porto-Novo Benin

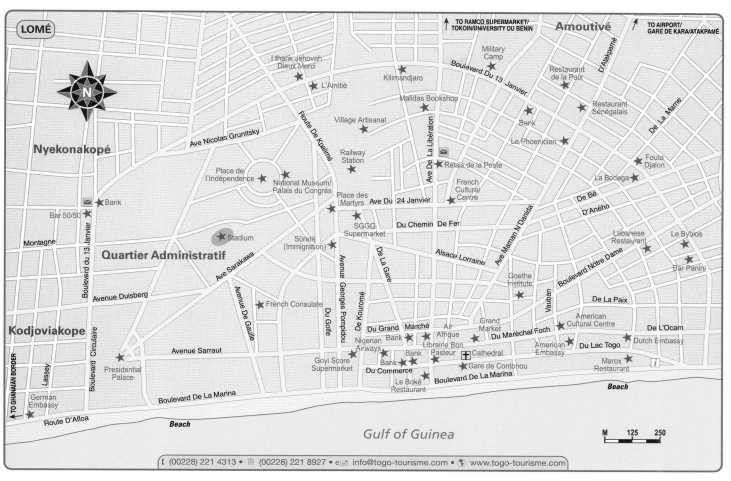

TO RAMCO SUPERMARKET/
TOKOIN/UNIVERSITY DU BENIN

TO AIRPORT/
GARE DE KARA/ATAKPAMÉ

Amoutivé

Nyekonakopé

I thank Jéhovah
Dieux Merci

L'Amitié

Kilimandjaro

Malidas Bookshop

Military
Camp

Boulevard Du 13 Janvier

Restaurant
de la Paix

D'Atakpamé

Restaurant
Sénégalais

De La Marne

Ave Nicolas Grunitsky

Route De Kpalimé

Village Artisanal

Railway
Station

Ave De La Libération

Bank

Le Phoenicien

Fouta
Djalon

La Bodega

Place de
l'Indépendence

National Museum/
Palais du Congrés

Place des
Martyrs

Relais de la Poste

French
Cultural
Centre

De Bé

D'Aného

Bank

Bar 50/50

Montagne

Boulevard du 13 Janvier

Stadium

Quartier Administratif

Sûreté
(Immigration)

Ave Sarakawa

Ave Du 24 Janvier

SGGG
Supermarket

Du Chemin De Fer

Alsace Lorraine

Ave Maman N'Danida

Lebanese
Restaurant

Le Byblos

Bar Panini

Goethe
Institute

De La Paix

Boulevard Nôtre Dame

Vauban

American
Cultural Centre

De L'Ocam

Avenue Duisberg

Kodjoviakope

Boulevard Circulaire

Avenue De Gaulle

French Consulate

Avenue Sarraut

Du Golfe

Avenue Georges Pompidou

De Koumoré

De La Gare

Du Grand
Bassin

Marché

Air
Afrique

Grand
Market

Du Maréchal Foch

American
Embassy

Du Lac Togo

Dutch Embassy

Nigerian
Airways

Bank

Bank

Librairie Bon
Pasteur

Cathedral

Marox
Restaurant

TO GHANAIAN BORDER

Lassey

Presidential
Palace

Goyi Score
Supermarket

Du Commerce

Le Boké
Restaurant

Gare de Contonou

Boulevard De La Marina

Beach

Boulevard De La Marina

German
Embassy

Route D'Afloa

Beach

Gulf of Guinea

M   125   250

(00228) 221 4313 • (00228) 221 8927 • e info@togo-tourisme.com • www.togo-tourisme.com

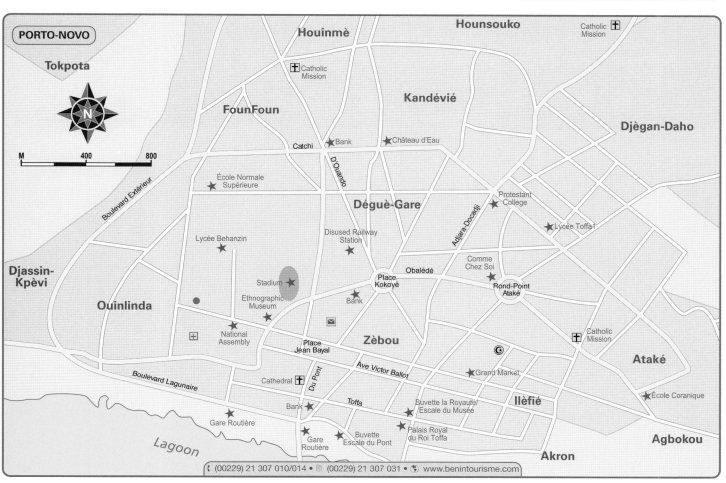

Tokpota

Houinmè

Hounsouko

Catholic
Mission

Catholic
Mission

FounFoun

Kandévié

Djègan-Daho

Catchi

Bank

Château d'Eau

M   400   800

Boulevard Extérieur

École Normale
Supérieure

D'Ouando

Déguè-Gare

Protestant
College

Lycée Toffa 1

Adjara-Docadji

Lycée Behanzin

Disused Railway
Station

Comme
Chez Soi

Djassin-
Kpèvi

Obalédé

Rond-Point
Ataké

Ouinlinda

Stadium

Ethnographic
Museum

Place
Kokoyé

Bank

Catholic
Mission

Ataké

National
Assembly

Place
Jean Bayal

Zèbou

Boulevard Lagunaire

Cathedral

Du Pont

Ave Victor Ballot

Grand Market

École Coranique

Ilèfié

Bank

Toffa

Buvette la Royauté/
Escale du Musée

Gare Routière

Gare
Routière

Buvette
Escale du Pont

Palais Royal
du Roi Toffa

Agbokou

Lagoon

Akron

(00229) 21 307 010/014 • (00229) 21 307 031 • www.benintourisme.com

59

Adventures

Adventure	Country	Duration
Windsurfing Guinea-Bissau's Coast	Guinea-Bissau	1 day +
Hiking the Fouta Djalon Plateau	Guinea	2 days +
Hiking the Man Region	Côte d'Ivoire	5 hours +
Touring the Banfora Region	Burkina Faso	1 day +
On the Waters of Lac Togo	Togo	1 day +
Driving scenic Accra	Ghana	1 day +

Windsurfing Guinea-Bissau's Coast (Bijagós Archipelago)

Requirements:
Apart from standard travel documents, most visitors need a one-month visa (easily extended). A yellow fever certificate is also required.

Climate:
Although generally hot, very high rainfall makes December-January the best time to visit the coast.

Risk factor:
There are few risks to windsurfing off Guinea Bissau – as long as you know what you are doing or have a local expert with you! These are unfamiliar waters with a temperament of their own — take no foolhardy chances.

Health:
Malaria is a real risk in Guinea Bissau — even on the offshore islands — and certain of the muddy waters have been known to carry bilharzia. Take all the necessary precautions.

Pack:
Water purification tablets, and a first-aid kit for emergencies. Take your own equipment and gear if you prefer.

Facilities:
Accommodation in and around the capital is rather good, but generally costly, with the less expensive options centred around the offshore islands, where the standard is quite high.

Contact:
Guiné Tours, Avenue Amíllcar, Bissau. Information Centre, Bissau.
Tel: 00245-213282 / 905 / 212844

Hiking the Fouta Djalon Plateau

Requirements:
A valid passport and visa are required, although you may also need an invitation from a citizen. Keep travel documents with you always, especially when travelling in 'unsafe' areas.

Climate:
Days can be very warm, but the valleys are moderate, particularly during the rains. Best hiking is early in the year.

Risk factor:
As long as travellers are prepared and do not take chances when hiking in this rugged and often precarious terrain, there should be few hazards.

Health:
Much of the abundant water may not be suitable for Western stomachs, so avoid drinking the water unless it has been boiled or purified.

Pack:
Hikers will probably need to take their own tent, camping equipment and food rations, with a set of warm clothing for chilly nights.

Facilities:
Facilities are rather basic and hikers should be self-reliant, and prepared for any eventuality. Some command of French will be useful.

Contact:
National Tourism Office,
B.P. 1275, Six Avenue de la Republique, Immeuble Al-aman, Conakry, Guinea.
Tel: 00224-455-161 / 3

Hiking the Man Region

Requirements:
Most visitors need a visa, but all require yellow fever vaccination. Visitors from the US who stay less than three months may not need a visa, but verify prior to departure.

Climate:
Harmattan winds plague the dry season, while rains fall April–July and again October–November; many of the national parks close during this time.

Risk factor:
Beyond the standard precautions for hiking in an unfamiliar terrain with a limited infrastructure, risks are few in the mountains around Man.

Health:
Although water is usually safe, take bottled water. There are few health risks, although AIDS is a growing concern, particularly in outlying areas.

Pack:
Lightweight clothing should be fine for days, but pack extra clothes for nights on the mountain, where temperatures drop steeply and quickly. Hiking boots and other essentials are needed.

Facilities:
Much of Côte d'Ivoire is well geared towards tourists, and many operators are well established. Do not to rely on facilities in Man, Danané and Biankouma.

Contact:
Bourse de Tourisme.
Tel: 00225-202-51600 / 202-0651

Touring the Banfora Region

Requirements:
Apart from the standard travel documents, all visitors will require a visa and proof of yellow fever vaccination.

Climate:
Best time to tour the Banfora region is in January or February, when the rains have largely passed and high temperatures and winds have not yet settled.

Risk factor:
Dehydration – the physical exertion combined with soaring temperatures can take their toll.

Health:
Much of the natural waters that flow in the region are contaminated with bilharzia. Malaria is ever-present.

Pack:
The standard hiking and camping equipment should suffice. Ensure that you have sunscreen and bottled drinking water.

Facilities:
Many of the principal towns offer adequate enough facilities for budget travellers, but take your own camping equipment and stock up on all the necessary supplies before heading off into the hills.

Contact:
Office du Tourisme Burkinabe, P.O. Box 2765, Bobo, Burkina Faso.
Tel: 00226-5030-6396

On the Waters of Lac Togo

Requirements:
Standard travel documents. Most visitors need a visa and proof of yellow fever vaccination.

Climate:
Rain falls largely mid-year, yet conditions around the lake area are generally moderate, with the average temperature 27°C December–January.

Risk factor:
Considered relatively safe, Togo is recovering from the turmoil it experienced towards the end of the 20th century. Blockades are still regular on prominent cross-country routes.

Health:
Lake Togo is considered to be free of bilharzia, but don't take chances.

Pack:
Pack only essentials, such as sunscreen and changes of clothing – travel light! What you don't have you will be able to buy in Lomé – what you don't find there, you probably don't need.

Facilities:
Few of the water-sport operators around Lac Togo will have up-to-date gear and equipment, but what they do stock and hire out should be sufficient. The area's market towns have adequate accommodation and food outlets.

Contact:
Lomé Tourism Office,
P.O. Box 1289, Lomé, Togo.
Tel: 00228-221-4313 / 215662

Driving scenic Accra

Requirements:
Standard travel documents. Most visitors need a visa and proof of yellow fever vaccination.

Climate:
Temperatures can climb to uncomfortable levels, but Accra is generally moderate.

Risk factor:
Although there have been reports of pickpocketing and other petty crime, safety is not really an issue in Accra. Police presence can be irritating, most often when hinting at a bribe for a minor transgression of the law.

Health:
There should be few health hazards, but although tap water in the city is drinkable it is safer to drink bottled water. Many of the beaches are plagued by volatile currents – never swim alone!

Pack:
Pack no more – and no less – than for any other African city. Standards such as sunscreen, bottled water and the like are readily available.

Facilities:
Despite the deterioration of the city towards the end of the 20th century, Accra has seen a turnaround, and facilities – along with their price tags – vary from adequate to luxurious.

Contact:
Scantravel,
P.O. Box 4969, Accra, Ghana.
Tel: 00233-21-663134 / 664456

The Equatorial Interior

The central region of West Africa is a land of extremes: prosperity versus dire poverty, harmony and reconciliation versus anarchy and disorder, peace and stability versus corruption and outright civil warfare. Whereas some of the towns and even the capital cities are lively places, with a warm, generous and welcoming reception for visitors, others are alarmingly hostile and dangerous to the uninitiated, where even the marketplaces – usually Africa's great melting pots of indigenous culture – have been taken over by gangs of thugs and thieves. In some instances, such as the Central African Republic (CAR), policies adopted by government have simply exacerbated these problems, with corruption and crime rife in CAR, posing a very real threat to the traveller – and the future of the nation's tourism industry. That said, cities such as Yaoundé in Cameroon and even Malabo in Equatorial Guinea are a delight, epitomizing the very best of what Africa has to offer the adventurer.

NIGERIA

ABUJA
Given its size and population – a phenomenal 130 million spread out over nearly a million square kilometres - Nigeria understandably exerts enormous clout over the entire region, affecting the broader economy and, to some degree, even the politics. Abuja acts as an influential powerhouse and is the economic heart of West Africa, as well as boasting the greatest number of museums in the world. Nigerians are, on average, the most highly educated people in Africa, yet the nation is still suffering the effects of a severe depression, a corrupt and inefficient government system, and a serious lack of basic commodities. Despite all it has to offer, Abuja is not a spot for extensive sightseeing. Its streets are tree lined and dotted with towering office blocks and some prestigious hotels, but inexpensive accommodation is hard to come by and the transport infrastructure is chaotic. As a multicultural centre, Abuja is so varied in flavour that it seems to lack the charm of other similar cities. One of the few reminders of its mystical past is provided by the distinctive profile of the landmark Central Mosque.

LAGOS
As the previous capital of Nigeria, Lagos's congested streets, crowded pavements and high levels of crime have made it Africa's most notorious city, a scattered settlement that includes a portion of the mainland and the islands of Lagos, Ikoyi and Victoria, originally separated by wetlands now filled in to form one seething mass of humanity. Lagos is a sad reflection of the continent and, although considered a vital cultural and economic centre, its more than eight million citizens live lives of despair, threatened daily by the global underworld of drugs. In the city's defence, there are a few highlights: a proliferation of markets, most notably the Jankara market; beautiful beaches; an intriguing Brazilian Quarter; and a fine selection of theatres and museums, including the Onikan National Museum. It is, however, the contagious rhythms and unique styles of Nigeria's music that remains Lagos's great asset, a vibrant music tradition that has evolved into one of the country's most significant cultural treasures.

KANO
On a continent where everything is ancient, it is no small feat for Kano (Nigeria's second-largest settlement) to be heralded as 'the oldest city in West Africa'. The bustling metropolis centres around the ramparts of the Old City, which is said to be about 1,000 years old and is one of the few attempts to preserve Nigeria's ancient culture. It is immense and overwhelmingly busy, yet the Kurmi market, the mosques, palaces and ancient dye pits of the Old City remain much as they have been for centuries. Within the crumbling clay walls of Kano is the Gidan Makama Museum, a palace of one of the chiefs and a fine example of the city's age-old architecture.

CAMEROON

YAOUNDÉ
Cameroon's capital, Yaoundé, is the great gem in the crown of Africa. Blessed with breathtaking beauty, Yaoundé is the lifeline of one of the continent's most prosperous nations. No fewer than 130 different ethnic groups have made their home here. Cameroon's capital – with its moderate clime and hospitable people – remains one of the most vital cities. Located on a dramatic plateau, Yaoundé was custom built as a national showcase and is easy to navigate. There is an exciting calendar of festivals, some fine local architecture, glorious beaches and impressive museums. The Musée d'Art Cameroonais, on the city's outskirts, displays the world's best West African art.

BANDJOUN
Just a little way from the provincial capital at Bafousam stands Bandjoun, one of the greatest centres of authentic Cameroonian culture – a boisterous and spirited nucleus of commercial activity. The ancient Bamileke settlement, some 3km beyond the limits of the town's boundaries, is the area's principal attraction. The imposing chief's compound – known as the chefferie – at Bandjoun is the best preserved of the age-old settlements that were home to the chiefs of the Bamileke, famed across the globe as one of the great trading nations of their time. The chief's compound at Bandjoun, the biggest of the remaining historical sites in Cameroon, comprises a fascinating series of ancient Bamileke homes – separated by squares and marketplaces – dotted around the picturesque countryside and fenced in by a bamboo enclosure for protection.

DOUALA
Douala (Cameroon's principal city) is not a favourite destination of travellers, but it remains an important hub for cross-country travelling in Cameroon. The nation's most prosperous urban centre, Douala is the epitome of a big African city: a magnificent location surrounded by a chain of starkly beautiful black-sand beaches counterbalanced by a steadily growing urban population, and all the crowds and crime. Hot and humid, with annual precipitation levels exceeding 4,000mm, the jostling city is a churning, blistering metropolitan centre. Despite being spread across a wide, open landscape that is scenically enchanting, the business districts of the huge inner city are generally the home territory of gangs of petty thieves and thugs. Visitors should not be discouraged and should make some effort to see the museums and markets of contemporary Akwa, a thriving modern centre structured around the Boulevard de la Liberté, with its landmark Catholic cathedral.

CENTRAL AFRICAN REPUBLIC

BANGUI
Bangui, a crime-ridden city situated on the Ubangi (alternatively Bangui or Oubangui), one of Africa's great rivers, is a quagmire of political tensions, lawlessness and destitution. It offers a vast contrast to the remarkable beauty of the country and the wealth of mineral deposits that lies beneath its soils, largely unexploited and virtually forgotten. The CAR is a truly beautiful country, its rugged splendour unexplored by masses of tourists, and vast stretches of its landscape remain as they have been for hundreds, if not thousands, of years. The ecological grandeur of its lush rainforest environment is not only a natural haven for an abundant and varied plant and animal life, but is also the home of some 15,000 native Pygmies, many of whom still adhere rather strictly to the nomadic lifestyle pursued by their hunter-gatherer forefathers. Bangui is one of the most crime-infested capitals in Central Africa. There are indeed highlights, many of which remain unexplored and unexploited. Plenty of venues in the west of Bangui are devoted entirely to the promotion of innovative indigenous music, and there are a number of enticing theatres, galleries and museums, the most significant of which must be the Musée de Boganda. Here the story of Pygmy culture is explained by knowledgeable guides. The city's principal attraction is the magnificent Centre Artisanal, which boasts an impressive collection of local artefacts and traditional items that is representative of most of the countries in Central Africa and the Congo Basin. There is also a remarkable assembly of local art in the unique collection of unusual art created using the wings of butterflies.

EQUATORIAL GUINEA

MALABO
The capital of beautiful but impoverished Equatorial Guinea, Malabo is situated on the attractive island of Bioko and is gentle but rustic, laid-back yet lively, nestling in an awe-inspiring landscape ringed by a selection of pretty beaches and charming little fishing hamlets. Exploring the formerly dilapidated little town is a richly rewarding adventure, and one that can be achieved in comfort. Malabo is upmarket and vibrant and local festivals are celebrated with verve, a spirited mix of traditional music and dance highlighted by Balélé performances. Beyond the city limits, the rich, dark soils and verdant vegetation are typical of a volcanic landscape. The mountainside is laced with walking paths and hiking trails, although making the 3,106m ascent to the summit of Pico Malabo (a military zone, so a permit is necessary) remains one of the most popular of the local adventures.

The western and central regions, although in large parts riddled with instability and corruption, are some of the most scenically spectacular in Africa, awash with vast stretches of lush rainforests, gently undulating hills, and endless sandy coastlines blessed with balmy beaches and lively and colourful locals.

Adobe House, Kano, Nigeria

Woodtrading schooners, Riaba, Bioko, Equatorial Guinea

Map labels:

Lake Chad

Kano

NIGERIA

RAMDOGAR VALLEY

BAUCHI PLATEAU

Niger

★ **ABUJA**

Chari

CHAÎNE DES BONGOS

MBANG MOUNTAINS

▲ 1605m

Goliath Bullfrog

CENTRAL AFRICAN REPUBLIC

Lagos

Cross River National Park

ADAMAWA

Bafoussam

Bandjoun

CAMEROON

★ **BANGUI**

Forest Pools

Mbaïki

Port Harcourt

MOUNT CAMEROON

Douala

★ **YAOUNDÉ**

Lomié

Niger Delta

Bight of Bonny

MALABO

Bioko

(EQUATORIAL GUINEA)

Riaba

ATLANTIC OCEAN

Bata

Temelon

Príncipe

Santo António

SAO TOME & PRINCIPE

EQUATORIAL GUINEA

★ **SÃO TOMÉ**

São Tomé

Santa Cruz

Km   150   300

Some water features have been exaggerated for detail

Forest pool, CAR

SAO TOME & PRINCIPE ★★

SÃO TOMÉ

The capital city is a dreamy destination: laid back and with a tiny population, lack of development has lent it an old-world charm, yet it is extremely pretty and clean. The largely unknown islands of Sao Tome and Principe offer an equatorial paradise, with lush jungles, pristine waters, volcanoes and abundant bird species.

63

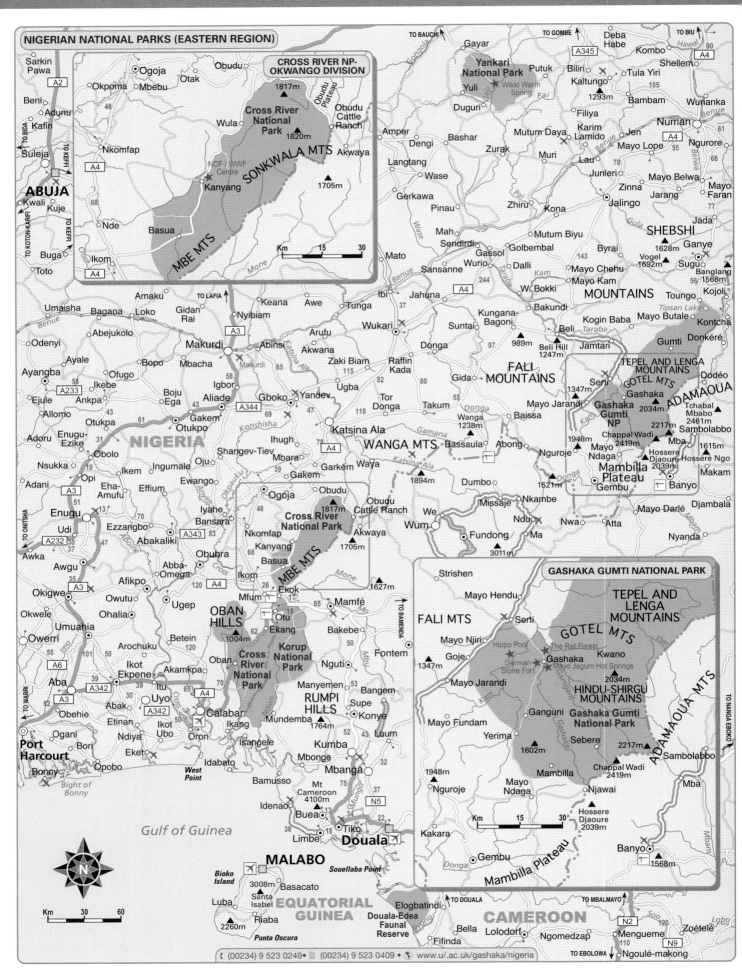

NIGERIAN NATIONAL PARKS (EASTERN REGION)

CROSS RIVER NP-
OKWANGO DIVISION

GASHAKA GUMTI NATIONAL PARK

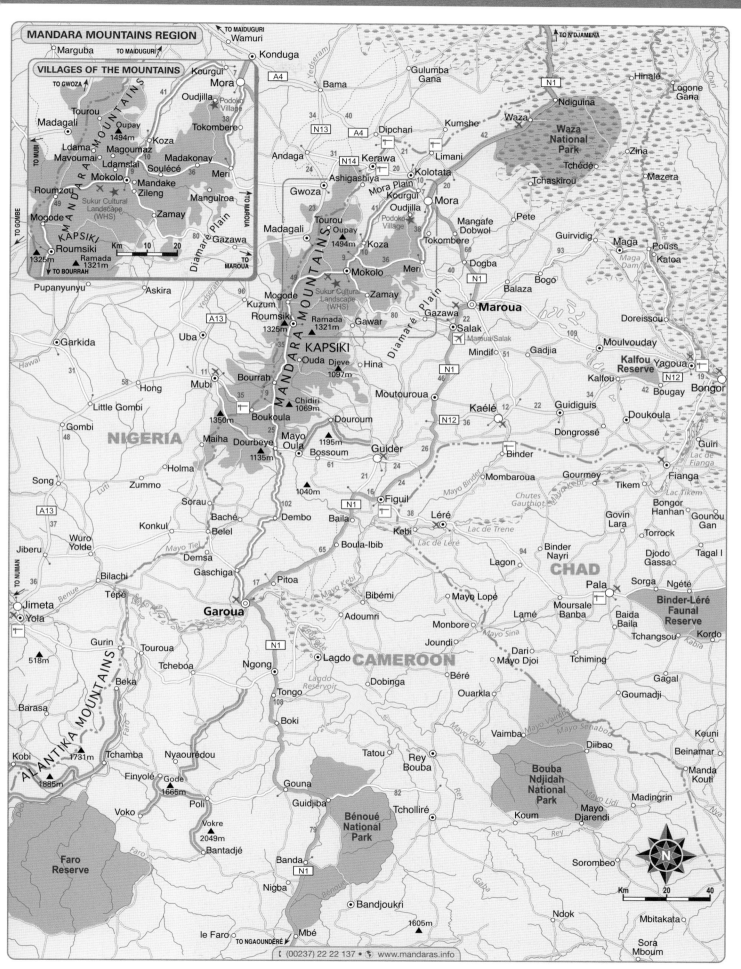

MANDARA MOUNTAINS REGION

VILLAGES OF THE MOUNTAINS

Marguba
TO MAIDUGURI
Wamuri
TO MAIDUGURI
Kourgui   7
Mora
TO GWOZA
Tourou
Oudjilla
Podoko Village
41
Madagali
Oupay
1494m
Koza
Tokombere
38
Ldama
Magoumaz
Madakonay
Mavoumai
Ldamslai
Souléce
Meri
TO MUBI
Mokolo
Mandake
Zileng
Mangulroa
Roumzou
Sukur Cultural Landscape (WHS)
Zamay
TO GOMBE
Mogode
KAPSIKI
Gazawa
Diamaré Plain
TO MAROUA
Roumsiki
1325m
Ramada
1321m
TO BOURRAH
TO MAROUA
Km 10 20

Konduga
Bama
Gulumba Gana
TO N'DJAMENA
Hinalé
Logone Gana
Chari
A4
Yedseram
N1
Ndiguina
Waza
Kourgui
Mora
Oudjilla
Podoko Village
34 40
N13
A4
Dipchari
Kumshe
42
Waza National Park
Zina
Tchédé
Mazera
Andaga
31
N14 Kerawa
21
Limani
Kolotata
Tchaskirou
24
20
10
20
Ashigashiya
Mora Plain
Kourgui
Mora
Mangafe Dobwol
Pete
Guirvidig
Maga
Pouss
Gwoza
Tourou
Oudjilla
41
Koza
Tokombere
60
Dogba
Bogo
Maga Dam
Katoa
Madagali
Oupay
1494m
9
10
36
Meri
40
N1
Balaza
93
Mokolo
Zamay
80
Gazawa
Maroua
Doreissou
Mogode
Kuzum
Roumsiki
Gawar
Diamaré Plain
Salak
109
Moulvouday
Pupanyunyu
Askira
96
Hina
Maroua/Salak
Gadjia
Kalfou Reserve
Yagoua
N12
19
Bongor
A13
Uba
35
Ouda
Dieve
1097m
N1
46
Mindif
51
Kalfou
42
Bougay
Doukoula
Garkida
Hawal
31
11
Bourrah
9
Chidiri
1069m
Douroum
Moutouroua
N12 36
Kaélé
12
22
Guidiguis
34
Dongrossé
Guiri
Lac de Fianga
Hong
58
Mubi
35
Boukoula
1350m
Maiha
Dourbeye
1135m
Mayo Oula
Bossoum
1195m
61
Guider
26
Binder
Mombaroua
Gourmey
Tikem
Fianga
Little Gombi
Lac Tikem
Gombi
48
Holma
1040m
21
24
Chutes Gauthiot
Bongor Hanhan
Govin Lara
Gounou Gan
Song
Zummo
Sorau
Baché
Dembo
102
Baila
Figuil
N1
16
24
Mayo Binder
Léré
Lac de Trene
94
Binder Nayri
Torrock
Djodo Gassa
Tagal I
Konkul
Belel
65
Boula-Ibib
Lac de Léré
Lagon
CHAD
Wuro Yolde
Jiberu
Demsa
Gaschiga
17
Pitoa
Bibémi
Mayo Lopé
Pala
Sorga
Ngété
TO NUMAN
36
Bilachi
Benue
Tépé
Jimeta
Yola
Garoua
Adoumri
Mayo Kebi
Monbore
Lamé
Moursale Banba
Baida Baila
Binder-Léré Faunal Reserve
Kordo
Tchangsou
Gurin
Touroua
Tcheboa
N1
Ngong
Lagdo
Lagdo Reservoir
CAMEROON
Joundi
Dari
Mayo Djoi
Tchiming
Mayo Sina
Gagal
Goumadji
518m
Barasa
Beka
Tongo
108
Boki
Dobinga
Béré
Ouarkla
ALANTIKA MOUNTAINS
1731m
Tchamba
Nyaourédou
Tatou
Rey Bouba
Vaimba
Mayo Vaimba
Mayo Senabo
Keuni
Beinamar
Kobi
Finyolé
Gode
1665m
Gouna
Bouba Ndjidah National Park
Diibao
Manda Kouti
1885m
Faro
Voko
Poli
Guidjiba
Bénoué National Park
Tchollire
Koum
Mayo Lidi
Mayo Djarendi
Madingrin
Deo
Vokre
2049m
Banda
Rey
Nva
Faro Reserve
Bantadjé
Nigba
N1
Sorombeo
Ndok
Mbitakata
le Faro
Mbé
1605m
Bandjoukri
Sora Mboum
TO NGAOUNDÉRÉ
Km 20 40

NIGERIA

KAPSIKI

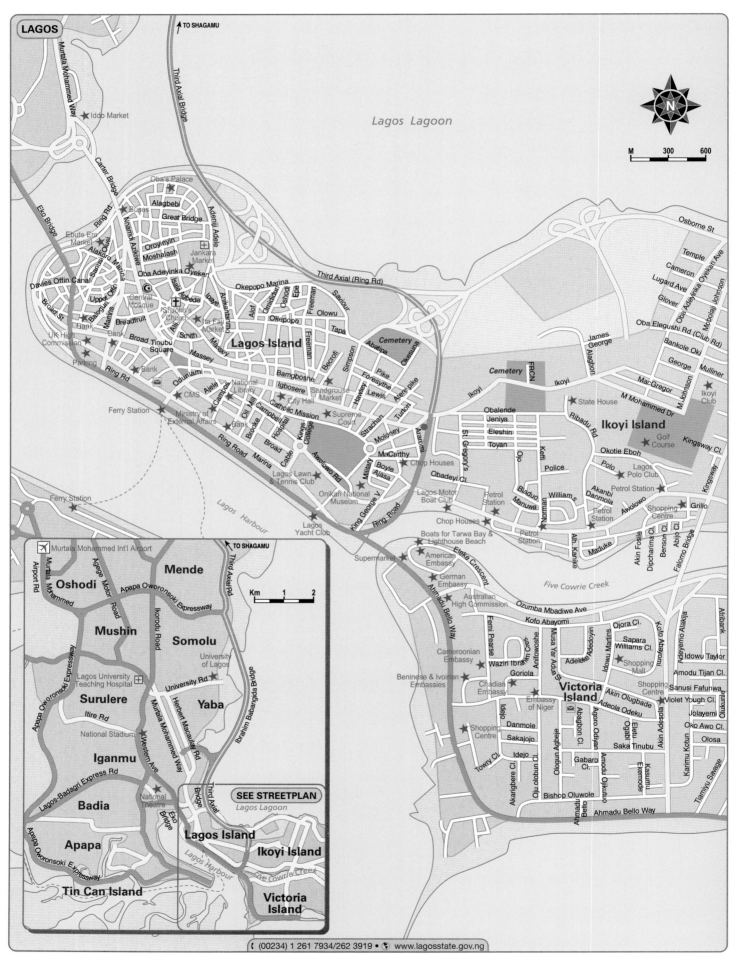

Lagos Nigeria

TO SHAGAMU

Lagos Lagoon

M 300 600

Murtala Mohammed Way
Iddo Market
Third Axial Bridge
Carter Bridge
Oba's Palace
Eko Bridge
Ring Rd
Buses
Alagbebi
Great Bridge
Adeniji Adele
Osborne St
Nnamdi Azikwe
Oroyinyin
Moshalash
Jankara Market
Temple
Cameron
Ebute Ero Market
Oba Adeyinka Oyekan
Alakoro Marina
Lugard Ave
Oba Adeyinka Oyekan Ave
Glover
Davies Offin Canal
Sanusi Olusi
Okepopo Marina
Third Axial (Ring Rd)
Oba Elegushi Rd (Club Rd)
Mbolaji Johnson
Upper Offin
Isale Agbede
Okepopo Marina
Omididun
Oshodi
Epe
Freeman
Saviour
Bankole Oki
George
Mulliner
Broad St
Balogun
Ipaya
Olowu
James George
Martins
Central Mosque
Aliu
Ita Faji Market
Tapa
Cemetery
Abatipa
Okesuna
Cemetery
Alagbon
MacGregor
Ikoyi Club
UK High Commission
Bank
St John's Church
Breadfruit
Smith
Lagos Island
Becrofi
Pike
FRCN
Ikoyi
State House
Parking
Bank
Broad
Tinubu Square
Massey
Foresythe
Lewis
Ikoyi Island
Odunlami
Ring Rd
Bank
Bamgboshe
Igbosere
Hawlay
Atere pike
Strachan
Obalende
Jeniya
Eleshin
Toyan
Obalende
Kingsway Cl
CMS
National Library
Sandgrouse Market
City Hall
St Gregory's
Ojo
Keffi
Police
Golf Course
Ferry Station
Ministry of External Affairs
Oil Mill
Campbell
Catholic Mission
Hospital
Supreme Court
Military
Boyle
Okotie Eboh
Polo
Lagos Polo Club
Petrol Station
Ring Road Marina
Booke
Broad
Cable
Kings College
Awolowo Rd
Ajasa
MaCarthy
Araromi
Bladuo
Manuwa
William s
Norman
Akanbi Danmola
Awolowo
Shopping Centre
Grillo
Ferry Station
Lagos Lawn & Tennis Club
Moloney
Chop Houses
Obadeyi Cl
Petrol Station
Petrol Station
Akin Fosile
Dipcharima Cl
Benson Cl
Abijo Cl
Falomo Bridge
Lagos Harbour
Onikan National Museum
King George V
Ring Road
Lagos Motor Boat Club
Petrol Station
Kingsway
Maduke
Alh Kanike
Lagos Yacht Club
Boats for Tarwa Bay & Lighthouse Beach
Eleke Crescent
Five Cowrie Creek
Supermarket
American Embassy
German Embassy
Ozumba Mbadiwe Ave
Ahmadu Bello Way
Australian High Commission
Kofo Abayomi
Ojora Cl
Afribank
Adeyemo Alakija
Femi Pearse
Musa Yar Adua St
Anifowoshe
Sapara Williams Cl
Shopping Mall
Idowu Taylor
Amodu Tijan Cl
Cameroonian Embassy
Waziri Ibra
Goriola
Adeleke
Shopping Centre
Sanusi Fafunwa
Beninese & Ivoirian Embassies
Chadian Embassy
Akin Olugbade
Adeola Odeku
Violet Yough Cl
Jolayemi
Embassy of Niger
Abagbon Cl
Agora Odivan
Elentu
Akin Adesola
Oko Awo Cl
Victoria Island
Shopping Centre
Danmole
Sakajojo
Ogabo
Saka Tinubu
Olosa
Idejo
Oloqun Agbele
Amodu Ojikutuo
Kasumu Ekemode
Karimu Kotun
Idejo
Towry Cl
Oju olobun Cl
Gabaro Cl
Akarigbere Cl
Bishop Oluwole
Ahmadu Bello
Ahmadu Bello Way

Inset Map

Murtala Mohammed Int'l Airport
TO SHAGAMU
Airport Rd
Murtala Mohammed
Agege Motor Road
Apapa Oworonsoki Expressway
Third Axial Rd
Mende
Oshodi
Ikorodu Road
Km 1 2
Mushin
Somolu
University of Lagos
Jewessway Expressway
Apapa Oworonsoki Expe
Lagos University Teaching Hospital
University Rd
Herbert Macaulay Rd
Ibrahim Babangida Bridge
Surulere
Itire Rd
Yaba
National Stadium
Western Ave
Iganmu
Murtala Mohammed Way
Badia
National Theatre
Bridge
Eko Bridge
Third Axial
SEE STREETPLAN
Lagos Lagoon
Lagos-Badagri Express Rd
Apapa
Lagos Island
Apapa Oworonsoki Expressway
Lagos Harbour
Ikoyi Island
Tin Can Island
Five Cowrie Creek
Victoria Island

(00234) 1 261 7934/262 3919 • www.lagosstate.gov.ng

ABUJA

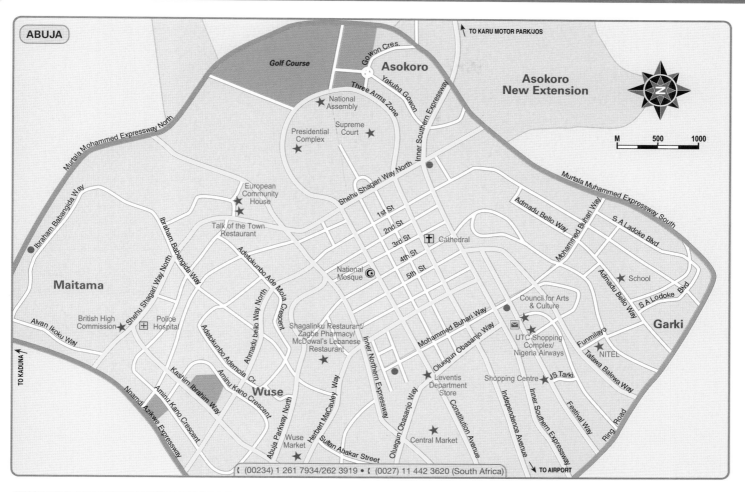

TO KARU MOTOR PARK/JOS

Golf Course

Gowon Cres.

Asokoro

Yakuba Gowon

Three Arms Zone

Asokoro
New Extension

National
Assembly

Presidential
Complex

Supreme
Court

Murtala Mohammed Expressway North

Inner Southern Expressway

Ibrahim Babangida Way

Shehu Shagari Way North

Murtala Muhammed Expressway South

European
Community
House

1st St

2nd St

Admadu Bello Way

S A Ladoke Blvd

Talk of the Town
Restaurant

Adetokunbo Ade Mola Crescent

3rd St

Cathedral

Mohammed Buhari Way

4th St

5th St

Admadu Bello Way

Maitama

Ibrahim Babangida Way

National
Mosque

School

S A Lodoke Blvd

British High
Commission

Shehu Shagari Way North

Ahmadu bello Way North

Police
Hospital

Council for Arts
& Culture

Garki

Alvan Ikoku Way

Adetokunbo Ademola Cr.

Shagalinku Restaurant/
Zagbé Pharmacy/
McDowal's Lebanese
Restaurant

Mohammed Buhari Way

UTC Shopping
Complex/
Nigeria Airways

Funmilayo

NITEL

TO KADUNA

Kashim Ibrahim Way

Aminu Kano Crescent

Wuse

Herbert McCauley Way

Inner Northern Expressway

Olusegun Obasanjo Way

Leventis
Department
Store

Shopping Centre

JS Tarki

Talawa Balewa Way

Nnamdi Azikwe Expressway

Aminu Kano Crescent

Abuja Parkway North

Wuse
Market

Sultan Abakar Street

Central Market

Constitution Avenue

Olusegun Obasanjo Way

Independence Avenue

Inner Southern Expressway

Festival Way

Ring Road

TO AIRPORT

((00234) 1 261 7934/262 3919 • ((0027) 11 442 3620 (South Africa)

YAOUNDÉ

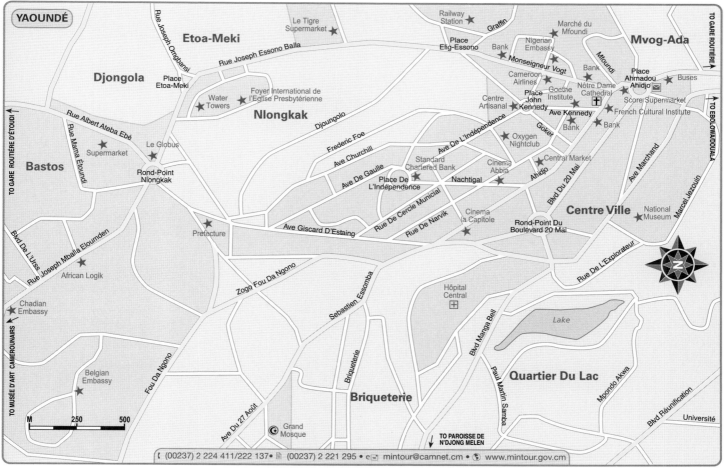

TO GARE ROUTIÈRE

Rue Joseph Omgbansi

Le Tigre
Supermarket

Railway
Station

Graffin

Marché du
Mfoundi

Mvog-Ada

Etoa-Meki

Rue Joseph Essono Balla

Place
Elig-Essono

Bank

Nigerian
Embassy

Bank

Mfoundi

Djongola

Place
Etoa-Meki

Monseigneur Vogt

Place
Ahmadou
Ahidjo

Buses

Foyer International de
l'Eglise Presbytérienne

Cameroon
Airlines

Goethe
Institute

Notre Dame
Cathedral

Score Supermarket

Water
Towers

Nlongkak

Centre
Artisanal

Place
John
Kennedy

French Cultural Institute

Rue Albert Ateba Ebé

Djoungolo

Ave Kennedy

TO EBOLOWA/DOUALA

Rue Mama Étoundi

Frederic Foe

Ave De L'Indépendence

Goker

Bank

Bank

Bastos

Supermarket

Le Globus

Frederic Foe

Ave Churchill

Oxygen
Nightclub

TO GARE ROUTIÈRE D'ÉTOUDI

Rond-Point
Nlongkak

Ave De Gaulle

Place De
L'Indépendence

Standard
Chartered Bank

Nachtigal

Cinema
Abbia

Ahidjo

Central Market

Ave Marchand

Blvd De L'Urss

Rue Joseph Mballa Eloumden

Prefecture

Ave Giscard D'Estaing

Rue De Cercle Municial

Rue De Narvik

Cinema
(a Capitole

Bld Du 20 Mai

Centre Ville

National
Museum

Marcel Jezoulin

Rue De L'Explorateur

Zogo Fou Da Ngono

Rond-Point Du
Boulevard 20 Mai

African Logik

Sebastien Essomba

Hôpital
Central

Lake

Chadian
Embassy

Fou Da Ngono

Zogo Fou Da Ngono

Briqueterie

Blvd Manga Bell

Quartier Du Lac

Paul Martin Samba

Mpondo Akwa

Blvd Réunification

TO MUSÉE D'ART CAMEROUNAIS

Belgian
Embassy

Ave Du 27 Août

Grand
Mosque

Briqueterie

TO PAROISSE DE
N'DJONG MELEN

Université

((00237) 2 224 411/222 137 • (00237) 2 221 295 • e mintour@camnet.cm • www.mintour.gov.cm

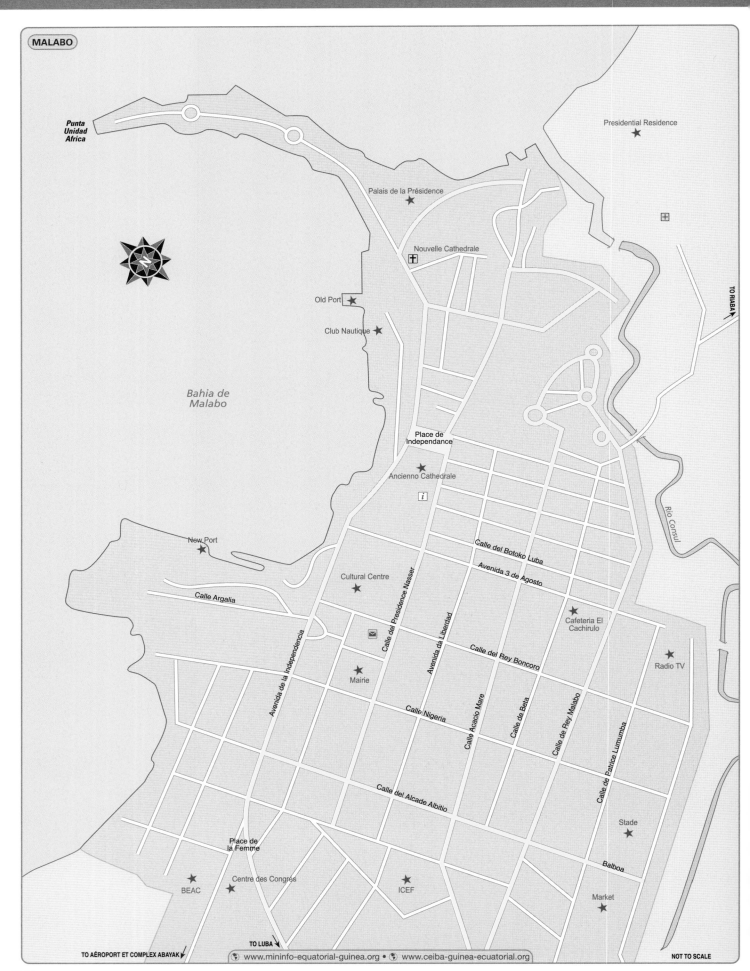

Adventures

Adventure	Country	Duration
Exploring Nigeria's Rainforests (Obudu Cattle Ranch)...	Nigeria	1 day +
Riding Nigeria's Dumbo Trek (Bassaula)...	Nigeria	2 days
Climbing Mount Cameroon...	Cameroon	2 days +
Walking the Mandara Mountains...	Cameroon	2 days +
Exploring the Dja Faunal Reserve...	Cameroon	1 day +
Exploring Bioko Island's Volcanoes...	Equatorial Guinea	1 day +

Exploring Nigeria's Rainforests (Obudu Cattle Ranch)

Requirements:
Most visitors will require a pre-arranged visa and proof of a yellow fever and (occasionally) cholera vaccination. If travelling by vehicle, special clearance by way of a Carnet de Passage en Douane is required.

Climate:
The southern regions are hot and wet, with rains falling March–November and the dry period December–March, when harmattan winds blow.

Risk factor:
Hitchhiking is potentially dangerous, but there are few other risks. You will inevitably need a local guide to help navigate the routes and to help you out of any trouble.

Health:
Malaria is particularly rampant in the hot, wet rainforest conditions.

Pack:
Take malaria medication, provisions and supplies, and all the necessary camping gear to be self-sufficient.

Facilities:
Visitors' amenities in Nigeria are appalling, and few of the 'luxuries' are operational. You need to be self-reliant, especially in 'undeveloped' areas such as the parks. English is widely spoken.

Contact:
Nigeria Tourist Board, P.O. Box 167, Abuja, Nigeria.
Tel: 00234-9-523-0420
www.nigeria.com

Riding Nigeria's Dumbo Trek (Bassaula)

Requirements:
Most visitors need a pre-arranged visa and proof of yellow fever and (occasionally) cholera vaccination. If travelling by vehicle, a Carnet de Passage en Douane is required.

Climate:
The southern regions are hot and wet, with rains falling March–November and the dry period December–March, when harmattan winds blow.

Risk factor:
Other than the overgrown route of the Dumbo Trek, there are few risks. Porters and guides know the route and may be of help when you enter Cameroon, where immigration authorities are not accustomed to tourists.

Health:
Malaria is particularly rampant in the hot, wet rainforest conditions.

Pack:
Take malaria medication, provisions and supplies, and all the necessary camping gear to be self-sufficient.

Facilities:
English is not widely spoken in the border region with Cameroon. Bassaula has basic accommodation, but most trekkers camp in villages en route. This is basic, but quite safe.

Contact:
Nigeria Tourist Board,
P.O. Box 167, Abuja, Nigeria.
Tel: 00234-9-523-0420
www.nigeria.com

Climbing Mount Cameroon

Requirements:
Virtually all Westerners need a passport and visa, although no particular immunizations are required.

Climate:
Although warm and humid, the best time to climb Mount Cameroon is December–April, when everything is dry.

Risk factor:
Guides will help to avoid any dangers you may encounter on the slopes of the mountain, and practical common sense should keep you out of danger.

Health:
Malaria is rife and the water is seldom drinkable, but prophylactic medication and bottled water are available in most of the larger towns.

Pack:
Your own rations, along with sturdy hiking shoes or boots and good quality camping gear – sleeping bag, tent, warm clothing, cooking equipment.

Facilities:
This is hiking and trekking country aimed largely at the budget traveller, and although some equipment and gear may be hired in Buea and similar settlements in the area, they offer only rudimentary accommodation at basic camp sites and the like.

Contact:
Mount Cameroon Intercommunal Ecotourism Board, Bura, Cameroon.
Tel: 00237-332-2038

Walking the Mandara Mountains

Requirements:
Virtually all Westerners need a passport and visa, although no particular immunizations are required.

Climate:
Although warm and humid, the best time to climb the Mandara Mountains is December to April, when everything is still reasonably dry.

Risk factor:
Guides should help to avoid dangers you may encounter on the mountain slopes, and practical common sense should keep you out of danger.

Health:
Malaria is rife throughout the country and the water is seldom drinkable, but prophylactic medication and bottled water are available in large towns.

Pack:
Your own rations, sturdy hiking shoes or boots, and good quality camping gear – sleeping bag, tent, warm clothing, cooking equipment.

Facilities:
This is hiking and trekking country aimed largely at the budget traveller. Some equipment and gear can be hired in Maroua and similar settlements in the area, but they offer only rudimentary accommodation at basic camp sites and the like.

Contact:
Star Voyages, Boulevard de la Renouveau, Maroua, Cameroon.
Tel: 00237-229-2522

Exploring the Dja Faunal Reserve

Requirements:
Virtually all Westerners need a passport and visa, although no particular immunisations are required.

Climate:
The southern areas can be wet and hot, and the tree canopy offers little respite even during the end-of-year rains. Humidity is high year-round.

Risk factor:
There are virtually no dangers in the Dja Reserve. The Baka are hospitable and well able to placate fears.

Health:
Malaria is rife and water is seldom drinkable, but prophylactic medication and bottled water are available in large towns. Stock up well beforehand.

Pack:
Although visitors to the reserve may want to pack camping gear and food, overnighting with the Baka means you may have little need for provisions.

Facilities:
Dja is somewhat isolated, resulting in the accommodation offered being rudimentary. Other options include camping at the existing camp or seeking out the basic hospitality of the pygmies.

Contact:
Ecosystem Forestier d'Afrique Centrale, P.O. Box 13844, Yaoundé, Cameroon.
Tel: 00237-220-9472 / 214 273
ecofac@tamnet.cm
www.ecofac.org

Exploring Bioko Island's Volcanoes

Requirements:
Virtually all visitors need a passport and visa, and those climbing the peaks of Bioko require a special permit from government authorities – expect delays!

Climate:
Humidity levels are high during the rains, with the heaviest rains falling the first three/four months of the year.

Risk factor:
Visitors should encounter no hazards on Bioko, as long as they remain sensible, keep an eye on prevailing conditions and plan their routes in advance.

Health:
The island habitat poses no health risks, apart from heat and exhaustion on the uphill trail. Visitors are advised to drink only bottled water.

Pack:
Sturdy hiking boots, sunscreen, water rations and warm clothes to protect you if a chill settles over the slopes.

Facilities:
Accommodation in Malabo varies from the basic to the comfortable – unless you are looking for the ultra-luxurious, you will find what you need here. Other essentials – such as food and water supplies – are generally readily available in the capital.

Contact:
Ministry of Culture, Tourism and Francophony, Malabo, Bioko Norte, Equatorial Guinea.
Tel: 00240-92903

The Horn of Africa

The Horn of Africa has, in recent years, seen untold misery, ranging from drought and famine to civil war and border disputes that resulted in a huge displacement of the population and a serious problem with refugees intent on escaping the turmoil of their home territories, and with Ethiopia surviving as the only African country never to be colonized. With the possible exclusion of Somalia – which remains a difficult, treacherous and unpredictable place for foreign visitors – it is a region that is slowly rejuvenating itself, rebuilding its infrastructure not only for its long-suffering citizens but also for the steady trickle of tourists slowly making their way back to an area that harbours considerable potential for peace and prosperity.

ETHIOPIA

ADDIS ABABA

Widely recognized as one of Africa's greatest capitals, Addis Ababa originated in pre-Christian times and was formally established just over 100 years ago. The city is the spiritual centre of the Land of Cush. Despite the pressures on its natural resources, Addis Ababa has a relatively stable economy based on agriculture that supports a population of about three million. Given its historical significance, the outskirts are scattered with archaeological sites, while the city confines have a collection of temples and churches decorated with medieval paintings, murals and mosaics, all of which make this the starting point for historical routes that wind across the country. Its international status is signified by the acclaimed Addis Ababa University and the headquarters of the Organisation of African Unity and United Nations Economic Commission for Africa. The hospitality industry is Ethiopia's second-largest income earner. Streets are dangerous at night, and markets popular among thieves and pickpockets, yet the capital can be a delight. Addis Ababa boasts a number of significant museums, notably the university's Ethnological Museum.

BLUE NILE

Virtually synonymous with Africa, the Nile is Africa's greatest asset and the Blue Nile Ethiopia's most significant watercourse. The mighty Blue Nile Falls is one of the continent's great waterfalls. Some 400m in width and plummeting an impressive 45-50m, the falls are known by the locals as Tis Isat, which translates as 'Smoke of the Nile' - an apt description of the spray that emanates from the gushing chasm. Although indeed an awesome spectacle year-round, the falls reach their full potential following the often torrential rain in November and December. The natural splendour of the Blue Nile Falls is, therefore, one of Ethiopia's premier drawcards, and the tourism infrastructure that has developed around the falls is one of the country's most advanced. Still in use is the bridge erected by the Portuguese nearly 400 years ago, and the surrounds are intertwined with a network of paths and trails, a popular walking route. Voyages are offered on the river in a vessel made almost entirely from papyrus. Further along the course of the Blue Nile, some 30km from the falls, is the lively port town of Bahir Dar on the southern banks of 3,600km^2 Lake Tana, both of which offer an equally rewarding experience.

AKSUM

The holy city of Aksum is acclaimed far and wide as the nation's most significant religious centre. Founded some 1,000 years ago by Menelik, apparently the bastard son of the legendary Queen of Sheba and wise King Solomon, Aksum has a vital Christian heritage that is very orthodox in nature. Ethiopians are devout believers and claim that the Arc of the Covenant remains hidden at Aksum. The history of the city is largely unexplored and many archaeological sites have yet to be excavated, but there is little doubt that Aksum is at least 500 years old, the collection of granite monoliths in the stele field on the outskirts of the town dating back some 2,000 years. The site is an impressive tribute to the history of the region, the adjacent museum providing a fascinating look at finds excavated from local sites. The 7th-century church of St Mary of Zion, the country's most sacred site, is said to house the elusive Arc of the Covenant. The landscape is further dotted with ancient monasteries, churches, palaces and a complex of meticulously crafted catacombs.

LALIBELA

Scattered across Ethiopia is a series of rugged cave-like churches painstakingly carved from the rock face by human hands. The most celebrated of these is the series of 11 churches dotted around ancient Lalibela. There are similar conglomerations of rock-hewn churches around Ethiopia - notably at Tigray - but those at Lalibela have been most widely acclaimed as great architectural gems. The chapel-like subterranean caverns house treasures of historical and religious significance. The labyrinth of stone, which took nearly 50,000 worshippers a decade to complete, still hums with the haunting chants of monks and other orthodox Ethiopians celebrating mass, while priests carefully guard the relics from desecration and theft. The largest of the churches, Bet Medhane Alem, looms 11.5m and covers an area of 800m^2. Other sites include the Bet Abba Libanos and Bet Giorgis, in the shape of a 15m cross.

DJIBOUTI

DJIBOUTI

The Monaco of Africa, Djibouti is a lively and bustling city-state barely 100 years old and peopled by an eclectic mix of cultures. Until 1977 the commercial port was a French colony and, despite being home to nearly 70 per cent of the nation's population, it retains some of its colonial flavour. Once little more than extensive pastures for itinerant herders that roamed the hinterland, the tranquil streets are lined with fine mansions and its harbour-cum-marina is dotted with traditional fishing boats, dhows and modern sailing vessels. Le Marché Centra, the city's principal market district, is its most enduring attraction, while an interesting drawcard is the African Quarter which, although seedy, is inexpensive and offers fascinating insight into the lives of the trading locals. Lack of luxuries aside, the tiny city-state is an undiscovered treasure of mainland Africa.

SOMALIA

MOGADISHU

As Hammawein, old Mogadishu was a sprawling spectacle of grand cathedrals and architectural masterpieces set amid a splendid African landscape of sweeping sands and pristine, cove-dotted beaches that should have made it a highlight of the continent. Founded by the Arabs approximately 1,000 years ago, Mogadishu reached its greatest potential in the 1200s, when much of the city's early wealth originated as a result of a flourishing trade with China, Persia and India. Today, Somalia is one of the least developed nations in the world, and the capital continues to suffer as a result of political, geographic and social problems. The once impressive architecture of an old African capital is now riddled with bullets and is steadily decaying, and tourist travel is extremely limited. This nation of traders and farmers is, however, slowly creeping towards some semblance of peace. Situated on the longest shoreline of any African country, Mogadishu's fishing industry remains vital to the local economy, and the city also has a relatively small but thriving industry in frankincense, myrrh, henna and a local perfume base known as unce, all of which may be found at Mogadishu's street markets. As a consequence of floods, famine, drought and political unrest, the southern reaches of the country remain far less accessible and rewarding than the northern stretch, which itself remains painfully susceptible to the turbulence permeating the rest of the country.

ERITREA

ASMARA

Established in 1993, Eritrea is the youngest nation on the continent, emerging from extended civil strife and a long-standing border dispute with Ethiopia. One of the shining lights in Africa, it has survived a tormented past to step boldly into a promising future. Its capital at Asmara is relaxed, friendly and peaceful, and the suburban thoroughfares of the old quarter are lined with gracious old buildings and flowering trees. The most valiant attempt at civil engineering is the great Massawa-Asmara highway: its extensive length (with 65 bridges and 30 tunnels) was all but destroyed during the war, but is being restored entirely by the Eritreans without Western assistance. The city is pleasantly uncrowded, remarkably uncluttered, clean, efficient and very safe by African standards.

Although the vast majority of its people are engaged almost exclusively in agriculture, the northeastern stretches of the continent, a region of desert dune and endless sands, has a surprising wealth of resources, much of which still needs to be harnessed.

Blue Nile Falls, Ethiopia

Bread queue, Somalia

St George Cross, Lalibela, Ethiopia

ERITREA

Red Sea

ASMARA

• Aksum

Gonder •

Lake Tana

Nakatalapa
Rock Church

• Lalibela

Bahir Dar •

Blue Nile Falls

Blue Nile

DJIBOUTI

Lake Assal

DJIBOUTI

Gulf of Aden

• Dire Dawa

⊙ Hargeysa

S O M A L I A

ADDIS ABABA ✪

• Nazret

E T H I O P I A

DISPUTED AND UNDEMARCATED BOUNDARY

I N D I A N   O C E A N

✪ MOGADISHU

• Marca
(Merca)

N

Km   100   200

Some water features have
been exaggerated for detail

• Kismaayo

71

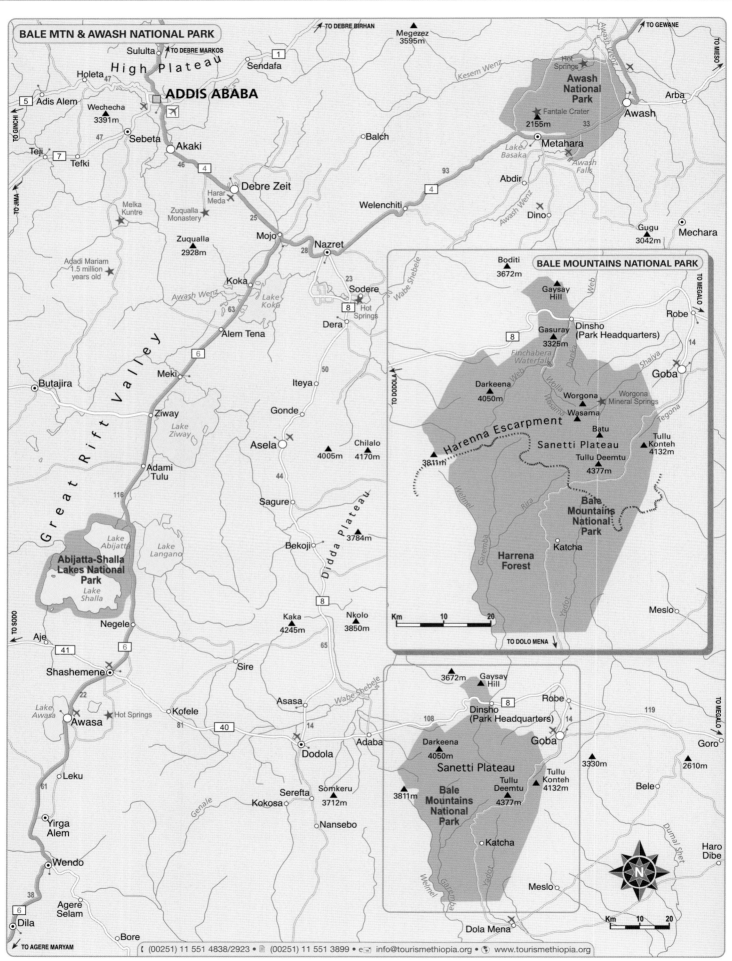

Great Rift Valley Region   Ethiopia

BALE MTN & AWASH NATIONAL PARK

High Plateau

TO DEBRE BIRHAN
TO DEBRE MARKOS
TO GEWANE
TO MIESO

Sululta
Sendafa
1
Megezez
3595m

Holeta
47
ADDIS ABABA

Awash National Park
Hot Springs

Adis Alem
5
Wechecha
3391m

Arba

TO GINCHI

Teji
Tefki
7

Sebeta
Akaki

Melka Kuntre

Balch

Fantale Crater
2155m

Awash

TO JIMA

46
4

Debre Zeit

Harar Meda

33

Metahara

Lake Basaka

Awash Falls

Zuqualla Monastery

25

Mojo

Koka

28

Nazret

Sodere

Welenchiti

4
93

Abdir

Dino

Gugu
3042m

Mechara

Zuqualla
2928m

Acadi Mariam
1.5 million
years old

63

Lake Koka

23

8

Hot Springs

Dera

BALE MOUNTAINS NATIONAL PARK

Boditi
3672m

Alem Tena

Wabe Shebele

Gaysay Hill

Gasuray
3325m

Dinsho
(Park Headquarters)

Robe

TO MEGALO

Meki

50

Iteya

TO DODOLA

8

Finchabera Waterfall

Web

Danka

Shaiya

14

Goba

Butajira

Gonde

Darkeena
4050m

Worgona

Worgona Mineral Springs

Lake Ziway

Ziway

Asela

Chilalo
4170m

4005m

Wasama

Batu

Tegona

Harenna Escarpment

3811m

Sanetti Plateau

Tullu Deemtu
4377m

Tullu Konteh
4132m

Adami Tulu

44

Sagure

116

Lake Abijatta

Lake Langano

Bekoji

Didda Plateau

3784m

Garemba

Rira

Bale Mountains National Park

Abijatta-Shalla Lakes National Park

Lake Shalla

Welmel

Harrena Forest

Katcha

Meslo

Negele

Kaka
4245m

Nkolo
3850m

Km
10
20

TO SODO

Aje

41

6

65

TO DOLO MENA

Shashemene

Sire

Asasa

Wabe Shebele

3672m

Gaysay Hill

Robe

22

Kofele

Dinsho
(Park Headquarters)

8

14

119

Lake Awasa

Awasa

Hot Springs

81
40

14

Adaba

108

Goba

TO MEGALO

Goro

Dodola

Darkeena
4050m

3330m

2610m

Leku

Serefta

Somkeru
3712m

Sanetti Plateau

Tullu Deemtu
4377m

Tullu Konteh
4132m

Bele

Genale

Kokosa

Bale Mountains National Park

3811m

61

Yirga Alem

Nansebo

Welmel

Katcha

Haro Dibe

Wendo

Dumal Shet

38

Agere Selam

6

Dila

Meslo

N

Yadot

Km
10
20

TO AGERE MARYAM

Dola Mena

Bore

✆ (00251) 11 551 4838/2923 • 📄 (00251) 11 551 3899 • ✉ info@tourismethiopia.org • 🌐 www.tourismethiopia.org

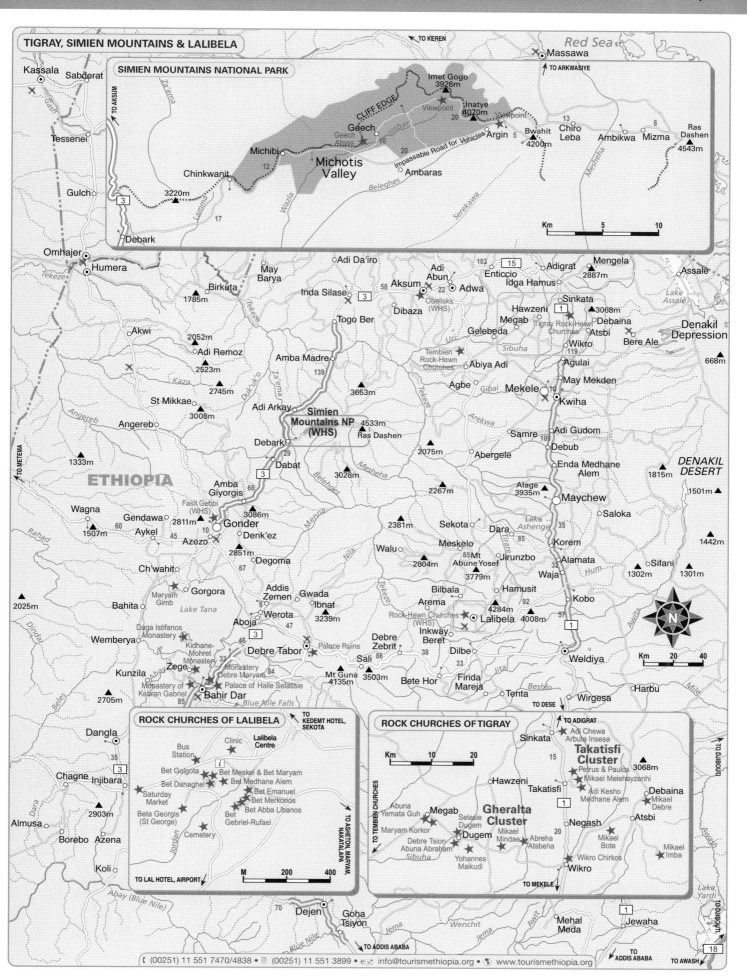

Asmara Eritrea

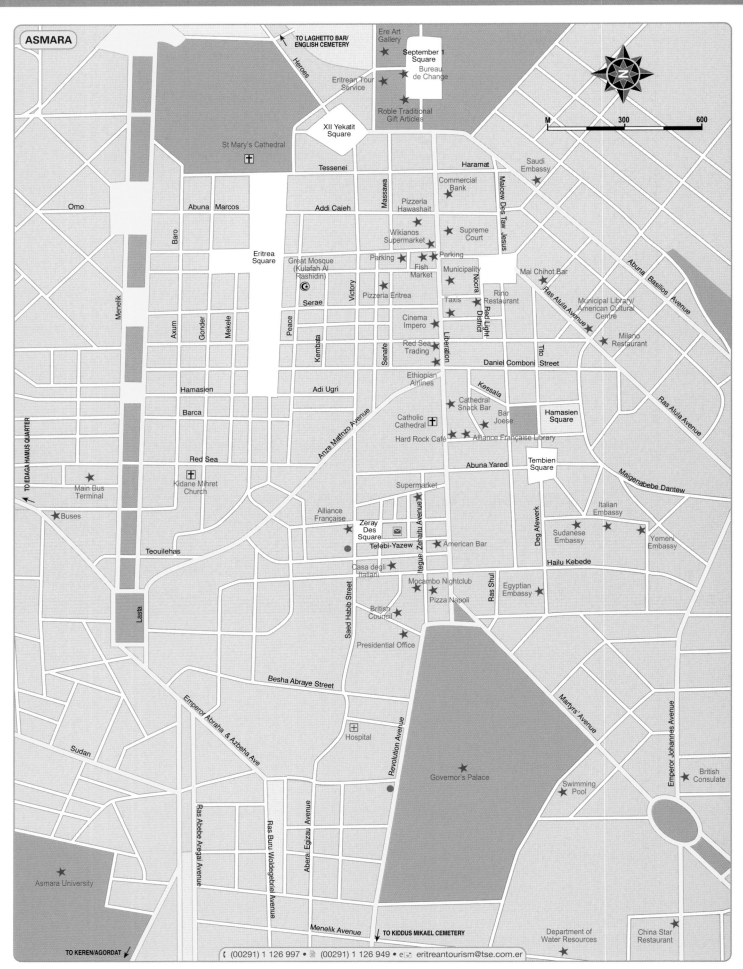

ASMARA

TO LAGHETTO BAR/
ENGLISH CEMETERY

Heroes

Ere Art
Gallery

September 1
Square

Eritrean Tour
Service

Bureau
de Change

Roble Traditional
Gift Articles

XII Yekatit
Square

St Mary's Cathedral

Tessenei

Haramat

Saudi
Embassy

Omo

Abuna Marcos

Addi Caieh

Massawa

Commercial
Bank

Maicew Des Taw. Jesus

Baro

Pizzeria
Hawashait

Abuna Basilios Avenue

Wikianos
Supermarket

Supreme
Court

Eritrea
Square

Great Mosque
(Kulafah Al
Rashidin)

Parking

Parking

Mai Chihot Bar

Ras Alula Avenue

Municipal Library/
American Cultural
Centre

Menelik

Fish
Market

Municipality

Nocra

Rino
Restaurant

Milano
Restaurant

Axum

Gonder

Mekele

Serae

Victory

Pizzeria Eritrea

Taxis

Liberation

Red Light
District

Ras Alula Avenue

Peace

Kembata

Senate

Cinema
Impero

Daniel Comboni Street

Tito
Street

Red Sea
Trading

Hamasien

Adi Ugri

Ethiopian
Airlines

Kessala

Barca

Catholic
Cathedral

Cathedral
Snack Bar

Bar
Joese

Hamasien
Square

Anzè Mafinzo Avenue

Hard Rock Café

Alliance Française Library

Red Sea

Kidane Mihret
Church

Abuna Yared

Tembien
Square

Maigenabebe Dantew

Main Bus
Terminal

Supermarket

Italian
Embassy

Buses

Alliance
Française

Itegue Zehaitu Avenue

Deg Atewerk

Sudanese
Embassy

Yemeni
Embassy

Teouilehas

Zeray
Des
Square

Tefebi-Yazew

American Bar

Hailu Kebede

Casa degli
Italiani

Lasta

Saed Habib Street

Mocambo Nightclub

Ras Shul

Egyptian
Embassy

Pizza Napoli

British
Council

Presidential Office

Besha Abraye Street

Emperor Abraha & Azbeha Ave

TO EDAGA HAMUS QUARTER

Hospital

Revolution Avenue

Martyrs' Avenue

Emperor Johannes Avenue

Sudan

Governor's Palace

British
Consulate

Ras Abebe Aregai Avenue

Ras Buru Woldegebriel Avenue

Abera Egizau Avenue

Swimming
Pool

Asmara University

Menelik Avenue

TO KIDDUS MIKAEL CEMETERY

Department of
Water Resources

China Star
Restaurant

TO KEREN/AGORDAT

((00291) 1 126 997 • (00291) 1 126 949 • e eritreantourism@tse.com.er

M   300   600

74

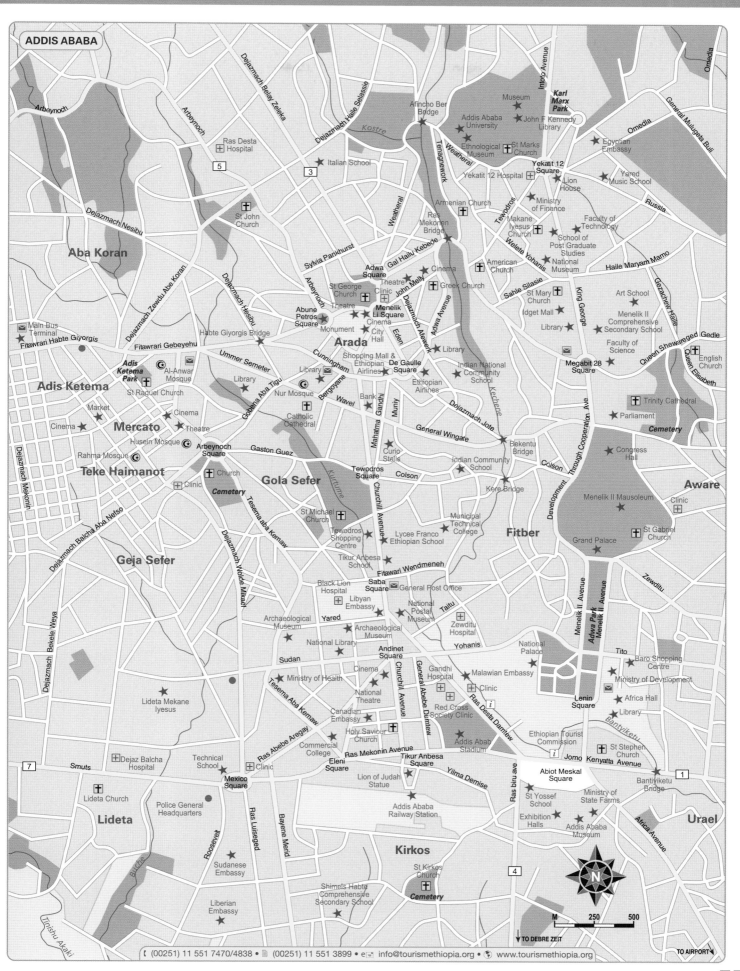

Addis Ababa
Ethiopia

ADDIS ABABA

Arbeynoch

Dejazmach Belay Zeleka

Arbeynoch

Dejazmach Haile Selassie

Intoto Avenue

Omedla

Karl Marx Park

Museum

Afincho Ber Bridge

Kostre

Addis Ababa University

John F Kennedy Library

General Mulugeta Buli

Omedla

Ras Desta Hospital

Italian School

5

3

Tenagnework

Weatheral

Ethnological Museum

St Marks Church

Egyptian Embassy

Yekatit 12 Square

Dejazmach Nesibu

St John Church

Yekatit 12 Hospital

Lion House

Yared Music School

Russia

Aba Koran

Sylvia Pankhurst

Weatheral

Armenian Church

Tewodros

Makane Iyesus Church

Ministry of Finance

Faculty of Technology

School of Post Graduate Studies

National Museum

Haile Maryam Mamo

Arbeynoch

Dejazmach Hesibu

Adwa Square

Gal Hailu Kebede

Cinema

Ras Mekonen Bridge

American Church

Welete Yohanis

King George

Gezachew Haile

Habte Giyorgis Bridge

St George Church

Theatre Clinic

John Mely

Greek Church

Sahle Silasie

St Mary Church

Art School

Queen Shewareged Gedle

Dejazmach Zewdu Abe Koran

Abune Petros Square

Theatre

Menelik Li Square

Dejazmach Atewerk

Idget Mall

Menelik II Comprehensive Secondary School

Queen Elisabeth

Main Bus Terminal

Fitawrari Habte Giyorgis

Fitawrari Gebeyehu

Monument

Cinema

City Hall

Eden

Library

Library

Faculty of Science

English Church

Adis Ketema Park

Al-Anwar Mosque

Arada

Shopping Mall & Ethiopian Airlines

Adwa Avenue

Megabit 28 Square

Trinity Cathedral

Adis Ketema

St Raguel Church

Ummer Semeter

Cunningham

De Gaulle Square

Indian National Community School

Ethiopian Airlines

Mercato

Market

Library

Library

Bergoyane

Bank

Gandhi

Muniy

Dejazmach Jote

Parliament

Cemetery

Cinema

Nur Mosque

Wavel

Mahatma

Dejazmach Jote

Bekentu Bridge

Congress Hall

Cinema

Theatre

Goba Aba Tigu

Catholic Cathedral

General Wingate

Aware

Husein Mosque

Arbeynoch Square

Gaston Guez

Curio Stalls

Colson

Indian Community School

Colson

Menelik II Mausoleum

Clinic

Rahma Mosque

Kurtume

Tewodros Square

Kere Bridge

Teke Haimanot

Church

Clinic

Cemetery

St Michael Church

Lycee Franco Ethiopian School

Municipal Technical College

Fitber

St Gabriel Church

Geja Sefer

Tesema aba Kemaw

Gola Sefer

Tewodros Shopping Centre

Tikur Anbesa School

Fitawari Wendmeneh

Grand Palace

Development Through Cooperation Ave

Dejazmach Balcha Aba Netso

Dejazmach Wolde Mikael

Black Lion Hospital

Saba Square

General Post Office

Zewditu

Libyan Embassy

Yared

National Postal Museum

Taitu

Menelik II Avenue

Menelik II Avenue

Baro Shopping Centre

Tito

Archaeological Museum

Archaeological Museum

Zewditu Hospital

Adwa Park

Ministry of Development

National Library

Andinet Square

Yohanis

National Palace

Africa Hall

Dejazmach Bekele Weya

Sudan

Cinema

Gandhi Hospital

Library

Tesema Aba Kemaw

Ministry of Health

National Theatre

Churchill Avenue

General Abebe Dumtew

Malawian Embassy

Red Cross Society Clinic

Clinic

Lenin Square

Lideta Mekane Iyesus

Ras Desta Damtew

Ethiopian Tourist Commission

St Stephen Church

Ras Abebe Aregay

Canadian Embassy

Holy Saviour Church

Addis Abab Stadium

Jomo Kenyatta Avenue

Bantiviketu

7

Smuts

Dejaz Balcha Hospital

Technical School

Commercial College

Eleni Square

Ras Mekonin Avenue

Tikur Anbesa Square

Yilma Demise

Ras biru ave

Abiot Meskal Square

Ministry of State Farms

Bantiviketu Bridge

1

Lideta Church

Mexico Square

Clinic

Lion of Judah Statue

St Yossef School

Africa Avenue

Urael

Lideta

Police General Headquarters

Roosevelt

Ras Luiseged

Bayene Merid

Addis Ababa Railway Station

Exhibition Halls

Addis Ababa Museum

Sudanese Embassy

Kirkos

St Kirkos Church

4

Liberian Embassy

Shimels Habte Comprehensive Secondary School

Cemetery

Batcha

Tinishu Akaki

N

M 250 500

TO DEBRE ZEIT

TO AIRPORT

(00251) 11 551 7470/4838 • (00251) 11 551 3899 • e info@tourismethiopia.org • www.tourismethiopia.org

Mogadishu　Somalia
Djibouti　Djibouti

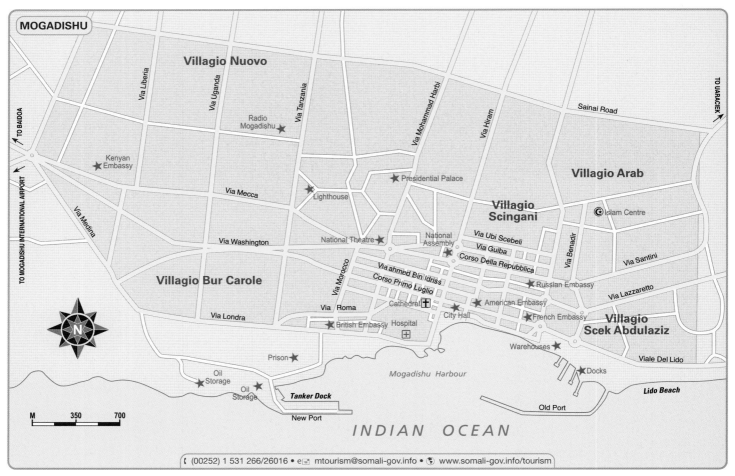

MOGADISHU

Villagio Nuovo

Via Liberia

Via Uganda

Via Tanzania

TO BAIDOA

Radio Mogadishu ★

Via Mohammad Harbi

Via Hiram

Sainai Road

TO URACIEK

Kenyan Embassy ★

Villagio Arab

★ Presidential Palace

Via Medina

Via Mecca

TO MOGADISHU INTERNATIONAL AIRPORT

★ Lighthouse

Villagio Scingani

ⓒ Islam Centre

Via Washington

National Theatre ★

National Assembly

Via Ubi Scebeli

Via Guiba

Via Benadir

Via Santini

Corso Della Repubblica

Villagio Bur Carole

Via Morocco

Via ahmed Bin Idriss

Corso Primo Luglio

★ Russian Embassy

Via Lazzaretto

Via Londra

Via Roma

Cathedral ✝

★ American Embassy

Villagio Scek Abdulaziz

★ British Embassy

Hospital

✚

★ City Hall

★ French Embassy

Prison ★

Warehouses

Viale Del Lido

★ Docks

Oil Storage

Mogadishu Harbour

Lido Beach

Oil Storage

Tanker Dock

Old Port

M　350　700

New Port

INDIAN OCEAN

☎ (00252) 1 531 266/26016 • e✉ mtourism@somali-gov.info • ⊕ www.somali-gov.info/tourism

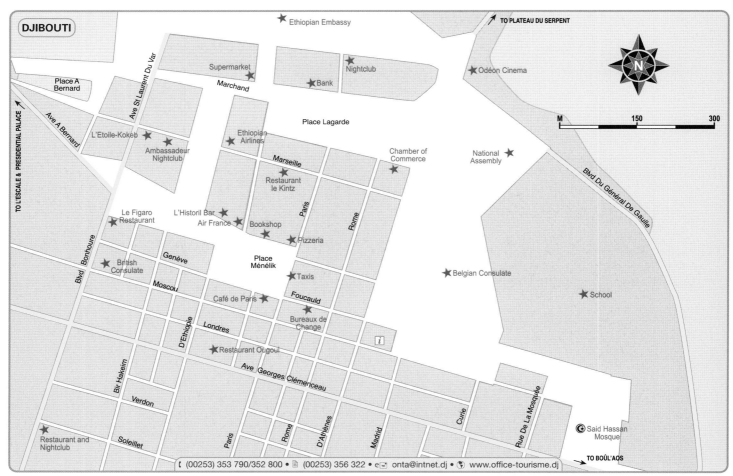

DJIBOUTI

★ Ethiopian Embassy

TO PLATEAU DU SERPENT

Ave St Laurent Du Var

Place A Bernard

Supermarket

Marchand

Nightclub

★ Odéon Cinema

Ave A Bernard

★ Bank

Place Lagarde

TO L'ESCALE & PRESIDENTIAL PALACE

L'Etoile-Kokeb ★

Ethiopian Airlines

Chamber of Commerce

National Assembly ★

M　150　300

Ambassadeur Nightclub ★

Marseille

Le Figaro Restaurant ★

L'Historil Bar

Air France

Restaurant le Kintz

Paris

Rome

Blvd Du Général De Gaulle

Bookshop

Blvd Bonhoure

Genève

Pizzeria

Place Ménélik

★ British Consulate

Moscou

Taxis

★ Belgian Consulate

Café de Paris

Foucauld

★ School

D'Ethiopie

Londres

Bureaux de Change

ⓘ

★ Restaurant Ougoul

Bir Hakeim

Ave Georges Clémenceau

Verdon

Paris

Rome

D'Athènes

Madrid

Curie

Rue De La Mosquée

ⓒ Said Hassan Mosque

★ Restaurant and Nightclub

Soleillet

TO BOÛL'AOS

☎ (00253) 353 790/352 800 • 🖨 (00253) 356 322 • e✉ onta@intnet.dj • ⊕ www.office-tourisme.dj

Adventures

Adventure	Country	Duration
Diving the Dahlak Archipelago	Eritrea	1 - 3 days
Hiking the Bale Mountains	Ethiopia	1 - 7 days
Mule Trekking in the Simien Mountains	Ethiopia	1 -10 days
Sailing Lake Tana	Ethiopia	1 - 5 hours
Exploring historic Lalibela	Ethiopia	4 hours
Exploring the Gulf of Tadjoura	Djibouti	1 day +

Diving the Dahlak Archipelago

Requirements:
Eritrean authorities are notoriously relaxed about documentation; nonetheless, all visitors require a valid passport and visa.

Climate:
Coastal conditions hot and, June–August extremely humid, with day temperatures averaging 40°C. Best times are December to February, when temperatures average 30°C.

Risk factor:
Apart from the usual risks of diving in unfamiliar waters, there are few other dangers, and much of Eritrea is relatively risk-free – apart from land mines that remain following the war.

Health:
Malaria and dengue fever are both prevalent in the coastal regions, and the sun can be fierce in summer.

Pack:
Unlike other areas along the Red Sea, not many dive operators work the Eritrean coast. Those who do are usually well equipped and knowledgeable. Equipment may be hired, but it may be best to take your own basics.

Facilities:
Diving amenities are modest but usually adequate, with a few dive centres offering courses and diving expeditions that are well serviced.

Contact:
Petros, Dahlak Sea Touring.
Tel: 00291-1-552489

Hiking the Bale Mountains

Requirements:
All travellers – except Kenyans – will need a valid passport and visa, in addition to permits to hike the mountain ranges. Cholera and yellow fever vaccinations may also be required.

Climate:
Temperatures are surprisingly moderate even in the interior, and the climate is generally comfortable year-round, apart from the heavy rains between July and September.

Risk factor:
Apart from the usual health risks (see below), there have been some reports of banditry in outlying areas, although not particularly in daylight.

Health:
Bilharzia (and other waterborne diseases) is prevalent throughout the country; extreme caution should be exercised with drinking water and fresh foods. AIDS is ever-present.

Pack:
Water purification tablets are essential, as are a sunscreen and comfortable but sturdy hiking gear. Do not depend on your guide for anything.

Facilities:
Access is limited and in need of some upgrading. Amenities are poor to adequate, with only a few basics.

Contact:
Bale Mountains National Park.
Tel: 00251-11-5514838 / 5512923

Mule Trekking in the Simien Mountains

Requirements:
All travelers – except Kenyans – need a passport and visa, in addition to permits to hike the mountain. Cholera and yellow fever vaccinations may also be required.

Climate:
Temperatures are moderate even in the interior and, apart from the heavy rains July–September, the climate is generally comfortable year-round.

Risk factor:
Apart from usual health risks (see below), there have been reports of banditry in outlying areas; this is not common, particularly not in daylight.

Health:
Bilharzia (and other waterborne diseases) is prevalent, and caution should be exercised with drinking water and fresh foods. AIDS is ever-present.

Pack:
Water purification tablets are essential, as are a sunscreen and comfortable but sturdy hiking gear. Do not depend on your guide for anything.

Facilities:
Amenities are rudimentary to adequate, but the experience is worth any discomfort travellers may experience as a result of spending too many hours on the back of a mule trudging across a rocky landscape.

Contact:
Ethiopia Tourism Commission.
Tel: 00251-11-5514838 / 5512923

Sailing Lake Tana

Requirements:
All travellers – except Kenyans – need a passport and visa. Cholera and yellow fever vaccinations may also be required.

Climate:
Temperatures are moderate, and the climate is comfortable year-round (heavy rains July–September).

Risk factor:
Apart from usual health risks (see below) associated with water-based pastimes, Tana holds few dangers.

Health:
Bilharzia (and other waterborne diseases) is prevalent throughout the country, and extreme caution should be exercised with drinking water and fresh foods. AIDS is ever-present.

Pack:
Water purification tablets are essential, as are a sunscreen and a set of warm, dry clothing. Do not depend on your guide for anything.

Facilities:
Facilities at Lake Tana are usually good, with a variety of options available to travellers. Accommodation varies from basic to comfortable, but prices are equally extreme, so it is best to plan through a reliable tour operator.

Contact:
Experience Ethiopia Travel.
Tel: 00251-11-4409716
eet@telecom.net.et
www.telecom.net.et/eet

Exploring historic Lalibela

Requirements:
All travellers – except Kenyans – need a passport and visa. Cholera and yellow fever vaccinations may also be required; church custodians may want to see a touring permit.

Climate:
Temperatures are moderate, and apart from heavy rains July–September, the climate is comfortable year-round.

Risk factor:
Apart from the usual health risks (see below), there have been reports of banditry in outlying areas.

Health:
Bilharzia (and other waterborne diseases) is prevalent and caution should be exercised with drinking water and fresh foods. AIDS is ever-present.

Pack:
Water purification tablets are essential, as are sunscreen and comfortable but sturdy hiking gear.

Facilities:
Because Lalibela is one of the top tourist attractions in Ethiopia, facilities are fair to good, with a number of private tour agents – and locals masquerading as such. Established operators will offer a far better service than the considerably cheaper fly-by-nighters.

Contact:
Experience Ethiopia Travel.
Tel: 00251-11-4409716
eet@telecom.net.et, www.telecom.net.et/eet

Exploring the Gulf of Tadjoura

Requirements:
All visitors (except French citizens) require a passport and the necessary one-month visas on entry.

Climate:
Humid and very hot, with day-time temperatures in even the moderate cooler months peaking at 25°C.

Risk factor:
There are almost no risks around the main centre, but venturing further afield – particularly the northern areas – may present some dangers.

Health:
There are few health risks, but it is safest to drink only bottled water and avoid sexual contact with the prostitutes operating in and around Djibouti City.

Pack:
Take light holiday clothing and plenty of sunscreen, particularly if much of the holiday is to be spent on the water. To avoid high hiring costs, take your own equipment, such as scuba gear.

Facilities:
Visitors' facilities in Djibouti are adequate, but are certainly no match even for countries such as Ethiopia. Because locals speak virtually no English at all, travel can be frustrating, and is very expensive – especially for the budget traveller.

Contact:
La Caravane du Sel (The Caravan of Salt),
P.O. Box 2098, Djibouti.
Tel: 00253-35-3752

The Congo Basin

With the exception of oil-rich Gabon, a prosperous and relatively stable nation, the south-central region of the continent – with its profusion of rainforest and swamps, perhaps the epitome of the romantic notions of the African jungle – is one that has seen great suffering among its people, due almost entirely to the series of civil wars, revolution and instability that have come to symbolize the temperament of the region. Even by African standards, Congo, the Democratic Republic of the Congo (DRC) and Angola – but, again, with the exception of Gabon – are vast countries, with a total population of some 70 million people. This results in much strain on existing natural resources and leads to extreme poverty, especially among rural peoples who rely almost entirely on what the earth yields. The high cost of travel and the issue of personal safety remain areas of concern for international visitors, but the rewards are no less gratifying.

DEMOCRATIC REPUBLIC OF THE CONGO

KINSHASA

Known by its colonists as Léopoldville, what is today Kinshasa became the capital of the Belgian Congo in 1929 and is now one of the most dynamic of Africa's modern cities. Set amid rainforests and volcanic mountains and peopled by over five million, the city vacillates between a thriving metropolis and a dusty little backwater, incorporating the good and the bad of virtually every contemporary urban settlement. It has a very reputable university, a number of impressive museums – most significantly the Musée de Kinshasa – and a proud heritage of fine art, the finest examples of which may be seen at the Académie des Beaux-Arts. The local music scene is Kinshasa's most enduring highlight. Musicians continue to perform at popular nightspots in the Cité area and the thumping music and laughter emanating from the ngandas (open-air dance venues) continue to draw crowds of revellers. Kinshasa's detractions include being hot, humid and chaotic with a horribly inept public transport system, an extremely intimidating (and often corrupt) military and police presence, and vast numbers of visitors reporting incidents of harassment.

GOMA

The town of Goma is a good base from which to explore national parks such as Kahuzi-Biega National Park. Although the outskirts are undeniably attractive and the shores of Lake Kivu are lined with grand, well-maintained private homes, the inner Cité still bears the scars left by marauding troops in the mid - late 1990s. More recently, Nyiragongo Volcano, which forms the majestic backdrop of the town, erupted in early 2002 and resulted in one of the country's most horrific tragedies. Goma is still struggling to overcome the massive geological as well as political and social devastation. It can, nevertheless, be a charming little stopover.

CONGO RIVER

The length of the Congo River's winding, 4,800km course delineates the political boundary between Congo and the DRC and lies in a basin of some 3,000,000km^2 lined with lush equatorial forest and punctuated intermittently with swamp and savanna plain. The great river, hailed as the second-longest in Africa, rises on the Katanga Plateau, where it is known locally as the Lualaba and, together with the Ubangi River, channels most of the DRC's run-off to the sea. One of the greatest benefactors of the waters of the Congo River is Kisangani, the all-important urban settlement nestling on the water's edge and an important crossroads for cross-country travellers. A large proportion of local travel centres on the much vaunted Stanley Falls (Boyoma Falls), one of the area's most significant tourism drawcards.

CONGO

BRAZZAVILLE

Following at least a decade of political turbulence and sustained bloodshed at the hands of revolutionaries, Brazzaville (located on the Congo River) has both its advantages and disadvantages for any tourist brave enough to venture into the very heart of Africa. Congo is famed for its short stretch of pristine coastline and its vibrant and innovative local music industry, yet the overriding feeling is one of despair. The capital of Congo is a spread-out mass of urban decay, where big city meets tiny village. Well greened, there are small pockets of tranquil solitude unblemished by the scars of war that ravaged the people and their environment, especially the Congo River. Just 10km from the city centre are the celebrated rapids on the Congo river.

POINTE-NOIRE

In a country best known for its tropical forest and hot and humid interior, it is a refreshing change to discover that large parts of its shoreline are little short of idyllic, such as Pointe-Noire. One of Congo's many popular beach towns, the laid-back milieu and breathtaking setting of turquoise waters and deserted beaches are incomparable. Pointe-Noire is relaxed and friendly, with a succession of beach clubs and pubs. The days are balmy, but the gentle sea breeze is refreshing. With the blue sea and pristine beaches dotted with thatched umbrellas just a few kilometres beyond the urban limits, it is little wonder that the resort town is enjoying increasing attention.

ANGOLA

LUANDA

Still bearing the evidence of its Portuguese colonial heritage and fighting a continuing battle against crime and civil unrest, Luanda – officially known as São Paulo de Loanda – was founded in 1576 and, in less than 100 years, had become the nucleus of the thriving slave trade to the plantations of Brazil. Originally established to accommodate no more than 30,000 settlers, what is now the capital of Angola is wholly unable to meet the needs of its 2.8 million citizens, many of whom made their way here from farmland during the civil war towards the end of the 20th century. The overcrowded city streets spill over into dirty and dusty shanty towns on its outskirts. Luanda has managed to retain at least some of its centuries-old charm. The old Portuguese Quarter, known as Cidade Alta, is undoubtedly the most picturesque, a series of Victorian- and Edwardian-style buildings housing museums and galleries, restaurants and even government offices. Sadly, this is virtually the only evidence of a profusion of indigenous cultures in the city, where most of the citizens have adopted Western lifestyles.

GABON

LIBREVILLE

Established as a French trading colony in the mid-1800s, Libreville saw considerable development following its lucrative slave trade to Brazil and other South American nations towards the end of the 19th century. Situated on an estuary of the Gabon River, it is one of the most modern capitals on the continent, and the principal city of one of the richest countries in Africa south of the Sahara – its more than one million people enjoy the fruits of Gabon's extensive oil reserves. The wide thoroughfares and leafy boulevards stand in stark contrast to the rustic little villages scattered on the outskirts. Although the charm of the rural settlements seems to have eluded Libreville's commercial districts, its African quarters are alive with a buzz more typical of the continent. Highlights are the impressive St-Michel's Church, with its mosaic and wood-carved façade, the traditional utensils and handiwork for sale at Le Village des Artisans, and the indigenous art on display at the Musée des Arts et Traditions. Along the northern coastal stretch is a series of truly beautiful beaches and resort towns, such as the famed Cap Estérias and Pointe-Dénis.

LAMBARÉNÉ

Steeped in a popular history that has become the focal point of the entire area, the town of Lambaréné – situated on the banks of an island in the Ogooué River – is gentle and laid-back, despite the fact that it is the third-largest settlement in Gabon. No more than a tiny rural community half buried in the lush rainforest that surrounds it, Lambaréné was put on the map by its most famous citizen, the doctor and philanthropist Albert Schweitzer, whose remains were laid to rest here in 1965. When he arrived in 1913, he set about establishing one of Gabon's finest medical facilities. The famed doctor's home, his original office, laboratory and treatment centre, some 8km outside of the town, are now a little dilapidated but the Schweitzer Hospital, its annex and the adjacent museum are still popular among visitors. Excursions in the immediate vicinity include a pirogue trip to see the wildlife in the famed lake region. Hippos – along with other animals and birds – are prolific here during the dry season, when they tend to congregate at the all-important water sources.

While Gabon has made best use of its mineral resources to build up considerable wealth from its oil fields, the vast oil reserves and diamond deposits to be found in Congo, Angola and the DRC (some 85 per cent of its foreign income) have remained largely unexploited while these countries have battled civil war and economic collapse.

Gabon, Congo, Democratic Republic of the Congo, Angola

Old Christian Church, Luanda, Angola

Virunga National Park, Democratic Republic of the Congo

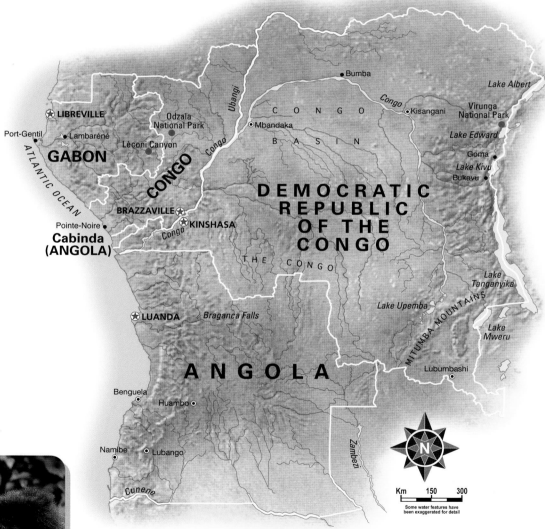

Mountain Gorillas, Odzala National Park, Congo

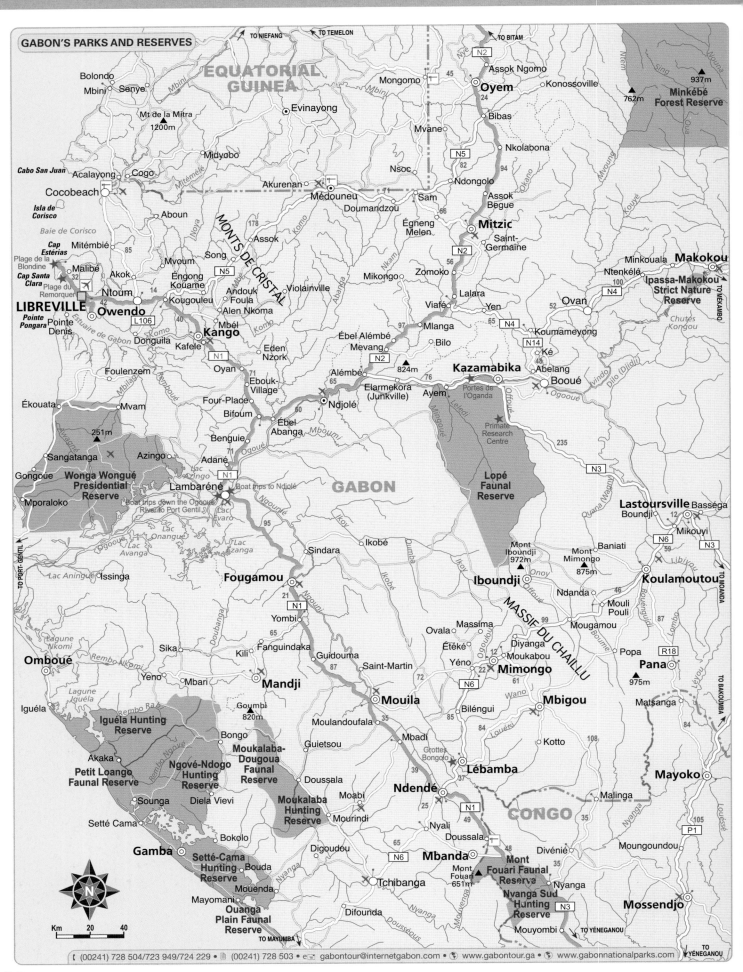

GABON'S PARKS AND RESERVES

EQUATORIAL GUINEA

GABON

CONGO

Libreville
Owendo
Kango
Ndjolé
Lambaréné
Fougamou
Mandji
Mouila
Ndendé
Mbanda
Tchibanga
Gamba
Omboué
Iguéla
Akaka
Sounga
Setté Cama
Bokolo
Bouda
Mouenda
Mayomani
Difounda
Oyem
Mitzic
Makokou
Boué
Kazamabika
Lastoursville
Koulamoutou
Iboundji
Mimongo
Mbigou
Mayoko
Pana
Lébamba
Mossendjo

Wonga Wongué Presidential Reserve
Lopé Faunal Reserve
Iguéla Hunting Reserve
Petit Loango Faunal Reserve
Ngové-Ndogo Hunting Reserve
Moukalaba-Dougoua Faunal Reserve
Moukalaba Hunting Reserve
Setté-Cama Hunting Reserve
Ouanga Plain Faunal Reserve
Mont Fouari Faunal Reserve
Nyanga Sud Hunting Reserve
Minkébé Forest Reserve
Ipassa-Makokou Strict Nature Reserve

MONTS DE CRISTAL
MASSIF DU CHAILLU

Km 20 40

TO MAYUMBA

☎ (00241) 728 504/723 949/724 229 • 📠 (00241) 728 503 • 📧 gabontour@internetgabon.com • 🌐 www.gabontour.ga • 🌐 www.gabonnationalparks.com

Eastern Congo Region DRC

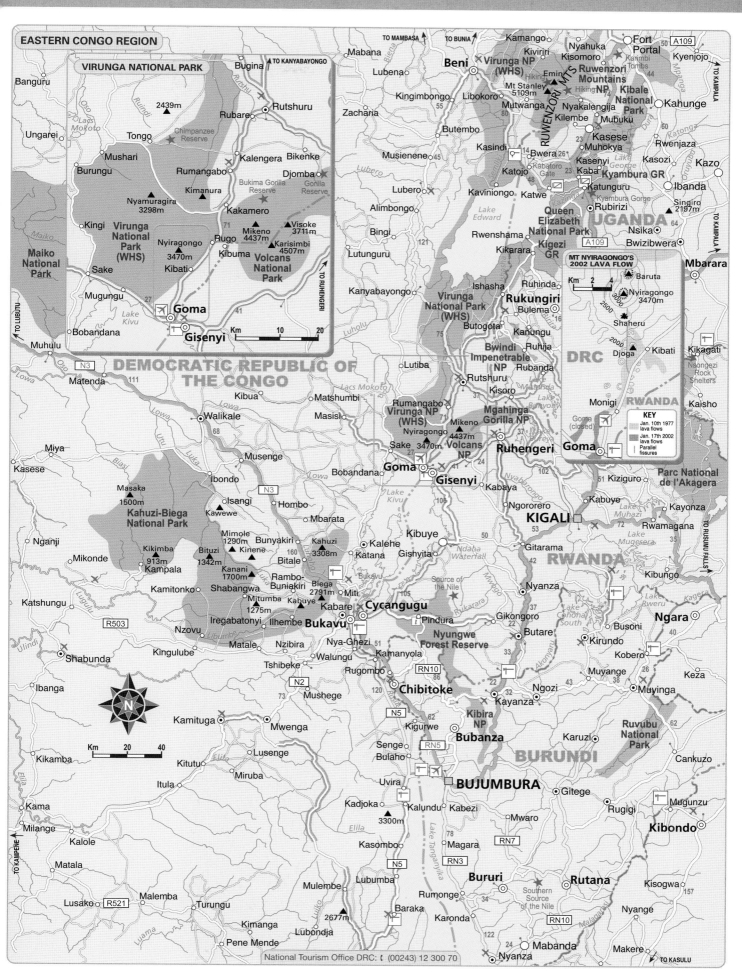

EASTERN CONGO REGION

VIRUNGA NATIONAL PARK

TO KANYABAYONGO

Banguru
Ungarei
Bangura
Muhulu
Matenda
Miya
Kasese
Nganji
Mikonde
Ibanga
Kikamba
Kama
Milange
Kalole
Matala
Lusako
R521
Malemba

Bugina
Mabana
Rubare
2439m
Tongo
Mushari
Burungu
Kingi
Sake
Mugungu
Bobandana
N3
Kibua
Walikale
68
Masaka
1500m
Isangi
Kawewe
Ibondo
Hombo
Mbarata
Kahuzi-Biega
National Park
Mimole
1290m
Bunyakiri
Kahuzi
3308m
Kikimba
913m
Bituzi
1342m
Kinene
Bitale
160
Kanani
1700m
Rambo-
Buniakiri
Shabangwa
Biega
2791m
Miti
Mjtumba
1275m
Kabuye
Kabare
Iregabatonyi
Ilhembe
Bukavu
R503
Nzovu
Matale
Nzibira
Kingulube
Tshibeke
Walungu
Kamitonko
Kampala
Katshungu

Rutshuru
Kalengera
Bikenke
Rumangabo
Djomba
Kimanura
Kakamero
Nyamuragira
3298m
Visoke
3711m
Mikeno
4437m
Karisimbi
4507m
Nyiragongo
3470m
Rugo
Kibuma
Kibati
Volcans
National
Park
27
Goma
41
Gisenyi
Km 10 20

Virunga
National
Park
(WHS)

Chimpanzee
Reserve
71
Bukima Gorilla
Reserve
Gorilla
Reserve
TO RUHENGERI

Lake
Kivu

Maiko
National
Park

DEMOCRATIC REPUBLIC OF
THE CONGO

111
Matshumbi
Masisi
Rumangabo
Virunga NP
(WHS)
71
Nyiragongo
4437m
3470m
Sake
27
Bobandana
Goma
41
Gisenyi
106

Lacs Mokoto
Lutiba
Rutshuru
37
Kisoro
Mikeno
Volcans
NP
24
Ruhengeri
Kabaya
102
Ngororero
Km 20 40

TO MAMBASA
TO BUNIA
Kamango
Kiviriri
Nyahuka
Nyakatsoro
Kisomoro
Fort
Portal
50 A109
TO KAMPALA
Beni
Virunga NP
(WHS)
Emin
Ruwenzori
Mountains
44
Kyenjojo
Libokoro
Mt Stanley
5109m
Hiking NP
Kibale
National
Park
Kingimbongo
55
Mutwanga
80
Nyakalengija
Kilembe
Mubuku
Kahunge
Butembo
Kasindi
14
Bwera
261
Muhokya
60
Musienene
45
Katojo
Kabatoro
Gate
23
Kasenyi
Kaba
Rwenjaza
Lubero
Kaviniongo
Katwe
Kasozi
Kazo
Alimbongo
Lake
Edward
Rubirizi
Singiro
2197m
Ibanda
Bingi
Rwenshama
Queen
Elizabeth
National Park
Kyamura GR
Katunguru
Lutunguru
Kikarara
Kigezi
GR
A109
UGANDA
64
Nsika
Bwizibwera
Kanyabayongo
Ishasha
Ruhinda
Rukungiri
Virunga
National
Park
(WHS)
Bulema
16
Mbarara
Butogota
75
Kanungu
Bwindi
Impenetrable
NP
Ruhija
Rubanda
DRC
Mgahinga
Gorilla NP
37
RWANDA
Monigi
Goma
(closed)
Goma
Kiziguro
Parc National
de l'Akagera
KIGALI
53
Kabuye
Kayonza
Rwamagana
72
35
Gitarama
42
Kibungo
Nyanza
Lake
Mugesera
TO RUSUMU FALLS
Kibuye
50
Gishyita
Katana
Kalehe
Source of
the Nile
105
Cyangugu
Pindura
Gikongoro
37
Lake
Cohoha
South
Ngara
Busoni
Kirundo
Kobero
Keza
Nya-Ghezi
51
Kamanyola
Rugombo
RN10
86
Walungu
N2
Mushege
73
120
Chibitoke
Kayanza
Ngozi
43
Muyange
38
26
Muyinga
Kamituga
Mwenga
N5
82
Kigurwe
Kibira
NP
Bubanza
Karuzi
Ruvubu
National
Park
62
Cankuzo
Lusenge
Senge
RN5
BURUNDI
Kitutu
Bulaho
Miruba
Itula
Uvira
BUJUMBURA
Gitete
Rugigi
Mugunzu
Kadjoka
Kalundu
Kabezi
Mwaro
Kibondo
3300m
Mwaro
Kasombo
Magara
RN7
Elila
Lake
Tanganyika
78
N5
Lubumba
RN3
Mulembe
Rumonge
Bururi
Rutana
Kisogwa
Baraka
Karonda
34
Southern
Source
of the Nile
Nyange
157
Turungu
2677m
Lubondja
Kimanga
122
24
RN10
Pene Mende
Mabanda
Makere
Nyanza
TO KASULU

National Tourism Office DRC: ((00243) 12 300 70

MT NYIRAGONGO'S
2002 LAVA FLOW
Km 2 4
Baruta
Nyiragongo
3470m
3000
2500
Shaheru
2000
Djoga
Kibati
Kikagati
Nsongezi
Rock
Shelters
KEY
Jan. 10th 1977
lava flows
Jan. 17th 2002
lava flows
Parallel
fissures

81

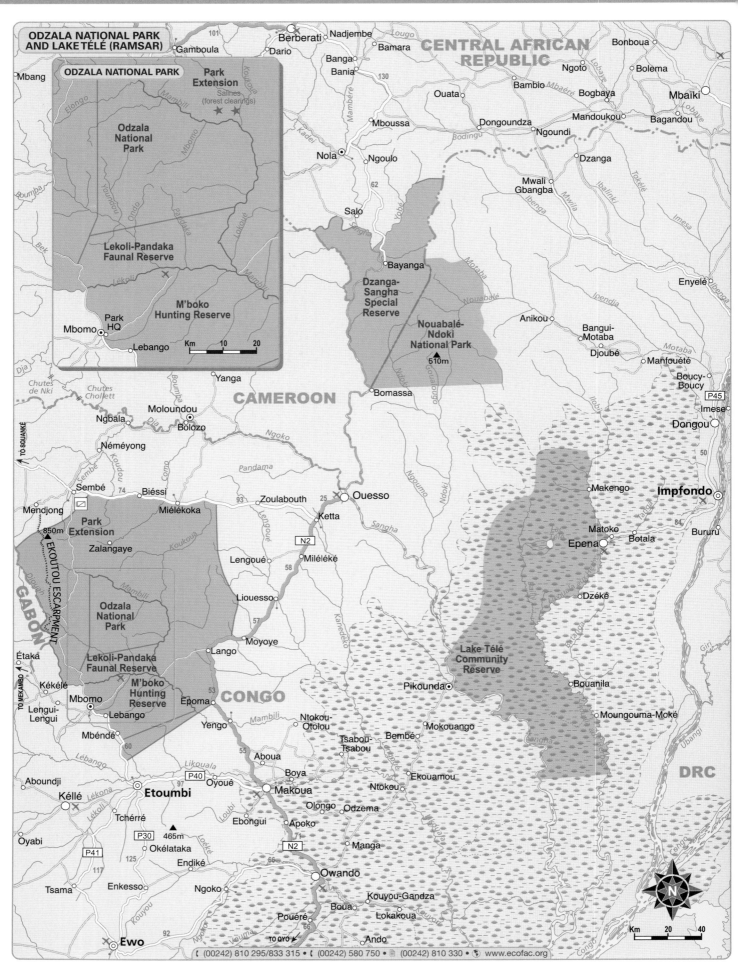

ODZALA NATIONAL PARK
AND LAKE TÉLÉ (RAMSAR)

ODZALA NATIONAL PARK

Park Extension
Salines (forest clearings)

Odzala National Park

Lekoli-Pandaka Faunal Reserve

M'boko Hunting Reserve

Park HQ

Mbomo

Lebango

Km   10   20

Mbang

Gamboula

Berberati

Nadjembe

Bamara

Dario

Banga

Bania

Mboussa

Nola

Ngoulo

Salo

Bayanga

Dzanga-Sangha Special Reserve

Nouabalé-Ndoki National Park

510m

Bomassa

CENTRAL AFRICAN REPUBLIC

Bonboua

Bolema

Ngoto

Bambio

Bogbaya

Mbaïki

Ouata

Mandoukou

Bagandou

Dongoundza

Ngoundi

Dzanga

Mwali Gbangba

Anikou

Enyelé

Bangui-Motaba

Djoubé

Manfouété

Boucy-Boucy

P45

Imese

Dongou

50

Chutes de Nki

Chutes Chollett

CAMEROON

Moloundou

Ngbala

Bolozo

Néméyong

Yanga

Ngoko

Pandama

TO SOUANKÉ

Sembé

Biéssi

Miélékoka

Zoulabouth

Ouesso

Ketta

Impfondo

Makengo

Matoko

Botala

Bururu

Mendjong

Park Extension

850m

EKOUTOU ESCARPMENT

Zalangaye

Lengoué

Miléléké

N2

58

Epena

Dzéké

GABON

Odzala National Park

Lekoli-Pandaka Faunal Reserve

M'boko Hunting Reserve

Mbomo

Lebango

Étaka

Kékélé

TO MEKAMBO

Lengui-Lengui

Mbéndé

60

Liouesso

57

Moyoye

Lango

Epoma

Yengo

Youé

55

Aboua

Boya

Lake Télé Community Reserve

Pikounda

Bouanila

Moungouma-Moké

CONGO

Ntokou-Otolou

Tsabou-Tsabou

Bembé

Mokouango

Ekouamou

Ntokeu

DRC

Aboundji

Kéllé

Etoumbi

Makoua

Odzema

P40

97

Oyoué

Olongo

Tchérré

P30

465m

Ebongui

Apoko

Manga

71

N2

Oyabi

Okélataka

Endiké

66

P41

125

117

Enkesso

Ngoko

Owando

Kouyou-Gandza

Tsama

Boua

Lokakoua

Ewo

92

Pouéré

TO OYO

Ando

N

Km   20   40

☎ (00242) 810 295/833 315 • ☎ (00242) 580 750 • 🖷 (00242) 810 330 • 🌐 www.ecofac.org

82

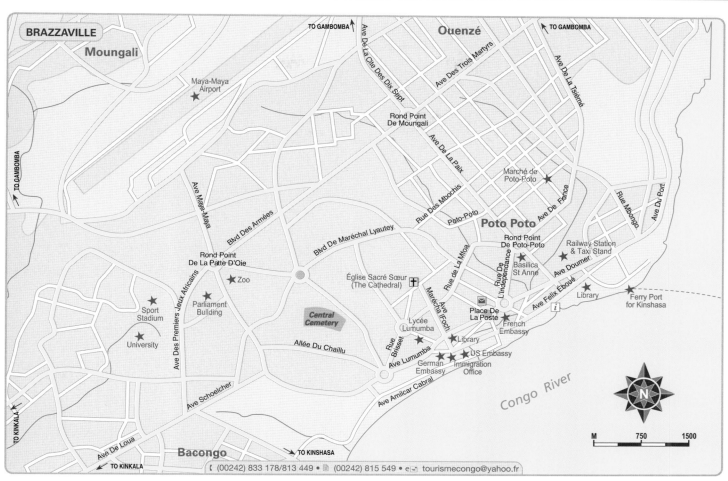

BRAZZAVILLE

Moungali

TO GAMBOMBA
TO GAMBOMBA
Ouenzé

Maya-Maya Airport

Ave De La Cité Des Dix Sept
Ave Des Trois Martyrs
Ave De La Tsiémé

Rond Point De Moungali

Ave De La Paix

Marché de Poto-Poto

Rue Des Mbochis
Poto-Poto

Ave De France
Rue Mbongo
Ave Du Port

Blvd Des Armées

Blvd De Maréchal Lyautey

Poto Poto

Rond Point De La Patte D'Oie

Blvd De Maréchal Lyautey

Rue de la Mfoa
Rond Point De Poto-Poto
Railway Station & Taxi Stand

Zoo

Église Sacré Sœur (The Cathedral)
Basilica St Anne
Ave Doumer

Ave Des Premiers Jeux Africains

Parliament Building

Rue De L'Independance

Sport Stadium

Central Cemetery

Lycée Lumumba

Place De La Poste
French Embassy
Ave Felix Éboué
Library
Ferry Port for Kinshasa

University

Allée Du Chaillu

Rue Brisset
Ave Maréchal Foch
Library

Ave Lumumba
US Embassy

German Embassy
Immigration Office

Ave Schoelcher

Ave Amilcar Cabral

Congo River

N

Ave De Loua

Bacongo
TO KINSHASA

TO KINKALA

M 750 1500

TO KINKALA

☎ (00242) 833 178/813 449 • 🖨 (00242) 815 549 • e 📧 tourismecongo@yahoo.fr

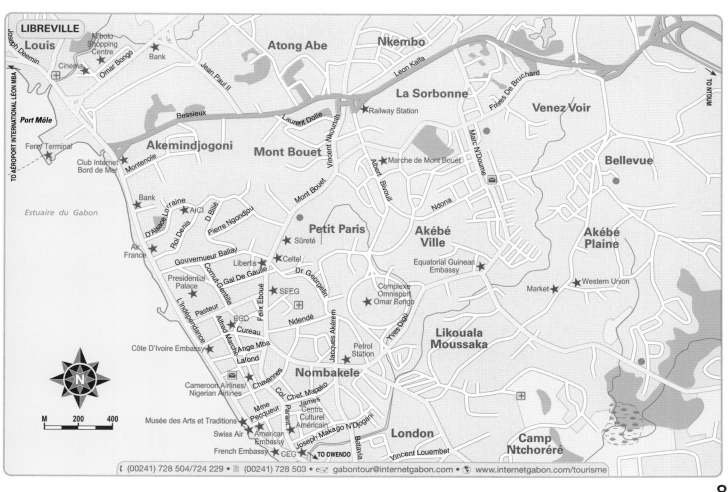

LIBREVILLE

Joseph Deemin
Louis
M'boto Shopping Centre
Cinema
Bank
Omar Bongo
Atong Abe
Nkembo
Jean Paul II
Leon Kalfa

La Sorbonne
Frères De Bruchard
Venez Voir

Bessieux
Laurent Dolle
Railway Station

TO NTOUM

Port Môle
Ferry Terminal
Club Internet Bord de Mer
Montenole
Akemindjogoni
Montenole
Mont Bouet
Vincent Nkouriah
Marc N'Doume

Estuaire du Gabon
Bank
D'Alsace Lorraine
AICI
D Bilié
Pierre Ngondiou
Roi Denis
Mont Bouet
Marche de Mont Bouët
Albert Bivouli
Ndona

Bellevue

Air France
Gouverneur Ballay
Petit Paris
Sûreté
Akébé Ville
Equatorial Guinean Embassy
Akébé Plaine

Presidential Palace
Libertis
Cornut-Gentille
Gal De Gaulle
Celtel
Dr Georgelin
Complexe Omnisport Omar Bongo
Western Union
Market

Pasteur
Alfred Marche
Felix Éboué
SEEG
Ndendé
Yves Digo
Likouala Moussaka

L'Independance
BGD
Cureau
Ange Mba
Lafond
Jacques Akérem
Petrol Station

Côte D'Ivoire Embassy
Chavannes
Nombakele

Cameroon Airlines/ Nigerian Airlines
Col Chef Mapako
James Centre Culturel Américain
London
Camp Ntchoréré

Musée des Arts et Traditions
Mme Pecqueur
Joseph Makago N'Dogani
Batavia
Vincent Louembet

Swiss Air
American Embassy
French Embassy
CEG
TO OWENDO

N
M 200 400

☎ (00241) 728 504/724 229 • 🖨 (00241) 728 503 • e 📧 gabontour@internetgabon.com • 🌐 www.internetgabon.com/tourisme

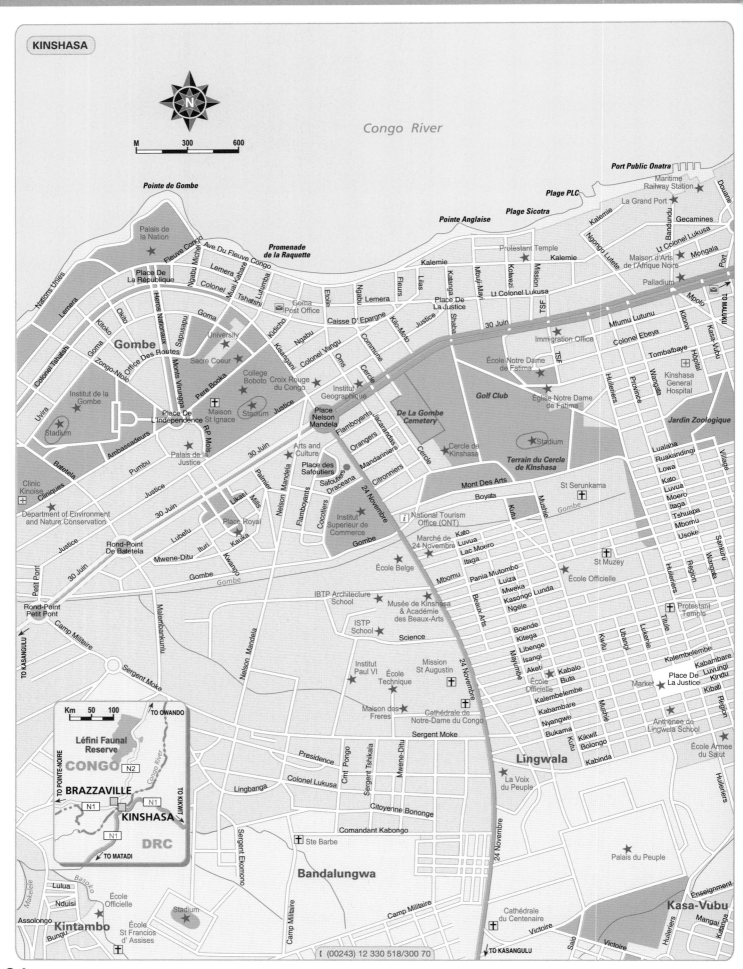

Kinshasa
Democratic Republic of the Congo

Congo River

M 300 600

Pointe de Gombe

Port Public Onatra

Plage PLC

Maritime
Railway Station

La Grand Port

Plage Sicotra

Douane

Pointe Anglaise

Palais de
la Nation

Promenade
de la Raquette

Protestant Temple

Kalemie

Lt Bandundu

Gecamines

Place De
La République

Ave Du Fleuve Congo

Kalemie

Ngongo Lutete

Lt Colonel Lukusa

Mongala

Maison d'Arts
de l'Afrique Noire

Lemera

Colonel Muriu Kabate

Lutumba

Etoile

Ngabu Lemera

Fleurs

Lilas

Kolwezi

Mbuji-Mayi

Kalemie

Palladium

Nations Unies

Lemera

Kiloko

Okito

Goma

Kidicho

Goma
Post Office

Caisse D' Epargne

Place De
La Justice

Katanga

Lt Colonel Lukusa

Mission

Kitona

Kasa-Vubu

TO MALUKU

Gombe

Office Des Routes

Heros Nationaux

Monts Virunga

University

Sacre Coeur

Kisangani

Ngabu

Colonel Vangu

Oms

Commune

Cercle

Justice

Shaba

30 Juin

Immigration Office

Mfumu Lutunu

Colonel Ebeya

Tombalbaye

Wangata

Hopital

Zongo-Ntolo

Pere Booka

College
Boboto

Croix Rouge
du Congo

Institut
Geographique

École Notre Dame
de Fatima

TSF

Kinshasa
General
Hospital

Institut de la
Gombe

Place De
L'Indépendance

Maison
St Ignace

Stadium

Justice

Place
Nelson
Mandela

De La Gombe
Cemetery

Golf Club

Église Notre Dame
de Fatima

Province

Jardin Zoologique

Uvira

R.P Mols

Flamboyants

Jacarandas

Cercle

Stadium

Lualaba

Stadium

Ambassadeurs

Palais de la
Justice

30 Juin

Arts and
Culture

Orangers

Mandariniers

Citronniers

Cercle

Cercle de
Kinshasa

Terrain du Cercle
de Kinshasa

Ruakandingi

Lowa

Pumbu

Nelson Mandela

Mills

Palmier

Place des
Safoutiers

Safoutiers

Draceana

24 Novembre

Mont Des Arts

St Serunkama

Kato

Luvua

Moero

Itaga

Batetela

Clinic
Kinoise

Justice

Cliniques

30 Juin

Likasi

Flamboyants

Cocotiers

Institut
Superieur de
Commerce

Gombe

Boyata

Kutu

Mushie

Gombe

National Tourism
Office (ONT)

Kato

Tshuapa

Mbomu

Usoke

Department of Environment
and Nature Conservation

Justice

Lubefu

Ituri

Place Royal

Kauka

Kwango

Gombe

Gombe

Marché de
24 Novembre

Luvua

Lac Moero

Itaga

École Belge

Mbomu

Pania Mutombo

Luiza

Mweka

St Muzey

École Officielle

Sankuru

Wangata

Rond-Point
De Batetela

Mwene-Ditu

Kasôngo Lunda

Ngele

Huileriers

Region

Titule

Petit Pont

Rond-Point
Petit Pont

TO KASANGULU

Camp Militaire

Nelson Mandela

Malembankulu

Gombe

IBTP Architecture
School

Musée de Kinshasa
& Académie
des Beaux-Arts

Mbomu

Beaux-Arts

Boende

Kitega

Libenge

Isangi

Aketi

École
Officielle

Kabalo

Buta

Kalembelembe

Protestant
Temple

Lukenie

Ubangi

Kalembelembe

Kabambare

Luvungi

Kindu

Place De
La Justice

Kibati

Sergent Moke

ISTP
School

Science

Institut
Paul VI

École
Technique

Mission
St Augustin

24 Novembre

Kabambare

Mushie

Nyangwe

Market

Kwilu

Anthenee de
Lingwala School

Maison des
Freres

Cathédrale de
Notre-Dame du Congo

Sergent Moke

Bukama

Kikwit

Bolongo

Kutu

École Armee
du Salut

TO OWANDO

Km 50 100

Léfini Faunal
Reserve

CONGO

N2

Presidence

Sergent Tshikala

Cmt Pongo

Mwene-Ditu

Sergent Moke

Kabinda

Lingwala

Huileriers

TO POINTE-NOIRE

BRAZZAVILLE

N1

N1

TO KIKWIT

Lingbanga

Colonel Lukusa

La Voix
du Peuple

Region

KINSHASA

N1

DRC

Sergent Ekomono

Citoyenne Bononge

Comandant Kabongo

24 Novembre

Palais du Peuple

TO MATADI

Makelele

Basoko

Ste Barbe

Kasa-Vubu

Lualaba

Lulua

Nduisi

École
Officielle

Bandalungwa

Cathédrale
du Centenaire

Mangai

Assolongo

Bungu

Stadium

Victoire

Enseignment

Kintambo

École
St Francios
d' Assises

Camp Militaire

Sato

Victoire

Katanga

TO KASANGULU

((00243) 12 330 518/300 70

84

Luanda   Angola

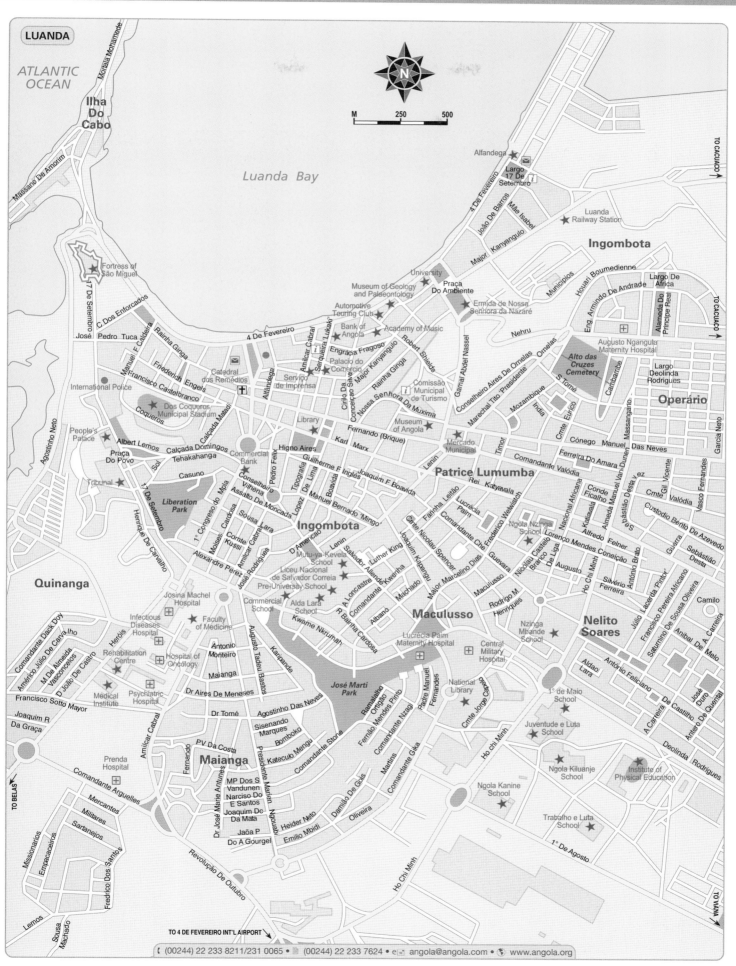

LUANDA

ATLANTIC OCEAN

Ilha Do Cabo

Luanda Bay

Massano De Amorim

Mortala Mohamede

Alfandega

Largo 17 De Setembro

4 De Fevereiro

João De Barros

Mãe Isabel

Luanda Railway Station

Ingombota

Fortress of São Miguel

17 De Setembro

C. Dos Enforcados

José   Pedro Tuca

Rainha Ginga

Manuel F. Caldeira

Friederich Engels

Francisco Castelbranco

International Police

Catedral dos Remédios

4 De Fevereiro

Serviço de Imprensa

Amilcar Cabral

Sequeira 'Lukaki'

Engrácia Fragoso

Palácio do Comércio

Conceição Silveira

Major Kanyangulo

Robert Shields

Cirilo Da

Academy of Music

Bank of Angola

Automotive Touring Club

Museum of Geology and Palaeontology

Praça Do Ambiente

University

Municípios

Major Kanyangulo

Houari Boumedienne

Eng. Armindo De Andrade

Largo De Africa

Alameda Do Príncipe Real

Ermida de Nossa Senhora da Nazaré

Nehru

Augusto Ngangula Maternity Hospital

Alto das Cruzes Cemetery

Carhbambe

Largo Deolinda Rodrigues

Operário

Gamal Abdel Nassel

Conselheiro Aires De Ornelas

Ornelas

S. Tomé

Nossa Senhora Da Muxima

Comissão Municipal de Turismo

Rainha Ginga

Marechal Tito 'Presidente'

Mozambique

India

Timor

Cónego   Manuel   Das Neves

Garcia Neto

Cmte Eurico

Cmte 'Gil' Vicente

Cmte   'Gil'   Valódia

People's Palace

Albert Lemos

Calçada Domingos

Tehakahanga

Sol

Casuno

Dos Coqueiros Municipal Stadium

Coqueiros

Calçada Matadi

Commercial Bank

Higno Aires

Library

Fernando (Brique)

Museum of Angola

Mercado Municipal

Ferreira Do Amara

Comandante Valódia

Nacional Africana

Almeida Manuel Van-Dunen

Bastião Desta

Conde Ficalho

Katiavala

Alfredo Felner

Custodio Bento De Azevedo

Praça Do Povo

Tribunal

17 De Setembro

Henrique De Carvalho

Liberation Park

Conselheiro Vilhena

Assalto De Moncada

Pedro Felix

Guilherme F Inglés

Tipografia

De Lima

Manuel Bernado 'Mingo'

Joaquim F Boavida

Karl Marx

Lenin

Patrice Lumumba

Rei Katyavala

Lucrécia Paim

Comandante Che   Frederico Welwitsch

Ngola Nzinga School

Lorenço Mendes Coneição

Branco

De Liga

Augusto

António Brato

Silvério Ferreira

Guerra

Sebastião Desta

Agostinho Neto

Quinanga

1° Congreso do Mpla

Moisés Cardosa

Cmte. Kussi

Amilcar Cabral

José Rodrigues

Alexandre Perez

Sousa Lara

D Américao

Mutu-ya-Kevela School

Liceu Nacional de Salvador Correia

Pre-University School

Lenin

Salvador Allende

'Luther King'

Kwertha

A Loncastre

Comandante

Machado

Joaquim Kabangu

Cmte Nicolau Spencer

Major Marcelino Dias

Guevara

Maculusso

Nicolau Casele

Rodrigo M Henriques

Nelito Soares

Júlio 'Lácerda Pintor'

Francisco Pereira Africano

Saturnino De Sousa Oliveira

Anibal De A Melo

Camilo

José Duro

De Castilho

Antero De Quental

A Carreira

Josina Machel Hospital

Faculty of Medicine

Commercial School

Alda Lara School

Albano

R Bainha Cardosa

Kwame Nkrumah

Ingombota

Maculusso

Lucrécia Paim Maternity Hospital

Central Military Hospital

Nzinga Mbande School

Aldao Lara

António Feliciano

Quinanga

Comandante Dack Doy

Américo Júlio De Carvalho

Heróis

M De Almeida Vasconcelos

D João De Castro

Francisco Sotto Mayor

Joaquim R Da Graça

Infectious Diseases Hospital

Rehabilitation Centre

Medical Institute

Psychiatric Hospital

Hospital of Oncology

Antonio Monteiro

Augusto Tadeu Bastos

Maianga

Dr Aires De Meneses

Karipende

Agostinho Das Neves

Dr Tomé

Maianga

José Marti Park

Ramalaho Ortigao

Fernão Mendes Pinto

Comandante Nzaji

Padre Manuel Fernandes

National Library

Cmte Jorge Cedo

Ho chi Minh

1° de Maio School

Juventude e Luta School

Ngola Kiluanje School

Institute of Physical Education

De Carreira

Deolinda Rodrigues

Prenda Hospital

Comandante Arguelles

Mercantes

Militares

Sartanejos

Missionarios

Empacaceiros

Fredrico Dos Santos

Lemos

Sousa Machado

Amilcar Cabral

Fernando

Presidente Marien

Kateculo Mengu

PV Da Costa

MP Dos S Vandunen

Narciso Do E Santos

Joaquim Do Da Mata

Jaôa P Do A Gourgel

Dr José Marie Antunes

Ngouati

Heider Neto

Emilio Mbidi

Sisenando Marques

Bomboko

Comandante Stone

Damião De Gois

Oliveira

Martins

Comandante Gika

Ngola Kanine School

Trabalho e Luta School

1° De Agosto

Ho chi Minh

Revolução De Outubro

TO BELAS

TO 4 DE FEVEREIRO INT'L AIRPORT

TO CACUACO

TO CACUACO

TO VIANA

M   250   500

℡ (00244) 22 233 8211/231 0065 • 🖷 (00244) 22 233 7624 • e🖂 angola@angola.com • 🕙 www.angola.org

85

Adventures

Adventure	Country	Duration
Exploring the Poubara Falls (Franceville)	Gabon	1 day +
Down the Ogooué River (Port-Gentil & Lamberene)	Gabon	1 - 2 days +
Hiking the Ruwenzori Mountains	Democratic Republic of the Congo	1 day +
Whitewater Rafting on the Congo (Kinshasa)	Democratic Republic of the Congo	2 days +
Trekking the Lowland Forests (Kahuzi-Biega NP)	Democratic Republic of the Congo	1 day
A Riverboat on the Congo	Democratic Republic of the Congo	3 days +

Exploring the Poubara Falls (Franceville)

Requirements:
All visitors require a visa – which can take weeks – and, theoretically, a written invitation from a resident to visit. Although not always essential, it is best to follow rules. Yellow fever and cholera immunizations are required.

Climate:
Hot and very humid virtually year-round throughout the country, especially in the forested zones.

Risk factor:
The wilds of Gabon are relatively safe – although a reliable guide will help facilitate matters – so it is the volatility of animal life that poses the most risks. Do not take chances.

Health:
The nature of the environment brings with it health risks, such as waterborne diseases; consult a doctor familiar with tropical conditions.

Pack:
Lightweight, waterproof clothing. Sturdy, protective shoes – preferably boots – if you intend doing a lot of walking (inevitable in Gabon's forests).

Facilities:
Facilities are usually extremely rudimentary, and few operators are able to offer anything other than the basics.

Contact:
Mistral Voyages, B.P. 2106, Libreville, Gabon.
Tel: 00241-760421
mistral.lbv@internetgabon.com

Down the Ogooué River (Port-Gentil & Lamberene)

Requirements:
All visitors require a visa – which can take weeks – and, theoretically, an invitation to visit, so it is best to follow rules to the letter. Yellow fever and cholera immunizations are required.

Climate:
Hot and very humid year-round, especially in the forests. Temperatures on the river are more moderate.

Risk factor:
Although generally safe, the Ogooué River is best experienced with a local at your side. The forests receive a very high rainfall (3,000mm), making the waters powerful.

Health:
The Ogooué does pose risks, including diseases carried by water used frequently for industry.

Pack:
Clothing must be waterproof and comfortable, as you will be spending a lot of time on the water.

Facilities:
Facilities are adequate, with Lamberene and Port Gentil well serviced by river-trip operators – be they 'official' or private. There is seldom any real difference between first- and second-class fares on the more formal excursions.

Contact:
Mistral Voyages, B.P. 2106, Libreville, Gabon.
Tel: 00241-760421
mistral.lbv@internetgabon.com

Hiking the Ruwenzori Mountains

Requirements:
Although standard entry conditions apply, be prepared for complications. The DRC is not an easy place in which to travel – and not particularly safe – so keep your visa-stamped passport and yellow fever vaccination certification with you at all times.

Climate:
Hot, humid and wet throughout the year, often uncomfortably so.

Risk factor:
Security remains risky and travellers should enquire beforehand.

Health:
Malaria is a real danger, and most Westerners may be susceptible to other diseases. Take precautions.

Pack:
Antimalarial medication, plus light, warm clothing that is waterproof as well as easily removable as the humidity increases and the temperature rises.

Facilities:
Facilities are simple, with no luxuries, although Virunga headquarters are well geared towards visitors. Specialized tours to see the gorillas can be expensive, but Virunga permits are usually valid for at least seven days.

Contact:
Uganda Tourist Board,
P.O. Box 722, Kampala, Uganda.
Tel: 00256-41-4342196 / 7

Whitewater Rafting on the Congo (Kinshasa)

Requirements:
Although standard entry conditions apply, be prepared for complications. The DRC is not an easy place in which to travel – and not particularly safe – so keep your visa-stamped passport and yellow fever vaccination certification with you at all times.

Climate:
Hot and humid, and exploring the Congo River can add to discomfort.

Risk factor:
Apart from the usual security risks, rapids are graded one to six (one being tame with few risks, six being virtually impassable) and much of the Congo falls dangerously close to the more challenging classification.

Health:
Malaria is a real danger, and most Westerners are susceptible to other diseases. Whitewater rafters should always carry a well-stocked first-aid kit.

Pack:
Antimalarial medication and comfortable, waterproof clothing, with a dry set for after a day on the water.

Facilities:
Facilities vary from good to very good, but are expensive. Sadly, this is the only option worth considering.

Contact:
ONATRA, B.P. 98, Kinshasa.
Tel: 00243-12-23424 / 30070

Trekking the Lowland Forests (Kahuzi-Biega National Park)

Requirements:
Although standard entry conditions apply, be prepared for complications. The DRC is not an easy place in which to travel – and not particularly safe – so keep your visa-stamped passport and yellow fever vaccination certification with you at all times.

Climate:
Hot, humid and wet throughout the year, often uncomfortably so.

Risk factor:
Security remains risky and travellers should enquire beforehand.

Health:
Malaria is a real danger, and most Westerners are susceptible to other diseases. Take precautions.

Pack:
Antimalarial medication, plus lightweight but waterproof clothing and comfortable but sturdy hiking boots.

Facilities:
Facilities are extremely basic and, even though the special gorilla tours are expensive, travellers should not expect any frills. Accommodation is limited and lacks even the most basic facilities. Take your own camping gear, food and water rations.

Contact:
National Tourism Office,
B.P. 9502, Kinshasa.
Tel: 00243-12-30070

A Riverboat on the Congo

Requirements:
Although standard entry conditions apply, be prepared for complications. The DRC is not an easy place in which to travel – and not particularly safe – so keep your visa-stamped passport and yellow fever vaccination certification with you at all times.

Climate:
Hot, humid and wet throughout the year, often uncomfortably so.

Risk factor:
A trip on the river means you will mix with people such as con artists. Watch your baggage, and keep a low profile. Cameras could cause trouble.

Health:
Malaria and other tropical diseases may be rife. Take precautions.

Pack:
Antimalarial medication, lightweight but waterproof clothing, as well as bedding if travelling third class.

Facilities:
Facilities in first and second class are adequate, but third class may be overwhelming for Westerners. Trading boats selling supplies visit the riverboat regularly, but treat the food and water bought from these locals with caution.

Contact:
ONATRA, B.P. 98, Kinshasa.
Tel: 00243-12-23424 / 30070

The Great Lakes

The warm, tropical climate and mostly fertile lands of Rwanda, Burundi and Uganda provide an ideal habitat for the gorillas and chimpanzees for which the region is justifiably famed, but it is also blessed with an abundance of other wild animals so characteristic of equatorial Africa and more than its fair share of avifauna. The rainforests of the west and savanna plains of the east create a surprising contrast in landscape and mood, but despite the flaming sunsets sinking over an unblemished wilderness, the recent history of its human inhabitants is unfortunately less inspiring. Although showing remarkable recovery, all three nations have been ravaged by war and drought and, as a result, famine and poverty. Today, Rwanda, Burundi and Uganda suffer the worst of the worldwide AIDS epidemic, and huge numbers of locals live with HIV/AIDS. As a result, population estimates are dramatically affected by low life expectancy, high infant mortality, and low population growth.

UGANDA

KAMPALA

Despite the crumbling walls of the ghetto areas, bullet-riddled and shrapnel-scarred, what was once considered the Pearl of Africa is re-emerging as one of the gems in Africa's crown. Located on the undulating landscape so typical of Central Africa, the seven hills on which Kampala stands are lush and fertile, and the city itself is fast becoming a burgeoning modern centre, along with the impressive National Museum and enthralling Kasubi Tombs. Grand places of worship for all the prominent faiths include the Kibuli Mosque, Rubaga Catholic Cathedral, Namirembe Anglican Cathedral and a typically ornate Hindu Temple. The city is peopled with an eclectic mix of colourful characters, a human parade of lively vendors and an avian population of marabou storks who alight on every conceivable vantage point. Kampala experienced pitiful degradation during the bloody reign of dictator Idi Amin, but its people have returned to the city, and brought with them a stability and even 'prosperity'. The streets are still filled with the widows, orphans and refugees that are Amin's legacy, but the broken windows are slowly being replaced, the buildings patched up and reinforced, and the inner city of Kampala is no longer a place to be avoided. In fact, it is lush, pretty, friendly and safe – something not many African capitals can claim.

MURCHISON FALLS

Unmistakable as one of Uganda's most recognizable faces, the Murchison Falls (or Kabalega Falls) on the Victoria Nile River lie at the heart of 3,900km^2 of natural splendour, neatly divided by the waters of the Victoria Nile as it snakes its way from Lake Kyoga to Lake Albert. The outlying countryside comprises mostly savanna and grassland, but along the banks of the river are stands of densely packed forest, including mahogany, with acacia trees and papyrus reeds filling in the gaps. The terrain is stalked by predators such as lion and leopard, trod by those great African giants, the elephant and the giraffe, and grazed by bushbuck and waterbuck, while crocodiles and hippos wallow in the river waters. Waders and other waterfowl are common and it is not unusual to spot shoebills, African skimmers, red-throated bee-eaters, herons and kingfishers among the more than 380 bird species to be found in the national park. However, the most enduring asset of the park is the spectacular falls, which tumble about 43m. Even more remarkable is the enormous force of the water of the usually 50m-wide Nile as it is thrust through a mere 7m gap between the rocks that form the Rift Valley escarpment. A three-hour boat trip from Paraa takes enthralled visitors right up to the foot of the falls, while an intriguing diversion may be to hunt for the latter-day survivor of the timeless African Queen, the humble vessel that carried Katherine Hepburn and Humphrey Bogart to the heights of stardom. The original vessel was unearthed from the banks of the Victoria Nile during the reclamation of the park and continues to ply the waters of the river.

LAKE VICTORIA

The papyrus-fringed shores and intermittent swamps along Lake Victoria have contributed considerably to its image as one of the most striking in all of Africa. As the largest of the continent's great lakes, Lake Victoria is delightfully free of fishing, sailing and water-sport enthusiasts. A vast, gentle and tranquil body of water that borders Kenya, Tanzania and Uganda, Lake Victoria lies a relatively short distance from both Rwanda and Burundi. It is into this great lake that the beginning of the mighty Nile empties, and then leaves again at Jinja as the Victoria Nile. The great river moves on to feed the swamplands of Lake Kyoga in the centre of the country and spills into Lake Albert in the northwest of Uganda en route to the north of Africa. Together with the Victoria Nile, Lake Victoria is at the heart of some of the best-watered lands on the African continent and is the home territory of an endless variety of wildlife, notably the black-and-white pied kingfishers at home in the bird sanctuaries dotting the shore, and the common Nile perch, which was introduced into Lake Victoria. Locals harvest the waters by casting fishing nets from small handcrafted rowboats to eke out their meagre living. Lake Victoria remains very much a place for the people of Uganda, offering little evidence of the tourist market.

BURUNDI

BUJUMBURA

Situated on hill slopes stretching up from the northern shore of Lake Tanganyika and blessed with a balmy climate, Bujumbura is a treasure house of cultural gems. Comparatively small, but beautiful, it has a rich history moulded by the developments of the entire country. Although it boasts magnificent views across Lake Tanganyika's northern reaches, the former colonial town remains unmistakably the capital of one of the world's most populated nations. Attractive and even beautiful in parts, its most intriguing tourist magnet is the Musée Vivant, a reconstruction of a model Burundian village with a reptile park and market.

GITEGA

One of the few centres that continue to attract Burundi's share of travellers is Gitega, Burundi's second-largest settlement. A certain charm infiltrates the multi-sensory streets. There is a small but interesting National Museum. The surrounds are rugged but picturesque, and dotted on the outskirts of town are a selection of diversions and day trips that offer a very pleasant glimpse of unspoilt Burundi. Among the natural splendours are the magnificent Kagera Falls, little more than a relaxed day trip from the town and its most popular drawcard. The falls are at their most striking during the rainy season from about October to January.

RWANDA

KIGALI

Despite the horrors of the genocide that took place in Rwanda, Kigali has emerged as a promising focal point of the country's rehabilitation process. Standing high on a ridge, Kigali lies in the centre of a country that is surrounded by other nations that have seen equally devastating conflict in recent times. With a relatively small citizenship of about a quarter million, the capital remains the nation's most important cultural, economic and academic centre. Although many of the buildings in the urban hub still bear the scars of the war, there has been a very real attempt to resurrect the beauty of the old city, and a number of small but pretty parks have been established to help enhance the face of Kigali. Although post-war Kigali boasts a mobile cellular service that connects the national capital with the capitals of the prefectures, the infrastructure is basic, and there are no more than 1,000 television sets in the city.

LAKE KIVU

Lake Kivu lies at 1,460m, covering an impressive 2,698km^2 and plunging to depths of 475m. The grand body of water is navigated by small vessels and shallow barges, many of which play no small role in the tea and cotton processing industries around Kamembe. The lake shore is equally spectacular. To the south lies the Nyungwe Forest. The surrounds are quite beautiful, dotted intermittently with the gems of Rwanda's natural attractions, including the 100m falls of Les Chutes de Ndaba, the waterfalls on the Rusizi River, Nyakabuye's hot springs, and the wildlife of Rugege Forest, including chimpanzees, leopard and even elephant. The shores are studded with pretty towns, from Cyangugu on Kivu's southernmost shore to Gisenyi in the north, noted for the 3,407m peaks of Nyiragongo.

The landmass covered by Uganda, Burundi and Rwanda is some of the most densely populated in the world and, although there are small pockets of valuable parks and reserves, much of it is given over to cultivation in order to feed the region's 37-odd million people.

Rwanda, Burundi, Uganda

Murchison Falls, Uganda

Gorilla, Volcans National Park, Rwanda

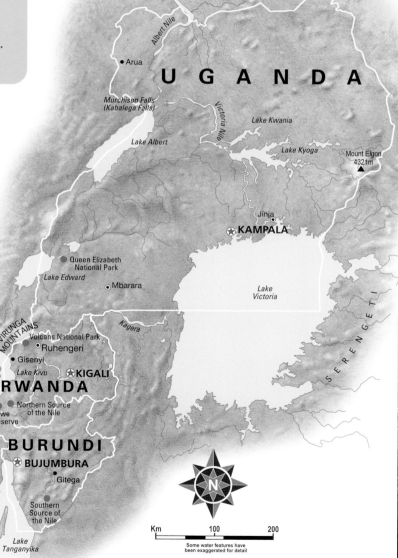

UGANDA

Albert Nile

Arua

Murchison Falls
(Kabalega Falls)

Victoria Nile

Lake Kwania

Lake Albert

Lake Kyoga

Mount Elgon
4321m

Jinja

KAMPALA

Queen Elizabeth
National Park

Lake Edward

Mbarara

Lake
Victoria

S E R E N G E T I

VIRUNGA
MOUNTAINS

Kagera

Volcans National Park

Ruhengeri

Gisenyi

Lake Kivu

KIGALI

RWANDA

Northern Source
of the Nile

Nyungwe
Forest Reserve

BURUNDI

BUJUMBURA

Gitega

Southern
Source
of the Nile

Lake
Tanganyika

N

Km   100   200

Some water features have
been exaggerated for detail

Hindu temple, Kampala, Uganda

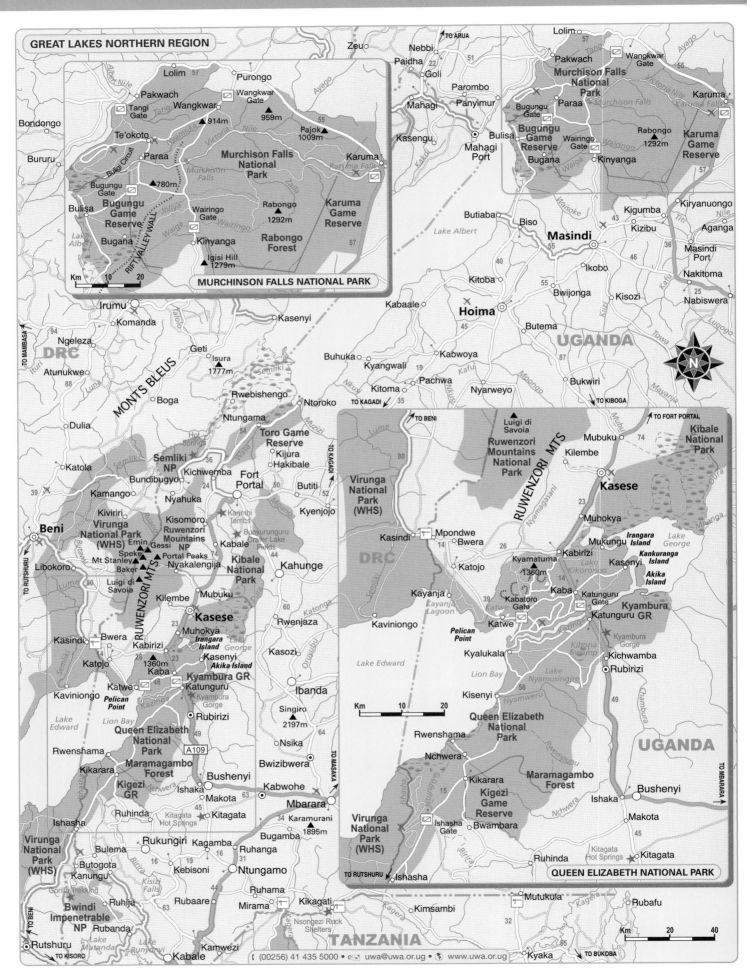

GREAT LAKES NORTHERN REGION

MURCHINSON FALLS NATIONAL PARK

QUEEN ELIZABETH NATIONAL PARK

✆ (00256) 41 435 5000 • e🖂 uwa@uwa.or.ug • 🌐 www.uwa.or.ug

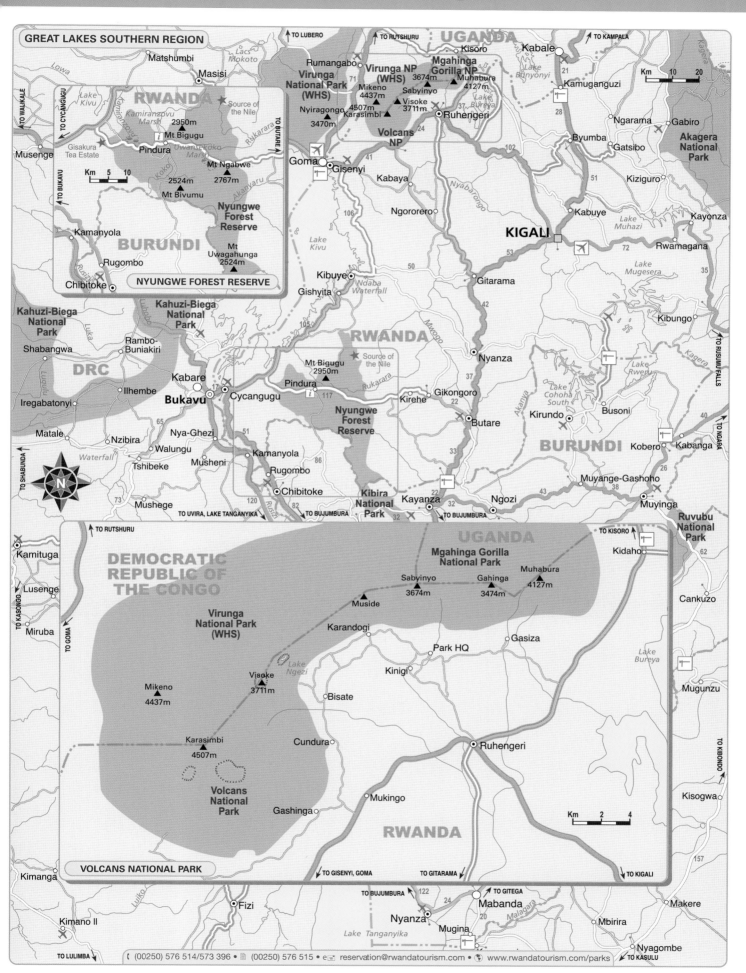

GREAT LAKES SOUTHERN REGION

TO WALIKALE
TO CYANGUGU
Lowa
Lacs
Mokoto
Matshumbi
Masisi
TO LUBERO
TO RUTSHURU
TO KAMPALA
UGANDA
Kisoro
Kabale
Lake
Bonyonyi
21
Km 10 20
Kamuganguzi

Rumangabo
Virunga
National Park
(WHS)
71
Virunga NP
(WHS)
Mikeno
4437m
Mgahinga
Gorilla NP
3674m
Muhabura
4127m
Lake
Bureya
28
Ngarama
Gabiro

RWANDA
Kamiranzovu
Marsh
2950m
Mt Bigugu
i
Source
of the
Nile
Nyiragongo
3470m
4507m
Karasimbi
Sabyinyo
Visoke
3711m
Ruhengeri
37
24
Byumba
51
Kiziguro
Akagera
National
Park

TO BUKAVU
Gisakura
Tea Estate
Pindura
Uwansekoko
Marsh
Rukarara
TO BUTARE
Goma
Gisenyi
Volcans
NP
41
Kabaya
102
Gatsibo

Km 5 10
Mt Ngabwe
2767m
Ngororero
Lake
Muhazi
Kayonza

Musenge
Lake
Kivu
Kamiranzovu
2524m
Mt Bivumu
Nyungwe
Forest
Reserve
106
KIGALI
53
Kabuye
Rwamagana
35

Kamanyola
BURUNDI
Mt
Uwagahunga
2524m
Lake
Kivu
50
Gitarama
Lake
Mugesera

Rugombo
NYUNGWE FOREST RESERVE
Kibuye
Ndaba
Waterfall
42
Kibungo

Chibitoke
Gishyita
105
RWANDA
Mwogo
Nyanza
37
TO RUSUMU FALLS

Kahuzi-Biega
National
Park
Kahuzi-Biega
National
Park
Mt Bigugu
2950m
Source
of the Nile
Lake
Cohoha
South
Lake
Rweru
40
TO NGARA

Shabangwa
Rambo-
Buniakiri
Pindura
i
117
Rukarara
Kirehe
Gikongoro
22
Kirundo
Busoni

DRC
Kabare
17
Cycangugu
Nyungwe
Forest
Reserve
Butare
33
BURUNDI
Kobero
Kabanga

Iregabatonyi
Ilhembe
Bukavu
Akanya
Kayanza
Kabanga

Matale
Nzibira
65
Nya-Ghezi
51
86
37
Koboro
26
Muyange-Gashoho
38

Waterfall
Walungu
Musheni
Kamanyola
Rugombo
33
22
43
Muyinga

N
Tshibeke
Mushege
73
120
Chibitoke
82
Kibira
National
Park
Kayanza
32
Ngozi
Ruvubu
National
Park

TO SHABUNDA
TO UVIRA, LAKE TANGANYIKA
TO BUJUMBURA
32
TO BUJUMBURA
62

TO RUTSHURU
UGANDA
TO KISORO
Kidaho

Kamituga
DEMOCRATIC
REPUBLIC OF
THE CONGO
Mgahinga Gorilla
National Park
Sabyinyo
3674m
Gahinga
3474m
Muhabura
4127m
Cankuzo

Lusenge
Virunga
National Park
(WHS)
Muside
Karandogi
Lake
Bureya

TO KASONGO
Miruba
TO GOMA
Visoke
3711m
Lake
Ngezi
Park HQ
Gasiza
Mugunzu

Mikeno
4437m
Kinigi
Bisate

Karasimbi
4507m
Cundura
Ruhengeri

Volcans
National
Park
Mukingo
Kisogwa

Gashinga
RWANDA
Km 2 4

VOLCANS NATIONAL PARK
TO GISENYI, GOMA
TO GITARAMA
TO KIGALI
157

Kimanga
TO BUJUMBURA
122
TO GITEGA
Mabanda
Makere

TO LULIMBA
Fizi
Nyanza
24
20
Mugina
Mbirira

Kimano II
Lake Tanganyika
Nyagombe
TO KASULU

((00250) 576 514/573 396 • (00250) 576 515 • e reservation@rwandatourism.com • www.rwandatourism.com/parks

Kigali Rwanda
Bujumbura Burundi

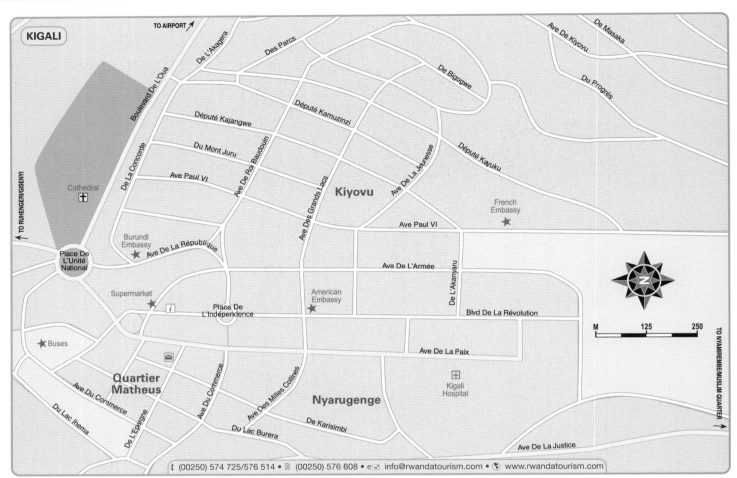

KIGALI

TO AIRPORT

De Masaka
Ave De Kiyovu
De L'Akagera
Des Parcs
Du Progrès
Boulevard De L'Oua
De Bigogwe
Député Kamuzinzi
Député Kajangwe
Député Kayuku
Du Mont Juru
Ave De La Jeunesse
Ave Paul VI
Ave De Roi Baudouin
Kiyovu
De La Concorde
Cathedral
French Embassy
Ave Des Grands Lacs
Ave Paul VI
TO RUHENGERI/GISENYI
Burundi Embassy
Ave De La République
Ave De L'Armée
De L'Akanyaru
Place De L'Unité National
N
Supermarket
Place De L'Indépendence
American Embassy
Blvd De La Révolution
M 125 250
TO NYAMIREMBE/MUSLIM QUARTER
Buses
Ave De La Paix
Quartier Matheus
Ave Du Commerce
Ave Du Commerce
Ave Des Mille Collines
Kigali Hospital
Du Lac Ihema
De L'Epargne
Nyarugenge
De Karisimbi
Du Lac Burera
Ave De La Justice

((00250) 574 725/576 514 • 🖨 (00250) 576 608 • e📧 info@rwandatourism.com • 🌐 www.rwandatourism.com

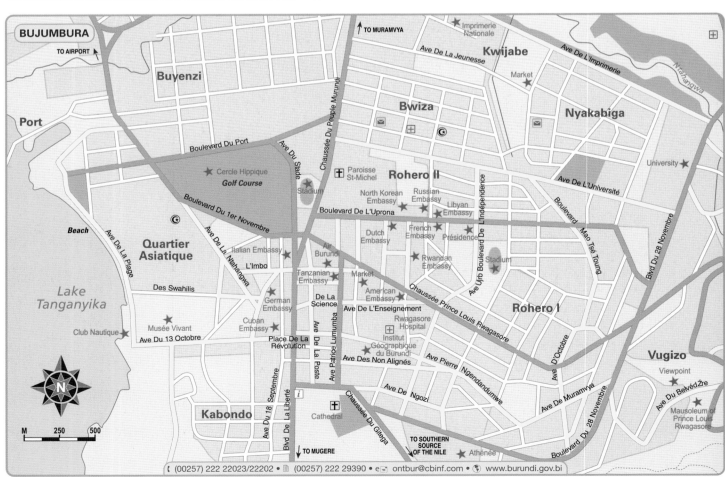

BUJUMBURA

TO AIRPORT
TO MURAMVYA
Imprimerie Nationale
Buyenzi
Ave De La Jeunesse
Kwijabe
Ave De L'Imprimerie
Market
Nyarugwa
Chaussée Du Peuple Murundi
Bwiza
Nyakabiga
Port
Boulevard Du Port
Ave Du Stade
Cercle Hippique
Golf Course
Paroisse St-Michel
Rohero II
University
Ave De L'Université
Stadium
North Korean Embassy
Russian Embassy
Libyan Embassy
L'Indépendence
Boulevard
Mao Tsé Toung
Boulevard Du 1er Novembre
Boulevard De L'Uprona
Dutch Embassy
French Embassy
Présidence
Blvd Du 28 Novembre
Beach
Ave De La Plage
Ave De La Nahangwa
Italian Embassy
L'Imbo
Air Burundi
Rwandan Embassy
Ave Ujrb Boulevard De
Stadium
Rohero I
Quartier Asiatique
Tanzanian Embassy
Market
De La Science
American Embassy
Chaussée Prince Louis Rwagasore
Lake Tanganyika
Des Swahilis
German Embassy
Ave De L'Enseignement
Vugizo
Club Nautique
Musée Vivant
Cuban Embassy
Ave Du 13 Octobre
Place De La Révolution
Rwagasore Hospital
Institut Géographique du Burundi
Ave Pierre Ngendandumwe
Viewpoint
Ave D'Octobre
Ave De Muramvya
N
Ave Du 18 Septembre
Blvd De La Liberté
Ave Patrice Lumumba
Ave De La Poste
Ave Des Non Alignés
Ave De Ngozi
Boulevard Du 28 Novembre
Ave Du Belvédère
M 250 500
Kabondo
Cathedral
Chaussée Du Gitega
Mausoleum of Prince Louis Rwagasore
TO MUGERE
TO SOUTHERN SOURCE OF THE NILE
Athénée

((00257) 222 22023/22202 • 🖨 (00257) 222 29390 • e📧 ontbur@cbinf.com • 🌐 www.burundi.gov.bi

92

Kampala   Uganda

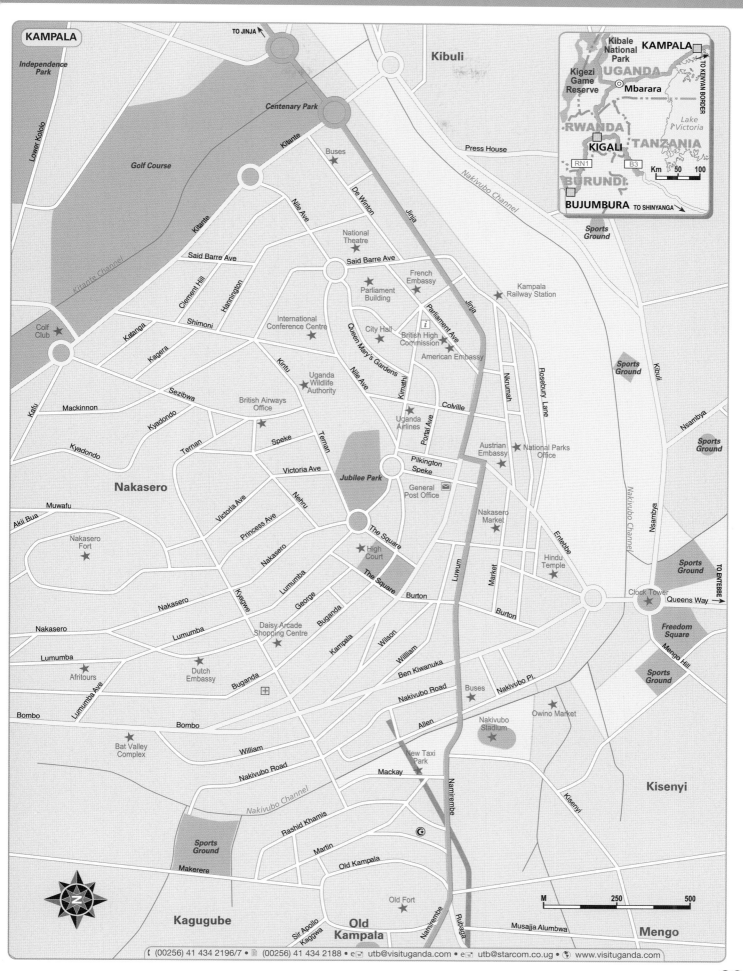

Adventures

Adventure	Country	Duration
Rafting Rwanda's Waterways (Lake Kivu)	Rwanda	1 day +
Hiking the Nyungwe Rainforest (Nyungwe NP)	Rwanda	1 day
Rafting Burundi's White Rivers (Luvironza River)	Burundi	1 day +
Climbing Mount Elgon	Uganda	1 day +
Trekking the Ruwenzori Mountains	Uganda	1 - 6 days
Gorilla Trekking in Uganda (Bwindi Impenetrable NP)	Uganda	1 day

Rafting Rwanda's Waterways (Lake Kivu)

Requirements:
Apart from standard documents (including yellow fever certification), visitors need a one-month visa.

Climate:
Hot and humid year-round. The best times are in the rains, March–May.

Risk factor:
Dangers posed by whitewater rafting are enormous, and sections of Rwanda's rivers are not even navigable for experts. Parts are still a security risk – enquire when planning your trip.

Health:
AIDS and malaria are rampant. Tap water is not safe, with bilharzia a problem in certain slow-moving waters.

Pack:
Take everything you need (apart from food) for a minimum stay of a week or two, as consumables are generally scarce and outlets for adventure gear are virtually non-existent.

Facilities:
Like most things in Rwanda, accommodation is expensive and few tour operators cater for budget travellers. Most operators rent out the most basic equipment, provide a guide and offer few other services.

Contact:
Rwandan National Tourism and Parks Office, P.O. Box 905, Kigali.
Tel: 00250-576514
ortpn@rwanda1.com, www.visitrwanda.gov.rw

Hiking the Nyungwe Rainforest (Nyungwe National Park)

Requirements:
Standard documents (including yellow fever certification), and visitors require a one-month visa.

Climate:
Hot and humid year-round. The best times are in the rains, March–May

Risk factor:
Parts of the country are still considered a security risk (check status before arriving) and, according to reports, land mines may still be found.

Health:
AIDS and malaria are rampant. Tap water is not safe, with bilharzia a problem in certain slow-moving waters.

Pack:
Take all the equipment and gear you will require for walks and hikes, which tend to vary greatly in difficulty and distance. Especially important are waterproof clothing and hiking shoes.

Facilities:
Good accommodation is expensive, and few tour operators cater for budget travellers. While operators in nearby towns and authorities at the forest station will provide a guide, forest camps offer nothing beyond the basic site and some toilet facilities.

Contact:
Rwandan National Tourism and Parks Office, P.O. Box 905, Kigali.
Tel: 00250-576514
www.visitrwanda.gov.rw

Rafting Burundi's White Rivers (Luvironza River)

Requirements:
Apart from standard documents, most visitors need a one-month visa and yellow-fever certification.

Climate:
Inevitably hot and humid throughout the year, temperatures can average some 30ºC, with the heaviest rains mid-October to April.

Risk factor:
Burundi's river waters are potentially hazardous to even experienced whitewater rafters, and every precaution should be taken. Political instability means independent travel beyond the capital also poses dangers.

Health:
Malaria is a serious problem, especially along rivers and lakes. Drink only bottled water. Parts of Lake Tanganyika may be bilharzia infected.

Pack:
Take all the gear and equipment you will need, rather than rely on the inevitably limited tourist infrastructure.

Facilities:
Facilities are generally poor, and are usually limited to catering for backpackers and budget travellers, all of whom would be well advised to be self-sufficient wherever possible.

Contact:
Burundi Tourist Office,
P.O. Box 902, Bujumbura, Burundi.
Tel: 00257-22-222023
ontbur@cbinf.com

Climbing Mount Elgon

Requirements:
Although all visitors will need a passport, some require a visa. Entry fee (starting at US$15) required to enter Mount Elgon National Park.

Climate:
Rains fall almost all year, and it is best to climb and hike from December to early March, and in mid-year.

Risk factor:
Apart from a few precarious climbs, risks are few. It can be cold and windy on the mountain at night.

Health:
High incidence of AIDS, bilharzia and malaria, but risks are low if you take precautions. Water should be purified or boiled, and expect mild altitude-related headaches and the like near summits.

Pack:
Pack only personal items and commodities such as sunscreen. Food can also be purchased in Mbale and camping gear may be hired in Kolongi.

Facilities:
The nearby settlements should serve the needs of climbers and hikers venturing onto the slopes of Mount Elgon, but aim to be self-sufficient – especially once in the mountain.

Contact:
Uganda Wildlife Authority,
P.O. Box 3530, Kampala, Uganda.
Tel: 00256-41-4355000
uwa@uwa.or.ug, www.uwa.or.ug

Trekking the Ruwenzori Mountains

Requirements:
Although all visitors need a passport, some require a visa for Uganda. Enquire well in advance.

Climate:
Despite their equatorial location, the Ruwenzoris can be cold and wet, with heavy rains mid-September to November and March to late April.

Risk factor:
Dangers are numerous and a very real part of hiking the Ruwenzoris – they should not be taken lightly. Only for the most skilled mountaineer.

Health:
Altitude sickness is a concern on the peaks; malaria, yellow fever and other mosquito-carried diseases (eg: sleeping sickness) have been recorded.

Pack:
Protective clothing is essential, and all items should be waterproof. Take sturdy hiking boots, protective headgear and rain gear.

Facilities:
Facilities are generally good when it comes to the actual hike, but accommodation and other amenities may be sorely lacking if you are not prepared to rough it, especially in the mountains.

Contact:
Ruwenzori Mountain Service (RMS),
P.O. Box 33, Kasese.
Tel: 00256-48344936 or 00256-41-341786
www.rwenzoriabruzzi.com

Gorilla Trekking in Uganda (Bwindi Impenetrable NP)

Requirements:
Although all visitors need a passport, some require a visa. A gorilla-tracking permit (US$150 or more) must be obtained at the National Parks Office in Kampala. Entry fee of US$15 is required for Bwindi.

Climate:
Rains fall almost all year, and hiking is best from December to early March and mid-year. Nights can be cold.

Risk factor:
Hazards are negligible, as treks are led by experienced guides. This is some of Uganda's most rugged terrain, so do not take chances.

Health:
To protect the gorillas anyone showing symptoms of illness will not be permitted within range of the animals.

Pack:
Clothing that will protect legs, arms and torso from the heavy — and often invasive — vegetation. Take sturdy boots, protective headgear and rain gear.

Facilities:
Facilities are generally good on the hike, but accommodation and other amenities may be lacking, especially in the depths of the park.

Contact:
Uganda Wildlife Authority,
P.O. Box 3530, Kampala, Uganda.
Tel: 00256-41-4355000
uwa@uwa.or.ug, www.uwa.or.ug

The Great Rift Valley

At its most dramatic in East Africa, the Great Rift Valley was formed some 20 million years ago when violent subterranean shifts resulted in the collapse of mammoth tracks of land situated along parallel fault lines, causing volcanic eruptions of molten rock. Today, this massive fissure in the earth's crust stretches 9,500km from Lebanon to Mozambique, and no less than 800km between Lake Manyara and the Red Sea. The dramatic inclines of its valley walls slice between 50km and 500km through the width of the African landscape. Apart from Ethiopia on the Horn of Africa, the two countries that are home to the most theatrical inclines of the great valley are Kenya and Tanzania, both of which are characterized by high-lying inland plateaux and fertile coastal belts dotted with tropical islands.

KENYA

NAIROBI

One of the most cosmopolitan and certainly one of the youngest of all of Africa's capitals, Nairobi is a metropolis of museums and malls interspersed with market stalls, galleries and game reserves, boutiques and bars, curios and criminals. The city's two million inhabitants come from a variety of tribal cultures, and the noise, colour and squalor of the older portions contrast greatly with modern structures such as the Kenyatta Conference Centre. Nairobi National Park lies on the city perimeter, with the Aberdare National Park nearby and river rafting on the Athi River.

MOUNT KENYA

Sacred Kirinyaga (Mount Kenya) on the central Highlands is a playground for hikers, mountaineers and climbers. The snowcapped summit of its three-million-year-old bulk stands at 5,199m, already eroded by 2,000m through glaciation. Topped by three main peaks – Batian, Nelion and Lenana – the slopes of this extinct volcano are covered in snow and ice, with 600km^2 of protected land above the 3,200m forest line. The region is the traditional home to the Kikuyu people, and the park is home to birds, elephant, buffalo, lion, black rhino and bushbuck.

LAKE TURKANA

Kenya's long, narrow lake covers 7,104km^2. Known by many locals as Basso Narok (Black Lake), in Kenya's colonial heyday it was known as Lake Rudolf, a ribbon of water 250km long and 56km wide, enclosed by the cliffs of the Rift Valley, cutting through the parched northern reaches of endless horizons and volcanic outcrops. Fed by Ethiopia's Omo River and, to some degree, by the Turkwel, Lake Turkana is the world's largest desert lake, and one of the largest alkaline lakes. Volcanic islands in the middle of the lake are the territory of hippos and some 22,000 crocodiles, while the waters shelter huge Nile perch. Migrant birds visit in such great numbers that their breeding sites on South and Central Island have been declared national parks.

LAKE VICTORIA

Also known as Victoria Nyanza, Lake Victoria falls within the boundaries of Kenya, Tanzania and Uganda. Covering 69,485km^2, Victoria is Africa's largest lake and the world's second largest. Lying at an altitude of 1,134m in the populated highlands of Kenya, it averages a depth of only 78m, and its waters are drained by the Victoria Nile. The lake is dotted with little islands such as Ndere (a national park in the middle of the lake) and Saa Nane (a reserve harbouring island wildlife like rock agamas and hyraxes), while the 240km^2 Rubondo Island reserve boasts sitatunga, elephant, bushbuck and chimps. The lake shore is lined with reeds, papyrus and flamingoes, while its banks are settled mostly by the Luo, farmers and fishermen who ply the lake for Nile perch.

MOMBASA

A romantic port on a coral island, Mombasa has retained much of its 12-centuries-old charm. Like Zanzibar, it has remained virtually unchanged for about 100 years, with its floating market skirting the shores of Mombasa Island. With a population of half a million, old Mombasa has a long history of conquerors and colonists. Guarding the Old Harbour is historic Fort Jesus, and beyond lie spectacular reefs only 640m offshore. These reefs are lined with white, pebble-free beaches such as Tiwi and Diani, circled by dhows and schools of tropical fish. This makes for excellent snorkelling and scuba diving.

LAMU ARCHIPELAGO

The islands of Lamu, Manda and Apte form the Lamu Archipelago, site of some of the best diving off East Africa. The lesser-known isles include Manda – best known for its Takwa Ruins covering 5ha – and Pate Island, home to the mystical 8ha Swahili state of Shanga. Most prominent of the trio is Lamu Island, a 9th-century settlement of cobbled streets and flagstoned courtyards. The island, 19km long, is a mix of traditional Islam and Swahili and offers a fascinating glimpse into old Africa. The lively harbour front is also the hunting ground of the island's many feral cats.

TANZANIA

DAR ES SALAAM

Established in 1870 by Sultan Majid of Zanzibar as his 'Haven of Peace', the spiritual heart of Tanzania is magical Dar es Salaam, the nation's most important harbour city and its largest urban settlement. More acclaimed for its splendid beaches such as at Oyster Bay and Kunduchi, dynamic Dar remains every inch the contemporary city. It has a wonderful mix of people and cultures (the legacy of German and English colonists), as well as noisy but mesmerizing markets and unparalleled, upmarket tourist facilities. It also boasts impressive historic sites that are, in the most part, only a few decades old.

MOUNT KILIMANJARO

Mighty Kilimanjaro, with an altitude of 5,895m emerged 750,000 years ago as a result of volcanic activity to create the world's highest freestanding mountain. The precise origin of Kili's name remains lost in time – the local word kilima (from which the name apparently stems) means 'hill' rather than 'mountain'. Rising from the plains of the Masai, the mountain peak – a dormant volcano – is snowcapped (although just 3° south of the equator) and the make-up of the slopes varies enormously. From the foot to about 1,800m, the inclines comprise volcanic soils, while the vegetation up to 2,800m is rainforest, which receives over 2,000mm of rain, followed — to an altitude of 4,000m — by a moorland of heather and giant lobelias.

ZANZIBAR

Zanzibar is a separate Swahili city-state within Tanzania and consists of two islands which lie about 40km off the coast – Unguja (or Zanzibar) is the more famous, but there is also Pemba. Both share a sad history of trade in ivory and slaves. Known as the Spice Island, Zanzibar is a beach idyll, at the centre of which stands Stone Town, the old quarter of Zanzibar Town, the island's largest settlement. The maze of narrow streets, paths and alleys is littered with the history of its Swahili, Arabic, Asian and European residents. Stone Town boasts a romantic skyline of towering minarets, an Arab fort, lavish 19th-century palaces, and Portuguese churches, the most prominent landmarks being St Joseph's Cathedral and the Victorian clock tower of the House of Wonders. The outskirts are ringed with clove plantations, and the harbour is dotted with Swahili fishing dhows that flit across the offshore reefs.

NGORONGORO CRATER

The Ngorongoro Crater, the largest intact volcanic caldera in the world, forms the heart of the Ngorongoro Conservation Area, the expansive tableland that covers the 265km^2 of the crater floor. Hedged in by 600m walls that tower high above the open savanna, this is a sweep of untamed wilderness across which herds numbering hundreds of zebra and wildebeest charge, and huge flocks of pink flamingoes wade the seasonal waters. The plains and montane forest are home to a breathtaking array of Africa's most recognized wildlife, with no fewer than a quarter million large mammals scattered across the emptiness. The abundance of antelope species means that this is also prime big cat country, with cheetah, leopard and the world's densest population of over 100 lions. The rest of the Big Five have also settled here: elephant bulls, 3,000 head of buffalo, and roughly 20 black rhinos.

SERENGETI

The dramatic natural arena in which Africa's greatest display plays itself out, the horizonless plains of the Serengeti are a spectacular wildlife sanctuary without parallel. Known by the local Masai as 'The Great Open Place', the plateau of the 15,000km^2 grassland is covered by the short grasses of the Serengeti National Park, acclaimed as the finest game reserve in Africa. This extraordinary ecosystem – adjoined by the Masai Mara Reserve, Maswa Game Reserve, Ngorongoro and Loliondo Controlled Area – is home to enormous populations of mammals. The Serengeti's annual wildebeest migration begins on the southern plateau during the summer rains (December to May) when herds of 100,000 animals – reaching 40km – begin their 800km trek to the western territories, only to make the gruelling return trip to the southern plains between October and November.

Cutting through the heart of both Kenya and Tanzania is the colossal trench of the Rift Valley, its extraordinarily vertical walls looming up from the wide golden plain below and the cliff-like ramparts broken by cross fractures. The length of the great scar that has been forged down one-sixth of the earth's circumference is characterized by a succession of great lakes.

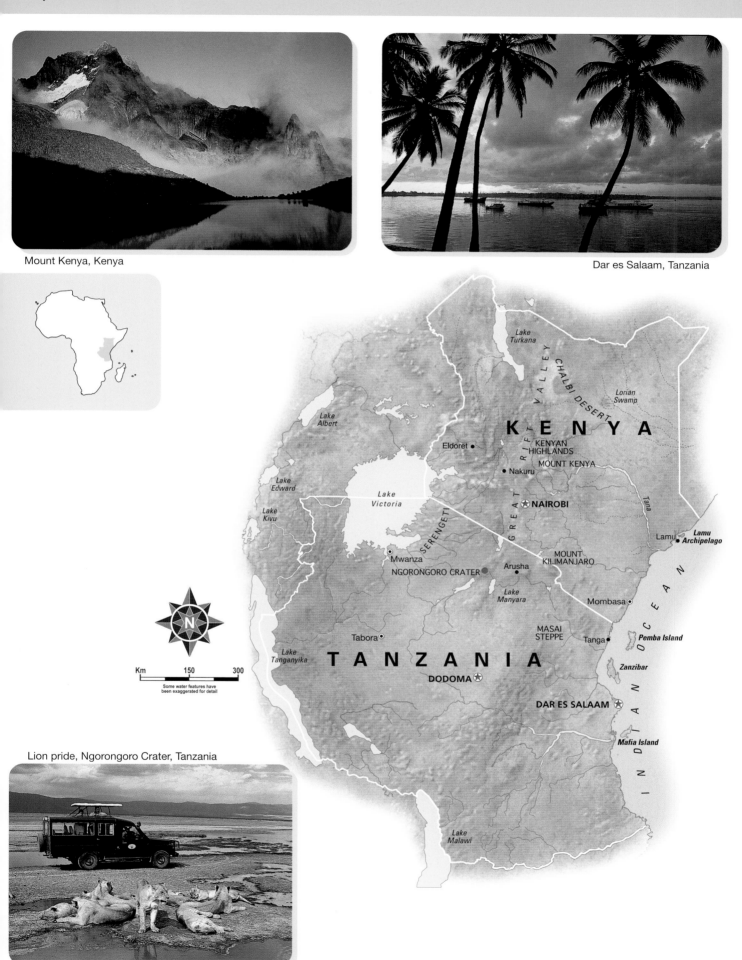

Mount Kenya, Kenya

Dar es Salaam, Tanzania

Lion pride, Ngorongoro Crater, Tanzania

Lake Turkana

CHALBI DESERT

Lorian Swamp

K E N Y A

Lake Albert

Eldoret •

KENYAN HIGHLANDS

MOUNT KENYA

• Nakuru

Lake Edward

Lake Kivu

Lake Victoria

GREAT RIFT VALLEY

⊕ NAIROBI

SERENGETI

Tana

Lamu •

Lamu Archipelago

Mwanza ⊙

NGORONGORO CRATER ●

Arusha •

MOUNT KILIMANJARO

Lake Manyara

Mombasa ⊙

MASAI STEPPE

Tanga •

Pemba Island

Tabora ⊙

T A N Z A N I A

Zanzibar

DODOMA ⊕

I N D I A N   O C E A N

Lake Tanganyika

DAR ES SALAAM ⊕

Mafia Island

N

Km   150   300

Some water features have been exaggerated for detail

Lake Malawi

Amboseli National Park   Kenya

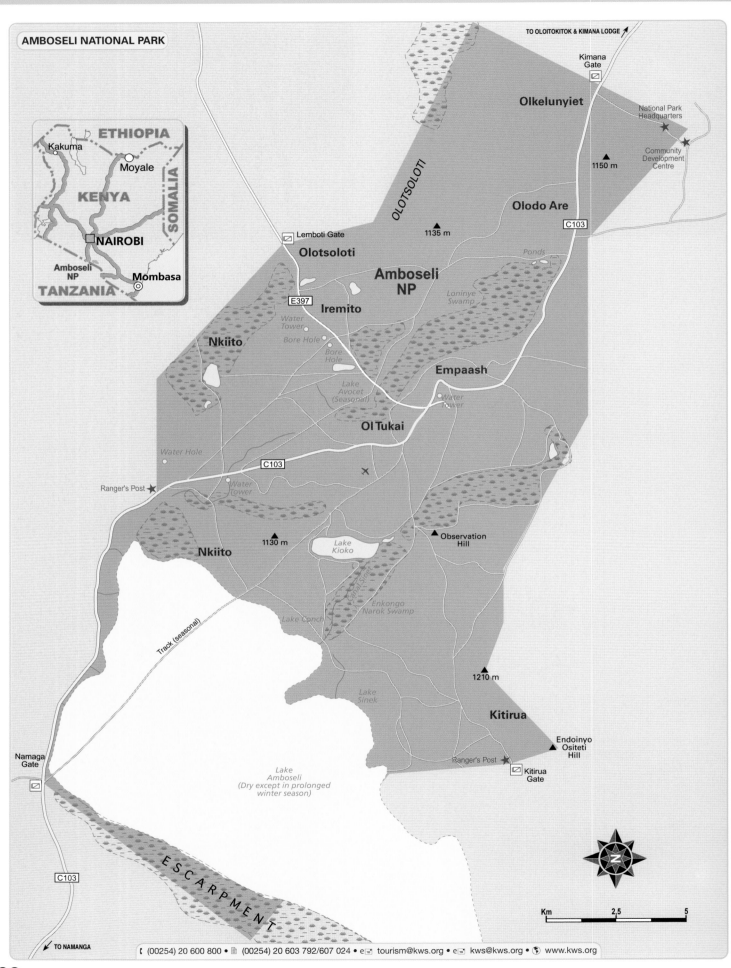

AMBOSELI NATIONAL PARK

TO OLOITOKITOK & KIMANA LODGE ↗

ETHIOPIA

Kakuma

Moyale

KENYA

SOMALIA

NAIROBI

Amboseli
NP

Mombasa

TANZANIA

Kimana
Gate

Olkelunyiet

National Park
Headquarters

Community
Development
Centre

1150 m

Olodo Are

OLOTSOLOTI

C103

Lemboti Gate

Olotsoloti

1135 m

Ponds

Amboseli
NP

Loninye
Swamp

E397

Iremito

Water
Tower

Bore Hole

Nkiito

Bore
Hole

Empaash

Lake
Avocet
(Seasonal)

Water
Tower

Ol Tukai

Water Hole

C103

Ranger's Post

Water
Tower

1130 m

Lake
Kioko

Observation
Hill

Nkiito

Canal River

Enkongo
Narok Swamp

Lake Conch

1210 m

Lake
Sinek

Kitirua

Track (seasonal)

Endoinyo
Ositeti
Hill

Ranger's Post

Kitirua
Gate

Namaga
Gate

Lake
Amboseli
(Dry except in prolonged
winter season)

C103

E S C A R P M E N T

N

Km   2,5   5

TO NAMANGA

☏ (00254) 20 600 800 • 🖷 (00254) 20 603 792/607 024 • e🖂 tourism@kws.org • e🖂 kws@kws.org • 🌐 www.kws.org

98

Arusha National Park Tanzania

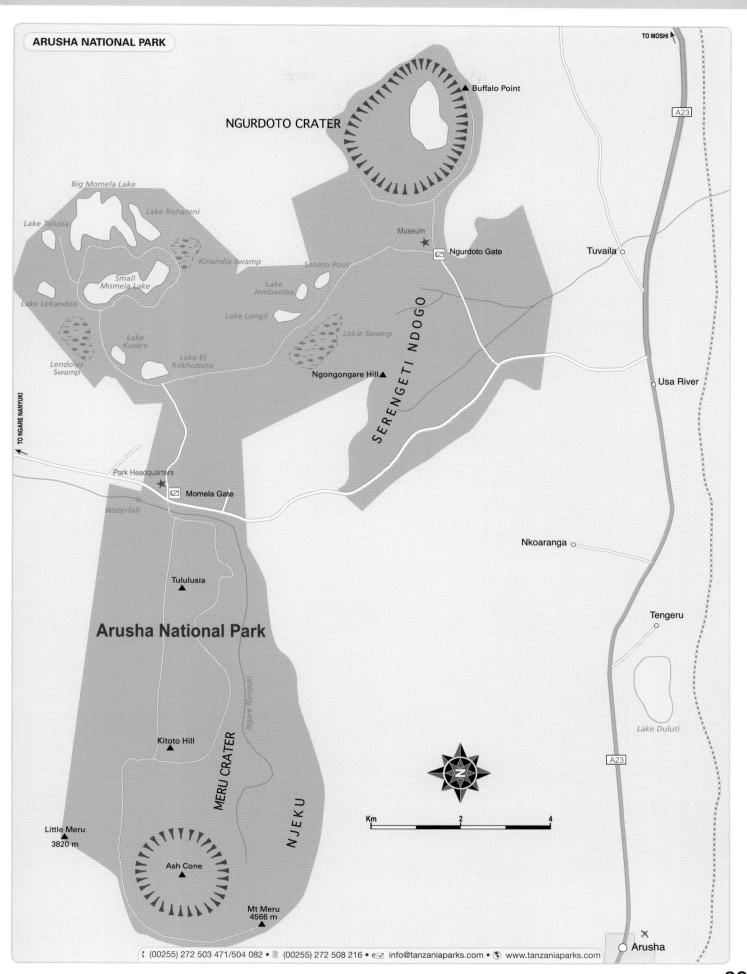

ARUSHA NATIONAL PARK

TO MOSHI

A23

NGURDOTO CRATER

▲ Buffalo Point

Big Momela Lake

Lake Rishateni

Lake Tulusia

Museum
★

Kinandia Swamp

☑ Ngurdoto Gate

Small
Momela Lake

Senato Pool

Lake
Jembamba

Tuvaila ○

Lake Lekandiro

Lake Longil

S E R E N G E T I   N D O G O

Lake
Kusare

Lokie Swamp

Lake El
Kekhotoito

Ngongongare Hill ▲

Usa River ○

Lendoiya
Swamp

TO NGARE NANYUKI

Park Headquarters
★

☑ Momela Gate

Nkoaranga ○

Waterfall

Tululusia
▲

Tengeru ○

Arusha National Park

M E R U   C R A T E R

N G A R E   N A N Y U K I

Kitoto Hill
▲

N J E K U

Lake Duluti

Little Meru
3820 m
▲

A23

Ash Cone
▲

Km   2   4

Mt Meru
4566 m
▲

✕

Arusha ○

☎ (00255) 272 503 471/504 082 • 🖷 (00255) 272 508 216 • e🖂 info@tanzaniaparks.com • 🌐 www.tanzaniaparks.com

99

SAMBURU & BUFFALO SPRINGS NATIONAL RESERVE

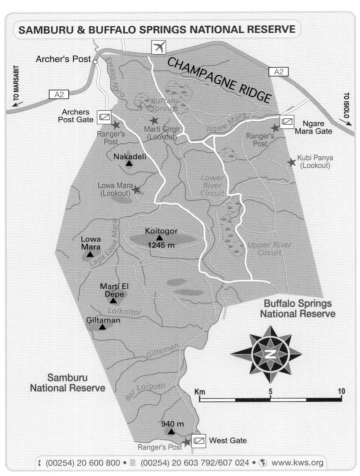

TO MARSABIT

Archer's Post

A2

CHAMPAGNE RIDGE

A2

TO ISIOLO

Archers Post Gate

Ranger's Post

Ewaso Nairo

Buffalo Springs

Marti Girgir (Lookout)

Ngare Mara

Ngare Mara Gate

Ranger's Post

Nakadeli

Kubi Panya (Lookout)

Lowa Mara (Lookout)

Lower River Circuit

Laga Lowa Mara

Koitogor
1245 m

Upper River Circuit

Lowa Mara

Marti El Depe

Lolkoitoi

Buffalo Springs National Reserve

Giltaman

Gilteman

Bar Lolgoto

Samburu National Reserve

Km   5   10

940 m

Ranger's Post   West Gate

((00254) 20 600 800 • (00254) 20 603 792/607 024 • www.kws.org

SHABA NATIONAL RESERVE

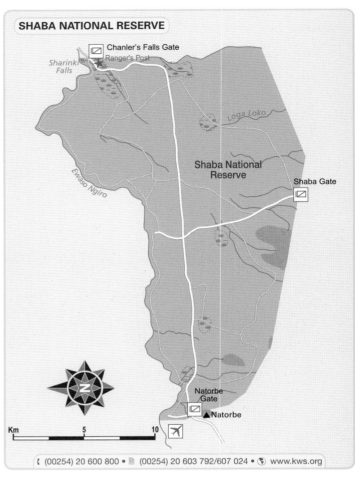

Chanler's Falls Gate
Ranger's Post

Sharinki Falls

Loga Loko

Ewaso Ngiro

Shaba National Reserve

Shaba Gate

Km   5   10

Natorbe Gate

Natorbe

((00254) 20 600 800 • (00254) 20 603 792/607 024 • www.kws.org

ABERDARE NATIONAL PARK

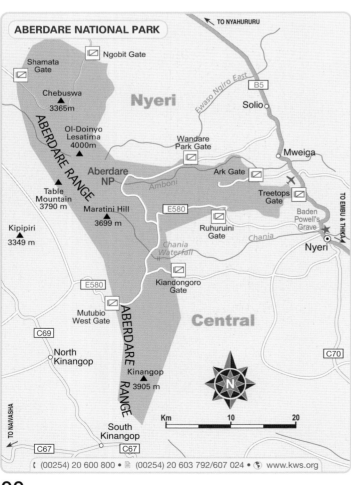

TO NYAHURURU

Ngobit Gate

Shamata Gate

Chebuswa
3365m

Nyeri

Ewaso Ngiro East

B5

Solio

Ol-Doinyo Lesatima
4000m

ABERDARE RANGE

Wandare Park Gate

Mweiga

Aberdare NP

Ark Gate

Amboni

Table Mountain
3790 m

Maratini Hill
3699 m

E580

Treetops Gate

TO EMBU & THIKA

Kipipiri
3349 m

Ruhuruini Gate

Baden Powell's Grave

Chania

Chania Waterfall

Nyeri

E580

Kiandongoro Gate

Central

Mutubio West Gate

ABERDARE RANGE

C69

North Kinangop

Kinangop
3905 m

C70

TO NAIVASHA

South Kinangop

C67   C67

N

Km   10   20

((00254) 20 600 800 • (00254) 20 603 792/607 024 • www.kws.org

MERU NATIONAL PARK

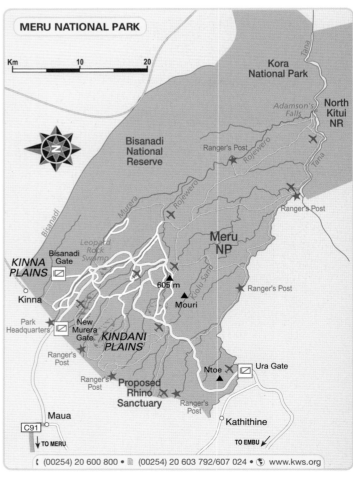

Km   10   20

Kora National Park

Tana

Adamson's Falls

North Kitui NR

Bisanadi National Reserve

Ranger's Post

Rojewero

Tana

Murera

Rojewero

Ranger's Post

Bisanadi

Leopard Rock Swamp

Meru NP

KINNA PLAINS

Bisanadi Gate

605 m

Kiolu Sand

Ranger's Post

Kinna

Mouri

Park Headquarters

New Murera Gate

KINDANI PLAINS

Ntoe

Ura Gate

Ranger's Post

Ranger's Post

Proposed Rhino Sanctuary

Ranger's Post

Maua

C91

TO MERU

Kathithine

TO EMBU

((00254) 20 600 800 • (00254) 20 603 792/607 024 • www.kws.org

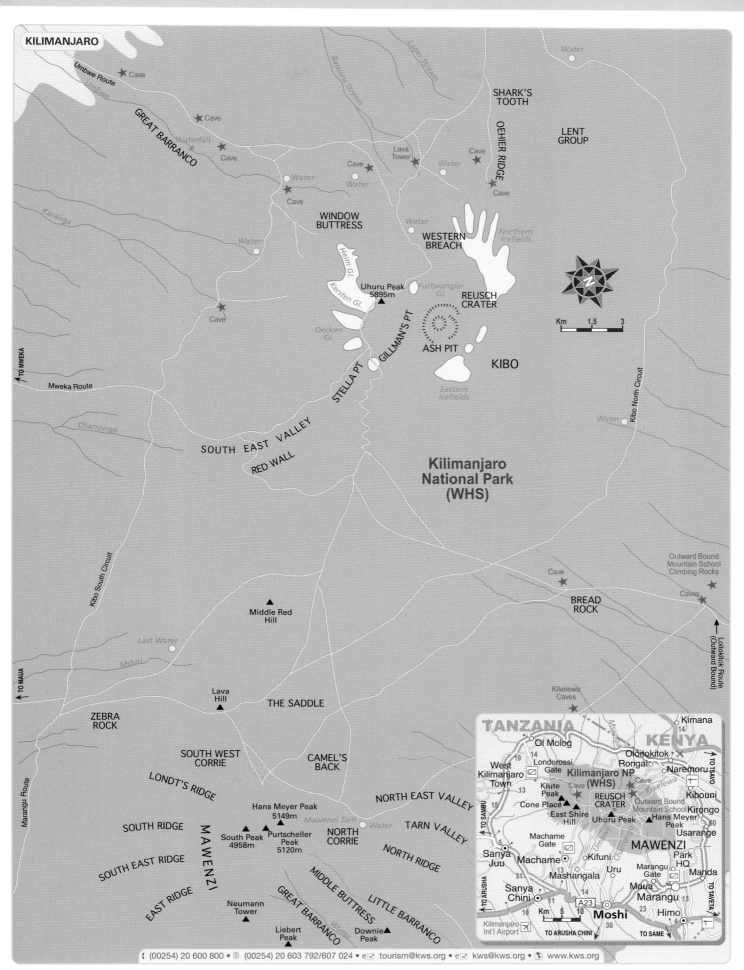

KILIMANJARO

Umbwe Route   ★ Cave

Cave ★

Waterfall

GREAT BARRANCO

Cave ★

Bastions Stream

Lager Stream

Water

SHARK'S TOOTH

LENT GROUP

Cave ★

Cave ★

Lava Tower ★

Water

OEHIER RIDGE

Cave

Karanga

Cave ★

Water

Water

WINDOW BUTTRESS

Water

WESTERN BREACH

Northern Icefields

Heim Gl.

Water

Kersten Gl.

Uhuru Peak ▲ 5895m

Furtwangler Gl.

REUSCH CRATER

Cave ★

Decken Gl.

GILLMAN'S PT

ASH PIT

KIBO

Eastern Icefields

N

Km   1,5   3

TO MWEKA →

Mweka Route

STELLA PT

SOUTH EAST VALLEY

RED WALL

Charrongo

Kilimanjaro National Park (WHS)

Kibo North Circuit

Water

Kibo South Circuit

Cave ★

BREAD ROCK

Outward Bound Mountain School Climbing Rocks

Caves ★★

TO MAUA →

Last Water

Middle Red Hill ▲

Mshiri

Loitokitok Route (Outward Bound) ↓

Lava Hill ▲

THE SADDLE

Kikelewa Caves ★

ZEBRA ROCK

SOUTH WEST CORRIE

CAMEL'S BACK

NORTH EAST VALLEY

LONDT'S RIDGE

Marangu Route

Hans Meyer Peak 5149m

Mawenzi Tarn

TARN VALLEY

SOUTH RIDGE

MAWENZI

South Peak 4958m

Purtscheller Peak 5120m

NORTH CORRIE

Water

NORTH RIDGE

SOUTH EAST RIDGE

EAST RIDGE

Neumann Tower ▲

GREAT BARRANCO

MIDDLE BUTTRESS

LITTLE BARRANCO

Worn

Liebert Peak ▲

Downie Peak ▲

Inset map:

TANZANIA

KENYA

Ol Molog

Kimana

14

West Kilimanjaro Town

19   14

Londorossi Gate

Oloitokitok

Rongai

TO TSAVO →

13

Kilimanjaro NP (WHS)

Cave ★

Cave ★

Naremoru

Klute Peak ▲

18

Cone Place ▲

Kibouni

East Shire Hill ▲

REUSCH CRATER

Outward Bound Mountain School

Kirongo

5

Uhuru Peak ▲

Hans Meyer Peak ▲

Usarange

60

Machame Gate

MAWENZI

Sanya Juu

Machame

Kifuni

Uru

Park HQ

Manda

13

Mashangala

Marangu Gate

Sanya Chini

11

Maua

Marangu

13

A23

23

Himo

10

Km

10

Moshi

30

14

Kilimanjaro Int'l Airport

TO ARUSHA CHINI

TO SAME

TO ARUSHA

☎ (00254) 20 600 800 • 🖨 (00254) 20 603 792/607 024 • e✉ tourism@kws.org • e✉ kws@kws.org • 🌐 www.kws.org

101

Mount Kenya National Park Kenya

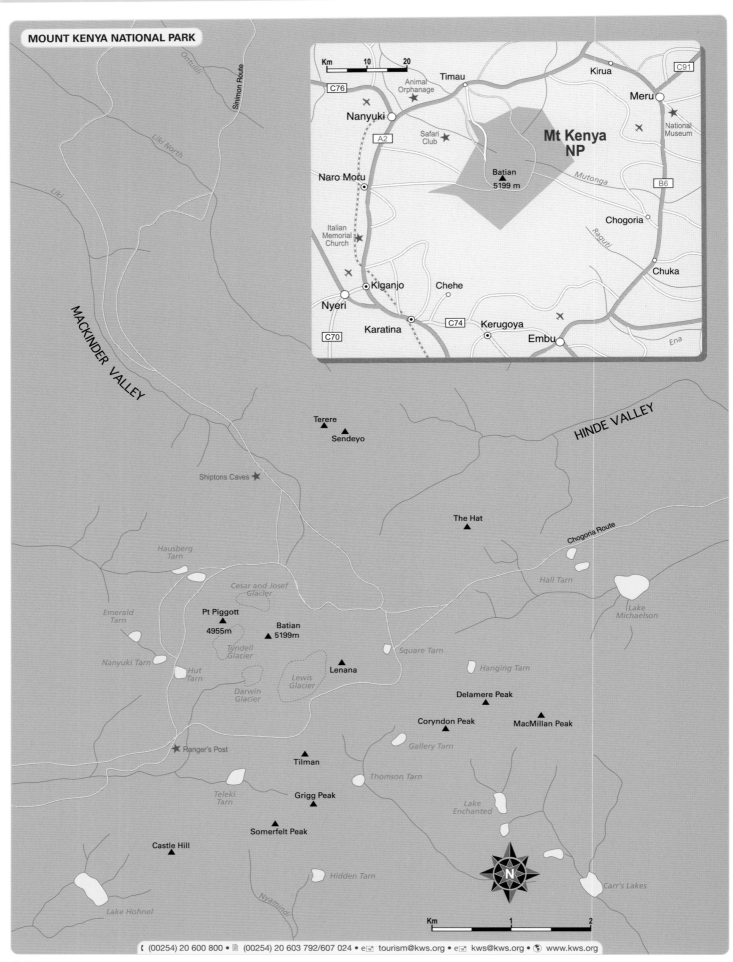

MOUNT KENYA NATIONAL PARK

Ontulili

Sirimon Route

Liki North

Liki

MACKINDER VALLEY

Km 10 20

C76

Animal Orphanage

Timau

Kirua

C91

Meru

Nanyuki

A2

Safari Club

National Museum

Naro Moru

Mt Kenya NP

Batian 5199 m

Mutonga

B6

Chogoria

Ragati

Italian Memorial Church

Chuka

Kiganjo

Chehe

Nyeri

Karatina

C74

Kerugoya

Ena

C70

Embu

Terere

Sendeyo

HINDE VALLEY

Shiptons Caves

The Hat

Chogoria Route

Hausberg Tarn

Hall Tarn

Cesar and Josef Glacier

Lake Michaelson

Emerald Tarn

Pt Piggott
4955m

Batian
▲ 5199m

Nanyuki Tarn

Tyndell Glacier

Hut Tarn

Square Tarn

Hanging Tarn

Delamere Peak

Lewis Glacier

Lenana

Darwin Glacier

Coryndon Peak

MacMillan Peak

Ranger's Post

Gallery Tarn

Tilman

Thomson Tarn

Teleki Tarn

Grigg Peak

Lake Enchanted

Somerfelt Peak

Castle Hill

Hidden Tarn

N

Carr's Lakes

Nyamindi

Lake Hohnel

Km 1 2

☎ (00254) 20 600 800 • 🖹 (00254) 20 603 792/607 024 • e🖂 tourism@kws.org • e🖂 kws@kws.org • 🌐 www.kws.org

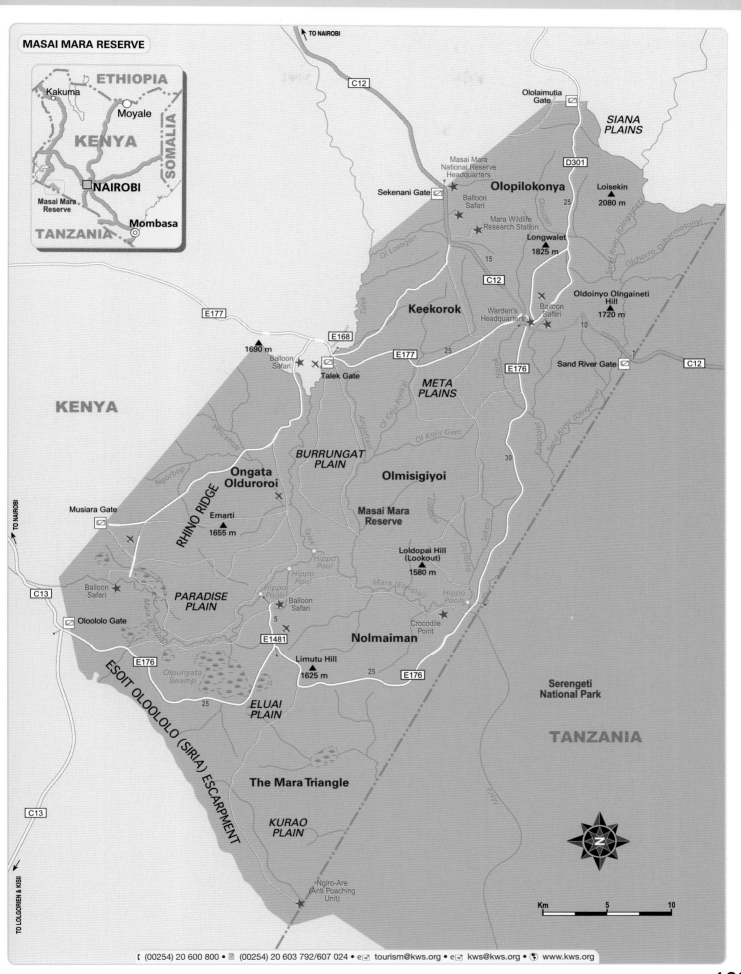

Tsavo National Park Kenya

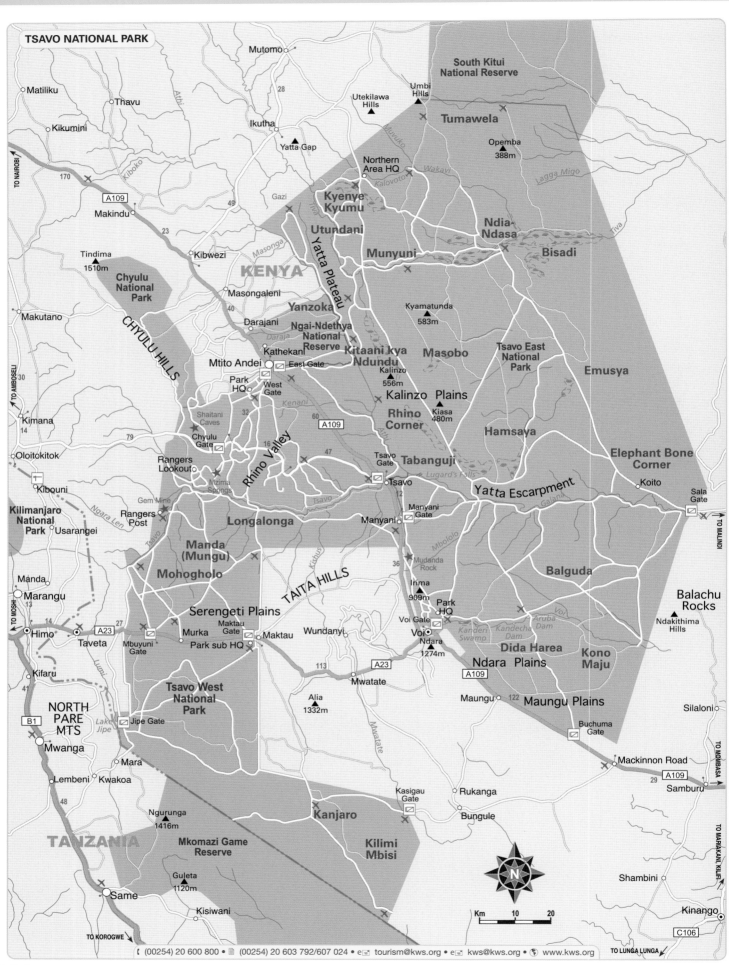

TSAVO NATIONAL PARK

Mutomo
Matiliku
Thavu
Kikumini
Ikutha
Yatta Gap
170
TO NAIROBI
Makindu
A109
23
Tindima
1510m
Kibwezi
Chyulu
National
Park
Masongaleni
KENYA
Makutano
40
Darajani
Kathekani
Mtito Andei
East Gate
Park
HQ
West
Gate
Shaitani
Caves
32
Chyulu
Gate
Rangers
Lookout
Rhino Valley
Mzima
Springs
Gem Mine
Rangers
Post
Kilimanjaro
National
Park
Usarangei
Kibouni
Ngara Len
Longalonga
Manda
(Mungu)
Mohogholo
Kimana
14
Oloitokitok
79
Kiboko
Masonga
CHYULU HILLS
TO AMBOSELI
30
Gazi
49
Utundani
Yanzoka
Yatta Plateau
Ngai-Ndethya
National
Reserve
Kitaani kya
Ndundu
Kenani
60
A109
47
16
Tsavo
Gate
Tsavo
12
Rhino
Corner
Tabanguji
Lugard's Falls
Yatta Escarpment
Galana
Manyani
Gate
Manyani
Mbololo
Kichua
TAITA HILLS
Serengeti Plains
Maktau
Gate
Murka
Maktau
Park sub HQ
Wundanyi
Mbuyuni
Gate
Tsavo West
National
Park
Alia
1332m
Mwatate
A23
113
Kiasa
480m
Kalinzo
Plains
Hamsaya
Elephant Bone
Corner
Koito
Sala
Gate
TO MALINDI
Mudanda
Rock
Irima
909m
Park
HQ
Voi Gate
Voi
Ndara
1274m
Aruba
Dam
Kandecha
Dam
Kanderi
Swamp
Balguda
Dida Harea
Ndara Plains
Kono
Maju
Balachu
Rocks
Ndakithima
Hills
South Kitui
National Reserve
Umbi
Hills
Utekilawa
Hills
Tumawela
Opemba
388m
Lagga Migo
Northern
Area HQ
Kalovoto
Kyenye
Kyumu
Munyuni
Ndia-
Ndasa
Bisadi
Tiva
Kyamatunda
583m
Masobo
Tsavo East
National
Park
Emusya
Kalinzo
556m
Wakavi
Muvuko
28
Mara
Lembeni
Kwakoa
48
Ngurunga
1416m
Mkomazi Game
Reserve
Guleta
1120m
Kanjaro
Kilimi
Mbisi
Kasigau
Gate
Rukanga
Bungule
Maungu
122
Maungu Plains
Buchuma
Gate
Silaloni
Mackinnon Road
29
A109
Samburu
TO MOMBASA
TO MARAKANI, KILIFI
Shambini
Kinango
C106
TO LUNGA LUNGA
Manda
Marangu
TO MOSH
13
Himo
A23
27
Taveta
14
Kifaru
41
NORTH
PARE
MTS
B1
Mwanga
Jipe Gate
Lake
Jipe
TANZANIA
Same
Kisiwani
TO KOROGWE

Km 10 20
N

((00254) 20 600 800 • (00254) 20 603 792/607 024 • e tourism@kws.org • e kws@kws.org • www.kws.org

104

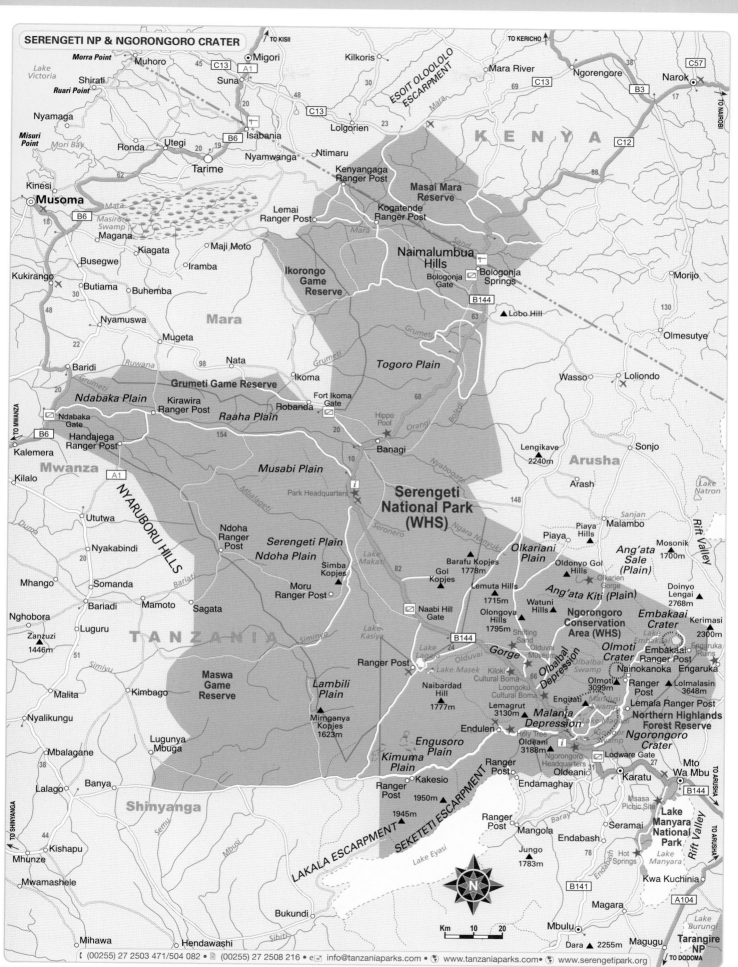

SERENGETI NP & NGORONGORO CRATER

TO KISII
TO KERICHO
TO NAIROBI
TO DODOMA
TO ARUSHA
TO MWANZA
TO SHINYANGA

Lake Victoria
Morra Point
Muhoro
Migori
Kilkoris
Mara River
Ngorengore
Narok
C13
A1
C57
C13
B3
C12

Shirati
Ruari Point
Suna
45
38
Nyamaga
48
Lolgorien
ESOIT OLOOLOLO ESCARPMENT
23
K E N Y A
Misuri Point
Mori Bay
Isabania
B6
Ntimaru
20
19
C13
20
30
69
88
Ronda
Utegi
Nyamwanga
Tarime
Kenyanga Ranger Post
Masai Mara Reserve
62
Kinesi
Musoma
Mara
Lemai Ranger Post
Kogatende Ranger Post
Naimalumbua Hills
Bologonja Springs
Morijo
B6
18
Masirori Swamp
Magana
Kiagata
Maji Moto
Bologonja Gate
B144
130
Busegwe
Iramba
Ikorongo Game Reserve
Olmesutye
Butiama
Buhemba
63
Lobo Hill
Kukirango
30
Mara
Nyamuswa
Mugeta
Nata
Grumeti
Togoro Plain
Wasso
Loliondo
22
48
Baridi
Ruwana
98
Ikoma
Bolodu
68
Arusha
20
Grumeti
Grumeti Game Reserve
Fort Ikoma Gate
Hippo Pool
Lengikave 2240m
Sonjo
Lake Natron
Ndabaka Plain
Kirawira Ranger Post
Robanda
Orangi
Ndabaka Gate
Raaha Plain
Arash
B6
Handajega Ranger Post
154
Banagi
Nyabogati
Arash
Kalemera
Mwanza
Musabi Plain
Mbalageti
10
Nyabogati
Serengeti National Park (WHS)
Piaya Hills
Malambo
Mosonik 1700m
Kilalo
A1
Park Headquarters
Seronera
148
Piaya
Ang'ata Sale (Plain)
Ututwa
NYARUBORU HILLS
Ndoha Ranger Post
Lake Makati
Barafu Kopjes 1778m
Olkariani Plain
Oldonyo Gol Hills
Olkarien Gorge
Doinyo Lengai 2768m
Nyakabindi
20
Serengeti Plain
Ndoha Plain
82
Gol Kopjes
Lemuta Hills 1715m
Ang'ata Kiti (Plain)
Kerimasi 2300m
Mhango
Somanda
Simba Kopjes
Watuni Hills
Ngorongoro Conservation Area (WHS)
Embakaai Crater
Bariati
Moru Ranger Post
Olongoya Hills 1795m
Embakaai
Engaruka Ruins
Mhango
Bariadi
Mamoto
Sagata
Naabi Hill Gate
Shifting Sand
Olmoti Crater
Engaruka
Nghobora
Luguru
Simiyu
Lake Kasiya
Lake Lagaja
24
Olduvai
Olduvai Museum
Olbalbal Depression
Nainokanoka
Lolmalasin 3648m
Zanzuzi 1446m
51
T A N Z A N I A
Siminyo
Ranger Post
Lake Masek
Kiloki Cultural Boma
66
Olbalbal Swamp
Olmoti 3099m
Ranger Post
Lemala Ranger Post
Malita
Kimbago
Lambili Plain
Naibardad Hill 1777m
Loongoku Cultural Boma
Engitati
Malduai Swamp
Northern Highlands Forest Reserve
Nyalikungu
Maswa Game Reserve
Lemagrut 3130m
Malania Depression
Lake Magadi
Goduer Swamp
Ngorongoro Crater
Mbalagane
Mimganya Kopjes 1623m
Endulen
Holy Tree
Oldeani 3188m
Ngorongoro Headquarters
Lodware Gate
Mto Wa Mbu
Lugunya Mbuga
Engusoro Plain
Ranger Post
Oldeani
Karatu
B144
Banya
Kimuma Plain
Kakesio
Endamaghay
Msasa Picnic Site
TO ARUSHA
Lalago
38
1950m
Ranger Post
Seramai
Lake Manyara National Park
Kishapu
Semu
1945m
Mangola
Endabash
Rift Valley
44
SEKETETI ESCARPMENT
Baray
78
Hot Springs
Lake Manyara
Mhunze
Mbusi
LAKALA ESCARPMENT
Lake Eyasi
Jungo 1783m
Kwa Kuchinia
Mwamashele
N
B141
Mihawa
Hendawashi
Sibiti
Km 10 20
Bukundi
Mbulu
Dara 2255m
Magugu
Tarangire NP
Mbulu
Lake Burungi
Magara
A104
TO DODOMA

℡ (00255) 27 2503 471/504 082 • 🖷 (00255) 27 2508 216 • e🖃 info@tanzaniaparks.com • 🌐 www.tanzaniaparks.com • 🕭 www.serengetipark.org

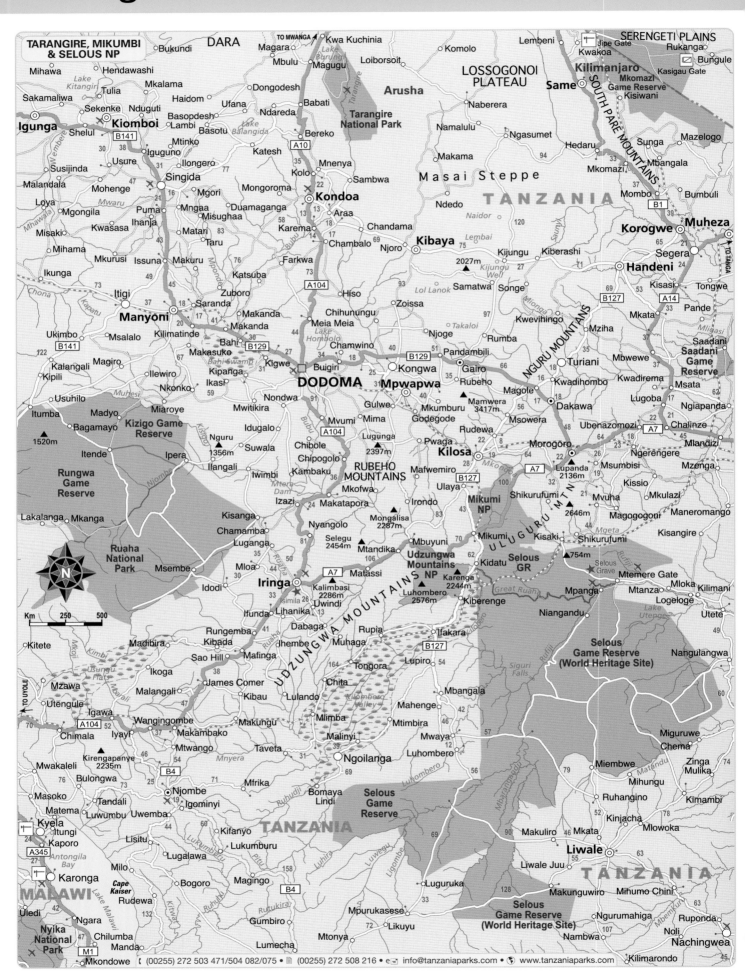

TARANGIRE, MIKUMBI
& SELOUS NP

DARA

TO MWANGA
SERENGETI PLAINS

Bukundi
Magara
Mbulu
Kwa Kuchinia
Komolo
Lembeni
Jipe Gate
Kwakoa
Rukanga
Bungule

Mihawa
Hendawashi
Mkalama
Magugu
Loiborsoit
LOSSOGONOI
PLATEAU
Same
Kilimanjaro
Mkomazi
Game Reserve
Kisiwani
Kasigau Gate

Lake
Kitangiri
Haidom
Dongodesh
Arusha
Naberera
Namalulu
Mkomazi
Mazelogo

Sakamaliwa
Sekenke
Nduguti
Ufana
Babati
Ngasumet
Hedaru
Sunga

Igunga
Kiomboi
Lambi
Basopdesh
Tarangire
National Park
Makama
94
Mkomazi
33
Mbangala

Shelul
B141
Mtinko
Basotu
Bereko
Masai Steppe
Mombo
Bumbuli

Usure
Iguguno
Ilongero
Katesh
A10
Mnenya
Kolo
TANZANIA
B1

Susijinda
Singida
Mgori
Mongoroma
Kondoa
Sambwa
Naidor
120
Korogwe
Muheza

Malandala
Mohenge
Mngaa
Duamaganga
Araa
Chandama
Njoro
Kibaya
Lembai
Kijungu
Kiberashi
Segera
Handeni

Loya
Mwaru
Matari
Karema
Chambalo
2027m
Kijungu
Well
Kisasi
Tongwe

Misaki
Kwasasa
Ihanja
Taru
83
Farkwa
Samatwa
Songe
B127
A14
Pande

Mihama
Issuna
Makuru
76
Katsuba
73
Lol Lanok
Mziha
Saadani
Game
Reserve

Mkurusi
49
Zuboro
A104
Hiso
93
Zoissa
Turiani
Mbwewe
Msata

Ikunga
73
Itigi
Saranda
Chihunungu
Njoge
Takaloi
97
Kwevihingo
NGURU MOUNTAINS
Kwadirema
Lugoba
Ngiapanda

Chona
Manyoni
Makanda
Meia Meia
Lake
Hombolo
Rumba
Gairo
Magole
Dakawa
Mlandizi

Ukimbo
Msalalo
Kilimatinde
Makanda
Chamwino
B129
Pandambili
Rubeho
Magole
Ubenazomozi
Chalinze

B141
Kalangali
Magiro
Bahi
B129
Kigwe
Buigiri
Kongwa
Gairo
Morogoro
Msumbisi
Mzenga

Kipili
Usuhilo
Ilewiro
Makasuko
Bahi Swamp
DODOMA
Mpwapwa
Mkumburu
Mamwera
3417m
Kilosa
A7
Lupanda
2136m
Kissio
Mkulazi

Itumba
Madyo
Miaroye
Nkonko
Ikasi
Nondwa
Gulwe
Mima
Godegode
Mtandika
Pwaga
Ulaya
B127
Shikurufumi
2646m
Mvuha
Magogogoni
Maneromango

Bagamayo
1520m
Kizigo Game
Reserve
Nguru
1356m
Suwala
Idugalo
Mvumi
Lugunga
2397m
Rudewa
Mikumi
NP
Kisaki
Shikurufumi
Kisangire

Itende
Ipera
Ilangali
Chibole
Chipogolo
Kambaku
RUBEHO
MOUNTAINS
Mafwemiro
Mkondo
Mikumi
Kidatu
Selous
GR
754m
Selous
Grave
Mtemere Gate
Mloka
Kilimani

Rungwa
Game
Reserve
Lakalanga
Mkanga
Kisanga
Chamamba
Izazi
Makatapora
Mkofwa
Irondo
Mongalisa
2287m
Mbuyuni
Udzungwa
Mountains
NP
Kiberenge
Mpanga
Mtanza
Logeloge
Utete

Ruaha
National
Park
Msembe
Luganga
Nyangolo
Selegu
2454m
Mtandika
106
Luhombero
2576m
Karenga
2244m
Great Ruaha
Niangandu
Lake
Utengwe
49

Mloa
Idodi
Iringa
Matassi
A7
Kalimbasi
2286m
Uwindi
Kiberenge
Selous
Game
Reserve
(World Heritage Site)
Nangulangwa

Kitete
Mzawa
Madibira
Kibada
Sao Hill
Mafinga
Isimila
Lihanika
Dabaga
Rupia
Ifakara
B127
Lupiro
Mbangala
Siguri
Falls
60

Utengule
Igawa
Wangingombe
Makungu
Ikoga
Malangali
James Comer
Kibau
Lulando
Chita
Tongora
164
Mahenge
Mwaya
42
Miguruwe
Chema

A104
Chimala
IyayP
Makambako
Mtwango
Taveta
Mlimba
Malinyi
Mtimbira
46
Luhombero
57
Miembwe
Zinga
Mulika

Mwakaleli
Bulongwa
Kirengapanye
2235m
B4
Mfrika
Ngoilanga
12
Mihungu

Masoko
Matema
Tandali
Njombe
Igominyi
Bomaya
Lindi
Selous
Game
Reserve
Makuliro
Mkata
Mlowoka
Kimambi

Kyela
Itungi
Kaporo
Luwumbu
Uwemba
Kifanyo
Lukumburu
TANZANIA
Liwale
Liwale Juu
Kinjacha

A345
Antongila
Bay
Lisitu
Lugalawa
Milo
Bogoro
Magingo
B4
Luguruka
128
Makunguwiro
Mihumo Chini
TANZANIA
Ruponda

Karonga
Cape
Kaiser
Rudewa
Gumbiro
Likuyu
72
Mpurukasese
Selous
Game
Reserve
(World Heritage Site)
Ngurumahiga
Noli
Nachingwea

MALAWI
Uledi
Ngara
Chilumba
Manda
Mkondowe
Mtonya
Lumecha
Nambwa
Kilimarondo
45

Nyika
National
Park
M1

Km   250   500

Mkondowe ✆ (00255) 272 503 471/504 082/075 • 🖷 (00255) 272 508 216 • e ✉ info@tanzaniaparks.com • 🌐 www.tanzaniaparks.com

Nairobi National Park   Kenya

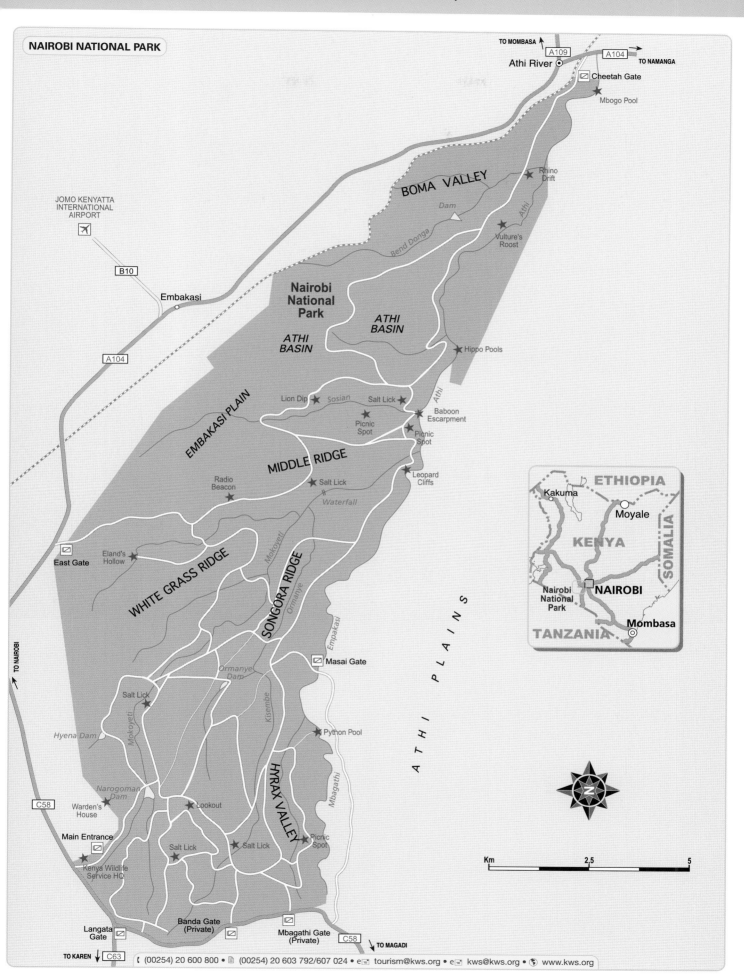

NAIROBI NATIONAL PARK

TO MOMBASA
A109
Athi River
A104
TO NAMANGA
Cheetah Gate
Mbogo Pool

BOMA VALLEY
Rhino Drift
Dam
Bend Donga
Vulture's Roost
Athi

JOMO KENYATTA INTERNATIONAL AIRPORT

B10

Embakasi

A104

Nairobi National Park

ATHI BASIN

ATHI BASIN

Hippo Pools

Athi

EMBAKASI PLAIN

Lion Dip
Sosian
Salt Lick
Baboon Escarpment
Picnic Spot
Picnic Spot

MIDDLE RIDGE

Radio Beacon
Salt Lick
Waterfall
Leopard Cliffs

East Gate
Eland's Hollow

WHITE GRASS RIDGE

SONGORA RIDGE

Mokoyeti
Ormanye

Empakasi

Masai Gate

ATHI PLAINS

TO NAIROBI

Ormanye Dam

Kisembe

Salt Lick
Mokoyeti

Python Pool

Hyena Dam

HYRAX VALLEY

Mbagathi

Narogoman Dam

C58
Warden's House

Lookout

Main Entrance

Salt Lick
Salt Lick
Picnic Spot

Kenya Wildlife Service HQ

Langata Gate
Banda Gate (Private)
Mbagathi Gate (Private)
C58
TO MAGADI

TO KAREN C63

ETHIOPIA
Kakuma
Moyale
KENYA
SOMALIA
NAIROBI
Nairobi National Park
Mombasa
TANZANIA

Km   2,5   5

((00254) 20 600 800 • ▤ (00254) 20 603 792/607 024 • e✉ tourism@kws.org • e✉ kws@kws.org • 🌐 www.kws.org

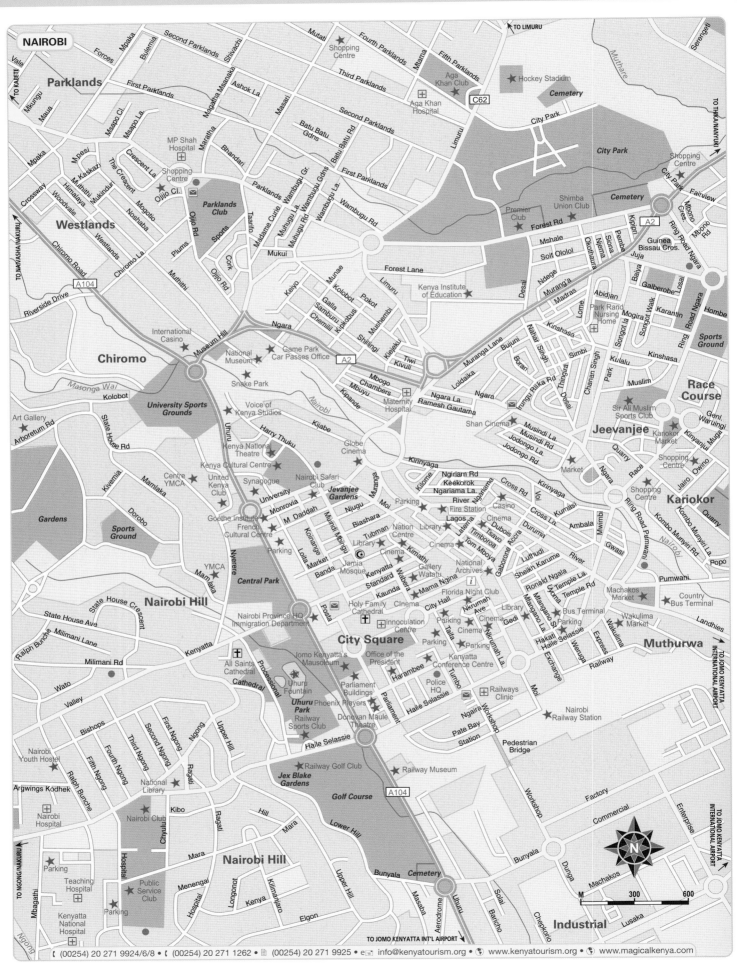

((00254) 20 271 9924/6/8 • ((00254) 20 271 1262 • 📄 (00254) 20 271 9925 • e✉ info@kenyatourism.org • 🌐 www.kenyatourism.org • 🌐 www.magicalkenya.com

108

Mombasa Island   Kenya

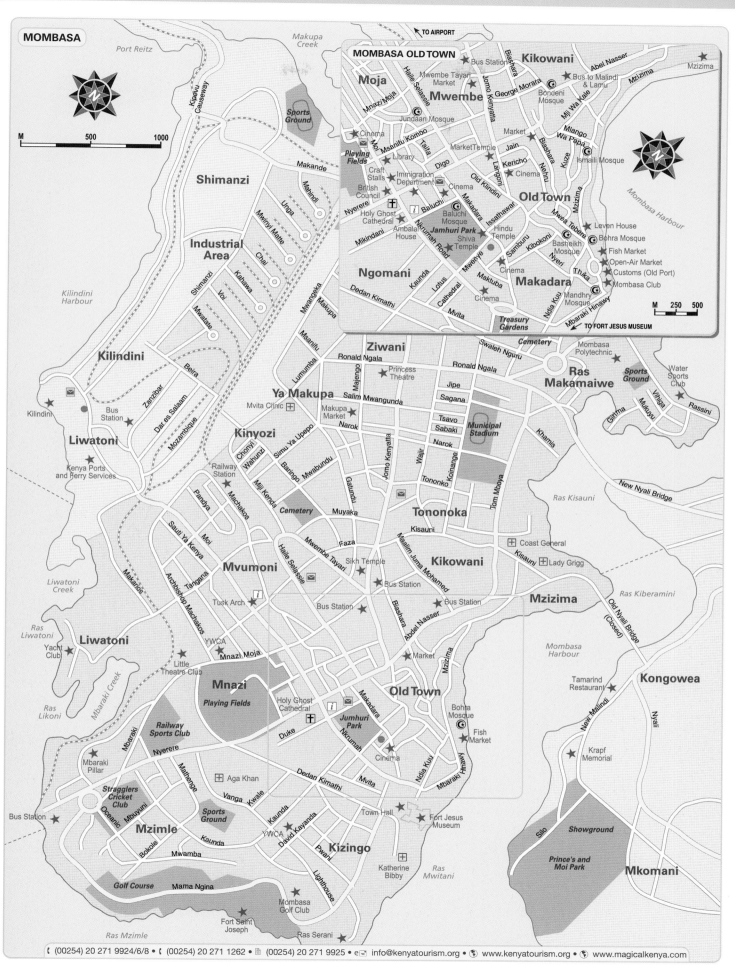

((00254) 20 271 9924/6/8 • ((00254) 20 271 1262 • ▤ (00254) 20 271 9925 • e⊠ info@kenyatourism.org • ⟳ www.kenyatourism.org • ⟳ www.magicalkenya.com

109

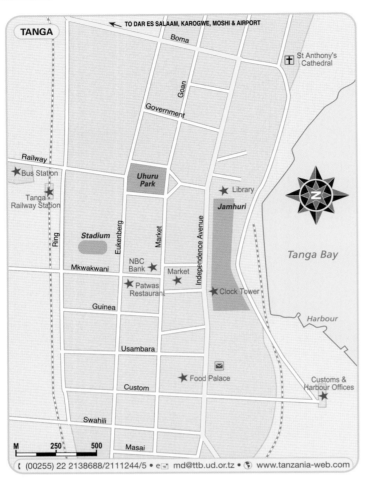

TANGA

TO DAR ES SALAAM, KAROGWE, MOSHI & AIRPORT

Boma

Goan

Government

St Anthony's Cathedral

Railway

Bus Station

Tanga Railway Station

Uhuru Park

Library

Jamhuri

Clock Tower

Stadium

Eukenberg

Market

Independence Avenue

Mkwakwani

NBC Bank

Market

Patwas Restaurant

Guinea

Tanga Bay

Usambara

Harbour

Food Palace

Custom

Customs & Harbour Offices

Swahili

Masai

M 250 500

((00255) 22 2138688/2111244/5 • e md@ttb.ud.or.tz • www.tanzania-web.com

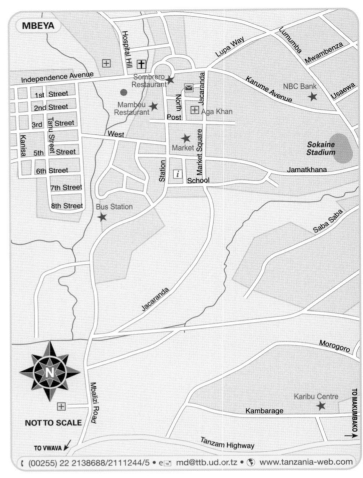

MBEYA

Hospital Hill

Lumumba

Lupa Way

Mwambenza

Independence Avenue

Sombrero Restaurant

Karume Avenue

NBC Bank

Usaewa

1st Street

2nd Street

Mambeu Restaurant

North Post

Jacaranda

Aga Khan

3rd Street

Taru Street

Kanisa

West

Market Square

Sokaine Stadium

5th Street

6th Street

Station

School

Jamatkhana

7th Street

8th Street

Bus Station

Saba Saba

Morogoro

Jacaranda

NOT TO SCALE

Mbalizi Road

Karibu Centre

TO MAKUMBAKO

Kambarage

TO VWAVA

Tanzam Highway

((00255) 22 2138688/2111244/5 • e md@ttb.ud.or.tz • www.tanzania-web.com

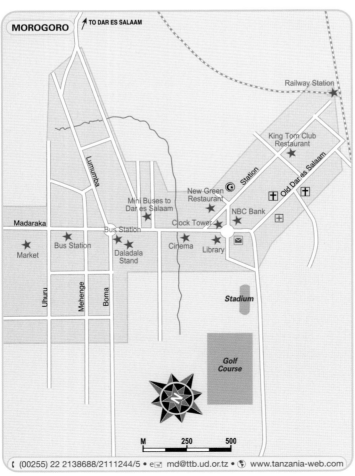

MOROGORO

TO DAR ES SALAAM

Railway Station

King Tom Club Restaurant

Station

Lumumba

New Green Restaurant

Old Dar es Salaam

Mini Buses to Dar es Salaam

NBC Bank

Madaraka

Bus Station

Clock Tower

Market

Bus Station

Cinema

Library

Daladala Stand

Uhuru

Mehenge

Boma

Stadium

Golf Course

M 250 500

((00255) 22 2138688/2111244/5 • e md@ttb.ud.or.tz • www.tanzania-web.com

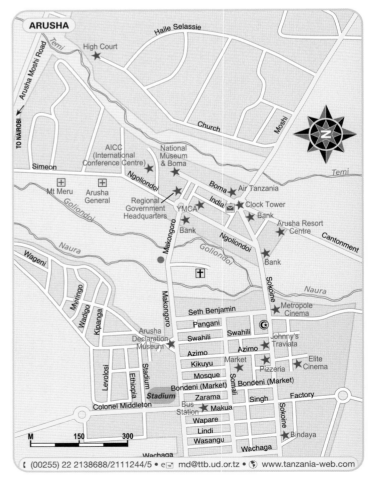

ARUSHA

Haile Selassie

Temi

High Court

Arusha Moshi Road

Church

Moshi

TO NAIROBI

AICC (International Conference Centre)

National Museum & Boma

Temi

Simeon

Ngoliondoi

Boma

Air Tanzania

Mt Meru

Goliondoi

Arusha General

Regional Government Headquarters

India

Clock Tower

YMCA

Bank

Arusha Resort Centre

Naura

Wageni

Makongoro

Bank

Ngoliondoi

Goliondoi

Cantonment

Bank

Mvitingo

Wadigo

Kipanga

Naura

Sokoine

Seth Benjamin

Metropole Cinema

Pangani

Swahili

Swahili

Johnny's Traviata

Arusha Declaration Museum

Azimo

Azimo

Isolovolo

Ethiopia

Stadium

Somali

Kikuyu

Market

Elite Cinema

Pizzeria

Mosque

Bondeni (Market)

Bondeni (Market)

Zarama

Singh

Factory

Colonel Middleton

Bus Station

Makua

Stadium

Wapare

Lindi

Sokoine

Wasangu

Bindaya

Wachaga

Wachaga

((00255) 22 2138688/2111244/5 • e md@ttb.ud.or.tz • www.tanzania-web.com

M 150 300

110

Dar es Salaam & Zanzibar Tanzania

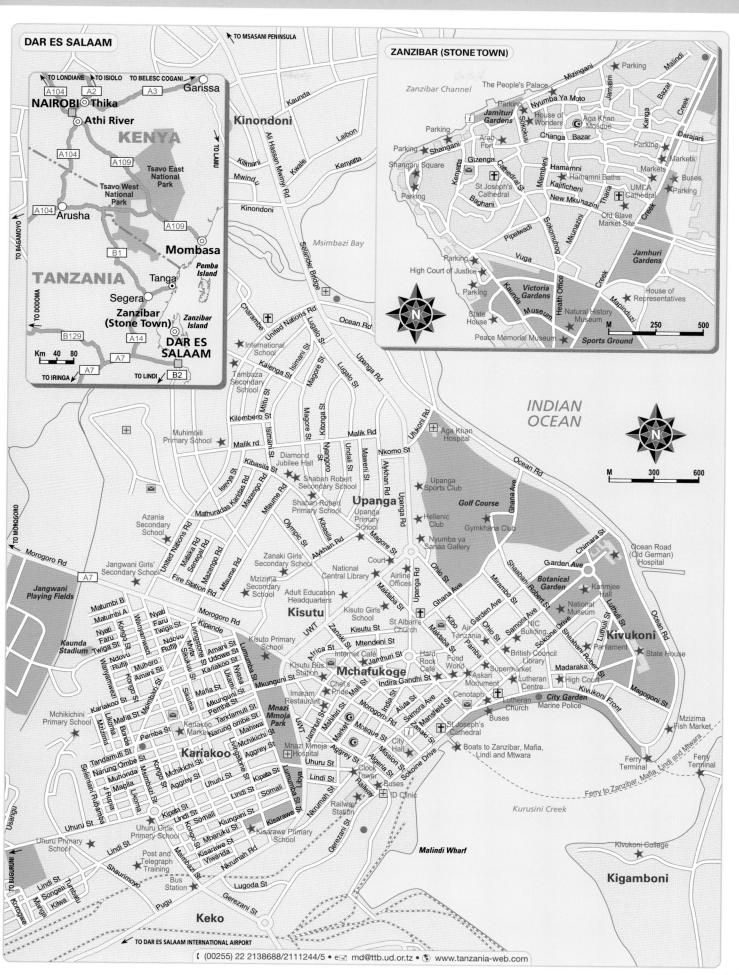

☎ (00255) 22 2138688/2111244/5 • e✉ md@ttb.ud.or.tz • 🌐 www.tanzania-web.com

Adventures

Adventure	Country	Duration
Ballooning over the Masai Mara Reserve	Kenya	1 hour +
Camel Safaris in Kenya	Kenya	4 days +
Dhow Sailing the Kenyan Coast	Kenya	3 hours +
Climbing Kilimanjaro	Tanzania	5 days
Walking the Serengeti NP	Tanzania	1 - 2 days
Exploring the Waters off Zanzibar	Tanzania	1 day +

Ballooning over the Masai Mara Reserve

Requirements:
Passports and, for citizens of some countries, visas are required. Only immunization required is for visitors travelling through or from countries with a recent history of yellow fever.

Climate:
Hot and dry, with heavy rains from December-April.

Risk factor:
No more risk than would usually be associated with adventure sports. Nerve-wracking, but safe.

Health:
Malaria is rife, except at Nairobi and on the highlands, where risk is lower. Seafood such as shellfish may be a little risky. Drink only bottled water.

Pack:
For safaris, light cotton clothes, a sun hat and solid walking boots should be sufficient, but early-morning balloon trips can be affected by wind-chill.

Facilities:
Luxury lodges and comfortable tented camps cater for an extremely upmarket tourist trade. Budget camp sites run by local Masai (such as Musiara, Talek, Olooloo, Sekenani and Ololaimutiek) are inexpensive but basic.

Contact:
Gametrackers, P.O. Box 62042, Nairobi.
Tel: 00254-20-251771
game@southafricaonline.co.ke
www.gametrackers.com

Camel Safaris in Kenya

Requirements:
Passports and, for citizens of some countries, visas are required. Only immunization required is for visitors travelling through or from countries with a recent history of yellow fever.

Climate:
Usually hot and dry throughout the country, and relatively humid along the coastal stretches.

Risk factor:
Generally risk-free and, besides stubborn camels and the usual dangers of nights in the bush, safari operators take good care of clients.

Health:
Malaria is rife throughout most of Kenya, except at Nairobi and on the highlands where the risk is considerably lower. Dehydration can be an issue, but be sure to drink only bottled water.

Pack:
Lightweight clothes, sun hat and sturdy walking boots are essential for trekking safaris.

Facilities:
Luxury lodges and very comfortable tented camps cater largely for the upmarket tourist visiting national parks and reserves. More basic and substantially cheaper options may be found throughout the country.

Contact:
Let's Go Travel Nairobi, Nairobi, Kenya.
Tel: 00254-20-4447151

Dhow Sailing the Kenyan Coast

Requirements:
Passports and, for citizens of some countries, visas are required. Only immunization required is for visitors travelling through or from countries with a recent history of yellow fever.

Climate:
Conditions are usually hot and humid along the tropical coast.

Risk factor:
Risks are minimal, but stick to basic hygiene with food and water.

Health:
Malaria is rife throughout most of Kenya, except at Nairobi and on the highlands, where the risk is considerably lower. Dehydration can be an issue when you are under the harsh sun all day, but be sure to drink only bottled water.

Pack:
You will need little more than standard touring clothes, which should include light cotton clothing, sunscreen and sun hat, as well as some form of cover if you will be cruising at night.

Facilities:
Lodges, resorts and upmarket hotels — the base for many tour operators — take very good care of clients, but dhow taxis and small, one-man businesses offer little in "creature comforts".

Contact:
Tamarind Dhow Safaris,
P.O. Box 95805, Mombasa.
Tel: 00254-41-474600 / 1

Climbing Kilimanjaro

Requirements:
Most visitors need passports and visas from their local embassy. Travellers from South America and most of Africa are required to present a yellow fever immunization certificate.

Climate:
Avoid the rains in April, May and November.

Risk factor:
Cheap package deals may be less reliable and less safe than established operators. Irresponsible tourists are degrading the trail in Kilimanjaro National Park through constant use.

Health:
Exhaustion, fatigue and altitude sickness are the most serious complaints. Be vaccinated against cholera, tetanus, hepatitis and polio. AIDS is prevalent.

Pack:
Warm, waterproof and windproof clothes, sturdy hiking boots, a sleeping bag, sunscreen and water. Sweets help maintain energy. A head torch for the early-morning stretch. A kikoi (sarong) that can act as a scarf and pillow.

Facilities:
Reliable operators offer the best service and provide equipment.

Contact:
Wild Frontiers (RSA-based), P.O. Box 844, Halfway House, 1685.
Tel: 011-702 2035
wildfront@icon.co.za, www.wildfrontiers.com

Walking the Serengeti NP

Requirements:
Most visitors will need passports and visas, so enquire at your local embassy before departure. Travellers from South America and most of Africa are required to present a yellow fever immunization certificate.

Climate:
Coolest June–October, but this is also the busiest and most expensive time. January–February may be better – although hot, it's the best time to see migration in the southern park.

Risk factor:
The day-to-day life is filled with the dangers of wildest Africa.

Health:
Be vaccinated against cholera, tetanus, hepatitis and polio. Malaria is rife in the lowlands. AIDS is prevalent.

Pack:
Most operators supply basics, but take light hiking gear, warm clothes, walking boots, and sun protection.

Facilities:
Expensive tented camps and lodges; 18 simple camp sites ('special' camp sites and wilderness camp sites, with reasonable amenities), and 12 public camps (including Seronera, Lobo, Ndabaka and Bologonja) where facilities are virtually non-existent.

Contact:
Tropical Tours, P.O. Box 727, Arusha, Tanzania.
Tel: 00255-27-2502417 / 2548907

Exploring the Waters off Zanzibar

Requirements:
Most visitors need passports and visas – enquire at your local embassy. Travellers from South America and most of Africa are required to present a yellow fever immunization certificate. Travel documentation is checked again on entry to Zanzibar. Some diving excursions may require qualifications.

Climate:
Best times are December–January (peak holiday season) and June–Oct. Ocean conditions vary according to location, and the best time to dive is Oct–Nov.

Risk factor:
Theft and mugging are becoming more frequent. Exposure to the sun exacerbated by wind and sea. Malaria remains a threat. Currents on the east coast may be dangerous.

Health:
Malaria is a risk. AIDS is prevalent.

Pack:
Zanzibar is Muslim, so exposed flesh is frowned upon beyond tourist spots.

Facilities:
Many hotels have local guides on call and a number of operators offering water-based excursions keep offices in Stone Town. Many offer PADI courses.

Contact:
Indian Ocean Divers,
Mizingani Road, P.O. Box 2370, Zanzibar.
Tel: 00255-24-2233860 or 00255-24-2234797

The Great Zambezi

Steeped in a long and erratic history of colonial occupation, Zambia and Zimbabwe were once known as Northern and Southern Rhodesia respectively, settler outposts that continue in many ways to struggle against the legacy left behind by empirical Britain after independence. Ethnically diverse and culturally extremely rich, both Zambia and Zimbabwe rely to a large degree on the land that has since been reclaimed from colonial powers. Zambia's greatest asset is its copper reserves and, although these are gradually declining, copper exports still account for some 80 per cent of the nation's foreign income. Zimbabwe, on the other hand, has historically relied almost entirely on the harvest of its cash crops, most notably tobacco, which have created one of the most broadly based economies of the region.

ZAMBIA

LUSAKA

Having originated as little more than a single general store serving workers building a railway siding in the early 1900s, the modern city – succeeding Livingstone as the nation's capital in 1930 – has mushroomed into a hub of activity conveniently situated at one of the most important crossroads in southern Africa. Lusaka is every inch a modern urban settlement with all the charm and scourges that entails: open-air markets, tree-lined boulevards and dusty side streets lurking with muggers and less innocuous criminals. In reality, apart from a network of travel-orientated facilities such as the airport, bus terminals and tourist offices, there is little to attract the casual sightseer. Lusaka's citizens are nevertheless widely acknowledged as the friendliest and most hospitable on the continent.

BAROTSELAND

Fiercely independent and devout followers of tradition, the people of Barotseland remain one of the most authentic indigenous groups in Zambia. Barotseland once extended far and wide, but now centres around the Zambezi's flood plains. The most engrossing feature of the region is the rituals of its people, epitomized in the Kuomboka, a lavish parade that sees the Lozi king take to the waters in an ornate barge in his ceremonial evacuation of the flood plain in favour of higher ground. The ritual is repeated every year as a highlight of the ceremonial calendar.

LUANGWA VALLEY

The Luangwa Valley follows the course of the Luangwa River: one side is wild, unpredictable and remote, the other an expanse of picturesque nature reserve abounding with wild animals. The northern reaches of the valley, occupied mostly by the Bemba people, is dominated by the untamed wilderness of North Luangwa National Park: difficult to access, nature reigns supreme in the Park. Predators and scavengers lurk in murky waters and scour the plains. It is from the fauna-rich miombo woodlands of the Zambian plateau that the escarpment dips 1,000m to the floor of the Luangwa Valley. Hippo and crocodile still inhabit the Luangwa River, but along the 200km that separate North Luangwa from its southern counterpart there is a noticeable change. South Luangwa National Park is one of Africa's best reserves and is far more developed than the north. Although no 'walk in the park', it is much more accessible, dry river beds and hard-baked soils opening into woodland and grassy plains populated with lion, leopard, elephant, buffalo, zebra and Thornicroft's giraffe. The Save the Rhino Trust continues to combat the poaching of elephant and rhino in the area.

SHIWA NGANDU

Virtually hidden in the miombo woodland, this 9,350-hectare grand private estate near Mpika is astonishing. In 1914 Stuart Gore-Brown, ex-soldier, mentor and explorer, laid claim to 4,900ha, later adding 4,450ha to the property. He went on to play a pivotal role in the story of Zambia and remains the only European settler to have been honoured with a state funeral and to be buried according to the ritual reserved for a tribal chief. The grand old Shiwa House is in a sad state of disrepair, but the surrounding wilderness is quite breathtaking.

VICTORIA FALLS

Located on the majestic Zambezi River (within the boundaries of Zambia and Zimbabwe), the dramatic Victoria Falls has been hailed as the greatest spectacle on earth. Situated amid a small rainforest, which forms part of the surrounding national park, Victoria Falls has become one of the continent's most enduring legacies and is today big business. Thousands of visitors flock here annually to look out over the spectacular 2km wide falls and down into the Zambezi Gorge: for the privilege they suffer the spray of water as it tumbles 100m. The rainforest that skirts the edge of Victoria Falls is washed in parts by 500m of spray and is laced with a convoluted network of walks and trails, at times stepping out onto the lip of the great basin and at others receding into the woods, or winding down the tracks to the gorge below. Zambia's vantage points offer a much closer look at the 545 million litres that gush down the rock face every minute during heavy rains. A rainbow hangs semi-permanently above the falls between April and June, enhancing the breathtaking view over the hinterland.

ZIMBABWE

HARARE

Founded just over 100 years ago, Zimbabwe's capital was once hailed as the most African of the continent's principal cities. Harare – known as Salisbury until independence in 1980 – was pronounced the official capital of Southern Rhodesia in 1923 and was declared a city in 1935. It has seen better days and is plagued intermittently with fuel shortages and near empty supermarket shelves. Despite the latter-day problems (including a growing urban crime rate), the capital remains a beautiful city that has retained at least some of its charm. Harare is an important centre of the country's arts and crafts industry, most notably the soapstone sculptures synonymous with Zimbabwe, the best of which may be found about 8km from town at Chapungu Kraal, a model Shona village that offers a glimpse of tribal life. Harare is set against an inspiring backdrop of bushveld savanna punctuated with a series of rock formations – the most famous of which are the Epworth Balancing Rocks – and an impressive number of rock-art sites.

LAKE KARIBA

Constructed between 1955 and 1958, and opened by Queen Elizabeth II in 1960, Lake Kariba remains one of the continent's most ambitious water projects, and is the third-largest artificial body of water in Africa. The massive walls span a perimeter of 579m and stretch 282km across the landscape to cover a total of 5,000km². The walls are 24m thick at the base and 128m high. A fascinating diversion is to take a walk along the top of the dam wall to feel the pounding of the massive turbines. The shores of the great lake are a wildlife haven and are surrounded by some of Zimbabwe's finest parks, reserves and wilderness areas, all of which are rich in game and popular drawcards.

GREAT ZIMBABWE

Perhaps the country's most significant legacy, the majestic stone-walled ruins of Great Zimbabwe comprise the most impressive medieval site in Africa south of the Sahara. This architectural and archaeological gem, about 30km from Masvingo, was established more than 1,000 years ago by the Karonga, ancestors of the local Shona, and comprises a fascinating series of stone walls. The walled city harboured no fewer than 10,000 citizens – a fatal mistake that led to overpopulation and the abandonment of the citadel in the 1450s. Excavation of the site has provided evidence that medieval Africa was indeed highly sophisticated. Guided tours take visitors through the Hill Complex – once known as the Acropolis – thought to have been the monarch's residence. The walls of the Great Enclosure are 5m thick and 11m high and were built with nearly a million stone 'bricks' over 100 years in the 14th and 15th centuries.

MATOBO HILLS

Despite the stark beauty of their horizonless vistas, the granite hills of Matobo are best known in the Western world as the final resting place of Cecil John Rhodes, the mining pioneer and statesman who played a significant role in the troubled history of southern Africa. His grave tablet stands in the middle of a wide circle created from the boulders that lie strewn across the hillsides. The spot at Malindidzimu is known as the View of the World and provides one of the most impressive panoramas in southwestern Zimbabwe. Backed by austere, cold-faced mountains weathered by rain and wind and sand, the Matobo National Park – 50km south of Bulawayo – is a breathtaking wilderness, home to a relatively small assortment of wild and rare animals. The giant granite outcrops and precariously balanced rock formations characterize the landscape, and boast arguably the world's most astounding collection of indigenous rock art.

Both Zambia and Zimbabwe are spectacular in their natural beauty and, despite the political turmoil in which they have been — and, in the case of Zimbabwe, still are — embroiled, the potential of the tourism industry remains virtually the only shining light on what may otherwise be rather bleak futures.

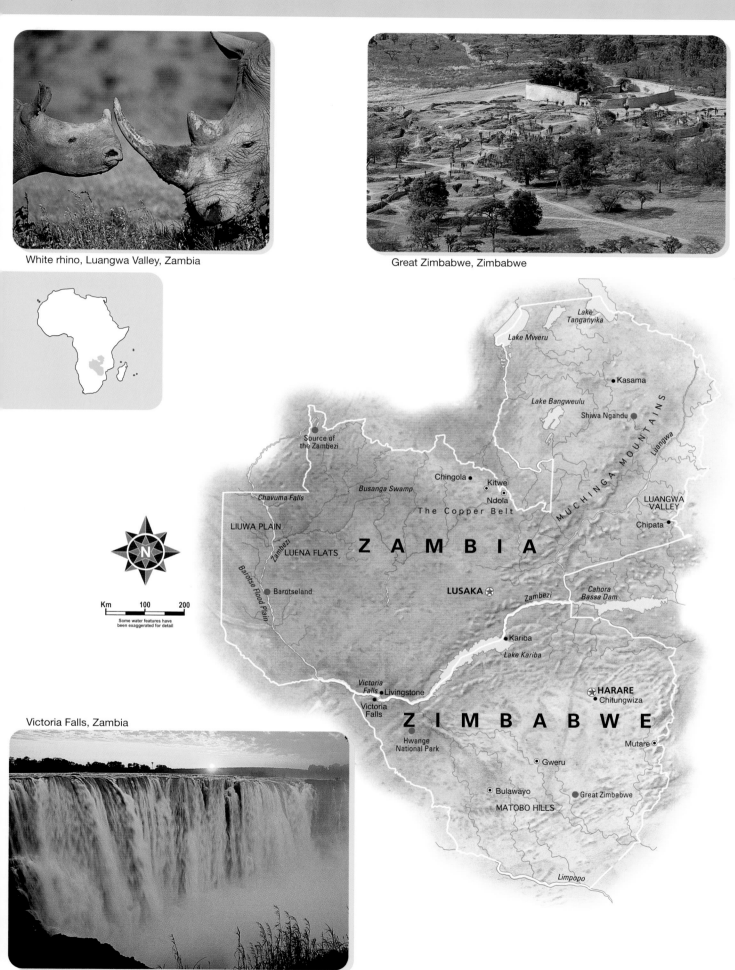

White rhino, Luangwa Valley, Zambia

Great Zimbabwe, Zimbabwe

Victoria Falls, Zambia

Lake Tanganyika

Lake Mweru

Kasama

Lake Bangweulu

Shiwa Ngandu

Source of
the Zambezi

Chingola

Kitwe

Ndola

The Copper Belt

MUCHINGA MOUNTAINS

Luangwa

LUANGWA
VALLEY

Chavuma Falls

Busanga Swamp

LIUWA PLAIN

Chipata

LUENA FLATS

Zambezi

Z A M B I A

Barotse Flood Plain

Barotseland

LUSAKA ✪

Zambezi

Cahora
Bassa Dam

Kariba

Lake Kariba

Victoria
Falls

Livingstone

Victoria
Falls

✪ **HARARE**
Chitungwiza

Z I M B A B W E

Hwange
National Park

Mutare

Gweru

Bulawayo

Great Zimbabwe

MATOBO HILLS

Limpopo

Km   100   200
Some water features have
been exaggerated for detail

N

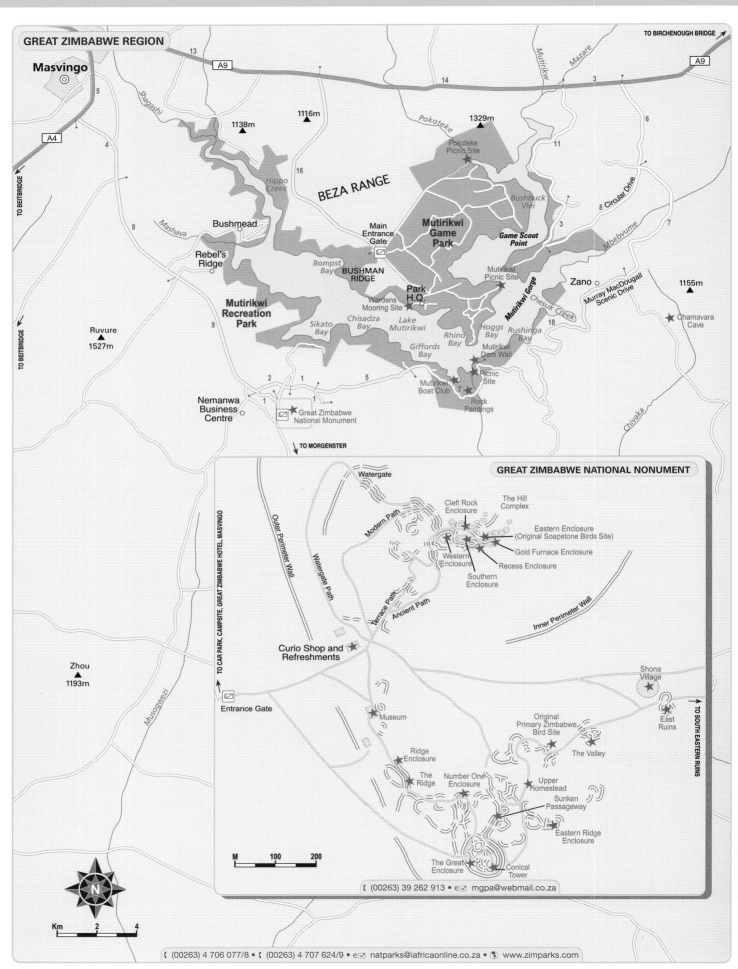

GREAT ZIMBABWE REGION

Masvingo

TO BIRCHENOUGH BRIDGE

A9

A4

TO BEITBRIDGE

TO BEITBRIDGE

1138m

1116m

1329m

1155m

Shagashi

Hippo Creek

BEZA RANGE

Pokoteke

Pokoteke Picnic Site

Mutirikwi

Mazare

Bushbuck Vlei

Mbebvume

8 Circular Drive

Bushmead

Mashava

Rebel's Ridge

Bompst Bay

Main Entrance Gate

BUSHMAN RIDGE

Mutirikwi Game Park

Game Scout Point

Mutirikwi Picnic Site

Zano

Murray MacDougall Scenic Drive

Chamavara Cave

Mutirikwi Recreation Park

Park H.Q.

Wardens Mooring Site

Sikato Bay

Chisadza Bay

Lake Mutirikwi

Rhino Bay

Hoggs Bay

Rushinga Bay

Mutirikwi Gorge

Chesuk Creek

Giffords Bay

Mutirikwi Dam Wall

Picnic Site

Mutirikwi Boat Club

Rock Paintings

Chivaka

Ruvure 1527m

Nemanwa Business Centre

Great Zimbabwe National Monument

TO MORGENSTER

GREAT ZIMBABWE NATIONAL NONUMENT

Watergate

TO CAR PARK, CAMPSITE, GREAT ZIMBABWE HOTEL, MASVINGO

Outer Perimeter Wall

Watergate Path

Modern Path

Cleft Rock Enclosure

The Hill Complex

Eastern Enclosure (Original Soapstone Birds Site)

Gold Furnace Enclosure

Western Enclosure

Recess Enclosure

Southern Enclosure

Terrace Path

Ancient Path

Inner Perimeter Wall

Curio Shop and Refreshments

Shona Village

Zhou 1193m

Musogwezi

Entrance Gate

Museum

Original Primary Zimbabwe Bird Site

East Ruins

TO SOUTH EASTERN RUINS

Ridge Enclosure

The Valley

The Ridge

Number One Enclosure

Upper Homestead

Sunken Passageway

Eastern Ridge Enclosure

The Great Enclosure

Conical Tower

M 100 200

((00263) 39 262 913 • e mgpa@webmail.co.za

N

Km 2 4

((00263) 4 706 077/8 • ((00263) 4 707 624/9 • e natparks@iafricaonline.co.za • www.zimparks.com

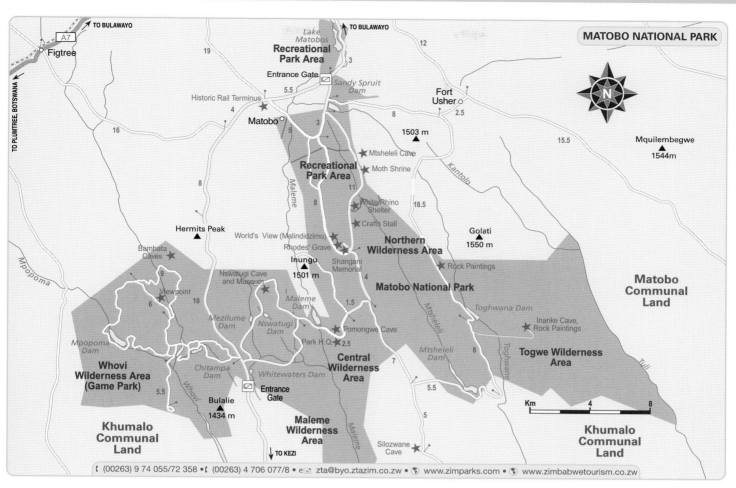

MATOBO NATIONAL PARK

TO BULAWAYO
A7
Figtree
TO PLUMTREE, BOTSWANA
19
Lake Matobos
Recreational Park Area
TO BULAWAYO
12
Entrance Gate
Sandy Spruit Dam
5.5
Fort Usher
2.5
Historic Rail Terminus
4
1503 m
Mtsheleli Cave
Mquilembegwe 1544m
Matobo
5
Mpopoma
16
3
8
15.5
Kantolo
8
Recreational Park Area
11
Moth Shrine
Hermits Peak
8
White Rhino Shelter
18.5
Crafts Stall
Bambata Caves
World's View (Malindidzimu)
Rhodes' Grave
Shangani Memorial
Golati 1550 m
9
Inungu 1501 m
Northern Wilderness Area
Rock Paintings
Viewpoint
Nswatugi Cave and Museum
4
Matobo National Park
6
10
Maleme Dam
1.5
Mezilume Dam
Nswatugi Dam
Pomongwe Cave
Toghwana Dam
Mpopoma Dam
Park H.Q.
2.5
Central Wilderness Area
7
Inanke Cave, Rock Paintings
Mtsheleli
Togwe Wilderness Area
Tuli
Whovi Wilderness Area (Game Park)
Chitampa Dam
Whitewaters Dam
Mtsheleli Dam
8
Toghwane
Khumalo Communal Land
5.5
Whovi
Entrance Gate
5.5
Bulalie 1434 m
5
Km   4   8
Maleme
Maleme Wilderness Area
Silozwane Cave
Khumalo Communal Land
TO KEZI

((00263) 9 74 055/72 358 • ((00263) 4 706 077/8 • e⊠ zta@byo.ztazim.co.zw • 🌐 www.zimparks.com • 🌐 www.zimbabwetourism.co.zw

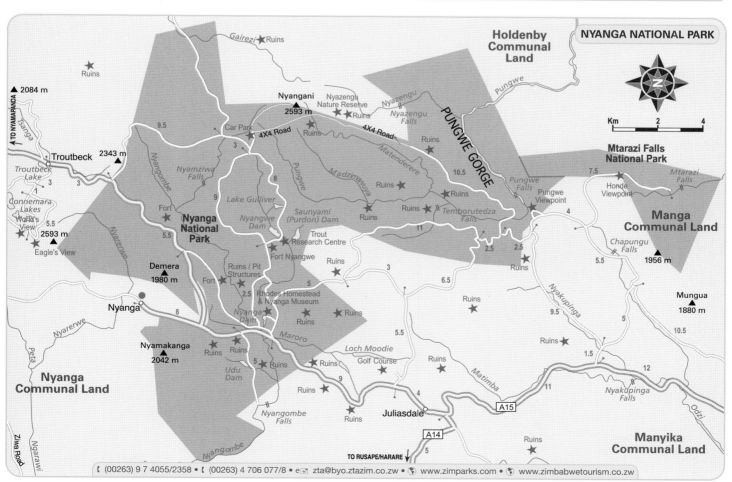

NYANGA NATIONAL PARK

Gairezi   Ruins
Holdenby Communal Land
Ruins
2084 m
Pungwe
TO NYAMAPANDA
Tsanga
Nyangani 2593 m
Nyazengu Nature Reserve
Nyazengu
Nyazengu Falls
9.5
Car Park
Ruins
PUNGWE GORGE
Troutbeck 2343 m
4X4 Road
4X4 Road
Mtarazi Falls National Park
Nyangombe
3
Matenderere
Ruins
10.5
7.5
Mtarazi Falls
Troutbeck Lake
Nyamziwa Falls
Pungwe
Madzimazuva
Ruins
Pungwe Falls
Honde Viewpoint
Connemara Lakes
9
Lake Gulliver
Ruins
Pungwe Viewpoint
Manga Communal Land
1
Nyangwe Dam
Saunyami (Purdon) Dam
Ruins
Temborutedza Falls
World's View 2593 m
5.5
Nyanga National Park
Fort
Ruins
11
Chapungu Falls
Eagle's View
Trout Research Centre
2.5
2.5
Nyarerwe
5.5
Fort Nyangwe
Ruins
5.5
1956 m
Demera 1980 m
Ruins / Pit Structures
Ruins
Nyakupinga
Mungua 1880 m
Fort
6.5
9.5
Nyanga
8
2.5
Rhodes Homestead & Nyanga Museum
Ruins
5
10.5
Nyanga Dam
Ruins
Nyamakanga 2042 m
Ruins
Ruins
5.5
Ruins
Maroro
Loch Moodie Golf Course
Ruins
Matimba
12
Nyakupinga Falls
Peta
Nyanga Communal Land
Udu Dam
5
Ruins
9
Ruins
Ruins
Nyangombe Falls
Ruins
Juliasdale
A15
11
Odzi
Ngarawi
Ziwa Road
Nyangombe
A14
TO RUSAPE/HARARE
5
Ruins
Manyika Communal Land

Km   2   4

((00263) 9 7 4055/2358 • ((00263) 4 706 077/8 • e⊠ zta@byo.ztazim.co.zw • 🌐 www.zimparks.com • 🌐 www.zimbabwetourism.co.zw

Hwange National Park Zimbabwe

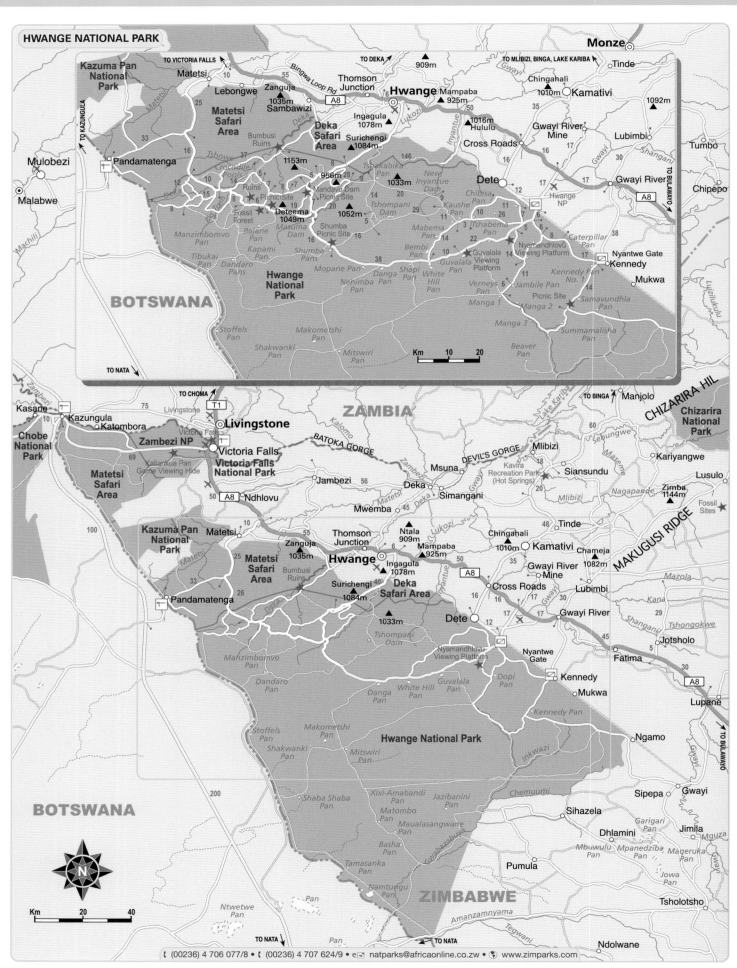

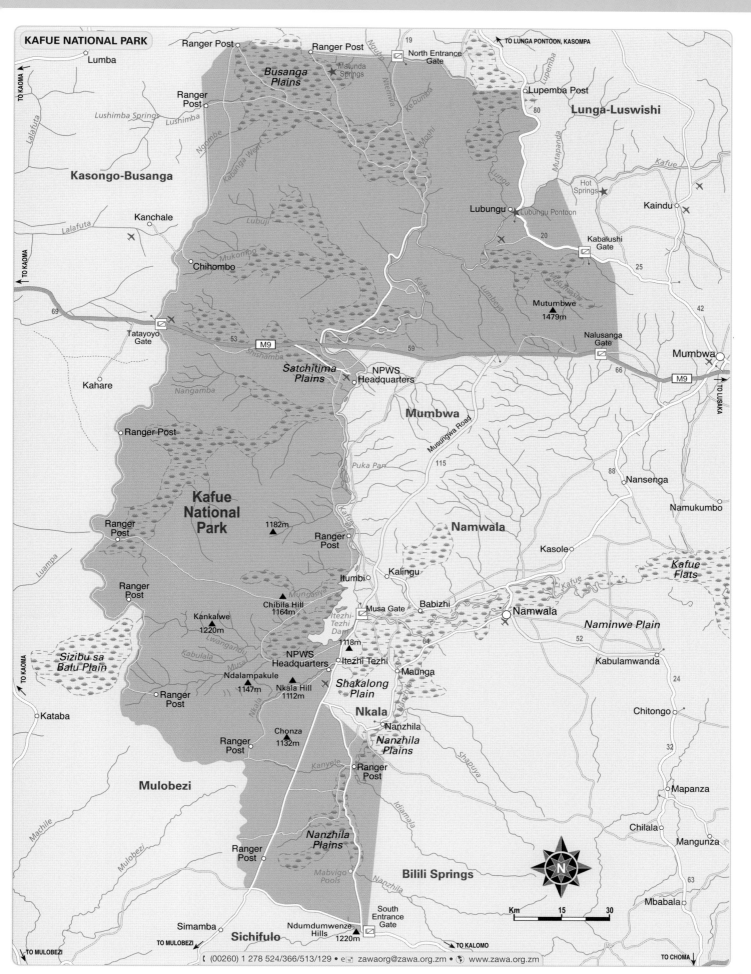

KAFUE NATIONAL PARK

TO KAOMA

Lumba

Ranger Post

Busanga Plains

Matunda Springs

Ranger Post

19

North Entrance Gate

TO LUNGA PONTOON, KASOMPA

Lupemba Post

Lunga-Luswishi

Ranger Post

Lushimba Springs

Lushimba

Ngombe

Ntemwa

Kebumba

Moshi

Mutapanda

Lupemba

80

Kasongo-Busanga

Lalafuta

Lalafuta

Kanchale

Kabanga West

Lubuji

Mukombo

Kafue

Lunga

Kafue

Hot Springs

Kaindu

Lubungu

Lubungu Pontoon

Lumbeva

20

Mukitnasha

Kabalushi Gate

25

Chihombo

Mutumbwe 1479m

42

69

TO KAOMA

Tatayoyo Gate

53

M9

Shishamba

59

Nalusanga Gate

66

M9

Mumbwa

TO LUSAKA

Kahare

Nangamba

Satchitima Plains

NPWS Headquarters

Mumbwa

Musungwa Road

Puka Pan

115

Namwala

Nansenga

Namukumbo

Ranger Post

Kafue National Park

1182m

Ranger Post

Kalingu

Kasole

Kafue Flats

Luampa

Ranger Post

Itumbi

Naminwe Plain

Ranger Post

Mungasiya

Chibila Hill 1164m

Musa Gate

Babizhi

Kafue

Namwala

52

Kankalwe 1220m

Itezhi-Tezhi Dam

1118m

64

Kabulamwanda

24

Sizibu sa Balu Plain

Kabulala

Lwangandu

Musa

NPWS Headquarters

Ndalampakule 1147m

Nkala Hill 1112m

Itezhi Tezhi

Maunga

Shakalong Plain

Chitongo

TO KAOMA

Ranger Post

Nkala

Nkala

Nanzhila

32

Katata

Chonza 1132m

Nanzhila Plains

Shapuya

Mapanza

Ranger Post

Kanyele

Ranger Post

Idiamaja

Mulobezi

Chilala

Mangunza

Machile

Nanzhila Plains

Mabvigo Pools

Nanzhila

Bilili Springs

N

63

Mulobezi

Mbabala

Ranger Post

Km   15   30

TO MULOBEZI

Simamba

TO MULOBEZI

Sichifulo

Ndumdumwenze Hills 1220m

South Entrance Gate

TO KALOMO

TO CHOMA

📞 (00260) 1 278 524/366/513/129 • e ✉ zawaorg@zawa.org.zm • 🌐 www.zawa.org.zm

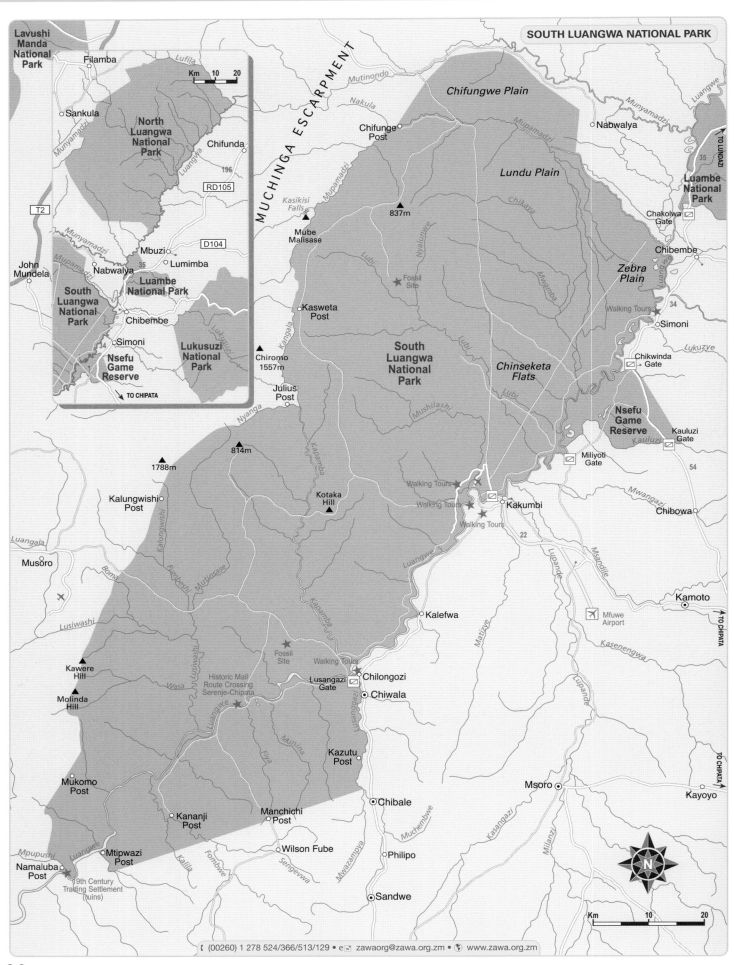

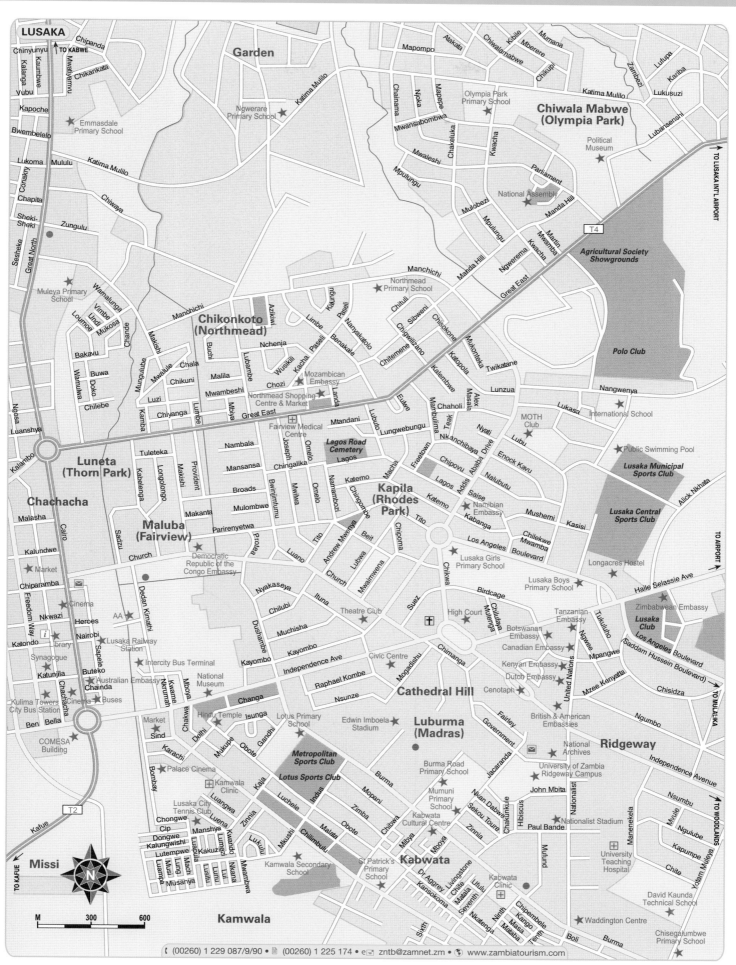

Lusaka   Zambia

Harare   Zimbabwe

HARARE

((00263) 4 758 730/12/24/28/34 • e info@ztazim.co.zw • www.zimbabwetourism.co.zw

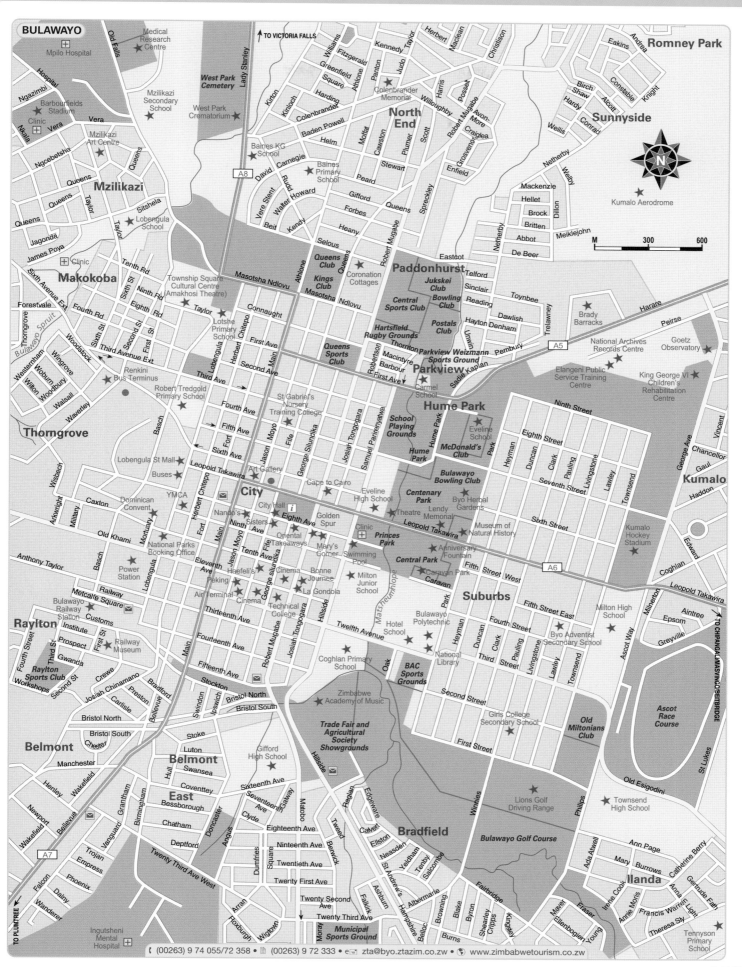

Bulawayo, Zimbabwe

✆ (00263) 9 74 055/72 358 • 🖹 (00263) 9 72 333 • e📧 zta@byo.ztazim.co.zw • 🌐 www.zimbabwetourism.co.zw

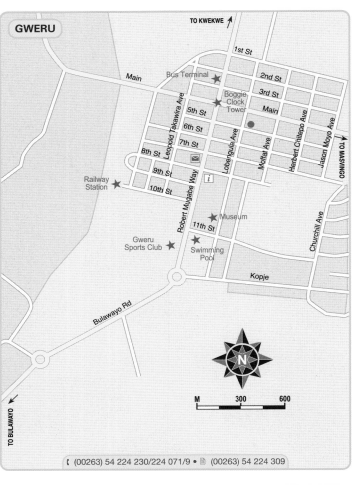

GWERU

TO KWEKWE

1st St
Main
Bus Terminal
2nd St
3rd St
Boggie Clock Tower
Main
5th St
Leopold Takawira Ave
6th St
Lobengula Ave
Moffat Ave
Herbert Chitepo Ave
Jason Moyo Ave
7th St
8th St
9th St
TO MASVINGO
Railway Station
10th St
Robert Mugabe Way
Museum
Churchill Ave
11th St
Gweru Sports Club
Swimming Pool
Kopje
Bulawayo Rd
TO BULAWAYO
M 300 600

☎ (00263) 54 224 230/224 071/9 • 🖹 (00263) 54 224 309

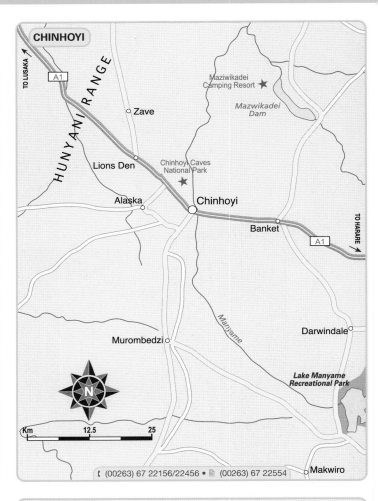

CHINHOYI

TO LUSAKA
A1
HUNYANI RANGE
Maziwikadei Camping Resort
Mazwikadei Dam
Zave
Lions Den
Chinhoyi Caves National Park
Alaska
Chinhoyi
Banket
A1
TO HARARE
Manyame
Darwindale
Murombedzi
Lake Manyame Recreational Park
Km 12.5 25
Makwiro

☎ (00263) 67 22156/22456 • 🖹 (00263) 67 22554

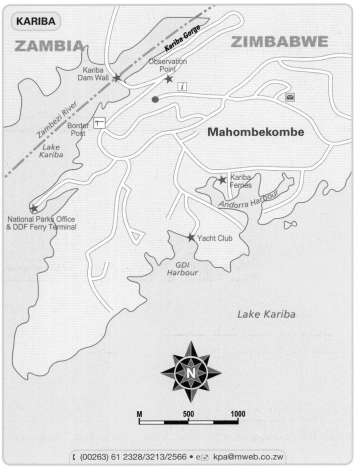

KARIBA

ZAMBIA
Kariba Gorge
ZIMBABWE
Kariba Dam Wall
Observation Point
Zambezi River
Border Post
Mahombekombe
Lake Kariba
Kariba Ferries
Andorra Harbour
National Parks Office & DDF Ferry Terminal
Yacht Club
GDI Harbour
Lake Kariba
M 500 1000

☎ (00263) 61 2328/3213/2566 • e✉ kpa@mweb.co.zw

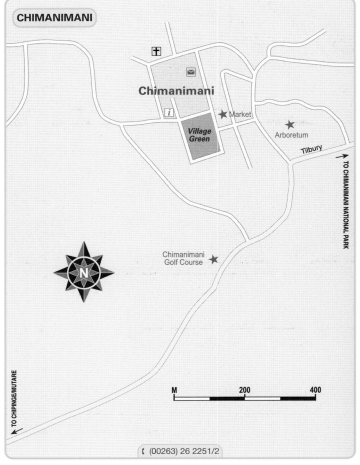

CHIMANIMANI

Chimanimani
Market
Village Green
Arboretum
Tilbury
TO CHIMANIMANI NATIONAL PARK
Chimanimani Golf Course
TO CHIPINGE/MUTARE
M 200 400

☎ (00263) 26 2251/2

124

Mutare Zimbabwe
Masvingo Zimbabwe
Kwekwe Zimbabwe

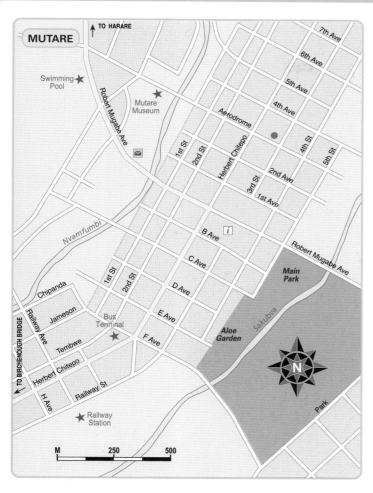

MUTARE

TO HARARE

Swimming Pool
Mutare Museum
7th Ave
6th Ave
5th Ave
4th Ave
Aerodrome
Robert Mugabe Ave
1st St
2nd St
Herbert Chitepo
3rd St
4th St
5th St
2nd Ave
1st Ave
B Ave
C Ave
D Ave
E Ave
F Ave
Nyamfumbi
1st St
2nd St
Chipanda
Railway Ave
Jameson
Bus Terminal
Tembwe
Herbert Chitepo
H Ave
Railway St
Railway Station
TO BIRCHENOUGH BRIDGE
Robert Mugabe Ave
Main Park
Aloe Garden
Sakubya
Park
N

M 250 500

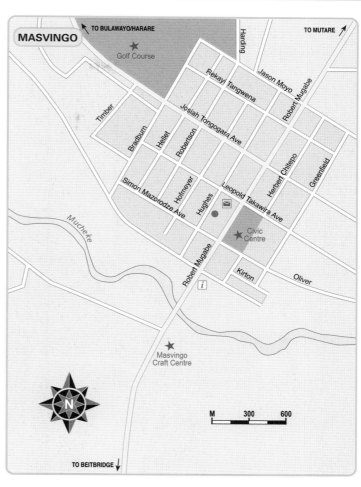

MASVINGO

TO BULAWAYO/HARARE
TO MUTARE
Golf Course
Harding
Rekayi Tangwena
Jason Moyo
Robert Mugabe
Timber
Bradburn
Hellet
Robertson
Josiah Tongogara Ave
Herbert Chitepo
Greenfield
Simon Mazorodze Ave
Hofmeyer
Hughes
Leopold Takawira Ave
Mucheke
Robert Mugabe
Civic Centre
Kirton
Oliver
Masvingo Craft Centre
N

M 300 600

TO BEITBRIDGE

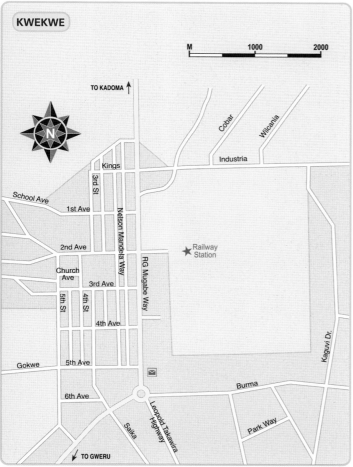

KWEKWE

M 1000 2000

TO KADOMA
N
Cobar
Wilcania
Industria
Kings
3rd St
School Ave
1st Ave
Nelson Mandela Way
2nd Ave
Church Ave
3rd Ave
5th St
4th St
4th Ave
RG Mugabe Way
Railway Station
Gokwe
5th Ave
Kaguvi Dr.
6th Ave
Burma
Leopold Takawira Highway
Salka
Park Way
TO GWERU

MUTARE: ☎ (00263) 20 64412/80 • 🗎 (00263) 20 61002

MASVINGO: ☎ (00263) 39 262 913 • e✉ mgpa@webmail.co.za

KWEKWE: ☎ (00263) 55 22301 • 🗎 (00263) 55 24301

125

Victoria Falls
Zimbabwe, Zambia

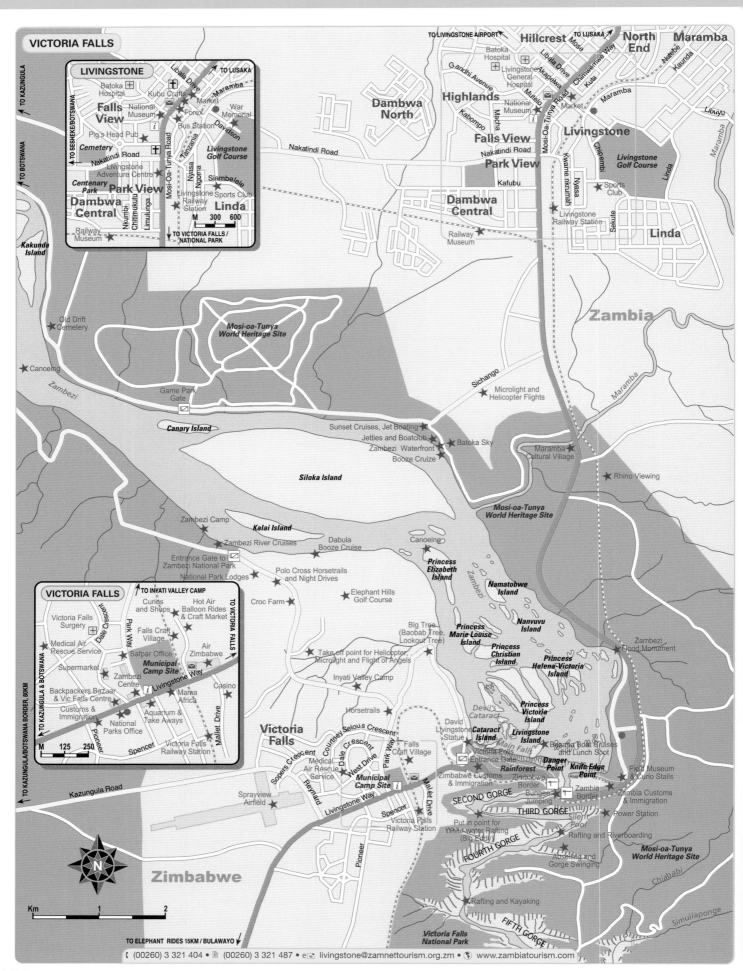

Adventures

Walking South Luangwa NP

Requirements:
Most visitors require visas, unless with an organized tour.

Climate:
September to November can be unbearably hot in the valley, but June to November are dry and thus provide the best game-viewing opportunities.

Risk factor:
Distances are vast and may be challenging in parts, with the usual risks posed by wilderness safaris, so it is best to take a pre-arranged tour with guides.

Health:
Malaria is rife throughout the country year-round, as are waterborne diseases.

Pack:
Antimalarial medication, water purification tablets, protective clothing and good hiking shoes. Tour operators should provide a list of essentials.

Facilities:
Facilities are generally very good – even impressive – in the lodges, but some hiking stopovers can be quite basic. Lodge service and amenities are beyond reproach.

Contact:
Lilongwe-based (Malawi) Ulendo Safaris.
Tel: 00265-1-754926
rob@ulendo.malawi.net

Sailing Lake Kariba

Requirements:
Few visitors will require a visa, but a valid passport is essential.

Climate:
Temperatures are the highest in the country and can be especially high on the water. Nights can, however, be cold, especially mid-year.

Risk factor:
Because the waters and shores of Kariba are well serviced by the local travel industry, risks are few – beware of the usual pickpockets and adhere to the standard safety precautions when on the water.

Health:
Malaria, bilharzia and, of course, AIDS are prevalent throughout much of the country, but drinking water is relatively safe.

Pack:
Malarial prophylactics, sunscreen and personal supplies if unsupervised.

Facilities:
Amenities are generally very good to excellent (especially at Kariba's upmarket lodges), but even the most rustic of camp sites and overnight accommodation will offer the basic facilities.

Contact:
Chete Island Camp,
Harare Lake Kariba
Tel: 09263-4-499783
Fax: 09263-4-499060
westisl@id.co.zw

Driving the Zambezi Valley

Requirements:
Zambia – Most visitors require visas, unless they are part of an organized tour; Zimbabwe – Few visitors require a visa; a valid passport is essential.

Climate:
The valley can be hot and humid, and is particularly wet in December.

Risk factor:
Summer rains in and around December can make driving hazardous.

Health:
Malaria is rife throughout the region year-round, as are waterborne diseases, such as bilharzia. AIDS is prevalent throughout.

Pack:
Lightweight clothing for driving, and warm clothes for cold nights. Drivers not part of an organized tour are well advised to take extra precautions and plan with great care, especially for the maintenance and repair of vehicles.

Facilities:
Beyond established and well-patronized tourist destinations such as Mana Pools in Zimbabwe, facilities may not be up to standard and refuelling and restocking may be problematic.

Contact:
Backpackers Africa, P.O. Box 44, Victoria Falls.
Tel: 00263-13-42208 / 9 / 42248
backpack@africaonline.co.zw
lvhwalkingsafaris@esmartbiz.com

On the Waters of the Zambezi

Requirements:
Zambia – Most visitors require visas, unless they are part of an organized tour; Zimbabwe – Few visitors require a visa, but a passport is essential.

Climate:
The Zambezi Valley is both hot and humid, and the summer rains mean that water levels rise, while certain areas can experience torrential flows.

Risk factor:
Risks are generally few, but some swimming ability is advised.

Health:
Malaria is rife throughout the region year-round, as are waterborne diseases, such as bilharzia. AIDS is prevalent throughout the region.

Pack:
Day trips require little planning as essentials are usually covered by operators. Overnight excursions and trips of a few days will require warm, waterproof clothing. Check with your tour operator.

Facilities:
Trips of two or three days or more are usually well established. Operators take good care of their guests, although some overnight stops may be a little more basic than some may expect, so be prepared to rough it.

Contact:
Shearwater Adventures.
Tel: 00263-13-44471 / 2 / 3 or 00263-13-43392
reservations@shearwater.co.zw

Victoria Falls Adventure

Requirements:
Zambia – Most visitors require visas, unless they are part of an organized tour; Zimbabwe – Few visitors require a visa, but a passport is essential.

Climate:
Hot and humid all year, but the falls are best February–August.

Risk factor:
Risks are plentiful, like dodging hippos and battling some of Africa's most fearsome rapids. Some excursions require little more than determination; others can be deadly and require considerable skill on the water.

Health:
Malaria is rife; AIDS remains a concern; waterborne diseases (bilharzia) are a risk; bumps, grazes and bruises are par for the course on the river.

Pack:
Antimalarial medication and water purification tablets and protective, waterproof clothing. Most reliable tour operators provide the necessities.

Facilities:
River operators tend to plan well to make the trip comfortable, and luxuries are few, but basics are covered.

Contact:
Safari Par Excellence,
P.O. Box 5920, Harare.
Tel: (Harare) 00263-4-443409 / 10
Tel: (Victoria Falls) 00263-13-44424 / 42190
speres@mweb.co.zw, www.safpar.com,
ziminfo@safpar.com

Exploring Chimanimani NP

Requirements:
Few visitors need a visa, but a passport is essential.

Climate:
Best time to hike is May–September, when it is sunny but not too hot. Can be windy and cold at night.

Risk factor:
It is generally safe to walk Chimanimani, but never hike alone or even in pairs and plan well. Keep to known routes as you may wander into Mozambique. Watch for sudden changes in weather. Give your itinerary to park authorities in case you don't return.

Health:
Malaria, bilharzia and AIDS are prevalent. Although drinking water is relatively safe even on the mountain, take purification tablets as a precaution.

Pack:
Take your own supplies such as food and equipment (collecting of firewood is prohibited, so you will need a gas cooker), plus warm clothes, sun protection and a sleeping bag.

Facilities:
Do not expect luxury accommodation, but amenities are generally good, and overnight stays comfortable.

Contact:
National Parks Central Booking Office,
P.O. Box CY 140, Causeway, Harare.
Tel: 00263-4-706077 / 707624 / 9
natparks@africaonline.co.zw

127

The Mozambique Coast

Mozambique and Malawi are desperately poor nations, with up to 80 per cent of their rural people engaged in farming, and the majority of citizens living on the shores of Lake Malawi depending on its waters for subsistence and livelihood. This vital body of water is called Lago Niassa in Mozambique and Lake Nyasa in Tanzania. Mozambique and Malawi are both covered by large stretches of endless savanna and have proven remarkable in their resilience. Malawi, the landlocked 'Warm Heart of Africa', and Mozambique — some of the continent's finest coastline makes it one of Africa's premier beach destinations — are a traveller's dream: wild animals crossing an unspoiled wilderness easily accessible to the visitor, and all very, very cheap. The diverse cultural heritage of both countries is an eclectic mix of fascinating customs and traditions still practised with enthusiasm by the vast majority of the population, making for a memorable exploration of the eastern reaches of southern Africa.

MOZAMBIQUE

MAPUTO

No more than a small, haphazard collection of temporary shelters in the 16th century, Maputo (known in fairly recent times as Lourenço Marques) is a lively port city criss-crossed with palm-fringed avenues lined with jacaranda and flame trees. Following a period of civil strife and political uncertainty that ended only in 1992, many of Maputo's grand palaces and synagogues, markets and museums, and even humble Creole-style homes - particularly in the larger urban centres - bear the physical scars of civil war to this day. However, Maputo is emerging from the ashes to slowly regain some of the glory of its heyday. Home to a thriving population of bohemian artists and a steady trickle of travellers, Maputo's vigorous nightlife centres around the late-night bars of Rua do Bagamoio, the revelry spilling over into the evening markets and brightly lit seafront. The city - rather dilapidated in parts - is dotted with historic Portuguese forts and highlighted by its must-see Museum of the Revolution.

INHACA ISLAND

The idyll that is Inhaca is a series of beautiful beaches lined with brightly coloured offshore reefs and shores dotted with stands of mango trees. About 24km from the mainland and easily accessible via the ferries departing from the capital, Inhaca Island is the largest in the Gulf of Maputo and its pretty village presents a fascinating look at island life. Dominated by the upgraded Inhaca Hotel, the narrow streets have a good selection of restaurants and cafés interspersed with the odd - laid-back - attraction. Situated in extraordinarily rich waters, the island's coastal attractions have proven its most popular drawcards. Apart from the marine research centre, which offers a different perspective to the conventional island idyll, Inhaca's shores are peppered with striking beaches and a fascinating reef life that offers some of the finest diving, snorkelling and underwater explorations on Africa's east coast.

ZAMBEZI DELTA

The 3,000km Zambezi River winds for 820km of its route across Mozambique before reaching the ocean. Its broad valley slices the country in two, beginning at Feira and ending, after having accumulated run-off waters from five other countries, in the wetlands of the delta. By the time the waters reach Mozambique they have been tamed by Zimbabwe's Lake Kariba and are again dammed by the 160m walls of the 270km-long Cahora Bassa, Mozambique's most ambitious dam. Having coursed through the hinterland, waters guarded by crocodiles and hippos, the Zambezi begins to disperse about 600km downstream on the buffalo plains of Marromeu, where it spreads into a network of streams, channels and tributaries covering 4,000km^2. Today, the delta spans only 100km, but is nevertheless breathtaking – especially from the air – and is home to big game such as elephant, buffalo, rhino and roan antelope.

IBO

Heavily fortified during its Portuguese occupation, Ibo has a history as the region's most important supplier of slaves to the sugar plantations of Île de France and, along with Ilha de Mozambique, was hailed as the colonists' most vital trading grounds off the African coast. Although the island has seen better days, its wide streets are lined with quaint Mediterranean-style buildings. Many of these stately structures were erected in the 1800s and, although the whitewashed walls of the once grand but long abandoned Portuguese villas and palaces are fading, it is the very isolation that is the island's charm. The centuries-old churches and ancient bulwarks that fringe the streets and line the waterfront are but half the attraction - the other is the surrounding ocean, alive with turtles and dolphins that can easily be spotted from the dhows that ferry visitors around Ibo's romantic coastline.

BARRA PENINSULA

Barra is the site of Inhambane (the capital of the province) and is one of Mozambique's most popular holiday meccas - the azure waters, coves, bays and sands provide a spectacular backdrop to the beach life. The landscape of Barra and the adjoining Cape Inhambane is dotted with coconut plantations and mangrove swamps, and the wave-washed shores are a vivid invitation to the marine wonderland. The waters are warm but unpredictable, and powerful rip currents and volatile waves make it an exhilarating but precarious water-sport base.

MALAWI

LILONGWE

Although it is Malawi's vast natural heritage that is its enduring drawcard, the appeal of its large centres – in particular its capital at Lilongwe – should not be underestimated. Blantyre stretches for about 20km into Limbe, and is the social and commercial heart of Malawi. Lilongwe, on the other hand, is gentle, laid-back and utterly predictable in character. Although only of limited interest to the casual visitor, the sprawling city - home to about a half million Malawians - is a refreshing mix of old and new, with little clutter, noise and commotion. The older sectors of Lilongwe have retained much of their original charm, while the modern parts are a sedate collection of malls, tourist traps and official buildings merging well with the islands of green that form the residential districts. A notable example is Capital City, initiated by President Banda with the financial assistance of the South African government during the height of the latter's apartheid regime. Not only is the climate of the city moderately warm, but Lilongwe is very accessible, very cheap and, in the heart of southern Africa, a convenient base from which to explore the subcontinent.

LAKE MALAWI

Known as Lake Nyasa or Lago Niassa, depending on which bank you are standing, the 23,000km^2. Lake Malawi is the third-largest inland body of water on the continent and covers nearly half the country's territory. The 585km of its length along the southern Rift Valley comprises a diversity of habitats for an array of wildlife. As a result, the waters of the lake - encircled by mountain slopes - have formed the mainstay of the nation's economy and the nucleus of Malawi's tourism industry. Blessed with tranquil beaches, the most important human settlement along the shore is the fishing community at Chember, who depend on Lake Malawi for their livelihood. Numerous dugout vessels ply the lake surface, netting fish that form the staple diet of Malawi. The lake has one of the world's richest populations of freshwater fish and many of the species found here are endemic. Casual angling is forbidden in areas, including Cape Maclear National Park and the surrounding islands, although water-based leisure activities are encouraged.

SHIRE RIVER

The 596km Shire, flowing from Lake Malawi through Malawi and Mozambique to the Zambezi, is the country's longest river. It winds through Malawi's Liwonde National Park, crossing some of the country's most abundant wildlife territories, and through wild open spaces. The river is the hunting and grazing waters of crocodile and hippo, while the surrounding wilderness has a small but healthy population of elephant and even two black rhinos, introduced into the area in recent years. The shallows, wooded shores and expansive sky are home to waders, waterfowl and migrant birds during the summer months. Although much of the Shire offers boat rides for visitors, the southern valley remains largely undiscovered, top attractions being the wild expanses of Majete Wildlife Reserve and Lengwe National Park.

LIKOMA ISLAND

Although Likoma lies just off Mozambique, the island remains the property of Malawi, its coastline - dotted with lone baobabs alongside crystal waters - taking on the flavour of the motherland. The sandy 17km^2 island, with its mango trees and rugged mountain peaks, is flat and unprepossessing, but its languid beaches are lapped by clear waters. Lying in splendid isolation off the mountain-backed beach of Mozambique's mainland, Likoma can be difficult to reach and the only proper - albeit rather unreliable - way to reach the island is via the MV Ilala II, the dilapidated but enchanting old lake steamer that once a week ferries passengers between Likoma and Mozambique. The island itself is tranquil and laid back and, apart from the weekly performance of the malipenga dancers pandering almost exclusively to a tourist audience, there are few notable landmarks. The most significant is the cavernous St Peter's Cathedral, built along the lines of Winchester Cathedral by Anglican missionaries in the early 1900s. St Peter's remains the focal point of the island today, with many of the locals working virtually all year every year on maintaining the colossal remnant of Likoma's past.

Although both Malawi and Mozambique are covered largely by extensive savanna plains, these are fringed by forested highlands and, in the case of Mozambique, a lush coast of lagoons and coral reefs that continue to attract travellers and adventurers to some of southern Africa's wildest and most undeveloped landscape.

Elephants, Lilongwe, Malawi

Pomene Beach, Inhaca Island, Mozambique

Cahora Bassa dam, Mozambique

MALAWI

Lake Malawi

MOZAMBIQUE

Ruvuma

Ibo

Likoma Island

LILONGWE

Lake Malombe

Shire

Lake Chilwa

Cahora Bassa Dam

Blantyre

Nacala

Nampula

Ilha de Mozambique

INDIAN OCEAN

Zambezi

Zambeze Delta

Beira

N

Km   100   200

Some water features have
been exaggerated for detail

Bazaruto Island

BARRA PENINSULA

Inhambane

LEBOMBO MTS

MAPUTO

Inhaca Island

129

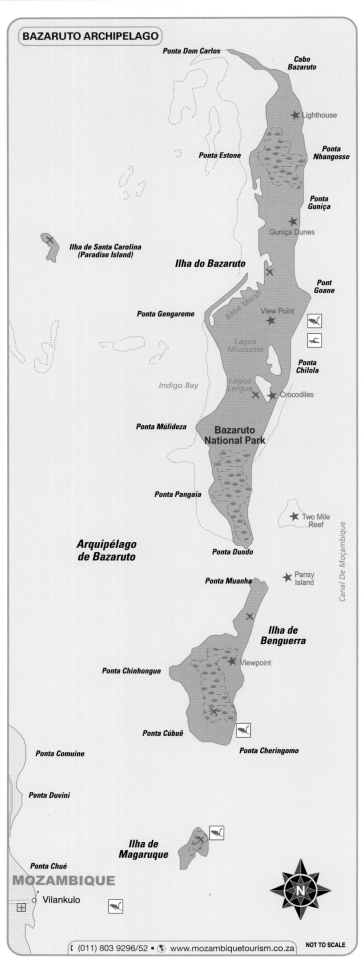

BAZARUTO ARCHIPELAGO

Ponta Dom Carlos
Cabo Bazaruto
Lighthouse
Ponta Estone
Ponta Nhangosse
Ponta Guniça
Guniça Dunes
Ilha de Santa Carolina (Paradise Island)
Ilha do Bazaruto
Pont Goane
Babé Marsh
View Point
Ponta Gengareme
Lagoa Nhassasse
Ponta Chilola
Indigo Bay
Lagoa Lergue
Crocodiles
Ponta Múlideza
Bazaruto National Park
Ponta Pangaia
Two Mile Reef
Arquipélago de Bazaruto
Ponta Dundo
Canal De Moçambique
Pansy Island
Ponta Muanha
Ilha de Benguerra
Viewpoint
Ponta Chinhongue
Ponta Cúbuê
Ponta Cheringomo
Ponta Comuine
Ponta Duvini
Ilha de Magaruque
Ponta Chué
MOZAMBIQUE
Vilankulo

NOT TO SCALE

(011) 803 9296/52 • www.mozambiquetourism.co.za

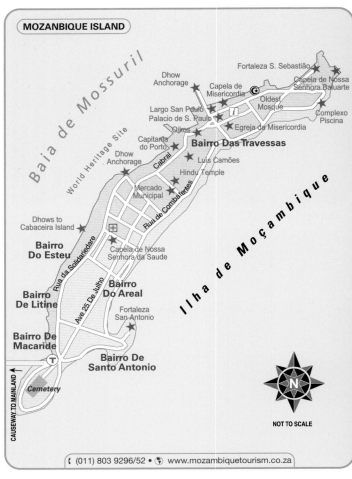

MOZANBIQUE ISLAND

Baia de Mossuril
Fortaleza S. Sebastião
Dhow Anchorage
Capela de Misericordia
Capela de Nóssa Senhora Baluarte
Largo San Paulo
Palacio de S. Paulo
Oldest Mosque
Complexo Piscina
Oijkos
Egreja da Misericordia
Capitania do Porto
Bairro Das Travessas
World Heritage Site
Cabral
Dhow Anchorage
Luis Camões
Hindu Temple
Mercado Municipal
Rua de Combatentes
Ilha de Moçambique
Dhows to Cabaceira Island
Bairro Do Esteu
Capela de Nóssa Senhora da Saude
Rua da Solidariedade
Bairro Do Areal
Bairro De Litine
Ave 25 De Julho
Fortaleza San Antonio
Bairro De Macaride
Bairro De Santo Antonio
CAUSEWAY TO MAINLAND
Cemetery

N
NOT TO SCALE

(011) 803 9296/52 • www.mozambiquetourism.co.za

MAPUTO BAY & INHACA ISLAND

TO MARRACUENE
Ilha Xefina Pequena
Costa do Sol
Ponta da Macaneta
Ilha Xefina do Meio
Ponta Languene
Costa do Sol
Ponta Manhapanga
Ponta Leitelete
Ilha Xefina Grande
Ponta Garapão

N
NOT TO SCALE

Ponta dos Elefantes
Ponta Samendene
Ponta Mazandue
Ilha dos Portugueses
Ponta Cigalo
Cabo Inhaca
Ponta Black Bluff
Inhaca
Baia de Maputo
Portinho da Inhaca
Barreira Vermelha
Reserva de Inhaca
Ilha da Inhaca
Marine Biological Station and Museum
Saco da Inhaca
Ponta Raza
Baia Capessuane
Ponta Punduine
Ponta Xohomane
Ponta Torres
Santa Maria
Cabo de Santa Maria
Ponta Abril
Peninsula de Santa Maria
Ponta da Três Marais
Lighthouse
Lagoa Buti
Lagoa Mandi
Ponta Goméni
Ponta Camandjuba
Lagoa Mahumse
Lagoa Mucumbe
Lagoa Manglindje
Maputo Elephant Reserve
Machangulo
Ponta Mucombo
Rio Maputo
Lagoa Chitenge
Lagoa Chavi
Baie de Machangula

(00258) 21 307 320/3 • (00258) 21 307 324 • www.futur.org.mz

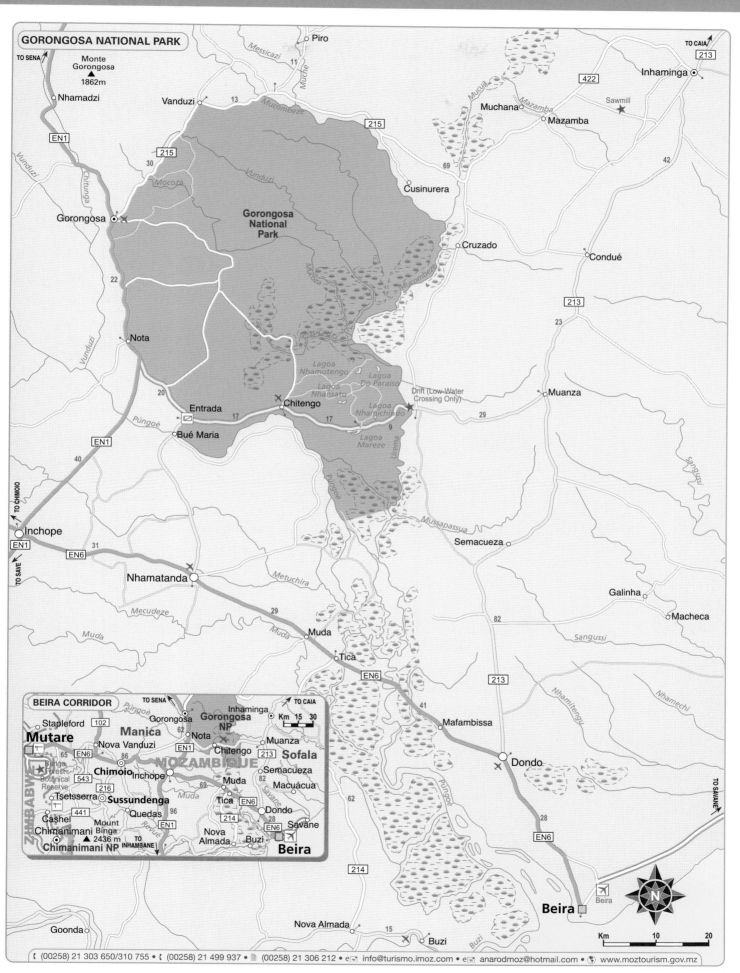

GORONGOSA NATIONAL PARK

TO SENA

Monte Gorongosa ▲ 1862m

Nhamadzi

EN1

Vunduzi

Chitunga

Mocoza

Gorongosa

Nota

22

20

Entrada

17

Bué Maria

EN1

40

TO CHIMOIO

Inchope

EN1

TO SAVE

EN6

31

Mecudeze

Muda

Nhamatanda

29

Muda

Piro

Messicazi

11

Muche

Mucombeze

13

Vanduzi

215

215

30

Vunduzi

Gorongosa National Park

Mussi

Lagoa Nhamutengo

Lagoa Nhansato

Chitengo

17

9

Lagoa Mareze

Pungoe

Metuchira

Muda

Muda

Lagoa Do Paraiso

Lagoa Nhamichindo

Urema

Pungoe

Mucua

Muchana

Mazamba

422

Sawmill

215

69

Cusinurera

Cruzado

Mucombeze

Drift (Low-Water Crossing Only)

29

Mussapassua

Semacueza

Sangussi

Muda

Tica

EN6

EN6

213

41

Mafambissa

Pungoe

Nhamitengu

213

82

Sangussi

Nhamechi

TO CAIA

213

Inhaminga

42

Condué

23

213

Muanza

Galinha

Macheca

Dondo

28

EN6

TO SAVANE

BEIRA CORRIDOR

TO SENA

TO CAIA

Km 15 30

Stapleford 102

Gorongosa

Gorongosa NP

Mutare

Manica

62

Nova Vanduzi

Nota

Inhaminga

EN6

65

86

EN1

Chitengo

213

Muanza

Binga Forest Botanical Reserve

Chimoio

Inchope

Sofala

Semacueza

543

216

Muda

69

82

Macuácua

ZIMBABWE

Tsetsserra

Sussundenga

Tica

EN6

MOZAMBIQUE

441

Quedas

96

214

Dondo

Cashel

Mount Binga

EN1

28

Savane

Chimanimani ▲ 2436 m

Nova Almada

Buzi

EN6

Beira

Chimanimani NP

TO INHAMBANE

Revue

214

Beira

Goonda

Nova Almada

15

Buzi

Buzi

Km 10 20

N

((00258) 21 303 650/310 755 • ((00258) 21 499 937 • (00258) 21 306 212 • info@turismo.imoz.com • anarodmoz@hotmail.com • www.moztourism.gov.mz

131

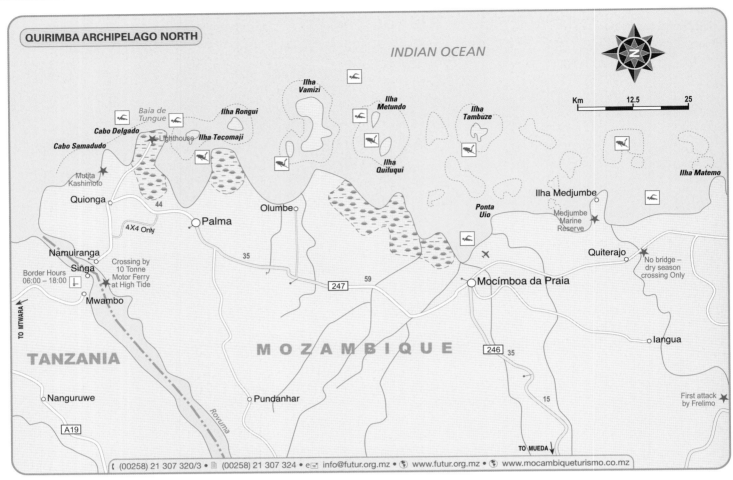

QUIRIMBA ARCHIPELAGO NORTH

INDIAN OCEAN

Km   12.5   25

Baía de Tungue

Ilha Vamizi

Ilha Rongui

Ilha Metundo

Ilha Tambuze

Cabo Delgado

Ilha Tecomaji

Cabo Samadudo

Lighthouse

Ilha Quifuqui

Ilha Matemo

Mutita Kashimoto

Ilha Medjumbe

Medjumbe Marine Reserve

Quionga

Olumbe

Ponta Uio

Quiterajo

No bridge – dry season crossing Only

Palma

4X4 Only

Namuiranga

35

Mocímboa da Praia

Singa

Border Hours 06:00 – 18:00

Crossing by 10 Tonne Motor Ferry at High Tide

247

59

TO MTWARA

Mwambo

MOZAMBIQUE

246   35

Iangua

TANZANIA

Rovuma

Nanguruwe

Pundanhar

15

First attack by Frelimo

A19

TO MUEDA

(00258) 21 307 320/3 • (00258) 21 307 324 • e info@futur.org.mz • www.futur.org.mz • www.mocambiqueturismo.co.mz

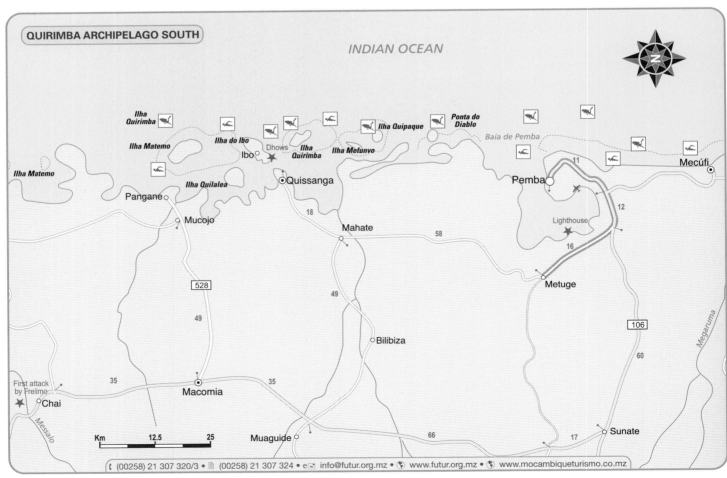

QUIRIMBA ARCHIPELAGO SOUTH

INDIAN OCEAN

Ilha Quirimba

Ilha do Ibo

Ilha Quipaque

Ponta do Diablo

Ilha Matemo

Dhows

Baía de Pemba

Ibo

Ilha Quirimba

Ilha Mefunvo

Mecúfi

Ilha Matemo

Ilha Quilalea

Quissanga

Pemba

11

Pangane

18

12

Mucojo

Mahate

58

Lighthouse

16

528

Metuge

49

49

106

Bilibiza

60

First attack by Frelimo

35

35

106

Chai

Macomia

60

Messalo

Megaruma

Km   12.5   25

Muaguide

66

Sunate

17

(00258) 21 307 320/3 • (00258) 21 307 324 • e info@futur.org.mz • www.futur.org.mz • www.mocambiqueturismo.co.mz

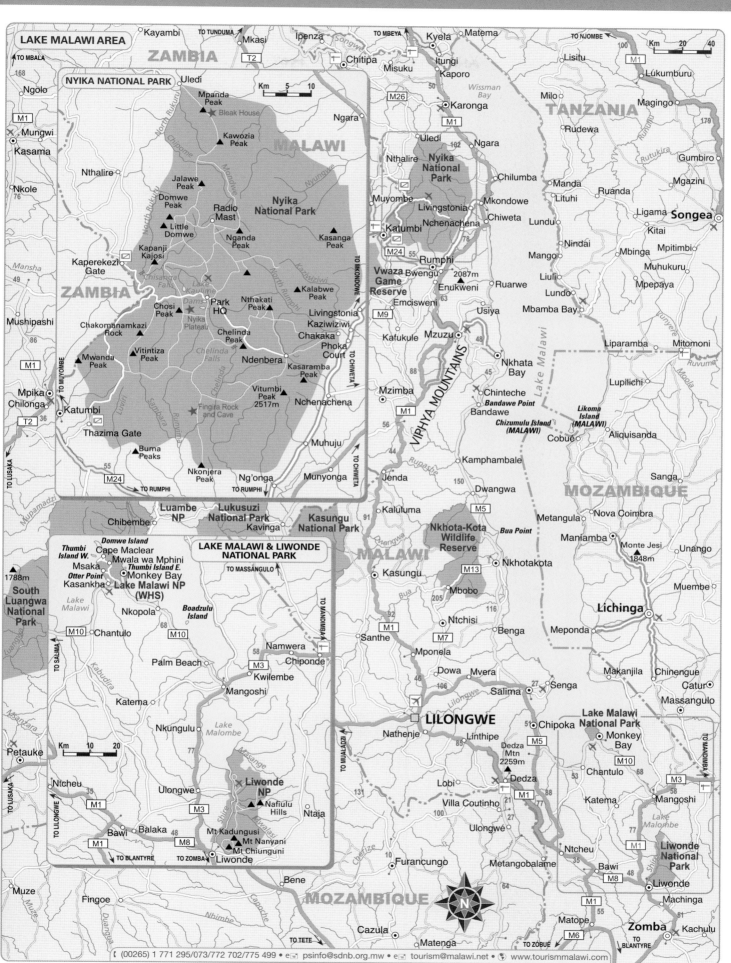

LAKE MALAWI AREA

ZAMBIA

TANZANIA

MALAWI

NYIKA NATIONAL PARK

Kayambi
TO TUNDUMA
Mkasi
Ipenza
Songwe
TO MBEYA
Kyela
Matema
TO NJOMBE
Lisitu
Km   20   40
M1
Chitipa
Misuku
Kaporo
Itungi
Lukumburu
TO MBALA
168
Ngolo
Uledi
Mpanda Peak
Bleak House
Ngara
Wissman Bay
M26
Karonga
Milo
Magingo
Mungwi
Kasama
Kawozia Peak
MALAWI
M1
Uledi
Rudewa
179
Nthalire
Nthalire
Ngara
Manda
Ligama
Songea
Jalawe Peak
Nyika National Park
Muyombe
Nyika National Park
Chilumba
Lituhi
Kitai
Domwe Peak
Radio Mast
Katumbi
Livingstonia
Mkondowe
Chiweta
Lundu
Mbinga
Mpitimbi
Little Domwe
Nganda Peak
Kasanga Peak
M24
Nchenachena
Chiweta
Nindai
Mango
Muhukuru
Kapanji Kajosi
Rumphi
78
Usiya
Liuli
Mpepaya
Kaperekezi Gate
Kalabwe Peak
Bwengu
2087m
Vwaza Game Reserve
Enukweni
Ruarwe
Lundo
ZAMBIA
Chisanga Falls
Lake Kaulime
Dams
Park HQ
Nthakati Peak
Emcisweni
63
Kafukule
Usiya
Mbamba Bay
Mansha
49
Chosi Peak
Nyika Plateau
Livingstonia
M9
Mzuzu
48
Chakomanamkazi Rock
Chelinda Peak
Kaziwiziwi
Chakaka
Mzimba
Nkhata Bay
Liparamba
Mitomoni
86
Vitintiza Peak
Chelinda Falls
Ndenbera
Phoka Court
M1
Ruvuma
Mushipashi
Mwanda Peak
Kasaramba Peak
56
Chinteche
Lupilichi
M1
Vitumbi Peak 2517m
Nchenachena
Bandawe Point
Likoma Island (MALAWI)
Mpika
Chilonga
Katumbi
Fingira Rock and Cave
44
Bandawe
Chizumulu Island (MALAWI)
Aliquisanda
T2   36
Thazima Gate
Muhuju
Jenda
150
Cobué
Buma Peaks
TO CHIWETA
Kamphambale
Sanga
55
Nkonjera Peak
Ng'onga
TO CHIWETA
Dwangwa
MOZAMBIQUE
M24
TO RUMPHI
TO RUMPHI
Kaluluma
M5
Metangula
Nova Coimbra
TO LUSAKA
Luambe NP
Lukusuzi National Park
Kavinga
Kasungu National Park
91
Nkhota-Kota Wildlife Reserve
Bua Point
Maniamba
Monte Jesi 1848m
Unango
Chibembe
MALAWI
Nkhotakota
Lichinga
Thumbi Island W.
Domwe Island
Cape Maclear
Mwala wa Mphini
LAKE MALAWI & LIWONDE NATIONAL PARK
Kasungu
Mbobo
Muembe
1788m
Msaka
Otter Point
Thumbi Island E.
Monkey Bay
TO MASSANGULO
205
116
South Luangwa National Park
Kasankha
Lake Malawi NP (WHS)
92
Ntchisi
Benga
Meponda
Nkopola
Boadzulu Island
M1
Santhe
M7
M10
Chantulo
68
Mponela
Makanjila
Chinengue
Catur
M10
Namwera
Dowa
Massangulo
Palm Beach
58
Chiponde
106
Mvera
Lake Malawi National Park
M3
Kwilembe
46
Senga
27
Monkey Bay
Katema
Mangoshi
Salima
51
Chipoka
M10
Petauke
Nkungulu
Lake Malombe
LILONGWE
Chantulo
68
Km   10   20
77
Nathenje
Linthipe
Dedza Mtn 2259m
M3
Ncheu
35
Ulongwe
85
Lobi
Dedza
53
Katema
58
TO LUSAKA
M1
M3
Liwonde NP
Villa Coutinho
M1
88
Mangoshi
TO LILONGWE
Nafiulu Hills
Ntaja
131
21
77
Lake Malombe
Bawi
Balaka
48
Mt Kadungusi
100
27
Liwonde National Park
M1
M8
Mt Nanyani
Ulongwé
M5
TO BLANTYRE
TO ZOMBA
Mt Chiunguni
Liwonde
Furancungo
10
Ntcheu
M1
Muze
Fingoe
Bene
MOZAMBIQUE
N
64
Metangobalame
35
Bawi
M8
Liwonde
Cazula
Matenga
TO ZÓBUE
M6
Matope
55
Machinga
51
Zomba
Kachulu
TO BLANTYRE

📞 (00265) 1 771 295/073/772 702/775 499 • e✉ psinfo@sdnb.org.mw • e✉ tourism@malawi.net • 🌐 www.tourismmalawi.com

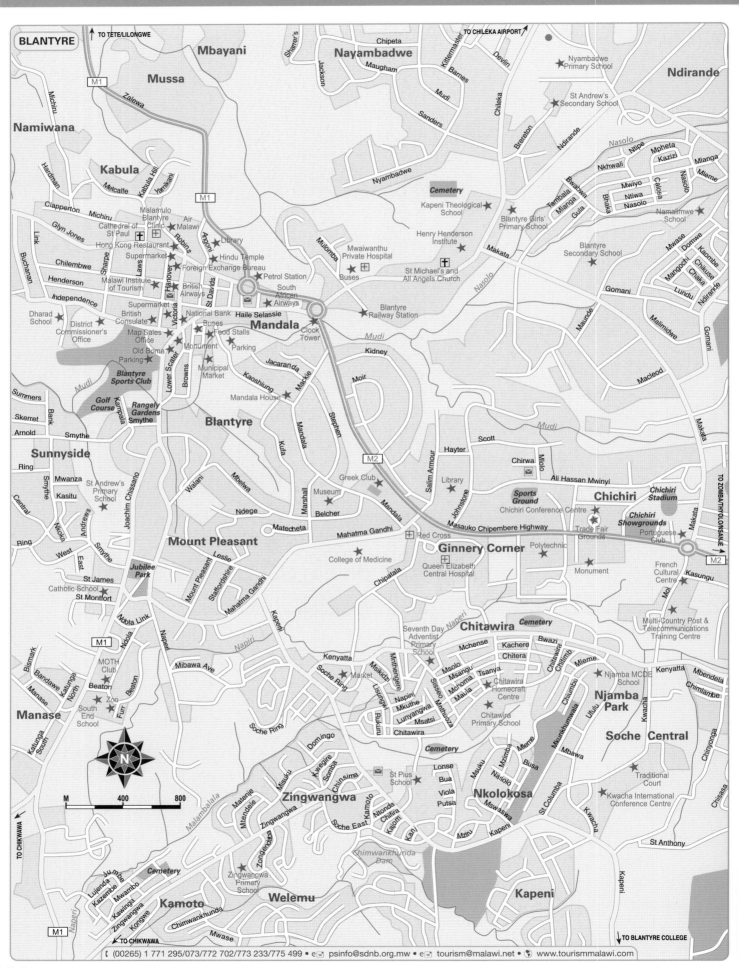

BLANTYRE

TO TETE/LILONGWE

Namiwana

Mbayani

Mussa

Mussa

Kabula

Nayambadwe

Chipeta

TO CHILEKA AIRPORT

Nyambadwe
Primary School

Ndirande

Michiru

Zalewa

Sharer's

Jackson

Maugham

Mudi

Sanders

Krittenmaster

Barnes

Devlin

Chileka

St Andrew's
Secondary School

Brereton

Ndirande

Nasolo

Ntipe

Mpheta

Kazizi

Mlanga

Hardiman

Metcalfe

Kabula Hill

Yamikani

Michiru

Nyambadwe

Cemetery

Kapeni Theological
School

Blantyre Girls'
Primary School

Makata

Nkhwali

Tambala

Bwabwa

Mlanga

Mwiyo

Bhaka

Gula

Ntiwa

Nasolo

Caloba

Nasolo

Mieme

Namalimwe
School

Clapperton

Glyn Jones

Link

Michiru

Malamulo
Blantyre
Clinic

Cathedral of
St Paul

Air
Malawi

Hong Kong Restaurant

Robins

Argon

Library

Hindu Temple

Mulomba

Mwaiwanthu
Private Hospital

Buses

Henry Henderson
Institute

St Michael's and
All Angels Church

Blantyre
Secondary School

Gomani

Mwase

Domwe

Mangochi

Chikuse

Chaka

Kaombe

Lundu

Ndirande

Buchanan

Chilembwe

Sharpe

Supermarket

Foreign Exchange Bureau

Petrol Station

South
African
Airways

Henderson

Malawi Institute
of Tourism

Hanover

British
Airways

St Davids

Victoria

Supermarket

National Bank

Haile Selassie

Blantyre
Railway Station

Mudi

Nasolo

Maunde

Gomani

Malimidwe

Macleod

Independence

Dharad
School

District
Commissioner's
Office

British
Consulate

Map Sales
Office

Old Boma

Parking

Laws

Buses

Food Stalls

Monument

Municipal
Market

Clock
Tower

Mandala

Kidney

Moir

Parking

Summers

Skerret

Arnold

Bank

Smythe

Blantyre
Sports Club

Golf
Course

Rangely
Gardens
Smythe

Kampala

Lower Sclater

Browns

Jacaranda

Kaoshiung

Mackie

Mandala House

Blantyre

Kufa

Mandala

Stephen

M2

Scott

Hayter

Chirwa

Mlolo

Ali Hassan Mwinyi

Chichiri
Stadium

Chichiri

Sunnyside

Ring

Smythe

Mwanza

Kasitu

St Andrew's
Primary School

Joachim Chissano

Walani

Mbelwa

Marshall

Museum

Belcher

Greek Club

Mandala

Library

Johnstone

Sports
Ground

Chichiri Conference Centre

Trade Fair
Grounds

Chichiri
Showgrounds

Portuguese
Club

TO ZOMBA/THYOLO/NSANJE

Central

Nkoka

Andrews

West

Smythe

East

Ndege

Matecheta

Mahatma Gandhi

College of Medicine

Red Cross

Ginnery Corner

Polytechnic

Masauko Chipembere Highway

Monument

French
Cultural
Centre

Kasungu

M2

Multi-Country Post &
Telecommunications
Training Centre

Mount Pleasant

Leslie

Mount Pleasant

Staffordshire

Mahatma Gandhi

Chipatala

Kapeni

Queen Elizabeth
Central Hospital

Cemetery

Chitawira

Bwazi

Chitumbu

Chilumb

Mleme

Njamba MCDE
School

Kenyatta

Mbendela

Jubilee
Park

St James

Catholic School

St Montfort

Ndola Link

M1

Napiri

Mibawa Ave

Napiri

Seventh Day
Adventist
Primary
School

Mchense

Kachere

Chitera

Mchoma

Kachere

Chimlambe

Njamba
Park

Soche Central

Bismark

Bandawe

Katunga
North

MOTH
Club

Beaton

Kenyatta

Soche Ring

Market

Msikidzi

Mnthengere

Msolo

Msangu

Tsanya

Chitawira
Homecraft
Centre

Mkunkhumwala

Chiumbu

Utulu

Kwacha

Chimlambe

Chinyonga

Manase

Manase

Zoo

Furr

South End
School

Soche Ring

Domingo

Misuku

Kwegire

Somba

Chinsima

Napini

Mkuthe

Lisungwi

Lunyangwa

Msatsi

Rukuru

Chitawira

Sisseo Mithkoza

Chitawira
Primary School

Cemetery

Mleme

Mbawa

Mkunkhumwala

Busa

Traditional
Court

Chisasa

Katunga
South

Jumbe

Lujenda

Kazembe

Mwambo

Katinga

Zingwangwa

Kongwe

Cemetery

Zingwangwa
Primary
School

Matenje

Mtendele

Zingwangwa

Zongendaba

Zingwangwa

Soche East

Kamoto

Chinsima

Chimwankhunda

St Pius
School

Lonse

Bua

Viola

Putsa

Ntonda

Chifira

Kaiom

Kani

Nkolokosa

Nasolo

Mzimba

St Columba

Kapeni

Mzu

Mswaswa

Kwacha

Kwacha International
Conference Centre

St Anthony

Kamoto

Welemu

Chimwankhunda

Mwase

Chimwankhunda
Dam

Kapeni

Kapeni

M1

TO CHIKWAWA

TO CHIKWAWA

TO BLANTYRE COLLEGE

M 400 800

N

(00265) 1 771 295/073/772 702/773 233/775 499 • e: psinfo@sdnb.org.mw • e: tourism@malawi.net • www.tourismmalawi.com

Beira Mozambique
Inhambane Mozambique Vilankulo Mozambique

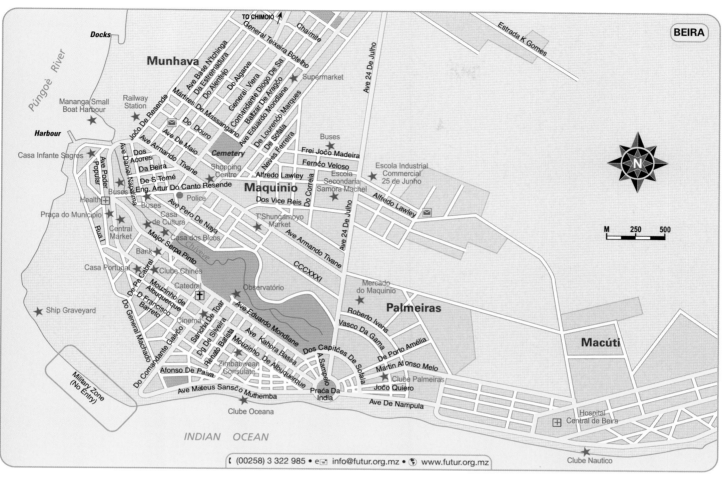

BEIRA

TO CHIMOIO

Docks

Púngoè River

Munhava

Mananga Small Boat Harbour

Railway Station

Harbour

Casa Infante Sagres

Praça do Município

Central Market

Bank

Casa Portugal

Casa de Cultura

Casa dos Bicos

Major Serpa Pinto

Clube Chinês

Catedral

Observatório

Cinema

Zimbabwean Consulate

Ship Graveyard

Military Zone (No Entry)

Afonso De Paiva

Clube Oceana

INDIAN OCEAN

Chaimite

General Teixeira Botelho

Ave Base N'chinga

Da Estremadura

Do Alentejo

Do Algarve

Mártires De Massangano

Generai Viera

Comandante Diogo De Sá

Baltzar De Aragão

Ave Eduardo Mondlane

Da Solala

Neves Ferreira

Joáo De Resende

Do Douro

Ave De Maio

Dos Açores

Da Beira

De S Tomé

Ave Armando Tivane

Ave Eng. Artur Do Canto Resende

Ave Poder Popular

Ave Daniel Napatima

Buses

Health

Buses

Buses

Police

Ave Pero De Naya

Rua 1

De Pa Cabral

Mouzinho de Albuquerque

De D Francisco Barreto

Do General Machado

Do Comandante Galvão

Sancha De Toar

Dg De Silveira

Renato Batista

Mouzinho De Albuquerque

Ave Kanora Bassa

Ave Mateus Sansão Muthemba

Ave Eduardo Mondiane

Maquinio

Alfredo Lawley

Dos Vice Reis

T'Shungamoyo Market

Dos Correia

Ave Armando Tivane

CCCXXXI

Dos Capitões De Solala

A Sampaio

Praça Da India

Supermarket

Buses

Frei João Madeira

Fernco Veloso

Escola Secondaria

Samora Machel

Escola Industrial Commercial 25 de Junho

Alfredo Lawley

Ave 24 De Julho

Mercado do Maquinio

Roberto Ivens

Vasco Da Gama

De Porto Amélia

Martin Afonso Melo

Clube Palmeiras

João Quiero

Ave De Nampula

Palmeiras

Macúti

Estrada K Gomes

Hospital Central de Beira

Clube Nautico

M   250   500

((00258) 3 322 985 • e✉ info@futur.org.mz • 🌐 www.futur.org.mz

---

INHAMBANE

Inhambane Bay

Inhambane Bay

Old Mosque

Josina Machel Park

Governor's Palace

Dhow Anchorage

Cathedral

Telecommunications Building

Ferry & Dhows to Maxixe

Jetty   Port

Ti Jamu Restaurant

Mariano's Bar (Prima Vera Restaurant)

Cinema

New Mosque

Museum

Xiphefo

3 De Fevereiro

Dos Continuadores

Ave Da Vigilancia

Ave Independância

Ave Acordos De Lusaka

Main Road

Main Road

Main Road

Supermarket

Market

Buses

Ave Revolução

Tic Tic Restaurant

Railway Station (Disused)

Market

M   150   300

TO EN1

TO AIRPORT/TOFO/ PONTA DA BARRA

((00258) 23 20 216 • e✉ turismo.inhambane@teledata.mz • 🌐 www.futur.org.mz

---

VILANKULO

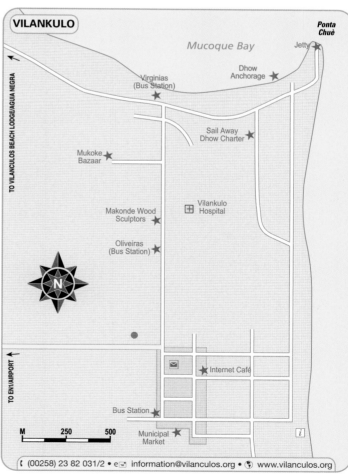

Ponta Chuè

Mucoque Bay

Jetty

Dhow Anchorage

Virginias (Bus Station)

Sail Away Dhow Charter

Mukoke Bazaar

Makonde Wood Sculptors

Oliveiras (Bus Station)

Vilankulo Hospital

TO VILANCULOS BEACH LODGE/AGUIA NEGRA

TO EN1/AIRPORT

Internet Café

Bus Station

Municipal Market

M   250   500

((00258) 23 82 031/2 • e✉ information@vilanculos.org • 🌐 www.vilanculos.org

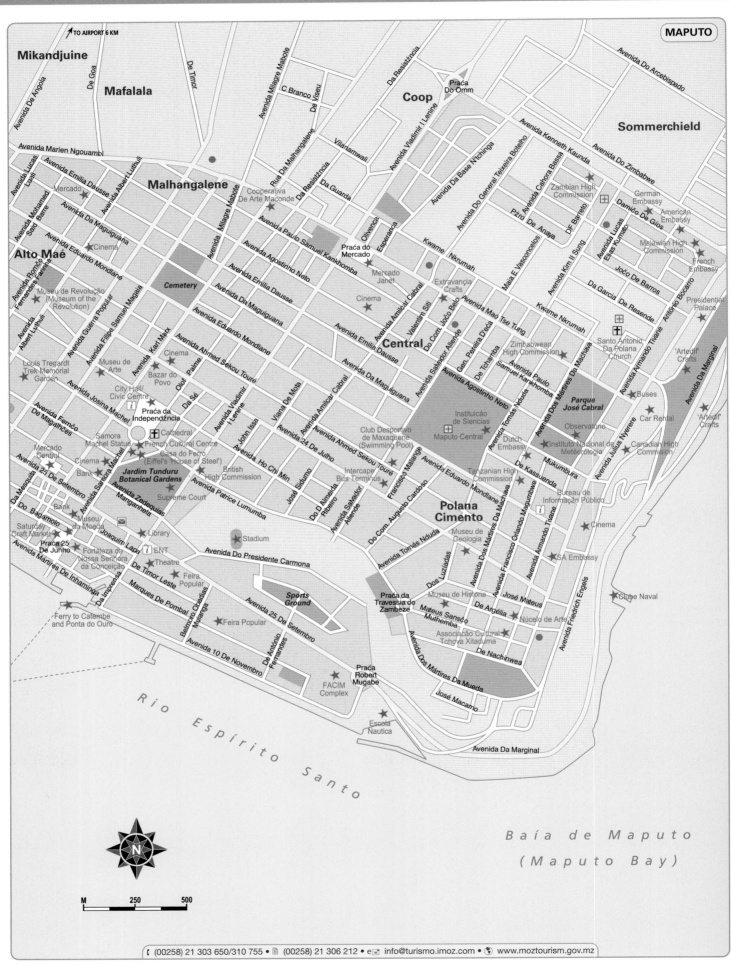

Maputo
Mozambique

TO AIRPORT 6 KM

Mikandjuine

Mafalala

Coop

Sommerchield

Avenida De Angola
De Goa
De Timor
Avenida Milagre Mabote
C Branco
De Viseu
Da Resistência
Praça Do Omm

Avenida Do Arcebispado
Avenida Do Zimbabwe

Avenida Marien Ngouambi

Rua Da Malhangalene
Vilanamwali
Avenida Vladimir I Lenine
Avenida Kenneth Kaunda

Avenida Lucas Luali
Avenida Emília Dausse
Avenida Albert Luthuli
Mercado
Malhangalene
Cooperativa De Arte Maconde
Da Guarda
Da Resistência
Avenida Da Base N'chinga
Zambian High Commission
German Embassy
Damião De Gios
American Embassy

Avenida Mohamed Said Barre
Avenida Da Maguiguana
Avenida Milagre Mabote
Olivenca
Esperanca
Avenida Do General Teixeira Botelho
Avenida Cahora Bassa
DF Barreto
Avenida Lucas Elias Kumato
Malawian High Commission

Alto Maé
Avenida Eduardo Mondlane
Avenida Paulo Samuel Kankhomba
Praça do Mercado
Pžro De Anaya
Avenida Kim Il Sung
João De Barros
French Embassy

Avenida Romão Fernandes Farinha
Museu de Revolução (Museum of the Revolution)
Cemetery
Avenida Agostinho Neto
Avenida Emília Dausse
Mercado Janet
Extravância Crafts
Kwame Nkrumah
Maia E Vasconcelos
Da Garcia De Resende
Presidential Palace

Avenida Albert Luthuli
Avenida Guerra Popular
Avenida Filipe Samuel Magaia
Avenida Eduardo Mondlane
Avenida Da Maguiguana
Cinema
Avenida Amilcar Cabral
Cinema
Avenida Mao Tse Tung
Valentim Siti
Kwame Nkrumah
Santo António Da Polana Church

Louis Tregardt Trek Memorial Garden
Museu de Arte
Karl Marx
Cinema
Avenida Ahmed Sekou Touré
Avenida Emília Dausse
Avenida Da Maguiguana
Central
Do Com. João Belo
Do Tchamba
Avenida Paulo Samuel Kankhomba
'Artedif' Crafts

City Hall/ Civic Centre
Bazar do Povo
Old Palme
Da Sé
Avenida Vladimir I Lenine
Viana De Mota
Avenida Amilcar Cabral
Avenida Salvador Allende
Gen. Pereira Deça
Zimbabwean High Commission
Observatorio
Buses

Praça da Independência
Cathedral
French Cultural Centre
John Issa
Avenida 24 De Julho
Avenida Ahmed Sekou Touré
Club Desportivo de Maxaquene (Swimming Pool)
Institução de Siencias
Maputo Central
Avenida Tomás Nduda
Avenida Dos Mártires Da Machava
Parque José Cabral
Car Rental
'Artedif' Crafts

Avenida Fernão De Magalhães
Samora Machel Statue
Casa do Ferro (Eiffel's 'House of Steel')
Avenida Ho Chi Min
Intercape Bus Terminus
Francisco Matange
Avenida Eduardo Mondlane
Dutch Embassy
Instituto Nacional de Meteorológia
Canadian High Commission

Mercado Central
Bank
Cinema
Avenida 25 De Setembro
Jardim Tunduru Botanical Gardens
British High Commission
Avenida Patrice Lumumba
José Sidumo
Do D Almeida Ribeiro
Avenida Salvador Allende
Do Com. Augusto Cardoso
Polana Cimento
Tanzanian High Commission
De Mukumbura
De Kassuenda
Avenida Julius Nyerere
Cinema

Da Mesquita
Bank
Avenida Samora Machel
Avenida Zedequias Manganhela
Supreme Court
Museu de Geologia
Bureau de Informação Público

Do Bagamoio
Museu da Moeda
Joaquim Lapa
Library
Stadium
Avenida Tomás Ndcuda
Avenida Dos Mártires Da Machava
Avenida Armando Tivane
USA Embassy

Saturday Craft Market
Praça 25 De Junho
Fortaleza da Nossa Senhora da Conceição
ENT
Theatre
Avenida Do Presidente Carmona
Dos Luziadas
Avenida Francisco Orlando Magumbwe
Clube Naval

Avenida Mártires De Inhaminga
De Timor Leste
Feira Popular
Museu de Historia
José Mateus
De Argélia
Nucleo de Arte
Avenida Friedrich Engels

Da Imprensa
Marques De Pombal
Belmico Obadias Muianga
Feira Popular
Sports Ground
Avenida 25 De Setembro
Praça da Travessia do Zambeze
Mateus Sansço Muthemba
Avenida Dos Mártires Da Mueda

Ferry to Catembe and Ponta do Ouro
Avenida 10 De Novembro
De António Fernandes
FACIM Complex
Praça Robert Mugabe
Associação Cultural Tchova Xitaduma
De Nachinwea
José Macamo

Rio Espírito Santo

Escola Nautica

Avenida Da Marginal

Baía de Maputo
(Maputo Bay)

N

M   250   500

(00258) 21 303 650/310 755 • (00258) 21 306 212 • e info@turismo.imoz.com • www.moztourism.gov.mz

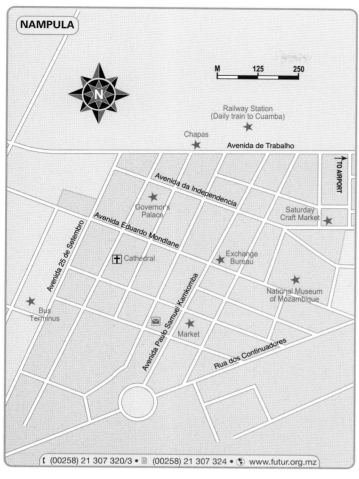

NAMPULA

M 125 250

Railway Station
(Daily train to Cuamba)

Chapas

Avenida de Trabalho

TO AIRPORT

Avenida da Independencia

Governor's Palace

Saturday Craft Market

Avenida Eduardo Mondlane

Avenida 25 de Setembro

Cathedral

Exchange Bureau

Avenida Paulo Samuel Kamkomba

National Museum of Mozambique

Bus Terminus

Market

Rua dos Continuadores

((00258) 21 307 320/3 • ▤ (00258) 21 307 324 • ☉ www.futur.org.mz

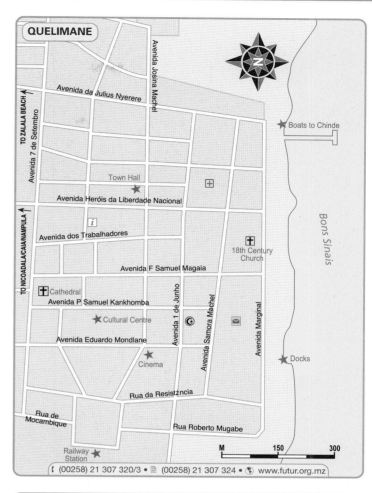

QUELIMANE

Avenida da Julius Nyerere

Avenida Josina Machel

TO ZALALA BEACH

Avenida 7 de Setembro

Boats to Chinde

Town Hall

Avenida Heróis da Liberdade Nacional

TO NICOADALA/CAIA/NAMPULA

i

Avenida dos Trabalhadores

18th Century Church

Avenida F Samuel Magaia

Bons Sinais

Cathedral

Avenida P Samuel Kankhomba

Avenida 1 de Junho

Avenida Samora Machel

Avenida Marginal

Cultural Centre

G

Avenida Eduardo Mondlane

Cinema

Docks

Rua da Resistźncia

Rua de Mocambique

Rua Roberto Mugabe

Railway Station

M 150 300

((00258) 21 307 320/3 • ▤ (00258) 21 307 324 • ☉ www.futur.org.mz

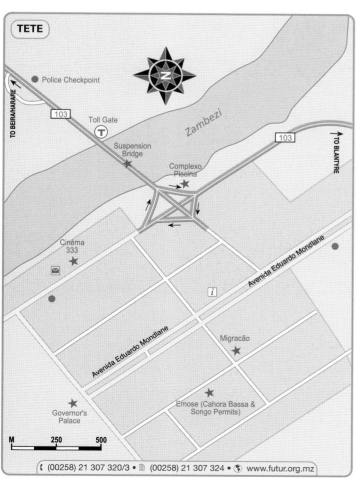

TETE

Police Checkpoint

TO BEIRA/HARARE

103

Toll Gate

T

Suspension Bridge

Zambezi

103

TO BLANTYRE

Complexo Piscina

Cinéma 333

Avenida Eduardo Mondlane

i

Avenida Eduardo Mondlane

Migração

Emose (Cahora Bassa & Songo Permits)

Governor's Palace

M 250 500

((00258) 21 307 320/3 • ▤ (00258) 21 307 324 • ☉ www.futur.org.mz

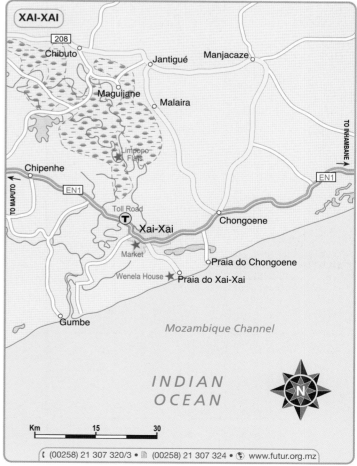

XAI-XAI

208

Chibuto

Jantigué

Manjacaze

Maguijane

Malaira

TO INHAMBANE

EN1

Chipenhe

Limpopo Flats

TO MAPUTO

EN1

Toll Road

T

Xai-Xai

Chongoene

Market

Praia do Chongoene

Wenela House

Praia do Xai-Xai

Gumbe

Mozambique Channel

INDIAN OCEAN

Km 15 30

((00258) 21 307 320/3 • ▤ (00258) 21 307 324 • ☉ www.futur.org.mz

137

Adventures

Adventure	Country	Duration
Diving at Bazaruto Archipelago......................................	Mozambique...	1 day +
Walking Ilha de Mozambique..	Mozambique...	3 hours +
Exploring Maputo Province...	Mozambique...	4 hours +
Kayaking on Lake Malawi...	Malawi...	3 hours +
Climbing Mount Mulanje..	Malawi...	1 day +
Horse Riding in Nyika National Park.............................	Malawi...	4 hours +

Diving at Bazaruto Archipelago

Requirements:
Passports, visas and, if travelling by car, a driver's licence, which may have to be presented on request. Visitors travelling through or from countries with a recent history of yellow fever need a vaccination certificate.
Climate:
Humid and tropical, with high summer temperatures and moderate rains.
Risk factor:
No real danger beyond the usual risks posed by ocean sports. Be prepared, take precautions, and be sensible, as rescue services are limited.
Health:
Malaria is rife and AIDS is a very real threat. Waterborne diseases include hepatitis, typhoid, cholera and dysentery. The local water is not drinkable.
Pack:
Winter evenings can be chilly, but carrying plenty of clothing should not be a priority. Take malarial prophylactics and sunscreen, as well as diving gear if you're on a budget (renting is costly).
Facilities:
Bazaruto is an upmarket destination and, although facilities are adequate, most lodges and resorts range from good to excellent, albeit pricey.
Contact:
Mozambique National Tourism Company, C.P. 2446, Maputo.
Tel: 00258-21-650001 / 307320 / 3
info@futur.org.mz

Walking Ilha de Mozambique

Requirements:
Passports and visas required. Visitors travelling through or from countries with a recent history of yellow fever need a vaccination certificate.
Climate:
Generally hot and humid, with cooler weather June–August.
Risk factor:
Petty crime may be a problem in the south of the island. Vandalizing historic sites is punishable.
Health:
Malaria is rife on the mainland and AIDS is a real threat. Waterborne diseases include hepatitis, typhoid, cholera and dysentery. The water is not drinkable.
Pack:
Lightweight clothing should be sufficient, but be sure to pack good walking shoes. The Muslim community will frown on female travellers who expose any flesh. Sunscreen is recommended and bottled water is essential.
Facilities:
Very, very basic to adequate. Harassment and theft means that the rudimentary lodgings are a better bet than camping. Reservations are advised.
Contact:
Mozambique Tourism
Tel: 011-8039296 / 52
travel@mozambiquetourism.co.za
www.mozambiquetourism.co.za

Exploring Maputo Province

Requirements:
Passports and visas are required. Visitors travelling through or from countries with a recent history of yellow fever will need a vaccination certificate. Beach driving requires a permit.
Climate:
Hot and humid, with cool weather and coastal breezes June–August.
Risk factor:
Experienced mechanics specializing in 4x4 maintenance are hard to come by, and language is an obstacle.
Health:
Malaria is rife and AIDS is a real threat. Waterborne diseases include hepatitis, typhoid, cholera and dysentery. Water is not drinkable.
Pack:
Lightweight summer clothing and sunscreen. Bottled water is essential. Ensure you are familiar with your vehicle's requirements (bring your own spares). Vehicle hire is not recommended.
Facilities:
Facilities vary from basic to very comfortable; out-of-the-way stops offer budget accommodation. Roads are navigable but are generally in poor condition and best suited for 4x4 vehicles.
Contact:
Mozambique Tours (RSA-based), P.O. Box 38359, Point, 4069.
Tel: 0027-31-303-2190
mit@iafrica.com
www.mozambiquetravel.co.za

Kayaking on Lake Malawi

Requirements:
Passports and, for citizens of some countries, visas are required. No health certificates are required.
Climate:
Warm and pleasant: temperatures average 24°C November–April and 30°C May–October.
Risk factor:
Health risks are considerable and crime is a problem: tents have been slashed during robberies and there has been an increase in muggings. Be alert.
Health:
Malaria is a very real threat, and few areas are entirely free of pollution and diseases such as bilharzia. Water-based activities are rewarding, but many medical advisors are reluctant to encourage swimming and snorkelling.
Pack:
Take malarial prophylactics and a mosquito net. Drink bottled water, and carry a supply of purification tablets.
Facilities:
Amenities are generally very good, and the area is serviced by well-established hotels and resorts as well as reliable tour operators, although camping facilities are very basic.
Contact:
Lake Malawi National Park.
Tel: 0027-21-7831955
let'sgo@kayakafrica.co.za, www.kayakafrica.co.za

Climbing Mount Mulanje

Requirements:
Passports and, for citizens of some countries, visas are required. No health certificates are required.
Climate:
Climbing is best in the dry months April–November, although temperatures, especially September/October, can be high. Summer rains render many roads impassable without a 4x4 vehicle.
Risk factor:
The climb can be demanding at times, but trekking Mount Mulanje is generally risk-free, and the only real dangers are those brought upon themselves by foolhardy hikers.
Health:
Malaria is a real threat and, like Lake Malawi, many water sources may contain diseases such as bilharzia.
Pack:
Water purification tablets, malarial prophylactics and a mosquito net, especially if you are overnighting on the mountain. Drink only bottled water.
Facilities:
Overnight accommodation in the mountain huts is basic but comfortable. Hikers and trekkers are well advised to be self-sufficient — even if you are using the services of a guide.
Contact:
Central African Safaris, P.O. Box 489, Lilongwe, Malawi.
Tel: 00265-1-771393

Horse Riding in Nyika National Park

Requirements:
Passports and, for citizens of some countries, visas are required. No health certificates required.
Climate:
Moderately warm to hot, with temperatures ranging from 20°C to 27°C throughout the year.
Risk factor:
Risks are few, but most horseback safari operators will insist clients have some skill on horseback.
Health:
Malaria is a real threat and water sources may contain bilharzia.
Pack:
Professional operators provide most of your needs and all necessary riding equipment, but for extended trips pack your own comfortable gear and footwear, malarial prophylactics and a mosquito net. Drink only bottled water, and keep a supply of purification tablets.
Facilities:
Private safari operators deservedly pride themselves on service excellence. Remember that the nature of a horseback safari means that you will be roughing it!
Contact:
Nyika Safari Company, P.O. Box 2338, Lilongwe, Malawi.
Tel: 00265-1-752379 / 1-330180
reservations@nyika.com, www.nyika.com

138

The Indian Ocean Islands

Virtually all the tropical islands that dot the Indian Ocean off the east coast of the continent have a long history of colonization that has had a deep and lasting influence on their local communities. These comprise a vast mix of people descended from African, Arab, European and Asian settlers who have made their home here over the centuries. The larger nations like Madagascar, Mauritius and Seychelles are multiparty republics, while Réunion remains a French Overseas Department, and their cultural legacies are extremely varied and contribute enormously to the social fabric of the island populations. The islands of the Seychelles (colonized first by the French and then the British) make up a relatively wealthy nation where poverty is rare and the standard of living one of the highest in the Third World. Nonetheless, some 80 per cent of the people of politically volatile Comoros depend exclusively on subsistence farming, making it one of Africa's poorest countries.

MADAGASCAR

ANTANANARIVO
'Tana' is charmingly dishevelled in appearance, its cobbled thoroughfares traversed by rickety carts and jampacked with French colonial-style buildings housing anything from souvenir shops to family-owned produce stores. Quaint and laid-back, Tana is the capital of Madagascar and boasts the Ivato international airport, its population of some 2 million citizens relying on income derived from a small but thriving tourism industry. Considering the extraordinary wildlife for which the island is renowned, many visitors are conservationists and wildlife enthusiasts, and it is the uniqueness of the indigenous flora and fauna that remains the principal attraction. This is despite the bustling urban development and the fact that Tana is relatively cheap as a holiday destination, and its zoological gardens provide fascinating insights into the wildlife. The centre is home to the prolific Madagascar nightjar as well as the hedgehog tenrec.

NOSY BE ARCHIPELAGO
The heart of Madagascar's hospitality industry, the island of Nosy Be is at the centre of the archipelago. Dotted with tourist hotels and amenities, the hilly 280km² island is easily accessible from the capital and, as such, has taken on many of its more popular elements: boat excursions to neighbouring islands, open-air markets and a vibrant nightlife. For a glimpse of the natural heritage of Madagascar, take a walk through the luxuriant vegetation that covers much of Nosy Be or visit the fascinating rainforest stand on the Lokobe Peninsula. Lokobe is home to the endemic thorn spider and Isoxya species, the Parson's chameleon, as well as subspecies of the black lemur.

FORT DAUPHIN
Relatively isolated by unforgiving terrain and an underdeveloped road network and infrastructure, Tôlañaro (Fort Dauphin) was the landing site of the first European travellers in the 16th century and is the centre of Madagascar's lobster industry. The scrubland and relatively high rainfall predominant in much of the area make it inhospitable to the casual tourist, although the beaches allow for a great adventure for naturalists, most notably at Libanona, the rugged slopes of Pic St Louis and the splendour of the nearby Berenty reserve. Those on the lookout for nocturnal species such as the greater dwarf lemur will be richly rewarded.

ISALO MOUNTAINS
The sandstone mountains of Isalo offer a different view to the conventional image of lush Madagascar. Small patches of grassland break the rather bleak landscape, and the occasional green belts are interspersed with strange rock configurations. Punctuated with a number of ancient burial sites held sacred by locals, the recently upgraded network of roads affords access to splendid views of the highlying landscape. Visitors' amenities are in a sad state and the region is (ISALO MOUNTAINS) largely the domain of hikers, campers and wildlife enthusiasts.They are able to take full advantage of the country's top trails and camp sites as well as the wildlife, especially the lemurs and the endemic Benson's rock thrush.

MAURITIUS

PORT LOUIS
As the heart of idyllic Mauritius, a democracy boasting a virtually non-existent crime rate and a literacy rate of more than 90 per cent among the under-30s, Port Louis is a quaint amalgamation of old and new, wild and sedate. Encircled by the craggy volcanic peaks of the Moka Mountains and overlooked by the 19th-century ramparts of La Citadelle, the few remaining clearings and gardens are lined with banyan trees and old colonial buildings, legacy of Victoria's Empire. Port Louis remains every inch the capital, home to 20 per cent of the island's population and bustling with pedestrian traffic. The city has retained a distinct village charm, yet the increasingly modern skyline is dotted with ever popular fast-food and souvenir shops. Its impressive Caudan Waterfront is a thoroughly contemporary tourist development.

TAMARIND FALLS
The hot and dry Sunset Coast is pummelled on occasion by tropical storms and lashed by waves that lure surfers of all abilities. Inland lie the decidedly more tranquil environs of Mare aux Vacoas, a mountain lake encircled by forests of pine and palm, green woods and tea plantations with breathtaking views of the Black River Gorges. The sometimes demanding forest trails are the domain of deer and monkey, and many visitors hike to the spectacular 295m Tamarind Falls, the island's biggest and most impressive waterfall. The area is restricted primarily because of the presence of all-important hydroelectric power stations. Hikers and trailists will need to obtain permission from the Forestry Department or the Electricity Board.

LE MORNE PENINSULA
In the early days of settlement, Le Morne was relatively isolated, inaccessible and unpopulated and a haven for runaway slaves. The scenic peninsula is widely considered the last remaining outpost of African-Creole culture. The rocky landscape, pinpointed by the 556m Le Morne Brabant, offers spectacular views of the 14km coast and is a popular tourist drawcard. Access to the mountain slopes is restricted and permission must be obtained. Fashionable hotels boast golf courses, horse-riding, big-game fishing, diving, water-sports and evening entertainment.

RÉUNION (FRANCE)

ST-DENIS
Located on the north coast of the island, Réunion's capital is most admired for its mountain and volatile volcano, yet boasts picturesque beaches and is a lively centre of social activity. The highest mountain in the Indian Ocean is Piton des Neiges – 3,069m – separating St-Denis from the urban hub of St-Pierre on the southern coast. St-Denis is a trendy town bordering foothills of the rugged hinterland and skirted by cultivated lands of grapevines, lentil crops and geraniums. Geranium oil is a vital element of Réunion's economy. The island's varied climate lends itself to an equally diverse landscape, from tropical lushness to more temperate vegetation. Most travellers visit the three cirques, the natural amphitheatres that form the island's heart.

COMOROS

MORONI
Moroni, the capital of Comoros, is situated on the island of Grande Comore, the most prominent of the three main volcanic islands surrounded by a number of picturesque coral atolls. Moroni and the islands are all scenically beautiful – heavily wooded and cultivated with aromatic crops such as cloves and vanilla that perfume Comoros. Although tourism is a burgeoning industry and a vital earner of foreign exchange, most of the 25,000 impoverished citizens of Moroni are involved in some way with the farming of cash crops. The capital is rustic in appearance and there is little urban lifestyle, yet it is lively and colourful – a true 'island paradise'. The magnificent scenery and the unspoiled island wilderness are Moroni's primary attractions.

SEYCHELLES

MAHÉ
The largest of the 40 islands and 75 low-lying atolls that make up the Seychelles, Mahé is home to 90 per cent of the population, the seat of the nation's capital, Victoria, and the nucleus of the all-important tourism industry. Visitors are drawn to Mahé by the picturesque environs, most notably exceptional beaches such as Beau Vallon, and the unique plant and animal life. Blessed with an old-world charm, the capital Victoria, has rapidly developed a sound infrastructure geared toward the hospitality industry.

ALDABRA ATOLL
Aldabra is the most removed atoll, situated 1,200km from the frenetic activity of Mahé and the capital. This small collection of 14 islets is best accessed via a three-hour boat trip from the nearest airstrip on Assumption. The large coral lagoon and the immediate environs of mangrove are a sanctuary for flora and fauna, including pemphis scrub and giant land tortoises. The crystal waters and well-preserved corals around the 100km coast of Aldabra's islands are a much admired haven for water adventurers, who consider the atoll to be the most pristine in all Seychelles.

The hot and humid conditions and varying topography of the Mascarenes (Mauritius, Rodrigues and Réunion) range from mountainous highlands to low-lying coral atolls. The other small islands of the Indian Ocean are ideally suited to the production of exotic crops such as vanilla, coffee, sugar and spices, the export of which forms the basis of local economies and the centre of the largely farming communities.

Antananarivo, Madagascar

Valley, St-Denis, Réunion

Silhouette   Praslin
VICTORIA ✪   La Digue
Mahé

Aldabra Atoll

Aldabra Islands

SEYCHELLES

Agalega Islands
(MAURITIUS)

MORONI ✪   Njazidja
(Grande Comore)
Fomboni •   COMOROS
Mwali   Nzwani
Mayotte   Nosy Be
(FRANCE)   Archipelago

Mahé, Seychelles

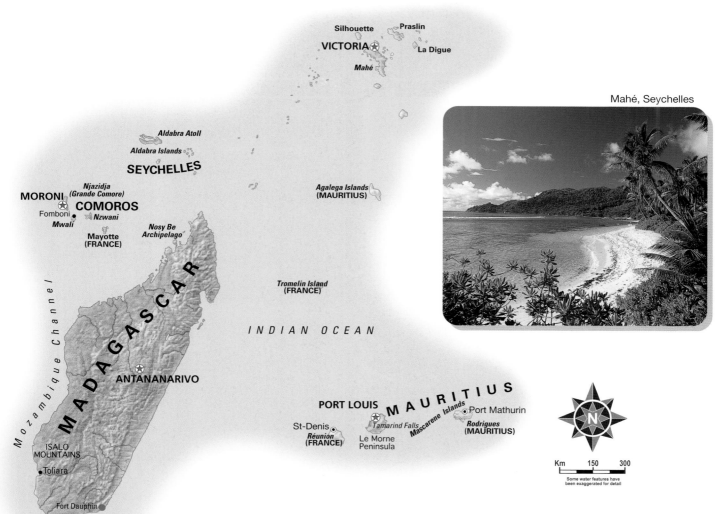

Tromelin Island
(FRANCE)

INDIAN OCEAN

MADAGASCAR

ANTANANARIVO ✪

ISALO
MOUNTAINS
• Toliara

Fort Dauphin

PORT LOUIS   MAURITIUS

St-Denis   ✪ Tamarind Falls   • Port Mathurin
Réunion   Le Morne   Mascarene Islands   Rodrigues
(FRANCE)   Peninsula   (MAURITIUS)

N

Km   150   300

Some water features have
been exaggerated for detail

141

Black River Gorges National Park
Mauritius

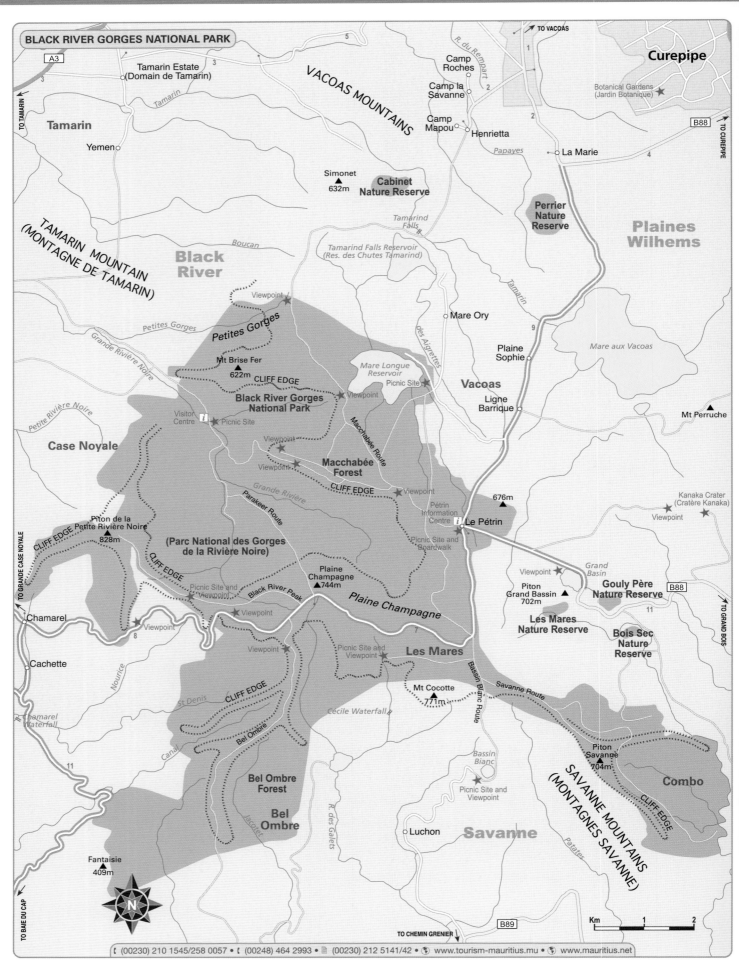

BLACK RIVER GORGES NATIONAL PARK

TO VACOAS

Curepipe

A3

Tamarin Estate
(Domain de Tamarin)

VACOAS MOUNTAINS

Camp Roches

Camp la Savanne

Botanical Gardens
(Jardin Botanique)

Tamarin

Yemen

Camp Mapou

Henrietta

B88

TO CUREPIPE

R. du Rempart

Papayes

La Marie

Simonet
632m

Cabinet Nature Reserve

Perrier Nature Reserve

Plaines Wilhems

TAMARIN MOUNTAIN
(MONTAGNE DE TAMARIN)

Boucan

Tamarind Falls

Tamarind Falls Reservoir
(Res. des Chutes Tamarind)

Black River

Petites Gorges

Viewpoint

Mare Ory

Petites Gorges

Mt Brise Fer
622m

CLIFF EDGE

Mare Longue Reservoir

Plaine Sophie

Mare aux Vacoas

Grande Rivière Noire

Black River Gorges National Park

Viewpoint

Picnic Site

Vacoas

Petite Rivière Noire

Visitor Centre

Picnic Site

Viewpoint

Ligne Barrique

Case Noyale

Viewpoint

Macchabée Forest

Macchabée Route

Mt Perruche

Grande Rivière

CLIFF EDGE

Viewpoint

676m

Kanaka Crater
(Cratère Kanaka)

Parakeer Route

Pétrin Information Centre

Le Pétrin

Viewpoint

Piton de la Petite Rivière Noire
828m

(Parc National des Gorges de la Rivière Noire)

Picnic Site and Boardwalk

Grand Basin

CLIFF EDGE

CLIFF EDGE

Plaine Champagne
744m

Viewpoint

Piton Grand Bassin
702m

Gouly Père Nature Reserve

B88

TO GRANDE CASE NOYALE

Picnic Site and Viewpoint

Black River Peak

Plaine Champagne

Les Mares Nature Reserve

Bois Sec Nature Reserve

Chamarel

Viewpoint

Nourice

Viewpoint

Picnic Site and Viewpoint

Les Mares

TO GRAND BOIS

Cachette

CLIFF EDGE

Viewpoint

Bassin Blanc Route

Savanne Route

Piton Savanne
704m

St Denis

Mt Cocotte
771m

Cécile Waterfall

To Chamarel Waterfall

Bel Ombre

Canal

Jacotet

Bel Ombre Forest

Bassin Blanc

SAVANNE MOUNTAINS
(MONTAGNES SAVANNE)

Combo

CLIFF EDGE

Bel Ombre

R. des Galets

Picnic Site and Viewpoint

Luchon

Savanne

Patates

Fantaisie
409m

TO BAIE DU CAP

N

TO CHEMIN GRENIER

B89

Km   1   2

℡ (00230) 210 1545/258 0057 • ℡ (00248) 464 2993 • 🖹 (00230) 212 5141/42 • 🌐 www.tourism-mauritius.mu • 🌐 www.mauritius.net

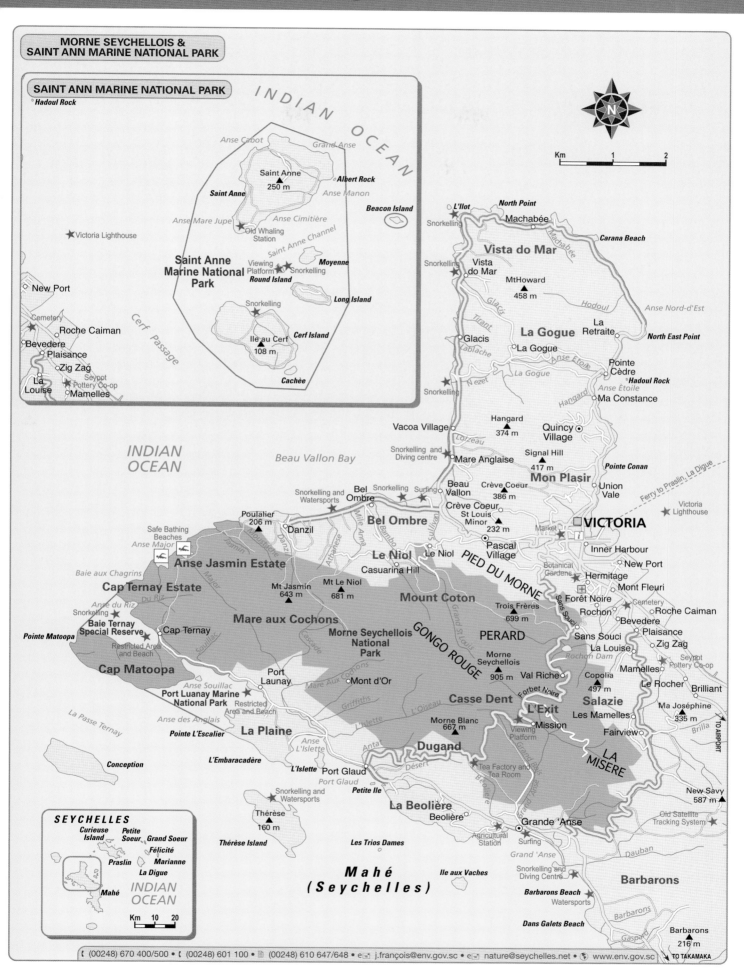

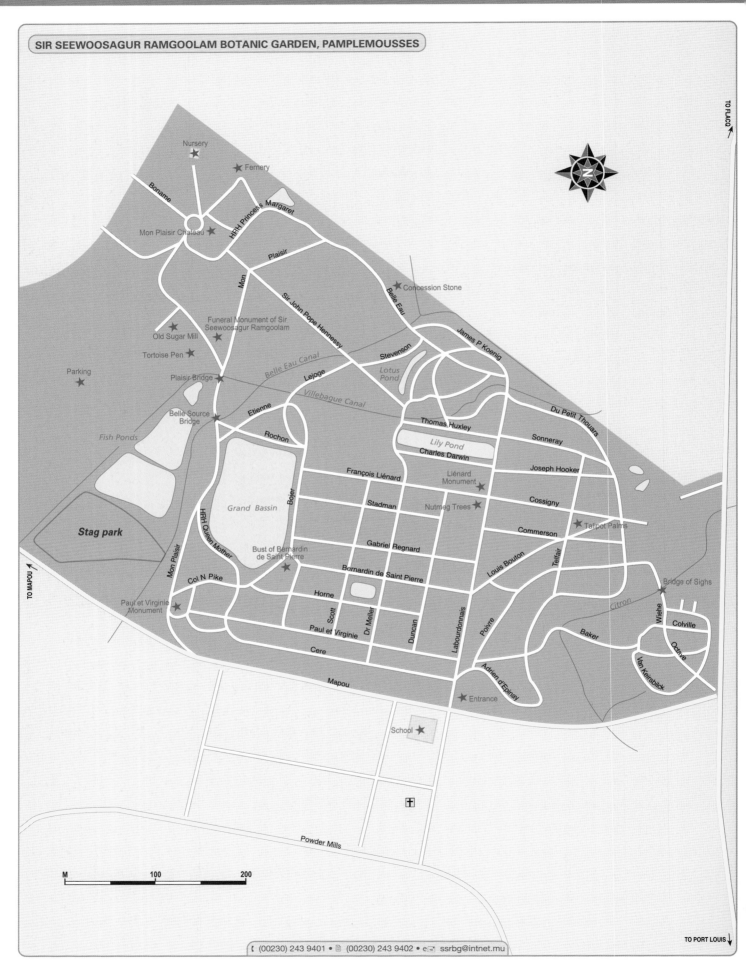

SIR SEEWOOSAGUR RAMGOOLAM BOTANIC GARDEN, PAMPLEMOUSSES

TO FLACQ

Nursery

Fernery

Boname

HRH Princess Margaret

Mon Plaisir Chateau

Plaisir

Mon

Concession Stone

Belle Eau

Sir John Pope Hennessy

James P Koenig

Funeral Monument of Sir Seewoosagur Ramgoolam

Old Sugar Mill

Tortoise Pen

Stevenson

Belle Eau Canal

Lejoge

Lotus Pond

Parking

Plaisir Bridge

Villebague Canal

Du Petit Thouars

Belle Source Bridge

Etienne

Thomas Huxley

Sonneray

Fish Ponds

Rochon

Lily Pond

Charles Darwin

Joseph Hooker

François Liénard

Liénard Monument

Cossigny

Bojer

Stadman

Nutmeg Trees

Commerson

Talipot Palms

Grand Bassin

HRH Queen Mother

Stag park

Bust of Bernardin de Saint Pierre

Gabriel Regnard

Louis Bouton

Telfair

Bridge of Sighs

Mon Plaisir

Col N Pike

Bernardin de Saint Pierre

Citron

Wiehe

Paul et Virginie Monument

Horne

Scott

Dr Meller

Duncan

Labourdonnais

Poivre

Baker

Colville

Octave

Paul et Virginie

Cere

Adrien d'Epinay

Van Keirsbilck

TO MAPOU

Mapou

Entrance

School

Powder Mills

M   100   200

TO PORT LOUIS

Madagascar's Parks & Reserves

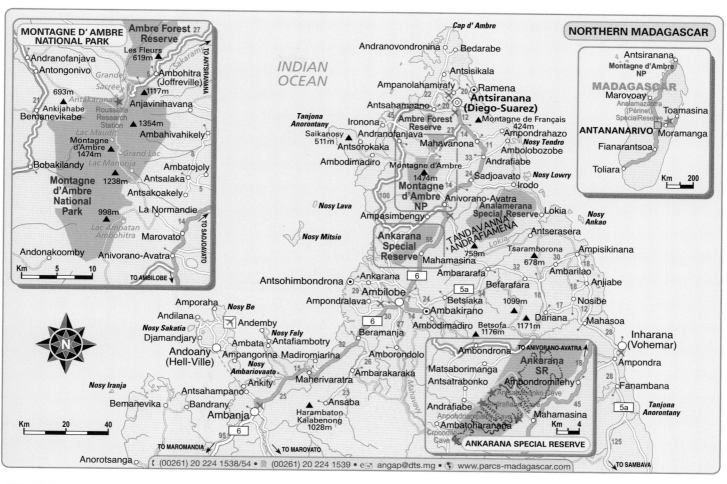

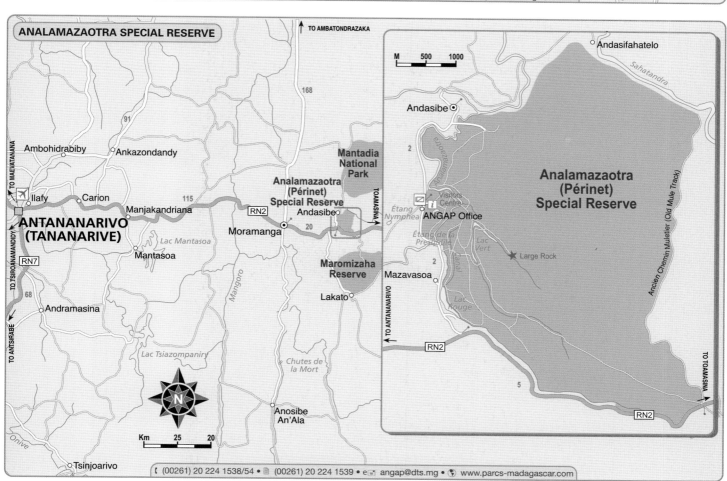

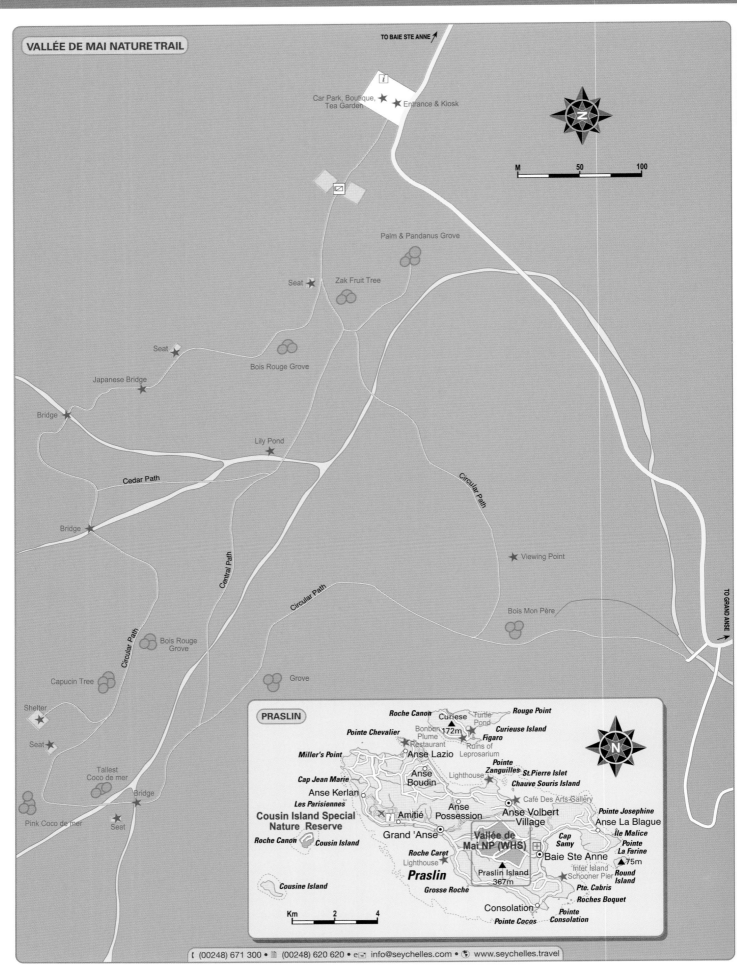

VALLÉE DE MAI NATURE TRAIL

TO BAIE STE ANNE

Car Park, Boutique,
Tea Garden
Entrance & Kiosk

M   50   100

Palm & Pandanus Grove

Seat   Zak Fruit Tree

Seat   Bois Rouge Grove

Japanese Bridge

Bridge

Lily Pond

Cedar Path

Circular Path

Bridge

Central Path

Viewing Point

Circular Path

Circular Path

Bois Mon Père

Bois Rouge
Grove

Grove

Capucin Tree

TO GRAND ANSE

Shelter

Seat

Tallest
Coco de mer

Bridge

Pink Coco de mer   Seat

PRASLIN

N

Roche Canon   Curiese   Turtle   Rouge Point
Pointe Chevalier   Bonben   Plume   172m   Curieuse Island
Figaro
Miller's Point   Restaurant   Ruins of
Anse Lazio   Leprosarium
Pointe
Cap Jean Marie   Anse   Lighthouse   Zanguilles   St.Pierre Islet
Boudin   Chauve Souris Island
Anse Kerlan   Café Des Arts Gallery
Les Parisiennes   Anse   Anse Volbert   Pointe Josephine
Possession   Village   Anse La Blague
Cousin Island Special   Amitié   Île Malice
Nature Reserve   Cap   Pointe
Grand 'Anse   Samy   La Farine
Roche Canon   Vallée de
Cousin Island   Mai NP (WHS)   Baie Ste Anne   75m
Roche Caret   Round
Lighthouse   Island
Praslin   Inter Island
Praslin Island   Schooner Pier
Cousine Island   367m   Pte. Cabris
Grosse Roche   Roches Boquet
Consolation   Pointe
Consolation
Pointe Cocos

Km   2   4

(00248) 671 300 • (00248) 620 620 • e info@seychelles.com • www.seychelles.travel

Antananarivo   Madagascar

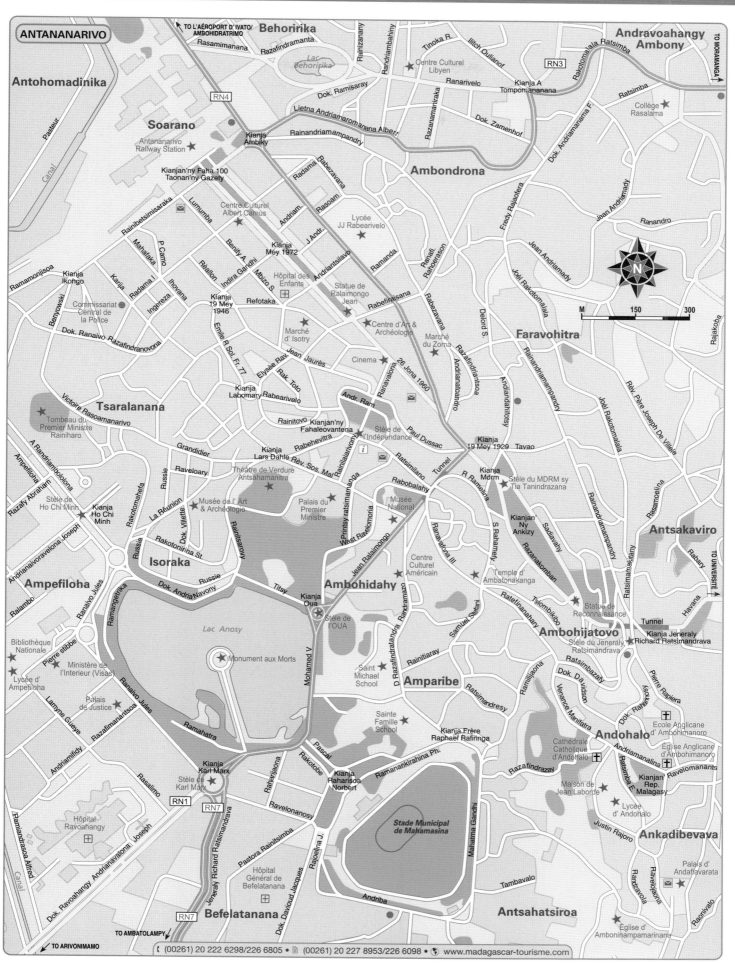

ANTANANARIVO

Port Louis Mauritius

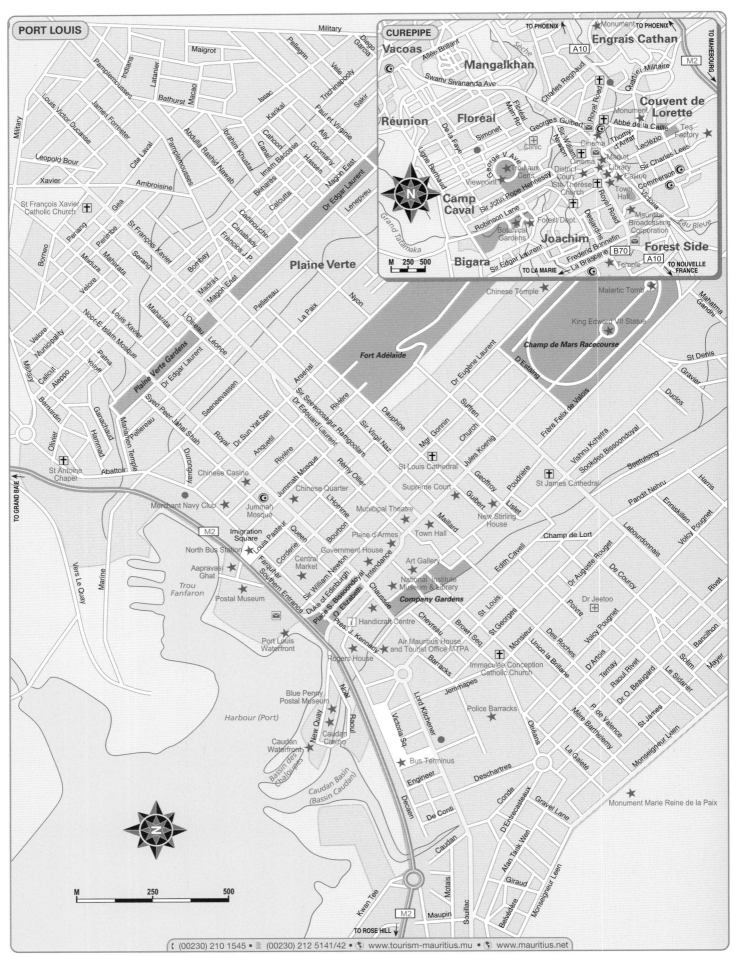

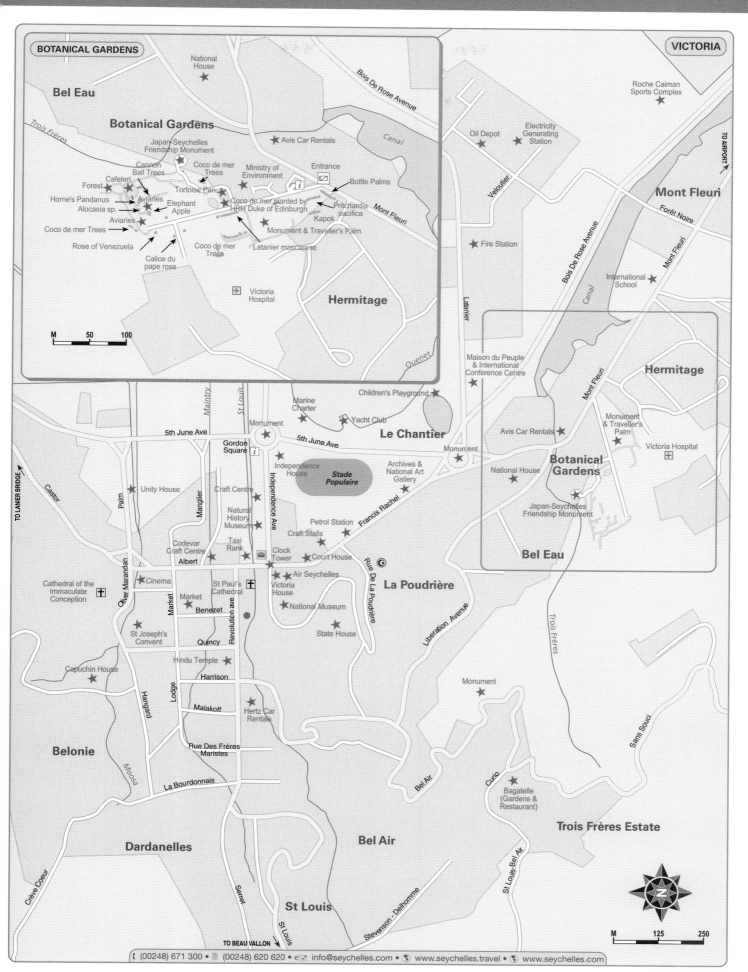

BOTANICAL GARDENS

VICTORIA

Bel Eau

National House

Roche Caiman Sports Complex

Botanical Gardens

Trois Frères

Japan-Seychelles Friendship Monument

Bois De Rose Avenue

Canal

Avis Car Rentals

Oil Depot

Electricity Generating Station

Cannon Ball Trees

Coco de mer Trees

Cafeteri

Forest

Ministry of Environment

Entrance

Bottle Palms

Veloutier

Mont Fleuri

Horne's Pandanus

Tortoise Pen

Aviaries

Alocasia sp.

Elephant Apple

Coco de mer planted by HRH Duke of Edinburgh

Pritchardia pacifica

Mont Fleuri

Forêt Noire

Aviaries

Kapok

Fire Station

Coco de mer Trees

Monument & Traveller's Palm

International School

Rose of Venezuela

Coco de mer Trees

Latanier mascarene

Calice du pape rose

Victoria Hospital

Hermitage

Maison du Peuple & International Conference Centre

Hermitage

M 50 100

Quenet

Children's Playground

Maintry

St Louis

Marine Charter

Yacht Club

Le Chantier

Monument & Traveller's Palm

5th June Ave

Monument

Gordon Square

5th June Ave

Archives & National Art Gallery

Monument

Avis Car Rentals

Victoria Hospital

Independence House

Stade Populaire

National House

Botanical Gardens

Bel Eau

TO LANIER BRIDGE

Unity House

Craft Centre

Japan-Seychelles Friendship Monument

Castor

Palm

Manglier

Natural History Museum

Petrol Station

Francis Rachel

Codevar Craft Centre

Taxi Rank

Craft Stalls

Albert

Clock Tower

Court House

Rue De La Poudrière

La Poudrière

Cinema

Air Seychelles

Olier Marandan

St Paul's Cathedral

Victoria House

Cathedral of the Immaculate Conception

Market

Benezet

National Museum

Liberation Avenue

Trois Frères

St Joseph's Convent

Quincy

Revolution ave

State House

Hindu Temple

Capuchin House

Hangard

Lodge

Harrison

Monument

Malakoff

Hertz Car Rentals

Sans Souci

Rue Des Frères Maristes

Belonie

Moosa

La Bourdonnais

Bel Air

Curio

Bagatelle (Gardens & Restaurant)

Dardanelles

Bel Air

Trois Frères Estate

Crève Cœur

Serret

St Louis

St Louis-Bel Air

St Louis

Stevenson - Delhomme

TO BEAU VALLON

M 125 250

((00248) 671 300 • (00248) 620 620 • e info@seychelles.com • www.seychelles.travel • www.seychelles.com

Indian Ocean Islands

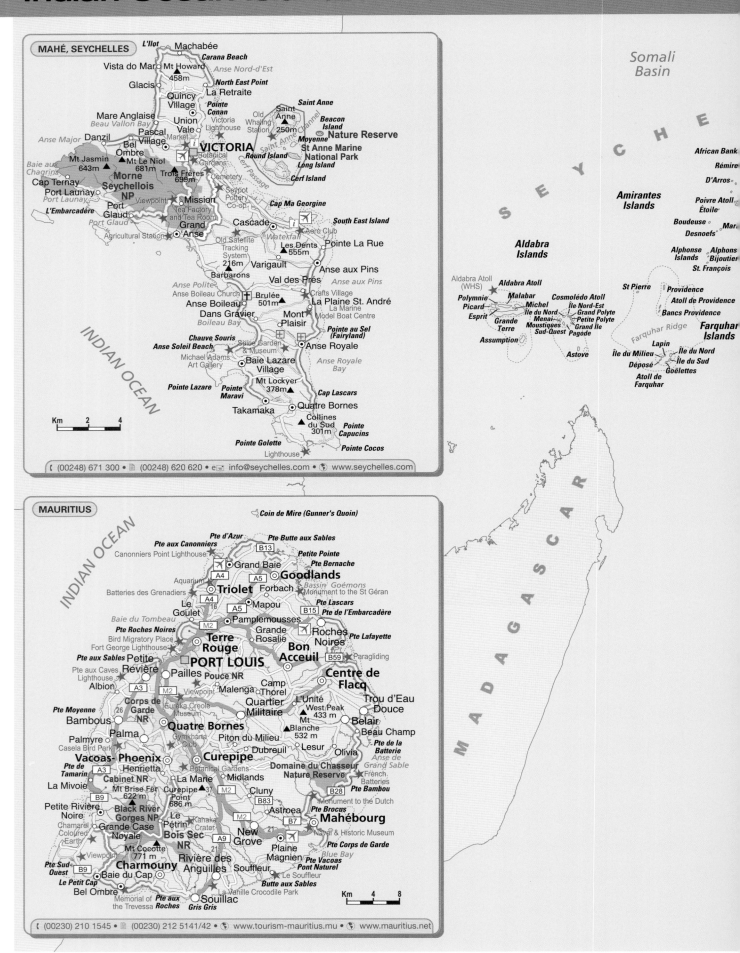

MAHÉ, SEYCHELLES

L'Ilot · Machabée
Carana Beach
Vista do Mar · Mt Howard · Anse Nord-d'Est
458m
Glacis · North East Point
Quincy · La Retraite
Village · Pointe
Conan
Mare Anglaise · Union · Victoria
Beau Vallon Bay · Vale · Lighthouse
Anse Major · Danzil · Pascal · Market
Bel · Village
Ombre
Mt Jasmin · Mt Le Niol · Trois Frères
Baie aux · 643m · 681m · 698m
Chagrins · Morne · Cemetery
Cap Ternay · Seychellois · Viewpoint · Mission
Port Launay · NP · Tea Factory
Port Launay · Port · and Tea Room
L'Embarcadère · Glaud · Grand
Port Glaud · 'Anse
Agricultural Station

Saint Anne
Saint · Beacon
Anne · Island
Old · 250m
Whaling · Moyenne · Nature Reserve
Station · St Anne Marine
Round Island · National Park
Long Island
Cerf Island
Cap Ma Georgine
Cascade
Aero Club · South East Island
Watekfall
Les Dents · Pointe La Rue
555m
Varigault · Anse aux Pins
216m · Val des Prés · Anse aux Pins
Barbarons
Anse Polite · Crafts Village
Anse Boileau Church · Brulée · La Plaine St. André
501m · La Marine
Anse Boileau · Model Boat Centre
Dans Gravier · Mont
Boileau Bay · Plaisir
Chauve Souris · Pointe au Sel
Spice Garden · (Fairyland)
Anse Soleil Beach · & Museum · Anse Royale
Michael Adams · Baie Lazare · Anse Royale
Art Gallery · Village · Bay
Pointe Lazare · Pointe · Mt Lockyer
Pointe · 378m
Maravi · Cap Lascars
Takamaka · Quatre Bornes
Collines · Pointe
du Sud · Capucins
301m
Pointe Golette
Lighthouse · Pointe Cocos

Km 2 4

INDIAN OCEAN

((00248) 671 300 · 🖨 (00248) 620 620 · e✉ info@seychelles.com · 🌐 www.seychelles.com

Somali
Basin

S E Y C H E

African Bank
Rémire
D'Arros
Amirantes · Poivre Atoll
Islands · Étoile
Boudeuse
Desnoefs · Mar
Aldabra · Alphonse · Alphons
Islands · Islands · Bijouiter
St. François
Aldabra Atoll · St Pierre · Providence
(WHS) · Aldabra Atoll · Atoll de Providence
Polymnie · Malabar · Bancs Providence
Picard · Michel · Cosmolédo Atoll · Farquhar Ridge · Farquhar
Esprit · Île du Nord · Île Nord-Est · Islands
Grande · Menai · Grand Polyte
Terre · Moustiques · Petite Polyte · Lapin
Sud-Quest · Grand Île · Île du Milieu
Assumption · Pagode · Île du Nord
Astove · Déposé · Île du Sud
Atoll de · Goëlettes
Farquhar

MAURITIUS

Coin de Mire (Gunner's Quoin)

Pte d'Azur · Pte Butte aux Sables
Pte aux Canonniers · B13
Canonniers Point Lighthouse · Petite Pointe
Grand Baie · Pte Bernache
Aquarium · A4 · A5 · Goodlands
Batteries des Grenadiers · Forbach · Pte Lascars
Le · A4 · Triolet · Mapou · Bassin Goémons
Goulet · 18 · A5 · Monument to the St Géran
Baie du Tombeau · M2 · Pamplemousses · Pte de l'Embarcadère
Pte Roches Noires · Grande · B15
Bird Migratory Place · Rosalie · Roches · Pte Lafayette
Terre · Noires
Fort George Lighthouse · Rouge · Pte Lafayette
Pte aux Sables · Petite · Bon · Paragliding
Pte aux Caves · Rivière · PORT LOUIS · Acceuil · B59
Lighthouse · Pailles · Pouce NR · Centre de
Albion · A3 · Viewpoint · Flacq
M2 · Malenga · Camp · L'Unité · Trou d'Eau
Corps de · Thorel · West Peak · Douce
Pte Moyenne · Garde · Eureka Creole · Quartier · 433 m
Bambous · NR · Museum · Militaire · Mt · Belair
Palma · Quatre Bornes · Blanche · Beau Champ
Palmyre · Gymkhana · Piton du Milieu · 532 m · Pte de la
Casela Bird Park · Club · Dubreuil · Lesur · Batterie
Vacoas- Phoenix · Curepipe · Olivia · Anse de
Pte de · Henrietta · Botanical Gardens · Domaine du Chasseur · Grand Sable
Tamarin · A3 · La Marie · Midlands · Nature Reserve · French
La Mivoie · Cabinet NR · Curepipe · 37 · Cluny · Batteries
Mt Brise Fer · Point · M2 · B28 · Pte Bambou
622 m · 686 m · B83 · Astroea · B7 · Monument to the Dutch
Petite Rivière · Black River · Le · Pte Brocus
Noire · Gorges NP · Pétrin · Kanaka · New · Naval & Historic Museum · Mahébourg
Chamarel · Grande Case · Crater · Grove · Pte Corps de Garde
Coloured · Noyale · Bois Sec · A9 · Plaine · Pte Vacoas
Earth · Mt Cocotte · NR · 21 · Magnien · Pont Naturel · Blue Bay
Viewpoint · 771 m · Rivière des · Le Souffleur
Pte Sud · Charmouny · Anguilles · Souffleur
Quest · B9 · Butte aux Sables
Baie du Cap · La Vanille Crocodile Park
Le Petit Cap · Km 4 8
Bel Ombre · Pte aux
Memorial of · Roches · Souillac
the Trevessa · Gris Gris

INDIAN OCEAN

M A D A G A S C A R

((00230) 210 1545 · 🖨 (00230) 212 5141/42 · 🌐 www.tourism-mauritius.mu · 🌐 www.mauritius.net

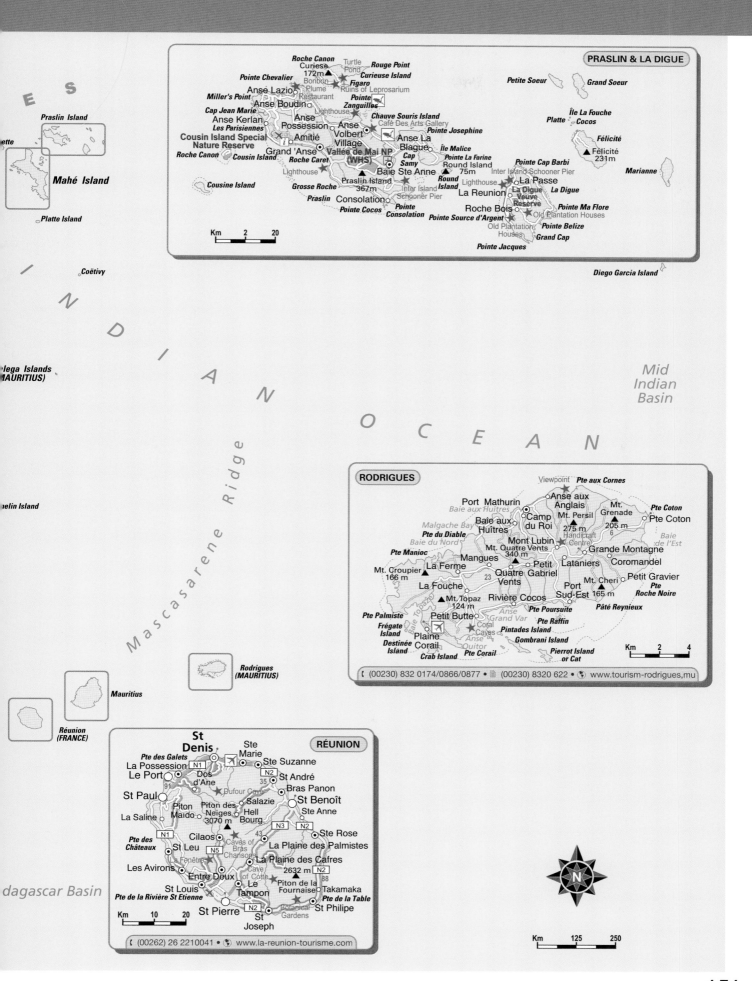

PRASLIN & LA DIGUE

Roche Canon
Curieuse
172m
Rouge Point
Turtle Pond
Curieuse Island
Pointe Chevalier
Bonbon
Plume
Figaro
Ruins of Leprosarium
Pointe Chevalier
Petite Soeur
Grand Soeur
Anse Lazio
Miller's Point
Anse Boudin
Restaurant
Pointe Zanguilles
Cap Jean Marie
Lighthouse
Île La Fouche
Platte
Cocos
Anse Kerlan
Chauve Souris Island
Les Parisiennes
Anse Possession
Anse Volbert
Café Des Arts Gallery
Pointe Josephine
Félicité
Cousin Island Special
Nature Reserve
Amitié
Anse La Blague
Anse Josephine
Félicité
231m
Roche Canon
Cousin Island
Grand 'Anse
Vallée de Mai NP (WHS)
Île Malice
Pointe La Farine
Pointe Cap Barbi
Marianne
Cousine Island
Roche Caret
Cap Samy
Round Island
Inter Island Schooner Pier
Grosse Roche
Baie Ste Anne
Round Island
La Passe
La Digue
Praslin Island
367m
Inter Island Schooner Pier
Lighthouse
La Reunion
La Digue
Veuve Reserve
Praslin
Consolation
Roche Bois
Pointe Ma Flore
Pointe Cocos
Pointe Consolation
Pointe Source d'Argent
Old Plantation Houses
Old Plantation Houses
Pointe Belize
Grand Cap
Pointe Jacques

Km 2 20

RODRIGUES

Viewpoint
Pte aux Cornes
Anse aux Anglais
Port Mathurin
Baie aux Huîtres
Camp du Roi
Mt. Persil
275 m
Mt. Grenade
205 m
Pte Coton
Pte Coton
Malgache Bay
Pte du Diable
Baie aux Huîtres
Mont Lubin
Handicraft Centre
Baie de l'Est
Baie du Nord
Pte Maniac
Mt. Quatre Vents
340 m
Grande Montagne
Mangues
Petit
Lataniers
Coromandel
Mt. Croupier
166 m
La Ferme
Quatre Gabriel
Vents
Petit Gravier
Pte Roche Noire
23
Mt. Cheri
165 m
La Fouche
Rivière Cocos
Port Sud-Est
Pâté Reynieux
Mt. Topaz
124 m
Pte Poursuite
Pte Palmiste
Petit Butte
Anse Grand Var
Pte Raffin
Frégate Island
Coral Caves
Pintades Island
Destinée Island
Plaine Corail
Anse Quitor
Gombrani Island
Crab Island
Pte Corail
Pierrot Island or Cat

Km 2 4

((00230) 832 0174/0866/0877 • (00230) 8320 622 • www.tourism-rodrigues.mu

RÉUNION

St Denis
Pte des Galets
Ste Marie
La Possession
Le Port
Dos d'Ane
Ste Suzanne
St André
St Paul
Dufour Cave
Salazie
Bras Panon
St Benoît
Piton Maido
Piton des Neiges
3070 m
Hell Bourg
Ste Anne
La Saline
Cilaos
Caves of Bras Chansons
La Plaine des Palmistes
Ste Rose
Pte des Châteaux
St Leu
La Fenêtre
Cave of Côte
La Plaine des Cafres
Les Avirons
Entre Deux
2632 m
Piton de la Fournaise
Takamaka
St Louis
Le Tampon
Pte de la Table
Pte de la Rivière St Etienne
St Pierre
Botanical Gardens
St Philipe
St Joseph

Km 10 20

((00262) 26 2210041 • www.la-reunion-tourisme.com

Praslin Island
Mahé Island
Platte Island

Coëtivy

INDIAN OCEAN

Mid Indian Basin

...lega Islands
(MAURITIUS)
...elin Island

Mascasarene Ridge

Rodrigues (MAURITIUS)

Mauritius

Réunion (FRANCE)

...dagascar Basin

Diego Garcia Island

N

Km 125 250

Adventures

Adventure	Country	Duration
Surfing the Seychelles (Grand 'Anse, Mahé).................	Seychelles...	2 hours +
Scuba Dive off the Seychelles (Mahé).........................	Seychelles...	2 hours +
Big-game Fishing in Mauritius...................................	Mauritius..	2 hours +
Flying around Réunion (St Gilles les Bains).................	Réunion...	1 hour
Diving off Mauritius (Grand Baie).............................	Mauritius..	2 hours +
Hiking Isalo National Park..	Madagascar...	1 day +

Surfing the Seychelles (Grand 'Anse, Mahé)

Requirements:
Valid passport only — and your surfboard, although local schools based on Mahé may provide them at a nominal cost.
Climate:
Generally warm to hot, with some tropical humidity. Trade winds offer the best surfing conditions from April to October.
Risk factor:
Virtually no risks, other than the occasional hungry shark and the breakneck speed of the waves.
Health:
No vaccinations are necessary and malaria poses no threat. The combination of wind and sea can cause severe dehydration and sunburn.
Pack:
Boardshorts and sunscreen are the most important, but be safe by taking a light beach shirt and/or sarong, as well as your own bottled water to the beach.
Facilities:
Waves are excellent, as are all the visitors' amenities on a group of islands that depends on its tourism income. Even the remotest of beaches has comfortable facilities for tourists.
Contact:
Travel Services Seychelles,
P.O. Box 356, Victoria.
Tel: 00248-32-2414
tss@tss.sc, www.tss.sc

Scuba Dive off the Seychelles (Mahé)

Requirements:
Valid passport only. Scuba-diving schools and operators do provide diving equipment.
Climate:
Weather is pleasantly hot all year, with sea temperatures seldom less than 18°C; November–February is humid, with heavy monsoon rains occasionally affecting water clarity. Diving is good all year, but best in October.
Risk factor:
The only risk is the inexperience of novice divers. Dangers from marine life are minimal – brush up on those presented by stone fish and the like.
Health:
No vaccinations required and malaria poses no threat.
Pack:
Swimwear and beach clothing should be enough, but pack your own scuba gear to avoid high costs of hiring.
Facilities:
Scuba facilities are good to excellent, and available through the main hotels and specialist operators. There are dive schools for novices as well as advanced dives for certified divers (take proof). Accommodation standards are high, and no camping is permitted.
Contact:
Indian Ocean Explorer Cruises,
P.O. Box 384, Victoria.
Tel: 00248-22-5844
info@ioexpl.com, www.ioexpl.com
divesy@seychelles.net

Big-game Fishing in Mauritius

Requirements:
A valid passport, as well as a return or onward air ticket. Visas, where required, are very easily obtained.
Climate:
Weather is generally good all year, but the west coast fishing grounds are dry and hot, especially from Jan–March, with Feb–March the wettest.
Risk factor:
Few to no risks, but big-game fishing is a specialized activity that demands both expertise and strength — novices should be accompanied by a skilled angler.
Health:
No vaccinations are necessary and malaria poses no threat, but sunburn can cause considerable discomfort.
Pack:
If travelling on a deep-sea fishing trip in a private capacity, make sure that you are fully prepared and well equipped. The services of a professional operator are highly recommended, and these will provide all the necessary gear.
Facilities:
Accommodation, be it budget or high-end, is seldom a problem, and hotels and private tour operators are generally extremely well equipped.
Contact:
Organisation de Pêche du Nord (Corsaire Club),
Trou aux Biches, Mauritius.
Tel: 00230-261-6267

Flying around Réunion (St Gilles les Bains)

Requirements:
Valid passport only, but some nationals may also require a visa. Consult your local embassy.
Climate:
Balmy to hot with seasonal rains and warm sea temperatures. Best time to visit May–October.
Risk factor:
Buckle up – and avoid the cyclone season January–March.
Health:
No immunizations are required, unless visitors are travelling through or from countries with a recent history of cholera or yellow fever.
Pack:
Light, summer clothing, and some rain gear if travelling in the warm wet period between November and April.
Facilities:
Generally good to very good visitors' amenities, and most of the independent helicopter companies are extremely knowledgeable and helpful.
Contact:
Helilagon, 97867 St Paul, CIDEX,
Altiport de l'Eperon, St Gilles les Hauts.
Tel: 00262-262-555555

Diving off Mauritius (Grand Baie)

Requirements:
A valid passport, as well as a return or onward air ticket. Visas, where required, are very easily obtained.
Climate:
Weather is generally good all year, but the west can be dry and hot, especially from Jan–March, with Feb–March the wettest.
Risk factor:
Deep-sea diving can be a very dangerous pastime; obey the rules of safety and etiquette, even in the idyllic waters of Mauritius, and employ the services of professional dive masters.
Health:
No vaccinations are necessary and malaria poses no threat. Sunburn can cause considerable discomfort.
Pack:
All equipment and accessories will be provided by established dive schools and dive operators; private diving trips are not recommended, especially for those who are not seasoned divers.
Facilities:
Accommodation is generally good to outstanding, and hotels and private tour operators are more than able to accommodate diving expeditions.
Contact:
Paradise Diving,
PLM. Mont Choisy, Coastal Rd,
Grand Baie, Mauritius.
Tel: 00230-265-6070

Hiking Isalo National Park

Requirements:
A valid passport and a visa are both required.
Climate:
Although the climate may vary considerably, tropical Madagascar is generally hot and humid throughout the year, particularly in the forested regions. September–December provides the best conditions for hikers, but avoid the rains between January and March.
Risk factor:
Malaria is rife, and rabies is common among wild dogs. The water is not drinkable, and bilharzia and giardia are present. AIDS is an increasing risk.
Health:
No immunizations are required, unless visitors are travelling through or from countries with a recent history of cholera or yellow fever.
Pack:
Comfortable but solid walking boots; lightweight clothing (days), warm clothing and a flashlight (nights), and waterproof gear for the rainy season.
Facilities:
The infrastructure is very modest, affording few luxuries.
Contact:
Unusual Destinations,
P.O. Box 97508, Petervale.
Tel: 0027-11-706-1991
info@unusualdestinations.com
www.unusualdestinations.com

The Skeleton Coast

The multiparty republics of neighbouring Botswana and Namibia cover the arid western and central interior of the southern subcontinent (including the Kalahari) and offer two rather different impressions of Africa. Botswana is entirely landlocked and punctuated with occasional pockets of bushveld, while Namibia is flanked by coastal desert plains. However, there are a number of important similarities that contribute to making this expansive region one of the wealthiest and most spectacular on the continent. Both countries have a long history of European settlement and domination, and the remnants of the colonial era continue to influence their latter-day sociopolitical landscape. The first to gain independence was Botswana, which until 1966 was known as the British protectorate of Bechuanaland. Namibia (formerly South West Africa) remained under the control of neighbouring South Africa until it gained independence in 1990, following protracted guerilla activity.

NAMIBIA

NAMIB DESERT

Namibia's most conspicuous drawcard is the Namib, an endless stretch of red sand interrupted with sparse vegetation. The desert comprises the Skeleton Coast and the Namib-Naukluft parks, covering 15 per cent of the country's landmass, including about 6.5 million hectares of some of the southern hemisphere's driest and most inhospitable terrain. These abandoned stretches of sand and gravel, hemmed in by relentless dune, are home to a range of unique flora and fauna, with nearly 200 vertebrates found nowhere else. Despite its desolation, it is a living desert, inhabited by gemsbok (oryx), bird flocks, succulent plants, insects and over 20 endemic reptiles.

SKELETON COAST

The most extraordinary of Namibia's many spectacles is the bone-white sands that comprise the great Skeleton Coast, an eerie expanse of beach that extends from the country's northern border to the Namib-Naukluft Park in the south. Hemmed in by the cold Atlantic in the west and the dry interior to the east, the 1.6 million hectares of the Skeleton Coast Park is an untamed wilderness divided into two main regions. The baking sand of the Namib covers the northern stretch, while the south is made up of dry gravel plains scattered with boulders and laced, in part, with seasonal rivers. Although there are few mammal species, it is renowned for its abundant bird life. The volatility of the elements and the relentless battering of wave and wind lend to this landscape an almost surreal beauty. The coast can be shrouded in mist for days, which helped to earn it the reputation as the world's largest shipping graveyard - over 100 vessels have run aground here.

WALVIS BAY

Positioned between the searing sands of the Namib in the south and the windswept shore of the Skeleton Coast in the north, Walvis Bay is the unofficial capital of Namibia's coastal stretch. Much of the social and economic activity of this thriving little city centres on its all-important natural harbour, the deepest in southwestern Africa. For centuries, small indigenous settlements remained undisturbed in this forgotten corner until Dutch, German and British colonial powers stumbled across the treasure that is its natural harbour. The town was only reincorporated into official national boundaries four years after independence, remaining an essential 'outpost' of South Africa until 1994. Walvis Bay acts as a vital instrument in the national economy, servicing the freight and fishing industries, and is an ideal base for adventure activities offered by its immediate environment, including four-wheel-drive and desert exploration, and bird-watching.

KAOKOLAND

Kaokoland refers to the vast rocky, mountainous terrain bordered in the north by the Cunene River and by the Hoanib in the south, and immediately inland of the northern Skeleton Coast. It is a wild and unpredictable wilderness populated largely by the Himba and Herero-speaking people, who gave the area its name. Kaokoland's river waters are the home of crocodiles, and small herds of Kaokoland elephant continue to roam this desolate landscape. The region fell victim to devastating drought in the 1970s and much of its wildlife was decimated, but the land is slowly recovering and Kaokoland remains a popular tourist drawcard, especially to view the lumbering great elephants.

WINDHOEK

The Namibian capital – although small and underdeveloped compared to other world capitals – is the great tourist centre and economic hub of the nation, a vibrant, colourful and modern city catering well for the international traveller. The nightlife is lively, the facilities adequate and the infrastructure impressive for such a small nation. The colours, cultures and panoramic vistas are a photographer's dream, and in recent years there has been a healthy resurgence in the tourism market. Windhoek lies at the very heart of this burgeoning industry and has, as a result, become every inch the modern city, with its fair share of attractions and detractions. Nonetheless, the city remains the gateway to the adventures promised by the coast, desert and wild expanse beyond waiting to be explored.

FISH RIVER CANYON

The Fish River Canyon comprises wind-carved depressions, inclines and rock formations moulded from the inland plateau. The Canyon is dramatic in its simplicity, with valleys and gullies slicing through its geological foundations laid 2,000 million years ago. The Canyon is some 160km long and, in parts, nearly 600m deep, putting it second in size only to the Grand Canyon in North America.

BOTSWANA

MAKGADIKGADI PANS

The Makgadikgadi Pans form part of Botswana's 7,000km[2] Makgadikgadi Pans Game Reserve and Nxai Pan National Park, and it is the world's largest natural salt pans, covering 12,000km[2]. The pans once formed part of a massive inland lake, but all that exists today on the remaining plains is an endless sea of cracked, empty, salt-encrusted pans, most notable among them the Sowa, Ntwetwe and Nxai pans of Makgadikgadi. Summer rains fill the depressions to create the lifeblood of the wildlife that flocks here during the rainless winter.

KALAHARI DESERT

The Kalahari is the largest continuous stretch of sand in the world. Flat, dry and empty, it covers more than 80 per cent of Botswana, stretching from the Orange River towards the more equatorial regions. This wide-open expanse – whipped by clouds of dust, lashed by the summer rains and baked by the sun – was formed 200 million years ago when the supercontinent Gondwana began to break up to form the landmasses of the southern hemisphere. The foundation of sandstone, shale and coal is 300 million years old, while some rocks date back three billion years.

OKAVANGO DELTA

The Okavango Delta is the world's largest, spreading over 15,000km[2]. This wetland wilderness creates a vast green oasis in the middle of otherwise inhospitable terrain. It is here that the waters of the country's only perennial river, the Okavango, spread across its flood plain, soaking deep into the surrounding lands. The river should fulfil all Botswana's water requirements, but not only is it shared with Namibia, much of the water is lost to evaporation. Drawing on the water supply for irrigation and domestic consumption also encroaches on the river and its delta. Conservationists are fighting to have the delta declared a World Heritage Site to secure its protection.

BAINES' BAOBABS

The stands of baobabs that dot pockets of the otherwise empty interior symbolize the grandeur of this sparse country. From the outskirts of settlements to the featureless pans, the horizon is broken by the silhouette of a baobab, indigenous resident for thousands of years. The most prominent of these are the Seven Sisters. Referred to as Baines' Baobabs, this cluster of 'upside down' trees is named in honour of the artist and explorer, Thomas Baines, who captured them on canvas in 1862. Baines' Baobabs stand on the rim of Kudiakam Pan.

GABORONE

The capital is a relatively small, compact city, and although there may be few conventional tourist sites, Gaborone has enjoyed phenomenal growth since it was appointed the capital of the new nation in the 1960s. Back then, the rather insignificant village had no more than a scattering of homes, but it boasted one important resource – water. As a result, it was declared a city within 20 months of becoming the capital and, largely because of its considerable mineral wealth, is one of the fastest-growing urban settlements on the African continent. Its road infrastructure lends Gaborone a modern appearance, with impressive restaurants, hotels, casinos and other entertainment centres. The modern city has retained at least some of its distinct African flavour – its side streets are filled with craft markets and vending stalls, and few other urban centres of similar status can boast the same number of small reserves and conservation land on its doorstep.

Although the portion of the southern African subcontinent covered by Namibia and Botswana is generally rather dry (and, in places, inhospitable) terrain, the land is rich in diamonds and other minerals (uranium, copper, nickel and coal). The national economies of both countries rely considerably on these valuable exports.

The Skeleton Coast, Namibia

Okavango Delta, Botswana

Baines' Baobabs, Botswana

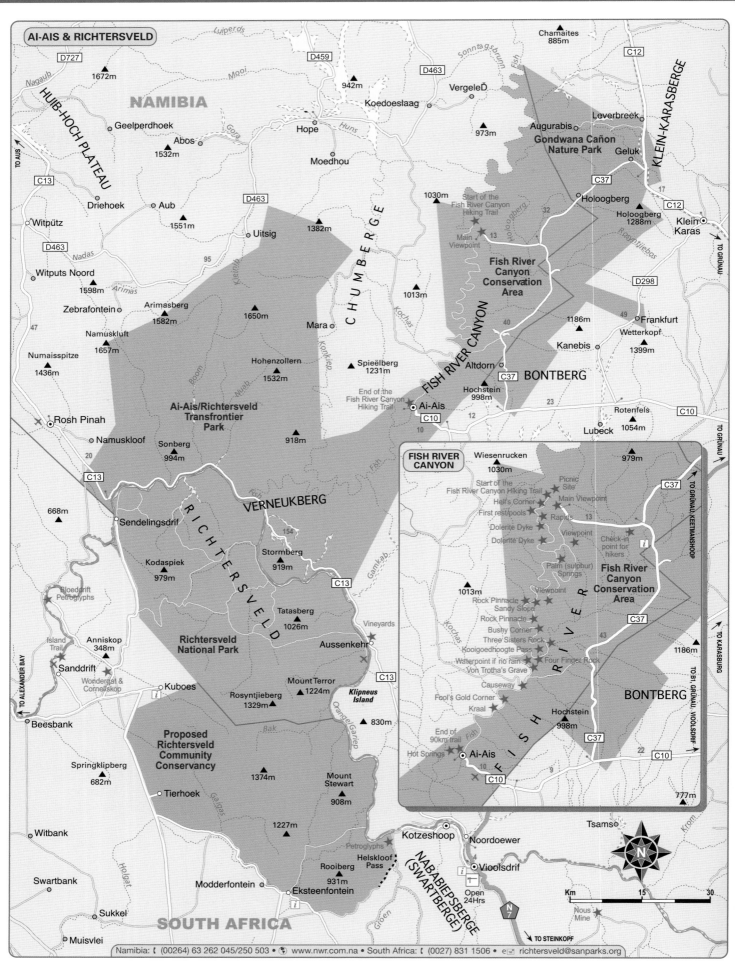

Ai-Ais & Richtersveld

Namibia, South Africa

AI-AIS & RICHTERSVELD

NAMIBIA

HUIB-HOCH PLATEAU

TO AUS

D727
1672m

Nagaub

Geelperdhoek

Abos
1532m

Hope

Moedhou

Koedoeslaag
942m

Luiperds

Mooi

D459

D463

VergeleD

Chamaites
885m

C12

KLEIN-KARASBERGE

Sonntagsbrunn

Fish

973m

Augurabis

Leverbreek

Gondwana Cañon
Nature Park

Geluk

C13

Driehoek

Witpütz

D463

Nadas

Aub
1551m

Uitsig

D463

1382m

C
H
U
M
B
E
R
G
E

Goa

Huns

1030m

Start of the
Fish River Canyon
Hiking Trail

Main
Viewpoint

C37

Holoogberg

Holoogberg
1288m

C12

17

Klein
Karas

TO GRÜNAU

Witputs Noord
1598m

Arimas

95

Kleinb

Hohenberg

Fish River
Canyon
Conservation
Area

13

32

D298

Zebrafontein

Arimasberg
1582m

1650m

Mara

Boom

Kochas

Konkiep

1013m

40

1186m

Kanebis

49

Frankfurt

Wetterkopf
1399m

Namuskluft
1657m

Numaisspitze
1436m

Hohenzollern
1532m

Nuab

Spieëlberg
1231m

FISH RIVER CANYON

Altdorn

C37

BONTBERG

Rosh Pinah

Ai-Ais/Richtersveld
Transfrontier
Park

Sonberg
994m

918m

End of the
Fish River Canyon
Hiking Trail

Ai-Ais
C10

Hochstein
998m

12

23

Rotenfels
1054m

Lubeck

C10

TO GRÜNAU

Namuskloof

20

C13

668m

Sendelingsdrif

R
I
C
H
T
E
R
S
V
E
L
D

VERNEUKBERG

154

Stormberg
919m

Fish

10

**FISH RIVER
CANYON**

Wiesenrucken
1030m

Start of the
Fish River Canyon Hiking Trail

Hell's Corner

First rest/pools

Dolerite Dyke

Dolerite Dyke

Picnic
Site

Main Viewpoint

Rapids

Viewpoint

13

Check-in
point for
hikers

C37

TO GRÜNAU, KEETMANSHOOP

979m

i

47

Kodaspiek
979m

Bloeddrift
Petroglyphs

Island
Trail

Anniskop
348m

TO ALEXANDER BAY

Sanddrift

Wondergat &
Cornellskop

Beesbank

Springklipberg
682m

Witbank

Swartbank

Sukkel

Muisvlei

Tatasberg
1026m

Richtersveld
National Park

Kuboes

i

Rosyntjieberg
1329m

Proposed
Richtersveld
Community
Conservancy

Tierhoek

1374m

Modderfontein

Gamkab

Vineyards

Aussenkehr

C13

Mount Terror
1224m

Klipneus
Island

830m

Mount
Stewart
908m

1227m

Petroglyphs

Rooiberg
931m

Eksteenfontein

i

Helskloof
Pass

NABABIEPSBERGE
(SWARTBERGE)

Bak

Gariep

Orange

Galgas

Holgat

Groen

Palm (sulphur)
Springs

1013m

Rock Pinnacle

Sandy Slope

Rock Pinnacle

Bushy Corner

Three Sisters Rock

Kooigoedhoogte Pass

Waterpoint if no rain

Von Trotha's Grave

Causeway

Fool's Gold Corner

Kraal

End of
90km trail

Hot Springs

Ai-Ais

Viewpoint

Kochas

F
I
S
H

R
I
V
E
R

Fish

Four Finger Rock

Fish River
Canyon
Conservation
Area

C37

43

C37

C37

1186m

BONTBERG

777m

Hochstein
998m

10

9

22

C10

TO KARASBURG

TO B1, GRÜNAU, VIOOLSDRIF

Kotzeshoop

Noordoewer

4

Vioolsdrif

Open
24Hrs

N7

TO STEINKOPF

Tsams

Krom

Nous
Mine

TO AUS

i

i

N

SOUTH AFRICA

Km   15   30

Namibia: ☎ (00264) 63 262 045/250 503 • 🌐 www.nwr.com.na • South Africa: ☎ (0027) 831 1506 • ✉ richtersveld@sanparks.org

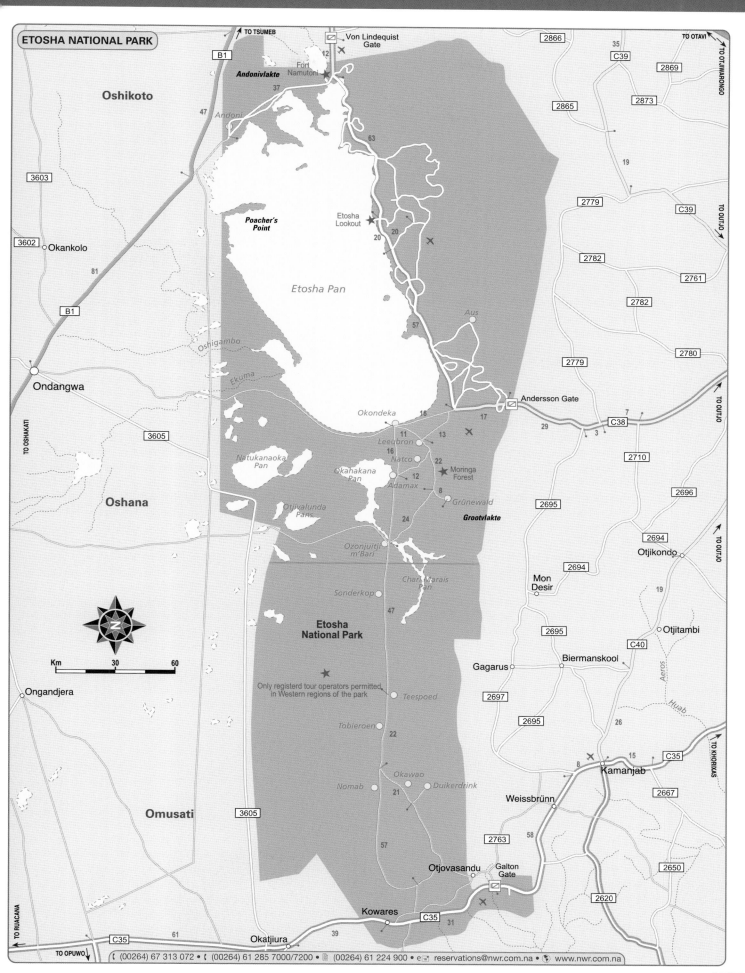

ETOSHA NATIONAL PARK

TO TSUMEB
B1

Oshikoto

Andonivlakte

Fort Namutoni

Von Lindequist Gate

TO OTAVI
TO OTJIWARONGO

2866
35
C39
2869

2865
2873

B1
47
Andoni
37
12

63
19

3603

2779
C39

Poacher's Point
Etosha Lookout
20
20

2782

3602 Okankolo
81
57

Etosha Pan
2761
2782

B1
Oshigambo
2780

Ondangwa
Ekuma
Aus

2779

Okondeka
16
Andersson Gate

3605
Leeubron
11
13
17
C38
29
7
3

Natukanaoka Pan
16
Natco
22
Moringa Forest
2710

Oshana
Okahakana Pan
12
Adamax
8
Grünewald

24
Grootvlakte
2695

Otjivalunda Pans
2694

Ozonjuitji m'Bari
2694

Otjikondo

Chari Marais Pan
Mon Desir
19

Sonderkop
47

Etosha National Park
2695
C40
Otjitambi

Gagarus
Biermanskool

Only registerd tour operators permitted in Western regions of the park
Teespoed
2697

Aeros

Huab
Tobieroen
22
2695
26

15
C35
TO KHORIXAS

Km   30   60

Nomab
21
Okawao
Duikerdrink
8
Kamanjab

Ongandjera
Weissbrünn
2667

Omusati
3605
2763
58
2650

Otjovasandu
Galton Gate

TO RUACANA
C35
61
Kowares
C35
31
2620

TO OPUWO
Okatjiura
39

((00264) 67 313 072 • ((00264) 61 285 7000/7200 • (00264) 61 224 900 • e reservations@nwr.com.na • www.nwr.com.na

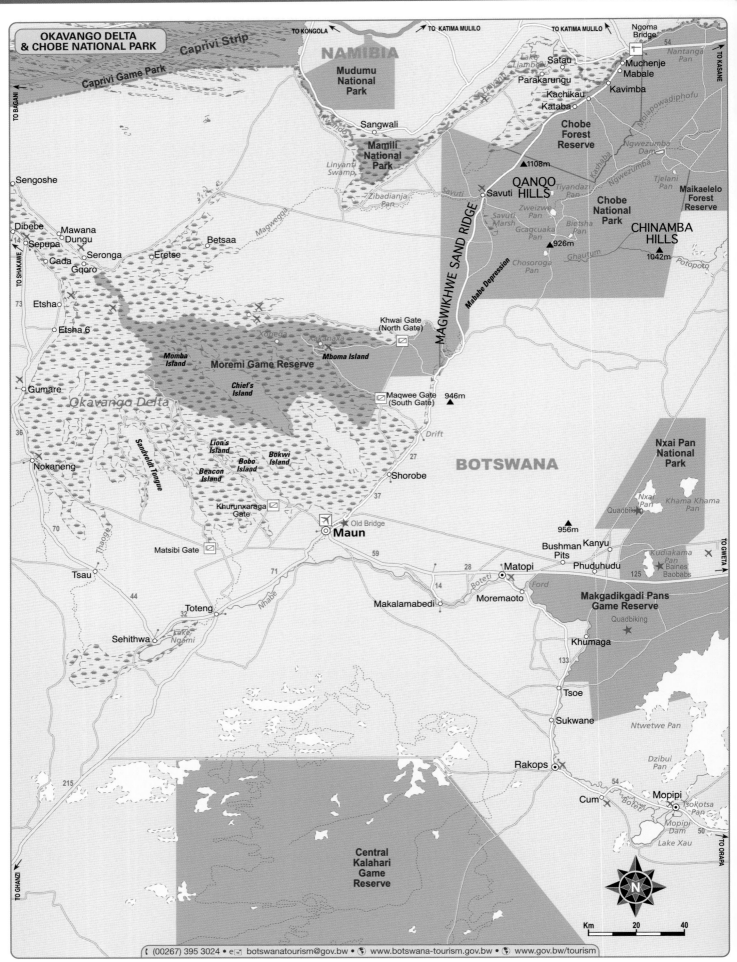

OKAVANGO DELTA
& CHOBE NATIONAL PARK

Caprivi Strip

TO KONGOLA
TO KATIMA MULILO
TO KATIMA MULILO

Ngoma
Bridge
54

Caprivi Game Park

NAMIBIA

Mudumu
National
Park

Nantanga
Pan

TO KASANE

TO BAGANI

Muchenje
Mabale

Lake
Liambezi

Satau
Parakarungu
Kachikau
Kataba

Kavimba

Sangwali

Mamili
National
Park

Chobe
Forest
Reserve

Ngwezumba
Dam

Sengoshe

Linyanti
Swamp

▲1108m

Tjelani
Pan

Maikaelelo
Forest
Reserve

Zibadianja
Pan

Savuti

QANQO
HILLS

Tiyandazi
Pan

Chobe
National
Park

Dibebe
Sepupa

Mawana
Dungu

Betsaa

Magwegqa

Savuti
Marsh

Zweizwe
Pan

CHINAMBA
HILLS

Cada
Seronga
Gqoro

Eretse

Gcagcuaka
Pan

Bietsha
Pan

926m

1042m

Chosoroga
Pan

Ghautum

Etsha

Khwai Gate
(North Gate)

Etsha 6

Xobega

Xakanaxa

Mboma Island

Momba
Island

Moremi Game Reserve

Chief's
Island

Maqwee Gate
(South Gate)

946m

Nxai Pan
National
Park

Gumare

Okavango Delta

Drift

Nxar
Pan

Khama Khama
Pan

Quadbiking

Lion's
Island

Bokwi
Island

Beacon
Island

Bobo
Island

27

BOTSWANA

Nokaneng

Sandveldt Tongue

Shorobe

37

Khurunxaraga
Gate

Matsibi Gate

Old Bridge

Maun

Bushman
Pits

Kanyu

Kudiakama
Pan

TO GWETA

Phuduhudu

Baines
Baobabs

125

Thaoge

59

Matopi

Tsau

71

28

Moremaoto

Makgadikgadi Pans
Game Reserve

Nhabe

14

Boteti

Ford

Quadbiking

Toteng

Makalamabedi

Khumaga

Sehithwa

Lake
Ngami

133

Tsoe

Sukwane

Ntwetwe Pan

Dzibui
Pan

Rakops

54

Mopipi

215

Cum

Boteti

Tsokotsa
Pan

Mopipi
Dam

50

Lake Xau

TO ORAPA

Central
Kalahari
Game
Reserve

TO GHANZI

N

Km   20   40

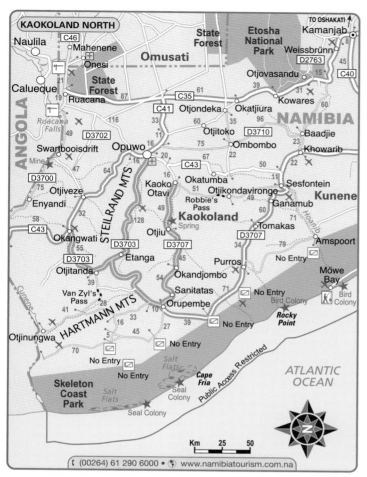

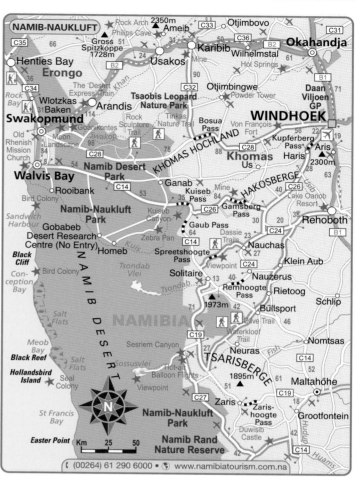

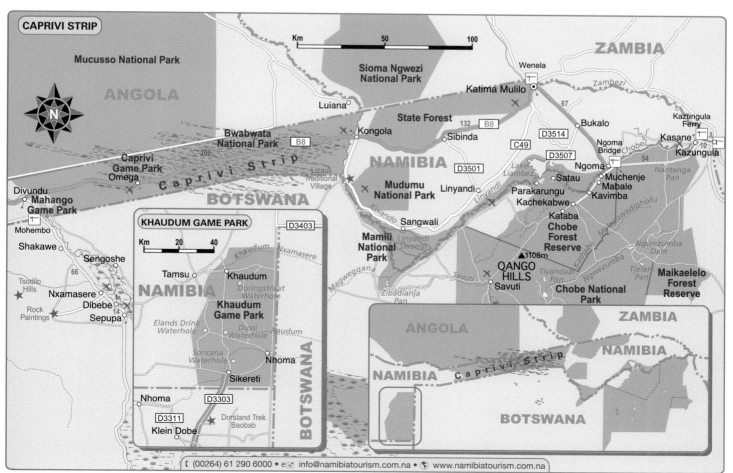

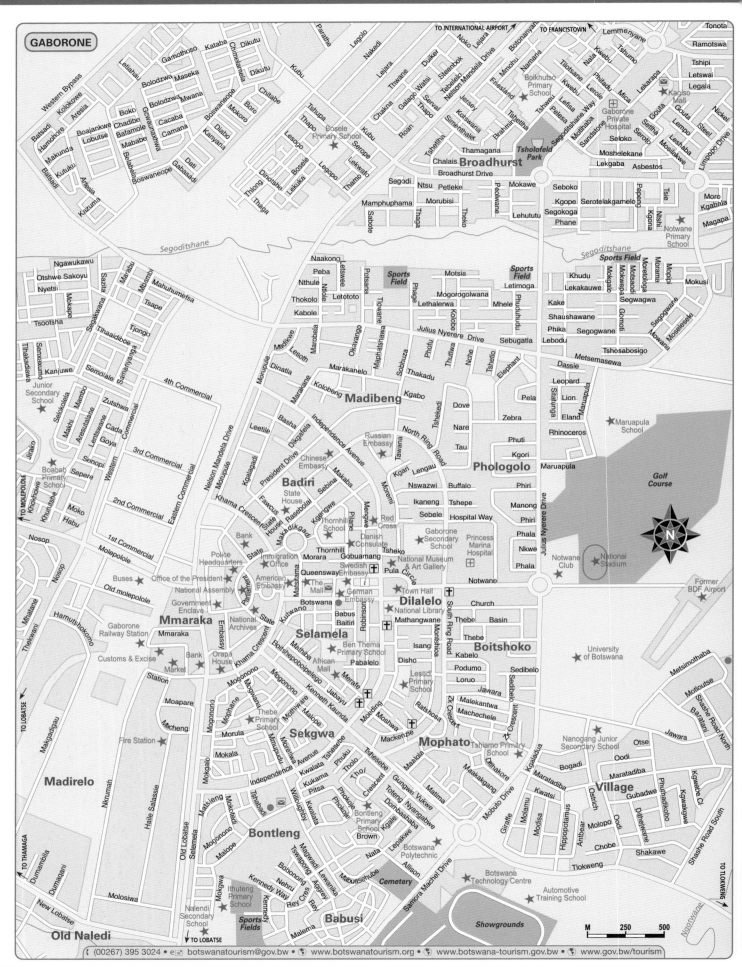

Swakopmund Namibia
Walvis Bay Namibia

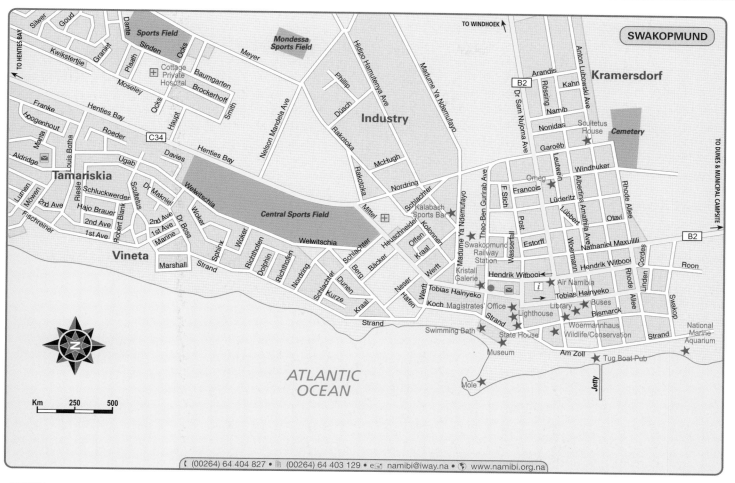

Kramersdorf

Industry

Tamariskia

Vineta

ATLANTIC OCEAN

Km 250 500

((00264) 64 404 827 • (00264) 64 403 129 • namibi@iway.na • www.namibi.org.na

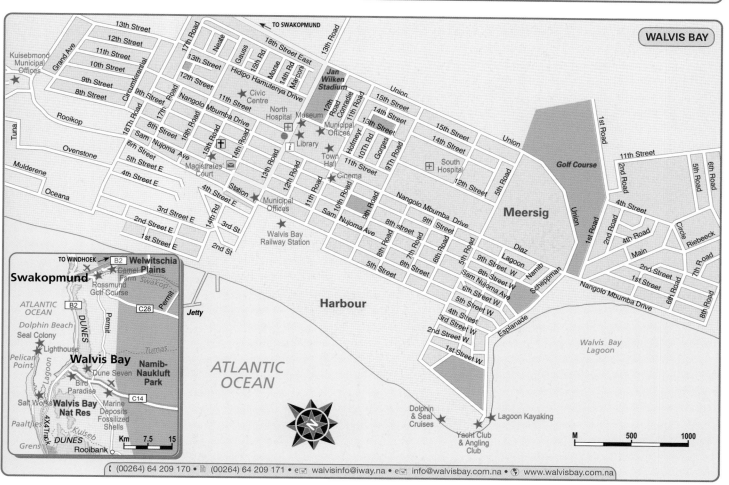

TO SWAKOPMUND

Jan Wilken Stadium

Meersig

Golf Course

Harbour

ATLANTIC OCEAN

Swakopmund

ATLANTIC OCEAN

Walvis Bay

Namib-Naukluft Park

Km 7.5 15

M 500 1000

((00264) 64 209 170 • (00264) 64 209 171 • walvisinfo@iway.na • info@walvisbay.com.na • www.walvisbay.com.na

Windhoek Namibia

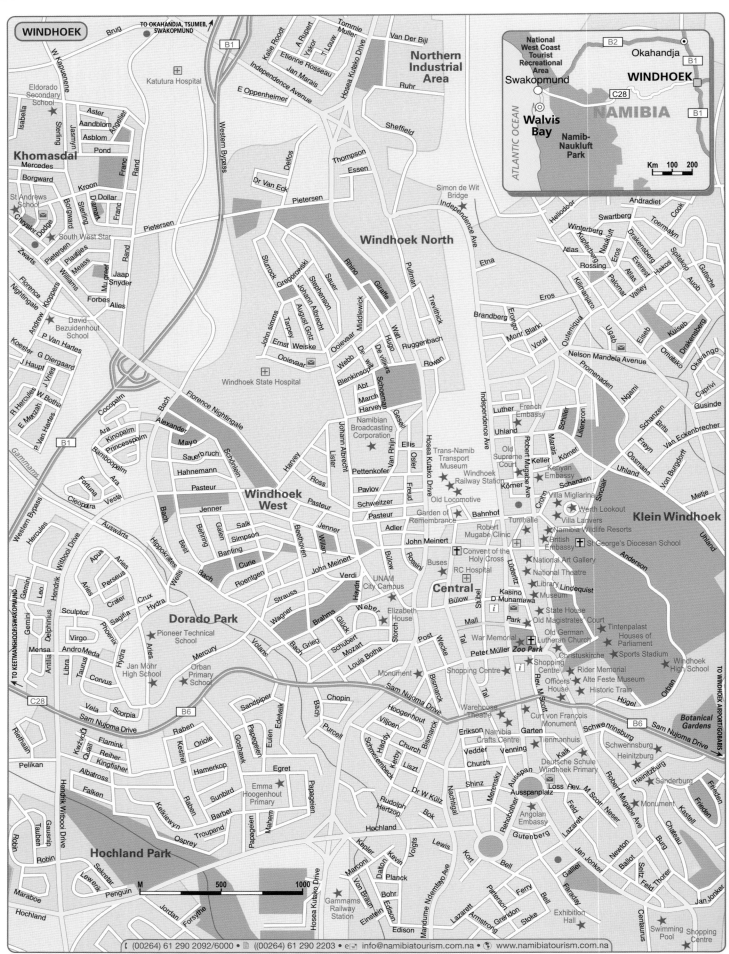

WINDHOEK

National West Coast Tourist Recreational Area

ATLANTIC OCEAN

Swakopmund

Walvis Bay

Namib-Naukluft Park

Okahandja

WINDHOEK

NAMIBIA

Km 100 200

TO OKAHANDJA, TSUMEB, SWAKOPMUND

Northern Industrial Area

Khomasdal

Eldorado Secondary School

Katutura Hospital

Windhoek North

St Andrews School

South West Star

David Bezuidenhout School

Simon de Wit Bridge

Windhoek State Hospital

Namibian Broadcasting Corporation

Windhoek West

Trans-Namib Transport Museum

Windhoek Railway Station

Old Locomotive

Garden of Remembrance

Old Supreme Court

French Embassy

Kenyan Embassy

Villa Migliarina

Werth Lookout

Villa Lanvers

Namibia Wildlife Resorts

British Embassy

St George's Diocesan School

Klein Windhoek

Dorado Park

Pioneer Technical School

Jan Möhr High School

Orban Primary School

UNAM City Campus

Elizabeth House

Robert Mugabe Clinic

John Meinert

Convent of the Holy Cross

RC Hospital

Buses

National Art Gallery

National Theatre

Library

Museum

Lindequist

Central

Kasino D Munamawa

State House

Old Magistrates' Court

War Memorial

Peter Müller

Zoo Park

Christuskirche

Rider Memorial

Tintenpalast

Houses of Parliament

Sports Stadium

Shopping Centre

Officers House

Alte Feste Museum

Historic Train

Windhoek High School

Monument

Warehouse Theatre

Curt von François Monument

Namibia Crafts Centre

Garten

Tienmanhuis

Schwennsburg

Schwennsburg

Heinitzburg

Hochland Park

Emma Hoogenhout Primary

Vedder Church

Deutsche Schule Windhoek Primary

Ausspanplatz

Angolan Embassy

Rehobother

Sanderburg

Monument

Kastell

Frieden

Gammams Railway Station

Exhibition Hall

Swimming Pool

Shopping Centre

Botanical Gardens

TO KEETMANSHOOP/SWAKOPMUND

TO WINDHOEK AIRPORT/GOBABIS

M 500 1000

KEETMANSHOOP

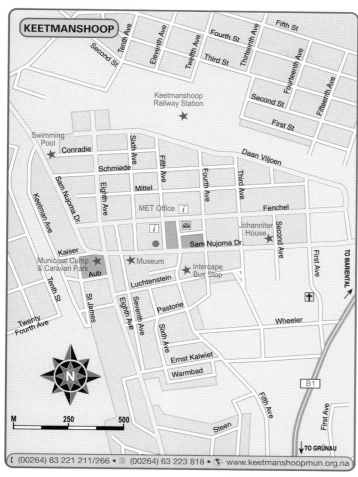

Tenth Ave · Second St · Eleventh Ave · Twelfth Ave · Fourth St · Third St · Thirteenth Ave · Fifth St · Fourteenth Ave · Fifteenth Ave · Second St · First St

Keetmanshoop Railway Station

Swimming Pool · Conradie · Sixth Ave · Daan Viljoen · Schmiede · Fifth Ave · Fourth Ave · Third Ave · Mittel · Fenchel · Eighth Ave · MET Office · Sam Nujoma Dr. · Johanniter House · Second Ave · Sam Nujoma Dr. · First Ave · Kaiser · Museum · Intercape Bus Stop · Municipal Camp & Caravan Park · Aub · Luchtenstein · Keetman Ave · St James · Pastorie · Wheeler · Tenth St · Seventh Ave · Sixth Ave · Eighth Ave · Twenty Fourth Ave · Ernst Kalwiet · Warmbad · Fifth Ave · B1 · Steen · First Ave · TO MARIENTAL · TO GRÜNAU

M 250 500

((00264) 63 221 211/266 • 🖹 (00264) 63 223 818 • 🌐 www.keetmanshoopmun.org.na

GOBABIS

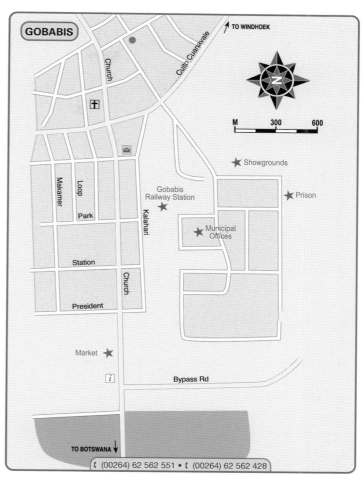

TO WINDHOEK · Church · Cuito Cuanavale · Showgrounds · Makamer · Loop · Park · Gobabis Railway Station · Kalahari · Prison · Municipal Offices · Station · Church · President · Market · Bypass Rd · TO BOTSWANA

M 300 600

((00264) 62 562 551 • ((00264) 62 562 428

HENTIES BAY

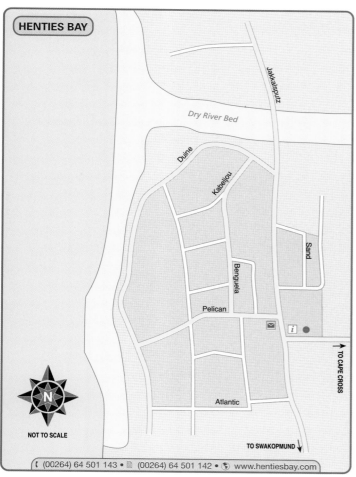

Jakkalsputz · Dry River Bed · Duine · Kabeljou · Sand · Benguela · Pelican · Atlantic · TO CAPE CROSS · TO SWAKOPMUND

N
NOT TO SCALE

((00264) 64 501 143 • 🖹 (00264) 64 501 142 • 🌐 www.hentiesbay.com

KATIMA MULILO

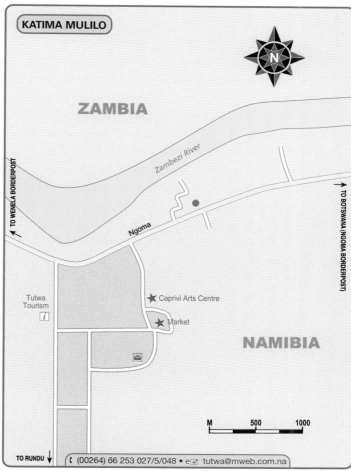

ZAMBIA · Zambezi River · TO WENELA BORDERPOST · TO BOTSWANA (NGOMA BORDERPOST) · Ngoma · Tutwa Tourism · Caprivi Arts Centre · Market · NAMIBIA · TO RUNDU

M 500 1000

((00264) 66 253 027/5/048 • e✉ tutwa@mweb.com.na

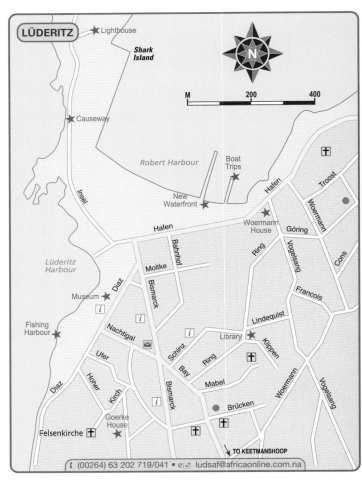

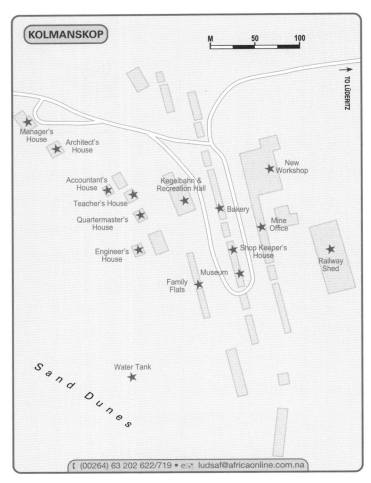

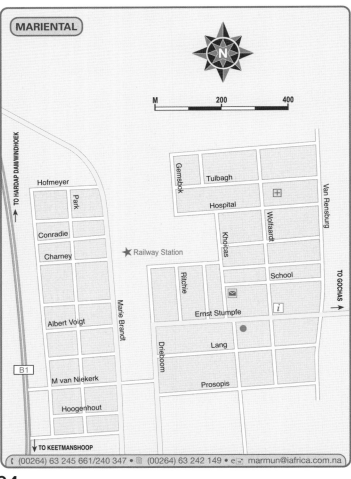

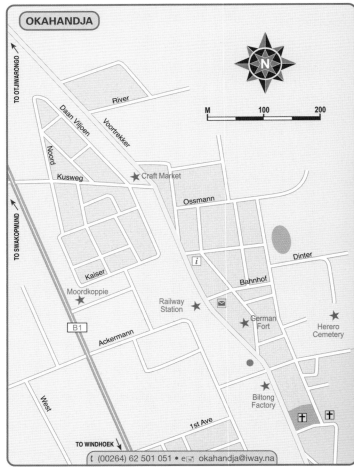

164

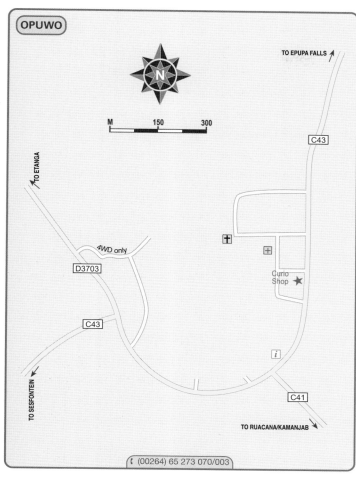

OPUWO

TO EPUPA FALLS

TO ETANGA

C43

4WD only

D3703

C43

Curio Shop

i

C41

TO SESFONTEIN

TO RUACANA/KAMANJAB

((00264) 65 273 070/003

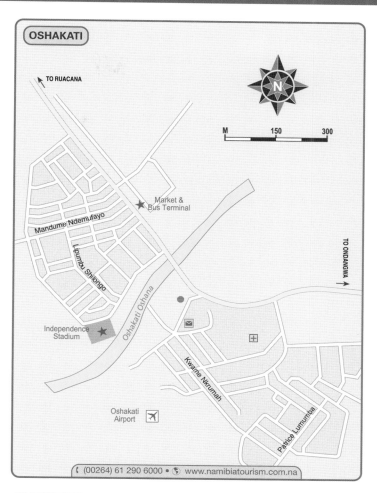

OSHAKATI

TO RUACANA

Market & Bus Terminal

Mandume Ndemufayo

Lipumbu Shiongo

Oshakati Oshana

Independence Stadium

Kwame Nkrumah

TO ONDANGWA

Patrice Lumumba

Oshakati Airport

((00264) 61 290 6000 • www.namibiatourism.com.na

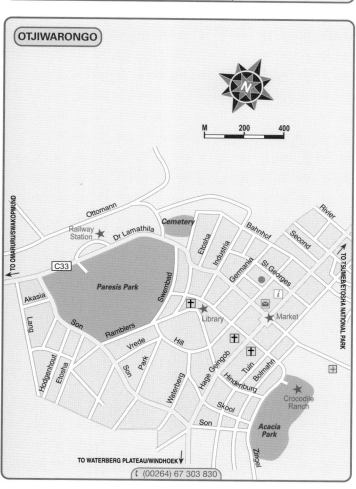

OTJIWARONGO

TO OMARURU/SWAKOPMUND

Ottomann

Railway Station

Dr Lamathila

Cemetery

Rivier

Bahnhof

Etosha

Industria

Germania

St Georges

Second

C33

Paresis Park

Swembad

i

Akasia

Library

Market

TO TSUMEB/ETOSHA NATIONAL PARK

Lang

Son

Ramblers

Vrede

Hill

Hage Geingob

Tuin

Bolmahn

Hodgenhout

Etosha

Son

Park

Waterberg

Hindenburg

Crocodile Ranch

Skool

Son

Zingel

Acacia Park

TO WATERBERG PLATEAU/WINDHOEK

((00264) 67 303 830

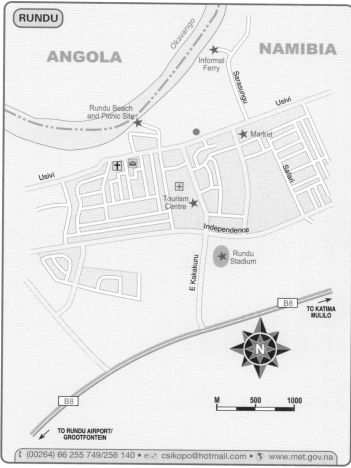

RUNDU

Okavango

ANGOLA

NAMIBIA

Informal Ferry

Sarasungu

Usivi

Rundu Beach and Picnic Site

Market

Usivi

Safari

Tourism Centre

Independence

E Kakakuru

Rundu Stadium

B8

TO KATIMA MULILO

B8

TO RUNDU AIRPORT/ GROOTFONTEIN

((00264) 66 255 749/256 140 • e csikopo@hotmail.com • www.met.gov.na

165

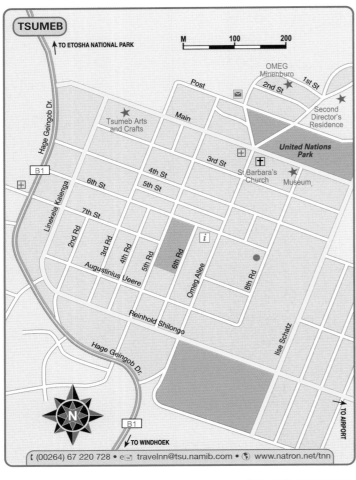

TSUMEB

TO ETOSHA NATIONAL PARK

M 100 200

OMEG Minenburo
1st St
2nd St
Post
Second Director's Residence
Main
Tsumeb Arts and Crafts
United Nations Park
3rd St
4th St
St Barbara's Church
5th St
Museum
6th St
7th St
Hage Geingob Dr.
Linekela Kalenga
B1
2nd Rd
3rd Rd
4th Rd
5th Rd
6th Rd
8th Rd
Augustinius Ueere
Omeg Allee
Ilse Schatz
Reinhold Shilongo
Hage Geingob Dr.
N
B1
TO WINDHOEK
TO AIRPORT

((00264) 67 220 728 • e travelnn@tsu.namib.com • www.natron.net/tnn

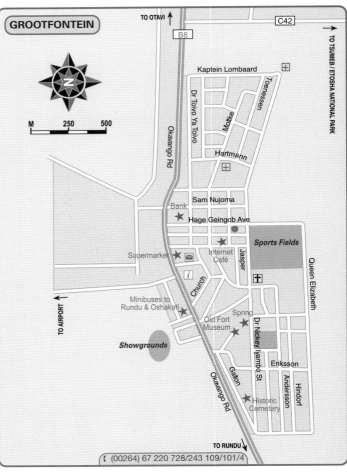

GROOTFONTEIN

TO OTAVI
C42
B8
TO TSUMEB / ETOSHA NATIONAL PARK
Kaptein Lombaard
Dr Toivo Ya Toivo
Toenessen
Moltke
Hartmann
N
M 250 500
Sam Nujoma
Bank
Hage Geingob Ave
Sports Fields
Okavango Rd
Supermarket
Internet Café
Jasper
Queen Elizabeth
Church
Minibuses to Rundu & Oshakati
Old Fort Museum
Spring
Dr Nickey Iyambo St
Eriksson
Showgrounds
Galton
Andersson
Hindorf
TO AIRPORT
Okavango Rd
Historic Cemetery
TO RUNDU

((00264) 67 220 728/243 109/101/4

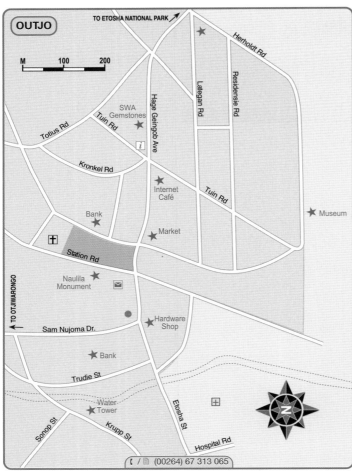

OUTJO

TO ETOSHA NATIONAL PARK
Herholdt Rd
M 100 200
Lategan Rd
Residensie Rd
SWA Gemstones
Tuin Rd
Hage Geingob Ave
Totius Rd
Kronkel Rd
Internet Café
Tuin Rd
Bank
Market
Museum
Station Rd
TO OTJIWARONGO
Naulila Monument
Hardware Shop
Sam Nujoma Dr.
Bank
Trudie St
Water Tower
Sonop St
Krupp St
Etosha St
Hospital Rd

(/ (00264) 67 313 065

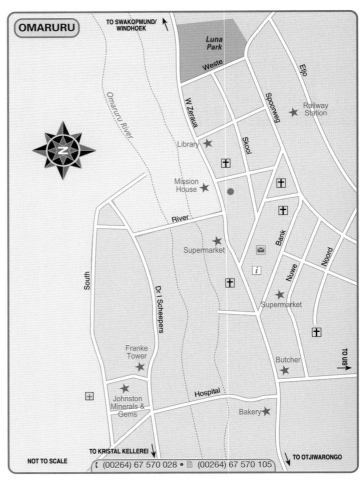

OMARURU

TO SWAKOPMUND/ WINDHOEK
Luna Park
Weste
Etjo
Omaruru River
W Zeraua
Spoorweg
Railway Station
Library
Skool
Mission House
N
River
Bank
Supermarket
South
Nuwe
Dr I Scheepers
Supermarket
Noord
Franke Tower
Butcher
Hospital
Johnston Minerals & Gems
TO UIS
Bakery
NOT TO SCALE
TO KRISTAL KELLEREI
TO OTJIWARONGO

((00264) 67 570 028 • (00264) 67 570 105

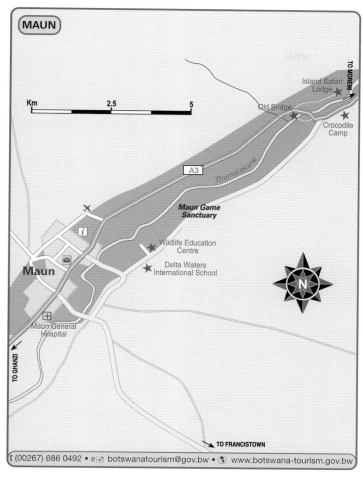

MAUN

Km 2.5 5

Island Safari Lodge
Old Bridge
Crocodile Camp
TO MOREMI
TO MAUN
A3
Thamalakane
Maun Game Sanctuary
Wildlife Education Centre
Delta Waters International School
Maun
Maun General Hospital
TO GHANZI
TO FRANCISTOWN

((00267) 686 0492 • e botswanatourism@gov.bw • www.botswana-tourism.gov.bw

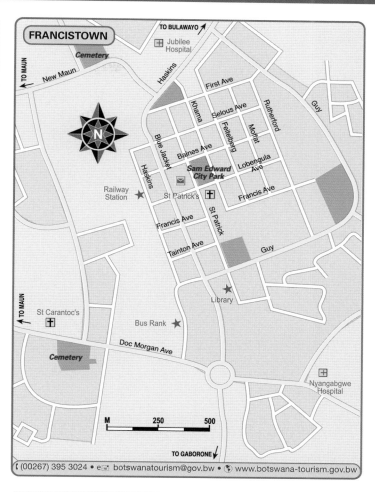

FRANCISTOWN

TO BULAWAYO
Jubilee Hospital
Cemetery
New Maun
Haskins
First Ave
Khama
Selous Ave
Rutherford
Moffat
Guy
Blue Jacket
Balnes Ave
Feitelberg
Lobengula Ave
Sam Edward City Park
Haskins
Railway Station
St Patrick's
Francis Ave
Francis Ave
St Patrick
Tainton Ave
Guy
Library
TO MAUN
St Carantoc's
Bus Rank
Doc Morgan Ave
Cemetery
Nyangabgwe Hospital
M 250 500
TO GABORONE

((00267) 395 3024 • e botswanatourism@gov.bw • www.botswana-tourism.gov.bw

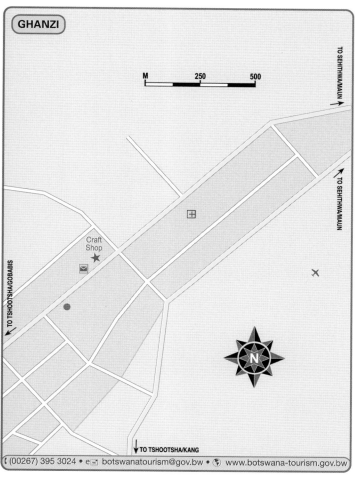

GHANZI

M 250 500
TO SEHTHWA/MAUN
TO SEHTHWA/MAUN
Craft Shop
TO TSHOOTSHA/GOBABIS
TO TSHOOTSHA/KANG

((00267) 395 3024 • e botswanatourism@gov.bw • www.botswana-tourism.gov.bw

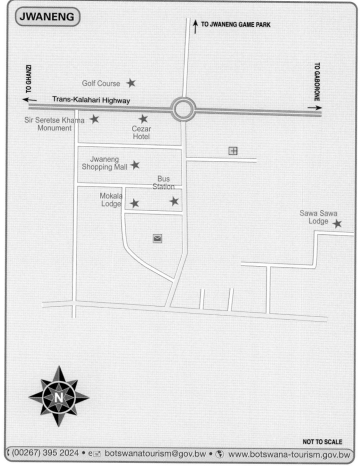

JWANENG

TO JWANENG GAME PARK
TO GHANZI
Golf Course
Trans-Kalahari Highway
TO GABORONE
Sir Seretse Khama Monument
Cezar Hotel
Jwaneng Shopping Mall
Bus Station
Mokala Lodge
Sawa Sawa Lodge
NOT TO SCALE

((00267) 395 2024 • e botswanatourism@gov.bw • www.botswana-tourism.gov.bw

Kanye Botswana Mahalapye Botswana
Nata Botswana Selebi Phikwe Botswana

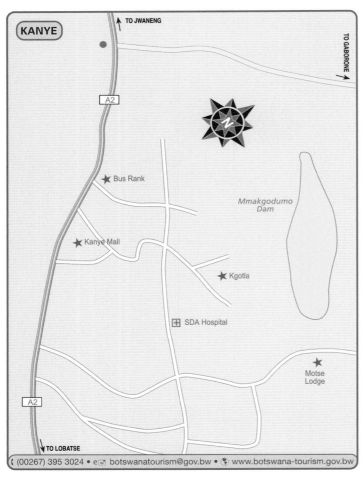

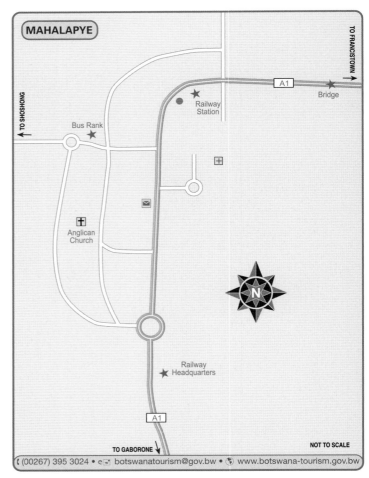

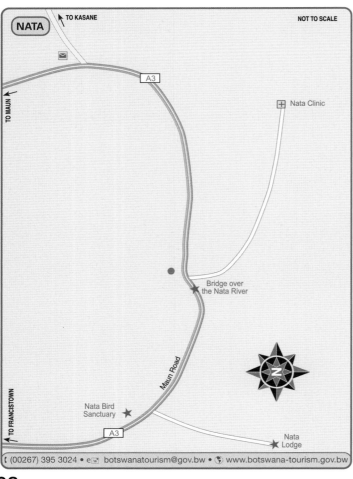

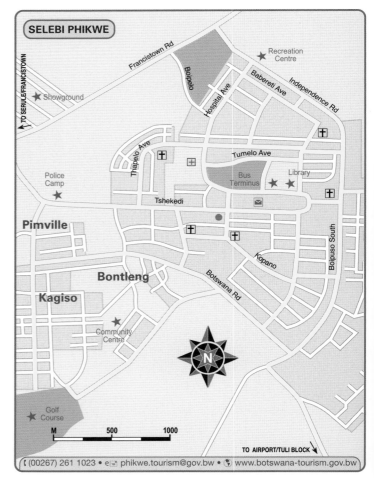

168

Adventures

Adventure	Country	Duration
Driving Namibia's Skeleton Coast Park	Namibia	2 days +
Driving through Kaokoland	Namibia	3 days
Hiking the Fish River Canyon	Namibia	2 days +
River-rafting on the Cunene	Namibia	2 days +
Quadbiking across Nxai and Makgadikgadi Pans	Botswana	2 days +
On Horseback through Tuli	Botswana	3 - 10 days

Driving Namibia's Skeleton Coast Park

Requirements:
Valid passport; visa for non-RSA, -US and -EU visitors (confirm with your travel agent).
Climate:
Generally moderate, often misty. Heavy summer rains (Jan–March) with flash floods and high temperatures.
Risk factor:
Private trips should be well planned, taking into account the volatility of desert and ocean.
Health:
Only visitors travelling from or through areas where yellow fever is endemic need to provide proof of vaccination; no other vaccinations are required. Malaria is endemic in the northern areas, so prophylactic treatment is essential. There is a risk of AIDS and bilharzia in this area.
Pack:
Warm clothing for the fog-laden coast; sunscreen is essential; comfortable lightweight clothing for hot days.
Facilities:
Some plush private operations, but generally simple to very rustic camping and overnight facilities.
Contact:
Wilderness Safaris Namibia.
P.O. Box 6850, Windhoek, Namibia.
Tel: 00264-61-225178
info@nts.com.na
www.wilderness/safaris.com

Driving through Kaokoland

Requirements:
Valid passport; visa for visitors other than those from RSA, US and EU.
Climate:
Winters are moderate but cool, with heavy summer rains January–March.
Risk factor:
Isolated and inhospitable to the ill-prepared traveller. Party of at least two 4x4s essential on roads that are essentially dust tracks. Professional assistance in planning is advised.
Health:
Only visitors travelling from or through areas where yellow fever is endemic need provide proof of vaccination. Malaria endemic to northern area. There is a risk of AIDS and bilharzia in this region.
Pack:
Sunscreen and comfortable lightweight clothing essential, as are first-aid supplies, water rations and vehicle parts.
Facilities:
Although locals are generally accommodating, guesthouses are few and far between — visitors need to be entirely self-sufficient. Some reliable tour operators service this area.
Contact:
Kaokohimba Safaris,
P.O. Box 11580, Windhoek, Namibia.
Tel: 00264-61-222378

Hiking the Fish River Canyon

Requirements:
Valid passport; visa for visitors not from RSA, US and EU. Hiking permits required from Nature Conservation.
Climate:
Summers are blistering, but winter night temperatures can plummet.
Risk factor:
Terrain is hard-going and tough, with plenty of dangers for the uninitiated. Professional assistance in planning is advised.
Health:
Only visitors travelling from or through areas where yellow fever is endemic need to provide proof of vaccination; no other vaccinations are required. AIDS and bilharzia in this area.
Pack:
Sunscreen and comfortable lightweight clothing are essential, as are comprehensive first-aid supplies and plenty of water rations.
Facilities:
Varying from comfortable to very simple, but there are plenty of agents operating from Lüderitz and Keetmanshoop. Hiking is seasonal and is permitted only from May–August.
Contact:
Namibia Tourism Board,
Private Bag 13306, Windhoek, Namibia.
Tel: 00264-61-2842111 / 2906000
info@namibiatourism.com.na

River-rafting on the Cunene

Requirements:
Valid passport; visa for visitors not from RSA, US and EU.
Climate:
Winters are moderate but cool, with heavy summer rains January– March, which may bring flash floods.
Risk factor:
Relatively dangerous to extremely dangerous in places, with a number of risks that may prove serious (if not fatal) if handled incorrectly. Professional operators are recommended.
Health:
Only visitors travelling from or through areas where yellow fever is endemic need to provide proof of vaccination. Malaria is endemic to the north, and there is a risk of AIDS and bilharzia.
Pack:
Sunscreen and comfortable, light clothing essential; waterproofing and safety equipment a must. First-aid supplies and water rations required in parts.
Facilities:
Rough and physically demanding, but most operations (many RSA-based) provide some simple comforts.
Contact:
Felix Unite,
P.O. Box 2807, Clareinch 7700.
Tel: 00264-63-297161
reservations@felixunite.co.za
www.felixunite.com

Quadbiking across Nxai and Makgadikgadi Pans

Requirements:
Valid passport; visa for visitors not from RSA, US and EU. A 4x4 vehicle is essential.
Climate:
Generally sunny and hot. Heavy summer rains December–February; freezing night-time temperatures in winter.
Risk factor:
Private excursions are ill-advised; thin-crusted pans are very dangerous; inexperienced bikers can cause severe environmental damage.
Health:
Malaria is endemic, so prophylactic treatment is essential. Tickbite fever is common after the first rains, and there have been reports of hepatitis A. AIDS and bilharzia are widespread.
Pack:
Sunscreen and lightweight protective clothing are essential.
Facilities:
Simple but comfortable private lodges and designated camp sites for self-drive visitors; luxury San and Jack's camps are in a concession area.
Contact:
Uncharted Africa Safari Company,
P.O. Box 173, Francistown, Botswana.
Tel: 00267-241-2277
office@unchartedafrica.com
www.unchartedafrica.com

On Horseback through Tuli

Requirements:
Valid passport; visa for visitors not from RSA, US and EU.
Climate:
Generally sunny and hot. Heavy summer rains December–February; freezing night-time temperatures in winter.
Risk factor:
Private excursions are ill-advised, and visitors are required to be competent riders – outfitters will refuse to take novices throughout what is essentially treacherous territory.
Health:
Malaria is endemic, so prophylactic treatment is essential. Tickbite fever is common after the first rains, and there have been reports of hepatitis A. AIDS and bilharzia are widespread in the area.
Pack:
Sunscreen and lightweight protective clothing is essential.
Facilities:
Mostly luxurious private lodges and safari-style tented camps, but also catered and self-catered operations for the budget-conscious.
Contact:
Mawana Horse Safaris,
Tel: 00267-72-320024 or 0027-11-442-2267
lvhs@infotech.co.za
www.lvhsafaris.co.za

Southern Africa

The southernmost sweep of the subcontinent comprises South Africa and the independent kingdoms of Lesotho and Swaziland that fall within its boundaries. For the most part this is a wilderness of wide-open spaces stretching from mountain to sea, desert to savanna. The undulating grasslands, wooded valleys, open bushveld and towering cityscapes combine to create a rich tapestry that forms a breathtaking backdrop to the natural wonder of southern Africa and the diverse cultural heritage of its many peoples - from the Zulu to the San - as they embrace full democracy. For intrepid travellers and adventurers, the prime attraction is the region's unrivalled wildlife heritage, at its most impressive in the big-game regions of Mpumalanga, KwaZulu-Natal and the Eastern Cape. The landscape is arid and desolate in parts, while other areas are verdant and bountiful. Such contrasting faces offer a unique look at a region that varies from First World sophistication to pastoralist Africa.

SOUTH AFRICA

TABLE MOUNTAIN
The distinctive flat-topped summit of Table Mountain is the most recognizable landmark in Cape Town (the Mother City) and lies in the heart of the Cape Floral Kingdom, the smallest but richest of the world's six broad floral regions. Fynbos (hardy, fine-leaved shrubs and plants that have taken root in these nutrient-poor soils) accounts for about 80 per cent of the 8,500-plus plant species on the mountain slopes. The world-famous Kirstenbosch National Botanical Garden lies on the slopes of Table Mountain. Many wild animals once roamed these rocky slopes, including Africa's great cats and a number of antelope species. It is currently the domain of the dassie, or rock hyrax, easily viewed from the ever popular revolving cable car that carries sightseers up the mountain. The highest point on Table Mountain is MacClear's Beacon, 1,086m above sea level, and at the foot lies Table Bay.

GARDEN ROUTE
The Garden Route is an extraordinarily beautiful stretch of countryside that winds along the southwestern contour of the subcontinent for some 200km between the town of Mossel Bay and the mouth of the Storms River. The route is dotted with charming little towns and villages, including some of the country's most notable holiday resorts, such as Knysna and Plettenberg Bay. The Garden Route boasts an astounding array of indigenous flora and fauna and attracts adventurers and holiday-makers from far afield. Flanked in the east by the warm Indian Ocean and in the west by the sometimes parched hinterland, the tranquil coves and sandy dunes are a traveller's paradise. The coastline is battered in parts by wind and pummelled by the ocean, yet much of it is traversed via well-developed roads, with only an occasional dirt road leading to out-of-the-way beachside havens.

ORANGE RIVER
The mighty Orange River is South Africa's longest, most prominent and most significant watercourse. Flowing approximately 2,250km across some of South Africa's most desolate terrain, the Orange is said to drain almost half the country's rainwater. Although much of the land through which it winds is treeless and relatively arid, the waters of the Orange are a vital resource for the farmlands that line its course, as well as a popular playground for river-rafters and other adventurers. Many of the abundant hikes and walking trails in the Orange River Valley date from a time when the region was originally settled by early farmers and prospectors. Located along the Orange's rugged path is Augrabies Falls, the sixth-largest waterfall in the world, with 19 individual cataracts cascading more than 90m. The Orange empties its vital resource on the Atlantic coastline, where South Africa borders Namibia. It is here that early explorers discovered some of the country's first diamond and gold deposits.

ROBBEN ISLAND
Less than 12km off the shores of Table Bay and Cape Town's bustling Waterfront lies tiny Robben Island, isolated from the mainland by the tumultuous waters of the Atlantic. Plagued by a sorrowful history (including ostracized lepers and political prisoners), Robben Island is best known as the place where former South African president Nelson Mandela spent much of his 27-year imprisonment. It is acclaimed throughout the Western world as the spiritual home of South Africa's struggle for democracy and is considered a remarkable human rights monument. The 570ha island is a World Heritage Site, and conservationists have hailed it as one of the world's few remaining unspoiled ecosystems.

DRAKENSBERG ESCARPMENT
The western boundary of KwaZulu-Natal is demarcated by a series of crests that comprise the spectacular Drakensberg range. This in turn forms the Great Escarpment that separates the province from the mountain kingdom of Lesotho beyond. The scenic splendour of these impressive mountain slopes and lush valleys is also the picturesque setting for some of the country's finest national parks and game reserves, which are characterized by towering peaks and rolling hills. Among the most spectacular of the towering ridges are Cathedral Peak (with streams and rivers coursing down its rocky inclines) and the magnificent Mont-Aux-Sources Amphitheatre, which in turn towers over the valleys of the Drakensberg's Royal Natal National Park. In stark contrast to the vision of sparkling waters gushing through the rocky gorges of the Drakensberg in the summer rainfall season, the winter landscape yields a blanket of snow that descends on the towns and villages that punctuate the craggy rise of the Great Escarpment. This 'Mountain of the Dragon' is the most significant of the Escarpment, and its age-old rock faces are dotted with caves painted by ancient San artists.

BLYDE RIVER CANYON
One of the most spectacular of the country's natural wonders is the Blyde River Canyon in Mpumalanga – an awesome conglomeration of impressive buttresses and forested inclines that forms the centrepoint of the 27,000ha nature reserve of the same name. Some 800m deep and 1.5km wide in places, the canyon comprises a series of sculptured bowl formations carved by the abrasive action of the Blyde River. The most unusual of these are the famed Bourke's Luck Potholes, named after a prospector who sought his fortune in the gold yielded by this stony ground.

LESOTHO

THABANA NTLENYANA
Part of the Drakensberg mountain range that formed over 150 million years ago, Thabana Ntlenyana in the northeastern corner of Lesotho is the highest peak in the southern subcontinent.Thabana Ntlenyana (ironically meaning 'beautiful little mountain') lies an impressive 3,480m above sea level, offering spectacular views over some of the most panoramic vistas in southern Africa. In winter, the snow-covered slopes are icy cold, a chilling wind whipping its way through every valley and down rock cliffs. Fortunately, the balmy summer months - the rain season - bring with them a green blanket that covers the rugged terrain. The hike to the top of Thabana Ntlenyana is along 25km of some of the roughest terrain in Lesotho, rising to an altitude of some 2,000m.

SANI PASS
High above some of the tiny nation's most magnificent scenery stands Sani Top, an eerily windswept haven for hikers and adventurers who have made their way up the treacherous pass through the rocky mountains – and the summit boasts the highest pub in Africa. Sani Pass, the highest in Lesotho and South Africa, snakes through the Mkhomazana River Valley in the Drakensberg from just beyond the tiny village of Himeville to Sani Top. Sani rises 1,000m over a distance of 7km, providing the only road link between Lesotho and KwaZulu-Natal. Established in 1955, the route is demanding at best and perilous at worst, and can only be undertaken in a four-wheel-drive. The broader region caters for hikers, trailists and 'pony trekkers', usually led by the blanket-clad local Basotho people.

SWAZILAND

FEAST OF THE FIRST FRUITS
Like all the indigenous peoples of southern Africa, the Swazi place enormous importance on traditional spiritual beliefs and ancient customs. One of the most significant of the age-old celebrations that plays a role in Swaziland is the Incwala, or Feast of the First Fruits, held annually after the last full moon in December. A group of traditional Swazi warriors makes its way to the Indian Ocean that skirts South Africa's eastern shore to collect sea water said to hold magical powers, while another band of warriors retrieves fresh water from the region's abundant rivers. This special water is used in a cleansing ceremony in which the Ngwenyama (the king) is blessed and sacrifices are made to the ancestors.

The spectacle of southern Africa's varied wildlife, the diversity of its extraordinary landscape and the rich cultural heritage of its indigenous peoples has ensured that the region has enjoyed an unprecedented resurgence in its tourism and hospitality industries. South Africa in particular has now emerged as one of the leading players in Africa's social, political and economic arena.

Ndebele artwork, Lesotho

Wilderness, Garden Route, South Africa

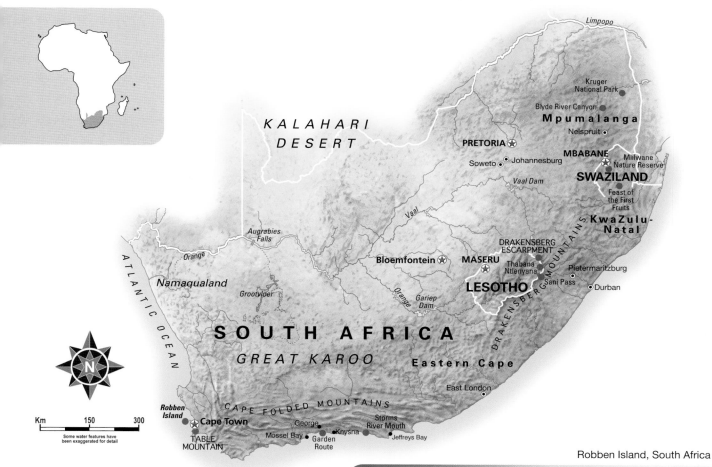

Limpopo

Kruger
National Park

Blyde River Canyon

Mpumalanga

Nelspruit

*KALAHARI
DESERT*

PRETORIA ☆

MBABANE ☆

Mlilwane
Nature Reserve

Soweto ◉ ● Johannesburg

SWAZILAND

Vaal Dam

Feast of
the First
Fruits

Vaal

**KwaZulu-
Natal**

Augrabies
Falls

DRAKENSBERG
ESCARPMENT

Orange

Bloemfontein ☆

MASERU ☆

Pietermaritzburg
◉

Namaqualand

Thabana
Ntlenyana

Sani Pass

● Durban

Grootvloer

Orange

Gariep
Dam

LESOTHO

SOUTH AFRICA

GREAT KAROO

Eastern Cape

East London
◉

A T L A N T I C   O C E A N

CAPE FOLDED MOUNTAINS

*Robben
Island*

☆ **Cape Town**

George

Storms
River Mouth

Mossel Bay ● ●
Garden
Route

● Knysna

● Jeffreys Bay

TABLE
MOUNTAIN

Km   150   300

Some water features have
been exaggerated for detail

Robben Island, South Africa

171

Blyde River Canyon South Africa

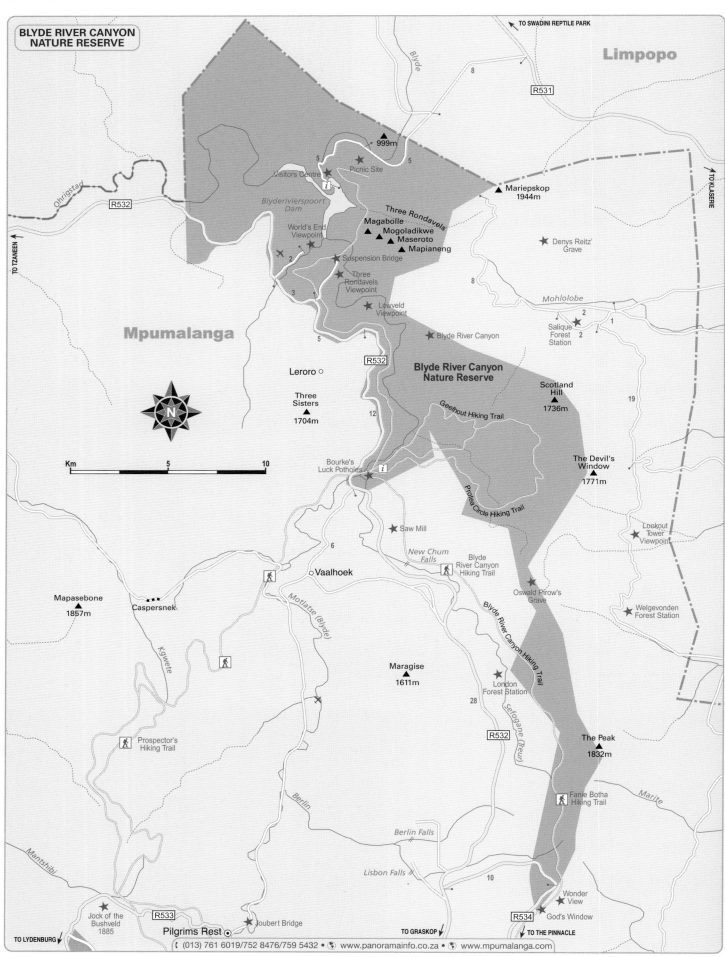

BLYDE RIVER CANYON
NATURE RESERVE

TO SWADINI REPTILE PARK

Blyde

Limpopo

R531

8

Ohrigstad

R532

TO TZANEEN

TO KLASERIE

999m

5

5

Picnic Site

Visitors Centre

i

Blyderivierspoort Dam

World's End Viewpoint

Three Rondavels

Mariepskop
1944m

Magabolle

Mogoladikwe

Maseroto

Mapianeng

Denys Reitz' Grave

2

Suspension Bridge

Three Rondavels Viewpoint

3

Mpumalanga

5

Lowveld Viewpoint

Blyde River Canyon

R532

Mohlolobe

8

Salique Forest Station

2

2

1

Leroro

Blyde River Canyon Nature Reserve

Scotland Hill
1736m

19

N

Three Sisters
1704m

12

Geelhout Hiking Trail

The Devil's Window
1771m

Km   5   10

Bourke's Luck Potholes

i

Protea Circle Hiking Trail

Lookout Tower Viewpoint

Saw Mill

New Chum Falls

6

Vaalhoek

Blyde River Canyon Hiking Trail

Oswald Pirow's Grave

Welgevonden Forest Station

Mapasebone
1857m

Caspersnek

Kgwete

Motlatse (Blyde)

Maragise
1611m

London Forest Station

28

Blyde River Canyon Hiking Trail

Sefogane (Treur)

R532

The Peak
1832m

Marite

Prospector's Hiking Trail

Berlin

Fanie Botha Hiking Trail

Berlin Falls

Mantshibi

Lisbon Falls

10

Wonder View

Jock of the Bushveld
1885

R533

Joubert Bridge

Pilgrims Rest

TO GRASKOP

R534

God's Window

TO LYDENBURG

TO THE PINNACLE

((013) 761 6019/752 8476/759 5432 • www.panoramainfo.co.za • www.mpumalanga.com

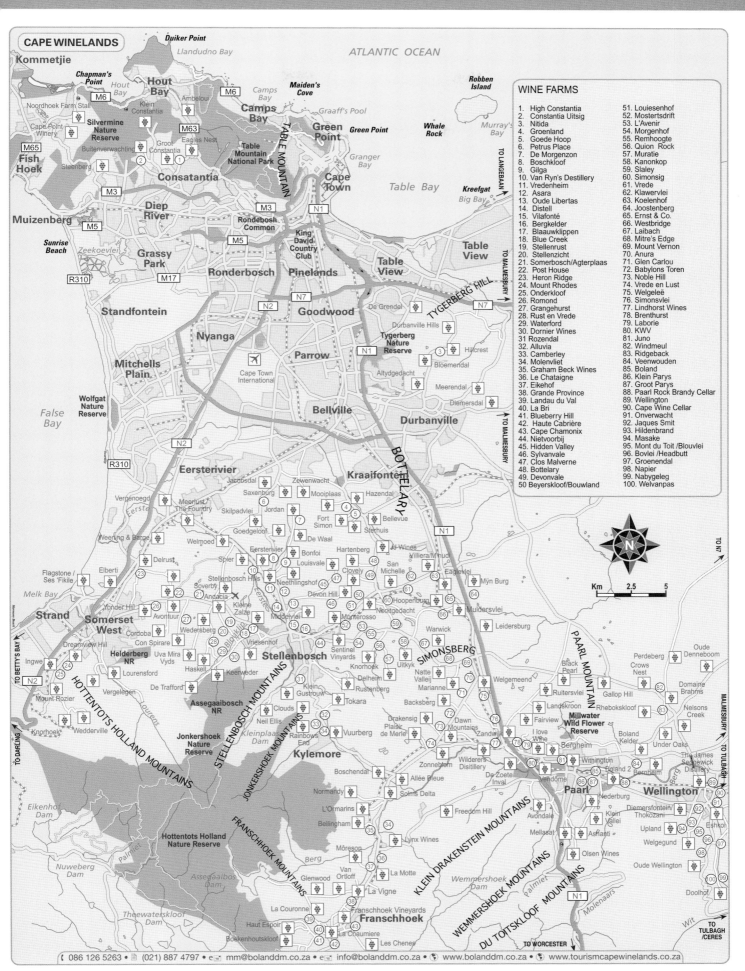

CAPE WINELANDS

ATLANTIC OCEAN

WINE FARMS

1.	High Constantia	51.	Louiesenhof
2.	Constantia Uitsig	52.	Mostertsdrift
3.	Nitida	53.	L'Avenir
4.	Groenland	54.	Morgenhof
5.	Goede Hoop	55.	Remhoogte
6.	Petrus Place	56.	Quion Rock
7.	De Morgenzon	57.	Muratie
8.	Boschkloof	58.	Kanonkop
9.	Gilga	59.	Slaley
10.	Van Ryn's Distillery	60.	Simonsig
11.	Vredenheim	61.	Vrede
12.	Asara	62.	Klawervlei
13.	Oude Libertas	63.	Koelenhof
14.	Distell	64.	Joostenberg
15.	Vilafonté	65.	Ernst & Co.
16.	Bergkelder	66.	Westbridge
17.	Blaauwklippen	67.	Laibach
18.	Blue Creek	68.	Mitre's Edge
19.	Stellenrust	69.	Mount Vernon
20.	Stellenzicht	70.	Anura
21.	Somerbosch/Agterplaas	71.	Glen Carlou
22.	Post House	72.	Babylons Toren
23.	Heron Ridge	73.	Noble Hill
24.	Mount Rhodes	74.	Vrede en Lust
25.	Onderkloof	75.	Welgeleë
26.	Romond	76.	Simonsvlei
27.	Grangehurst	77.	Lindhorst Wines
28.	Rust en Vrede	78.	Brenthurst
29.	Waterford	79.	Laborie
30.	Dornier Wines	80.	KWV
31.	Rozendal	81.	Juno
32.	Alluvia	82.	Windmeul
33.	Camberley	83.	Ridgeback
34.	Molenvliet	84.	Veenwouden
35.	Graham Beck Wines	85.	Boland
36.	Le Chataigne	86.	Klein Parys
37.	Eikehof	87.	Groot Parys
38.	Grande Province	88.	Paarl Rock Brandy Cellar
39.	Landau du Val	89.	Wellington
40.	La Bri	90.	Cape Wine Cellar
41.	Blueberry Hill	91.	Onverwacht
42.	Haute Cabrière	92.	Jaques Smit
43.	Cape Chamonix	93.	Hildenbrand
44.	Nietvoorbij	94.	Masake
45.	Hidden Valley	95.	Mont du Toit /Blouvlei
46.	Sylvanvale	96.	Bovlei /Headbutt
47.	Clos Malverne	97.	Groenendal
48.	Bottelary	98.	Napier
49.	Devonvale	99.	Nabygeleg
50	Beyerskloof/Bouwland	100.	Welvanpas

Km   2.5   5

(086 126 5263 • ☎ (021) 887 4797 • e✉ mm@bolanddm.co.za • e✉ info@bolanddm.co.za • 🌐 www.bolanddm.co.za • 🌐 www.tourismcapewinelands.co.za)

173

Cederberg Wilderness Area   South Africa

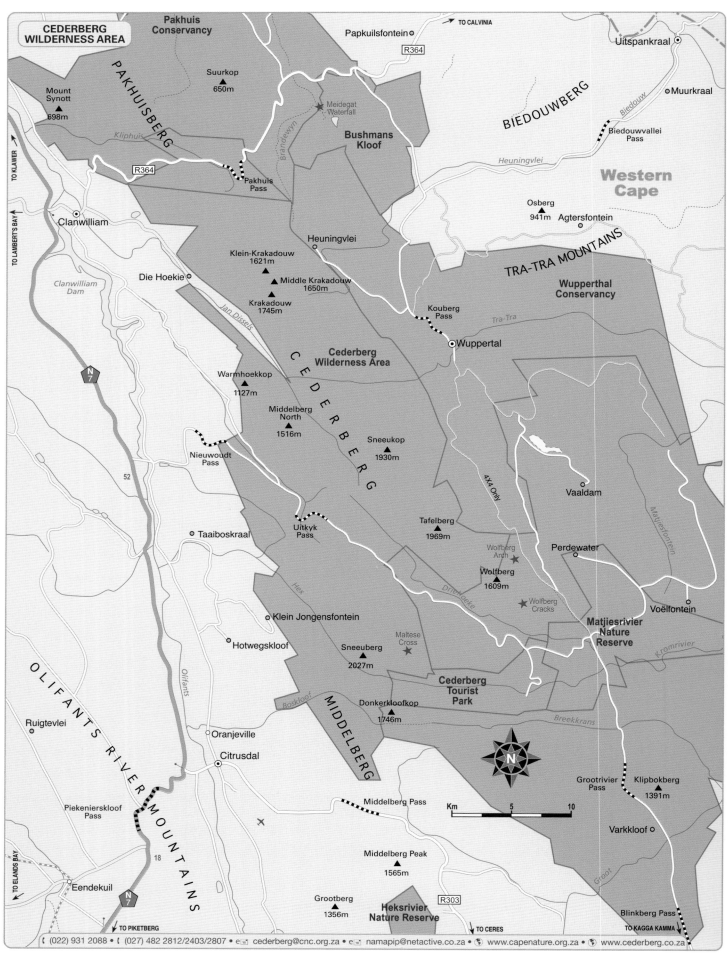

CEDERBERG
WILDERNESS AREA

Pakhuis
Conservancy

TO CALVINIA

Papkuilsfontein

R364

Uitspankraal

PAKHUISBERG

Suurkop
650m

Meidegat
Waterfall

Bushmans
Kloof

BIEDOUWBERG

Muurkraal

Biedouw

Biedouwvallei
Pass

Mount
Synott
698m

Kliphuis

R364

Pakhuis
Pass

Heuningvlei

Western
Cape

Clanwilliam

Osberg
941m   Agtersfontein

Heuningvlei

TRA-TRA MOUNTAINS

Die Hoekie

Klein-Krakadouw
1621m

Middle Krakadouw
1650m

Wupperthal
Conservancy

Clanwilliam
Dam

Jan Dissels

Krakadouw
1745m

Kouberg
Pass

Tra-Tra

Wuppertal

CEDERBERG

Cederberg
Wilderness Area

N7

Warmhoekkop
1127m

Middelberg
North
1516m

Sneeukop
1930m

52

Nieuwoudt
Pass

4x4 Only

Vaaldam

Taaiboskraal

Uitkyk
Pass

Tafelberg
1969m

Matjiesfontein

Wolfberg
Arch

Perdewater

Hex

Wolfberg
1609m

Wolfberg
Cracks

Voëlfontein

Klein Jongensfontein

Driehoeke

Matjiesrivier
Nature
Reserve

OLIFANTS RIVER

Hotwegskloof

Maltese
Cross

Kromrivier

Sneeuberg
2027m

Boskloof

MIDDELBERG

Cederberg
Tourist
Park

Breekkrans

Ruigtevlei

Donkerkloofkop
1746m

Oranjeville

Olifants

N

Citrusdal

Grootrivier
Pass

Klipbokberg
1391m

MOUNTAINS

Piekenierskloof
Pass

Middelberg Pass

Km   5   10

Varkkloof

18

Middelberg Peak
1565m

Eendekuil

N7

Grootberg
1356m

Heksrivier
Nature Reserve

R303

Groot

Blinkberg Pass

TO ELANDS BAY

TO PIKETBERG

TO CERES

TO KAGGA KAMMA

TO KLAWER

TO LAMBERT'S BAY

((022) 931 2088 • ((027) 482 2812/2403/2807 • e cederberg@cnc.org.za • e namapip@netactive.co.za • www.capenature.org.za • www.cederberg.co.za

174

Hluhluwe-iMfolozi Park   South Africa

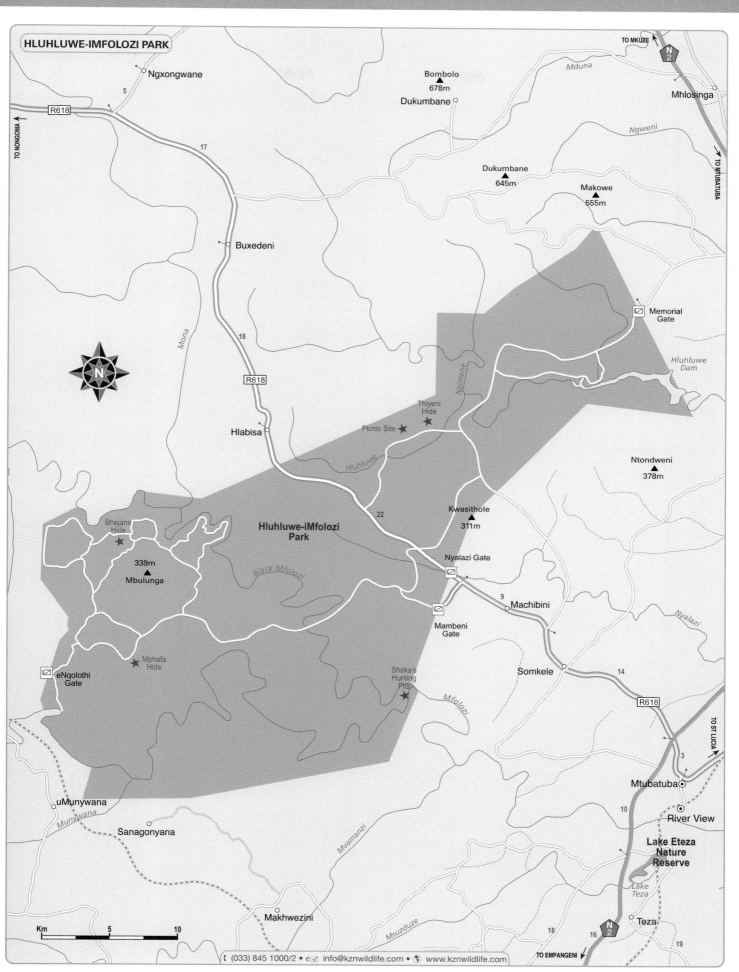

HLUHLUWE-IMFOLOZI PARK

TO MKUZE

TO NONGOMA

R618

Ngxongwane

5

17

Buxedeni

Mona

18

R618

Hlabisa

N

Bombolo
678m
Dukumbane

Dukumbane
645m

Makowe
555m

Mduna

Ngweni

TO MTUBATUBA

Memorial
Gate

Hluhluwe
Dam

Thiyeni
Hide

Picnic Site

Nzimane

Hluhluwe

22

Ntondweni
378m

Kwasithole
311m

Nyalazi Gate

Bhejane
Hide

Hluhluwe-iMfolozi
Park

Black Mfolozi

339m
Mbulunga

Mphafa Hide

eNqolothi
Gate

9   Machibini

Mambeni
Gate

Nyalazi

Somkele

14

Shaka's
Hunting
Pits

Mfolozi

R618

TO ST LUCIA

3

uMunywana

Munywana

Sanagonyana

Mvamanzi

Mtubatuba

10

River View

Lake Eteza
Nature
Reserve

Lake Teza

Makhwezini

Msuzduze

18

16

N2

Teza

19

Km   5   10

TO EMPANGENI

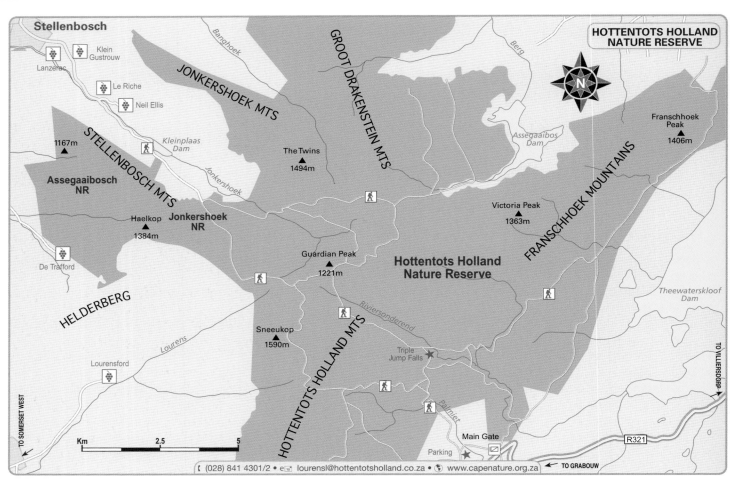

HOTTENTOTS HOLLAND NATURE RESERVE

Stellenbosch

Banghoek

JONKERSHOEK MTS

GROOT DRAKENSTEIN MTS

Berg

Klein Gustrouw

Lanzerac

Le Riche

Neil Ellis

1167m

STELLENBOSCH MTS

Kleinplaas Dam

Jonkershoek

Assegaaibosch NR

The Twins
1494m

Assegaaibos Dam

Franschhoek Peak
1406m

FRANSCHHOEK MOUNTAINS

Victoria Peak
1363m

Haelkop
1384m

Jonkershoek NR

De Trafford

Guardian Peak
1221m

Hottentots Holland Nature Reserve

Theewaterskloof Dam

HELDERBERG

Riviersonderend

HOTTENTOTS HOLLAND MTS

Sneeukop
1590m

Lourens

Triple Jump Falls

Lourensford

Palmiet

Main Gate

Parking

TO SOMERSET WEST

Km   2.5   5

R321

TO VILLIERSDORP

TO GRABOUW

☏ (028) 841 4301/2 • ✉ lourensl@hottentotsholland.co.za • 🌐 www.capenature.org.za

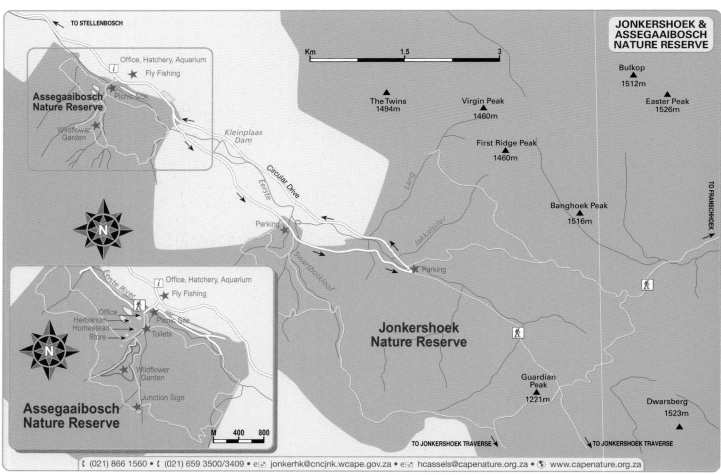

JONKERSHOEK & ASSEGAAIBOSCH NATURE RESERVE

TO STELLENBOSCH

Office, Hatchery, Aquarium

ℹ Fly Fishing

Assegaaibosch Nature Reserve

Picnic Site

Wildflower Garden

Kleinplaas Dam

Eerste

Circular Drive

Parking

Swartboskloof

Eerste River

ℹ Office, Hatchery, Aquarium

Fly Fishing

Office
Herbarium
Homestead
Store
Picnic Site
Toilets

Wildflower Garden

Junction Sign

Assegaaibosch Nature Reserve

M   400   800

Km   1.5   3

Bulkop
1512m

The Twins
1494m

Virgin Peak
1460m

Easter Peak
1526m

First Ridge Peak
1460m

Lang

Banghoek Peak
1516m

Jakkalsvlei

Parking

TO FRANSCHHOEK

Jonkershoek Nature Reserve

Guardian Peak
1221m

Dwarsberg
1523m

TO JONKERSHOEK TRAVERSE

TO JONKERSHOEK TRAVERSE

☏ (021) 866 1560 • ☏ (021) 659 3500/3409 • ✉ jonkerhk@cncjnk.wcape.gov.za • ✉ hcassels@capenature.org.za • 🌐 www.capenature.org.za

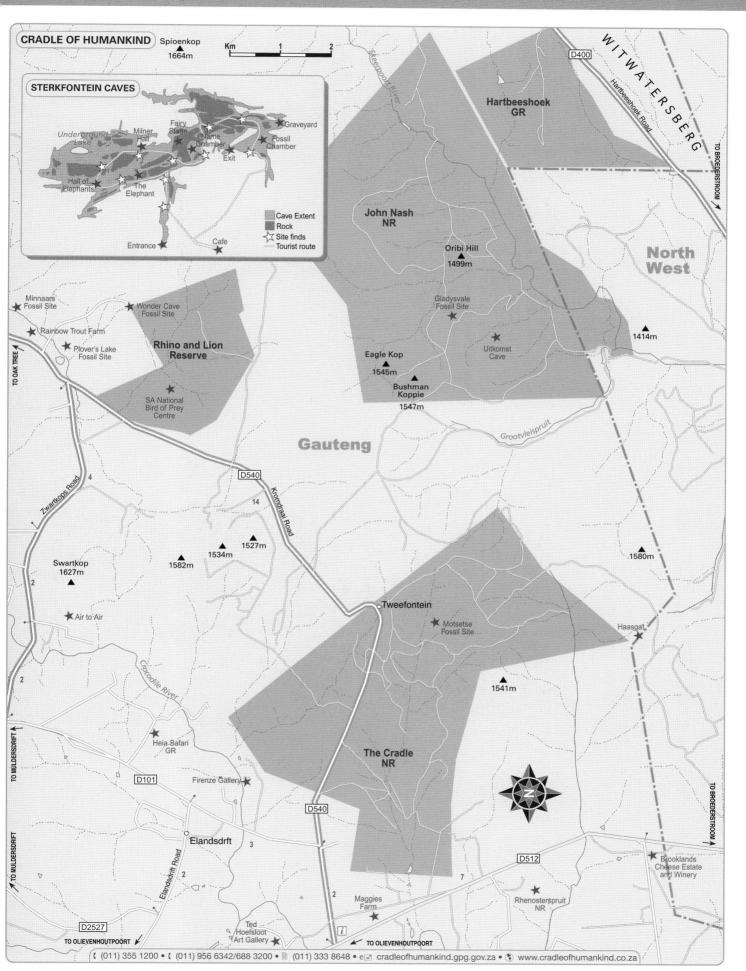

Cradle of Humankind South Africa

CRADLE OF HUMANKIND

Spioenkop
1664m

Km 1 2

STERKFONTEIN CAVES

Underground Lake

Milner Hall

Fairy Stage

Name Chamber

Graveyard

Fossil Chamber

Exit

Hall of Elephants

The Elephant

Entrance

Cafe

Cave Extent
Rock
Site finds
Tourist route

WITWATERSBERG

D400

Hartbeeshoek GR

Hartbeeshoek Road

TO BROEDERSTROOM

Skeerpoort River

John Nash NR

Oribi Hill
1499m

North West

Gladysvale Fossil Site

1414m

Minnaars Fossil Site

Wonder Cave Fossil Site

Rainbow Trout Farm

Rhino and Lion Reserve

Plover's Lake Fossil Site

TO OAK TREE

SA National Bird of Prey Centre

Eagle Kop
1545m

Uitkomst Cave

Bushman Koppie
1547m

Grootvleispruit

Gauteng

Zwartkops Road

4

D540

14

Kromdraai Road

1527m

1534m

1582m

1580m

Swartkop
1627m

2

Air to Air

Tweefontein

Motsetse Fossil Site

Haasgat

1541m

2

Crocodile River

Heia Safari GR

2

The Cradle NR

D101

Firenze Gallery

TO MULDERSDRIFT

Elandsdrft

3

D540

TO BROEDERSTROOM

2

D512

Brooklands Cheese Estate and Winery

TO MULDERSDRIFT

2

7

Rhenosterspruit NR

Elandsdrift Road

Maggies Farm

D2527

Ted Hoefsloot Art Gallery

i

TO OLIEVENHOUTPOORT

TO OLIEVENHOUTPOORT

(011) 355 1200 • (011) 956 6342/688 3200 • (011) 333 8648 • e cradleofhumankind.gpg.gov.za • www.cradleofhumankind.co.za

177

De Hoop Nature Reserve South Africa

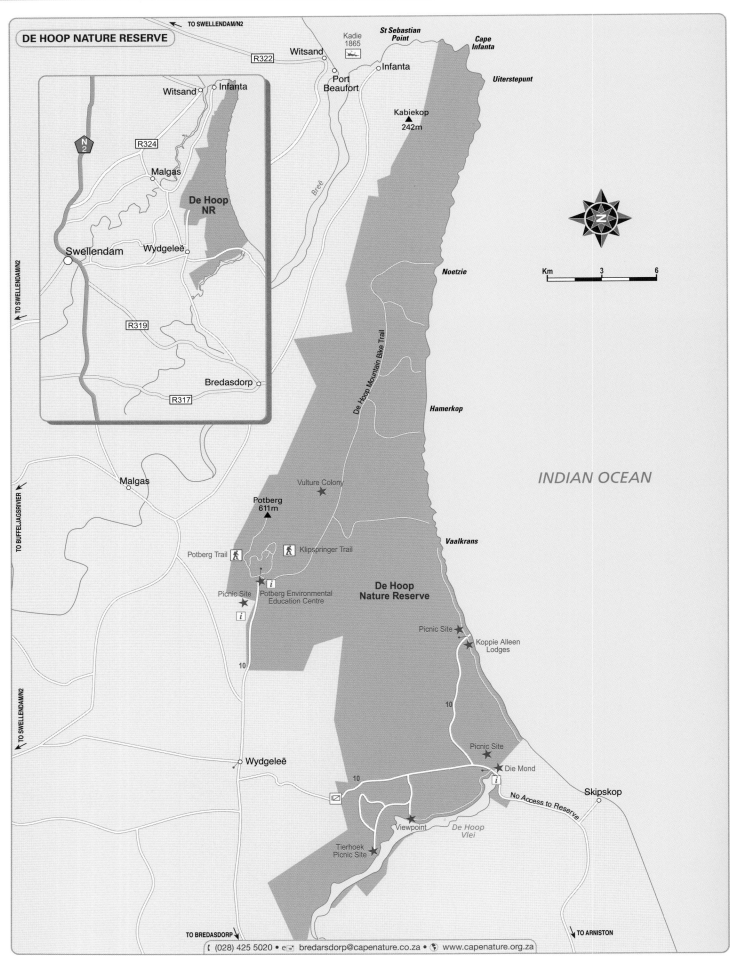

DE HOOP NATURE RESERVE

TO SWELLENDAM/N2

R322

Witsand

Kadie 1865

St Sebastian Point

Cape Infanta

TO ARNISTON

Infanta

Uiterstepunt

Port Beaufort

Kabiekop ▲ 242m

Breë

Witsand

Infanta

N2

R324

Malgas

De Hoop NR

Swellendam

Wydgeleë

R319

Bredasdorp

R317

Noetzie

De Hoop Mountain Bike Trail

Hamerkop

INDIAN OCEAN

Vaalkrans

Vulture Colony ★

Potberg 611m ▲

TO BUFFELJAGSRIVIER

Malgas

Potberg Trail 🚶

🚶 Klipspringer Trail

De Hoop Nature Reserve

Picnic Site

Potberg Environmental Education Centre

Picnic Site ★

Koppie Alleen Lodges ★

TO SWELLENDAM/N2

10

10

Picnic Site ★

Die Mond ★

Skipskop

No Access to Reserve

Wydgeleë

10

10

Viewpoint ★

De Hoop Vlei

Tierhoek Picnic Site ★

TO BREDASDORP

TO ARNISTON

📞 (028) 425 5020 • ✉ bredarsdorp@capenature.co.za • 🌐 www.capenature.org.za

Km 3 6

iSimangaliso Wetland Park (Greater St Lucia) South Africa

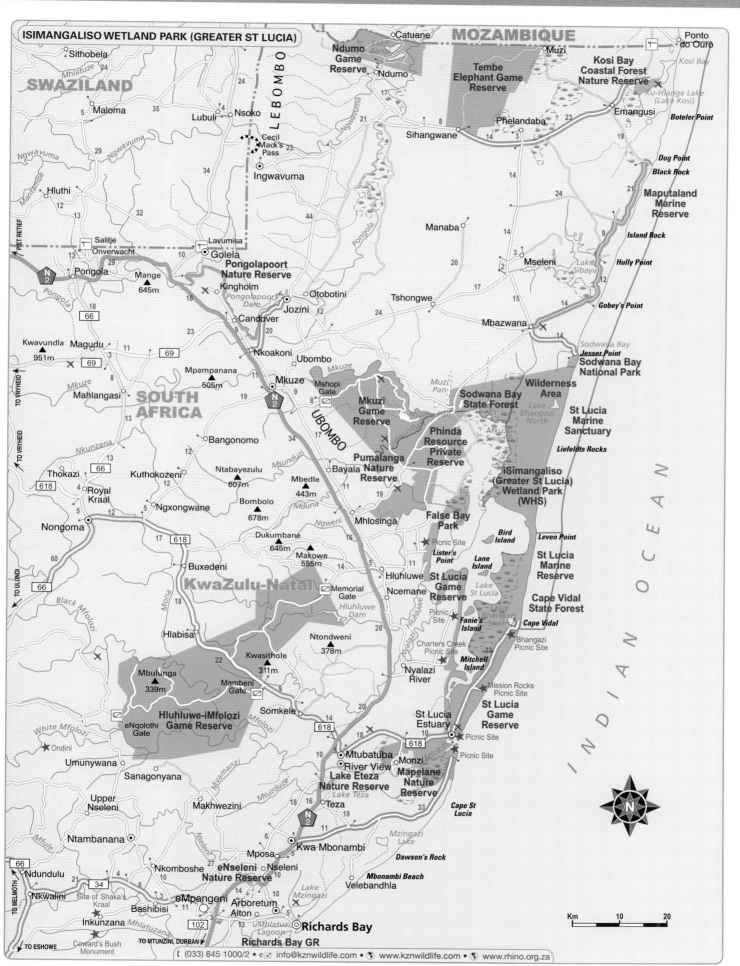

ISIMANGALISO WETLAND PARK (GREATER ST LUCIA)

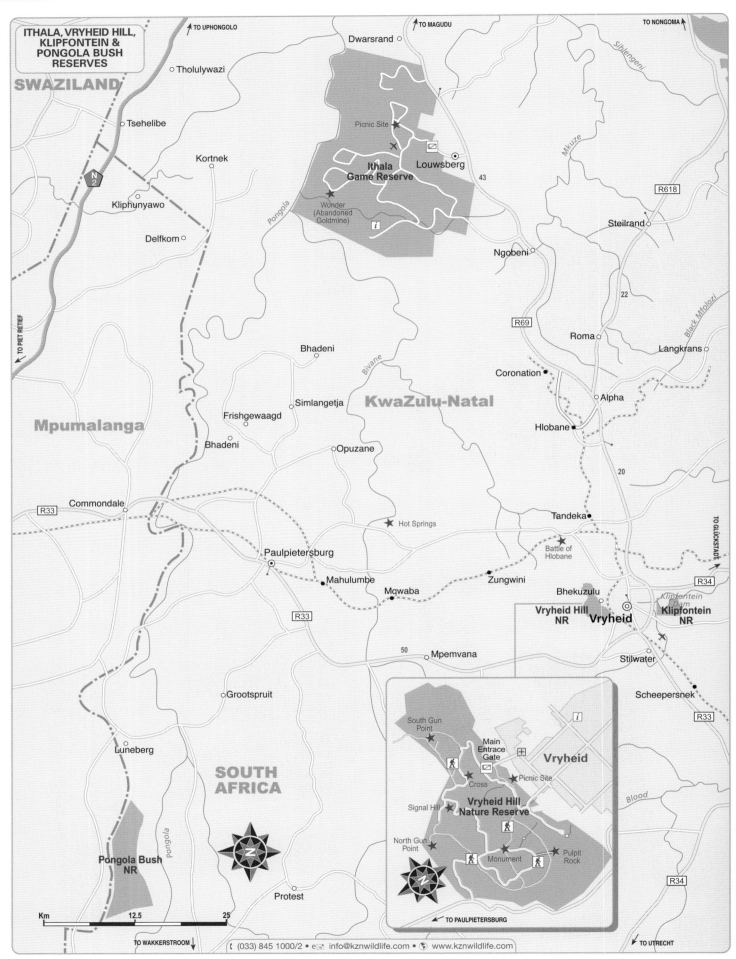

Ithala, Vryheid Hill, Klipfontein & Pongola Bush

South Africa

ITHALA, VRYHEID HILL, KLIPFONTEIN & PONGOLA BUSH RESERVES

SWAZILAND

TO UPHONGOLO

TO MAGUDU

TO NONGOMA

Dwarsrand

Tholulywazi

Tsehelibe

Kortnek

Kliphunyawo

Delfkom

Picnic Site

Ithala Game Reserve

Louwsberg

43

Wonder (Abandoned Goldmine)

Pongola

Mkuze

R618

Steilrand

Ngobeni

22

Sihlengeni

TO PIET RETIEF

Bhadeni

Frishgewaagd

Bhadeni

Simlangetja

Opuzane

KwaZulu-Natal

Bivane

R69

Roma

Langkrans

Coronation

Alpha

Hlobane

20

Black Mfolozi

Mpumalanga

R33

Commondale

Hot Springs

Paulpietersburg

Mahulumbe

Mqwaba

Zungwini

Battle of Hlobane

Tandeka

TO GLÜCKSTADT

R34

Bhekuzulu

Vryheid Hill NR

Vryheid

Klipfontein Dam

Klipfontein NR

50

Mpemvana

Stilwater

Scheepersnek

R33

Grootspruit

SOUTH AFRICA

Luneberg

Pongola

Pongola Bush NR

Protest

Blood

R34

Km   12.5   25

TO WAKKERSTROOM

(033) 845 1000/2 • e info@kznwildlife.com • www.kznwildlife.com

TO UTRECHT

South Gun Point

Main Entrace Gate

Cross

Signal Hill

Vryheid Hill Nature Reserve

Picnic Site

Vryheid

North Gun Point

Monument

Pulpit Rock

TO PAULPIETERSBURG

N2

180

West Coast

South Africa

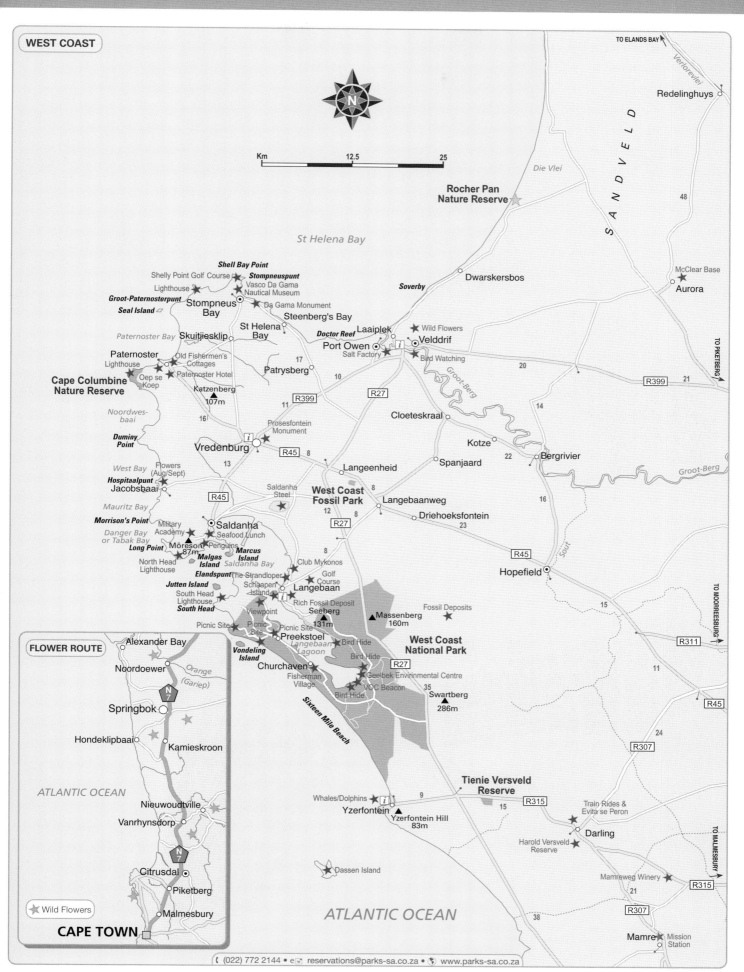

WEST COAST

TO ELANDS BAY

Verlorevlei

SANDVELD

Redelinghuys

Km 12.5 25

Die Vlei

Rocher Pan
Nature Reserve

St Helena Bay

McClear Base

Dwarskersbos

Aurora

Shell Bay Point
Shelly Point Golf Course
Lighthouse
Stompneuspunt
Vasco Da Gama
Nautical Museum
Groot-Paternosterpunt
Stompneus
Bay
Seal Island
Da Gama Monument
Steenberg's Bay

Soverby

Wild Flowers
Laaiplek
Doctor Reef
Port Owen
Salt Factory
Velddrif
Bird Watching

20

TO PIKETBERG

R399 21

Paternoster Bay
Skuitjesklip
St Helena
Bay
Patrysberg
17
10

Paternoster
Lighthouse
Old Fishermen's
Cottages
Paternoster Hotel
Cape Columbine
Nature Reserve
Oep se
Koep
Katzenberg
107m
11
R399

Groot-Berg

Cloeteskraal

14

Kotze
Bergrivier
Spanjaard
22

Noordwes-
baai
Duminy
Point
16
Prosesfontein
Monument
Vredenburg
13
R45 8
Langeenheid
West Coast
Fossil Park
Langebaanweg
16

Groot-Berg

West Bay
Flowers
(Aug/Sept)
Hospitaalpunt
Jacobsbaai
Saldanha
Steel
R45
8
12
8
Driehoeksfontein
23

Mauritz Bay
Morrison's Point
Danger Bay
or Tabak Bay
Long Point
Military
Academy
Saldanha
Seafood Lunch
Môreson
87m
Penguins
Malgas
Island
Marcus
Island
North Head
Lighthouse
Elandspunt
Jutten Island
South Head
Lighthouse
South Head
Schaapen
Island
The Strandloper
Club Mykonos
Golf
Course
Langebaan
R27
8
R45
Hopefield
15

R311

Viewpoint
Picnic Site
Picnic
Site
Picnic Site
Preekstoel
Vondeling
Island
Churchaven
Fisherman
Village
Bird Hide
Seeberg
131m
Rich Fossil Deposit
Langebaan
Lagoon
Bird Hide
Bird Hide
Massenberg
160m
Fossil Deposits
West Coast
National Park
Geelbek Environmental Centre
VOC Beacon
35
Swartberg
286m
R27
11

FLOWER ROUTE

Alexander Bay
Noordoewer
Orange
(Gariep)
N7
Springbok
Hondeklipbaai
Kamieskroon

ATLANTIC OCEAN

Nieuwoudtville
Vanrhynsdorp
N7
Citrusdal
Piketberg
Wild Flowers
Malmesbury
CAPE TOWN

Sixteen Mile Beach

Tienie Versveld
Reserve

Whales/Dolphins
Yzerfontein
Yzerfontein Hill
83m
9
15
R315

Train Rides &
Evita se Peron

Harold Versveld
Reserve

Darling

TO MOORREESBURG

R45
24
R307

TO MALMESBURY

R311
R315

Mamreweg Winery
21
R307
38
Mamre
Mission
Station

Dassen Island

ATLANTIC OCEAN

((022) 772 2144 • e reservations@parks-sa.co.za • www.parks-sa.co.za

TABLE MOUNTAIN NATIONAL PARK

Km   3   6

Table Bay

TO MALMESBURY

Canal Walk

Thermopylae 1899
Athens 1865
SA Seafarer 1966
Lighthouse
Three Anchor Bay 11
Noon Gun
Victoria & Alfred Waterfront
Cape Town Convention Centre
Sea Point
Bantry Bay
Lion's Head 670m
Clifton Bay
SIGNAL HILL
Castle of Good Hope
Rhodes Memorial
Devil's Peak 1001m
Camps Bay
Camps Bay
M6
TABLE MOUNTAIN
Theatre on the Bay
Orion's Cave
Kirstenbosch National Botanical Garden
Boshof Gateway
Het Huis te Kraaiestein 1698
Bellsfontein Kramat
TWELVE APOSTLES
Antipolis 1977
Oudekraal
M6
Table Mountain National Park
Van Riebeeck's Hedge
Kenilworth Race Course
Llandudno Bay
Little Lion's Head
World of Birds
Alphen 1714
Maynardville Open Air Theatre
Romelia 1977
7 M63
Sandy Bay
436m
CONSTANTIABERG
Constantia
M41
Oude Schip
Suther Peak 614m
Maori 1909
Boss 400
Hout Bay
Mariner's Wharf
The Leopard
Groot Constantia 1685
M42 M3
M41 M5
Rondevlei
Zeekoevlei
Karbonkelberg Sanctuary Zone
Constantiaberg 928m
The Lonely Bridge
Duiker Island
West Fort 1781
Hout Bay
M6
Elephant's Eye Cave
Spotty Dog
Rondevlei Bird Sanctuary
Vulcan Rock
Astor
Katzmaru 1970
11
Tokai Forest
Die Josie
Chapman's Peak 592m
Higher Steenberg Peak 537m
Muizenberg Cave
M4
Chapman's Point
Silvermine 1687
10
Muizenberg
Neptune's Corner
Noordhoek Toll Booth
Silvermine Nature Reserve
Rhodes Cottage
Chapman's Bay
M6
1.5 1
Peer's Cave
Kalk Bay Cave
M5
R310
Tunnel Cave
Kakapo 1900
5
5.5
Tidal Lagoon
Trappies Caves
Klein Slangkop Point
1
M65
Fish Hoek
False Bay
Kommetjie Bay
M65 10.5
Rooikrans 364m
Fish Hoek Bay
Slangkop Point
M65
Else Peak 303m
Skeleton Rock
Clan Munroe 1905
Slangkop 174m
Else Bay
M4
The Anchor
Hartenberg Circa 1730
Clan Stuart 1914
5
Simon's Town
Die Eiland
Table Mountain National Park
Simon's Bay
Lighthouse
Phoenix 1829
Witsand Bay
8
Camel Rock
7.5
Just Nuisance Statue
Schuster's Bay
Red Hill 256m
SWARTKOP MOUNTAINS
Schusterskraal
Simonsberg 548m
M4
Miller's Point
Bonteberg 227m
Dassiekop 314m
14
Lookout Post
Viewpoint
Menskop Point
Smitswinkel Bay
Olifantsbos Bay
Olifantsbos Cottage
Thomas T Tucker 1942
Judas Peak 319m
Blaasbalk Cave
Cape of Good Hope Nature Reserve
Nolloth 1965
14
Old Cannon
Phyllisia 1968
Kommetjieberg 114m
Da Gama Monument 1497
Hoek van Bobbejaan
Dias Monument 1488
Bordjiesrif
107m
Tania 1972
Blouberstrand
GROOT-BLOUBERG
Matrooskop
Viewpoint
Rooikrans
Platboom Bay
Viewpoint
Lighthouse
Cape Point
Shir-Yib 1970
Cape of Good Hope

M5 N1 R102
GrandWest Casino
N1 SA Astronomical Observatory
N2
6
TO BELLVILLE
TO SOMERSET WEST
M17
M9

ATLANTIC OCEAN

KIRSTENBOSCH NATIONAL BOTANICAL GARDEN

TO SKELETON GORGE
Kirstenbosch National Botanical Garden
Yellowwood Trail
Reservoirs (No Access)
Nursery Stream
Skeleton Track
Stinkwood Trail
Fynbos Walk
Education Centre
Proteas
Buchus
Smuts Track
Braille
Toilets
Garden Centre
Gate 2 Garden Centre Entrance
Parking
Fynbos Walk
Ericas
Proteas
The Koppie
Bookshop
Tea Room
Lecture Hall
Xhosa Hut
Lawn
Water-wise Garden
Pearson House
Cycads
Toilets
Colonel Bird's Bath
Fragrance Garden
Medicinal Plants
Peninsula Garden
Vlei Garden
NBI Admin Office
Irrigation Dam (No Entry)
Pearson's Grave
Useful Plants Garden
Vygies
Pond
Nedbank Lodge
TO CAPE TOWN
Mathew's Rockery
Silver Tree Restaurant & Deli
Sculpture Garden
Fynbos Lodge
Seed Orchard
Restios
Concert Stage
Annuals
Parking
Van Riebeeck's Hedge
Toilets
Gate 1 Visitor's Centre Entrance
i Info & tickets
M63
Church of the Good Shepherd
TO HOUT BAY
Gate 3 Rycroft Entrance
Conservatory
Visitor's Centre
Toilets
Coffee Shop
Gift Shop
Rhodes Drive
M63
Liesbeek
Rhodes Drive
Nursery (no entry)
Bookshop
Garden Office
Klaassen's Road
Parking

The Garden is open all year
08:00 – 19:00 (Sept to Mar)
08:00 – 18:00 (Apr to Aug)

℡ (021) 799 88 99/8783 • 🖶 (021) 797 6570 • 🌐 www.sanb.org

℡ (021) 701 8692 • e🖂 tablemountain@sanparks.org • 🌐 www.tmnp.co.za

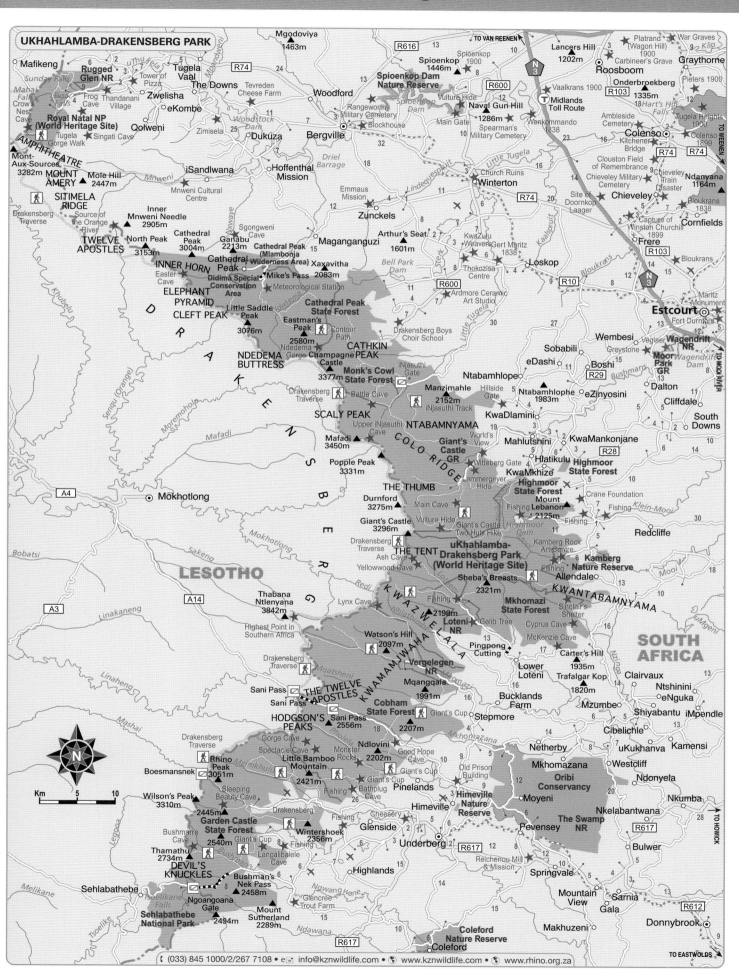

Karoo National Park South Africa

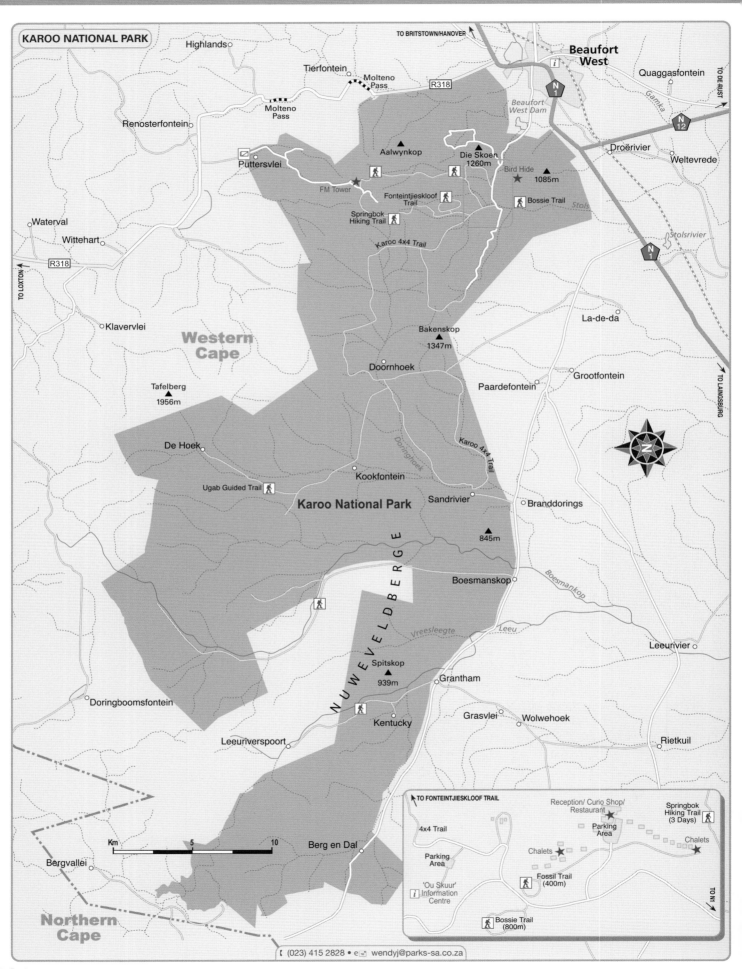

KAROO NATIONAL PARK

Highlands
Tierfontein
Molteno Pass
R318
TO BRITSTOWN/HANOVER
Beaufort West
Quaggasfontein
TO DE RUST
Molteno Pass
Renosterfontein
Beaufort West Dam
N1
Droërivier
Weltevrede
Gamka
Puttersvlei
Aalwynkop
Die Skoen 1260m
Bird Hide
1085m
N12
FM Tower
Fonteintjieskloof Trail
Bossie Trail
Stols
Waterval
Springbok Hiking Trail
Stolsrivier
Wittehart
R318
Karoo 4x4 Trail
N1
TO LOXTON
Western Cape
La-de-da
Klavervlei
Bakenskop 1347m
Grootfontein
Doornhoek
Paardefontein
Tafelberg 1956m
Karoo 4x4 Trail
De Hoek
Doringhoek
Kookfontein
Branddorings
Ugab Guided Trail
Karoo National Park
Sandrivier
845m
NUWEVELDBERGE
Boesmanskop
Boesmankop
Leeu
Leeurivier
Vreesleegte
Doringboomsfontein
Spitskop 939m
Grantham
Grasvlei
Wolwehoek
Kentucky
Rietkuil
Leeuriverspoort
TO LAINGSBURG

Km 5 10

Bergvallei
Berg en Dal
Northern Cape

TO FONTEINTJIESKLOOF TRAIL
Reception/ Curio Shop/ Restaurant
Springbok Hiking Trail (3 Days)
4x4 Trail
Parking Area
Parking Area
Chalets
Chalets
'Ou Skuur' Information Centre
Fossil Trail (400m)
Bossie Trail (800m)
TO N1

((023) 415 2828 • e✉ wendyj@parks-sa.co.za

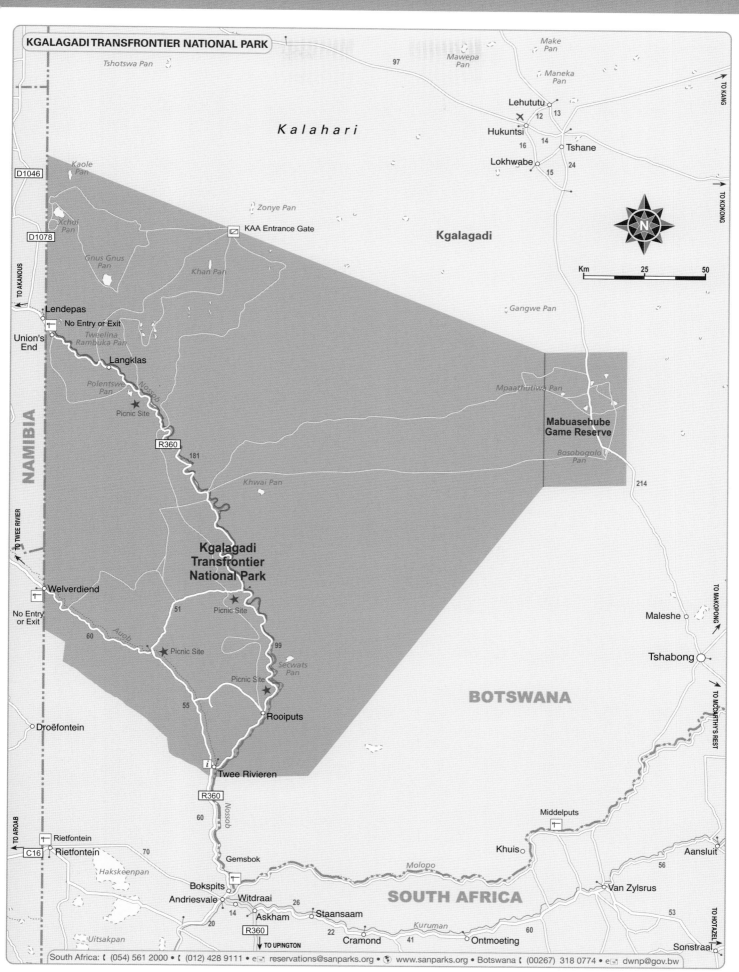

KGALAGADI TRANSFRONTIER NATIONAL PARK

Tshotswa Pan

Make Pan

Mawepa Pan

97

Maneka Pan

Lehututu ✕ 12 13

Kalahari

Hukuntsi 14

16 Tshane

Lokhwabe 24

15

Kaole Pan

D1046

Kgalagadi

Zonye Pan

D1078

Xchoi Pan

KAA Entrance Gate

Gnus Gnus Pan

Khan Pan

Km 25 50

Gangwe Pan

Lendepas

No Entry or Exit

Union's End

Tweelina Rambuka Pan

Langklas

Mpaathutlwa Pan

Polentswe Pan

Nossob

Picnic Site

R360

Mabuasehube Game Reserve

181

Bosobogolo Pan

Khwai Pan

214

Kgalagadi Transfrontier National Park

Welverdiend

51 Picnic Site

No Entry or Exit

60

Auob

Maleshe

Picnic Site

99

Secwats Pan

Tshabong

Picnic Site

55

BOTSWANA

Rooiputs

Droëfontein

i

Twee Rivieren

R360

60

Nossob

Middelputs

Rietfontein

Khuis

Aansluit

C16 Rietfontein

70

Gemsbok

Van Zylsrus

56

Hakskeenpan

Molopo

Bokspits

SOUTH AFRICA

Andriesvale Witdraai 26

Staansaam

Uitsakpan

14

Askham

Kuruman

60

53

20

22 Cramond

41 Ontmoeting

R360

Sonstraal

TO UPINGTON

NAMIBIA

TO AKANOUS

TO TWEE RIVIER

TO AROAB

TO KANG

TO KOKONG

TO MAKOPONG

TO MCCARTHY'S REST

TO HOTAZEL

South Africa: ((054) 561 2000 • ((012) 428 9111 • e✉ reservations@sanparks.org • 🌐 www.sanparks.org • Botswana ((00267) 318 0774 • e✉ dwnp@gov.bw

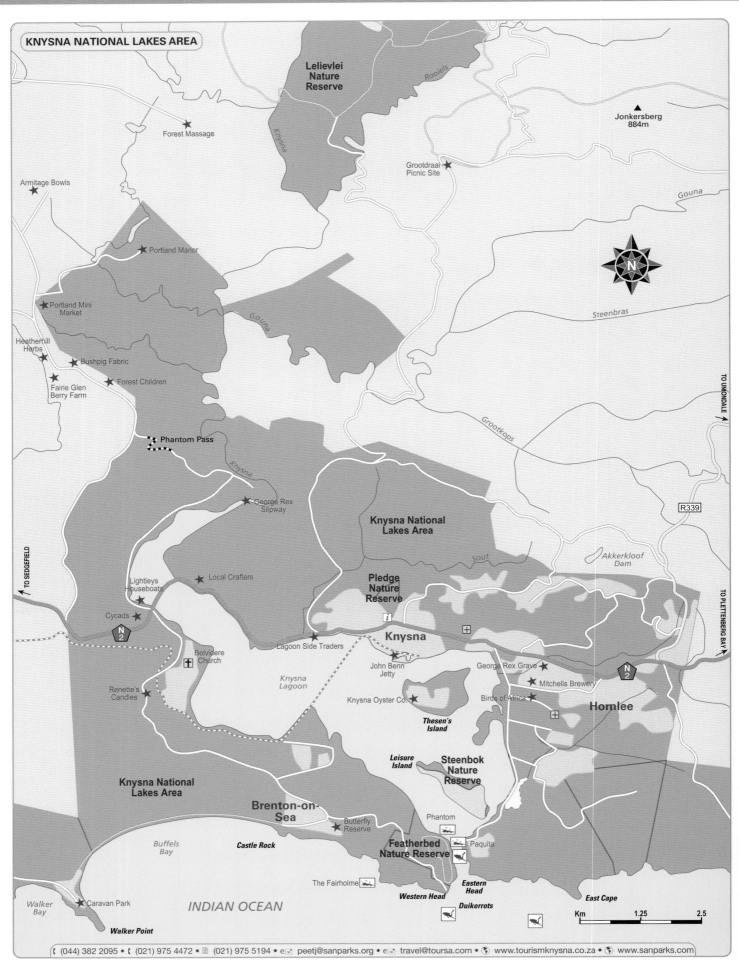

Knysna National Lakes Area   South Africa

KNYSNA NATIONAL LAKES AREA

Lelievlei Nature Reserve

Jonkersberg 884m

Rooiels

Knysna

Gouna

Forest Massage

Grootdraai Picnic Site

Armitage Bowls

Steenbras

Portland Manor

N

Gouna

Portland Mini Market

Heatherhill Herbs

Bushpig Fabric

Fairie Glen Berry Farm

Forest Children

Grootkops

TO UNIONDALE

Phantom Pass

Knysna

R339

George Rex Slipway

Knysna National Lakes Area

Akkerkloof Dam

Sout

Pledge Nature Reserve

TO SEDGEFIELD

Lightleys Houseboats

Local Crafters

i

Knysna

TO PLETTENBERG BAY

Cycads

N2

Lagoon Side Traders

John Benn Jetty

George Rex Grave

N2

Belvidere Church

Mitchells Brewery

Renette's Candles

Knysna Lagoon

Knysna Oyster Co.

Birds of Africa

Hornlee

Thesen's Island

Knysna National Lakes Area

Leisure Island

Steenbok Nature Reserve

Brenton-on-Sea

Butterfly Reserve

Phantom

Buffels Bay

Castle Rock

Featherbed Nature Reserve

Paquita

INDIAN OCEAN

The Fairholme

Eastern Head

Walker Bay

Caravan Park

Western Head

Duikerrots

East Cape

Walker Point

Km   1.25   2.5

((044) 382 2095 • ((021) 975 4472 • 🗎 (021) 975 5194 • e🖳 peetj@sanparks.org • e🖳 travel@toursa.com • 🌐 www.tourismknysna.co.za • 🌐 www.sanparks.com

Kruger National Park   South Africa

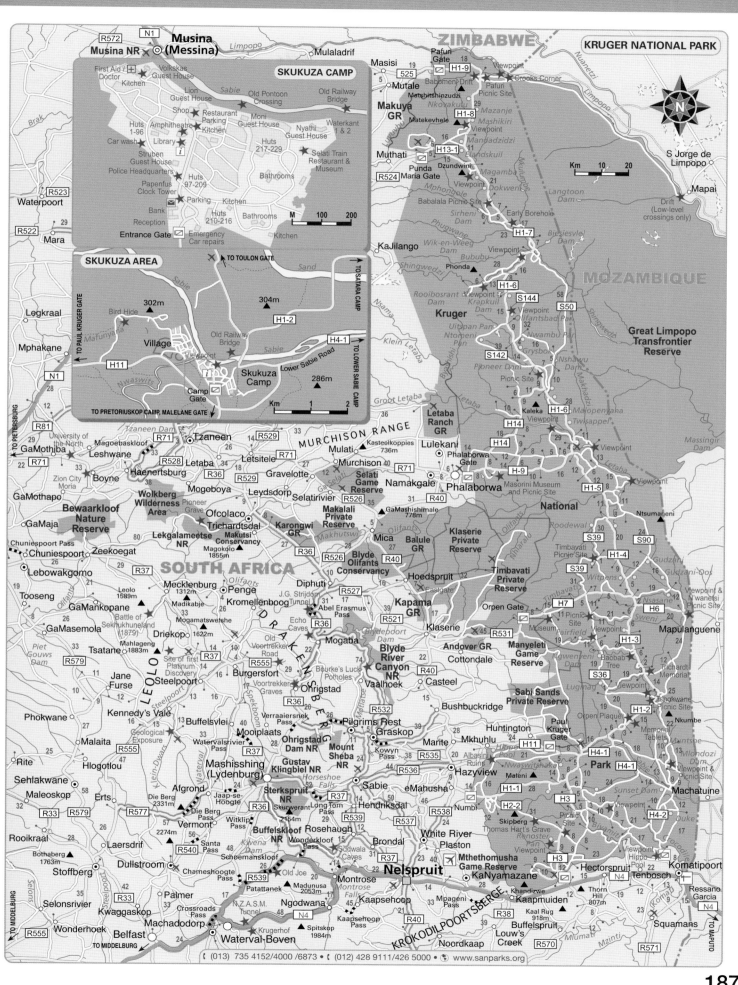

Maseru Lesotho
Mbabane Swaziland

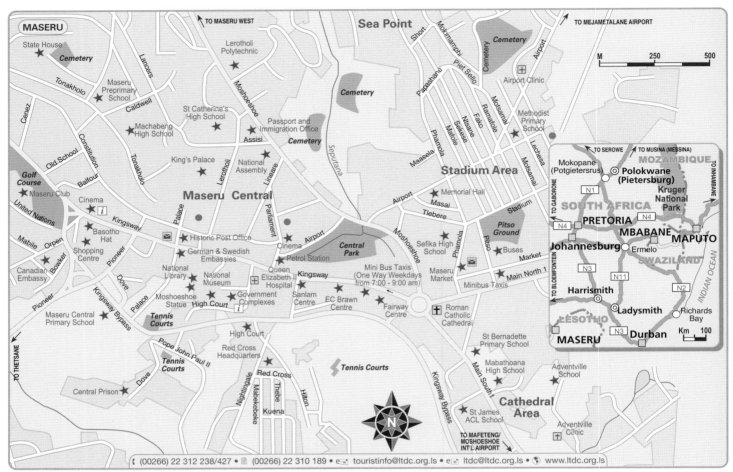

MASERU

TO MASERU WEST

Sea Point

TO MEJAMETALANE AIRPORT

State House

Cemetery

Lerotholi Polytechnic

Cemetery

Cemetery

Airport Clinic

Methodist Primary School

M 250 500

Tonakholo

Maseru Preprimary School

Caldwell

St Catherine's High School

Cenez

Machabeng High School

Assisi

Passport and Immigration Office

Cemetery

Stadium Area

Old School

Constitution

Tonakholo

King's Palace

Balfour

National Assembly

Lerotholi

Lineare

Maseru Central

Memorial Hall

Masai

TO SEROWE TO MUSINA (MESSINA)

Mokopane (Potgietersrus)

Polokwane (Pietersburg)

MOZAMBIQUE

Golf Course

Maseru Club

Cinema

Kingsway

Basotho Hat

Shopping Centre

Palace

Airport

Tlebere

Pitso Ground

Stadium

N1

SOUTH AFRICA

N4

Kruger National Park

PRETORIA

N4

MBABANE

MAPUTO

United Nations

Mabile Orpen

Pioneer

Historic Post Office

German & Swedish Embassies

Petrol Station

Cinema Airport

Moshoeshoe

Sefika High School

Phamola

Pitso

Buses

Market

Johannesburg

Ermelo

SWAZILAND

Canadian Embassy

Bowker

Dove

National Library

Queen Elizabeth II Hospital

Kingsway

Central Park

Mini Bus Taxis (One Way Weekdays from 7:00 - 9:00 am)

Maseru Market

Main North 1

N3

Harrismith

N11

N2

Richards Bay

Pioneer

Kingsway Bypass

Palace

National Museum

Moshoeshoe Statue

High Court

Government Complexes

Sanlam Centre

EC Brawn Centre

Fairway Centre

Minibus Taxis

Roman Catholic Cathedral

Ladysmith

LESOTHO

INDIAN OCEAN

Maseru Central Primary School

Tennis Courts

High Court

St Bernadette Primary School

MASERU

N3

Durban

Km 100

TO THETSANE

Pope John Paul II

Tennis Courts

Red Cross Headquarters

Red Cross

Tennis Courts

Mabathoana High School

Adventville School

Central Prison

Nightingale

Mabekebeke

Thebe

Kuena

Hilton

Kingsway Bypass

Main South

Cathedral Area

Adventville Clinic

St James ACL School

TO MAFETENG/ MOSHOESHOE INT'L AIRPORT

📞 (00266) 22 312 238/427 • 📠 (00266) 22 310 189 • ✉ touristinfo@ltdc.org.ls • ✉ ltdc@ltdc.org.ls • 🌐 www.ltdc.org.ls

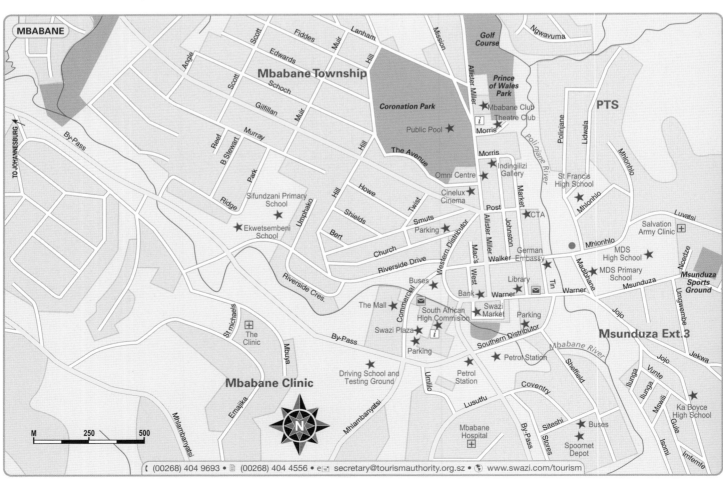

MBABANE

Scott Fiddes Lanham

Muir

Hill

Mission

Golf Course

Ngwavuma

Angle

Edwards

Allister Miller

Prince of Wales Park

PTS

Scott

Schoch

Mbabane Township

Coronation Park

Mbabane Club

Theatre Club

Morris

Polinjane

Lidwala

Mhlonhlo

TO JOHANNESBURG

By-Pass

Gilfillan

Muir

Reef

B Stewart

Murray

Hill

Public Pool

Morris

Indingilizi Gallery

St Francis High School

Park

The Avenue

Omni Centre

Market

Ridge

Sifundzani Primary School

Umphako

Howe

Twist

Cinelux Cinema

Post

CTA

Mhlonhlo

Luvatsi

Salvation Army Clinic

Ekwetsembeni School

Hill

Shields

Smuts

Parking

Allister Miller

Johnston

MDS High School

Bert

Church

Western Distributor

Mac's

Walker

German Embassy

Madibhane

MDS Primary School

Msunduza

Ncedze

Umgwembe

Msunduza Sports Ground

Riverside Drive

West

Library

Tin

Warner

Riverside Cres.

Buses

Bank

Warner

Jojo

Msunduza Ext.3

St michaels

The Clinic

The Mall

Commercial

South African High Commision

Swazi Market

Swazi Plaza

Parking

Southern Distributor

Mbabane River

Jojo

Mbuya

By-Pass

Parking

Petrol Station

Sheffield

Ilunga

Vunte

Jekwa

Mbabane Clinic

Mhlambanyatsi

Ernajika

Driving School and Testing Ground

Umlilo

Mhlambanyatsi

Lusutfu

Petrol Station

Petrol Station

Coventry

Siteshi

Stores

Ilunga

Gule

Mswili

Isoni

Imfemie

Mbabane Hospital

Buses

Spoornet Depot

Ka Boyce High School

M 250 500

📞 (00268) 404 9693 • 📠 (00268) 404 4556 • ✉ secretary@tourismauthority.org.sz • 🌐 www.swazi.com/tourism

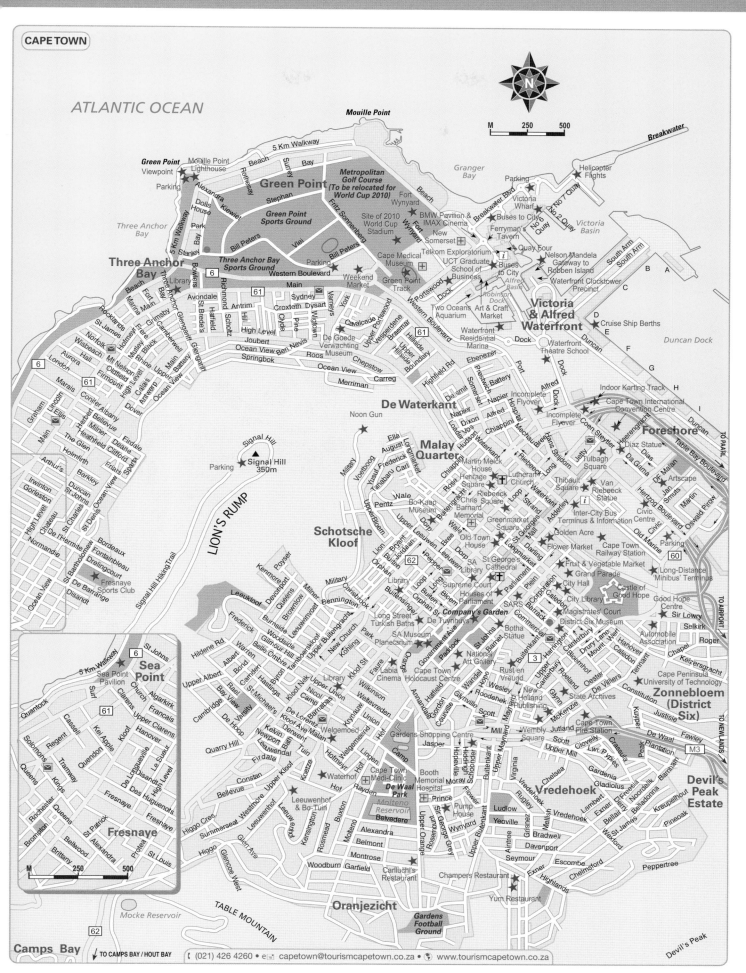

Cape Town
South Africa

CAPE TOWN

ATLANTIC OCEAN

M 250 500

Breakwater

Mouille Point

Granger Bay

Green Point
Viewpoint
Mouille Point
Lighthouse
Parking

Green Point

Metropolitan
Golf Course
(To be relocated for
World Cup 2010)

Site of 2010
World Cup
Stadium

Green Point
Sports Ground

Fort
Wynyard

Helicopter
Flights

Parking

Victoria
Wharf

No 7 Quay

No 2 Quay

Victoria
Basin

Three Anchor
Bay

Three Anchor
Bay

Three Anchor Bay
Sports Ground

BMW Pavilion &
IMAX Cinema

New
Somerset

Telkom Exploratorium
UCT Graduate
School of
Business

Buses to City

Ferryman's
Tavern

Quay Four

Nelson Mandela
Gateway to
Robben Island

Waterfront Clocktower
Precinct

South Arm

South Arm

Library

Weekend
Market

Green Point
Track

Cape Medical
Museum

Dock

Robinson
Dock

Buses
to City

Alfred
Basin

Cruise Ship Berths

Western Boulevard

Two Oceans
Aquarium

Art & Craft
Market

Victoria
& Alfred
Waterfront

Duncan Dock

Waterfront
Residential
Marina

Waterfront
Theatre School

Duncan Dock

De Waterkant

Noon Gun

Malay
Quarter

Indoor Karting Track

Cape Town International
Convention Centre

Incomplete
Flyover

Incomplete
Flyover

Foreshore

Signal Hill

Signal Hill
350m

Parking

LION'S RUMP

Schotsche
Kloof

Martin Melck
House

Lutheran
Church

Heritage
Square

Bo-Kaap
Museum

Rose

Chris
Barnard
Memorial

Riebeeck
Square

Greenmarket
Square

Old Town
House

SA
Library

St George's
Cathedral

Thibault
Square

Van
Riebeeck
Statue

Tulbagh
Square

Diaz Statue
Da Gama

Artscape

Civic
Centre

Civic

Golden Acre

Flower Market

Cape Town
Railway Station

Fruit & Vegetable Market

Grand Parade

City Hall

Castle of
Good Hope

Parking

Long-Distance
'Minibus' Terminus

Good Hope
Centre

Company's Garden

Supreme Court

Houses of
Parliament

SARS
Barrack

City Library

Magistrates' Court

District Six Museum

Sir Lowry

Selkirk

Roger

Long Street
Turkish Baths

De Tuynhuys

SA Museum
Planetarium

Botha
Statue

Automobile
Association

Chapel

Keizersgracht

National
Art Gallery

Labia
Cinema

Cape Town
Holocaust Centre

Rust en
Vreugd

New
Holland
Publishing

State Archives

Cape Peninsula
University of Technology

Zonnebloem
(District
Six)

TO NEWLANDS

Sea
Point

Fresnaye
Sports Club

M 250 500

Fresnaye

Gardens Shopping Centre

Wembly
Square

Cape Town
Fire Station

De Waal
Plantation

Devil's
Peak
Estate

Cape Town
Medi-Clinic

De Waal
Park

Molteno
Reservoir

Cape Town
Medi-Clinic

Booth
Memorial
Hospital

Pump
House

Vredehoek

Gardens
Football
Ground

Mocke Reservoir

TABLE MOUNTAIN

Oranjezicht

Carluchi's
Restaurant

Champers Restaurant

Yum Restaurant

Devil's Peak

Camps Bay

TO CAMPS BAY / HOUT BAY

(021) 426 4260 • capetown@tourismcapetown.co.za • www.tourismcapetown.co.za

189

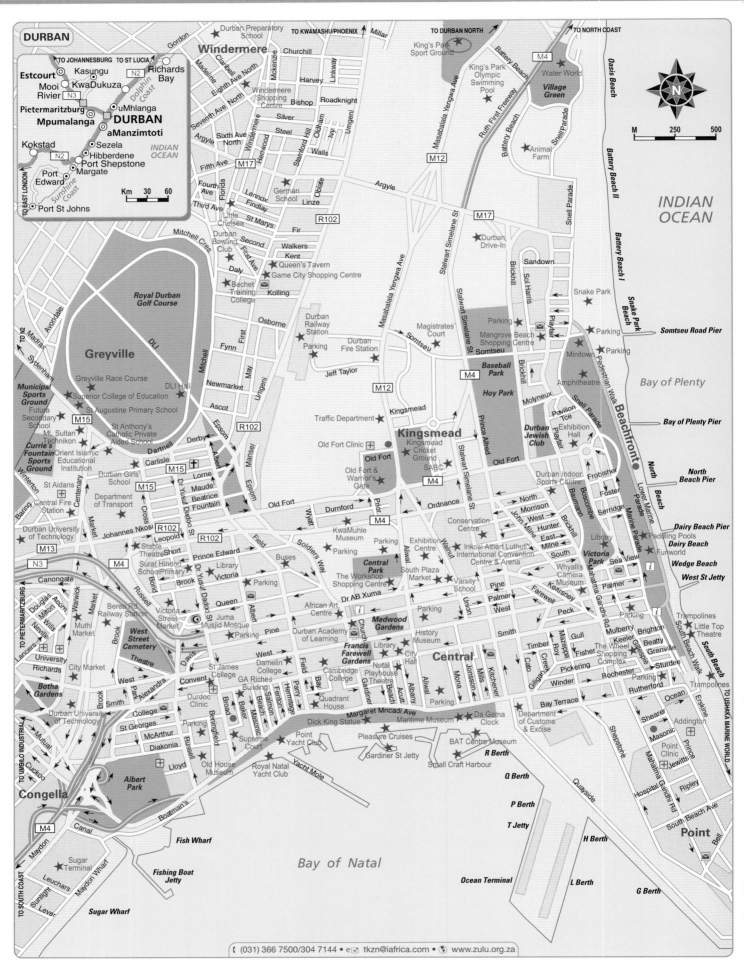

Durban South Africa

Windermere

Greyville

Royal Durban Golf Course

Greyville Race Course

Kingsmead

Central

Congella

Point

INDIAN OCEAN

Bay of Plenty

Beachfront

Bay of Natal

TO KWAMASHU/PHOENIX
TO DURBAN NORTH
TO NORTH COAST
TO JOHANNESBURG
TO ST LUCIA

Estcourt
Kasungu
Richards Bay
Mooi Rivier
KwaDukuza
uMhlanga
Pietermaritzburg
DURBAN
Mpumalanga
aManzimtoti
Kokstad
Sezela
Hibberdene
Port Shepstone
Margate
Port Edward
TO EAST LONDON
Port St Johns

INDIAN OCEAN

Dolphin Coast
Sunshine Coast

Km 30 60

N2 N3

☎ (031) 366 7500/304 7144 • e✉ tkzn@iafrica.com • 🌐 www.zulu.org.za

Johannesburg & Surrounds   South Africa

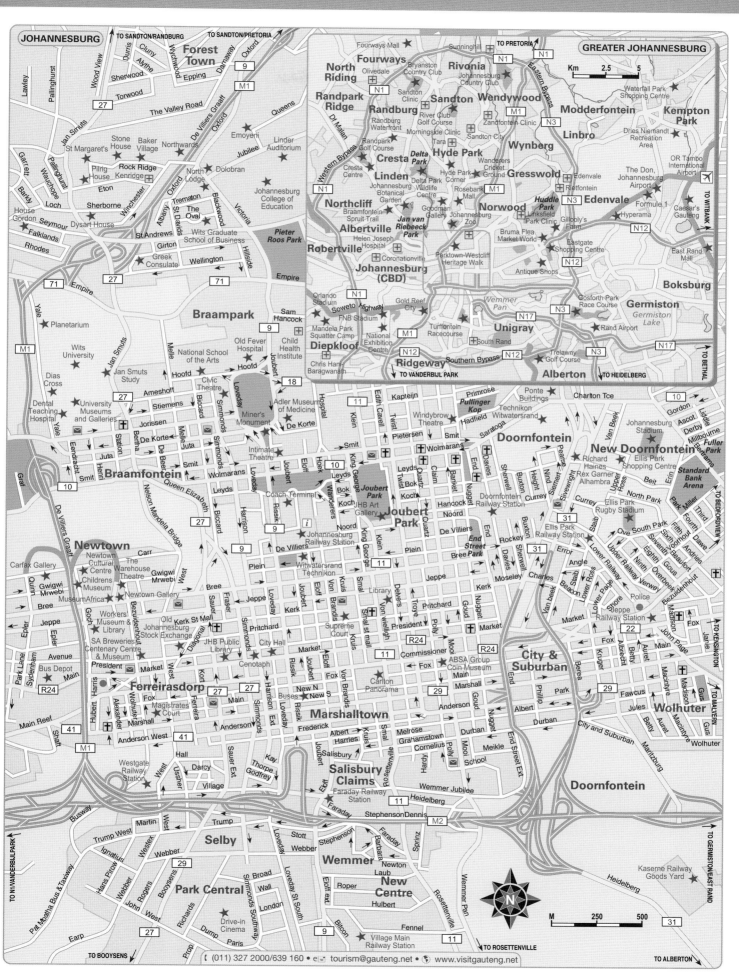

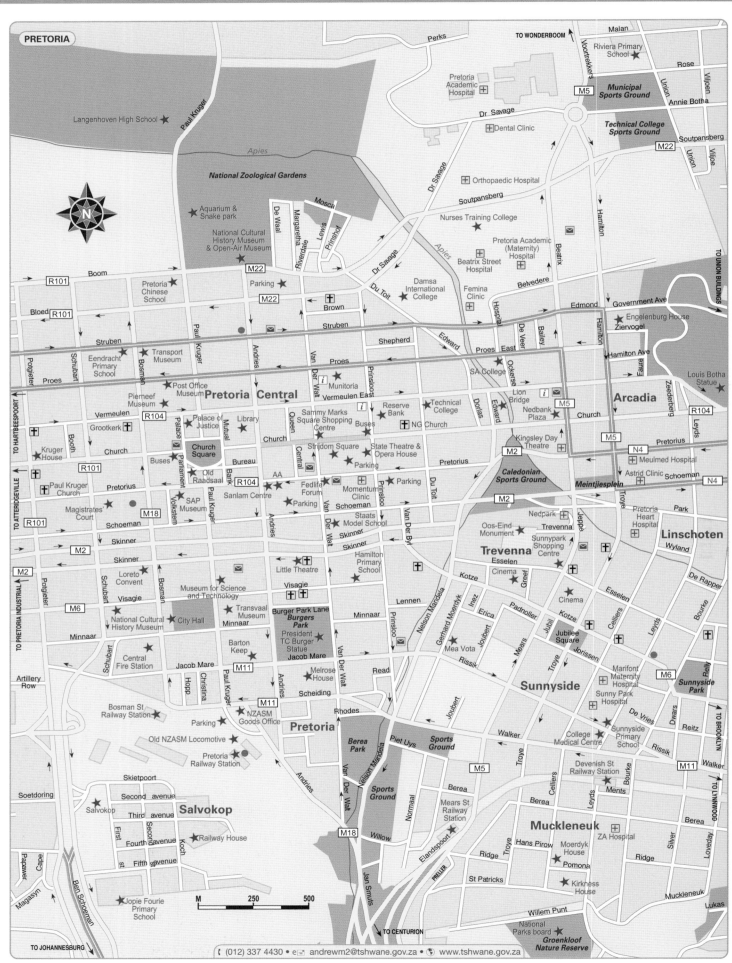

PRETORIA

TO WONDERBOOM

Malan

Perks

Pretoria Academic Hospital

Riviera Primary School

M5

Voortrekkers

Rose

Municipal Sports Ground

Union

Viljoen

Annie Botha

Dr. Savage

Technical College Sports Ground

Soutpansberg

Langenhoven High School

Paul Kruger

Dental Clinic

M22

Union

Viljoe

Apies

Dr Savage

Orthopaedic Hospital

Soutpansberg

Hamilton

Beatrix

TO UNION BUILDINGS

National Zoological Gardens

Nurses Training College

Aquarium & Snake park

Mosca

De Waal

Margaretha

Rissik

Lewis

Prinshof

Pretoria Academic (Maternity) Hospital

Belvedere

National Cultural History Museum & Open-Air Museum

Dr Savage

Apies

Beatrix Street Hospital

Femina Clinic

Hospital

De Veer

Bailey

Edmond

Government Ave

Engelenburg House

Ziervogel

Louis Botha Statue

M22

Boom

R101

Parking

M22

Brown

Struben

Damsa International College

Proes

East

Hamilton Ave

Eeufees

Zeederberg

R104

Bloed

R101

Pretoria Chinese School

Struben

Shepherd

Edward

Proes

SA College

Leyds

Struben

Andries

Van Der Walt

Proes

Ockerse

Dorias

Edward

Lion Bridge

Church

M5

Arcadia

Potgieter

Schubart

Transport Museum

Bosman

Paul Kruger

Munitoria

Vermeulen East

Nedbank Plaza

Kingsley Day Theatre

M5

Pretorius

R104

Proes

Pierneef Museum

Pretoria Central

Sammy Marks Square Shopping Centre

Reserve Bank

Technical College

M5

Meulmed Hospital

Astrid Clinic

N4

Vermeulen

R104

Palace of Justice

Library

Queen

Buses

NG Church

Pretorius

M2

Caledonian Sports Ground

Meintjiesplein

Schoeman

N4

Kruger House

Church

Grootkerk

Palace

Mutual

Church

Central

Strijdom Square

State Theatre & Opera House

Parking

Pretorius

M2

Nedpark

Jeppe

Pretoria Heart Hospital

Park

Linschoten

Booth

Parliament

Church Square

Bureau

AA

Parking

Trevenna

Buses

Old Raadsaal

Bank

R104

Fedlife Forum

Momentum Clinic

Oos-Eind Monument

Sunnypark Shopping Centre

Wyland

Paul Kruger Church

Pretorius

SAP Museum

Volkstem

Sanlam Centre

Parking

Schoeman

Staats Model School

Trevenna

Esselen

De Rapper

R101

Schoeman

Skinner

Skinner

Kotze

Cinema

Esselen

M18

Magistrates' Court

Van Der Walt

Hamilton Primary School

Cinema

Bourke

M2

Skinner

Skinner

Greef

Kotze

Loreto Convent

Bosman

Little Theatre

Lennen

Nelson Mandela

Gerhard Moerdyk

Erica

Padholler

Joubert

Jubil

Celliers

Leyds

M6

Visagie

Visagie

Museum for Science and Technology

Visagie

Burger Park Lane

Burgers Park

Minnaar

Inez

Mears

Jubilee Square

Jorissen

TO PRETORIA INDUSTRIAL

National Cultural History Museum

City Hall

Transvaal Museum

President TC Burger Statue

Mea Vota

Marifont Maternity Hospital

M6

Sunnyside Park

Minnaar

Minnaar

Jacob Mare

Rissik

Sunnyside

Sunny Park Hospital

Barton Keep

Jacob Mare

Read

Troye

Central Fire Station

Schubart

Christina

Paul Kruger

Andries

Van Der Walt

Melrose House

Scheiding

Joubert

De Vries

Reitz

Rissik

TO BROOKLYN

Artillery Row

Hopp

M11

Rhodes

Nelson Mandela

Piet Uys

Sports Ground

College Medical Centre

Sunnyside Primary School

Bosman St Railway Station

Parking

NZASM Goods Office

Pretoria

Berea Park

Walker

Dwars

TO LYNWOOD

Old NZASM Locomotive

Van Der Walt

Sports Ground

M5

Devenish St Railway Station

M11

Walker

Skietpoort

Pretoria Railway Station

Berea

Ments

Soetdoring

Second avenue

Berea

Berea

Salvokop

Third avenue

Salvokop

Mears St Railway Station

Mucleneuk

Leyds

Silver

Berea

Lovapsa

First

Fourth avenue

Second avenue

ZA Hospital

Hans Pirow

Moerdyk House

Ridge

Magasyn

Fifth avenue

Koch

Willow

M18

Elandspoort

Troye

Ridge

Pomona

Ben Schoeman

TO CENTURION

Jan Smuts

Preller

St Patricks

Celliers

Kirkness House

Mucleneuk

Lukas

Cape

Papenea

Jopie Fourie Primary School

M

250

500

Willem Punt

TO JOHANNESBURG

National Parks board

Groenkloof Nature Reserve

(012) 337 4430 • e andrewm2@tshwane.gov.za • www.tshwane.gov.za

Port Elizabeth South Africa
East London South Africa

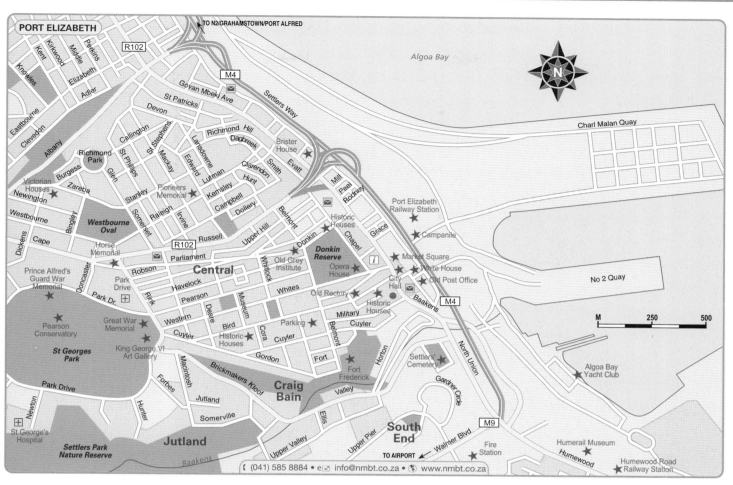

PORT ELIZABETH

TO N2/GRAHAMSTOWN/PORT ALFRED
R102
M4
Algoa Bay

Kent
Knowles
Kirkwood
Middle
Perkins
Eastbourne
Clevedon
Albany
Adler
Elizabeth
Govan Mbeki Ave
St Patricks
Devon
Callington
St Stephens
Richmond Hill
Settlers Way
Dagbreek
Brister House
Charl Malan Quay

Victorian Houses
Newington
Westbourne
Burgess
Zareba
Richmond Park
St Phillips
Glen
MacKay
Lansdowne
Edward
Clarendon
Smith
Evatt
Pioneers Memorial
Kemsley
Hunt
Dickens
Cape
Bingley
Westbourne Oval
Somerset
Raleigh
Irvine
Stanley
Russell
Upper Hill
Belmont
Donkin
Chapel
Grace
Mill
Peel
Rodney
Port Elizabeth Railway Station
Campanile

No 2 Quay

Prince Alfred's Guard War Memorial
Horse Memorial
Parliament
Robson
Old Grey Institute
Donkin Reserve
Market Square
White House
Old Post Office
Doncaster
Park Drive
Rink
Havelock
Whitlock
Opera House
City Hall
Baakens
M4

Pearson Conservatory
Great War Memorial
Western
Pearson
Depre
Bird
Whites
Old Rectory
Historic Houses
Military
Cuyler
No 2 Quay

St Georges Park
King George VI Art Gallery
Cuyler
Historic Houses
Cora
Cuyler
Parking
Belmont
Horton
North Union
M 250 500

Park Drive
Forbes
MacIntosh
Brickmakers Kloof
Gordon
Fort
Craig Bain
Fort Frederick
Valley
Settlers' Cemetery
Gardner Circle
Algoa Bay Yacht Club

Newton
Hunter
Jutland
Somerville
Ellis
Upper Pier
South End
M9
Humerail Museum
Humewood
Humewood Road Railway Station

St George's Hospital
Settlers Park Nature Reserve
Jutland
Upper Valley
Baakens
TO AIRPORT
Walmer Blvd
Fire Station

℅ (041) 585 8884 • e✉ info@nmbt.co.za • 🌐 www.nmbt.co.za

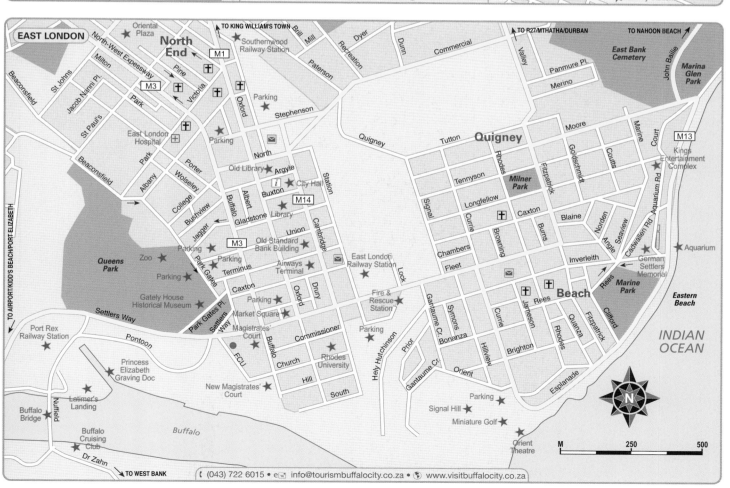

EAST LONDON

TO KING WILLIAM'S TOWN
Oriental Plaza
North End
Southernwood Railway Station
Brill
Mill
Dyer
Recreation
Dunn
Commercial
TO R27/MTHATHA/DURBAN
Valley
TO NAHOON BEACH
East Bank Cemetery
John Baillie
Marina Glen Park

Beaconsfield
St Johns
Milton
North-West Expressway
Pine
Victoria
Oxford
Parking
Stephenson
Paterson
Quigney
Panmure Pl.
Merino
Quigney
Moore
Marine
M13
Kings Entertainment Complex

Jacob Namhi Pl.
St Paul's
Park
East London Hospital
Parking
North
Old Library
Argyle
Station
Tutton
Rhodes
Tennyson
Milner Park
Goldschmidt
Fitzpatrick
Coutts

Beaconsfield
Park
Albany
Porter
Wolseley
College
Bushview
Jagger
Buxton
City Hall
M14
Library
Buffalo
Albert
Gladstone
Union
Cambridge
Signal
Longfellow
Currie
Caxton
Blaine
Browning
Burns
Norden
Inverleith
Angle
Seaview
Cadwallen Rd
Aquarium Rd
German Settlers Memorial
Aquarium

Queens Park
Zoo
Parking
Park Gates
Old Standard Bank Building
Airways Terminal
Terminus
Caxton
Drury
Oxford
East London Railway Station
Fire & Rescue Station
Chambers
Fleet
Lock
Marine Park
Beach
Rees
Jameson
Rees
Clifford
Esplanade
Eastern Beach
INDIAN OCEAN

Gately House Historical Museum
Settlers Way
Park Gates Pl.
Settlers Way
Market Square
Magistrates Court
Buffalo
Commissioner
Church
Rhodes University
Parking
Helga Hutchinson
Prior
Symons
Bonanza
Gantaume Cr.
Currie
Hillview
Brighton
Quanza
Fitzpatrick

Port Rex Railway Station
Pontoon
Princess Elizabeth Graving Doc
New Magistrates' Court
Hill
South
Gantaume Cr
Orient
Parking
Signal Hill
Miniature Golf

Buffalo Bridge
Nuffield
Latimer's Landing
Buffalo Cruising Club
Dr Zahn
FCU
Buffalo
Orient Theatre
M 250 500
TO WEST BANK

℅ (043) 722 6015 • e✉ info@tourismbuffalocity.co.za • 🌐 www.visitbuffalocity.co.za

193

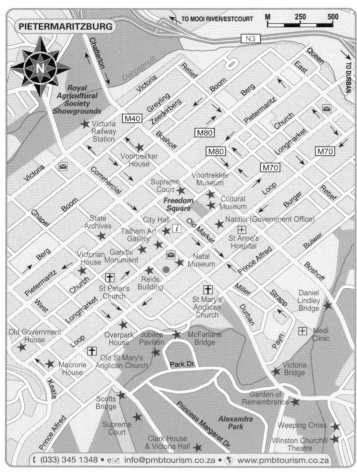

PIETERMARITZBURG

TO MOOI RIVER/ESTCOURT
N3
TO DURBAN

Dorpspruit
Chatterton
Victoria
Greyling
Zeederberg
Boshoft
Retief
Victoria
Boom
Berg
Pietermaritz
Boom
Church
East
Queen
Berg

Royal Agricultural Society Showgrounds
Victoria Railway Station
Voortrekker House
Voortrekker Museum
Supreme Court
Cultural Museum
Freedom Square
State Archives
City Hall
Tatham Art Gallery
Gandhi Monument
Victorian House
Reids Building
St Peter's Church
Commercial
Chapel
Berg
Pietermaritz
Church
West
Longmarket
Loop
Old Market
Natalia (Government Office)
St Anne's Hospital
Natal Museum
Prince Alfred
Miller
Durban
Strapp
Payn
Bulwer
Boshoft
Retief
Daniel Lindley Bridge
Medi Clinic

Old Government House
Overpark House
Jubilee Pavilion
McFarlane Bridge
St Mary's Anglican Church
Old St Mary's Anglican Church
Macrorie House
Keate
Prince Alfred
Loop
Park Dr
Scotts Bridge
Supreme Court
Clark House & Victoria Hall
Princess Margaret Dr
Alexandra Park
Garden of Remembrance
Weeping Cross
Victoria Bridge
Winston Churchill Theatre

M40 M80 M80 M70 M70

☎ (033) 345 1348 • e✉ info@pmbtourism.co.za • 🌐 www.pmbtourism.co.za

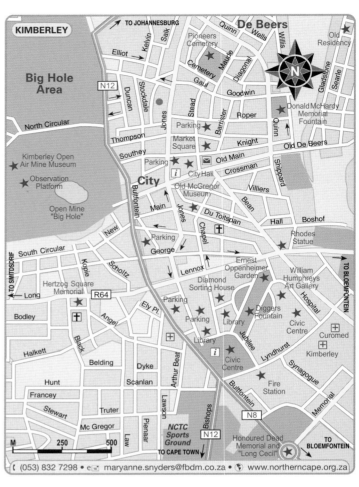

KIMBERLEY

TO JOHANNESBURG
N12

Big Hole Area
North Circular
Kimberley Open Air Mine Museum
Observation Platform
Open Mine "Big Hole"
TO SMITSDRIF
South Circular
Hertzog Square Memorial
Bodley
Halkett
Belding
Hunt
Francey
Stewart
Truter
Mc Gregor
Long
Kopie
Scholtz
Black
Dyke
Scanlan
Pienaar
Law

De Beers
Pioneers Cemetery
Old Residency
Quinn
Kelvin
Elliot
Cemetery
Gaul
Duncan
Stockdale
Thompson
Southey
New
Jones
Du Toitspan
Scholtz
Angel
Ely Pl.
Arthur Beat
Lawson
Bistops
Maude
Diagonal
Stead
Selous
Barkner
Roper
Knight
Old Main
Crossman
Main
George
Lennox
Diamond Sorting House
Parking
Parking
Library
Library
Civic Centre
Wells
Willis
Gladstone
Searle
Goodwin
Quinn
Donald McHardy Memorial Fountain
Old De Beers
Shippard
Villiers
Bean
Hall
Boshof
Rhodes Statue
Ernest Oppenheimer Garden
William Humphreys Art Gallery
Hospital
Diggers Fountain
Civic Centre
Curomed Kimberley
Jubilee
Lyndhurst
Synagogue
Fire Station
Buttonfontein
Memorial
TO BLOEMFONTEIN

City
City Hall
Market Square
Parking
Parking
Buttonfontein
Old McGregor Museum
Parking
Parking
Civic Centre
NCTC Sports Ground
Honoured Dead Memorial and "Long Cecil"
N8
N12
TO CAPE TOWN
TO BLOEMFONTEIN

R64
R521

☎ (053) 832 7298 • e✉ maryanne.snyders@fbdm.co.za • 🌐 www.northerncape.org.za

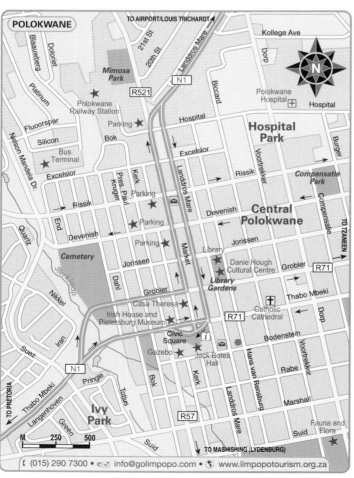

POLOKWANE

TO AIRPORT/LOUIS TRICHARDT
21st St
20th St
Kollege Ave
Landdros Mare
Dorp
Biccard
Polokwane Hospital
Hospital

Blaauwberg
Doloriet
Platinum
Fluoorspar
Silicon
Nelson Mandela Dr
Quartz
Suez
Iran
Thabo Mbeki
Langenhoven
Green
Mimosa Park
Polokwane Railway Station
Parking
Bus Terminal
Excelsior
Rissik
Devenish
Cemetery
Sterkloop
Casa Theresa
Irish House and Pietersburg Museum
Civic Square
Gazebo
Jack Botes Hall
Nikkel
Pringle
Tollus
Bok
Ivy Park
Suid

Bok
Hospital
Excelsior
Rissik
Devenish
Jorissen
Jorissen
Grobler
Kerk
Pres. Paul Kruger
Parking
Parking
Parking
Library
Danie Hough Cultural Centre
Library Gardens
Thabo Mbeki
Catholic Cathedral
Bodenstein
Hans van Rensburg
Landdros Mare
Market
Kerk
Voortrekker
Hospital Park
Compensatie Park
Central Polokwane
Compensatie
Grobler
Dorp
Rabe
Marshall
Suid
Fauna and Flora
TO TZANEEN
TO MASHISHING (LYDENBURG)

N1
R521
N1
R71
R71
R57

☎ (015) 290 7300 • e✉ info@golimpopo.com • 🌐 www.limpopotourism.org.za

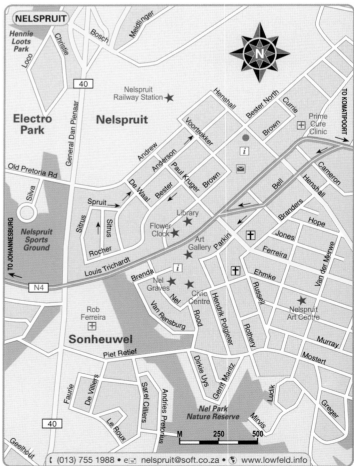

NELSPRUIT

Hennie Loots Park
Bosch
Meidlinger
Christie
Loco
Electro Park
General Dan Pienaar
Nelspruit Railway Station
Nelspruit
Henshall
Bester North
Currie
Prime Cure Clinic
TO KOMATIPOORT

Old Pretoria Rd
Silva
Nelspruit Sports Ground
Sittus
Sittus
Sittus
Rocher
Louis Trichardt
TO JOHANNESBURG
N4

Andrew
Anderson
Paul Kruger
Brown
Da Waal
Bester
Spruit
Voortrekker
Flower Clock
Library
Art Gallery
Parkin
Brenda
Nel Graves
Nel
Civic Centre
Hendrik Potgieter
Van Rensburg
Rob Ferreira
Sonheuwel
Piet Retief
Dinkie Uys
Faurie
De Villiers
Le Roux
Geelhout
Safel Cilliers
Andries Pretorius
Gert Maritz
Nel Park Nature Reserve
Mirvis
Ludik

Bell
Cameron
Henshall
Branders
Hope
Jones
Ferreira
Ehmke
Russell
Rothery
Van der Merwe
Nelspruit Art Centre
Murray
Mostert
Greger

40
40

☎ (013) 755 1988 • e✉ nelspruit@soft.co.za • 🌐 www.lowfeld.info

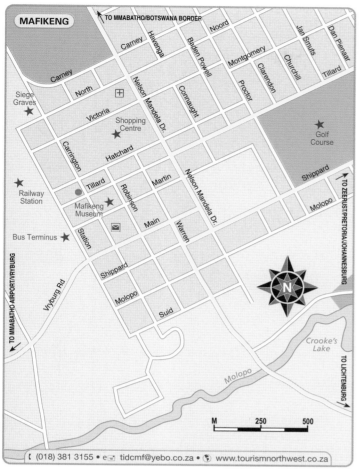

MAFIKENG

TO MMABATHO/BOTSWANA BORDER

Carney
Havenga
Baden Powell
Noord
Montgomery
Clarendon
Churchill
Tillard
Jan Smuts
Dan Pienaar
Carney
North
Victoria
Connaught
Proctor
Siege Graves
Shopping Centre
Nelson Mandela Dr.
Hatchard
Carrington
Tillard
Martin
Robinson
Nelson Mandela Dr.
Railway Station
Mafikeng Museum
Shippard
Molopo
Main
Warren
Bus Terminus
Station
Shippard
Molopo
Golf Course
Suid
Vryburg Rd
TO MMABATHO AIRPORT/VRYBURG
Crooke's Lake
TO ZEERUST/PRETORIA/JOHANNESBURG
TO LICHTENBURG
Molopo

M 250 500

((018) 381 3155 • e tidcmf@yebo.co.za • www.tourismnorthwest.co.za

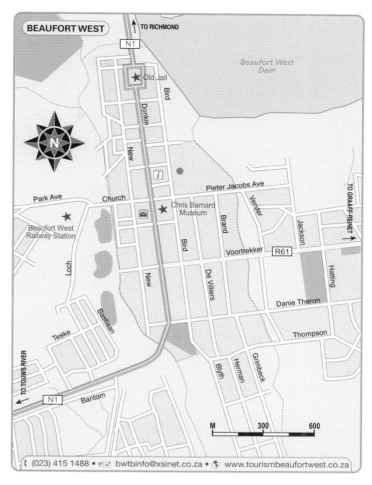

BEAUFORT WEST

TO RICHMOND
N1
Old Jail
Bird
Donkin
New
Park Ave
Church
Beaufort West Railway Station
Pieter Jacobs Ave
Chris Barnard Museum
Brand
Verster
Jackson
TO GRAAFF-REINET
Loch
Bird
Voortrekker
R61
Hatting
New
De Villiers
Danie Theron
Teske
Bastiaan
Thompson
TO TOUWS RIVER
Blyth
Herman
Grimbeck
N1
Bantom
Beaufort West Dam

M 300 600

((023) 415 1488 • e bwtbinfo@xsinet.co.za • www.tourismbeaufortwest.co.za

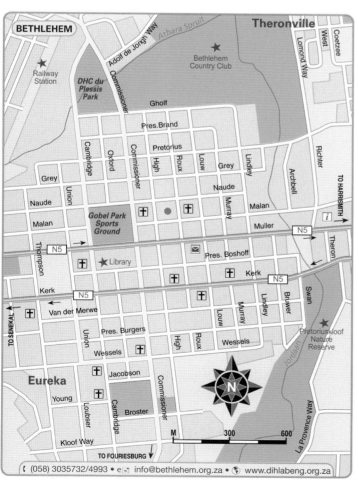

BETHLEHEM

Atbara Spruit
Adolf de Jongh Way
Theronville
West
Coetzee
Lomond Way
Railway Station
Bethlehem Country Club
DHC du Plessis Park
Commissioner
Gholf
Pres. Brand
Pretorius
Richter
Archbell
TO HARRISMITH
Cambridge
Oxford
Commissioner
High
Roux
Louw
Grey
Lindley
Naude
Grey
Union
Naude
Murray
Malan
Malan
Gobel Park Sports Ground
Muller
N5
Thompson
N5
Pres. Boshoff
Theron
Kerk
N5
Library
Kerk
Van der Merwe
Swan
Brouwer
TO SENEKAL
Kerk
Union
Pres. Burgers
Louw
Murray
Lindley
Pretoriuskloof Nature Reserve
High
Roux
Wessels
Wessels
Jordan
Eureka
Jacobson
Young
Loubser
Broster
Cambridge
Commissioner
La Provence Way
Kloof Way
TO FOURIESBURG

M 300 600

((058) 3035732/4993 • e info@bethlehem.org.za • www.dihlabeng.org.za

CITRUSDAL

TO CLANWILLIAM
Kooperasie
Citrusdal Wine Cellars
Kelders
N7
Skool
Voortrekker
Golf Course
Muller
Citrusdal Museum
Muller
Olifants
Prinsloo
Kerk
Prinsloo
Park
Dankaart
Oranje
Oranje
Qewer
Paul de Villiers
Hoop
Paul de Villiers
TO PIKETBERG
Loop
Craig Royston Country Museum
De Klerk
The Baths Road
Vrede
Keerom/Bo-river Rd

M 250 500

((022) 921 3210 • e info@citrusdal.info • www.citrusdal.info

195

Colesberg   South Africa
Graaff-Reinet   South Africa

George   South Africa
Estcourt   South Africa

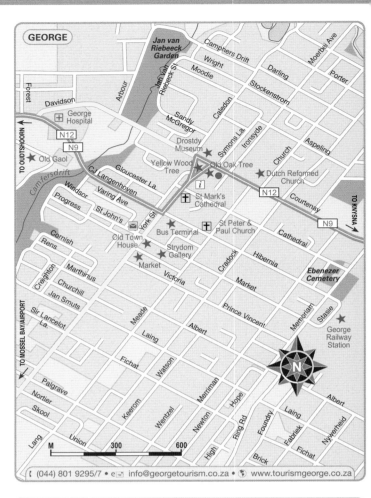

COLESBERG

((051) 753 0777/0678 • e colesbergourism@shisas.co.za • www.colesberg.co.za

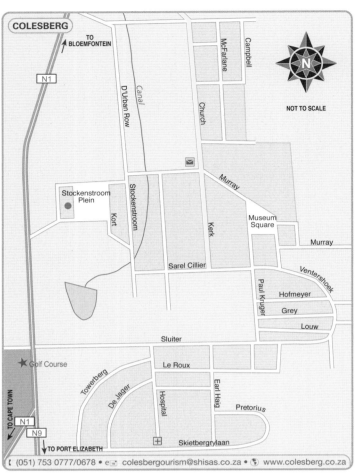

GEORGE

((044) 801 9295/7 • e info@georgetourism.co.za • www.tourismgeorge.co.za

GRAAFF-REINET

((049) 892 4248 • e info@graaffreinet.co.za • www.graaffreinet.co.za

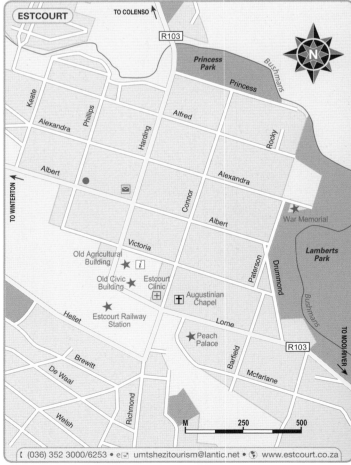

ESTCOURT

((036) 352 3000/6253 • e umtshezitourism@lantic.net • www.estcourt.co.za

Grahamstown South Africa
Kroonstad South Africa

Knysna South Africa
Ladysmith South Africa

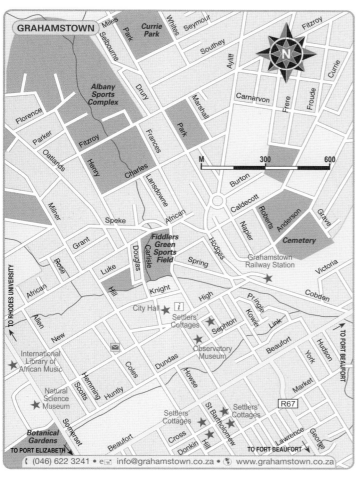

GRAHAMSTOWN

Miles, Selbourne, Whites, Seymour, Fitzroy
Currie Park
Park, Southey, Ayliff, Carnarvon, Currie
Albany Sports Complex, Drury, Marshall, Park, Froude, Frere
Florence, Fitzroy, Frances, Park, Burton
Parker, Henry, Charles, Lansdowne, Caldecott, Roberts, Napier, Anderson, Grave
Oatlands, Milner, Speke, African, Cemetery
Grant, Ross, Luke, Douglas, Carlisle, Fiddlers Green Sports Field, Spring, Hodges, Grahamstown Railway Station, Victoria
African, Allen, Hill, Knight, High, Pr Ingle, Kowie, Link, Cobden
City Hall, Settlers' Cottages, Sephton, Beaufort, Hudson, York
New, Coles, Dundas, Howse, Observatory Museum, Market, TO FORT BEAUFORT
International Library of African Music, Scotts, Huntly, St Bartholomew, R67
Natural Science Museum, Settlers' Cottages, Settlers' Cottages, Lawrence, George
Botanical Gardens, Somerset, Beaufort, Cross, Donkin, Hill, TO FORT BEAUFORT
TO PORT ELIZABETH, TO RHODES UNIVERSITY

M 300 600

((046) 622 3241 • e info@grahamstown.co.za • www.grahamstown.co.za

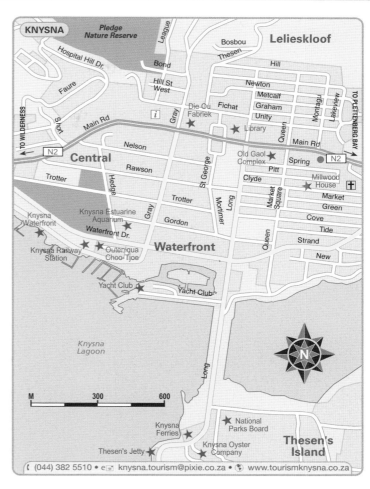

KNYSNA

Pledge Nature Reserve, Bosbou, Thesen, Lelieskloof
Hospital Hill Dr., Bond, Hill, Newton, Metcalf, Graham, Unity
Faure, Hill St West, Die Ou Fabriek, Fichat, Library, Montagu, Lakeview
Short, Main Rd, Gray, Queen, Main Rd, TO PLETTENBERG BAY
N2, Central, Nelson, Old Gaol Complex, Spring, N2
Trotter, Rawson, Clyde, Pitt, Millwood House
Knysna Waterfront, Knysna Estuarine Aquarium, Trotter, Gong, Market Square, Market, Green
Knysna Railway Station, Waterfront Dr., Gordon, Cove, Tide
Outeniqua Choo-Tjoe, Waterfront, Queen, Strand, New
Yacht Club, Yacht Club
Knysna Lagoon, Long
TO WILDERNESS
Knysna Ferries, National Parks Board
Thesen's Jetty, Knysna Oyster Company, Thesen's Island

M 300 600

((044) 382 5510 • e knysna.tourism@pixie.co.za • www.tourismknysna.co.za

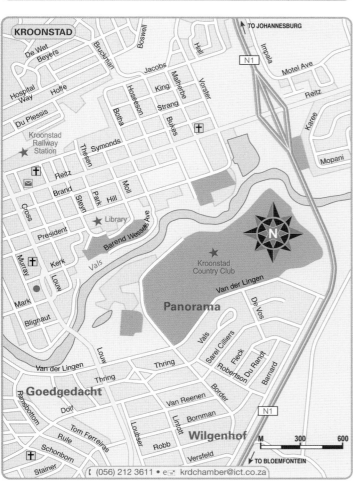

KROONSTAD

TO JOHANNESBURG
De Wet, Beyers, Bruckman, Ilawson, Bosch, Hall, Impala, Motel Ave
Hospital Way, Hoffe, Jacobs, Malherbe, Vorster, Reitz
Du Plessis, King, Hoseeson, Strang, Karee, N1
Kroonstad Railway Station, Botha, Symonds, Bukes, Mopani
Thesen, Reitz, Moll, Park, Hill
Brand, Steyn, Library
Cross, President, Barend Wessel Ave
Murray, Kerk, Vals, Kroonstad Country Club
Mark, Louw, Van der Lingen
Blignaut, Panorama, De Vos
Vals, Sarel Cilliers, Fleck, Du Randt
Van der Lingen, Louw, Thring, Robertson, Barnard
Goedgedacht, Thring, Van Reenen, Border
Ransbothm, Dolf, Lintott, Bornman, N1
Rule, Tom Ferreira, Loubser, Robb
Schonborn, Wilgenhof, Versfeld
Stainer, TO BLOEMFONTEIN

M 300 600

((056) 212 3611 • e krdchamber@ict.co.za

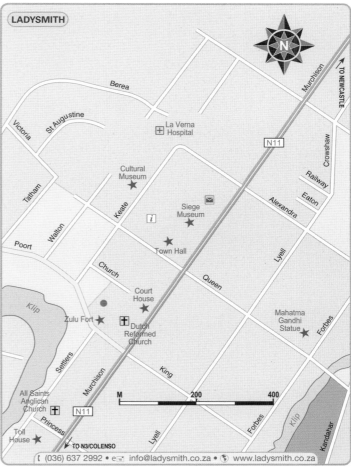

LADYSMITH

Berea, Murchison, TO NEWCASTLE
Victoria, St Augustine, La Verna Hospital, N11, Crowshaw
Tatham, Cultural Museum, Keate, Railway, Eaton
Poort, Walton, Siege Museum, Alexandra
Town Hall, Queen, Lyell
Church, Court House, Klip
Zulu Fort, Dutch Reformed Church, Mahatma Gandhi Statue, Forbes
All Saints Anglican Church, Settlers, Murchison, King, Forbes
Toll House, Princess, N11, Lyell, Kandahar
TO N3/COLENSO

M 200 400

((036) 637 2992 • e info@ladysmith.co.za • www.ladysmith.co.za

Lamberts Bay South Africa
Mossel Bay South Africa

Mashishing (Lydenburg) South Africa
Musina South Africa

LAMBERTS BAY

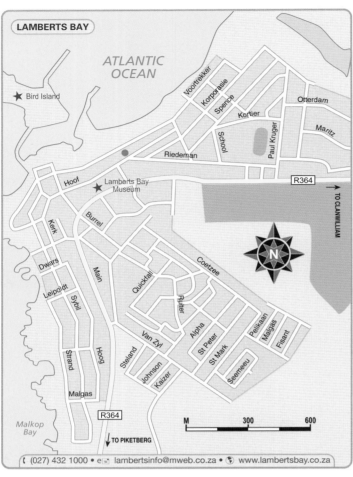

ATLANTIC OCEAN

★ Bird Island

Voortrekker
Korporasie
Spence
Kortier
Otterdam
Maritz
Paul Kruger
School
Riedeman

R364

TO CLANWILLIAM →

Hoof
★ Lamberts Bay Museum

Kerk
Burrel
Main
Coetzee
Dwars
Leipoldt
Sybil
Quickfall
Ruiter
Alpha
Pelikaan
Malgas
Fisant
Strand
Hoog
Van Zyl
Steland
Johnson
Kaizer
St Peter
St Mark
Seemeeu
Malgas

Malkop Bay

R364

M 300 600

→ TO PIKETBERG

☎ (027) 432 1000 • e ✉ lambertsinfo@mweb.co.za • 🌐 www.lambertsbay.co.za

MASHISHING (LYDENBURG)

↗ TO TZANEEN/ PILGRIMS REST

Noord
Fourie

★ Golf Course

Old Voortrekker School ★
Old Dutch Reformed Church ★
Kerk
St Johns Anglican Church ✝
Old Voortrekker Church ★
Dutch Reformed Church ✝
Viljoen
De Beer
Buhrmann
Coetzer
Eeufees
Marren

TO NELSPRUIT/SABIE VIA LONG TOM PASS

Lange
Kantoor
Burger
Rensburg
✉
ℹ
Old Municipal Offices
Johannes Coetzer
Voortrekker
Lehman
Potgieter
★ Powder Magazine
Fort Mary Monument
Long Tom
Greyling
Marren

Sterkspruit
Brug
★ Lydenburg Fly-fishing Club
Finsbury Cres
Nel
Van Staden
Schulze
Goodman

Schoeman
Viljoen
Jansen
Marais
Goud
Lydenburg
Kriel
Buiten
De Vos
Chris Lombard
Brown

Berg
Maasdorp
Marren La
McGee
Ruiter

Lydenburg Hospital ✚

↙ TO MACHADODORP

M 250 500

☎ (013) 235 2213/082 779 3748 • e ✉ jcilliers@thabachweu.org.za • 🌐 www.lydenburg.org

MOSSEL BAY

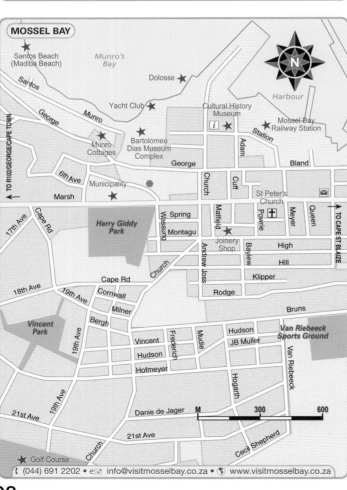

Santos Beach (Madiba Beach)
Munro's Bay
★ Dolosse
Harbour

Santos
George
Munro
★ Yacht Club
Cultural History Museum ℹ ★
Mossel Bay Railway Station ★
Station
Adam

TO R102/GEORGE/CAPE TOWN

Munro Cottages ★
Bartolomeu Dias Museum Complex ★
George
Bland

6th Ave
Municipality ★
Church
Cuff
St Peter's Church ✝
✉
Marsh
Spring
Matfield
Powrie
Meyer
Queen

TO CAPE ST BLAIZE →

17th Ave
Cape Rd
Harry Giddy Park
Wassung
Montagu
Joinery Shop ★
Bayview
High
Andrew Joss
Church
Hill
Klipper
18th Ave
19th Ave
Cornwall
Milner
Rodge
Bruns
19th Ave
Vincent Park
Bergh
Vincent
Frederick
Mudie
Hudson
JB Muller
Van Riebeeck Sports Ground
Hofmeyer
Hogarth
Van Riebeeck

21st Ave
19th Ave
Danie de Jager
M 300 600
21st Ave
Church
Cecil Shepherd
★ Golf Course

☎ (044) 691 2202 • e ✉ info@visitmosselbay.co.za • 🌐 www.visitmosselbay.co.za

MUSINA

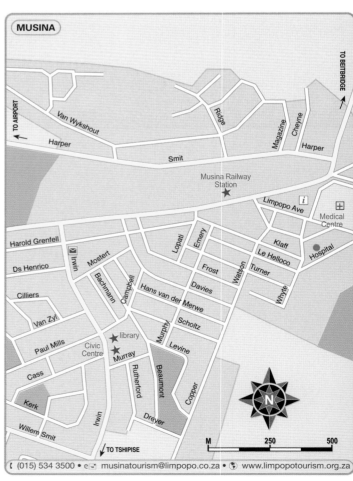

TO BEITBRIDGE ↗

TO AIRPORT
Van Wykshout
Ridge
Cheyne
Harper
Harper
Smit

Musina Railway Station ★

Limpopo Ave ℹ
✚ Medical Centre

Harold Grenfell
Irwin ✉
Mostert
Lonati
Emery
Klaff
Le Helloco
Hospital ●
Ds Henrico
Bachmann
Campbell
Frost
Watson
Turner
Cilliers
Hans van der Merwe
Davies
Whyte
Van Zyl
Scholtz
Paul Mills
★ library
Murphy
Levine
Civic Centre ★
Murray
Rutherford
Beaumont
Copper
Cass
Kerk
Irwin
Dreyer
Willem Smit

↓ TO TSHIPISE

M 250 500

☎ (015) 534 3500 • e ✉ musinatourism@limpopo.co.za • 🌐 www.limpopotourism.org.za

198

Newcastle
Pilgrims Rest
South Africa
South Africa

Oudtshoorn
Port Shepstone
South Africa
South Africa

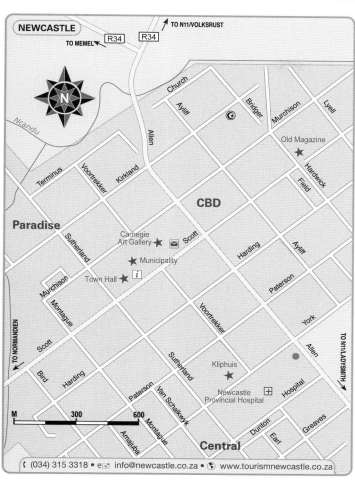

NEWCASTLE

TO N11/VOLKSRUST
TO MEMEL
R34
R34

Church
Aylift
Bridger
Murchison
Lyell
Allen
Kirkland
Voortrekker
Terminus
Old Magazine
Hardwick
Field
CBD
Paradise
Carnegie Art Gallery
Scott
Municipality
Harding
Town Hall
Sutherland
Paterson
Aylift
Murchison
Montague
York
Voortrekker
Scott
Bird
Harding
Kliphuis
Sutherland
Paterson
Van Schalkwyk
Newcastle Provincial Hospital
Hospital
Montague
Amajuba
Dunton
Earl
Greaves
Central

TO NORMANDIEN
TO N11/LADYSMITH
Ncandu

M 300 600

(034) 315 3318 • e info@newcastle.co.za • www.tourismnewcastle.co.za

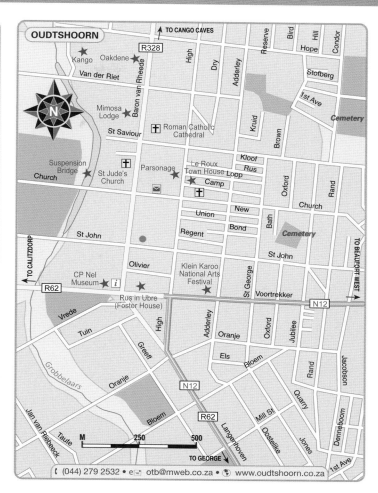

OUDTSHOORN

TO CANGO CAVES
R328

Kango
Oakdene
Van der Riet
Reserve
Bird
Hill
Condor
Hope
Stofberg
1st Ave
High
Dry
Adderley
Brown
Cemetery
Mimosa Lodge
Baron van Rheede
Kruid
St Saviour
Roman Catholic Cathedral
Kloof
Rus
Suspension Bridge
St Jude's Church
Parsonage
Le Roux Town House Loop
Camp
Oxford
Rand
Church
Church
New
Union
Bond
Bath
St John
Regent
Cemetery
Olivier
Klein Karoo National Arts Festival
St John
CP Nel Museum
St George
Voortrekker
N12
TO CALITZDORP
R62
Rus in Urbe (Foster House)
Vrede
Tuin
High
Adderley
Oranje
Oxford
Jubilee
Greeff
Els
Bloem
Rand
Oranje
N12
Jacobson
Grobbelaars
Bloem
Quarry
Mill St
Denneboom
Jan van Riebeeck
Taute
Langenhoven
Oostelike
Jones
1st Ave
R62
TO GEORGE
TO BEAUFORT WEST

M 250 500

(044) 279 2532 • e otb@mweb.co.za • www.oudtshoorn.co.za

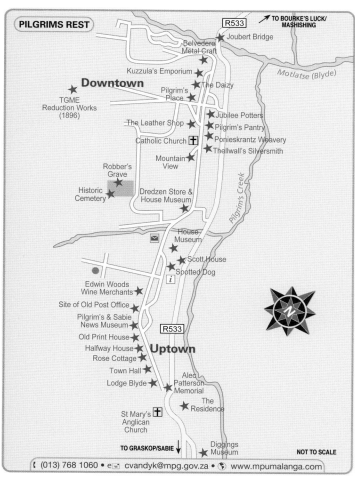

PILGRIMS REST

R533
TO BOURKE'S LUCK/ MASHISHING
Joubert Bridge
Belvedere Metal Craft
Kuzzula's Emporium
Motlatse (Blyde)
Downtown
The Daizy
Pilgrim's Place
TGME Reduction Works (1896)
Jubilee Potters
The Leather Shop
Pilgrim's Pantry
Catholic Church
Ponieskrantz Weavery
Thellwall's Silversmith
Mountain View
Robber's Grave
Historic Cemetery
Dredzen Store & House Museum
Pilgrim's Creek
House Museum
Scott House
Spotted Dog
Edwin Woods Wine Merchants
Site of Old Post Office
Pilgrim's & Sabie News Museum
Old Print House
R533
Halfway House
Rose Cottage
Uptown
Town Hall
Lodge Blyde
Alec Patterson Memorial
The Residence
St Mary's Anglican Church
TO GRASKOP/SABIE
Diggings Museum
NOT TO SCALE

(013) 768 1060 • e cvandyk@mpg.gov.za • www.mpumalanga.com

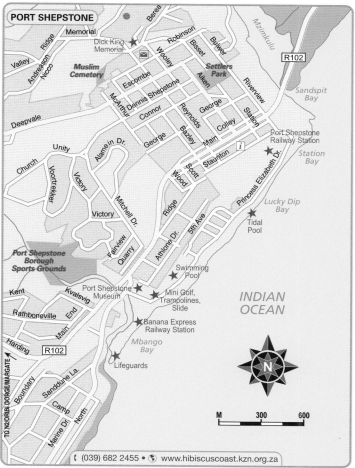

PORT SHEPSTONE

Memorial
Berea
Mzimkulu
Ridge
Valley
Robinson
Bisset
Bulwer
R102
Andreason
Nicco
Dick King Memorial
Wooley
Muslim Cemetery
Settlers Park
Sandspit Bay
Escombe
Aiken
Riverview
Deepvale
McArthur
Dennis Shepstone
Reynolds
George
Station
Connor
Bazley
Main
Colley
Port Shepstone Railway Station
Unity
Alamein Dr.
George
Wood
Scott
Staunton
Station Bay
Church
Victory
Voortrekker
Mitchell Dr.
Ridge
Princess Elizabeth Dr.
Lucky Dip Bay
Victory
Fairview
Quarry
Athlone Dr.
5th Ave
Tidal Pool
Port Shepstone Borough Sports Grounds
Swimming Pool
INDIAN OCEAN
Kent
Kvalsvig
Port Shepstone Museum
Mini Golf, Trampolines, Slide
Rathboneville
End
Banana Express Railway Station
Mbango Bay
Harding
Main
R102
TO N2/ORIBI GORGE/MARGATE
Lifeguards
Boundary
Sanddune La.
Camp
North
Marine Dr.

N

M 300 600

(039) 682 2455 • www.hibiscuscoast.kzn.org.za

199

Richards Bay South Africa
Sishen South Africa
Rustenburg South Africa
Springbok South Africa

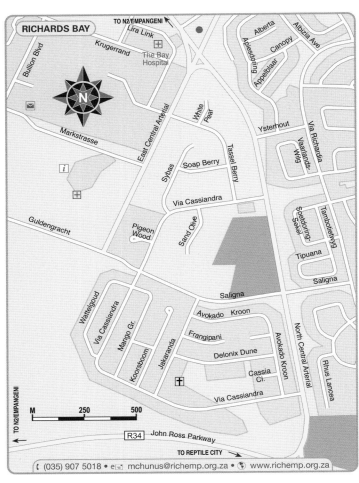

RICHARDS BAY

((035) 907 5018 • e⌷ mchunus@richemp.org.za • ⓢ www.richemp.org.za

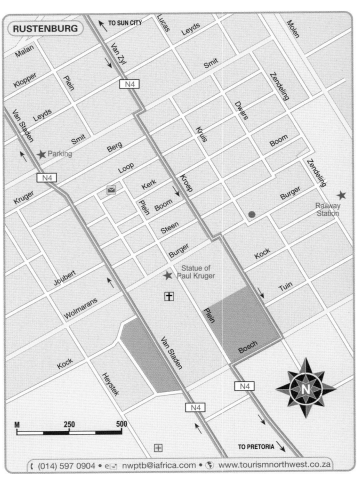

RUSTENBURG

((014) 597 0904 • e⌷ nwptb@iafrica.com • ⓢ www.tourismnorthwest.co.za

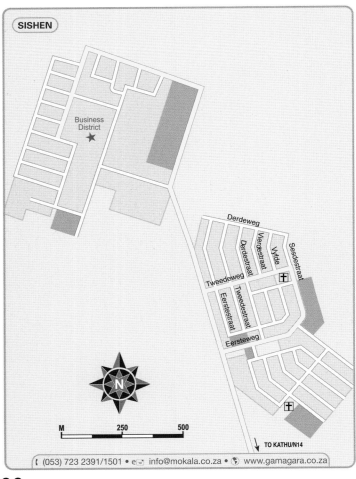

SISHEN

((053) 723 2391/1501 • e⌷ info@mokala.co.za • ⓢ www.gamagara.co.za

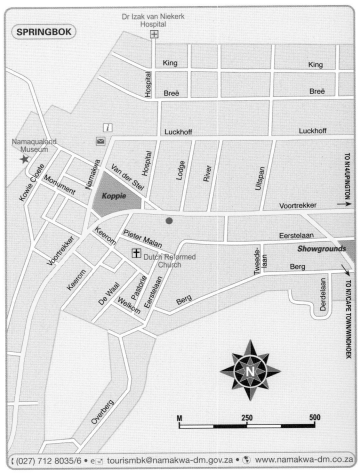

SPRINGBOK

((027) 712 8035/6 • e⌷ tourismbk@namakwa-dm.gov.za • ⓢ www.namakwa-dm.co.za

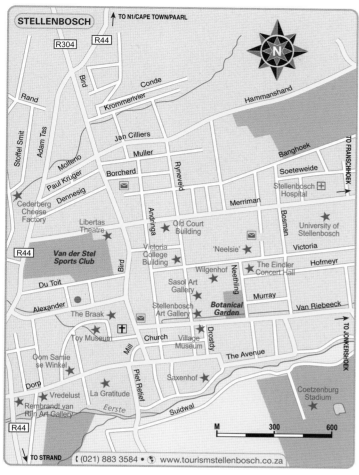

STELLENBOSCH

TO N1/CAPE TOWN/PAARL

R304   R44

Bird
Rand
Conde
Krommenvier
Hammanshand
Stoffel Smit
Adam Tas
Jan Cilliers
Molteno
Muller
Banghoek
Paul Kruger
Borcherd
Ryneveld
Soeteweide
Dennesig
Stellenbosch Hospital
Cederberg Cheese Factory
Merriman
Bosman
Libertas Theatre
Andringa
Old Court Building
University of Stellenbosch
R44
Van der Stel Sports Club
Victoria College Building
'Neelsie'
Victoria
Bird
Wilgenhof
Neethling
The Eindler Concert Hall
Hofmeyr
Du Toit
Sasol Art Gallery
Murray
Alexander
Stellenbosch Art Gallery
Botanical Garden
Van Riebeeck
The Braak
Church
Village Museum
Drostdy
Toy Museum
Mill
The Avenue
Oom Samie se Winkel
Dorp
Saxenhof
Vredelust
La Gratitude
Piet Relief
Suidwal
Coetzenburg Stadium
Rembrandt van Rijn Art Gallery
Eerste
R44

M   300   600

TO STRAND

((021) 883 3584 • ⊕ www.tourismstellenbosch.co.za

TO FRANSCHHOEK
TO JONKERSHOEK

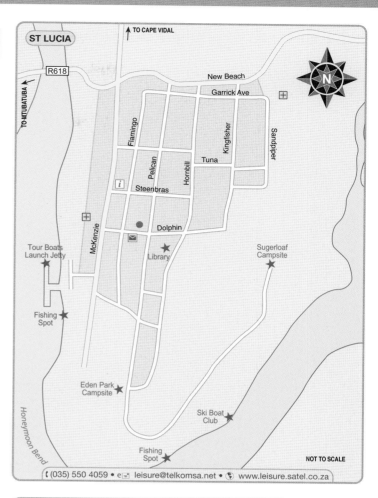

ST LUCIA

TO CAPE VIDAL

R618
New Beach
Garrick Ave
TO MTUBATUBA
Flamingo
Kingfisher
Sandpiper
Pelican
Hornbill
Tuna
Steenbras
i
McKenzie
Dolphin
Tour Boats Launch Jetty
Library
Sugerloaf Campsite
Fishing Spot
Eden Park Campsite
Ski Boat Club
Honeymoon Bend
Fishing Spot

NOT TO SCALE

((035) 550 4059 • e✉ leisure@telkomsa.net • ⊕ www.leisure.satel.co.za

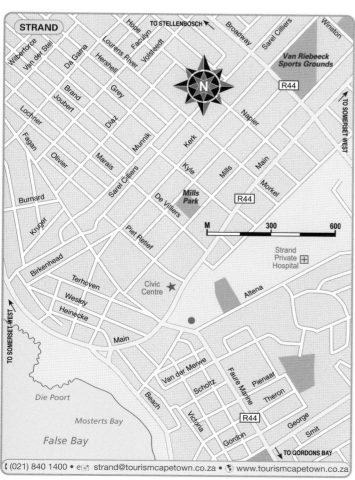

STRAND

TO STELLENBOSCH
Broadway
Winston
Hode
Faoulyn
Volsteedt
Sarel Cilliers
Wilberforce
Van der Stel
Da Gama
Lourens River
Hershell
Van Riebeeck Sports Grounds
Brand
Grey
Joubert
Napier
R44
Lochner
Diaz
Fagan
Olivier
Munnik
Kerk
Main
Burnard
Marais
Kyle
Mills
Morkel
Sarel Cilliers
De Villiers
Mills Park
R44
Kruger
Birkenhead
Piet Retief
Terhoven
Strand Private Hospital
Civic Centre
Wesley
Heinecke
Altena
Main
Van der Merwe
Scholtz
Faure Marine
Pienaar
Theron
Die Poort
Beach
Victoria
Gordon
George
Smit
R44
Mosterts Bay
False Bay
TO SOMERSET WEST
TO GORDONS BAY

M   300   600

((021) 840 1400 • e✉ strand@tourismcapetown.co.za • ⊕ www.tourismcapetown.co.za

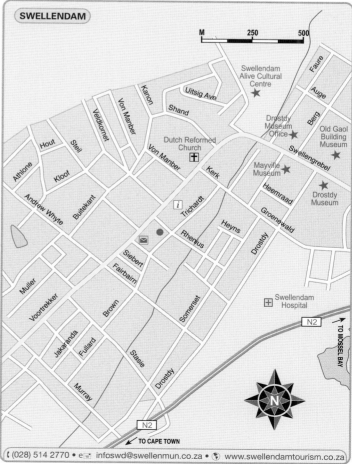

SWELLENDAM

M   250   500

Swellendam Alive Cultural Centre
Faure
Uitsig Ave
Auge
Karton
Shand
Berg
Veldkornet
Von Manber
Drostdy Museum Office
Old Gaol Building Museum
Hout
Steil
Dutch Reformed Church
Swellengrebel
Athlone
Kloof
Von Manber
Kerk
Mayville Museum
Heemraad
Andrew Whyte
Buitekant
Trichardt
Heyns
Drostdy Museum
i
Heyns
Groenewald
Rhenius
Drostdy
Siebert
Fairbairn
Muller
Voortrekker
Brown
Somerset
Swellendam Hospital
Jakaranda
Fullard
Stasie
N2
Drostdy
TO MOSSEL BAY
Murray
N2
TO CAPE TOWN

((028) 514 2770 • e✉ infoswd@swellenmun.co.za • ⊕ www.swellendamtourism.co.za

201

Tzaneen
South Africa
Upington
South Africa

Mthatha
South Africa
Vryburg
South Africa

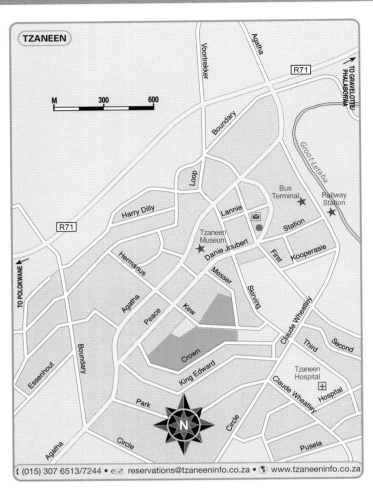

TZANEEN

M — 300 — 600

R71

TO GRAVELOTTE/PHALABORWA →

Voortrekker

Agatha

Boundary

Loop

Groot-Letaba

Harry Dilly

Lannie

Bus Terminal

Railway Station

Station

Tzaneen Museum

Danie Joubert

Kooperasie

First

Hermanus

Messer

Skirving

Claude Wheatley

R71

Agatha

Peace

Kew

Third

Second

Crown

King Edward

Tzaneen Hospital

Claude Wheatley

Hospital

Essenhout

Boundary

Park

Circle

Pusela

TO POLOKWANE →

Agatha

Circle

N

((015) 307 6513/7244 • e✉ reservations@tzaneeninfo.co.za • 🌐 www.tzaneeninfo.co.za

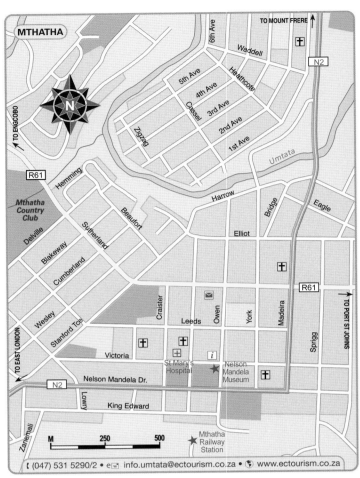

MTHATHA

TO MOUNT FRERE →

6th Ave

Waddell

N2

5th Ave

Heathcote

4th Ave

3rd Ave

Cassel

2nd Ave

Zigzag

1st Ave

Umtata

N

R61

Hemming

Harrow

Bridge

Eagle

Mthatha Country Club

Delville

Sutherland

Beaufort

Elliot

Blakeway

Cumberland

R61

Craister

Leeds

Owen

York

Madeira

TO ENGCOBO →

Wesley

Stanford Tce

Spring

TO EAST LONDON

Victoria

St Mary's Hospital

Nelson Mandela Museum

TO PORT ST JOHNS →

N2

Nelson Mandela Dr.

Zanemali

Lowry

King Edward

Mthatha Railway Station

M — 250 — 500

((047) 531 5290/2 • e✉ info.umtata@ectourism.co.za • 🌐 www.ectourism.co.za

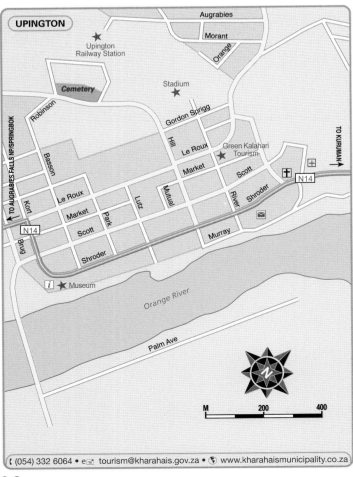

UPINGTON

Augrabies

Morant

Orange

Upington Railway Station

Cemetery

Stadium

Robinson

Gordon Sprigg

Hill

Le Roux

Green Kalahari Tourism

TO KURUMAN →

Basson

Market

Scott

N14

Le Roux

Lutz

Mutual

River

Shroder

TO ALGRABIES FALLS NP/SPRINGBOK

Kort

Market

Park

Murray

N14

Scott

Brug

Shroder

Museum

Orange River

Palm Ave

N

M — 200 — 400

((054) 332 6064 • e✉ tourism@kharahais.gov.za • 🌐 www.kharahaismunicipality.co.za

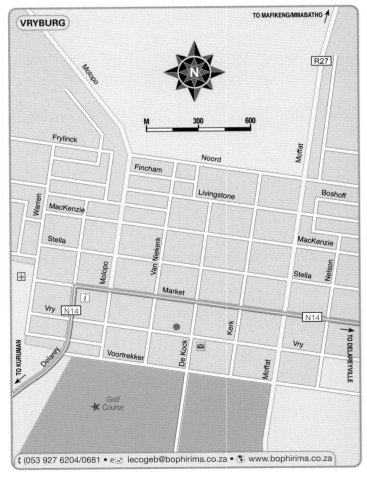

VRYBURG

TO MAFIKENG/MMABATHO →

Molopo

R27

N

M — 300 — 600

Frylinck

Noord

Moffat

Fincham

Livingstone

Boshoff

Warren

MacKenzie

MacKenzie

Stella

Van Niekerk

Stella

Nelson

Molopo

Market

TO KURUMAN

Vry

N14

Kerk

N14

Vry

Delarey

Voortrekker

De Kock

Moffat

TO DELAREYVILLE →

Golf Course

((053) 927 6204/0681 • e✉ lecogeb@bophirima.co.za • 🌐 www.bophirima.co.za

Vryheid South Africa
Worcester South Africa
Witbank (Emalahleni) South Africa
Bhisho South Africa

VRYHEID

Ntinginono Environment Centre
Vryheid Hill Nature Reserve
Vryheid Provincial Hospital
Noord
Boom
Klip
Shepstone
Hird
Brecher
Oos
Hoog
Republiek
Deputasie
President
Kommissie
Landdrost
Utrecht
Wes
Hlobane
The Old Carnegie Museum/ Raadsaal & Nieuwe Republiek Museum
Kommissie
Dutch Reformed Church
Kerk
Hlobane
Utrecht
Mark
Kerk
Boeren
President
Afrikaner
Landdrost
Heeren
Mark
Hoog
Boeren
Afrikaner
Republiek
Deputasie
Uitlander
Suid
Njala
Emmett
Park
Heeren
Emmett
Wes
Spoor
TO PAUL PIETERSBURG R33
TO DUNDEE R33/R34
TO LOUWSBURG
R69
TO MELMOTH N3
M 250 500

((034) 982 2133 • e⬛ information@vhd.dorea.co.za • 🌐 www.vryheid.co.za

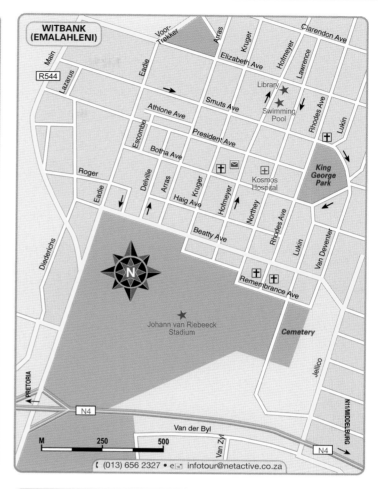

WITBANK (EMALAHLENI)

Voor-Trekker
Main
Arras
Kruger
Clarendon Ave
Hofmeyer
Lawrence
Elizabeth Ave
R544
Lazarus
Eadie
Smuts Ave
Library
Rhodes Ave
Swimming Pool
Lukin
Athlone Ave
President Ave
Escombe
Botha Ave
Roger
Delville
Arras
Kruger
Kosmos Hospital
King George Park
Eadie
Haig Ave
Hofmeyer
Northey
Rhodes Ave
Van Deventer
Lukin
Beatty Ave
Diederichs
Remembrance Ave
Cemetery
Johann van Riebeeck Stadium
Jellico
PRETORIA
N4
Van der Byl
Van Zyl
N4
N11/MIDDELBURG
M 250 500

((013) 656 2327 • e⬛ infotour@netactive.co.za

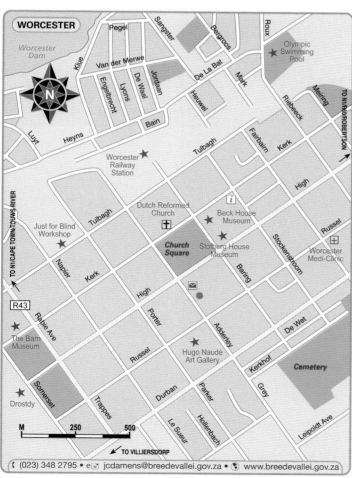

WORCESTER

Worcester Dam
Pegel
Sangster
Roux
Bergroos
Klue
Van der Merwe
De La Bat
Olympic Swimming Pool
Engelbrecht
Lyons
Jordaan
Mark
De Waal
Heuwel
Bain
Riebeeck
Meiring
Luyt
Heyns
Fairbairn
Kerk
Tulbagh
Worcester Railway Station
High
Tulbagh
Russel
Just for Blind Workshop
Dutch Reformed Church
Beck House Museum
Napier
Church Square
Stofberg House Museum
Stockenstroom
Worcester Medi-Clinic
Kerk
High
Baring
Porter
Russel
Hugo Naudé Art Gallery
De Wet
The Barn Museum
Adderley
Kerkhof
Cemetery
Rabie Ave
Durban
Parker
Grey
Somerset
Trappes
Le Sueur
Hollenbach
Leipoldt Ave
Drostdy
R43
TO N1/CAPE TOWN/TOUWS RIVER
TO N1/R60/ROBERTSON
TO VILLIERSDORP
M 250 500

((023) 348 2795 • e⬛ jcdamens@breedevallei.gov.za • 🌐 www.breedevallei.gov.za

BHISHO

TO KEI ROAD/ N6
Mafani
King William's Town/Komga Rd
Amatola Pl.
Khawuta Dr. Cres.
Mabona
Amatola Cres.
Matwa Ave
Mangaliso
TO KING WILLIAM'S TOWN
Sarhili
Anita Ave
Bhisho Township Ext. 1
Circular Dr.
Khama Ave
Nolambe Ave
Sandlie Ave
Ngoika Ave
Mlawu Ave
Civic Centre
Bhisho CBD
Phalo Ave
Rharhabe Ave
Hintsa Cres.
Independence Ave
Swani Ave
Hintsa Cres.
Circular Dr.
Main Rd
Ncgika Ave
Main Rd
Tapa Ln.
Sogwana Pl.
Tynall Ave
Tshatshu La.
Main Dr.
Matl Dr.
Bambo Ave
Chungwa
Tyutyu Central Ext. 1
Tyutyu South

((043) 722 6015• e⬛ info@tourismbuffalocity.co.za • 🌐 www.visitbuffalocity.co.za

Adventures

Adventure	Country	Duration
Crossing the Richtersveld National Park	South Africa	2 - 5 days
Hiking the Drakensberg	South Africa	2 days +
Rafting the Orange River	South Africa	1 - 5 days +
Kayaking the Garden Route	South Africa	1 - 5 days
Pony Trekking in the Maluti Mountains	Lesotho	2 - 5 days
Driving Sani Pass	South Africa & Lesotho	1 - 4 days

Crossing the Richtersveld National Park

Requirements:
Valid passport only. Permits for hiking, angling and 4x4 trails in the Richtersveld National Park can be obtained from the park warden.
Climate:
Winter (May–August) is best, as summer heat can be oppressive, with sandstorms and strong winds.
Risk factor:
Moderate to high-risk driving, and easy to physically demanding hiking routes.
Health:
Visitors travelling through areas where yellow fever is endemic need to provide proof of vaccination; no other vaccinations are required. There is no malaria risk in the dry Richtersveld.
Pack:
Sunscreen is essential, along with a high fluid intake. Strong winds and very basic facilities necessitate a tent that can be sealed.
Facilities:
Amenities within the park vary from basic camp sites with no facilities at all to comfortable self-catering, fully equipped accommodation. Official routes and trails are clearly signposted.
Contact:
Park Warden, Richtersveld National Park, P.O. Box 406, Alexander Bay 8290.
Tel: 0027-27-831-1506

Hiking the Drakensberg

Requirements:
Valid passport only. Permits, where required, are available at the various park entrances. Booking is essential virtually throughout the area.
Climate:
Snowfalls in the icy winters and heavy downpours in the hot summer, so spring (August–November) is best.
Risk factor:
Simple walking trails to very demanding hikes across varied terrain.
Health:
Visitors travelling through areas where yellow fever is endemic need to provide proof of vaccination; no other vaccinations are required.
Pack:
Camping equipment, comfortable and solid hiking boots, warm, protective clothing and sleeping bags for the freezing winters or lightweight clothing and rain gear for blistering summer days.
Facilities:
Relatively sophisticated, varying from basic camp sites with ablutions to very comfortable overnight huts and private lodges. Many routes and trails are well signposted.
Contact:
KwaZulu-Natal Wildlife, P.O. Box 1750, Winterton 3200.
Tel: 0027-33-845-1000
info@kznwildlife.com
www.kznwildlife.com

Rafting the Orange River

Requirements:
Valid passport. All necessary documentation and permits to raft are obtained via commercial operators. Booking is essential.
Climate:
Best during the summer rains (November–January) when waters are high. Intense heat can cause discomfort.
Risk factor:
Moderate to challenging, but professional river guides provide valuable instruction and guidance.
Health:
Visitors travelling through areas where yellow fever is endemic need to provide proof of vaccination; no other vaccinations are required. Basic swimming ability recommended.
Pack:
Protective, waterproof clothing adds to your comfort levels; tour operators will provide most of your requirements. Sunscreen is essential.
Facilities:
Facilities offered by operators are generally good to very good, although the nature of the adventure means that participants should be willing to rough it in the wilderness.
Contact:
Felix Unite, P.O. Box 2807, Clareinch 7700.
Tel: 0027-21-670-1300
reservations@felixunite.co.za
www.felixunite.com

Kayaking the Garden Route

Requirements:
Valid passport only. Permits obtained via commercial operators. Booking is essential.
Climate:
Conditions are generally good year-round, but winter rains can be bothersome. Summer is the peak holiday period and can be terribly crowded.
Risk factor:
Usually gentle, but the warm ocean can pose a shark risk.
Health:
Visitors travelling through areas where yellow fever is endemic need to provide proof of vaccination; no other vaccinations are required. Basic swimming ability and some kayaking experience are recommended (not essential).
Pack:
Some waterproof clothing may be a good idea, but operators should provide the necessary equipment. Sunscreen is recommended, especially in summer.
Facilities:
Facilities offered by operators are generally good to very good, although the nature of the adventure means that participants should be prepared to get at least a little wet, with some discomfort in cold winter months.
Contact:
Real Cape Adventures, P.O. Box 51508, Waterfront, Cape Town.
Cell: 082 556 2520
john@mweb.co.za
www.seakayak.co.za

Pony Trekking in the Maluti Mountains

Requirements:
Valid passport only. Border crossings can be problematic without the correct documentation, so thorough planning is essential.
Climate:
Winter temperatures can be icy, with a formidable wind-chill factor contributing enormously to freezing conditions. Summers are moderate to hot.
Risk factor:
At least some riding ability is recommended, but pony-trekking is generally risk-free.
Health:
Visitors travelling through areas where yellow fever is endemic need to provide proof of vaccination; no other vaccinations are required.
Pack:
Warm clothing for winter, and lightweight clothing for summer. Solid walking and/or riding boots are advisable. Bottled water is recommended.
Facilities:
Facilities are virtually non-existent; those available are extremely simple, yet charming. Be prepared.
Contact:
Basotho Pony Trekking, P.O. Box 12118, Brandhof, 9324.
Cell: 082 552 4215
malealea@mweb.co.za
www.malealea.co.ls
www.malealea.com

Driving Sani Pass

Requirements:
Valid passport only. Border crossings require all the proper documentation, so planning is essential. Permits, where required, can be arranged by operators in Himeville and Underberg.
Climate:
Snowfalls in the icy winters and heavy downpours in the hot summers make spring (Aug–Nov) the best bet.
Risk factor:
Not for the uninitiated, anyone with less than impressive driving skills or with no head for heights. Route may close in adverse conditions.
Health:
Visitors travelling through areas where yellow fever is endemic need to provide proof of vaccination.
Pack:
Warm clothing is essential for overnight stays during the freezing winter months. You should carry every conceivable necessary spare vehicle part.
Facilities:
Comfortable overnight amenities in foothill towns, but accommodation in Lesotho is rudimentary.
Contact:
Sani Pass Tours, P.O. Box 12, Himeville 3256.
Tel: 0027-33-701-1064
info@sanipasstours.co.za
www.sanipasstours.com

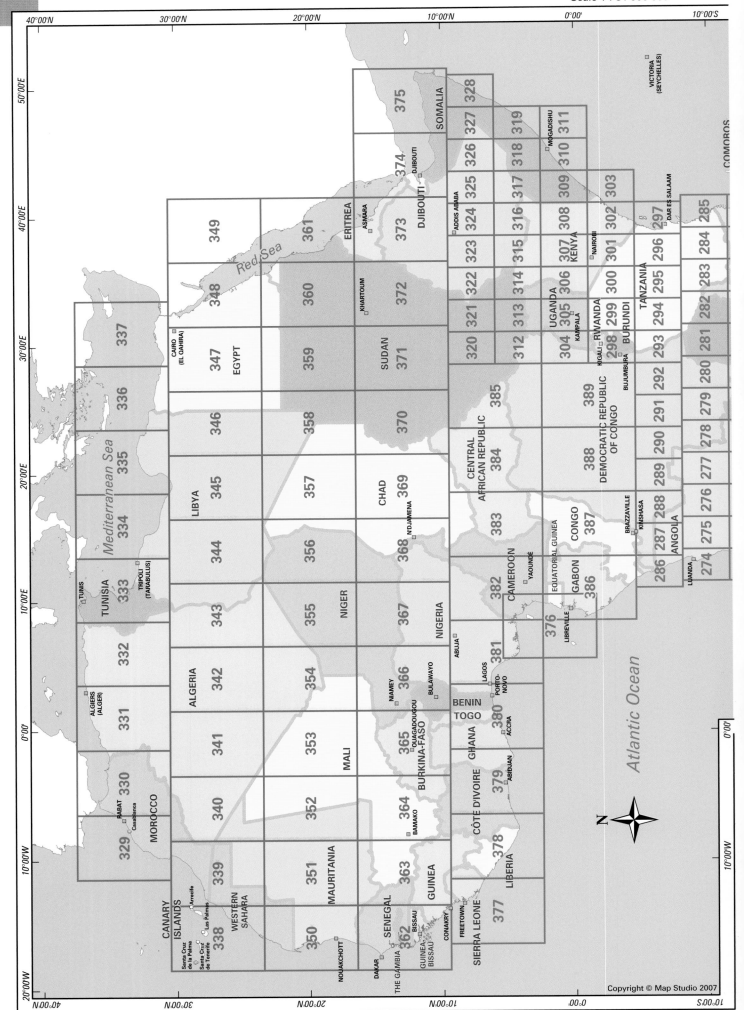

Scale 1 : 31 500 000

0   200   400   800   1,200   1,600 Km

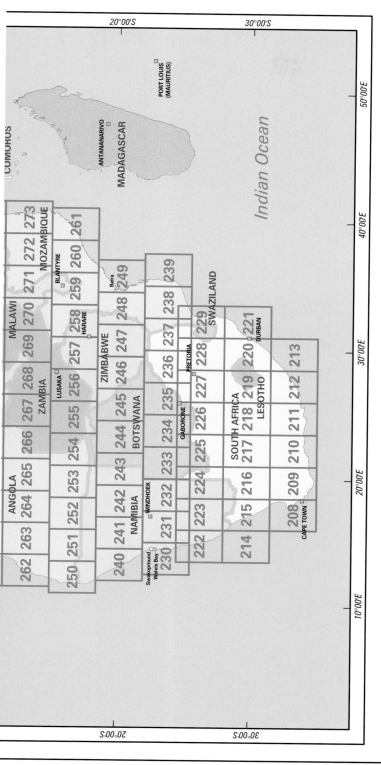

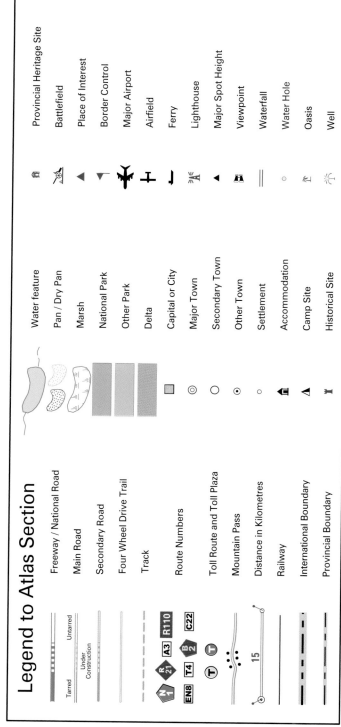

Legend to Atlas Section

Freeway / National Road	
Main Road	
Secondary Road	
Four Wheel Drive Trail	
Track	
Route Numbers	
Toll Route and Toll Plaza	
Mountain Pass	
Distance in Kilometres	
Railway	
International Boundary	
Provincial Boundary	

Water feature	
Pan / Dry Pan	
Marsh	
National Park	
Other Park	
Delta	
Capital or City	
Major Town	
Secondary Town	
Other Town	
Settlement	
Accommodation	
Camp Site	
Historical Site	

Provincial Heritage Site	
Battlefield	
Place of Interest	
Border Control	
Major Airport	
Airfield	
Ferry	
Lighthouse	
Major Spot Height	
Viewpoint	
Waterfall	
Water Hole	
Oasis	
Well	

Elevation

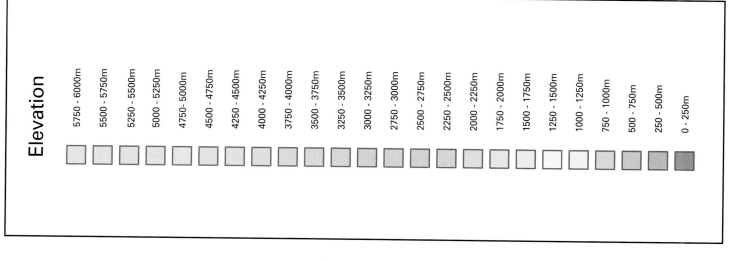

	5750 - 6000m
	5500 - 5750m
	5250 - 5500m
	5000 - 5250m
	4750 - 5000m
	4500 - 4750m
	4250 - 4500m
	4000 - 4250m
	3750 - 4000m
	3500 - 3750m
	3250 - 3500m
	3000 - 3250m
	2750 - 3000m
	2500 - 2750m
	2250 - 2500m
	2000 - 2250m
	1750 - 2000m
	1500 - 1750m
	1250 - 1500m
	1000 - 1250m
	750 - 1000m
	500 - 750m
	250 - 500m
	0 - 250m

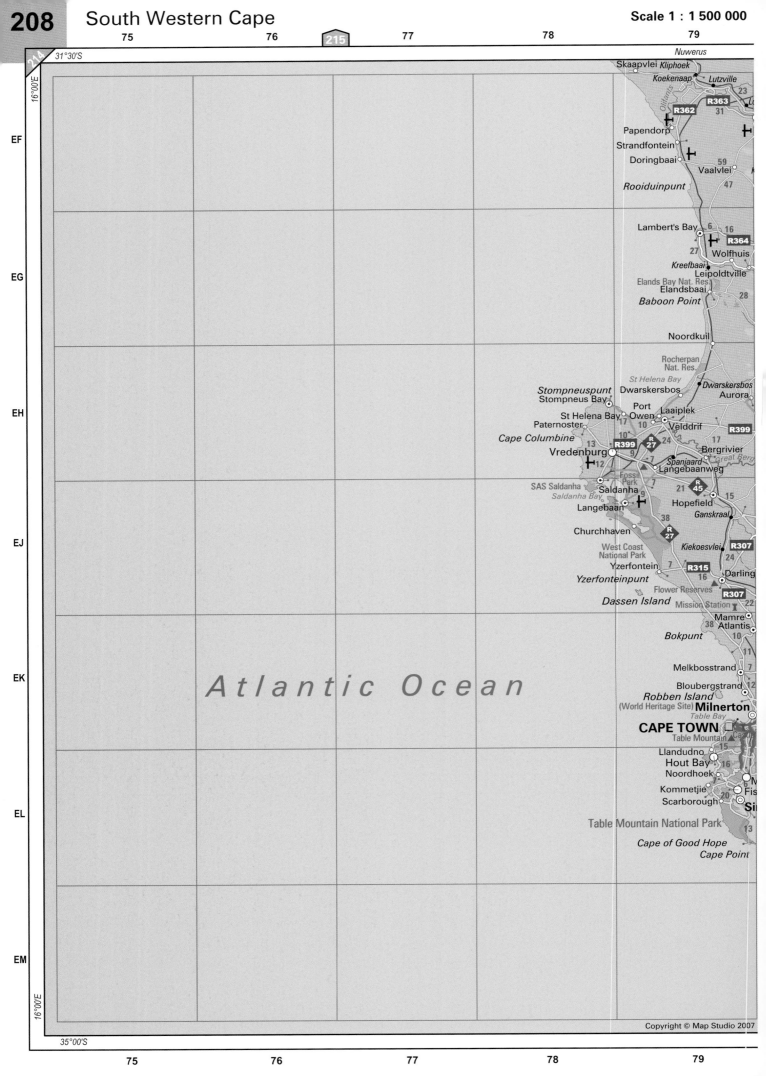

Atlantic Ocean

Nuwerus
Skaapvlei Kliphoek
Koekenaap   Lutzville
23
R362   R363   31
Papendorp
Strandfontein
Doringbaai
Vaalvlei   59
Rooiduinpunt   47

Lambert's Bay   6   16
R364
27   Wolfhuis
Kreefbaai
Leipoldtville
Elands Bay Nat. Res.
Elandsbaai
Baboon Point   28

Noordkuil

Rocherpan
Nat. Res.
St Helena Bay
Stompneuspunt Dwarskersbos   • Dwarskersbos
Stompneus Bay   Aurora
Port   Laaiplek
St Helena Bay Owen   10
Paternoster   Velddrif
Cape Columbine   0°   17
13 R399   R399   24   Bergrivier
Vredenburg   27   *Spanjaard* Great Berg
12   9 7   Langebaanweg
Fossil
Park   7
SAS Saldanha   21 R45   15
Saldanha Bay Saldanha   9   Hopefield
Langebaan   *Ganskraal*
38
Churchhaven   R27
West Coast   *Kiekoesvlei* R307
National Park   24
Yzerfontein   R315   Darling
16
Yzerfonteinpunt   R307
Flower Reserves   22
Dassen Island   Mission Station
Mamre
38 Atlantis
Bokpunt   10
11
Melkbosstrand   7
Bloubergstrand   12
Robben Island
(World Heritage Site) **Milnerton**
Table Bay
CAPE TOWN
Table Mountain
15
Llandudno
Hout Bay   16
Noordhoek
Kommetjie   20 Fis
Scarborough   Si
Table Mountain National Park
Cape of Good Hope   13
Cape Point

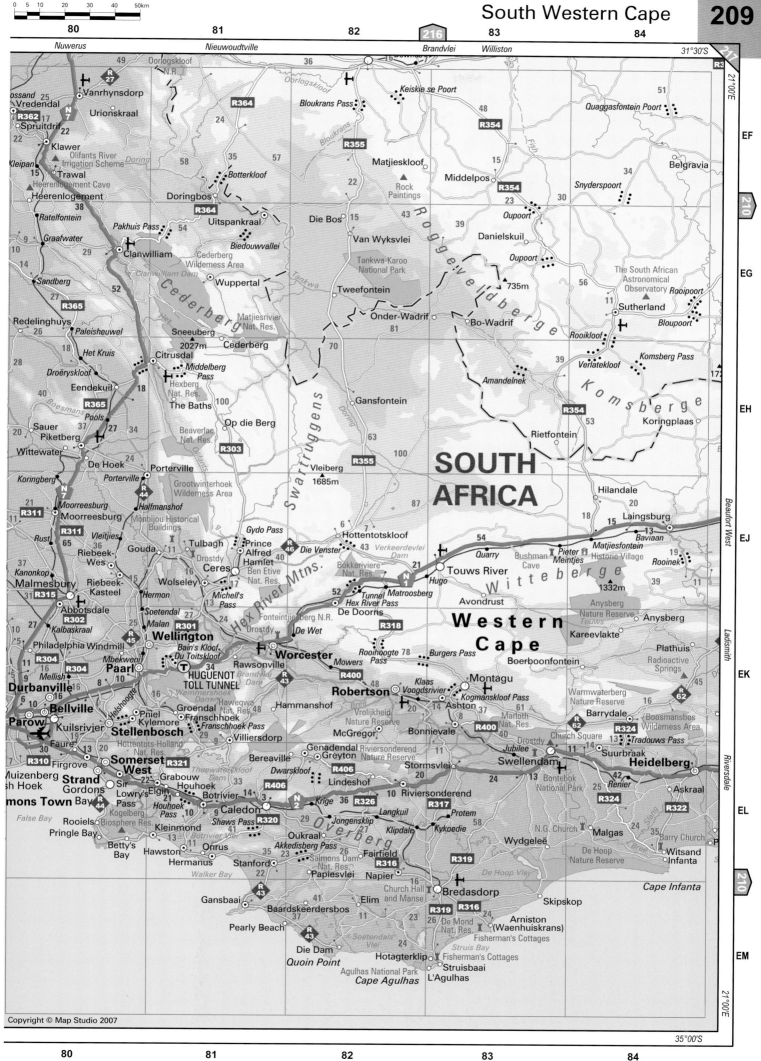

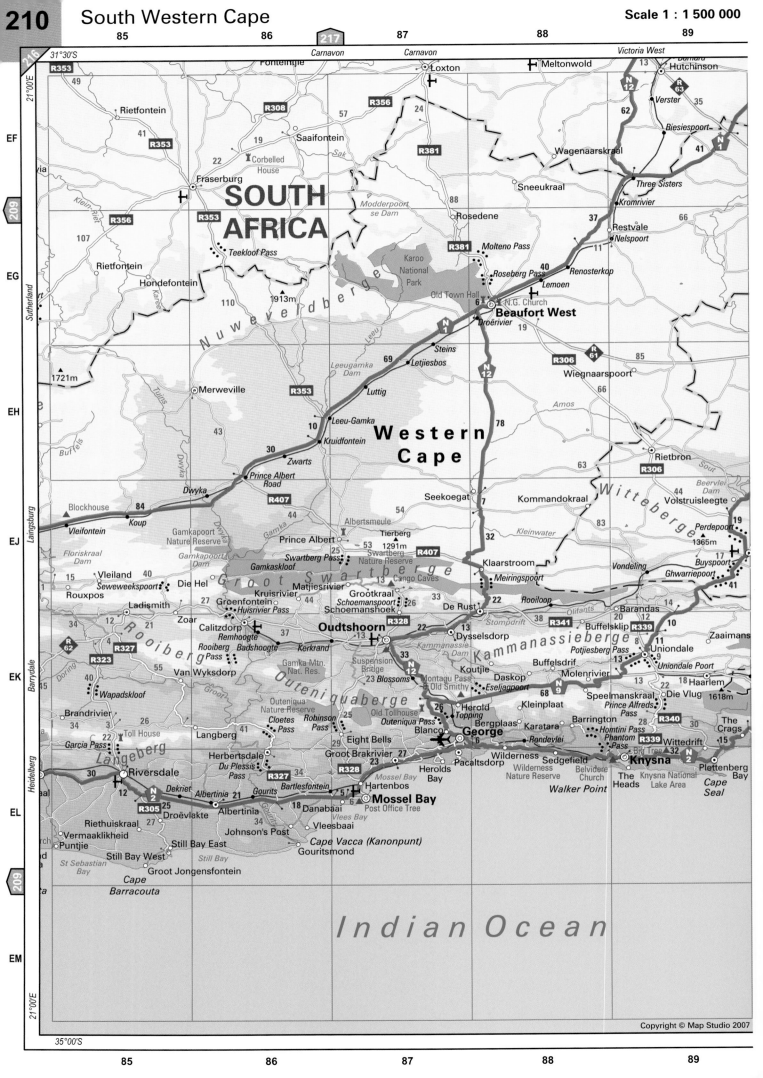

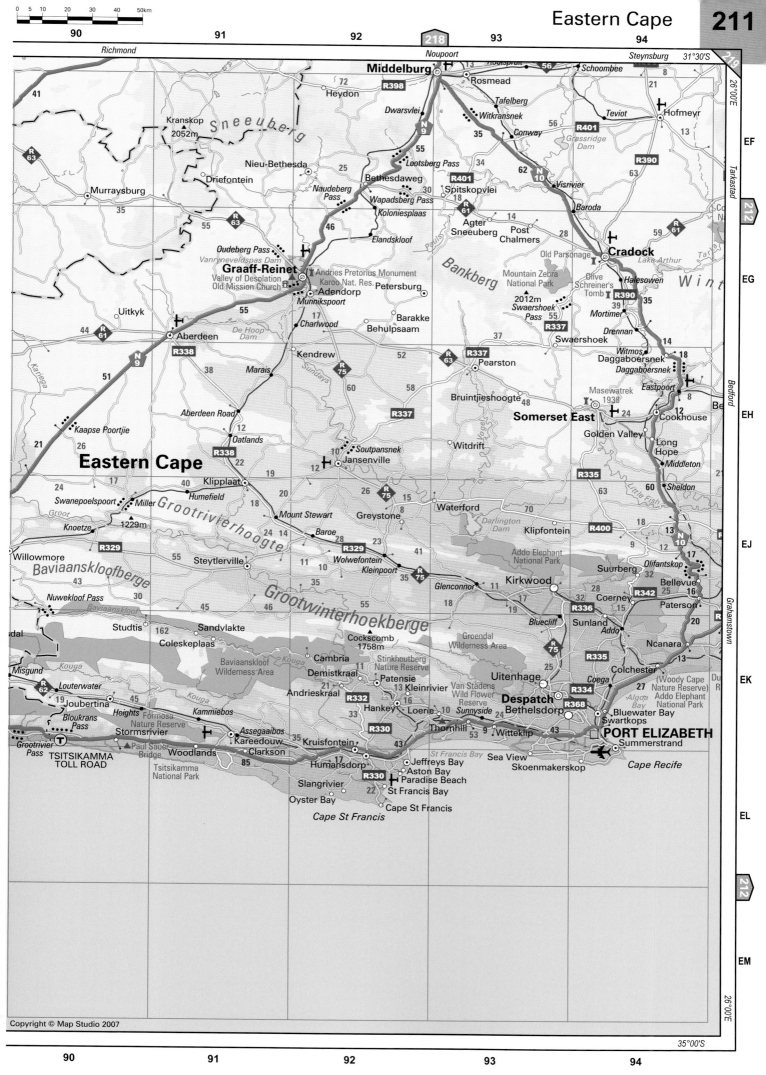

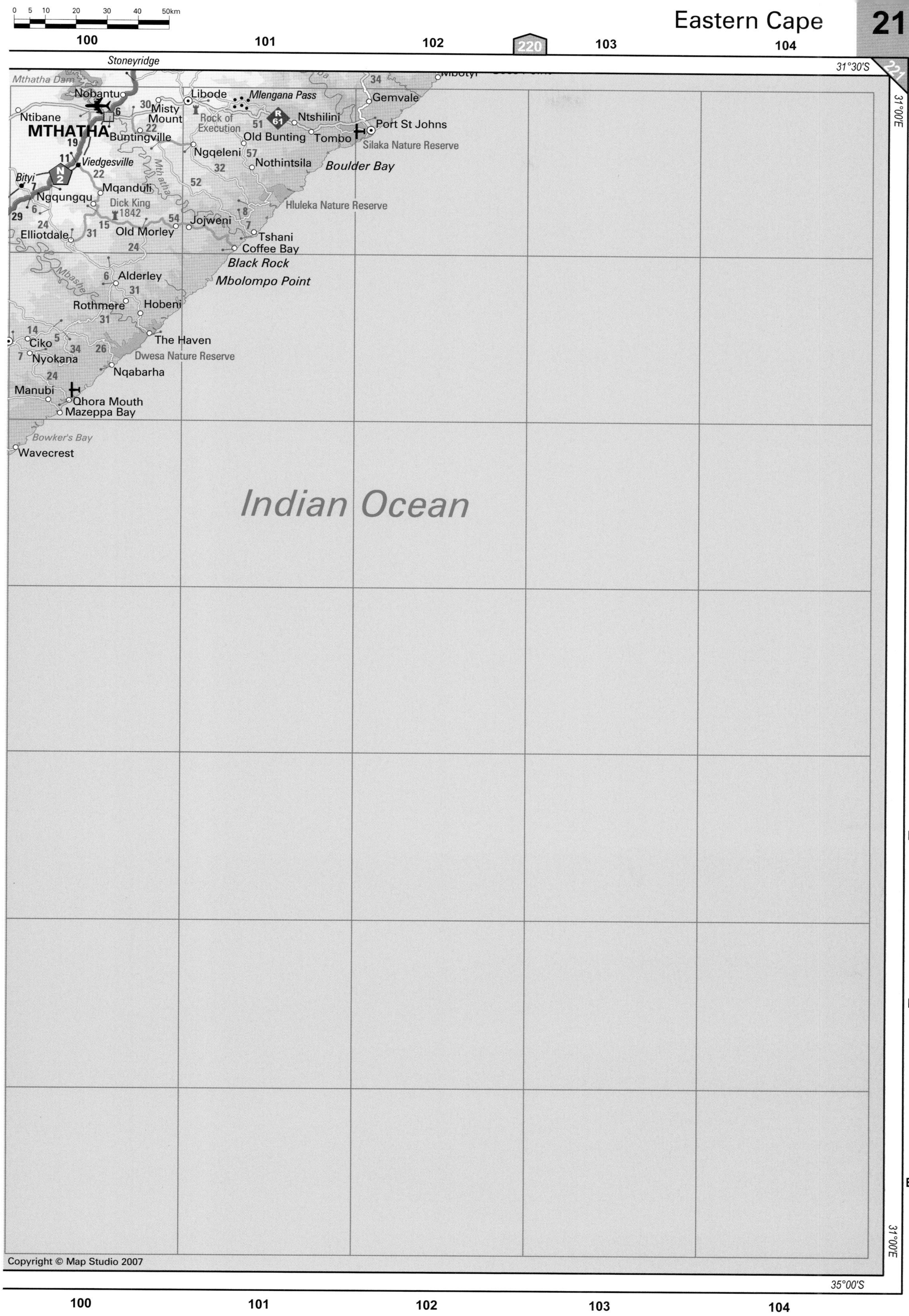

0 5 10   20   30   40   50km

Stoneyridge

31°30'S

221

31°00'E

Mthatha Dam

Nobantu
Ntibane
MTHATHA 19
Buntingville 22
Misty Mount 30
Libode
Rock of Execution
Mlengana Pass
R 61 51
Ntshilini
Gemvale
Mbotyi
Gosel Point

6

11 Viedgesville
Bityi 7
Ngqungqu 6
29 24 6
Elliotdale 31 15
Old Morley
24
Mqanduli
Dick King 1842
54
Jojweni 8
Ngqeleni 57
Nothintsila
32
52
Old Bunting Tombo
Port St Johns
Silaka Nature Reserve
Boulder Bay

7
Tshani
Coffee Bay

Black Rock
Mbolompo Point

Alderley 6
31
Rothmere Hobeni
31
Ciko 14 5
7 34 26
Nyokana
24
Nqabarha
Manubi
Qhora Mouth
Mazeppa Bay

The Haven
Dwesa Nature Reserve

Hluleka Nature Reserve

Bowker's Bay
Wavecrest

EF

EG

Indian Ocean

EH

EJ

EK

EL

EM

31°00'E

35°00'S

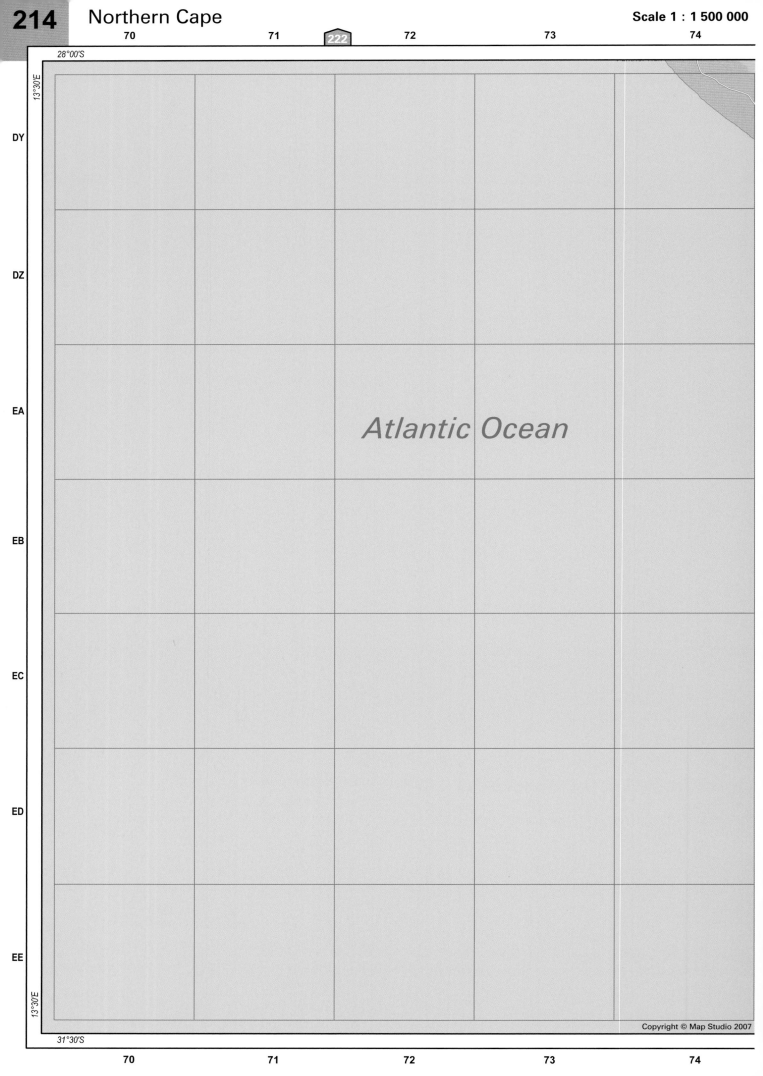

Atlantic Ocean

28°00'S

31°30'S

13°30'E

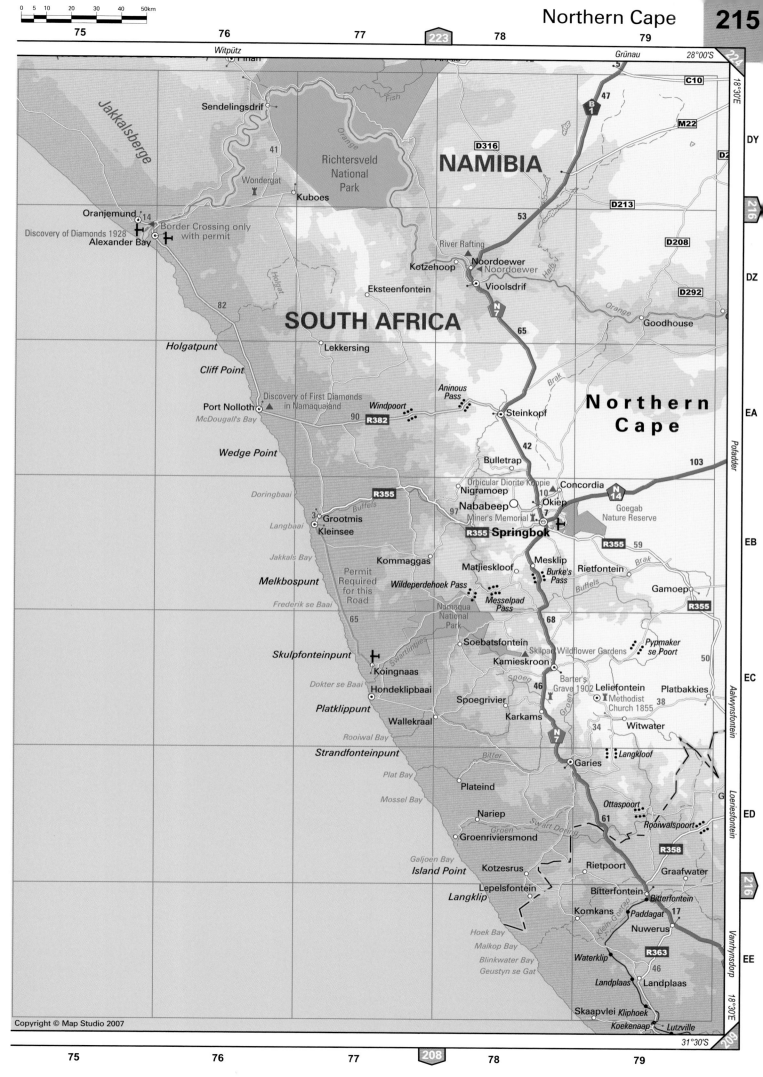

0 5 10 20 30 40 50km

75   76   77   223   78   79

28°00'S

Witpütz

Pinah

Grünau

224

18°30'E

C10

DY

Sendelingsdrif

Fish

B1   47

M22

D2

Jakkalsberge

Orange

Richtersveld National Park

41

Wondergat

D316

NAMIBIA

D213

D208

DZ

Kuboes

Oranjemund 14

Discovery of Diamonds 1928

Border Crossing only with permit

53

D292

Alexander Bay

Holgat

River Rafting

Noordoewer

Kotzehoop

Noordoewer

Eksteenfontein

SOUTH AFRICA

Vioolsdrif

Halby

Orange

Goodhouse

82

N7

EA

Holgatpunt

Cliff Point

Lekkersing

65

Brak

N o r t h e r n C a p e

Pofadder

Discovery of First Diamonds in Namaqualand

Aninous Pass

Port Nolloth

90 R382

Windpoort

Steinkopf

103

McDougall's Bay

Wedge Point

42

Doringbaai

Buffels

Bulletrap

Orbicular Diorite Koppie

Concordia

N14

EB

R355

Nigramoep

10

Okiep

Goegab Nature Reserve

Langbaai

3

Grootmis

97

Nababeep

7

Miner's Memorial

Kleinsee

Jakkals Bay

R355 **Springbok**

R355

59

Mesklip

Brak

Kommaggas

Matjieskloof

Burke's Pass

Rietfontein

Buffels

Gamoep

Melkbospunt

Permit Required for this Road

Wildeperdehoek Pass

Messelpad Pass

R355

Frederik se Baai

Namaqua National Park

68

Pypmaker se Poort

EC

65

Soebatsfontein

Skilpad Wildflower Gardens

50

Skulpfonteinpunt

Swartlintjies

Kamieskroon

Koingnaas

Spoeg

Barter's Grave 1902

Leliefontein

Platbakkies

Dokter se Baai

46

Methodist Church 1855

38

Hondeklipbaai

Spoegrivier

Green

Platklippunt

Karkams

34

Witwater

Wallekraal

N7

Rooiwal Bay

Langkloof

ED

Strandfonteinpunt

Bitter

Garies

Plat Bay

Plateind

Mossel Bay

Ottaspoort

G

Nariep

Groen

61

Rooiwalspoort

Loeriesfontein

Groenriviersmond

Swart Doring

Galjoen Bay

R358

Island Point

Kotzesrus

Rietpoort

Graafwater

216

Langklip

Lepelsfontein

Bitterfontein

Bitterfontein

Komkans

Paddagat

17

Nuwerus

Hoek Bay

Klein Goetap

Malkop Bay

Blinkwater Bay

R363

Geustyn se Gat

Waterklip

46

Vanrhynsdorp

EE

18°30'E

Landplaas

Landplaas

Skaapvlei Kliphoek

Koekenaap Lutzville

31°30'S

209

208

75   76   77   78   79

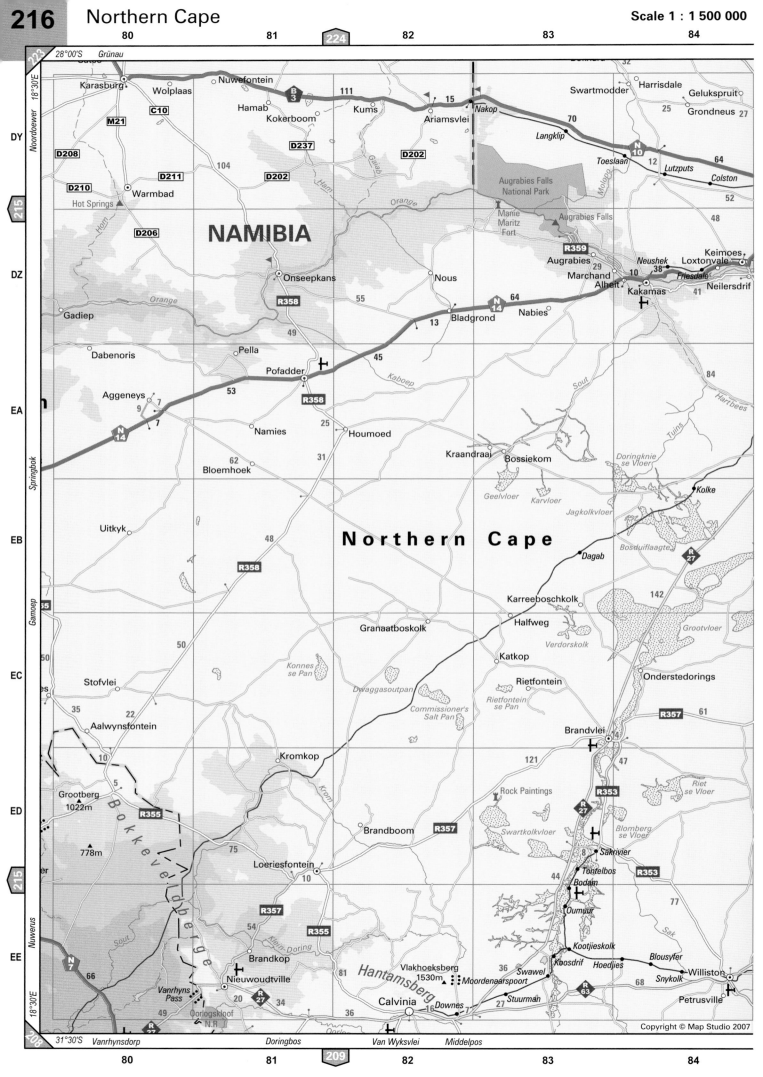

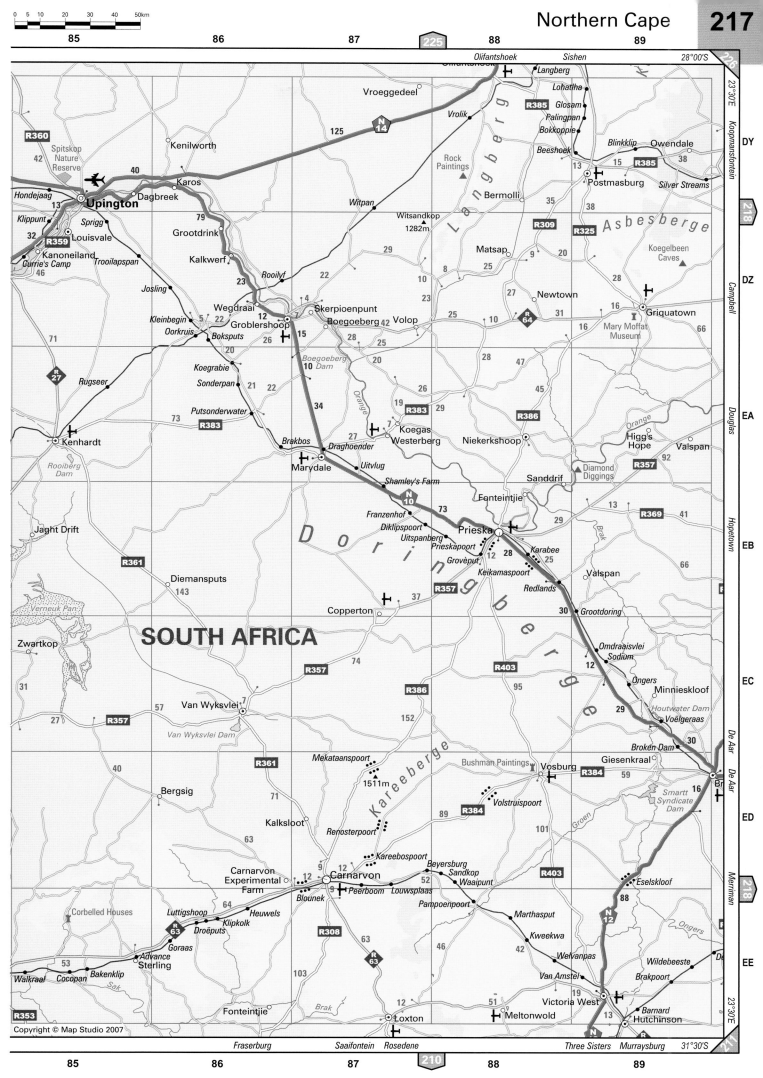

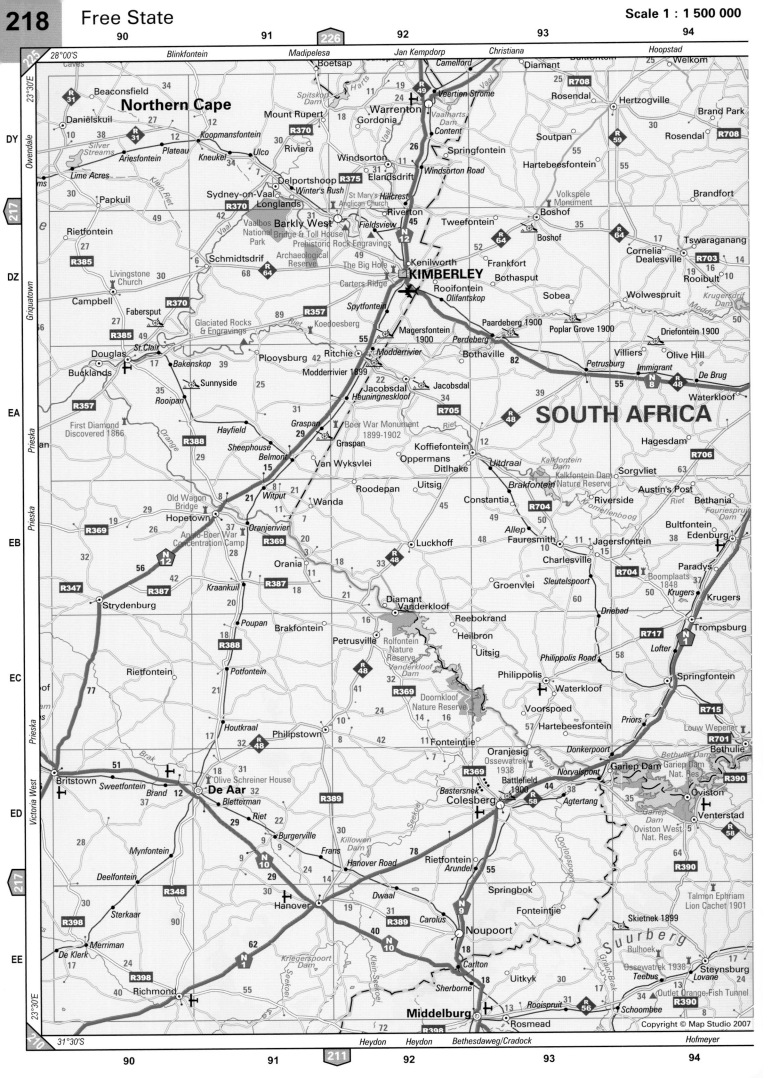

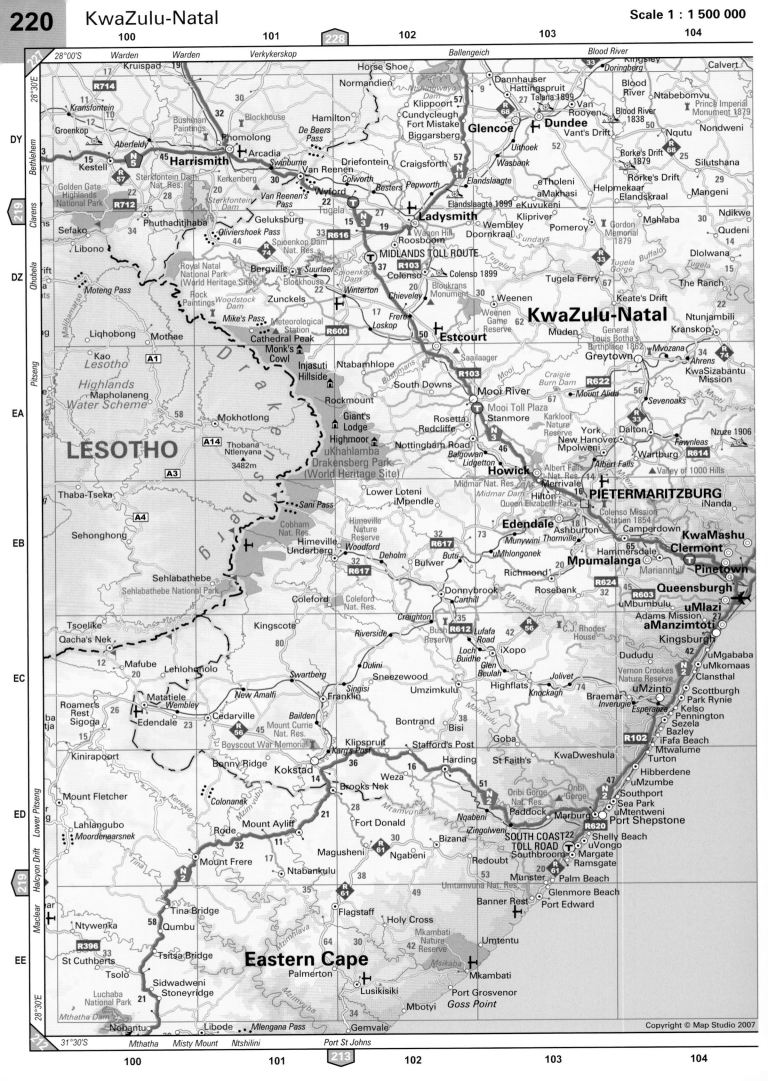

0 5 10 20 30 40 50km

105   106   107   229   108   109

Nongoma   Nongoma   Mkuze   Mbazwana   28°00'S

Glückstadt   KwaCeza   25   33   Bird Island

Ngogweni   Hluhluwe   Lake St Lucia

Bayeni   Sigubudu   Hluhluwe   Fanie's Island

Bloubank   Nhlazatshe   R 66 29   Hlabisa   Hilltop/Mtwazi   Hluhluwe Game Reserve   Fanie's Island   Cape Vidal   Cape Vidal

70   uMfolozi   Mahlabathini   Black Mfolozi   Bushlands   Fanie's Island

R 34   uLoliwe   uLundi   iLangakazi   Hluhluwe Dam   28   Charters Creek   St Lucia Marine Reserve

Nsubeni   uLundi 1879   23   Nodwengu   iMfolozi Game Reserve   Fernwood   Makhakhathana Point

Babanango   Dingaan's Kraal   Piet Retief's Grave 1838   19   oNdini   White Mfolozi   Mdindi   50   Machibini   22   Mtubatuba   R618   St Lucia

Osborn   41   Munywana   uMunywana   River View   Mapelane Nature Reserve

Randalhurst   Melmoth   27   R 66   eMakwezini   23   Teza   Lake Eteza Nature Reserve

Nkandla   Mabhensa   Dondotsha   Ntambanana   Nhlabane Lake (Lake Mzingazi)

Fossils   Ndundulu   45   Heatonville   15   KwaMbonambi

R 34   Nkwalini   Mposa   13   Dawson's Rock

Bulawayo Site of Shaka's Kraal   N 2   19   eNseleni Nature Reserve

Cetshwayo's Grave   eMpangeni   Richards Bay

eNtumeni   21   Felixton   29   Mhlatuzi Lagoon

Coward's Bush Monument   45   Richards Bay Nature Reserve

eShowe   Fort Nongqai   Fort KwaMondi   uMlalazi Nature Reserve

Gingindlovu   21   R102 17   Mtunzini

aMatikulu   Gingindlovu

Fort Mtombeni   Nyoni   Fort Trealork

Mapumulo   Nyathini   22   T   NORTH COAST TOLL ROUTE

oTimati   Mandini   Tugela   Tugela 1838

Mpumulwane   46   12   Tugela Mouth   Fort Pearson

Darnall   Ultimatum Tree   Zinkwazi Beach

Shaka's Memorial   Mvoti   Stanger

Aldinville   17   80

Shakaskraal   Sheffield Beach

uMhlali   15   Salt Rock

Tongaat   Shaka's Rock

Ndwedwe   Ballito   T

Verulam   NORTH COAST TOLL ROUTE

Phoenix   uMdloti

uMhlanga

DURBAN
The Bluff

Indian Ocean

DY

DZ

EA

EB

EC

ED

EE

33°30'E

33°30'E

31°30'S

105   106   107   108   109

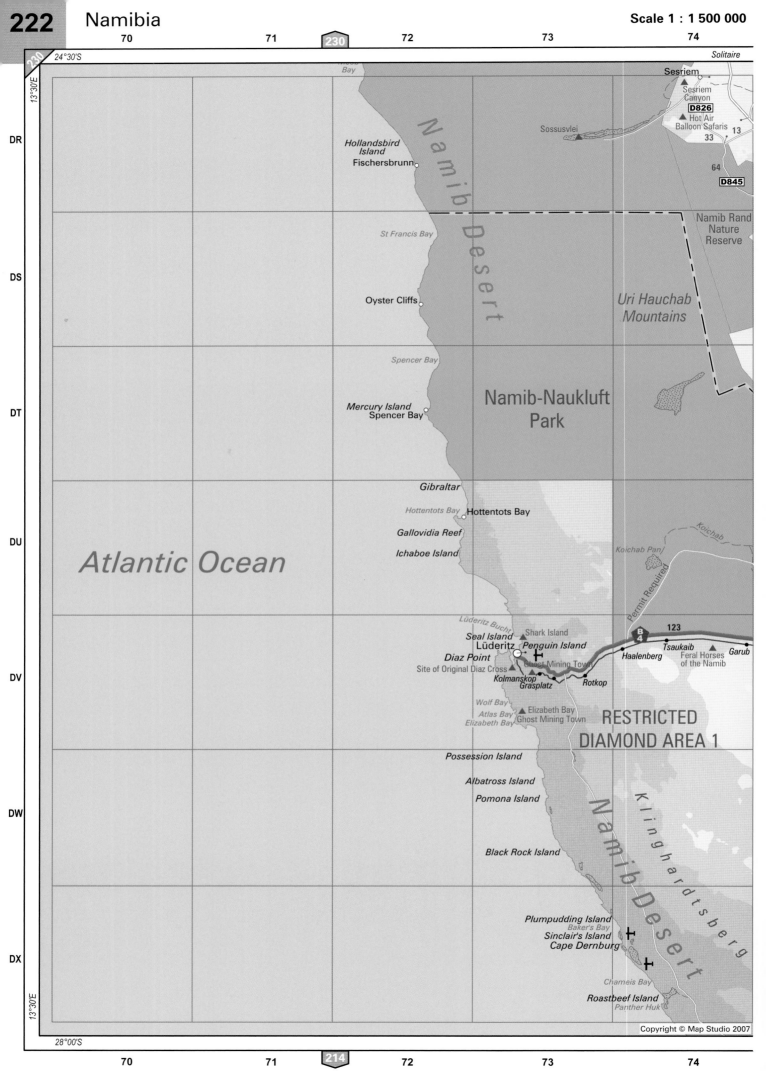

70   71   230   72   73   74

24°30'S   *Solitaire*

230

13°30'E

DR

Hollandsbird Island
Fischersbrunn

Namib Desert

Sossusvlei

Sesriem
Sesriem Canyon
D826
Hot Air Balloon Safaris
33   13
64
D845

St Francis Bay

Namib Rand Nature Reserve

DS

Oyster Cliffs

Uri Hauchab Mountains

Spencer Bay

DT

Mercury Island
Spencer Bay

Namib-Naukluft Park

Gibraltar

Hottentots Bay   **Hottentots Bay**

DU

Atlantic Ocean

Gallovidia Reef
Ichaboe Island

Koichab
Koichab Pan
Permit Required

Lüderitz Bucht
Shark Island
Seal Island
Lüderitz
Penguin Island
Diaz Point
Ghost Mining Town
Site of Original Diaz Cross

123
B4
Tsaukaib
Haalenberg   Feral Horses of the Namib   Garub

DV

Kolmanskop
Grasplatz
Rotkop

Wolf Bay
Atlas Bay   Elizabeth Bay
Elizabeth Bay   Ghost Mining Town

RESTRICTED DIAMOND AREA 1

Possession Island

Albatross Island
Pomona Island

DW

Namib Desert

Klinghardtsberg

Black Rock Island

Plumpudding Island
Baker's Bay
Sinclair's Island
Cape Dernburg

DX

Chameis Bay

Roastbeef Island
Panther Huk

13°30'E

28°00'S

70   71   214   72   73   74

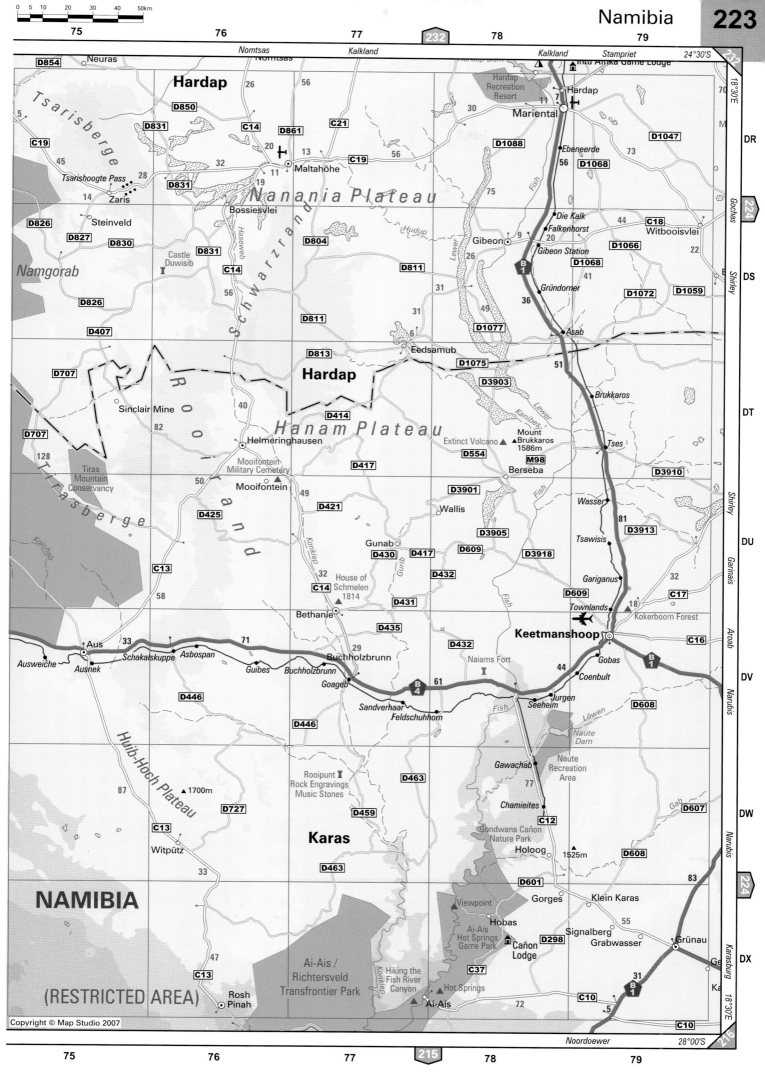

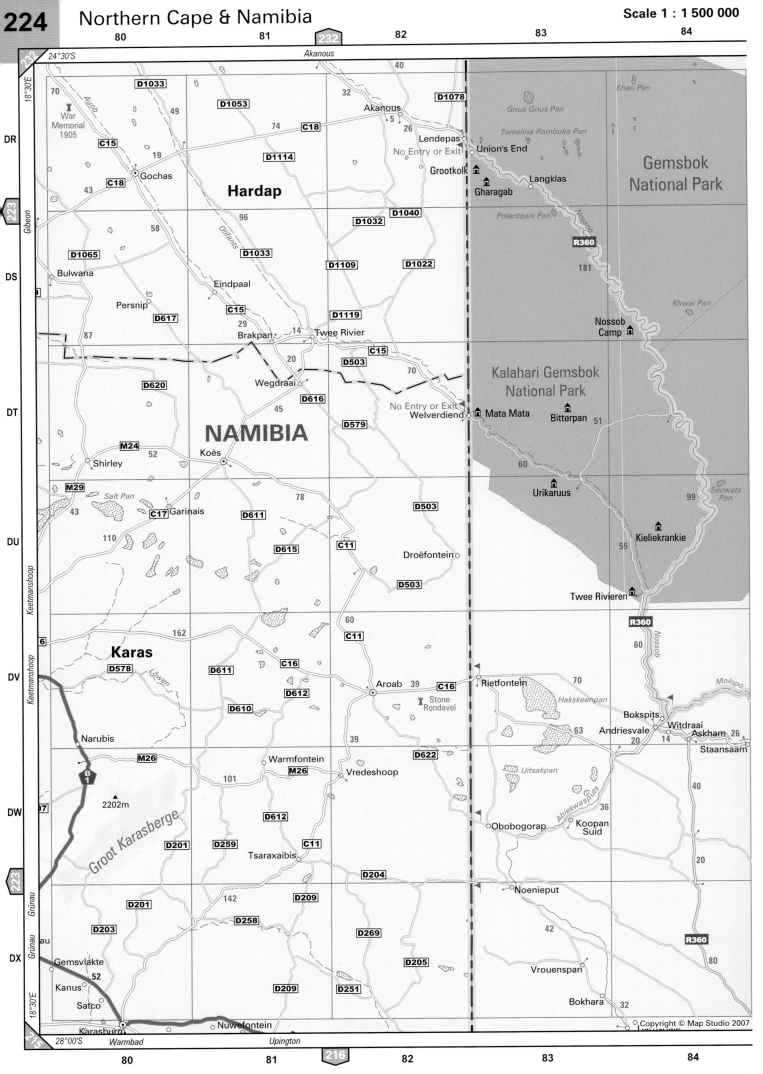

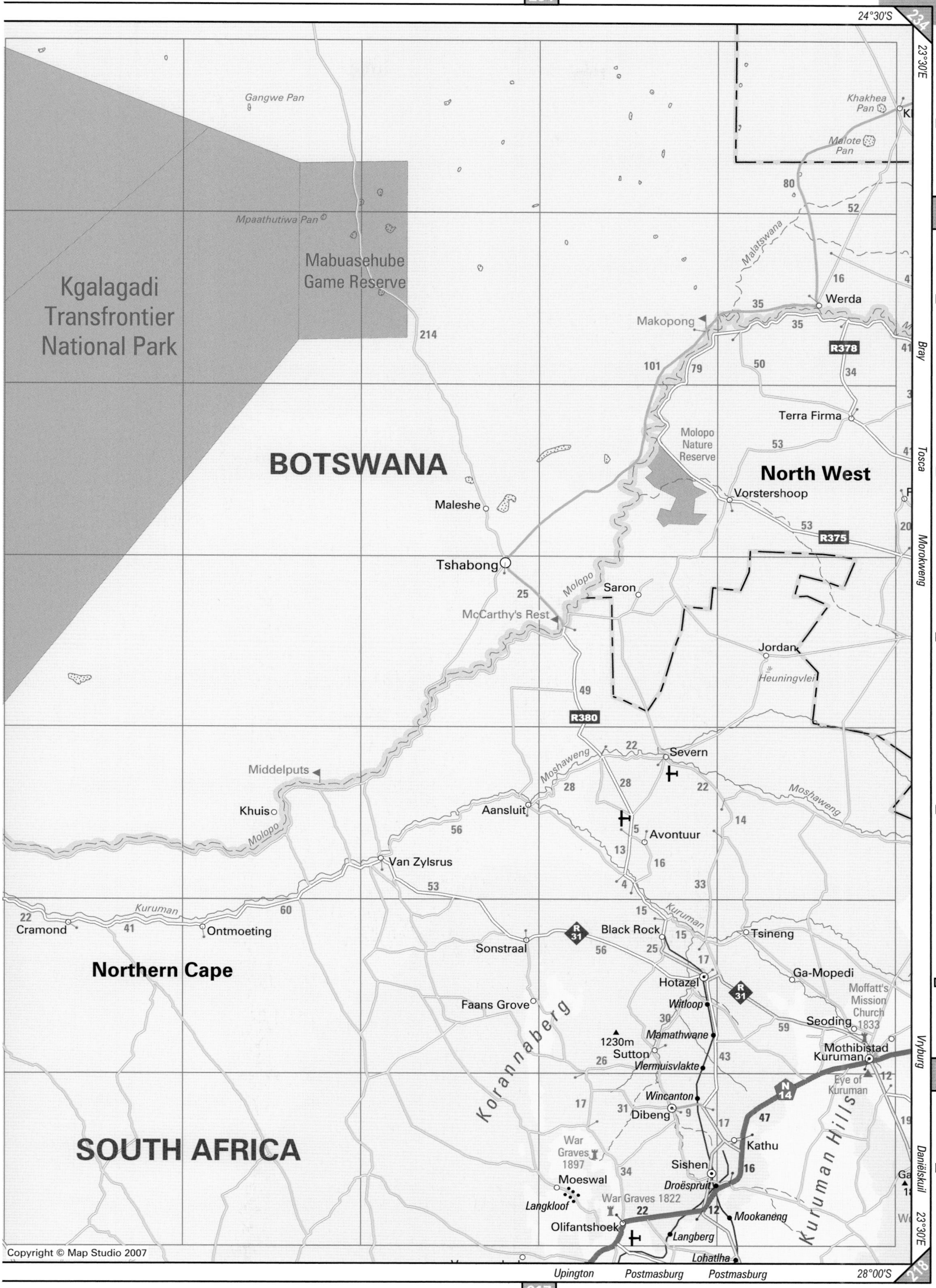

0 5 10 20 30 40 50km

85   86   87   234   88   89

24°30'S

23°30'E

Gangwe Pan

DR

Khakhea Pan

K

Malote Pan

80

52

226

16   4

Mpaathutiwa Pan

Mabuasehube
Game Reserve

Werda

DS

Malatswana

35

35

**Kgalagadi
Transfrontier
National Park**

214

35

Makopong

101   79

50

R378

41

Bray

34

3

53

Molopo
Nature
Reserve

North West

Terra Firma

Tosca

DT

Vorstershoop

53   R375

20

Morokweng

Maleshe

BOTSWANA

Tshabong

Molopo

Saron

25

McCarthy's Rest

Jordan

Heuningvlei

DU

49

R380

Moshaweng

22

Severn

28

28

22

DV

Middelputs

Moshaweng

Khuis

Aansluit

28

14

56

5

Avontuur

13

16

Van Zylsrus

4

33

53

15

Kuruman

60

Black Rock

15

Tsineng

22

41

Ontmoeting

R31

25

17

Cramond

Sonstraal

56

Hotazel

Ga-Mopedi

Northern Cape

Witloop

R31

Moffatt's
Mission
Church
1833

DW

Faans Grove

30

Mamathwane

59

Seoding

Korannaberg

1230m

Sutton

43

Mothibistad
Kuruman

26

Vlermuisvlakte

12

17

Wincanton

N14

*Eye of
Kuruman*

Dibeng

9

17

47

19

War Graves
1897

Kathu

Kuruman Hills

SOUTH AFRICA

DX

Moeswal

34

Sishen

16

Langkloof

War Graves 1822

Droëspruit

Ga

Vryburg

Daniëlskuil

22

12

Mookaneng

Olifantshoek

Langberg

Lohatlha

23°30'E

28°00'S

Upington   Postmasburg   Postmasburg

85   86   87   217   88   89

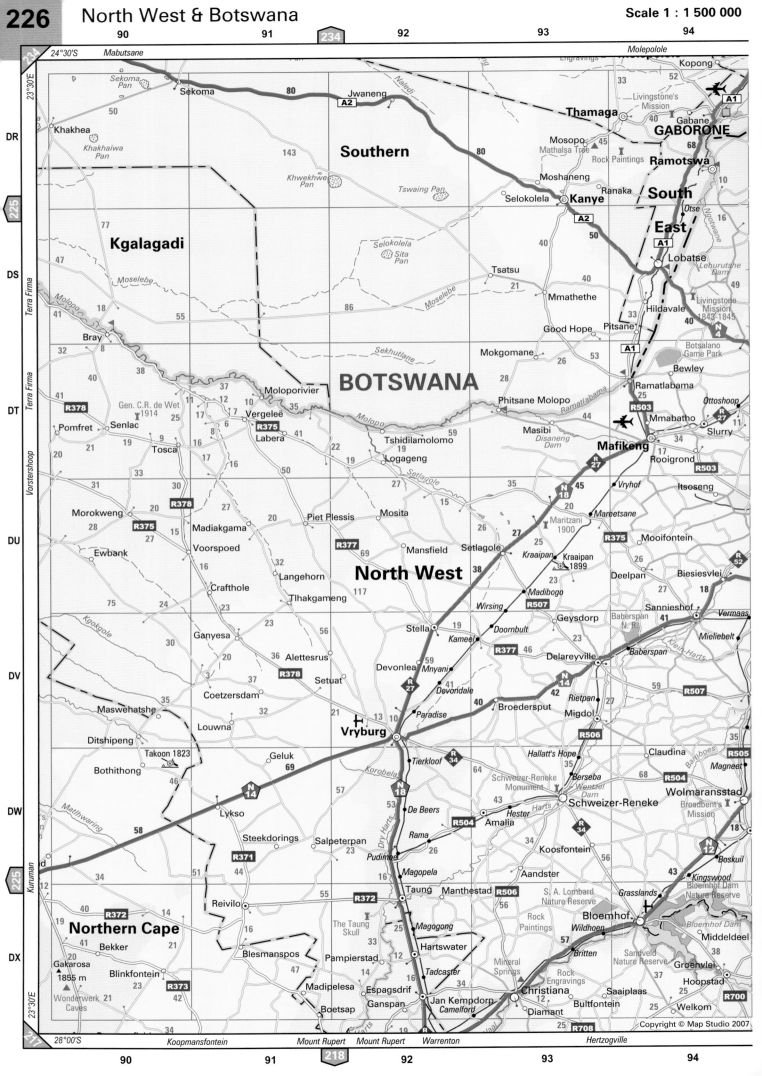

0 5 10 20 30 40 50km

Mochudi | Lephalale | Vaalwater | 24°30'S

28°30'E Mokopane / Polokwane | 236

DR

Medipane | Sikwane | Silent Valley | 17 | 18 | Thabazimbi | 45 | Rankin's Pass | Alma | Veldslag | 50 | Loubad
Kopfontein Gate | Derdepoort | 12 | 16 | 18 | Oostermoed | 33 | 31 | Modimolle (Nylstroom)
Madikwe Game Reserve | 35 | 16 | Dwaalboom | 15 | en Alberts N. R. | 1345m | 9
Chonuane 1846-1847 | 23 | Kaya se put | 21 | Ganskuil | Middelwit | Tussenin | Rooiberg | 43 | 19 | R101
Zwingli | 31 | Bierspruit | Bier | 39 | 38 | Koedoeskop | Leeupoort | Hot Mineral Springs | 27 | T | 19
18 | Brakfontein | Dwarsberg | Northam | 22 | R516 | 33 | Mabula | Bela-Bela (Warmbaths) | KRANSKOP TOLL ROAD
Nietverdiend | Silkaatskop Monument | Silkaatskop | SOUTH AFRICA | 26 | Willem | R101 | 23 | Radium | 20
11 | 49 | Mabeskraal | Pilanesberg Game Reserve | 33 | Mogwase | Assen | Atlanta | Borakalalo Game Reserve | Pienaarsrivier | R576
21 | Sand | 35 | Straatsdrif | Mabaalstad | Sun City / Lost City | Motshikiri | 22 | Vaalkop Dam | Roodekopjes Dam | Rust de Winter Dam | N | Rust de Winter N. R.
Blairbeth | 31 | Skuinsdrif | Lindleyspoort | R565 | Paul | 24 | Beesteskraal | Winterveld | Temba | Carousel | T | 31 | Babelegi
Pienaar Nature Reserve | Kromellenboog Dam | Riekertsdam | 36 | Rusverby | Boekenhoutfontein 1873 | Boshoek | 53 | Bethanie | Pansdrif | Tswaing | Hammanskraal
28 | Zeerust | Woodbine | Marico Bosveld N.R. | Ga-Luka | Bospoort Dam | Sonop | De Wildt | Mabopane | Ga-Rankuwa | Roodeplaat | R573
17 | Anglican Church | Groot Marico | 24 | 7 | Swartruggens | R510 | Bleskop | Maroelakop | Hartbeespoort | Brits | 80 | Bon Accord | Roodeplaat Dam | R513
Swartruggens | 19 | Millvale | N4 | 35 | Rustenburg | Marikana | Marikana | Kosmos | N4 | R513 | PRETORIA
Wondermere | 23 | Twinbrook | R52 | Rustenburg N. R. | Olifantsnek Dam | Magaliesberg | Hartbeespoort Dam | Pelindaba | N4 | T | Mamelodi | N4
Lead Mine | 29 | Koster | Dessing | Heldina | 24 | Maanhaarrand | Skeerpoort | Atteridgeville | Centurion | R50
10 | 23 | 38 | R53 | Derby | Boons | Magaliesburg | Hekpoort | Cradle of Humankind (World Heritage Site) | Midrand | 41 | Tembisa
R505 | Carlsonia | Grootpan | R509 | 14 | R563 | R24 | Randburg | Sandton | Bapsfontein | Kempton Park
Bakerville | 50 | R52 | Swartplaas | 36 | Klerkskraal | R500 | Krugersdorp | Roodepoort | Edenvale | Benoni
Lichtenburg | 44 | R53 | 10 | R500 | Randfontein | JOHANNESBURG | Boksburg | Brakpan
28 | Ga-Ramodingwana | Ventersdorp | 37 | Carletonville | Soweto | Germiston | Springs
Groot-Harts | R505 | N14 | Bodenstein | 53 | Makokskraal | Mooi | Westonaria | Alberton | R23 | Nigel
22 | 25 | Coligny | Dovesdale | Bank | Lenasia | Gauteng | Jameson Park | 40
Gerdau | 25 | Mesa | Welverdiend | Grasmere | Walkerville | Heidelberg
Doringbult | Hauptrus | R501 | Daleside | Suikerbosrand Nature Reserve | Transport Museum
42 | Bospoort | Brakspruit | Danie Theron Monument | Fochville | R26 | Sebokeng | Randvaal | Midvaal Motor Race Track | N3
Hartbeesfontein | R503 | Werda | N12 | POTCHEFSTROOM | Venterskroon | Meyerton | R42 | R549 | 61
R507 | Ottosdal | KLERKSDORP | New Machavie | Vanderbijlpark | Vereeniging
Bamboesspruit | Sendelingsfontein | Orkney | Stilfontein | Parys | Sasolburg | Viljoensdrif | R59 | Dasville
43 | Renosterspruit | R502 | Reitzburg | KROONVAAL TOLL ROUTE | Deneysville | R54
Harrisburg | Vierfontein | Vredefort | Dover | R82 | Wolwehoek | Oranjeville | R716
Witpoort | R76 | Spes Bona | R720 | N1 | Koppies | Koppies Dam | Heilbron
25 | R502 | Leeudoringstad | Oasis | N1/14 | R723 | R34
Makwassie | R504 | Viljoenskroon | Mirage | Groeneblloem | R721 | Koppies | Rooiwal | Syferkuil | Hoogte
R505 | Bothaville | R727 | Rustig | Heuningspruit | R720 | Vechtkop | R707
Doornkraal Memorial | Schuttesdraai | R713 | Westleigh | Edenville | Petrus Steyn
R719 | Ancona | R30 | Maokeng | R76 | Prehistoric Stone Huts | R725 | R707
Wesselsbron | R34 | Allanridge | Prospectors Borehole Monument | Kroonstad | R34 | Lindley | Reitz
Besempan | R34 | Odendaalsrus | Kutlwanong | Geneva | Wonderkop | Allemansspek | R76 | R26 | Bolivia
Tierfontein | WELKOM | Thabong | Riebeeckstad | Hennenman | Steynsrus | Komspruit | R707 | R76 | Danielsrus
Whites | Mooigeleë | Arlington | Blyd

28°30'E

DS | DT | DU | DV | DW | DX

0 5 10 20 30 40 50km

105 106 107 238 108 109

Macarretane
24°30'S
33°30'E

Orpen Game Res.
N'wanetsi
Mapulanguene
Canicado
Chókwè
208
Mohambe
205

Acornhoek
Cottondale
R531
Andover Game Reserve
H1-3
Macaena
Govero
Mazivila
24

Hokwe
R40
Manyeleti Game Reserve
Sabi Sand Game Reserve
Tshokwane
Trichardt Memorial
Orpen Dam
70
Lagoa Chuáli
Chissano
EN1

Bushbuckridge
Matshaye
Newington
Londolozi Game Reserve
H10
Magude
Xinavane
Macia
Magul
408
Gumbe

R533
Marite
H11
Skukuza
H4-1
Lower Sabie
Taninga
Palmeira
Praia do Bilene
Zongo Lod

Hazyview
S1
Paul Kruger Gate
Machatuine
Chinhanguanine
Manhiça

Kiepersol
H1-1
Pretoriuskop
Jock of the Bushveld
H4-2
Sabie
Esperança
Maluana

Numbi Gate
R538
Legogote
White River
Plaston
Kruger National Park
Afsaal
Crocodile Bridge
Mthethomusha Game Reserve
Hectorspruit
Komatipoort
Lebombo
Ressano Garcia
Moamba
Mevedja
Vundica
Passene
EN1
Marracuene
Lagoa Manje

Crocodile
Karino
KaNyamazane
Malelane
Hectorspruit
N4
MAPUTO CORRIDOR
EN4
Machava
Chicabela
Ilha Xefinha Grande

Kaapmuiden
R38
Nkomazi
R570
Kaalrug
Lebomboberg
Samora Machel Aircraft Accident Site
EN4
Matola
MAPUTO
Ilha da Inhaca

Avoca
Jeppe's Reef
R571
Matsomo
Lake Matsamo
Mananga
Namaacha
EN251
EN2
Cátembe
Inhaca

First Stock Exchange
Hhohho
Ngonini
Sihhoye
Mananga
Sand River Reservoir
EN5
Boane
Ponta Maona
Cabo de Santa Maria
Santa Maria

Barberton
R40
Herefords
Tshaneni
Mhlume
Lomahasha
Vuvulane
Goba
Machangulo
Ponta Mucombo ou Majumbo

Bulembu
Piggs Peak
Croydon
Mlawula
Baie de Maputo

Josefsdal
Malanoela
1231m
Mnjoli Dam
Mlawula Ndzindza Nat. Res.
Changalane
Ponta Chemucane

Forbes Reef
MBABANE
Bushman Paintings
Malolotja Nature Res
Hlane Game Sanctuary
Bela Vista
Maputo Elephant Game Reserve
Ponta Milibangalala

Mlilwane Wildlife Sanctuary
Mpaka
Siteki
Salamanga
Lagoa Xingute
Lagoa Piti

Mhlambanyatsi
Mafutseni
Mkhaya Nature Reserve
MOZAMBIQUE
Zitundo
Ponta Madejanine

Bhunya
Malkerns
Manzini
Lubhuku
Catuane
Manhoca
Ponta do Ouro
Ponta do Oura

Loyengo
Sidvokodvo
Siphofaneni
Phuzumoya
Mboyi
Manyiseni
Ndumo
Tembe Elephant Game Reserve
Mloli
Emangusi
Kosi Bay
Kosi Bay Coastal Forest Nature Reserve
Ku-Hlange Lake (Lake Kosi)

Mankayane
SWAZILAND
Big Bend
Sithobela
Nsoko
Nkungwini
Shemula
Boteler Point
Malangeni

Mantola
1392m
Kubutsa
Maloma
Mboza
Mpophomeni
Mvelabusha

Gege
Hlathikhulu
iNgwavuma
Mthonjeni
R22

Mozane
1171m
Nhlangano
Mzama Royal Graves
Mlokloma Royal Graves
Hluthi
Golela
Lavumisa
Mseleni
Hully Point
Sodwana Bay

Mahamba
Berbice
Mhlosheni
Onverwacht
Golela
Pongola
Ndabeni
Jozini
Tshongwe
Mbazwana

Kortnek
Pongolapoort Dam
Kingholm
Candover
Pongolapoort N. R.
uBombo
Malobeni
Jesser Point
Sodwana Bay National Park

Louwsburg
Magudu
R69
Nkonkoni
Ndabeni
Jozini
St Lucia Marine Reserve

Itala Game Reserve
R66
R69
R66
Mahlangasi
Mkuze
Nhlohlela
Malomeni
Phinda Resource Reserve
The Greater St Lucia Wetland Park (World Heritage Site)

Kranskop
Thokazi
Bayala
Msunduzi
Leven Point
Bird Island

Alpha
Steilrand
Ngome
R618
Zihlakenpele
Dukumbane
False Bay Park

Brakfontein
Swart uMfolozi
KwaCeza
Nongoma
N2
Hluhluwe
Lake St Lucia

Indian Ocean

Incomáti
Massintonto
Tembe
Umbuluzi
Lebombo
Ubombo
Pongola
Maputo
Msikazi

28°00'S
33°30'E

Copyright © Map Studio 2007
Goedgeloof
Bayeni
Hlabisa
KwaMbonambi
221
105 106 107 108 109

DR DS DT DU DV DW DX

Scale 1 : 1 500 000

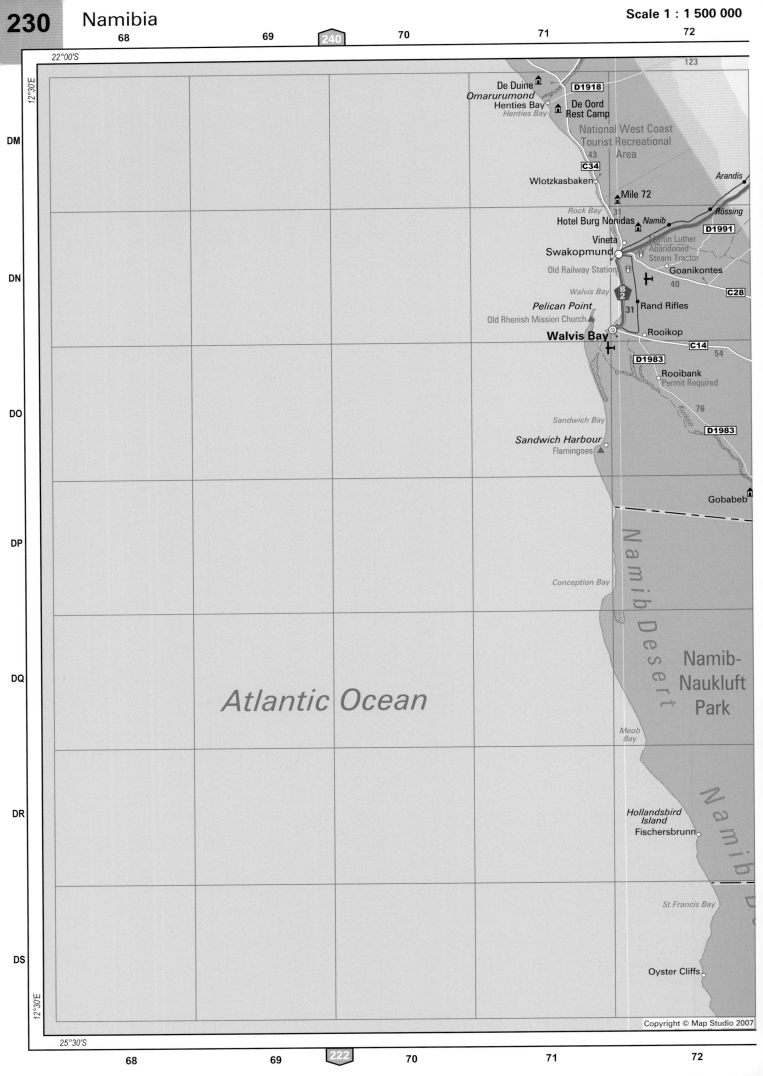

68   69   240   70   71   72

22°00'S

12°30'E

DM

123

De Duine
Omarurumond   D1918
Henties Bay   De Oord
Henties Bay   Rest Camp

National West Coast
Tourist Recreational
Area

Arandis

C34

Wlotzkasbaken   43

Mile 72   31   *Rössing*

Rock Bay   *Namib*

Hotel Burg Nonidas   D1991

Vineta   Martin Luther
Swakopmund   Abandoned
Steam Tractor

Old Railway Station   Goanikontes

40   C28

DN

Walvis Bay

Pelican Point   B2   Rand Rifles

Old Rhenish Mission Church   31   Rooikop

Walvis Bay   C14   54

D1983

Kuiseb   Rooibank
Permit Required

DO

Sandwich Bay

Sandwich Harbour   76   D1983

Flamingoes

Gobabeb

DP

Conception Bay

N
a
m
i
b   D
e
s
e
r
t

Namib-
Naukluft
Park

DQ

Atlantic Ocean

*Meob
Bay*

DR

*Hollandsbird
Island*

Fischersbrunn

N
a
m
i
b

DS

St Francis Bay

Oyster Cliffs

12°30'E

25°30'S

68   69   222   70   71   72

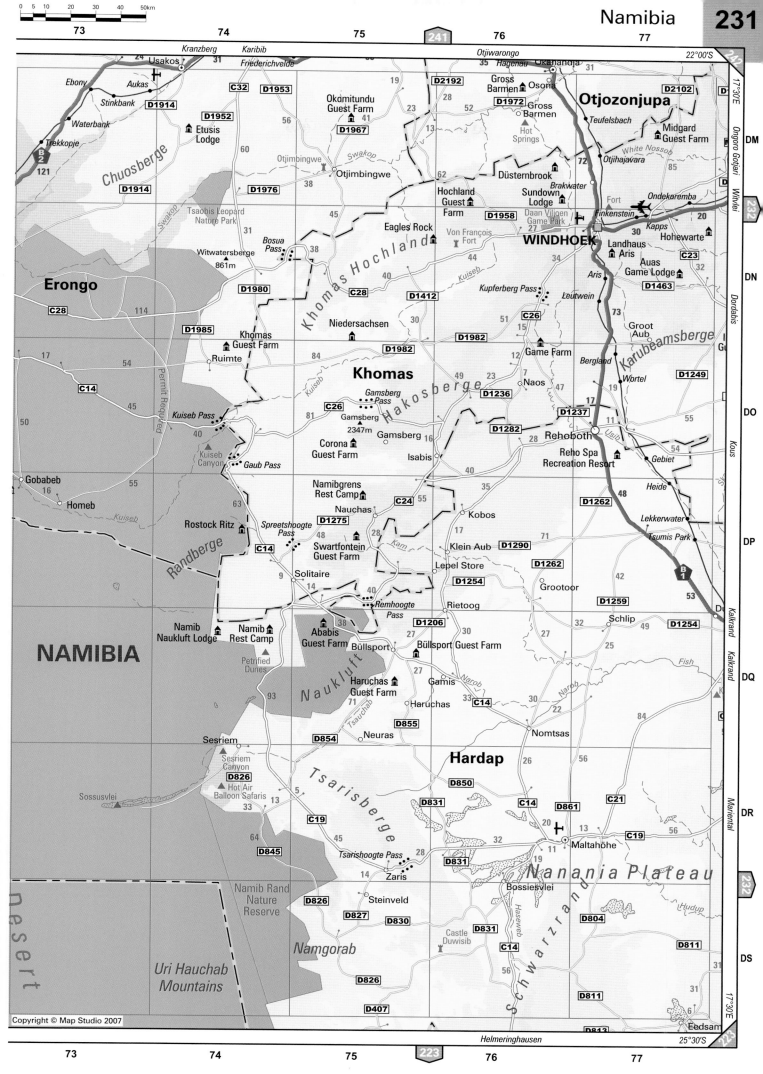

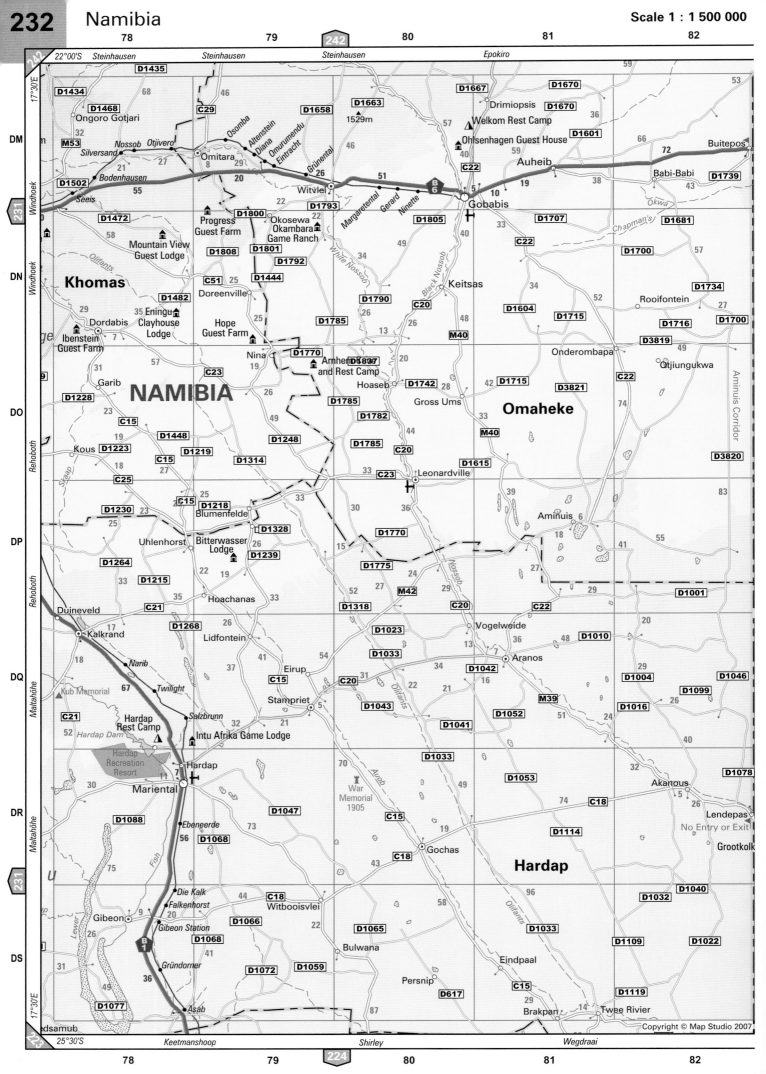

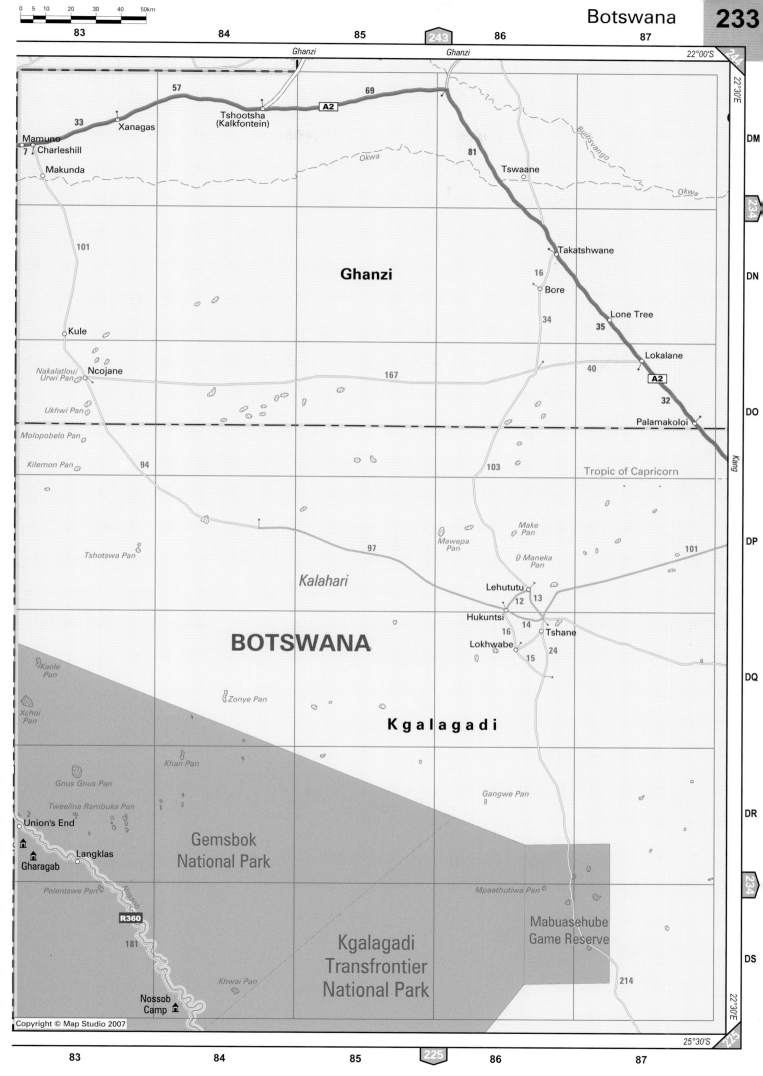

0 5 10   20   30   40   50km

83   84   85   243   86   87

Ghanzi   *Ghanzi*   22°00'S

22°30'E

57   69   A2

33   Xanagas   Tshootsha
                             (Kalkfontein)
Mamuno
7   Charleshill   81   Tswaane   DM
                                      Okwa
Makunda

Okwa

101   Takatshwane   DN

Ghanzi   16
                                         Bore
Kule   34   Lone Tree
                                                                     35   DO
Nakalatlou/   Ncojane   167   Lokalane
Urwi Pan   40
Ukhwi Pan   A2
                                                                                  32
Molopobelo Pan   Palamakoloi

Kilemon Pan   94   103   *Tropic of Capricorn*   DP
                                                                                  101
Tshotswa Pan   97   Mawepa   Make
                                                    Pan   Pan
                                                            Maneka
Kalahari   Pan

                                                    Lehututu   DP
BOTSWANA   12 13
                                                    Hukuntsi
Kaole   16   14
Pan   Lokhwabe   Tshane   DQ
Xchoi   15   24
Pan   Zonye Pan

          K g a l a g a d i

Gnus Gnus Pan   Khan Pan

Tweelina Rambuka Pan   Gangwe Pan   DR

Union's End
          Langklas
Gharagab   **Gemsbok
          National Park**

Polentswe Pan   Mpaathutiwa Pan   234
          R360   **Mabuasehube
          181   **Kgalagadi   Game Reserve**   DS
                                         Transfrontier
          Khwai Pan   National Park**   214
Nossob
Camp   25°30'S

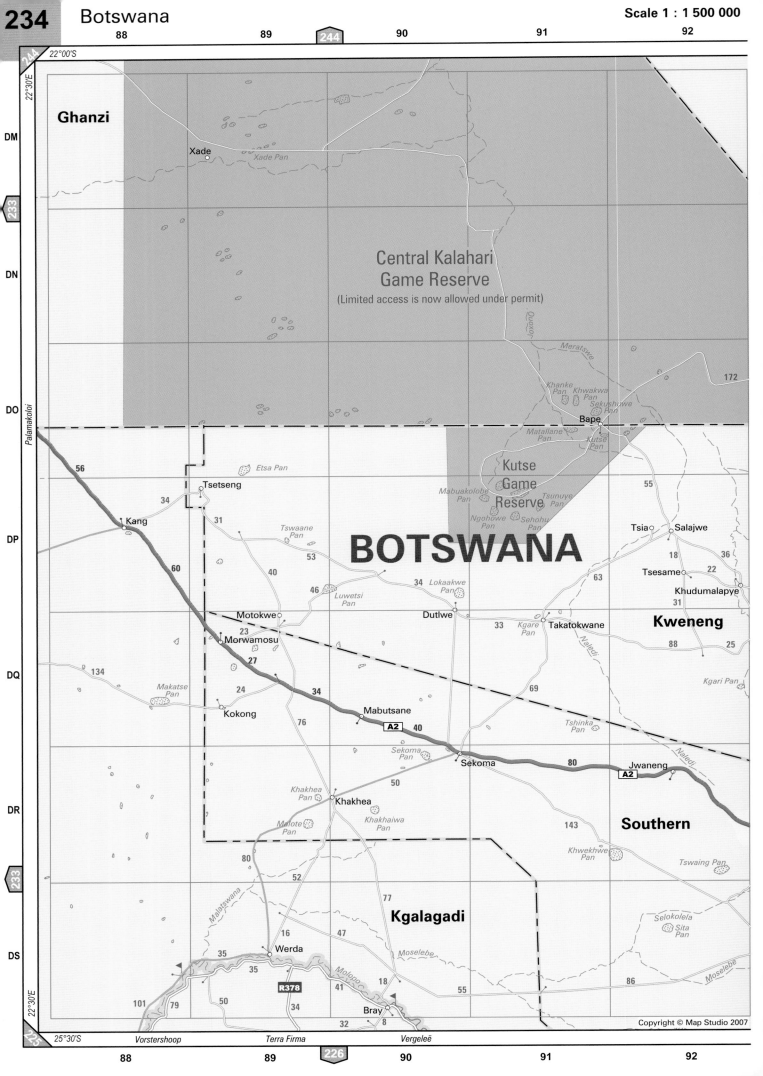

Ghanzi

Xade

Xade Pan

Central Kalahari
Game Reserve
(Limited access is now allowed under permit)

Joxono

Meratswe

172

Khanke Pan *Khwakwa Pan*

Sekushuwe Pan

Bape

Matallane Pan

Kutse Pan

Kutse
Game
Reserve

Mabuakolobe Pan

Tsunuye Pan

Ngohowe Pan *Sehohu Pan*

BOTSWANA

55

Tsia Salajwe

18   36

Tsesame   22

Khudumalapye

31

Kweneng

56

Etsa Pan

Tsetseng

34

Kang

31

Tswaane Pan

53

40

46

Luwetsi Pan

34 *Lokaakwe Pan*

Motokwe

Dutlwe

33 *Kgare Pan*

Takatokwane

63

60

Palamakoloi

23

Morwamosu

27

134

Makatse Pan

24

Kokong

34

76

Mabutsane

A2 40

69

88   25

Kgari Pan

Tshinka Pan

Sekoma Pan

Sekoma

80

Jwaneng

A2

Naledi

Naledi

50

Khakhea Pan

Khakhea

Malote Pan

Khakhaiwa Pan

143

Southern

Khwekhwe Pan

Tswaing Pan

80

52

77

Kgalagadi

Selokolela

Sita Pan

16

47

Malatswana

35

Werda

Moselebe

18

55

86

Moselebe

35

R378 34

Molopo

41

101 79 50

32

Bray

8

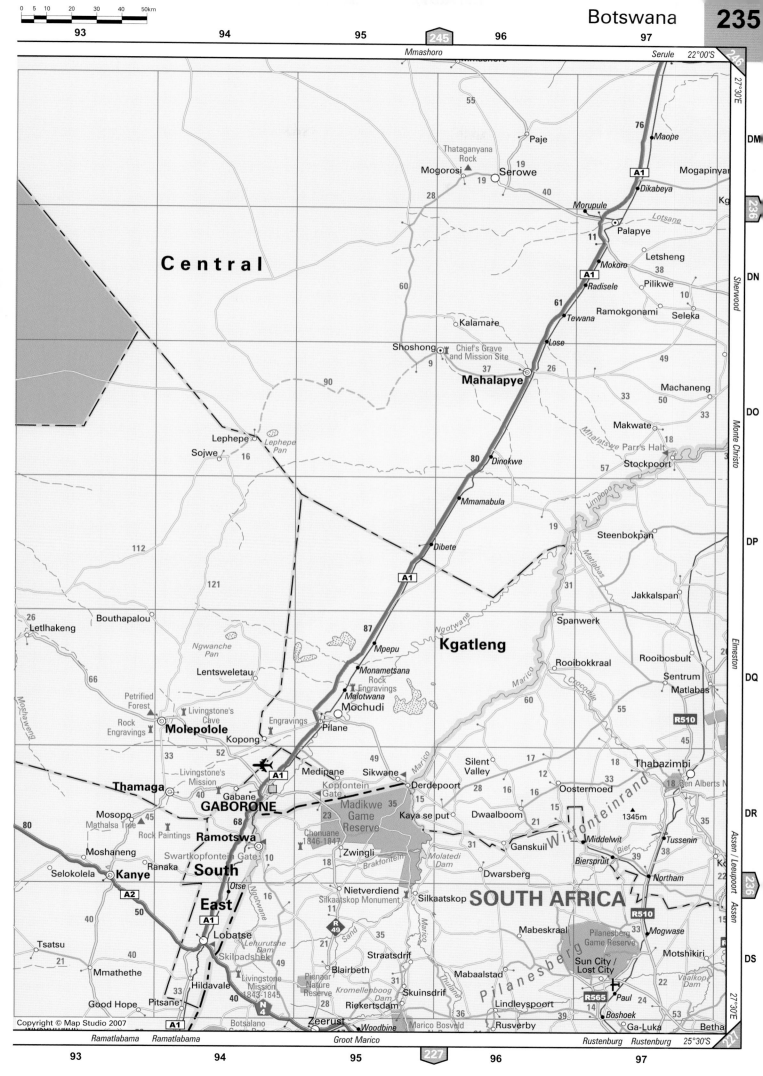

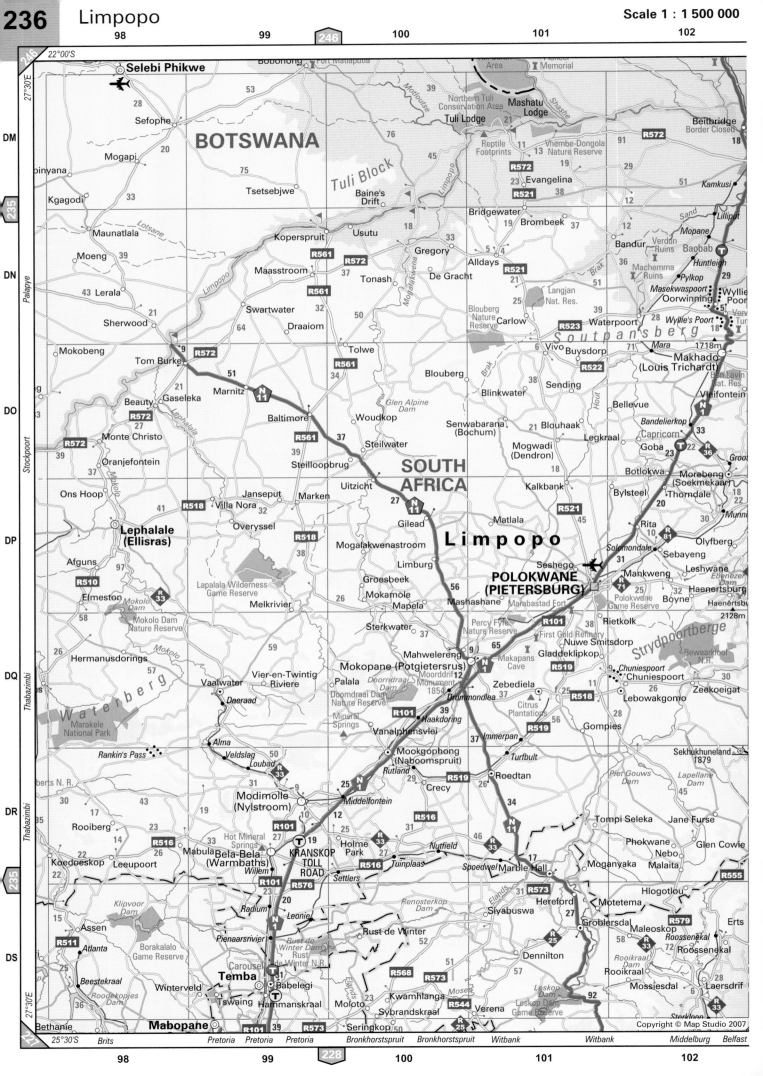

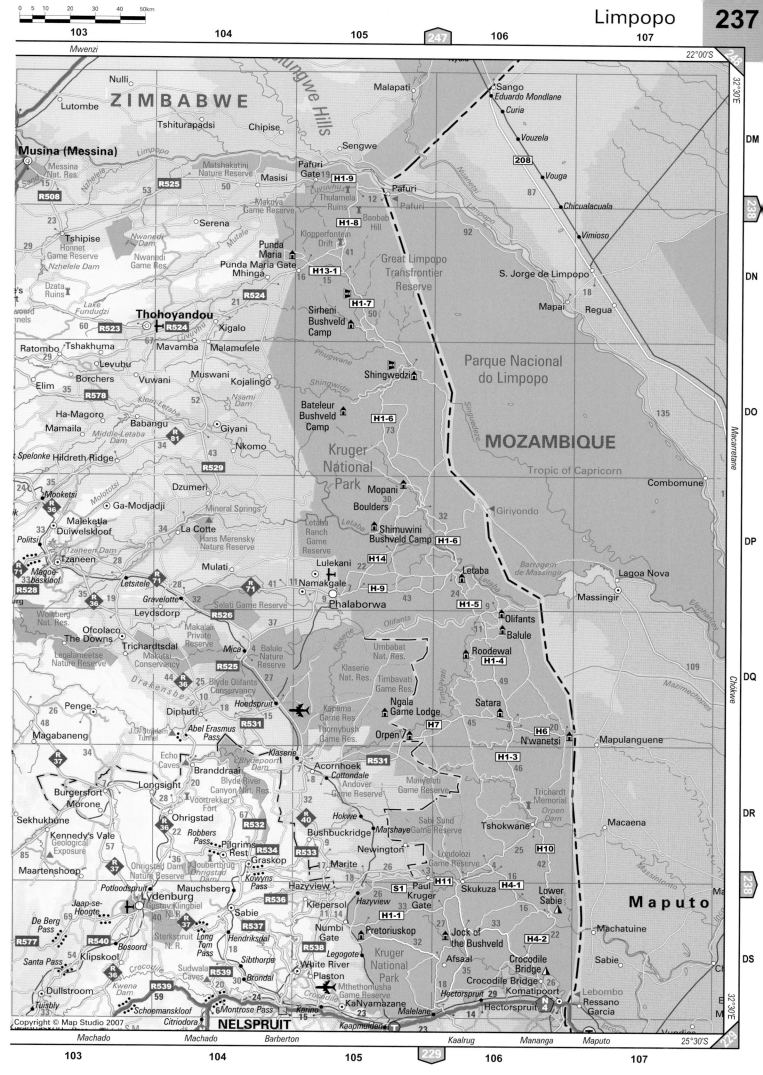

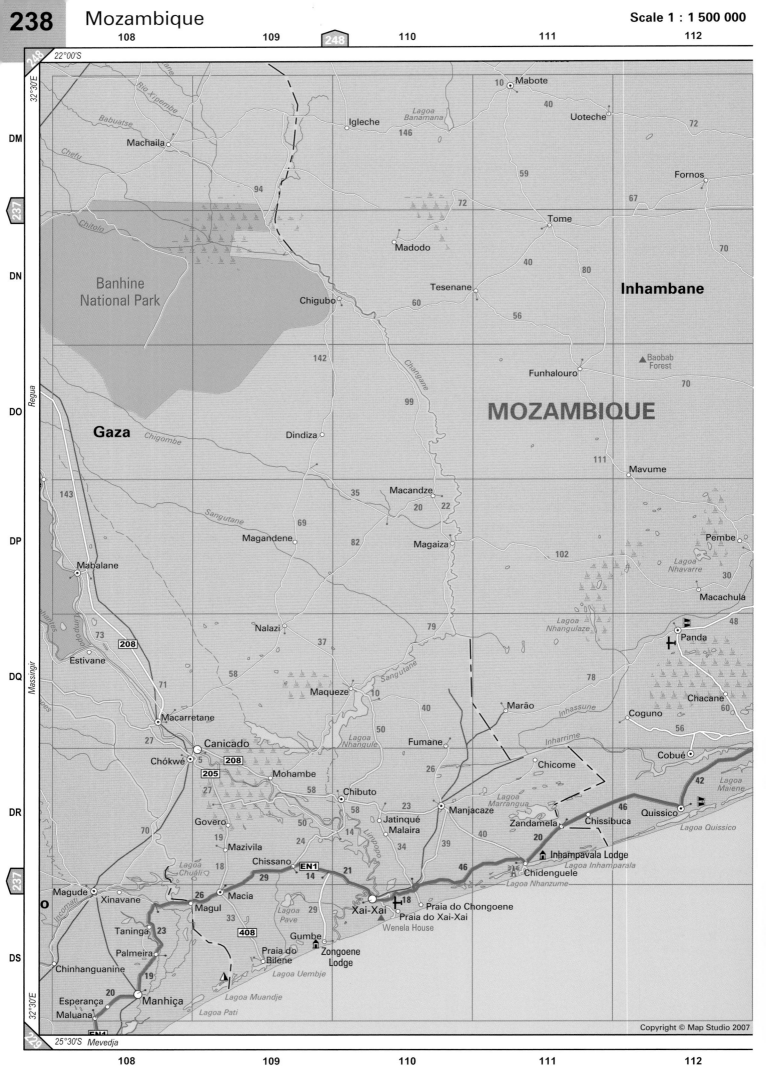

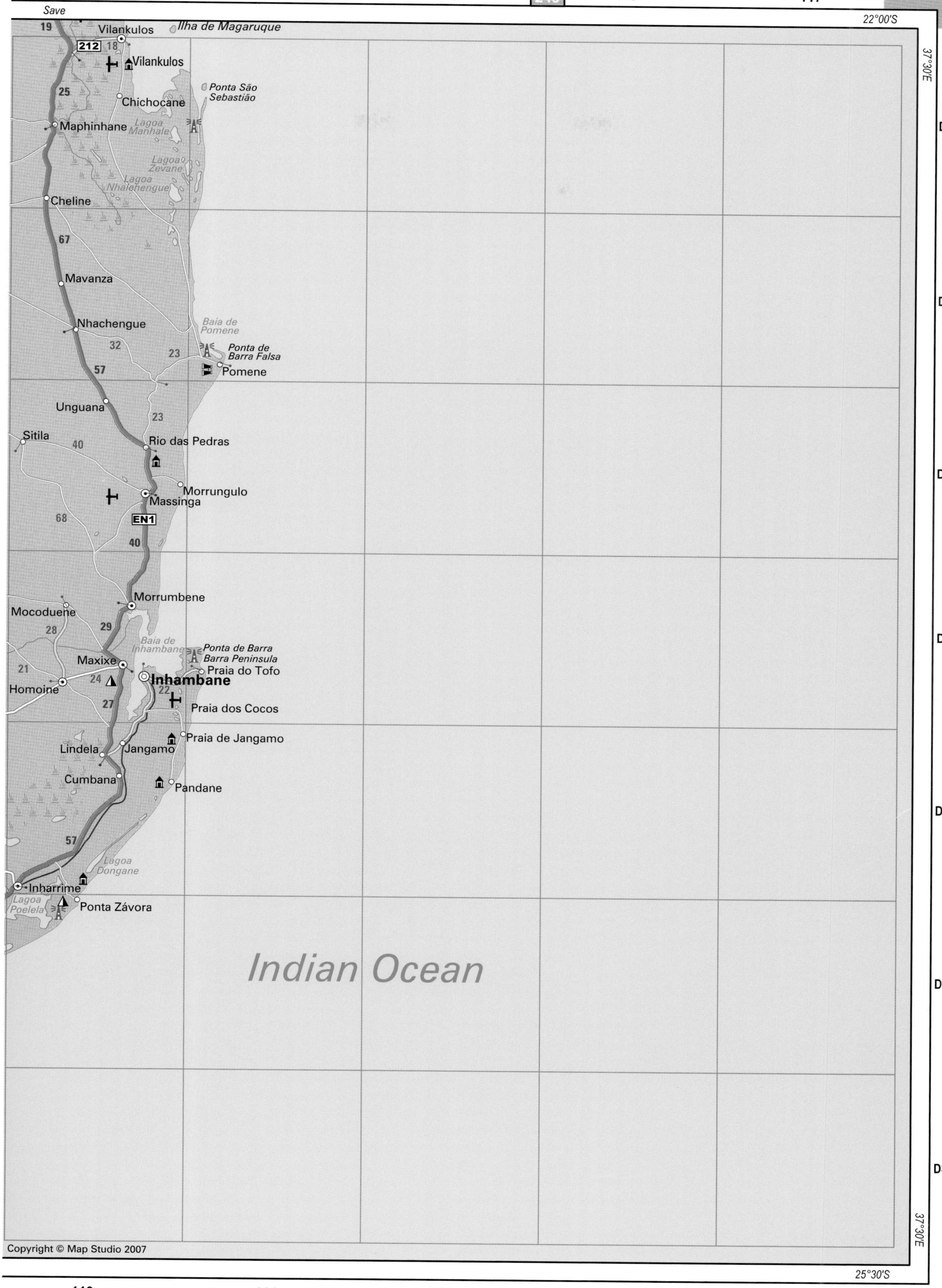

0 5 10 20 30 40 50km

Save

22°00'S

37°30'E

19

Vilankulos   *Ilha de Magaruque*

212   **18**

Vilankulos

25

Chichocane

DM

Maphinhane   *Lagoa Manhale*   *Ponta São Sebastião*

Lagoa Zevane

Lagoa Nhalehengue

Cheline

67

DN

Mavanza

Nhachengue   *Baia de Pomene*

32   **23**   *Ponta de Barra Falsa*

57   Pomene

Unguana

23

DO

Sitila   **40**   Rio das Pedras

Morrungulo

Massinga

68   **EN1**

40

Morrumbene

Mocoduene

28   **29**   *Baia de Inhambane*   *Ponta de Barra*

DP

21   Maxixe   *Barra Peninsula*

Homoine   **24**   **Inhambane**   Praia do Tofo

27   **22**   Praia dos Cocos

Lindela   Jangamo   Praia de Jangamo

Cumbana   Pandane

57

DQ

Lagoa Dongane

Inharrime

Lagoa Poelela   Ponta Závora

DR

Indian Ocean

DS

37°30'E

25°30'S

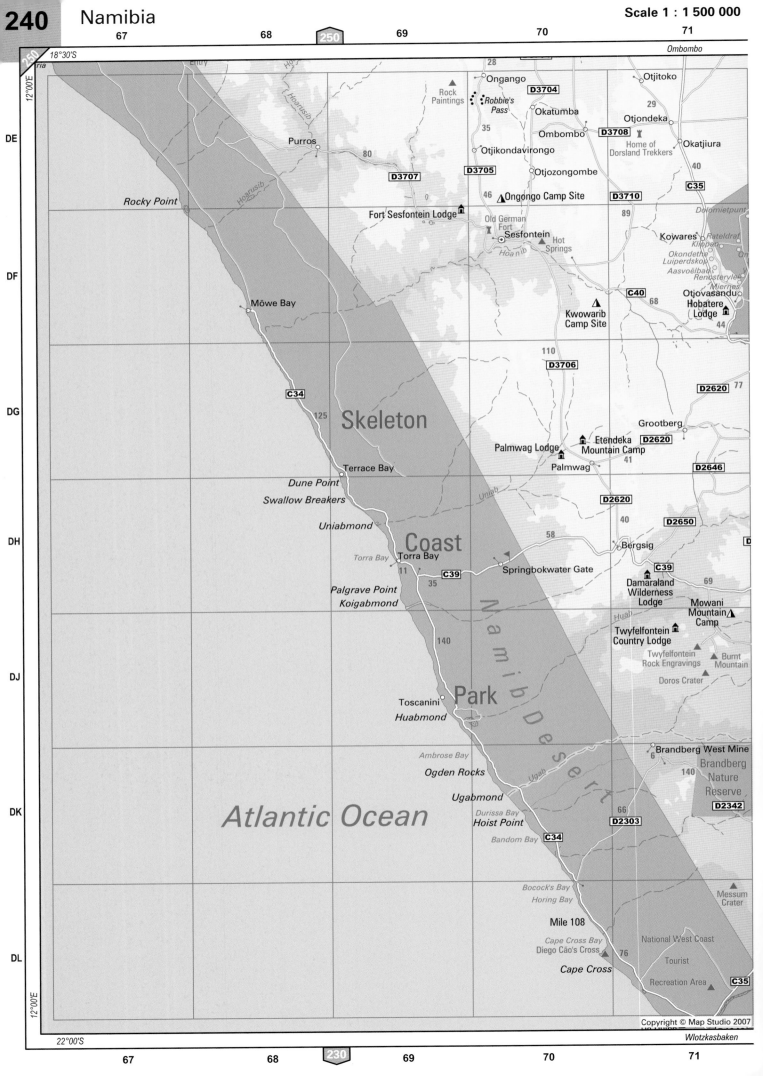

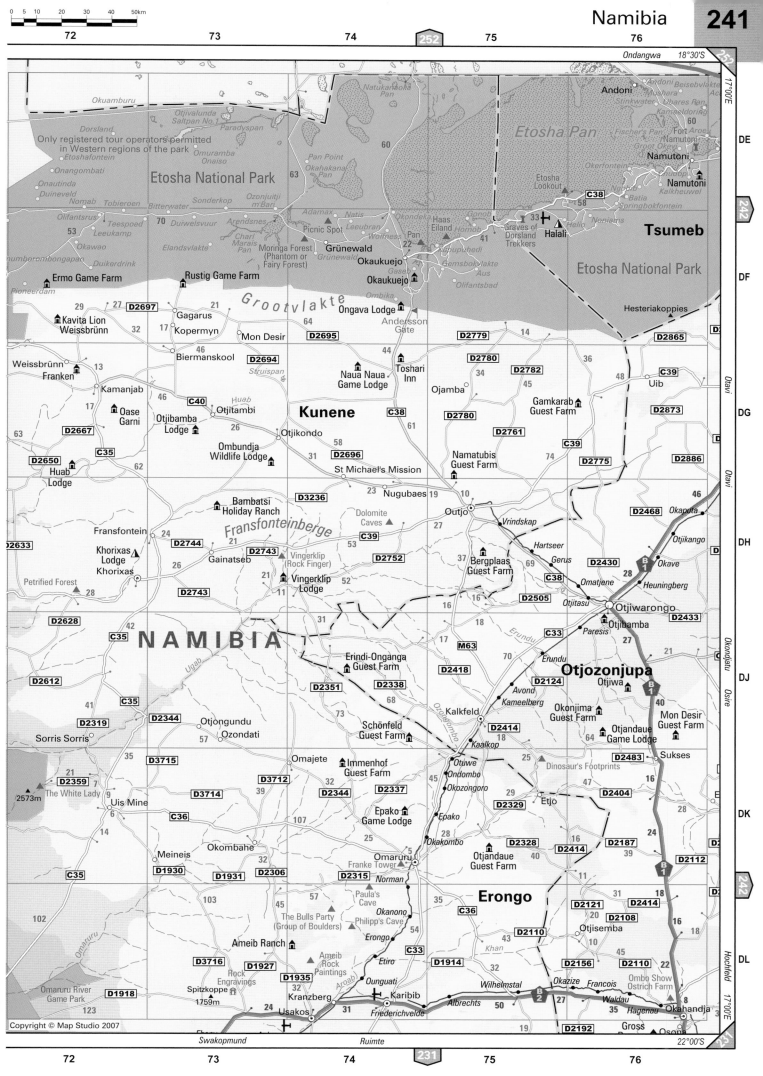

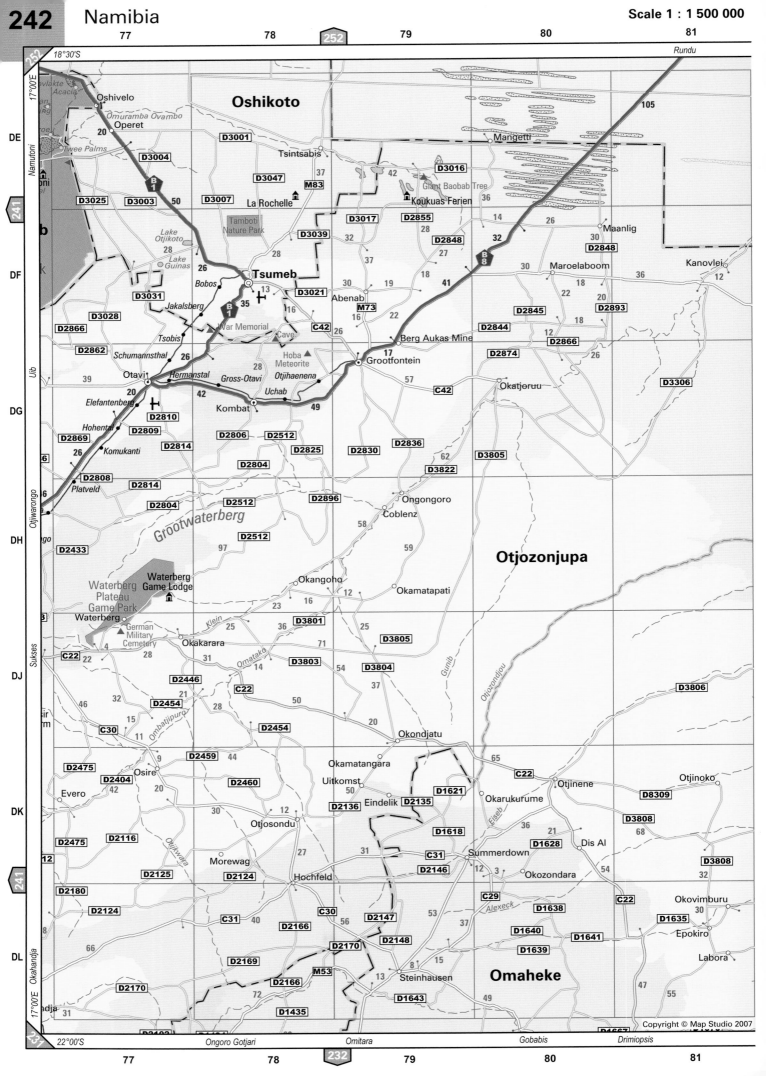

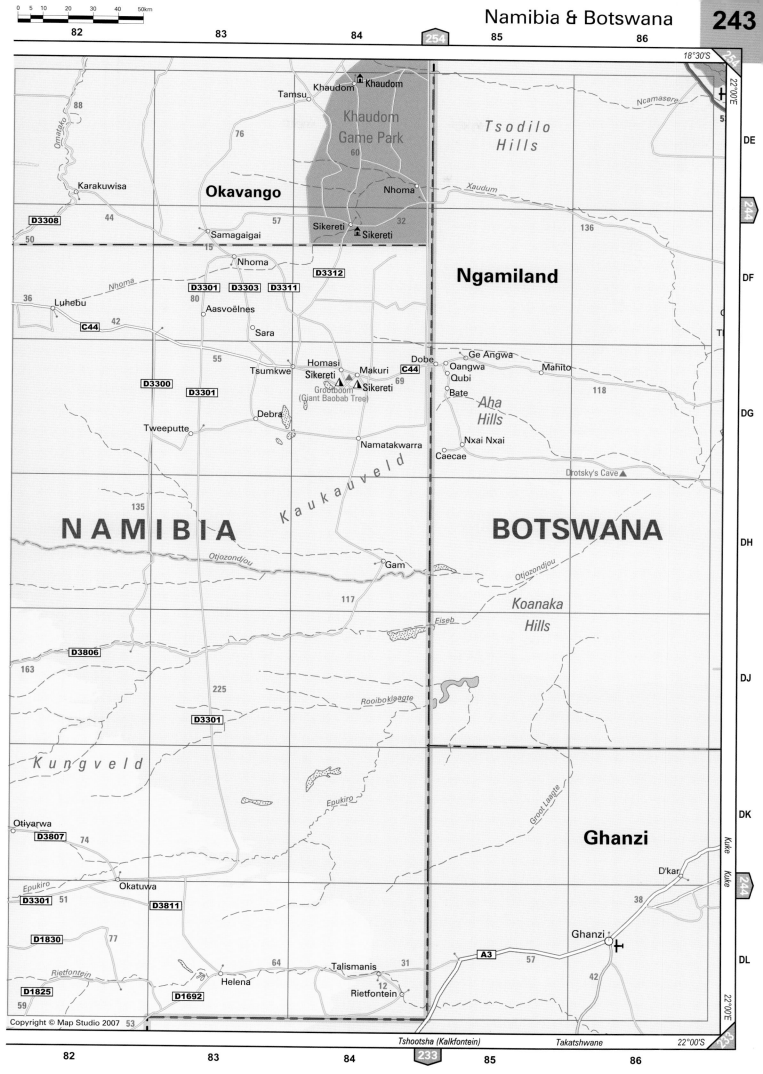

0 5 10 20 30 40 50km

254

18°30'S

22°00'E

254

244

DE

88

Omatako

Karakuwisa

Okavango

Khaudom Khaudom
Tamsu

76

Khaudom
Game Park

60

Nhoma

*Tsodilo
Hills*

Ncamasere

D3308   44

50   15

Samagaigai

57

Sikereti   Sikereti   32

136

DF

Nhoma

Nhoma

D3312

Ngamiland

36   Luhebu

C44   42

D3301 D3303 D3311
80

Aasvoëlnes

Sara

55

Homasi
Sikereti   Makuri   Dobe   C44
Grootboom   Sikereti   69
(Giant Baobab Tree)

Ge Angwa
Oangwa   Mahito
Qubi
Bate

*Aha
Hills*

118

Xaudum

DG

Tsumkwe

D3300

D3301

Debra

Tweeputte

Namatakwarra

Nxai Nxai

Caecae

Drotsky's Cave ▲

Kaukauveld

135

N A M I B I A

Otjozondjou

Gam

B O T S W A N A

DH

117

Otjozondjou

*Koanaka
Hills*

D3806

163

Eiseb

DJ

Rooiboklaagte

D3301

K u n g v e l d

Epukiro

DK

Groot Laagte

Otiyarwa

D3807   74

Ghanzi

Kuke
Kuke

244

Epukiro

D3301   51

Okatuwa

D3811

D'kar

38

D1830   77

Rietfontein

64

Helena

Talismanis   31

12
Rietfontein

Ghanzi

A3   57

42

DL

22°00'E

233

53

Tshootsha (Kalkfontein)   *Takatshwane*   22°00'S

D1825   59

D1692

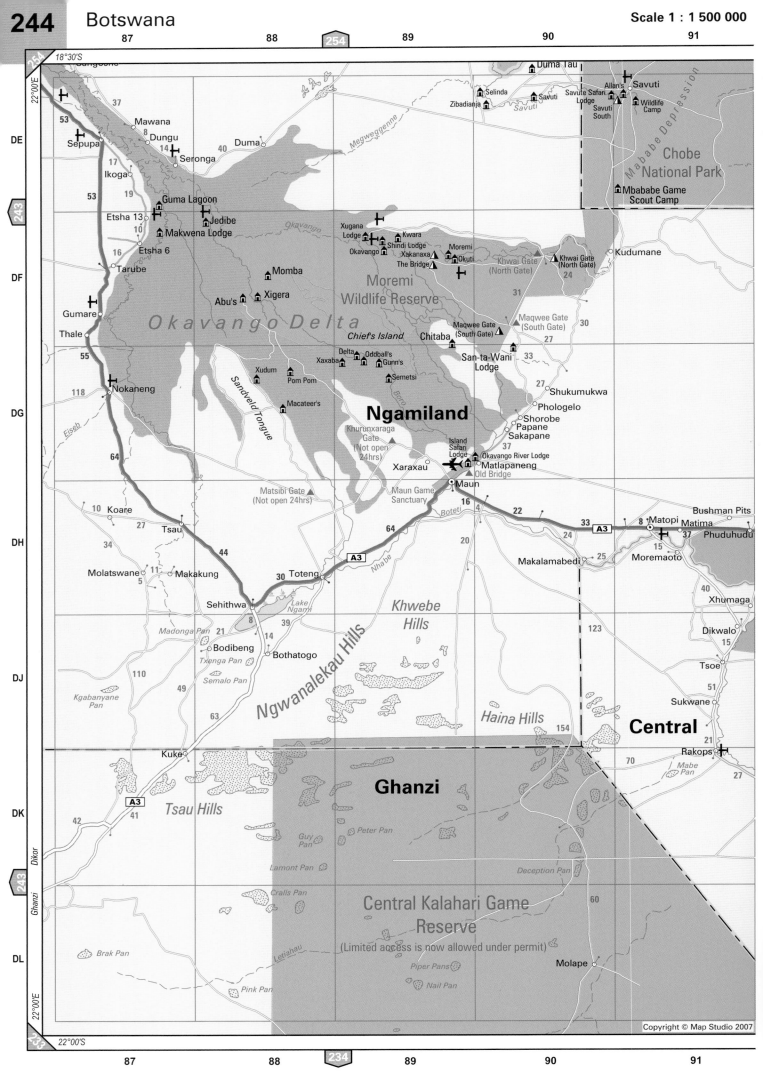

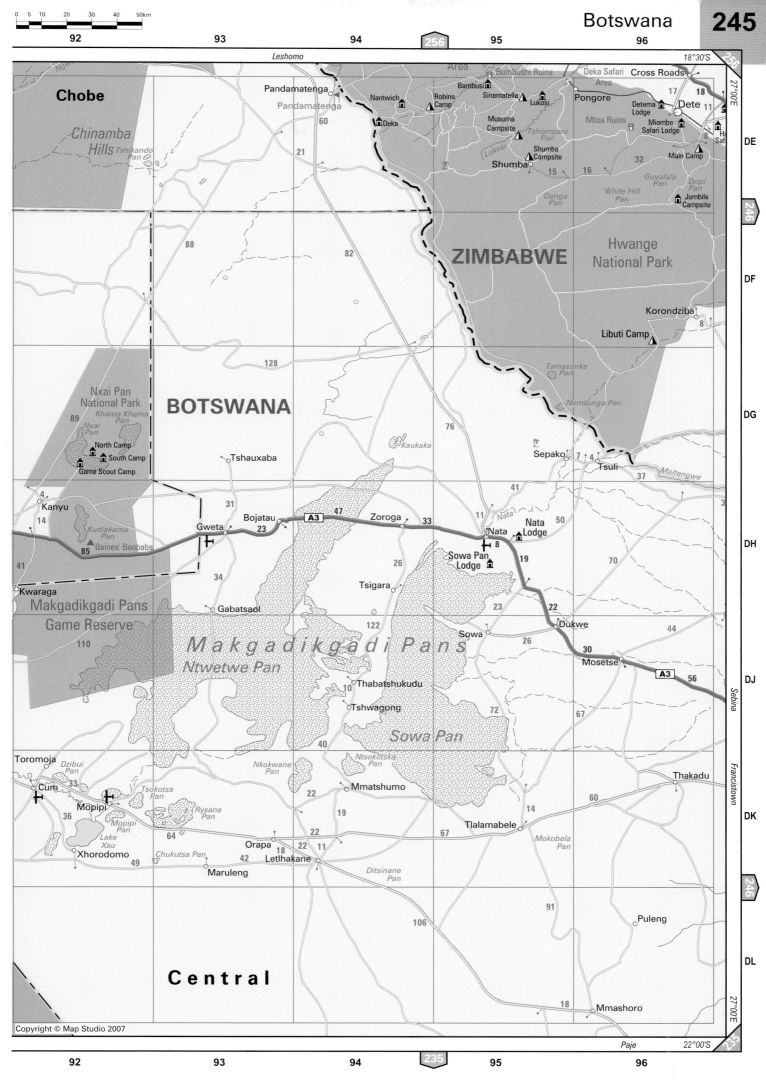

92   93   94   256   95   96

256

246

27°00'E

DE

246

DF

DG

DH

DJ

246

DK

DL

27°00'E

235

Leshomo

18°30'S

Chobe

Chinamba
Hills
Tshikando
Pan

Pandamatenga
Pandamatenga

60

21

Nantwich

Deka

Bambusi
Bumbushi Ruins
Robins
Camp
Sinamatella
Lukosi
Musuma
Campsite
Tshompani
Pan
Shumba
Campsite
Shumba

Deka Safari
Area

Cross Roads

Pongore

17

18

11

Detema
Lodge

Miombe
Safari Lodge
Dete

8

Main Camp

Mtoa Ruins

Danga
Pan

15

16

32

White Hill
Pan

Guvalala
Pan

Dopi
Pan

Jumbile
Campsite

88

82

ZIMBABWE

**Hwange
National Park**

Korondziba

8

Libuti Camp

128

BOTSWANA

*Khama Khama
Pan*

76

Kaukaka

Tamasanka
Pan

Nemtungu Pan

**Nxai Pan
National Park**

89

Nxai
Pan

North Camp

South Camp

Game Scout Camp

Tshauxaba

Sepako

7 4

Tsuli

37

Maitengwe

4

Kanyu

14

*Kudiakama
Pan*

Baines' Baobabs

85

31

Gweta

Bojatau

A3

23

47

Zoroga

33

41

11 Nata

Nata
Lodge

50

3

8

Sowa Pan
Lodge

19

70

41

Kwaraga

34

26

Tsigara

23

22

Dukwe

44

**Makgadikgadi Pans
Game Reserve**

110

Gabatsaol

122

Sowa

26

30

Mosetse

A3

56

M a k g a d i k g a d i   P a n s

Ntwetwe Pan

Thabatshukudu

10

Tshwagong

72

67

Sowa Pan

40

Toromoja

*Dzibui
Pan*

Cum

33

Mopipi

36

*Tsokotsa
Pan*

*Mopipi
Pan*

*Rysana
Pan*

Nkokwane
Pan

Ntsokotska
Pan

Mmatshumo

22

19

Thakadu

60

14

Tlalamabele

Mokobela
Pan

64

*Lake
Xau*

Xhorodomo

49

Chukutsa Pan

Maruleng

42

Orapa

18

22 11

Letlhakane

67

*Ditsinane
Pan*

91

106

Puleng

C e n t r a l

18

Mmashoro

Paje

22°00'S

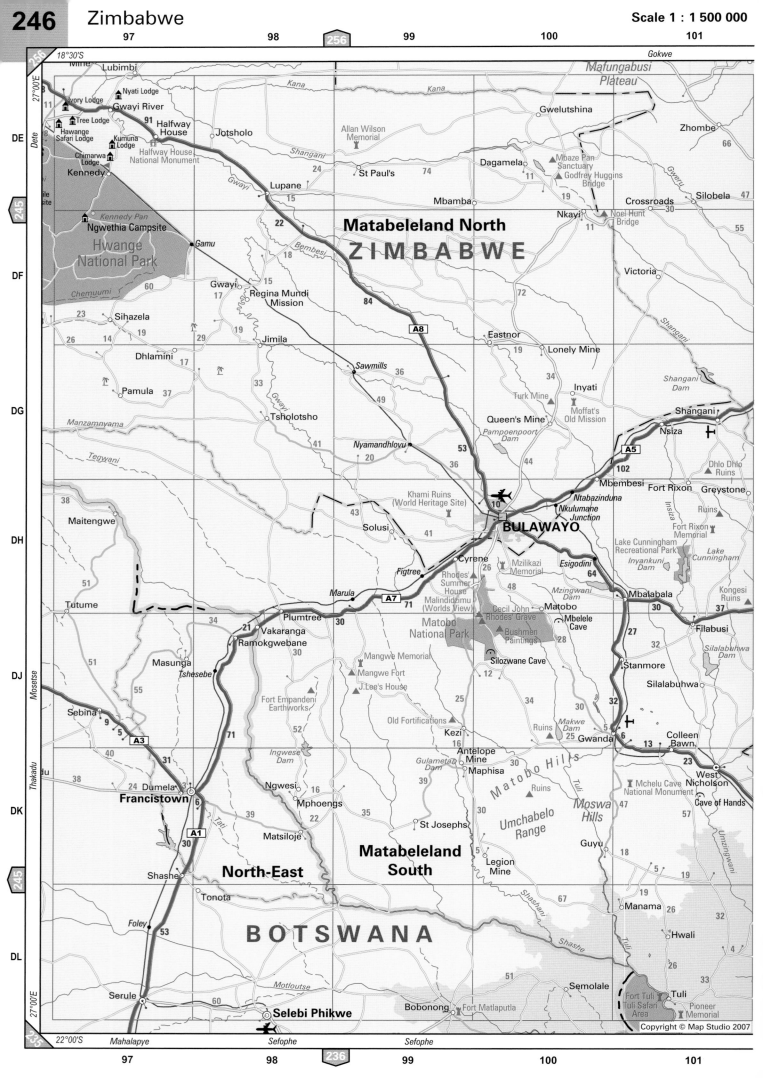

ZIMBABWE

Matabeleland North

Matabeleland South

BOTSWANA

North-East

Hwange National Park

Matobo National Park

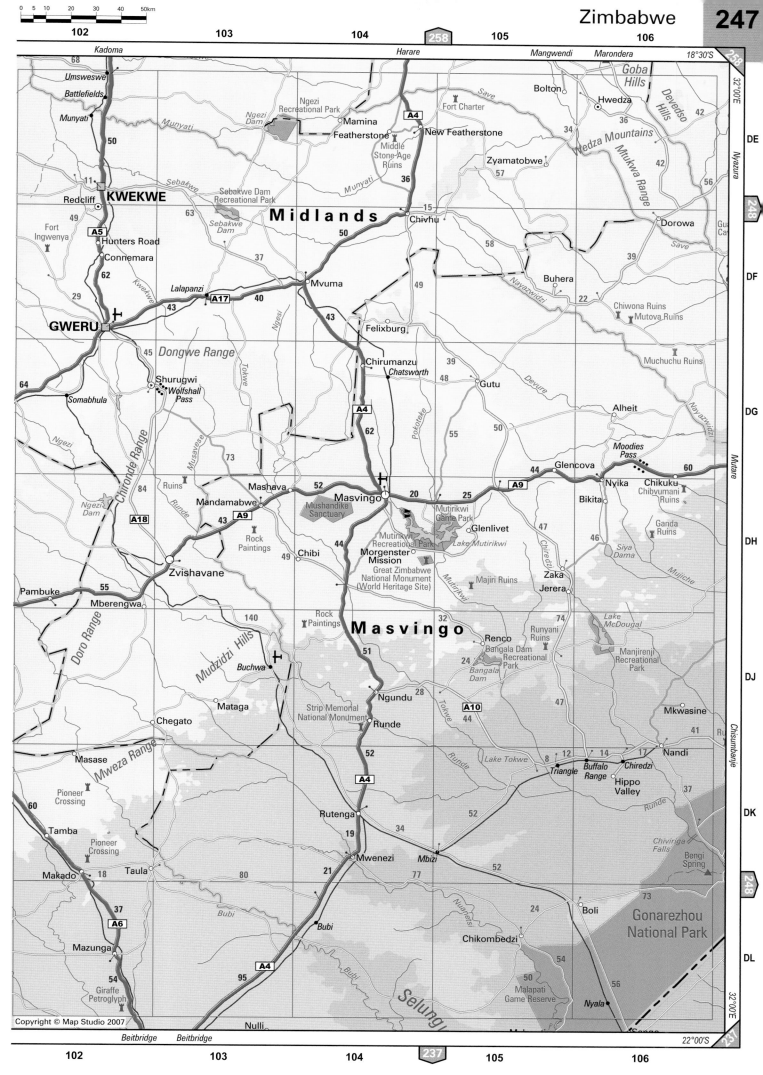

0 5 10 20 30 40 50km

258

Kadoma
68
Umsweswe
Battlefields
Munyati
50

11
Redcliff
KWEKWE
49
Fort
Ingwenya
A5 Hunters Road
Connemara
62
29
GWERU
64
Somabhula
45 *Dongwe Range*
Shurugwi
Wolfshall
Pass

Munyati
Ngezi
Dam
Ngezi
Recreational Park
Sebakwe
Sebakwe Dam
Recreational Park
Sebakwe
Dam
63
50
37
Lalapanzi **A17** 40
43
Ngesi
Tokwe

M i d l a n d s
15
Chivhu
50
58
49
Mvuma
43
Felixburg
A4
Chirumanzu
Chatsworth
39
62
48
Gutu

Harare *Mangwendi* *Marondera*   18°30'S
Bolton
Fort Charter Hwedza
36
Save
34
Zyamatobwe
57
55
50
Alheit
Devure
Nayazwidzi
Buhera
22 *Chiwona Ruins*
Mutova Ruins
Muchuchu Ruins

Goba
Hills
Devedso
Hills
42
42
56
Wedza Mountains
Mhukwa Range
Dorowa
39
Save
Nayazwidzi

DE
DF
DG

A4
A4
Middle
Stone Age
Ruins
36
Mamina
Featherstone
New Featherstone

248

32°00'E
Nyazura

Mutare

Musavese
73
84
Ruins
Runde
Ngezi
Dam
A18
Chironde Range
Mashava
52
Mandamabwe
A9 43
Rock
Paintings
49
Chibi
44
Pambuke
55
Mberengwa
Zvishavane

Masvingo
20 25
A9
44 Glencova
Nyika
Bikita
Mushandike
Sanctuary
Mutirikwi
Game Park
Glenlivet
Mutirikwi
Recreational Park
47
Lake Mutirikwi
Morgenster
Mission
Great Zimbabwe
National Monument
(World Heritage Site)
Majiri Ruins
Zaka
Jerera
Mutirikwi
Chiredzi
46

Moodies
Pass
60
Chikuku
Chibvumani
Ruins
Ganda
Ruins
Siya
Dama
Mujiche

DH

Doro Range
Mudzidzi Hills
140
Buchwa
Mweza Range
Mataga
Chegato
Masase
60
Pioneer
Crossing
Tamba
Pioneer
Crossing
Makado 18 Taula
37
A6
Mazunga
54
Giraffe
Petroglyph

M a s v i n g o
51
Ngundu
28 *Tokwe*
Strip Memorial
National Monument
Runde
52
A4
Rutenga
19
34
Mwenezi
Mbizi
21
80
77
Bubi
Bubi
95
Nulli

32
Renco
Runyani
Ruins
Bangala Dam
Recreational
Park
24 *Bangala*
Dam
A10
44
Lake
McDougal
47
Lake Tokwe
8 12 14 17
Triangle *Buffalo*
Range
Hippo
Valley
52
52
24 Boli
Nuanetsi
Chikombedzi
54
50
Malapati
Game Reserve
56
Nyala

Mkwasine
41
Nandi
Chiredzi
37
Runde
Chiviriga
Falls
Bengi
Spring
73
Gonarezhou
National Park

DJ
DK
248
DL

32°00'E

Chisumbanje
Mujiche

Copyright © Map Studio 2007

Beitbridge *Beitbridge*
22°00'S
237

Selungu

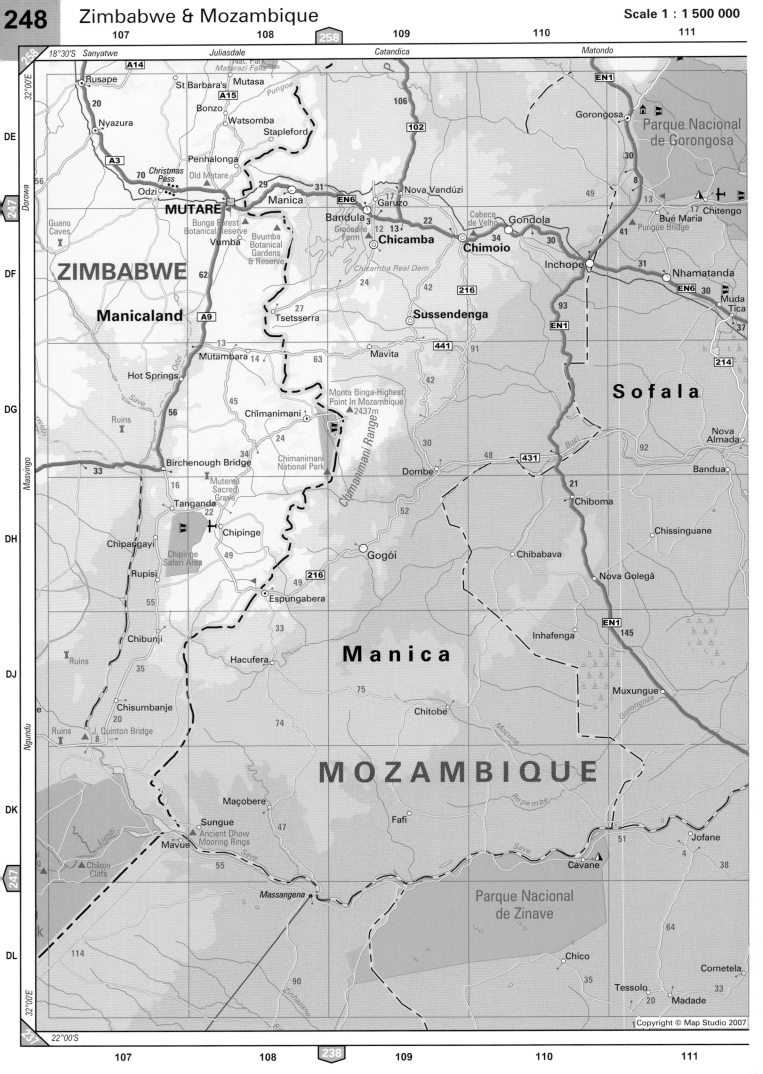

107 258 108 109 110 111

18°30'S Sanyatwe   Juliasdale   Catandica   Matondo

258

A14
Rusape
St Barbara's   Mutasa
20   Bonzo   A15
Nyazura   Watsomba
Stapleford

DE

EN1
Gorongosa
Parque Nacional
de Gorongosa
30
8
49
13
17   Chitengo
Bué Maria

A3
Penhalonga
70   Christmas   Old Mutare
Pass   ⚊⚊⚊
Odzi
MUTARE   29   Manica   31
Bunga Forest   EN6   Garuzo
Botanical Reserve   17
Vumba   Bandula   3
Bvumba   Crocodile   12 13
Botanical   Farm
Gardens   Chicamba   22   Cabeça
& Reserve   de Velho   Gondola
Chimoio   34   30
41   Pungue Bridge
Inchope   31
93   Nhamatanda
EN6   30   Muda
Tica
37
214

247
Dorowa

DF

ZIMBABWE
62
Manicaland   A9
Chicamba Real Dam   24
42   216
Sussendenga
EN1

Masvingo

Sofala

27
Tsetsserra
13   441   91
Mutambara   14   63   Mavita
Hot Springs   42
45
56   Monta Binga–Highest
Chimanimani   Point In Mozambique
24   ▲2437m   30   48   431   92   Nova
Almada
Chimanimani   Dombe   Bandua
National Park   21
Birchenough Bridge   34   Chiboma
33   16   Mutema   52
Sacred   Chissinguane
Tanganda   Grave
22   Chibabava
Chipinge   Nova Golegã

DG

DH

Ruins

Chipangayi   Chipinge
49   Safari Area
Rupisi   216   Gogói
55   49   Inhafenga   EN1   145
Espungabera
33   Muxungue
Chibunji   Manica
Ruins   35   Hacufera
20   Chitobe
Chisumbanje   75
Ruins   J. Quinton Bridge   74
8   Jofane
51   4   38

247
Ngundu

DJ

MOZAMBIQUE
Maçobere   Fafi
Sungue   47   Cavane
Ancient Dhow
Mavue   Mooring Rings
Chilojo   55
Cliffs   Save   64
Massangena   Parque Nacional   Chico
de Zinave   35
114   90   Cometela
20   Tessolo   33
Madade

DK

DL

22°00'S
32°00'E

107 238 108 109 110 111

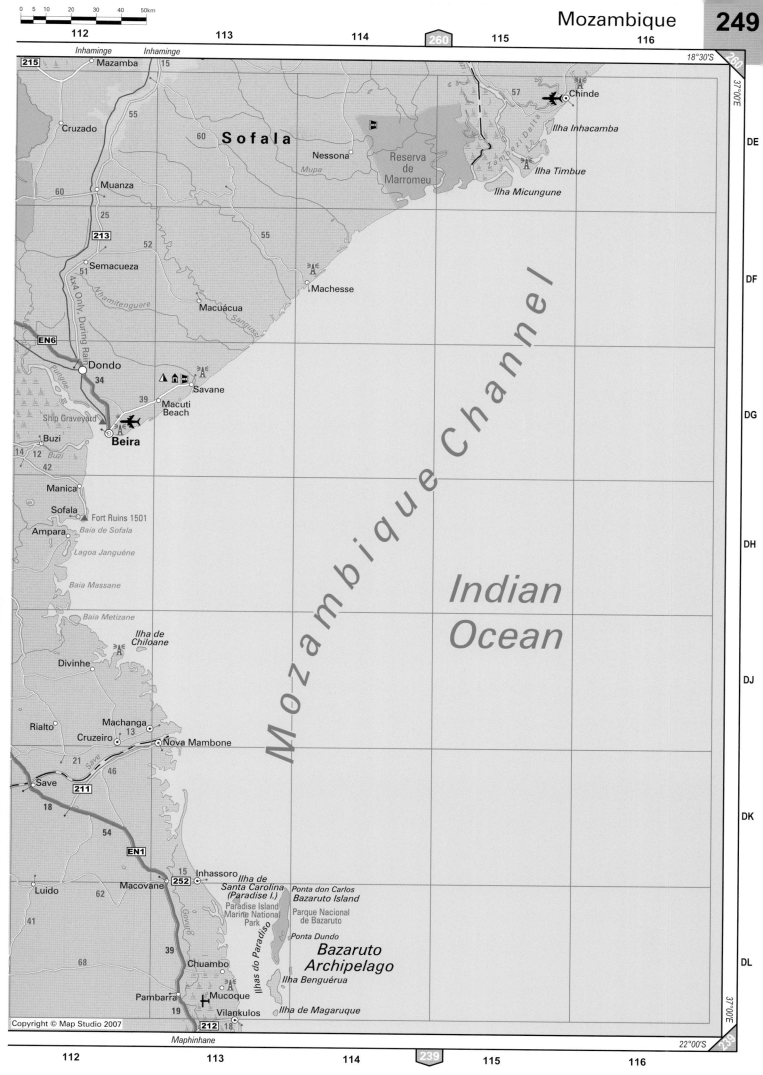

0 5 10   20   30   40   50km

112   113   114   260   115   116

Inhaminge   Inhaminge   18°30'S

215   Mazamba   15   Chinde

DE

Cruzado   55   60   **S o f a l a**   *Ilha Inhacamba*

                 Nessona   Reserva   *Ilha Timbue*

Muanza   60   *Mupa*   de   *Ilha Micungune*
                     Marromeu

60   25

213   52   55

DF

Semacueza   Machesse

51   Macuácua

EN6   *Sanguss*

Dondo   *M o z a m b i q u e   C h a n n e l*

34   Savane

DG

39   Macuti

Ship Graveyard   Beach

Buzi   **Beira**

14   12   *Buzi*

42

Manica   *Indian*

Sofala

Ampara   ▲ Fort Ruins 1501   *Ocean*

      Baia de Sofala

DH

     Lagoa Janguéne

     Baia Massane

     Baia Metizane

     Ilha de
     Chiloane

Divinhe

DJ

Rialto   Machanga

Cruzeiro   13

21   *Save*   Nova Mambone

46

Save   211

18   DK

54

EN1

15   Inhassoro

Luido   62   Macovane   252   *Ilha de*
                 Santa Carolina   Ponta don Carlos
41   *(Paradise I.)*   *Bazaruto Island*
                Paradise Island   Parque Nacional
                Marine National   de Bazaruto
                Park
39   *Govuro*   *Ponta Dundo*

68   Chuambo   *Bazaruto*
                   Archipelago

DL

Pambarra   Mucoque   *Ilha Benguérua*

19   Vilankulos

212   18   *Ilha de Magaruque*

Ilhas do Paradiso

Pungoe

Nhamitenguere

4x4 Only During Rain

Copyright © Map Studio 2007   22°00'S

Maphinhane   239

57

Zambezi Delta

37°00'E

37°00'E

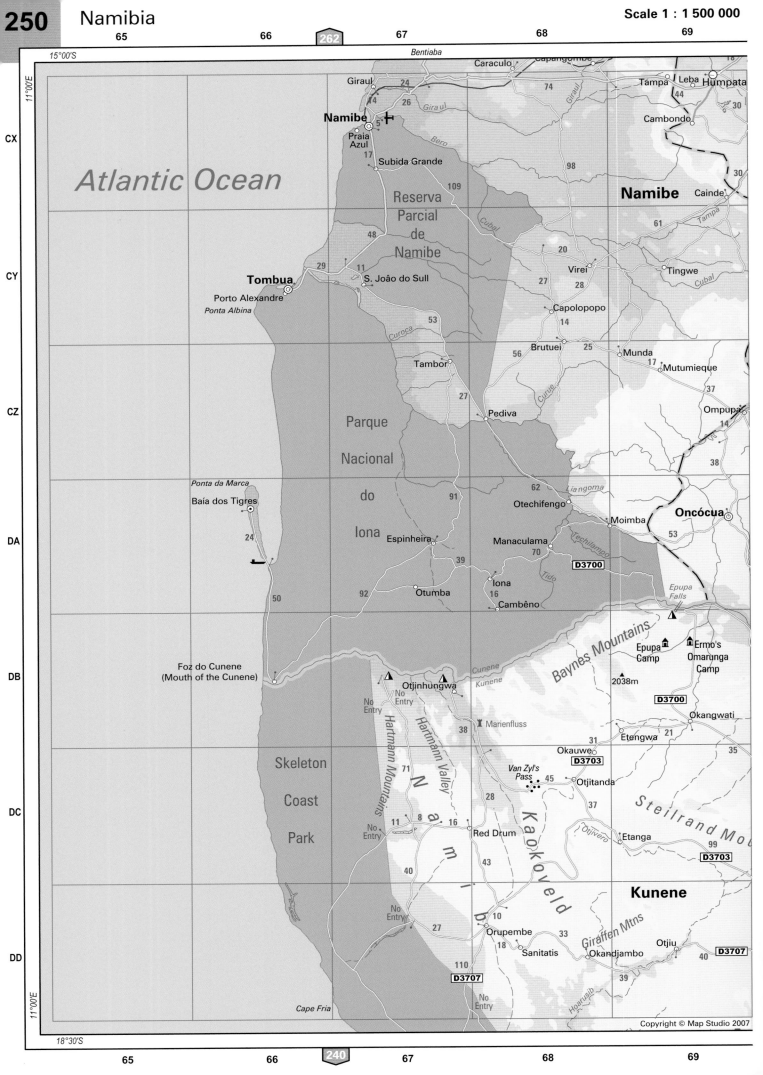

Atlantic Ocean

Bentiaba

Caraculo · Capangombe

Giraul · 24 · 74 · Tampa · Leba · **Humpata**
14 · 26 · 44 · 30

Namibe · 5 · Cambondo

Praia Azul · 98 · 30

17 · **Namibe** · Cainde

Subida Grande · 61

Reserva Parcial de Namibe · 109

48 · 20 · Virei · Tingwe

29 · 27 · 28

11 · 14 · Capolopopo

Tombua
Porto Alexandre
Ponta Albina · S. Joâo do Sull

53 · 56 · Brutuei · 25 · Munda
17 · Mutumieque

Curoca · Tambor · 37

27 · Ompupa
14

Ponta da Marca
Baía dos Tigres · Pediva

Parque · 62 · *Liangoma*

Nacional · 91 · Otechifengo · Moimba · 53 · **Oncócua**

24 · do · Espinheira · Manaculama · 70 · *Techilampo* · **D3700**

50 · Iona · 39 · *Tido* · *Epupa Falls*

92 · Otumba · Iona · 16
Cambêno

Foz do Cunene
(Mouth of the Cunene) · *Cunene* · *Baynes Mountains*
Epupa Camp · Ermo's Omarunga Camp

Otjinhungwa · No Entry · *Kunene* · 2038m · **D3700**

No Entry · 38 · Marienfluss · Okangwati

Skeleton · 31 · Etengwa · 21 · 35

Coast · 71 · Okauwe · **D3703**

Park · Van Zyl's Pass · 45 · Otjitanda · 37 · *Steilrand Mo*

28

No Entry · 11 · 8 · 16 · 43 · Etanga · 99 · **D3703**
Red Drum · *Otjivero*

40 · **Kunene**

No Entry · 10 · *Giraffen Mtns*

27 · Orupembe · 33 · Otjiu

18 · Sanitatis · Okandjambo · 40 · **D3707**

110 · 39 · *Hoarusib*

D3707

Cape Fria · No Entry

Copyright © Map Studio 2007

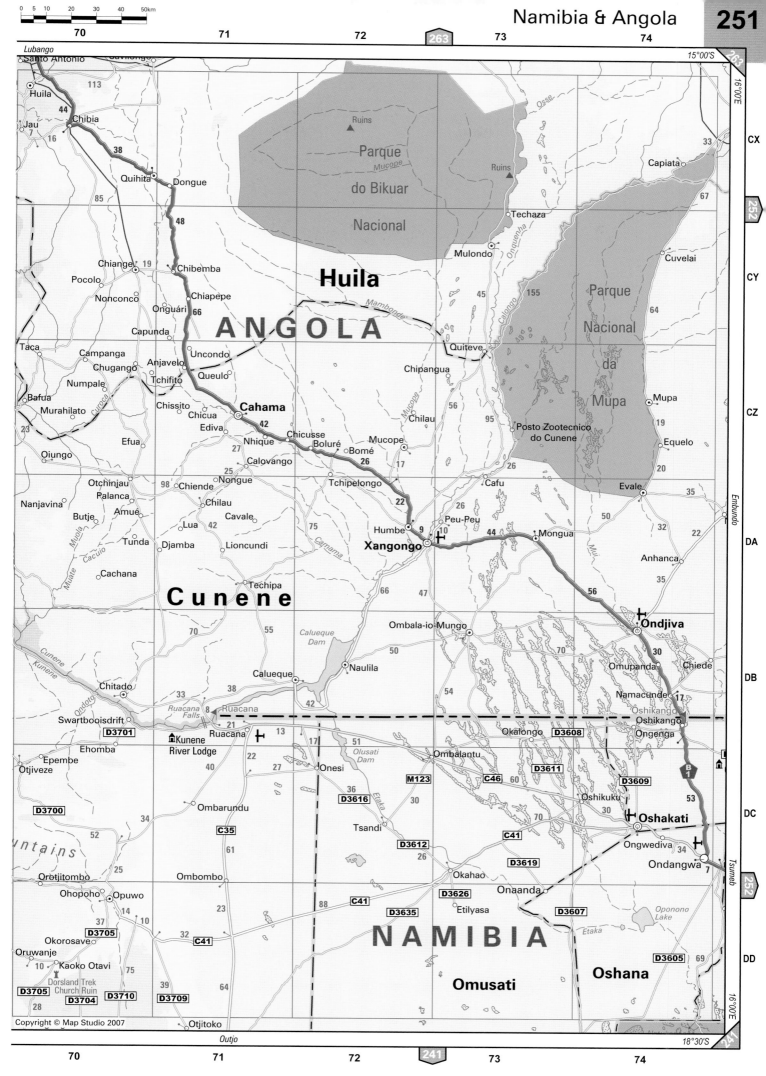

0 5 10   20   30   40   50km

70   71   72   263   73   74

Lubango
Santo Antonio
Huila
113
44
Jau
7   Chibia
16
38
Quihita   Dongue
85
48
Chiange   19   Chibemba
Pocolo
Nonconco   Chiapepe
Onguári   66
Capunda
Taca   Uncondo
Campanga   Anjavelo   Queulo
Chugango   Tchifito
Numpale
Bafua   Chissito
Murahilato   Chicua
Efua   Ediva   **Cahama**
Oiungo   42
Nhique   Chicusse
27   Boluré
Calovango   Bomé   26
25   Mucope
Otchinjau   98   Chiende   Nongue   17
Palanca   Chilau   Tchipelongo
Nanjavina   Amué   Cavale   75   22
Butje   Lua   42
Tunda   Djamba   Lioncundi   Humbe   9   10   Peu-Peu
Xangongo   44   Mongua
Cachana   66   47   56
Cunene   Techipa
70   55   *Calueque Dam*
Chitado   Naulila   50
Swartbooisdrift   38   Calueque   54
D3701   33   42   Ombala-io-Mungo   70
Ruacana Falls   8   Ruacana   50
Ehomba   21   Ruacana   13   Okalongo   D3608
Epembe   17   51   Ongenga
Otjiveze   22   *Olusati Dam*   Ombalantu   Oshikango
40   27   Onesi   D3611
Ombarundu   36   M123   C46   60
D3700   34   C35   D3616   30   Tsandi   70
52   61   D3612   Oshikuku
Orotjitombo   25   26   C41   Oshakati
Ohopoho   Opuwo   Ombombo   D3619   Ongwediva   34
14   23   Okahao   Ondangwa   7
37   10   88   C41   D3626   Onaanda
Okorosave   D3705   32   C41   D3635   Etilyasa   D3607
Oruwanje   10   **NAMIBIA**   *Oponono Lake*
Kaoko Otavi   75   *Etaka*   D3605   69
Dorsland Trek   39   D3709   64   **Omusati**   **Oshana**
Church Ruin   D3704   D3710
28   Otjitoko

Outjo   241

70   71   72   241   73   74

Copyright © Map Studio 2007

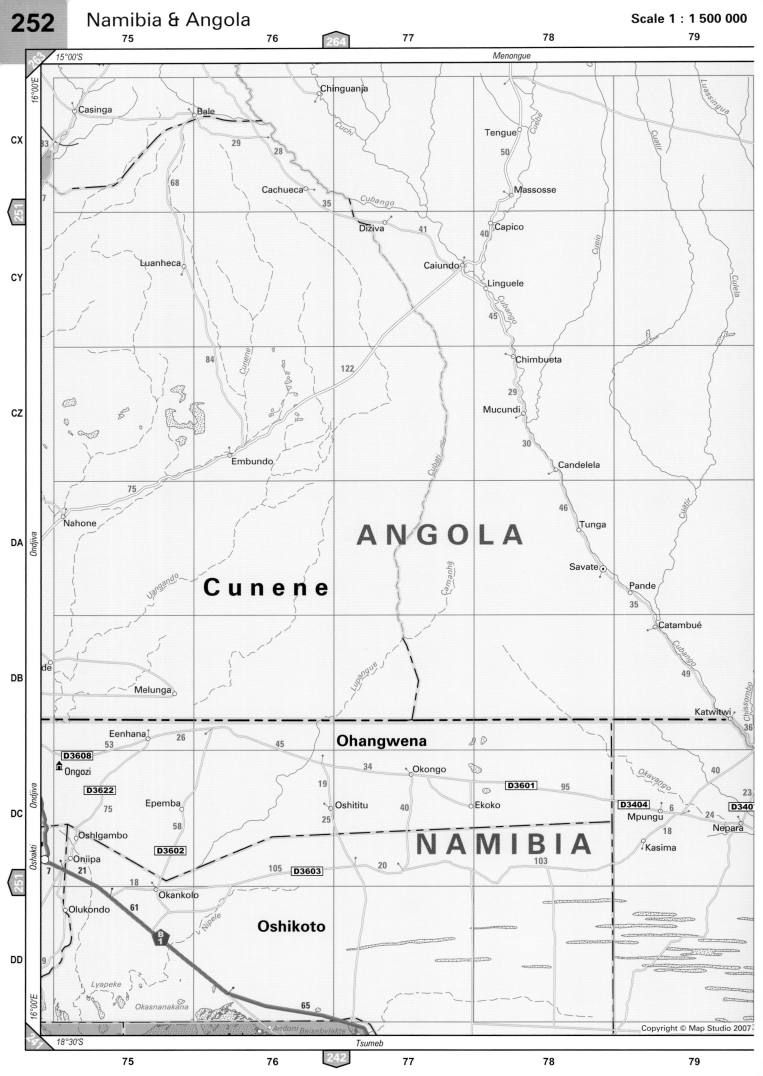

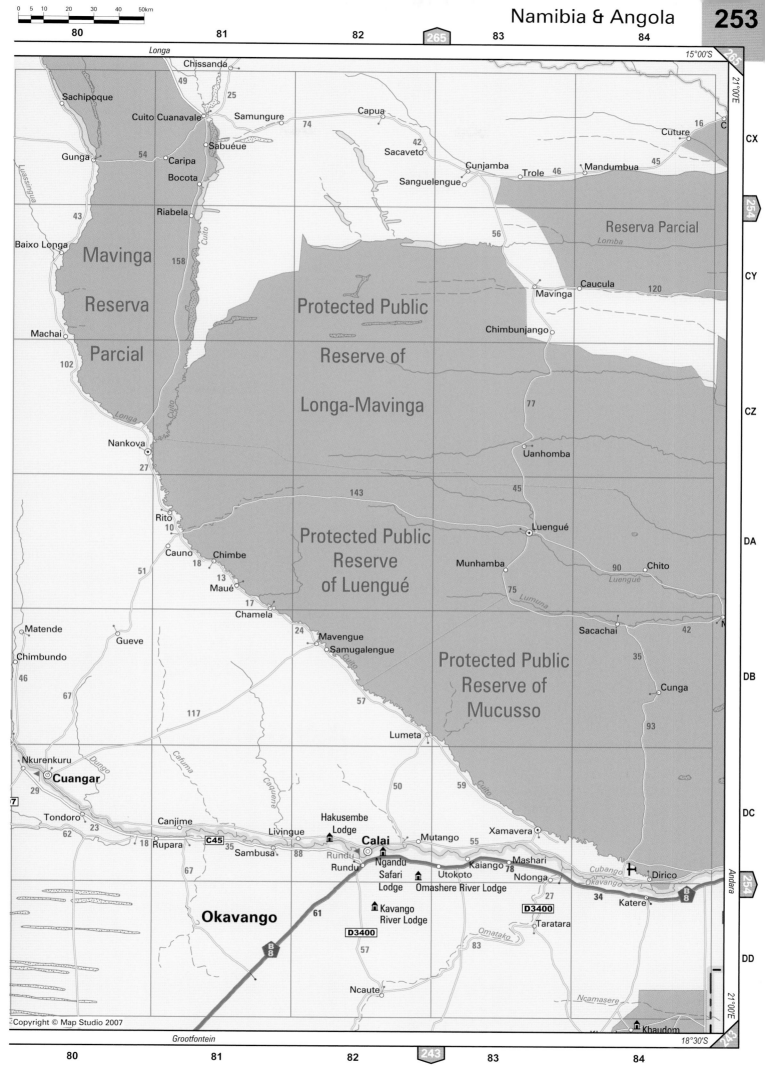

Longa

Chissanda

49

25

Sachipoque

Cuito Cuanavale

Samungure

Capua

Cuture   16
C

CX

Gunga   54

Caripa

Bocota

Sabuéue

42

Sacaveto

Sanguelengue

Cunjamba
Trole   46

Mandumbua   45

Luassingua

Riabela

Baixo Longa

43

56

Reserva Parcial
Lomba

CY

Mavinga
Reserva

158

Cuito

Protected Public

Mavinga

Caucula   120

Machai

102

Parcial

Longa

Reserve of

Chimbunjango

Longa-Mavinga

77

CZ

Nankova

27

Uanhomba

45

143

Rito
10

Protected Public

Luengué

DA

Cauno
18

Chimbe

Reserve
of Luengué

Munhamba

75

90

Chito

Luengué

Maué   13

Chamela   17

Lumuna

24

Mavengue

Samugalengue

Sacachai   42

35

N

Matende

Gueve

Protected Public

Cunga

Chimbundo

46

67

117

Cuito

57

Reserve of
Mucusso

93

DB

Lumeta

Dungo

Catuma

Caquene

50

59

Cuito

Nkurenkuru

Cuangar

29

DC

7

Tondoro

62   23

Canjime

18   Rupara

C45

35

Livingue

Sambusa

88

Hakusembe
Lodge

Calai

Mutango   55

Xamavera

Cubango

Dirico

Andara

254

67

Rundu
Rundu

Ngandu
Safari
Lodge

Utokoto

Kaiango   78
Ndonga

Mashari

Okavango

27

34

Katere

B
8

Omashere River Lodge

D3400

Okavango

61

Kavango
River Lodge

Taratara

Omatako

83

B
8

D3400

57

Ncaute

Ncamasere

DD

Khaudom

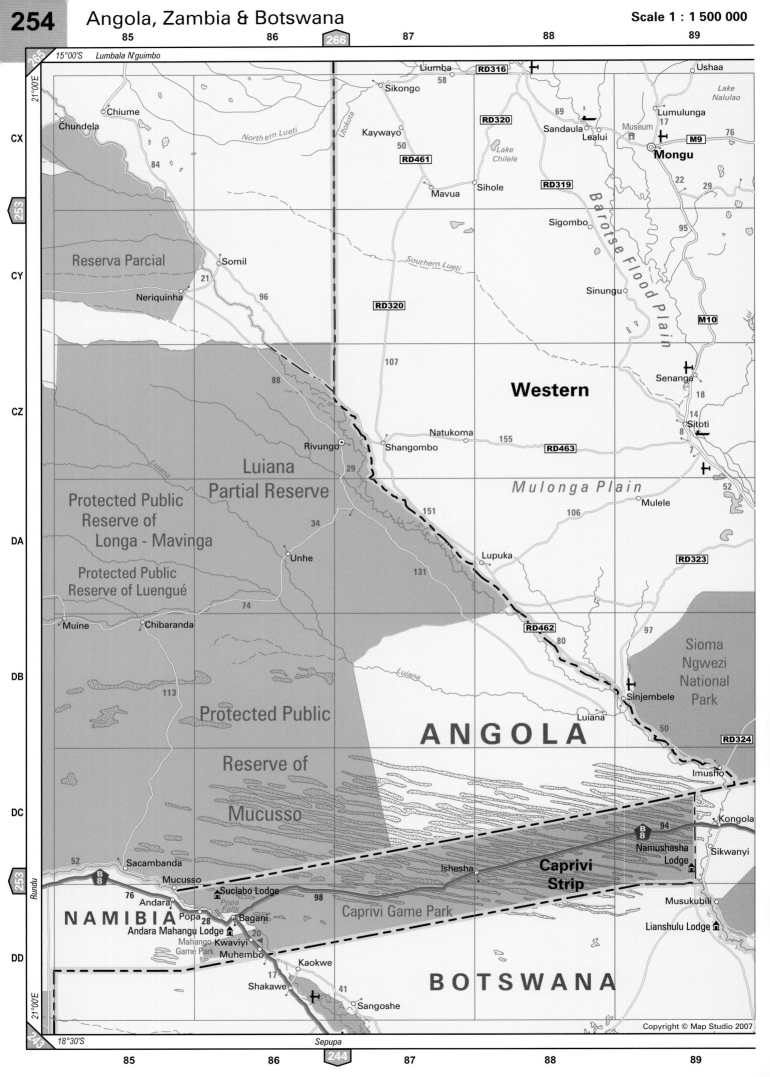

85   86   266   87   88   89

265 15°00'S   *Lumbala N'guimbo*

21°00'E

Chundela

Chiume

84

CX

Northern Lueti

Liumba

58

RD316

Sikongo

RD320

Kaywayo

Lumulunga

17

Ushaa

Lake
Nalulao

M9

76

Sandaula

Lealui

Museum

Mongu

69

Mavua

Sihole

50

RD461

22

29

Somil

21

CY

Sigombo

95

Neriquinha

96

Southern Lueti

Barotse Flood Plain

Sinungu

M10

Reserva Parcial

107

Western

Senanga

18

88

CZ

14

Sitoti

Rivungo

Natukoma

8

155

RD319

7

Luiana
Partial Reserve

Shangombo

RD463

Mulonga Plain

52

29

Mulele

DA

151

106

Luiana

Protected Public
Reserve of
Longa - Mavinga

34

Lupuka

RD323

Unhe

131

Protected Public
Reserve of Luengué

74

RD462

80

97

Muine

Chibaranda

DB

113

Sioma
Ngwezi
National
Park

Protected Public

Luiana

ANGOLA

Sinjembele

Luiana

50

RD324

Reserve of

Imusho

DC

Mucusso

94

Kongola

B8

52

Sacambanda

Namushasha
Lodge

Sikwanyi

253 Rundu

B8

Mucusso

Ishesha

**Caprivi
Strip**

76

Andara

98

Musukubili

Popa

Suclabo Lodge

Popa
Falls

28

Bagani

Caprivi Game Park

NAMIBIA

20

Lianshulu Lodge

Andara Mahangu Lodge

Mahango
Game Park

Kwaviyi

DD

Muhembo

Kaokwe

17

BOTSWANA

Shakawe

41

Sangoshe

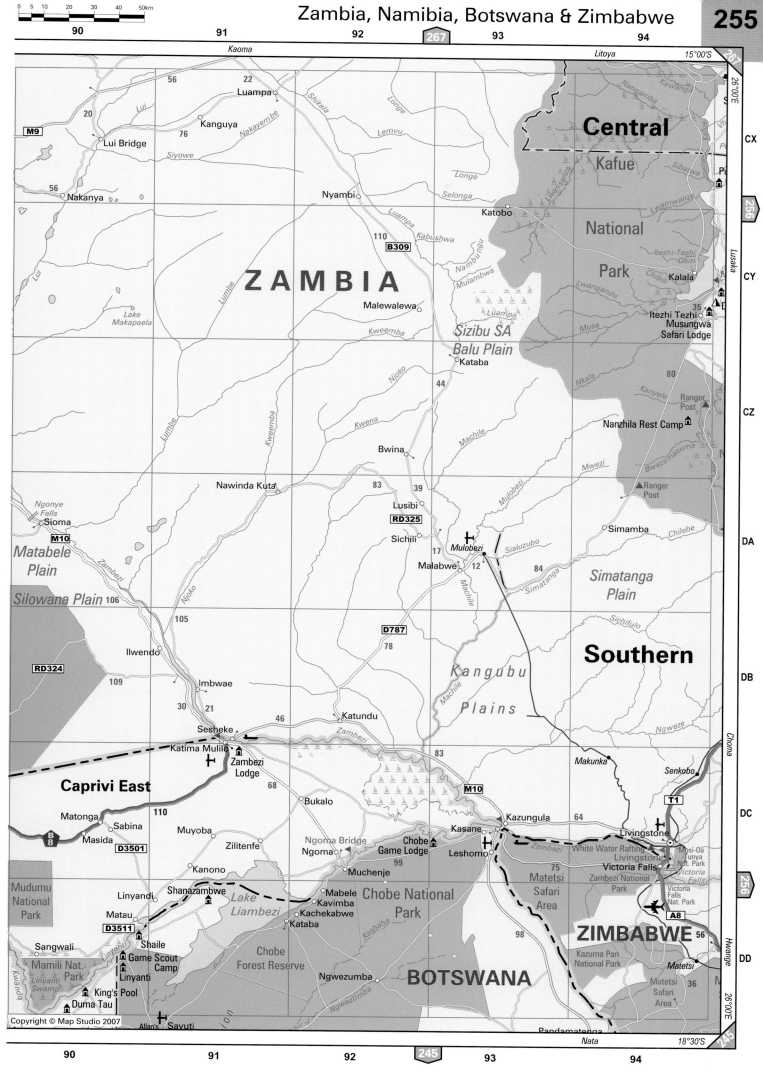

0 5 10 20 30 40 50km

90   91   92   267   93   94

Kaoma

Litoya   15°00'S

56

20

M9

22

Luampa

Kanguya

76

Lui Bridge

Siyowe

Nakayembe

Shikela

Longe

Lemvu

Central

Kafue

56

Nakanya

Nyambi

Luampa

Selonga

Longe

Katobo

National

Park

Itezhi-Tezhi
Dam

Kalala

110

B309

Kabushwa

Nambungu

Mulambwa

CX

CY

Lusaka

Pu

35

Itezhi Tezhi
Musungwa
Safari Lodge

ZAMBIA

Malewalewa

Kweemba

*Sizibu SA
Balu Plain*

Luampa

Musa

Kataba

Nkala

80

Njoko

Kwena

44

Machile

Mwezi

CZ

Nanzhila Rest Camp

Bwina

Lumbe

Kweemba

83

39

Lusibi

RD325

Sichili

17

Mulobezi

Mulobezi

Sialuzubo

84

Simamba

Chilebe

DA

Ranger
Post

Nawinda Kuta

*Ngonye
Falls*

Sioma

M10

*Matabele
Plain*

Silowana Plain 106

Zambezi

Malabwe   12

Simatanga

*Simatanga
Plain*

Sichifulo

Ranger
Post

105

RD324

Ilwendo

109

Njoko

Imbwae

Kangubu

Southern

DB

30   21

46

Katundu

Zambezi

Plains

Machile

Ngweze

D787

78

Makunka

Senkobo

Sesheke

Katima Mulilo

Zambezi
Lodge

83

M10

Choma

T1

DC

Caprivi East

68

Bukalo

Kazungula

64

Livingstone

110

Matonga

Sabina

Masida

B8

D3501

Muyoba

Zilitenfe

Ngoma Bridge

Ngoma

Chobe
Game Lodge

Kasane

Leshomo

Zambezi

White Water Rafting
Livingstone

75

Victoria Falls

*Mosi-Oa-
Tunya
Nat. Park*

256

A8

Kanono

99

Muchenje

*Matetsi
Safari
Area*

*Zambezi National
Park*

Victoria
Falls
Nat. Park

*Mudumu
National
Park*

Linyandi

Shanazambwe

*Lake
Liambezi*

Mabele

Kavimba

Kachekabwe

Kataba

Chobe National

Park

Kashaba

ZIMBABWE   56

Matau

D3511

Sangwali

Shaile

*Chobe
Forest Reserve*

98

*Kazuma Pan
National Park*

Matetsi

DD

*Mamili Nat.
Park*

Game Scout
Camp

Linyanti

Ngwezumba

BOTSWANA

*Matetsi
Safari
Area*

36

*Linyanti
Swamp*

King's Pool

Duma Tau

Ngwezumba

26°00'E

Allan's Sayuti

Nata   18°30'S

245

Copyright © Map Studio 2007

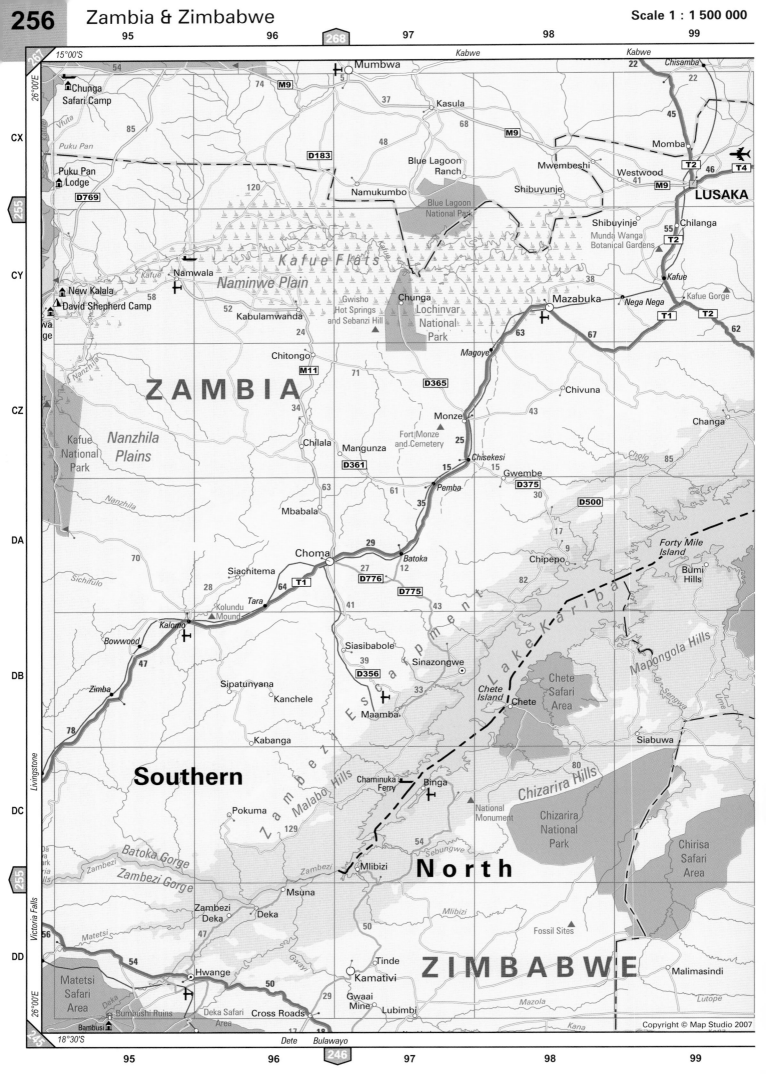

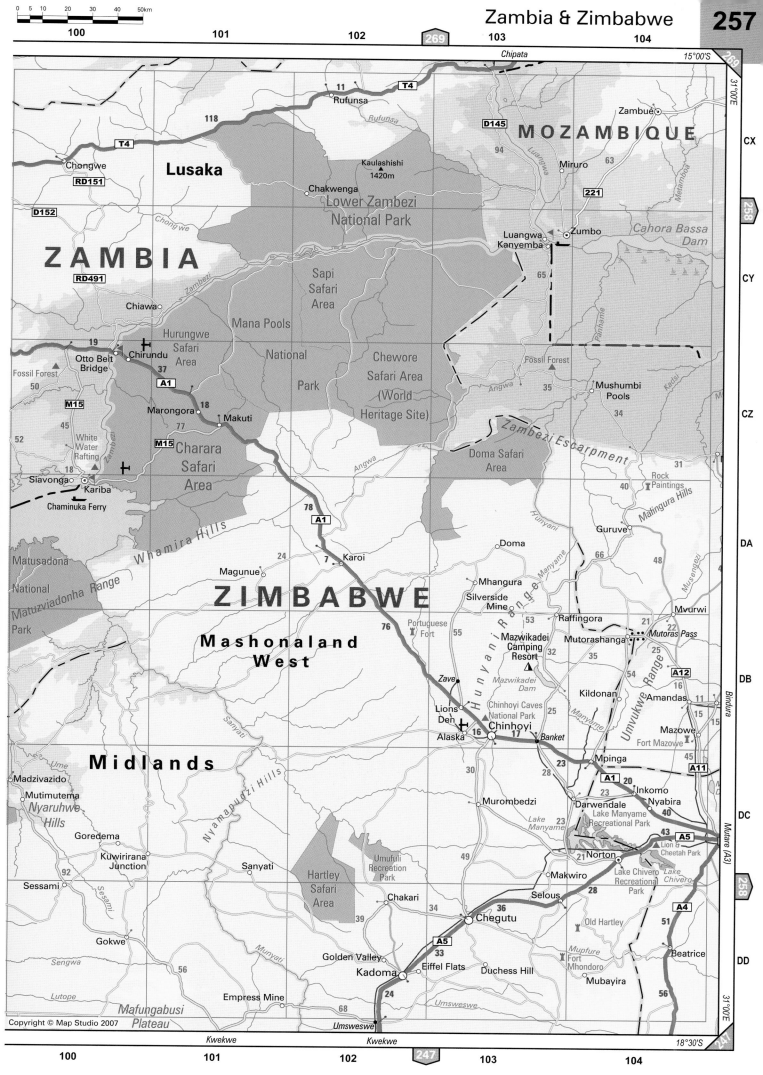

15°00'S

269
258
CX
CY
CZ
DA
DB
DC
258
DD

31°00'E

MOZAMBIQUE

Chipata

Zambué

Miruro

D145
94
63
221
Luangwa
Kanyemba
Zumbo
Cahora Bassa Dam
65

Fossil Forest
Mushumbi Pools
35
34

Zambezi Escarpment
Angwa
Doma Safari Area

Rock Paintings
40
31
Malingura Hills

ZAMBIA

Lusaka

Chongwe

RD151
D152
RD491

Chiawa

T4
118
11
Rufunsa
T4
Rufunsa

Kaulashishi 1420m
Chakwenga

Lower Zambezi National Park

Sapi Safari Area

Mana Pools

Hurungwe Safari Area

National Park

Chewore Safari Area (World Heritage Site)

Chirundu
19
Otto Beit Bridge
37
A1
Marongora
18
Makuti
77
M15
M15
Charara Safari Area

Fossil Forest
50
M15
45
52
White Water Rafting
18
Siavonga
Kariba
Chaminuka Ferry

Matusadona National Park
Matuzviadonha Range

Whamira Hills

78
A1

Guruve

Hunyani
66
48

ZIMBABWE

Doma

Mhangura
Silverside Mine
53
Raffingora
Mvurwi
21
22 Mutoras Pass
Mutorashanga
25
A12
54
16

Mashonaland West

24
7
Karoi
Magunue
76
Portuguese Fort
55
Mazwikadei Camping Resort
32
35

Kildonan
Amandas
11
A12
15
Bindura

Zave
Mazwikadei Dam
Mazowe
Fort Mazowe

Lions Den
Chinhoyi Caves National Park
25
Alaska
16
Chinhoyi
17
Banket
23
Mpinga
A11
28
A1
20
Inkomo
Nyabira
23
40

Midlands

Madzivazido
Mutimutema
Nyaruhwe Hills

Goredema
Kuwirirana Junction
92
Sessami

Ume

Nyamapudzi Hills

Sanyati

Sanyati

Hartley Safari Area

Umufuli Recreation Park
30
49
Murombedzi
Lake Manyame
23
Darwendale
Lake Manyame Recreational Park
21
Norton
43
A5
Lion & Cheetah Park
Lake Chivero Recreational Park
Lake Chivero
A4

Goredema
Gokwe

Sessami

Sengwa

56

Lutope

Mafungabusi Plateau

Empress Mine

Golden Valley
A5
33
Eiffel Flats
Kadoma
24
68
Umsweswe

Chakari
34
39
Chegutu
36
Duchess Hill
Makwiro
Selous
28
Old Hartley
Mupfure Fort Mhondoro
Mubayira
Beatrice
51
56

Kwekwe
Kwekwe
247
18°30'S

31°00'E

100   101   102   103   104

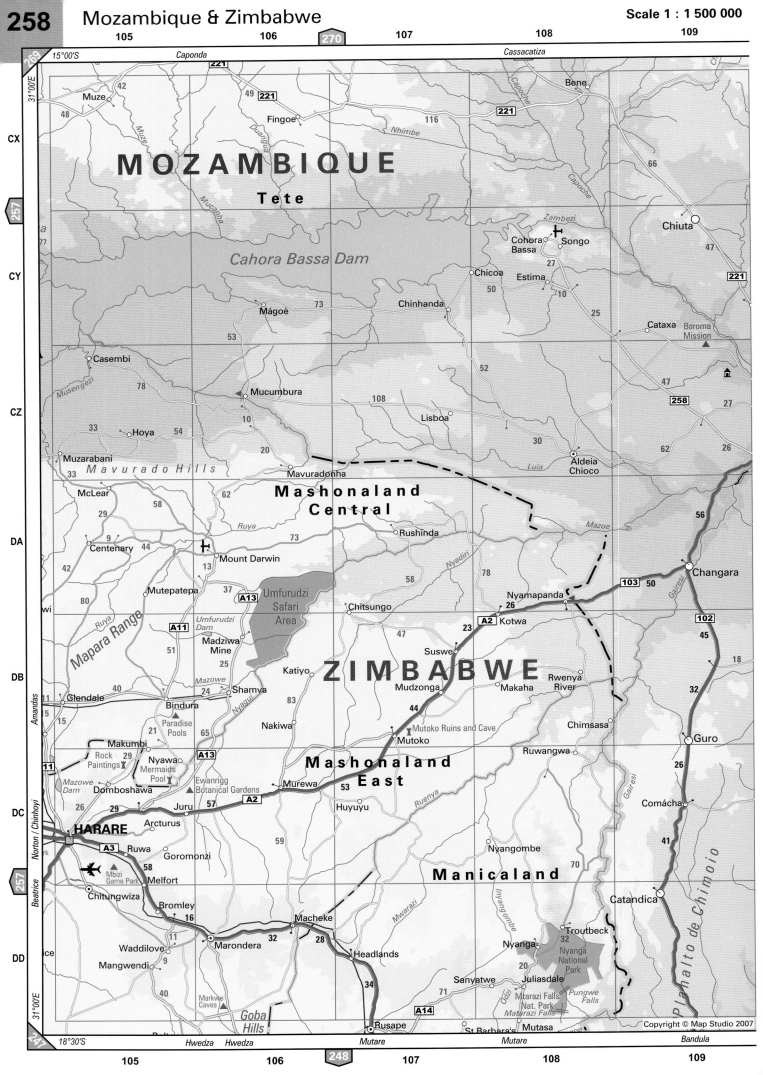

105   106   270   107   108   109

269

15°00'S   Caponda   Cassacatiza

31°00'E

CX

257

CY

M O Z A M B I Q U E

T e t e

Cahora Bassa Dam

CZ

DA

M a s h o n a l a n d C e n t r a l

DB

Z I M B A B W E

M a s h o n a l a n d E a s t

DC

HARARE

257

M a n i c a l a n d

DD

31°00'E

18°30'S   Hwedza   Hwedza   Mutare   Mutare   Bandula

241   105   248   106   107   108   109

Copyright © Map Studio 2007

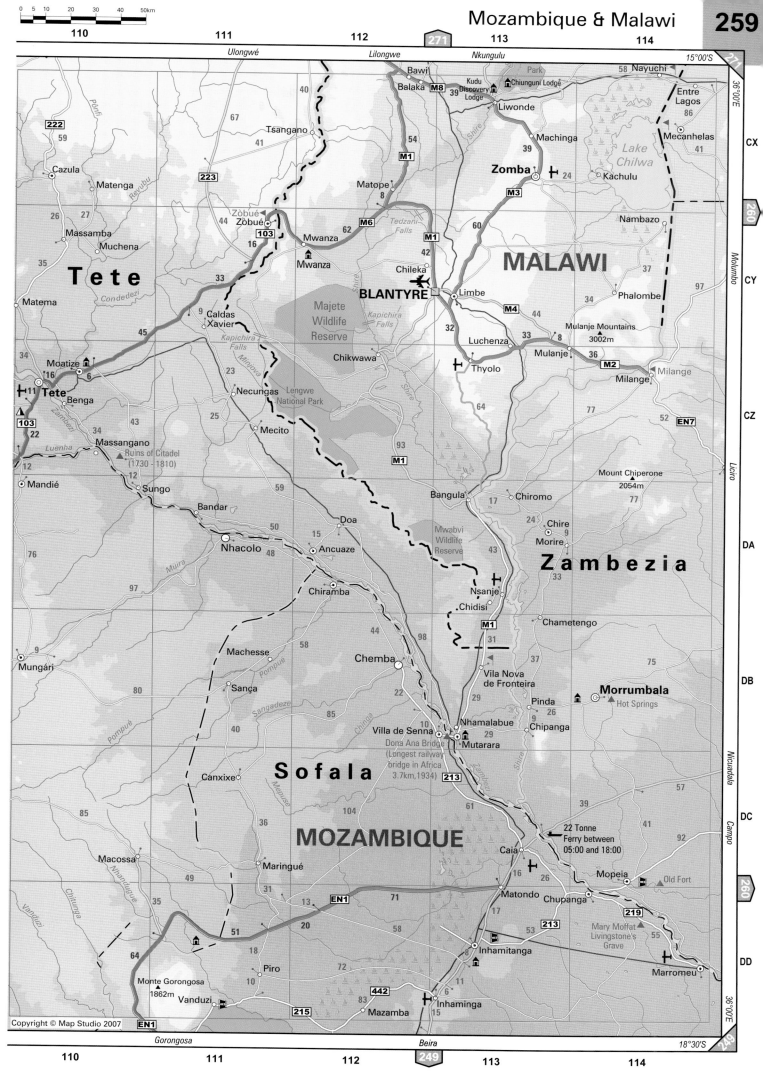

0 5 10   20   30   40   50km

Ulongwé   Lilongwe   Nkungulu   15°00'S

Bawi
Balaka   M8   39
Kudu Discovery Lodge   Chiunguni Lodge
58   Nayuchi

40
67
Tsangano
41
54
M1
Liwonde
Machinga
39
Zomba
M3

Entre Lagos
86
Mecanhelas
41

222
59
Cazula
Matenga
Muchena
26   27
Massamba

223
44   Zòbué
103
16
Mwanza
62   M6
Matope
8
42
M1
Chileka
BLANTYRE
Limbe

Nambazo

MALAWI
37
97
Phalombe
34
24   Kachulu

Tete
35
Matema
Condedezi
45

9   Caldas Xavier
Kapichira Falls
23
Necungas
Minyova

Majete Wildlife Reserve
Kapichira Falls
Chikwawa
Lengwe National Park

32
M4   44
Luchenza
33
8
Mulanje
Mulanje Mountains
3002m
36   M2   Milange
Milange

34
16   Moatize
6
11   Tete
Benga
103
22
Luenha
12
34   Massangano
Ruins of Citadel (1730 - 1810)
12   Sungo
43
25
Mecito

64
77
52   EN7
93
M1

Mandié
76
9   Mungári

59
Bandar
50
Nhacolo
48
15
Doa
Ancuaze

Mount Chiperone
2054m
77
Bangula
17   Chiromo
24   Chire
9
Morire
43
33
Zambezia

80
97
Chiramba
Machesse
58
44
98
Chemba
Nsanje
Chidisi
M1
Chametengo
31
37
75

Sança
Sangadeze
85
22
Villa de Senna
Dona Ana Bridge (Longest railway bridge in Africa 3.7km,1934)
213
Mutarara
Nhamalabue
29
Vila Nova de Fronteira
29
Pinda
26
Chipanga

Morrumbala
Hot Springs

Canxixe
Mepuase
40
10
104
61
39
57
41
92

Sofala
36
49
Macossa
Maringué
31
13   EN1
71
MOZAMBIQUE
Caia
16   26
22 Tonne Ferry between 05:00 and 18:00
Mopeia
Old Fort

35
51
20
58
Matondo
Chupanga
53   213
219
55
Mary Moffat Livingstone's Grave

64
18
Piro
10
72
83
442
215
Mazamba
Inhaminga
15
11
6
Inhamitanga
17

Monte Gorongosa
1862m
Vanduzi
EN1
Marromeu

Gorongosa   Beira   18°30'S

CX
CY
CZ
DA
DB
DC
DD
271
260
260
249
36°00'E
36°30'E
Molumbo
Liciro
Nicuadala
Campo

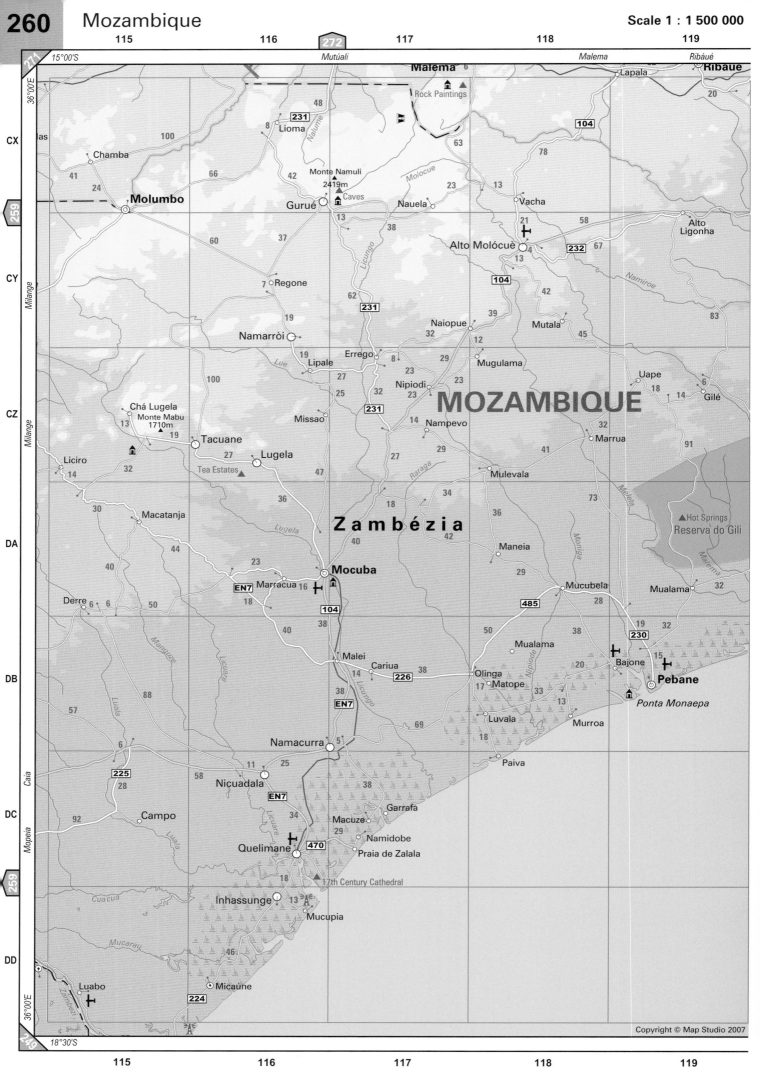

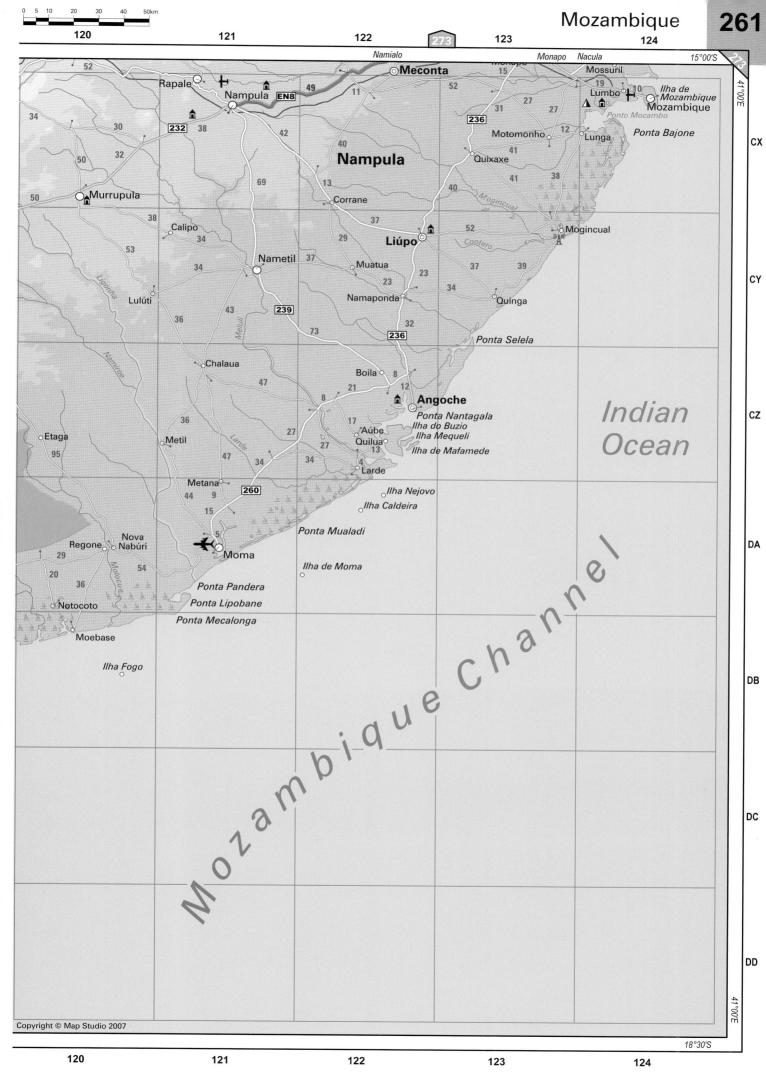

0 5 10 20 30 40 50km

Namialo

Monapo   Nacula

15°00'S

273

41°00'E

Meconta

Monopo

Mossuril

15

19

CX

Rapale

Nampula   EN8

52

49

11

52

Motomonho

31   27

27

Lumbo

10

Ilha de
Mozambique

Ponto Mocambo

Mozambique

34

30

232   38

42

40

236

12

Lunga

Ponta Bajone

50

32

69

13

Quixaxe

41

41

38

50

Murrupula

Corrane

40

Mogincual

CY

38

Calipo

37

37

Liúpo

52

Mogincual

53

34

Nametil   37

Muatua

29

Contero

Mogincual

34

Lulúti

34

23

23

37   39

36

43

239

Namaponda

34

Quinga

73

236

32

CZ

Chalaua

Ponta Selela

47

Boila   8

36

21

12

Metil

8

Angoche

Larde

27

17

Ponta Nantagala

Ilha do Buzio

Ilha Mequeli

Etaga

95

47

Aúbe

34

Quilua

13

Ilha de Mafamede

34   34

4

Metana

260

Larde

DA

44   9

Ilha Nejovo

15

Ilha Caldeira

Nova
Nabúri

5

Ponta Mualadi

Regone

29

Moma

Ilha de Moma

20

36

54

Ponta Pandera

Notocoto

Ponta Lipobane

Moebase

Ponta Mecalonga

Ilha Fogo

**Indian
Ocean**

DB

Mozambique Channel

DC

DD

18°30'S

41°00'E

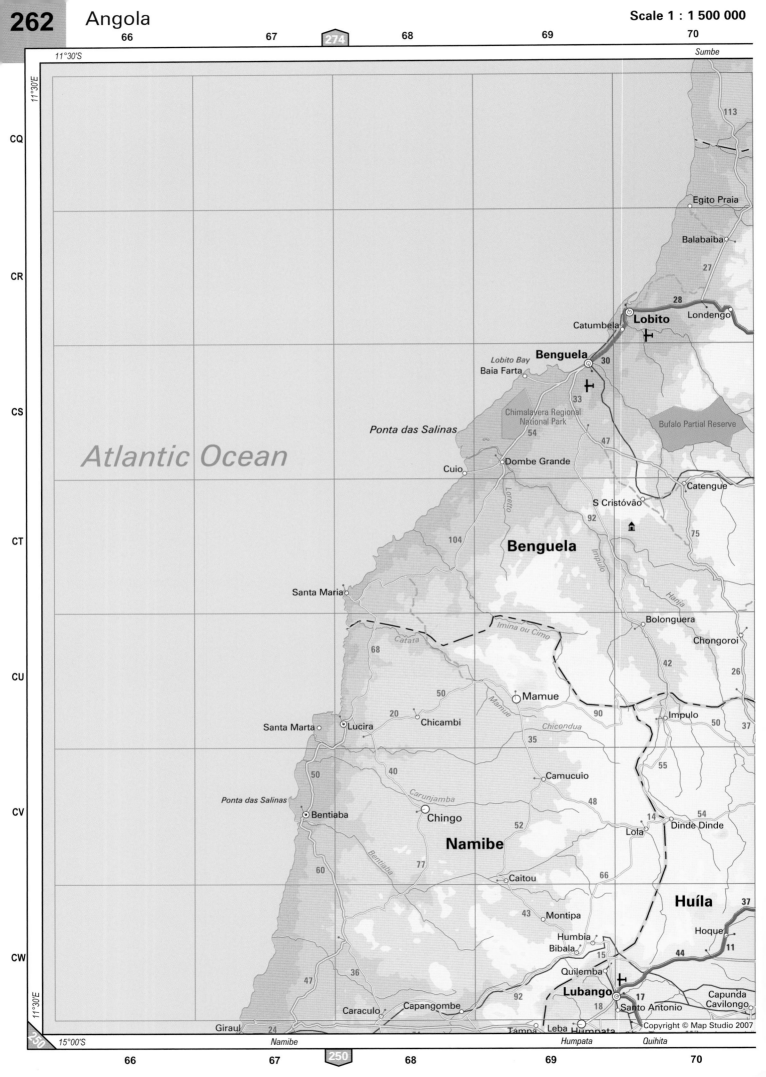

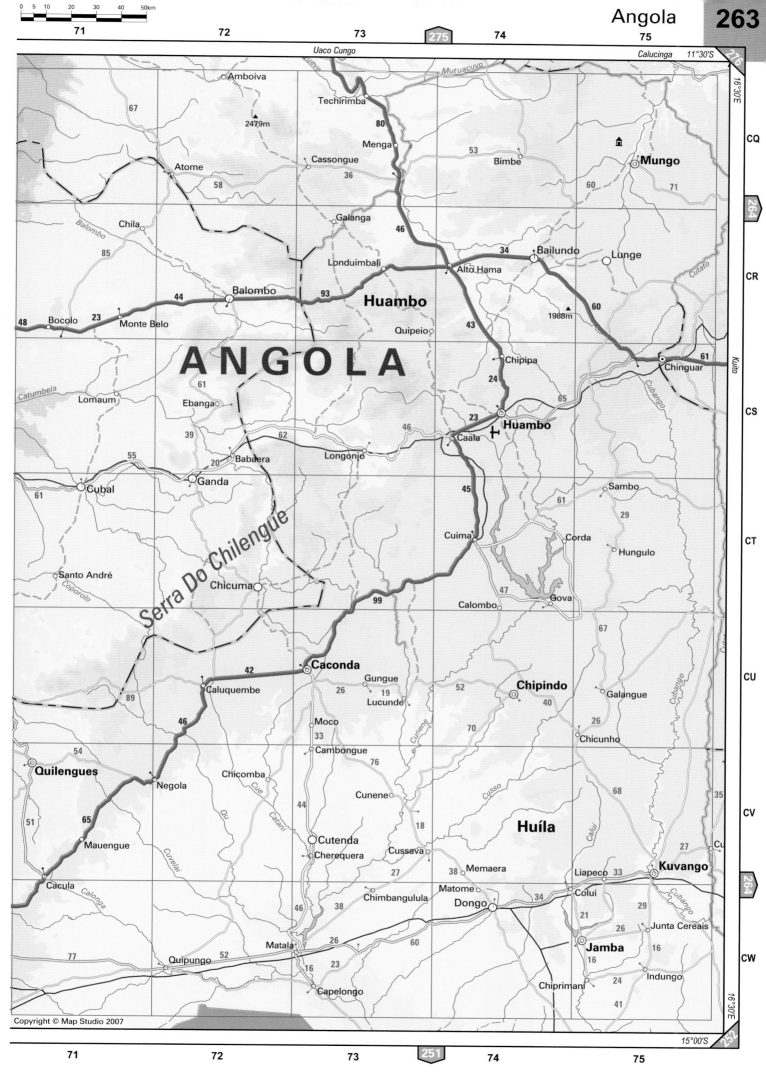

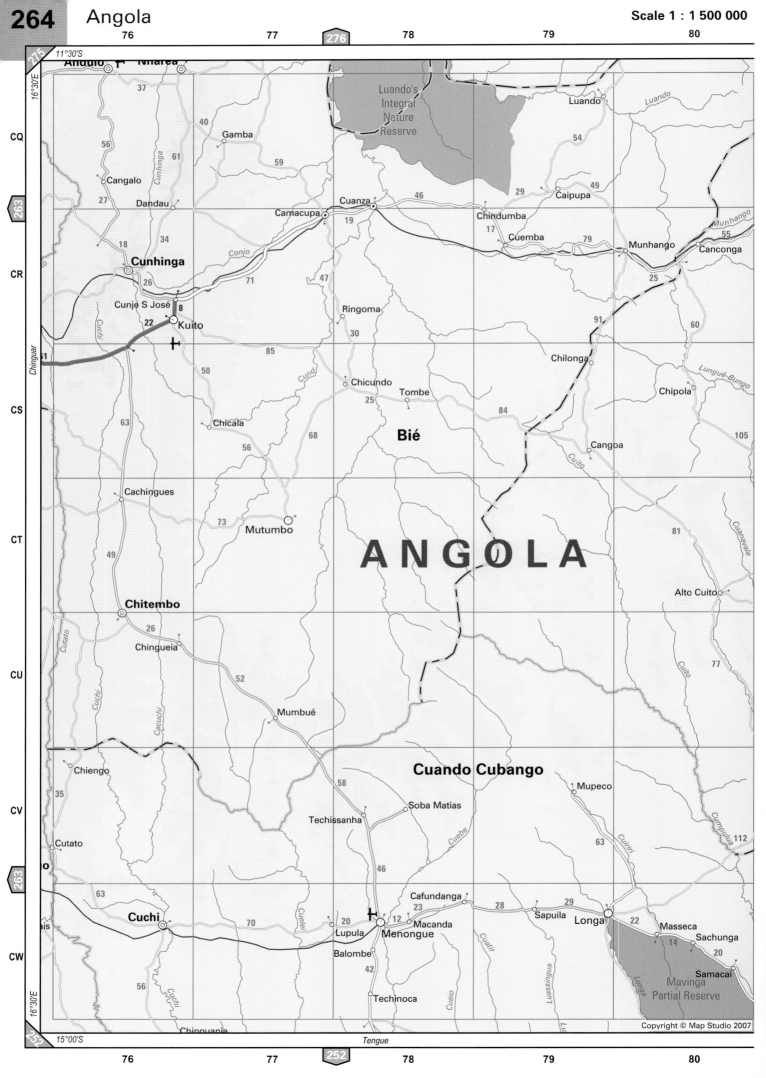

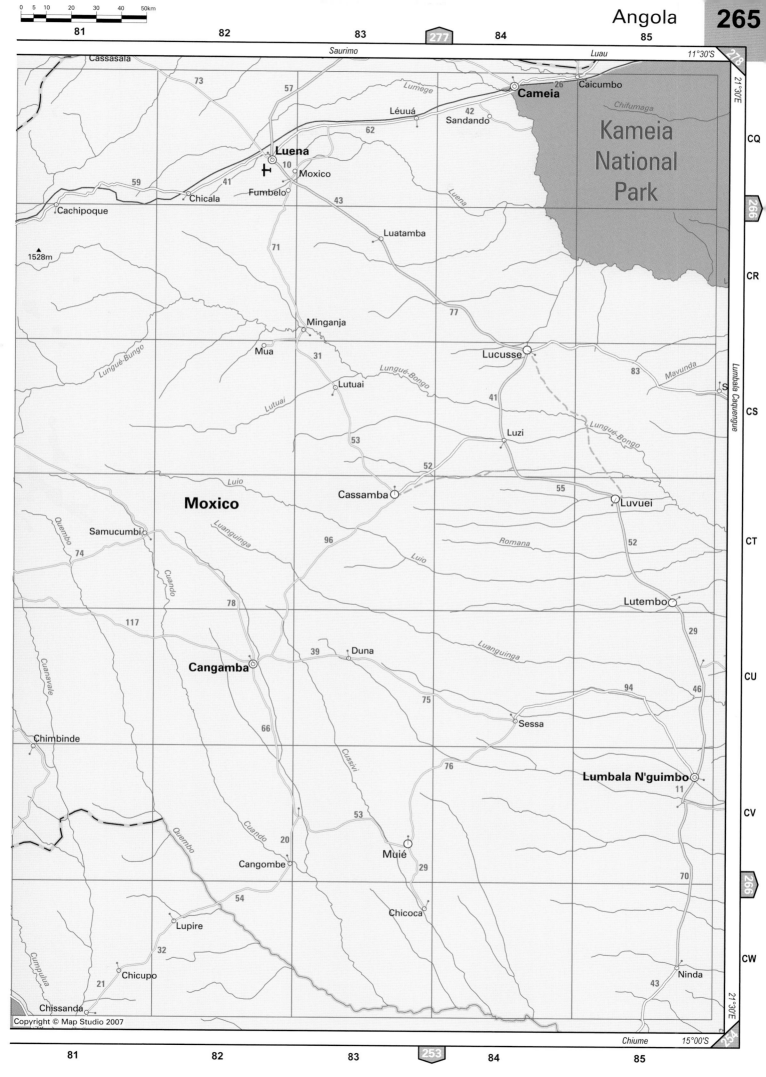

0 5 10   20   30   40   50km

81   82   83   277   84   85

Saurimo   Luau   11°30'S

Cassasala

73   57   Lumège   26 Caicumbo

Léuuá   42 Cameia

62   Sandando

Luena   Kameia
10   National
Mosico   Park

59   41   Chicala

Cachipoque   Fumbelo   43

71   Luatamba

1528m

77

Minganja

Mua   31   Lucusse   83 Mavunda

Lutuai   Lungué-Bongo   41 S

53   Luzi   Lungué-Bongo

52   55 Luvuei

Luio   Cassamba

Moxico   96   Luio Romana

Samucumbi

74   Luanguinga   52

Lutembo

78   29

117

39 Duna   Luanguinga

Cangamba   75   94 46

66   Sessa

Chimbinde

76

Lumbala N'guimbo
11

53   Muié

20   29   70

Cangombe

54

Lupire   Chicoca

32   43 Ninda

21 Chicupo

Chissanda   Chiume   15°00'S

81   82   83   253   84   85

CQ
266
CR
CS
CT
CU
CV
266
CW

21°30'E
Lumbala Caquengue
21°30'E

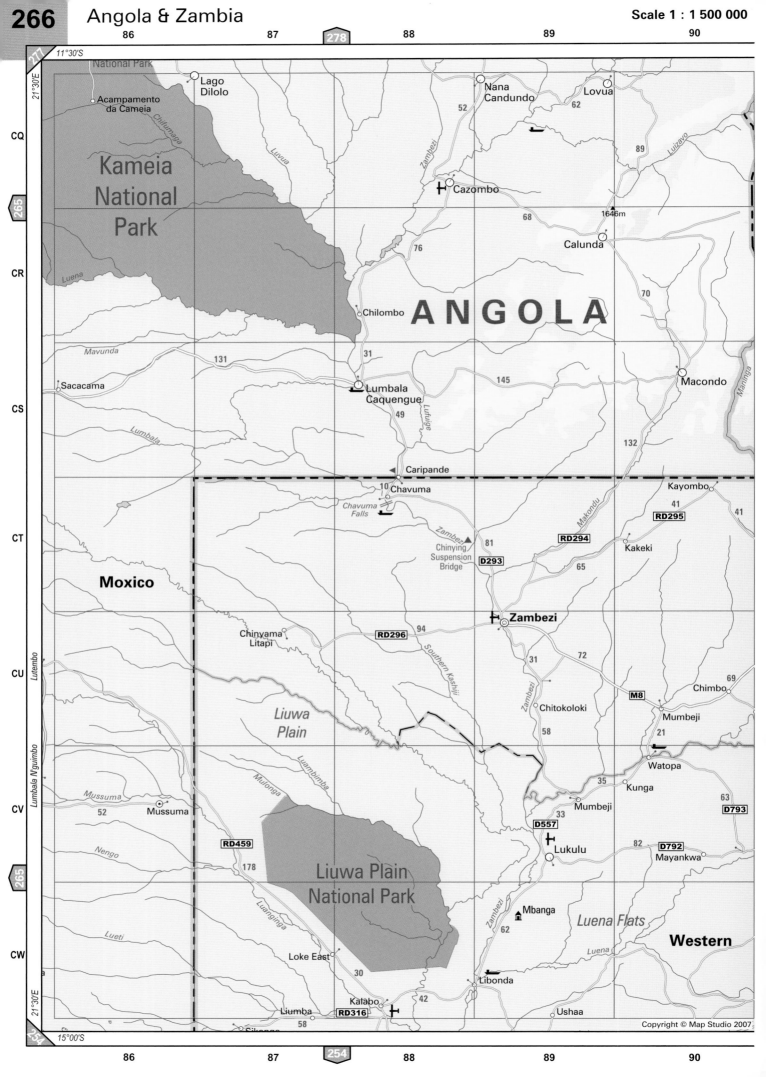

11°30'S
21°30'E

National Park

Lago Dilolo

Acampamento da Cameia

Chifumaga

Luvua

Kameia National Park

52

Nana Candundo

Lovua

62

Zambezi

89

Luizavo

Luena

Cazombo

68

1646m

Calunda

70

76

Chilombo

A N G O L A

Mavunda

131

31

145

Macondo

Maninga

Sacacama

Lumbala Caquengue

49

Lufuige

132

Lumbala

Caripande

10 Chavuma

Kayombo

Chavuma Falls

Zambezi

Chinying Suspension Bridge

81

Makondu

41

RD295

41

D293

RD294

Kakeki

65

Moxico

Lutembo

Zambezi

94

RD296

Chinyama Litapi

Southern Kashiji

31

72

Chimbo

69

M8

Mumbeji

21

Chitokoloki

Watopa

58

Liuwa Plain

Luambimba

Kunga

35

Lumbala Nguimbo

Mussuma

52

Mussuma

Mulonga

Mumbeji

63

D793

D557

82

D792

Mayankwa

Nengo

RD459

178

Liuwa Plain National Park

Luanginga

Lukulu

Mbanga

Zambezi

62

Luena Flats

Lueti

Loke East

Luena

Western

30

Libonda

Kalabo

42

Liumba

RD316

58

Sikonga

Ushaa

15°00'S
21°30'E

Copyright © Map Studio 2007

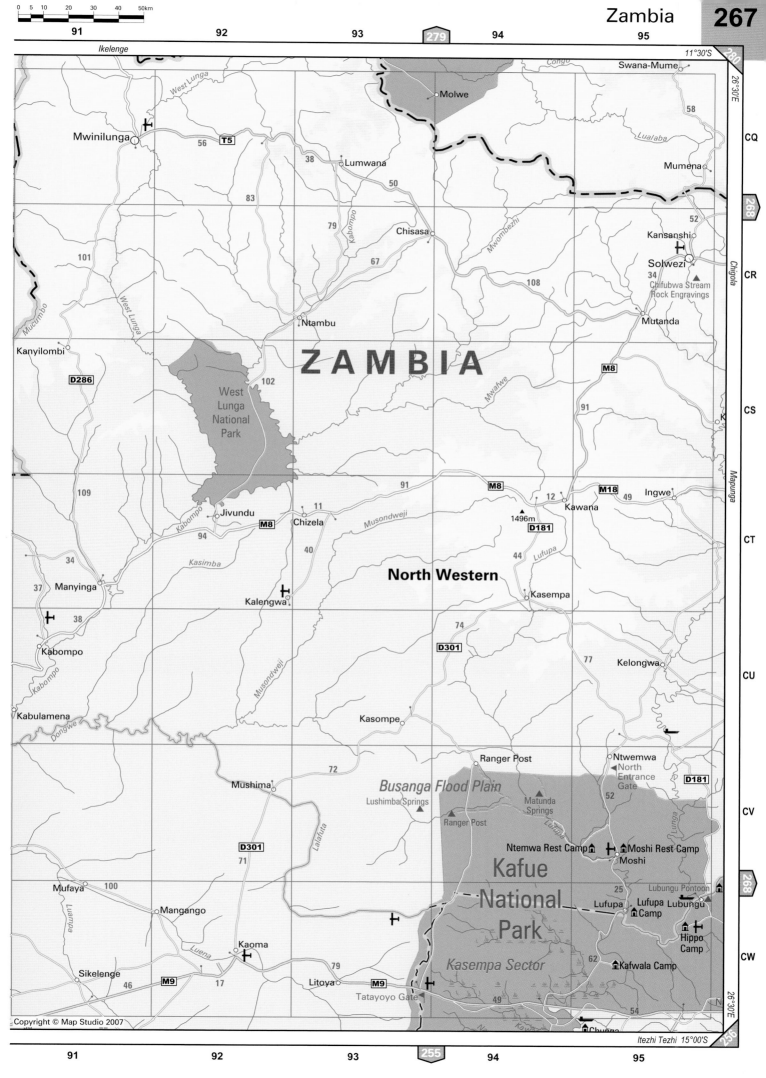

ZAMBIA

West Lunga National Park

North Western

Kafue National Park

Kasempa Sector

Busanga Flood Plain

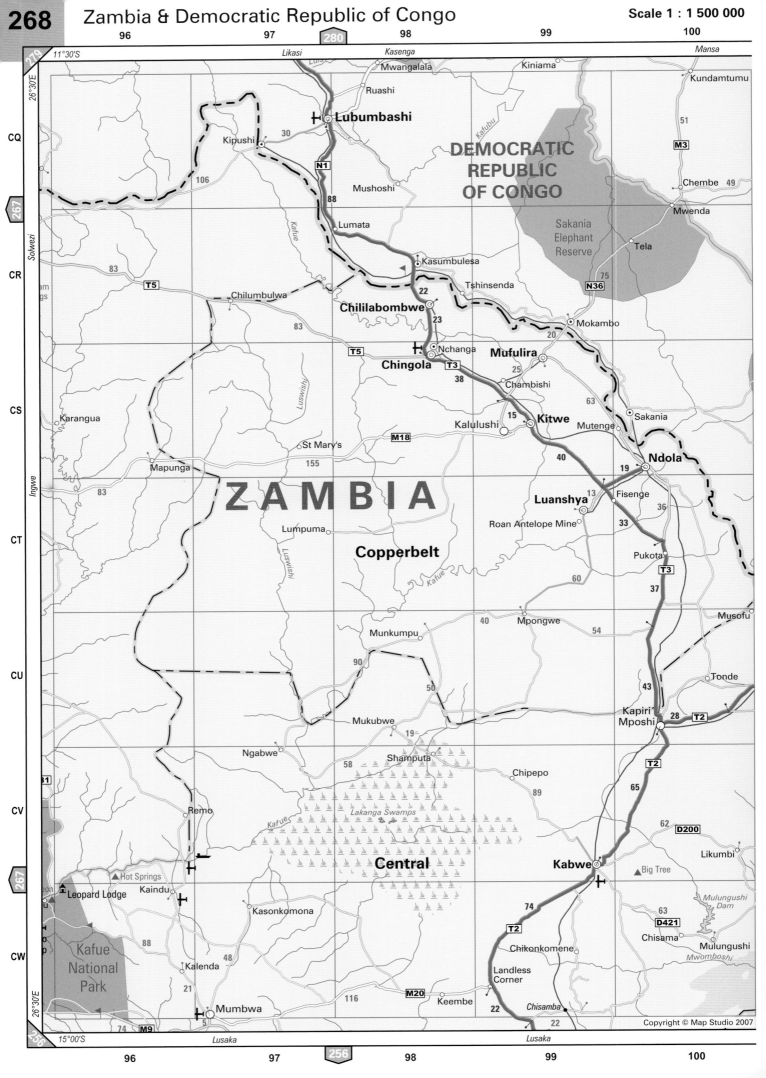

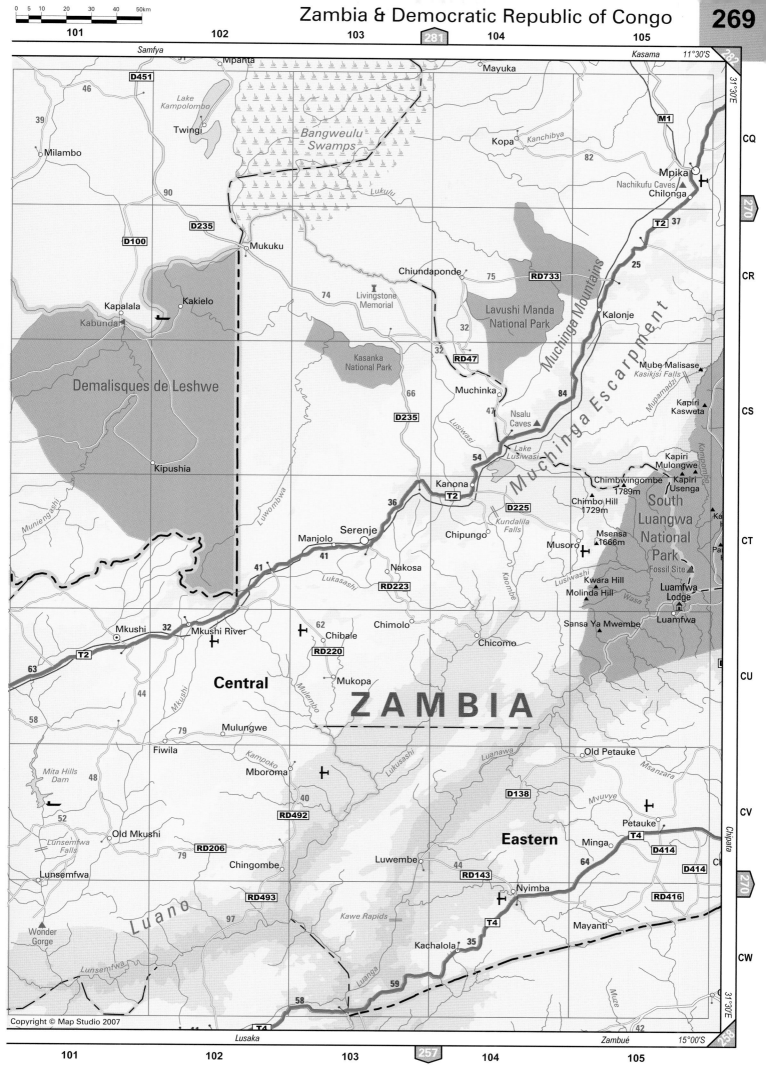

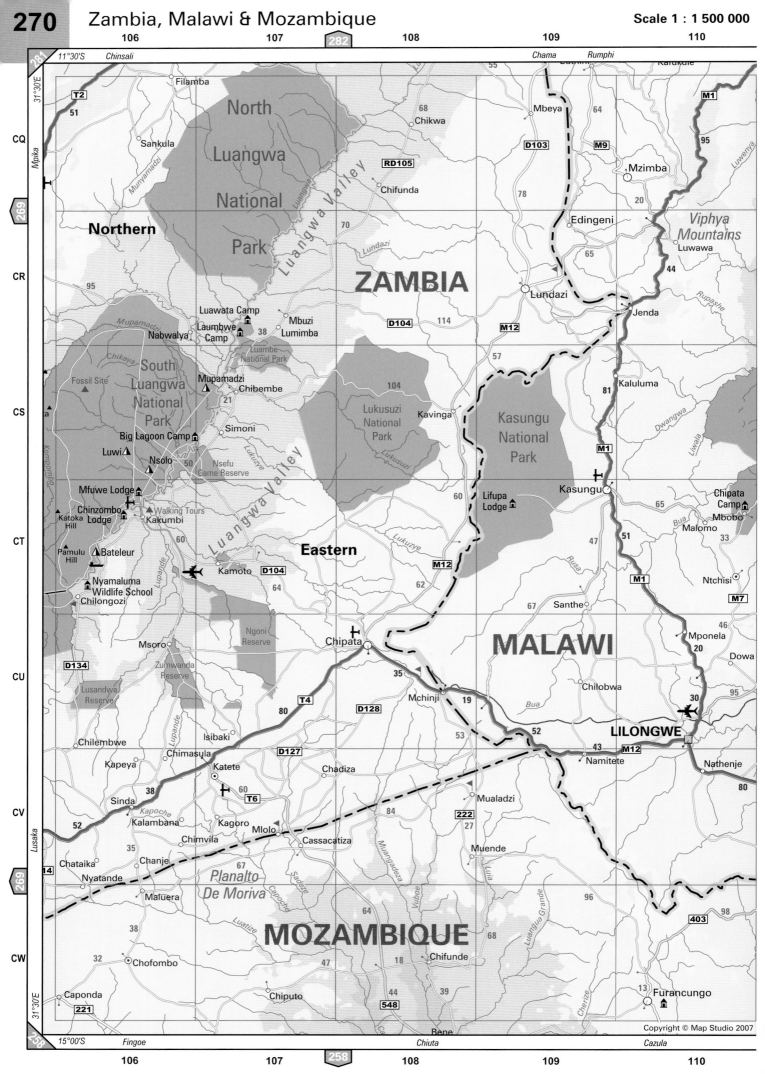

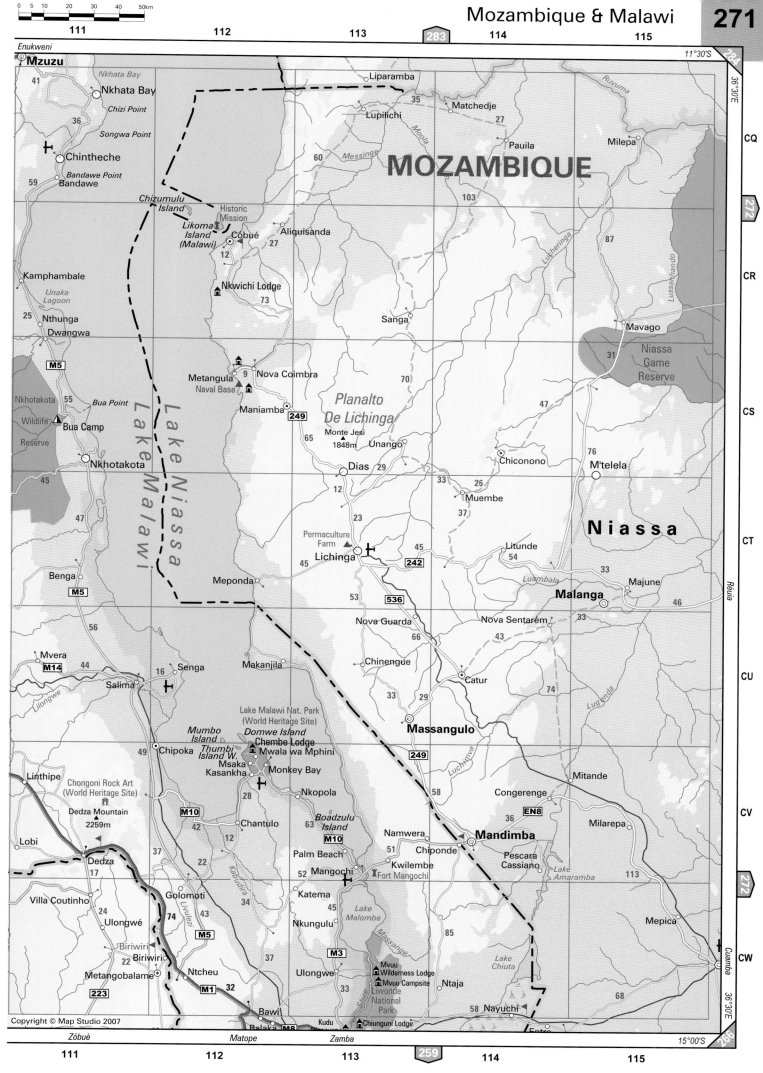

Scale 1 : 1 500 000

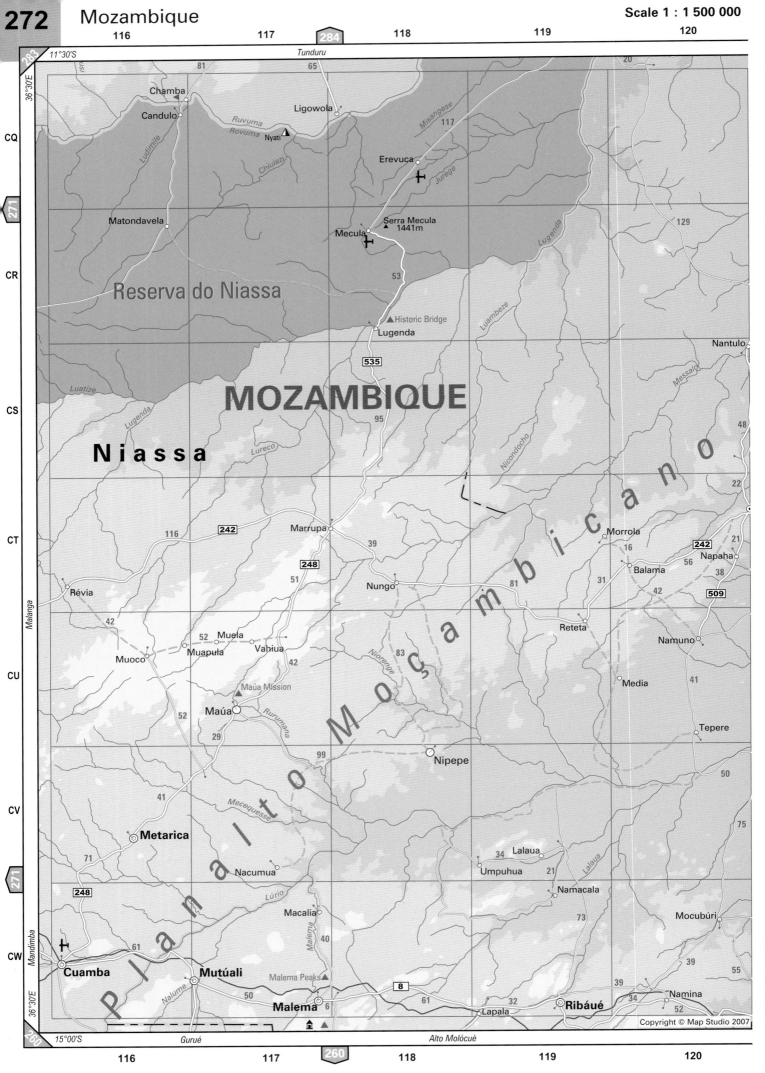

Tunduru

Chamba
Candulo
Ligowola
Nyati
Ruvuma
Rovuma
Ludimile
Chiulezi
Misangese

CQ

Erevuça
Jurege

Matondavela
Serra Mecula
1441m
Mecula
Lugenda

271

CR

Reserva do Niassa
53

Nantulo

Historic Bridge
Lugenda
Luambeze
Messalo

CS

535

MOZAMBIQUE
95

48

Luatize
Lugenda
Lureco

N i a s s a

Nicondocho

22

CT

116
242
Marrupa
39
248
51

Morrola
16
242
21
Napaha
56
Balama
38
509
Nungo
81
31
42

Révia

Malanga
42

52 Muela
Muapula Vahiua
Muoco
42

Reteta

Namuno

CU

52

Maúa Mission
Maúa
29
Rurumaria

Niorenge
83

Media
41

Tepere

99

Nipepe

50

CV

41

Mecequesse

75

Metarica

34 Lalaua
Umpuhua 21

271

71

Lalaua

Nacumua

248

Lúrio
Macalia

Namacala

73

Mocubúri

Malema
40

CW

61
Cuamba
Mutúali
Malema Peaks
Nalume
50
Malema
6
8
61
Lapala
32
Ribáué
39
Namina
34
52
55

Mandimba

Gurué
Alto Molócuè

P l a n a l t o   M o ç a m b i c a n o
M o ç a m b i c a n o

283
284
271
260
260

11°30'S
36°30'E
15°00'S
36°30'E

116 117 118 119 120

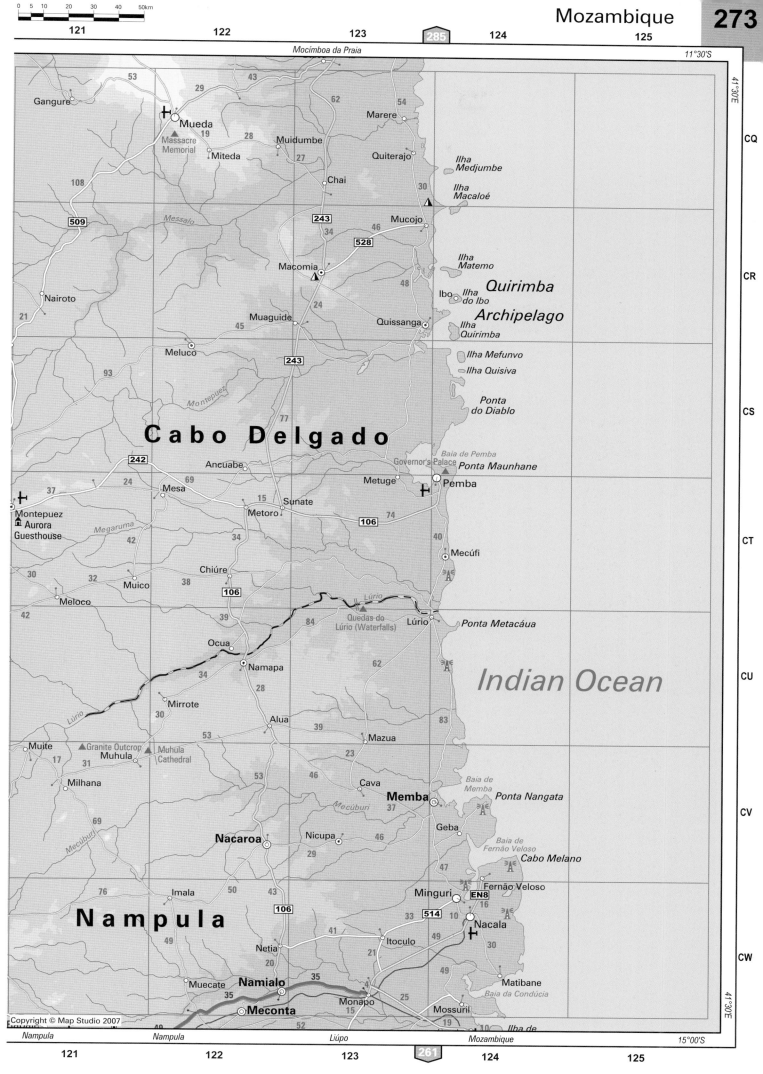

0 5 10 20 30 40 50km

121   **122**   **123**   285   **124**   **125**

Mocímboa da Praia

11°30'S

Gangure

53

29

43

CQ

Mueda
19

Massacre
Memorial

28

Miteda

108

Muidumbe

27

62

Marere

54

Quiterajo

30

*Ilha
Medjumbe*

*Ilha
Macaloé*

509

Messalo

Nairoto

243

34

46

528

Mucojo

CR

*Ilha
Matemo*

21

93

Macomia

24

Muaguide

45

48

Ibo

*Ilha
do Ibo*

Quirimba

Archipelago

Quissanga

*Ilha
Quirimba*

Meluco

243

Montepuez

77

Ilha Mefunvo

Ilha Quisiva

CS

*Ponta
do Diablo*

C a b o   D e l g a d o

242

Ancuabe

Baia de Pemba

Governor's Palace

Ponta Maunhane

37

24

Mesa

69

Metuge

Pemba

Montepuez

Aurora
Guesthouse

Megaruma

15

Sunate

Metoro

106

74

CT

42

34

40

Mecúfi

30

32

Muico

38

Chiúre

106

Meloco

39

Lúrio

84

*Quedas do
Lúrio (Waterfalls)*

Lúrio

Ponta Metacáua

42

Ocua

62

Indian Ocean

Lúrio

34

Namapa

CU

Mirrote

28

83

30

Alua

39

53

Mazua

Muite

Granite Outcrop

Muhula

*Muhula
Cathedral*

23

17

31

53

46

Cava

*Baia de
Memba*

Ponta Nangata

Milhana

Memba

37

Mecúburi

Geba

CV

69

Nacaroa

Nicupa

46

*Baia de
Fernão Veloso*

29

Cabo Melano

47

Fernão Veloso

76

Imala

50

43

Minguri

EN8

16

Nampula

106

33

514

10

Netia

41

Itoculo

49

Nacala

30

20

21

CW

49

Muecate

Namialo

35

Matibane

35

Monapo

25

Baia da Condúcia

Meconta

52

15

Mossuril

19

10

Ilha de

Copyright © Map Studio 2007

Nampula   *Nampula*   *Liúpo*   *Mozambique*   15°00'S

41°30'E

66   67   286   68   69   70

8°00'S

11°30'E

N'zeto

CJ

Protected Reserve

Zotto

Ambriz
Protected
Reserve

Quicabo

38

Barra do Dande

CK

Baia do Bengo

Caxito

39

LUANDA

21 Cacuaco

58

Ponta das Palmeirinhas

Viana

61

Bengo

40

Belas

Catete

Palmeirinhas

49

CL

62

Atlantic
Ocean

Muxima

143

Galinda

CM

Quiçama

National

Park

CN

Calamba

Pacuária da Barra do Longa

62

Mercado

CO

Porto Amboim

Cabo das
Tres Pontas

49

Quedas de Agua da Binga

23

Sumbe

CP

11°30'E

11°30'S

Lobito

66   67   262   68   69   70

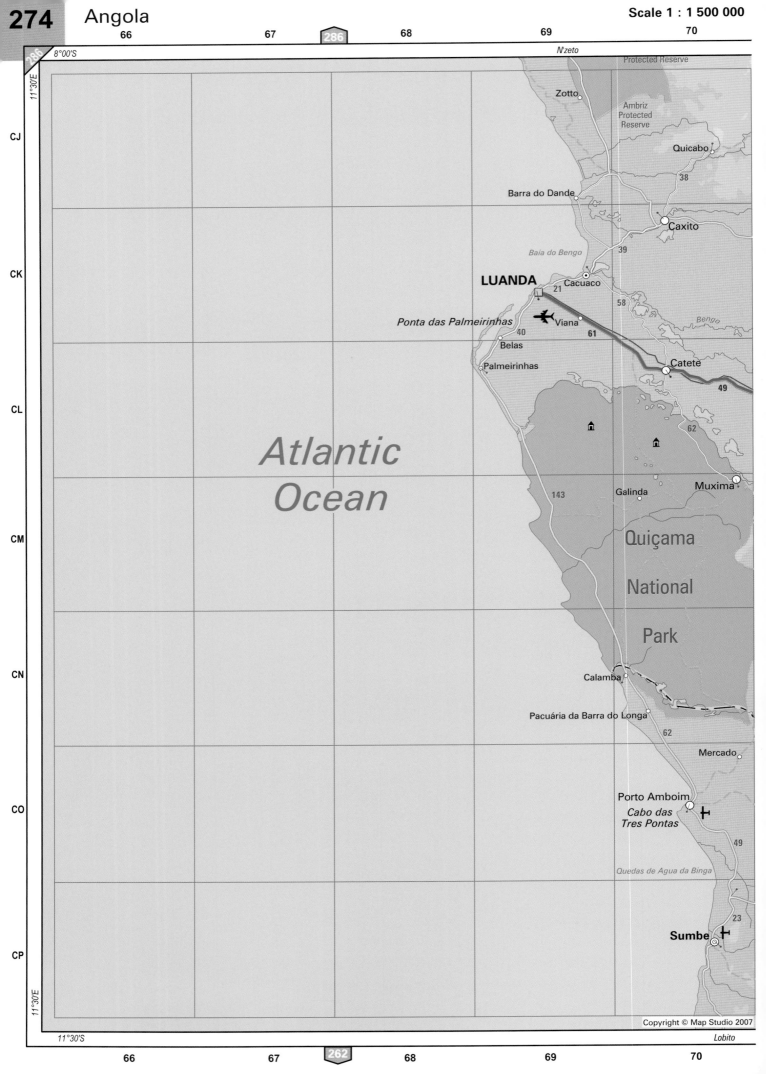

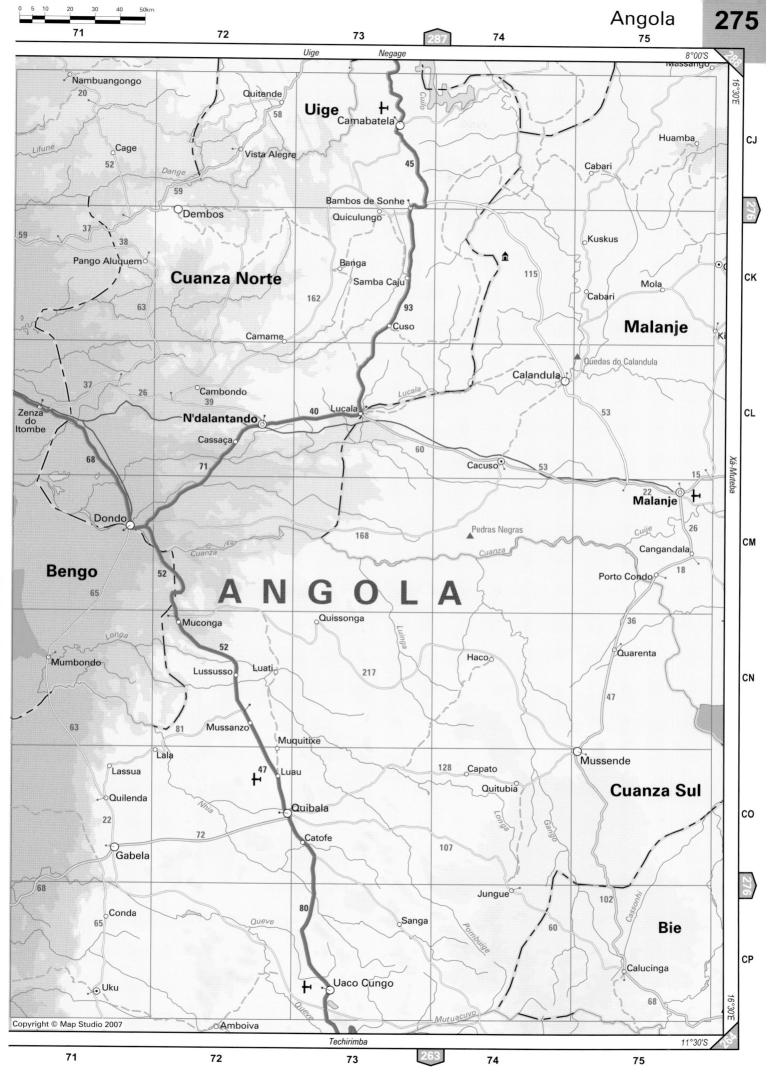

0 5 10 20 30 40 50km

71 72 73 **287** 74 75

288

16°30'E

Uige *Negage* 8°00'S

Massango

CJ

Nambuangongo

20

Quitende

58

Uige

Camabatela

Cuilo

Huamba

Cage

52

Vista Alegre

Dange

59

Cabari

Kuskus

45

Cuanza Norte

Dembos

Bambos de Sonhe

Quiculungo

115

276

37

38

Banga

Samba Caju

Mola

CK

59

Pango Aluquem

162

93

Cabari

Malanje

Ki

63

Cuso

Lucala

Camame

Quedas do Calandula

37

26

Cambondo

39

Calandula

CL

Zenza
do
Itombe

N'dalantando

40

Lucala

53

Xá-Muteba 15'S

68

Cassaça

60

Cacuso

53

22

Malanje

71

Ki

Bengo

Dondo

Cuanza

168

Cuanza

Pedras Negras

Cuije

Cangandala

CM

52

26

Porto Condo

18

65

A N G O L A

Muconga

Quissonga

36

Longa

52

Quarenta

Mumbondo

Lussusso

Luati

Luinga

217

Haco

47

CN

81

Mussanzo

Muquitixe

Lala

Luau

128

Capato

Mussende

Lassua

47

Quitubia

Cuanza Sul

Quilenda

Quibala

CO

22

72

Catofe

107

Gabela

80

Jungue

102

276

68

Conda

Queve

60

Bie

65

Sanga

Pombuíge

Calucinga

CP

Uku

Uaco Cungo

68

Amboiva

Techirimba *Queve* *Mutuacuvo* 11°30'S

16°30'E

71 72 73 **263** 74 75

294

Scale 1 : 1 500 000

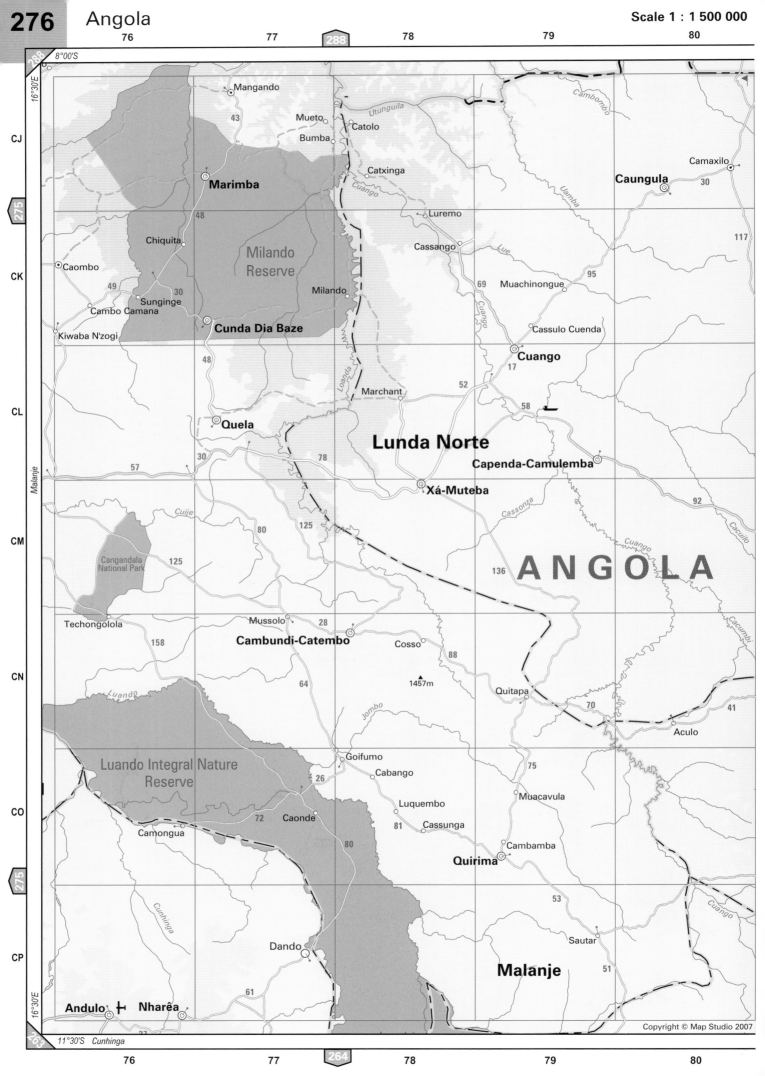

76   77   78   79   80

8°00'S
16°30'E

CJ

Mangando

Mueto
Catolo
Bumba

Catxinga

Utunguila

Cambombo

275

Marimba

43

48

Luremo

Cassango

Cuango

Camaxilo

Caungula

30

117

CK

Chiquita

Caombo

49

Sunginge   30

Cambo Camana

Milando

Milando
Reserve

Muachinongue

69

Lue

95

Cuango

Cassulo Cuenda

Kiwaba N'zogi

Cunda Dia Baze

48

Cuango

17

CL

Quela

Marchant

52

58

Lunda Norte

Capenda-Camulemba

Malanje

30

57

78

Xá-Muteba

Cassonza

92

CM

Cuije

Cangandala
National Park

125

80

125

136

A N G O L A

Cuango

Cacuilo

CN

Techongolola

158

Mussolo

Cambundi-Catembo

28

64

Cosso

88

▲
1457m

Jombo

Quitapa

70

41

Aculo

Luando

CO

Luando Integral Nature
Reserve

26

72

Caonde

Goifumo

Cabango

Luquembo

81

Cassunga

75

Muacavula

Cambamba

80

Camongua

Quirima

275

Cunhinga

53

Cuango

Sautar

CP

Dando

Malanje

51

61

Andulo   Nharêa

27

263

11°30'S   *Cunhinga*

16°30'E

264

76   77   78   79   80

Copyright © Map Studio 2007

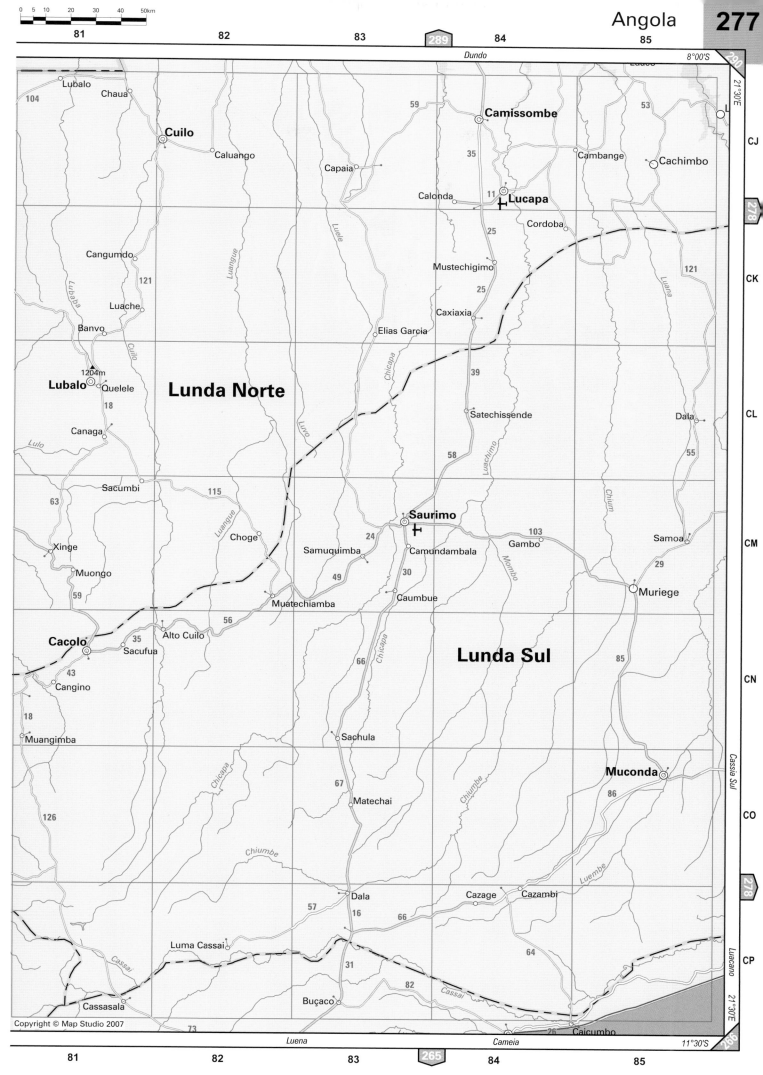

Dundo
8°00'S

0 5 10 20 30 40 50km

81 82 83 84 85

Lubalo
Chaua
104
Cuilo
Caluango
Capaia
59
Camissombe
Cambange
Cachimbo
53
35
Calonda
Lucapa
11
Cordoba
25
Cangumdo
121
Mustechigimo
25
Luache
Banvo
Caxiaxia
Elias Garcia
39
1204m
Lubalo Quelele
Lunda Norte
Satechissende
Dala
18
58
55
Canaga
Sacumbi
115
63
Choge
Saurimo
103
Samoa
Xinge
Samuquimba
24
Camundambala
Gambo
29
Muongo
49
30
59
Muatechiamba
Caumbue
Muriege
56
Cacolo 35
Alto Cuilo
66
Lunda Sul
85
Sacufua
43
Cangino
18
Muangimba
Sachula
126
67
Muconda
Matechai
86
Chiumbe
Dala
Cazage
Cazambi
57
16
66
64
Luma Cassai
31
Cassai
82
Buçaco
Cassasala
73
26
Caicumbo

Luena
Cameia
11°30'S

81 82 83 84 85

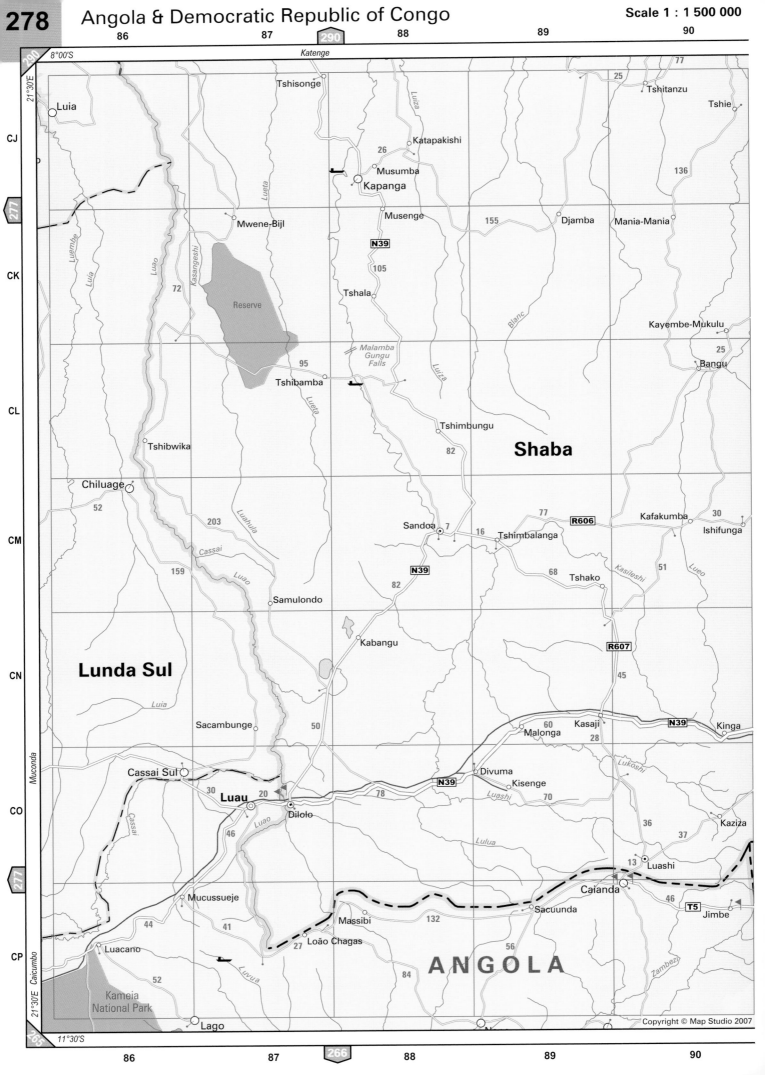

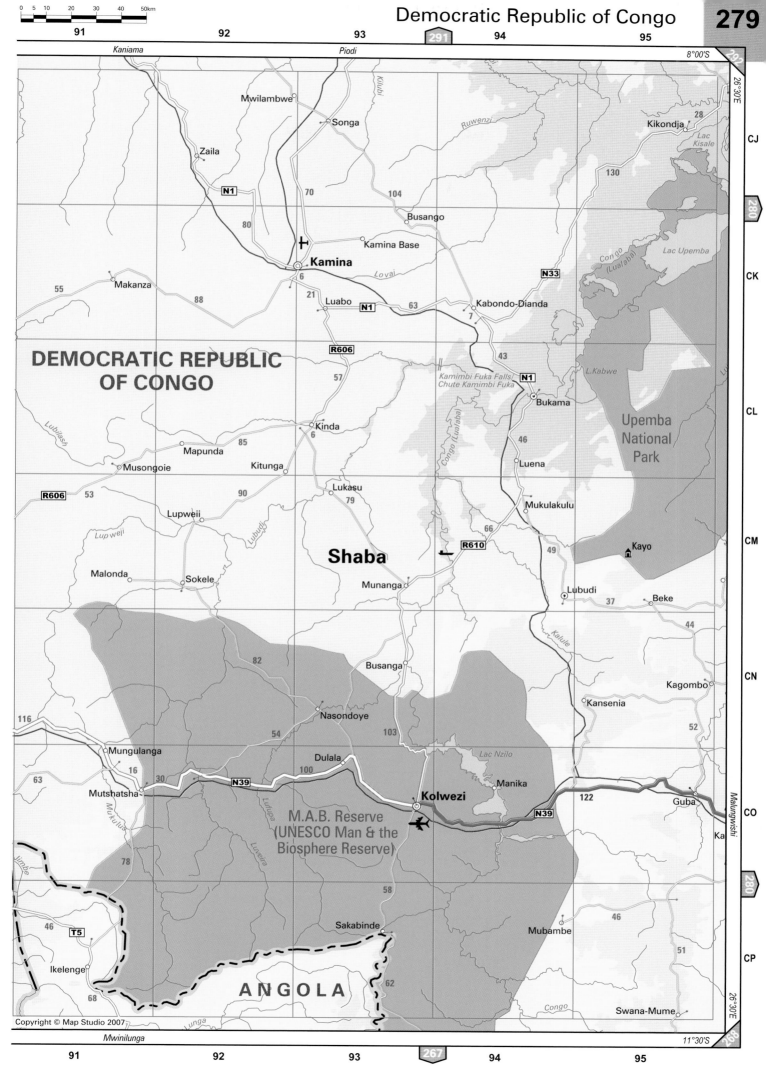

0 5 10 20 30 40 50km

91 92 93 **291** 94 95

Kaniama Piodi 8°00'S

CJ

Mwilambwe

Songa Kikondja 28

Zaila Lac Kisale

70 104 130

N1

80 Busango

CK

Kamina Base **N33**

Kamina Lovoi

6 63 Kabondo-Dianda

21 Luabo **N1** 7

Makanza 55 88

43

DEMOCRATIC REPUBLIC OF CONGO **R606** Kamimbi Fuka Falls/ Chute Kamimbi Fuka **N1** L.Kabwe

57 Bukama

CL

Kinda Upemba National Park

6 46

Mapunda 85 Luena

Musongoie Kitunga

Lukasu Mukulakulu

R606 53 90 79

66

Lupweii **R610** 49 Kayo CM

Shaba

Malonda Sokele Lubudi 37 Beke

Munanga 44

82 Kagombo CN

Busanga

52

116 Nasondoye Kansenia

54 103

Mungulanga Dulala Lac Nzilo

16 30 **N39** 100 Manika Guba

Mutshatsha **Kolwezi** 122 **N39** Ka CO

M.A.B. Reserve (UNESCO Man & the Biosphere Reserve)

78 58

46 **T5** Mubambe 46

Sakabinde

Ikelenge 51 CP

68 62

A N G O L A Congo Swana-Mume

Copyright © Map Studio 2007 11°30'S

Mwinilunga

91 92 93 **267** 94 95

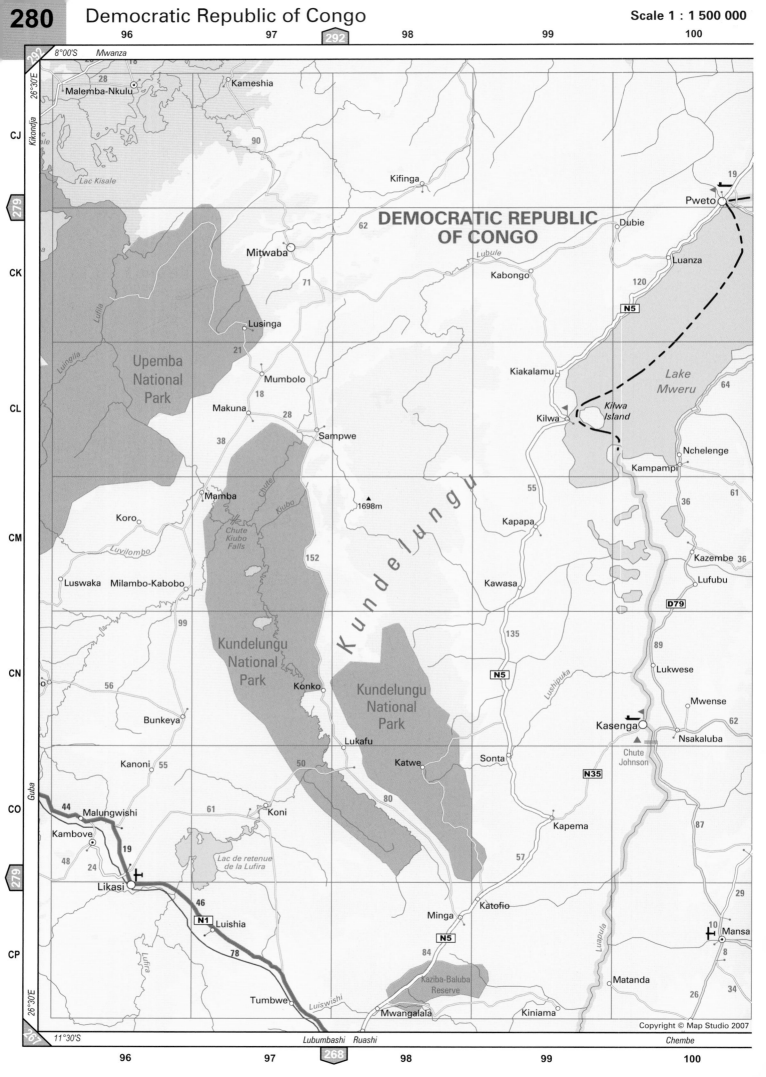

DEMOCRATIC REPUBLIC
OF CONGO

Upemba
National
Park

Kundelungu
National
Park

Kundelungu
National
Park

Kundelungu

*Lake
Mweru*

*Kilwa
Island*

Mwanza

Malemba-Nkulu

Kameshia

Kifinga

Pweto

Dubie

Luanza

Lac Kisale

Mitwaba

Kabongo

Lusinga

Kiakalamu

Mumbolo

Makuna

Kilwa

Nchelenge

Sampwe

Kampampi

Mamba

1698m

Kapapa

Kazembe

Koro

Lufubu

*Chute
Kiubo
Falls*

Kawasa

Luswaka Milambo-Kabobo

Lukwese

Konko

Mwense

Bunkeya

Kasenga

Nsakaluba

Lukafu

*Chute
Johnson*

Kanoni

Katwe

Sonta

Koni

Kapema

Malungwishi

Kambove

Likasi

Katofio

Minga

Mansa

Luishia

Tumbwe

Matanda

Mwangalala

Kiniama

*Kaziba-Baluba
Reserve*

Lubumbashi Ruashi

Chembe

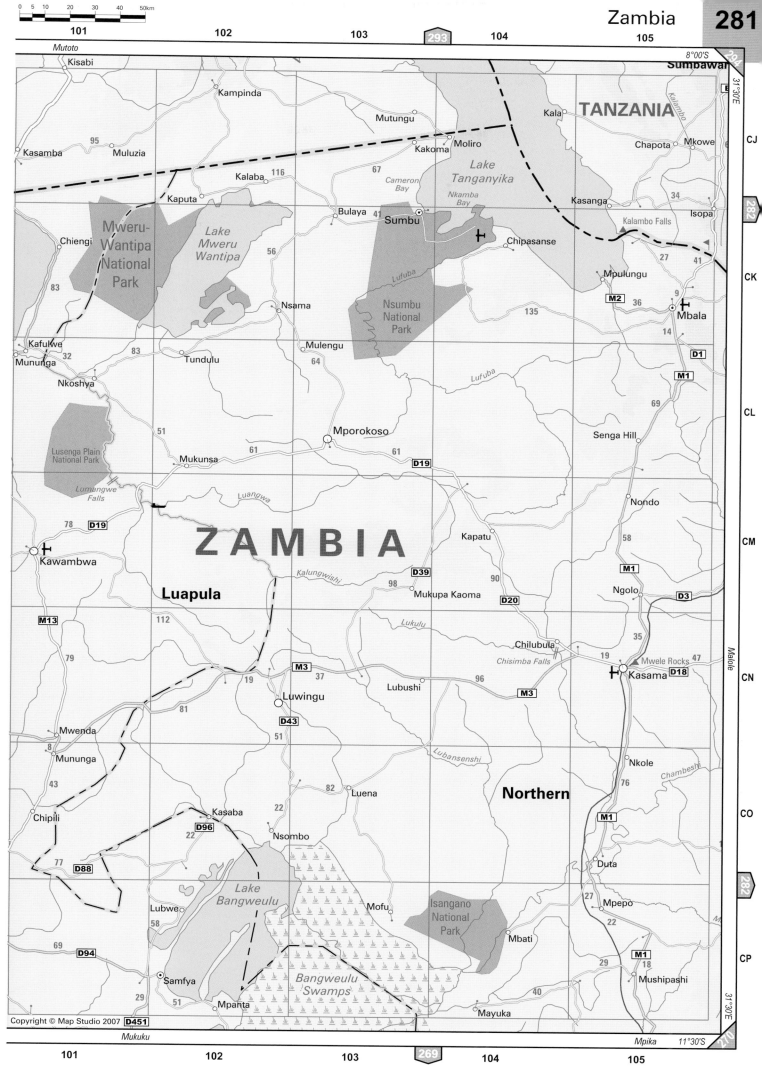

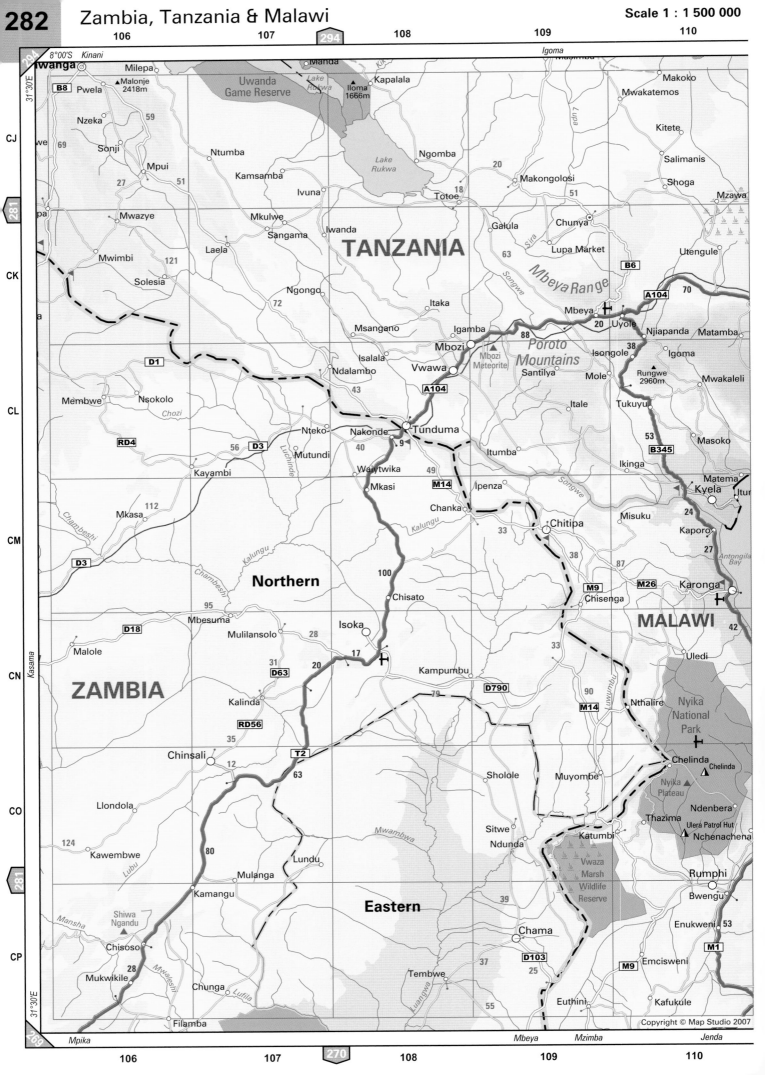

0 5 10   20   30   40   50km

Iringa   8°00'S

36°30'E

296

284

CJ

CK

CL

CM

CN

CO

CP

Ifunda
Lihanika
13
Rungemba
41
Dabaga
Uletelwa
Ngagau
Muhaga
Rupia
Kibada
A104
Mafinga
Ihembe
Njagi
Madibira
Sao Hill
164
Tongora
Chita
Little Ruaha
38
Ikoga
Kalinga
Iringa
Mdabulo
Usungu Flats
James Comer
Kilombero Valley
Malangali
Kasanga
Lulando
Mlimba
Mtimbira
Mkoji
Krimbi
Kibau
Isunura
Makungu
Morogo
Mbarali
Igawa
Itengule
Malinyi
Sofi Majiji
A104
52
Wangingombe
37
Itete
Chimala
Iyayi
Makambako
Mdervi
39
Usango
Mtwango
46
Taveta
31
Ngoilanga
54
B4
Mdandu
69
Mnyera
Njogonjwa
Kirengapanye
2235m
25
Matakankoro
71
Lupembe
76
Mfrika
Pitu
73
Bulongwa
Kipengere
Bomaya
Lindi
Tandali
Nganda
Njombe
19
Igominyi
Selous Game Reserve
Luwumbu
Ikombe
Uwemba
Itoni
60
Ruhudji
44
Kifanyo
Lisitu
Lukumburu
TANZANIA
Lugalawa
Lukumburu
Milo
Pitu
B4
Luhira
Luwegu
Bogoro
Magingo
158
Ligombe
Rudewa
Ruhuru
Ruvuma
Mulale Bay
Cape Kaiser
132
Ukenju Bay
Kilwat
Rutukira
Ngara
Mpurukasese
Lake Malawi
47
Gumbiro
72
Likuyu
Chilumba
Amelia Bay
Manda
Mtonya
Young's Bay
Lumecha
Nyamtumbo
M1
Lituhi
66
49
67
Mkondowe
Livingstonia
Ligama
Peramiho
Likonde
Chiweta
A19
52
Songea
23
Matimira
Ndombi Bay
66
34
Ruvuma
Mango
Mpitimbo
Lukimwa
66
Tumbi Point
Liuli
62
Mpepaya
Muhukuru
81
Njungo
92
Lusewa
Usisya Bay
Dankhayo Bay
Usiya
Mbamba Bay
Mitomoni
Rovuma
Cape Manula
Chikwina
Lukoma Bay

Mzuzu

Nkhata Bay

Liparamba
Ruvu

11°30'S

36°30'E

Jumbe Salim's

284

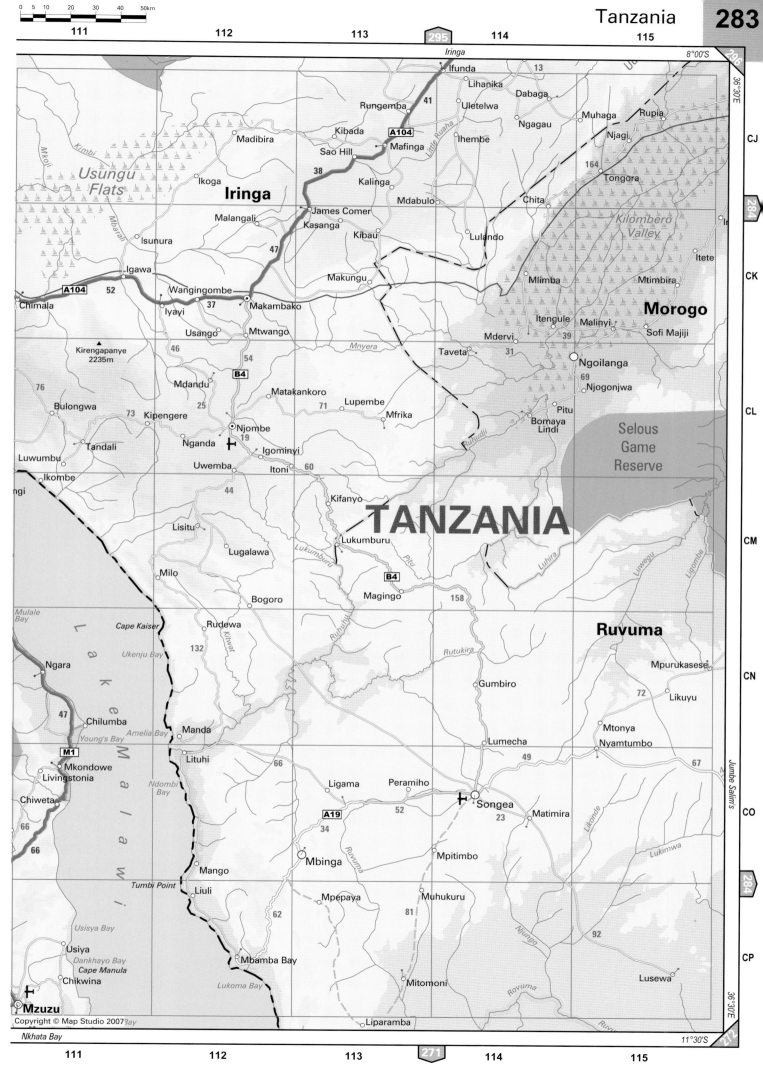

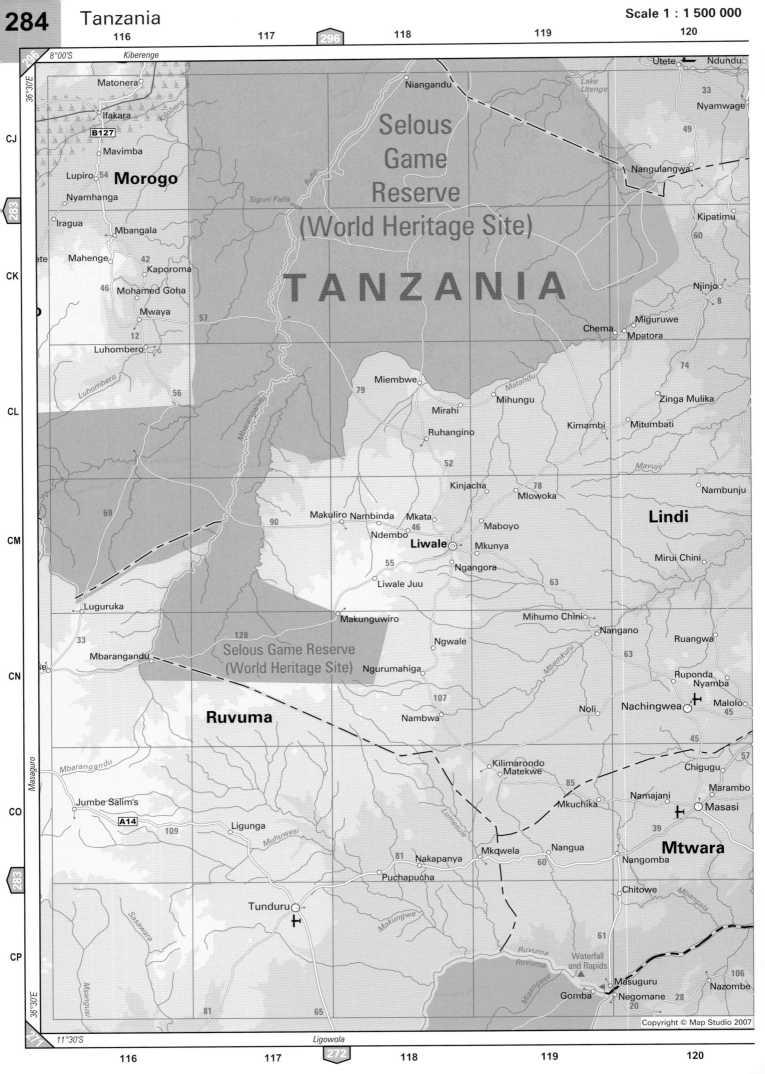

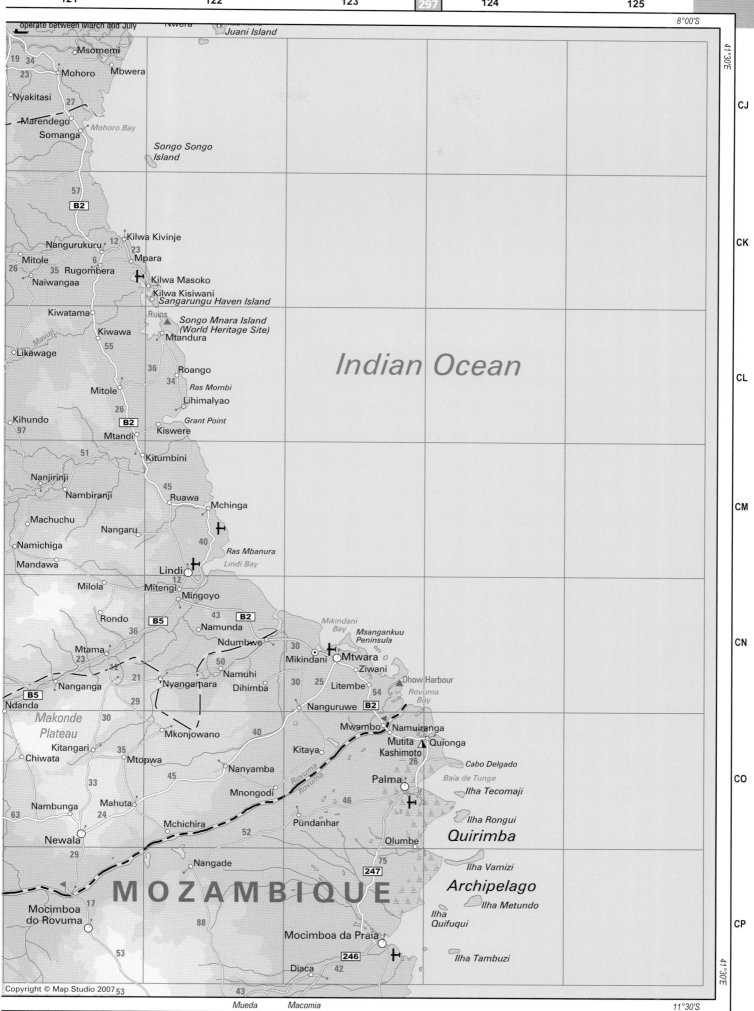

8°00'S
41°30'E

CJ

CK

CL

CM

CN

CO

CP

41°30'E
11°30'S

Indian Ocean

operate between March and July

Nwera
Juani Island
Msomemi
Mbwera
19 34
23
Mohoro
Nyakitasi
27
Marendego
Somanga
Mohoro Bay
Songo Songo Island

57
B2

Nangurukuru
12
Kilwa Kivinje
23
Mpara
Mitole
6
26
35 Rugombera
Naiwangaa
Kilwa Masoko
Kilwa Kisiwani
Sangarungu Haven Island

Kiwatama
Ruins
Songo Mnara Island (World Heritage Site)
Kiwawa
55
Mtandura
Likawage
36
Roango
Mitole
34 *Ras Mombi*
Lihimalyao
26
B2
Grant Point
Kihundo
97
Mtandi
Kiswere

51
Kitumbini

Nanjirinji
45
Nambiranji
Ruawa
Mchinga
Machuchu
Nangaru
40
Namichiga
Ras Mbanura
Mandawa
Lindi Bay
Milola
Lindi
Mitengi
12
Rondo
Mingoyo
B5
43 **B2**
36
Namunda
Mtama
Ndumbwe
23
30 *Mikindani Bay*
50
Msangankuu Peninsula
Nanganga
21
Namuhi
Mikindani
Mtwara
B5
Nyangamara
Dihimba
Ziwani
Ndanda
29
30 25
Litembe
54
Dhow Harbour
Naguruwe
B2
Rovuma Bay
Makonde Plateau
30
Mkonjowano
40
Mwambo
Namuiranga
Kitangari
35
Mutita
Quionga
Chiwata
Mtopwa
Kitaya
Kashimoto
33
45
Nanyamba
26
Cabo Delgado
Nambunga
Mahuta
Mnongodi
Palma
Baia de Tunge
63
24
46
Ilha Tecomaji
Newala
Mchichira
Ruvuma
Pundanhar
Ilha Rongui
29
52
Olumbe
Quirimba
Nangade
75
Ilha Vamizi
247
M O Z A M B I Q U E
Archipelago
Ilha Metundo
Mocìmboa do Rovuma
17
88
Ilha Quifuqui
53
Mocìmboa da Praia
Ilha Tambuzi
246
Diaca
42
43
Mueda Macomia

0 5 10 20 30 40 50km

Scale 1 : 1 500 000

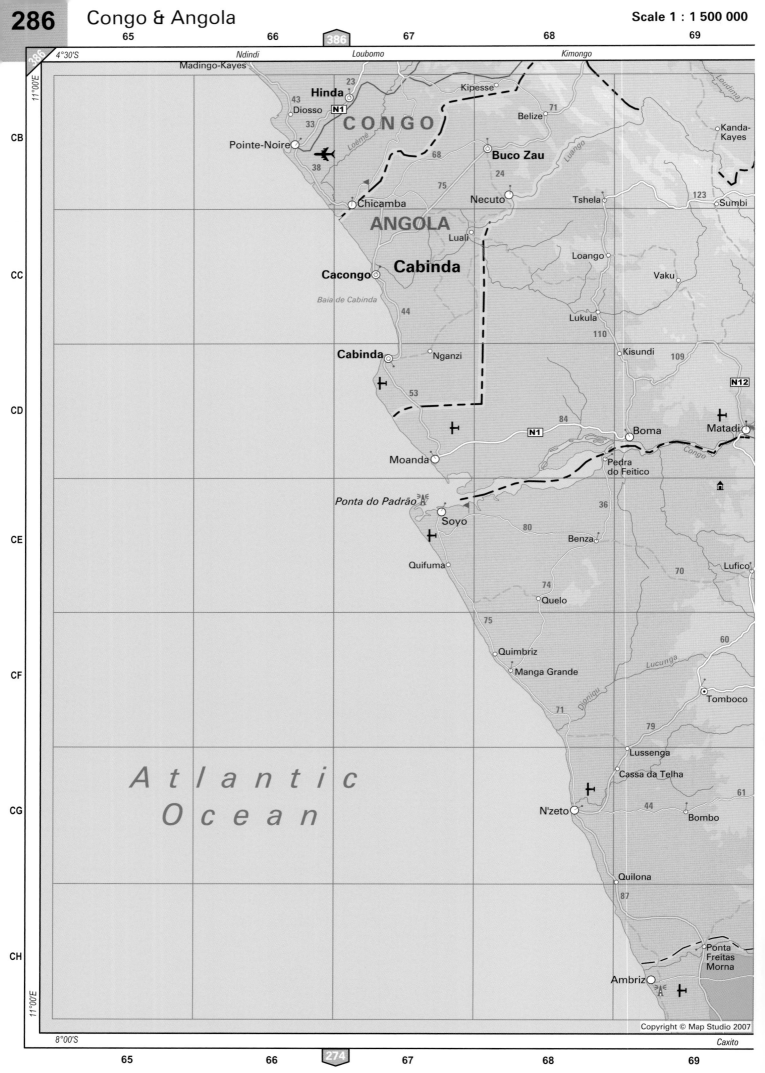

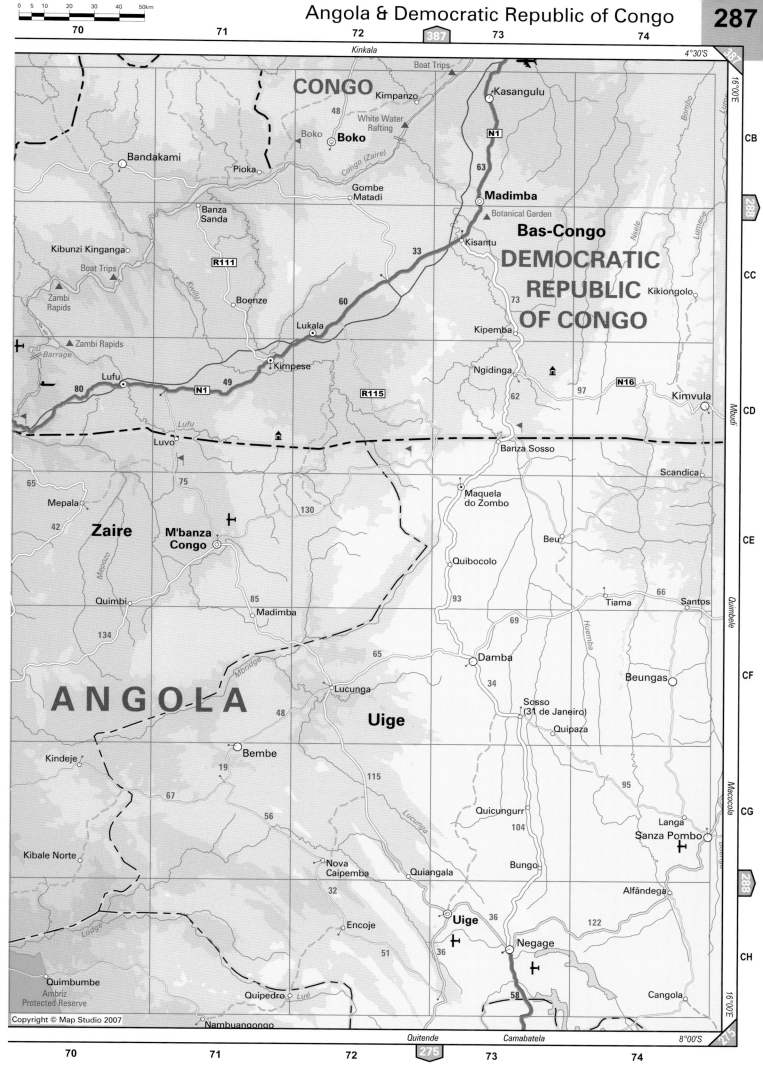

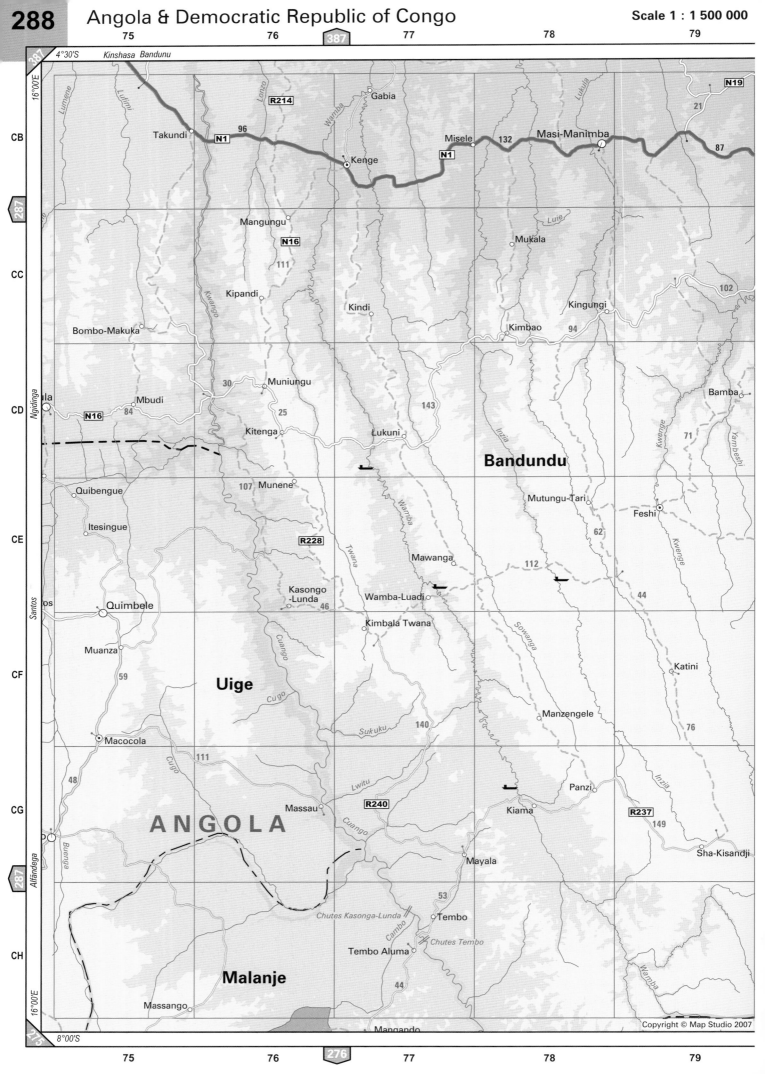

75 76 77 78 79

4°30'S *Kinshasa Bandunu*

16°00'E

N19

21

CB

Gabia

R214

Lonzo *Lufimi* *Lumene* Takundi **N1** 96

132 Masi-Manimba 87

Misele

Wamba Kenge **N1** *Lukula*

287

Mangungu

Luie

N16

Mukala

111

CC

Kwango Kipandi

Kindi Kingungi

102

Bombo-Makuka Kimbao 94

Ngidinga Muniungu

CD la 30

Mbudi **N16** 84 25 143 **Bandundu** Bamba

Kitenga *Inzia* *Kwenge* 71 *Yambeshi*

Lukuni

Quibengue Mutungu-Tari

107 Munene Feshi 62

CE Itesingue

R228

Mawanga 112 44

Twana *Santos*

os Kasongo Wamba-Luadi

Quimbele -Lunda 46 *Wamba* *Kwenge*

Kimbala Twana *Sowanga* Katini

Muanza

CF 59 Manzengele 76

Cuango **Uige**

Cugo

Sukuku 140

Macocola *Cugo*

111 Panzi

48 *Lwitu* Kiama **R237**

CG Massau **R240** 149

A N G O L A *Cuango* Sha-Kisandji

Buenga Mayala

287 *Alfândega*

53

Chutes Kasonga-Lunda Tembo

Cambo *Chutes Tembo*

Tembo Aluma

CH **Malanje**

16°00'E 44

275

Massango *Wamba*

8°00'S Copyright © Map Studio 2007

Mangando

75 76 276 77 78 79

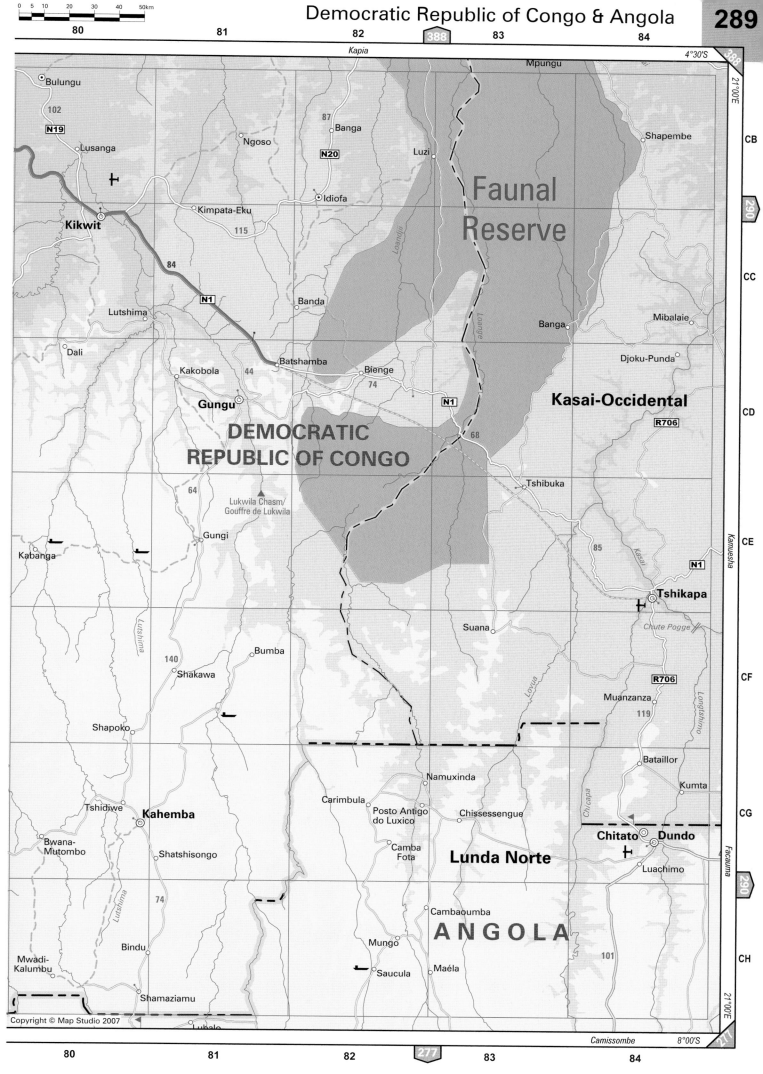

0 5 10 20 30 40 50km

80 81 82 **388** 83 84

Kapia 4°30'S

Mpungu

Bulungu

102

N19

Banga

87

Luzi

Shapembe

Ngoso

Lusanga

N20

Idiofa

Faunal Reserve

Kimpata-Eku

Kikwit

115

84

N1

Banda

Banga

Mibalaie

Lutshima

Djoku-Punda

Dali

Batshamba

Bienge

44

74

Kasai-Occidental

Kakobola

N1

R706

Gungu

68

DEMOCRATIC REPUBLIC OF CONGO

Tshibuka

64

Lukwila Chasm/
Gouffre de Lukwila

85

Gungi

N1

Kabanga

Tshikapa

Chute Pogge

Kamuesha

Suana

Bumba

140

Shakawa

Muanzanza

R706

119

Shapoko

Bataillor

Namuxinda

Kumta

Carimbula

Tshidiwe

Posto Antigo
do Luxico

Chissessengue

Kahemba

Chitato

Dundo

Bwana-
Mutombo

Camba
Fota

Lunda Norte

Luachimo

Shatshisongo

74

Cambaoumba

Facauma

Bindu

Mungo

A N G O L A

Mwadi-
Kalumbu

Saucula

Maéla

101

Shamaziamu

21°00'E

Luhalo

Camissombe 8°00'S

80 81 82 **277** 83 84

21°00'E

Lutshima

Lovua

Kasai

Longtshimo

Chicapa

Loandji

Loange

CB

CC

CD

CE

CF

CG

CH

290

290

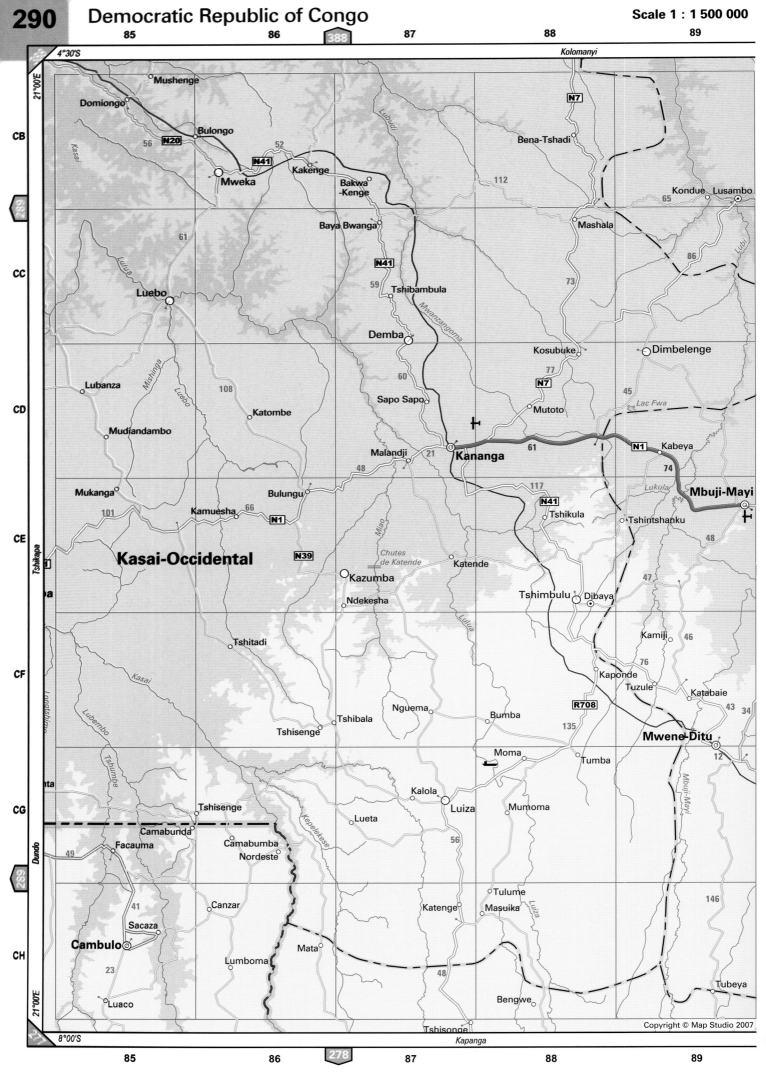

Kolomanyi

4°30'S
21°00'E

388

85   86   87   88   89

Mushenge

Domiongo
N20
Bulongo
56
N41
52
Kakenge
Mweka
Bakwa-Kenge
Kasai

CB

Baya Bwanga

N7
Bena-Tshadi

112

Kondue Lusambo
65

Mashala

86

N41
59
Tshibambula
73

CC

Luebo
61
Lulua
Mishinga
Luebo

Mwanzangoma

Demba

Kosubuke
Dimbelenge

CD

Lubanza
108
60
Sapo Sapo
77
N7
45
Lac Fwa

Mudiandambo
Katombe
Mutoto

Malandji
21
Kananga
61
N1
Kabeya
74

CD

Mukanga
101
48
Bulungu
117
Mbuji-Mayi

Kamuesha
66
N1
N41
Lukula

CE

Tshikapa
Kasai-Occidental
N39
Miao
Chutes de Katende
Katende
Tshikula
Tshintshanku
48

Kazumba
47

Ndekesha
Tshimbulu
Dibaya

CE

Tshitadi
Kamiji
46

Lulua
76

CF

Kaponde
Tuzule
Katabaie
43 34

Nguema
Bumba
R708
135

Tshibala
Mwene-Ditu
12

Tshisenge
Moma
Tumba

Lubembo
Kalola
Mbuji-Mayi

Tshumbe
Luiza
Mumoma

CG

Tshisenge
Lueta
56

Camabunda
Facauma
49
Camabumba
Nordeste

Dundo

289

Tulume

Canzar
Katenge
Masuika
Luiza
146

41
Sacaza

CH

Cambulo
Mata

Luaco
23
Lumboma
48
Bengwe
Tubeya

8°00'S
21°00'E
Kapanga

278

85   86   87   88   89

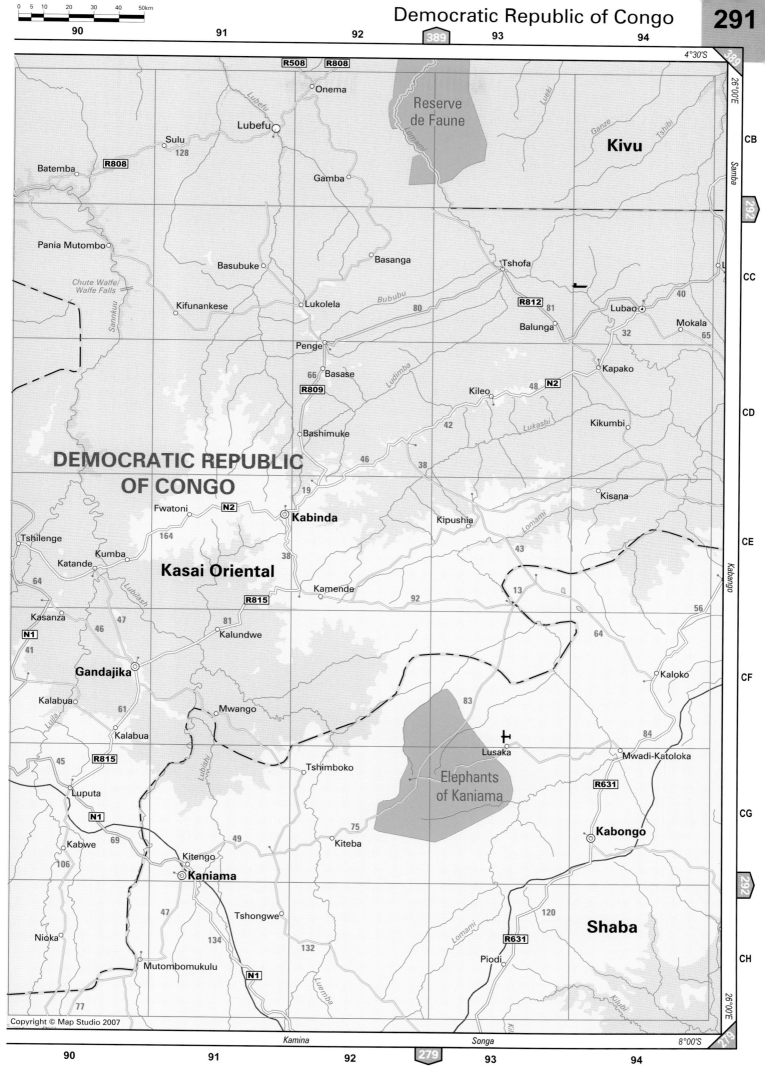

0 5 10   20   30   40   50km

90   91   92   389   93   94

4°30'S

26°00'E

Kivu

Reserve
de Faune

R508   R808

Onema

Lubefu

Sulu
128

Batemba   R808

Gamba

Pania Mutombo

Basanga

Tshofa

Basubuke

Lubao

Chute Walfe/
Walfe Falls

Kifunankese

Lukolela   Bububu   80   R812   81   Mokala

Balunga   32   65

Penge   Ludimba   Kapako

66 Basase   48 N2

R809   Kileo

42   Kikumbi

Lukashi

Bashimuke

46   38

**DEMOCRATIC REPUBLIC
OF CONGO**

19   Kisana

Fwatoni   N2   Kipushia   Lomami

Kabinda   43

164   **Kasai Oriental**   38   13

Tshilenge   Kamende   92   56

Kumba   R815

Katande   81   64

0   Kalundwe

64   Kaloko

Kasanza   47   46

N1   83

41

Gandajika   Mwadi-Katoloka

Kalabua   84

61

Kalabua   Lusaka   R631

45   R815   Mwango   **Elephants
of Kaniama**

Luputa   Tshimboko

N1   **Kabongo**

Kabwe   69   75

106   Kiteba   120

Kitengo   49

Kaniama   **Shaba**

47   Tshongwe

Nioka   134   132   R631

Piodi

Mutombomukulu   N1

77

26°00'E

Copyright © Map Studio 2007

Kamina   Songa   8°00'S

90   91   92   279   93   94

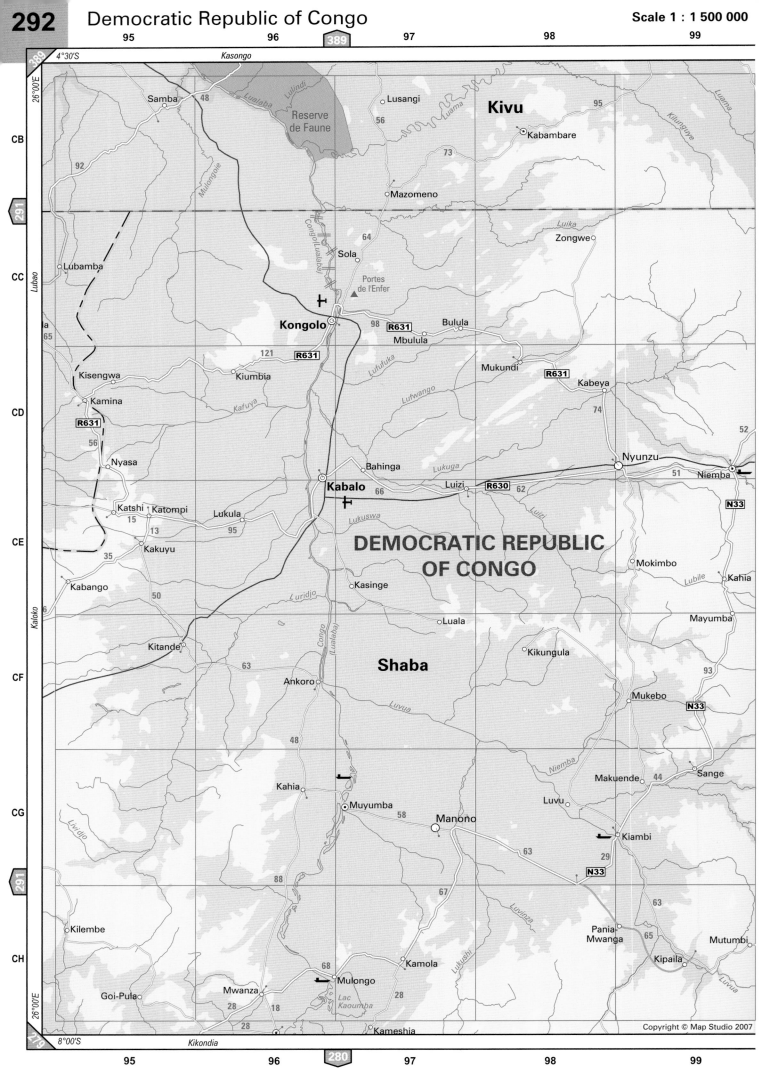

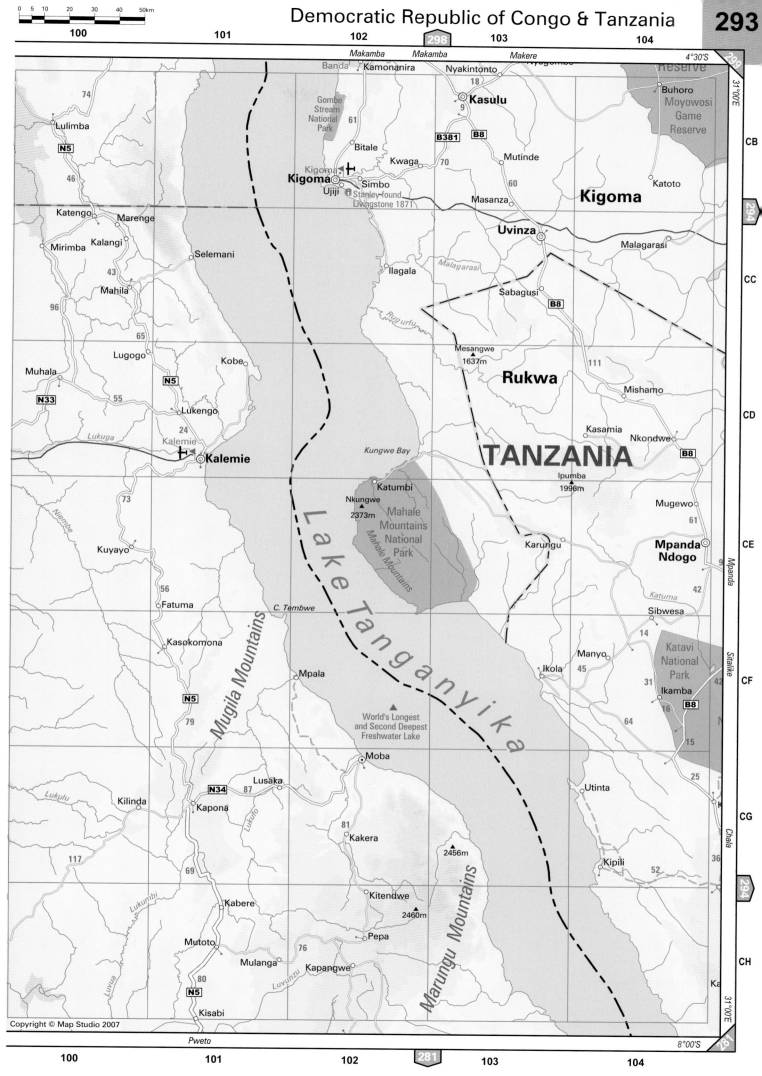

Makamba   Makamba   Makere   4°30'S

Banda   Kamonanira   Nyakintonto   Nyagombe

Gombe
Stream   18
National   **Kasulu**
Park   9
61   CB
Bitale   Kwaga   Mutinde
Kigoma ✠   70
Kigoma ⊙   Simbo   Masanza   60
Ujiji   Stanley-found   **Kigoma**
Livingstone 1871   Katoto

B381   B8   294

Uvinza ⊙   Malagarasi

Malagarasi   Sabagusi   CC
B8
Ilagala

Rugurfu
Mesangwe   111
1637m   Mishamo
Rukwa
CD
Kasamia   Nkondwe
Kungwe Bay   B8
Ipumba
Katumbi   1996m   **TANZANIA**
Nkungwe ▲   Mugewo
2373m   **Mahale**   61
Mountains
National   CE
Park   Karungu   **Mpanda**
Mahale Mountains   **Ndogo** ⊚

Katuma
42
C. Tembwe   Sibwesa

Mugila Mountains   14
Katavi
Manyo   National
Fatuma   Park
Ikola   45   31
Ikamba
Kasokomona   16   B8
64
N5
79   15
Mpala
World's Longest
and Second Deepest   25
Freshwater Lake   Utinta
Moba   CG

Lusaka   52
N34   87   Kipili   36
Kilinda   Kapona
2456m
81
Kakera   294

117
69   Kitendwe
2460m
Kabere   **Marungu Mountains**

Mutoto
76
Mulanga   Kapangwe
80
N5
31°00'E
Kisabi

Lake Tanganyika

Lukuga   *Niembe*   *Lukulu*   *Lukumbi*   *Lukuo*   *Luvua*   *Luvunzu*   *Mpanda*   *Sitalike*   *Chala*

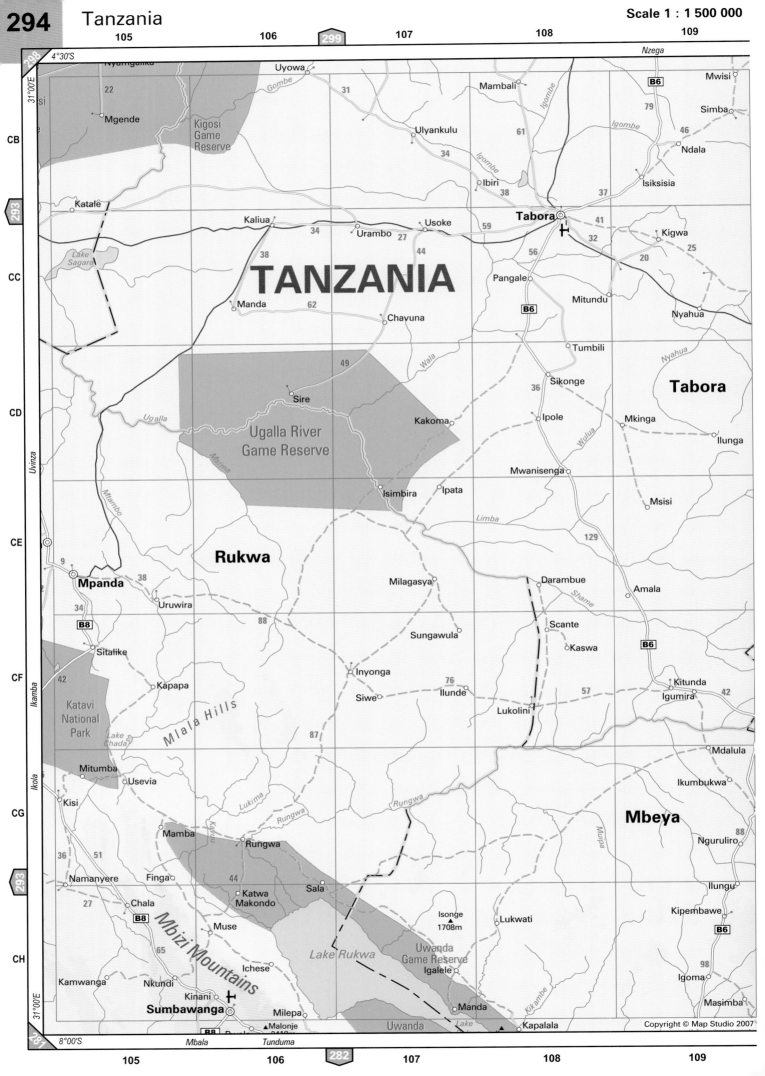

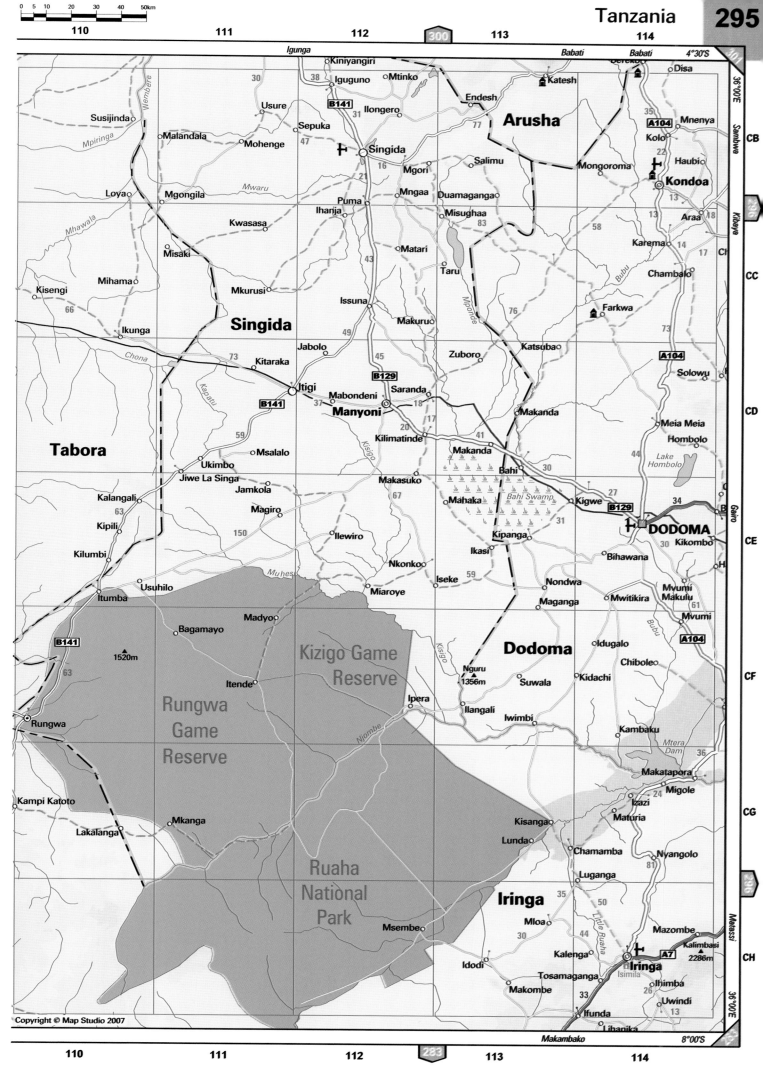

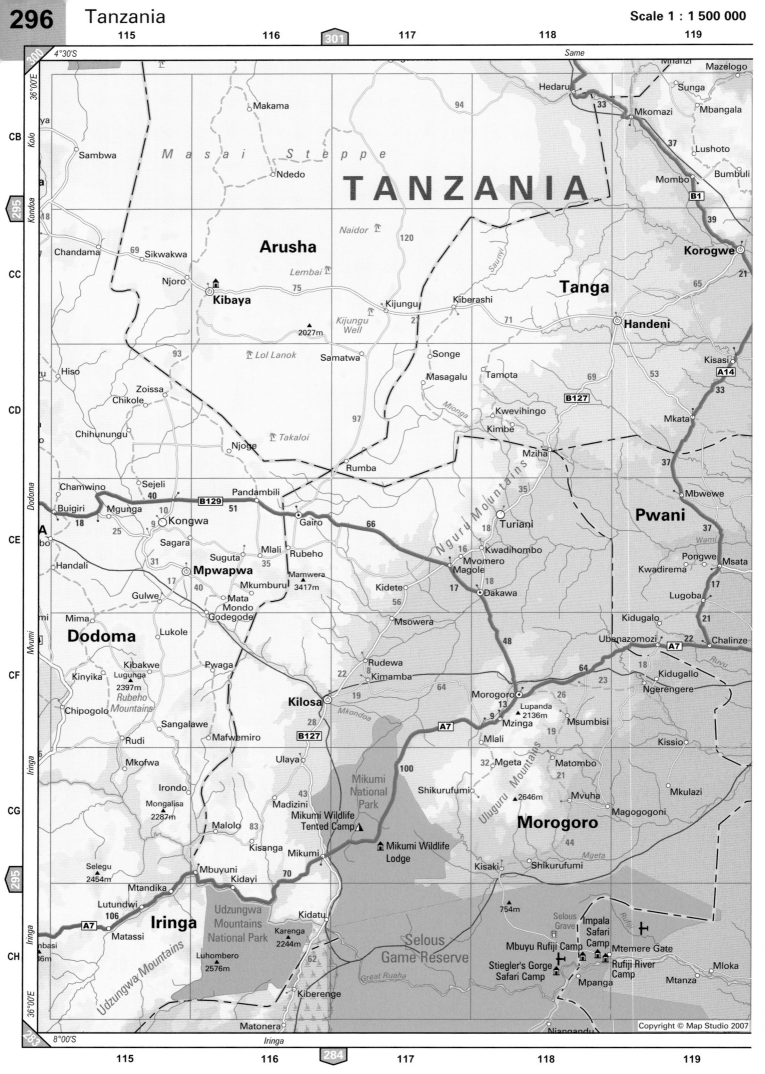

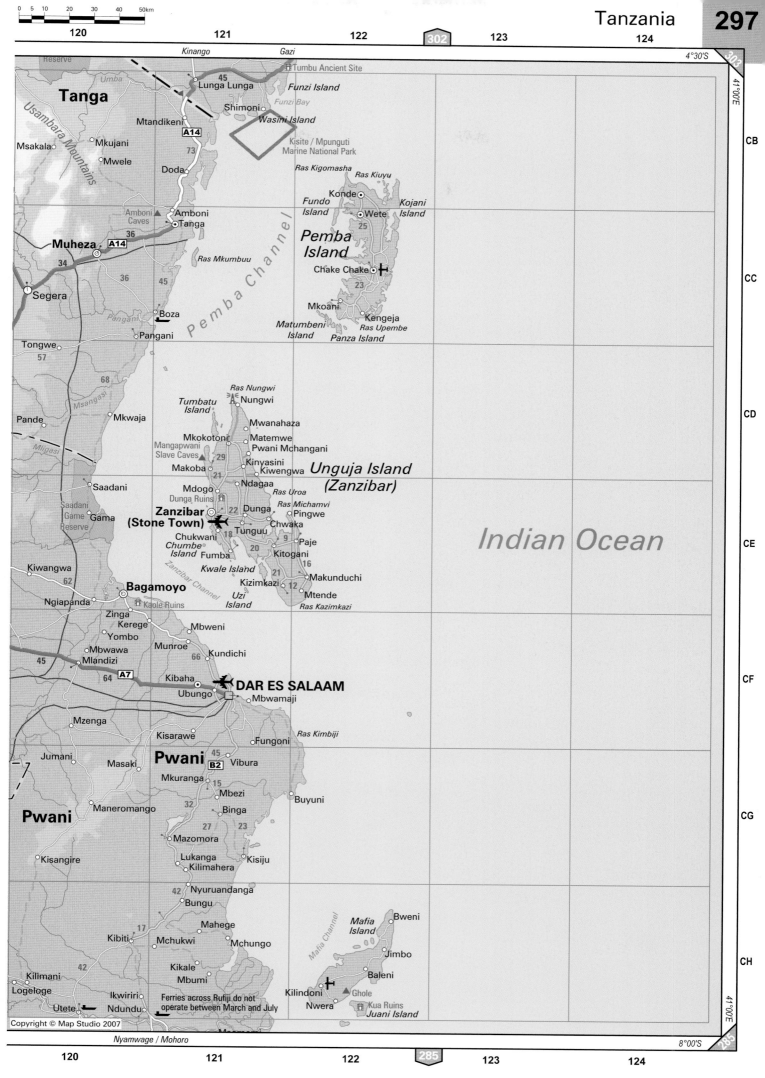

0 5 10 20 30 40 50km

4°30'S
303
41°00'E

Kinango
Gazi
Tumbu Ancient Site

Tanga

Reserve
Umba

Lunga Lunga
45
Funzi Island
Funzi Bay

Shimoni

Mtandikeni
A14
Wasini Island

Msakala
Mkujani

Mwele
73

Doda

*Kisite / Mpunguti
Marine National Park*

Ras Kigomasha
Ras Kiuyu

Konde

CB

Amboni
Caves
Amboni
Tanga

Muheza A14
36

*Fundo
Island*
Wete
25
*Kojani
Island*

*Pemba
Island*

Ras Mkumbuu

34

36
45

Segera

Chake Chake
23

Boza

Pangani
Pangani

Mkoani
Kengeja

*Matumbeni
Island*
Ras Upembe
Panza Island

CC

Tongwe
57

68

Msangasi

Pande

Miigasi

Mkwaja

Ras Nungwi
Nungwi

*Tumbatu
Island*

Mwanahaza

Matemwe
Mkokotoni
Pwani Mchangani

*Mangapwani
Slave Caves*
29
Kinyasini
Kiwengwa
21
Makoba

*Unguja Island
(Zanzibar)*

CD

Saadani

*Saadani
Game
Reserve*
Gama

Mdogo
Dunga Ruins

**Zanzibar
(Stone Town)**
22
Ndagaa
Dunga
Ras Uroa
Ras Michamvi
Pingwe

18
Tunguu

Chukwani
*Chumbe
Island*
Fumba
20
Chwaka
9
Paje
Kitogani

Kiwangwa
62

Bagamoyo
Kaole Ruins

Kwale Island

Kizimkazi
21
16
Makunduchi

CE

Indian Ocean

Ngiapanda

*Uzi
Island*
12
Mtende
Ras Kazimkazi

Zinga
Kerege
Mbweni

Yombo
Munroe
Kundichi

Mbwawa
66
Mlandizi
45

64
A7
Kibaha
DAR ES SALAAM

Ubungo
Mbwamaji

CF

Mzenga

Kisarawe
Ras Kimbiji

Fungoni

Jumani
45
Pwani
Vibura

Masaki
B2

Mkuranga
15

Mbezi
Buyuni

Maneromango
32
Binga

Pwani
27
23

Mazomora

CG

Kisangire
Lukanga
Kilimahera
Kisiju

42
Nyuruandanga
Bungu

Mahege
*Mafia
Island*
Bweni

Kibiti
Mchukwi
Mchungo
Mafia Channel

Jimbo

17

CH

Kilimani
Kikale
Mbumi

Logeloge
Baleni

Utete
Ikwiriri
Ndundu
Ferries across Rufiji do not
operate between March and July
Kilindoni
Ghole
Nwera
Kua Ruins
Juani Island

Copyright © Map Studio 2007

41°00'E
285

Nyamwage / Mohoro
8°00'S

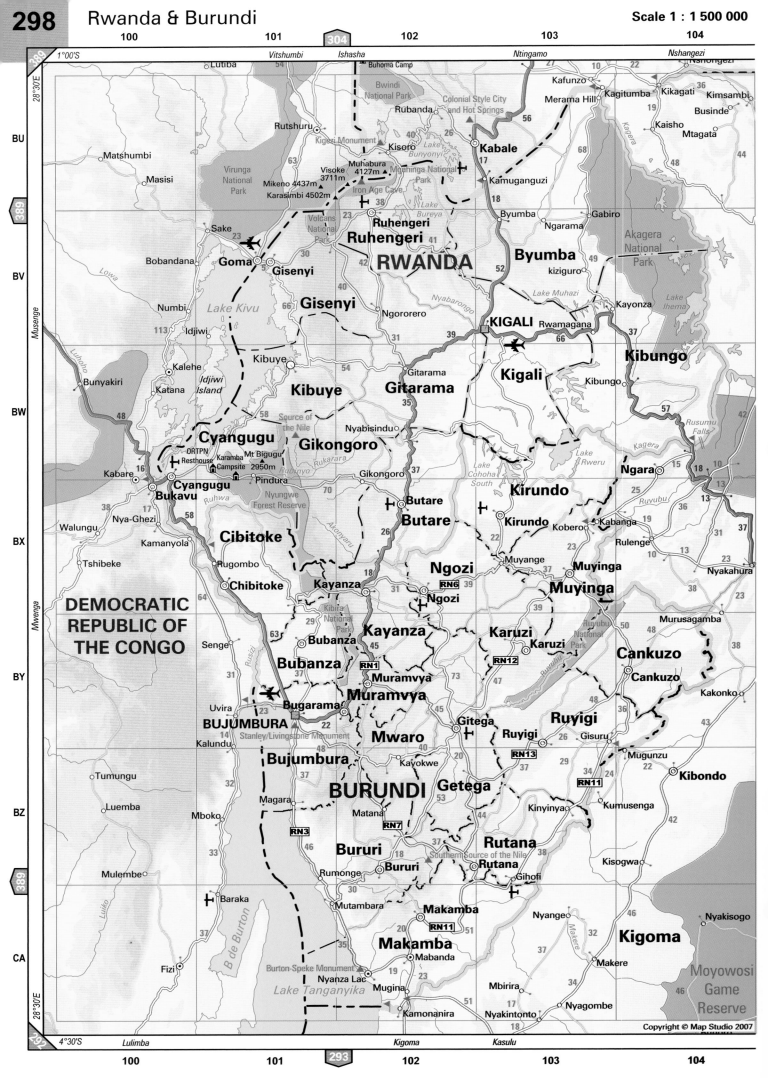

100   101   304   102   103   104

1°00'S   Vitshumbi   Ishasha   Ntingamo   Nshangezi

BU

Lutiba   54   Buhoma Camp   27   10   22   Nshongezi

Bwindi National Park   Kafunzo   Kagitumba   Kikagati   Kimsambi

Colonial Style City and Hot Springs   Merama Hill   56   19   Businde   36

Matshumbi   Rutshuru   Rubanda   40   26   Kabale   17   68   Kaisho   Mtagata   48   44

Masisi   Kigezi Monument   Kisoro   Kamuganguzi

Virunga National Park   63   Visoke 3711m   Muhabura 4127m   Mgahinga National Park   18

Mikeno 4437m   Karasimbi 4502m   Iron Age Cave   38   Byumba   Gabiro

BV

Sake   23   Volcans National Park   23   Ruhengeri   Lake Bureya   Ngarama   Akagera National Park

Goma   30   Ruhengeri   41   RWANDA   52   Byumba   49   Lake Ihema

Bobandana   5   Gisenyi   42   kiziguro

Numbi   Gisenyi   40   Lake Muhazi   Kayonza

Lowa   66   Ngororero   Nyabarongo

113   Idjiwi   KIGALI   Rwamagana   37

Luhoho   31   39   66

BW

Bunyakiri   Kalehe   Kibuye   54   Gitarama   Kigali   Kibungo   Kibungo

Katana   Idjiwi Island   Kibuye   Gitarama   35   57

58   Source of the Nile   Nyabisindu   Rusumu Falls   42

Cyangugu   Gikongoro   Rukarara   Kagera

Kabare   16   ORTPN Resthouse   Karamba Campsite   Mt Bigugu 2950m   Gikongoro   37   Lake Cohoha South   Lake Rweru   Ngara   15   18   10

BX

Cyangugu   Pindura   70   13

Bukavu   Ruhwa   17   Nyungwe Forest Reserve   Butare   Kirundo   25   13

Nya-Ghezi   58   Akonyaru   Butare   Kirundo   Kobero   Kabanga   19   36   31

Walungu   38   Cibitoke   26   22   Rulenge   10   37

Kamanyola   18   Muyange   23   Nyakahura

Tshibeke   Rugombo   Kayanza   Ngozi   37   Muyinga   38   23

BY

DEMOCRATIC REPUBLIC OF THE CONGO   64   Chibitoke   31   RN6   39   Muyinga

Senge   29   Kibira National Park   Ngozi   39   Murusagamba

63   Bubanza   Kayanza   Karuzi   Ruvubu National Park   50   48

Mwenga   31   Bubanza   45   Karuzi   Cankuzo   38

RN1   Muramvya   73   RN12   47   Cankuzo   Kakonko

Uvira   37   Muramvya   45   48   36   43

Bugarama   23   Mwaro   Gitega   Ruyigi   Gisuru

BUJUMBURA   22   40   20   RN13   Mugunzu

Kalundu   14   Stanley/Livingstone Monument   Kayokwe   29   34   24   22   Kibondo

Tumungu   48   Bujumbura   37   Getega   Kinyinya   RN11   Kumusenga

BZ

Luemba   32   Magara   BURUNDI   53   44   42

Mboko   Matana   RN7   Rutana   Kisogwa

Mulembe   33   RN3   46   Bururi   18   Southern Source of the Nile   Rutana   38   Gihofi

Bururi   Rumonge   Makamba   Kigoma

CA

Baraka   30   Mutambara   RN11   51   Nyange   46   Nyakisogo

37   B de Burton   20   Makamba   32   37   Kigoma

Fizi   35   Burton-Speke Monument   Mabanda   Makere   Moyowosi Game Reserve

Lake Tanganyika   Nyanza Lac   19   23   Mbirira   34   Nyagombe

Mugina   51   17   Nyakintonto   46

Kamonanira   18

4°30'S   Lulimba   Kigoma   Kasulu

100   101   293   102   103   104

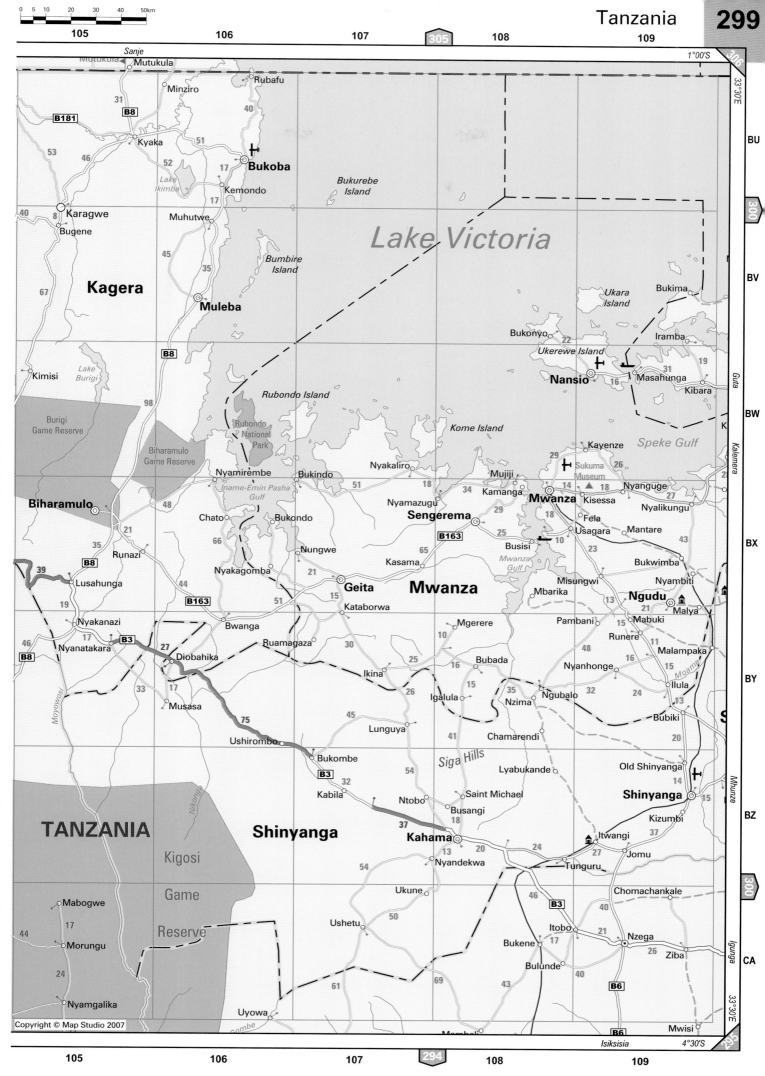

0 5 10 20 30 40 50km

105 106 107 | 305 | 108 109

Sanje
Mutukula ◄ ○ Mutukula
○ Minziro
○ Rubafu

BU

B181
31 **B8**
53 46
○ Kyaka
51
40

33°30'E
306

1°00'S

BV

52
17
✈ **Bukoba**
○ Kemondo
17

Lake Ikimba

40 8
○ Karagwe
○ Bugene

○ Muhutwe

Bukurebe Island

67

Kagera
45

35

Bumbire Island

Lake Victoria

○ Bukonyo
22
Ukara Island
○ Bukima

○ Iramba

BW

B8
Muleba ○

Lake Burigi

○ Kimisi
98

Burigi Game Reserve

Rubondo Island

Rubondo National Park

○ Nyamirembe

Iname-Emin Pasha Gulf

○ Bukindo

○ Nyakaliro

○ Mujiji
○ Kamanga

✈ **Nansio**
16
Ukerewe Island

○ Nyanguge

29 ✈ *Sukuma Museum* 26
14 ▲ 18
○ Kisessa
○ Masahunga
31
○ Kibara
19

Speke Gulf

Guta
Kalemera

Biharamulo ○
21

48

○ Chato

51

18

○ Nyamazugu

34

Sengerema ○
29

B163
25

○ Fela

Mwanza

○ Nyalikungu

Mwanza Gulf

○ Mbarika

○ Usagara
10

○ Misungwi
23

○ Mantare
43

○ Bukwimba

BX

35
○ Runazi

Biharamulo Game Reserve

○ Bukondo

○ Nungwe

○ Kasama
65

○ Busisi

13

○ Pambani
15

Ngudu ○
21
○ Malya

○ Nyambiti

39
○ Lusahunga
44

66

○ Nyakagomba
21

Geita ○
15

Mwanza

○ Mabuki

○ Runere
11

○ Malampaka

BY

19

B163
51

○ Kataborwa

○ Mgerere
10

○ Bubada
16

○ Nyanhonge
48
16

○ Ilula

15

Moame

17 **B3**
○ Nyakanazi

○ Bwanga

○ Ruamagaza
30

○ Igalula
15

○ Nzima
35

○ Ngubalo
32

24

13

○ Bubiki

46
B8
○ Nyanatakara
27
○ Diobahika
33
17

○ Ikina
25

26

○ Chamarendi
41

○ Musasa
75

○ Lunguya
45

20

○ Ushirombo

○ Bukombe

Siga Hills

○ Lyabukande

○ Old Shinyanga
14
✈

Shinyanga ✈
15

BZ

B3
32
○ Kabila
37

○ Ntobo
18

○ Saint Michael
○ Busangi

○ Kizumbi

S
Mhunze

TANZANIA

Shinyanga

○ Itwangi
27
○ Jomu

○ Tunguru

Kigosi

○ Nyandekwa
13 20
24

Kahama ○

○ Chomachankale

Game

○ Mabogwe
17

○ Ukune

54

46 **B3**
○ Itobo
40

○ Nzega

300

Reserve

○ Ushetu
50

21

○ Ziba
26

CA

44
○ Morungu

○ Bukene
17

B6

24

○ Bulunde
40

○ Nyamgalika
61

○ Uyowa
69

43

B6
○ Mwisi

33°30'E

Isiksisia
4°30'S

105 106 107 | 294 | 108 109

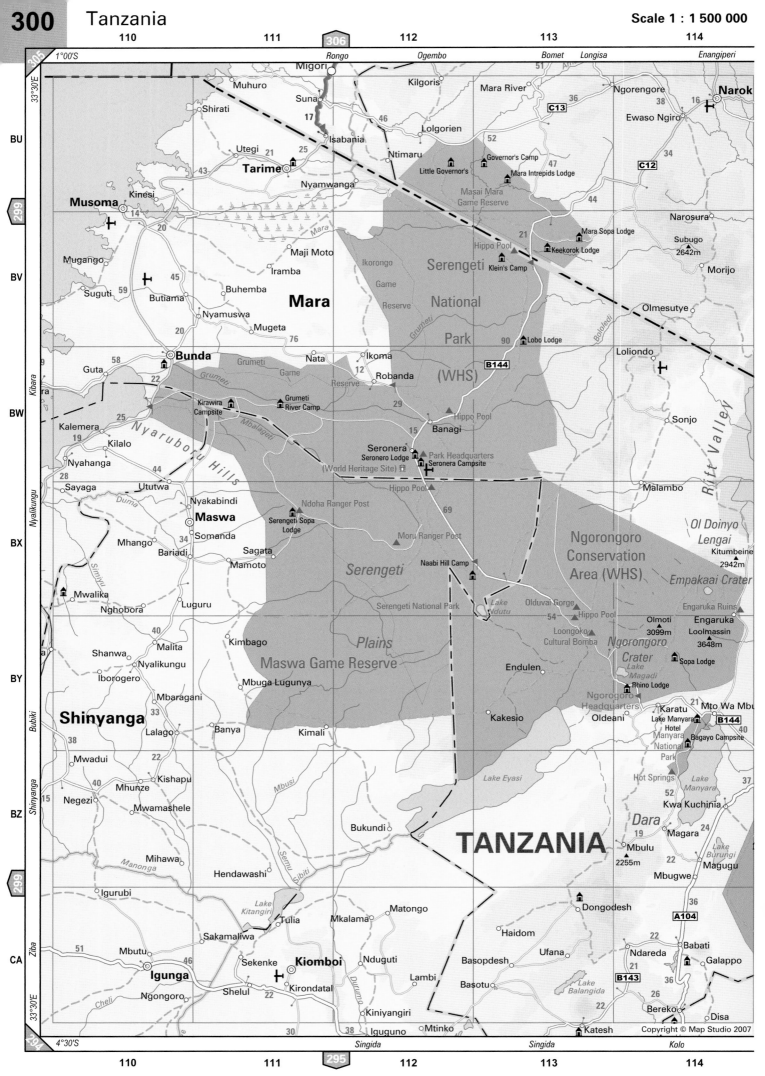

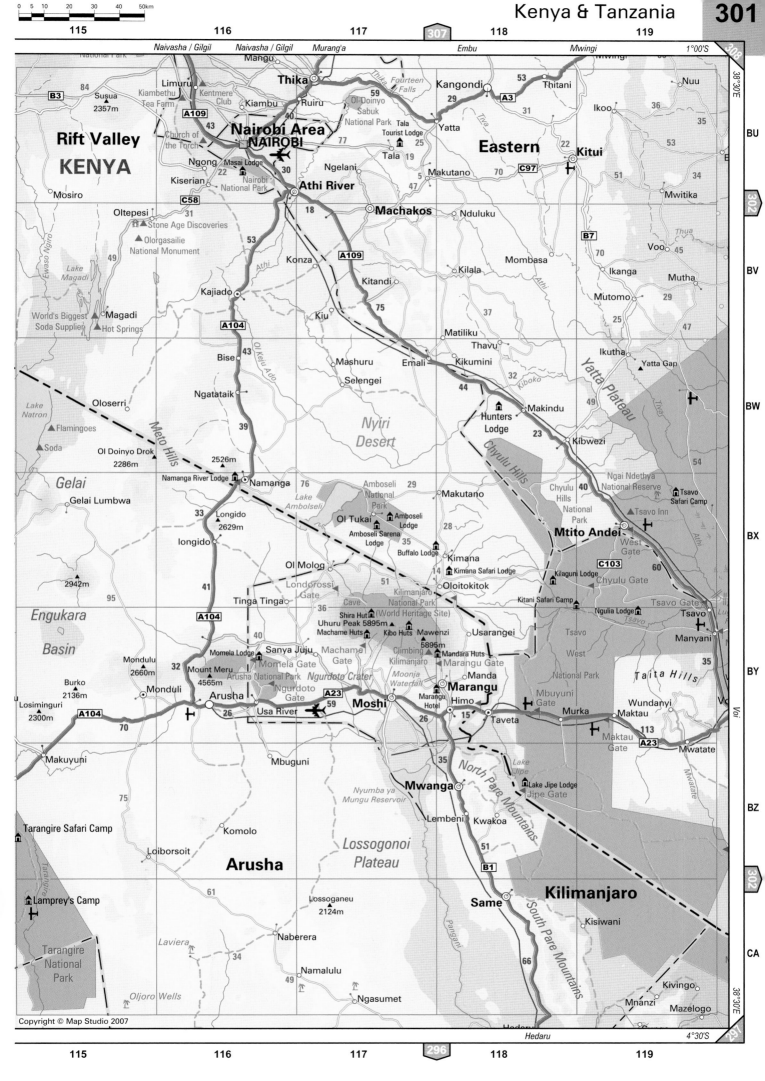

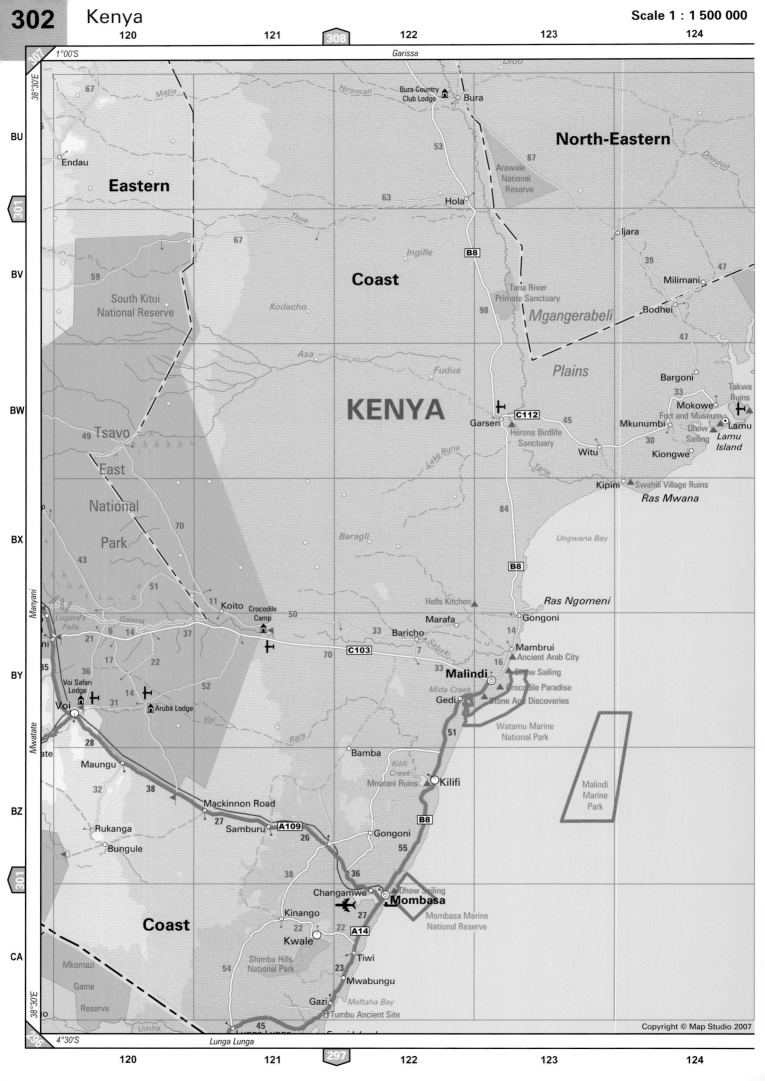

120   121   308   122   123   124

307

1°00'S   *Garissa*   *Dido*

38°30'E

67   *Matia*   *Hiraman*   Bura Country Club Lodge   Bura

BU   Endau   **North-Eastern**

Eastern   53   87   *Dondon*

301   63   Hola   Arawale National Reserve

Thua   B8   Ijara

BV   59   67   *Ingille*   **Coast**   Tana River Primate Sanctuary   39   47   Milimani

South Kitui National Reserve   *Kodacho*   98   *Mgangerabeli*   Bodhei

Asa   *Plains*   47

BW   49   **Tsavo**   *Fudua*   **KENYA**   33   Bargoni   Takwa Ruins

East   Garsen   C112   45   Mkunumbi   Fort and Museum   Mokowe   Lamu

Herons Birdlife Sanctuary   Witu   30   Dhow Sailing   *Lamu Island*   Kiongwe

National   *Lake Buna*   Kipini   Swahili Village Ruins

BX   43   **Park**   70   *Baragli*   84   *Ras Mwana*

Manyani   51   *Ungwana Bay*

11 Koito   Crocodile Camp   Hells Kitchen   *Ras Ngomeni*

Lugard's Falls   *Galana*   50   B8   Gongoni

21   6   14   37   33   Baricho   Marafa   14

70   C103   7   *Sabaki*   Mambrui   Ancient Arab City

BY   35   17   22   52   33   **Malindi**   16   Dhow Sailing

36   Voi Safari Lodge   14   Aruba Lodge   *Mida Creek*   Gedi   Crocodile Paradise / Stone Age Discoveries

Voi   31   *Voi*   Watamu Marine National Park

Mwatate   *Rare*   51

28   Bamba   *Kilifi Creek*   Malindi Marine Park

Maungu   Mnarani Ruins   Kilifi

BZ   32   38   Mackinnon Road   B8

Rukanga   27   Samburu   A109   Gongoni

Bungule   26   55

38   36   Dhow Sailing

Changamwe   **Mombasa**

Kinango   27   Mombasa Marine National Reserve

301   22   22   A14

CA   *Mkomazi Game Reserve*   Kwale   Tiwi

Coast   54   Shimba Hills National Park   23   Mwabungu

38°30'E   Gazi   *Maftaha Bay*

Tumbu Ancient Site

4°30'S   *Lunga Lunga*   45

Umba

296   297

120   121   122   123   124

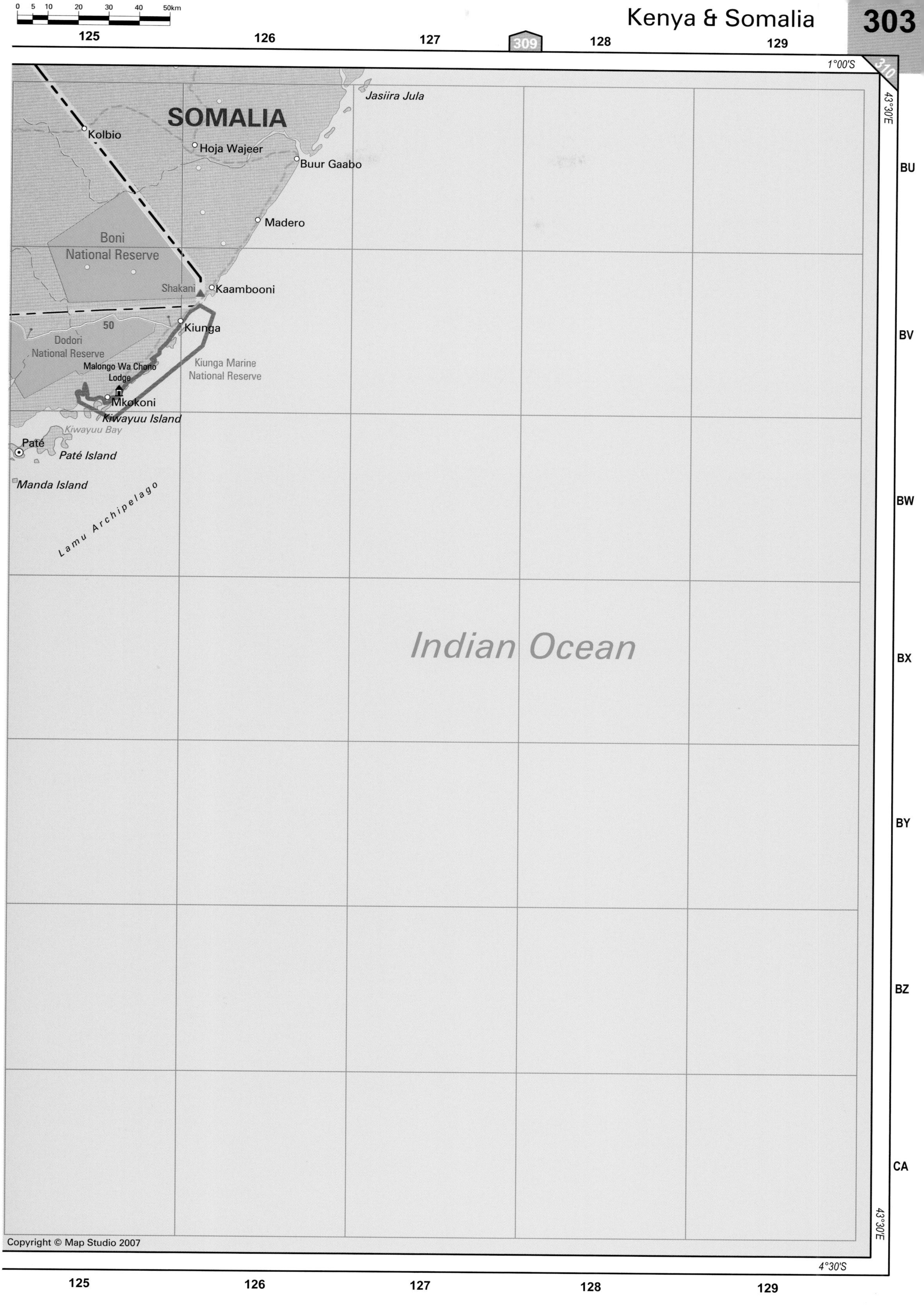

0 5 10 20 30 40 50km

125 126 127 309 128 129

1°00'S

43°30'E

310

SOMALIA

Jasiira Jula

BU

Kolbio

Hoja Wajeer

Buur Gaabo

4°30'S

Madero

Boni National Reserve

BV

Shakani Kaambooni

50 Kiunga

Dodori National Reserve

Kiunga Marine National Reserve

BW

Malongo Wa Chono Lodge

Mkokoni

Kiwayuu Island

Kiwayuu Bay

Paté

Paté Island

Manda Island

Lamu Archipelago

Indian Ocean

BX

BY

BZ

CA

43°30'E

125 126 127 128 129

4°30'S

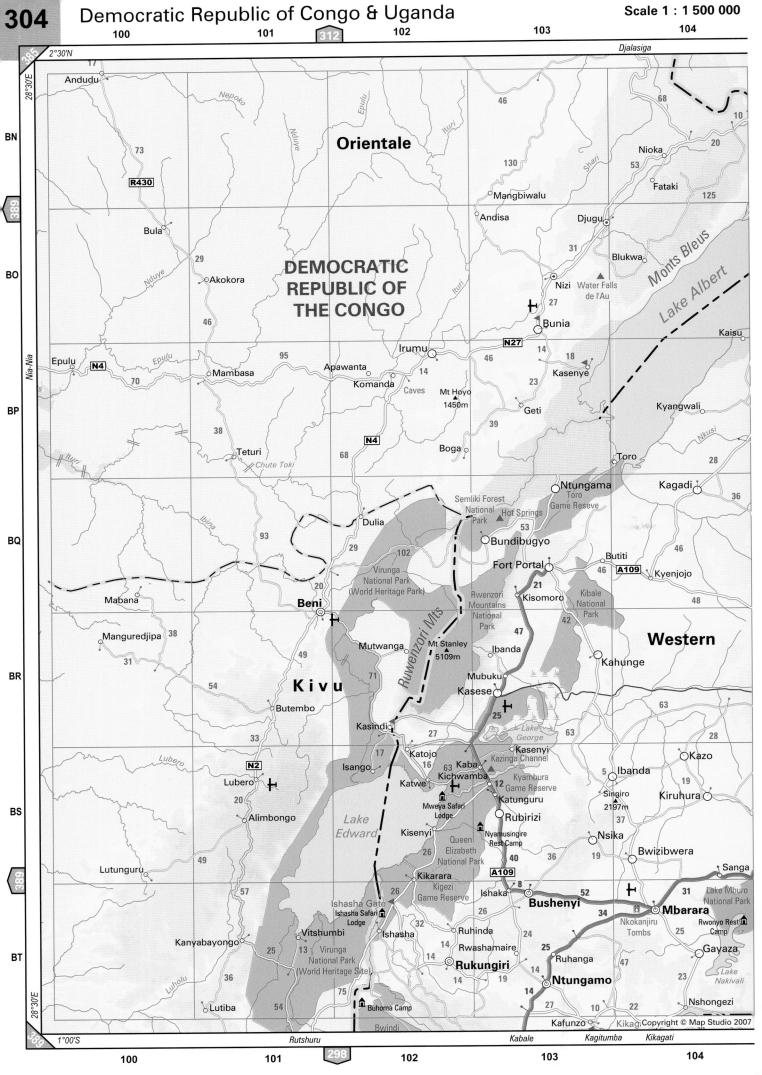

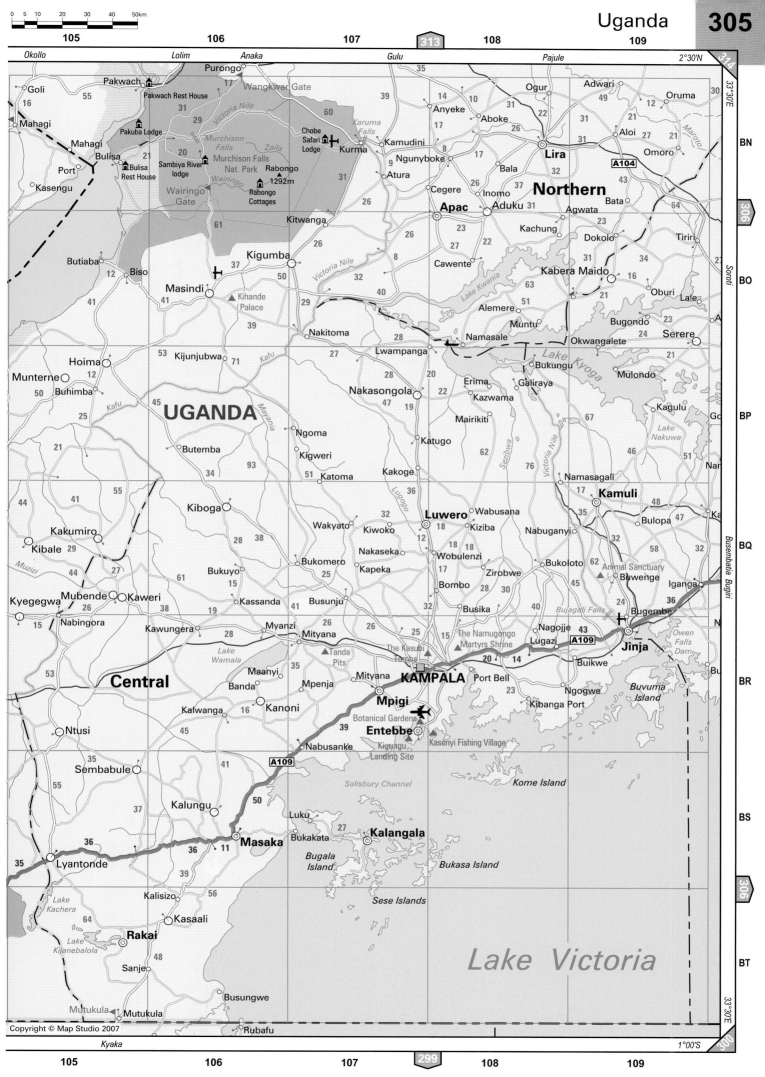

0 5 10   20   30   40   50km
105   106   107   313   108   109

Okollo   Lolim   Anaka   Gulu   Pajule   2°30'N

Goli
16   Pakwach
55   Pakwach Rest House   Wangkwar Gate   35
Mahagi
Port   31   Victoria Nile   39   14   10   Ogur   Adwari   Oruma   30
Mahagi   Pakuba Lodge   29   60   Anyeke   31   22   31   12
Kasengu   Bulisa   21   20   Murchison   Zaila   Chobe   Kurma   26   Kamudini   8   17   Aloi   27   21   Omoro
                  Sambiya River   Falls   Safari   Ngunyboke   17   Lira   A104
            Bulisa   lodge   Murchison Falls   Rabongo   31   Atura   9   Bala   32
            Rest House   Nat. Park   1292m   26   Cegere   Inomo   37   43   Bata   64
Butiaba   Wairingo   Rabongo   Apac   Aduku   31   Agwata
            Biso   Gate   Cottages   Kitwanga   26   23   Kachung   Dokolo   23
12   37   61   23   22   Kabera Maido   31   34   Tiriri
Masindi   41   50   Kigumba   26   Victoria Nile   8   63   51   16   Oburi   Lale
            41   Kihande   29   32   40   Cawente   Alemere   21   Bugondo   23
                  Palace   39   Namasale   Muntu   Okwangalete   24   Serere
Hoima   Nakitoma   27   Lwampanga   Lake Kwania   Bukungu   Mulondo   Lake
Munterne   12   53   Kijunjubwa   71   Kafu   28   20   Erima   Galiraya   67   Nakuwa   51
50   Buhimba   Nakasongola   47   19   Kazwama   76   Namasagali   Kamuli   48
            25   Ngoma   22   Mairikiti   Sezibwa   17   Bulopa   47
21   Butemba   Kigweri   Katugo   62   Victoria Nile   35   58   32
44   41   34   93   Katoma   Kakoge   Luwero   Wabusana   Nabuganyi   Bukoloto   62   Buwenge   Iganga
Kakumiro   Kiboga   51   36   Kiwoko   18   Kiziba   Animal Sanctuary
Kibale   29   28   38   Wakyato   32   12   18   Zirobwe   45   24   36
Kyegegwa   Mubende   Kaweri   61   Bukomero   Nakaseka   18   Wobulenzi   Bukoloto   Bugembe
15   26   44   27   15   Bukuyo   25   Kapeka   17   Bombo   28   30   Busika   Bujagali Falls   Jinja   Owen
Nabingora   38   19   Kassanda   41   Busunju   26   32   Nagojje   43   Falls
Kawungera   28   Myanzi   26   25   15   20   Lugazi   A109   Dam
53   Maanyi   35   Mityana   The Kasubi   The Namugongo   14   Buikwe   Buvuma
Central   Banda   Mpenja   Mityana   Tombs   Martyrs Shrine   Kibanga Port   Island   BR
Ntusi   Kalwanga   16   Kanoni   KAMPALA   Port Bell   23   Ngogwe
45   39   Mpigi   Botanical Gardens   Kasenyi Fishing Village
Sembabule   41   Nabusanke   Entebbe   Kigungu   Kome Island
35   Landing Site   Salisbury Channel
55   Kalungu   50   Luku   Bukasa Island
37   Masaka   Bukakata   27   Kalangala
Lyantonde   36   11   Bugala   Lake Victoria
35   36   39   Island   Bukasa Island
Kalisizo   56   Sese Islands
Lake   64   Kasaali
Kachera   Rakai
Lake   48
Kijanebalola   Sanje
Mutukula   Busungwe
Mutukula   Rubafu
Kyaka   1°00'S
105   106   107   299   108   109

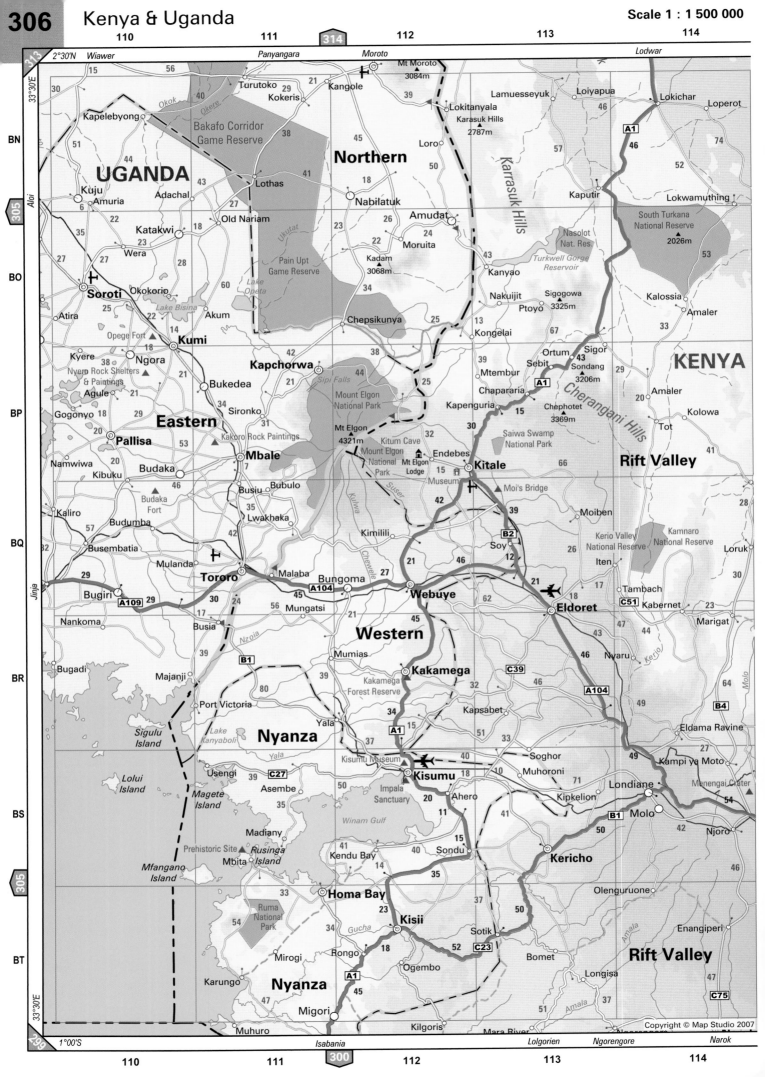

Scale 1 : 1 500 000

UGANDA

Northern

KENYA

Eastern

Rift Valley

Western

Nyanza

Rift Valley

Nyanza

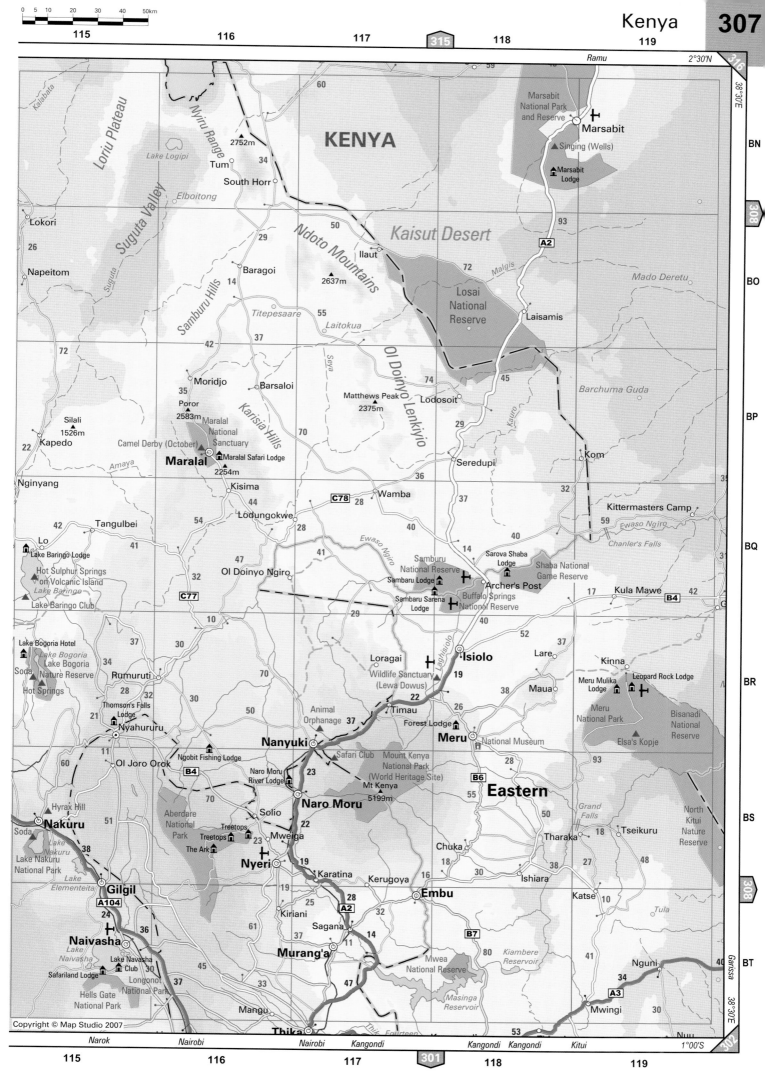

0 5 10 20 30 40 50km

115 116 117 315 118 119

Ramu 2°30'N

38°30'E

316

BN

Loriu Plateau

Nyiru Range

Lake Logipi

2752m

Tum

34

South Horr

Elboitong

Ndoto Mountains

KENYA

60

59

Marsabit National Park and Reserve

Marsabit

▲ Singing (Wells)

🏠 Marsabit Lodge

308

Lokori

26

Napeitom

72

50

29

Ilaut

2637m

Baragoi

Titepesaare

55

Laitokua

Kaisut Desert

72

A2

93

Losai National Reserve

Laisamis

Mado Deretu

Malgis

BO

Samburu Hills

14

37

42

Seya

Ol Doinyo Lenkiyio

Moridjo

35

Poror

2583m ▲

Maralal National Sanctuary

Camel Derby (October)

Maralal

🏠 Maralal Safari Lodge

2254m

Kisima

Silali

1526m ▲

22

Kapedo

Barsaloi

Karisia Hills

70

Matthews Peak 2375m ▲

74

Lodosoit

45

29

Kom

Barchuma Guda

Kauro

BP

35

Nginyang

Amaya

44

C78 28

Wamba

36

Seredupi

37

32

Kittermasters Camp

59

Ewaso Ngiro

Chanler's Falls

Tangulbei

42

54

Lodungokwe

28

40

40

14

31

BQ

Lo 🏠

Lake Baringo Lodge

41

47

C77

41

Ol Doinyo Ngiro

29

Ewaso Ngiro

Samburu National Reserve

Samburu Lodge 🏠

Samburu Sarena Lodge 🏠

Sarova Shaba Lodge 🏠

Archer's Post

Buffalo Springs National Reserve

Shaba National Game Reserve

17

Kula Mawe

B4

42

Hot Sulphur Springs Volcanic Island

Lake Baringo

Lake Baringo Club

10

52

40

BR

Lake Bogoria Hotel 🏠

Lake Bogoria

Soda

Lake Bogoria Nature Reserve

Hot Springs

37

34

30

30

70

Loragai

Wildlife Sanctuary (Lewa Dowus)

22

Isiolo

19

Lare

Maua

38

26

Kinna

Meru Mulika Lodge 🏠

Leopard Rock Lodge 🏠

Meru National Park

Bisanadi National Reserve

Rumuruti

32

Thomson's Falls Lodge 🏠

21

Nyahururu

28

50

Animal Orphanage

37

Timau

Forest Lodge 🏠

Meru

National Museum 🏛

28

Elsa's Kopje 🏠

93

Grand Falls

North Kitui Nature Reserve

BS

Soda

Nakuru

Hyrax Hill ▲

51

11

60

Ol Joro Orok

B4

Ngobit Fishing Lodge

70

Naro Moru River Lodge

23

Naro Moru

Safari Club

Mount Kenya National Park (World Heritage Site)

Mt Kenya 5199m ▲

55

Eastern

50

Tharaka

18

Tseikuru

Lake Nakuru National Park

Lake Nakuru

38

Solio

22

Treetops

Treetops 🏠

The Ark 🏠

Mweiga

23

Nyeri

19

Karatina

Kerugoya

16

18

Chuka

38

Ishiara

27

48

Lake Elementeita

Gilgil

A104

24

Lake Naivasha

Naivasha

Lake Navasha Club 🏠

36

45

37

19

Kiriani

25

Sagana

A2

28

32

11

14

Murang'a

80

Kiambere Reservoir

Katse

10

Tula

B7

41

Nguni

40

Garissa

38°30'E

BT

Safariland Lodge 🏠

Longonot National Park

Hells Gate National Park

30

33

47

Mangu

61

Mwea National Reserve

Masinga Reservoir

A3

34

Mwingi

302

Copyright © Map Studio 2007

Thika

53

Nuu

1°00'S

Narok Nairobi Nairobi Kangondi Kangondi Kangondi Kitui

115 116 117 301 118 119

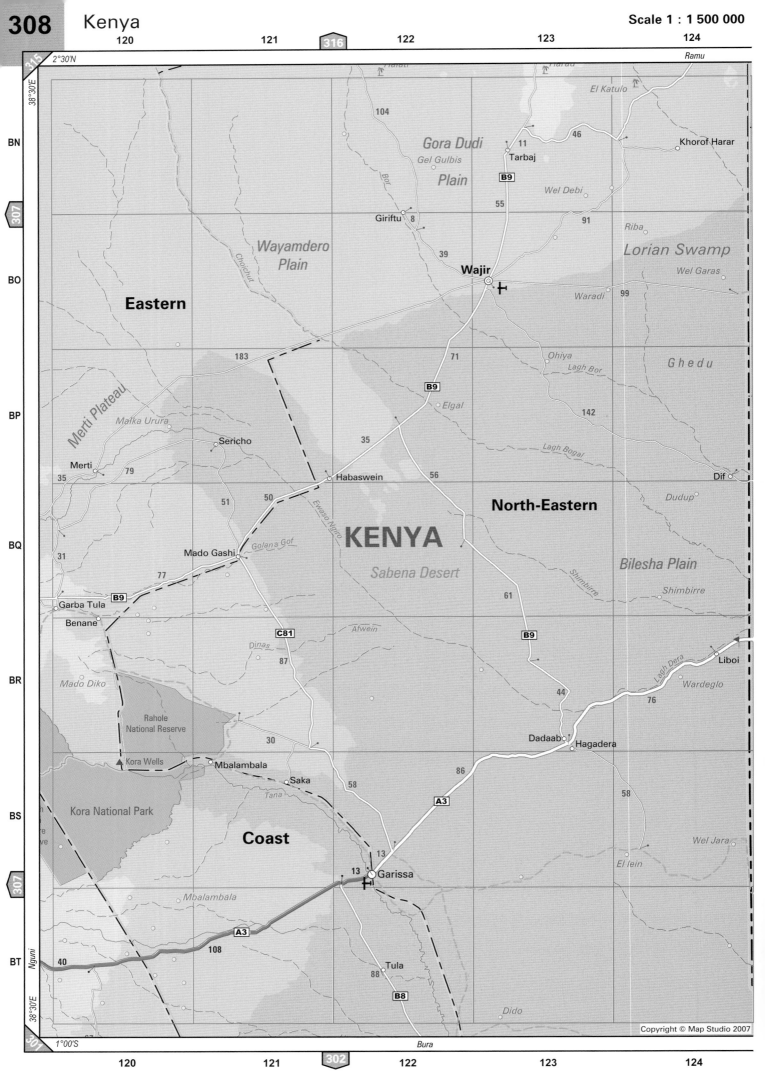

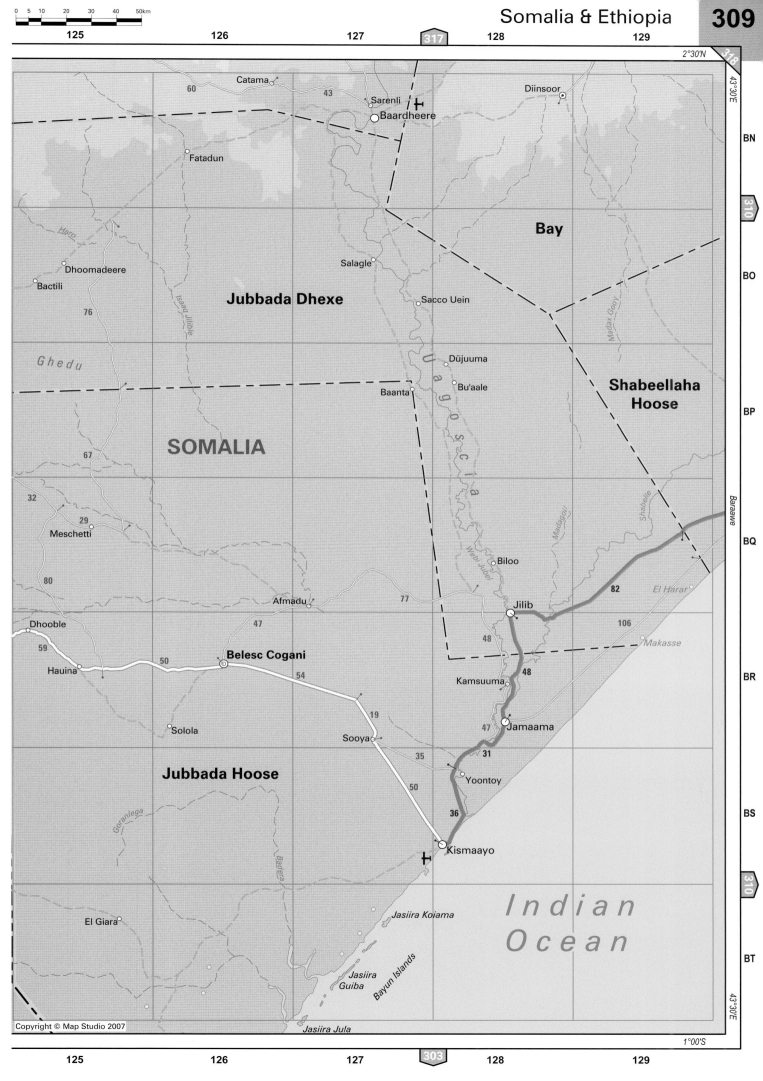

0 5 10 20 30 40 50km

125 126 127 **317** 128 129

2°30'N

43°30'E

BN

Catama

60 43

Sarenli

Baardheere

Diinsoor

Bay

BO

Fatadun

Dhoomadeere

Haro

Salagle

Sacco Uein

Bactili

76

Isaaq Jilible

Ghedu

Düjuuma

Madax Gooy

Jubbada Dhexe

Bu'aale

BP

U a g o s c i a

Shabeellaha Hoose

Baanta

SOMALIA

67

Barawe

32

Welbi Jubei

Madagoii

Shabelle

29

Meschetti

Biloo

El Harar

BQ

80

82

Afmadu

77

106

47

Jilib

Makasse

Dhooble

48

59

Belesc Cogani

50 54

48

BR

Hauina

Kamsuuma

19

48

Solola

Sooya

47

Jamaama

Jubbada Hoose

35

31

50

Yoontoy

BS

36

Goranlega

Kismaayo

Badera

310

El Giara

Jasiira Koiama

I n d i a n

BT

Jasiira Guiba

Bayun Islands

O c e a n

Jasiira Jula

1°00'S

43°30'E

125 126 127 **303** 128 129

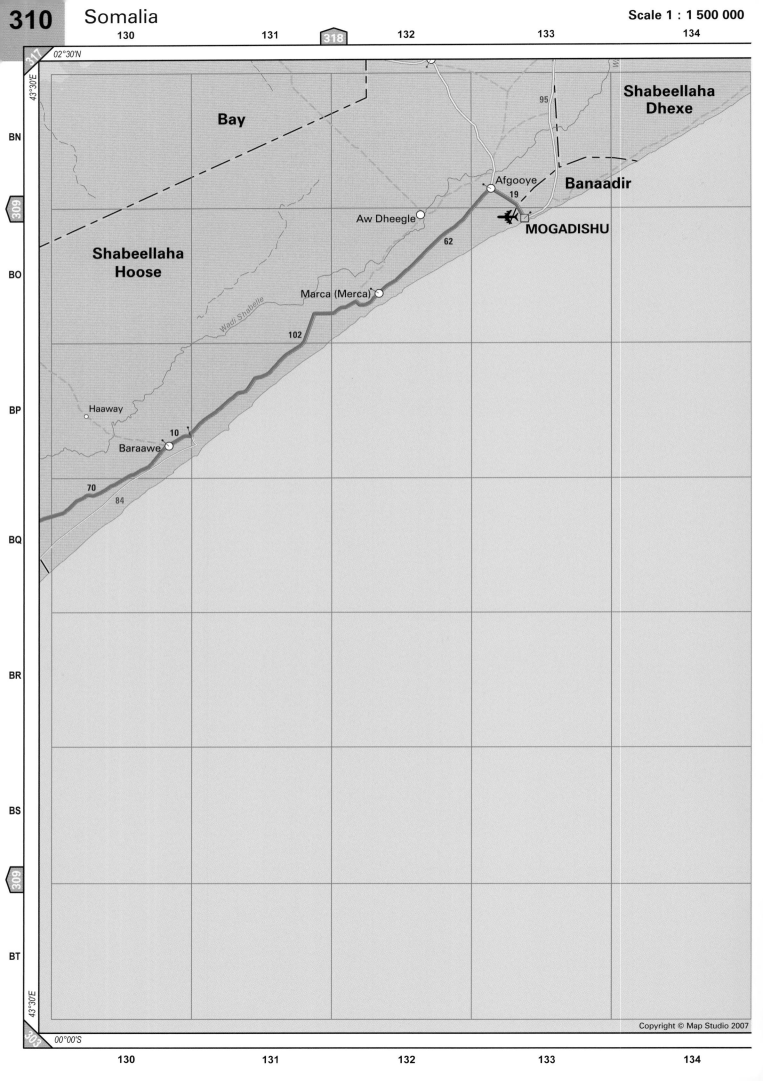

130   131   318   132   133   134

02°30'N
43°30'E
317
309

BN

Bay

Shabeellaha Dhexe

95

Afgooye
19
Banaadir

Aw Dheegle

MOGADISHU

BO

Shabeellaha Hoose

62

Marca (Merca)

102

Wadi Shabelle

BP

Haaway

10

Baraawe

70
84

BQ

BR

BS

309

BT

43°30'E

00°00'S
303

Copyright © Map Studio 2007

130   131   132   133   134

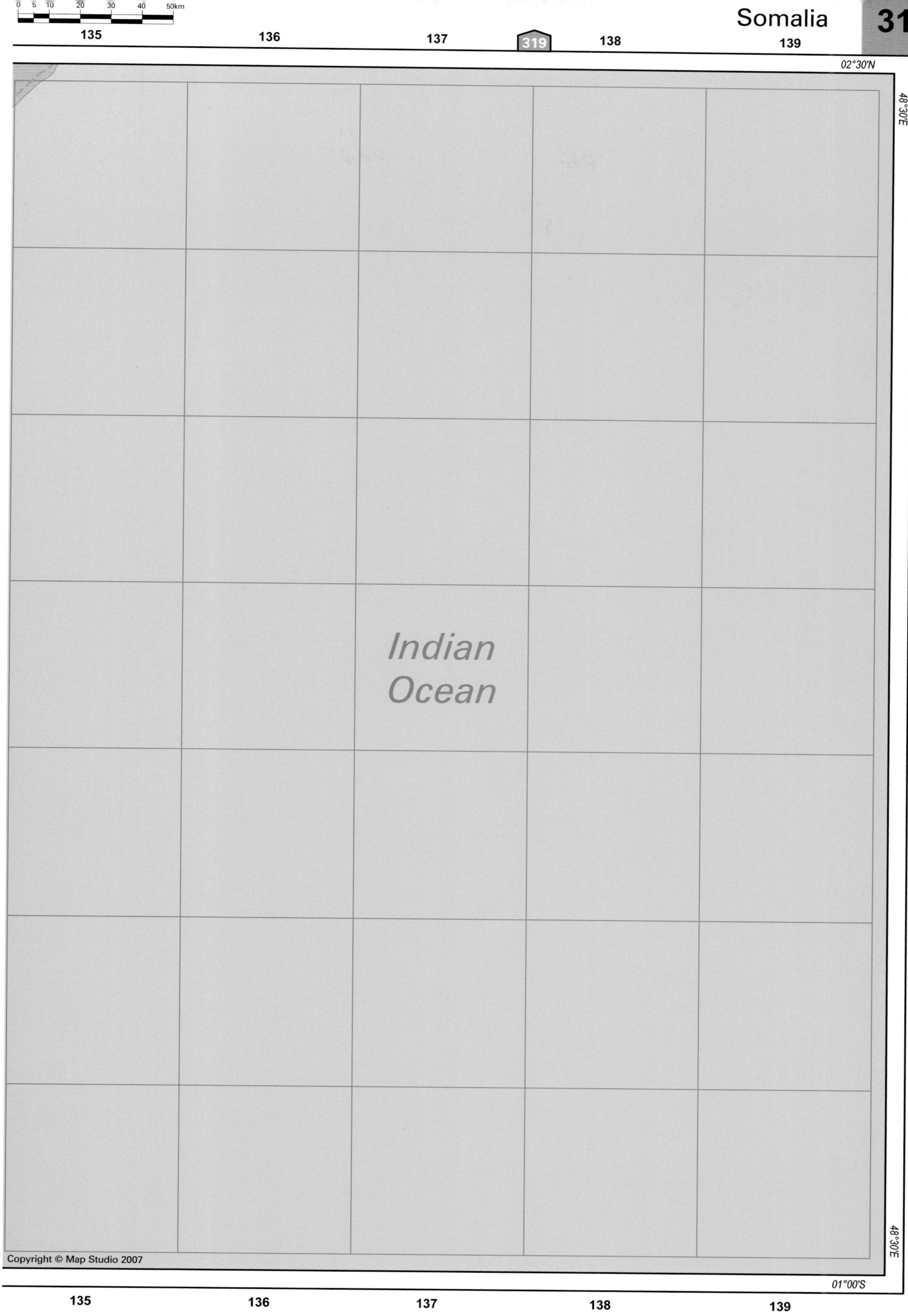
0 5 10 20 30 40 50km
135
136
137
319
138
139
02°30'N
48°30'E
BN
BO
BP
Indian
Ocean
BQ
BR
BS
BT
48°30'E
01°00'S
135
136
137
138
139

100   101   320   102   103   104

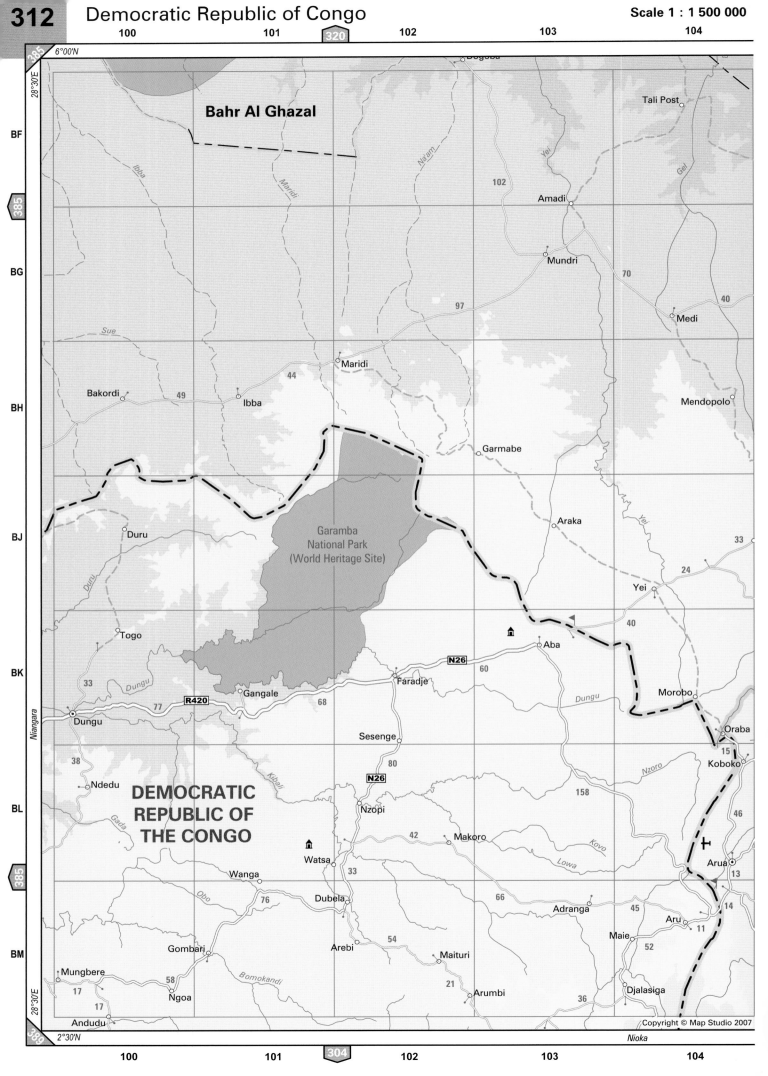

6°00'N

28°30'E

BF

Bahr Al Ghazal

Ibba

Maridi

Na'am

Yei

102

Gel

Tali Post

Amadi

BG

Mundri

70

Medi

40

Sue

97

BH

Bakordi

49

44

Maridi

Mendopolo

Ibba

Garmabe

BJ

Duru

Duru

Garamba
National Park
(World Heritage Site)

Araka

Yei

33

24

Yei

40

Togo

BK

33

Dungu

Gangale

R420

77

68

Faradje

N26

60

Aba

Dungu

Dungu

Morobo

Niangara

Dungu

Oraba

Sesenge

15

Koboko

38

Ndedu

80

N26

Kibali

Nzoro

BL

**DEMOCRATIC
REPUBLIC OF
THE CONGO**

Nzopi

158

46

42

Makoro

Kovo

Watsa

33

Lowa

Arua

Wanga

13

Obo

76

Dubela

66

Adranga

45

14

54

Aru

Gombari

Arebi

Maituri

Maie

52

BM

Mungbere

Bomokandi

21

Arumbi

36

Djalasiga

17

Ngoa

58

Andudu

17

2°30'N

Nioka

28°30'E

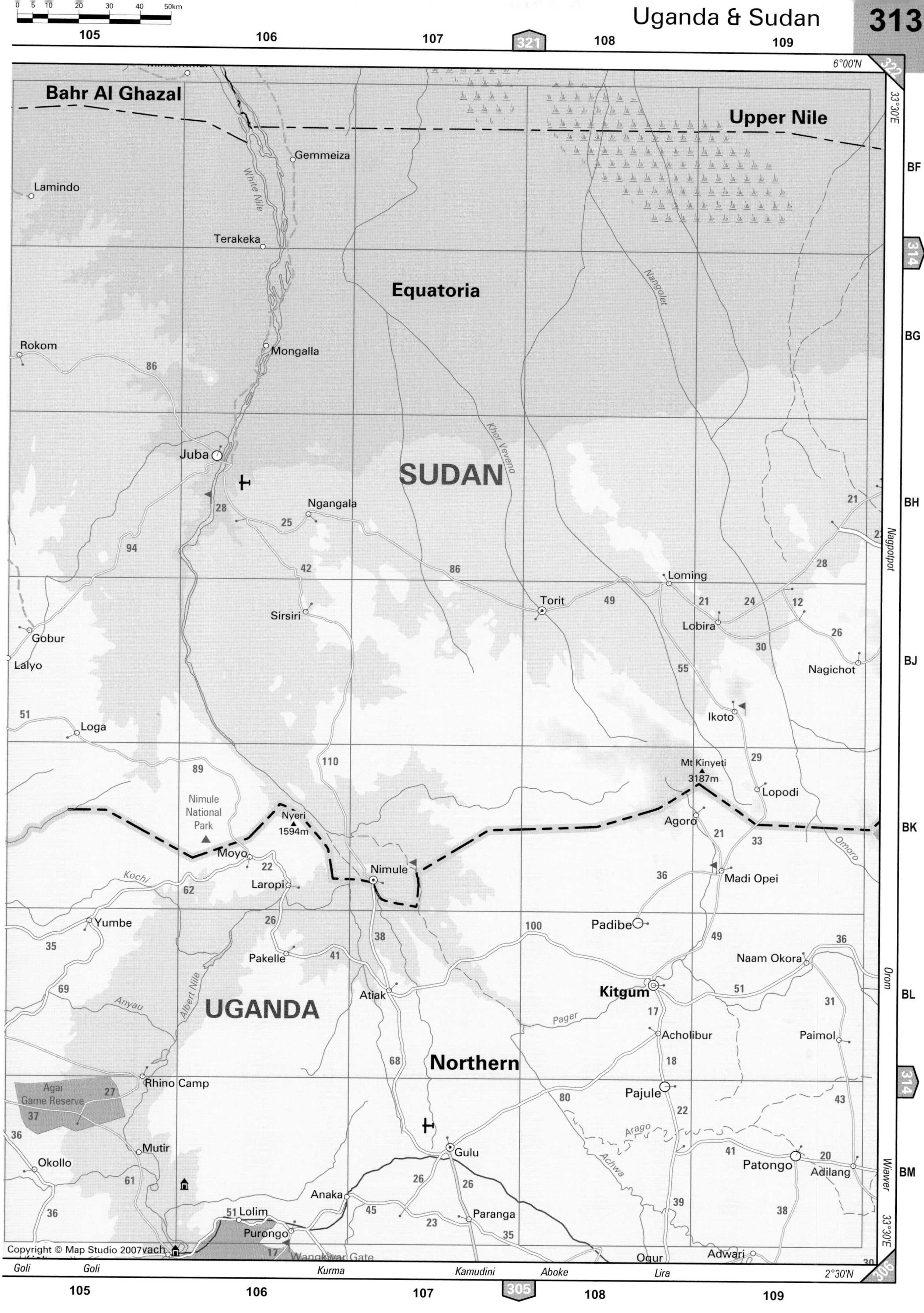

0 5 10   20   30   40   50km

6°00'N

Bahr Al Ghazal

Upper Nile

Lamindo

Gemmeiza

BF

Rokom

Terakeka

Equatoria

BG

Mongalla

86

Juba

SUDAN

28

Ngangala

BH

21

25

94

42

86

Sirsiri

Loming

28

Torit

49

21   24   12

Lobira

26

30

55

Nagichot

BJ

51

Loga

Ikoto

29

110

Mt Kinyeti
3187m

Lopodi

89

Nimule
National Park

Nyeri
1594m

Agoro

BK

Moyo

21   33

22

Nimule

36

Madi Opei

62

Laropi

Kochi

26

100

Padibe

49

36

Yumbe

38

41

Naam Okora

35

Pakelle

UGANDA

Atiak

Kitgum

51

31

69

Acholibur

Paimol

Anyau

17

18

Northern

BL

68

Pajule

43

Rhino Camp

80

22

**Agai
Game Reserve** 27

37

41

Patongo

20

Adilang

36

Mutir

Gulu

BM

Okollo

61

26   26

39

38

36

Anaka

45

Paranga

51 Lolim

23

35

Purongo

17

Wanokwar Gate

Goli   Goli   Kurma   Kamudini   Aboke   Lira   2°30'N

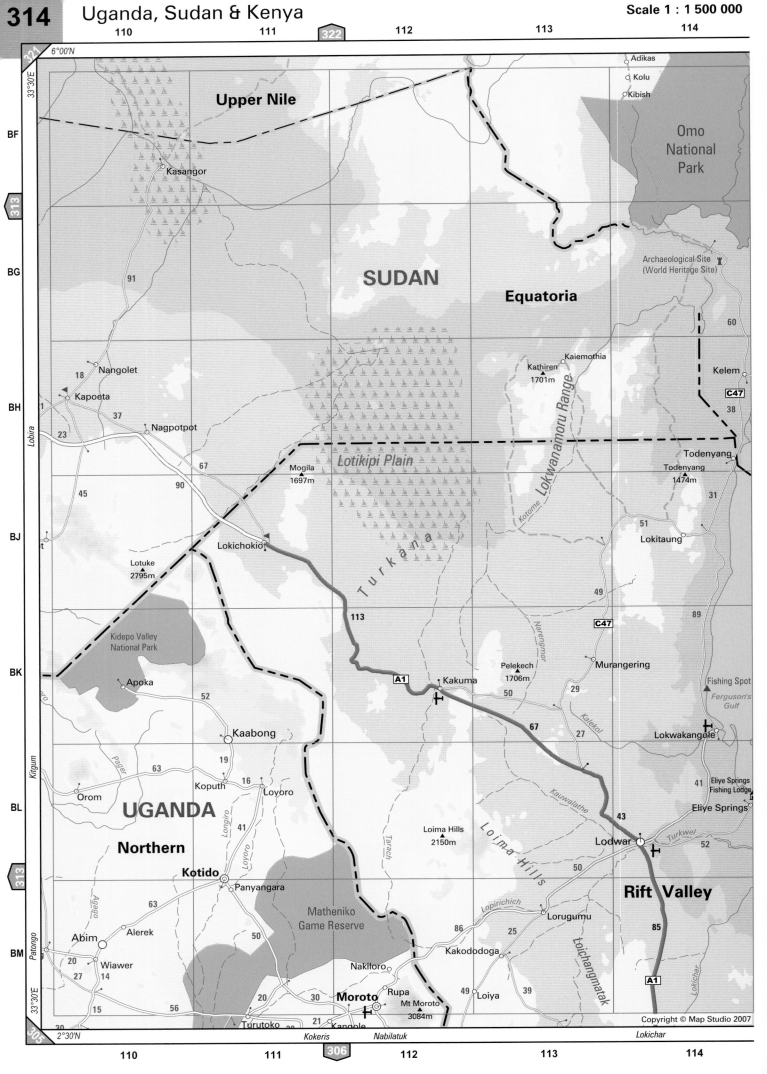

321

6°00'N

33°30'E

BF

Upper Nile

Kasangor

313

BG

SUDAN

Equatoria

Adikas

Kolu

Kibish

Omo
National
Park

Archaeological Site
(World Heritage Site)

60

Nangolet

18

Kapoeta

1

37

23

Nagpotpot

67

90

45

Mogila
1697m

Lotikipi Plain

Kathiren
1701m

Kaiemothia

Kelem

C47

38

Todenyang

Todenyang
1474m

31

BH

Lobira

BJ

t

Lotuke
2795m

Lokichokio

Turkana

51

Lokitaung

49

89

113

Kidepo Valley
National Park

Apoka

52

Kaabong

19

63

Koputh

16

Loyoro

Orom

41

Narengmor

Pelekech
1706m

Kalekol

C47

Murangering

29

Fishing Spot

Ferguson's
Gulf

A1

Kakuma

50

67

27

Lokwakangole

41

Eliye Springs
Fishing Lodge

Eliye Springs

BK

Kitgum

Pager

Longiro

Loyoro

UGANDA

Northern

Kotido

Panyangara

63

Agago

Matheniko
Game Reserve

Tarach

Loima Hills
2150m

Loima Hills

Kauwalathe

Lopirichich

Lorugumu

25

43

Lodwar

Turkwel

52

50

Rift Valley

85

313

BL

Abim

Alerek

20

27

14

Wiawer

Patongo

50

Nakiloro

86

Kakododoga

Toichangmatak

Lokichar

A1

BM

33°30'E

15

30

56

20

30

21

Turutoko

Kangole

Moroto

Rupa

Mt Moroto
3084m

49

Loiya

39

305

2°30'N

Kokeris

Nabilatuk

Lokichar

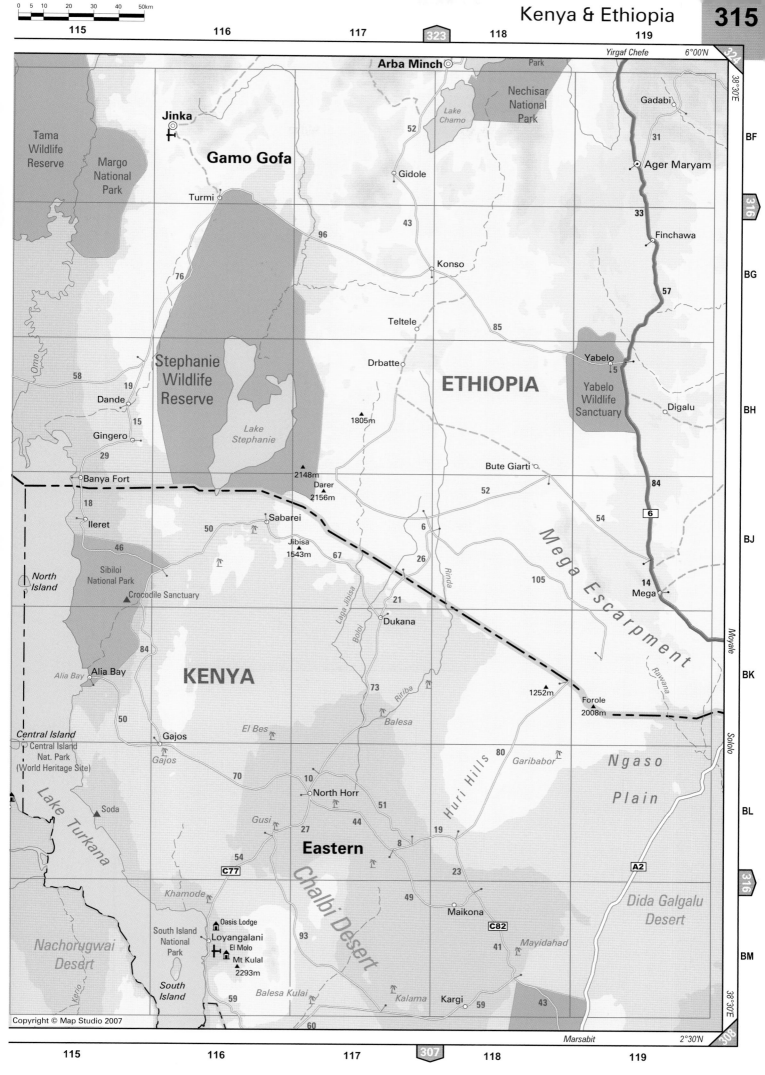

0 5 10   20   30   40   50km

Yirgaf Chefe   6°00'N   38°30'E

Arba Minch

Park

Nechisar
National
Park

Gadabi

BF

31

Jinka

Lake
Chamo

52

Ager Maryam

Tama
Wildlife
Reserve

Margo
National
Park

Gamo Gofa

Gidole

33

316

Turmi

43

Finchawa

BG

96

57

76

Konso

ETHIOPIA

58

Stephanie
Wildlife
Reserve

Teltele

85

Yabelo

BH

19

Drbatte

15

Dande

Yabelo
Wildlife
Sanctuary

Digalu

15

Lake
Stephanie

1805m

Gingero

29

Bute Giarti

84

Banya Fort

2148m

52

6

BJ

18

Darer
2156m

54

Ileret

50

Sabarei

6

Mega Escarpment

46

Jibisa
1543m

67

26

14

North
Island

Sibiloi
National Park

Laga Jibisa

21

105

Mega

Moyale

Crocodile Sanctuary

Bolol

Dukana

Rinda

BK

84

1252m

Rawana

KENYA

73

Forole
2008m

Alia Bay

Ririba

Sololo

Alia Bay

50

El Bes

Balesa

Central Island

Gajos

Ngaso

Central Island
Nat. Park
(World Heritage Site)

Gajos

80

Plain

Garibabor

BL

70

10

Soda

Eastern

North Horr

51

Huri Hills

19

Lake Turkana

Gusi

44

8

23

A2

27

49

316

54

C77

Maikona

Dida Galgalu
Desert

Khamode

93

C82

Oasis Lodge

41

Mayidahad

Nachorugwai
Desert

South Island
National Park

Loyangalani
El Molo

Mt Kulal
2293m

BM

South
Island

Balesa Kulai

Kalama

Kargi

59

43

59

60

Marsabit   2°30'N   38°30'E

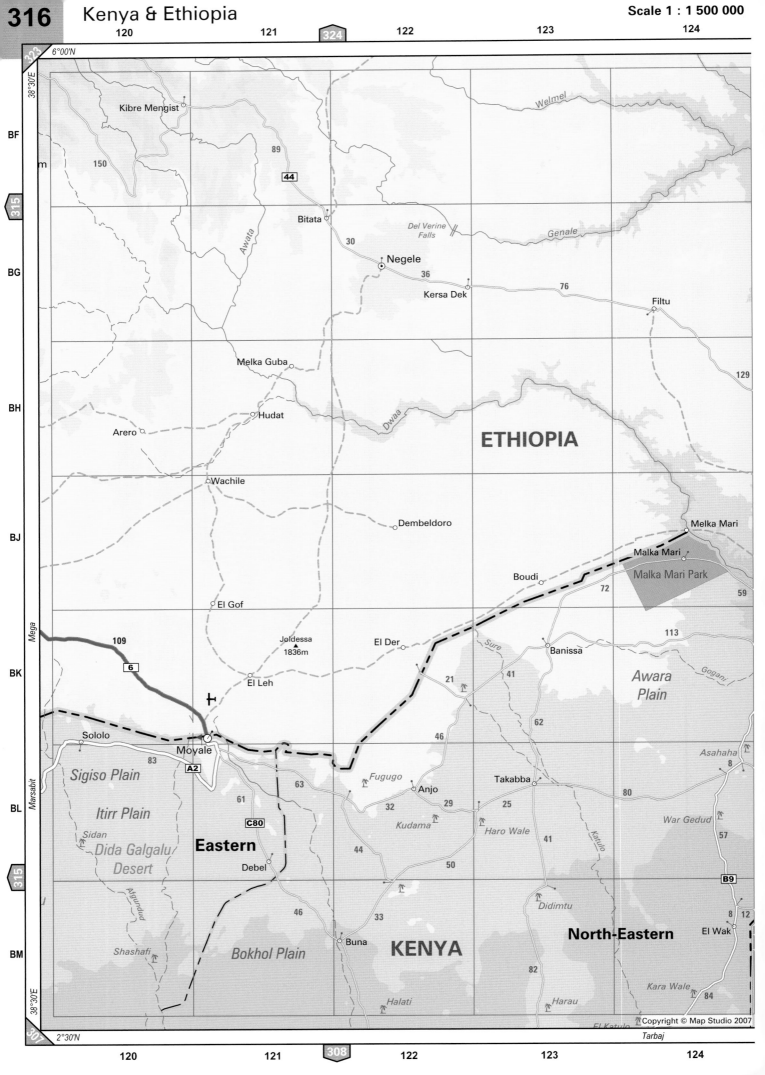

6°00'N

38°30'E

120   121   324   122   123   124

BF

150

Kibre Mengist

89

44

Bitata

30

BG

Negele

36

Kersa Dek

76

Filtu

Melka Guba

129

BH

Dwaa

Hudat

Arero

ETHIOPIA

Genale

Del Verine Falls

Welmel

Awata

Wachile

Dembeldoro

Melka Mari

BJ

Malka Mari

Malka Mari Park

Boudi

72

59

El Gof

Sure

113

Goganu

Mega

109

Joldessa
1836m

El Der

Banissa

6

21

41

Awara Plain

BK

El Leh

62

46

Marsabit

Sololo

83

Moyale

A2

61

63

Fugugo

Anjo

Takabba

Asahaha

80

8

Sigiso Plain

32

29

25

War Gedud

57

BL

Itirr Plain

C80

Kudama

Haro Wale

41

Sidan

44

50

B9

Dida Galgalu Desert

Eastern

Debel

46

33

Didimtu

8   12

Afgundud

Didimtu

El Wak

BM

Shashafi

Bokhol Plain

Buna

KENYA

North-Eastern

82

84

Halati

Harau

Kara Wale

El Katulo

2°30'N

Tarbaj

120   121   308   122   123   124

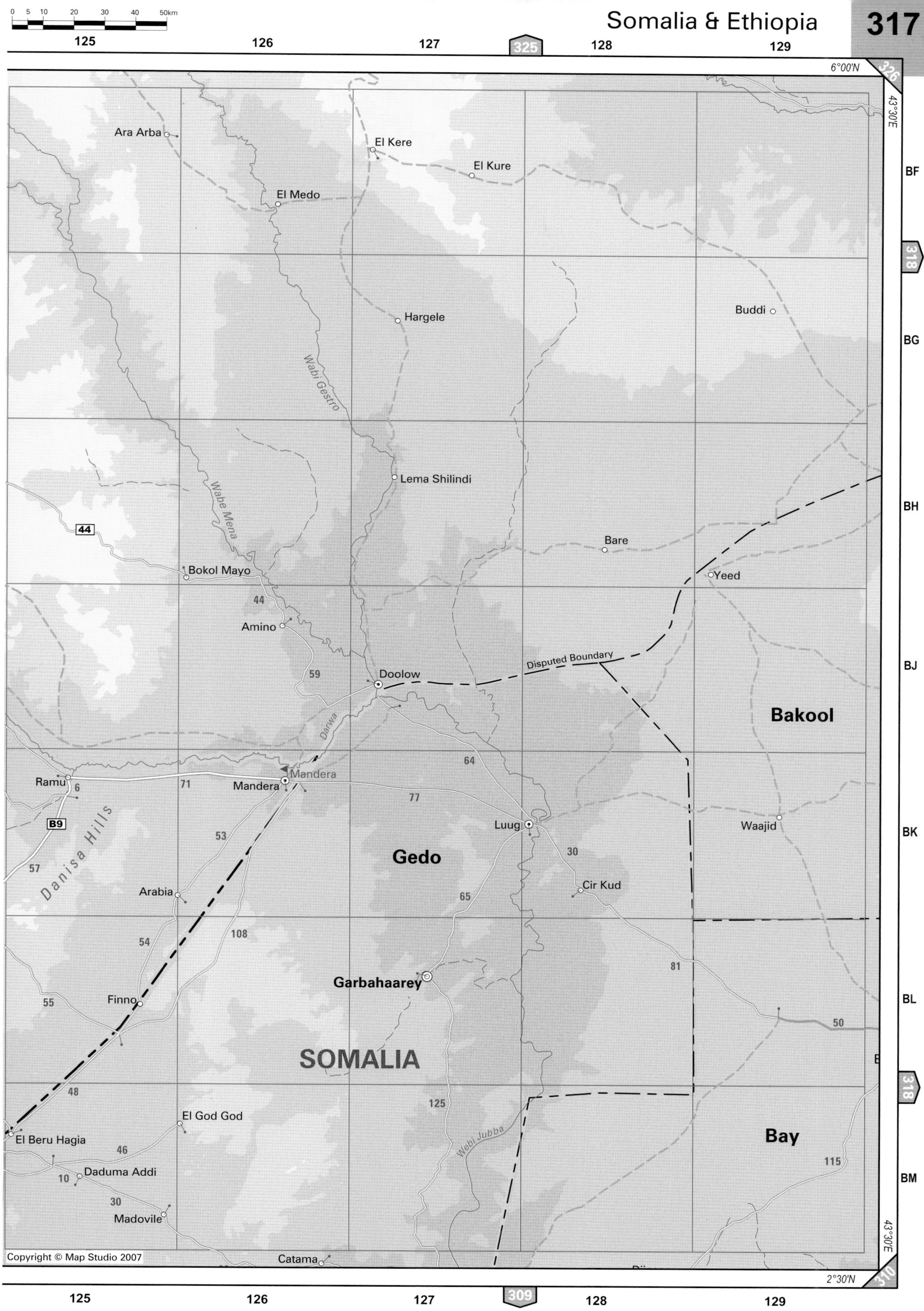

0 5 10   20   30   40   50km

125   126   127   325   128   129

6°00'N
326
43°30'E

Ara Arba ○

El Kere ○

El Kure ○

BF

El Medo ○

Hargele ○

Buddi ○

318

BG

Wabi Gestro

Lema Shilindi ○

BH

Wabe Mena

Bare ○

44

Yeed ○

Bokol Mayo ○

44

Amino ○

Disputed Boundary

BJ

59

Doolow ⊙

Bakool

Dariwa

64

Mandera ◄

Luug ⊙

Ramu ○ 6

71   Mandera ○

77

Waajid ○

BK

B9

53

Gedo

30

57 *Danisa Hills*

Arabia ○

Cir Kud ○

65

54   108

81

55   Finno ○

Garbahaarey ⊙

BL

48

50

SOMALIA

El God God ○

125

Webi Jubba

Bay

El Beru Hagia ○

46

115

BM

Daduma Addi ○

10

30

Madovile ○

43°30'E

Catama ○

2°30'N
310

125   126   127   309   128   129

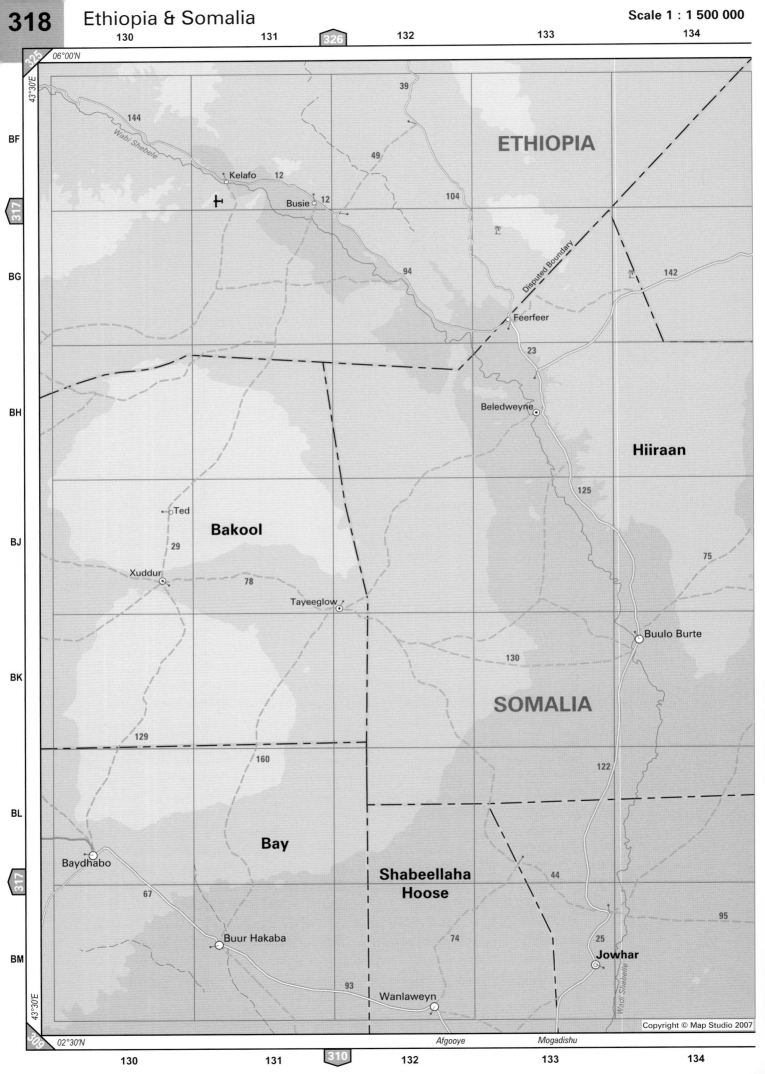

130 131 326 132 133 134

06°00'N
43°30'E
325
317

BF
BG
BH
BJ
BK
BL
BM

144
Wabi Shebele
Kelafo 12
Busie 12
39
49
104
ETHIOPIA
Disputed Boundary
142
94
Feerfeer
23
Beledweyne
Hiiraan
125
Ted
Bakool
29
Xuddur
78
Tayeeglow
75
Buulo Burte
130
SOMALIA
129
160
122
Bay
Shabeellaha
Hoose
Baydhabo
67
44
Buur Hakaba
74
95
25
Jowhar
93
Wanlaweyn
Wadi Shabelle

317
309
02°30'N
43°30'E

130 131 310 132 133 134

Afgooye Mogadishu

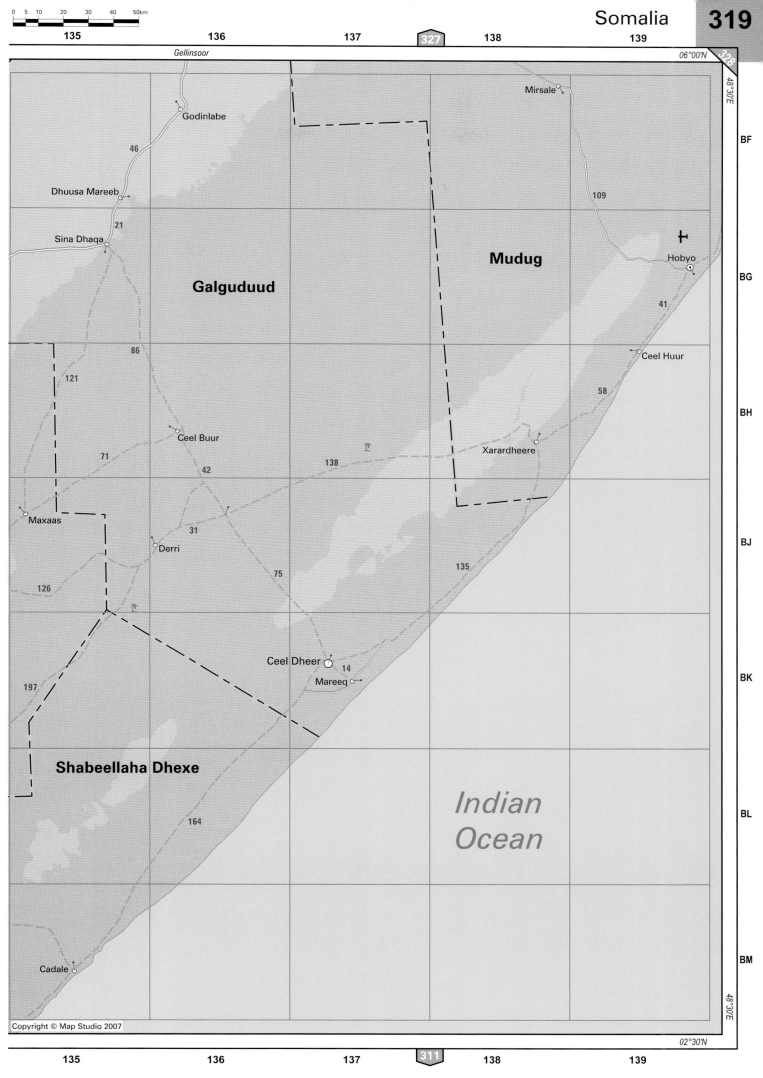

0 5 10 20 30 40 50km

135   136   137   327   138   139

Gellinsoor

06°00'N

48°30'E

328

Mirsale

BF

Godinlabe

46

109

Dhuusa Mareeb

21

Sina Dhaqa

Hobyo

BG

Mudug

Galguduud

41

86

Ceel Huur

BH

121

58

71

Ceel Buur

Xarardheere

42

138

Maxaas

BJ

31

Derri

75

126

135

BK

Ceel Dheer   14

197

Mareeq

Shabeellaha Dhexe

BL

Indian
Ocean

164

BM

Cadale

48°30'E

02°30'N

135   136   137   311   138   139

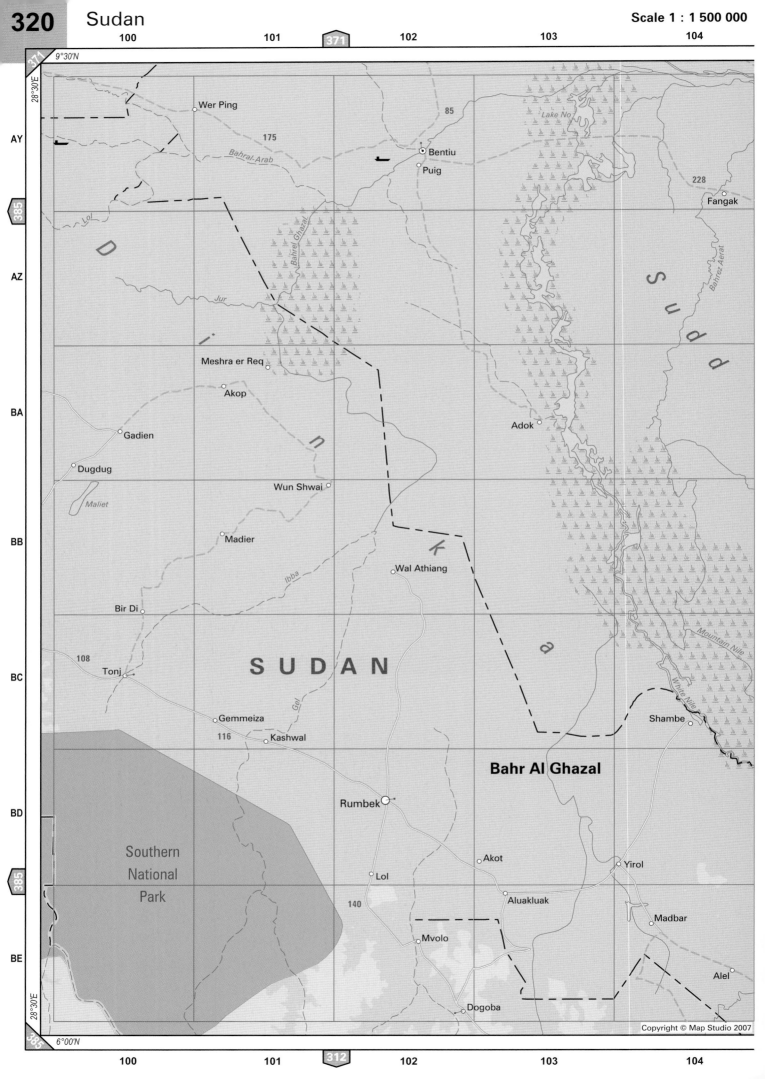

Map labels

- 100
- 101
- 371
- 102
- 103
- 104

- 9°30'N
- 28°30'E
- Wer Ping
- 175
- 85
- Lake No
- Bentiu
- Puig
- 228
- Fangak
- AY
- 385
- Bahral-Arab
- Lol
- D
- Bahrel Ghazal
- S
- u
- d
- d
- Bahrez Aerat
- AZ
- Jur
- i
- Meshra er Req
- n
- Akop
- BA
- Gadien
- Adok
- Dugdug
- Maliet
- Wun Shwai
- BB
- Madier
- Ibba
- Wal Athiang
- k
- Bir Di
- Mountain Nile
- 108
- Tonj
- a
- BC
- Gel
- SUDAN
- White Nile
- Shambe
- Gemmeiza
- 116
- Kashwal
- **Bahr Al Ghazal**
- Rumbek
- BD
- Southern National Park
- Akot
- Yirol
- 385
- Lol
- 140
- Aluakluak
- Madbar
- Mvolo
- BE
- Alel
- 28°30'E
- Dogoba
- Copyright © Map Studio 2007
- 6°00'N
- 385
- 100
- 101
- 312
- 102
- 103
- 104

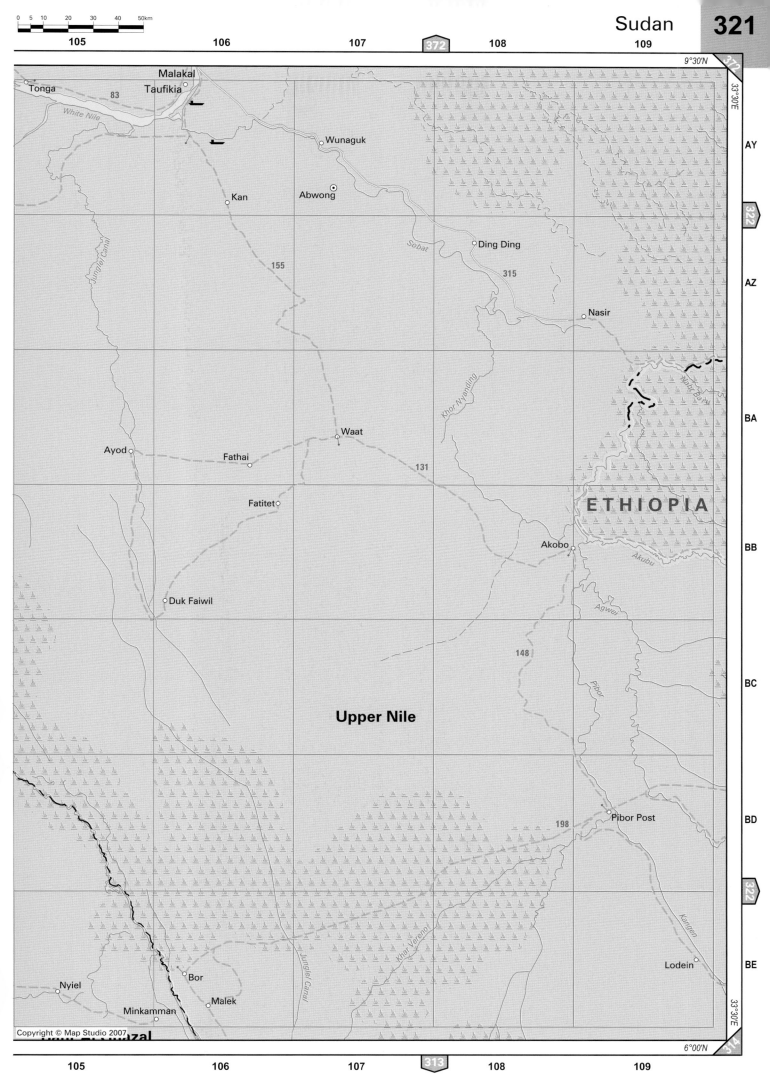

0 5 10 20 30 40 50km

105 106 372 107 108 109

9°30'N

372

33°30'E

AY

Tonga
Malakal
Taufikia
White Nile
83

Wunaguk

Kan
Abwong

Jungle Canal

322

AZ

Sobat
Ding Ding
155
315

Nasir

Malakal

BA

Khor Nyanding

Waat
131

ETHIOPIA

Ayod
Fathai

Fatitet

BB

Akobo
Akubu

Agwei

Duk Faiwil

148

BC

Pibor

Upper Nile

BD

198
Pibor Post

322

BE

Khor Verenor

Jungle Canal

Kangen

Lodein

Nyiel
Bor

Malek

Minkamman

Copyright © Map Studio 2007

33°30'E

6°00'N

314

313

105 106 107 108 109

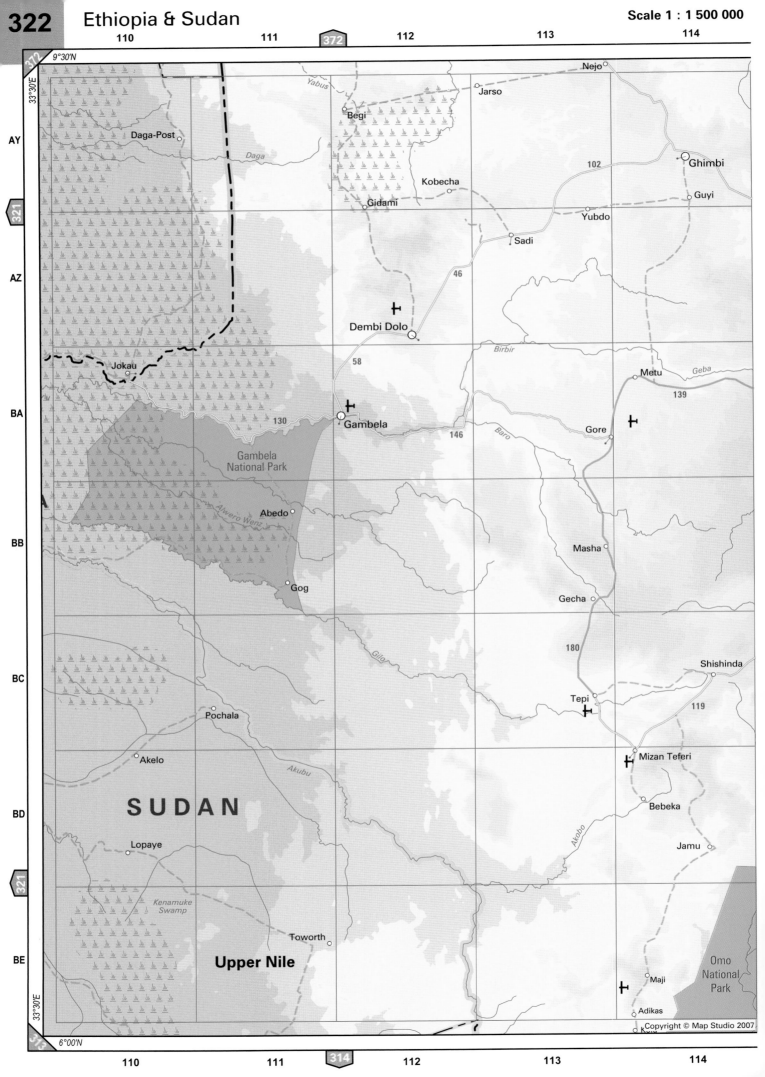

AY

AZ

BA

BB

BC

BD

BE

110

111

372

112

113

114

9°30'N

33°30'E

6°00'N

33°30'E

321

321

314

372

314

S U D A N

Upper Nile

Gambela
National Park

Omo
National
Park

Kenamuke
Swamp

Daga-Post

Jokau

Begi

Jarso

Nejo

Kobecha

Gidami

Ghimbi

Guyi

102

Yubdo

Sadi

46

Dembi Dolo

58

Birbir

Metu

Geba

139

Gore

Gambela

130

146

Baro

Abedo

Alwero Wenz

Gog

Masha

Gecha

Gilo

180

Shishinda

Tepi

119

Pochala

Akobu

Mizan Teferi

Akelo

Bebeka

Jamu

Akobo

Lopaye

Toworth

Maji

Adikas

Daga

Yabus

Copyright © Map Studio 2007

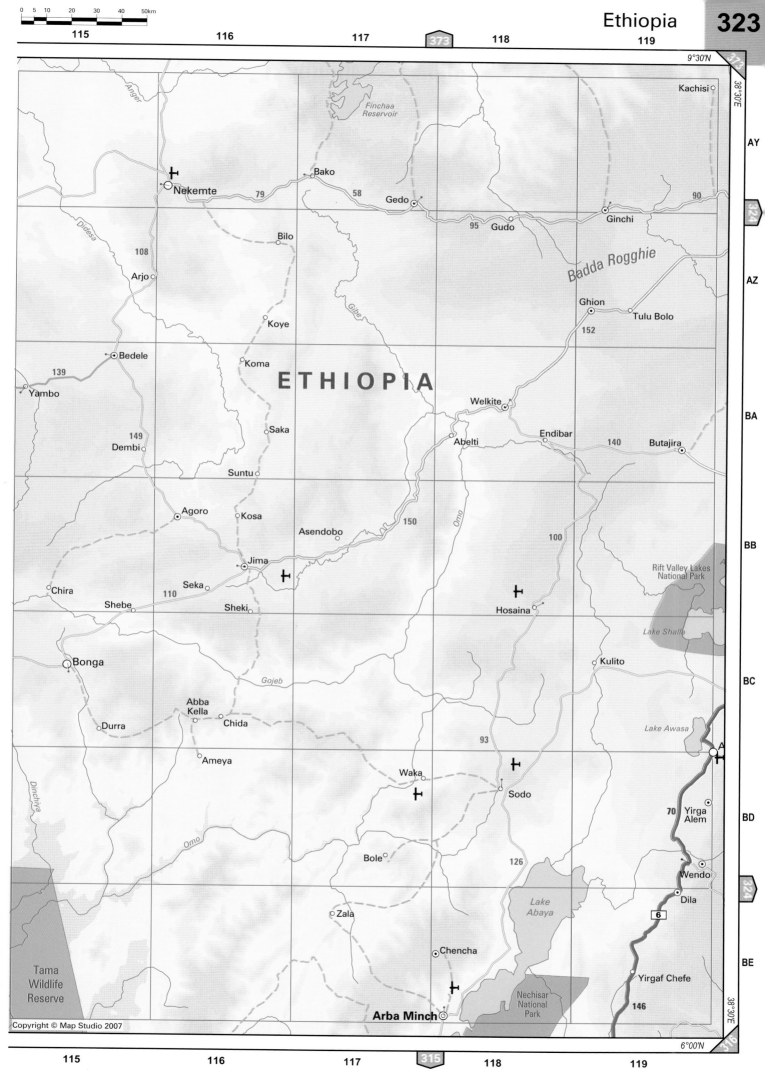

0 5 10 20 30 40 50km

9°30'N

38°30'E

373

AY

324

Kachisi

Anger

Finchaa
Reservoir

Bako

Nekemte   79   58   Gedo

90

Didesa

Gudo   95   Ginchi

AZ

Bilo

108

Badda Rogghie

Arjo

Ghion

Koye

Tulu Bolo

152

Gibe

Bedele

139

Koma

E T H I O P I A

Welkite

BA

Yambo

Abelti

Endibar

140

Butajira

Saka

149

Dembi

Suntu

Agoro

Kosa

Asendobo

150

Omo

100

BB

Jima

Rift Valley Lakes
National Park

Chira

110

Seka

Lake Shalla

Shebe

Sheki

Hosaina

Bonga

Gojeb

Kulito

BC

Abba
Kella

Chida

Lake Awasa

Durra

A

Ameya

93

Waka

Sodo

BD

Dinchiya

70   Yirga
Alem

Omo

Bole

126

Wendo

Zala

Dila

324

6

Chencha

*Lake
Abaya*

Tama
Wildlife
Reserve

BE

Yirgaf Chefe

Nechisar
National
Park

146

Arba Minch

38°30'E

6°00'N

316

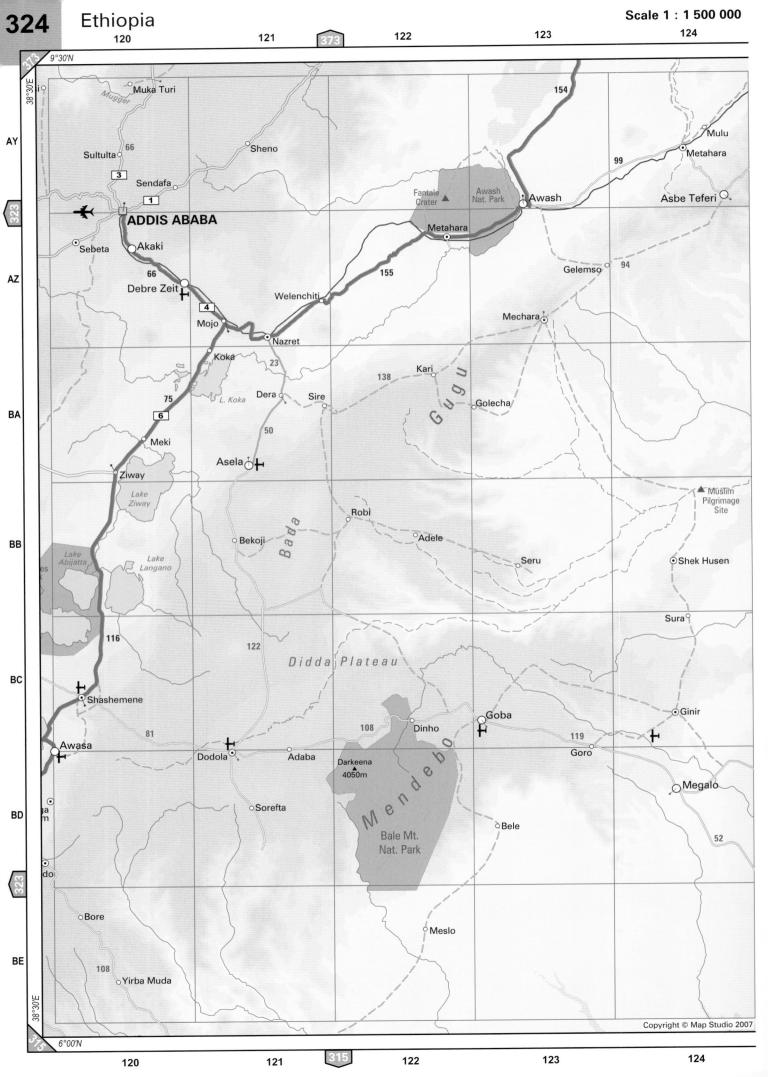

9°30'N

38°30'E

AY

AZ

BA

BB

BC

BD

BE

6°00'N

38°30'E

120   121   373   122   123   124

Muka Turi

Mugger

Sheno

154

Mulu

Metahara

Sultulta   66

3

Sendafa

1

99

Asbe Teferi

Fantale Crater

Awash Nat. Park

Awash

ADDIS ABABA

Metahara

Sebeta

Akaki

66

Debre Zeit

4

Welenchiti

155

Gelemso   94

Mojo

Nazret

Mechara

Koka

23

Kari

G u g u

L. Koka

138

Golecha

75

6

Dera

Sire

50

Meki

Asela

Muslim Pilgrimage Site

Ziway

Robi

Lake Ziway

Bekoji

Adele

B a d a

Lake Abijatta

Lake Langano

Seru

Shek Husen

116

Sura

122

D i d d a   P l a t e a u

BC

Shashemene

Goba

Ginir

Awasa

81

Dinho

108

119

Dodola

Adaba

Goro

Darkeena 4050m

M e n d e b o

Megalo

Sorefta

52

Bele

Bale Mt. Nat. Park

Bore

Meslo

108

Yirba Muda

120   121   315   122   123   124

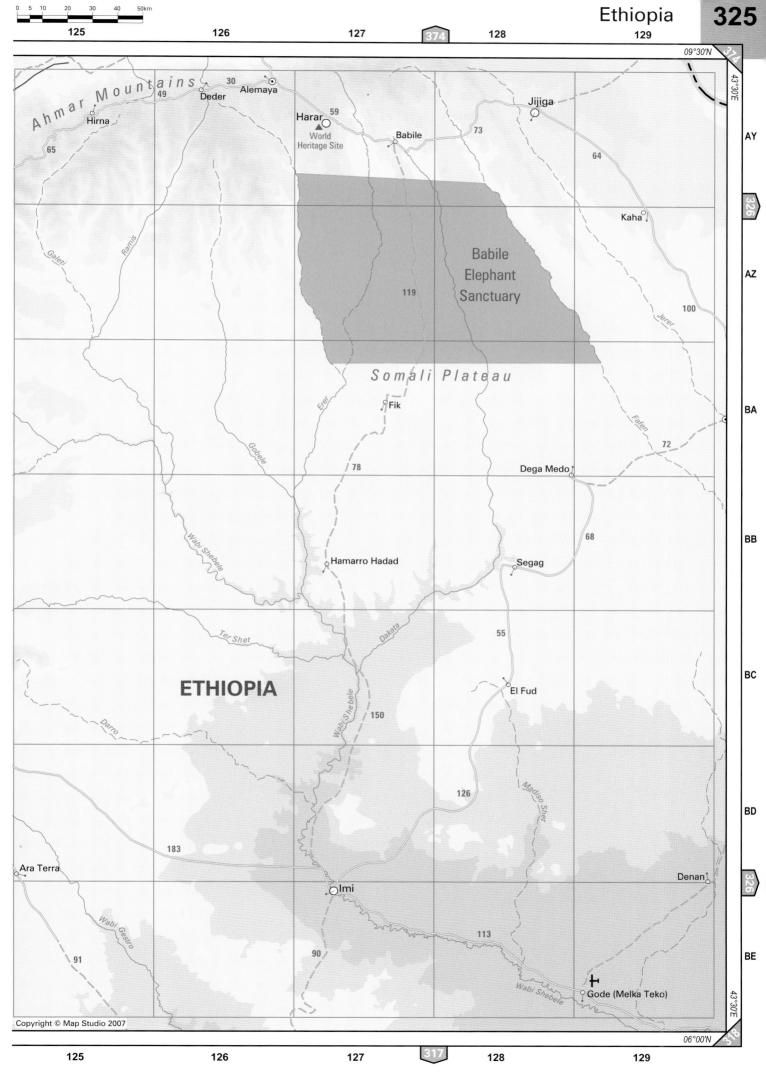

0 5 10 20 30 40 50km

09°30'N

43°30'E

AY

AZ

BA

BB

BC

BD

326

BE

43°30'E

Ahmar Mountains

Hirna

65

Galeti

Ramis

Deder

49

30

Alemaya

Harar
World
Heritage Site

59

Babile

78

Erer

Gobele

Fik

Wabi Shebele

Hamarro Hadad

Ter Shet

ETHIOPIA

Darro

Dakata

Wabi Shebele

150

183

Ara Terra

Wabi Gestro

91

90

Imi

113

Wabi Shebele

Jijiga

73

64

100

Kaha

Babile
Elephant
Sanctuary

119

Somali Plateau

Jerer

Fafen

72

Dega Medo

68

Segag

55

El Fud

126

Madiso Sher

Denan

Gode (Melka Teko)

06°00'N

374

371

326

317

318

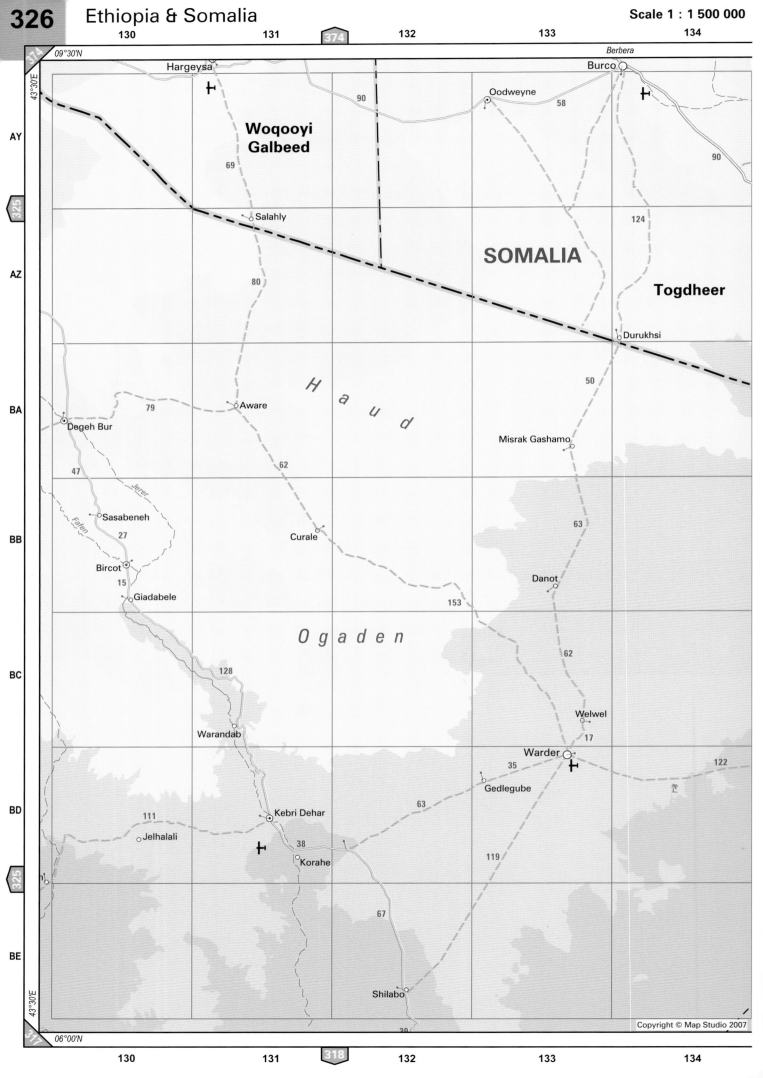

09°30'N

43°30E

Hargeysa

Berbera

Burco

90

Oodweyne

58

**Woqooyi
Galbeed**

69

AY

124

SOMALIA

Salahly

AZ

80

Togdheer

Durukhsi

50

BA

79

Aware

H a u d

Degeh Bur

Misrak Gashamo

47

62

Jerer

Sasabeneh

63

Faren

27

Curale

BB

Bircot

15

Danot

Giadabele

153

O g a d e n

62

BC

128

Welwel

17

Warandab

Warder

122

35

Gedlegube

BD

111

63

Jelhalali

Kebri Dehar

119

38

Korahe

67

BE

43°30'E

Shilabo

30

06°00'N

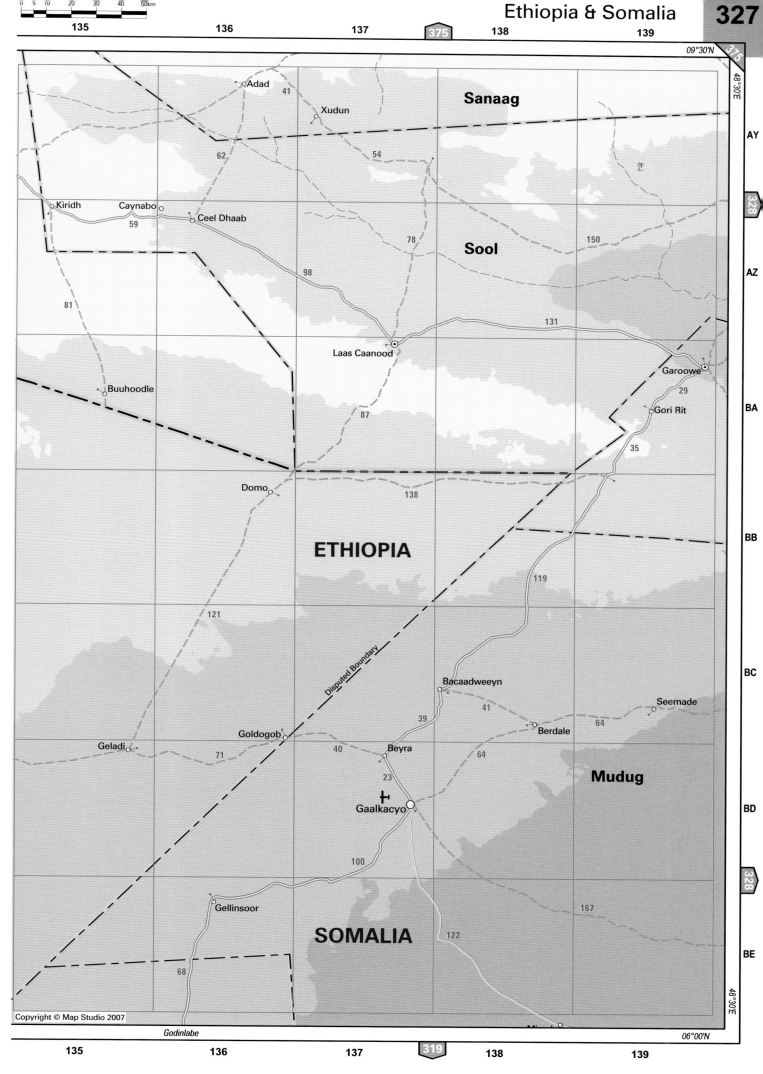

0 5 10 20 30 40 50km

135   136   137   375   138   139

09°30'N
48°30'E

Adad 41

Xudun

Sanaag

62

54

Kiridh

Caynabo

59   Ceel Dhaab

78

150

Sool

98

81

131

Laas Caanood

Garoowe

29

Buuhoodle

Gori Rit

87

35

Domo

138

ETHIOPIA

BB

119

121

Disputed Boundary

Bacaadweeyn

Seemade

41

39

Berdale

64

Geladi

Goldogob

71

40   Beyra

64

Mudug

23

Gaalkacyo

100

167

Gellinsoor

SOMALIA

122

68

Copyright © Map Studio 2007

Godinlabe

06°00'N
48°30'E

135   136   137   319   138   139

AY

328

AZ

BA

BC

BD

328

BE

375

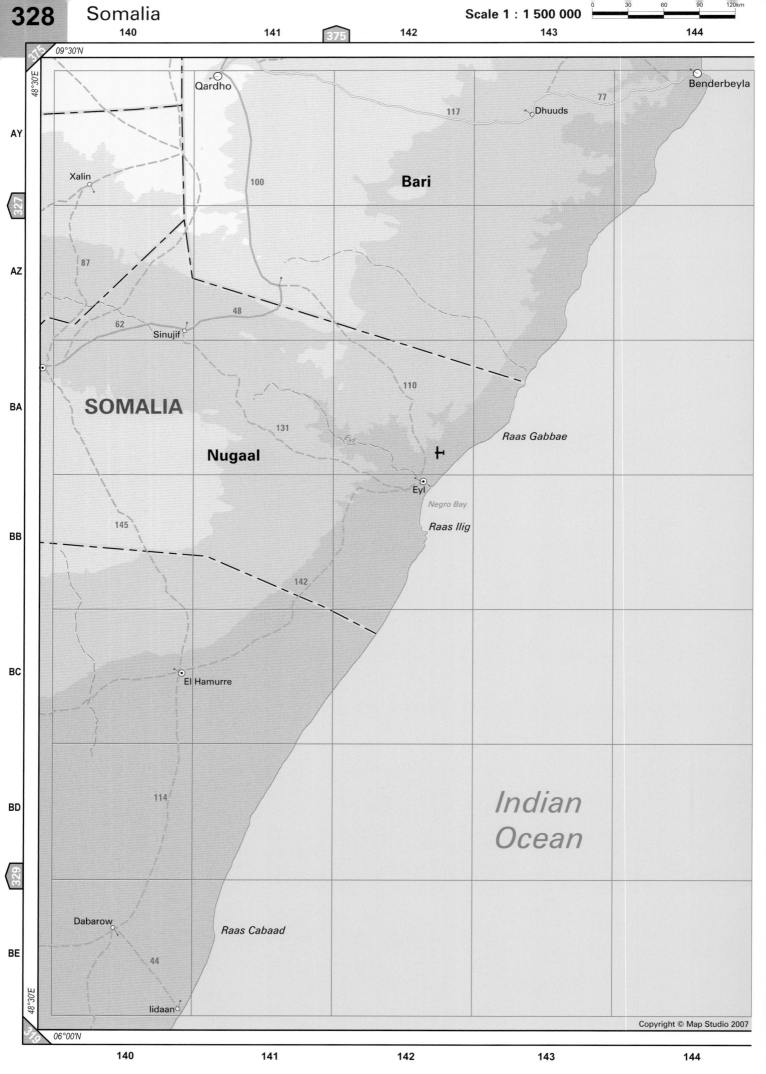

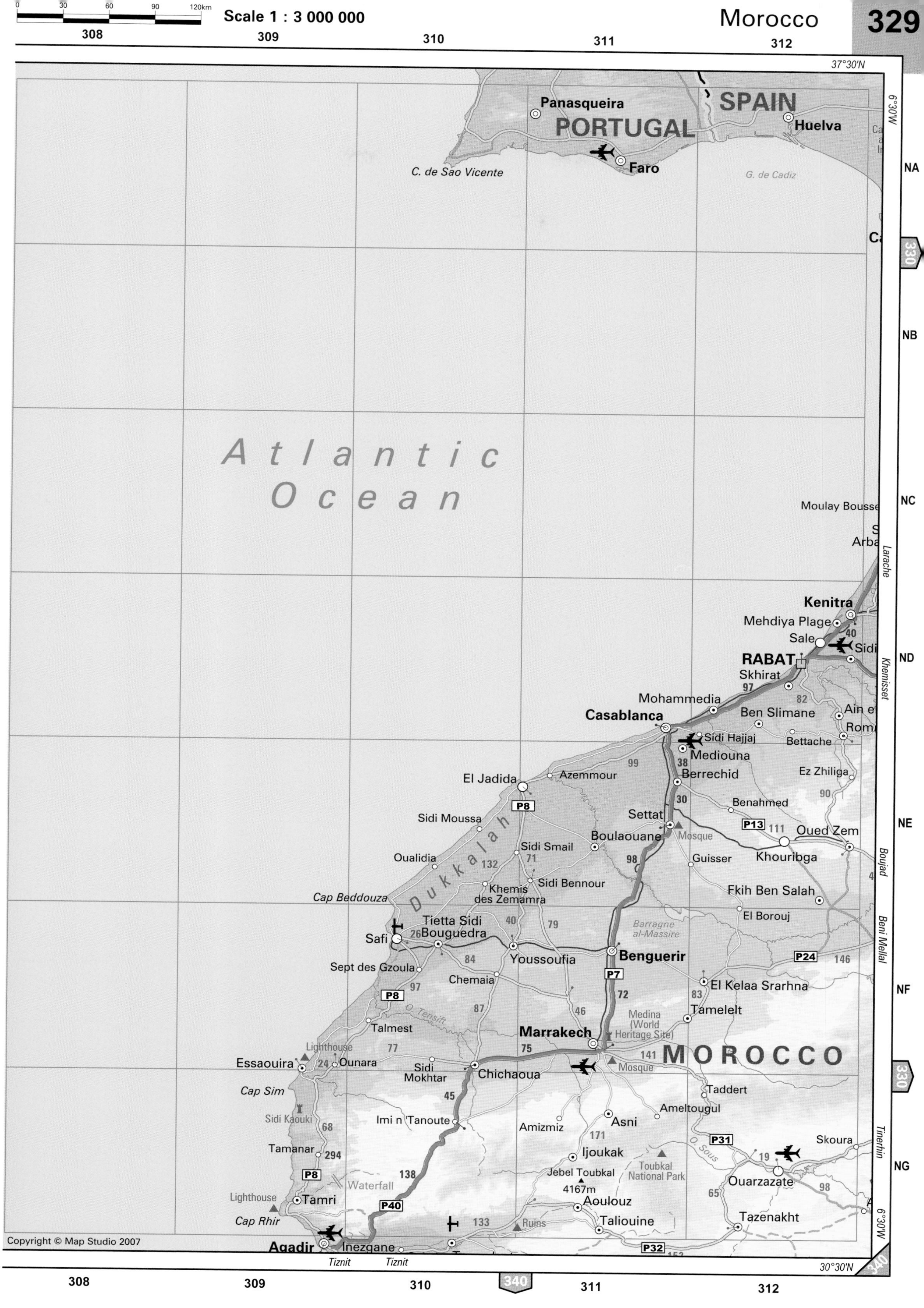

0 30 60 90 120km

308   309   310   311   312

37°30'N

6°30'W

NA

Panasqueira

SPAIN

PORTUGAL

Huelva

C. de Sao Vicente

Faro

G. de Cadiz

C

330

NB

Atlantic
Ocean

NC

Moulay Bousse

S
Arba

Larache

Kenitra

Mehdiya Plage

Sale

40

RABAT

Sidi

Khemisset

ND

Skhirat

97

82

Mohammedia

Ben Slimane

Ain e
Rom

Casablanca

Sidi Hajjaj

Bettache

Medphouna

Ez Zhiliga

Azemmour

99

38

Berrechid

El Jadida

30

Benahmed

90

P8

Settat

P13

111

Sidi Moussa

Boulaouane

Mosque

Oued Zem

NE

Oualidia

132

Sidi Smail

71

98

Guisser

Khouribga

Khemis
des Zemamra

Sidi Bennour

Fkih Ben Salah

Boujad

Cap Beddouza

40

79

Barragne
al-Massire

El Borouj

Beni Mellal

Tietta Sidi

Safi

26

Bouguedra

84

Youssoufia

Benguerir

P24

146

Sept des Gzoula

P7

72

El Kelaa Srarhna

NF

Chemaia

83

Tamelelt

P8

97

87

46

Talmest

77

Marrakech

75

M O R O C C O

Essaouira

Lighthouse

24

Ounara

Sidi
Mokhtar

Chichaoua

Mosque

141

Cap Sim

45

Taddert

330

Ameltougul

Sidi Kaouki

68

Imi n Tanoute

Amizmiz

Asni

171

P31

Skoura

Tamanar

294

Ijoukak

O. Sous

19

Ouarzazate

NG

P8

138

Jebel Toubkal

Toubkal
National Park

65

98

Lighthouse

Waterfall

4167m

Tazenakht

Tamri

P40

Aoulouz

Tinerhin

Cap Rhir

133

Ruins

Taliouine

6°30'W

Agadir

Inezgane

P32

340

30°30'N

Tiznit

Tiznit

308   309   310   340   311   312

313 314 315 316 317

37°30'N

NA

Sevilla
Dos Hermanas
Cathedral Alcazar and Archivo dé Indias in Seville
Utrera   Morón de la Frontera

SPAIN

Granada
Genil
Alhambra Generalife and Albayzin Granada
Mulhacén ▲ 3482

Jerez de la Frontera
Malaga
Cádiz
San Fernando
Chiclana de la Frontera

Málaga   Motril   Almeria

C. de Gata

329

NB

C Trafalgar
Algeciras
Gibraltar (U.K.)

M e d i t e r r a n e a n   S e a

Alboran (Spain)

Tangier (Tanger)
Strait of Gibraltar   *Pointe Almina*
Ceuta (Spain)
28   Restinga
Regaia   37   Smir
27   Medina (World Heritage Site)
Asilah   88   Tetouan
51   Bou Hamed

Cap des Trois Fourches

NC

Arba des Beni Hassan   66
Larache **P2**
P28   Chechaouene
Ksar el Kebir   Bab Taza
housselham Réserve de Merdja Zerga 73 **P39**   99
Souk el **121**   Ouezzane   Ketama
Arba du Rharb 148
P2 Mechra Bel Ksiri
Allal Tazi 60 Mjara
Rafsai
Taounate

Al Hoceima
113 Lighthouse
Targuist Midar
126
Aknoul
Taharsouk 112
Saka

Melilla
24 Nador
Zelouane
14 **P39** 126
P27 Berkane
El Aioun

Beni
Ghazaouet 117
Saidia Ahfir
Maghnia
108 Oujda
83

ND

Rabat   Mehdya Plage
Rharo
62 **P3**
Sidi Slimane
Sidi Kacem
32
P6
Sidi Allal el Babraoui 46
Khemisset **P1**
82 63
Tiflet 58
Ain el Auoda
Rommani

Mjara 52
Tissa 162
Medina (World Heritage Site)
Fez 48
Volubilis (World Heritage Site)
Abjelil 120
Bir Tam Tam
Meknes
El Hajeb 67 78
Sefrou
Imouzzer du Kandar
Ifrane 179

Taza 65
Taourirt 54
Guercif **P1**
Qued Za **P19**
Waterfall
Debdou
Ain Benimathar
Sidi Brahim
Zeroulilet *Q. El-Betoun* *Q. Bou-Rouhat*
115
Djenen Krater

Jerada
Magoure

NE

Oued Zem
Boujad
Kasba Tadla 47
El Ksiba 99

Oulmes
P24 Azrou
Mrirt 82
Timahdite
96
Itzer
Bouma 55
Boulemane
Enjil
Ksabi
Midelt
Missour
Outat Oulad el Hajj 256
Chebket bou Abssira ▲ 1678m
Tendrara 70
Bou Arfa Iche
P19

NF

El Kelaa Salah
Beni Mellal

M O R O C C O

P21
Gourrama
Rich 126
58 23
Er Rachidia
127
Boudenib
Bou Anane
Mengoub **P32** 108
141
Boukas
Lahmas 109
N6
Bechar
Kenadsa
Meridja 101
N6 92
Menouarar

329

Goulmima
79 Aoufous 60
Tinerhin
Boumaine du Dades **P32**
169 118
Erfoud
Rissani
Abadla
Taghit

NG

Ouarzazate
Agdz
Nkob Alnif
135 Ait Saadaut
Tazzarine
Hamaguir
Gur
96 94

Dades Valley

N50
Hassiel Khebi   El Ouata

Copyright © Map Studio 2007

30°30'N

340

313 314 315 316 317

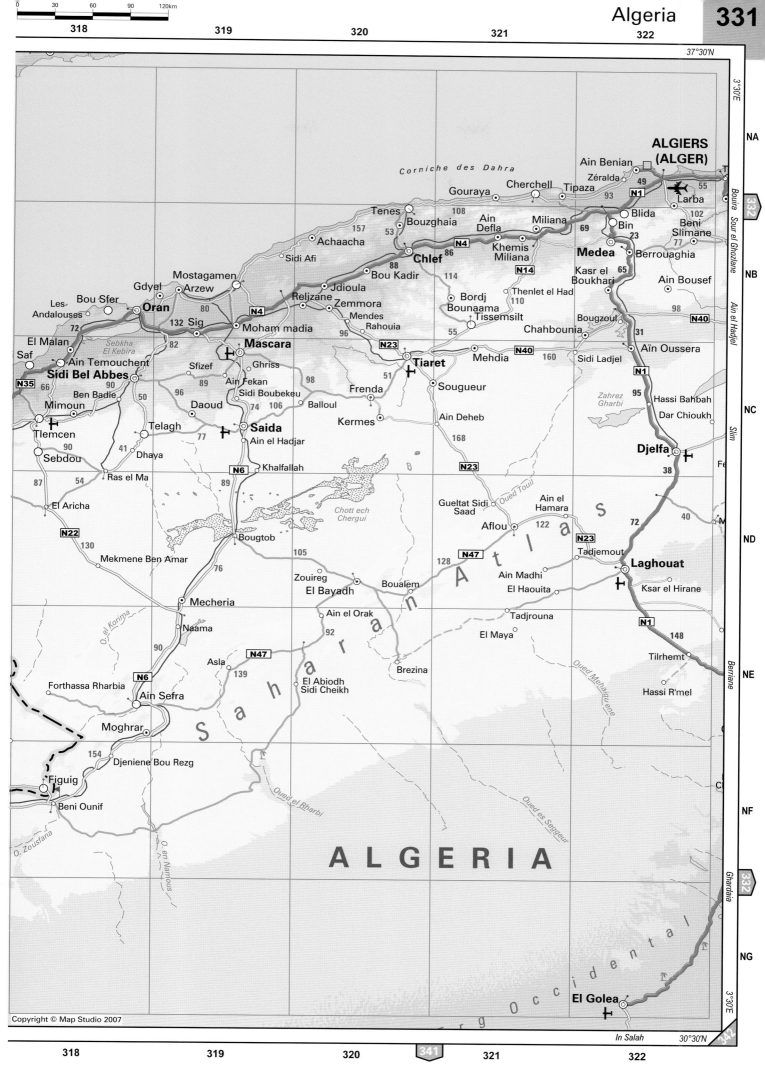

323 324 325 326 327

37°30'N
3°30'E

NA

Bejaia **Skikda** **Annaba** El Kala

Cap Bougaroun Cap de Fer
Zitouna Collo Chetaibi
Dellya Jijel Berrahal Ben Mehidi
Thenia Tizi Ouzou Azazga El Kseur El Milia El Tarf
Lakhdaria Ain el Hammoth Kherrata El Arrouch El Hadjar Ghardimaou
Algiers

NB
Bouira Akbou Bougaa Ferdjioua Mila Guelma Mechroha Souk Ahras
66 Sour el Ghozlane Djemila Setif El Bulma Chelghoum El Aid **Qacentina (Constantine)** Sedrata Sakiet Sidi Yussef
35 39 77 N5 64 131 N5 El Khroub Ain M'lila El Aouinet
Sidi Aissa Bordj Bou Arreridj Ain Oulmene Oum el Bouaghi Ain Beida El Kala
Larba 81 60 74 109 106 Haidra
Bougzoul N8 67 **M'Sila** Magra Merouana Gar et Tarf 48 N10
Ain el Hadjel Chelal N40 55 Batna Timgad 103 Khenchela 117 Tebessa
65 81 39 Aim Touta 118 Cheria
Zahrez Chergui 68 Barika N28 Menaa Babar El Ogla Gasses Elma Labiod 75

NC
El Hamel Bou Saada Ben S'Rour 73 Rhoufi Taberdga Bir el Ater 149
Slim Am el Melh 113 M'Chouneche Khangar Sidi Nadji N16
117 61 Biskra 115 Zeribet el Oued Negrine Moulares Redeyef
Feidh el Botma 181 Tolga N8 Oumache 79 99 Metlaoui
Djelfa Sidi Khaled Chegga Stile Chott Melrhir Chott El Gharsa 93

ND
Messaad **A L G E R I A** Ouled Djellal N48 147 Nefta 58 **Tozeur**
O. Retem El Meghaier N3 Hazoua 64 5
93 Chott Merouane

NE
Delaa Djamaa
51 El Oued
Dzioua 96
Berriane Guerara Touggourt N16
39 Ghardaia Chegguet El Ftaiet 80
26 Zelfana El Alia N3

NF
Metlili Chaamba N49 100
156 108
Ouargla 85 Haoud el Hamra
239
N1 Hassi Messaoud

NG
331
O. el Fahl Rhoard el Baguel 239
El Golea O. Bou Ali Belhirane

30°30'N
3°30'E

o r i e n t a l

Tin Fouye

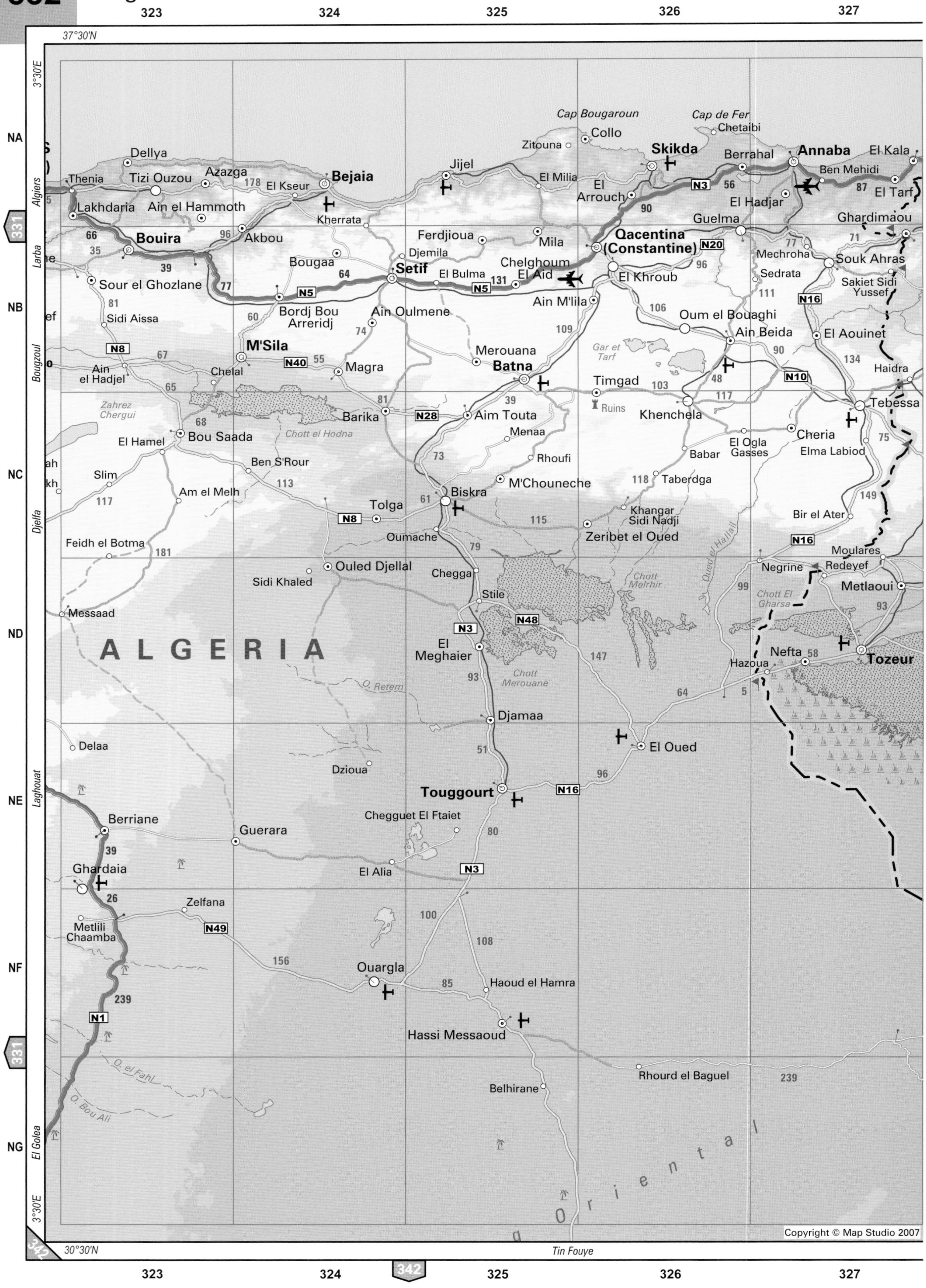

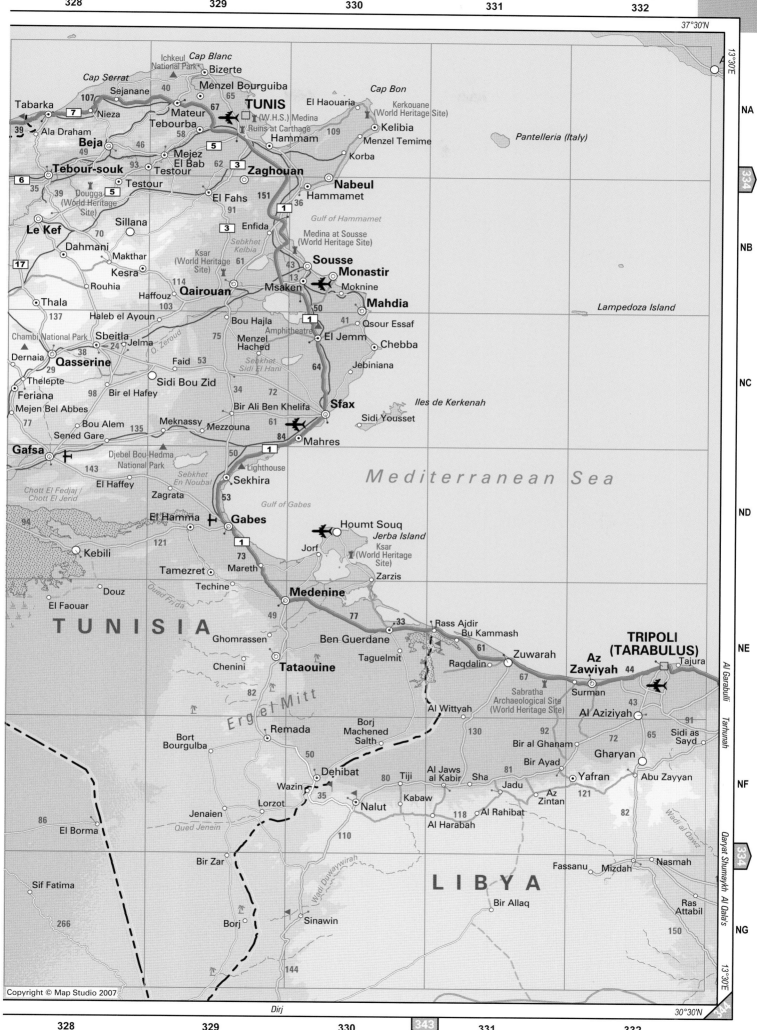

37°30'N
13°30'E

NA

334

Cap Blanc
Ichkeul
Cap Serrat
National Park   Bizerte
Tabarka   107   Sejanane   40   Menzel Bourguiba
39   Nieza   65
Ala Draham   67
Mateur   **TUNIS**   Cap Bon   El Haouaria
Beja   46   Tebourba   58   (W.H.S.) Medina   Kerkouane
49   5   Ruins at Carthage   (World Heritage Site)
Tebour-souk   93   Mejez   62   3   Testour   Hammam   Kelibia
6   El Bab   Zaghouan   109   Menzel Temime
35   39   Dougga   5   Testour   Korba
Sillana   (World Heritage   El Fahs   151   36   **Nabeul**   Pantelleria (Italy)
Site)   91   1   Hammamet
Le Kef   70   3   Enfida   Gulf of Hammamet
Dahmani   Medina at Sousse
17   Makthar   Ksar   (World Heritage Site)
Kesra   (World Heritage   61   43   **Sousse**
Rouhia   Site)   114   13   **Monastir**
Thala   Haffouz   **Qairouan**   Msaken   Moknine   Lampedoza Island
137   103   50   Mahdia
Chambi National Park   Haleb el Ayoun   Bou Hajla   Amphitheatre   41   Qsour Essaf
Sbeitla   75   Menzel   El Jemm   Chebba
Dernaia   38   Jelma   Hached   Sebkhet   64
29   24   Sidi El Hani   Jebiniana
Qasserine   Faid   53
Thelepte   34   72
Feriana   98   Bir el Hafey   Sidi Bou Zid   Iles de Kerkenah
Mejen Bel Abbes   Bir Ali Ben Khelifa   61   **Sfax**
77   Bou Alem   135   Meknassy   Mezzouna   Sidi Yousset
Sened Gare   50   84   Mahres
Gafsa   Djebel Bou-Hedma   1
143   National Park   Lighthouse   *M e d i t e r r a n e a n   S e a*
Chott El Fedjaj /   El Haffey   Sebkhet   Sekhira
Chott El Jerid   Zagrata   En Noubal   53
94   El Hamma   **Gabes**   Gulf of Gabes
121   1   Houmt Souq   Jerba Island
Kebili   73   Jorf   Ksar
Tamezret   Mareth   (World Heritage
Douz   Techine   Zarzis   Site)
El Faouar   **Medenine**
T U N I S I A   49   77   Rass Ajdir
Ghomrassen   33   Bu Kammash
Chenini   Taguelmit   61   Zuwarah   **TRIPOLI**
Tataouine   Raqdalin   **(TARABULUS)**
82   67   **Az**   44   Tajura
Al Wittyah   Sabratha   Surman   **Zawiyah**   43
Bort   Remada   Borj   Archaeological Site   Al Aziziyah   91
Bourgulba   Machened   (World Heritage Site)   130   92   72   65   Sidi as
Salth   Bir al Ghanam   Gharyan   Sayd
50   Bir Ayad
Dehibat   Al Jaws   81   Yafran   Abu Zayyan
Wazin   80   Tiji   al Kabir   Sha   Jadu   Az   121
35   Kabaw   118   Zintan   82
Jenaien   Lorzot   Nalut   Al Rahibat
86   Al Harabah
El Borma   Qued Jenein   Fassanu   Mizdah   Nasmah
Bir Zar
266   **L I B Y A**   Ras
Borj   Sinawin   Bir Allaq   Attabil
Sif Fatima   150
144

13°30'E   30°30'N

333   334   335   336   337

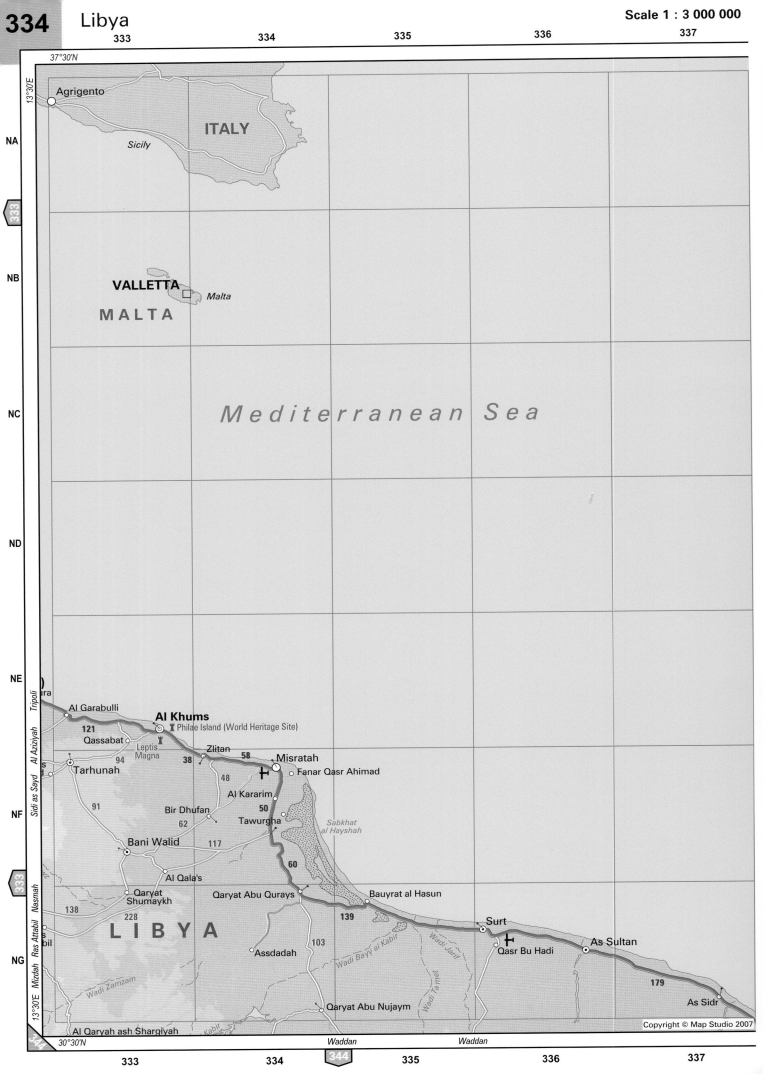

37°30'N

NA

Agrigento

ITALY

Sicily

NB

VALLETTA   *Malta*

M A L T A

NC

M e d i t e r r a n e a n   S e a

ND

NE

Tripoli

Al Garabulli

Al Khums

121   ♦ Philae Island (World Heritage Site)

Qassabat   *Leptis*   Zlitan   **58**

Al Aziziyah   *Magna*   **38**   Misratah

94   **48**   Fanar Qasr Ahimad

Tarhunah   Al Kararim

Sidi as Sayd   **91**   Bir Dhufan   **50**

NF   **62**   Tawurgha   *Sabkhat*

al Hayshah

Bani Walid   **117**

Al Qala's   **60**

Qaryat   Qaryat Abu Qurays   Bauyrat al Hasun

Shumaykh

Nasmah   **138**   **139**   Surt

228   Qasr Bu Hadi   As Sultan

Ras Attabil   **L I B Y A**   **103**

NG   Assdadah

Wadi Bayy al Kabir   *Wadi Jarif*   **179**   As Sidr

Mizdah   13°30'E   *Wadi Zamzam*   *Wadi Ta met*   Qaryat Abu Nujaym

30°30'N   Al Qaryah ash Shargiyah   *Kabir*   Waddan   Waddan

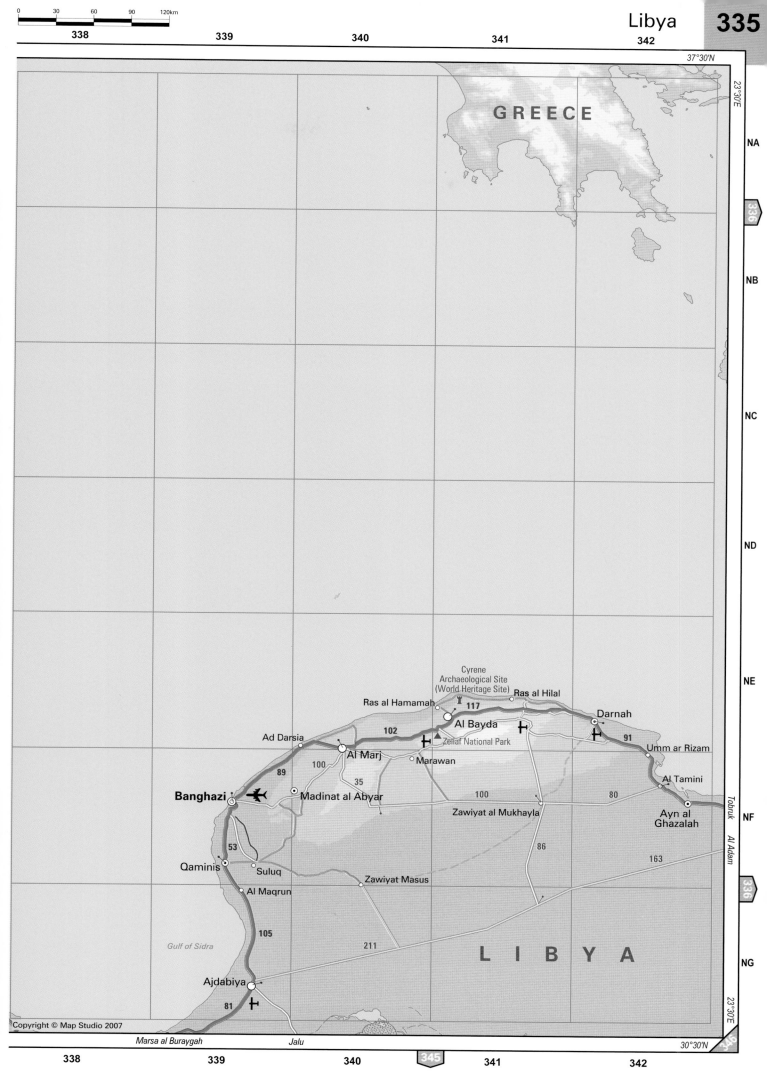

338   339   340   341   342

0   30   60   90   120km

GREECE

NA

336

NB

NC

ND

NE

Cyrene
Archaeological Site
(World Heritage Site)   Ras al Hilal

Ras al Hamamah   117   Darnah

102   Zellaf National Park   91

Ad Darsia   Al Bayda   Umm ar Rizam

Al Marj   Marawan   Al Tamini

89   100   35

Banghazi   Madinat al Abyar   100   80

Zawiyat al Mukhayla   Ayn al
Ghazalah

NF

53   86

Qaminis   163

Suluq

Al Maqrun   Zawiyat Masus

336

105

Gulf of Sidra   211   L I B Y A

NG

Ajdabiya

81

37°30'N

23°30'E

Tobruk

Al Adam

23°30'E

30°30'N

Marsa al Buraygah   Jalu

338   339   341   342

Scale 1 : 3 000 000

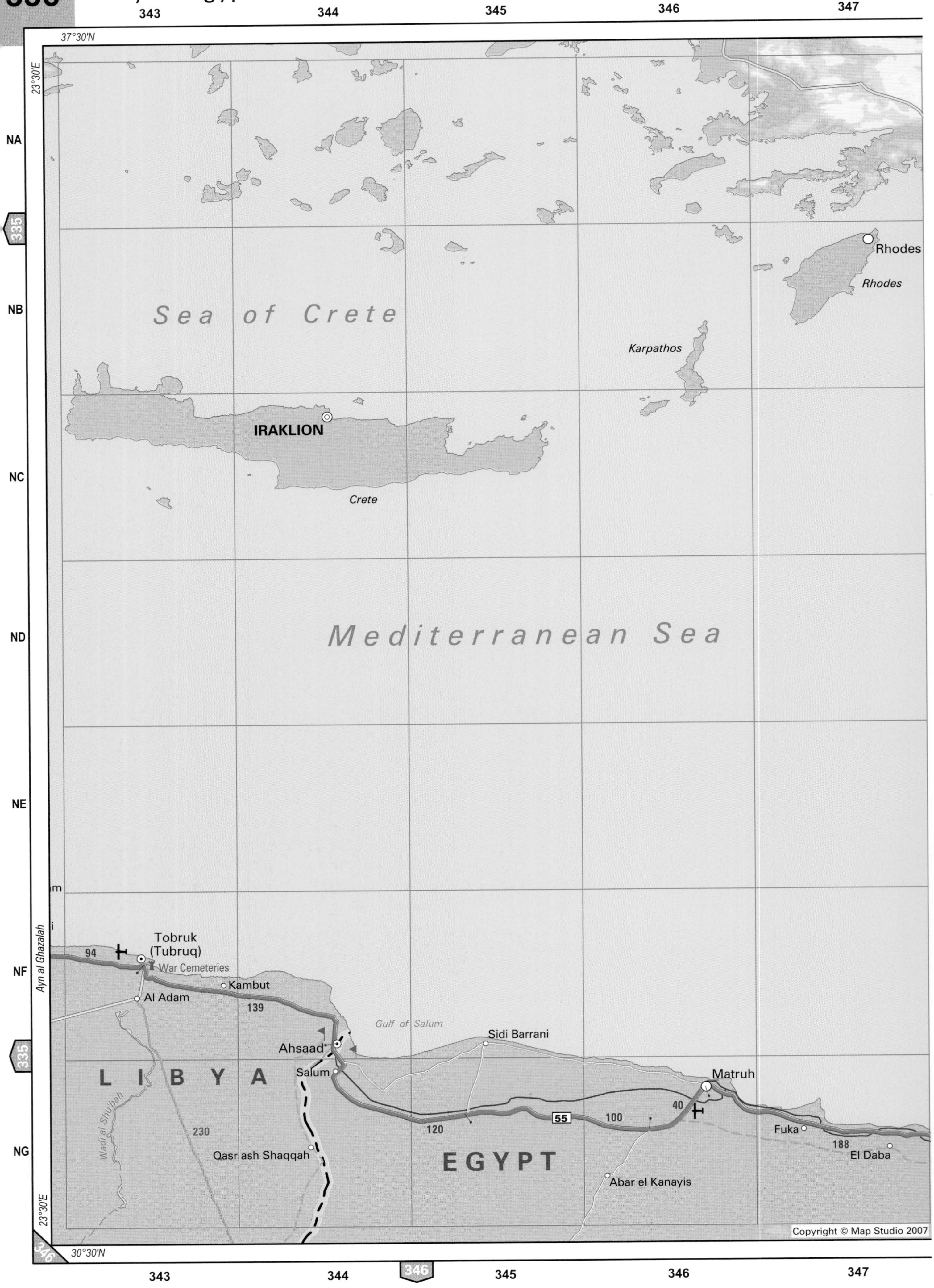
343
344
345
346
347
37°30'N
23°30'E
NA
NB
NC
ND
NE
NF
NG
335
Rhodes
Rhodes
Sea of Crete
Karpathos
IRAKLION
Crete
Mediterranean Sea
Tobruk
(Tubruq)
94
War Cemeteries
Kambut
Al Adam
139
Ayn al Ghazalah
Gulf of Salum
Sidi Barrani
Ahsaad
Salum
Matruh
40
55
100
120
Fuka
188
El Daba
LIBYA
EGYPT
230
Wadi al Shubah
Qasr ash Shaqqah
Abar el Kanayis
30°30'N
346
Copyright © Map Studio 2007

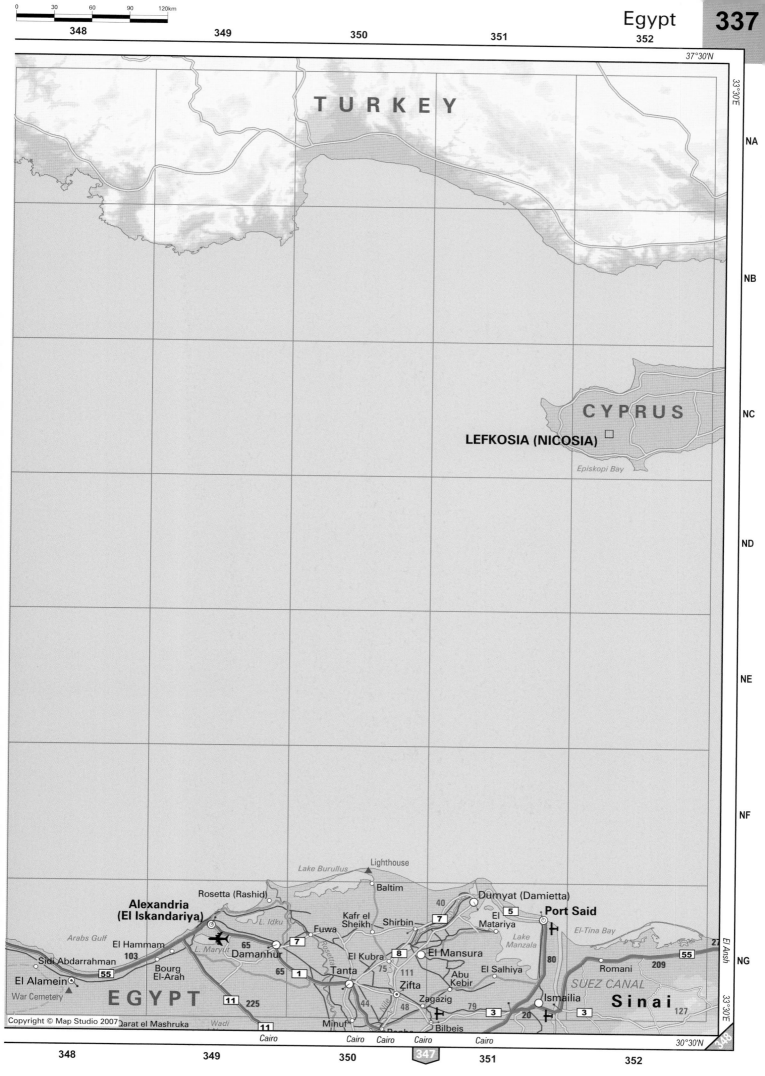

0 30 60 90 120km

348   349   350   351   352

37°30'N

33°30'E

NA

T U R K E Y

NB

NC

C Y P R U S

LEFKOSIA (NICOSIA) □

Episkopi Bay

ND

NE

NF

Lake Burullus   Lighthouse

Rosetta (Rashid)   Baltim

Alexandria   Dumyat (Damietta)
(El Iskandariya)   40   **5**   **Port Said**
                                                      El Matariya
Arabs Gulf   *L. Idku*   Kafr el   Shirbin   **7**   *El-Tina Bay*
                                    Sheikh   *Lake*   27
El Hammam   *L. Maryut* Fuwa   1   *Manzala*   55
103   **65**   80
Sidi Abdarrahman   Damanhur **7**   El Kubra **8** El Mansura   Romani   **209**
              Bourg   75 El Salhiya   *SUEZ CANAL*
El Alamein **55** El-Arah **65** **1** Tanta 111 Abu   20 Ismailia Sinai
War Cemetery   Zifta Kebir
▲   **E G Y P T**   **11** **225**   44   48   Zagazig 79 **3**   **3**   127
Qarat el Mashruka   *Wadi* **11**   Minuf   Bilbeis
                                Cairo   *Cairo* *Cairo* *Cairo*   *Cairo*   30°30'N

348   349   350   **347**   351   352

33°30'E

Scale 1 : 3 000 000

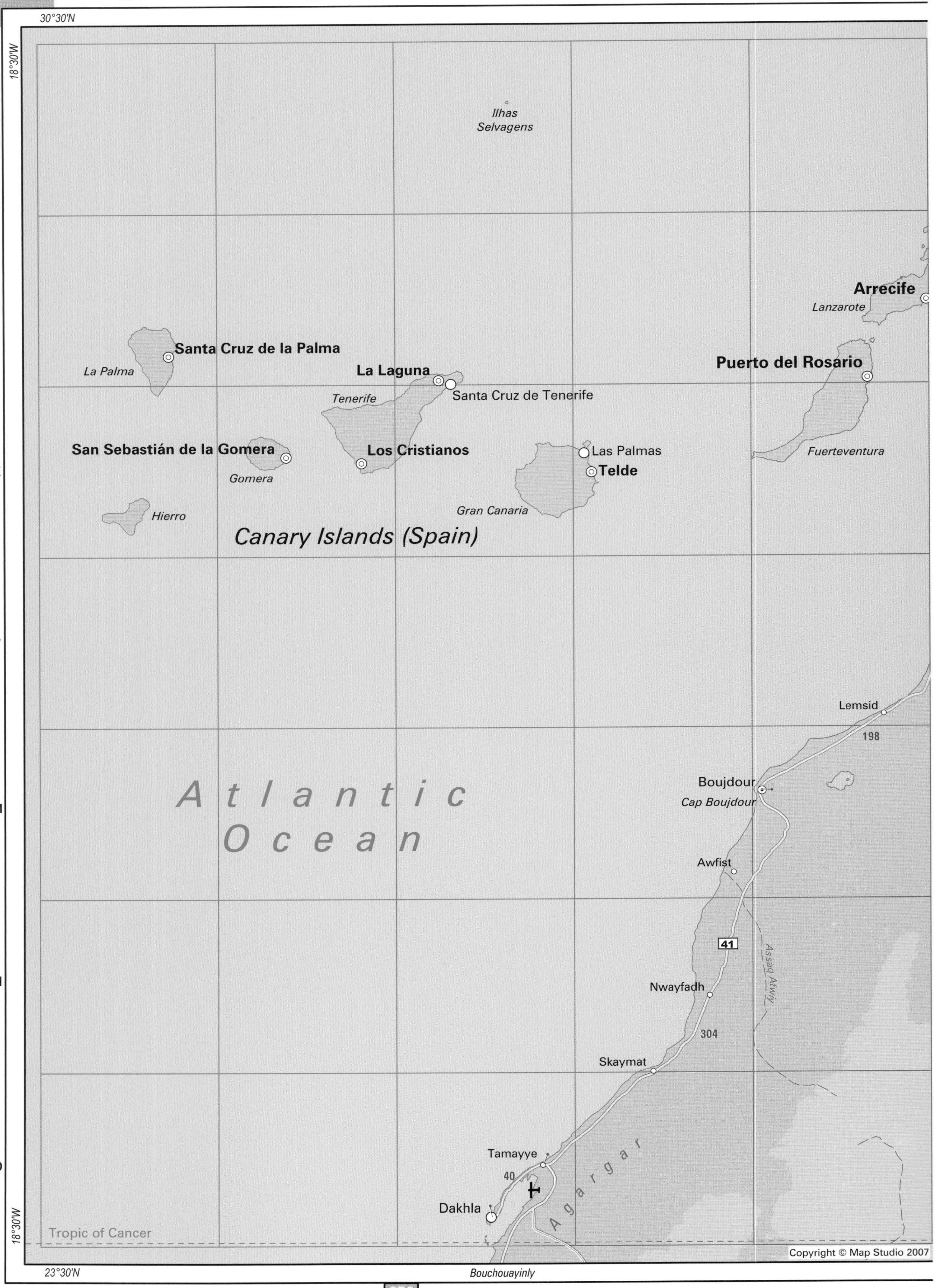
301
302
303
304
305
30°30'N
18°30'W
NH
NJ
NK
NL
NM
NN
NO
Ilhas Selvagens
Arrecife
Lanzarote
Santa Cruz de la Palma
La Palma
La Laguna
Puerto del Rosario
Santa Cruz de Tenerife
Tenerife
San Sebastián de la Gomera
Los Cristianos
Las Palmas
Telde
Fuerteventura
Gomera
Hierro
Gran Canaria
Canary Islands (Spain)
Lemsid
198
Boujdour
Cap Boujdour
Atlantic Ocean
Awfist
41
Assaq Atwiy
Nwayfadh
304
Skaymat
Tamayye
40
Dakhla
Agargar
Tropic of Cancer
18°30'W
23°30'N
Bouchouayinly
301
302
303
304
305

350

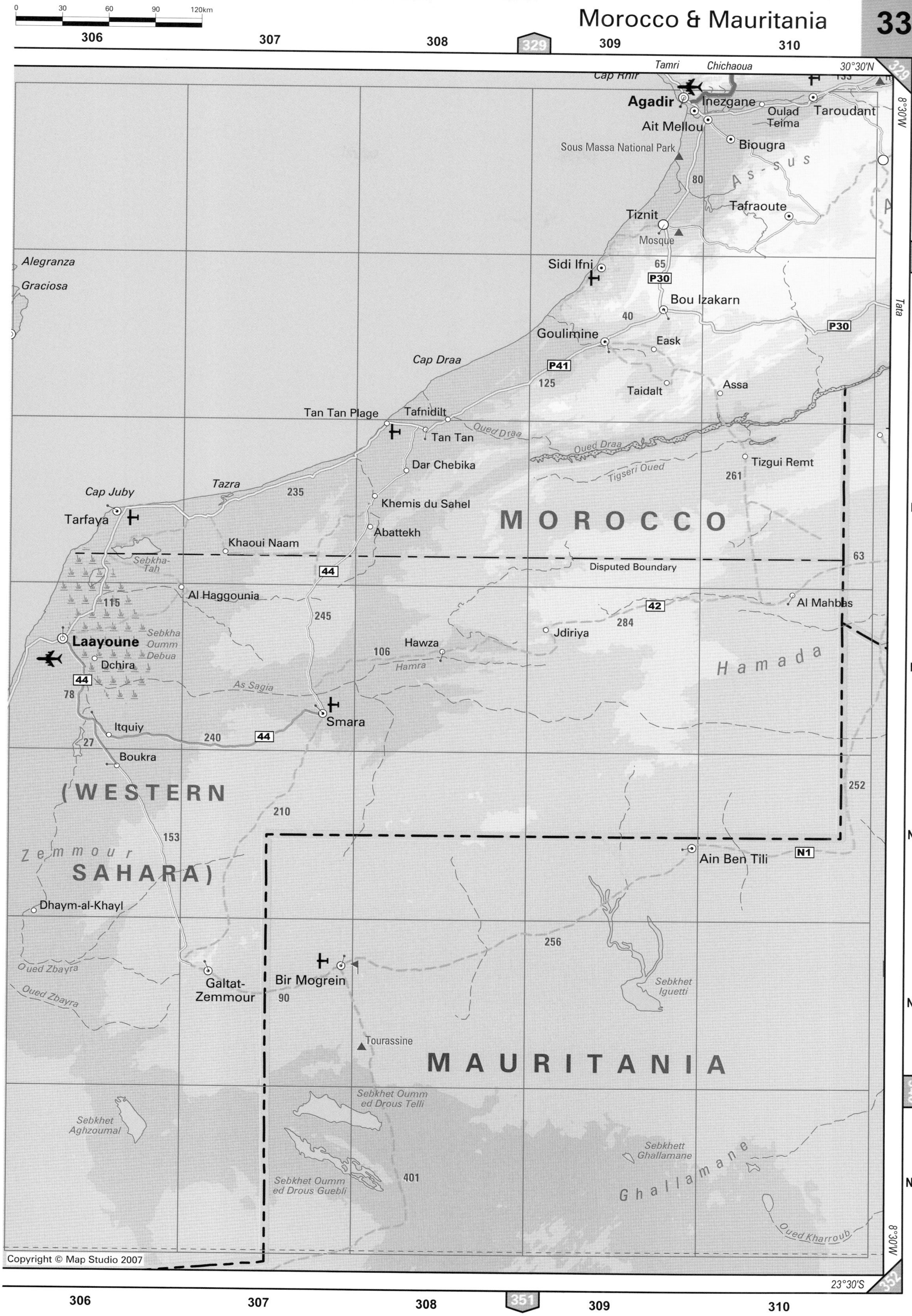

Tamri Chichaoua 30°30'N

Cap Rhir

Agadir Inezgane Oulad Taroudant
Teima

Ait Mellou Biougra

Sous Massa National Park

80 NH

Tiznit Tafraoute

Mosque

Sidi Ifni 65 **P30**

Bou Izakarn NJ

40 **P30**

Goulimine Eask

Cap Draa **P41**

125 Taidalt Assa

Tan Tan Plage Tafnidilt

Tan Tan Oued Draa Tizgui Remt

Dar Chebika Oued Draa 261 NK

Cap Juby Tazra 235 Khemis du Sahel **M O R O C C O**

Tarfaya Abattekh

Khaoui Naam Disputed Boundary 63

44

Al Haggounia **42** Al Mahbas

245 Jdiriya 284

Sebkha- Hawza NL
Tah

Laayoune 106 *Hamra* *H a m a d a*

Dchira Sebkha
Oumm
44 Debua

78 As Sagia

Itquiy Smara **44**

27 240 **44**

Boukra

(W E S T E R N 210 252

153 NM

Z e m m o u r Ain Ben Tili **N1**

S A H A R A)

Dhaym-al-Khayl

Oued Zbayra 256

Galtat- Bir Mogrein *Sebkhet NN
Zemmour* 90 *Iguetti*

Oued Zbayra

Tourassine

M A U R I T A N I A

*Sebkhet Oumm
ed Drous Telli*

*Sebkhet
Aghzoumal* *Sebkhett
Ghallamane*

NO

*Sebkhet Oumm 401 *G h a l l a m a n e*
ed Drous Guebli*

Oued Kharroub

23°30'S

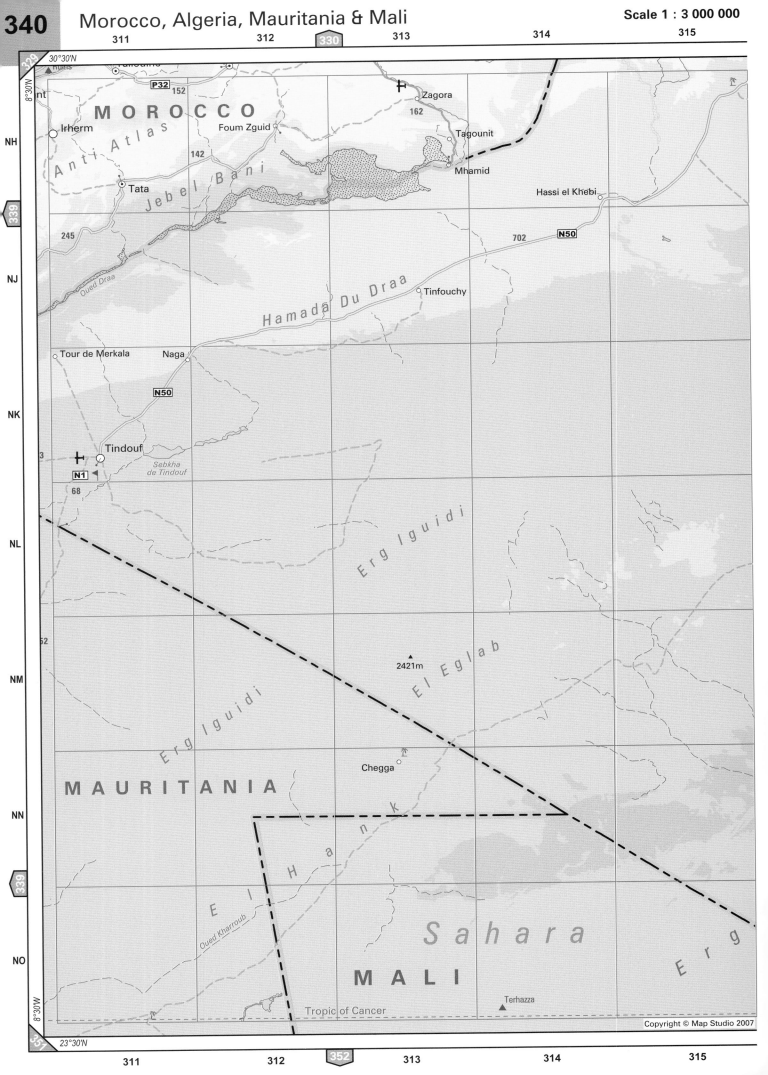

MOROCCO

Anti Atlas

Irherm

Tata

Jebel Bani

Foum Zguid

Zagora

Tagounit

Mhamid

Hassi el Khebi

N50

702

Hamada Du Draa

Tinfouchy

Oued Draa

Tour de Merkala

Naga

N50

Tindouf

Sebkha
de Tindouf

N1

Erg Iguidi

2421m

El Eglab

Erg Iguidi

MAURITANIA

Chegga

El Hank

NN

Oued Kharroub

Sahara

Erg

MALI

Terhazza

Tropic of Cancer

P32

152

162

142

245

3

68

52

30°30'N

23°30'N

8°30'W

8°30'N

NH

NJ

NK

NL

NM

NN

NO

311 312 330 313 314 315

339

352

357

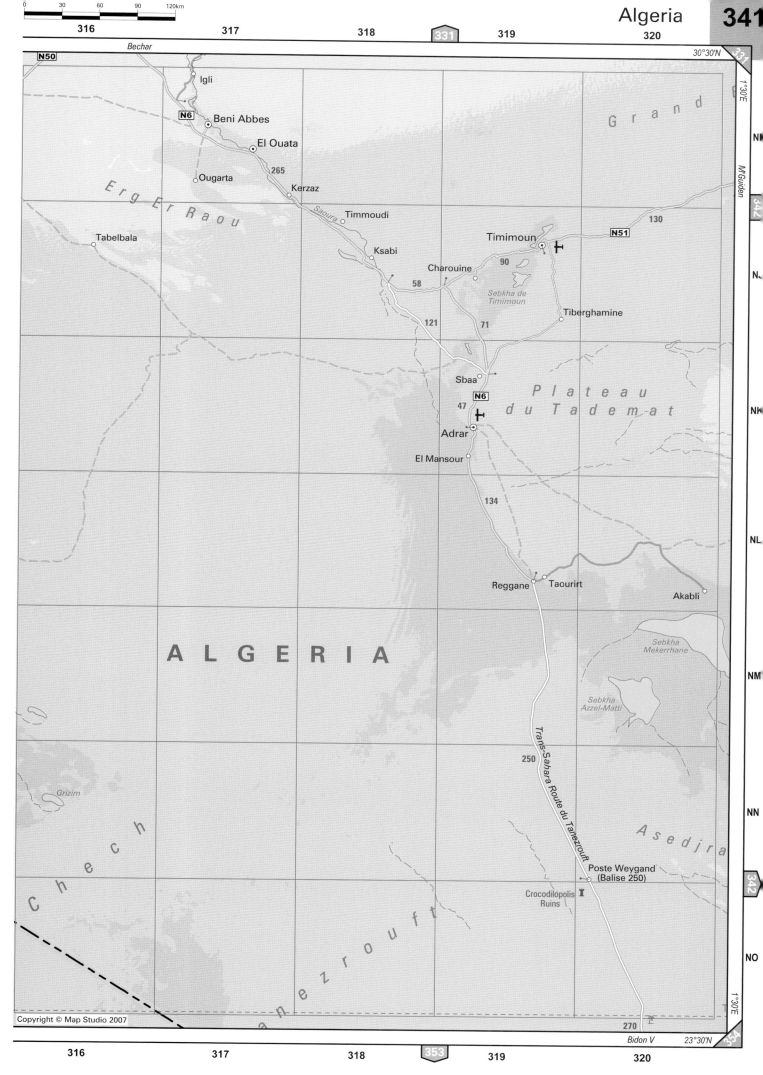

0 30 60 90 120km

N50

Bechar

30°30'N

1°30'E

331

Igli

N6

Beni Abbes

El Ouata

NK

342

Ougarta

265

Kerzaz

Saoura

Timmoudi

130

NJ

Erg Er Raou

Timimoun

N51

Tabelbala

Ksabi

90

Charouine

58

Sebkha de
Timimoun

Tiberghamine

121

71

NK

Plateau
du Tademat

Sbaa

N6

47

NL

Adrar

El Mansour

134

Reggane

Taourirt

Akabli

NM

Sebkha
Mekerrhane

ALGERIA

Sebkha
Azzel-Matti

Trans-Sahara Route du Tanezrouft

250

Grizim

NN

Asedjra

342

Poste Weygand
(Balise 250)

Chech

Crocodilopolis
Ruins

Tanezrouft

NO

1°30'E

270

Bidon V

23°30'N

354

M'Guiden

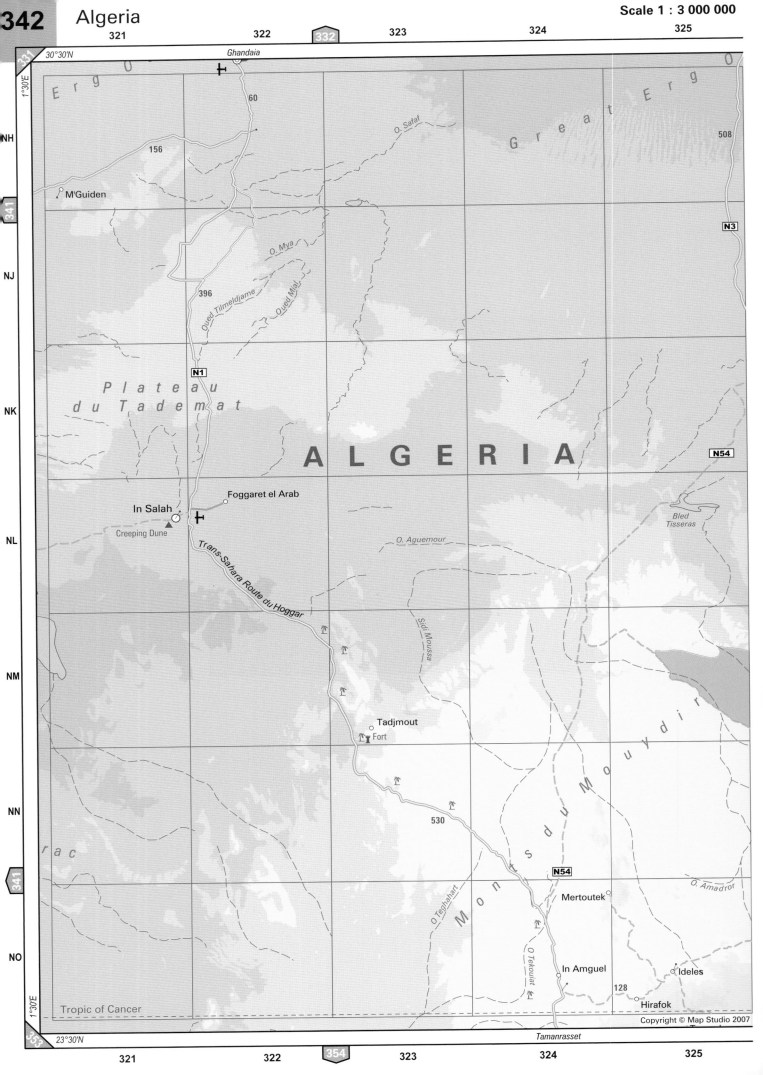

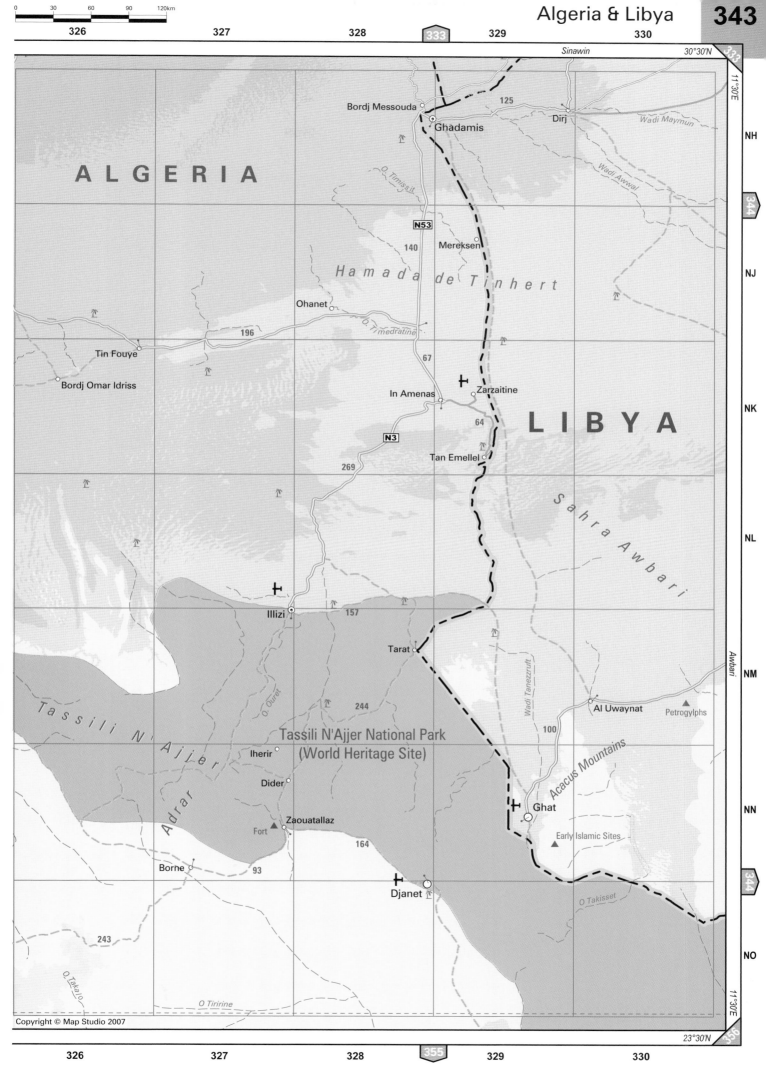

0 30 60 90 120km

326 327 328 **333** 329 330

Sinawin 30°30'N

11°30'E

NH

Bordj Messouda
125
Ghadamis Dirj
Wadi Maymun

ALGERIA

Wadi Awwal

NJ

N53

140 Mereksen

Hamada de Tinhert

Ohanet

O. Timissit

O. Timedratine

196 67

Tin Fouye

LIBYA

NK

Bordj Omar Idriss

In Amenas Zarzaitine

N3 64

Sahra Awbari

269 Tan Emellel

NL

Awbari

Illizi 157

Tarat NM

Wadi Tanezzruft

244 Al Uwaynat
100 Petrogylphs

Tassili N'Ajjer

Tassili N'Ajjer National Park
(World Heritage Site)

Iherir

Acacus Mountains

Adrar Dider

Zaouatallaz Ghat NN
Fort

Early Islamic Sites

Borne 164

93

Djanet

O Takisset

344

243

O. Takalo

O Tiririne 11°30'E

23°30'N

NO

355

326 327 328 329 330

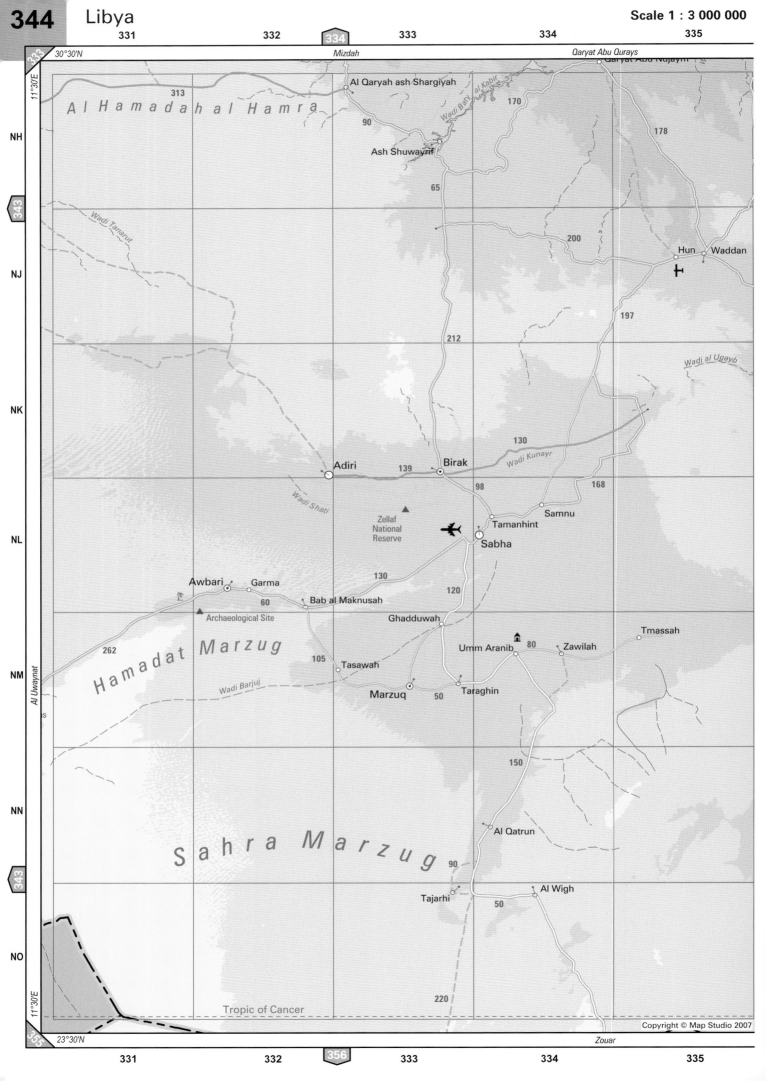

331 332 334 333 334 335

30°30'N Mizdah Qaryat Abu Qurays

Qaryat Abu Nujaym

NH

Al Hamadah al Hamra

313

Al Qaryah ash Shargiyah

170

90

178

Ash Shuwayrif

65

NJ

Wadi Tanarut

200

Hun Waddan

212

197

Wadi al Ugayb

NK

130

Adiri 139 Birak Wadi Kunayr

98 168

Samnu

Zellaf National Reserve Tamanhint

NL Sabha

130

Awbari Garma 120

60 Bab al Maknusah

Archaeological Site Ghadduwah Tmassah

262 105 Umm Aranib 80 Zawilah

NM Tasawah

Wadi Barjuj Marzuq 50 Taraghin

Hamadat Marzug

150

NN

Al Qatrun

Sahra Marzug

90

343

Al Wigh

Tajarhi 50

NO

11°30'E

220

Tropic of Cancer

23°30'N Zouar

331 332 333 334 335

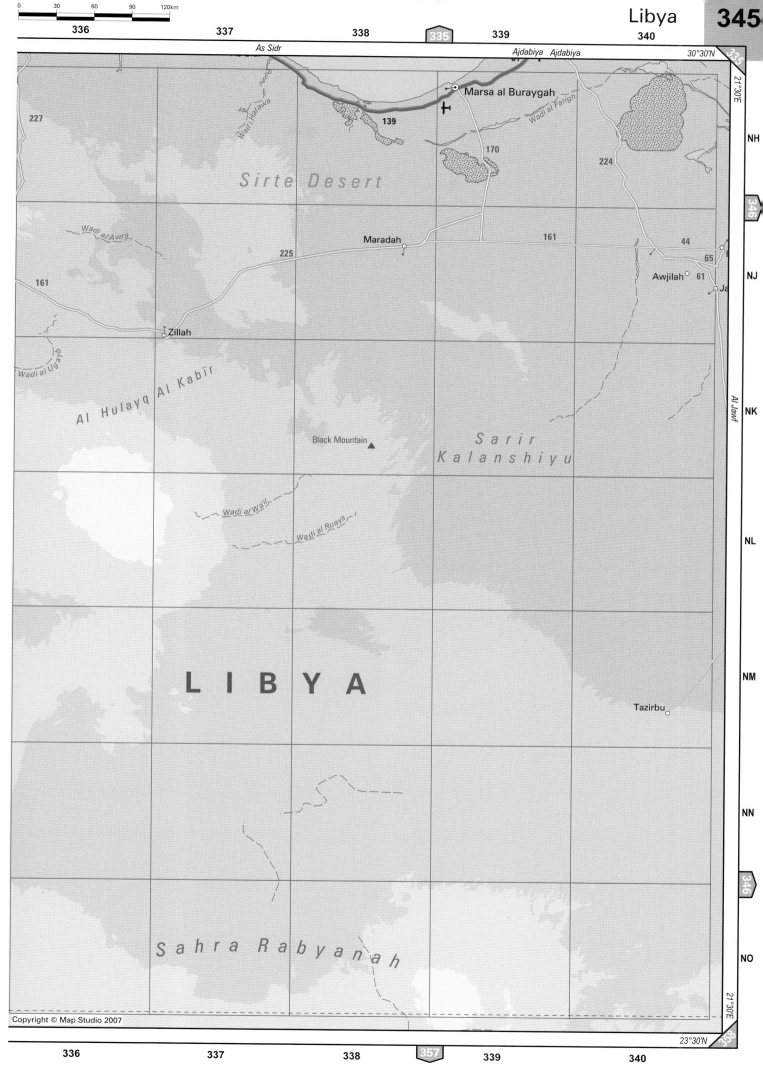

0 30 60 90 120km

As Sidr   Ajdabiya Ajdabiya   30°30'N

227

Marsa al Buraygah

139

170

224

Sirte Desert

NH

NJ

NK

NL

NM

NN

NO

346

346

Wadi al Awra

Wadi al Harawa

Maradah

161

44

65

225

Awjilah   61   Ja

161

Zillah

Wadi al Ugayb

Al Hulayq Al Kabir

Black Mountain ▲

S a r i r
K a l a n s h i y u

Wadi al Wa'ir

Wadi al Ruays

L I B Y A

Tazirbu

S a h r a   R a b y a n a h

23°30'N

21°30'E

21°30'E

23°30'E

Al Jawf

335

338

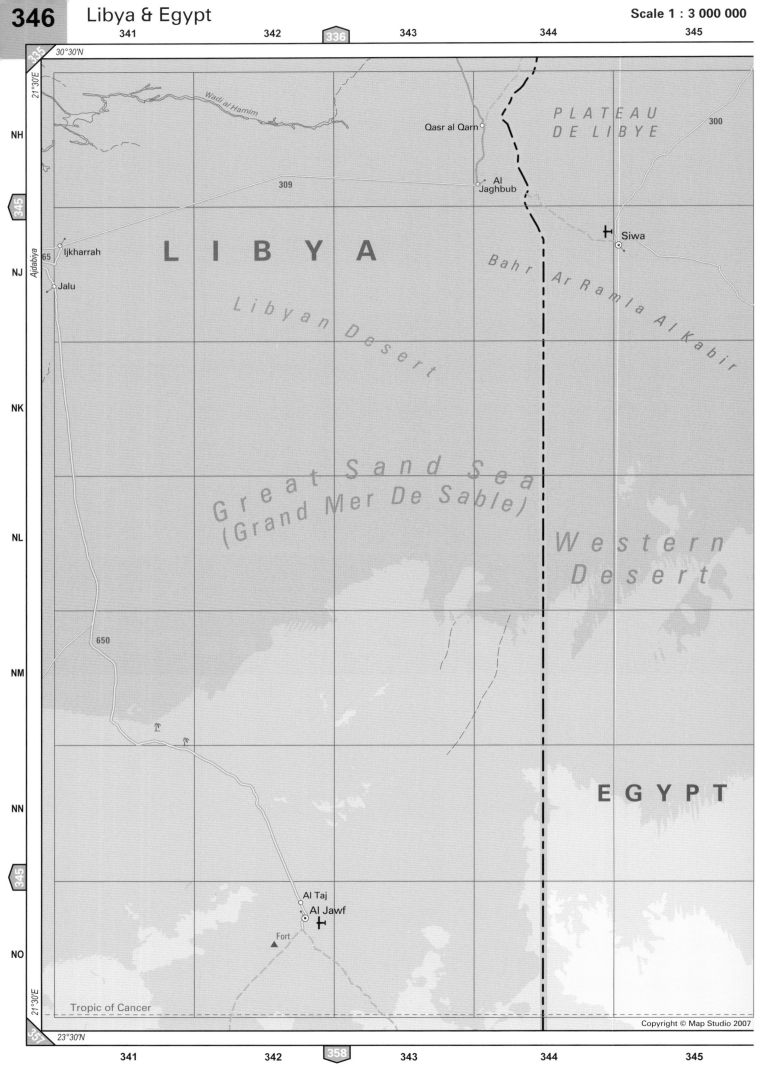

341   342   336   343   344   345

30°30'N
21°30'E

NH

Wadi al Hamim

Qasr al Qarn

PLATEAU
DE LIBYE

300

309

Al
Jaghbub

345

Ajdabiya

65 Ijkharrah

LIBYA

Siwa

NJ

Jalu

Bahr Ar Ramla Alkabir

Libyan Desert

NK

Great Sand Sea
(Grand Mer De Sable)

Western
Desert

NL

650

NM

NN

EGYPT

345

Al Taj

Al Jawf

Fort

NO

Tropic of Cancer

21°30'E
23°30'N

351

Copyright © Map Studio 2007

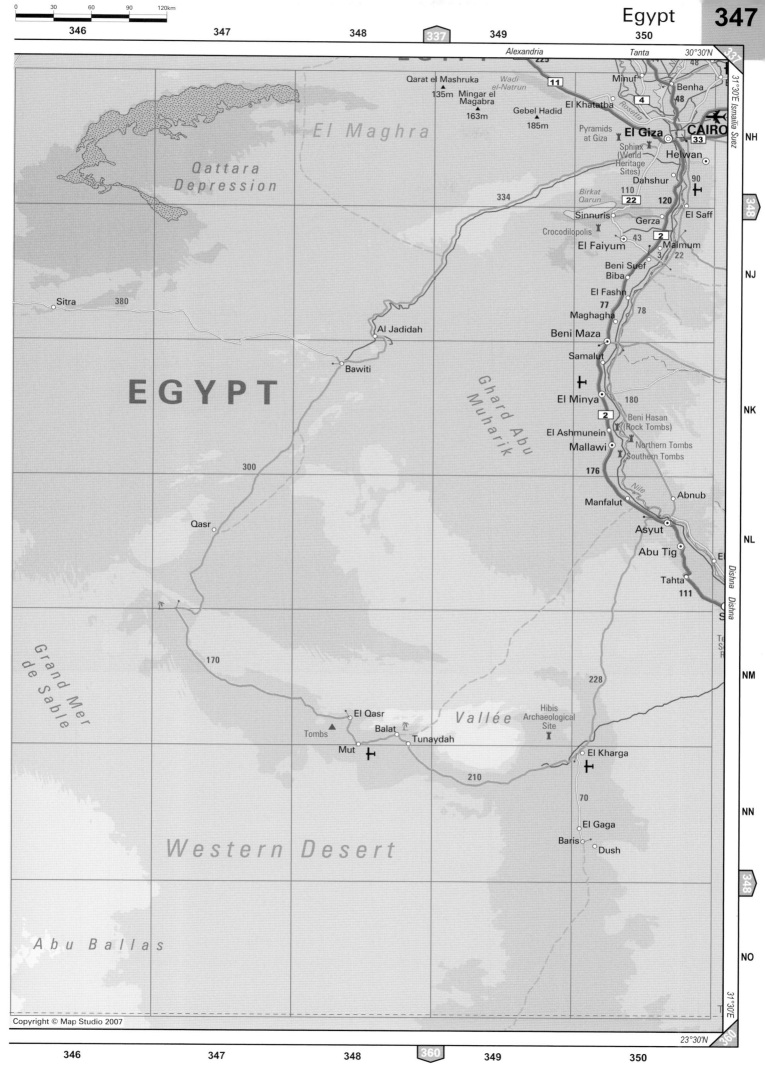

0 30 60 90 120km

346 347 348 337 349 350

NH

NJ

NK

NL

NM

NN

NO

Alexandria   Tanta   30°30'N

31°30'E Ismailia Suez

Qarat el Mashruka
135m   Mingar el
Magabra
163m
Gebel Hadid
185m

El Maghra

Wadi
el-Natrun

11

El Khatatba

Minuf   48

Benha
48

4

El Giza

El Giza

Pyramids
at Giza

Sphinx
(World
Heritage
Sites)

CAIRO
33

Helwan

Qattara
Depression

334

Dahshur

90

110
22   120

El Saff

Sinnuris
Gerza

Birkat
Qarun

El Faiyum
Crocodilopolis
43   2

Maimum

3   22

Beni Suef
Biba

El Fashn

77   78

Maghagha

Beni Maza

Samalut

El Minya   180

2

Beni Hasan
(Rock Tombs)

El Ashmunein

Mallawi

Northern Tombs
Southern Tombs

176

Nile

Abnub

Manfalut

Asyut

Abu Tig

Tahta
111

Sitra   380

Al Jadidah

Bawiti

EGYPT

Ghard Abu
Muharik

300

Qasr

Dishna Dishna

NM

170

228

Grand Mer
de Sable

El Qasr

Balat

Tombs

Mut

Tunaydah

Vallée

Hibis
Archaeological
Site

El Kharga

210

70

Western Desert

El Gaga

Baris   Dush

Abu Ballas

31°30'E

23°30'N

351 352 353 354 355

30°30'N Port Said

Bilbeis
3 20
3
44
120 91 98 127
CAIRO (EL-QAHIRA)
83 33
51
60 55
140
Suez (El-Suneis)
Sudr
Ain Sukhna
65
44
66
Zafarana
St Anthony's Monastery
170
St Paul's Monastery
135
Ras Gharib
Khasm el Raqaba
483m
245
O. Tarfa
EGYPT
Eastern
Desert

Bir Hasana
Pillars of Solomon
ISRAEL
80
Maan
Nakhl
33 119
El Thamad
37
Elat
40
108
JORDAN
164
Taba
Al Aqabah
104
65
85
394 109
S i n a i
Coloured Canyon
Nuweiba
171
Ras Abu Gallum Reserve
Abu Durba
Jebel Musa
2285m
152
137
SAUDI ARABIA
66
Ras al Ushsh
44
Tiran-Sanafir Islands Natural Protectorate
222
Sharm el Sheikh
Ras Muhammed National Park
Ras Muhammad
222

Gez Shadwan
Duba
Hurghada
Bur Safaga
Red Sea
161
77
85
Bir Seiyala
Quseir
88
Gebel el Shalui
697m
44

Asyut
El Badari
Antaeopolis
Akhmim
Tahta
Sohag
Temples of Sethos I & Rames II
57
Dishna
2
El Araba el Madfuna
145
Valley of the Kings & Queens
Necropolis of Thebes (World Heritage Site)
El Karnak
Qena
63
Qift
Qus
Luxor
Armant
El Rizeiqat
El Bayadiya
El Idisat
125
El Deir
Aphroditopolis
El Mahamid
Isna
El Basaliya Qibli
El Kanayis
99 230
Idfu
Temple of Horus
El Kanayis Temple
65
El Nasser
Kom Ombo
145
Marsa Alam
145
44
45
2
1st Cataract
Tombs of the Nobles
Aswan
El Shalla
Elephantine Island
Aswan High Dam
Kalabsha Temple
Lake Nasser
369
Berenice
Ras Banas
Eastern Desert
Foul Bay
Tropic of Cancer
31°30'E
23°30'N
Abu Simbel
Bab el Kalabsha
Temple of Hathor

351 352 360 353 354 355

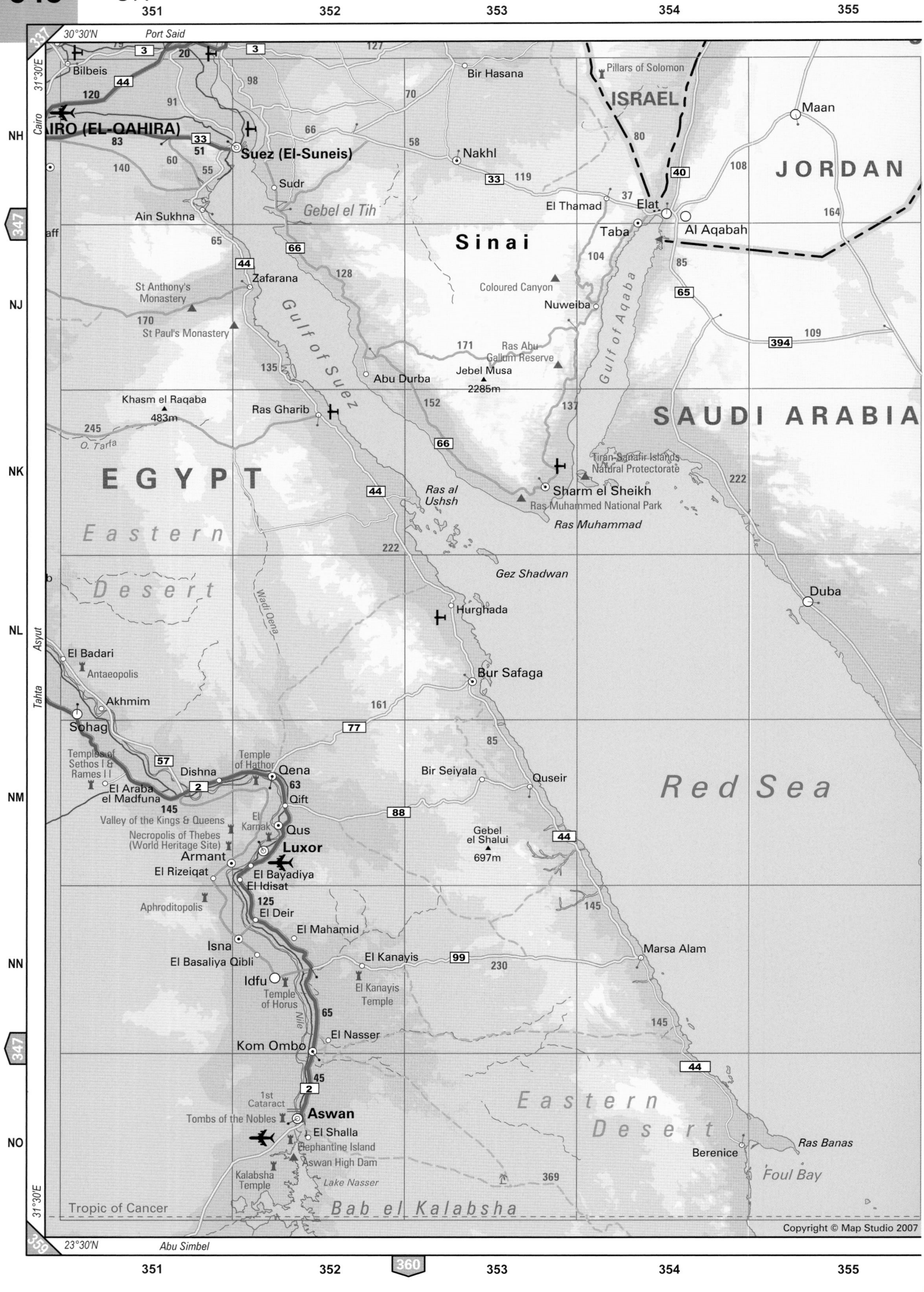

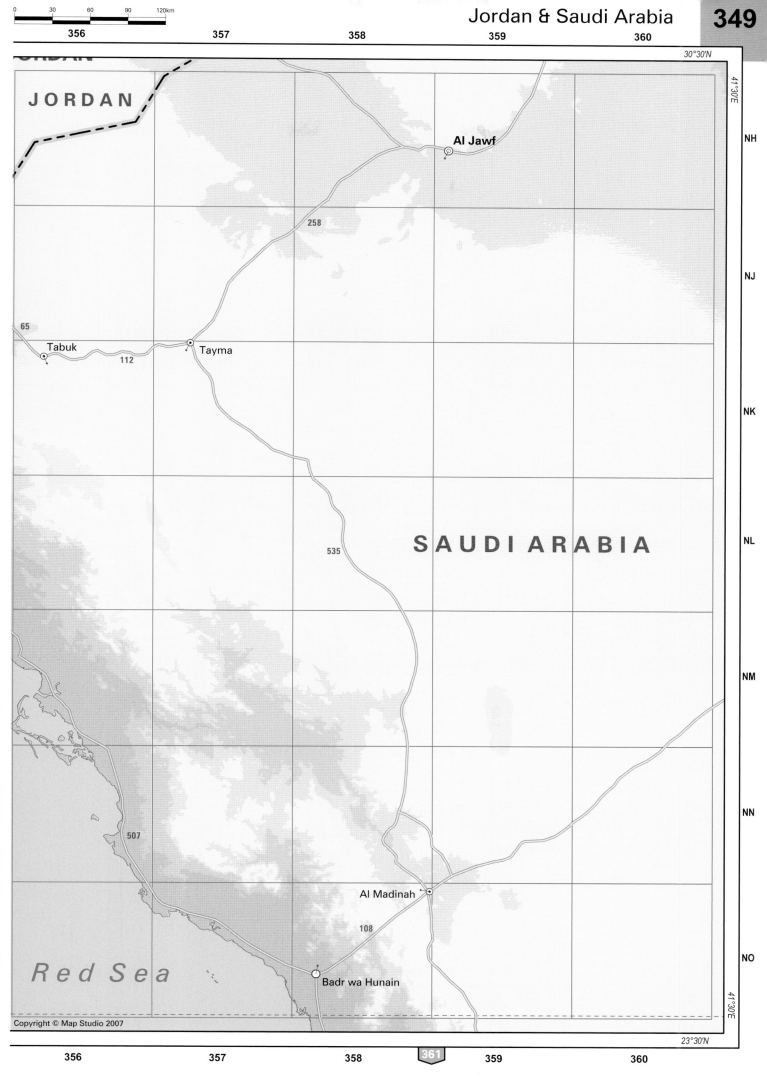

0 30 60 90 120km

356   357   358   359   360

30°30'N

41°30'E

JORDAN

NH

○ Al Jawf

258

NJ

65

NK
Tabuk
○
112   ○ Tayma

NL
535   SAUDI ARABIA

NM

NN
507

Al Madinah ○

108

NO

Red Sea

○ Badr wa Hunain

41°30'E

23°30'N

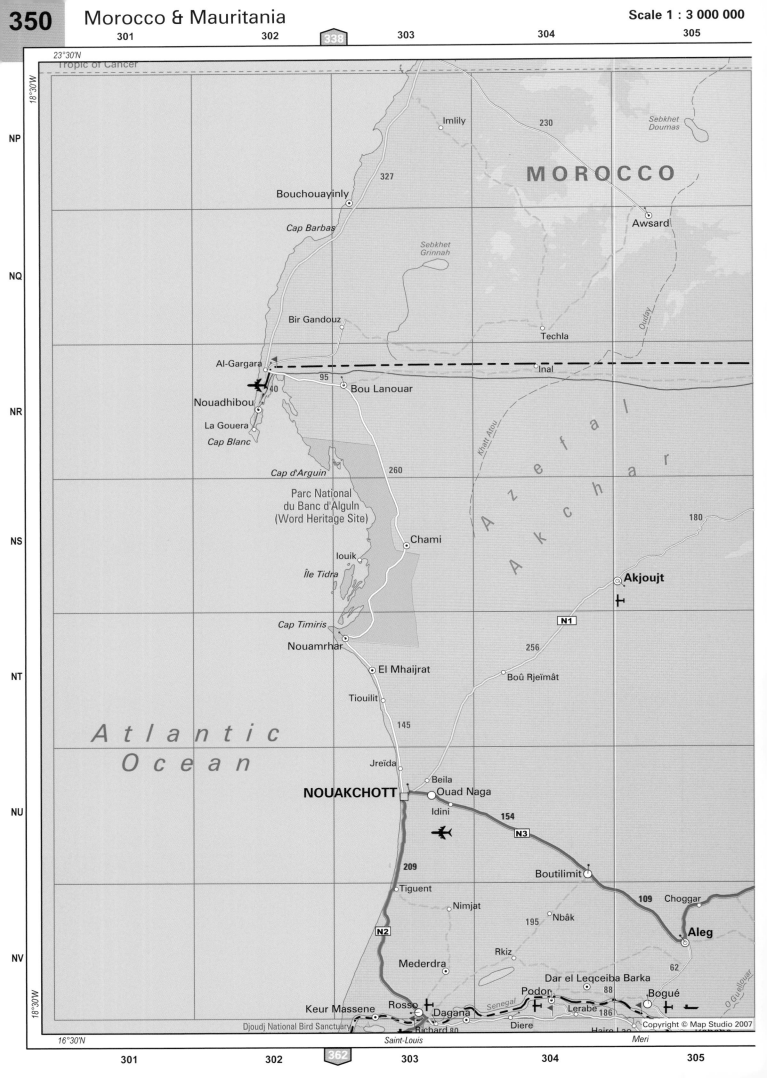

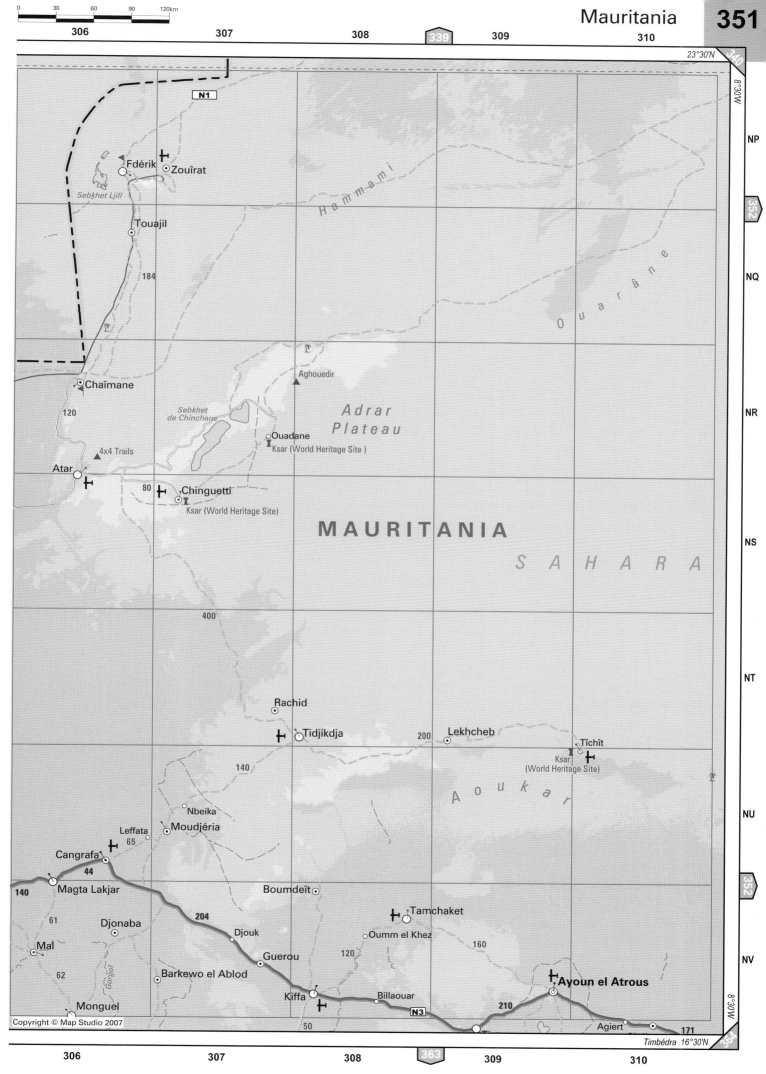

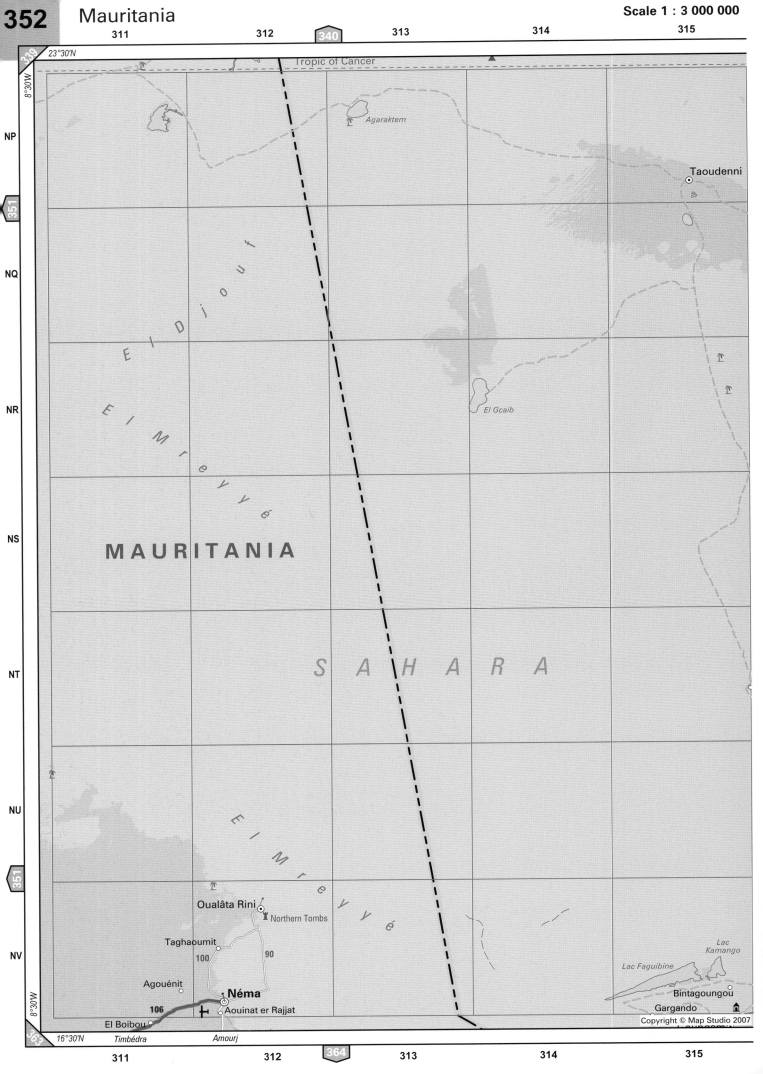

MAURITANIA

S A H A R A

E l   D j o u f

E l   M r e y y é

E l   M r e y y é

Tropic of Cancer

23°30'N

16°30'N

Agaraktem

Taoudenni

El Gcaib

Oualâta Rini
Northern Tombs

Taghaoumit

Agouénit

Néma

Aouinat er Rajjat

El Boibou

Timbédra

Amourj

Lac Kamango

Lac Faguibine

Bintagoungou

Gargando

100

90

106

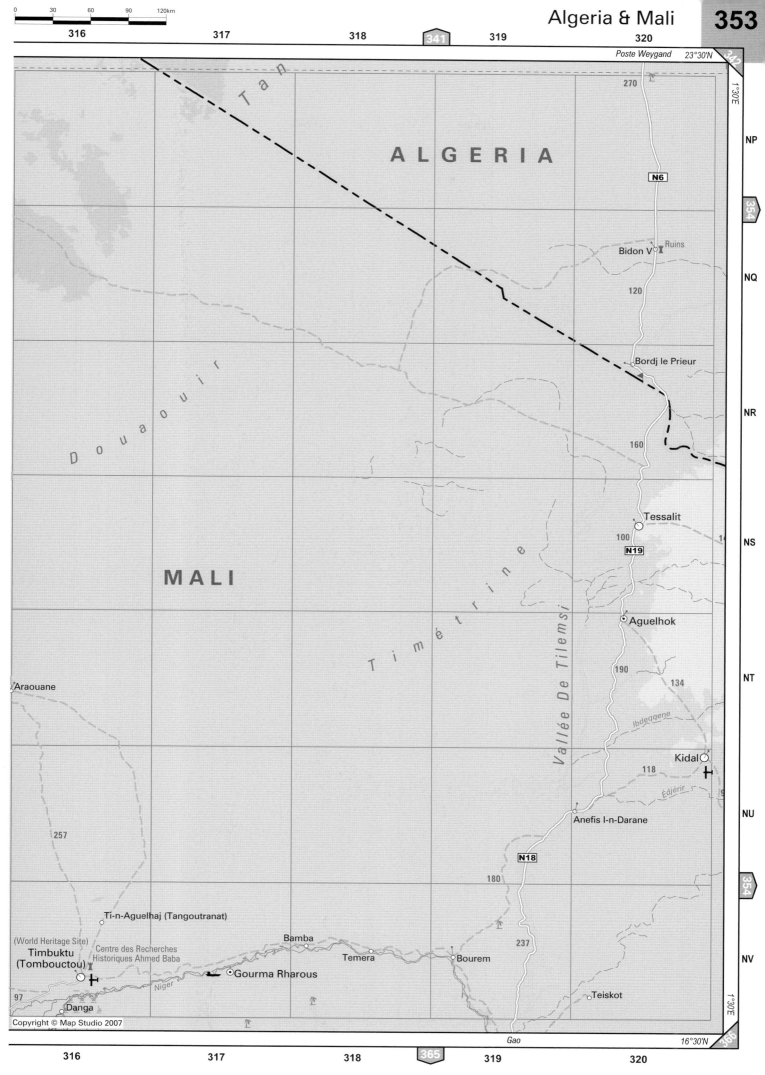

A L G E R I A

MALI

Poste Weygand   23°30'N

270

N6

Bidon V   ⚓ Ruins

120

Bordj le Prieur

160

Tessalit

100
N19

14

Aguelhok

190

134

Ibdeqqene

Kidal

118

Édjérir

9

Anefis I-n-Darane

N18

180

257

Araouane

Timétrine

Vallée De Tilemsi

Douaouir

Tan

Ti-n-Aguelhaj (Tangoutranat)

Bamba

237

(World Heritage Site)
Centre des Recherches
Historiques Ahmed Baba

Temera

Bourem

Timbuktu
(Tombouctou)

Gourma Rharous

Niger

97

Danga

Teiskot

Gao   16°30'N

NP

NQ

NR

NS

NT

NU

NV

342
354
354
366

0   30   60   90   120km

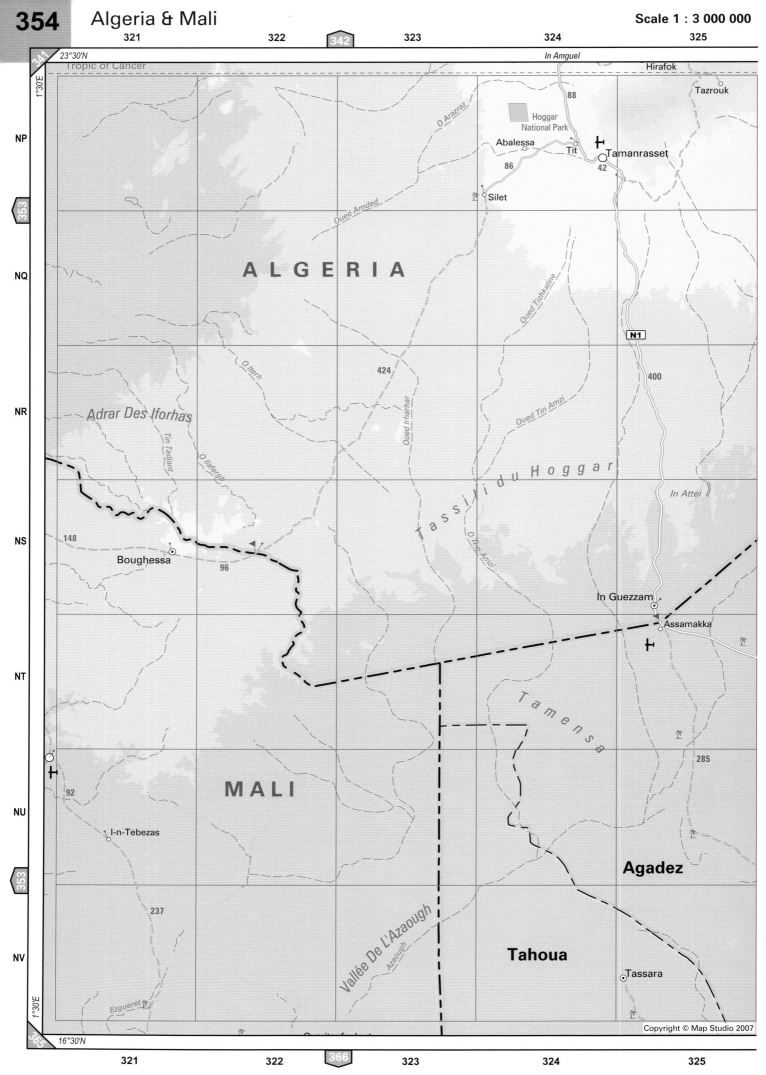

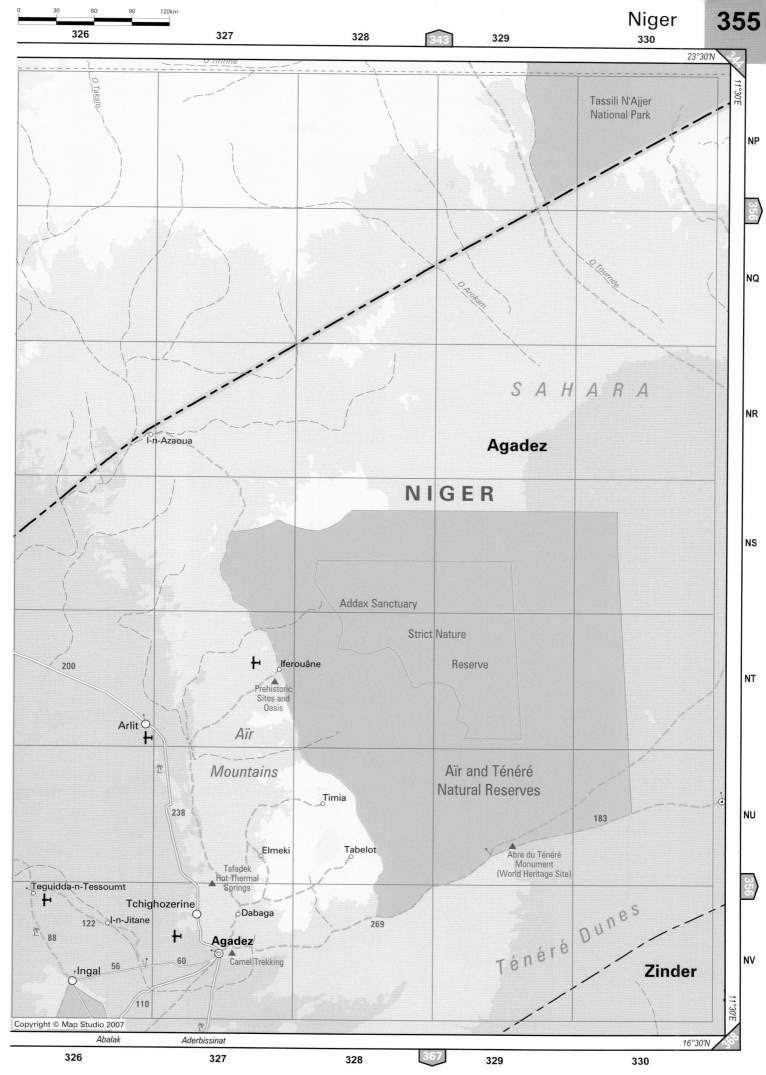

0 30 60 90 120km

326 327 343 328 329 330

23°30'N

11°30'E

NP

O Tinirine

O Takalo

Tassili N'Ajjer
National Park

356

NQ

O Tournde

O Arokam

S A H A R A

NR

I-n-Azaoua

Agadez

NIGER

NS

Addax Sanctuary

Strict Nature

Reserve

200

Iferouâne

NT

Prehistoric
Sites and
Oasis

Arlit

Aïr

Aïr and Ténéré
Natural Reserves

Mountains

Timia

183

NU

238

Elmeki

Tabelot

Abre du Ténéré
Monument
(World Heritage Site)

Teguidda-n-Tessoumt

Tafadek
Hot Thermal
Springs

122

Tchighozerine

356

I-n-Jitane

Dabaga

269

88

Ténéré Dunes

Ingal

56

Agadez

60

NV

Camel Trekking

Zinder

110

Copyright © Map Studio 2007

Abalak

Aderbissinat

16°30'N

11°30'E

326 327 367 328 329 330

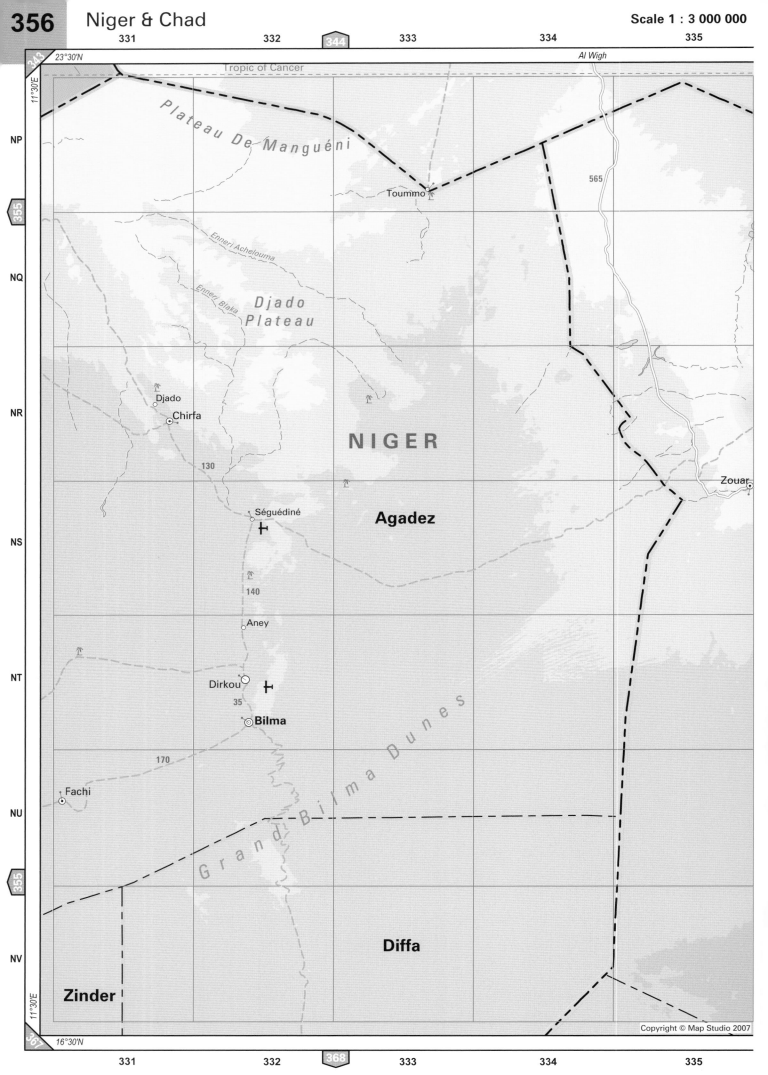

331 332 344 333 334 335

NP

NQ

NR

NS

NT

NU

NV

23°30'N
Tropic of Cancer
Al Wigh

Plateau De Manguéni

565

Enneri Achelouma

Enneri Blaka

Djado
Plateau

Toummo

NIGER

Djado
Chirfa

130

Zouar

Séguédiné

Agadez

140

Aney

Dirkou
35

Bilma

170

Grand Bilma Dunes

Fachi

Diffa

Zinder

11°30'E
16°30'N

331 332 368 333 334 335

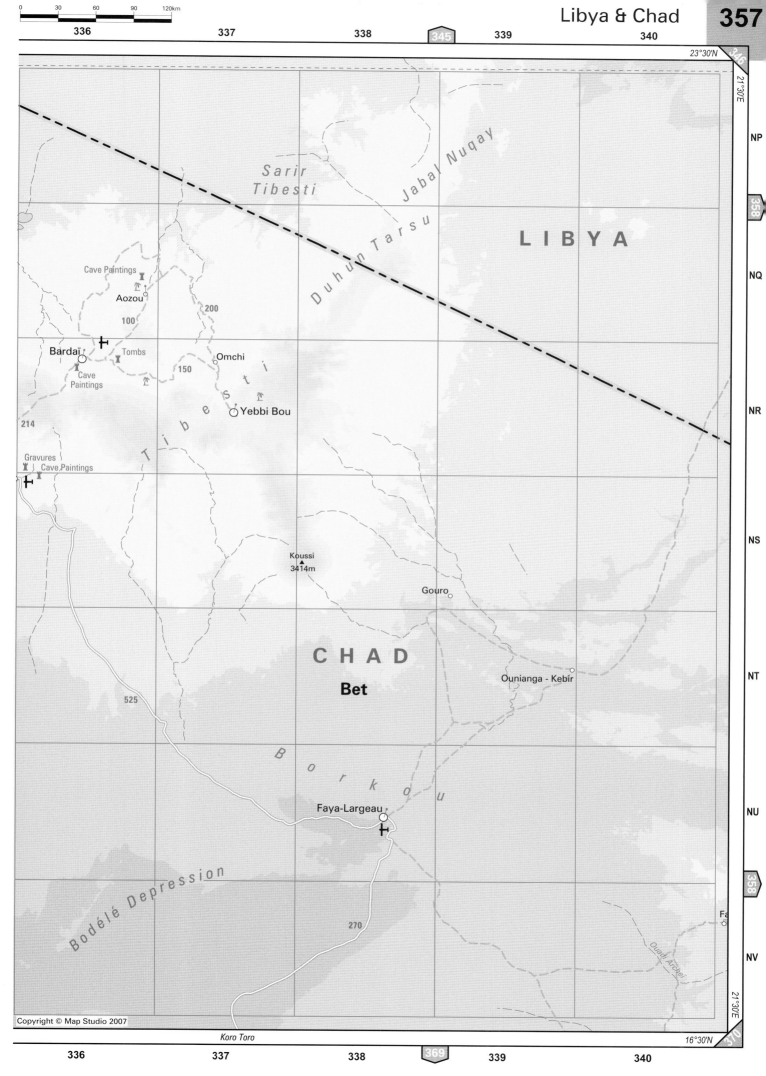

0 30 60 90 120km

23°30'N

21°30'E

346

NP

S a r i r
T i b e s t i

Jabal Nuqay

358

NQ

Cave Paintings

Aozou

L I B Y A

Duhun Tarsu

200

100

Bardaï

Tombs

NR

Omchi

Cave
Paintings

150

T i b e s t i

214

Yebbi Bou

Gravures Cave Paintings

NS

Koussi
3414m

Gouro

21°3'0E

C H A D

NT

Bet

Ounianga - Kebir

525

B o r k o u

Faya-Largeau

NU

358

Bodélé Depression

Fa

NV

270

Ouad Archei

21°3'0E

Koro Toro

16°30'N

370

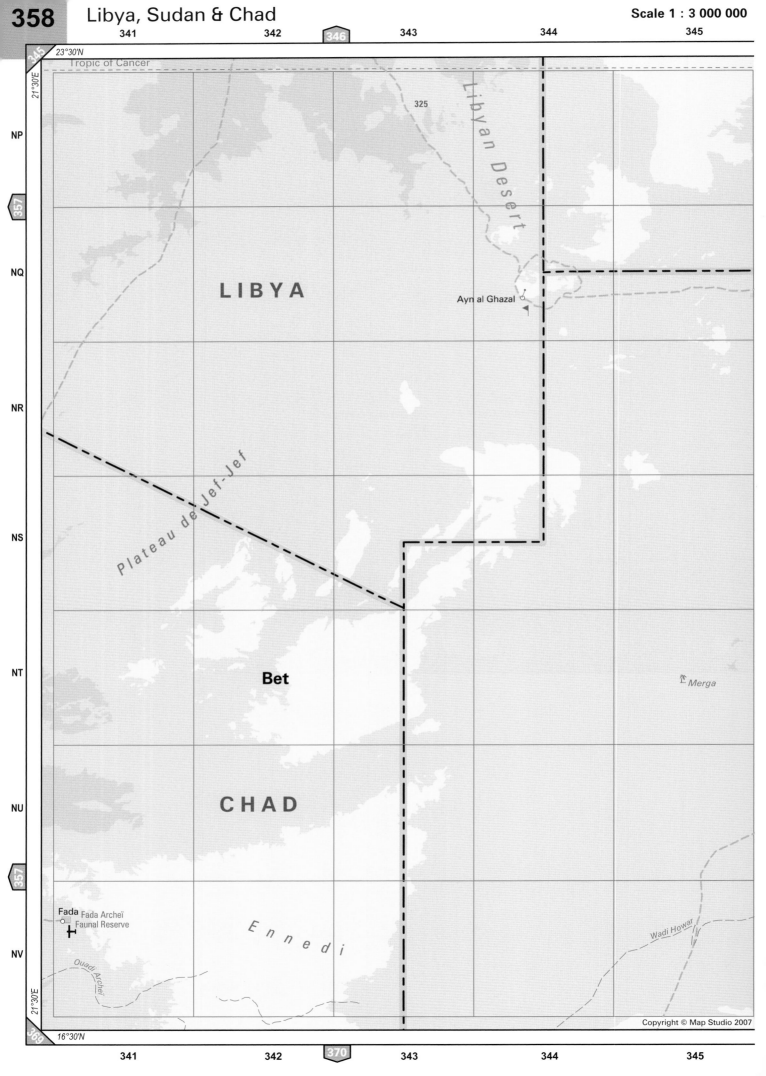

341 342 346 343 344 345

23°30'N
21°30'E
Tropic of Cancer

NP

357

NQ

325

Libyan Desert

LIBYA

Ayn al Ghazal

NR

Plateau de Jef-Jef

NS

Bet

NT

Merga

CHAD

NU

357

Fada
Fada Archeï
Faunal Reserve

Ennedi

Wadi Howar

NV

Ouadi Archeï

21°30'E
16°30'N

369 341 342 370 343 344 345

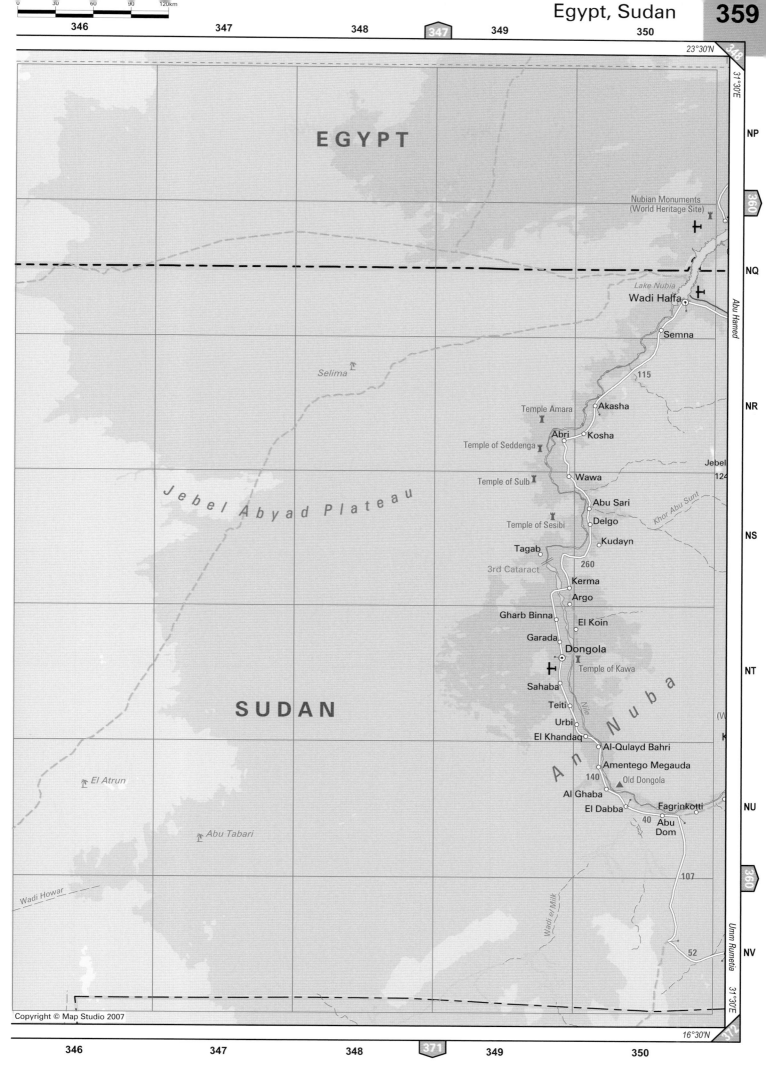

0 30 60 90 120km

23°30'N
31°30'E

NP

Nubian Monuments
(World Heritage Site)

360

EGYPT

NQ

Lake Nubia

Wadi Halfa

Semna

115

NR

Selima

Akasha

Temple Amara

Abri   Kosha

Temple of Seddenga

Jebel
124

J e b e l   A b y a d   P l a t e a u

Temple of Sulb   Wawa

Abu Sari

Khor Abu Sunt

NS

Temple of Sesibi   Delgo

Kudayn

Tagab

260

3rd Cataract

Kerma

Argo

Gharb Binna   El Koin

Garada

NT

Dongola

Temple of Kawa

Sahaba

S U D A N

Teiti

Urbi

A n   N u b a

El Khandaq

Al-Qulayd Bahri

El Atrun

Amentego Megauda

140   Old Dongola

Al Ghaba

El Dabba   Fagrinkotti

NU

Abu Tabari

40   Abu
Dom

107

Wadi Howar

360

Umm Rumeila

52

NV

16°30'N
31°30'E

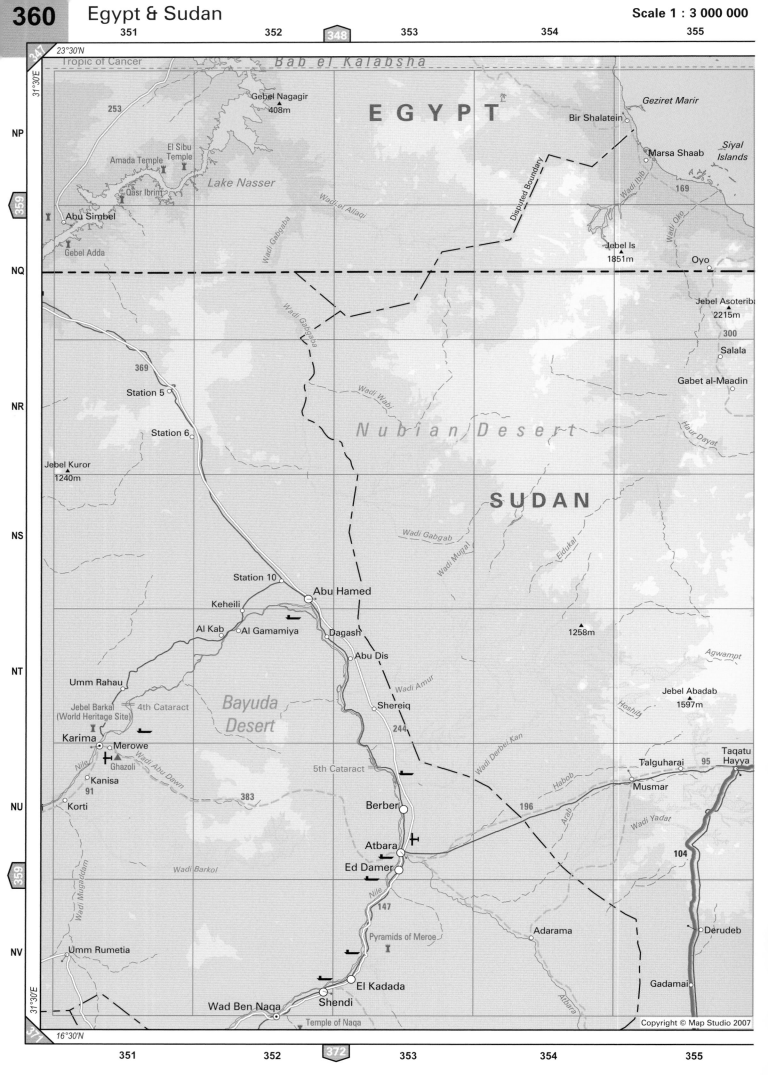

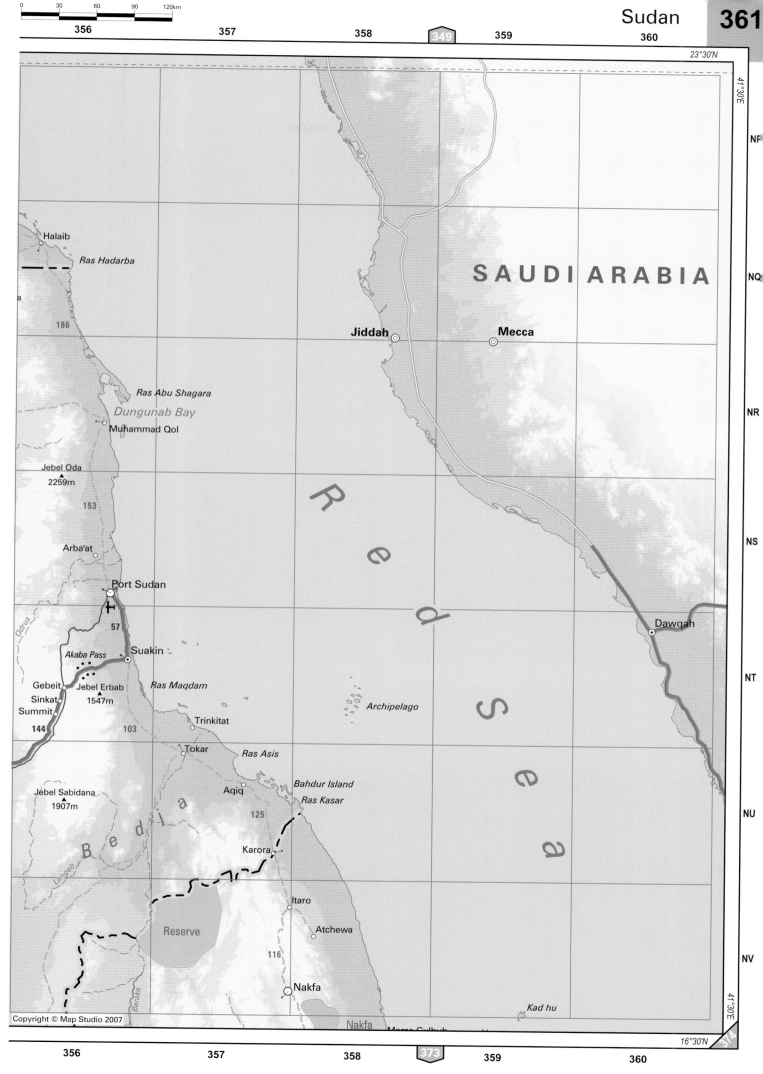

0   30   60   90   120km

356   357   358   349   359   360

23°30'N

41°30'E

NP

Halaib

Ras Hadarba

186

NQ

SAUDI ARABIA

Ras Abu Shagara

Dungunab Bay

Muhammad Qol

Jiddah   **Mecca**

Jebel Oda
▲
2259m

153

NR

Arba'at

NS

Port Sudan

⊞

57

Suakin

Akaba Pass

Gebeit   Jebel Erbab
Sinkat   ▲
Summit   1547m

144   103

Ras Maqdam

Trinkitat

Tokar

Ras Asis

R   e   d

S   e   a

Archipelago

Dawqah

NT

Odrus

Jebel Sabidana
▲
1907m

Bahdur Island

Aqiq   *Ras Kasar*

125

Bedia

NU

Karora

Langeb

Itaro

Atchewa

Reserve

116

NV

Baraka

Nakfa

Kad hu

Nakfa

Marsa Gulbub

Copyright © Map Studio 2007

41°30'E

16°30'N

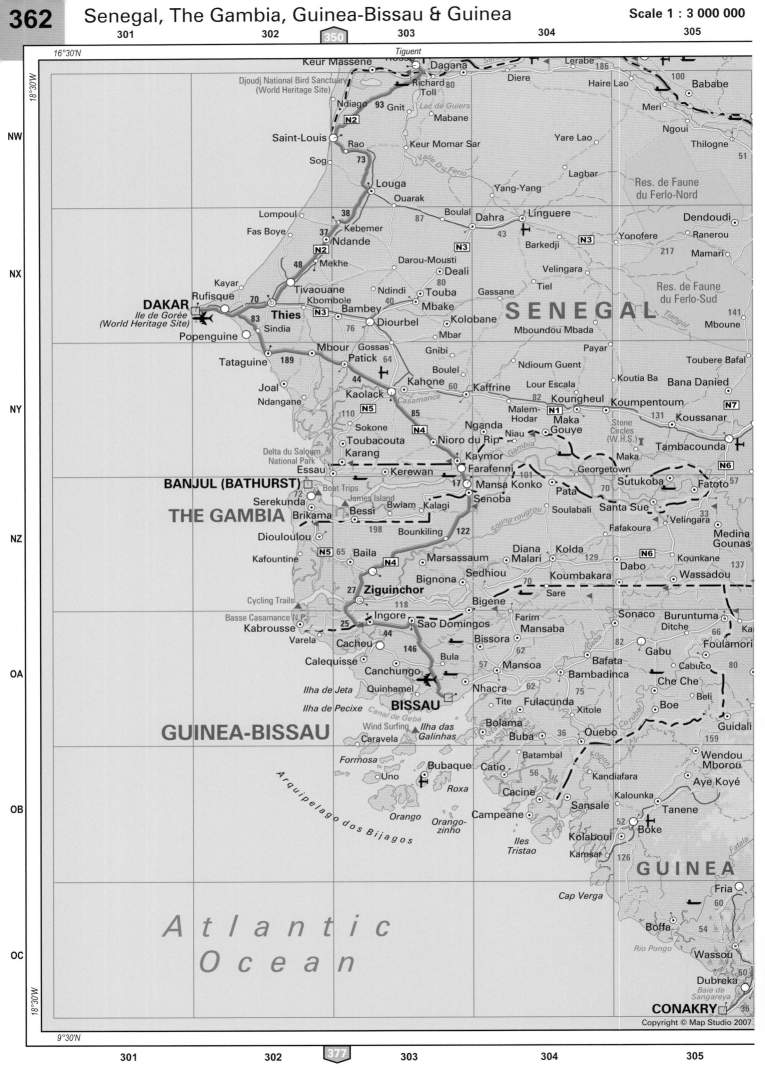

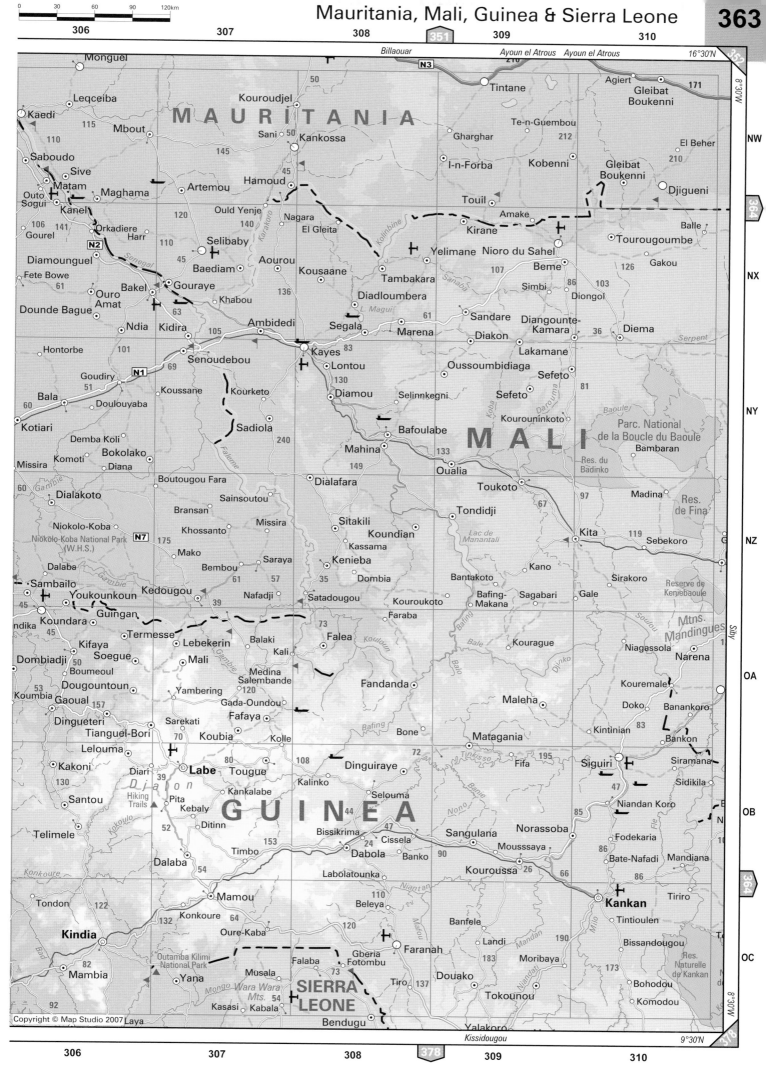

306   307   308   351   309   310

MAURITANIA

Monguel   Kouroudjel   50   Billaouar   N3   Tintane   210   Ayoun el Atrous   Ayoun el Atrous   16°30'N   8°30'W   171   NW
Leqceiba   115   Sani   50   Kankossa   Te-n-Guembou   Agiert   Gleibat Boukenni
Kaedi   Mbout   145   45   Gharghar   I-n-Forba   Kobenni   212   Gleibat   El Beher   210
Saboudo   Artemou   Hamoud   Touil   Amake   Boukenni   Djigueni   NX
Sive   120   Ould Yenje   140   Nagara   Kirane   Tourougoumbe   Balle
Outo Sogui   Matam   Maghama   El Gleita   Yelimane   Nioro du Sahel   Beme   126   Gakou
Kanel   106   141   Orkadiere   110   45   Baediam   Aourou   Kousaane   107   Simbi   86   Diongol   103
Diamounguel   61   Harr   Selibaby   136   Diadloumbera   Tambakara   Sandare   Diangounte-   Diema   NY
Fete Bowe   Bakel   Gouraye   Khabou   L. Magui   Marena   61   Diakon   Kamara   36   Serpent
Dounde Bague   Ouro Amat   63   Ambidedi   Segala   Lakamane   Sefeto   81
Ndia   Kidira   105   Kayes   83   Oussoumbidiaga   Sefeto   Baoule
Hontorbe   101   Senoudebou   Lontou   Selinnkegni   Kourouninkoto   Parc. National   NZ
Goudiry   N1   69   Koussane   130   Diamou   de la Boucle du Baoule
Bala   51   Doulouyaba   Kourketo   Diamou   Res. du   Bambaran
60   Kotiari   Demba Koli   Sadiola   240   Bafoulabe   Badinko   MALI
Missira   Komoti   Bokolako   Mahina   133   Madina   Res.
Dialakoto   Diana   Boutougou Fara   149   Oualia   de Fina
Niokolo-Koba   Sainsoutou   Dialafara   Toukoto   67   97
Niokolo-Koba National Park   Bransan   Missira   Sitakili   Tondidji   119   Kita   Sebekoro
(W.H.S.)   N7   175   Khossanto   Koundian   Lac de   Sirakoro   Reserve de
Dalaba   Mako   Kassama   Manantali   Kano   Keniebaoule
Sambailo   Bembou   Saraya   Kenieba   35   Bantakoto   Sagabari   Gale
Youkounkoun   Kedougou   61   57   Dombia   Bafing-   Mtns.
45   Guingan   39   Nafadji   Satadougou   Kouroukoto   Makana   Mandingues
ndika   Koundara   Termesse   Lebekerin   Balaki   Faraba   Kourague   Niagassola   Narena
Kifaya   Mali   Kali   Falea   73   Bale   Kouremale
Dombiadji   Soegue   Medina   Fandanda   Doko   Banankoro
Koumbia   Boumeoul   Yambering   Salembande   120   Maleha   83   Bankon
53   Dougountoun   Gada-Oundou   Bone   Matagania   Kintinian   Siramana
Gaoual   157   Sarekati   Fafaya   Bafing   Siguiri   Sidikila
Dingueteri   Tianguel-Bori   70   Koubia   Kolle   47   Niandan Koro
Lelouma   80   Dinguiraye   72   Fifa   195   85   Fodekaria
Kakoni   130   Diari   Labe   Tougue   Kalinko   Norassoba   Bate-Nafadi   Mandiana
Santou   39   Pita   Kankalabe   Selouma   Moussaya   86   86
Telimele   Hiking Trails   Kebaly   Bissikrima   Cissela   Sangulana   Kouroussa   26   66
Djalon   Ditinn   GUINEA   24   Dabola   90   Kankan
Tondon   122   52   Timbo   153   Labolatounka   Banko   110   Tiriro
Mamou   Dalaba   54   Beleya   Banfele   Landi   190   Tintioulen
Kindia   132   Konkoure   64   Oure-Kaba   120   Gberia   Faranah   183   Moribaya   Bissandougou
Mambia   82   Yana   Musala   Fotombu   Tiro   137   Douako   173   Bohodou   Res. Naturelle
92   Laya   Kasasi   Kabala   54   Bendugu   Yalakoro   Tokounou   Komodou   de Kankan
SIERRA LEONE   Kissidougou   9°30'N   8°30'W

306   307   308   378   309   310

Copyright © Map Studio 2007

N2   Senegal   Karakoro   Kolinbine   Sanaba   Koba   Darouma   Soulou   Siby   352   364
Gambie   Faleme   Gambie   Kokoulo   Djalon   Bafing   Dinko   Balo   Kouloun   Tinkisso   Bante   Nono   Niantan   Marou   Mandan   Niandan   Milo   364
Bad   Konkoure   Mongo Wara Wara Mts.   378

Mali, Mauritania, Burkina Faso & Côte D'Ivoire

16°30'N
Néma

MALI

Aouinat er Rajjat
Gargando
Lac Tele
Goundam
Lac Fati
El Boibou
Houeiriye
Lac Oro
90
Timbédra
Kataouana
Tonka
Bou Gadoum
Amourj
122
Houeiriye
Niafounke
Saraféré
Koumbi Salem
Ruins
191
Sah
78
135

MAURITANIA
193
84
Bassikounou
Léré
Gati-Loumo
Lac Tanda
Youvarou
Médala
89
Korientze
Adel Bagrou
16
Nampala
Lac Debo
46
Koronga
Kona
Sanpaka
Dali
Boulel
65
169
Nara
55
Dilli
Goumbou
Dioura
Komoguel
Sevaré
Akor
168
108
Mosque
Falou
89
Sokolo
Mopti
30
Ban-
diagara
Mourdiah
50
Soma-
dougou
Bankass
111
Warde
Niono
Kouakourou
156
79
Mercoya
Doura
110
Djafarabe
Djénné
(World Heritage Site)
Sofara
Didieni
Taïmana
Sansanding
Massina
Say
130
41
Sonanga
Dioro
91
Sarro
N6
Kolokani
Togou
Fatine
Si
69
Banamba
Ségou
Banankoro
San
Tominian
Ouenkoro
Réserve
de Bay
Tioribougou
56
Komodimini
Zinzana
41
Bénéna
Barani
Niamina
Tamani
46
111
53
Mandiakui
Djibasso
100
94
Baraoueli
88
Yallo
81
Nossombougou
Koula
110
Sanando
Bla
Kamparana
Ben
Soin
Guissoumale
30
Konobougou
Falo
74
Mpessoba
82
Nouna
57
Negala
Koulikoro
Fana
Kouniana
Kaledougou
38
28
125
Dioïla
84
Konina
Koutiala
82
Sanaba
47
Kati
Santiguila
Belako
Konseguela
91
Yorosso
15
BAMAKO
Baguineda
Zàngasso
Karangana
Kouri
20
Solenzo
77
127
Siby
Sanankoroba
Mena
Kouoro
Faramana
43
118
Ouarkoye
67
Banko
157
130
Koundougou
Kouka
Haho
Kourouba
Dogo
Massigui
Sara
Kangaba
Ouelessebougou
Sanso
Blendio
Kignan
Kléla
BURKINA FASO
Kangare
Lac del
Séllingue
Sido
Kourouma
75
Bekuy
99
Bougouni
Sirakoro
Niéna
N9
Satiri
Faragouaran
134
Nkourala
78
Sikasso
BOBO
137
Zantie-
bougou
Kebila
50
DIOULASSO
Badogo
Kolondieba
Koloko
45
Tjera
73
Res. Partielle
de Nabere
136
Yanfolila
Yorobougoula
Garalo
A5
Lobougoula
Loulouni
136
Orodara
101
Sidéradougou
Niantanina
146
154
Foulabala
Kadiana
Fourou
Tourni
Banfora
Kalana
A7
34
Kadiolo
Sindou
Douna
Tiefora
Pilemane
Manankoro
Tingréla
Soubaka-
niedougou
Kouéré
Tindlla
Tienko
Bolona
Misseni
A300
Niangoloko
96
Toumoundjila
Kotoula
117
Ngandana
Nielle
Yendéré
Loropeni
Mininian
Sianhala
40
Diawala
61
Kaouara
Kampti
Res.
Naturelle
de Kapkan
Goulia
Mbengue
Kaloa
Ouangolo-
dougou
45
Noumou-
kiedoumou
Samatiguila
Samakona
Kouto
Kassera
Tiebila
Nambolkaha
Mangodara
168
Kimbirila Sud
Kaniasso
Kadiaso
Kolia
75
Gbodonon
53
Kafolo
Téhini
Gebeledan
Madinani
57
Pono-
dougou
98
Ferkéssédougou
Bombela
Koebonou
Odienné
30
Tieme 49
Boundiali
Korhogo
Sirana
34
Bako
9°30'N
Gbadikaha

CÔTE D'IVOIRE

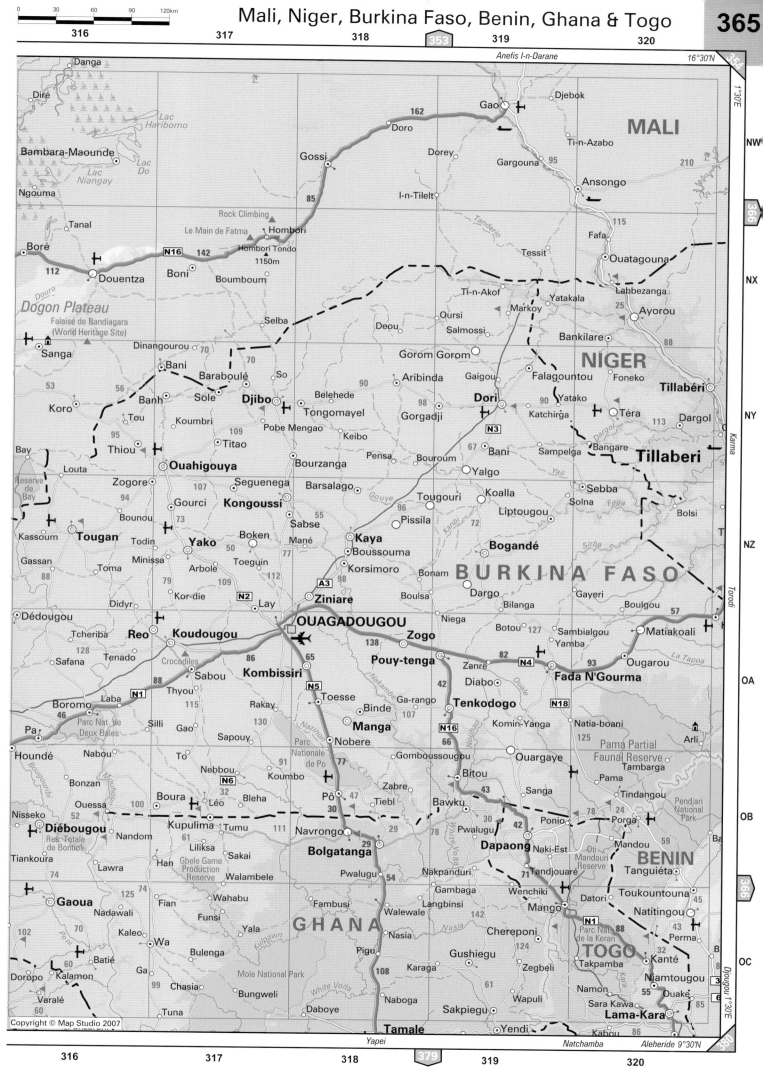

0   30   60   90   120km

Anefis I-n-Darane   16°30'N

1°30'E   354   NW

Danga
Diré
Bambara-Maounde
Ngouma
Lac Haribomo
Lac Do
Lac Niangay
Tanal
Boré
112
Douentza
N16   142
Boni
Boumboum
Gossi
85
Doro
162
Gao
Djebok
MALI
Dorey
Ti-n-Azabo
Gargouna   95
I-n-Tilelt
Ansongo
210
115
Fafa
Tessit
Ouatagouna
Labbezanga
25
Ayorou

NX

Rock Climbing
Le Main de Fatma
Hombori
Hombori Tondo
1150m
Selba
Ti-n-Akof
Yatakala
Markoy
Bankilare
88

NX

Dogon Plateau
Falaise de Bandiagara
(World Heritage Site)
Sanga
Dinangourou   70
Bani
Baraboulé
So
70
Deou
Oursi
Salmossi
Gorom Gorom
Gaigou
Falagountou
Yatako
Foneko
Tillabéri

NY

53
56
Koro
Banh
Sole
Djibo
Belehede
Tongomayel
Keibo
90
Aribinda
Gorgadji
98
Dori
N3
90
Katchirga
Sampelga
Bangare
Tillaberi
Téra
113
Dargol
Karma

NY

Tou
Koumbri
Pobe Mengao
Pensa
Bouroum
67
Bani
Yali
Dargol

95
Thiou
Titao
109
Bourzanga
Yalgo
Koalla

Bay
Louta
Ouahigouya
Seguenega
107
Barsalago
Gouye
Tougouri
96
Pissila
72
Sebba
Solna
Liptougou
Bolsi
Faga

NZ

Reserve de Bay
Zogore
94
Gourci
Kongoussi
55
Sabse
Tougan
Bounou
73
Yako
Boken
Mané
Kaya
Boussouma
Korsimoro
Bonam
Bogandé
Dargo
Sirba

Kassoum
Todin
50
Arbole
Toeguin
77
BURKINA FASO

Gassan
88
Toma
Minissa
79
Kor-die
109
112
98
Boulsa
Bilanga
Gayeri
Boulgou
57
Matiakoali

NZ

Didyr
N2
Lay
A3
Ziniare
Botou   127
Sambialgou
Yamba
Ougarou
La Tapoa
Torodi

Dédougou
Tcheriba
128
Tenado
Crocodiles
Koudougou
86
65
OUAGADOUGOU
138
Zogo
Niega
82
N4
93
Fada N'Gourma

OA

Reo
Sabou
Kombissiri
Pouy-tenga
Zanre
Diabo

Safana
88
Thyou
N5
Toesse
42
Ga-rango
Tenkodogo
N18
Natia-boani
Arli

N1
Laba
115
Silli
Rakay
Binde
107
Manga
Komin-Yanga
125
Pama Partial Faunal Reserve

Boromo
46
Gao
130
Nobere
66
Gomboussougou
Ouargaye
Tambarga

Pa
Parc Nat. de Deux Bales
Nabou
To
Sapouy
Parc Nationale de Po
77
N16
Bitou
Pama

Houndé
Bonzan
N6
Nebbou
Koumbo
Zabre
43
Sanga
Tindangou

OB

Bougouriba
Ouessa
Boura
Léo
Bleha
Pô
47
Tiebl
Bawku
30
Ponio
42
Porga
Pendjari National Park

Nisseko
52
100
Kupulima
Tumu
111
Navrongo
29
78
Pwalugu
Naki-Est
Mandou
59

Diébougou
Res. Totale de Bontioli
Nandom
Liliksa
Sakai
Bolgatanga
White Volta
Dapaong
Oti Mandouri Reserve
BENIN

Tiankoura
Lawra
Han
Gbele Game Production Reserve
Walambele
Pwalugu
54
Nakpanduri
71
Tandjouaré
Tanguiéta

74
Gaoua
125
74
Wahabu
Fian
Fambusi
Gambaga
Wenchiki
Datori
Toukountouna
45

102
Nadawali
Kaleo
Funsi
Walewale
142
Mango
N1
88
Natitingou
43
Perma

60
Batié
Wa
Yala
Pigu
Nasia
124
Chereponi
Parc Nat. de la Keran
32
Kanté
TOGO

Doropo
Kalamon
Ga
Bulenga
108
Karaga
Gushiegu
Zegbeli
Namon
Quake
85

Varalé
60
Chasia
Bungweli
Mole National Park
Daboye
Naboga
Sakpiegu
61
Wapuli
Sara Kawa
55
Lama-Kara

OC

Tamale
Yapei
Yendi
Natchamba
Aleheride   9°30'N
Djougou 1°30'E

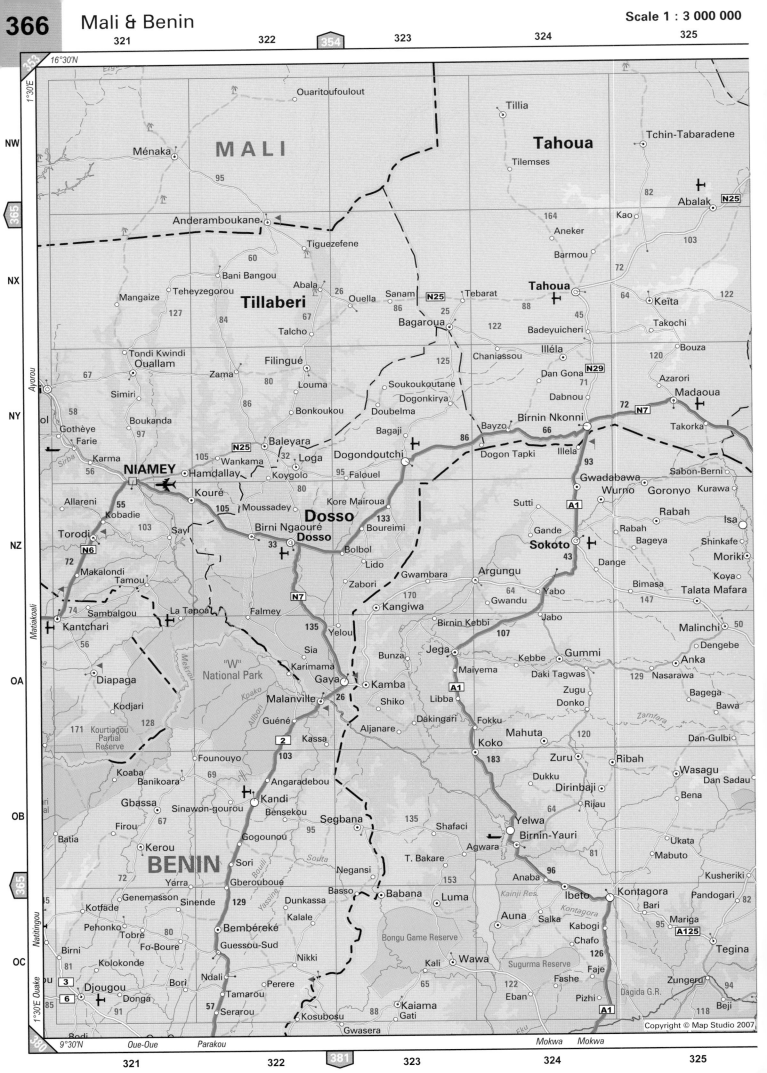

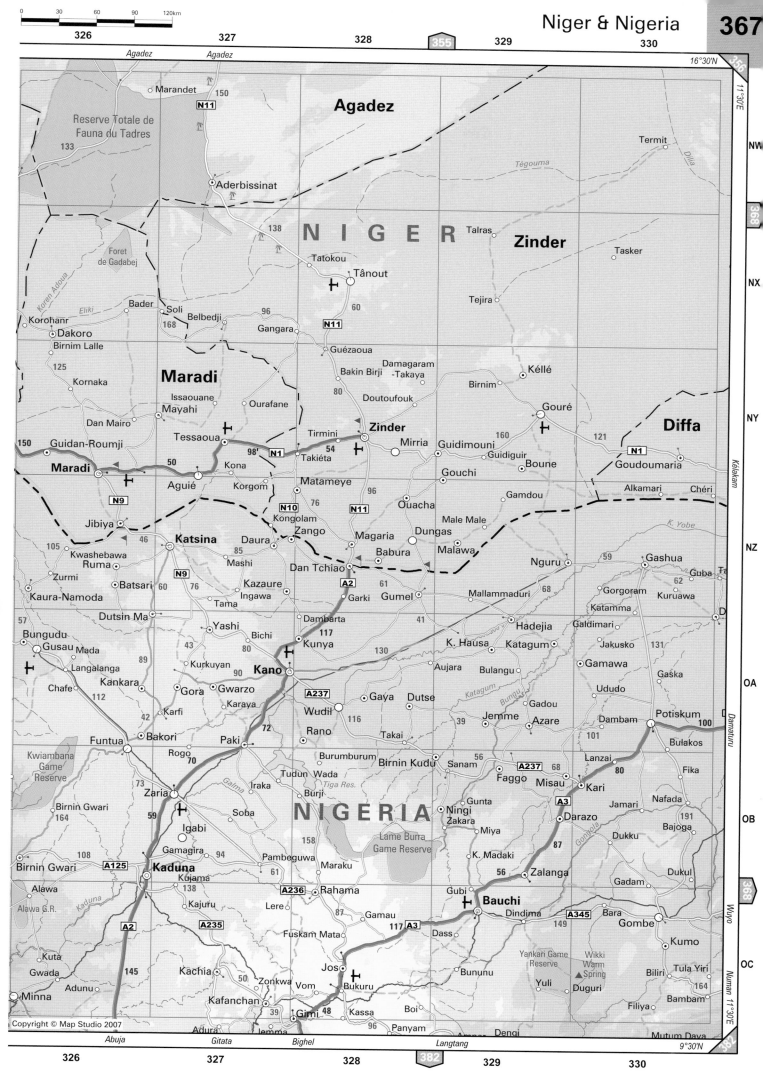

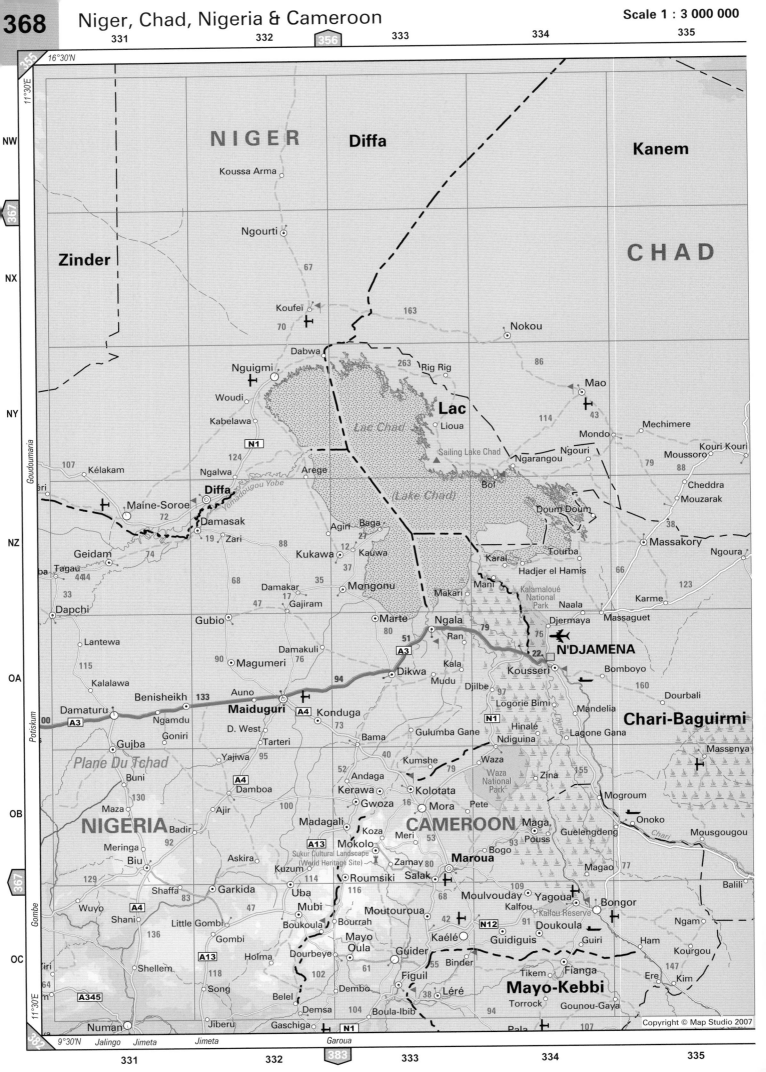

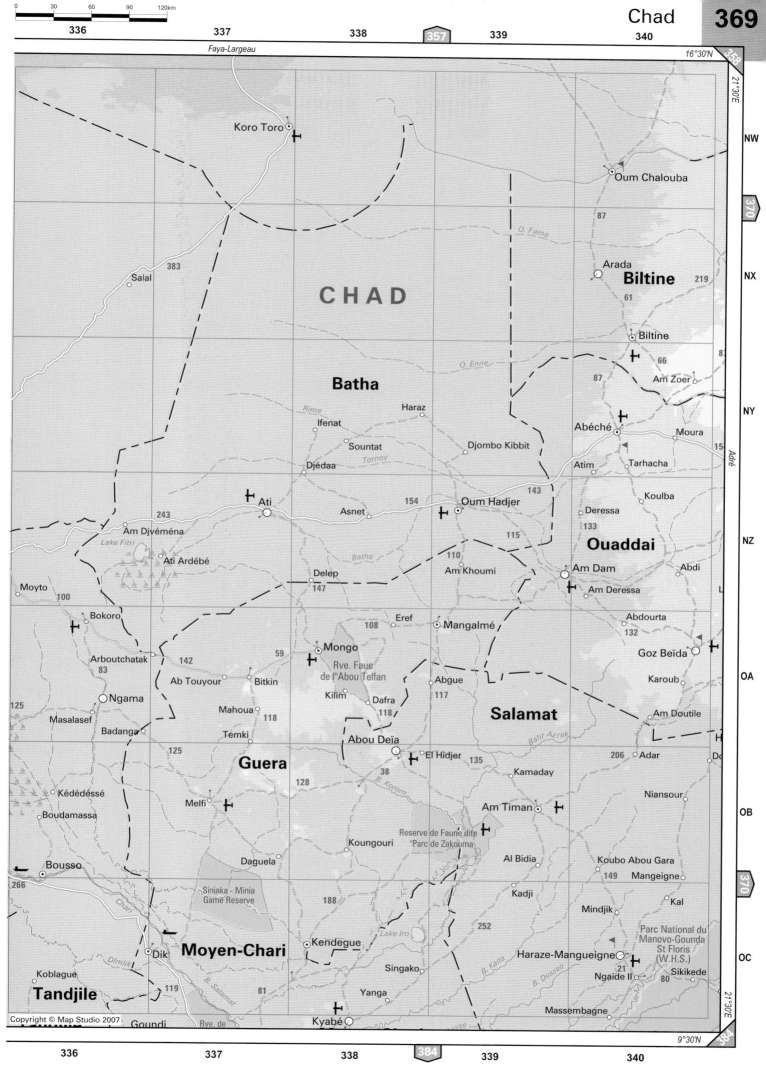

0   30   60   90   120km

336   337   357   338   339   340

Faya-Largeau

16°30'N

21°30'E

358

370

Koro Toro

NW

Oum Chalouba

87

Arada

Biltine

NX

61

383

Salal

CHAD

Biltine

66

Am Zoer

87

87

15

Batha

Haraz

O. Enne

O. Fama

Ifenat

Abéché

Moura

Sountat

Djombo Kibbit

NY

Djédaa

Tornoy

Rime

Atim

Tarhacha

Ati

154

Oum Hadjer

143

Koulba

243

Asnet

Deressa

Am Djéména

Lake Fitri

115

133

Ouaddai

NZ

Ati Ardébé

110

Am Khoumi

Abdi

Moyto

100

Delep

147

Am Dam

Batha

Am Deressa

Bokoro

108

Eref

Mangalmé

Abdourta

132

Arboutchatak

142

59

Mongo

Goz Beïda

83

Rve. Faue

de l"Abou Telfan

Karoub

OA

Ngama

Ab Touyour

Bitkin

Abgue

117

125

Kilim

Dafra

Am Doutile

Masalasef

Mahoua

118

118

Salamat

Badanga

Témki

Abou Deïa

Bahr Azrak

H

125

El Hidjer

135

Adar

Do

Guera

38

206

128

Kamaday

Niansour

Kédédéssé

Melfi

B. Korom

Am Timan

OB

Boudamassa

Reserve de Faune dite

"Parc de Zakouma"

Al Bidia

Koubo Abou Gara

Bousso

Koungouri

149

Mangeigne

266

Daguela

Kadji

Kal

Siniaka - Minia

Game Reserve

188

Mindjik

370

252

Parc National du

Manovo-Gounda

St Floris

(W.H.S.)

Chari

Lake Iro

Moyen-Chari

Kendegue

Haraze-Mangueigne

OC

Dik

Dimlik

Singako

B. Kéita

21

Sikikede

Koblagué

B. Salamat

119

81

Yanga

Ngaide II

80

Tandjile

Massembagne

B. Dosseo

Goundi   Rve. de

Kyabé

9°30'N

21°30'E

384

336   337   384   338   339   340

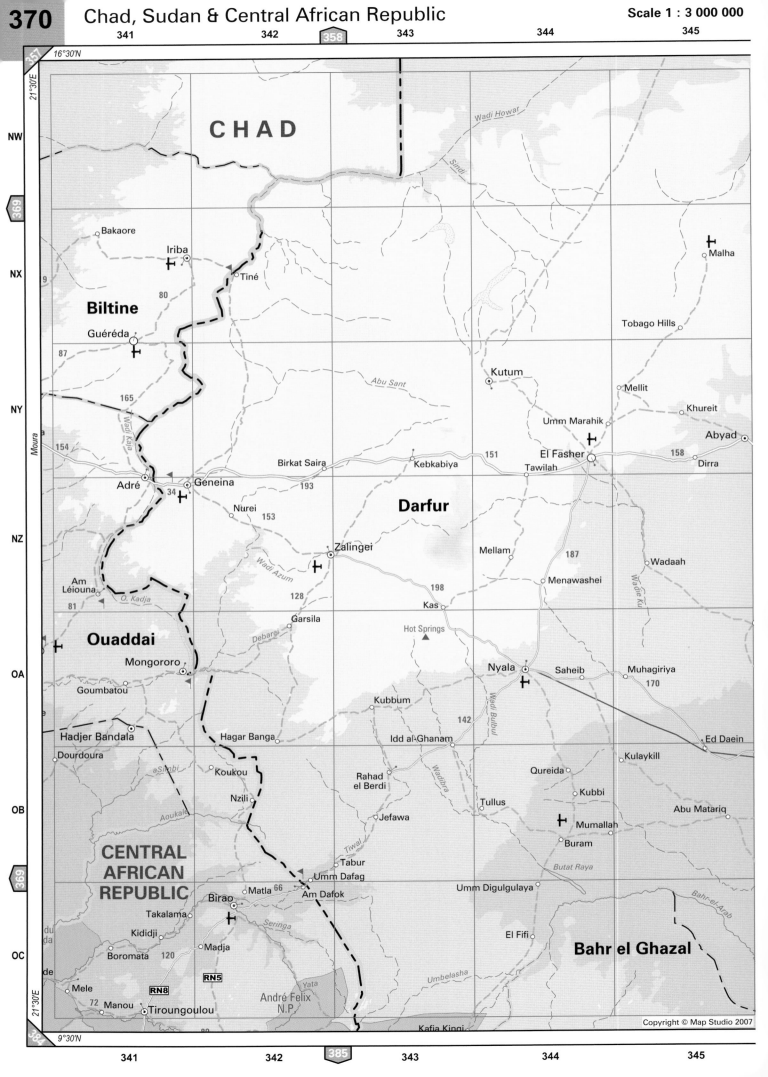

16°30'N
21°30'E

357
369

C H A D

NW

Wadi Howar

Sindi

Bakaore

Iriba
80

NX

Malha

Tiné

Biltine

Guéréda
87

Tobago Hills

165

Wadi Kaja

Abu Sant

Kutum

NY

Mellit

Khureit

Umm Marahik

Abyad

154

Moura

Birkat Saira

Kebkabiya

El Fasher

158

Tawilah

Dirra

Adré

34

Geneina
193

Darfur

Nurei
153

NZ

Zalingei

Mellam

Wadaah

187

Wadi Azum

Menawashei

Wadie Ku

Am
Léiouna
81

128

198

O. Kadja

Garsila

Kas

Debarei

Hot Springs

Ouaddai

Mongororo

Nyala

Saheib

Muhagiriya

OA

Goumbatou

170

Kubbum

142

Wadi Bulbul

Hadjer Bandala

Hagar Banga

Idd al-Ghanam

Ed Daein

Dourdoura

Kulaykill

aSinbi

Koukou

Qureida

Kubbi

Abu Matariq

Nzili

Rahad
el Berdi

Wadibra

OB

Aoukale

Jefawa

Tullus

Mumallah

Buram

**CENTRAL
AFRICAN
REPUBLIC**

Tiwal

Tabur

Umm Dafag

Butat Raya

369

Matla
66

Am Dafok

Umm Digulgulaya

Birao

Takalama

Seringa

Kididji

El Fifi

Bahr el Ghazal

Madja
120

Boromata

Bahr-el-Arab

OC

*du
da*

Mele

RN5

72
Manou

RN8

Tiroungoulou

André Felix
N.P

Yata

Umbelasha

Kafia Kingi

Copyright © Map Studio 2007

384
385

9°30'N
21°30'E

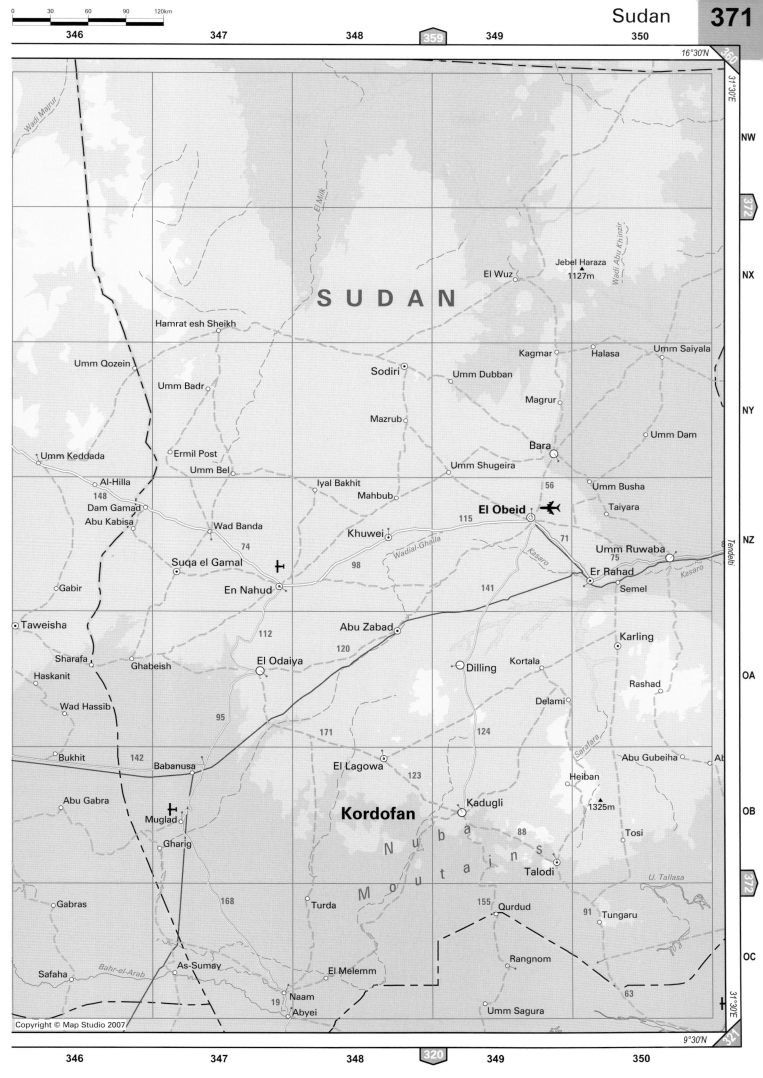

0 30 60 90 120km

346   347   348   359   349   350

16°30'N

31°30'E

NW

372

NX

S U D A N

Jebel Haraza
▲
1127m

Wadi Abu Khinzir

El Wuz

Hamrat esh Sheikh

Kagmar ○   Halasa   Umm Saiyala

NY

Umm Qozein

Sodiri ⊙   Umm Dubban

Umm Badr ○   Magrur

Mazrub   Umm Dam

Ermil Post   Bara ⊙

Umm Keddada   Umm Shugeira

Al-Hilla   Umm Bel ○   Iyal Bakhit   56   Umm Busha

148   Mahbub   115   El Obeid ⊙ ✈   Taiyara

Dam Gamad   Wad Banda   Khuwei ○   71

Abu Kabisa   74   Wadial-Ghaila   Kasaro   Umm Ruwaba ⊙

Suqa el Gamal ○   98   75

En Nahud   141   Er Rahad ⊙   Kasaro

Gabir ○   Semel

NZ

Taweisha ⊙   112   Abu Zabad   Karling ⊙

Sharafa   120   Dilling ○   Kortala

Haskanit   Ghabeish ○   El Odaiya ⊙   Rashad

Wad Hassib   95   171   124   Delami   OA

Bukhit ○   142   Sarafara

Babanusa   El Lagowa   Abu Gubeiha

Abu Gabra   123   Heiban

Muglad   **Kordofan**   Kadugli ⊙   1325m ▲   OB

Gharig   88   Tosi

N u b a   Talodi ⊙   U. Tallasa

Gabras   168   M o u n t a i n s

Turda   155   Qurdud   91   Tungaru

OC

Safaha   As-Sumay   El Melemm   Rangnom

Bahr-el-Arab   19   Naam   Umm Sagura   63

Abyei

9°30'N

31°30'E

346   347   348   320   349   350

372

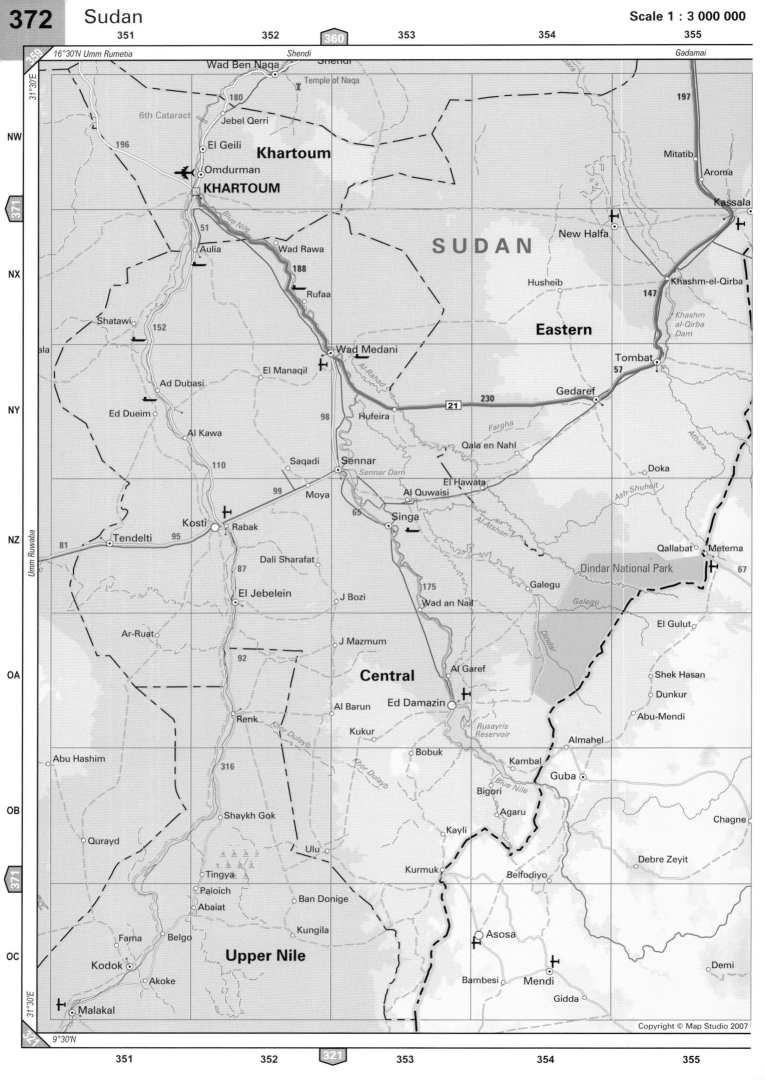

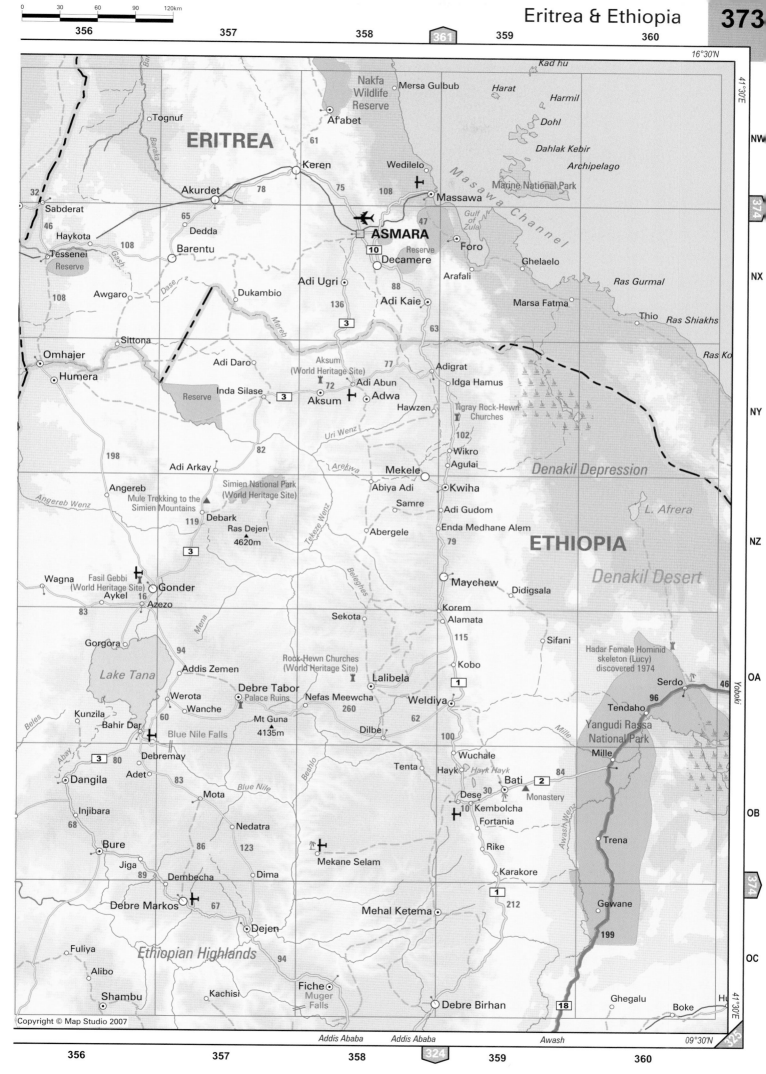

0   30   60   90   120km

356   357   358   361   359   360

16°30'N

41°30'E

NW

ERITREA

Tognuf

Kad hu

Mersa Gulbub

Nakfa
Wildlife
Reserve

Harat

Harmil

Af'abet

61

Dohl

Keren

Wedilelo

Dahlak Kebir
Archipelago

Akurdet   78

75   108

32

Sabderat

46   65

Dedda

Massawa

Marine National Park

374

Haykota   108

Barentu

ASMARA   47

Gulf
of
Zula

NX

Tessenei
Reserve

108

Awgaro

Dukambio

Adi Ugri

10   Reserve
Decamere

Foro

Ghelaelo

Ras Gurmal

Sittona

136   Adi Kaie

Arafali

Marsa Fatma

108

Omhajer

Adi Daro

Aksum
(World Heritage Site)

3

88

63

Thio   Ras Shiakhs

NY

Humera

Reserve

Inda Silase   3

72   Adi Abun
Aksum   Adwa

Hawzen

77   Adigrat
Idga Hamus

Ras Ko

Tigray Rock-Hewn
Churches

Uri Wenz

102

198

Adi Arkay

82

Arekwa

Mekele

Wikro
Agulai

Denakil Depression

L. Afrera

Angereb

Simien National Park
(World Heritage Site)

Abiya Adi

Kwiha

NZ

Angereb Wenz

Mule Trekking to the
Simien Mountains

119   Debark

Samre

Abergele

Adi Gudom

Enda Medhane Alem

ETHIOPIA

Denakil Desert

Ras Dejen
4620m   3

Teteze Wenz

79

Wagna

Fasil Gebbi
(World Heritage Site)

Gonder

16   Azezo

Beleghes

Maychew

Didigsala

Aykel

83

Korem
Alamata

Gorgora

94

Sekota

115

Sifani

Hadar Female Hominid
skeleton (Lucy)
discovered 1974

OA

Mena

Rock-Hewn Churches
(World Heritage Site)

Kobo

Serdo   46

Lake Tana

Addis Zemen

Lalibela

1

96

Yoboki

Kunzila

Beles

Werota
Wanche

Debre Tabor
Palace Ruins

Nefas Meewcha
260

Weldiya   62

Tendaho

Yangudi Rassa
National Park

Bahir Dar

60

Mt Guna
4135m

Dilbe

100

Mille   Mille

Blue Nile Falls

Wuchale

Mille

3   80
Debremay

Tenta   Hayk Hayk

Abay

84

Dangila   Adet

83

Mota

Blue Nile

Hayk   Bati   2   Monastery

Dese   30

Trena

Injibara

Beshlo

Nedatra

Kembolcha

Fortania

OB

68

86   123

Rike

Bure

Mekane Selam

Karakore

Jiga

Dima

Mehal Ketema

1

212

Gewane

Dembecha

Awash Wenz

Debre Markos   67

Dejen

199

374

Fuliya

Ethiopian Highlands

94

OC

Alibo

Fiche
Muger
Falls

Debre Birhan   18

Ghegalu   Boke

Shambu

Kachisi

Hu

Copyright © Map Studio 2007

Addis Ababa   Addis Ababa   Awash   09°30'N

41°30'E

356   357   358   324   359   360

325

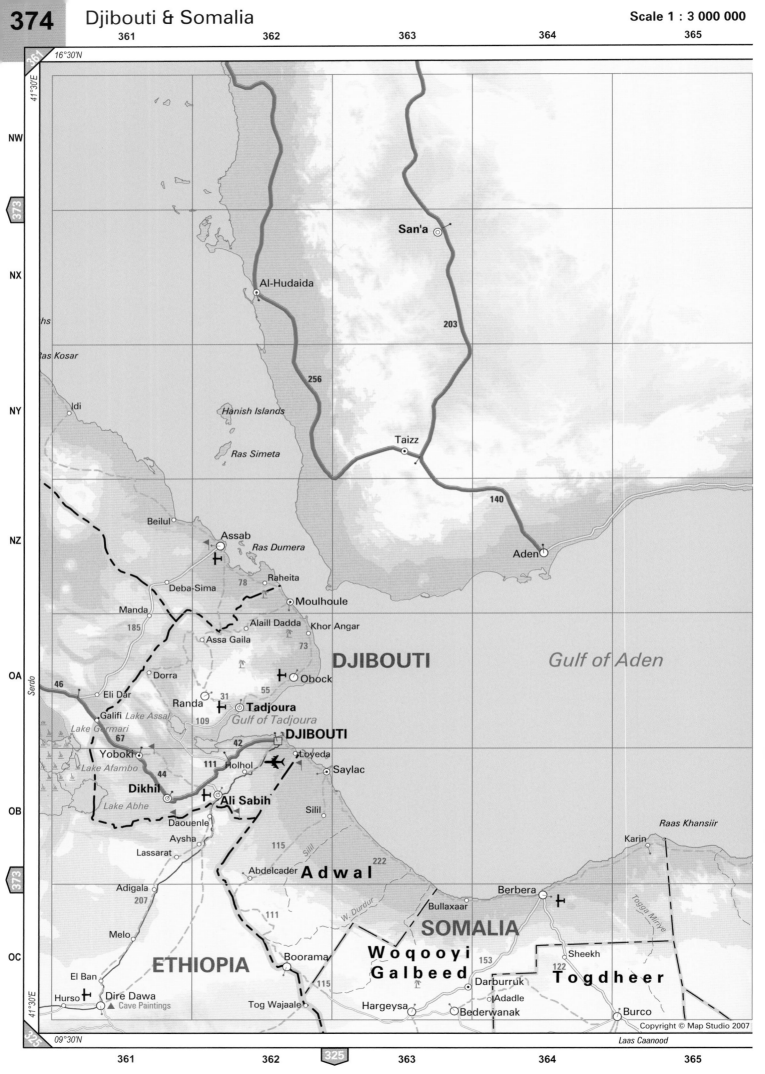

361
362
363
364
365

16°30'N

NW

NX

San'a

NY
Al-Hudaida

256
203

Ras Kosar

Idi

Taizz

NZ
Beilul

140
Assab
Ras Dumera
Aden

Deba-Sima
78
Raheita

Manda
185
Moulhoule

Alaill Dadda
Khor Angar
Assa Gaila

73
DJIBOUTI
Gulf of Aden

OA
Dorra
Obock

46
Eli Dar
Randa
31
55

Galifi *Lake Assal*
Tadjoura
109
Gulf of Tadjoura

Lake Germari
67
42
DJIBOUTI

Yoboki
111
Holhol
Loyeda

Raas Khansiir
Lake Afambo
44
Saylac

Dikhil
Silil
Karin

OB
Lake Abhe
Ali Sabih
Daouenle

Aysha
115
Silil

Lassarat
222

Abdelcader
A d w a l

Adigala
Berbera

207
Bullaxaar

Melo
111
W. Durdur
SOMALIA

OC
Boorama
W o q o o y i
Sheekh

G a l b e e d
153

E T H I O P I A
Darburruk
122
T o g d h e e r

El Ban
115
Adadle

Hurso Dire Dawa
Tog Wajaale
Hargeysa
Bederwanak
Burco
▲ Cave Paintings

09°30'N

Laas Caanood

361
362
363
364
365

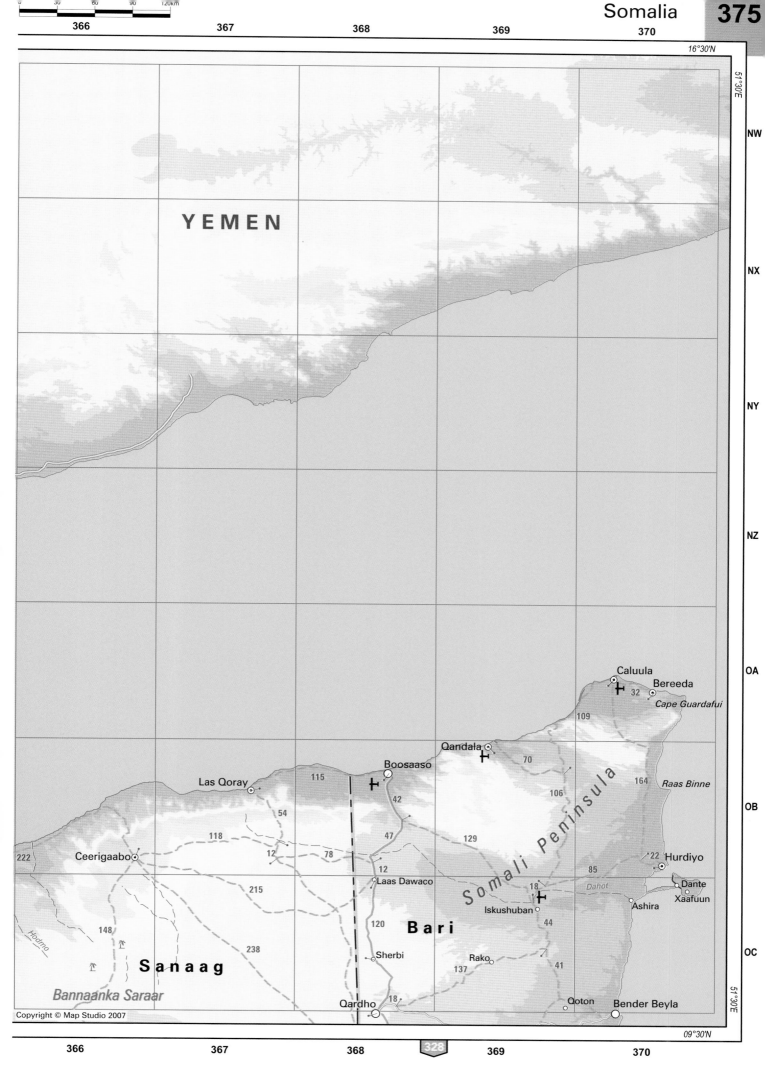

16°30'N

51°30'E

NW

YEMEN

NX

NY

NZ

OA

Caluula
Bereeda
32
Cape Guardafui
109

Qandala
70
Somali Peninsula
164 Raas Binne

OB

Boosaaso
115
42
106
Las Qoray
54
118
129
222
Ceerigaabo
12 78
47
12
85
22 Hurdiyo
Laas Dawaco
18
Dante
215
Iskushuban Dahot Ashira Xaafuun
Bari
120
44
148
238
137
41
Sanaag
Sherbi
Rako
Hodmo
Bannaanka Saraar
Qardho
18
Qoton Bender Beyla

OC

51°30'E

09°30'N

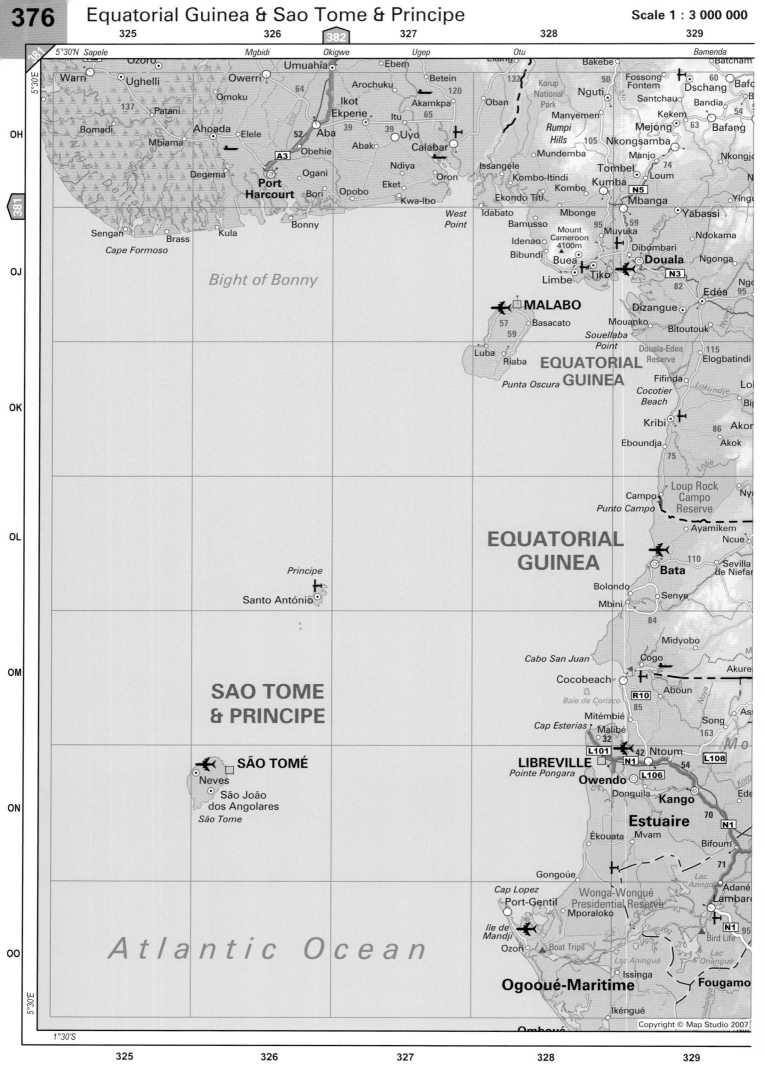

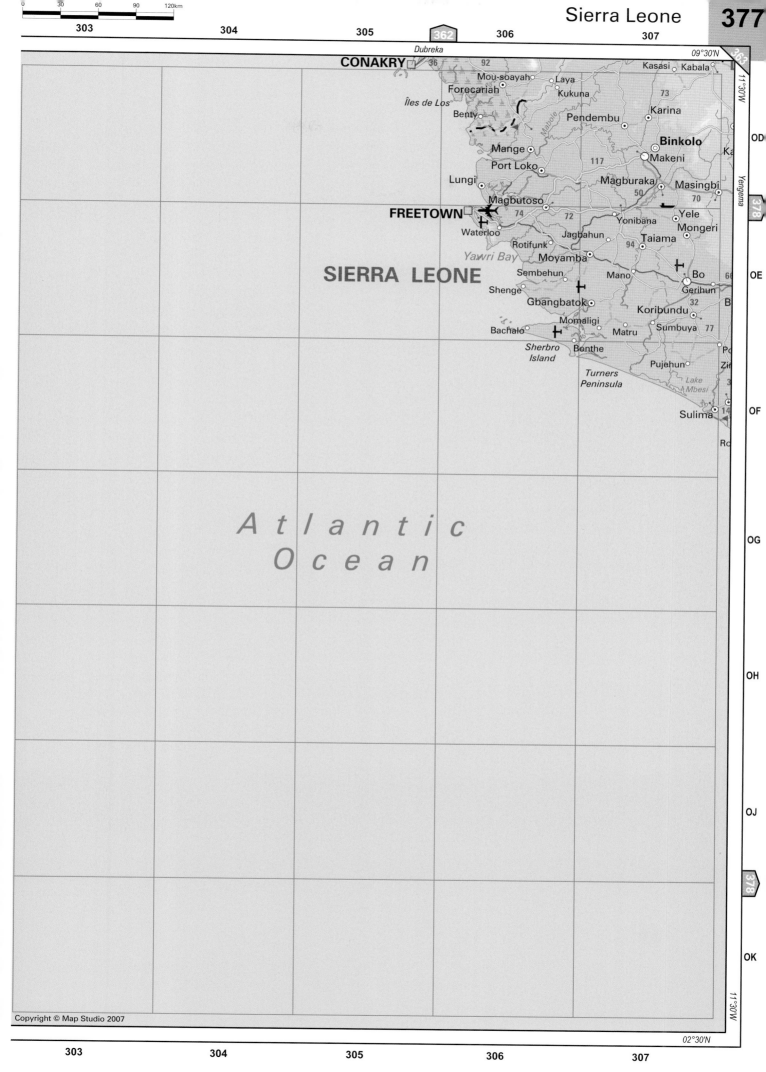

0 30 60 90 120km

303 304 305 **362** 306 307

Dubreka 09°30'N

CONAKRY 36 92

Mou-soayah Laya Kasasi Kabala

Forecariah Kukuna 73

Îles de Los Karina

Benty Pendembu **Binkolo**

Mange Makeni

Port Loko 117 Masingbi

Lungi Magburaka 50 70

Magbutoso 74 72 Yonibana Yele

FREETOWN Jagbahun Taiama Mongeri

Waterloo Rotifunk 94 Mano

Moyamba Bo

SIERRA LEONE Sembehun Gerihun 60

Shenge Koribundu 32

Gbangbatok Momaligi Matru Sumbuya 77

Bachalo Bonthe

Sherbro Island Pujehun

Turners Lake
Peninsula Mbesi

Sulima

*A t l a n t i c
O c e a n*

OD
OE
OF
OG
OH
OJ
OK

363 378 378

Yawri Bay

02°30'N

303 304 305 306 307

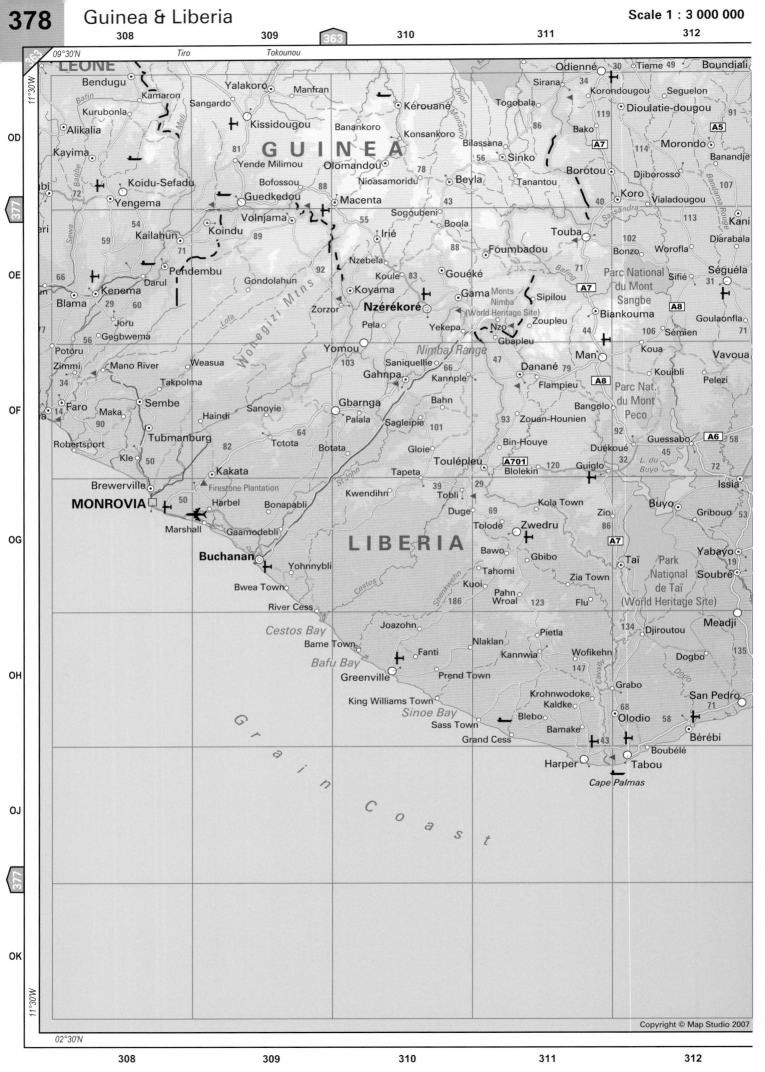

308   309   363   310   311   312

09°30'N   Tiro   Tokounou

LEONE
Bendugu
Kamaron
Sangardo
Yalakoro
Manfran
Odienné 30 Tieme 49 Boundiali
Sirana 34
Korondougou
Seguelon
Kurubonla
Kissidougou
Banankoro
Kérouané
Togobala
Bako
Dioulatie-dougou
A5 91
Alikalia
Yende Milimou
Konsankoro
Bilassana
119
A7
114
Morondo
Kayima
81
GUINEA
Olomandou
78
Sinko
Borotou
Banandje
Koidu-Sefadu
Bofossou
Nioasamoridu
Beyla
Tanantou
40
Koro
Djiborosso
107
72
Yengema
88
Macenta
43
Vialadougou
Kani
54
Guedkedou
Sogoubeni
Touba
113
Kailahun
Volnjama
Irié
Boola
71
Bonzo
Worofla
Diarabala
59
Koindu
89
Nzebela
88
Foumbadou
A7
Séguéla 31
66
Pendembu
92
Koule 83
Gouéké
Gama
Sipilou
Sifié
Darul
Koyama
Nzérékoré
Monts Nimba (World Heritage Site)
Zoupleu
Biankouma
A8
Goulaonfla 71
Kenema
Gondolahun
Zorzor
Pela
Yekepa
Nzo
Gbapleu
44
Koua
106
Sémien
Blama 29 60
Joru
Gegbwema
Yomou
Nimba Range
Man
Vavoua
56
Potoru
Weasua
103
Saniquellie
66
47
Danané 79
Kouibli
Pelezi
Zimmi
Mano River
Gahnpa
Kannple
Bahn
Flampieu
A8
Parc Nat. du Mont Peco
34
Takpolma
Sanoyie
Bangolo
14 Faro
Maka
Haindi
Gbarnga
Sagleipie
101
93
Zouan-Hounien
92
Guessabo
A6 58
90
Palala
Botata
Gloie
Bin-Houye
Duékoué
45
72
Sembe
64
Totota
Touleupleu
A701
Guiglo
32 L. du Buyo
Tubmanburg
82
Kakata
Tapeta
Blolekin
120
Brewerville
50
Harbel
Bonapabli
Kwendih
39
29
Tobli
Kola Town
Zio
Buyo
Issia
MONROVIA 50
Duge
69
86
Gribouo 53
Marshall
Gaamodebli
Tolode
Zwedru
Taï
Yabayo
Buchanan
Yohnnybli
Bawo
Gbibo
Zia Town
Park National de Taï (World Heritage Site)
Soubré 19
Bwea Town
Tahomi
Kuoi
Flu
Meadji
River Cess
Joazohn
Pahn Wroal
123
134
Djiroutou
Cestos Bay
Bame Town
Nlaklan
Pietla
Dogbo
135
Bafu Bay
Fanti
Kannwia
Wofikehn
Greenville
Prend Town
147
Grabo
King Williams Town
Krohnwodoke
Kaldke
San Pedro
Sinoe Bay
Blebo
68
Sass Town
Bamake
Olodio 58
Bérébi
Grand Cess
43
Boubélé
Grain Coast
Harper
Tabou
Cape Palmas

02°30'N

308   309   310   311   312

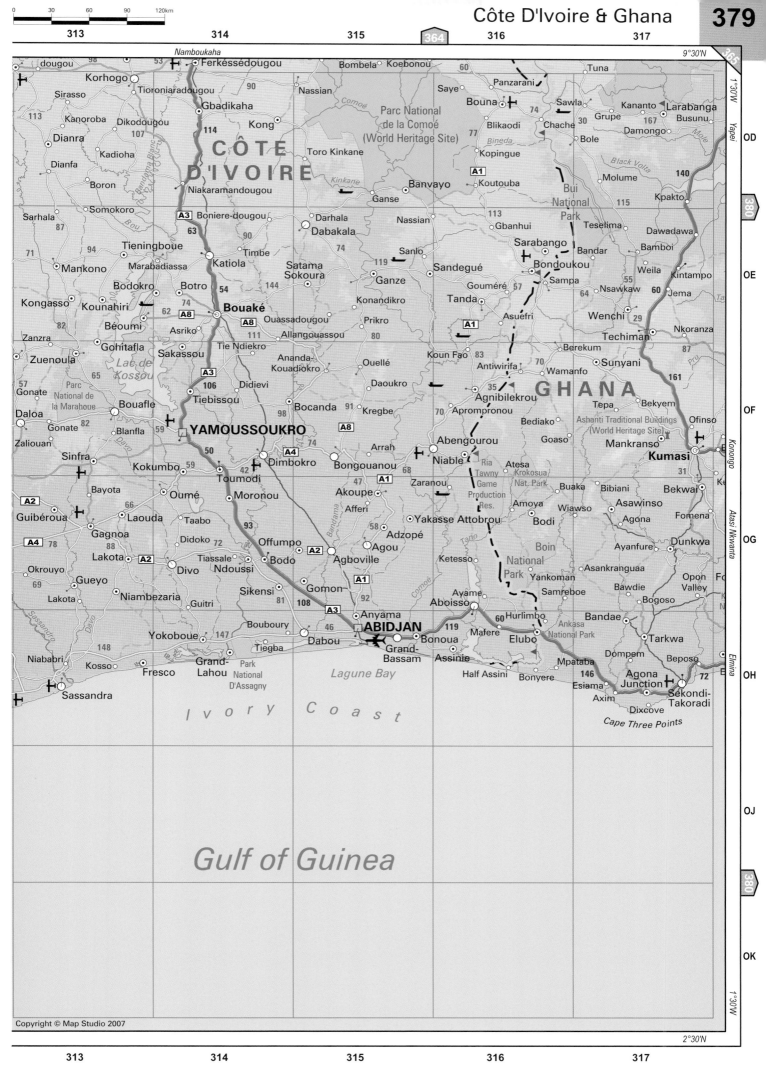

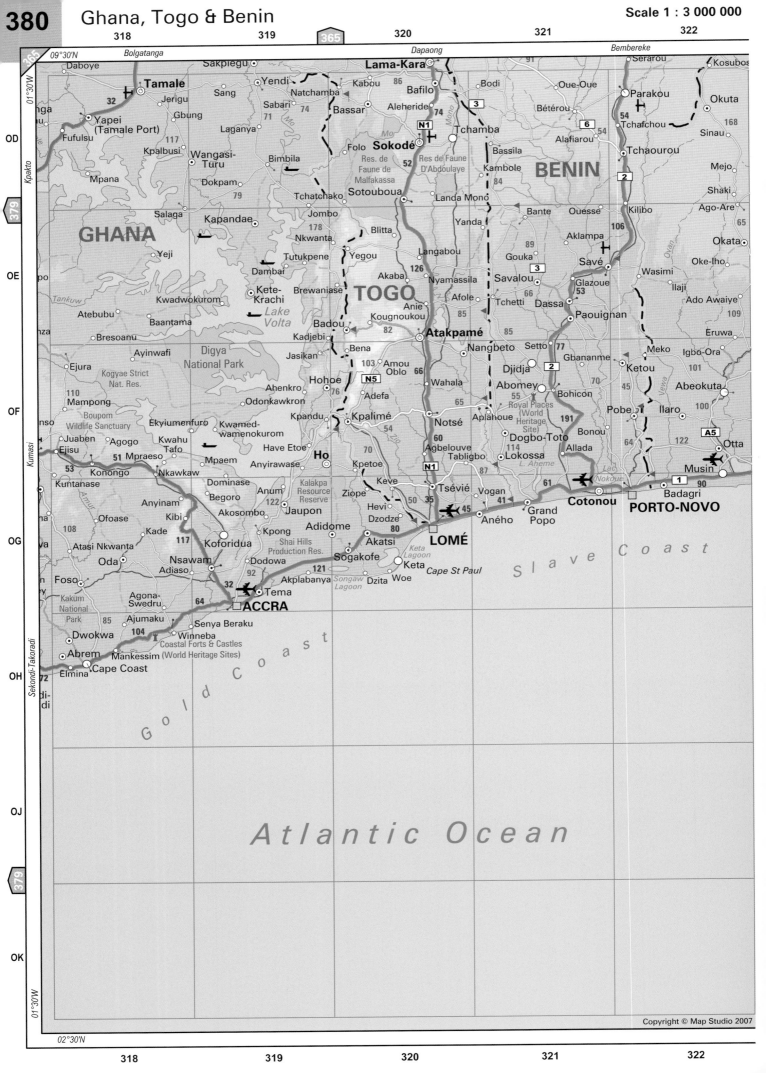

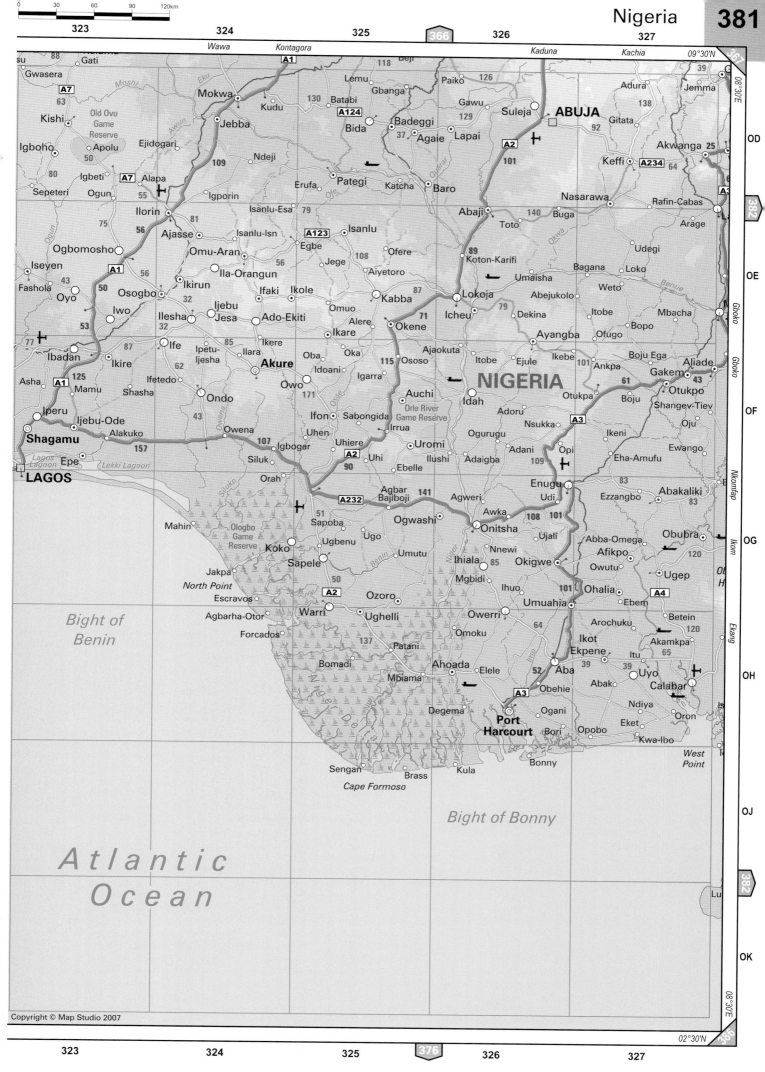

0 30 60 90 120km

Wawa   Kontagora   Kaduna   Kachia   09°30'N

Gwasera Gati 88 A1 118 Beji   Adura Jemma 39
A7 63 Mokwa 130 Lemu Gbanga Paiko 126   138
Kishi   Jebba Kudu Batabi Gbanga Gawu Suleja ABUJA Gitata Akwanga 25
Igboho Apolu Old Ovu Game Reserve A124 Badeggi 129 A2 92 Keffi A234 64
50 Ejidogari Bida 37 Agaie Lapai 101 Nasarawa Rafin-Cabas
Igbeti 80 Ndeji Pategi Katcha Baro Abaji 140 Buga Arage
Sepeteri Ogun Alapa 109 Igporin Erufa Ofe   Toto Udegi
A7 55 Ilorin 81 Isanlu-Esa 79   89 Koton-Karifi Bagana Loko
56 Ajasse A123 Isanlu Umaisha Weto Mbacha
Iseyen Ogbomosho Omu-Aran Egbe Ofere Abejukolo Itobe Bopo
43 A1 56 Ila-Orangun 108 Aiyetoro Lokoja Dekina Ofugo Boju Ega
Fashola 50 Osogbo Ikirun Ifaki Ikole Kabba 87 79 Ankpa 101 Aliade
Oyo 53 Iwo 32 Ilesha Ijebu Jesa Ado-Ekiti Omuo Alere Okene 71 Icheu Ayangba Ikebe Gakem 43
77 87 Ife 85 Ikere Ikare 61 Otukpo
Ibadan Ikire 62 Ipetu-Ijesha Ilara Akure Oba Oka 115 Ososo Ajaokuta Itobe Ejule Boju Shangev-Tiev
A1 125 Ifetedo Idoani Igarra NIGERIA Nsukka Oju
Asha Mamu Shasha Owo 171 Auchi Idah Adoru A3 Ikeni Ewango
Iperu Ondo 43 Ifon Sabongida Orle River Game Reserve Ogurugu Adani Opi Eha-Amufu
Shagamu Ijebu-Ode Owena Uhen Irrua Uromi Adaigba 109 83
Alakuko 157 107 Igbogar Uhiere A2 Ilushi Enugu Ezzangbo Abakaliki
LAGOS Epe Lekki Lagoon Siluk Uhi 90 Ebelle Udi 83
Lagos Lagoon Orah Agbar 141 Agweri 108 101 Abba-Omega Obubra
Mahin Ologbo Game Reserve 51 Sapoba Bajiboji Ogwashi Awka Onitsha Afikpo 120
Koko Ugbenu Ugo Umutu Ujali Owutu Ugep
A232 Sapele Nnewi Okigwe Ohalia
Jakpa A2 50 Ozoro Ihiala 85 Mgbidi Ihuo 101 A4
North Point Escravos Umuahia Ebem
Agbarha-Otor Warri Ughelli Owerri 64 Arochuku Betein
Forcados Omoku Ikot Ekpene Itu 120
137 Patani Ahoada Elele 52 Aba 39 Akamkpa
Bomadi Mbiama A3 Obehie Abak Uyo 65
Bight of Benin Degema Ogani Calabar
Port Harcourt Ndiya Oron
Sengan Brass Kula Bori Opobo Eket Kwa-Ibo
Cape Formoso Bonny West Point

Bight of Bonny

Atlantic Ocean

OD OE OF OG OH OJ OK

08°30'N

02°30'N

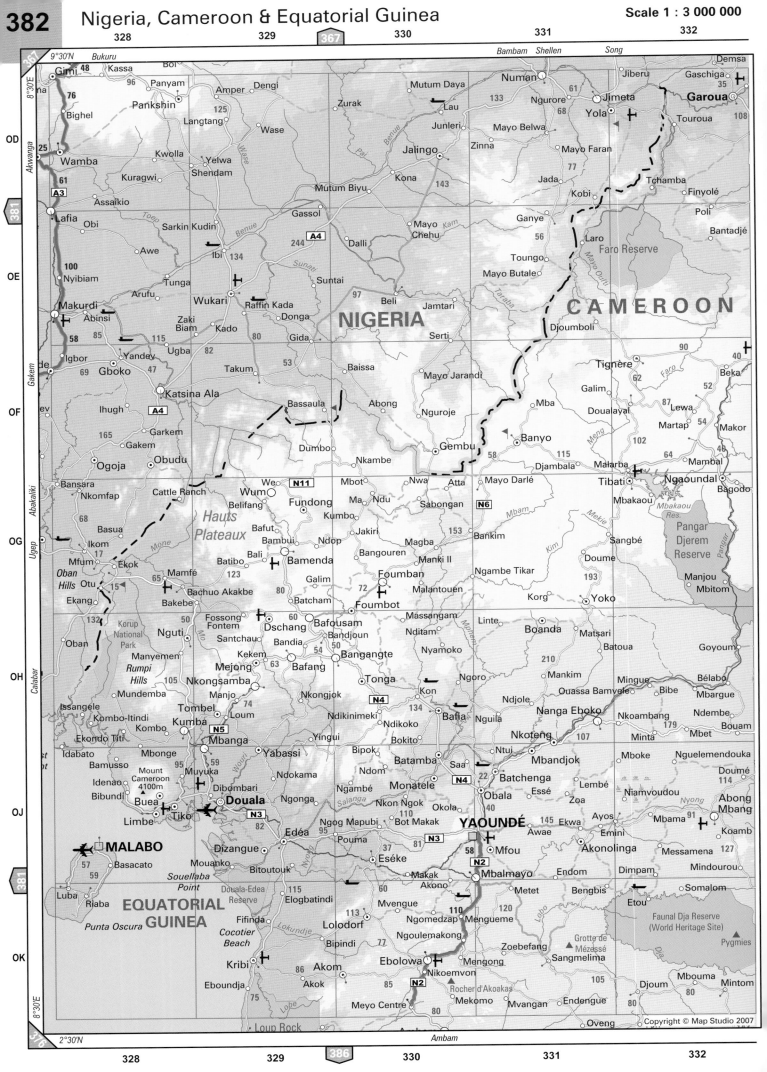

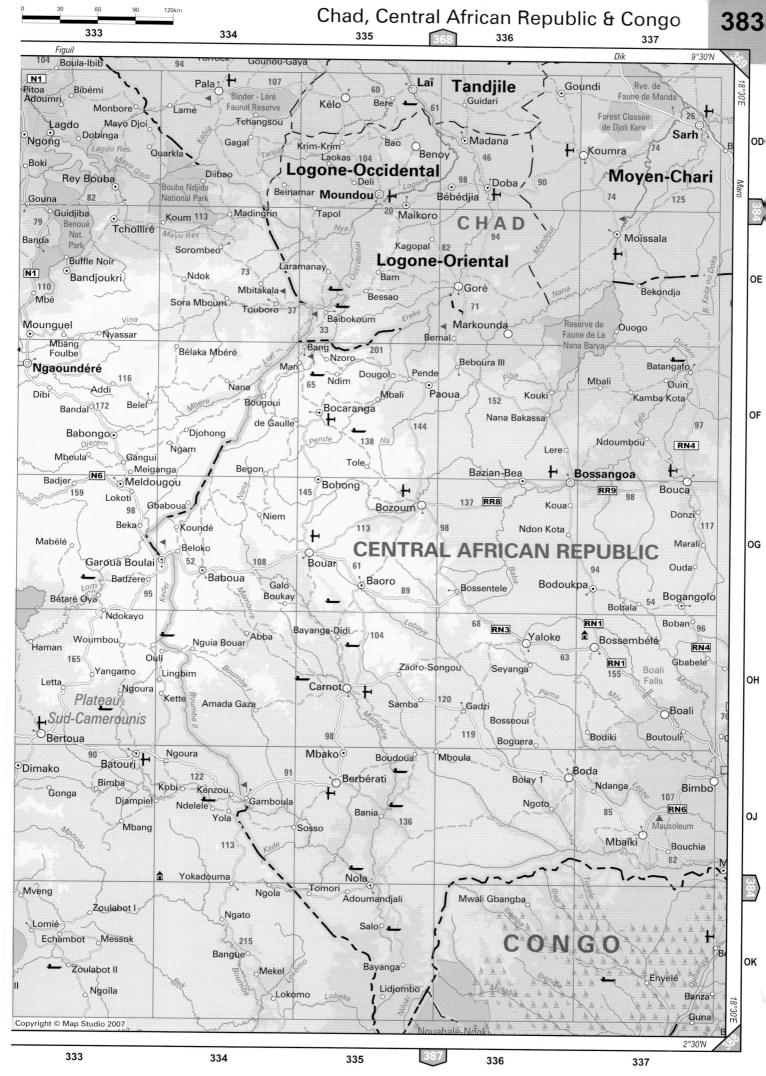

0   30   60   90   120km

N1
Pitoa
Adoumri
Boula-Ibib
Bibémi
Monbore
Lagdo
Ngong
Boki
Rey Bouba
Gouna
Guidjiba
Banda
Tchollire
Buffle Noir
Bandjoukri
Mbé
Mbé
Mounguel
Nyassar
Mbang
Foulbe
Ngaoundéré
Dibi
Addi
Bandal
Belel
Babongo
Mboula
Gangui
Meiganga
Badjer
Meldougou
Lokoti
Beka
Gbaboua
Mabélé
Garoua Boulai
Badzere
Bétaré Oya
Ndokayo
Woumbou
Haman
Yangamo
Letta
Ngoura
Ouli
Lingbim
Kette
Plateau
Sud-Camerounis
Bertoua
Dimako
Batouri
Bimba
Gonga
Kobi
Djampiel
Mbang
Kénzou
Ndelele
Yola
Mveng
Zoulabot I
Lomié
Echambot
Messok
Zoulabot II
Ngoïla
Yokadouma
Mbako
Ngoura
Mekel
Bangue
Ngato
Salo
Bangui
Lomé

Figuil
104
94
Yorrock
Gounou-Gaya
Pala
Binder - Léré
Faunal Reserve
Lamé
107
Kélo
Laokas
Krim-Krim
Gagal
Tchangsou
Diibao
Beinamar
Bouba Ndjida
National Park
Madingrin
Tapol
Koum 113
Sorombeo
Ndok
Mbitakala
Laramanay
Mayo Rey
Sora Mboum
Touboro
Baibokoum
Bang
Nzoro
Man
Ndim
Dougol
Pende
Mbali
Nana
Bougoui
de Gaulle
Bocaranga
Tole
Begon
Bohong
Niem
Koundé
Beloko
Baboua
Galo
Boukay
Baoro
Bayanga-Didi
Abba
Nguia Bouar
Amada Gaza
Carnot
Samba
Gadzi
Bosseoui
Boguera
Mbaïki

CHAD

Logone-Occidental
Moundou
Logone-Oriental
Bessao
Bam
Gore
Markounda
Bemal
Beboura III
Paoua
Nana Bakassa
Lere
Bazian-Bea
Bozoum
Koua
Ndon Kota

CENTRAL AFRICAN REPUBLIC

Bossentele
Bodoukpa
Bobala
Yaloke
Seyanga
Bossembélé
Boali
Falls
Boda
Bolay 1
Ngoto
Bouchia
Nola
Tomori
Adoumandjali
Mwali Gbangba
Bayanga
Lidjombo
Lokomo

CONGO

Enyélé
Banza
Guna

Tandjile
Laï
Guidari
Goundi
Sarh
Madana
Benoy
Doba
Bébédjia
Moissala
Bekondja
Koumra
Moyen-Chari

Sosso
Bania
Berbérati
Gamboula
Mbaïki
Mbako
Boudoua
Mboula

2°30'N
9°30'N
18°30'E

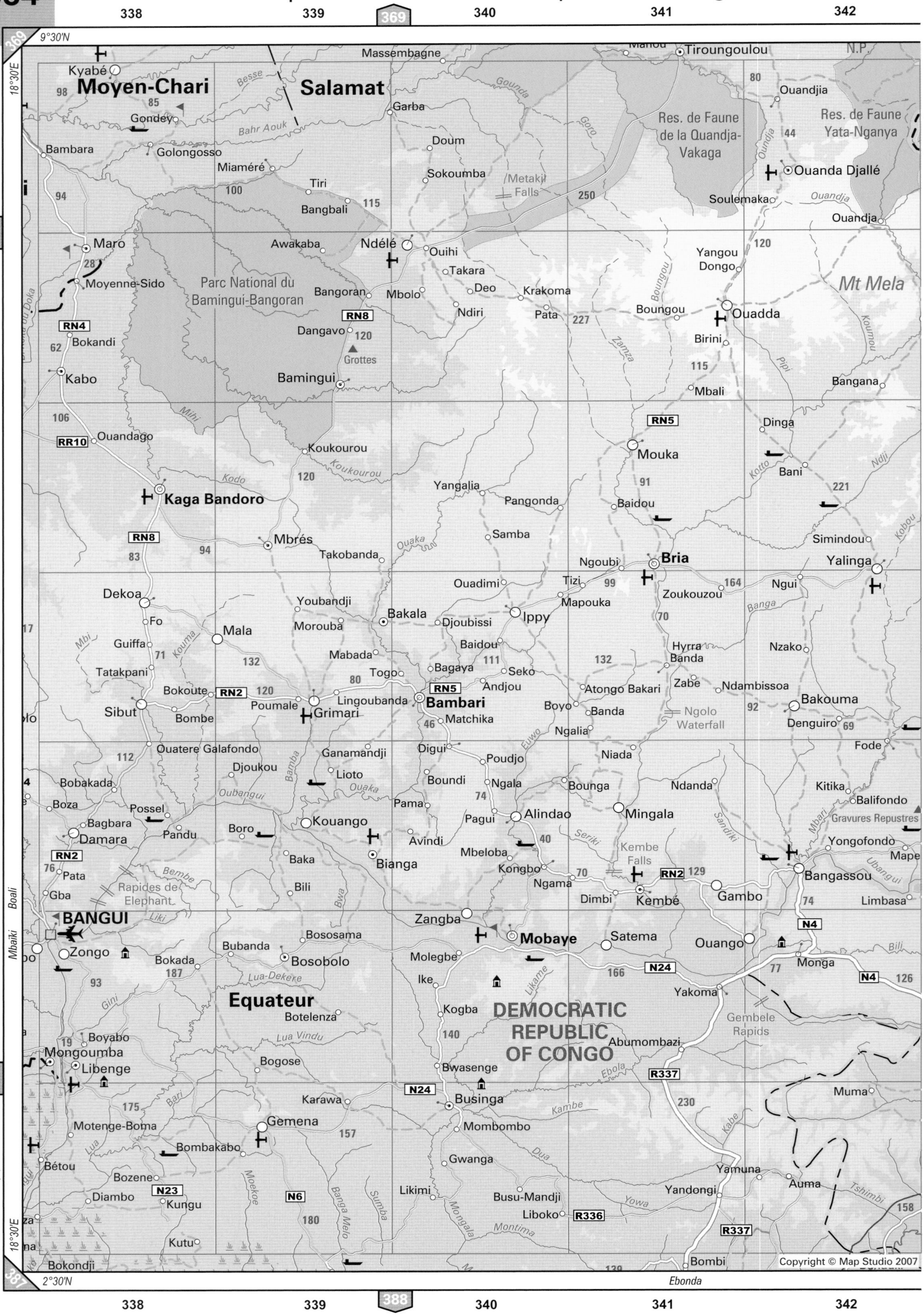

338 339 369 340 341 342

9°30'N
18°30'E
OD

Kyabé
Moyen-Chari **Salamat**
Massembagne
Mahou Tiroungoulou N.P.
98 85
Gondey
Garba
Ouandjia
80
Bambara Golongosso
Miaméré
Doum
Res. de Faune
de la Quandja-Vakaga
Res. de Faune
Yata-Nganya
94 100
Tiri
Sokoumba
44
Ouanda Djallé
Bangbali 115
Metakil
Falls
250
Soulemaka Ouandja

OE
Maro
Awakaba
Ndélé Ouihi
Takara
Krakoma
227
Yangou
Dongo
120
Mt Mela
28
Moyenne-Sido
Bangoran
Mbolo
Deo
Pata
Boungou
Ouadda
RN4
62 Bokandi
**Parc National du
Bamingui-Bangoran**
Dangavo 120
Ndiri
Birini
Kabo
Grottes
Bamingui
115
Mbali
Bangana

OF
106
Ouandago
RN5
Dinga
RR10
Koukourou
Mouka
Bani
Kodo 120
Yangalia
91
221
Kaga Bandoro
Pangonda
Baidou
Simindou Yalinga
RN8 Mbrés
Ouaka Samba
Ngoubi **Bria**
83 94
Takobanda
Tizi 99
Ngui 164

OG
Dekoa
Youbandji
Ouadimi
Mapouka
Zoukouzou
Nzako
Fo
Moroubá
Bakala Djoubissi **Ippy**
70
Guiffa 71
Mabada
Baidou
Hyrra
Banda
Zabe
Ndambissoa
Tatakpani
132
Togo
Bagaya 111
Seko
132
92 Bakouma
Bokoute RN2 120
Poumale 80
Lingoubanda Andjou
Atongo Bakari
Denguiro 69
Sibut
Grimari **Bambari**
Boyo
Banda
Ngolo
Waterfall
Fode
Bombe
46 Matchika
Ngalia

OH
Ouatere Galafondo
Ganamandji
Digui
Poudjo
Niada
Ndanda
Kitika
112
Djoukou
Lioto
Boundi
Ngala
Bounga
Balifondo
Bobakada
74
Gravures Repustres
Boza
Pama
Pagui
Alindao
Mingala
Yongofondo
Bagbara Possel
Kouango
Avindi
Mbeloba
40
Kembe
Falls
Mape
Damara Pandu
Boro
Baka
Kongbo
70
RN2 129
Bangassou
RN2
Bianga
Bili
Ngama
Dimbi Kembé
Gambo 74
Limbasa
76 Pata
Gba
Rapides de
Elephant
Zangba
N4

OJ
BANGUI
Bososama
Mobaye
Satema
Ouango
Monga
N4 126
Zongo
Bubanda
Molegbe
166
N24
Yakoma
77
Bokada 187
Bosobolo
Ike
**DEMOCRATIC
REPUBLIC
OF CONGO**
Gembele
Rapids
93
Lua-Dekere
Equateur
Kogba
140
Abumombazi
R337
Boyabo
Botelenza
230
Mongoumba
Bogose
Bwasenge
Muma
Libenge
Karawa
N24 Businga

OK
175 Gemena 157
Mombombo
Motenge-Boma
Bombakabo
Gwanga
Yamuna
Auma
Bétou
N23
N6
Likimi
Busu-Mandji
Yandongi
158
Bozene
Liboko R336
Diambo Kungu
180
Bombi
R337

2°30'N
Ebonda

338 339 388 340 341 342

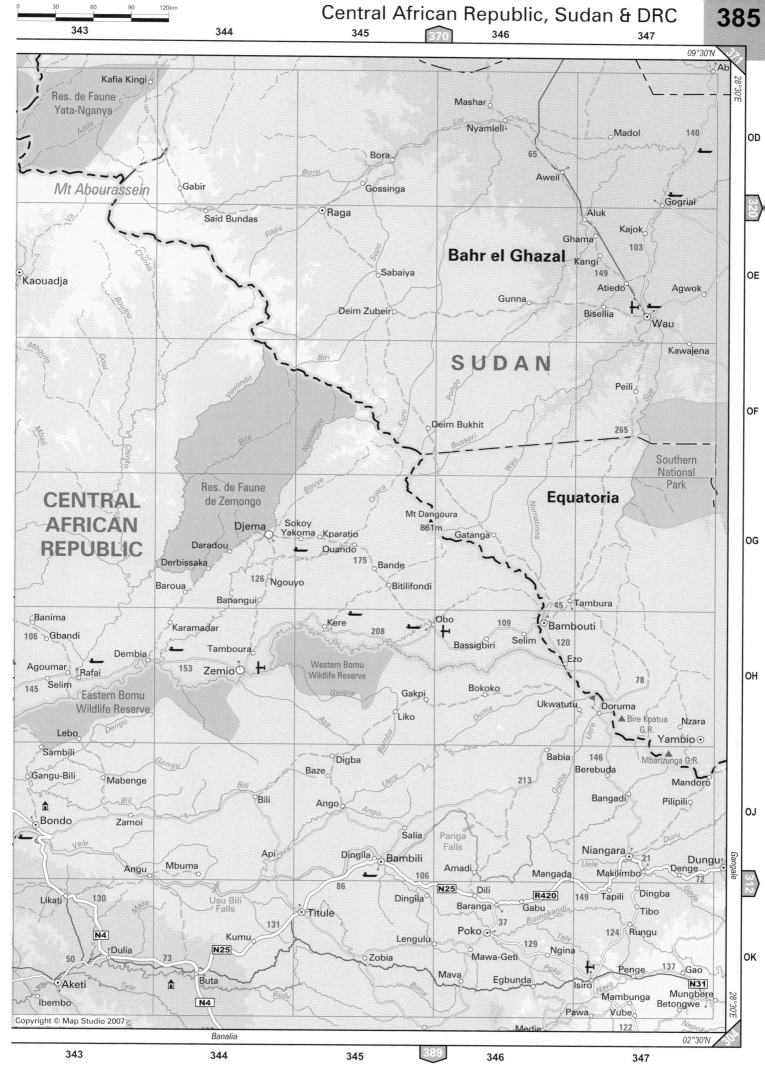

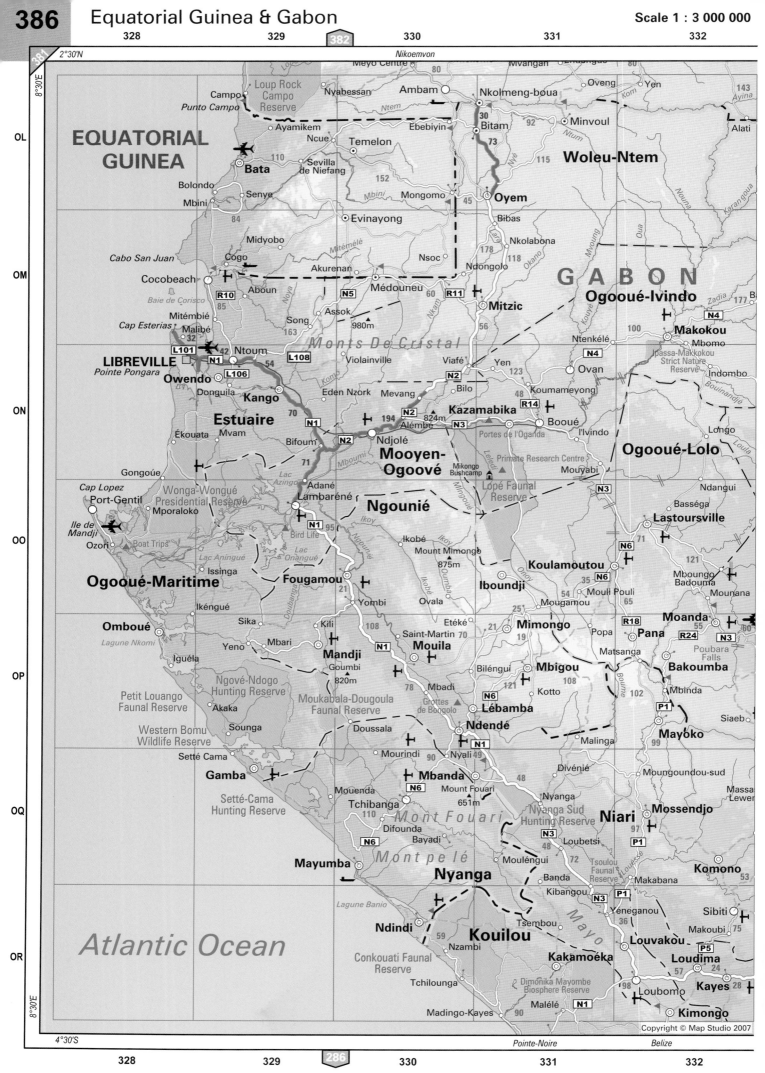

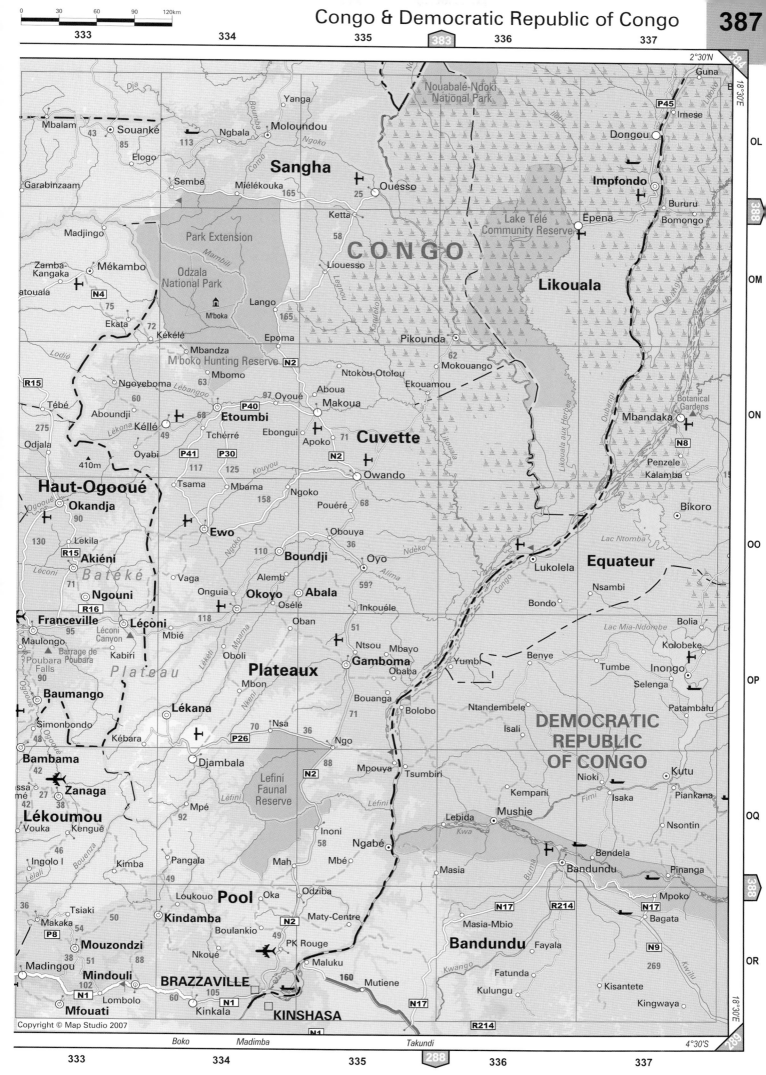

0   30   60   90   120km

2°30'N

18°30'E

OL

388

OM

ON

OO

OP

388

OQ

OR

18°30'E

289

Congo

Mbalam   43   Souanké   85   Elogo

Garabinzaam

Madjingo   113   Ngbala   Yanga   Moloundou

Zamba-Kangaka   Mékambo   N4   75   atouala   Ekata   72   Kékélé

Sangha   Sembé   Miélékouka   165   25   Ouesso   Ketta   58

Nouabalé-Ndoki National Park

Lake Télé Community Reserve   Epena

Impfondo   Bururu   Bomongo

Dongou   P45   Imese   Guna

Park Extension

Odzala National Park   M'boka   Lango   165   Epoma

C O N G O   Liouesso

Likouala   Pikounda

R15   Ngoyeboma   60   63   Mbandza   M'boko Hunting Reserve   N2   Mbomo

Tébé   275   Aboundji   68   P40   Etoumbi   97   Oyoué   Aboua   Makoua   Ntokou-Otolou   62   Mokouango   Ekouamou

Odjala   Kéllé   49   Tchérré   Ebongui   Apoko   71   **Cuvette**

410m   Oyabi   P41   P30   117   125   N2   Owando

Haut-Ogooué   Okandja   90   Tsama   Mbama   158   Ngoko   Pouéré   68

Mbandaka   N8   Penzele   Kalamba

Botanical Gardens

130   Lekila   Ewo   Obouya   36

R15   Akiéni   71   *Batéké*   Vaga   110   **Boundji**   Oyo   *Ndéko*   Lukolela   **Equateur**

Ngouni   R16   Alemb   **Okoyo**   **Abala**   Osélé   59?   *Alima*   Bondo

Bikoro

Lac Ntomba

Nsambi

Onguia   Inkouéle

Franceville   95   Léconi   118   Oban   51   Mbayo   Yumbi   Benye   Tumbe   Inongo   Kolobeke

Maulongo   Léconi Canyon   Mbié   Oboli   Ntsou   **Gamboma**   Obaba   Selenga   Bolia

Barrage de Poubara Poubara Falls   Kabiri   *Plateau*   **Plateaux**   Mbon   Bouanga   Bolobo   Ntandembele   Patambalu

90   **Baumango**   Lékana   Isali   **DEMOCRATIC REPUBLIC OF CONGO**

48   Simonbondo   Kébara   70   Nsa   36   71   P26   Ngo   Mpouya   Tsumbiri   Kutu

Bambama   42   Zanaga   88   Nioki   Piankana

ssa   mé   27   42   38   Djambala   N2   Lefini Faunal Reserve   *Léfini*   Kempani   Isaka   Nsontin

Lékoumou   Mpé   92   Mushie

Vouka   Kengué   Inoni   58   Ngabé   Lebida   *Kwa*   Bendela   Pinanga

46   Kimba   Pangala   Mah   Mbé   Masia   Bandundu   Mpoko

Ingolo I   *Lélali*   *Bouenza*   49   269

36   Tsiaki   50   **Pool**   Loukouo   Oka   Odziba   N17   R214   N17   Bagata

Makaka   54   **Kindamba**   Maty-Centre   Masia-Mbio   **Bandundu**   Fayala   N9

P8   Boulankio   49   N2   Fatunda

Mouzondzi   Nkoué   PK Rouge   Kulungu   Kisantete

38   51   88   Maluku   160   Mutiene   Kingwaya

Madingou   **Mindouli**   102   **BRAZZAVILLE**   N17

N1   Lombolo   60   N1   Kinkala

Mfouati   Kinkala   **KINSHASA**   R214

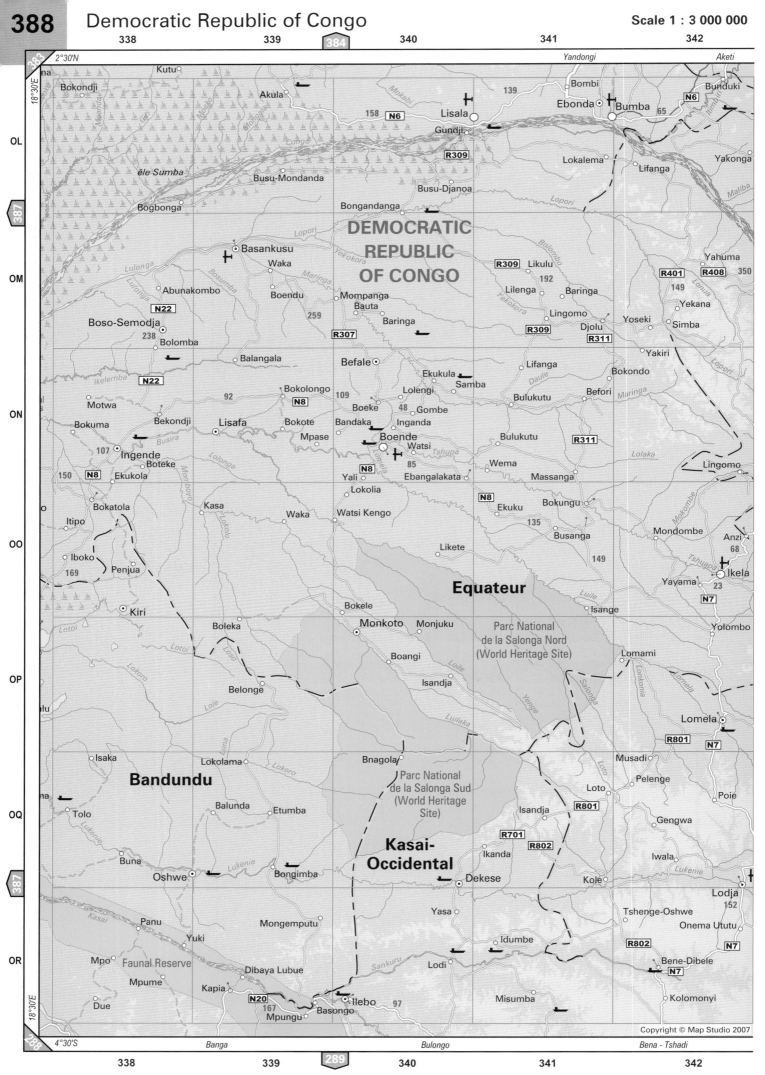

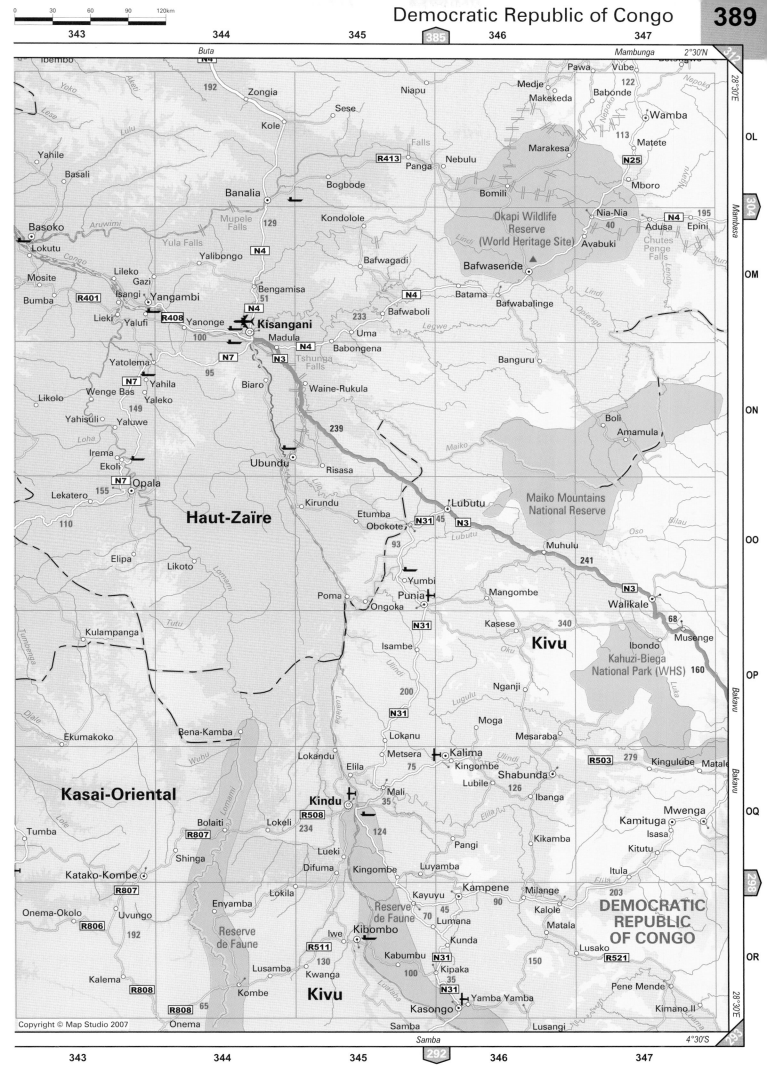

Aalwynsfontein > Bere

PLACE NAME	PG	GRID
Aalwynsfontein	216	EC 80
Aandster	226	DW 93
Aansluit	225	DV 87
Aasvoëlnes	243	DF 83
Ab Touyour	369	OA 337
Aba (DRC)	312	BK 103
Aba (Nig.)	376	OH 326
Abadla	330	NG 316
Abaiat	372	OC 352
Abaji	381	OE 326
Abak	376	OH 327
Abakaliki	381	OG 327
Abala (Ben.)	366	NX 322
Abala (Con.)	387	OO 335
Abalak	366	NX 325
Abalessa	354	NP 324
Abar el Kanayis	336	NG 346
Abattekh	339	NK 308
Abba	383	OH 334
Abba Kella	323	BC 116
Abba-Omega	381	OG 327
Abbotsdale	209	EK 80
Abdelcader	374	OB 362
Abdi	369	NZ 340
Abdourta	369	OA 340
Abéché	369	NY 340
Abedo	322	BB 111
Abejukolo	381	OE 326
Abelti	323	BA 118
Abenab	242	DF 79
Abengourou	379	OF 316
Abeokuta	380	OF 322
Aberdeen	211	EG 91
Aberdeen Road	211	EH 91
Aberfeldy	220	DY 100
Abergele	373	NZ 358
Abgue	369	OA 339
Abidjan	379	OH 315
Abim	314	BM 110
Abinsi	382	OE 328
Abiya Adi	373	NZ 358
Abjelil	330	ND 315
Abnub	347	NL 350
Aboisso	379	OG 316
Aboke	305	BN 108
Abomey	380	OF 321
Abong	382	OF 330
Abong Mbang	382	OJ 332
Abou Deia	369	OB 338
Aboua	377	ON 335
Aboun	376	OM 329
Aboundji	387	ON 333
Abrem	380	OH 318
Abri	359	NR 349
Abu Kebir	337	NG 351
Abu Dis	360	NT 353
Abu Dom	359	NU 350
Abu Durba	348	NJ 352
Abu Gabra	371	OB 346
Abu Gubeiha	371	OB 350
Abu Hamed	360	NS 353
Abu Hashim	372	OB 351
Abu Kabisa	371	NZ 346
Abu Matariq	370	OB 345
Abu Sari	359	NS 350
Abu Simbel	360	NO 351
Abu Tig	347	NL 350
Abu Zabad	371	OA 348
Abu Zayyan	333	NF 332
Abuja	381	OD 326
Abu-Mendi	372	OA 355
Abumombazi	384	OJ 341
Abunakombo	388	OM 338
Abwong	321	AY 107
Abyad	370	NY 345
Abyei	371	OC 348
Acampamento da Cameia	266	CQ 86
Accra	380	OH 319
Achaacha	331	NB 320
Acholibur	313	BL 108
Acornhoek	229	DR 105
Aculo	276	CN 80
Ad Darsia	335	NE 339
Ad Dubasi	372	NY 351
Adaba	324	BD 121
Adachal	306	BN 110
Adad	327	AY 136
Adadle	374	OC 364
Adaigba	381	OF 326
Adams Mission	220	EC 104
Adané	376	OO 329
Adani	381	OF 326
Adar	369	OB 340
Adarama	360	NV 354
Addi	383	OF 333
Addis Ababa	324	AZ 120
Addis Zemen	373	OA 357
Addo	211	EK 94
Adefa	380	OF 320
Adel Bagrou	364	NX 312
Adelaide	212	EH 95
Adele	324	BB 122
Aden	374	NZ 364
Adendorp	211	EG 92
Aderbissinat	367	NW 327
Adet	373	OB 356
Adi Abun	373	NY 358
Adi Arkay	373	NY 357
Adi Daro	373	NY 357
Adi Gudom	373	NZ 359
Adi Kaie	373	NX 358
Adi Ugri	373	NX 358
Adiaso	380	OG 318
Adidome	380	OG 319
Adigala	372	OC 361
Adigrat	373	NY 359
Adikas	322	BE 114
Adilang	313	BM 109
Adiri	344	NK 333
Ado Awaiye	380	OE 322
Ado-Ekiti	381	OE 324
Adok	320	BA 103
Adoru	381	OF 326
Adoumandjali	383	OK 335
Adoumri	383	OD 333
Adranga	312	BM 103
Adrar	341	NK 319
Adré	370	NZ 341
Aduku	305	BN 108
Adunu	367	OC 326
Adura	381	OD 327
Adusa	389	OM 347
Advance	217	EE 86
Adwa	373	NY 358
Adwari	305	BN 109
Adzopé	379	OG 315
Af'abet	373	NW 358
Afferi	379	OG 315
Afgooye	310	BN 133
Afguns	236	DP 98
Afikpo	381	OG 327
Aflou	331	ND 321
Afmadu	309	BQ 126
Afole	380	OE 320
Afsaal	229	DS 106
Agadez	355	NV 327
Agadir	339	NH 309
Agaie	381	OD 325
Agaro	372	OB 354
Agbar Bajiboji	381	OG 325
Agbarha-Otor	381	OH 324
Agbelouve	380	OF 320
Agboville	379	OG 315
Agdz	330	NG 313
Ager Maryam	315	BF 119
Aggeneys	216	EA 80
Agiert	363	NW 310
Agiri	368	NZ 333
Agnibilekrou	379	OF 316
Ago-Are	380	OE 322
Agogo (Sud.)	380	OF 318
Agona (Eth.)	379	OG 317
Agona Junction	379	OH 317
Agona-Swedru	380	OG 318
Agoro	313	BK 108
Agoro	323	BB 116
Agou	379	OG 315
Agouénit	352	NV 311
Agoumar	385	OH 343
Agrigento	334	NA 333
Agter Sneeuberg	211	EG 93
Agtertang	218	ED 93
Aguelhok	353	NT 320
Aguié	367	NZ 327
Agulai	373	NY 359
Agule	306	BP 110
Agwara	366	OB 324
Agwata	305	BO 109
Agweri	381	OG 326
Agwok	385	OE 347
Ahenkro	380	OF 319
Ahero	306	BS 112
Ahfir	330	NC 317
Ahoada	376	OH 326
Ahrens	220	EA 104
Ahsaad	336	NF 344
Ai-Ais	223	DX 78
Aim Touta	332	NC 325
Ain Beida	332	NB 327
Ain Ben Tili	339	NM 310
Ain Benian	331	NA 322
Ain Benimathar	330	ND 317
Ain Bousef	331	NB 322
Ain Defla	331	NB 321
Ain Deheb	331	NC 321
Ain el Auoda	330	ND 313
Ain el Hadjar	330	NC 319
Ain el Hadjel	332	NB 323
Ain el Hamara	331	ND 321
Ain el Hammoth	332	NA 323
Ain el Orak	331	NE 320
Ain Fekan	331	NC 319
Ain Madhi	331	NE 321
Ain M'lila	332	NB 325
Ain Oulmene	332	NB 325
Ain Oussera	331	NC 322
Ain Sefra	331	NE 319
Ain Sukhna	348	NH 351
Ain Temouchent	331	NC 318
Ait Mellou	339	NH 309
Aiyetoro	381	OE 325
Ajaokuta	381	OF 326
Ajasse	381	OE 324
Ajdabiya	335	NG 339
Ajir	368	OB 332
Ajumaku	380	OH 318
Akaba	380	OG 320
Akabli	341	NL 320
Akaka	386	OP 329
Akaki	324	AZ 120
Akamkpa	376	OH 327
Akanous	224	DR 82
Akasha	359	NR 350
Akatsi	380	OG 320
Akbou	332	NB 324
Akelo	332	BD 110
Aketi	385	OK 343
Akhmim	348	NL 351
Akiéni	387	OO 333
Akjoujt	350	NS 305
Aklampa	380	OE 321
Aknoul	330	NC 315
Akobo	321	BB 108
Akok	376	OK 329
Akoke	372	OC 351
Akokora	304	BO 101
Akom	376	OK 329
Akono	382	OK 330
Akonolinga	382	OJ 331
Akop	320	BA 101
Akor	364	NX 312
Akosombo	380	OG 319
Akot	320	BD 103
Akoupe	379	OG 315
Akplabanya	380	OG 319
Aksum	373	NY 358
Akula	388	OL 339
Akum	306	BO 111
Akurdet	373	NW 357
Akure	381	OF 324
Akurenan	376	OM 329
Akwanga	381	OD 327
Al Adam	336	NF 343
Al Aqabah	348	NJ 354
Al Aziziyah	333	NF 332
Al Barun	372	OA 353
Al Bayda	335	NE 341
Al Bidia	369	OB 339
Al Gamamiya	360	NT 352
Al Garabulli	334	NE 333
Al Garef	372	OA 353
Al Ghaba	359	NU 350
Al Haggounia	339	NL 307
Al Harabah	333	NF 331
Al Hoceima	330	NC 315
Al Jadidah	347	NJ 348
Al Jaghbub	336	NH 344
Al Jawf	346	NO 342
Al Jaws al Kabir	333	NF 331
Al Kab	360	NT 352
Al Kararim	334	NF 334
Al Kawa	372	NY 352
Al Khums	334	NE 333
Al Mahbas	339	NL 310
Al Maqrun	335	NG 339
Al Marj	335	NF 340
Al Qala's	334	NF 333
Al Qaryah ash Shargiyah	344	NH 333
Al Qatrun	344	NN 334
Al Quwaisi	372	NZ 353
Al Rahibat	333	NF 331
Al Taj	346	NO 342
Al Tamini	335	NF 342
Al Uwaynat	343	NM 330
Al Wigh	344	NO 334
Al Wittyah	333	NE 331
Ala Draham	333	NA 328
Alafiarou	380	OD 321
Alaill Dadda	374	OA 362
Alakuko	381	OF 323
Alamata	373	OA 359
Alapa	381	OD 323
Alaska	257	DB 103
Alati	386	OL 332
Alawa	367	OC 326
Albert Falls	220	EA 103
Albertinia	210	EL 86
Alberton	227	DU 99
Albrechts	241	DL 75
Aldam	219	DY 97
Aldeia Chioco	258	CZ 108
Alderley	213	EG 100
Aldinville	221	EA 105
Aleg	350	NV 305
Aleheride	380	OD 320
Alel	320	BE 104
Alemaya	325	AY 126
Alemb	387	OO 334
Alémbé	386	ON 330
Alemere	305	BO 108
Alere	381	OE 325
Alerek	314	BM 110
Alettesrus	226	DV 91
Alexander Bay	215	DZ 75
Alexandria	212	EK 95
Alexandria (El Iskandariya)	337	NG 349
Alfândega	287	CH 74
Al-Gargara	350	NR 302
Algeciras	330	NB 314
Algiers (Alger)	331	NA 322
Alheit (N.C.)	216	DZ 83
Alheit (Zim.)	247	DG 106
Al-Hilla	371	NZ 346
Al-Hudaida	374	NX 362
Ali Sabih	374	OB 362
Alia Bay	315	BK 115
Aliade	381	OF 327
Alibo	373	OC 356
Alice	212	EH 96
Alicedale	212	EJ 95
Alikalia	378	OD 308
Alimbongo	304	BS 101
Alindao	384	OH 340
Aliquisanda	271	CR 113
Aliwal North	219	ED 96
Aljanare	366	OA 323
Alkamari	367	NZ 330
Allada	380	OF 321
Allal Tazi	330	ND 313
Allangouassou	379	OE 315
Allanridge	227	DX 96
Allareni	366	NZ 322
Alldays	236	DN 101
Alleman	219	DZ 95
Allep	218	EB 93
Alma	236	DQ 99
Almahel	372	OA 354
Almería	330	NA 316
Alnif	330	NG 315
Aloi	305	BN 109
Alpha	229	DX 105
Al-Qulayd Bahri	359	NU 350
Altenstein	232	DM 79
Alto Cuilo (Ang.)	277	CN 82
Alto Cuito (Ang.)	264	CT 80
Alto Hama	263	CR 74
Alto Ligonha	260	CY 119
Alto Molócuè	260	CY 118
Alua	273	CU 122
Aluakluak	320	BE 103
Aluk	385	OE 347
Am Dafok	370	OC 342
Am Dam	369	NZ 340
Am Deressa	369	NZ 340
Am Djéména	369	NZ 337
Am Doutile	369	OA 340
Am el Melh	332	NC 323
Am Khoumi	369	NZ 339
Am Léiouna	370	NZ 341
Am Timan	369	OB 339
Am Zoer	369	NY 340
Amabele	212	EH 98
Amada Gaza	383	OH 334
Amadi (DRC)	312	BF 103
Amadi (DRC)	385	OJ 346
Amake	363	NX 309
aMakhasi	220	DY 103
Amala	294	CE 109
Amaler (Ken.)	320	BO 114
Amaler (Ken.)	306	BP 114
Amalia	226	DW 93
Amamula	389	ON 347
Amandas	257	DB 104
aManzimtoti	220	EC 104
aMatikulu	221	EA 105
Ambam	386	OL 330
Ambidedi	363	NX 307
Amboiva	263	CQ 72
Amboni	297	CC 121
Ambriz	276	CH 69
Ameltougul	329	NG 312
Amentego Megauda	359	NU 350
Amersfoort	228	DW 102
Ameya	323	BD 116
Amino	317	BJ 126
Aminuis	232	DP 81
Amizmiz	329	NG 311
Amou Oblo	380	OF 320
Amourj	364	NW 312
Amoya	379	OG 316
Ampara	249	DH 112
Amper	382	OD 329
Amsterdam	228	DV 104
Amudat	306	BO 112
Amué (Ang.)	251	DA 70
Amuria	306	BN 110
Anaba	366	OB 324
Anaka	313	BM 106
Ananda-Kouadiokro	379	OF 315
Ancona	227	DX 95
Ancuabe	273	CS 122
Ancuaze	259	DA 112
Andaga	368	OB 333
Andara	254	DD 85
Anderamboukane	366	NX 322
Andisa	304	BO 103
Andjou	384	OG 340
Andoni	241	DE 76
Andrieskraal	211	EK 92
Andriesvale	224	DV 84
Andudu	304	BN 100
Andulo	276	CP 76
Anefis I-n-Darane	353	NU 320
Aného	380	OG 321
Aneker	366	NX 324
Aney	356	NT 332
Angaradebou	366	OB 322
Angereb	373	NZ 356
Ango	385	OJ 345
Angoche	261	CZ 123
Angu	385	OJ 343
Anhanca	251	DA 74
Anie	380	OE 320
Anjavelo	251	CZ 71
Anjo	316	BL 122
Anka	366	OA 325
Ankoro	292	CF 96
Ankpa	381	OF 327
Annaba	332	NA 327
Ansongo	365	NW 320
Antelope Mine	246	DK 100
Antiwirifa	379	OF 316
Anum	380	OG 319
Anyama	379	OH 315
Anyeke	305	BN 108
Anyinam	380	OG 318
Anyirawase	380	OF 319
Anysberg	209	EK 84
Anysspruit	228	DW 104
Anzi	388	OO 342
Aoufous	330	NF 315
Aouinat er Rajjat	352	NV 312
Aoulouz	329	NG 311
Aourou	363	NX 307
Aozou	357	NQ 336
Apac	305	BO 108
Apawanta	304	BP 102
Api	385	OJ 344
Aplahoue	380	OF 321
Apoka	314	BK 110
Apoko	387	ON 335
Apolu	381	OD 323
Apromproonou	379	OF 316
Aqiq	361	NU 357
Ara Arba	317	BF 125
Ara Terra	325	BD 125
Araa	295	CC 114
Arabia	317	BK 125
Arada	369	NX 340
Arafali	373	NX 359
Arage	381	OE 327
Araka	312	BJ 103
Arandis	230	DM 72
Aranos	232	DQ 81
Araouane	353	NT 316
Arba des Beni Hassan	330	NC 313
Arba Minch	315	BF 117
Arba'at	361	NS 356
Arbole	365	NZ 317
Arboutchatak	369	OA 336
Arcadia	220	DY 101
Archer's Post	307	BQ 118
Arcturus	256	DC 105
Arebi	312	BM 102
Arege	368	NY 332
Arero	316	BH 120
Argent	228	DU 100
Argo	359	NS 350
Argungu	366	NZ 324
Ariamsvlei	216	DY 82
Aribinda	365	NY 318
Ariesfontein	218	DY 90
Aris	231	DN 77
Arjo	323	AZ 115
Arli	365	OA 320
Arlington	219	DY 98
Arlit	355	NT 326
Armant	348	NM 351
Arniston (Waenhuiskrans)	209	EM 83
Aroab	224	DV 82
Arochuku	376	OH 327
Aroma	372	NW 355
Arrah	379	OF 315
Arrecife	338	NJ 305
Ar-Ruat	372	OA 351
Artemou	363	NW 307
Aru	312	BM 104
Arua	312	BL 104
Arufu	382	OE 328
Arumbi	312	BM 103
Arundel	218	ED 92
Arusha	301	BY 116
Arzew	331	NB 319
As Sidr	334	NG 337
As Sultan	334	NG 336
Asab	223	DS 79
Asankranguaa	379	OG 317
Asawinso	379	OG 317
Asbe Teferi	324	AY 124
Asbospan	223	DV 76
Asela	324	BA 121
Asembe	306	BS 111
Asendobo	323	BB 117
Ash Shuwayrif	344	NH 333
Asha	381	OF 323
Ashburton	220	EB 103
Ashira	375	OC 370
Ashton	209	EK 83
Asilah	330	NC 313
Askeaton	212	EF 98
Askham	224	DV 84
Askira	368	OB 332
Askraal	209	EL 84
Asla	331	NE 319
Asmara	373	NX 358
Asnet	369	NZ 338
Asni	329	NG 311
Asosa	372	OC 354
Asriko	379	OE 314
Assa	339	NJ 310
Assa Gaila	374	OA 362
Assab	374	NZ 362
Assaikio	382	OD 328
Assamakka	354	NT 325
Assdadah	334	NG 334
Assegaaibos	211	EK 91
Assen	227	DS 98
Assinie	379	OH 316
Assok	386	OM 330
As-Sumay	371	OC 347
Aston Bay	211	EL 92
Asuefri	379	OE 316
Aswan	348	NO 352
Asyut	347	NL 350
Atakpamé	380	OF 320
Atar	351	NS 306
Atasi Nkwanta	380	OG 318
Atbara	360	NU 353
Atchewa	361	NV 358
Atebubu	380	OE 318
Atesa	379	OF 316
Athi River	301	BU 117
Ati	369	NZ 337
Ati Ardébé	369	NZ 337
Atiak	313	BL 107
Atiedo	385	OE 347
Atim	369	NY 340
Atira	306	BO 110
Atlanta	227	DS 98
Atlantis	208	EK 79
Atome	263	CQ 72
Atongo Bakari	380	OG 341
Atta	382	OG 330
Atteridgeville	227	CR 74
Atura	305	BN 107
Aúbe	261	CZ 122
Auchi	381	OF 325
Augrabies	216	DZ 83
Auheib	232	DM 81
Aujara	367	OA 329
Aukas	231	DM 73
Aulia	372	NX 352
Auma	384	OK 342
Auna	366	OC 324
Auno	368	OA 333
Aurora	208	EH 79
Aus	223	DV 75
Ausnek	223	DV 75
Austin's Post	218	EB 94
Ausweiche	223	DV 75
Avabuki	389	OM 347
Avindi	384	OH 340
Avoca	229	DT 105
Avond	241	DJ 75
Avondrust	209	EJ 83
Avontuur	225	DV 88
Aw Dheegle	310	BO 132
Awae	382	OJ 331
Awakaba	384	OE 339
Aware	326	BA 131
Awasa	324	BC 120
Awash	324	AY 123
Awbari	344	NL 332
Awe	382	OE 328
Aweil	385	OD 348
Awfist	338	NM 304
Awgaro	373	NX 356
Awjilah	345	NJ 340
Awka	381	OG 326
Awsard	350	NQ 305
Axim	379	OH 317
Ayame	379	OG 316
Ayamikem	376	OL 329
Ayanfure	379	OG 317
Ayangba	381	OE 326
Aye Koyé	362	OB 305
Ayinwafi	380	OF 318
Aykel	373	NZ 356
Ayn al Ghazal	358	NQ 344
Ayn al Ghazalah	335	NF 342
Ayod	321	BA 105
Ayorou	365	NX 320
Ayos	382	OJ 331
Ayoun el Atrous	351	NV 310
Aysha	374	OB 361
Az Zawiyah	333	NE 68
Az Zintan	333	NF 331
Azare	367	OA 329
Azarori	366	NY 325
Azazga	332	NA 323
Azemmour	329	NE 311
Azezo	373	OA 357
Azrou	330	NE 314
Baanta	309	BP 127
Baantama	380	OE 318
Baardheere	309	BN 127
Baard-skeerdersbos	209	EM 82
Bab al Maknusah	344	NL 333
Bab Taza	330	NC 314
Bababe	362	NW 305
Babaera	263	CS 72
Babana	366	OC 323
Babanango	221	DY 105
Babangu	237	DO 103
Babanusa	371	OB 347
Babar	332	NC 326
Babati	300	CA 114
Babelegi	227	DS 99
Baberspan	226	DV 94
Babia	385	OJ 346
Babi-Babi	232	DM 82
Babile	325	AY 127
Babonde	389	OL 347
Babongena	389	ON 345
Babongo	383	OF 333
Baboua	383	OG 334
Babura	367	NZ 328
Bacaadweeyn	327	BC 138
Bachalo	377	OE 306
Bachuo Akakbe	382	OG 329
Bactili	309	BO 125
Badagri	380	OG 322
Badanga	369	OA 336
Badeggi	381	OD 325
Bader	367	NX 326
Badeyuicheri	366	NX 324
Badir	368	OB 331
Badjer	383	OG 333
Badogo	364	OB 311
Badou	380	OE 319
Badplaas	228	DT 104
Badshoogte	210	EK 86
Badzere	383	OG 335
Baediam	363	NX 307
Bafang	376	OH 329
Bafata	362	OA 304
Bafia	382	OH 330
Bafilo	380	OD 320
Bafing-Makana	363	NZ 309
Bafoulabe	363	NY 308
Bafousam	382	OH 330
Bafua	251	CZ 70
Bafut	382	OG 329
Bafwabalinge	389	OM 346
Bafwaboli	389	OM 345
Bafwagadi	389	OM 345
Bafwasende	389	OM 346
Baga	368	NZ 331
Bagaji	366	NY 323
Bagamayo (Tan.)	295	CF 111
Bagamoyo (Tan.)	297	CE 121
Bagana	381	OE 327
Bagani	254	DD 86
Bagaroua	366	NX 323
Bagata	387	OR 337
Bagaya	384	OG 340
Bagbara	384	OH 338
Bagega	366	OA 325
Bageya	366	NZ 325
Bagodo	382	OG 332
Baguineda	364	NZ 311
Bahi	295	CD 113
Bahinga	292	CD 97
Bahir Dar	373	OA 356
Bahn	378	OF 310
Baía dos Tigres	250	DA 66
Baia Farta	262	CS 69
Baibokoum	383	OE 335
Baidou (CAR)	384	OF 341
Baidou (CAR)	384	OG 340
Baila	362	NZ 303
Bailden	220	EC 101
Bailey	212	EF 96
Bailundo	263	CR 74
Baine's Drift	236	DM 100
Baissa	382	OF 330
Baixo Longa	253	CY 80
Bajoga	367	OB 330
Bajone	260	DB 119
Baka	384	OH 339
Bakala	384	OG 340
Bakaore	370	NX 341
Bakebe	382	OG 328
Bakel	363	NX 306
Bakenklip	217	EE 85
Bakenskop	218	EA 91
Bakerville	227	DU 95
Bakin Birji	367	NY 328
Bako	323	AY 117
Bako	378	OD 311
Bakordi	312	BH 100
Bakori	367	OA 327
Bakouma	384	OG 342
Bakumba	386	OP 332
Bakwa Kenge	290	CB 87
Bala (Ugd.)	305	BN 108
Bala (Sen.)	363	NY 306
Balabaiba	262	CR 70
Balaka	259	CX 112
Balaki	303	OA 307
Balama	272	CT 120
Balangala	388	ON 339
Balat	347	NM 348
Bale	252	CX 76
Baleni	297	CH 122
Baleyara	366	NY 322
Balfour (E.C.)	212	EH 96
Balfour (Mpum.)	228	DV 100
Balgowan	220	EA 102
Bali	382	OG 329
Balifondo	384	OH 340
Balili	368	OC 335
Balle	363	NX 310
Ballengeich	228	DX 103
Ballito	221	EB 105
Balloul	331	NC 320
Balombe	264	CW 78
Balombo	263	CR 72
Baltim	337	NG 350
Baltimore	236	DO 99
Balunda	388	OQ 339
Balunga	291	CC 93
Bam	383	OE 335
Bama	368	OA 333
Bamake	378	OH 311
Bamako	364	NZ 311
Bamba (Mal.)	353	NV 318
Bamba (DRC)	288	CD 79
Bamba (Ken.)	302	BZ 122
Bambadinca	362	OA 304
Bambam	367	OC 330
Bambama	387	OQ 333
Bambara	384	OD 338
Bambara-Maounde	365	NW 316
Bambaran	363	NY 310
Bambari	384	OG 340
Bambesi	372	OC 354
Bambey	362	NX 303
Bambili	385	OJ 345
Bamboeskloof	219	ED 97
Bamboesspruit	227	DV 95
Bamboi	379	OE 317
Bambos de Sonhe	275	CJ 73
Bambouti	385	OH 346
Bambui	382	OG 329
Bame Town	378	OH 309
Bamenda	382	OG 329
Bamingui	384	OE 339
Bamusso	376	OJ 328
Ban Donige	372	OC 352
Bana Danied	371	NY 305
Banagi	300	BW 112
Banalia	389	OL 344
Banamba	364	NY 312
Banandje	378	OD 312
Banangui	385	OG 344
Banankoro (Gui.)	378	OD 310
Banankoro (Mali)	363	OA 310
Banankoro (Mali)	364	NZ 313
Banda (Cam.)	383	OE 333
Banda (CAR)	384	OG 341
Banda (Con.)	386	OQ 331
Banda (DRC)	289	CC 82
Banda (Uga.)	305	BR 106
Bandae	379	OH 317
Bandaka	388	ON 340
Bandakami	287	CB 70
Bandal	383	OF 333
Bandar (Moz.)	259	DA 111
Bandar (Gha.)	379	OF 317
Bandawe	271	CQ 111
Bande	385	OG 345
Bandelierkop	236	DO 102
Bandia	376	OH 329
Ban-diagara	364	NY 315
Bandjoukri	383	OE 333
Bandjoun	383	OH 330
Bandua	248	DH 111
Bandundu	387	OQ 337
Bandur	236	DN 102
Banfele	363	OC 309
Banfora	364	OB 314
Bang	383	OF 335
Banga (Ang.)	275	CK 73
Banga (DRC)	289	CB 82
Banga (DRC)	289	CC 83
Bangadi	385	OJ 347
Bangana	384	OE 342
Bangangte	382	OH 330
Bangare	365	NY 320
Bangassou	384	OH 342
Bangbali	384	OD 339
Banghazi	335	NF 339
Bangolo	378	OF 311
Bangoran	384	OE 339
Bangouren	382	OG 330
Bangu	278	CL 90
Bangue	383	OK 334
Bangui	384	OJ 338
Bangula	259	DA 113
Banguru	389	ON 346
Banh	365	NY 316
Bani (BF)	365	NY 319
Bani (CAR)	384	OF 342
Bani (Mali)	365	NY 317
Bani Bangou	366	NX 322
Bani Walid	334	NF 333
Bania	383	OJ 335
Banikoara	366	OB 321
Banima	385	OH 343
Banissa	316	BK 123
Banjul (Bathurst)	362	NZ 302
Bank	227	DU 99
Bankass	364	NY 315
Banket	257	DB 103
Bankilare	365	NX 320
Bankim	382	OG 331
Bankkop	228	DV 103
Banko (Gui.)	363	OB 308
Banko (Mali)	364	OA 312
Bankon	363	OA 310
Banner Rest	220	EE 103
Bansara	382	OG 328
Bantadjé	382	OE 332
Bantakoto	363	NZ 309
Bante	380	OE 321
Banvayo	379	OD 315
Banvo	277	CK 81
Banya	300	BY 111
Banya Fort	315	BJ 115
Banyo	382	OF 331
Banza	383	OK 337
Banza Sanda	287	CC 71
Banza Sosso	287	CD 73
Bao	383	OD 335
Baoro	383	OG 335
Bape	234	DO 91
Bapsfontein	227	DU 99
Bara (Nig.)	367	OC 330
Bara (Sud.)	371	NY 349
Baraawe	310	BP 130
Baraboulé	365	NY 317
Baragoi	307	BO 116
Baraka	298	CA 101
Barakke	211	EG 92
Barandas	210	EK 89
Baranga	385	OK 346
Barani	364	NZ 315
Baraouéli	364	NZ 312
Barberton	229	DT 105
Bardaï	357	NR 336
Bare	317	BH 128
Barentu	373	NX 357
Bargoni	302	BW 124
Bari	366	OC 325
Bariadi	300	BX 110
Baricho	302	BY 122
Barika	332	NC 324
Baringa (DRC)	388	OM 340
Baringa (DRC)	388	OM 341
Baris	347	NN 349
Barkedji	362	NX 304
Barkewo el Ablod	351	NV 307
Barkly East	219	ED 98
Barkly Pass	219	EE 98
Barkly West	218	DZ 91
Barmou	366	NX 324
Barnard	217	EE 89
Barnea	219	DY 99
Baro	381	OD 325
Baroda	211	EF 94
Baroe	211	EJ 92
Baroua	385	OG 344
Barra do Dande	274	CJ 69
Barra Peninsula	239	DP 114
Barrington	210	EK 88
Barrydale	209	EK 84
Barsalago	365	NZ 318
Barsaloi	307	BP 116
Bartlesfontein	210	EL 86
Basacato	376	OJ 328
Basali	389	OL 343
Basanga	291	CC 90
Basankusu	388	OM 339
Basase	291	CD 92
Bashimuke	291	CD 92
Basoko	389	OM 343
Basongo	388	OR 340
Basopdesh	300	CA 113
Basotu	300	CA 113
Bassar	380	OD 320
Bassaula	382	OF 329
Basséga	386	OO 332
Bassigbiri	385	OH 346
Bassikounou	364	NW 313
Bassila	380	OD 321
Basso	366	OC 323
Basua	382	OG 328
Basubuke	291	CC 91
Bata	305	BN 109
Bata	376	OL 329
Batabi	381	OD 325
Bataillor	289	CG 84
Batama	389	OM 346
Batamba	382	OJ 330
Batambal	362	OB 304
Batangafo	383	OF 337
Batcham	382	OG 330
Batchenga	382	OJ 331
Bate	243	DG 85
Batemba	291	CB 90
Bate-Nafadi	363	OB 310
Bathurst	212	EK 96
Bati	373	OB 359
Batia	366	OB 321
Batibo	382	OG 329
Batié	383	OH 330
Batna	332	NB 325
Batoka	256	DA 97
Batoua	382	OH 334
Batouala	387	OM 333
Batouri	383	OJ 333
Batsari	367	NZ 326
Batshamba	289	CD 82
Bauchi	367	OC 329
Baumango	387	OP 333
Bauta	388	OM 340
Bauyrat al Hasun	334	NF 332
Baviaan	209	EJ 84
Bawa	366	OA 325
Bawdie	379	OG 317
Bawi	259	CX 112
Bawiti	347	NK 348
Bawku	365	OB 319
Bawo	378	OG 311
Bay	365	NY 316
Baya Bwanga	290	CC 87
Bayadi	386	OQ 330
Bayala	229	DX 107
Bayanga	383	OK 335
Bayanga-Didi	383	OH 335
Baydhabo	318	BL 130
Bayeni	221	DY 106
Bayota	379	OG 313
Bayzo	366	NY 324
Baze	385	OJ 345
Bazian-Bea	383	OF 336
Bazley	220	EC 104
Beacon Bay	212	EH 99
Beaconsfield	218	DY 90
Beatrice	257	DD 104
Beaufort West	210	EG 88
Beauty	236	DO 98
Bébédjia	383	OD 336
Bebeka	322	BD 114
Beboura III	383	OF 336
Bechar	330	NF 317
Bedele	323	BA 115
Bederwanak	374	OC 364
Bedford	212	EH 95
Bediako	379	OF 316
Beerley	219	ED 97
Beeshoek	217	DY 88
Beestekraal	227	DS 98
Befale	388	ON 340
Befori	388	ON 341
Begi	322	AY 112
Begon	383	OF 334
Begoro	380	OG 319
Behulpsaam	211	EG 92
Beila	350	NU 303
Beilul	374	NZ 361
Beinamar	383	OD 334
Beira	249	DG 112
Beitbridge	236	DM 102
Beja	333	NA 328
Bejaia	332	NA 324
Beji	366	OC 325
Beka (Cam.)	382	OF 332
Beka (Cam.)	383	OG 333
Beke	279	CM 95
Bekker	226	DX 90
Bekoji	324	BB 121
Bekondja	383	OE 337
Bekondji	388	ON 338
Bekuy	364	OA 315
Bekwai	379	OG 317
Bekyem	379	OF 317
Bela Vista	229	DU 108
Bela-Bela (Warmbaths)	227	DR 99
Bélabo	382	OH 332
Bélaka Mbéré	383	OF 334
Belako	364	OA 312
Belas	274	CL 69
Belbedji	367	NX 327
Bele	324	BD 123
Beledweyne	318	BH 133
Belehede	365	NY 318
Belel (Cam.)	383	OF 333
Belel (Nig.)	368	OC 332
Belesc Cogani	309	BR 126
Beleya	363	OC 308
Belfast	228	DT 102
Belfodiyo	372	OB 354
Belgo	372	OC 351
Belgravia	209	EF 84
Belhirane	332	NG 325
Beli (Gui-B.)	362	OA 305
Beli (Nig.)	362	OE 330
Belifang	382	OG 329
Belize	286	CB 68
Bell	212	EJ 97
Bellevue (E.C.)	211	EJ 94
Bellevue (Lim.)	236	DO 102
Bellville	209	EK 80
Belmont	218	EA 91
Beloko	383	OF 335
Belonge	388	OP 339
Bemal	383	OE 335
Bembe	287	CG 71
Bembéréké	366	OC 322
Bembou	363	NZ 307
Beme	363	NX 309
Ben	364	NZ 315
Ben Badie	331	NC 318
Ben Guerdane	333	NE 330
Ben Mehidi	332	NA 327
Ben Slimane	329	ND 312
Ben S'Rour	331	NC 324
Bena (Nig.)	366	OB 325
Bena (Togo)	380	OF 320
Benahmed	329	NE 312
Bena-Kamba	389	OP 344
Benane	308	BR 120
Bena-Tshadi	290	CB 88
Bendela	387	OQ 337
Bender Beyla (Som.)	375	OC 370
Benderbeyla (Som.)	328	AY 144
Bendugu	378	OD 308
Bene	258	CX 108
Bene-Dibele	388	OR 342
Bénéna	364	NZ 315
Benga (Mal.)	259	CZ 110
Benga (Moz.)	271	CT 111
Bengamisa	389	OM 344
Bengbis	382	OK 331
Benguela	262	CS 69
Benguerir	329	NF 311
Bengwe	290	CH 88
Benha	347	NH 350
Beni	304	BQ 101
Beni Slimane	331	NB 322
Beni Abbes	341	NH 317
Beni Mazar	347	NJ 350
Beni Mellal	330	NF 313
Beni Ounif	331	NF 318
Beni Saf	330	NC 317
Beni Suef	347	NJ 350
Benisheikh	368	OA 331
Benoni	227	DU 99
Benoy	383	OE 335
Bensekou	366	OB 322
Bentiaba	262	CV 67
Bentiu	320	AY 102
Benty	377	OD 306
Benye	387	OP 336
Benza	286	CE 68
Béoumi	379	OE 313
Beposo	379	OH 317
Berber	360	NU 353
Berbera	374	OC 364
Berbérati	383	OJ 335
Berbice	229	DW 105
Berdale	327	BC 138
Bere	383	OD 335

Bereaville > Chimsasa

PLACE NAME	PG	GRID
Bereaville	209	EL 81
Bérébi	378	OH 312
Berebuda	385	OJ 347
Bereeda	375	OA 370
Bereko	300	CA 114
Berekum	379	OF 317
Berenice	348	NO 354
Berg Aukas Mine	242	DG 79
Bergland	231	DO 77
Bergplaas	210	EK 88
Bergrivier	208	EH 79
Bergsig (N.C.)	217	ED 86
Bergsig (Nam.)	240	DH 71
Bergville	220	DZ 101
Berkane	330	NC 317
Berlin	212	EH 98
Bermolli	217	DY 88
Berrahal	332	NA 326
Berrechid	329	NE 312
Berriane	332	NE 323
Berrouaghia	331	NB 322
Berseba (N.W.)	226	DW 93
Berseba (Nam.)	223	DT 78
Bertoua	383	OH 333
Besempan	227	DX 95
Bessao	383	OE 335
Bessi	362	NZ 303
Besters	220	DY 102
Bétaré Oya	383	OG 333
Betein	376	OH 327
Bétérou	380	OD 321
Bethal	228	DU 102
Bethania	218	EB 94
Bethanie (N.W.)	227	DT 98
Bethanie (Nam.)	223	DV 77
Bethelsdorp	211	EK 93
Bethesdaweg	211	EF 92
Bethlehem	219	DY 99
Bethulie	218	ED 94
Betongwe	385	OK 347
Bétou	384	OK 338
Bettache	329	NE 312
Bettiesdam	228	DV 102
Betty's Bay	209	EL 80
Beu	287	CE 73
Beungas	287	CF 74
Bewley	226	DT 94
Beyersburg	217	ED 88
Beyla	378	OD 310
Beyra	327	BD 137
Bhisho	212	EH 98
Bholo	212	EG 98
Bholothwa	212	EF 97
Bhunya	229	DV 105
Bianga	384	OH 340
Biankouma	378	OE 312
Biaro	389	ON 344
Biba	347	NJ 350
Bibala	262	CW 69
Bibas	386	OM 331
Bibe	382	OH 332
Bibémi	383	OD 333
Bibiani	379	OG 317
Bibundi	376	OJ 328
Bichi	367	OA 327
Bida	381	OD 325
Biddulph	219	DY 98
Bidon V	353	NQ 320
Bienge	289	CD 82
Biermanskool	241	DG 73
Bierspruit	227	DR 97
Biesiespoort	210	EF 89
Biesiesvlei	226	DU 94
Bifoum	376	ON 329
Big Bend	229	DV 106
Bigene	362	NZ 304
Biggarsberg	220	DY 102
Bighel	382	OD 328
Bignona	362	NZ 303
Bigori	372	OB 354
Biharamulo	299	BX 105
Bihawana	295	CE 114
Bikita	247	DH 106
Bikoro	387	OO 337
Bilanga	365	NZ 319
Bilassana	378	OD 311
Bilbeis	348	NH 351
Bildemar	219	EC 96
Biléngui	386	OP 331
Bili (DRC)	384	OH 339
Bili (DRC)	385	OJ 344
Biliri	367	OC 330
Billaouar	351	NV 308
Bilma	356	NT 332
Bilo (Eth.)	323	AZ 116
Bilo (Gab.)	386	ON 330
Biloo	309	BQ 128
Biltine	369	NX 340
Bimasa	366	NZ 325
Bimba	383	OJ 333
Bimbe	263	CQ 74
Bimbila	380	OD 319
Bimbo	383	OJ 337
Bin	331	NB 322
Binde	365	OA 318
Binder	368	OC 333
Bindu	289	CH 80
Bindura	258	DB 105
Binga (Tan.)	297	CG 121
Binga (Zim.)	256	DC 97
Bin-Houye	378	OF 311
Binkolo	377	OD 307
Bintagoungou	352	NV 315
Biougra	339	NH 310
Bipindi	382	OK 330
Bipok	382	OJ 330
Bir al Ghanam	333	NF 331
Bir Ali Ben Khelifa	333	NC 329
Bir Allaq	333	NG 331
Bir Ayad	333	NF 331
Bir Dhufan	334	NF 333
Bir Di	320	BB 100
Bir el Ater	332	NC 327
Bir el Hafey	333	NC 328
Bir Gandouz	350	NQ 302
Bir Hasana	348	NH 353
Bir Mogrein	339	NN 307
Bir Seiyala	348	NM 353
Bir Shalatein	360	NP 354
Bir Tam Tam	330	ND 315
Bir Zar	333	NG 329
Birak	344	NK 333
Birao	370	OC 342
Birchenough Bridge	248	DG 108
Bircot	326	BB 130
Birini	384	OE 341
Biriwiri	271	CW 111
Birkat Saira	370	NY 342
Birni	366	OC 321
Birni Ngaouré	366	NZ 322
Birnim	367	NY 329
Birnim Lalle	367	NY 326
Birnin Gwari (Nig.)	367	OB 326
Birnin Gwari (Nig.)	367	OB 326
Birnin Kebbi	366	OA 323
Birnin Kudu	367	OB 328
Birnin Nkonni	366	NY 324
Birnin-Yauri	366	OB 324
Bise	301	BW 116
Bisellia	385	OE 347
Bisi	220	EC 102
Biskra	332	NC 325
Biso	305	BO 105
Bissandougou	363	OC 310
Bissau	362	OA 303
Bissikrima	363	OB 308
Bissora	362	OA 304
Bitale	293	CB 102
Bitam	386	OL 331
Bitata	316	BG 121
Bitilifondi	385	OG 345
Bitkin	369	OA 337
Bitou	365	OB 319
Bitoutouk	376	OJ 329
Bitterfontein	215	EE 79
Bityi	213	EF 100
Biu	368	OB 331
Bivane	228	DX 104
Bizana	220	ED 102
Bizerte	333	NA 329
Bla	364	NZ 313
Black Rock	225	DW 88
Bladgrond	216	DZ 82
Blairbeth	227	DS 95
Blama	378	OE 308
Blanco	210	EK 87
Blanfla	379	OF 313
Blantyre	259	CY 112
Blebo	378	OH 311
Bleha	365	OB 317
Blendio	364	OA 313
Bleskop	227	DT 97
Blesmanspos	226	DX 91
Bletterman	218	ED 91
Blida	331	NB 322
Blikaodi	379	OD 316
Blinkfontein	226	DX 90
Blinkklip	217	DY 89
Blinkwater (E.C.)	212	EH 95
Blinkwater (Lim.)	236	DO 101
Blitta	380	OE 320
Bloemfontein	219	EA 95
Bloemhoek	216	EA 81
Bloemhof	226	DX 93
Blolekin	378	OF 311
Blood River (KZN)	220	DY 104
Blood River (KZN)	228	DX 103
Blossoms	210	EK 87
Bloubank	221	DY 105
Blouberg	236	DO 100
Bloubergstrand	208	EK 79
Blouhaak	236	DO 101
Blousyfer	216	EE 84
Blue Lagoon Ranch	256	CX 97
Bluecliff	211	EK 93
Bluegums	219	ED 97
Bluewater Bay	211	EK 94
Blukwa	304	BO 104
Blumenfelde	232	DP 79
Blydskap	228	DX 100
Bnagola	388	OQ 340
Bo	377	OE 307
Boali	383	OH 337
Boanda	382	OH 331
Boane	229	DU 107
Boangi	388	OP 340
Bobakada	384	OH 338
Bobala	383	OG 337
Boban	383	OH 337
Bobandana	298	BV 100
Bobo Dioulasso	364	OB 314
Bobonong	246	DL 99
Bobos	242	DF 78
Bobuk	372	OB 353
Bocanda	379	OF 315
Bocaranga	383	OF 335
Bocolo	263	CR 71
Bocota	253	CX 81
Boda	383	OJ 337
Bodam	216	EE 83
Bodenhausen	232	DM 78
Bodenstein	227	DU 96
Bodhei	302	BV 124
Bodi (Ben.)	380	OD 321
Bodi (Gha.)	379	OG 316
Bodibeng	244	DJ 88
Bodiki	383	OH 337
Bodo	379	OG 314
Bodokro	379	OE 313
Bodoukpa	383	OG 336
Boe	362	OA 305
Boegoeberg	217	DZ 87
Boeke	388	ON 340
Boende	388	ON 340
Boendu	388	OM 339
Boenze	287	CC 71
Boerboonfontein	209	EK 83
Boesmanskop	219	EC 97
Boesmans-riviermond	212	EK 96
Boetsap	226	DX 92
Boffa	362	OC 305
Bofossou	378	OD 309
Boga	304	BP 102
Bogandé	365	NZ 319
Bogangolo	383	OG 337
Bogbode	389	OL 345
Bogbonga	388	OL 338
Bogo	368	OB 334
Bogoro	283	CM 112
Bogose	384	OJ 339
Bogoso	379	OG 317
Bogué	350	NV 305
Boguera	383	OH 336
Bohicon	380	OF 321
Bohlokong	219	DY 99
Bohodou	363	OC 310
Bohong	383	OG 335
Boi	367	OC 328
Boila	261	CZ 122
Bojatau	245	DH 93
Boju	381	OF 327
Boju Ega	381	OF 327
Bokada	384	OJ 338
Bokandi	384	OE 338
Bokatola	388	OO 338
Boke (Eth.)	373	OC 360
Boke (Gui.)	362	OB 305
Bokele	388	OO 340
Boken	365	NZ 317
Bokhara	224	DX 83
Boki	383	OD 333
Bokito	382	OJ 330
Bokkoppie	217	DY 88
Boknes	212	EK 96
Boko	287	CB 72
Bokoko	385	OH 346
Bokol Mayo	317	BH 126
Bokolako	363	NY 306
Bokolongo	388	ON 339
Bokondji	388	OL 338
Bokondo	388	ON 342
Bokoro	369	OA 336
Bokote	388	ON 339
Bokoute	384	OG 338
Boksburg	227	DU 99
Bokspits	224	DV 84
Boksputs	217	DZ 86
Bokuma	388	ON 338
Bokungu	388	OO 341
Bol	368	NZ 334
Bolaiti	389	OQ 344
Bolama	362	OA 304
Bolay 1	383	OJ 336
Bolbol	366	NZ 323
Bole (Zim.)	323	BD 117
Bole (DRC)	379	OD 317
Boleka	388	OP 339
Bolgatanga	365	OB 318
Boli	247	DL 106
Boli	389	ON 347
Boli	383	OF 334
Bolia	387	OP 337
Bolivia	227	DX 99
Bolobo	387	OP 335
Bolomba	388	OM 338
Bolona	364	OC 312
Bolondo	376	OL 328
Bolonguera	262	CU 70
Bolsi	365	NZ 320
Bolton	247	DE 105
Boluré	251	CZ 72
Boma	286	CD 69
Bomadi	376	OH 325
Bomaya Lindi	283	CL 114
Bombakabo	384	OK 338
Bombe	384	OG 338
Bombela	364	OC 315
Bombi	388	OL 341
Bombo (Ang.)	286	CG 69
Bombo (Uga.)	305	BQ 108
Bombo-Makuka	288	CC 75
Bomboyo	368	OA 335
Bomé	251	CZ 72
Bomet	306	BT 113
Bomili	389	OL 346
Bomongo	387	OM 337
Bon Accord	227	DT 99
Bonam	365	NZ 319
Bonapabli	378	OG 309
Bondo (DRC)	385	OJ 343
Bondo (DRC)	387	OO 336
Bondoukou	379	OE 316
Bondoukui	364	OA 315
Bone	363	OA 308
Bonga	323	BC 115
Bongandanga	388	OL 340
Bongimba	388	OQ 339
Bongor	368	OC 335
Bongouanou	379	OF 315
Boni	365	NX 317
Boniere-dougou	379	OE 314
Bonkoukou	366	NY 322
Bonnievale	209	EK 83
Bonny	376	OJ 326
Bonny Ridge	220	ED 101
Bonou	380	OF 321
Bonoua	379	OH 316
Bonthe	377	OF 307
Bontrand	220	EC 102
Bonyere	379	OH 316
Bonza Bay	212	EJ 99
Bonzan	365	OB 316
Bonzo (Zim.)	248	DE 108
Bonzo (Ken.)	378	OE 312
Boola	378	OE 310
Boons	227	DT 97
Boorama	374	OC 362
Boord	228	DT 102
Boosaaso	375	OB 368
Booué	386	ON 331
Bopo	381	OE 327
Bor	321	BE 106
Bora	385	OD 345
Borchers	237	DO 103
Bordj Bou Arreridj	332	NB 324
Bordj Bounaama	331	NB 321
Bordj le Prieur	353	NR 320
Bordj Messouda	343	NH 328
Bordj Omar Idriss	343	NK 326
Bore (Bot.)	233	DN 86
Bore (Eth.)	324	BE 120
Boré	365	NX 316
Bori (Ben.)	366	OC 321
Bori (Nig.)	376	OH 326
Borj	333	NG 329
Borj Machened Salth	333	NF 330
Borne	343	NN 327
Boro	384	OH 339
Boromata	370	OC 341
Boromo	365	OA 316
Boron	379	OD 313
Borotou	378	OD 311
Bort Bourgulba	333	NF 329
Boshoek	227	DS 97
Boshof	218	DZ 93
Boskuil	226	DW 94
Bosobolo	384	OJ 339
Bosoord	228	DS 103
Bososama	384	OJ 339
Boso-Semodja	388	OM 338
Bospoort	227	DV 95
Bossangoa	383	OF 337
Bossembélé	383	OH 337
Bossentele	383	OG 336
Bosseoui	383	OH 336
Bossiekom	216	EA 83
Bossiesvlei	223	DS 76
Bot Makak	382	OJ 330
Botata	378	OF 310
Boteke	388	ON 338
Botelenza	384	OJ 339
Bothasput	218	DZ 93
Bothatogo	244	DJ 88
Bothaville (F.S.)	218	EA 93
Bothaville (F.S.)	227	DW 96
Bothithong	226	DW 90
Botlokwa	236	DP 102
Botou	365	OA 319
Botrivier	209	EL 81
Botro	379	OE 314
Botshabelo	219	EA 96
Bou Alem	333	NC 328
Bou Anane	330	NF 316
Bou Arfa	330	NE 317
Bou Gadoum	364	NW 311
Bou Hajla	333	NC 329
Bou Hamed	330	NC 314
Bou Izakarn	339	NJ 310
Bou Kadir	331	NB 320
Bou Lanouar	350	NR 303
Boû Rjeïmât	350	NT 304
Bou Saada	332	NC 323
Bou Sfer	331	NB 318
Bouafle	379	OF 313
Bouaké	379	OE 314
Boualem	331	ND 320
Bouam	382	OH 332
Bouanga	387	OP 335
Bouar	383	OG 335
Boubélé	378	OJ 312
Bouboury	379	OH 314
Bouca	383	OG 337
Bouchia	383	OJ 337
Bouchouayinly	350	NP 302
Boudamassa	369	OB 336
Boudenib	330	NF 315
Boudi	316	BJ 123
Boudoua	383	OJ 335
Bougaa	332	NB 324
Boughessa	354	NS 321
Bougoui	383	OF 334
Bougouni	364	OB 311
Bougtob	331	ND 319
Bougzoul	331	NB 322
Bouira	332	NB 323
Boujad	330	NE 313
Boujdour	338	NM 304
Boukanda	366	NY 321
Boukas	330	NF 316
Boukoula	368	OC 332
Boukra	339	NM 306
Boula-Ibib	368	OC 333
Boulal	362	NX 303
Boulankio	387	OR 334
Boulaouane	329	NE 311
Boulel (Sen.)	362	NY 303
Boulel (Mal.)	364	NX 314
Boulemane	330	NE 314
Boulgou	365	NZ 320
Boulsa	365	NZ 318
Bouma	330	NE 314
Boumaine du Dades	330	NG 313
Boumboum	365	NX 317
Boumdeït	351	NV 307
Boumeoul	363	OA 306
Bouna	379	OD 316
Boundi	384	OH 340
Boundiali	364	OC 312
Boundji	387	OO 335
Boune	367	NY 329
Bounga	384	OH 341
Boungou	384	OE 341
Bounkiling	362	NZ 303
Bounou	365	NZ 316
Boura	365	OB 317
Boureimi	366	NZ 323
Bourem	353	NV 319
Bourg El-Arah	337	NG 349
Bouroum	365	NY 319
Bourrah	368	OC 333
Bourzanga	365	NY 318
Bousso	369	OB 336
Boussouma	365	NZ 318
Bouthapalou	235	DQ 93
Boutilimit	350	NU 304
Boutougou Fara	363	NZ 307
Boutouli	383	OH 337
Bouza	366	NY 325
Bouzghaia	331	NB 320
Bo-Wadrif	209	EG 83
Bowker's Park	212	EF 96
Bowwood	256	DB 95
Boyabo	384	OJ 338
Boyne	236	DP 102
Boyo	384	OG 340
Boza (Tan.)	297	CC 121
Boza (DRC)	384	OH 338
Bozene	384	OK 338
Bozoum	383	OG 335
Braamspruit	219	ED 96
Braemar	220	EC 103
Brakbos	217	EA 87
Brakfontein (F.S.)	218	EB 93
Brakfontein (KZN)	229	DX 105
Brakfontein (N.C.)	218	EC 91
Brakkloof	212	EJ 95
Brakpan (Gau.)	224	DS 81
Brakpan (Nam.)	227	DU 99
Brakpoort	217	EE 89
Brakspruit	227	DV 96
Brakwater	231	DM 76
Brand	218	ED 90
Brand Park	218	DY 94
Brandberg West Mine	240	DK 71
Brandboom	216	ED 82
Branddraai	228	DR 104
Brandfort (F.S.)	218	DY 94
Brandfort (F.S.)	219	DZ 96
Brandkop	216	EE 81
Brandlaagte	219	DY 99
Brandrivier	210	EK 85
Brandvlei	216	EC 83
Brandwag	219	EA 95
Bransan	363	NZ 307
Brass	376	OJ 325
Braunschweig (E.C.)	212	EH 97
Braunschweig (Mpum.)	228	DW 104
Braunville	212	EF 97
Bray	226	DS 90
Brazzaville	387	OR 334
Breakfast Vlei	212	EJ 97
Bredasdorp	209	EM 83
Breidbach	212	EH 98
Breipaal	219	EC 95
Bresoanu	380	OE 318
Brewaniase	380	OE 319
Brewerville	378	OG 308
Breyten	228	DU 103
Brezina	331	NE 320
Bria	384	OF 341
Bridgewater	236	DN 101
Brikama	362	NZ 302
Brits	227	DT 98
Britstown	218	ED 90
Britten	226	DX 93
Broedersput	226	DV 93
Broken Dam	217	EC 89
Brombeek	236	DN 101
Bromley	258	DD 105
Brondal	228	DS 104
Bronkhorstspruit	228	DT 100
Brooks Nek	220	ED 102
Brughalte	219	ED 96
Bruintjieshoogte	211	EH 93
Brukkaros	223	DT 79
Brutuei	250	CZ 68
Bu Kammash	333	NE 331
Bu'aale	309	BP 128
Buaka	379	OG 316
Buba	362	OA 304
Bubada	299	BY 108
Bubanda	384	OJ 339
Bubanza	298	BY 101
Bubaque	362	OB 303
Bubi	247	DL 104
Bubiki	299	BY 109
Bubulo	306	BQ 111
Buçaco	277	CP 83
Buchanan	378	OG 309
Buchholzbrunn	223	DV 77
Buchwa	247	DJ 103
Bucklands	218	EA 90
Buco Zau	286	CB 68
Budaka	306	BP 110
Buddi	317	BG 129
Budumba	306	BQ 110
Bué Maria	248	DF 111
Buea	376	OJ 328
Buffalo Range	247	DK 106
Buffelsdrif	210	EK 88
Buffelsklip	210	EK 88
Buffle Noir	383	OE 333
Buga	381	OE 326
Bugadi	306	BR 110
Bugarama	298	BY 101
Bugembe	305	BQ 109
Bugene	299	BV 105
Bugiri	306	BQ 110
Bugondo	305	BO 109
Buhemba	300	BV 111
Buhera	247	DF 105
Buhimba	305	BP 105
Buhoro	293	CB 104
Buigiri	296	CE 115
Buikwe	305	BR 109
Buitepos	232	DM 82
Bujumbura	298	BY 101
Bukakata	305	BS 107
Bukalo	255	DC 92
Bukama	279	CL 94
Bukavu	298	BX 100
Bukedea	306	BP 111
Bukene	299	CA 108
Bukhit	371	OB 346
Bukima	299	BV 109
Bukindo	299	BX 107
Bukoba	299	BU 106
Bukoloto	305	BQ 108
Bukombe	299	BZ 107
Bukomero	305	BQ 107
Bukondo	299	BX 106
Bukonyo	299	BV 108
Bukundi	300	BZ 112
Bukungu	305	BP 108
Bukuru	367	OC 328
Bukuyo	305	BQ 106
Bukwimba	299	BX 109
Bula (DRC)	304	BO 100
Bula (Gui. B)	362	OA 303
Bulakos	367	OA 330
Bulangu	367	OA 329
Bulawayo	246	DH 100
Bulaya	281	CK 103
Bulembu	229	DT 105
Bulenga	365	OC 317
Bulisa	305	BN 105
Bullaxaar	374	OC 363
Bulletrap	215	EA 78
Büllsport	231	DQ 75
Bulongo	290	CB 86
Bulongwa	283	CL 111
Bulopa	305	BQ 109
Bultfontein (F.S.)	218	EB 94
Bultfontein (F.S.)	219	DY 95
Bultfontein (F.S.)	226	DX 93
Bulukutu (DRC)	388	ON 341
Bulukutu (DRC)	388	ON 341
Bulula	292	CC 97
Bulunde	299	CA 108
Bulungu (DRC)	289	CB 80
Bulungu (DRC)	290	CE 86
Bulwana	224	DS 80
Bulwer	220	EB 102
Bumba (Ang.)	276	CJ 77
Bumba (DRC)	289	CF 81
Bumba (DRC)	290	CF 88
Bumba (DRC)	388	OL 342
Bumba (DRC)	389	OM 343
Bumbuli	296	CB 119
Bumi Hills	256	DA 99
Buna (Kenya)	316	BM 122
Buna (DRC)	388	OQ 338
Bunda	300	BW 111
Bundibugyo	304	BQ 103
Bunduki	388	OL 342
Bungo	287	CG 73
Bungoma	306	BQ 112
Bungu	297	CH 121
Bungudu	367	OA 326
Bungule	302	BZ 120
Bungweli	365	OC 317
Buni	368	OB 331
Bunia	304	BO 103
Bunkeya	280	CN 96
Buntingville	213	EF 100
Bununu	367	OC 329
Bunyakiri	298	BW 100
Bunza	366	OA 323
Bur Safaga	348	NL 353
Bura	302	BU 122
Buram	370	OB 344
Burco	374	OC 365
Bure	373	OB 356
Burgersdorp	219	ED 95
Burgersfort	228	DR 103
Burgerville	218	ED 91
Burji	367	OB 328
Burumburum	367	OB 328
Buruntuma	362	OA 305
Bururi	298	BZ 102
Bururu	387	OL 337
Busanga (DRC)	279	CN 93
Busanga (DRC)	388	OO 341
Busangi	299	BZ 108
Busango	279	CK 93
Busembatia	306	BQ 110
Bushbuckridge	229	DR 105
Bushenyi	304	BT 103
Bushlands	221	DY 107
Bushman Pits	244	DH 91
Busia	306	BR 111
Busie	318	BF 131
Busika	305	BQ 108
Businde	298	BU 104
Businga	384	OK 340
Busisi	299	BX 108
Busiu	306	BQ 111
Busu-Djanoa	388	OL 340
Busu-Mandji	384	OK 340
Busu-Mondanda	388	OL 339
Busungwe	305	BT 106
Busunju	305	BQ 107
Busunu	379	OD 317
Buta	385	OK 344
Butajira	323	BA 119
Butare	298	BX 102
Bute Giarti	315	BH 118
Butemba	305	BP 106
Butembo	304	BR 101
Butha-Buthe	219	DZ 99
Butiaba	305	BO 105
Butiama	300	BV 110
Butiti	304	BQ 104
Butje	251	DA 70
Butterworth	212	EG 99
Butu	220	EB 102
Buuhoodle	327	BA 135
Buulo Burte	318	BK 134
Buur Gaabo	303	BU 126
Buur Hakaba	318	BM 131
Buwenge	305	BQ 109
Buyo	378	OG 312
Buysdorp	236	DO 101
Buyuni	297	CG 122
Buzi	249	DG 112
Bwana- Mutombo	289	CG 80
Bwanga	299	BY 106
Bwasenge	384	OJ 340
Bwea Town	378	OG 309
Bwengu	282	CP 110
Bweni	297	CH 122
Bwiam	362	NZ 303
Bwina	255	CZ 92
Bwizibwera	304	BS 104
Bylsteel	236	DP 102
Byumba	298	BV 103
Caala	263	CS 74
Cabango	276	CO 78
Cabari (Ang.)	275	CJ 75
Cabari (Ang.)	275	CK 75
Cabinda	286	CD 67
Cabuco	362	OA 305
Cachana	251	DA 70
Cacheu	362	OA 303
Cachimbo	277	CJ 85
Cachingues	264	CT 76
Cachipoque	265	CR 81
Cachueca	252	CX 76
Cacine	362	OB 304
Cacolo	277	CN 81
Caconda	263	CU 73
Cacongo	286	CC 67
Cacuaco	274	CK 69
Cacula	263	CW 71
Cacuso	275	CL 74
Cadale	319	BM 135
Caecae	243	DG 85
Cafu	251	DA 73
Cafundanga	264	CW 78
Cage	275	CJ 71
Cahama	251	CZ 71
Caia	259	DC 113
Caianda	278	CP 89
Caicumbo	265	CQ 85
Cainde	250	CX 69
Caipupa	264	CQ 79
Cairo (El-Q ahira)	348	NH 351
Caitou	262	CV 69
Caiundo	252	CY 77
Cala	212	EF 98
Cala Road	219	EE 98
Calabar	376	OH 327
Calai	253	DC 82
Calamba	274	CN 69
Calandula	275	CL 74
Caldas Xavier	259	CY 111
Caledon	209	EL 81
Calequisse	362	OA 302
Calipo	261	CY 121
Calitzdorp	210	EK 86
Calombo	263	CT 74
Calonda	277	CJ 83
Calovango	251	CZ 71
Caluango	277	CJ 82
Calucinga	275	CP 75
Calueque	251	DB 71
Calunda	266	CR 89
Caluquembe	263	CU 72
Caluula	375	OA 370
Calvert	228	DX 104
Calvinia	216	EE 82
Camabatela	275	CJ 73
Camabumba	290	CG 86
Camabunda	290	CG 85
Camacupa	264	CR 77
Camame	275	CK 72
Camaxilo	276	CJ 80
Camba Fota	289	CG 82
Cambamba	276	CO 79
Cambange	277	CJ 85
Cambaoumba	289	CH 83
Cambêno	250	DA 68
Cambo Camana	276	CK 76
Cambondo (Ang.)	250	CX 69
Cambondo (Ang.)	275	CL 72
Cambongue	263	CV 73
Cambria	211	EK 92
Cambulo	290	CH 85
Cambundi-Catembo	276	CN 77
Camden	228	DV 103
Cameia	265	CQ 84
Camelford	226	DX 92
Cameron's Glen	212	EG 95
Camissombe	277	CJ 84
Camongua	276	CO 76
Campanga	251	CZ 70
Campbell	218	DZ 90
Campeane	362	OB 304
Camperdown	220	EB 104
Campo	260	DC 115
Campo	376	OL 329
Camucuio	262	CV 69
Camundambala	277	CM 84
Canaga	277	CL 81
Canchungo	362	OA 303
Canconga	264	CR 80
Candelela	252	CZ 78
Candover	229	DW 106
Candulo	272	CQ 116
Cangalo	264	CQ 76
Cangamba	265	CU 82
Cangandala	275	CM 75
Cangino	277	CN 81
Cangoa	264	CS 79
Cangola	287	CH 74
Cangombe	265	CV 82
Cangrafa	351	NU 306
Cangumdo	277	CK 81
Canicado	238	DR 109
Canjime	253	DC 81
Cankuzo	298	BY 104
Canxixe	259	DC 111
Canzar	290	CH 86
Caombo	276	CK 76
Caonde	276	CO 77
Capaia	277	CJ 83
Capangombe	262	CW 68
Capato	275	CO 74
Cape Coast	380	OH 318
Cape St Francis	211	EL 92
Cape Town	208	EK 79
Capelongo	263	CW 73
Capenda-Camulemba	276	CL 79
Capiata	251	CX 74
Capico	252	CY 78
Capolopopo	250	CY 68
Caponda	270	CW 106
Capua	253	CX 82
Capunda	251	CY 70
Capunda Cavilongo	262	CW 70
Caraculo	262	CW 68
Caravela	362	OA 303
Carimbula	289	CG 82
Caripa	253	CX 81
Caripande	266	CS 88
Cariua	260	DB 117
Carlchew	228	DU 102
Carletonville	227	DU 97
Carlisle Bridge	212	EJ 95
Carlow	236	DN 101
Carlsonia	227	DT 95
Carlton	218	EE 93
Carnarvon	217	ED 87
Carnarvon Experimental Farm	217	EE 86
Carnot	383	OH 335
Carolina	228	DU 103
Carolus	218	EE 92
Carthill	220	EB 102
Casablanca	329	ND 311
Casembi	258	CZ 105
Casinga	252	CX 75
Cassa da Telha	286	CG 69
Cassaça	275	CL 72
Cassacatiza	270	CV 107
Cassai Sul	278	CO 86
Cassamba	265	CT 83
Cassango	276	CK 78
Cassasala	277	CP 81
Cassongue	263	CQ 73
Cassulo Cuenda	276	CK 79
Cassunga	276	CO 78
Catama	309	BN 126
Catambué	252	DB 79
Catandica	258	DD 109
Cataxa	258	CY 109
Catembe	229	DU 107
Catengue	262	CT 70
Catete	274	CL 70
Cathcart	212	EG 97
Cathedral Peak	220	DZ 101
Catio	362	OB 304
Catofe	275	CO 73
Catolo	276	CJ 78
Cattle Ranch	382	OG 328
Catuane	229	DV 107
Catumbela	262	CR 69
Catur	271	CU 114
Catxinga	276	CJ 78
Caucula	253	CY 84
Caumbue	277	CM 83
Caungula	276	CJ 80
Cauno	253	DA 81
Cava	273	CV 123
Cavale	251	DA 71
Cavane	248	DK 110
Cawente	305	BO 108
Caxiaxia	277	CK 84
Caxito	274	CK 70
Caynabo	327	AZ 135
Cazage	277	CP 84
Cazambi	277	CP 84
Cazombo	266	CQ 89
Cazula	259	CX 110
Cedarville	220	EC 101
Cederberg	209	EH 81
Ceel Buur	319	BH 136
Ceel Dhaab	327	AZ 136
Ceel Dheer	319	BK 137
Ceel Huur	319	BH 139
Ceerigaabo	375	OB 366
Cegere	305	BN 108
Centani	212	EH 99
Centenary	258	DA 105
Centurion	227	DT 99
Ceres	209	EJ 81
Ceuta (Spain)	330	NB 314
Chá Lugela	260	CZ 115
Chacane	238	DQ 112
Chache	379	OD 316
Chadiza	270	CV 108
Chafe	367	OA 326
Chafo	366	OC 324
Chagne	372	OB 355
Chahbounia	331	NB 321
Chai	273	CQ 123
Chaïmane	351	NR 306
Chakari	257	DD 102
Chake Chake	297	CC 122
Chakwenga	257	CX 102
Chala	294	CH 105
Chalaua	261	CZ 121
Chalinze	296	CF 119
Chalumna	212	EJ 97
Chama	282	CP 109
Chamamba	295	CG 114
Chamarendi	299	BY 108
Chamba (Moz.)	260	CX 115
Chamba (Tan.)	272	CQ 116
Chambalo	295	CC 114
Chambishi	268	CS 99
Chamela	253	DB 81
Chametengo	259	DB 113
Chami	350	NS 303
Chamieites	223	DW 78
Chamwino	296	CE 115
Chandama	296	CC 115
Changa	256	CZ 99
Changalane	229	DU 107
Changamwe	302	CA 122
Changara	258	DA 109
Chaniassou	366	NY 324
Chanje	270	CV 106
Chanka	282	CM 108
Chantulo	271	CV 112
Chapararia	306	BP 113
Chapota	281	CJ 105
Charl Cilliers	228	DV 101
Charleshill	233	DM 83
Charlestown	228	DW 103
Charlesville	218	EB 93
Charlwood	211	EG 92
Charouine	341	NJ 319
Chasia	365	OC 317
Chataika	270	CV 106
Chato	299	BX 106
Chatsworth	247	DG 104
Chaua	277	CJ 81
Chavuma	266	CT 88
Chavuna	294	CC 107
Che Che	362	OA 305
Chebba	333	NC 330
Chechaouene	330	NC 314
Cheddra	368	NZ 335
Chegato	247	DJ 103
Chegga (Alg.)	332	ND 325
Chegga (Mrt.)	340	NN 313
Chegguet El Ftaiet	332	NE 325
Chegutu	257	DD 103
Chelal	332	NB 323
Chelghoum El Aid	332	NB 325
Chelinda	282	CO 110
Cheline	239	DM 113
Chema	284	CK 119
Chemaia	329	NF 310
Chemba	259	DB 112
Chembe	268	CQ 100
Chencha	323	BE 118
Chenini	333	NE 329
Chepsikunya	306	BO 112
Cherchell	331	NA 321
Chereponi	365	OC 319
Cherequera	263	CV 73
Chéri	367	NZ 330
Cheria	332	NC 327
Chetaibi	332	NA 326
Chete	256	DB 98
Chiange	251	CY 70
Chiapepe	251	CY 71
Chiawa	257	CY 100
Chibabava	248	DH 110
Chibale	269	CU 103
Chibaranda	254	DB 85
Chibemba	251	CY 71
Chibembe	270	CS 107
Chibi	247	DH 104
Chibia	251	CX 70
Chibitoke	298	BX 101
Chibole	295	CF 114
Chiboma	248	DH 110
Chibunji	248	DJ 107
Chibuto	238	DR 110
Chicabela	229	DT 108
Chicala (Ang.)	264	CS 77
Chicala (Ang.)	265	CQ 82
Chicamba (Ang.)	286	CB 67
Chicamba (Moz.)	248	DF 109
Chicambi	262	CU 68
Chichaoua	329	NG 310
Chichocane	239	DM 113
Chiclana de la Frontera	330	NB 313
Chico	248	DL 110
Chicoa	258	CY 108
Chicoca	265	CW 83
Chicomba	263	CV 72
Chicome	238	DR 111
Chicomo	269	CU 104
Chicono no	271	CS 114
Chicua	251	CZ 71
Chicualacuala	237	DN 107
Chicuma	263	CT 72
Chicundo	264	CS 78
Chicunho	263	CU 75
Chicupo	265	CW 81
Chicusse	251	CZ 72
Chida	323	BC 116
Chidenguele	238	DR 111
Chidisi	259	DA 113
Chiede	251	DB 74
Chiende	251	DA 71
Chiengi	281	CK 101
Chiengo	264	CV 76
Chieveley	220	DZ 102
Chifunda	270	CQ 108
Chifunde	270	CW 108
Chigubo	238	DN 109
Chigugu	284	CO 120
Chihunungu	296	CD 115
Chikole	296	CD 115
Chikombedzi	247	DL 105
Chikonkomene	268	CW 99
Chikuku	247	DH 106
Chikwa	270	CQ 108
Chikwawa	259	CZ 112
Chikwina	283	CP 111
Chila	263	CR 71
Chilala	256	CZ 96
Chilanga	256	CY 99
Chilau (Ang.)	251	CZ 72
Chilau (Ang.)	251	DA 71
Chileka	259	CY 112
Chilembwe	270	CU 106
Chililabombwe	268	CR 98
Chilobwa	270	CU 109
Chilombo	266	CR 88
Chilonga (Ang.)	264	CS 79
Chilonga (Zam.)	269	CQ 105
Chilongozi	270	CT 106
Chiluage	278	CM 86
Chilubula	281	CN 104
Chilumba	283	CN 111
Chilumbulwa	268	CR 97
Chimala	283	CK 111
Chimanimani	248	DG 108
Chimasula	270	CV 106
Chimbangulula	263	CW 73
Chimbe	253	DA 81
Chimbinde	265	CV 81
Chimbo	266	CU 90
Chimbueta	252	CZ 78
Chimbundo	253	DB 80
Chimbunjango	253	CY 83
Chimoio (Moz.)	248	DF 110
Chimolo (Zam.)	269	CU 103
Chimsasa	258	DB 108

PLACE NAME	PG	GRID
Chimvila	270	CV 107
Chinde	249	DE 116
Chindumba	264	CR 79
Chinengue	271	CU 113
Chingo	262	CV 68
Chingola	268	CS 98
Chingombe	269	CV 102
Chinguanja	252	CX 77
Chinguar	263	CS 75
Chingueia	264	CU 76
Chinguetti	351	NS 307
Chinhanda	258	CY 107
Chinhanguanine	238	DS 108
Chinhoyi	257	DB 103
Chinsali	282	CO 106
Chintheche	271	CQ 111
Chintsa East	212	EH 99
Chintsa West	212	EH 99
Chinyama Litapi	266	CU 87
Chipanga	259	DB 113
Chipangayi	248	DH 107
Chipangua	251	CZ 72
Chipasanse	281	CK 104
Chipata	270	CU 108
Chipepo (Zam.)	256	DA 98
Chipepo (Zam.)	268	CV 99
Chipili	281	CO 101
Chipindo	263	CU 74
Chipinge	248	DH 108
Chipipa	263	CS 74
Chipise	237	DM 104
Chipogolo	296	CF 115
Chipoka	271	CV 112
Chipola	264	CS 80
Chiponde	271	CV 114
Chiprimani	263	CW 74
Chipungo	269	CT 104
Chiputo	270	CW 107
Chiquita	276	CK 76
Chira	323	BB 115
Chiramba	259	DA 112
Chire	259	DA 113
Chiredzi	247	DK 106
Chirfa	356	NR 331
Chiromo	259	DA 113
Chirumanzu	247	DG 104
Chirundu	257	CZ 100
Chisama	268	CW 100
Chisamba	268	CW 99
Chisasa	267	CR 93
Chisato	282	CM 108
Chisekesi	256	CZ 98
Chisenga	282	CM 109
Chisoso	282	CP 106
Chissanda	265	CW 81
Chissano	238	DR 109
Chissessengue	289	CG 83
Chissibuca	238	DR 111
Chissinguane	248	DH 111
Chissito	251	CZ 71
Chisumbanje	248	DJ 107
Chita	283	CJ 114
Chitado	251	DB 70
Chitato	289	CG 84
Chitembo	264	CT 76
Chitengo	248	DF 111
Chitipa	282	CM 109
Chito	253	DA 84
Chitobe	248	DJ 109
Chitokoloki	266	CU 89
Chitongo	256	CZ 96
Chitowe	284	CP 120
Chitsungo	258	DA 107
Chitungwiza	258	DD 105
Chiume	254	CX 85
Chiundaponde	269	CR 103
Chiúre	273	CT 122
Chiuta	258	CY 109
Chivhu	247	DF 104
Chivuna	256	CZ 98
Chiwata	285	CO 121
Chiweta	283	CO 111
Chizela	267	CT 93
Chlef	331	NB 320
Chofombo	270	CW 106
Choge	277	CM 82
Choggar	350	NV 305
Chókwé	238	DR 108
Choma	256	DA 96
Chomachankale	299	CA 109
Chongoroi	262	CU 70
Chongwe	257	CX 100
Chrissiesmeer	228	DU 103
Christiana	226	DX 93
Chuambo	249	DL 113
Chugango	251	CZ 70
Chuka	307	BS 118
Chukwani	297	CE 121
Chundela	254	CX 85
Chunga (Zam.)	256	CY 97
Chunga (Zam.)	282	CP 107
Chuniespoort	236	DQ 102
Chunya	282	CK 109
Chupanga	259	DD 113
Churchhaven	208	EJ 78
Chwaka	297	CE 121
Ciko	213	EG 100
Cir Kud	317	BK 128
Cissela	363	OB 308
Citriodora	228	DT 104
Citrusdal	209	EH 81
Clansthal	220	EC 104
Clanville	219	EE 97
Clanwilliam	209	EG 80
Clarens	219	DZ 99
Clarkebury	212	EF 99
Clarkson	211	EL 91
Claudina	226	DW 94
Clermont	220	EB 104
Clewer	228	DT 101
Clifford	219	EE 97
Clocolan	219	DZ 98
Coalville	228	DU 101
Coblenz	242	DH 79
Cobué (Moz.)	238	DR 112
Cóbué (Moz.)	271	CR 112
Cocobeach	376	OM 328
Cocopan	217	EE 85
Coega	211	EK 94
Coenbult	223	DV 79
Coerney	211	EJ 94
Coetzersdam	226	DV 91
Coffee Bay	213	EG 101
Cofimvaba	212	EF 98
Coghlan	212	EF 99
Cogo	376	OM 329
Coguno	238	DQ 112
Cohora Bassa	258	CY 108
Colchester	211	EK 94
Coleford	220	EB 101
Colenso	220	DZ 102
Colesberg	218	ED 92
Coleskeplaas	211	EK 91
Coligny	227	DU 95
Colleen Bawn	246	DK 101
Collo	332	NA 326
Colston	216	DY 84
Colui	263	CW 75
Colworth	220	DY 102
Comácha	258	DC 109
Combomune	237	DP 107
Cometela	248	DL 111
Committees	212	EJ 96
Commondale	228	DW 104
Conakry	377	OD 305
Concordia	215	EB 79
Conda	275	CP 71
Congerenge	271	CV 114
Connemara	247	DF 102
Constantia	218	EB 93
Content	218	DY 92
Conway	211	EF 93
Cookhouse	211	EH 94
Copperton	217	EB 87
Corda	263	CT 75
Cordoba	277	CK 84
Corn Exchange	219	DZ 98
Cornelia (F.S.)	218	DZ 94
Cornelia (F.S.)	228	DW 100
Corrane	261	CX 122
Cosso	276	CN 78
Cotonou	380	OG 321
Cottondale	229	DR 105
Cradock	211	EG 94
Crafthole	226	DU 91
Craigsforth	220	DY 102
Cramond	225	DW 85
Crecy	228	DR 100
Creighton	220	EC 102
Crocodile Bridge	229	DS 106
Cross Roads (Zim.)	256	DD 96
Crossroads (Zim.)	246	DE 101
Croydon	229	DU 105
Cruzado	249	DE 112
Cruzeiro	249	DJ 112
Cuamba	272	CW 116
Cuangar	253	DC 80
Cuango	276	CL 79
Cuanza	264	CQ 78
Cubal	263	CT 71
Cuchi	264	CW 76
Cuemba	264	CR 79
Cuilo	277	CJ 82
Cuima	263	CT 74
Cuio	262	CS 68
Cuito Cuanavale	253	CX 81
Cullinan	228	DT 100
Cum	245	DK 92
Cumbana	239	DQ 113
Cunda Dia Baze	276	CK 77
Cundycleugh	220	DY 102
Cunene	263	CV 73
Cunga	253	DB 84
Cunhinga	264	CR 76
Cunjamba	253	CX 83
Cunje S José	264	CR 76
Curale	326	BB 131
Curia	237	DM 106
Currie's Camp	217	DZ 85
Cuso	275	CK 73
Cussava	263	CV 73
Cutato	264	CV 76
Cutenda	263	CV 73
Cutting Camp	219	EC 98
Cuture	253	CX 84
Cuvelai	251	CY 74
Cyangugu	298	BX 101
Cyrene	246	DH 99
D. West	368	OA 332
Dabaga (Tan.)	283	CJ 114
Dabaga (Nig.)	355	NV 327
Dabakala	379	OE 315
Dabarow	328	BE 140
Dabenoris	216	EA 80
Dabnou	366	NY 324
Dabo	362	NZ 305
Dabola	363	OB 308
Dabou	379	OH 315
Daboye	365	OC 318
Dabwa	368	NY 332
Dadaab	308	BR 123
Daduma Addi	317	BM 125
Daeraad	236	DQ 99
Dafra	369	OA 338
Dagab	216	EB 83
Dagamela	246	DE 100
Dagana	350	NV 303
Daga-Post	322	AY 110
Dagash	360	NT 353
Dagbreek	217	DY 86
Daggaboersnek	211	EH 94
Daguela	369	OB 337
Dahmani	333	NB 328
Dahra	362	NX 304
Dahshur	347	NH 350
Dakar	362	NX 301
Dakawa	296	CE 118
Dakhla	338	NO 303
Daki Tagwas	366	OA 324
Dakingari	366	OA 323
Dakoro	367	NX 326
Dala (Ang.)	277	CL 85
Dala (Ang.)	277	CP 83
Dalaba (Gui.)	363	OB 307
Dalaba (Mali)	363	NZ 306
Daleside	227	DU 99
Dali (DRC)	289	CD 80
Dali (Mal.)	364	NX 311
Dali Sharafat	372	NZ 352
Dalli	382	OE 330
Dalmanutha	228	DT 103
Daloa	379	OF 313
Dalton	220	EA 104
Dam Gamad	371	NZ 346
Damagaram-Takaya	367	NY 328
Damakar	368	NZ 332
Damakuli	368	OA 332
Damanhur	337	NG 349
Damara	384	OH 338
Damasak	368	NZ 332
Damaturu	368	OA 331
Damba	287	CF 73
Dambai	380	OE 319
Dambam	367	OA 330
Dambarta	367	OA 328
Damboa	368	OB 332
Damongo	379	OD 317
Dan Gona	366	NY 324
Dan Mairo	367	NY 326
Dan Sadau	366	OB 325
Dan Tchiao	367	NZ 328
Danabaai	210	EL 86
Danané	378	OF 311
Dandau	264	CQ 76
Dande	315	BH 115
Dando	276	CP 77
Danga	353	NV 316
Dangavo	384	OE 339
Dange	366	NZ 324
Dangila	373	OB 356
Dan-Gulbi	366	OA 325
Danielskuil (W.C.)	209	EG 83
Daniëlskuil (W.C.)	218	DY 90
Danielsrus	219	DY 99
Dannhauser	220	DY 103
Danot	326	BB 133
Dante	375	OC 370
Daoud	331	NC 319
Daouenle	374	OB 361
Daoukro	379	OF 315
Dapaong	365	OB 319
Dapchi	368	NZ 331
Dar Chebika	339	NK 308
Dar Chioukh	331	NC 322
Dar el Leqceiba Barka	350	NV 304
Dar es Salaam	297	CF 121
Daradou	385	OG 344
Darambue	294	CE 108
Darazo	367	OB 330
Darburruk	374	OC 364
Dargo	365	NZ 319
Dargol	365	NY 320
Darhala	379	OE 315
Darling	208	EJ 79
Darnah	335	NE 342
Darnall	221	EA 105
Darou-Mousti	362	NX 303
Darul	378	OE 308
Darwendale	257	DC 104
Daskop	210	EK 88
Dass	367	OC 329
Dassa	380	OE 321
Dasville	227	DV 99
Datori	365	OC 320
Daura	367	NZ 327
Davel	228	DU 102
Dawadawa	379	OE 317
Dawn	212	EH 98
Dawqah	361	NT 360
Dchira	339	NL 306
De Aar	218	ED 91
De Beers	226	DW 92
De Brug	218	EA 94
De Doorns	209	EK 82
de Gaulle	383	OF 334
De Gracht	236	DN 100
De Hoek	209	EH 80
De Klerk	218	EE 90
De Rust	210	EJ 87
De Wet	209	EK 82
De Wildt	227	DT 98
Dealesville	218	DZ 94
Deali	362	NX 303
Debark	373	NZ 357
Deba-Sima	374	NZ 362
Debdou	330	ND 316
Debel	316	BL 121
Debra	243	DG 83
Debre Birhan	373	OC 359
Debre Markos	373	OC 356
Debre Tabor	373	OA 357
Debre Zeit	324	AZ 120
Debre Zeyit	372	OB 355
Debremay	373	OB 357
Decamere	373	NX 358
Dedda	373	NX 357
Deder	325	AY 126
Dédougou	365	OA 316
Dedza	271	CV 111
Deelfontein	218	ED 90
Deelpan	226	DU 94
Deelspruit	219	DY 96
Dega Medo	325	BA 128
Degeh Bur	326	BA 130
Degema	376	OH 326
Dehibat	333	NF 330
Deholm	220	EB 102
Deim Bukhit	385	OF 346
Deim Zubeir	385	OE 345
Dejen	373	OC 357
Deka	256	DD 96
Dekese	388	OQ 341
Dekina	381	OE 326
Dekoa	384	OG 338
Dekriet	210	EL 85
Delaa	332	NE 323
Delami	371	OA 349
Delareyville	226	DV 93
Delep	369	NZ 338
Delgo	359	NS 350
Deli	383	OD 335
Dellya	332	NA 323
Delmas	228	DU 100
Delportshoop	218	DY 91
Demba	290	CC 87
Demba Koli	363	NY 306
Dembecha	373	OC 357
Dembeldoro	316	BJ 122
Dembi	323	BA 115
Dembi Dolo	322	AZ 112
Dembia	385	OH 343
Dembo	368	OC 333
Dembos	275	CK 72
Demi	372	OC 355
Demistkraal	211	EK 92
Demsa	368	OC 332
Denan	325	BD 129
Dendoudi	362	NX 305
Deneysville	227	DV 99
Denge	385	OJ 347
Dengebe	366	OA 325
Dengi	382	OD 329
Denguiro	384	OG 342
Dennilton	228	DS 101
Deo	384	OE 340
Deou	365	NX 318
Dera	324	BA 121
Derbissaka	385	OG 344
Derby	227	DT 96
Derdepoort	227	DR 96
Dereham	219	EB 97
Deressa	369	NZ 340
Derm	232	DP 79
Dernaia	333	NC 328
Derre	260	DA 115
Derri	319	BJ 136
Derudeb	360	NV 355
Dese	373	OB 359
Despatch	211	EK 93
Dessing	227	DT 97
Dete	245	DE 96
Devon	228	DU 100
Devondale	226	DV 92
Devonlea	226	DV 92
Dewetsdorp	219	EB 96
Dhaya	331	NC 318
Dhaym-al-Khayl	339	NM 306
Dhlamini	246	DG 97
Dhooble	309	BR 125
Dhoomadeere	309	BO 125
Dhuuds	328	AY 143
Dhuusa Mareeb	319	BF 135
Diabo	365	OA 319
Diaca	285	CP 123
Diadloumbera	363	NX 308
Diakon	363	NY 309
Dialafara	363	NZ 308
Dialakoto	363	NZ 306
Diamant (F.S.)	218	EB 92
Diamant (F.S.)	226	DX 93
Diambo	384	OK 338
Diamou	363	NY 308
Diamounguel	363	NX 306
Diana (Nam.)	232	DM 79
Diana (Sen.)	363	NY 306
Diana Malari	362	NZ 304
Dianfa	379	OD 313
Diangounte-Kamara	363	NX 309
Dianra	379	OD 313
Diapaga	366	OA 321
Diarabala	378	OE 312
Diari	363	OB 306
Dias	271	CS 113
Diawala	364	OC 313
Dibaya	290	CE 88
Dibaya Lubue	388	OR 339
Dibeng	225	DX 88
Dibete	235	DP 96
Dibi	383	OF 333
Dibombari	376	OJ 329
Dider	343	NN 327
Didieni	364	NY 311
Didievi	379	OF 314
Didigsala	373	NZ 359
Didoko	379	OG 314
Didyr	365	NZ 316
Die Bos	209	EG 82
Die Dam	209	EM 82
Die Hel	210	EJ 86
Die Kalk	223	DS 78
Die Vlug	210	EK 89
Diébougou	365	OB 316
Diema	363	NX 310
Diemansputs	217	EB 86
Diere	362	NW 304
Dif	308	BQ 124
Diffa	368	NZ 332
Difounda	386	OQ 330
Difuma	389	OQ 345
Digalu	315	BH 119
Digba	385	OJ 345
Digui	384	OH 340
Dihimba	285	CN 122
Diibao	383	OD 334
Diinsoor	309	BN 128
Dik	369	OC 337
Dikabeya	235	DM 97
Dikhil	374	OB 361
Diklipspoort	217	EB 87
Dikodougou	379	OD 313
Dikwa	368	OA 333
Dikwalo	244	DJ 91
Dila	323	BE 119
Dilbe	373	OA 358
Dili	385	OK 346
Dilli	364	NX 311
Dilling	371	OA 349
Dilolo	278	CO 87
Dima	373	OB 357
Dimako	383	OJ 333
Dimbelenge	290	CD 89
Dimbi	384	OH 341
Dimbokro	379	OF 314
Dimpam	382	OJ 332
Dinangourou	365	NY 317
Dinde Dinde	262	CV 70
Dindima	367	OC 329
Dindiza	238	DO 109
Ding Ding	321	AZ 108
Dinga	384	OF 342
Dingba	385	OK 347
Dingila (DRC)	385	OJ 345
Dingila (DRC)	385	OK 345
Dingueteri	363	OA 306
Dinguiraye	363	OB 308
Dinho	324	BC 122
Dinokwe	235	DO 96
Diobahika	299	BY 106
Dioïla	364	NZ 312
Diongol	363	NX 310
Dioro	364	NY 313
Diosso	286	CB 66
Dioulatie-dougou	378	OD 312
Diouloulou	362	NZ 302
Dioura	364	NX 314
Diourbel	362	NX 303
Diphuti	237	DQ 104
Diré	365	NW 316
Dire Dawa	374	OC 361
Dirico	253	DC 84
Dirinbaji	366	OB 324
Dirj	343	NH 329
Dirkiesdorp	228	DW 103
Dirkou	356	NT 332
Dirra	370	NY 345
Dis Al	242	DK 80
Disa	300	CA 114
Dishna	348	NM 351
Ditche	362	OA 305
Ditinn	363	OB 307
Ditlhake	218	EA 92
Ditshipeng	226	DV 90
Divénié	386	OQ 331
Divinhe	249	DJ 112
Divo	379	OG 314
Divuma	278	CO 89
Dixcove	379	OH 317
Dizangue	376	OJ 329
Diziva	252	CY 77
Djado	356	NR 331
Djafarabe	364	NY 314
Djalasiga	312	BM 104
Djamaa	332	ND 325
Djamba (Ang.)	251	DA 71
Djamba (DRC)	278	CK 89
Djambala (Cam.)	382	OF 331
Djambala (DRC)	387	OQ 334
Djampiel	383	OJ 333
Djanet	343	NO 328
Djebok	365	NW 319
Djédaa	369	NY 338
Djelfa	331	NC 322
Djema	385	OG 344
Djemila	332	NB 325
Djenen Krater	330	ND 317
Djeniene Bou Rezg	331	NF 319
Djénné (World Heritage Site)	364	NY 314
Djermaya	368	OA 334
Djibasso	364	NZ 315
Djibo	365	NY 317
Djiborosso	378	OD 312
Djibouti	374	OA 362
Djidja	380	OF 321
Djigueni	363	NW 310
Djilbe	368	OA 334
Djiroutou	378	OH 312
Djohong	383	OF 334
Djoku-Punda	289	CD 84
Djolu	388	OM 341
Djombo Kibbit	369	NY 339
Djonaba	351	NV 306
Djoubissi	384	OG 340
Djougou	366	OC 321
Djouk	351	NV 307
Djoukou	384	OH 339
Djoum	382	OK 332
Djoumboli	382	OE 331
Djugu	304	BO 103
D'kar	243	DK 86
Dlolwana	220	DZ 104
Doa	259	DA 112
Doba	383	OD 336
Dobe	243	DG 84
Dobinga	383	OD 333
Doda	297	CB 121
Dodola	324	BD 121
Dodoma	295	CE 114
Dodowa	380	OG 319
Dogbo	378	OH 312
Dogbo-Toto	380	OF 321
Dogo	364	OA 312
Dogoba	320	BE 103
Dogon Tapki	366	NY 324
Dogondoutchi	366	NY 323
Dogonkirya	366	NY 323
Dohne	212	EH 98
Doka	372	NY 355
Doko	363	OA 310
Dokolo	305	BO 109
Dokpam	380	OD 319
Doma	257	DA 103
Dombe	248	DH 109
Dombe Grande	262	CS 69
Dombia	363	NZ 308
Dombiadji	363	OA 306
Domboshawa	258	DC 105
Dominase	380	OG 319
Domiongo	290	CB 85
Domo	327	BB 136
Dompem	379	OH 317
Dondo (Ang.)	275	CM 71
Dondo (Moz.)	249	DG 112
Dondotsha	221	DZ 106
Donga (Ben.)	366	OC 321
Donga (Nig.)	382	OE 329
Dongo	263	CW 74
Dongodesh	300	CA 113
Dongola	359	NT 350
Dongou	387	OL 337
Dongue	251	CX 71
Donguila	376	ON 329
Donkerpoort	218	ED 93
Donko	366	OA 324
Donnybrook	220	EB 102
Donzi	383	OG 337
Doolow	317	BJ 127
Doornbult	226	DV 93
Doornkraal	220	DZ 103
Dordabis	232	DN 78
Dordrecht	219	EE 97
Doreenville	232	DN 79
Dorey	365	NW 319
Dori	365	NY 319
Doringbaai	208	EF 79
Doringberg	228	DX 104
Doringbos	209	EF 81
Doringbult	227	DV 95
Doro	365	NW 318
Doropo	365	OC 316
Dorowa	247	DF 106
Dorra	374	OA 361
Doruma	385	OH 347
Dosso	366	NZ 322
Douako	363	OC 309
Douala	376	OJ 329
Doualayal	382	OF 331
Doubelma	366	NY 323
Douentza	365	NX 316
Douglas	218	EA 90
Dougol	383	OF 335
Dougountoun	363	OA 306
Doukoula	368	OC 334
Doulouyaba	363	NY 306
Doum	384	OD 340
Doum Doum	368	NZ 334
Doume	382	OG 331
Doumé	382	OJ 332
Douna	364	OB 314
Dounde Bague	363	NX 306
Doura	364	NY 313
Dourbali	368	OA 335
Dourbeye	368	OC 332
Dourdoura	370	OB 341
Doussala	386	OP 330
Doutoufouk	367	NY 328
Douz	333	NE 328
Dover	227	DW 98
Dovesdale	227	DU 97
Dowa	270	CU 110
Downes	216	EE 82
Draaiom	236	DN 99
Draghoender	217	EA 87
Drbatte	315	BH 117
Drennan	211	EG 94
Driebad	218	EC 94
Driefontein (E.C.)	211	EF 91
Driefontein (KZN)	220	DY 102
Drimiopsis	232	DM 81
Driver's Drift	212	EF 97
Droëfontein	224	DU 82
Droëputs	217	EE 86
Droërivier	210	EG 88
Droëryskloof	209	EH 80
Droëspruit	225	DX 88
Droëvlakte	210	EL 85
Drummondlea	236	DQ 101
Dschang	376	OH 329
Duamaganga	295	CB 113
Duba	348	NL 355
Dubela	312	BM 101
Dubie	280	CK 100
Dubreka	362	OC 305
Duchess Hill	257	DD 103
Dududu	220	EC 104
Due	388	OR 338
Duékoué	378	OF 311
Dugdug	320	BA 100
Duge	378	OG 310
Duguri	367	OC 330
Duineveld	232	DQ 78
Duiwelskloof	237	DP 103
Düjuuma	309	BP 128
Duk Faiwil	321	BB 106
Dukambio	373	NX 357
Dukana	315	BK 117
Dukku (Nig.)	366	OB 324
Dukku (Nig.)	367	OB 330
Dukul	367	OB 330
Dukumbane	229	DX 106
Dukwe	245	DJ 96
Dulala	279	CO 93
Dulia (DRC)	304	BQ 102
Dulia (CAR)	385	OK 343
Dulini	220	EC 102
Dullstroom	228	DS 103
Duma	244	DE 88
Dumbo	382	OF 329
Dumela	246	DK 97
Dumyat (Damietta)	337	NG 351
Duna	265	CU 83
Dundee	220	DY 103
Dundo	289	CG 84
Dunga	297	CE 121
Dungas	367	NZ 328
Dungu	385	OJ 347
Dungu (Bot.)	244	DE 87
Dungu (DRC)	312	BK 100
Dunkassa	366	OC 322
Dunkur	372	OA 355
Dunkwa	379	OG 317
Dupleston	219	EC 95
Durban	221	EB 105
Durbanville	209	EK 80
Durra	323	BC 115
Duru	312	BJ 100
Durukhsi	326	AZ 134
Dush	347	NN 350
Duta	281	CO 105
Dutlwe	234	DQ 90
Dutse	367	OA 328
Dutsin Ma	367	OA 326
Dutywa	212	EG 99
Dwaa	316	BH 122
Dwaal	218	EE 92
Dwaalboom	227	DR 96
Dwangwa	271	CS 111
Dwarsberg	227	DR 96
Dwarskersbos	208	EH 79
Dwarsvlei	211	EF 92
Dwokwa	380	OH 318
Dwyka	210	EJ 86
Dysselsdorp	210	EK 88
Dzioua	332	NE 324
Dzita	380	OG 320
Dzodze	380	OG 320
Dzumeri	237	DP 104
Eask	339	NJ 309
East London	212	EJ 99
Eastnor	246	DF 100
Eastpoort	211	EH 94
Eban	366	OC 324
Ebanga	263	CS 72
Ebangalakata	388	ON 340
Ebebiyin	386	OL 330
Ebelle	381	OF 325
Ebem	381	OG 327
Ebende	212	EG 99
Ebeneerde	223	DR 79
Ebolowa	382	OK 330
Ebonda	388	OL 341
Ebongui	387	ON 334
Ebony	231	DM 73
Eboundja	376	OK 329
Echambot	383	OK 333
Ed Daein	370	OB 345
Ed Damazin	372	OA 353
Ed Damer	360	NU 353
Ed Dueim	372	NY 351
Edéa	376	OJ 329
Eden Nzork	386	ON 330
Edenburg	218	EB 94
Edendale (KZN)	220	EB 103
Edendale (KZN)	220	EC 100
Edenvale	227	DU 99
Edenville	227	DX 98
Edingeni	270	CR 109
Ediva	251	CZ 71
Eduardo Mondlane	237	DM 106
Eedsamub	223	DT 78
Eendekuil	209	EH 80
Eenhana	252	DB 75
Eensgevonden	219	DZ 96
Efua	251	CZ 70
Egbe	381	OE 325
Egbunda	385	OK 346
Egito Praia	262	CQ 70
Eha-Amufu	381	OF 327
Ehomba	251	DC 70
Eiffel Flats	257	DD 103
Eight Bells	210	EK 87
Eindelik	242	DK 79
Eindpaal	224	DS 81
Eintracht	232	DM 79
Eirup	232	DQ 79
Ejidogari	381	OD 324
Ejisu	380	OF 318
Ejule	381	OF 326
Ejura	380	OF 318
Ekang	382	OG 328
Ekangala	228	DT 100
Ekata	387	OM 333
Eket	376	OH 327
Ekok	382	OG 328
Ekoko	252	DC 78
Ekoli	389	ON 343
Ekondo Titi	376	OH 328
Ekouamou	387	ON 335
Ékouata	376	ON 328
Eksteenfontein	215	DZ 77
Ekukola	388	ON 338
Ekuku	388	OO 341
Ekukula	388	ON 340
Ekumakoko	389	OP 343
eKuvukeni	220	DZ 103
Ekwa	382	OJ 331
Ekyiumenfuro	380	OF 318
El Abiodh Sidi Cheikh	331	NE 320
El Aioun	330	NC 317
El Alamein	337	NG 348
El Alia	332	NE 324
El Aouinet	332	NB 327
El Araba el Madfuna	348	NM 351
El Aricha	331	ND 318
El Arrouch	332	NA 326
El Ashmunein	347	NK 350
El Badari	348	NL 351
El Ban	374	OC 361
El Basaliya Qibli	348	NN 351
El Bayadh	331	ND 320
El Bayadiya	348	NM 352
El Beher	363	NW 310
El Beru Hagia	317	BM 125
El Boibou	364	NW 311
El Borma	333	NF 328
El Borouj	329	NF 312
El Bulma	332	NB 325
El Daba	336	NG 347
El Dabba	359	NU 350
El Deir	348	NN 352
El Der	316	BK 122
El Fahs	333	NB 329
El Faiyum	347	NJ 350
El Faouar	333	NE 328
El Fasher	370	NY 344
El Fashn	347	NJ 350
El Fifi	370	OC 344
El Fud	325	BC 128
El Gaga	347	NN 350
El Geili	372	NW 352
El Giara	309	BT 125
El Giza	347	NH 350
El Gleita	363	NX 308
El God God	317	BM 126
El Gof	316	BK 121
El Golea	331	NG 322
El Gulut	372	OA 355
El Hadjar	332	NA 327
El Haffey	333	ND 328
El Hajeb	330	ND 314
El Hamel	332	NC 323
El Hamma	333	ND 329
El Hammam	337	NG 348
El Hamurre	328	BC 141
El Haouaria	333	NA 330
El Haouita	331	ND 321
El Hawata	372	NZ 353
El Hidjer	369	OB 339
El Idisat	348	NN 352
El Jadida	329	NE 310
El Jebelein	372	NZ 352
El Jemm	333	NC 330
El Kadada	360	NV 353
El Kala	332	NA 327
El Kanayis	348	NN 352
El Kelaa Srarhna	329	NF 312
El Kere	317	BF 127
El Khandaq	359	NU 349
El Kharga	347	NN 350
El Khatatba	347	NH 350
El Khroub	332	NB 326
El Koin	359	NT 350
El Kseur	332	NA 324
El Ksiba	330	NE 313
El Kubra	337	NG 350
El Kure	317	BF 127
El Lagowa	371	OB 348
El Leh	316	BK 121
El Mahamid	348	NN 352
El Malan	331	NC 318
El Manaqil	372	NY 352
El Mansour	341	NK 318
El Mansura	337	NG 351
El Matariya	337	NG 351
El Maya	331	NE 321
El Medo	317	BF 126
El Meghaier	332	ND 325
El Melemm	371	OC 348
El Mhaijrat	350	NT 303
El Milia	332	NA 325
El Minya	347	NK 350
El Nasser	348	NN 352
El Obeid	371	NZ 349
El Odaiya	371	OA 347
El Ogla Gasses	332	NC 326
El Ouata	341	NH 317
El Oued	332	NE 326
El Qasr	347	NM 348
El Rizeiqat	348	NM 351
El Saff	347	NJ 350
El Salhiya	337	NG 351
El Shalla	348	NO 352
El Tarf	332	NA 327
El Thamad	348	NH 353
El Wak	316	BM 124
El Wuz	371	NX 349
Elands Height	219	ED 99
Elandsbaai	208	EG 79
Elandsdrift	218	DY 92
Elandskloof	211	EG 92
Elandskraal	220	DY 104
Elandslaagte	220	DY 103
Elat	348	NH 354
Eldama Ravine	306	BR 114
Eldoret	306	BQ 113
Elefantenberg	242	DG 77
Elele	376	OH 326
Elgin	209	EL 81
Eli Dar	374	OA 361
Elias Garcia	277	CK 83
Elila	389	OQ 345
Elim (Lim.)	237	DO 103
Elim (W.C.)	209	EM 82
Elipa	389	OO 343
Eliye Springs	314	BL 114
Elliot	219	EE 98
Elliotdale	213	EF 100
Elma Labiod	332	NC 327
Elmeki	355	NU 327
Elmeston	236	DP 98
Elmina	380	OH 318
Eloff	228	DU 100
Elogbatindi	376	OK 329
Elogo	387	OL 333
Elubo	379	OH 316
eMakwezini	221	DZ 106
Emali	301	BW 117
Emangusi	229	DW 108
Embu	307	BT 118
Embundo	252	CZ 76
Emcisweni	282	CP 110
Emini	382	OJ 331
eMpangeni	221	DZ 106
Empress Mine	257	DD 101
En Nahud	371	NZ 347
Enangiperi	306	BT 114
Encoje	287	CH 72
Enda Medhane Alem	373	NZ 359
Endau	302	BU 120
Endebes	306	BP 112
Endengue	382	OK 331
Endesh	295	CB 113
Endibar	323	BA 118
Endom	382	OJ 331
Endulen	300	BY 113
Enfida	333	NB 329
Engaruka	300	BY 114
Enjil	330	NE 314
Entebbe	305	BR 107
Entre Lagos	259	CX 114
eNtumeni	221	DZ 105
Enugu	381	OG 326
Enukweni	282	CP 110
Enyamba	389	OR 344
Enyelé	383	OK 337
Epako	241	DK 75
Epe	381	OF 323
Epemba	252	DC 75
Epembe	251	DC 70
Epena	387	OM 337
Epini	389	OM 347
Epokiro	242	DL 81
Epoma	387	OM 334
Epulu	304	BP 100
Equelo	251	CZ 74
Er Rachidia	330	NF 314
Er Rahad	371	NZ 350
Ere	368	OC 335
Eref	369	OA 338
Erevuca	272	CQ 118
Erfoud	330	NG 315
Erima	305	BP 108
Ermelo	228	DV 103
Ermil Post	371	NY 347
Erongo	241	DL 74
Errego	260	CZ 117
Erts	228	DS 102
Erufa	381	OD 325
Erundu	241	DJ 75
Eruwa	380	OE 322
Escravos	381	OG 324
Eséke	382	OJ 330
eShowe	221	DZ 105
Esiama	379	OH 317
Esigodini	246	DH 100
Espagsdrif	226	DX 92
Esperança	238	DS 108
Esperanza	220	EC 104
Espinheira	250	DA 67
Espungabera	248	DH 108
Essaouira	329	NG 309
Essau	362	NY 302
Essé	382	OJ 331
Estcourt	220	EA 102
Estima	258	CY 108
Estivane	238	DQ 108
Etaga	261	CZ 120
Etanga	250	DC 69
Etéké	386	OP 330
Etengwa	250	DB 69
eTholeni	220	DY 103
Etilyasa	251	DD 73
Etiro	241	DL 74
Etjo	241	DK 75
Etou	382	OK 332
Etoumbi	387	ON 334
Etsha 13	244	DF 87
Etsha 6	244	DF 87
Etumba (DRC)	388	OQ 339
Etumba (DRC)	389	OO 345
Eureka	228	DW 100
Euthini	282	CP 109
Evale	251	DA 74
Evander	228	DU 101
Evangelina	236	DM 101
Evero	242	DK 77
Evinayong	386	OM 330
Ewango	381	OF 327
Ewaso Ngiro	300	BU 114
Ewbank	226	DU 90
Ewo	387	OO 334
Excelsior	219	DZ 97
Eyl	328	BB 142
Ez Zhiliga	329	NE 312
Ezo	385	OH 346
Ezzangbo	381	OG 327
Faans Grove	225	DW 87
Facauma	290	CG 85
Fachi	356	NU 331
Fada	358	NV 341
Fada N'Gourma	365	OA 320
Fafa	365	NX 320
Fafakoura	362	NZ 305
Fafaya	363	OA 307
Fafi	248	DK 109
Faggo	367	OB 329
Fagrinkotti	359	NU 350
Faid	333	NC 329
Fairfield	209	EL 82
Faje	366	OC 324
Falaba	363	OC 308
Falagountou	365	NY 319
Falea	363	OA 308
Falkenhorst	223	DS 78
Fallodon	212	EJ 97
Falmey	366	OA 322
Falo	364	NZ 313
Falou	364	NX 311
Falouel	366	NY 323
Fama	372	OC 351
Fambusi	365	OC 318
Fana	364	NZ 312
Fanar Qasr Ahimad	334	NF 335
Fandanda	363	OA 308
Fangak	320	AY 104
Fanti	378	OH 310
Faraba	363	OA 308
Faradje	312	BK 102
Farafenni	362	NY 304
Faragouaran	364	OB 311
Faramana	364	OA 315
Faranah	363	OC 308
Farie	366	NY 321
Farim	362	OA 304
Farkwa	295	CC 114
Faro	378	OF 308
Fas Boye	362	NX 302
Fashe	366	OC 324
Fashola	381	OE 323
Fassanu	333	NG 332
Fatadun	309	BN 126
Fataki	304	BN 104
Fathai	321	BA 106
Fatine	364	NY 314
Fatitet	321	BB 106
Fatoto	362	NZ 305
Fatuma	293	CE 101
Fatunda	387	OR 336
Faure	209	EL 80
Fauresmith	218	EB 93

PLACE NAME	PG	GRID
Fawnleas	220	EA 104
Fayala	387	OR 336
Faya-Largeau	357	NU 338
Fdérik	351	NP 306
Featherstone	247	DE 104
Feerfeer	318	BG 133
Feidh el Botma	332	NC 323
Fela	299	BX 109
Feldschuhhorn	223	DV 77
Felixburg	247	DF 104
Felixton	221	DZ 106
Ferdjioua	332	NB 325
Feriana	333	NC 328
Ferkéssédougou	364	OC 314
Fernão Veloso	273	CW 124
Fernwood	221	DY 107
Ferreira	219	EA 95
Feshi	288	CE 79
Fete Bowe	363	NX 306
Fez	330	ND 314
Fian	365	OC 317
Fianga	368	OC 334
Fiche	373	OC 358
Ficksburg	219	DZ 98
Fieldsview	218	DZ 92
Fifa	363	OB 309
Fifinda	376	OK 329
Figtree	246	DH 99
Figuig	331	NF 318
Figuil	368	OC 333
Fik	325	BA 127
Fika	367	OB 330
Filabusi	246	DJ 101
Filamba	270	CQ 106
Filingué	366	NY 322
Filiya	367	OC 330
Filtu	316	BG 124
Finchawa	315	BG 119
Finga	294	CG 105
Fingoe	258	CX 106
Finkenstein	231	DN 77
Finno	317	BL 125
Finyolé	382	OD 332
Firgrove	209	EL 80
Firou	366	OB 321
Fischersbrunn	222	DR 72
Fisenge	268	CT 100
Fish Hoek	209	EL 80
Fiwila	269	CV 102
Fizi	298	CA 100
Fkih Ben Salah	329	NE 312
Flagstaff	220	EE 102
Flampieu	378	OF 311
Flint	228	DX 103
Flora	219	DZ 97
Florisbad	219	DZ 95
Flu	378	OG 311
Fo	384	OG 338
Fo-Boure	366	OC 321
Fochville	227	DU 98
Fode	384	OH 342
Fodekaria	363	OB 310
Foggaret el Arab	342	NH 322
Fokku	366	OA 324
Foley	246	DL 97
Folo	380	OD 320
Fomena	379	OG 317
Foneko	365	NY 320
Fonteintjie (E.C.)	218	ED 92
Fonteintjie (N.C.)	217	EB 88
Fonteintjie (N.C.)	217	EE 86
Fonteintjie (N.C.)	218	EE 93
Forbes Reef	229	DU 105
Forcados	381	OH 324
Forecariah	377	OD 306
Fornos	238	DM 112
Foro	373	NX 359
Fort Beaufort	212	EH 96
Fort Brown	212	EJ 96
Fort Donald	220	ED 102
Fort Hare	212	EH 96
Fort Mistake	220	DY 102
Fort Mtombeni	221	EA 105
Fort Portal	304	BQ 103
Fort Rixon	246	DH 101
Fortania	373	OB 359
Forthassa Rharbia	331	NE 318
Foso	380	OG 318
Fossong Fontem	376	OH 329
Fougamou	376	OO 329
Foulabala	364	OB 312
Foulamori	362	OA 305
Foum Zguid	340	NH 312
Foumbadou	378	OE 311
Foumban	382	OG 330
Foumbot	382	OG 330
Founouyo	366	OB 322
Fouriesburg	219	DZ 99
Fourou	364	OB 313
Foz do Cunene (Mouth of the...)	250	DB 66
Franceville	387	OP 333
Francistown	246	DK 97
Francois	241	DL 76
Frankfort (F.S.)	218	DZ 93
Frankfort (F.S.)	219	EA 97
Frankfort (F.S.)	228	DW 100
Franklin	220	EC 102
Frans	218	ED 91
Franschhoek	209	EK 81
Fransfontein	241	DH 72
Franzenhof	217	EB 87
Fraserburg	210	EF 86
Freetown	377	OE 305
Frenda	331	NC 320
Frere	220	DZ 102
Fresco	379	OH 314
Fria	362	OC 305
Friederichvelde	241	DL 74
Friesdale	216	DZ 84
Fufulsu	380	OD 318
Fuka	336	NG 347
Fulacunda	362	OA 304
Fuliya	373	OC 356
Fumane	238	DQ 110
Fumba	297	CE 121
Fumbelo	265	CQ 82
Fundong	382	OG 329
Fungoni	297	CF 121
Funhalouro	238	DO 111
Funsi	365	OC 317
Funtua	367	OB 326
Furancungo	270	CW 110
Fuskam Mata	367	OC 328
Fuwa	337	NG 350
Fwatoni	291	CE 91
Ga	365	OC 316
Gaalkacyo	327	BD 137
Gaamodebli	378	OG 309
Gabane	226	DR 94
Gabatsaol	245	DH 93
Gabela	275	CO 71
Gabes	333	ND 329
Gabet al-Maadin	360	NR 355
Gabia	288	CB 77
Gabir (Sud.)	371	NZ 346
Gabir (Sud.)	385	OD 344
Gabiro	298	BV 103
Gaborone	226	DR 94
Gabras	371	OC 346
Gabu (CAR)	385	OK 346
Gabu (Gui-B.)	362	OA 305
Gadabi	315	BF 119
Gadam	367	OB 330
Gadamai	360	NV 355
Gada-Oundou	363	OA 307
Gadien	320	BA 100
Gadiep	216	DZ 80
Gadou	367	OA 329
Gadzi	383	OH 336
Gafsa	333	ND 328
Gagal	383	OD 334
Gagarus	241	DF 73
Gagnoa	379	OG 313
Gahnpa	378	OF 310
Gaigou	365	NY 319
Gainatseb	241	DH 73
Gairo	296	CE 116
Gajiram	368	NZ 332
Gajos	315	BK 116
Gakem (Nig.)	381	OF 327
Gakem (Nig.)	382	OF 328
Gakou	363	NX 310
Gakpi	385	OH 345
Galanga	263	CR 73
Galangue	263	CU 75
Galappo	300	CA 114
Galdimari	367	OA 330
Gale	363	NZ 310
Galegu	372	NZ 354
Galifi	374	OA 361
Galim (Cam.)	382	OF 331
Galim (Cam.)	382	OG 329
Galinda	274	CM 70
Galiraya	305	BP 108
Galo Boukay	383	OG 334
Galtat-Zemmour	339	NN 307
Ga-Luka	227	DT 97
Galula	282	CK 109
Gam	243	DH 84
Gama (Tan.)	297	CE 120
Gama (Gui.)	378	OE 311
Gamagira	367	OB 327
Gamau	367	OC 328
Gamawa	367	OA 330
Gamba (Gab.)	386	OQ 329
Gamba (Ang.)	264	CQ 77
Gamba (DRC)	291	CB 92
Gambaga	365	OC 319
Gambela	322	BA 112
Gambo (Ang.)	277	CM 84
Gambo (CAR)	384	OH 341
Gamboma	387	OP 335
Gamboula	383	OJ 334
Gamdou	367	NZ 329
Gamis	231	DQ 76
Ga-Modjadji	237	DP 103
Gamoep	215	EB 79
Ga-Mopedi	225	DW 89
Gamsberg	231	DO 75
Gamu	246	DF 98
Ganamandji	384	OH 339
Ganda	263	CT 72
Gandajika	291	CF 90
Gande	366	NZ 324
Gangale	312	BK 101
Gangara	367	NX 327
Gangu-Bili	385	OJ 343
Gangui	383	OF 333
Gangure	273	CQ 121
Gansbaai	209	EM 81
Gansfontein	209	EH 82
Ganskraal	208	EJ 79
Ganskuil	227	DR 96
Ganspan	226	DX 92
Ganye	382	OE 331
Ganyesa	226	DV 91
Ganze	379	OE 315
Gao (BF)	365	OA 317
Gao (DRC)	385	OK 347
Gao (Mali)	365	NW 319
Gaoua	365	OC 316
Gaoual	363	OA 306
Garabinzaam	387	OL 333
Garada	359	NT 349
Garalo	364	OB 312
Ga-Ramodingwana	227	DU 96
Ga-rango	365	OA 318
Ga-Rankuwa	227	DT 99
Garba	384	OD 340
Garba Tula	308	BQ 120
Garbahaarey	317	BL 127
Gargando	352	NV 315
Gargouna	365	NW 319
Garib	232	DO 78
Gariep Dam	218	ED 94
Garies	215	EC 79
Gariganus	223	DU 79
Garinais	224	DU 80
Garissa	308	BS 122
Garkem	367	OF 328
Garki	367	NZ 328
Garkida	368	OC 332
Garma	344	NL 332
Garmabe	312	BH 103
Garner's Drift	212	EF 98
Garoowe	327	BA 139
Garoua	382	OD 332
Garoua Boulai	383	OG 333
Garrafa	260	DC 117
Garryowen	212	EF 98
Garsen	302	BW 123
Garsila	370	OA 342
Garub	222	DV 74
Garuzo	248	DF 109
Gaschiga	382	OD 332
Gaseleka	236	DO 98
Gashua	367	NZ 330
Gaska	367	OA 330
Gassan	365	NZ 316
Gassane	362	NX 304
Gassol	382	OE 329
Gatanga	385	OG 346
Gati	366	OC 323
Gati-Loumo	364	NW 314
Gawachab	223	DW 78
Gawu	381	OD 326
Gaya (Ngr.)	366	OA 322
Gaya (Nig.)	367	OA 329
Gayaza	304	BT 104
Gayeri	365	NZ 320
Gazi (Ken.)	302	CA 121
Gazi (DRC)	389	OM 343
Gba	384	OH 338
Gbabele	383	OH 337
Gbaboua	383	OG 334
Gbadikaha	379	OD 314
Gbananme	380	OF 321
Gbandi	385	OH 343
Gbanga	381	OD 325
Gbangbatok	377	OE 306
Gbanhui	379	OE 316
Gbapleu	378	OF 311
Gbarnga	378	OF 310
Gbassa	366	OB 321
Gberia Fotombu	363	OC 308
Gberouboue	366	OC 322
Gbibo	378	OG 311
Gbodonon	364	OC 313
Gboko	382	OF 328
Gbung	380	OD 318
Gdyel	331	NB 318
Ge Angwa	243	DG 85
Geba	273	CV 124
Gebeit	361	NT 356
Gebeledan	364	OC 311
Gebiet	231	DO 77
Gecha	322	BB 113
Gedaref	372	NY 354
Gedi	302	BY 122
Gedlegube	326	BD 133
Gedo	323	AY 117
Gegbwema	378	OE 308
Gege	229	DV 105
Geidam	368	NZ 331
Geita	299	BX 107
Geladi	327	BD 135
Gelai Lumbwa	301	BX 115
Gelemso	324	AZ 123
Gellinsoor	327	BE 136
Geluk	226	DW 91
Geluksburg	220	DZ 101
Gelukspruit	216	DY 84
Gelukwaarts	219	EB 96
Gembu	382	OF 330
Gemena	384	OK 339
Gemmeiza (Sud.)	313	BF 106
Gemmeiza (Sud.)	320	BC 101
Gemsvlakte	224	DX 80
Gemvale	213	EF 102
Genadeberg	219	EC 96
Genadendal	209	EL 82
Geneina	370	NZ 342
Genemasson	366	OC 321
Generaalsnek	219	DZ 98
Geneva	227	DX 97
Genwa	388	OQ 342
George	210	EK 88
Georgetown	362	NY 304
Gerard	232	DN 80
Gerdau	227	DU 95
Gerihun	377	OE 307
Germiston	227	DU 99
Gerus	241	DH 75
Gerza	347	NJ 350
Gesukkel	228	DT 103
Geti	304	BP 103
Gewane	373	OC 360
Geysdorp	226	DV 93
Ghabeish	371	OA 346
Ghadamis	343	NH 329
Ghadduwah	344	NM 333
Ghama	385	OE 347
Ghanzi	243	DL 86
Gharb Binna	359	NT 349
Ghardaia	332	NE 323
Ghardimaou	332	NB 327
Gharghar	363	NW 309
Gharig	371	OB 347
Gharyan	333	NF 332
Ghat	343	NN 329
Ghazaouet	330	NC 317
Ghegalu	373	OC 360
Ghelaelo	373	NX 359
Ghimbi	322	AY 114
Ghion	323	AZ 119
Ghomrassen	333	NE 329
Ghriss	331	NC 319
Giadabele	326	BB 130
Gibeon	223	DS 78
Gibeon Station	223	DS 78
Gibraltar (U.K.)	330	NB 314
Gida	382	OE 329
Gidami	322	AY 112
Gidda	372	OC 354
Gidole	315	BF 117
Giesenkraal	217	ED 89
Gihofi	298	BZ 103
Gikongoro	298	BW 102
Gilé	260	CZ 119
Gilead	236	DP 100
Gilgil	307	BT 115
Gimi	382	OD 328
Ginchi	323	AZ 119
Gingero	315	BH 115
Gingindlovu	221	EA 106
Ginir	324	BC 124
Giraul	250	CX 67
Giriftu	308	BO 122
Gisenyi	298	BV 101
Gisuru	298	BY 103
Gitarama	298	BW 102
Gitata	381	OD 327
Gitega	298	BY 103
Giyani	237	DO 104
Gladdeklipkop	236	DQ 101
Glazoue	380	OE 321
Gleibat Boukenni (Mrt.)	363	NW 310
Glen	219	DZ 95
Glen Beulah	220	EC 103
Glen Cowie	228	DR 102
Glencoe	220	DY 103
Glenconnor	211	EJ 93
Glencova	247	DG 106
Glendale	258	DB 105
Glenlivet	247	DH 105
Glenmore Beach	220	EE 103
Glenrock	212	EG 95
Gloie	378	OF 310
Gloria	228	DU 102
Glosam	217	DY 88
Glückstadt	229	DX 105
Gnibi	362	NY 303
Gnit	362	NW 303
Goageb	223	DV 77
Goanikontes	230	DN 72
Goaso	379	OF 316
Goba (Eth.)	324	BC 123
Goba (KZN)	220	EC 103
Goba (Lim.)	236	DO 102
Goba (Moz.)	229	DU 107
Gobabeb	230	DP 72
Gobabis	232	DN 81
Gobas	223	DV 79
Gobur	313	BJ 105
Gochas	224	DR 80
Gode (Melka Teko)	325	BE 129
Godegode	296	CF 116
Godinlabe	319	BF 136
Goedemoed	219	ED 96
Gog	322	BB 111
Gogói	248	DH 109
Gogonyo	306	BP 110
Gogounou	366	OB 322
Gogrial	385	OD 347
Gohitafla	379	OF 313
Goifumo	276	CO 78
Goi-Pula	292	CH 95
Gokwe	257	DD 100
Golden Valley (E.C.)	211	EH 94
Golden Valley (Zim.)	257	DD 102
Goldogob	327	BC 136
Golecha	324	BA 123
Golela	229	DW 106
Goli	305	BN 105
Golomoti	271	CW 112
Golongosso	384	OD 338
Goma	298	BV 101
Gomba	284	CP 119
Gombari	312	BM 100
Gombe (DRC)	388	ON 340
Gombe (Nig.)	367	OC 330
Gombe Matadi	287	CB 72
Gombi	368	OC 332
Gomboussougou	365	OB 319
Gomon	379	OG 315
Gompies	236	DQ 101
Gomvlei	219	EB 95
Gonate	379	OF 313
Gonder	373	NZ 357
Gondey	384	OD 338
Gondola	248	DF 110
Gondolahun	378	OE 309
Gonga	383	OJ 333
Gongoni (Tan.)	302	BY 123
Gongoni (Tan.)	302	BZ 122
Gongoue	376	ON 328
Goniri	368	OA 331
Gonubie	212	EH 99
Good Hope	226	DS 93
Goodhouse	215	DZ 79
Gora	367	OA 327
Goraas	217	EE 86
Gordonia	218	DY 92
Gordons Bay	209	EL 80
Gore (Eth.)	322	BA 113
Goré (Cha.)	383	OE 336
Goredema	257	DC 100
Gorgadji	365	NY 318
Gorges	223	DX 78
Gorgora	373	OA 356
Gorgoram	367	NZ 330
Gori Rit	327	BA 139
Goro	324	BD 123
Gorom Gorom	365	NY 319
Goromonzi	258	DC 105
Gorongosa	248	DE 110
Goronyo	366	NZ 325
Gossas	362	NY 303
Gossi	365	NW 318
Gossinga	385	OD 345
Gothèye	366	NY 321
Gouchi	367	NY 329
Gouda	209	EJ 80
Goudiry	363	NY 306
Goudoumaria	367	NY 330
Gouéké	378	OE 310
Gouka	380	OE 321
Goulaonfla	378	OE 312
Goulia	364	OC 312
Goulimine	339	NJ 309
Goulmima	330	NF 314
Goumbatou	370	OA 341
Goumbou	364	NX 312
Gouméré	379	OE 316
Gouna	383	OD 333
Goundam	364	NW 315
Goundi	383	OD 337
Gounou-Gaya	368	OC 334
Gouraya	331	NA 321
Gouraye	363	NX 307
Gourci	365	NZ 317
Gouré	367	NY 329
Gourel	363	NX 306
Gourits	210	EL 86
Gouritsmond	210	EL 86
Gourma Rharous	353	NV 317
Gouro	357	NS 338
Gourrama	330	NF 315
Gova	263	CT 74
Govero	228	DR 109
Goyoum	382	OH 332
Goz Beïda	369	OA 340
Graaff-Reinet	211	EG 91
Graafwater (W.C.)	215	ED 79
Graafwater (W.C.)	209	EG 80
Grabo	378	OH 312
Grabouw	209	EL 81
Grabwasser	223	DX 79
Grahamstown	212	EJ 95
Granaatboskolk	216	EC 82
Granada	330	NA 315
Grand Cess	378	OH 311
Grand Popo	380	OG 321
Grand-Bassam	379	OH 315
Grand-Lahou	379	OH 314
Graskop	228	DR 104
Grasmere	227	DU 98
Graspan	218	EA 91
Grasplatz	222	DV 73
Grasslands	226	DX 94
Gravelotte	237	DP 104
Grays	212	EH 98
Greenville	378	OH 310
Gregory	236	DN 100
Greylingstad	228	DV 100
Greystone (E.C.)	211	EJ 92
Greystone (Zim.)	246	DH 101
Greyton	209	EL 82
Greytown	220	EA 103
Gribouo	378	OG 312
Grimari	384	OG 339
Griquatown	217	DZ 89
Groblersdal	228	DS 101
Groblershoop	217	DZ 86
Groendal	209	EK 81
Groenebloem	227	DW 97
Groenfontein	210	EJ 86
Groenriviersmond	215	ED 78
Groenvlei (F.S.)	218	EB 93
Groenvlei (F.S.)	228	DX 94
Groenvlei (KZN)	228	DW 103
Groesbeek	236	DP 100
Grondneus	216	DY 84
Groot Aub	231	DN 77
Groot Brakrivier	210	EL 87
Groot Jongensfontein	210	EL 86
Groot Marico	227	DT 96
Groot Spelonke	237	DO 103
Grootberg	240	DG 71
Grootdoring	217	EB 89
Grootdrink	217	DZ 86
Grootfontein	242	DG 79
Grootkraal	210	EJ 87
Grootmis	215	EB 77
Grootoor	231	DP 76
Grootpan	227	DT 96
Grootspruit	228	DW 104
Grootvlei	228	DV 100
Gross Barmen	231	DM 76
Gross Ums	232	DO 80
Gross-Otavi	242	DG 78
Grovéput	217	EB 88
Grünau	223	DX 79
Gründorner	223	DS 78
Grünental	232	DM 79
Grünewald	241	DF 74
Grupe	379	OD 317
Guba (DRC)	279	CO 95
Guba (Eth.)	372	OB 354
Guba (Nig.)	367	NZ 330
Gubi	367	OC 329
Gubio	368	OA 332
Gudo	323	AZ 118
Guedkedou	378	OD 309
Guelengdeng	368	OB 334
Guelma	332	NB 326
Gueltat Sidi Saad	331	ND 321
Guéné	366	OA 322
Guerara	332	NE 324
Guercif	330	ND 316
Guéréda	370	NX 341
Gueriou	351	NV 307
Guessabo	378	OF 312
Guessou-Sud	366	OC 322
Gueve	253	DB 80
Gueyo	379	OG 313
Guézaoua	367	NY 328
Guibéroua	379	OG 313
Guibes	223	DV 76
Guidali	362	OA 305
Guidan-Roumji	367	NY 326
Guidari	383	OD 336
Guider	368	OC 333
Guidiguir	367	NY 329
Guidiguis	368	OC 334
Guidimouni	367	NY 329
Guidjiba	383	OE 333
Guiffa	384	OG 338
Guiglo	378	OF 311
Guingan	363	OA 306
Guiri	368	OC 334
Guisser	329	NE 312
Guissoumale	364	NZ 311
Guitri	379	OG 314
Gujba	368	OB 331
Gulu	313	BM 107
Gulumba Gane	368	OA 333
Gulwe	296	CE 115
Gumare	244	DF 87
Gumbe	238	DS 109
Gumbiro	283	CN 114
Gumel	367	NZ 328
Gumi	366	OA 324
Gumtree	219	DZ 98
Guna	383	OK 337
Gunab	223	DU 77
Gundji	388	OL 340
Gunga	253	CX 80
Gungu	289	CE 81
Gungue	263	CU 73
Gunna	385	OE 346
Gunta	367	OB 329
Guro	258	DB 109
Gurué	260	CX 116
Guruve	257	DA 104
Gusau	367	OA 326
Gushiegu	365	OC 319
Guta	300	BW 110
Guti	247	DG 105
Guyi	322	AY 114
Guyu	246	DK 100
Gwaai Mine	256	DD 97
Gwada	367	OC 326
Gwadabawa	366	NZ 324
Gwambara	366	NZ 323
Gwanda	246	DJ 100
Gwandu	366	NZ 324
Gwanga	384	OK 340
Gwarzo	367	OA 327
Gwasera	381	OD 323
Gwayi	246	DF 98
Gwayi River	246	DE 97
Gwelutshina	246	DE 100
Gwembe	256	DA 98
Gweru	247	DF 102
Gweta	245	DH 93
Gwoza	368	OB 333
Haakdoring	236	DQ 100
Haalenberg	222	DV 74
Haarlem	210	EK 89
Haaway	310	BP 130
Habaswein	308	BQ 122
Haco	275	CN 74
Hacufera	248	DJ 108
Hadejia	367	OA 329
Hadjer Bandala	370	OA 341
Hadjer el Hamis	368	NZ 334
Haenertsburg	236	DP 102
Haffouz	333	NB 329
Hagadera	308	BR 123
Haga-Haga	212	EH 99
Hagar Banga	370	OA 342
Hagenau	241	DL 76
Hagesdam	218	EA 94
Haho	364	OA 315
Haidom	300	CA 113
Haidra	332	NB 327
Haindi	378	OF 309
Haire Lao	362	NW 304
Halaib	361	NQ 356
Halasa	371	NY 350
Halcyon Drift	219	ED 99
Haleb el Ayoun	333	NC 328
Halesowen	211	EG 94
Half Assini	379	OH 316
Halfgewonnen	228	DU 102
Halfmanshof	209	EJ 81
Halfway House	246	DE 97
Halfweg	216	EC 83
Hallatt's Hope	226	DW 93
Halseton	219	EE 96
Ham	368	OC 335
Hamab	216	DY 81
Ha-Magoro	237	DO 103
Hamaguir	330	NG 316
Haman	383	OH 333
Hamarro Hadad	325	BB 127
Hamburg	212	EJ 98
Hamdallay	366	NY 322
Hamilton	220	DY 101
Hammam	333	NA 330
Hammamet	333	NB 330
Hammanshof	209	EK 82
Hammanskraal	227	DS 99
Hammersdale	220	EB 104
Hamoud	363	NW 307
Hamrat esh Sheikh	371	NX 347
Han	365	OB 317
Handali	296	CE 115
Handeni	296	CC 119
Hange	212	EG 98
Hankey	211	EK 92
Hanover	218	EE 91
Hanover Road	218	ED 92
Haoud el Hamra	332	NF 325
Harar	325	AY 127
Harare	258	DC 105
Haraz	369	NY 338
Haraze-Mangueigne	369	OC 339
Harbel	378	OG 309
Hardap	223	DR 79
Harding	220	ED 102
Hargele	317	BG 127
Hargeysa	374	OC 363
Harmony	228	DW 100
Harper	378	OJ 311
Harr	363	NX 306
Harrisburg	227	DW 95
Harrisdale	216	DY 84
Harrismith	220	DY 101
Hartbeesfontein	227	DV 95
Hartbeeskop	228	DU 104
Hartbeespoort	227	DT 98
Hartebeesfontein (F.S.)	218	DY 93
Hartebeesfontein (F.S.)	218	EC 93
Hartenbos	210	EL 87
Hartseer	241	DH 75
Hartswater	226	DX 92
Haruchas	231	DQ 75
Haskanit	371	OA 346
Hassi Bahbah	331	NC 322
Hassi el Khebi	340	NH 314
Hassi Messaoud	332	NF 325
Hassi R'mel	331	NE 322
Hattingspruit	220	DY 103
Haubi	295	CB 114
Hauina	309	BR 125
Hauptrus	227	DV 95
Have Etoe	380	OF 319
Hawston	209	EL 81
Hawza	339	NL 308
Hawzen	373	NY 358
Hayfield	218	EA 91
Hayk	373	OB 359
Haykota	373	NX 356
Hazoua	332	ND 326
Hazyview	229	DS 105
Headlands	258	DD 107
Heatonville	221	DZ 106
Hectorspruit	229	DS 106
Hedaru	296	CB 118
Heerenlogement	209	EF 80
Heiban	371	OB 350
Heide	231	DP 77
Heidelberg (Gau.)	227	DU 99
Heidelberg (W.C.)	209	EL 84
Heights	211	EK 90
Heilbron (F.S.)	218	EC 93
Heilbron (F.S.)	227	DW 99
Hekpoort	227	DT 98
Heldina	227	DT 97
Helena	243	DL 83
Helmeringhausen	223	DT 76
Helpmekaar	220	DY 104
Helvetia	219	EB 96
Helwan	347	NH 350
Hemlock	228	DT 104
Hendawashi	300	BZ 111
Hendriksdal	228	DS 104
Hendrina	228	DU 102
Hennenman	227	DX 97
Henning	219	EE 95
Henties Bay	230	DM 71
Herbertsdale	210	EL 86
Hereford	228	DS 101
Herefords	229	DT 105
Hermanstal	242	DG 76
Hermanus	209	EL 81
Hermanusdorings	236	DQ 98
Hermon	209	EJ 81
Herold	210	EK 88
Herolds Bay	210	EL 87
Herschel	219	EE 97
Hertzogville	218	DY 94
Hester	226	DW 93
Het Kruis	209	EH 80
Heuningberg	241	DH 76
Heuningneskloof	218	EA 92
Heuningspruit	227	DW 98
Heuwels	217	EE 86
Hevi	380	OG 320
Heydon	211	EF 92
Hhohho	229	DT 105
Hibberdene	220	ED 104
Higg's Hope	217	EA 89
Highflats	220	EC 103
Hilandale	209	EJ 84
Hildavale	226	DS 94
Hildreth Ridge	237	DO 103
Hillcrest	218	DY 92
Hilton	220	EB 103
Himeville	220	EB 101
Himo	301	BY 118
Hinalé	368	OA 334
Hinda	286	CB 66
Hippo Valley	247	DK 106
Hirafok	342	NO 325
Hirna	325	AY 125
Hiso	296	CD 115
Hlabisa	221	DY 106
Hlathikhulu	229	DV 105
Hlobane	228	DX 104
Hlogotlou	228	DS 102
Hlotse (Leribe)	219	DZ 99
Hluhluwe	221	DY 107
Hluthi	229	DW 106
Ho	380	OF 319
Hoachanas	232	DP 79
Hoaseb	232	DO 80
Hobas	223	DX 78
Hobeni	213	EG 100
Hobhouse	219	EB 97
Hobyo	319	BG 139
Hochfeld	242	DK 78
Hoedjies	216	EE 83
Hoedspruit	237	DQ 104
Hofmeyr	211	EF 94
Hogsback	212	EH 97
Hohental	242	DG 77
Hohoe	380	OF 319
Hoima	305	BP 105
Hoja Wajeer	303	BU 126
Hokwe	229	DR 105
Hola	302	BU 122
Holbank	228	DV 103
Holhol	374	OB 362
Holma	368	OC 332
Holmdene	228	DV 101
Holme Park	228	DR 100
Holomi	229	DV 106
Holoog	223	DW 78
Holy Cross	220	EE 102
Homa Bay	306	BT 112
Homasi	243	DG 84
Hombolo	295	CD 114
Hombori	365	NX 317
Homeb	231	DP 73
Homoine	239	DP 113
Hondefontein	210	EG 85
Hondejaag	217	DY 85
Hondeklipbaai	215	EC 77
Hontorbe	363	NY 306
Hoogte	227	DW 99
Hoopstad	226	DX 94
Hopefield	208	EJ 79
Hopetown	218	EB 90
Hoque	262	CW 70
Horse Shoe	228	DX 102
Hosaina	323	BB 118
Hot Springs	248	DG 107
Hotagterklip	209	EM 82
Hotazel	225	DW 88
Hottentots Bay	222	DU 73
Hottentotskloof	209	EJ 82
Houeiriye	364	NW 312
Houhoek	209	EL 81
Houmoed	216	EA 82
Houmt Souq	333	ND 330
Houndé	365	OB 316
Hout Bay	208	EL 79
Houtenbeck	219	DZ 96
Houtkraal	218	EC 91
Howick	220	EA 103
Hoya	258	CZ 105
Huamba	275	CJ 75
Huambo	263	CS 74
Hudat	316	BH 121
Hufeira	372	NY 353
Hugo	209	EJ 83
Huila	251	CX 70
Hukuntsi	233	DQ 86
Humansdorp	211	EL 92
Humbe	251	DA 72
Humbia	262	CW 69
Humefield	211	EJ 91
Humera	373	NY 356
Humpata	251	CY 69
Hun	344	NJ 335
Hungulo	263	CT 75
Hunters Road	247	DF 102
Huntleigh	236	DN 102
Hurdiyo	375	OB 370
Hurghada	348	NL 353
Hurlimbo	379	OH 316
Hurso	374	OC 361
Husheib	372	NX 354
Hutchinson	210	EF 89
Huyuyu	258	DC 107
Hwali	246	DL 101
Hwange	256	DD 96
Hwedza	247	DE 106
Hyrra Banda	384	OG 341
Ibadan	381	OF 323
Ibanda (Uga.)	304	BR 103
Ibanda (Uga.)	304	BS 104
Ibanga	389	OQ 346
Ibba	312	BH 101
Ibembo	385	OK 343
Ibeto	366	OC 324
Ibi	382	OE 329
Ibiri	294	CB 108
Ibo	273	CR 124
Iboko	388	OO 338
Ibondo	389	OP 347
Iborogero	300	BY 110
Iboundji	386	OO 331
Iche	330	NE 317
Ichese	294	CH 106
Icheu	381	OE 326
Ida	219	EE 98
Idabato	376	OJ 328
Idah	381	OF 326
Idd al-Ghanam	370	OA 343
Ideles	342	NO 325
Idenao	376	OJ 328
Idfu	348	NN 352
Idga Hamus	373	NY 359
Idi	374	NY 361
Idini	350	NU 303
Idiofa	289	CB 82
Idjiwi	298	BV 101
Idoani	381	OF 325
Idodi	295	CH 113
Idugalo	295	CF 114
Idumbe	388	OR 341
iFafa Beach	220	EC 104
Ifakara	284	CJ 116
Ifaki	381	OE 324
Ife	381	OF 324
Ifenat	369	OA 337
Iferouâne	355	NT 328
Ifetedo	381	OF 324
Ifon	381	OF 325
Ifrane	330	ND 314
Ifunda	283	CJ 114
Igabi	367	OB 327
Igalele	294	CH 107
Igalula	282	CK 109
Igamba	298	BZ 102
Iganga	305	BQ 109
Igarra	381	OF 325
Igawa	283	CK 111
Igbeti	381	OD 323
Igbogar	381	OF 324
Igboho	381	OD 323
Igbo-Ora	380	OF 322
Igbor	382	OF 328
Igleche	238	DM 110
Igli	341	NH 317
Igoma (Tan.)	282	CL 110
Igoma (Tan.)	294	CH 109
Igominyi	283	CL 112
Igporin	381	OD 324
Iguéla	386	OP 328
Iguguno	295	CB 112
Igumira	294	CF 109
Igunga	300	CA 110
Igurubi	300	CA 110
Ihanja	295	CC 112
Ihembe	283	CJ 114
Iherir	343	NN 327
Ihiala	381	OG 326
Ihimba	295	CH 114
Ihugh	382	OF 328
Ihuo	381	OG 326
Iidaan	328	BE 140
Ijara	302	BV 124
Ijebu Jesa	381	OE 324
Ijebu-Ode	381	OF 323
Ijkharrah	346	NJ 341
Ijoukak	329	NG 311
Ikamba	293	CF 104
Ikanda	388	OQ 341
Ikanga	301	BV 119
Ikare	381	OE 325
Ikasi	295	CE 113
Ike	384	OJ 340
Ikebe	381	OF 326
Ikela	388	OO 342
Ikelenge	279	CP 91
Ikéngué	376	OO 329
Ikeni	381	OF 327
Ikere	381	OF 324
Ikina	299	BY 107
Ikinga	282	CL 110
Ikire	381	OF 323
Ikirun	381	OE 324
Ikobé	386	OO 330
Ikoga (Bot.)	244	DE 87
Ikoga (Tan.)	283	CJ 112
Ikola	293	CF 103
Ikole	381	OE 325
Ikom	382	OG 328
Ikoma	300	BW 112
Ikombe	283	CM 111
Ikoo	301	BU 119
Ikot Ekpene	376	OH 327
Ikoto	313	BJ 109
Ikumbukwa	294	CG 109
Ikunga	295	CC 110
Ikutha	301	BW 119
Ikwiriri	297	CH 120
Ilagala	293	CC 102
Ilaji	380	OE 322
iLangakazi	221	DY 106
Ilangali	295	CF 113
Ila-Orangun	381	OE 324
Ilara	381	OF 324
Ilaro	380	OF 322
Ilaut	307	BO 117
Ilebo	388	OR 340
Ileret	315	BJ 115
Ilesha	381	OE 324
Ilewiro	295	CE 112
Illéla	366	NY 324
Illizi	343	NM 327
Ilongero	295	CB 112
Ilorin	381	OE 323
Ilula	299	BY 109
Ilunde	294	CF 107
Ilungu	294	CD 109
Ilungu	294	CH 109
Ilushi	381	OF 326
Ilwendo	255	DB 90
Imala	273	CW 122
Imbwae	255	DB 91
Imese	387	OL 337
Imi	325	BE 127
Imi n 'Tanoute	329	NG 310
Imlily	350	NP 303
Immerpan	236	DQ 101
Immigrant	218	EA 94
Imouzzer du Kandar	330	ND 314
iMpendle	220	EB 102
Impfondo	387	OL 337
Impulo	262	CU 70
Imusho	254	DC 89
In Amenas	343	NK 328
In Amguel	342	NO 324
In Guezzam	354	NS 325
In Salah	342	NL 321
Inal	350	NR 304
iNanda	220	EB 104
I-n-Azaoua	355	NR 327
Inchope	248	DF 110
Inda Silase	373	NY 357
Indombo	386	ON 332
Indungo	263	CW 75
Indwe	219	EE 97
Inezgane	339	NH 310
Infanta	209	EL 84
I-n-Forba	363	NW 309
Ingal	355	NV 326
Inganda	388	ON 340
Ingawa	367	NZ 327
Ingende	388	ON 338
Ingogo	228	DX 102
Ingolo I	387	OQ 333
Ingore	362	OA 303
iNgwavuma	229	DW 107
Ingwe	267	CT 95
Inhaca	229	DU 108
Inhafenga	248	DJ 110
Inhambane	239	DP 114
Inhaminga	259	DD 113
Inhamitanga	259	DD 113
Inharrime	239	DQ 113
Inhassoro	249	DK 113
Inhassunge	260	DD 116
Injibara	373	OB 356
I-n-Jitane	355	NV 326
Inkomo	257	DC 104
Inkouéle	387	OO 335
Inomo	305	BN 108
Inongo	387	OP 337
Inoni	387	OQ 335
I-n-Tebezas	354	NU 321
I-n-Tilelt	365	NW 318
Inverugie	220	EC 103
Inxu	219	EE 99
Inyati	246	DG 100
Inyonga	294	CF 107
Iona	250	DA 68
Iongido	301	BX 116
Iouik	350	NS 303
Ipata	294	CE 107
Ipenza	282	CM 109
Ipera	295	CF 112

Iperu > Kola Town

PLACE NAME	PG	GRID
Iperu	381	OF 323
Ipetu-Ijesha	381	OF 324
Ipole	294	CD 108
Ippy	384	OG 340
Iragua	284	CK 116
Iraka	367	OB 327
Iraklion	336	NC 344
Iramba (Tan.)	299	BV 109
Iramba (Tan.)	300	BV 111
Irema	389	ON 343
Irherm	340	NH 311
Iriba	370	NX 341
Irié	378	OE 310
Iringa	295	CH 114
Irondo	296	CG 115
Irrua	381	OF 325
Irumu	304	BP 102
Isa	366	NZ 325
Isabania	300	BU 112
Isabis	231	DO 76
Isaka (DRC)	387	OQ 337
Isaka (DRC)	388	OQ 338
Isalala	282	CL 108
Isali	387	OP 336
Isambe	389	OP 345
Isandja (DRC)	388	OP 340
Isandja (DRC)	388	OQ 341
Isange	388	OO 341
Isangi	389	OM 343
Isango	304	BS 102
Isanlu	381	OE 325
Isanlu-Esa	381	OE 324
Isanlu-Isn	381	OE 324
Isasa	389	OQ 347
Iseke	295	CE 113
Iseyen	381	OE 323
Ishaka	304	BT 103
Ishasha	304	BT 102
Ishesha	254	DC 87
Ishiara	307	BS 118
Ishifunga	278	CM 90
Isibaki	270	CU 107
Isiksisia	294	CB 109
Isimbira	294	CE 107
Isiolo	307	BR 118
Isiro	385	OK 347
Iskushuban	375	OC 369
Ismailia	337	NG 351
Isna	348	NN 351
Isoka	282	CN 108
Isongole	282	CL 110
Isopa	281	CK 105
Issangele	376	OH 328
Issaouane	367	NY 327
Issia	378	OG 312
Issinga	376	OO 329
Issuna	295	CC 112
Isunura	283	CK 112
Iswepe	228	DV 103
Itaka	282	CK 108
Itale	282	CL 109
Itaro	361	NV 358
Iten	306	BQ 113
Itende	295	CF 111
Itengule	283	CK 114
Itesingue	288	CE 75
Itete	283	CK 115
Itezhi Tezhi	255	CY 94
Itigi	295	CD 112
Itipo	388	OO 338
Itobe (Nig.)	381	OE 327
Itobe (Nig.)	381	OF 326
Itobo	299	CA 108
Itoculo	273	CW 123
Itoni	283	CM 112
Itquiy	339	NL 306
Itsoseng	226	DU 94
Itu	376	OH 327
Itula	389	OQ 347
Itumba (Tan.)	282	CL 109
Itumba (Tan.)	295	CE 110
Itungi	282	CM 110
Itwangi	299	BZ 109
Itzer	330	NE 314
Ivuna	282	CJ 107
Iwala	388	OQ 342
Iwanda	282	CK 108
Iwe	389	OR 345
Iwimbi	295	CF 113
Iwo	381	OE 323
iXopo	220	EC 103
Iyal Bakhit	371	NZ 348
Iyayi	283	CK 112
Izazi	295	CG 114
iZingolweni	220	ED 103
J Bozi	372	NZ 353
J Mazmum	372	OA 353
Jabo	366	OA 324
Jabolo	295	CD 112
Jacobsdal	218	EA 92
Jada	382	OD 331
Jadu	333	NF 331
Jagbahun	377	OE 307
Jagersfontein	218	EB 94
Jaght Drift	217	EB 85
Jakalsberg	242	DF 77
Jakiri	382	OG 330
Jakkalspan	235	DP 97
Jakpa	381	OG 324
Jakusko	367	OA 330
Jalingo	382	OD 330
Jalu	346	NJ 341
Jamaama	309	BR 128
Jamari	367	OB 330
Jamba	263	CW 75
Jambila	228	DT 104
James Comer	283	CK 113
Jameson Park	227	DU 99
Jamestown	219	EE 96
Jamkola	295	CE 111
Jammerdrif	219	EB 96
Jamtari	382	OE 330
Jamu	322	BD 114
Jan Kempdorp	226	DX 92
Jane Furse	228	DR 102
Jangamo	239	DQ 113
Jansenville	211	EH 92
Janseput	236	DP 99
Jarso	322	AY 113
Jasikan	380	OF 319
Jatinqué	238	DR 110
Jau	251	CX 70
Jaupon	380	OG 319
Jdioula	331	NB 320
Jdiriya	339	NL 309
Jebba	381	OD 324
Jebel Qerri	372	NW 352
Jebiniana	333	NC 330
Jefawa	370	OB 343
Jeffreys Bay	211	EL 93
Jega	366	OA 323
Jege	381	OE 325
Jelhalali	326	BD 130
Jelma	333	NC 328
Jema	379	OE 317
Jemma	381	OD 327
Jemme	367	OA 329
Jenaien	333	NF 329
Jenda	270	CR 110
Jerada	330	ND 317
Jerera	247	DH 105
Jerigu	380	OD 318
Jiberu	382	OD 332
Jibiya	367	NZ 326
Jiddah	361	NQ 358
Jiga	373	OB 356
Jijel	332	NA 325
Jijiga	325	AY 128
Jilib	309	BQ 128
Jima	323	BB 116
Jimbe	278	CP 90
Jimbo	297	CH 122
Jimeta	382	OD 332
Jimila	246	DF 98
Jinja	305	BR 109
Jinka	315	BF 116
Jivundu	267	CT 92
Jiwe La Singa	295	CE 111
Joal	362	NY 302
Joazohn	378	OH 310
Joel's Drift	219	DZ 99
Jofane	248	DK 111
Johannesburg	227	DU 98
Johnson's Post	210	EL 86
Jojweni	213	EF 101
Jokau	322	BA 110
Jolivet	220	EC 103
Jombo	380	OE 319
Jomu	299	BZ 109
Jongensklip	209	EL 82
Jordan	225	DU 89
Jorf	333	ND 330
Joru	378	OE 308
Jos	367	OC 328
Josling	217	DZ 86
Jotsholo	246	DE 98
Joubertina	211	EK 90
Jowhar	318	BM 134
Jozini	229	DW 107
Jreïda	350	NU 303
Juaben	380	OF 318
Juba	313	BH 105
Jubilee	209	EL 83
Juliasdale	258	DD 108
Jumani	297	CG 120
Jumbe Salim's	284	CO 116
Jungue	275	CP 74
Junleri	382	OD 330
Junta Cereais	263	CW 75
Jurgen	223	DV 78
Juru	258	DC 105
Jwaneng	226	DR 92
K. Hausa	367	OA 329
K. Madaki	367	OB 329
Kaabong	314	BK 111
Kaalkop	241	DK 75
Kaalrug	229	DT 105
Kaambooni	303	BV 126
Kaapmuiden	229	DT 105
Kaapsehoop	228	DT 104
Kaba	304	BS 102
Kabala	363	OC 307
Kabale	298	BU 103
Kabalo	292	CE 97
Kabambare	292	CB 98
Kabanga (DRC)	289	CE 80
Kabanga (Tan.)	298	BX 104
Kabanga (Zam.)	256	DB 96
Kabango	292	CE 95
Kabangu	278	CN 88
Kabare	298	BW 100
Kabaw	333	NF 330
Kabba	381	OE 325
Kabelawa	368	NY 332
Kabera Maido	305	BO 109
Kabere	293	CH 101
Kabernet	306	BQ 114
Kabeya (DRC)	290	CD 89
Kabeya (DRC)	292	CD 98
Kabila	299	BZ 107
Kabinda	291	CE 92
Kabiri	387	OP 333
Kabo	384	OE 338
Kabogi	366	OC 324
Kabompo	267	CU 91
Kabondo-Dianda	279	CK 94
Kabongo (DRC)	280	CK 99
Kabongo (DRC)	291	CG 94
Kabou	380	OD 320
Kabrousse	362	OA 302
Kabulamena	267	CU 91
Kabulamwanda	256	CY 96
Kabumbu	389	OR 345
Kabwe (DRC)	291	CG 90
Kabwe (Zam.)	268	CV 99
Kachalola	269	CW 104
Kachekabwe	255	DD 92
Kachia	367	OC 327
Kachisi (Eth.)	323	AY 119
Kachisi (Eth.)	373	OC 357
Kachulu	259	CX 114
Kachung	305	BO 108
Kade	380	OG 318
Kadiana	364	OB 312
Kadiaso	364	OC 312
Kadioha	379	OD 313
Kadiolo	364	OB 313
Kadjebi	380	OE 319
Kadji	369	OC 339
Kado	382	OE 329
Kadoma	257	DD 102
Kadugli	371	OB 349
Kaduna	367	OB 327
Kaedi	363	NW 306
Kaélé	368	OC 333
Kafakumba	278	CM 90
Kafanchan	367	OC 327
Kaffrine	362	NY 304
Kafia Kingi	385	OD 343
Kafolo	364	OC 315
Kafountine	362	NZ 302
Kafr el Sheikh	337	NG 350
Kafue	256	CY 99
Kafukule	282	CP 110
Kafulwe	281	CL 101
Kafunzo	298	BU 103
Kaga Bandoro	384	OF 338
Kagadi	304	BQ 104
Kagitumba	298	BU 104
Kagmar	371	NY 349
Kagombo	279	CN 95
Kagopal	383	OE 335
Kagoro	270	CV 107
Kagulu	305	BP 109
Kaha	325	AZ 129
Kahama	299	BZ 107
Kahemba	289	CG 81
Kahia (DRC)	292	CE 99
Kahia (DRC)	292	CG 96
Kahone	362	NY 303
Kahunge	304	BR 104
Kaiama	366	OC 323
Kaiango	253	DC 83
Kaiemothia	314	BH 113
Kailahun	378	OE 308
Kaindu	268	CW 96
Kaisho	298	BU 104
Kaisu	304	BO 104
Kajiado	301	BV 116
Kajok	385	OE 347
Kajuru	367	OC 327
Kakamas	216	DZ 84
Kakamega	306	BR 112
Kakamoéka	386	OR 331
Kakata	378	OF 309
Kakeki	266	CT 90
Kakenge	290	CB 86
Kakera	293	CG 102
Kakesio	300	BY 113
Kakielo	269	CR 102
Kakobola	289	CD 81
Kakododoga	314	BM 112
Kakoge	305	BP 107
Kakoma (Tan.)	294	CD 107
Kakoma (Zam.)	281	CJ 103
Kakoni	363	OB 306
Kakonko	298	BY 104
Kakuma	314	BK 112
Kakumbi	270	CT 106
Kakumiro	305	BQ 105
Kakuyu	292	CE 95
Kal	369	OC 340
Kala (Tan.)	281	CJ 104
Kala (Nig.)	368	OA 333
Kalaba	281	CJ 102
Kalabo	266	CW 88
Kalabua	291	CF 90
Kalagi	362	NZ 303
Kalala	255	CY 94
Kalalawa	368	OA 331
Kalale	366	OC 322
Kalamare	235	DN 96
Kalamba	387	ON 337
Kalambana	270	CV 106
Kalamon	365	OC 316
Kalana	364	OB 311
Kalangala	305	BS 107
Kalangali	295	CE 110
Kalangi	293	CC 100
Kalbaskraal	209	EK 80
Kaldke	378	OH 311
Kaledougou	364	NZ 314
Kalehe	298	BW 100
Kalema	389	OR 343
Kalemera	300	BW 110
Kalemie	293	CD 101
Kalenda	268	CW 97
Kalenga	295	CH 113
Kalengwa	267	CT 92
Kaleo	365	OC 316
Kalfou	368	OC 334
Kali (Gui.)	363	OA 307
Kali (Nig.)	366	OC 323
Kalima	389	OQ 346
Kalinda	282	CN 107
Kalinga	283	CJ 113
Kalinko	363	OB 308
Kaliro	306	BQ 110
Kalisizo	305	BT 106
Kaliua	294	CC 106
Kalkbank	236	DP 101
Kalkfeld	241	DJ 75
Kalkrand	232	DQ 78
Kalksloot	217	ED 86
Kalkwerf	217	DZ 86
Kaloa	364	OC 313
Kaloko	291	CF 94
Kalola	290	CG 87
Kalole	389	OR 346
Kalomo	256	DB 95
Kalonje	269	CR 105
Kalossia	306	BO 114
Kalounka	362	OB 305
Kaluluma	270	CS 110
Kalulushi	268	CS 99
Kalundu	298	BZ 101
Kalundwe	291	CF 91
Kalungu	305	BS 106
Kalwanga	305	BR 106
Kamaday	369	OB 339
Kamanga	299	BX 108
Kamangu	282	CP 107
Kamanjab	241	DG 72
Kamanyola	298	BX 100
Kamaron	378	OD 308
Kamativi	256	DD 97
Kamba	366	OA 323
Kamba Kota	383	OF 337
Kambaku	295	CF 114
Kambal	372	OB 354
Kambole	380	OD 321
Kambove	280	CO 96
Kambut	336	NF 344
Kameel	226	DV 92
Kameelberg	241	DJ 75
Kamende	291	CE 92
Kameshia	280	CJ 97
Kamieskroon	215	EC 78
Kamiji	290	CF 89
Kamina (DRC)	279	CK 93
Kamina (DRC)	292	CD 95
Kamina Base	279	CK 93
Kamituga	389	OQ 347
Kamkusi	236	DM 102
Kammiebos	211	EK 91
Kamola	292	CH 97
Kamonanira	298	CA 102
Kamoto	270	CT 107
Kampala	305	BR 108
Kampampi	280	CL 100
Kamparana	364	NZ 314
Kampene	389	OR 346
Kamphambale	271	CR 111
Kampi Katoto	295	CG 110
Kampi ya Moto	306	BS 114
Kampinda	281	CJ 102
Kampti	364	OC 315
Kampumbu	282	CN 108
Kamsamba	282	CJ 107
Kamsar	362	OB 304
Kamsuuma	309	BR 128
Kamudini	305	BN 107
Kamuesha	290	CE 86
Kamuganguzi	298	BU 103
Kamuli	305	BQ 109
Kamwanga	294	CH 105
Kan	321	AY 106
Kananga	290	CD 88
Kananto	379	OD 317
Kanchele	256	DB 96
Kanda- Kayes	286	CB 69
Kandi	366	OB 322
Kandiafara	362	OB 305
Kandika	363	OA 306
Kanel	363	NX 306
Kang	234	DP 88
Kangaba	364	OA 311
Kangare	364	OA 311
Kangi	385	OE 347
Kangiwa	366	NZ 323
Kango	376	ON 329
Kangole	306	BN 112
Kangondi	301	BU 118
Kanguya	255	CX 91
Kani	378	OE 312
Kaniama	291	CH 91
Kaniasso	364	OC 312
Kanisa	360	NU 351
Kankalabe	363	OB 307
Kankan	363	OC 310
Kankara	367	OA 326
Kankossa	363	NW 308
Kannple	378	OF 310
Kannwia	378	OH 311
Kano (Mali)	363	NZ 309
Kano (Nig.)	367	OA 327
Kanona	269	CT 104
Kanoneiland	217	DZ 85
Kanoni (DRC)	280	CO 96
Kanoni (Uga.)	305	BR 106
Kanonkop	209	EJ 80
Kanono	255	DC 91
Kanoroba	379	OD 313
Kanovlei	242	DF 81
Kansanshi	267	CR 95
Kansenia	279	CN 95
Kantchari	366	OA 321
Kanté	365	OC 320
Kanus	224	DX 80
Kanyabayongo	304	BT 101
KaNyamazane	229	DS 105
Kanyao	306	BO 113
Kanye	226	DR 93
Kanyemba	257	CY 103
Kanyilombi	267	CS 91
Kanyu	245	DH 92
Kao (Les.)	220	EA 100
Kao (Ben.)	366	NX 325
Kaoko Otavi	251	DD 70
Kaokwe	254	DD 86
Kaolack	362	NY 303
Kaoma	267	CW 92
Kaouadja	385	OE 343
Kaouara	364	OC 314
Kapako	291	CD 94
Kapalala (DRC)	269	CR 101
Kapalala (Tan.)	282	CJ 108
Kapandae	380	OE 319
Kapanga	278	CJ 88
Kapangwe	293	CH 102
Kapapa (DRC)	280	CM 99
Kapapa (Tan.)	294	CF 105
Kapatu	281	CM 104
Kapchorwa	306	BP 111
Kapedo	307	BP 115
Kapeka	305	BQ 107
Kapelebyong	306	BN 110
Kapema	280	CO 99
Kapenguria	306	BP 112
Kapeya	270	CV 106
Kapia	388	OR 339
Kapiri Mposhi	268	CU 100
Kapoeta	314	BH 110
Kapona	293	CG 101
Kaponde	290	CF 89
Kaporo	282	CM 110
Kaporoma	284	CK 116
Kapps	231	DN 77
Kapsabet	306	BR 113
Kaputa	281	CJ 102
Kaputir	306	BN 113
Karabee	217	EB 88
Karaga	365	OC 318
Karagwe	299	BV 105
Karakore	373	OB 359
Karakuwisa	243	DE 82
Karal	368	NZ 334
Karamadar	385	OH 344
Karang	362	NY 303
Karangana	364	OA 314
Karangua	268	CS 96
Karasburg	216	DY 80
Karatara	210	EK 88
Karatina	307	BS 117
Karatu	300	BY 114
Karawa	384	OK 339
Karaya	367	OA 327
Karee	219	DZ 95
Kareedouw	211	EK 91
Kareevlakte	209	EK 84
Karema	295	CC 114
Karfi	367	OA 327
Kargi	315	BM 118
Karg's Post	220	ED 102
Kari (Eth.)	324	BA 122
Kari (Nig.)	367	OB 330
Kariba	257	DA 100
Karibib	241	DL 74
Kariega	212	EK 96
Karima	360	NU 351
Karimama	366	OA 322
Karin	374	OB 365
Karina	377	OD 307
Karino	229	DS 105
Karkams	215	EC 78
Karling	371	OA 350
Karma	366	NY 321
Karme	368	NZ 335
Karoi	257	DA 102
Karonga	282	CM 110
Karora	361	NU 357
Karos	217	DY 86
Karoub	369	OA 340
Karreeboschkolk	216	EB 83
Karringmelkspruit	219	ED 97
Karungo	306	BT 111
Karungu	293	CE 103
Karuzi	298	BY 103
Kas	370	NZ 343
Kasa	388	OO 339
Kasaali	305	BT 106
Kasaba	281	CO 102
Kasaji	278	CN 89
Kasama (Tan.)	281	CN 105
Kasama (Tan.)	299	BX 107
Kasamba	281	CJ 101
Kasamia	293	CD 104
Kasane	255	DC 93
Kasanga (Tan.)	281	CJ 105
Kasanga (Tan.)	283	CK 113
Kasangor	314	BF 110
Kasangulu	287	CB 73
Kasankha	271	CV 112
Kasanza	291	CF 90
Kasasi	363	OC 307
Kasba Tadla	330	NE 313
Kasempa	267	CT 94
Kasenga	280	CN 100
Kasengu	305	BN 105
Kasenye	304	BP 103
Kasenyi	304	BS 103
Kasese (Uga.)	304	BR 103
Kasese (DRC)	389	OP 346
Kashwal	320	BC 101
Kasima	252	DC 79
Kasindi	304	BR 102
Kasinge	292	CE 97
Kasokomona	293	CF 101
Kasompe	267	CU 93
Kasongo	389	OR 345
Kasongo -Lunda	288	CE 76
Kasonkomona	268	CW 97
Kasouga	212	EK 96
Kasr el Boukhari	331	NB 322
Kassa (Ben.)	366	OA 322
Kassa (Nig.)	367	OC 328
Kassala	372	NW 355
Kassama	363	NZ 308
Kassanda	305	BQ 106
Kassera	364	OC 313
Kassoum	365	NZ 316
Kasula	256	CX 97
Kasulu	293	CB 103
Kasumbulesa	268	CR 98
Kasungu	270	CT 109
Kaswa	294	CF 108
Kataba (Bot.)	255	DD 92
Kataba (Zam.)	255	CZ 93
Katabaie	290	CF 89
Kataborwa	299	BX 107
Katagum	367	OA 329
Katako-Kombe	389	OQ 343
Katakwi	306	BO 110
Katale	294	CB 105
Katamma	367	NZ 330
Katana	298	BW 100
Katande	291	CE 90
Kataouana	364	NW 312
Katapakishi	278	CJ 88
Katcha	381	OD 325
Katchirga	365	NY 319
Katema	271	CW 113
Katende (DRC)	290	CE 87
Katenge (DRC)	290	CH 87
Katengo	293	CC 100
Katere	253	DD 84
Katesh	295	CB 113
Katete	270	CV 107
Kathu	225	DX 89
Kati	364	NZ 311
Katima Mulilo	255	DC 91
Katini	288	CF 79
Katiola	379	OE 314
Katiyo	258	DB 106
Katkop	216	EC 83
Katobo	255	CY 93
Katofio	280	CP 99
Katojo	304	BS 102
Katoma	305	BQ 107
Katombe	290	CD 86
Katompi	292	CE 95
Katoto	293	CB 104
Katse	307	BT 119
Katshi	292	CE 95
Katsina	367	NZ 327
Katsina Ala	382	OF 329
Katsuba	295	CD 113
Katugo	305	BP 108
Katumbi (Mal.)	282	CO 109
Katumbi (Tan.)	293	CE 102
Katundu	255	DB 92
Katunguru	304	BS 103
Katwa Makondo	294	CH 106
Katwe (DRC)	280	CO 98
Katwe (Uga.)	304	BS 102
Katwitwi	252	DB 79
Kaura-Namoda	367	NZ 326
Kauwa	368	NZ 333
Kavimba	255	DD 92
Kavinga	270	CS 108
Kawajena	385	OF 347
Kawambwa	281	CM 101
Kawana	267	CT 95
Kawasa	280	CM 99
Kawembwe	282	CO 106
Kaweri	305	BQ 105
Kawungera	305	BR 106
Kaya	365	NZ 318
Kaya se put	227	DR 95
Kayambi	282	CM 107
Kayanza	298	BX 102
Kayar	362	NX 302
Kayembe-Mukulu	278	CK 90
Kayenze	299	BW 109
Kayes (Con.)	386	OR 332
Kayes (Mali)	363	NY 308
Kayima	378	OD 308
Kayli	372	OB 353
Kaymor	362	NY 304
Kayokwe	298	BZ 102
Kayombo	266	CT 90
Kayonza	298	BV 104
Kayser's Beach	212	EJ 98
Kayuyu	389	OR 345
Kaywayo	254	CX 87
Kazamabika	386	ON 331
Kazaure	367	NZ 327
Kazembe	280	CM 100
Kaziza	278	CO 90
Kazo	304	BS 104
Kazumba	290	CE 87
Kazungula	255	DC 93
Kazwama	305	BP 108
Kbombole	362	NX 302
Keate's Drift	220	DZ 104
Kebaly	363	OB 307
Kébara	387	OP 333
Kebbe	366	OA 324
Kebemer	362	NX 303
Kebila	364	OB 312
Kebili	333	ND 328
Kebkabiya	370	NY 343
Kebri Dehar	326	BD 131
Kédédéssé	369	OB 336
Kedougou	363	NZ 307
Keembe	268	CW 98
Keetmanshoop	223	DV 78
Keffi	381	OD 327
Keheili	360	NT 352
Kei Mouth	212	EH 99
Kei Road	212	EH 98
Keibo	365	NY 318
Keimoes	216	DZ 84
Keiskammahoek	212	EH 97
Keïta	366	NX 325
Keitsas	232	DN 80
Kékélé	387	OM 334
Kekem	376	OH 329
Kelafo	318	BF 131
Kélakam	368	NY 331
Kelem	314	BH 114
Kelibia	333	NA 330
Kéllé (Con.)	387	ON 333
Kéllé (Ngr.)	367	NY 329
Kélo	383	OD 335
Kelongwa	267	CU 95
Kelso	220	EC 104
Kembé	384	OH 341
Kembolcha	373	OB 359
Kemondo	299	BU 106
Kempani	387	OQ 336
Kempton Park	227	DU 99
Kenadsa	330	NF 316
Kendal	228	DU 100
Kendegue	369	OC 338
Kendrew	211	EH 92
Kendu Bay	306	BS 112
Kenekou	364	NZ 312
Kenema	378	OE 308
Kenge	288	CB 77
Kengeja	297	CC 122
Kengué	387	OQ 333
Kenhardt	217	EA 85
Kenieba	363	NZ 308
Kenilworth (N.C.)	217	DY 86
Kenilworth (N.C.)	218	DZ 92
Kenitra	329	ND 312
Kennedy	246	DE 97
Kennedy's Vale	228	DR 103
Kenton-on-Sea	212	EK 96
Kenzou	383	OJ 334
Kerawa	368	OB 333
Kere	385	OH 345
Kerege	297	CF 120
Keren	373	NW 358
Kerewan	362	NZ 303
Kericho	306	BS 113
Kerkrand	210	EK 86
Kerma	359	NS 350
Kermes	331	NC 320
Kerou	366	OB 321
Kérouané	378	OD 310
Kersa Dek	316	BG 122
Kerugoya	307	BS 117
Kerzaz	341	NH 318
Kesra	333	NB 328
Kestell	220	DY 100
Keta	380	OG 320
Ketama	330	NC 314
Ketane	219	EC 98
Kete-Krachi	380	OE 319
Ketesso	379	OG 316
Ketou	380	OF 322
Ketta	387	OM 335
Kette	383	OH 334
Keur Massene	350	NV 303
Keur Momar Sar	362	NW 303
Keve	380	OG 320
Kezi	246	DJ 99
Kgagodi	236	DM 98
Khabo	219	DZ 99
Khabou	363	NX 307
Khakhea	226	DR 90
Khalfallah	331	NC 319
Khangar Sidi Nadji	332	NC 326
Khaoui Naam	339	NK 307
Khartoum	372	NW 352
Khashm-el-Qirba	372	NX 355
Khaudom	243	DE 84
Khemis des Zemamra	329	NE 310
Khemis du Sahel	339	NK 308
Khemis Miliana	331	NB 321
Khemisset	330	ND 313
Khenchela	332	NC 326
Khenifra	330	NE 313
Kherrata	332	NA 324
Khor Angar	374	OA 363
Khorixas	241	DH 72
Khorof Harar	308	BN 124
Khossanto	363	NZ 307
Khouribga	329	NE 312
Khudumalapye	234	DP 92
Khuis	225	DV 86
Khureit	370	NY 345
Khuwei	371	NZ 348
Kiakalamu	280	CL 99
Kiama	288	CG 78
Kiambi	292	CG 99
Kiambu	301	BU 116
Kibada	283	CJ 113
Kibaha	297	CF 121
Kibakwe	296	CF 115
Kibale	305	BQ 105
Kibale Norte	287	CG 70
Kibanga Port	305	BR 108
Kibangou	386	OR 331
Kibara	299	BW 109
Kibau	283	CK 113
Kibaya	296	CC 116
Kiberashi	296	CC 118
Kiberenge	296	CH 116
Kibi	380	OG 318
Kibish	314	BF 114
Kibiti	297	CH 120
Kiboga	305	BQ 106
Kibombo	389	OR 345
Kibondo	298	BZ 104
Kibre Mengist	316	BF 120
Kibuku	306	BP 110
Kibungo	298	BW 103
Kibunzi Kinganga	287	CC 70
Kibuye	298	BW 101
Kibwezi	301	BW 119
Kichwamba	304	BS 102
Kidachi	295	CF 114
Kidal	353	NU 320
Kidatu	296	CH 116
Kidayi	296	CH 116
Kidd's Beach	212	EJ 98
Kidete	296	CE 117
Kididji	370	OC 341
Kidira	363	NX 307
Kidugallo	296	CF 119
Kidugalo	296	CF 119
Kiekoesvlei	208	EJ 79
Kiepersol	229	DS 105
Kifanyo	283	CM 113
Kifaya	363	OA 306
Kiffa	351	NV 308
Kifinga	280	CJ 98
Kifunankese	291	CC 91
Kigali	298	BV 103
Kignan	364	OA 313
Kigoma	293	CB 102
Kigumba	305	BO 106
Kigwa	294	CC 109
Kigwe	295	CE 114
Kigweri	305	BP 107
Kihundo	285	CL 121
Kijungu	296	CC 117
Kijunjubwa	305	BP 106
Kikagati	298	BU 104
Kikale	297	CH 121
Kikamba	389	OQ 346
Kikarara	304	BS 102
Kikiongolo	287	CC 74
Kikombo	295	CE 114
Kikondja	279	CJ 95
Kikumbi	291	CD 94
Kikumini	301	BW 118
Kikungula	292	CF 98
Kikwit	289	CC 80
Kilala	301	BV 118
Kilalo	300	BW 110
Kildonan	257	DB 104
Kilembe	292	CH 95
Kileo	291	CD 93
Kilgoris	300	BU 112
Kili	386	OP 329
Kilibo	380	OE 322
Kilifi	302	BZ 122
Kilim	369	OA 338
Kilimahera	297	CG 121
Kilimani	297	CH 120
Kilimarondo	284	CO 119
Kilimatinde	295	CD 112
Kilinda	293	CG 100
Kilindoni	297	CH 122
Kilosa	296	CF 116
Kilumbi	295	CE 110
Kilwa	280	CL 99
Kilwa Kisiwani	285	CK 122
Kilwa Kivinje	285	CK 122
Kilwa Masoko	285	CK 122
Kim	368	OC 335
Kimali	300	BY 111
Kimamba	296	CF 117
Kimambi	284	CL 119
Kimana	301	BX 118
Kimano II	389	OR 347
Kimba	387	OQ 333
Kimbago	300	BY 111
Kimbala Twana	288	CF 77
Kimbao	288	CC 78
Kimbe	296	CD 118
Kimberley	218	DZ 92
Kimbirila Sud	364	OC 311
Kimilili	306	BQ 112
Kimisi	299	BW 105
Kimongo	386	OR 332
Kimpanzo	287	CB 72
Kimpata-Eku	289	CC 81
Kimpese	287	CD 71
Kimsambi	298	BU 104
Kimvula	287	CD 74
Kinango	302	CA 121
Kinani	294	CH 106
Kinda	279	CL 93
Kindamba	387	OR 334
Kindeje	287	CG 70
Kindi	288	CC 77
Kindia	363	OC 306
Kindu	389	OQ 345
Kinesi	300	BU 110
King William's Town (E.C.)	212	EH 97
King Williams Town (Lib)	378	OH 310
Kinga	278	CN 90
Kingholm	229	DW 106
Kingombe (DRC)	389	OQ 345
Kingombe (DRC)	389	OQ 346
Kingsburgh	220	EC 104
Kingscote	220	EC 101
Kingsley	228	DX 104
Kingswood	226	DW 94
Kingulube	389	OQ 347
Kingungi	288	CC 78
Kingwaya	387	OR 337
Kiniama	280	CP 99
Kinirapoort	220	ED 100
Kiniyangiri	300	CA 112
Kinjacha	284	CM 118
Kinkala	387	OR 334
Kinna	307	BR 119
Kinross	228	DU 101
Kinshasa	287	CB 74
Kintampo	379	OE 317
Kintinian	363	OA 310
Kinyasini	297	CD 121
Kinyika	296	CF 115
Kinyinya	298	BZ 103
Kiomboi	300	CA 111
Kiongwe	302	BW 124
Kipaila	292	CH 99
Kipaka	389	OR 346
Kipandi	288	CC 76
Kipanga	295	CE 113
Kipatimu	284	CK 120
Kipemba	287	CC 73
Kipembawe	294	CH 109
Kipengere	283	CL 112
Kipesse	286	CB 68
Kipili (Tan.)	293	CG 104
Kipili (Tan.)	295	CE 110
Kipini	302	BX 123
Kipkelion	306	BS 113
Kipushi	268	CQ 97
Kipushia (DRC)	269	CS 102
Kipushia (DRC)	291	CE 93
Kirane	363	NX 309
Kiri	388	OP 338
Kiriani	307	BT 117
Kiridh	327	AZ 135
Kirkwood	211	EJ 93
Kirondatal	300	CA 111
Kiruhura	304	BS 104
Kirundo	298	BX 103
Kirundu	389	OO 345
Kisabi	293	CH 101
Kisaki	296	CG 118
Kisana	291	CE 94
Kisanga (Tan.)	295	CG 113
Kisanga (Tan.)	296	CG 116
Kisangani	389	OM 344
Kisangire	297	CG 120
Kisantete	387	OR 337
Kisantu	287	CC 73
Kisarawe	297	CF 121
Kisasi	296	CD 119
Kisenge	278	CO 89
Kisengi	295	CC 110
Kisengwa	292	CD 95
Kisenyi	304	BS 102
Kiserian	301	BU 116
Kisessa	299	BX 109
Kishapu	300	BZ 110
Kishi	381	OD 323
Kisi	294	CG 105
Kisii	306	BT 112
Kisiju	297	CG 121
Kisima	307	BQ 116
Kisiwani	301	CA 119
Kismaayo	309	BS 128
Kisogwa	298	BZ 104
Kisomoro	304	BQ 103
Kisoro	298	BU 102
Kissidougou	378	OD 309
Kissio	296	CG 119
Kisumu	306	BS 112
Kisundi	286	CD 69
Kiswere	285	CL 122
Kita	363	NZ 310
Kitale	306	BP 113
Kitande	292	CF 95
Kitandi	301	BV 117
Kitangari	285	CO 121
Kitaraka	295	CD 111
Kitaya	285	CO 123
Kiteba	291	CG 92
Kitendwe	293	CH 102
Kitenga	288	CD 76
Kitengo	291	CG 91
Kitete	282	CJ 110
Kitgum	313	BL 108
Kitika	384	OH 342
Kitogani	297	CE 121
Kittermasters Camp	307	BQ 119
Kitui	301	BU 119
Kitumbini	285	CM 122
Kitunda (Tan.)	294	CF 109
Kitunga (DRC)	279	CL 92
Kitutu	389	OQ 347
Kitwanga	305	BO 107
Kitwe	268	CS 99
Kiu	301	BV 117
Kiumbia	292	CD 96
Kiunga	303	BV 126
Kivingo	301	CA 119
Kiwaba N'zogi	276	CK 76
Kiwangwa	297	CE 120
Kiwatama	285	CL 121
Kiwawa	285	CL 121
Kiwengwa	297	CD 121
Kiwoko	305	BQ 107
Kiziba	305	BQ 108
Kiziguro	298	BV 103
Kizimkazi	297	CE 121
Kizumbi	299	BZ 109
Klaarstroom	210	EJ 88
Klaas Voogdsrivier	209	EK 82
Klaserie	228	DR 104
Klawer	209	EF 80
Kle	378	OF 308
Klein Aub	231	DP 76
Klein Karas	223	DX 79
Kleinbegin	217	DZ 86
Kleinmond	209	EL 81
Kleinplaat	210	EK 88
Kleinpoort	211	EJ 92
Kleinrivier	211	EK 92
Kleinsee	215	EB 77
Kleipan	209	EF 80
Kléla	364	OA 313
Klerksdorp	227	DV 96
Klerkskraal	227	DU 97
Klesso	364	OB 315
Klipdale	209	EL 82
Klipfontein (E.C.)	211	EJ 93
Klipfontein (Mpum.)	228	DV 100
Kliphoek	215	EE 79
Klipkolk	217	EE 86
Klipplaat	211	EJ 91
Klippoort	220	DY 102
Klippunt	217	DZ 85
Klipriver	220	DZ 103
Klipskool	228	DS 103
Klipspruit (E.C.)	220	EC 102
Klipspruit (KZN)	228	DX 103
Knapdaar	219	ED 95
Kneukel	218	DY 91
Knockagh	220	EC 103
Knoetze	211	EJ 90
Knysna	210	EL 89
Koaba	366	OB 321
Koalla	365	NZ 319
Koamb	382	OJ 332
Koare	244	DH 87
Kobadie	366	NZ 321
Kobe	293	CD 101
Kobecha	322	AY 112
Kobenni	363	NW 309
Kobero	298	BX 103
Kobi (Nig.)	382	OD 331
Kobi (CAR)	383	OJ 334
Koblague	369	OC 336
Kobo	373	OA 359
Koboko	312	BL 104
Kobos	231	DP 76
Kodjari	366	OA 321
Kodok	372	OC 351
Koebonou	364	OC 315
Koedoeskop	227	DR 98
Koegas	217	EA 87
Koegrabie	217	EA 86
Koekenaap	208	EF 79
Koenong	219	EA 99
Koës	224	DT 81
Koffiefontein	218	EA 92
Koforidua	380	OG 319
Kogba	384	OJ 340
Koidu-Sefadu	378	OD 308
Koindu	378	OE 309
Koingnaas	215	EC 77
Koito	302	BX 121
Kojalingo	237	DO 104
Koka	324	BA 121
Kokerboom	216	DY 81
Kokeris	306	BN 111
Koko (Nig.)	366	OB 324
Koko (Nig.)	381	OG 324
Kokong	234	DQ 89
Kokstad	220	ED 101
Kokumbo	379	OF 314
Kola Town	378	OG 311

Makasuko > Mosiro

PLACE NAME	PG	GRID
Makasuko	295	CE 112
Makatapora	295	CG 114
Makekeda	389	OL 346
Makeni	377	OD 307
Makere	298	CA 103
Makhado (Louis Trichardt)	236	DO 102
Makilimbo	385	OJ 347
Makindu	301	BW 118
Mako	363	NZ 307
Makoba	297	CD 121
Makoko	282	CJ 110
Makokou	386	OM 332
Makokskraal	227	DU 96
Makombe	295	CH 113
Makongolosi	282	CJ 109
Makor	382	OF 332
Makoro	312	BL 102
Makoua	387	ON 335
Makoubi	386	OR 332
Maktau	301	BY 119
Makthar	333	NB 328
Makuende	292	CG 99
Makuliro	284	CM 117
Makumbi	258	DC 105
Makuna	280	CL 97
Makunda	233	DM 83
Makunduchi	297	CE 122
Makungu	283	CK 113
Makunguwiro	284	CN 118
Makunka	255	DC 94
Makurdi	382	OE 328
Makuri	243	DG 84
Makuru	295	CC 112
Makutano (Ken.)	301	BU 118
Makutano (Ken.)	301	BX 118
Makuti	257	CZ 101
Makuyuni	301	BZ 115
Makwassie	227	DW 95
Makwate	235	DO 97
Makwiro	257	DC 104
Mal	351	NV 306
Mala	384	OG 339
Malaba	306	BQ 111
Malabo	376	OJ 328
Malabwe	255	DA 93
Málaga	330	NA 315
Malagarasi	293	CC 104
Malaira	238	DR 110
Malaita	228	DR 102
Malakal	372	OC 351
Malambo	300	BX 114
Malampaka	299	BY 109
Malamulele	237	DO 104
Malan	209	EK 81
Malandala	295	CB 111
Malandji	290	CD 87
Malanga	271	CT 115
Malangali	283	CK 112
Malangeni	229	DW 108
Malanje	275	CM 75
Malantouen	382	OG 330
Malanville	366	OA 322
Malapati	237	DM 105
Malarba	382	OF 331
Malawa	367	NZ 329
Male Male	367	NZ 329
Maleha	363	OA 309
Malei	260	DB 117
Malek	321	BE 106
Maleketla	237	DP 103
Malelane	229	DS 105
Malélé	386	OR 331
Malema	272	CW 117
Malemba-Nkulu	280	CJ 96
Malem-Hodar	362	NY 304
Maleoskop	228	DS 102
Maleshe	225	DT 87
Malewalewa	255	CY 92
Malgas	209	EL 84
Malha	370	NX 345
Mali (Gui.)	363	OA 307
Mali (DRC)	389	OQ 345
Malibé	376	OM 328
Malimasindi	256	DD 99
Malinchi	366	OA 325
Malindi	302	BY 122
Malinga	386	OP 331
Malinyi	283	CK 115
Malita	300	BY 110
Malka Mari	316	BJ 124
Malkerns	229	DV 105
Mallammaduri	367	NZ 329
Mallawi	347	NK 350
Malmesbury	209	EJ 80
Malobeni	229	DX 107
Malole	282	CN 106
Malolo (Tan.)	284	CN 120
Malolo (Tan.)	296	CG 116
Maloma	229	DW 106
Malomeni	229	DX 106
Malomo	270	CT 110
Malonda	279	CM 91
Malonga	278	CN 89
Malotwana	235	DQ 95
Maltahöhe	223	DR 77
Maluana	238	DS 108
Maluera	270	CW 106
Maluku	387	OR 335
Malungwishi	280	CO 96
Malya	299	BY 109
Mamaila	237	DO 103
Mamari	362	NX 305
Mamates	219	EA 98
Mamathwane	225	DW 88
Mamba (DRC)	280	CM 97
Mamba (Tan.)	294	CG 105
Mambal	382	OF 332
Mambali	294	CB 108
Mambasa	304	BP 101
Mambia	363	OC 306
Mambrui	302	BY 123
Mambunga	385	OK 347
Mamelodi	227	DT 99
Mamfé	382	OG 328
Mamina	247	DE 104
Mamoto	300	BX 111
Mamou	363	OC 307
Mampong	380	OF 318
Mamre	208	EK 79
Mamu	381	OF 323
Mamue	262	CU 69
Mamuno	233	DM 83
Man (Lib.)	378	OF 311
Man (CAR)	383	OF 334
Manaculama	250	DA 68
Manama	246	DL 101
Mananga	229	DT 106
Manankoro	364	OC 312
Manda (Eth.)	374	OA 361
Manda (Tan.)	283	CN 112
Manda (Tan.)	294	CC 106
Manda (Tan.)	294	CH 107
Manda (Tan.)	301	BY 118
Mandamabwe	247	DH 103
Mandawa	285	CM 121
Mandelia	368	OA 334
Mandera	317	BK 126
Mandiakui	364	NZ 314
Mandiana	363	OB 310
Mandié	259	DA 110
Mandimba	271	CV 114
Mandini	221	EA 105
Mandji	386	OP 330
Mandoro	385	OJ 347
Mandou	365	OB 320
Mandumbua	253	CX 84
Mané	365	NZ 318
Maneia	260	DA 118
Maneromango	297	CG 120
Manfalut	347	NL 350
Manfran	378	OD 309
Manga	365	OA 318
Manga Grande	286	CF 68
Mangada	385	OJ 346
Mangaize	366	NX 321
Mangalmé	369	OA 339
Mangando	276	CJ 77
Mangango	267	CW 92
Mangbiwalu	304	BN 103
Mange	377	OD 306
Mangeigne	369	OB 340
Mangeni	220	DY 104
Mangetti	242	DE 80
Mango (Tan.)	283	CO 112
Mango (Tog.)	365	OC 319
Mangochi	271	CV 113
Mangodara	364	OC 314
Mangombe	389	OO 346
Mangu	307	BT 116
Mangungu	288	CC 76
Mangunza	256	CZ 97
Manguredjipa	304	BR 100
Mangwendi	258	DD 105
Manhiça	238	DS 108
Manhoca	229	DV 108
Mani	368	NZ 334
Mania-Mania	278	CK 90
Maniamba	271	CS 112
Manica (Moz.)	248	DE 108
Manica (Moz.)	249	DH 112
Manika	279	CO 94
Manjacaze	238	DR 110
Manjo	376	OH 329
Manjolo	269	CT 103
Manjou	382	OG 332
Mankayane	229	DV 105
Mankessim	380	OH 318
Manki II	382	OG 330
Mankim	382	OH 331
Mankono	379	OE 313
Mankranso	379	OF 317
Mankweng	236	DP 102
Mano	377	OE 307
Mano River	378	OF 308
Manono	292	CG 97
Manou	370	OC 341
Mansa	280	CP 100
Mansa Konko	362	NZ 304
Mansaba	362	OA 304
Mansfield	226	DU 92
Mansoa	362	OA 304
Mantare	299	BX 109
Manthestad	226	DX 92
Manubi	213	EG 100
Manyani	301	BY 119
Manyemen	376	OH 328
Manyinga	267	CT 91
Manyiseni	229	DV 107
Manyo	293	CF 104
Manyoni	295	CD 112
Manzengele	288	CF 78
Manzini	229	DV 105
Mao	368	NY 334
Maokeng	227	DX 97
Maope	235	DM 97
Mapai	237	DN 106
Mape	384	OH 342
Mapela	236	DP 100
Maphinhane	239	DM 113
Maphisa	246	DK 100
Mapholaneng	220	EA 100
Mapoteng	219	EA 98
Mapouka	384	OG 341
Mapulanguene	237	DQ 107
Mapumulo	221	EA 105
Mapunda	279	CL 92
Mapunga	268	CS 96
Maputo	229	DU 108
Maputsoe	219	DZ 98
Maquela do Zombo	287	CE 73
Maqueze	238	DQ 109
Mara	236	DO 102
Mara River	300	BU 113
Marabadiassa	379	OE 314
Maradah	345	NJ 338
Maradi	367	NY 326
Marafa	302	BY 122
Marais	211	EH 91
Marakesa	389	OL 346
Maraku	367	OB 328
Maralal	307	BP 116
Marali	383	OG 337
Marambo	284	CO 120
Marandet	367	NW 327
Marangu	301	BY 118
Marão	238	DQ 111
Marawan	335	NF 341
Marble Hall	228	DR 101
Marburg	220	ED 103
Marca (Merca)	310	BO 132
Marchand	216	DZ 83
Marchant	276	CL 78
Mareeq	319	BK 137
Mareetsane	226	DU 94
Marena	363	NX 308
Marendego	285	CJ 121
Marenge	293	CC 100
Marere	273	CQ 123
Mareth	333	ND 329
Margaretental	232	DN 80
Margate	220	ED 103
Maridi	312	BH 102
Mariental	223	DR 78
Mariga	366	OC 325
Marigat	306	BR 114
Marikana	227	DT 98
Marimba	276	CJ 77
Maringué	259	DC 111
Marite	229	DR 105
Marken	236	DP 99
Markounda	383	OE 336
Markoy	365	NX 319
Marnitz	236	DO 99
Maro	384	OE 338
Maroelaboom	242	DF 80
Maroelakop	227	DT 98
Marondera	258	DD 106
Marongora	257	CZ 101
Maroua	368	OB 333
Marquard	219	DZ 97
Marracua	260	DA 116
Marracuene	229	DT 108
Marrakech	329	NF 311
Marromeu	259	DD 114
Marrua	260	CZ 119
Marrupa	272	CT 117
Marsa al Buraygah	345	NH 339
Marsa Alam	348	NN 354
Marsa Fatma	373	NX 359
Marsa Shaab	360	NP 355
Marsabit	307	BN 119
Marsassaum	362	NZ 303
Marseilles	219	EA 97
Marshall	378	OG 308
Martap	382	OF 332
Marte	368	OA 333
Marthasput	217	EE 88
Marula	246	DH 99
Maruleng	245	DK 93
Marydale	217	EA 87
Marzuq	344	NM 333
Masagalu	296	CD 117
Masahunga	299	BW 109
Masaka	305	BS 106
Masaki	297	CG 120
Masalasef	369	OA 336
Masango	219	ED 96
Masanza	293	CB 103
Masase	247	DK 102
Masasi	284	CO 120
Mascara	331	NC 319
Maselspoort	219	EA 96
Maseru	219	EA 97
Masha	322	BB 113
Mashala	290	CC 88
Mashar	385	OD 346
Mashari	253	DC 83
Mashashane	236	DP 101
Mashava	247	DH 103
Mashi	367	NZ 327
Mashuru	301	BW 117
Masia	387	OQ 336
Masia-Mbio	387	OR 336
Masibi	226	DT 93
Masida	255	DC 90
Masi-Manimba	288	CB 78
Masimba	294	CH 109
Masindi	305	BO 106
Masingbi	377	OD 307
Masisi (DRC)	298	BU 100
Masisi (Lim.)	237	DM 104
Masoko	282	CL 110
Massaguet	368	OA 335
Massakory	368	NZ 335
Massamba	259	CY 110
Massanga	388	ON 341
Massangam	382	OH 330
Massangano	259	CZ 110
Massangena	248	DL 108
Massango	288	CH 75
Massangulo	271	CU 114
Massassa Lewemé	386	OQ 332
Massau	288	CG 76
Massawa	373	NW 359
Masseca	264	CW 80
Massembagne	369	OC 340
Massenya	368	OB 335
Massibi	278	CP 88
Massigui	364	OA 312
Massina	364	NY 314
Massinga	239	DO 113
Massingir	237	DP 107
Massosse	252	CX 78
Masuguru	284	CP 120
Masuika	290	CH 88
Masunga	246	DJ 97
Masvingo	247	DH 104
Maswa	300	BX 111
Maswehatshe	226	DV 90
Mata	290	CH 86
Mata Mondo	296	CE 116
Matadi	286	CD 69
Mataga	247	DJ 103
Matagania	363	OA 309
Matakankoro	283	CL 113
Matala (Ang.)	263	CW 72
Matala (DRC)	389	OR 346
Matale	298	BX 100
Matam	363	NW 306
Matamba	282	CK 110
Matameye	367	NZ 328
Matana	298	BZ 102
Matanda	280	CP 100
Matari	295	CC 112
Matassi	296	CH 115
Matatiele	220	EC 100
Matau	255	DD 90
Matchedje	271	CQ 114
Matchika	384	OG 340
Matechai	277	CO 83
Matekwe	284	CO 119
Matema (Moz.)	259	CY 110
Matema (Tan.)	282	CM 110
Matemwe	297	CD 121
Matende	253	DB 80
Matenga	259	CX 110
Matete	389	OL 347
Matetsi	255	DD 94
Mateur	333	NA 329
Matiakoali	365	OA 320
Matibane	273	CW 124
Matiliku	301	BV 118
Matima	244	DH 91
Matimira	283	CO 114
Matjiesfontein	209	EJ 84
Matjieskloof (N.C.)	209	EF 82
Matjieskloof (N.C.)	215	EB 78
Matjiesrivier	210	EJ 86
Matla	370	OC 342
Matlabas	235	DQ 97
Matlala	236	DP 101
Matlameng	219	DZ 99
Matlapaneng	244	DG 90
Matobo	246	DH 100
Matola	229	DT 107
Matombo	296	CG 118
Matome	263	CW 74
Matondavela	272	CR 116
Matondo	259	DD 113
Matonera	284	CJ 116
Matonga	255	DC 90
Matongo	300	CA 112
Matope (Mal.)	259	CX 112
Matope (Moz.)	260	DB 118
Matopi	244	DH 91
Matroosberg	209	EJ 82
Matru	377	OE 307
Matruh	336	NG 346
Matsanga	386	OP 332
Matsap	217	DZ 88
Matsari	382	OH 331
Matshaye	229	DR 105
Matshumbi	298	BU 100
Matsieng	219	EB 98
Matsiloje	246	DK 98
Maturia	295	CG 114
Maty-Centre	387	OR 335
Maua	307	BR 118
Maúa	272	CU 117
Mauchsberg	228	DS 104
Maué	253	DA 81
Mauengue	263	CV 71
Maulongo	387	OP 333
Maun	244	DH 89
Maunatlala	236	DN 98
Maungu	302	BZ 120
Mava	385	OK 346
Mavago	271	CR 115
Mavamba	237	DO 104
Mavanza	239	DN 113
Mavengue	253	DB 82
Mavimba	284	CJ 116
Mavinga	253	CY 83
Mavita	248	DG 109
Mavua	254	CX 87
Mavue	248	DK 107
Mavume	238	DO 112
Mavuradonha	258	DA 106
Mawa-Geti	385	OK 346
Mawana	244	DE 87
Mawanga	288	CE 77
Maxaas	319	BJ 135
Maxixe	239	DP 113
Mayahi	367	NY 327
Mayala	288	CG 78
Mayankwa	266	CV 90
Mayanti	269	CW 105
Maychew	373	NZ 359
Mayo Belwa	382	OD 331
Mayo Butale	382	OE 331
Mayo Chehu	382	OE 330
Mayo Darlé	382	OG 331
Mayo Djoi	383	OD 333
Mayo Faran	382	OD 331
Mayo Jarandi	382	OF 330
Mayo Oula	368	OC 333
Mayoko	386	OP 332
Mayuka	269	CP 104
Mayumba (DRC)	292	CF 99
Mayumba (Gab.)	386	OQ 329
Maza	368	OB 331
Mazabuka	256	CY 98
Mazamba	259	DD 112
Mazelogo	301	CA 119
Mazenod	219	EA 97
Mazeppa Bay	213	EG 100
Mazivila	238	DR 109
Mazombe	295	CH 114
Mazomeno	292	CB 97
Mazomora	297	CG 121
Mazowe	257	DB 104
Mazrub	371	NY 348
Mazua	273	CU 123
Mazunga	247	DL 102
Mba	382	OF 331
Mbabala	256	DA 96
Mbabane	229	DU 105
Mbacha	381	OE 327
Mbadi	386	OP 330
Mbaïki	383	OJ 337
Mbakaou	382	OG 332
Mbake	362	NX 303
Mbako	383	OJ 335
Mbala	281	CK 105
Mbalabala	246	DH 101
Mbalam	387	OL 333
Mbalambala	308	BS 121
Mbale	306	BP 111
Mbali (CAR)	383	OF 335
Mbali (CAR)	383	OF 337
Mbali (CAR)	384	OE 341
Mbalmayo	382	OJ 331
Mbama (Cam.)	382	OJ 332
Mbama (Con.)	387	OO 334
Mbamba	246	DE 99
Mbamba Bay	283	CP 112
Mbanda	386	OQ 330
Mbandaka	387	ON 337
Mbandjok	382	OJ 331
Mbandza	387	ON 334
Mbang	383	OJ 333
Mbang Foulbe	383	OF 333
Mbanga	376	OH 329
Mbangala (Tan.)	284	CK 116
Mbangala (Tan.)	296	CB 119
M'banza Congo	287	CE 71
Mbar	362	NX 303
Mbaragani	300	BY 110
Mbarangandu	284	CN 116
Mbarara	304	BT 104
Mbargue	382	OH 332
Mbari	386	OP 329
Mbarika	299	BX 108
Mbashe	212	EF 99
Mbashe Bridge	212	EF 99
Mbati	281	CP 104
Mbayo	387	OP 335
Mbazwana	229	DW 108
Mbé (Cam.)	383	OE 333
Mbé (Con.)	387	OQ 335
Mbekweni	209	EK 80
Mbeloba	384	OH 340
Mbembesi	246	DH 101
Mbengue	364	OC 313
Mberengwa	247	DJ 102
Mbesuma	282	CN 107
Mbet	382	OH 332
Mbeya (Tan.)	282	CK 109
Mbeya (Zam.)	270	CQ 109
Mbezi	297	CG 121
Mbiama	376	OH 325
Mbié	387	OP 334
Mbigou	386	OP 331
Mbinda	386	OP 332
Mbinga	283	CO 113
Mbini	376	OL 328
Mbirira	298	CA 103
Mbita	306	BS 111
Mbitakala	383	OE 334
Mbitom	382	OG 332
Mbizi	247	DK 104
Mbobo	270	CT 110
Mboke	382	OJ 332
Mboko	298	BZ 101
Mbolo	384	OE 340
Mbomo (Gab.)	386	ON 332
Mbomo (Con.)	387	ON 334
Mbon	387	OP 334
Mbonge	376	OJ 328
Mboro	389	OL 347
Mboroma	269	CV 102
Mbot	382	OG 330
Mbotyi	220	EE 102
Mboula (Cam.)	383	OF 333
Mboula (CAR)	383	OJ 336
Mbouma	382	OK 332
Mboundou Mbada	362	NX 304
Mboune	362	NX 305
Mboungo Badouma	386	OO 332
Mbour	362	NY 303
Mbout	363	NW 306
Mboyi	229	DV 107
Mboza	229	DW 107
Mbozi	282	CL 108
Mbrés	384	OF 339
Mbudi	288	CD 75
Mbuga Lugunya	300	BY 111
Mbuguni	301	BZ 116
Mbugwe	300	BZ 114
Mbuji-Mayi	290	CE 89
Mbulu	300	BZ 114
Mbulula	292	CD 97
Mbuma	385	OJ 344
Mbumi	297	CH 121
Mbutu	300	CA 110
Mbuyuni	296	CG 116
Mbuzi	270	CR 107
Mbwamaji	297	CF 121
Mbwawa	297	CF 120
Mbweni	297	CF 121
Mbwera	285	CJ 121
Mbwewe	296	CE 119
McGregor	209	EK 82
Mchichira	285	CO 122
Mchinga	285	CM 122
Mchinji	270	CU 108
M'Chouneche	332	NC 325
Mchukwi	297	CH 121
Mchungo	297	CH 121
McLear	258	DA 105
Mdabulo	283	CJ 113
Mdalula	294	CG 109
Mdandu	283	CL 112
Mdantsane	212	EH 98
Mdervi	283	CK 114
Mdogo	297	CE 121
Meadji	378	OH 312
Meadows	219	EA 96
Mecanhelas	259	CX 114
Mecca	361	NQ 359
Mechara	324	AZ 123
Mecheria	331	NE 319
Mechimere	368	NY 335
Mechra Bel Ksiri	330	NC 313
Mechroha	332	NB 327
Mecito	259	CZ 111
Meconta	261	CX 122
Mecúfi	273	CT 124
Mecula	272	CR 118
Médala	364	NW 313
Medea	331	NB 322
Medenine	333	NE 330
Mederdra	350	NV 303
Medi	312	BG 104
Media	272	CU 120
Medina Gounas	362	NZ 305
Medina Salembande	363	OA 307
Mediouna	329	NE 312
Medipane	227	DR 95
Medje	389	OL 346
Médouneu	386	OM 330
Mega	315	BJ 119
Megalo	324	BD 124
Mehal Ketema	373	OC 358
Mehdia	331	NC 321
Mehdiya Plage	329	ND 312
Meia Meia	295	CD 114
Meiganga	383	OF 333
Meineis	241	DK 73
Mejen Bel Abbes	333	NC 328
Mejez El Bab	333	NA 329
Mejo	380	OD 322
Mejong	376	OH 329
Mékambo	387	OM 333
Mekane Selam	373	OB 358
Mekel	383	OK 334
Mekele	373	NY 358
Mekhe	362	NX 303
Meki	324	BA 120
Mekmene Ben Amar	331	ND 318
Meknassy	333	NC 329
Meknes	330	ND 314
Meko	380	OF 322
Mekomo	382	OK 330
Meldougou	383	OG 333
Mele	370	OC 341
Melfi	369	OB 337
Melfort	258	DD 105
Melilla	330	NC 316
Melka Guba	316	BH 121
Melka Mari	316	BJ 124
Melkbosstrand	208	EK 79
Melkrivier	236	DP 99
Mellam	370	NZ 344
Mellish	209	EK 80
Mellit	370	NY 345
Melmoth	221	DZ 105
Melo	374	OC 361
Meloco	273	CU 121
Meltonwold	217	EE 88
Meluco	273	CS 122
Melunga	252	DB 75
Memaera	263	CV 74
Memba	273	CV 123
Membwe	282	CL 106
Memel	228	DX 102
Mena	364	OA 313
Menaa	332	NC 325
Ménaka	366	NW 321
Menawashei	370	NZ 344
Mendes	331	NB 320
Mendi	372	OC 354
Mendopolo	312	BH 104
Menga	263	CQ 73
Mengong	382	OK 331
Mengoub	330	NF 317
Mengueme	382	OK 331
Menongue	264	CW 78
Menouarar	330	NG 317
Menzel Hached	333	NC 329
Menzel Bourguiba	333	NA 329
Menzel Temime	333	NA 330
Mepala	287	CE 70
Mepica	271	CW 115
Meponda	271	CT 112
Merama Hill	298	BU 103
Mercado	274	CO 70
Mercoya	364	NY 311
Mereksen	343	NJ 329
Meri (Sen.)	362	NW 305
Meri (Cam.)	368	OB 333
Meridja	330	NF 316
Meringa	368	OB 331
Merino	228	DW 100
Merouana	332	NB 325
Merowe	360	NU 351
Merriman	218	EE 90
Merrivale	220	EB 103
Mersa Gulbub	373	NW 358
Merti	308	BP 120
Mertoutek	342	NO 324
Meru	307	BR 118
Merweville	210	EH 86
Mesa (Moz.)	273	CT 122
Mesa (N.W.)	227	DV 96
Mesaraba	389	OP 346
Meschetti	309	BQ 125
Meshra er Req	320	BA 101
Mesklip	215	EB 78
Meslo	324	BE 122
Messaad	332	ND 323
Messamena	382	OJ 332
Messok	383	OK 333
Metahara (Eth.)	324	AY 124
Metahara (Eth.)	324	AZ 122
Metana	261	DA 121
Metangobalame	271	CW 111
Metangula	271	CS 112
Metarica	272	CV 116
Metema	372	NZ 355
Metet	382	OK 331
Metil	261	CZ 121
Metlaoui	332	ND 327
Metlili Chaamba	332	NF 323
Metoro	273	CT 122
Metsera	389	OQ 345
Metu	322	BA 114
Metuge	273	CT 123
Mevang	386	ON 330
Mevedja	229	DT 108
Meyerton	227	DV 99
Meyerville	228	DV 101
Meyo Centre	382	OK 330
Mezzouna	333	NC 329
Mfou	382	OJ 331
Mfouati	387	OR 333
Mfrika	283	CL 113
Mfum	382	OG 328
Mgbidi	381	OG 326
Mgende	294	CB 105
Mgerere	299	BY 108
Mgeta	296	CG 118
Mgongila	295	CB 111
Mgori	295	CB 112
M'Guiden	342	NH 321
Mgunga	296	CE 115
Mgwali	212	EH 98
Mhamid	340	NH 314
Mhango	300	BX 110
Mhangura	257	DA 103
Mhinga	237	DN 104
Mhlambanyatsi	229	DU 105
Mhlosheni	229	DW 105
Mhlume	229	DU 106
Mhluzi	228	DT 101
Mhunze	300	BZ 110
Miaméré	384	OD 339
Miaroye	295	CE 112
Mibalaie	289	CC 84
Mica	237	DQ 104
Micaúne	260	DD 116
Midar	330	NC 315
Middelburg (E.C.)	211	EF 92
Middelburg (Mpum.)	228	DT 102
Middeldeel (F.S.)	219	DY 95
Middeldeel (F.S.)	226	DX 94
Middelfontein	228	DR 100
Middelpos	209	EF 83
Middelwit	227	DR 97
Middledrift	212	EH 96
Middleton	211	EH 94
Midelt	330	NE 314
Midrand	227	DT 99
Midyobo	376	OM 329
Miélékouka	387	OL 334
Mieliebelt	226	DV 94
Miembwe	284	CL 118
Migdol	226	DV 93
Migole	295	CG 114
Migori	306	BT 111
Miguruwe	284	CK 120
Mihama	295	CC 110
Mihawa	300	BZ 110
Mihumo Chini	284	CN 119
Mihungu	284	CL 119
Mikindani	285	CN 123
Mikumi	296	CG 116
Mila	332	NB 325
Milagasya	294	CE 107
Milambo	269	CQ 101
Milambo-Kabobo	280	CM 96
Milando	276	CK 77
Milange (Moz.)	259	CZ 114
Milange (DRC)	389	OR 346
Milarepa	271	CV 115
Milepa	294	CH 106
Milepa (Moz.)	271	CQ 115
Milhana	273	CV 121
Miliana	331	NB 321
Milimani	302	BV 124
Mille	373	OB 360
Miller	211	EJ 90
Millvale	227	DT 96
Milnerton	208	EK 79
Milo	283	CM 112
Milola	285	CN 121
Mima	296	CF 115
Mimongo	386	OP 331
Mimoun	331	NC 318
Mindjik	369	OC 340
Mindouli	387	OR 333
Mindourou	382	OJ 332
Minga (DRC)	280	CP 98
Minga (Zam.)	269	CV 105
Mingala	384	OH 341
Minganja	265	CR 83
Mingoyo	285	CN 122
Mingue	382	OH 332
Minguri	273	CW 124
Mininian	364	OC 311
Minissa	365	NZ 316
Minkamman	321	BE 105
Minna	367	OC 326
Minnaar	228	DU 101
Minnieskloof	217	EC 89
Minta	382	OH 332
Mintom II	382	OK 332
Minuf	347	NH 350
Minvoul	386	OL 331
Minziro	299	BU 106
Mirage	227	DW 96
Mirahi	284	CL 118
Mirimba	293	CC 100
Mirogi	306	BT 111
Mirria	367	NY 328
Mirrote	273	CU 122
Mirsale	319	BF 138
Mirui Chini	284	CM 120
Miruro	257	CX 104
Misaki	295	CC 111
Misau	367	OB 329
Misele	288	CB 77
Misgund	211	EK 90
Mishamo	293	CD 104
Misrak Gashamo	326	BA 133
Misratah	334	NF 334
Missao	260	CZ 116
Misseni	364	OC 313
Missira (Sen.)	363	NY 306
Missira (Sen.)	363	NZ 307
Missour	330	NE 315
Misty Mount	213	EF 100
Misughaa	295	CC 113
Misuku	282	CM 110
Misumba	388	OR 341
Misungwi	299	BX 109
Mitande	271	CV 115
Mitatib	372	NW 355
Miteda	273	CQ 122
Mitémbié	376	OM 328
Mitengi	285	CN 122
Mitole (Tan.)	285	CK 121
Mitole (Tan.)	285	CL 121
Mitomoni	283	CP 113
Mitumba	294	CG 105
Mitumbati	284	CL 120
Mitundu	294	CC 108
Mitwaba	280	CK 97
Mityana	305	BR 107
Mitzic	386	OM 331
Miya	367	OB 329
Mizan Teferi	322	BD 114
Mizdah	333	NG 332
Mjara	330	NC 314
Mkalama	300	CA 112
Mkambati	220	EE 103
Mkanga	295	CG 111
Mkasa	282	CM 106
Mkasi	282	CM 108
Mkata (Tan.)	284	CM 118
Mkata (Tan.)	296	CD 119
Mkinga	294	CD 109
Mkoani	297	CC 122
Mkofwa	296	CG 115
Mkokoni	303	BV 125
Mkokotoni	297	CD 121
Mkomazi	296	CB 119
Mkondowe	283	CO 111
Mkonjowano	285	CO 122
Mkowe	281	CJ 105
Mkowela	284	CO 119
Mkuchika	284	CO 119
Mkujani	297	CB 120
Mkulazi	296	CG 119
Mkulwe	282	CK 107
Mkumburu	296	CE 116
Mkunumbi	302	BW 124
Mkunya	284	CM 119
Mkuranga	297	CG 121
Mkurusi	295	CC 111
Mkushi	269	CU 101
Mkushi River	269	CU 102
Mkuze	229	DX 106
Mkwaja	297	CD 120
Mkwasine	247	DJ 106
Mlali (Tan.)	296	CE 116
Mlali (Tan.)	296	CF 118
Mlandizi	297	CF 120
Mlawula	229	DU 106
Mlibizi	256	DC 97
Mlimba	283	CK 114
Mloa	295	CH 113
Mloka	296	CH 119
Mloli	229	DV 108
Mlolo	270	CV 107
Mlowoka	284	CM 119
Mmabatho	226	DT 94
Mmamabula	235	DP 96
Mmashoro	245	DL 96
Mmathethe	226	DS 93
Mmatshumo	245	DK 94
Mnanzi	301	CA 119
Mnenya	295	CB 114
Mngaa	295	CB 112
Mnongodi	285	CO 122
Mnyani	226	DV 92
Moamba	229	DT 107
Moanda (Ang.)	286	CD 67
Moanda (Gab.)	386	OP 332
Moatize	259	CZ 110
Moba	293	CG 102
Mobaye	384	OJ 340
Mochudi	235	DQ 95
Mocimboa da Praia	285	CP 123
Mocimboa do Rovuma	285	CP 121
Moco	263	CU 73
Mocoduene	239	DP 113
Mocuba	260	DA 117
Mocubúri	272	CW 120
Modderrivier	218	EA 92
Modimolle (Nylstroom)	227	DR 99
Moebase	261	DB 120
Moeng	236	DN 98
Moeswal	225	DX 88
Mofu	281	CP 103
Moga	389	OP 346
Mogadishu	310	BO 133
Mogalakwenastroom	236	DP 100
Moganyaka	228	DR 102
Mogapi	236	DM 98
Mogapinyana	235	DM 97
Moghrar	331	NE 318
Mogincual	261	CY 124
Mogorosi	235	DM 96
Mogroum	368	OB 335
Mogwadi(Dendron)	236	DO 101
Mogwase	227	DS 97
Mohales Hoek	219	EC 97
Moham madia	331	NB 319
Mohambe	238	DR 109
Mohamed Goha	284	CK 116
Mohammedia	329	ND 311
Mohenge	295	CB 111
Mohoro	285	CJ 121
Moiben	306	BQ 113
Moimba	250	DA 69
Moïssala	383	OE 337
Mojo	324	AZ 121
Mokala	291	CC 94
Mokambo	268	CR 99
Mokamole	236	DP 100
Mokgomane	226	DT 93
Mokhotlong	220	EA 101
Mokimbo	292	CE 99
Moknine	333	NB 330
Mokobeng	236	DO 98
Mokolo	368	OB 333
Mokopane (Potgietersrus)	236	DQ 100
Mokopung	219	EB 98
Mokoro	235	DN 97
Mokouango	387	ON 336
Mokowe	302	BW 124
Mokwa	381	OD 324
Mola	275	CK 75
Molape	244	DL 90
Molatswane	244	DH 87
Mole	282	CL 109
Molegbe	384	OJ 340
Molenrivier	210	EK 88
Molepolole	235	DQ 94
Moletsane	219	EA 99
Moliro	281	CJ 104
Molo	306	BS 114
Moloporivier	226	DT 91
Moloto	228	DS 100
Moloundou	387	OL 334
Molteno	219	EE 95
Molumbo	260	CX 115
Molume	379	OD 317
Molwe	267	CQ 94
Moma (DRC)	290	CG 88
Moma (Moz.)	261	DA 121
Momaligi	377	OE 306
Momba	256	CX 99
Mombasa (Ken.)	301	BV 118
Mombasa (Ken.)	302	CA 122
Mombo	296	CB 119
Mombombo	384	OK 340
Mompanga	388	OM 340
Mon Desir	241	DF 73
Monametsana	235	DQ 95
Monapo	273	CW 123
Monastir	333	NB 330
Monatele	382	OJ 330
Monbore	383	OD 333
Mondo	368	NY 334
Mondombe	388	OO 342
Monduli	301	BY 116
Monga	384	OJ 342
Mongalla	313	BG 106
Mongemputu	388	OR 339
Mongeri	377	OE 307
Mongo	369	OA 338
Mongomo	386	OL 330
Mongonu	368	NZ 333
Mongoroma	295	CB 114
Mongororo	370	OA 341
Mongoumba	384	OJ 338
Mongu	254	CX 89
Mongua	251	DA 73
Monguel	351	NV 306
Monjuku	388	OP 340
Monkey Bay	271	CV 113
Monkoto	388	OP 340
Monrovia	378	OG 308
Montagu	209	EK 83
Monte Belo	263	CR 71
Monte Christo	236	DO 98
Montepuez	273	CT 121
Montevideo	219	DY 98
Montipa	262	CW 69
Monze	256	CZ 97
Mooi River	220	EA 103
Mooifontein (N.W.)	226	DU 94
Mooifontein (Nam.)	223	DU 76
Mooigeleë	227	DX 98
Mooivlei	228	DU 102
Mookaneng	225	DX 89
Mooketsi	237	DP 103
Mookgophong (Naboomspruit)	228	DR 100
Moolman	228	DW 104
Moorreesburg	209	EJ 80
Mopane	236	DN 102
Mopeia	259	DC 114
Mopipi	245	DK 92
Mopti	364	NY 315
Mora	368	OB 333
Morebeng (Soekmekaar)	236	DP 102
Moremaoto	244	DH 91
Morewag	242	DK 78
Morgan's Bay	212	EH 99
Morgenster Mission	247	DH 104
Morgenzon	228	DV 102
Moribaya	363	OC 309
Moridjo	307	BP 116
Morija	219	EB 98
Morijo	300	BV 114
Moriki	366	NZ 325
Morire	259	DA 113
Morobo	312	BK 104
Morogoro	296	CF 118
Morokweng	226	DU 90
Morondo	378	OD 312
Morone	228	DR 103
Moronou	379	OG 314
Moroto	314	BM 112
Morouba	384	OG 339
Morristown	219	EE 97
Morrola	272	CT 120
Morrumbala	259	DB 114
Morrumbene	239	DP 113
Morrungulo	239	DO 114
Mortimer	211	EG 94
Moruita	306	BO 112
Morungu	299	CA 105
Morupule	235	DM 97
Morwamosu	234	DQ 89
Mosetse	245	DJ 96
Moshaneng	226	DR 93
Moshesh's Ford	219	ED 98
Moshi (Zam.)	267	CV 95
Moshi (Tan.)	301	BY 117
Mosiro	301	BU 115

Mosita > Oasis

PLACE NAME	PG	GRID
Mosita	226	DU 92
Mosite	389	OM 343
Mosopo	226	DR 93
Mossel Bay	210	EL 87
Mossendjo	386	OQ 332
Mossiesdal	228	DS 102
Mossuril	273	CW 124
Mostagamen	331	NB 319
Mota	373	OB 357
Motenge-Boma	384	OK 338
Motetema	228	DS 102
Mothae	220	DZ 100
Mothibistad	225	DW 89
Motkop	219	ED 97
Motokwe	234	DQ 89
Motomonho	261	CX 123
Motril	330	NA 315
Motshikiri	227	DS 97
Motwa	388	ON 338
Mouanko	376	OJ 329
Moudjéria	351	NU 307
Mouenda	386	OQ 330
Mougamou	386	OO 331
Mouila	386	OP 330
Mouka	384	OF 341
Moulares	332	NC 327
Moulay Bousselham	329	NC 312
Mouléngui	386	OQ 331
Moulhoule	374	NZ 362
Mouli Pouli	386	OO 331
Moulvouday	368	OC 334
Mounana	386	OO 332
Moundou	383	OD 335
Moungoundou-sud	386	OQ 332
Mounguel	383	OE 333
Mount Alida	220	EA 103
Mount Ayliff	220	ED 101
Mount Darwin	258	DA 106
Mount Fletcher	220	ED 100
Mount Frere	220	ED 101
Mount Pelaan	228	DX 101
Mount Rupert	218	DY 91
Mount Stewart	211	EJ 92
Moura	369	NY 340
Mourdiah	364	NY 312
Mourindi	386	OQ 330
Mousgougou	368	OB 335
Mou-soayah	377	OD 306
Moussadey	366	NZ 322
Moussoro	368	NY 335
Mousssaya	363	OB 309
Moutouroua	368	OC 333
Mouyabi	386	ON 331
Mouzarak	368	NZ 335
Mouzondzi	387	OR 333
Möwe Bay	240	DF 68
Mowers	209	EK 82
Moxico	265	CQ 83
Moya	372	NZ 352
Moyale	316	BL 121
Moyamba	377	OE 306
Moyeni (Quthing)	219	EC 98
Moyenne-Sido	384	OE 338
Moyo	313	BK 106
Moyto	369	NZ 336
Mozambique	261	CX 124
Mpaem	380	OF 319
Mpaka	229	DU 106
Mpala	293	CF 102
Mpana	380	OD 318
Mpanda	294	CE 105
Mpanda Ndogo	293	CE 104
Mpanga	296	CH 118
Mpanta	281	CP 102
Mpara	285	CK 122
Mpase	388	ON 339
Mpataba	379	OH 317
Mpatora	284	CL 120
Mpé	387	OQ 334
Mpemvana	228	DX 104
Mpenja	305	BR 107
Mpepaya	283	CP 113
Mpepo	281	CP 105
Mpepu	235	DQ 95
Mpessoba	364	NZ 313
Mpethu	212	EH 99
Mphaki	219	EC 99
Mphoengs	246	DK 98
Mpigi	305	BR 107
Mpika	269	CQ 105
Mpinga	257	DC 104
Mpitimbo	283	CO 114
Mpo	388	OR 338
Mpoko	387	OR 337
Mpolweni	220	EA 103
Mponela	270	CU 110
Mpongwe	268	CU 99
Mpophomeni	229	DW 108
Mporaloko	376	OO 328
Mporokoso	281	CL 103
Mposa	221	DZ 107
Mpouya	387	OQ 335
Mpraeso	380	OF 318
Mpui	282	CJ 106
Mpulungu	281	CK 105
Mpumalanga	220	EB 103
Mpume	388	OR 338
Mpumulwane	221	EA 105
Mpungu (Nam.)	252	DC 79
Mpungu (DRC)	388	OR 339
Mpurukasese	283	CN 115
Mputi	212	EG 99
Mpwapwa	296	CE 116
Mqanduli	213	EF 100
Mqwabe	228	DX 104
Mrirt	330	NE 313
Msaka	271	CV 112
Msakala	297	CB 120
Msaken	333	NB 329
Msalalo	295	CD 111
Msangano	282	CK 108
Msata	296	CE 119
Mseleni	229	DW 108
Msembe	295	CH 112
M'Sila	332	NB 324
Msisi	294	CE 109
Msomemi	285	CJ 121
Msoro	270	CU 106
Msowera	296	CF 117
Msumbisi	296	CF 118
Msuna	256	DD 96
Mtagata	298	BU 104
Mtama	285	CN 121
Mtandi	285	CM 121
Mtandika	296	CH 115
Mtandikeni	297	CB 121
Mtandura	285	CL 122
Mtanza	296	CH 119
M'telela	271	CS 115
Mtembur	306	BP 113
Mtemere Gate	296	CH 119
Mtende	297	CE 122
Mthatha	213	EF 100
Mthonjeni	229	DW 107
Mtimbira	283	CK 115
Mtinko	295	CB 112
Mtito Andei	301	BX 119
Mto Wa Mbu	300	BY 114
Mtonya	283	CN 115
Mtopwa	285	CO 122
Mtubatuba	221	DY 107
Mtunzini	221	DZ 106
Mtwalume	220	ED 104
Mtwango	283	CK 112
Mtwara	285	CN 123
Mua	265	CS 82
Muacavula	276	CO 79
Muachinongue	276	CK 79
Muaguide	273	CR 122
Mualadzi	270	CV 109
Mualama (Moz.)	260	DA 119
Mualama (Moz.)	260	DB 118
Muangimba	277	CN 81
Muanza (Ang.)	288	CF 75
Muanza (Moz.)	249	DE 112
Muanzanza	289	CF 84
Muapula	272	CU 117
Muatechiamba	277	CM 83
Muatua	261	CY 122
Mubambe	279	CP 94
Mubayira	257	DD 104
Mubende	305	BQ 105
Mubi	368	OC 332
Mubuku	304	BR 103
Muchena	259	CY 110
Muchenje	255	DC 92
Muchinka	269	CS 104
Mucojo	273	CR 123
Muconda	277	CO 85
Muconga	275	CN 72
Mucope	251	CZ 72
Mucoque	249	DL 113
Mucubela	260	DA 118
Mucumbura	258	CZ 106
Mucundi	252	CZ 78
Mucupia	260	DD 116
Mucusso	254	DD 85
Mucussueje	278	CP 87
Muda	248	DF 111
Muden	220	DZ 103
Mudiandambo	290	CD 85
Mudu	368	OA 333
Mudzonga	258	DB 107
Muecate	273	CW 122
Mueda	273	CQ 122
Muela	272	CU 117
Muembe	271	CT 114
Muende	270	CV 109
Mueto	276	CJ 77
Mufaya	267	CW 91
Mufulira	268	CS 99
Mugango	300	BV 110
Mugeta	300	BV 111
Mugewo	293	CE 104
Mugina	298	CA 102
Muglad	371	OB 347
Mugulama	260	CZ 118
Mugunzu	298	BZ 104
Muhaga	283	CJ 115
Muhagiriya	370	OA 345
Muhala	293	CD 100
Muhammad Qol	361	NR 356
Muhembo	254	DD 86
Muheza	297	CC 120
Muhoroni	306	BS 113
Muhukuru	283	CP 114
Muhula	273	CV 121
Muhulu	389	OO 346
Muhuro	300	BU 111
Muhutwe	299	BV 106
Muico	273	CT 121
Muidumbe	273	CQ 123
Muié	265	CV 83
Muine	254	DB 85
Muite	273	CV 121
Muizenberg	209	EL 80
Mujiji	299	BW 108
Muka Turi	324	AY 120
Mukala	288	CC 78
Mukanga	290	CE 85
Mukebo	292	CF 99
Mukopa	269	CU 103
Mukubwe	268	CU 98
Mukuku	269	CR 102
Mukulakulu	279	CM 94
Mukundi	292	CD 98
Mukunsa	281	CL 102
Mukupa Kaoma	281	CM 104
Mukwikile	282	CP 106
Mulanda	306	BQ 110
Mulanga (DRC)	293	CH 101
Mulanga (Zam.)	282	CO 107
Mulanje	259	CZ 113
Mulati	237	DP 104
Muleba	299	BV 106
Mulele	254	DA 89
Mulembe	298	BZ 100
Mulengu	281	CL 103
Mulevala	260	CZ 118
Mulilansolo	282	CN 107
Mulobezi	255	DA 93
Mulondo (Ang.)	251	CY 73
Mulondo (Uga.)	305	BP 109
Mulongo	292	CH 97
Mulu	324	AY 124
Mulungushi	268	CW 100
Mulungwe	269	CU 102
Muluzia	281	CJ 101
Muma	384	OK 342
Mumallah	370	OB 344
Mumbeji (Zam.)	266	CU 90
Mumbeji (Zam.)	266	CV 89
Mumbolo	280	CL 97
Mumbondo	275	CN 71
Mumbué	264	CU 77
Mumbwa	268	CW 97
Mumena	267	CQ 95
Mumias	306	BR 112
Mumoma	290	CG 88
Munanga	279	CM 93
Munda	250	CZ 69
Mundemba	376	OH 328
Mundri	312	BG 103
Munene	288	CE 76
Mungári	259	DB 110
Mungatsi	306	BQ 111
Mungbere (DRC)	312	BM 100
Mungbere (DRC)	385	OK 347
Mungo (Ang.)	263	CQ 75
Mungo (Ang.)	289	CH 82
Mungulanga	279	CO 91
Munhamba	253	DA 83
Munhango	264	CR 80
Muniungu	288	CD 76
Munkumpu	268	CU 98
Munnik	236	DP 102
Munroe	297	CF 121
Munster	220	ED 103
Munterne	305	BP 105
Muntu	305	BO 108
Mununga (Zam.)	281	CL 101
Mununga (Zam.)	281	CO 101
Munyu	212	EF 99
Munywini	220	EB 103
Muoco	272	CU 116
Muongo	277	CM 81
Mupa	251	CZ 74
Mupeco	264	CV 79
Muquitixe	275	CN 73
Murahilato	251	CZ 70
Muramvya	298	BY 102
Murang'a	307	BT 117
Murangering	314	BK 114
Murewa	258	DC 106
Muriege	277	CM 85
Murka	301	BY 118
Murombedzi	257	DC 103
Murraysburg	211	EF 90
Murroa	260	DB 118
Murrupula	261	CX 120
Murusagamba	298	BY 104
Musadi	388	OQ 342
Musala	363	OC 307
Musasa	299	BY 106
Muse	294	CH 106
Musenge (DRC)	278	CK 88
Musenge (DRC)	389	OP 347
Mushenge	290	CB 85
Mushie	387	OQ 336
Mushima	267	CV 92
Mushipashi	281	CP 105
Mushoshi	268	CQ 98
Mushumbi Pools	257	CZ 104
Musin	380	OG 322
Musina (Messina)	237	DM 103
Musmar	360	NU 355
Musofu	268	CU 100
Musoma	300	BU 110
Musongoie	279	CL 91
Musoro	269	CT 104
Mussanzo	275	CN 72
Mussende	275	CO 75
Mussolo	276	CN 77
Mussuma	266	CV 86
Mustechigimo	277	CK 84
Musukubili	254	DD 89
Musumba	278	CJ 88
Muswani	237	DO 104
Mut	347	NN 348
Mutala	260	CY 118
Mutambara (Bur.)	298	CA 102
Mutambara (Zim.)	248	DG 108
Mutanda	267	CR 95
Mutango	253	DC 83
Mutarara	259	DB 113
Mutare	248	DF 108
Mutasa	248	DE 108
Mutenge	268	CS 99
Mutepatepa	258	DA 105
Mutha	301	BV 119
Mutiene	387	OR 335
Mutimutema	257	DC 100
Mutinde	293	CB 103
Mutir	313	BM 105
Mutoko	258	DB 107
Mutombomukulu	291	CH 91
Mutomo	301	BV 119
Mutorashanga	257	DB 104
Mutoto (DRC)	290	CD 88
Mutoto (DRC)	293	CH 101
Mutshatsha	279	CO 91
Mutúali	272	CW 117
Mutukula	305	BT 105
Mutum Biyu	382	OD 330
Mutum Daya	382	OD 330
Mutumbi	292	CH 99
Mutumbo	264	CT 77
Mutumieque	250	CZ 69
Mutundi	282	CL 107
Mutungu	281	CJ 103
Mutungu-Tari	288	CE 78
Mutwanga	304	BR 102
Muxima	274	CM 70
Muxungue	248	DJ 111
Muyange	298	BX 103
Muyinga	298	BX 103
Muyoba	255	DC 91
Muyombe	282	CO 109
Muyuka	376	OJ 329
Muyumba	292	CG 97
Muzarabani	258	CZ 105
Muze	258	CX 105
Mvam	376	ON 329
Mvangan	382	OK 331
Mvelabusha	229	DW 108
Mveng	383	OK 333
Mvengue	382	OK 330
Mvera	271	CU 111
Mvolo	320	BE 102
Mvomero	296	CE 118
Mvozana	220	EA 104
Mvuha	296	CG 118
Mvuma	247	DF 104
Mvumi	295	CF 114
Mvumi Makulu	295	CE 114
Mvurwi	257	DA 104
Mwabungu	302	CA 122
Mwadi- Kalumbu	289	CH 80
Mwadi-Katoloka	291	CG 94
Mwadui	300	BZ 110
Mwakaleli	282	CL 110
Mwakatemos	282	CJ 110
Mwala wa Mphini	271	CV 113
Mwali Gbangba	383	OK 336
Mwalika	300	BX 110
Mwamashele	300	BZ 110
Mwambo	285	CO 123
Mwanahaza	297	CD 121
Mwanga	301	BZ 117
Mwangalala	280	CP 98
Mwango	291	CF 91
Mwanisenga	294	CD 108
Mwanza (DRC)	292	CH 96
Mwanza (Mal.)	259	CY 112
Mwanza (Tan.)	299	BX 108
Mwatate	301	BZ 119
Mwaya	284	CK 116
Mwazye	282	CK 106
Mweiga	307	BS 116
Mweka	290	CB 86
Mwele	297	CB 120
Mwembeshi	256	CX 98
Mwenda (DRC)	268	CR 100
Mwenda (Zam.)	281	CN 101
Mwene-Bijl	278	CK 87
Mwene-Ditu	290	CF 89
Mwenezi	247	DK 104
Mwenga	389	OQ 347
Mwense	280	CN 100
Mwilambwe	279	CJ 92
Mwimbi	282	CK 106
Mwingi	307	BT 119
Mwinilunga	267	CQ 91
Mwisi	294	CB 109
Mwitika	301	BU 119
Mwitikira	295	CE 114
Myanzi	305	BR 106
Mynfontein	218	ED 90
Mzawa	282	CJ 110
Mzenga	297	CF 120
Mziha	296	CD 118
Mzimba	270	CQ 110
Mzinga	296	CF 118
Mzuzu	271	CQ 111
Naala	368	NZ 334
Naam	371	OC 348
Naam Okora	313	BL 109
Naama	331	NE 319
Nababeep	215	EB 78
Naberera	301	CA 117
Nabeul	333	NB 330
Nabies	216	DZ 83
Nabilatuk	306	BN 112
Nabingora	305	BR 105
Naboga	365	OC 318
Nabou	365	OB 316
Nabuganyi	305	BQ 108
Nabusanke	305	BS 107
Nabwalya	270	CR 106
Nacala	273	CW 124
Nacaroa	273	CV 122
Nachingwea	284	CN 120
Nacumua	272	CV 117
Nadawali	365	OC 316
Nador	330	NC 316
Nafada	367	OB 330
Nafadji	363	NZ 307
Naga	340	NK 311
Nagara	363	NX 308
Nagichot	313	BJ 109
Nagojje	305	BR 108
Nagpotpot	314	BH 110
Nahone	252	DA 75
Naiopue	260	CY 117
Nairobi	301	BU 116
Nairoto	273	CR 121
Naivasha	307	BT 115
Naiwangaa	285	CK 121
Nakanya	255	CX 90
Nakapanya	284	CO 118
Nakaseka	305	BQ 107
Nakasongola	305	BP 107
Nakfa	361	NV 358
Nakhl	348	NH 353
Naki-Est	365	OB 319
Nakiloro	314	BM 112
Nakitoma	305	BO 107
Nakiwa	258	DB 106
Nakonde	282	CL 108
Nakop	216	DY 83
Nakosa	269	CT 103
Nakpanduri	365	OB 319
Nakuijit	306	BO 113
Nakuru	307	BS 115
Nalazi	238	DQ 109
Nalut	333	NF 330
Namaacha	229	DT 107
Namacala	272	CW 119
Namacunde	251	DB 74
Namacurra	260	DB 116
Namajani	284	CO 120
Namakgale	237	DP 105
Namalulu	301	CA 117
Namanga	301	BX 116
Namanyere	294	CG 105
Namapa	273	CU 122
Namaponda	261	CY 122
Namarròi	260	CY 116
Namasagali	305	BP 109
Namasale	305	BO 108
Namatakwarra	243	DG 84
Nambazo	259	CY 114
Nambinda	284	CM 118
Nambiranji	285	CM 121
Namboukaha	364	OC 314
Nambuangongo	275	CJ 71
Nambunga	285	CO 121
Nambunju	284	CM 120
Nambwa	284	CN 118
Nametil	261	CY 121
Namialo	273	CW 122
Namib	230	DN 72
Namibe	250	CX 67
Namichiga	285	CM 121
Namidobe	260	DC 117
Namies	216	EA 81
Namina	272	CW 120
Namitete	270	CV 109
Namon	365	OC 320
Nampala	364	NX 314
Nampevo	260	CZ 117
Nampula	261	CX 121
Namuhi	285	CN 122
Namuiranga	285	CO 123
Namukumbo	256	CX 97
Namunda	285	CN 122
Namuno	272	CU 120
Namutoni	241	DE 76
Namuxinda	289	CG 83
Namwala	256	CY 95
Namwera	271	CV 113
Namwiwa	306	BP 110
Nana	383	OF 334
Nana Bakassa	383	OF 336
Nana Candundo	266	CQ 89
Nandi	247	DK 106
Nandom	365	OB 316
Nanga Eboko	382	OH 331
Nangade	285	CP 122
Nanganga	285	CN 121
Nangano	284	CN 120
Nangaru	285	CM 121
Nangbeto	380	OF 321
Nangolet	314	BH 110
Nangomba	284	CO 120
Nangua	284	CO 119
Nangulangwa	284	CJ 120
Nangurukuru	285	CK 121
Nanguruwe	285	CO 123
Nanjavina	251	DA 70
Nanjirinji	285	CM 121
Nankoma	306	BR 110
Nankova	253	CZ 80
Nansio	299	BW 108
Nantulo	272	CS 120
Nanyamba	285	CO 122
Nanyuki	307	BR 116
Naos	231	DO 76
Napaha	272	CT 120
Napeitom	307	BO 115
Napier	209	EM 82
Nara	364	NX 312
Narena	363	OA 310
Narib	232	DQ 78
Nariep	215	ED 78
Naro Moru	307	BS 117
Narok	300	BU 114
Narosura	300	BV 114
Narubis	224	DV 80
Nasarawa (Nig.)	366	OA 325
Nasarawa (Nig.)	381	OD 327
Nasia	365	OC 318
Nasir	321	AZ 109
Nasmah	333	NG 332
Nasondoye	279	CN 93
Nassian (Ct'l.)	379	OD 315
Nassian (Ct'l.)	379	OE 315
Nata (Bot.)	245	DH 95
Nata (Tan.)	300	BW 111
Natchamba	380	OD 319
Nathenje	270	CV 110
Natia-boani	365	OA 320
Natitingou	365	OC 320
Natukoma	254	CZ 87
Nauchas	231	DP 75
Nauela	260	CX 117
Naulila	251	DB 72
Navrongo	365	OB 318
Nawinda Kuta	255	DA 91
Nayuchi	271	CW 114
Nazombe	284	CP 120
Nazret	324	AZ 121
Nbâk	350	NV 304
Nbeika	351	NU 307
Ncanara	211	EK 94
Ncaute	253	DD 82
Nchanga	268	CS 98
Nchelenge	280	CL 100
Nchenachena	282	CO 110
Ncojane	233	DO 83
Ncue	376	OL 329
Ndabeni	229	DW 107
Ndagaa	297	CE 121
Ndala	294	CB 109
Ndalambo	282	CL 108
N'dalantando	275	CL 72
Ndali	366	OC 322
Ndambissoa	384	OG 342
Ndanda (Tan.)	285	CO 121
Ndanda (CAR)	384	OH 341
Ndande	362	NX 303
Ndanga	383	OJ 337
Ndangane	362	NY 302
Ndangui	386	OO 332
Ndareda	300	CA 114
Ndedo	296	CB 116
Ndedu	312	BL 100
Ndeji	381	OD 324
Ndekesha	290	CE 87
Ndélé	384	OE 339
Ndelele	383	OJ 334
Ndembe	382	OH 332
Ndembo	284	CM 118
Ndenbera	282	CO 110
Ndendé	386	OP 331
Ndia	363	NX 306
Ndiago	362	NW 303
Ndiguina	368	OA 334
Ndikinimeki	382	OH 330
Ndikoko	382	OH 330
Ndikwe	220	DZ 104
Ndim	383	OF 335
Ndindi (Sen.)	362	NX 303
Ndindi (Gab.)	386	OR 330
Ndioum Guent	362	NY 304
Ndiri	384	OE 340
Nditam	382	OH 330
Ndiya	376	OH 327
N'djamena	368	OA 334
Ndjole	382	OH 331
Ndjolé	386	ON 330
Ndok	383	OE 334
Ndokama	376	OJ 329
Ndokayo	383	OH 333
Ndola	268	CS 100
Ndom	382	OJ 330
Ndon Kota	383	OG 336
Ndonga	253	DC 83
Ndongolo	386	OM 331
Ndop	382	OG 329
Ndoumbou	383	OF 337
Ndoussi	379	OG 314
Ndu	382	OG 330
Nduguti	300	CA 112
Nduluku	301	BV 118
Ndumbwe	285	CN 122
Ndumo	229	DV 107
Ndunda	282	CO 109
Ndundu	297	CH 120
Ndundulu	221	DZ 106
Ndwedwe	221	EB 105
Nebbou	365	OB 317
Nebo	228	DR 102
Nebulu	389	OL 346
Necungas	259	CZ 111
Necuto	286	CB 68
Nedatra	373	OB 357
Nefas Meewcha	373	OA 358
Nefta	332	ND 327
Nega Nega	256	CY 99
Negage	287	CH 73
Negala	364	NZ 311
Negansi	366	OB 323
Negele	316	BG 122
Negezi	300	BZ 110
Negola	263	CV 72
Negomane	284	CP 120
Negrine	332	ND 327
Neilersdrif	216	DZ 84
Nekemte	323	AY 116
Nelspoort	210	EG 89
Nelspruit	228	DT 104
Néma	352	NV 312
Nepara	252	DC 79
Neriquinha	254	CY 85
Nessona	249	DE 114
Netia	273	CW 122
Neuras	231	DQ 75
Neushek	216	DZ 84
Nevada	219	EB 96
Neves	376	ON 326
New Amalfi	220	EC 101
New England	219	ED 98
New Featherstone	247	DE 105
New Halfa	372	NX 354
New Hanover	220	EA 103
New Machavie	227	DV 96
Newala	285	CO 121
Newcastle	228	DX 102
Newington	229	DR 105
Newtown	217	DZ 88
Ngabé	387	OQ 335
Ngabeni	220	ED 102
Ngabwe	268	CV 97
Ngagau	283	CJ 114
Ngaide II	369	OC 340
Ngala (Alg.)	368	OA 333
Ngala (CAR)	384	OH 340
Ngalia	384	OG 341
Ngalwa	368	NY 332
Ngam (Cha.)	368	OC 335
Ngam (Cam.)	383	OF 334
Ngama (Cha.)	369	OA 336
Ngama (DRC)	384	OH 340
Ngambé	382	OJ 330
Ngambe Tikar	382	OG 331
Ngamdu	368	OA 331
Nganda (Tan.)	283	CL 112
Nganda (Sen.)	362	NY 304
Ngandana	364	OC 313
Ngangala	313	BH 106
Ngangora	284	CM 119
Nganji	389	OP 346
Nganzi	286	CD 67
Ngaoundal	382	OG 332
Ngaoundéré	383	OF 333
Ngara (Mal.)	283	CN 111
Ngara (Tan.)	298	BW 104
Ngarama	298	BV 103
Ngarangou	368	NY 334
Ngasumet	301	CA 117
Ngatataik	301	BW 116
Ngato	383	OK 334
Ngbala	387	OL 334
Ngcobo	212	EF 98
Ngelani	301	BU 117
Ngerengere	296	CF 119
Nghobora	300	BX 110
Ngiapanda	297	CE 120
Ngidinga	287	CD 73
Ngina	385	OK 346
Nginyang	307	BQ 115
Ngo	387	OP 335
Ngoa	312	BM 100
Ngog Mapubi	382	OJ 330
Ngogwe	305	BR 109
Ngogweni	221	DY 105
Ngoila	383	OK 333
Ngoilanga	283	CL 115
Ngoko	387	OO 335
Ngola	383	OK 334
Ngolo	281	CM 105
Ngoma (Nam.)	255	DC 92
Ngoma (Uga.)	305	BP 107
Ngomba	282	CJ 108
Ngome	229	DX 105
Ngomedzap	382	OK 330
Ngong (Ken.)	301	BU 116
Ngong (Cam.)	383	OD 333
Ngonga	376	OJ 329
Ngongo	282	CK 107
Ngongoro	300	CA 110
Ngonini	229	DT 105
Ngora	306	BP 110
Ngorengore	300	BU 114
Ngoro	382	OH 330
Ngororero	298	BV 102
Ngoso	289	CB 81
Ngoto	383	OJ 336
Ngoubi	384	OF 341
Ngoui	362	NW 305
Ngoulemakong	382	OK 330
Ngouma	365	NW 316
Ngouni	387	OO 333
Ngoura (Cha.)	368	NZ 335
Ngoura (Cam.)	383	OH 333
Ngoura (Cam.)	383	OJ 334
Ngouri	368	NY 334
Ngourti	368	NX 332
Ngouyo	385	OG 344
Ngoyeboma	387	ON 333
Ngozi	298	BX 102
Ngqeleni	213	EF 101
Ngqungqu	213	EF 100
Ngubalo	299	BY 108
Ngudu	299	BX 109
Nguelemendouka	382	OJ 332
Nguema	290	CF 87
Ngui	384	OG 342
Nguia Bouar	383	OH 334
Nguigmi	368	NY 332
Nguila	382	OH 331
Ngundu	247	DJ 104
Nguni	307	BT 119
Ngunyboke	305	BN 107
Nguroje	382	OF 330
Ngurore	382	OD 331
Nguru	367	NZ 329
Nguruliro	294	CG 109
Ngurumahiga	284	CN 118
Nguti	376	OH 328
Ngwale	284	CN 118
Ngwesi	246	DK 98
Ngwezumba	255	DD 92
Nhachengue	239	DN 113
Nhacolo	259	DA 111
Nhacra	362	OA 304
Nhamalabue	259	DB 113
Nhamatanda	248	DF 111
Nharêa	276	CP 76
Nhique	251	CZ 71
Nhlangano	229	DW 105
Nhlazatshe	221	DY 105
Nhlohlela	229	DX 107
Nhoma (Nam.)	243	DE 84
Nhoma (Nam.)	243	DF 83
Niababri	379	OH 313
Niable	379	OF 316
Niada	384	OH 341
Niafounke	364	NW 315
Niagassola	363	OA 310
Niakaraman-dougou	379	OD 314
Niambezaria	379	OG 313
Niamey	366	NY 321
Niamina	364	NZ 312
Niamtougou	365	OC 320
Niamvoudou	382	OJ 332
Niandan Koro	363	OB 310
Niangandu	284	CJ 118
Niangara	385	OJ 347
Niangoloko	364	OC 314
Nia-Nia	389	OM 347
Niansour	369	OB 340
Niantanina	364	OB 311
Niapu	389	OL 345
Niau	362	NY 304
Nicuadala	260	DC 116
Nicupa	273	CV 123
Niega	365	OA 319
Niekerkshoop	217	EA 88
Nielle	364	OC 314
Niem	383	OG 334
Niemba	292	CE 99
Niéna	364	OB 313
Nietverdiend	227	DS 95
Nieu-Bethesda	211	EF 91
Nieuwoudtville	216	EE 81
Nieza	333	NA 328
Nigel	227	DU 99
Nigramoep	215	EB 78
Nikki	366	OC 322
Nikoemvon	382	OK 330
Nimjat	350	NV 303
Nimule	313	BK 107
Nina	232	DO 79
Ninda	265	CW 85
Ninette	232	DN 80
Ningi	367	OB 329
Nioasamoridu	378	OD 310
Nioka (DRC)	291	CH 90
Nioka (DRC)	304	BN 104
Nioki	387	OQ 337
Niokolo-Koba	363	NZ 306
Niono	364	NY 313
Nioro du Rip	362	NY 303
Nioro du Sahel	363	NX 309
Nipepe	272	CV 118
Nipiodi	260	CZ 117
Nisseko	365	OB 316
Nizi	304	BO 103
Njagi	283	CJ 115
Njiapanda	282	CK 110
Njinjo	284	CK 120
Njoge	296	CD 116
Njogonjwa	283	CL 115
Njombe	283	CL 112
Njoro (Ken.)	306	BS 114
Njoro (Tan.)	296	CC 115
Nkambe	382	OF 330
Nkandla	221	DZ 105
Nkawkaw	380	OF 318
Nkayi	246	DF 100
Nkhata Bay	271	CQ 111
Nkhotakota	271	CS 111
Nkoambang	382	OH 332
Nkob	330	NG 313
Nkolabona	386	OM 331
Nkole	281	CO 105
Nkolmeng-boua	386	OL 331
Nkomfap	382	OG 328
Nkomo	237	DO 104
Nkon Ngok	382	OJ 330
Nkondwe	293	CD 104
Nkongjok	376	OH 329
Nkongsamba	376	OH 329
Nkonko	295	CE 112
Nkonkoni	229	DX 106
Nkopola	271	CV 113
Nkoranza	379	OE 317
Nkoshya	281	CL 101
Nkoteng	382	OH 331
Nkoué	387	OR 334
Nkourala	364	OB 313
Nkulumane Junction	246	DH 100
Nkundi	294	CH 105
Nkungulu	271	CW 113
Nkungwini	229	DW 107
Nkurenkuru	253	DC 80
Nkwalini	221	DZ 105
Nkwanta	380	OE 319
Nlaklan	378	OH 311
Nnewi	381	OG 326
Nobantu	213	EF 100
Nobere	365	OB 318
Nobokhwe	212	EF 98
Noenieput	224	DX 83
Nohana	219	EB 98
Nokaneng	244	DG 87
Nokong	219	EA 99
Nokou	368	NX 334
Nola	383	OK 335
Noli	284	CN 119
Nomtsas	231	DQ 76
Nonconco	251	CY 70
Nondo	281	CM 105
Nondwa	295	CE 113
Nondweni	220	DY 104
Nongoma	229	DX 106
Nongue	251	DA 71
Noordhoek	208	EL 79
Noordkaap	228	DT 104
Noordkuil	208	EG 79
Noordoewer	215	DZ 78
Norassoba	363	OB 309
Nordeste	290	CG 86
Norman	241	DL 74
Normandien	220	DY 102
North Horr	315	BL 117
Northam	227	DR 97
Norton	257	DC 104
Norvalspont	218	ED 93
Nossob	232	DM 78
Nossombougou	364	NZ 311
Nothintsila	213	EF 101
Notocoto	261	DA 120
Notsé	380	OF 320
Nottingham Road	220	EA 102
Nouadhibou	350	NR 302
Nouakchott	350	NU 303
Nouamrhar	350	NT 302
Noumou-kiedoumou	364	OC 315
Nouna	364	NZ 315
Noupoort	218	EE 93
Nous	216	DZ 82
Nova Almada	248	DG 111
Nova Caipemba	287	CG 72
Nova Coimbra	271	CS 112
Nova Golegã	248	DH 111
Nova Guarda	271	CU 113
Nova Mambone	249	DK 113
Nova Nabúri	261	DA 120
Nova Sentarém	271	CU 114
Nova Vandúzi	248	DE 109
Nqabarha	213	EG 100
Nqabeni	220	ED 102
Nqamakhwe	212	EG 98
Nqutu	220	DY 104
Nsa	387	OP 334
Nsakaluba	280	CN 100
Nsama	281	CK 103
Nsambi	387	OO 337
Nsanje	259	DA 113
Nsawam	380	OG 318
Nsawkaw	379	OE 317
Nshongezi	304	BT 104
Nsika	304	BS 103
Nsiza	246	DG 101
Nsoc	386	OM 330
Nsoko	229	DW 106
Nsokolo	282	CL 106
Nsombo	281	CO 103
Nsontin	387	OQ 337
Nsubeni	221	DY 105
Nsukka	381	OF 326
Ntabamhlope	220	EA 102
Ntabankulu	220	ED 101
Ntabazinduna	246	DH 100
Ntabebomvu	220	DY 104
Ntaja	271	CW 114
Ntambanana	221	DZ 106
Ntambu	267	CR 93
Ntandembele	387	OP 336
Ntcheu	271	CW 112
Ntchisi	270	CT 110
Nteko	282	CL 107
Ntenkélé	386	OM 331
Nthalire	282	CN 110
Nthunga	271	CR 111
Ntibane	213	EF 100
Ntimaru	300	BU 112
Ntisana	212	EG 99
Ntobo	299	BZ 107
Ntokou-Otolou	387	ON 335
Ntoum	376	ON 329
Ntshilini	213	EF 101
Ntsou	387	OP 335
Ntui	382	OJ 331
Ntumba	282	CJ 107
Ntungama	304	BQ 103
Ntungamo	304	BT 103
Ntunjambili	220	DZ 104
Ntusi	305	BR 105
Ntwemwa	267	CV 95
Ntywenka	220	EE 100
Nugubaes	241	DH 74
Nulli	237	DM 103
Numan	382	OD 331
Numbi	298	BV 100
Numbi Gate	229	DS 105
Numpale	251	CZ 70
Nungo	272	CT 118
Nungwe	299	BX 107
Nungwi	297	CD 121
Nurei	370	NZ 342
Nutfield	228	DR 100
Nuu	301	BU 119
Nuwe Smitsdorp	236	DQ 101
Nuwefontein	216	DY 81
Nuweiba	348	NJ 353
Nuwerus	215	EE 79
Nwa	382	OG 330
Nwayfadh	338	NN 304
Nwera	297	CH 122
Nxai Nxai	243	DG 85
Nyabessan	386	OL 330
Nyabira	257	DC 104
Nyabisindu	298	BW 102
Nya-Ghezi	298	BX 100
Nyagombe	298	CA 103
Nyahanga	300	BW 110
Nyahua	294	CC 109
Nyahururu	307	BR 115
Nyakabindi	300	BX 111
Nyakagomba	299	BX 106
Nyakahura	298	BX 104
Nyakaliro	299	BW 107
Nyakanazi	299	BY 105
Nyakintonto	298	CA 103
Nyakisogo	298	CA 104
Nyakitasi	285	CJ 121
Nyala (Zim.)	247	DL 106
Nyala (Sud.)	370	OA 344
Nyali	386	OQ 330
Nyalikungu (DRC)	299	BX 109
Nyalikungu (DRC)	300	BY 110
Nyamandhlovu	246	DG 99
Nyamapanda	258	DA 108
Nyamassila	380	OE 320
Nyamazugu	299	BX 107
Nyamba	284	CN 120
Nyambi	255	CX 92
Nyambiti	299	BX 109
Nyamgalika	299	CA 105
Nyamhanga	284	CJ 116
Nyamirembe	299	BX 106
Nyamlell	385	OD 346
Nyamoko	382	OH 330
Nyamtumbo	283	CO 115
Nyamuswa	300	BV 111
Nyamwage	284	CJ 120
Nyamwanga	300	BU 111
Nyanatakara	299	BY 105
Nyandekwa	299	BZ 108
Nyanga (Zim.)	258	DD 108
Nyanga (Con.)	386	OQ 331
Nyangamara	285	CN 122
Nyange	298	CA 103
Nyangolo	295	CG 114
Nyangombe	258	DC 108
Nyanguge	299	BX 109
Nyanhonge	299	BY 109
Nyanza Lac	298	CA 102
Nyaru	306	BR 114
Nyasa	292	CD 95
Nyassar	383	OE 333
Nyatande	270	CV 106
Nyathini	221	EA 105
Nyawa	258	DC 105
Nyazura	248	DE 107
Nyeri	307	BS 116
Nyibiam	382	OE 328
Nyiel	321	BE 105
Nyika	247	DH 106
Nyimba	269	CW 104
Nyokana	213	EG 100
Nyoni	221	EA 105
Nyunzu	292	CD 99
Nyuruandanga	297	CH 121
Nzako	384	OG 342
Nzambi	386	OR 330
Nzara	385	OH 347
Nzebela	378	OE 310
Nzega	299	CA 109
Nzeka	282	CJ 106
Nzérékoré	378	OE 310
N'zeto	286	CG 68
Nzili	370	OB 342
Nzima	299	BY 108
Nzo	378	OE 311
Nzopi	312	BL 102
Nzoro	383	OF 335
Oakdene	212	EH 97
Oangwa	243	DG 85
Oasis	227	DW 96

Oatlands > Sakabinde

PLACE NAME	PG	GRID
Oatlands	211	EH 91
Oba	381	OF 325
Obaba	387	OP 335
Obala	382	OJ 331
Oban (Mpuma.)	228	DU 101
Oban (Nig.)	376	OH 328
Oban (Con.)	387	OP 335
Obehie	376	OH 326
Obi	382	OE 328
Obo	385	OH 346
Obobogorap	224	DW 83
Obock	374	OA 362
Obokote	389	OO 345
Oboli	387	OP 334
Obouya	387	OO 335
Obubra	381	OG 327
Obudu	382	OF 328
Oburi	305	BO 109
Ocua	273	CU 122
Oda	380	OG 318
Odendaalsrus	227	DX 96
Odienné	378	OD 311
Odjala	387	ON 333
Odonkawkron	380	OF 319
Odzi	248	DE 107
Odziba	387	OR 335
Ofcolaco	237	DQ 103
Ofere	381	OE 325
Offumpo	379	OG 314
Ofinso	379	OF 317
Ofoase	380	OG 318
Ofugo	381	OE 327
Ogani	376	OH 326
Ogbomosho	381	OE 323
Ogembo	306	BT 112
Ogies	228	DU 101
Ogoja	382	OF 328
Ogun	381	OD 323
Ogur	305	BN 108
Ogurugu	381	OF 326
Ogwashi	381	OG 325
Ohalia	381	OG 327
Ohanet	343	NJ 328
Ohopoho	251	DD 70
Ohrigstad	228	DR 104
Oiungo	251	CZ 70
Ojamba	241	DG 75
Oju	381	OF 327
Oka (Nig.)	381	OF 325
Oka (Con.)	387	OR 334
Okahandja	241	DL 76
Okahao	251	DC 73
Okakarara	242	DJ 78
Okakombo	241	DK 75
Okalongo	251	DB 73
Okamatangara	242	DK 79
Okamatapati	242	DH 79
Okandja	387	OO 333
Okandjambo	250	DD 69
Okangoho	242	DH 78
Okangwati	250	DB 69
Okankolo	252	DD 75
Okanono	241	DL 74
Okaputa	241	DH 76
Okarukurume	242	DK 80
Okata	380	OE 322
Okatjiura	240	DE 71
Okatjoruu	242	DG 80
Okatumba	240	DE 70
Okatuwa	243	DL 82
Okaukuejo	241	DF 74
Okauwe	250	DC 68
Okave	241	DH 76
Okazize	241	DL 75
Oke-Iho	380	OE 322
Okene	381	OE 325
Okiep	215	EB 78
Okigwe	381	OG 326
Okokorio	306	BO 110
Okola	382	OJ 330
Okollo	313	BM 105
Okombahe	241	DK 73
Okondjatu	242	DJ 79
Okongo	252	DC 77
Okorosave	251	DD 70
Okosewa	232	DN 79
Okovimburu	242	DL 81
Okoyo	387	OO 334
Okozondara	242	DK 80
Okozongoro	241	DK 75
Okrouyo	379	OG 313
Okuta	380	OD 322
Okwangalete	305	BO 109
Ol Doinyo Ngiro	307	BQ 116
Ol Joro Orok	307	BS 115
Ol Molog	301	BX 117
Ol Tukai	301	BX 117
Old Bunting	213	EF 101
Old Mkushi	269	CV 101
Old Morley	213	EF 100
Old Nariam	306	BO 111
Old Petauke	269	CV 105
Old Shinyanga	299	BZ 109
Oldeani	300	BY 113
Olenguruone	306	BT 114
Olifantshoek	225	DX 88
Olifantskop	218	DZ 92
Olinga	260	DB 118
Olive	219	ED 95
Olive Hill	218	EA 94
Olmesutye	300	BV 114
Olodio	378	OH 312
Oloitokitok	301	BX 118
Olomandou	378	OD 310
Oloserri	301	BW 115
Oltepesi	301	BV 115
Olukondo	252	DD 75
Olumbe	285	CO 123
Olyfberg	236	DP 102
Omajete	241	DK 74
Omaruru	241	DK 74
Omatjene	241	DH 76
Ombala-io-Mungo	251	DB 72
Ombalantu	251	DC 73
Ombarundu	251	DC 71
Ombombo (Nam.)	240	DE 70
Ombombo (Nam.)	251	DD 71
Omboué	386	OP 328
Omchi	357	NR 337
Omdraaisvlei	217	EC 89
Omdurman	372	NW 352
Omhajer	373	NY 356
Omitara	232	DM 79
Omoku	376	OH 326
Omoro	305	BN 109
Ompupa	250	CZ 69
Omu-Aran	381	OE 324
Omuo	381	OE 325
Omupanda	251	DB 74
Omurumendu	232	DM 79
Onaanda	251	DD 73

PLACE NAME	PG	GRID
Oncócua	250	DA 69
Ondangwa	251	DC 74
Ondekaremba	231	DM 77
Onderombapa	232	DO 81
Onderstedorings	216	EC 84
Onder-Wadrif	209	EG 82
Ondjiva	251	DB 74
Ondo	381	OF 324
Ondombo	241	DK 75
Onema	291	CB 92
Onema Ututu	388	OR 342
Onema-Okolo	389	OR 343
Onesi	251	DC 72
Ongango	240	DE 70
Ongenga	251	DB 74
Ongers	217	EC 89
Ongoka	389	OP 345
Ongongoro	242	DH 79
Ongoro Gotjari	232	DM 78
Ongoári	251	CY 71
Onguia	387	OO 334
Ongwediva	251	DC 74
Oniipa	252	DC 75
Onitsha	381	OG 326
Onoko	368	OB 335
Onrus	209	EL 81
Ons Hoop	236	DP 98
Onseepkans	216	DZ 81
Ontmoeting	225	DW 86
Ontspringen	219	ED 95
Oodweyne	326	AY 133
Ooreenkoms	219	DY 98
Oorkruis	217	DZ 86
Oorwinning	236	DN 102
Oostermoed	227	DR 97
Op die Berg	209	EH 81
Opala	389	OO 343
Operet	242	DE 77
Opi	381	OF 326
Opobo	376	OH 327
Opon Valley	379	OG 317
Oppermans	218	EA 92
Opuwo	251	DD 70
Oraba	312	BK 104
Orah	381	OG 324
Oran	331	NB 319
Orania	218	EB 91
Oranjefontein	236	DO 98
Oranjemund	215	DZ 75
Oranjerivier	218	EB 91
Oranjesig	218	ED 93
Oranjeville	227	DW 99
Orapa	245	DK 93
Orkadiere	363	NX 306
Orkney	227	DV 96
Orodara	364	OB 314
Orom	314	BL 110
Oron	376	OH 327
Orotjitombo	251	DD 70
Ortum	306	BP 113
Oruma	305	BN 109
Orupembe	250	DD 68
Oruwanje	251	DD 70
Osborn	221	DZ 105
Osélé	387	OO 334
Osfontein	219	ED 95
Oshakati	251	DC 74
Oshikango	251	DB 74
Oshikuku	251	DC 74
Oshititu	252	DC 77
Oshivelo	242	DE 77
Oshigambo	252	DC 75
Oshwe	388	OQ 338
Osire	242	DK 77
oSizweni	228	DX 103
Osogbo	381	OE 323
Osomba	232	DM 79
Osona	231	DM 76
Ososo	381	OF 325
Otavi	242	DG 77
Otchinjau	251	DA 70
Otechifengo	250	DA 68
oTimati	221	EA 105
Otiyarwa	243	DK 82
Otjihaenena	242	DG 78
Otjihajavara	231	DM 77
Otjikango	241	DH 76
Otjikondavirongo	240	DE 70
Otjikondo	241	DG 74
Otjimbingwe	231	DM 75
Otjinene	242	DK 80
Otjinhungwa	250	DB 67
Otjinoko	242	DK 81
Otjisemba	241	DL 76
Otjitambi	241	DG 73
Otjitanda	250	DC 68
Otjitasu	241	DH 76
Otjitoko	240	DE 71
Otjiu	250	DD 69
Otjiungukwa	232	DO 82
Otjivero	232	DM 78
Otjiveze	251	DC 70
Otjiwarongo	241	DH 76
Otjondeka	240	DE 71
Otjongundu	241	DJ 73
Otjosondu	242	DK 78
Otjovasandu	240	DF 71
Otjozongombe	240	DE 70
Otse	226	DS 94
Otta	380	OF 322
Otto Beit Bridge	257	CZ 100
Ottosdal	227	DV 95
Ottoshoop	226	DT 94
Otu	382	OG 328
Otukpa	381	OF 327
Otukpo	381	OF 327
Otumba	250	DA 67
Otuwe	241	DK 75
Ouacha	367	NZ 328
Ouad Naga	350	NU 303
Ouadane	351	NR 307
Ouadda	384	OE 342
Ouadimi	384	OG 340
Ouagadougou	365	OA 318
Ouahigouya	365	NY 317
Ouahire	364	OC 312
Ouake	365	OC 320
Oualâta Rini	352	NV 312
Oualia	363	NZ 309
Oualidia	329	NE 310
Ouallam	366	NY 321
Ouanda Djallé	384	OD 342
Ouandago	384	OF 338
Ouandja	384	OD 342
Ouandjia	384	OD 342
Ouando	385	OG 345
Ouango	384	OJ 341
Ouangolo-dougou	364	OC 314
Ouarak	362	NW 303
Ouargaye	365	OB 319
Ouargla	332	NF 324

PLACE NAME	PG	GRID
Ouaritoufoulout	366	NW 323
Ouarkla	383	OD 334
Ouarkoye	364	OA 315
Ouarzazate	329	NG 312
Ouassa Bamvele	382	OH 331
Ouassadougou	379	OE 315
Ouatagouna	365	NX 320
Ouatere Galafondo	384	OH 338
Ouda	383	OG 337
Oudtshoorn	210	EK 87
Ouebo	362	OA 304
Oued Zem	329	NE 312
Ouelessebougou	364	OA 311
Ouella	366	NX 323
Ouellé	379	OF 315
Ouenkoro	364	NZ 315
Oue-Oue	380	OD 321
Ouessa	365	OB 316
Ouesse	380	OE 321
Ouesso	387	OL 335
Ouezzane	330	NC 313
Ougarou	365	OA 320
Ougarta	341	NH 317
Ouihi	384	OE 340
Ouin	383	OF 337
Oujda	330	NC 317
Oukraal	209	EL 82
Ould Teima	339	NH 310
Ould Yenje	363	NX 307
Ouled Djellal	332	ND 324
Ouli	383	OH 333
Oulmes	330	NE 313
Oum Chalouba	369	NW 340
Oum el Bouaghi	332	NB 326
Oum Hadjer	369	NZ 339
Oumache	332	NC 325
Oumé	379	OG 314
Oumm el Khez	351	NV 308
Oumuur	216	EE 83
Ounara	329	NF 310
Ounguati	241	DL 74
Ounianga-Kebir	357	NT 339
Ouogo	383	OE 337
Ourafane	367	NY 327
Oure-Kaba	363	OC 307
Ouro Amat	363	NX 306
Oursi	365	NX 319
Oussoumbidiaga	363	NY 309
Outat Oulad el Hajj	330	NE 315
Outjo	241	DH 75
Outo Sogui	363	NX 306
Ovala	386	OO 330
Ovan	386	ON 331
Oveng	386	OL 331
Over-Vaal	228	DV 103
Overyssel	236	DP 99
Oviston	218	ED 94
Owando	387	OO 335
Owena	381	OF 324
Owendale	217	DY 89
Owendo	376	ON 328
Owerri	376	OH 326
Owo	381	OF 324
Owutu	381	OG 327
Oyabi	387	ON 333
Oyem	386	OL 331
Oyo (Egy.)	360	NQ 355
Oyo (Nig.)	381	OE 323
Oyo (Con.)	387	OO 335
Oyoué	387	ON 334
Oyster Bay	211	EL 92
Oyster Cliffs	222	DS 72
Ozondati	241	DJ 73
Ozori	376	OO 328
Ozoro	381	OG 325
Pa	365	OA 316
Paarl	209	EK 80
Pacaltsdorp	210	EL 88
Pacuária da Barra do Longa	274	CN 69
Paddagat	215	EE 79
Paddock	220	ED 103
Padibe	313	BL 108
Pafuri	237	DM 105
Pafuri Gate	237	DM 105
Pagui	384	OH 340
Pahn Wroal	378	OG 311
Paiko	381	OD 326
Paimol	313	BL 109
Paiva	260	DC 118
Paje (Bot.)	235	DM 96
Paje (Tan.)	297	CE 122
Pajule	313	BM 108
Pakele	313	BL 106
Paki	367	OA 327
Pakwach	305	BN 105
Pala	383	OD 334
Palala (LIM)	236	DQ 100
Palala (Gui.)	378	OF 310
Palamakoloi	233	DO 87
Palanca	251	DA 70
Palapye	235	DN 97
Paleisheuwel	209	EG 80
Palingpan	217	DY 88
Pallisa	306	BP 110
Palm Beach (KZN)	220	EE 103
Palm Beach (Mal.)	271	CV 113
Palma	285	CO 123
Palmeira	238	DS 108
Palmeirinhas	274	CL 69
Palmerton	220	EE 101
Palmietfontein	219	EC 97
Palmwag	240	DG 70
Paloich	372	OC 352
Pama (Bur.F)	365	OB 320
Pama (Bur.F)	384	OH 340
Pambani	299	BY 109
Pambarra	249	DL 113
Pambeguwa	367	OB 327
Pambuke	247	DH 102
Pampierstad	226	DX 92
Pampoenpoort	217	EE 88
Pamula	246	DG 97
Pana	386	OP 332
Panbult	228	DV 103
Panda	238	DQ 112
Pandamatenga	245	DE 94
Pandambili	296	CE 116
Pandane	239	DQ 114
Pande (Ang.)	252	DA 79
Pande (Tan.)	297	CD 120
Pandogari	366	OC 325
Pandu	384	OH 338
Pangala	387	OQ 334
Pangale	294	CC 108
Pangani	297	CC 121
Pangi	389	OQ 346
Pango Aluquem	275	CK 71
Pangonda	384	OF 340

PLACE NAME	PG	GRID
Pania Mutombo	291	CC 90
Pania-Mwanga	292	CH 98
Pankshin	382	OD 328
Pansdrif	227	DT 98
Panu	388	OR 338
Panyam	382	OD 328
Panyangara	314	BM 111
Panzarani	379	OD 316
Panzi	288	CG 78
Paoua	383	OF 336
Paouignan	380	OE 321
Papane	244	DG 90
Papendorp	208	EF 79
Papiesvlei	209	EL 82
Papkuil	218	DY 90
Paradise	226	DV 92
Paradise Beach	211	EL 93
Paradys (F.S.)	218	EB 94
Paradys (F.S.)	219	EA 96
Parakou	380	OD 322
Paranga	313	BM 107
Paresis	241	DJ 76
Park Rynie	220	EC 104
Parow	209	EK 80
Parys (F.S.)	219	DY 97
Parys (F.S.)	227	DV 97
Passene	229	DT 107
Pata (Sen.)	362	NZ 304
Pata (CAR)	384	OE 340
Pata (CAR)	384	OH 338
Patambalu	387	OP 337
Patani	376	OH 325
Paté	303	BW 125
Pategi	381	OD 325
Patensie	211	EK 92
Paternoster	208	EH 78
Paterson	211	EJ 94
Patick	362	NY 303
Patlong	219	EC 99
Patongo	313	BM 109
Pauila	271	CQ 114
Paul	227	DS 97
Paul Kruger Gate	229	DS 105
Paul Roux	219	DY 97
Paulpietersburg	228	DW 104
Pawa	385	OK 347
Payar	362	NY 304
Pearly Beach	209	EM 81
Pearston	211	EH 93
Pebane	260	DB 119
Peddie	212	EJ 97
Pedisa	250	CZ 68
Pedra do Feitico	286	CD 68
Peerboom	217	EE 87
Pehonko	366	OC 321
Peili	385	OF 347
Peka	219	EA 98
Pela	378	OE 310
Pelenge	388	OQ 342
Pelezi	378	OF 312
Pella	216	EA 81
Pemba (Moz.)	256	DA 97
Pemba (Zam.)	273	CT 124
Pembe	238	DP 112
Pende	387	OF 335
Pendembu (Sie.L)	377	OD 307
Pendembu (Sie.L)	378	OE 309
Pene Mende	389	OR 347
Penge (DRC)	385	OK 347
Penge (DRC)	291	CD 92
Penge (L.P.)	237	DQ 103
Penhalonga	248	DE 108
Penjua	388	OO 338
Pennington	220	EC 104
Pensa	365	NY 318
Penzele	387	ON 337
Pepa	293	CH 102
Pepworth	220	DY 102
Perdeberg	218	DZ 93
Perdekop	228	DW 102
Perere	366	OC 322
Perma	365	OC 320
Persnip	224	DS 80
Pescara Cassiano	271	CV 114
Petauke	269	CV 105
Pete	368	OB 334
Petersburg	211	EG 92
Petrus Steyn	227	DX 99
Petrusburg	218	EA 93
Petrusville (N.C.)	216	EE 84
Petrusville (N.C.)	218	EC 92
Peu-Peu	251	DA 73
Phalaborwa	237	DP 105
Phalombe	259	CY 114
Phamong	219	EC 98
Philadelphia	209	EK 80
Philippolis	218	EC 93
Philippolis Road	218	EC 93
Philipstown	218	EC 91
Phitsane Molopo	226	DT 93
Phoenix	221	EB 105
Phokwane	228	DR 102
Phologelo	244	DG 90
Phomolong	220	DY 101
Phuduhudu	244	DH 91
Phuthaditjhaba	220	DZ 100
Phuzumoya	229	DV 106
Piankana	387	OQ 337
Pibor Post	321	BD 109
Pienaarsrivier	227	DS 99
Piet Plessis	226	DU 92
Piet Retief	228	DW 104
Pieter Meintjes	209	EJ 84
Pietermaritzburg	220	EB 104
Pietla	378	OH 311
Piggs Peak	229	DT 105
Pigu	365	OC 318
Piketberg	209	EH 80
Pikounda	387	OM 335
Pilane	235	DQ 95
Pilemane	364	OC 311
Pilgrims Rest	228	DR 104
Pilikwe	235	DN 97
Pilipili	385	OJ 347
Pinanga	387	OQ 335
Pinda	259	DB 113
Pindura	298	BX 101
Pinetown	220	EB 104
Pingwe	297	CE 122
Piodi	291	CH 93
Pioka	287	CB 71
Piro	259	DD 111
Pissila	365	NZ 318
Pita	363	OB 307
Pitoa	383	OD 333
Pitsane	226	DS 94
Pitseng	219	EA 99
Pitu	283	CL 114
Pizhi	366	OC 324
PK Rouge	387	OR 335

PLACE NAME	PG	GRID
Plaston	229	DS 105
Platbakkies	215	EC 79
Plateau	218	DY 90
Plateind	215	ED 78
Plathuis	209	EK 84
Platrand	228	DW 102
Platveld	242	DH 77
Plettenberg Bay	210	EL 89
Plooysburg	218	EA 91
Plumtree	246	DJ 98
Pniel	209	EK 81
Pô	365	OB 318
Pobe	380	OF 322
Pobe Mengao	365	NY 317
Pochala	322	BC 111
Pocolo	251	CY 70
Podor	350	NV 304
Pofadder	216	EA 81
Poie	388	OQ 342
Pointe-Noire	286	CB 66
Poko	385	OK 346
Pokuma	256	DC 96
Poli	382	OE 332
Politsi	237	DP 103
Polokwane (Pietersburg)	236	DP 101
Poma	389	OO 345
Pomene	239	DN 114
Pomeroy	220	DZ 103
Pomfret	226	DT 90
Pongola	229	DW 106
Pongore	245	DE 96
Pongwe	296	CE 119
Ponio	365	OB 319
Ponon-dougou	364	OC 313
Ponta de Barra	239	DP 114
Ponta de Barra Falsa	239	DN 114
Ponta do Ouro	229	DV 109
Ponta Freitas Morna	286	CH 69
Ponta Závora	239	DR 113
Pools	209	EH 80
Popa (Nam.)	254	DD 85
Popa (Gab.)	386	OP 331
Popenguine	362	NX 302
Porga	365	OB 320
Port	305	BN 105
Port Alfred	212	EK 96
Port Bell	305	BR 108
Port Edward	220	EE 103
Port Elizabeth	211	EK 94
Port Grosvenor	220	EE 103
Port Harcourt	376	OH 326
Port Loko	377	OD 306
Port Nolloth	215	EA 76
Port Owen	208	EH 79
Port Said	337	NG 352
Port Shepstone	220	ED 104
Port St Johns	213	EF 102
Port Sudan	361	NS 356
Port Victoria	306	BR 111
Porterville	209	EJ 80
Port-Gentil	376	OO 328
Porto Alexandre	250	CY 66
Porto Amboim	274	CO 70
Porto Condo	275	CM 75
Porto-Novo	380	OG 322
Possel	384	OH 338
Post Chalmers	211	EG 93
Poste Weygand (Balise 250)	341	NO 320
Postmasburg	217	DY 89
Posto Antigo do Luxico	289	CG 82
Posto Zootecnico do Cunene	251	CZ 73
Potchefstroom	227	DV 97
Potfontein	218	EC 91
Potiskum	367	OA 330
Potloodspruit	228	DS 103
Potoru	378	OF 308
Potsdam	212	EH 98
Poudjo	384	OH 340
Pouéré	387	OO 335
Pouma	382	OJ 330
Poumale	384	OG 339
Poupan	218	EC 91
Pouss	368	OB 334
Pouy-tenga	365	OA 318
Praia Azul	250	CX 67
Praia de Jangamo	239	DQ 114
Praia de Zalala	260	DC 117
Praia do Bilene	238	DS 109
Praia do Chongoene	238	DS 110
Praia do Tofo	239	DP 114
Praia do Xai-Xai	238	DS 110
Praia dos Cocos	239	DP 114
Prend Town	378	OH 310
Pretoria	227	DT 99
Prieska	217	EB 88
Prikro	379	OE 315
Prince Albert	210	EJ 86
Prince Albert Road	210	EJ 86
Prince Alfred Hamlet	209	EJ 81
Pringle Bay	209	EL 80
Priors	218	EC 94
Protem	209	EL 83
Ptoyo	306	BO 113
Puchapucha	284	CP 118
Pudimoe	226	DW 92
Puerto del Rosario	338	NJ 305
Puig	320	AY 102
Pujehun	377	OF 307
Pukota	268	CT 100
Puleng	245	DL 96
Pullen's Hope	228	DU 102
Puma	295	CC 112
Punda Maria Gate	237	DN 104
Pundanhar	285	CO 123
Punia	389	OO 345
Puntjie	210	EL 85
Purongo	313	BM 106
Purros	240	DE 68
Putsonderwater	217	EA 86
Pweka	296	CF 116
Pwalugu (Gha.)	365	OB 318
Pwalugu (Gha.)	365	OB 318
Pwani Mchangani	297	CD 121
Pwela	282	CJ 106
Pweto	280	CJ 100
Pylkop	236	DN 102
Qacentina (Constantine)	332	NB 326
Qacha's Nek	220	EC 100
Qairouan	333	NB 329
Qala en Nahl	372	NY 354

PLACE NAME	PG	GRID
Qallabat	372	NZ 355
Qamata	212	EF 97
Qaminis	335	NF 339
Qandala	375	OB 369
Qardho (Som.)	328	AY 141
Qardho (Som.)	375	OC 368
Qaryat Shumaykh	334	NG 333
Qaryat Abu Nujaym	334	NG 335
Qaryat Abu Qurays	334	NG 334
Qasr	347	NL 347
Qasr al Qarn	346	NH 343
Qasr ash Shaqqah	336	NG 344
Qasr Bu Hadi	334	NG 336
Qassabat	334	NE 333
Qasserine	333	NC 328
Qemada	348	NM 352
Qena	333	NF 330
Qhobela	219	DZ 99
Qholora Mouth	212	EH 99
Qhora Mouth	213	EG 100
Qiba	219	EE 98
Qift	348	NM 352
Qobong	219	EC 98
Qombolo	212	EG 98
Qoqodala	212	EF 96
Qoton	375	OC 370
Qsour Essaf	333	NC 330
Quarenta	275	CN 75
Quarry	209	EJ 83
Qubi	243	DG 85
Qudeni	220	DZ 104
Queen's Mine	246	DG 100
Queensburgh	220	EB 104
Queenstown	212	EF 97
Quela	276	CL 77
Quelele	277	CL 81
Quelimane	260	DC 116
Quelo	286	CE 68
Queulo	251	CZ 71
Quiangala	287	CG 73
Quibala	275	CO 73
Quibengue	288	CE 75
Quibocolo	287	CE 73
Quicabo	274	CJ 70
Quiculungo	275	CK 73
Quicungurr	287	CG 73
Quifuma	286	CE 67
Quiiba	251	CX 70
Quilemba	262	CW 69
Quilenda	275	CO 71
Quilengues	263	CV 71
Quilona	286	CG 69
Quilua	261	CZ 122
Quimbele	288	CE 75
Quimbi	287	CF 70
Quimbriz	286	CF 68
Quimbumbe	287	CH 70
Quinga	261	CY 123
Quinhamel	362	OA 305
Quionga	285	CO 124
Quipaza	287	CF 73
Quipedro	287	CH 71
Quipeio	263	CR 73
Quipungo	263	CW 72
Quirima	276	CO 79
Quissanga	273	CR 123
Quissico	238	DR 112
Quissonga	275	CN 73
Quitapa	276	CN 79
Quitende	275	CJ 72
Quiterajo	273	CQ 123
Quiteve	251	CZ 73
Quitubia	275	CO 74
Quixaxe	261	CX 123
Quko	212	EH 99
Qumbu	220	EE 100
Qurayd	372	OB 351
Qurdud	371	OC 349
Qureida	370	OB 344
Qus	348	NM 352
Quseir	348	NM 353
Rabah	366	NZ 325
Rabak	372	NZ 352
Rabat	329	ND 312
Rachid	351	NT 307
Radisele	235	DN 97
Radium	227	DS 99
Rafai	385	OH 343
Raffin Kada	382	OE 329
Raffingora	257	DB 104
Rafin-Cabas	381	OD 327
Rafsai	330	NC 314
Raga	385	OE 345
Rahad el Berdi	370	OB 343
Rahama	367	OC 328
Raheita	374	NZ 362
Rahouia	331	NB 320
Rakai	305	BT 105
Rakay	365	OA 317
Rakhoi	219	EA 96
Rako	375	OC 369
Rakops	244	DK 91
Ralebona	219	EC 98
Rama	226	DW 92
Ramatlabama	226	DT 94
Ramokgonami	235	DN 97
Ramokgwebane	246	DJ 98
Ramotswa	226	DR 94
Ramsgate	220	ED 103
Ramu	317	BK 125
Ran	368	OA 333
Ranaka	226	DR 94
Rand Rifles	230	DN 72
Randa	374	OA 361
Randalhurst	221	DZ 105
Randburg	227	DU 98
Randfontein	227	DU 97
Randvaal	227	DV 98
Ranerou	362	NX 305
Ranger Post	267	CV 94
Rangnom	371	OC 349
Rano	367	OA 330
Rao	362	NW 303
Rapale	261	CX 121
Raqdalin	333	NE 331
Ras al Hamamah	335	NE 340
Ras al Hilal	335	NE 341
Ras Attabil	333	NG 332
Ras el Ma	331	ND 318
Ras Gharib	348	NK 352
Rashad	371	OA 350
Rass Ajdir	333	NE 331
Ratelfontein	209	EG 80
Ratombo	237	DO 103
Rawsonville	209	EK 81
Rayton	228	DT 100
Red Drum	250	DC 68
Redcliff	247	DF 102
Redcliffe	220	EA 102

PLACE NAME	PG	GRID
Reddersburg	219	EB 95
Redelinghuys	209	EG 80
Redeyef	332	ND 327
Redlands	217	EB 88
Redoubt	220	ED 103
Reebokrand	218	EC 93
Regaia	330	NB 313
Reggane	341	NL 319
Regina Mundi Mission	246	DF 98
Regone (Moz.)	260	CY 116
Regone (Moz.)	261	DA 120
Regua	237	DN 107
Rehoboth	231	DO 76
Reitz	227	DX 99
Reitzburg	227	DW 97
Reivilo	226	DX 91
Relizane	331	NB 320
Remada	333	NF 330
Remhoogte	210	EK 86
Remo	268	CV 97
Renco	247	DJ 105
Renier	209	EL 84
Renk	372	OA 352
Renosterkop	210	EG 88
Renostersspruit	227	DV 95
Reo	365	OA 316
Ressano Garcia	229	DS 107
Restinga	330	NB 314
Restvale	210	EG 89
Reteta	272	CU 119
Révia	272	CT 116
Rey Bouba	383	OD 333
Rhino Camp	313	BM 105
Rhodes	219	ED 98
Rhodes	336	NB 347
Rhoufi	332	NC 325
Rhourd el Baguel	332	NG 326
Riaba	376	OK 328
Riabela	253	CY 81
Rialto	249	DJ 112
Ribah	366	OB 325
Ribáué	272	CW 119
Rich	330	NF 314
Richard Toll	362	NW 303
Richards Bay	221	DZ 107
Richmond (KZN.)	220	EB 103
Richmond (N.C.)	218	EE 90
Riebeeck-East	212	EJ 95
Riebeeckstad	227	DX 96
Riebeek-Kasteel	209	EJ 80
Riebeek-Wes	209	EJ 80
Riekertsdam	227	DS 95
Riet	218	ED 91
Rietbron	210	EH 89
Rietfontein (N.C.)	209	EH 83
Rietfontein (N.C.)	210	EF 85
Rietfontein (N.C.)	210	EG 85
Rietfontein (N.C.)	215	EB 79
Rietfontein (N.C.)	216	EC 83
Rietfontein (N.C.)	218	EC 90
Rietfontein (N.C.)	218	ED 92
Rietfontein (N.C.)	224	DV 83
Rietfontein (Nam.)	243	DL 84
Riethuiskraal	210	EL 85
Rietkolk	236	DQ 102
Rietkuil (F.S.)	228	DX 101
Rietkuil (Mpum.)	228	DT 102
Rietpan	226	DV 93
Rietpoort	215	ED 79
Rig Rig	368	NY 333
Rijau	366	OB 324
Rike	373	OB 359
Ringoma	264	CR 78
Rio das Pedras	239	DO 114
Risasa	389	ON 345
Rissani	330	NG 315
Rita	236	DP 102
Ritchie	218	EA 92
Rito	253	DA 81
River Cess	378	OH 309
River View	221	DY 107
Riversdale	210	EL 85
Riverside (E.C.)	220	EC 102
Riverside (F.S.)	218	EB 94
Riverton	218	DZ 92
Riviera	218	DY 91
Riviersonderend	209	EL 83
Rivungo	254	CZ 86
Rkiz	350	NV 304
Roamer's Rest	220	EC 100
Roan Antelope Mine	268	CT 99
Roango	285	CL 122
Robanda	300	BW 112
Roberts Drift	228	DV 100
Robertson	209	EK 82
Robertsport	378	OF 308
Robi	324	BB 122
Rockmount	220	EA 102
Rode	220	ED 101
Rodenbeck	219	EA 95
Roedtan	228	DR 101
Rogo	367	OB 327
Rokom	313	BG 105
Roma	219	EA 98
Romani	337	NG 352
Rommani	330	ND 313
Rondevlei	210	EK 86
Rondo	285	CN 121
Rongo	306	BT 112
Roodebank	228	DV 101
Roodepan	218	EB 92
Roodepaal	227	DT 99
Roodepoort	227	DU 98
Rooibank	230	DO 72
Rooiberg	227	DR 98
Rooibokkraal	235	DQ 97
Rooibosbult	235	DQ 97
Rooibult	218	DZ 94
Rooiels	209	EL 80
Rooifontein (F.S.)	218	DZ 92
Rooifontein (Nam.)	232	DN 82
Rooigrond	226	DT 94
Rooikop	230	DN 72
Rooikraal	228	DS 102
Rooiloop	210	EJ 88
Rooilyf	217	DZ 86
Rooipan	218	EA 90
Rooisspruit	218	EE 92
Rooiwal	227	DW 98
Roosboom	220	DZ 102
Roossenekal	228	DS 102
Rorke's Drift	220	DY 104
Rosebank	220	EB 103
Rosedene	210	EG 88
Rosendal (F.S.)	218	DY 98
Rosendal (F.S.)	219	DY 94
Rosendal (F.S.)	219	DZ 99

PLACE NAME	PG	GRID
Rosetta	220	EA 102
Rosetta (Rashid)	337	NG 349
Rosh Pinah	223	DX 76
Rosmead	211	EF 93
Rössing	230	DN 72
Rosso	350	NV 303
Rossouw	219	EE 97
Rothmere	213	EG 100
Rotifunk	377	OE 306
Rotkop	222	DV 73
Rouhia	333	NB 328
Roumsiki	368	OC 333
Rouxpos	210	EJ 85
Rouxville	219	EC 96
Ruacana	251	DB 71
Ruamagaza	299	BY 106
Ruangwa	284	CN 120
Ruashi	268	CQ 98
Ruawa	285	CM 122
Rubafu	299	BU 106
Rubanda	298	BU 102
Rubeho	296	CE 116
Rubida	219	EC 97
Rubirizi	304	BS 103
Rudewa (Tan.)	283	CN 112
Rudewa (Tan.)	296	CF 117
Rudi	296	CF 115
Rufaa	372	NX 352
Rufisque	362	NX 302
Rufunsa	257	CX 102
Rugombera	285	CK 121
Rugombo	298	BX 101
Rugseer	217	EA 85
Ruhanga	304	BT 103
Ruhangino	284	CL 118
Ruhengeri	298	BV 102
Ruhinda	304	BT 103
Ruimte	231	DO 74
Ruiru	301	BU 117
Rukanga	302	BZ 120
Rukungiri	304	BT 103
Rulenge	298	BX 104
Ruma	367	NZ 326
Rumba	296	CD 117
Rumbek	320	BD 102
Rumonge	298	BZ 102
Rumphi	282	CO 110
Rumuruti	307	BR 115
Runazi	299	BX 105
Runde	247	DJ 104
Rundu	253	DC 82
Runere	299	BY 109
Rungemba	283	CJ 113
Rungu	385	OK 347
Rungwa (Tan.)	294	CG 106
Rungwa (Tan.)	295	CF 110
Rupa	314	BM 112
Rupara	253	DC 81
Rupia	283	CJ 115
Rupisi	248	DH 107
Ruponda	284	CN 120
Rusape	248	DE 107
Rushinda	258	DA 107
Rust	209	EJ 80
Rust de Winter	228	DS 100
Rustenburg	227	DT 97
Rustig	227	DW 97
Rusverby	227	DT 96
Rutana	298	BZ 103
Rutenga	247	DK 104
Rutland	228	DR 100
Rutshuru	298	BU 101
Ruwa	258	DC 105
Ruwangwa	258	DC 108
Ruyigi	298	BY 103
Rwamagana	298	BV 103
Rwashamaire	304	BT 103
Rwenya River	258	DB 108
S Cristóvão	262	CT 70
S. João do Sull	250	CY 67
S. Jorge de Limpopo	237	DN 106
Saa	382	OJ 330
Saadani	297	CE 120
Saaifontein	210	EF 86
Saaiplaas (F.S.)	219	DY 95
Saaiplaas (F.S.)	226	DX 94
Sabagusi	293	CC 103
Sabaiya	385	OE 345
Sabarei	315	BJ 116
Sabari	380	OD 319
Sabderat	373	NX 356
Sabha	344	NL 334
Sabie (Moz.)	229	DS 107
Sabie (Mpum.)	228	DS 104
Sabina	255	DC 90
Sabon-Berni	366	NY 325
Sabongan	382	OG 330
Sabongida	381	OF 325
Sabou	365	OA 317
Saboudo	363	NW 306
Sabse	365	NZ 318
Sabuéue	253	CX 81
Sacacama	266	CS 86
Sacachai	253	DB 84
Sacambanda	256	DC 85
Sacambunge	278	CN 87
Sacaveto	253	CX 82
Sacaza	290	CH 85
Sacco Uein	309	BO 128
Sachipoque	253	CX 80
Sachula	277	CN 83
Sachunga	264	CW 80
Sacufua	277	CN 81
Sacumbi	277	CM 81
Sacuunda	278	CP 89
Sada	212	EG 96
Sadi	322	AZ 113
Sadiola	363	NY 307
Safaha (Sud.)	371	OC 346
Safaha (Bur.F)	365	OA 316
Safi	329	NF 310
Sagabari	363	NZ 309
Sagana	307	BT 117
Sagara	295	CE 115
Sagata	300	BX 111
Sagleipie	378	OF 310
Sah	364	NW 315
Sahaba	359	NT 349
Saheib	370	OA 344
Said Bundas	385	OE 344
Saida	331	NC 319
Saidia	330	NC 317
Sainsoutou	363	NZ 307
Saint Michael	299	BZ 108
Saint-Louis	362	NW 302
Saint-Martin	386	OP 330
Saka (Ken.)	308	BS 121
Saka (Eth.)	323	BA 116
Saka (Mor.)	330	NC 315
Sakabinde	279	CP 93

PLACE NAME	PG	GRID
Sakai	365	OB 317
Sakamaliwa	300	CA 111
Sakania	268	CS 100
Sakapane	244	DG 90
Sakassou	379	OF 314
Sake	298	BV 101
Sakiet Sidi Yussef	332	NB 327
Sakpiegu	365	OC 319
Sakrivier	216	ED 84
Sala	294	CH 106
Salaga	380	OE 318
Salagle	309	BO 127
Salahly	326	AZ 131
Salajwe	234	DP 92
Salak	368	OB 333
Salal	369	NX 336
Salala	360	NR 355
Salamanga	229	DU 108
Saldanha	208	EJ 79
Sale	329	ND 312
Salem	212	EJ 95
Salia	385	OJ 345
Salima	271	CU 111
Salimanis	282	CJ 110
Salimu	295	CB 113
Salka	366	OC 324
Salmossi	365	NX 319
Salo	383	OK 335
Salpeterpan	226	DW 92
Salt Rock	221	EB 105
Salum	336	NG 344
Salzbrunn	232	DQ 79
Samacai	264	CW 80
Samagaigai	243	DF 83
Samakona	364	OC 312
Samalut	347	NK 350
Samatiguila	364	OC 311
Samatwa	296	CD 117
Samba (DRC)	292	CB 95
Samba (CAR)	383	OH 335
Samba (CAR)	384	OF 340
Samba (DRC)	388	ON 340
Samba Caju	275	CK 73
Sambailo	363	NZ 306
Sambalgou	366	OA 321
Sambialgou	365	OA 320
Sambili	385	OJ 343
Sambo	263	CT 75
Samburu	302	BZ 121
Sambusa	253	DC 81
Sambwa	296	CB 115
Same	301	CA 118
Samfya	281	CP 102
Samnu	344	NL 334
Samoa	277	CM 85
Sampa	379	OE 316
Sampelga	365	NY 319
Sampwe	280	CL 98
Samre	373	NZ 358
Samreboe	379	OG 316
Samucumbi	265	CT 81
Samugalengue	253	DB 82
Samulondo	278	CM 87
Samungure	253	CX 81
Samuquimba	277	CM 83
San	364	NZ 314
San Pedro	378	OH 312
San Sebastián de la Gomera	338	NK 301
San'a	374	NX 363
Sanaba	364	OA 315
Sanam	366	NX 323
Sanam	367	OB 329
Sanando	364	NZ 313
Sanankoroba	364	OA 311
Sança	259	DB 111
Sandando	265	CQ 84
Sandare	363	NX 309
Sandaula	254	CX 88
Sandberg	209	EG 80
Sanddrif	217	EB 88
Sandegué	379	OE 316
Sandkop	217	ED 88
Sandoa	278	CM 88
Sandton	227	DU 99
Sandverhaar	223	DV 77
Sandvlakte	211	EK 91
Sang	380	OD 319
Sanga (Ang.)	275	CP 73
Sanga (Bur.F)	365	OB 319
Sanga (Mali)	365	NY 316
Sanga (Moz.)	271	CR 113
Sanga (Uga.)	304	BS 104
Sangalawe	296	CF 115
Sangama	282	CK 107
Sangardo	378	OD 309
Sangbé	382	OG 332
Sange	292	CG 99
Sangmelima	382	OK 331
Sango	237	DM 106
Sangoshe	254	DD 87
Sanguelengue	253	CX 82
Sangulana	363	OB 309
Sangwali	255	DD 90
Sani	363	NW 307
Saniquellie	378	OF 310
Sanitatis	250	DD 68
Sanje	305	BT 105
Sankula	270	CQ 106
Sanlo	379	OE 315
Sannaspos	219	EA 96
Sannieshof	226	DV 94
Sanoyie	378	OF 309
Sanpaka	364	NX 311
Sansale	362	OB 304
Sansanding	364	NY 313
Sanso	364	OA 312
Santa Cruz de la Palma	338	NJ 302
Santa Cruz de Tenerife	338	NK 303
Santa Maria (Ang.)	262	CT 67
Santa Maria (Moz.)	229	DU 109
Santa Marta	262	CU 67
Santa Sue	362	NZ 305
Santchau	376	OH 329
Santhe	270	CT 109
Santiguila	364	NZ 312
Santilya	282	CL 109
Santo André	263	CT 71
Santo Antonio	262	CW 70
Santos	287	CE 74
Santou	363	OB 306
Sanya Juju	301	BY 116
Sanyati	257	DC 101
Sanyatwe	258	DD 107
Sanza Pombo	287	CG 74
São Antonio	376	OL 326
Sao Domingos	362	OA 303
Sao Hill	283	CJ 113
São João dos Angolares	376	ON 326
São Tomé	376	ON 326
Sapele	381	OG 325
Sapo Sapo	290	CD 87
Sapoba	381	OG 325
Sapouy	365	OA 317
Sapuila	264	CW 79
Saqadi	372	NY 352
Sara (Nam.)	243	DF 83
Sara (Bur.F)	364	OA 315
Sara Kawa	365	OC 320
Sarabango	379	OE 316
Saraféré	364	NW 315
Saranda	295	CD 112
Saraya	363	NZ 307
Sare	362	NZ 304
Sarekati	363	OA 307
Sarenli	309	BN 127
Sarh	383	OD 337
Sarhala	379	OE 313
Sarkin Kudin	382	OE 328
Saron	225	DU 88
Sarro	364	NY 314
Sasabeneh	326	BB 130
Sasolburg	227	DV 98
Sass Town	378	OH 310
Sassandra	379	OH 313
Satadougou	363	NZ 308
Satama Sokoura	379	OE 315
Satco	224	DX 80
Satechissende	277	CL 84
Satema	384	OJ 341
Satiri	364	OB 315
Saucula	289	CH 82
Sauer	209	EH 80
Saurimo	277	CM 83
Sautar	276	CP 79
Savalou	380	OE 321
Savane	249	DG 113
Savate	252	DA 78
Save	249	DK 112
Savé	380	OE 321
Savuti	244	DE 91
Sawla	379	OD 316
Sawmills	246	DG 99
Say (Mali)	364	NY 314
Say (Benin)	366	NZ 321
Sayaga	300	BX 110
Saye	379	OD 316
Saylac	374	OB 363
Sbaa	341	NK 319
Sbeitla	333	NC 328
Scandica	287	CE 74
Scante	294	CF 108
Scarborough	208	EL 79
Schakalskuppe	223	DV 75
Scheepersnek	228	DX 104
Schlip	231	DQ 77
Schmidtsdrif	218	DZ 91
Schoemanshoek	210	EK 87
Schoombee	218	EE 94
Schumannsthal	242	DG 77
Schuttesdraai	227	DX 96
Schweizer-Reneke	226	DW 94
Scottburgh	220	EC 104
Sea Park	220	ED 104
Sea View	211	EL 93
Sebapala	219	EC 98
Sebayeng	236	DP 102
Sebba	365	NZ 320
Sebdou	331	NC 318
Sebekoro	363	NZ 310
Sebeta	324	AZ 120
Sebina	246	DJ 97
Sebit	306	BP 113
Sebokeng	227	DV 98
Secunda	228	DV 101
Sedgefield	210	EL 88
Sedhiou	362	NZ 304
Sediba	219	EA 96
Sedrata	332	NB 327
Seeheim	223	DV 78
Seeis	232	DM 78
Seekoegat	210	EJ 87
Seemade	327	BC 139
Sefako	220	DZ 100
Sefeto	363	NY 309
Sefophe	236	DM 98
Sefrou	330	ND 314
Segag	325	BB 128
Segala	363	NX 308
Segbana	366	OB 323
Segera	297	CC 120
Ségou	364	NZ 313
Séguédiné	356	NS 332
Séguéla	378	OE 312
Seguelon	378	OD 312
Seguenega	365	NZ 317
Sehithwa	244	DH 88
Sehlabathebe	220	EB 100
Sehonghong	220	EB 100
Sejanane	333	NA 328
Sejeli	296	CE 115
Seka	323	BB 116
Sekenke	300	CA 111
Sekhira	333	ND 329
Sekhukhune	228	DR 103
Seko	384	OG 340
Sekoma	226	DR 91
Sekondi-Takoradi	379	OH 317
Sekota	373	OA 358
Selba	365	NX 317
Selebi Phikwe	236	DM 98
Seleka	235	DN 97
Selemani	293	CC 101
Selengi	387	OP 337
Selengei	301	BW 117
Selibaby	363	NX 307
Selim (CAR)	385	OH 343
Selim (CAR)	385	OH 346
Selinnkegni	363	NX 308
Selokolela	226	DR 93
Selonsrivier	228	DT 102
Selouma	363	OB 308
Selous	257	DD 103
Semacueza	249	DF 112
Sembabule	305	BS 105
Sembe (Lib.)	378	OF 308
Sembé (Congo)	387	OL 334
Sembehun	377	OE 306
Semel	371	NZ 350
Semien	378	OE 312
Semna	359	NR 350
Semolale	246	DL 100
Semonkong	219	EB 98
Senanga	254	CZ 89
Sendafa	324	AY 120
Sendelingsdrif	215	DY 76
Sendelingsfontein	227	DV 95
Sending	236	DO 101
Sened Gare	333	NC 328
Senekal	219	DY 98
Senga	271	CU 112
Senga Hill	281	CL 105
Sengan	376	OJ 325
Senge	298	BY 101
Sengerema	299	BX 108
Sengwe	237	DM 105
Senkobo	255	DC 94
Senlac	226	DT 90
Sennar	372	NY 353
Senoba	362	NZ 304
Senoudebou	363	NY 307
Sentrum	235	DQ 97
Senwabarana (Bochum)	236	DO 101
Senya Beraku	380	OH 319
Senye	376	OL 329
Seoding	225	DW 89
Sepako	245	DG 95
Sepane	219	EA 96
Sepeteri	381	OD 323
Sept des Gzoula	329	NF 310
Sepuka	295	CB 112
Sepupa	244	DE 87
Serarou	366	OC 322
Serdo	373	OA 360
Seredupi	307	BP 118
Serekunda	362	NZ 302
Serena	237	DN 104
Serenje	269	CT 103
Serere	305	BO 109
Sericho	308	BP 121
Seringkop	228	DT 100
Seronera	300	BW 112
Seronga	244	DE 88
Serowe	235	DM 96
Serti	382	OE 330
Seru	324	BB 123
Serule	246	DL 97
Sese	389	OL 345
Sesenge	312	BK 102
Sesfontein	240	DF 70
Seshego	236	DP 101
Sesheke	255	DB 91
Sesriem	222	DR 74
Sessa	265	CU 84
Sessami	257	DD 100
Setif	332	NB 325
Setlagole	226	DU 93
Settat	329	NE 311
Setté Cama	386	OQ 329
Settlers	228	DR 100
Setto	380	OF 321
Setuat	226	DV 91
Sevare	364	NX 315
Sevenoaks	220	EA 104
Severn	225	DV 88
Sevilla de Niefang	376	OL 329
Seyanga	383	OH 336
Seymour	212	EH 96
Sezela	220	EC 104
Sfax	333	NC 330
Sfizef	331	NC 319
Sha	333	NF 331
Shabunda	389	OQ 346
Shafaci	366	OB 323
Shaffa	368	OC 331
Shagamu	381	OF 323
Shaka's Rock	221	EB 105
Shakaskraal	221	EA 105
Shakawa	289	CF 81
Shakawe	254	DD 86
Shaki	380	OD 322
Sha-Kisandji	288	CG 79
Shamaziamu	289	CH 81
Shambe	320	BC 104
Shambu	373	OC 356
Shamley's Farm	217	EB 87
Shamputa	268	CV 98
Shamva	258	DB 106
Shangani	246	DG 101
Shangev-Tiev	381	OF 327
Shangombo	254	CZ 87
Shani	368	OC 331
Shannon	219	EA 95
Shanwa	300	BY 110
Shapembe	289	CG 83
Shapoko	289	CF 80
Sharafa	371	OA 346
Sharm el Sheikh	348	NK 354
Shasha	381	OF 323
Shashe	246	DK 97
Shashemene	324	BC 120
Shatawi	372	NX 351
Shatshisongo	289	CG 81
Shaykh Gok	372	OB 352
Shebe	323	BB 115
Sheekh	374	OC 364
Sheephouse	218	EA 91
Sheepmoor	228	DV 103
Sheffield Beach	221	EA 105
Shek Hasan	372	OA 355
Shek Husen	324	BB 124
Sheki	323	BB 116
Sheldon	211	EJ 94
Shellem	368	OC 331
Shelly Beach	220	ED 104
Shelui	300	CA 111
Shemula	229	DW 107
Shendam	382	OD 329
Shendi	360	NV 353
Shenge	377	OE 306
Sheno	324	AY 121
Sherbi	375	OC 368
Sherborne	218	EE 92
Shereiq	360	NT 353
Sherwood	236	DN 98
Shibuyinje	256	CY 99
Shibuyunje	256	CX 98
Shiko	366	OA 323
Shikurufumi (Tan.)	296	CG 117
Shikurufumi (Tan.)	296	CG 118
Shilabo	326	BE 132
Shimoni	297	CB 121
Shinga	389	OQ 344
Shinkafe	366	NZ 325
Shinyanga	299	BZ 109
Shirati	300	BU 111
Shirbin	337	NG 350
Shirley	224	DT 80
Shishinda	322	BC 114
Shoga	282	CJ 110
Sholole	282	CO 109
Shorobe	244	DG 90
Shoshong	235	DO 95
Shukumukwa	244	DG 90
Shumba	245	DE 95
Shurugwi	247	DG 103
Si	364	NY 314
Sia	366	OA 322
Siabuwa	256	DB 99
Siachitema	256	DA 96
Siaeb	386	OP 332
Sianhala	364	OC 312
Siasibabole	256	DB 97
Siavonga	257	DA 100
Sibiti	386	OR 332
Sibthorpe	228	DS 104
Sibut	384	OG 338
Sibwesa	293	CF 104
Siby	364	OA 311
Sichili	255	DA 92
Sidéradougou	364	OB 315
Sidi Mokhtar	329	NG 310
Sidi Abdarrahman	337	NG 348
Sidi Afi	331	NB 320
Sidi Aissa	332	NB 323
Sidi Allal el Babraoui	330	ND 313
Sidi as Sayd	333	NF 332
Sidi Barrani	336	NF 345
Sidi Bel Abbes	331	NC 318
Sidi Bennour	329	NE 311
Sidi Bou Zid	333	NC 329
Sidi Boubekeu	331	NC 319
Sidi Brahim	330	ND 316
Sidi Hajjaj	329	NE 312
Sidi Ifni	339	NJ 309
Sidi Kacem	330	ND 314
Sidi Khaled	332	ND 324
Sidi Ladjel	331	NC 322
Sidi Moussa	329	NE 310
Sidi Slimane	330	ND 313
Sidi Smail	329	NE 311
Sidi Yousset	333	NC 330
Sidikila	363	OB 310
Sido	364	OA 311
Sidvokodvo	229	DV 105
Sidwadweni	220	EE 100
Sif Fatima	333	NG 328
Sifani	373	OA 359
Sifié	378	OE 312
Sig	331	NB 319
Signalberg	223	DX 79
Sigoga	220	EC 100
Sigombo	254	CY 88
Sigor	306	BP 113
Sigubudu	221	DY 106
Siguiri	363	OB 310
Sihazela	246	DF 97
Sihhoye	229	DT 106
Sihole	254	CX 88
Sika	386	OP 329
Sikasso	364	OB 314
Sikelenge	267	CW 91
Sikensi	379	OG 314
Sikhwane	227	DR 95
Sikikede	369	OC 340
Sikonge	294	CD 108
Sikongo	254	CX 87
Sikwakwa	296	CC 115
Sikwane	227	DR 95
Sikwanyi	254	DC 89
Silalabuhwa	246	DJ 101
Silent Valley	227	DR 96
Silet	354	NP 324
Silil	374	OB 362
Silkaatskop	227	DS 96
Sillana	333	NB 328
Silli	365	OA 317
Silobela	246	DE 101
Siluk	381	OF 324
Silutshana	220	DY 104
Silver Streams	217	DY 89
Silversand	232	DM 78
Silverside Mine	257	DA 103
Simamba	255	DA 94
Simba (Tan.)	294	CB 109
Simba (DRC)	388	OM 342
Simbi	363	NX 309
Simbo	293	CB 102
Simindou	384	OF 342
Simiri	366	NY 321
Simonbondo	387	OP 333
Simoni	270	CS 107
Simons Town	209	EM 80
Sina Dhaqa	319	BG 135
Sinau	380	OD 322
Sinawin	333	NG 330
Sinawon-gourou	366	OB 322
Sinazongwe	256	DB 97
Sinclair Mine	223	DT 75
Sinda	270	CV 106
Sindia	362	NX 302
Sindou	364	OB 314
Sinende	366	OC 322
Sinfra	379	OF 313
Singa	372	NZ 353
Singako	369	OC 338
Singida	295	CB 112
Singisi	220	EC 102
Sinjembele	254	DB 89
Sinkat	361	NT 356
Sinko	378	OD 311
Sinnuris	347	NJ 350
Sinujif	326	BB 133
Sinungu	254	CY 88
Sioma	255	DA 90
Sipatunyana	256	DB 96
Siphofaneni	229	DV 106
Sipilou	378	OE 311
Sir Lowry's Pass	209	EL 80
Sirakoro (Mal.)	362	NZ 310
Sirakoro (Mal.)	364	OB 312
Siramana	363	OB 310
Sirana	378	OD 311
Sirasso	379	OD 313
Sire (Tan.)	294	CD 106
Sire (Eth.)	324	BA 121
Sironko	306	BP 111
Sirsiri	313	BJ 106
Sishen	225	DX 88
Sitakili	363	NZ 308
Sitalike	294	CF 105
Siteki	229	DU 106
Sithobela	229	DV 106
Sitila	239	DO 113
Sitoti	254	CZ 89
Sitra	347	NJ 346
Sittingbourne	212	EJ 97
Sittona	373	NY 356
Sitwe	282	CO 109
Sive	363	NW 306
Siwa	346	NJ 345
Siwe	294	CF 107
Siyabuswa	228	DS 101
Skaapvlei	215	EE 79
Skaymat	338	NN 304
Skeerpoort	227	DT 98
Skerpioenpunt	217	DZ 87
Skhirat	329	ND 312
Skikda	332	NA 326
Skipskop	209	EM 83
Skoenmakerskop	211	EL 93
Skoura	329	NG 312
Skuinsdrif	227	DS 95
Skukuza	229	DS 106
Slangrivier	211	EL 92
Sleutelspoort	218	EB 93
Slim	332	NC 323
Slurry	226	DT 94
Smara	339	NL 307
Smir	330	NB 314
Smithfield	219	EC 96
Sneeukraal	210	EF 88
Sneezewood	220	EC 102
Snykolk	216	EE 84
So	365	NY 317
Soba	367	OB 327
Soba Matias	264	CV 78
Sobea	218	DZ 93
Sodiri	371	NY 348
Sodium	217	EC 89
Sodo	323	BD 118
Soebatsfontein	215	EC 78
Soegue	363	OA 306
Soetendal	209	EK 81
Sofala	249	DH 112
Sofara	364	NY 315
Sofi Majiji	283	CK 115
Soi	362	NW 302
Sogakofe	380	OG 320
Soghor	306	BS 113
Sogoubeni	378	OE 310
Sohag	348	NM 351
Soin	364	NZ 315
Sojwe	235	DO 94
Sokele	279	CM 92
Sokodé	380	OD 320
Sokolo	364	NX 313
Sokone	362	NY 303
Sokoto	366	NZ 324
Sokoumba	384	OD 340
Sokoy Yakoma	385	OG 345
Sola	292	CC 97
Sole (E.C.)	212	EG 97
Sole (Bur.F)	365	NY 317
Solenzo	364	OA 315
Solesia	282	CK 106
Soli	367	NX 327
Solio	307	BS 116
Solitaire	231	DP 75
Solna	365	NZ 320
Solola	309	BR 126
Sololo	316	BK 120
Solomondale	236	DP 102
Solowu	295	CD 114
Solusi	246	DH 99
Solwezi	267	CR 95
Somabhula	247	DG 102
Soma-dougou	364	NY 315
Somalom	382	OK 332
Somanda	300	BX 111
Somanga	285	CJ 121
Somerset East	211	EH 93
Somerset West	209	EL 80
Somil	254	CY 86
Somokoro	379	OE 313
Sonaco	362	OA 305
Sonanga	364	NY 312
Sonderpan	217	EA 86
Sondu	306	BS 112
Song	360	NR 351
Song	376	OM 329
Songa	279	CJ 93
Songe	296	CD 117
Songea	283	CO 114
Songo	258	CY 108
Sonji	282	CJ 106
Sonjo	300	BW 114
Sonop	227	DT 98
Sonstraal	225	DW 87
Sonta	280	CO 99
Sooya	309	BR 127
Sora Mboum	383	OE 334
Sorefta	324	BD 121
Sorgvliet	218	EA 94
Sori	366	OB 322
Sorombeo	383	OE 334
Soroti	306	BO 110
Sorris Sorris	241	DJ 72
Sosso	383	OJ 335
Sosso (31 de Janeiro)	287	CF 73
Sotik	306	BT 113
Sotouboua	380	OD 320
Souanké	387	OL 333
Soubaka-niedougou	364	OC 314
Soubré	378	OG 312
Sougueur	331	NC 321
Souk Ahras	332	NB 327
Souk el Arba du Rharb	330	NC 313
Soukoukoutane	366	NY 323
Soulabali	362	NZ 304
Soulemaka	384	OD 341
Sounga	386	OP 329
Sountat	369	NY 338
Sour el Ghozlane	332	NB 323
Sousse	333	NB 330
South Downs	220	EA 102
South Horr	307	BN 116
Southbroom	220	ED 103
Southeyville	212	EF 98
Southport	220	ED 104
Southwell	212	EK 96
Soutpan (F.S.)	218	DY 93
Soutpan (F.S.)	219	DZ 95
Sowa	245	DJ 95
Soweto	227	DU 98
Soy	306	BQ 113
Soyo	286	CE 67
Spanjaard	208	EH 79
Spanwerk	235	DQ 97
Speelmanskraal	210	EK 89
Spencer Bay	222	DT 72
Spes Bona	227	DW 97
Spitskop	219	EA 96
Spitskopvlei	211	EF 93
Spoedwel	228	DR 101
Spoegrivier	215	EC 78
Sprigg	217	DZ 85
Spring Valley	212	EG 95
Springbok (E.C.)	218	EE 93
Springbok (N.C.)	215	EB 78
Springbokwater Gate	240	DH 70
Springfontein (F.S.)	218	DY 93
Springfontein (F.S.)	218	EC 94
Springs	227	DU 99
Spruitdrif	209	EF 80
Spytfontein	218	DZ 92
St Marks	212	EG 97
St Barbara's	248	DE 107
St Clair	218	EA 90
St Cuthberts	220	EE 100
St Faith's	220	ED 103
St Francis Bay	211	EL 92
St Helena Bay	208	EH 78
St Josephs	246	DK 99
St Lucia	221	DY 107
St Mary's	268	CS 97
St Michael's Mission	241	DG 74
St Paul's	246	DE 99
Staansaam	224	DW 84
Stafford's Post	220	ED 102
Stampriet	232	DQ 79
Standerton	228	DV 101
Stanford	209	EL 81
Stanger	221	EA 105
Stanmore (KZN)	220	EA 103
Stanmore (Zim.)	246	DJ 101
Stapleford	248	DE 108
Station 10	360	NS 352
Station 5	360	NR 351
Station 6	360	NR 351
Steekdorings	226	DW 91
Steenbokpan	235	DP 97
Steilloopbrug	236	DO 99
Steilrand	229	DX 105
Steilwater	236	DO 100
Steinhausen	242	DL 79
Steinkopf	215	EA 78
Steins	210	EH 87
Steinveld	223	DS 75
Stella	226	DV 92
Stellenbosch	209	EK 81
Sterkaar	218	EE 90
Sterkloop	228	DT 102
Sterkspruit	219	ED 97
Sterkstroom	212	EF 95
Sterkwater	236	DQ 100
Sterling	217	EE 86
Steynsburg	218	EE 94
Steynsrus	227	DX 97
Steytlerville	211	EJ 91
Stile	332	ND 325
Stilfontein	227	DV 96
Still Bay East	210	EL 86
Still Bay West	210	EL 85
Stinkbank	231	DM 73
Stockpoort	235	DO 97
Stofvlei	216	EC 80
Stompneus Bay	208	EH 78
Stoneyridge	220	EE 100
Stormberg	219	EE 95
Stormsrivier	211	EK 90
Stormsvlei	209	EL 83
Straatsdrif	227	DS 95
Strand	209	EL 80
Strandfontein	208	EF 79
Struisbaai	209	EM 83
Strydenburg	218	EB 90
Studtis	211	EK 90
Stutterheim	212	EH 97
Stuurman	216	EE 83
Suakin	361	NT 356
Suana	289	CF 83
Subida Grande	250	CX 67
Sudr	348	NH 352
Suez (El-Suneis)	348	NH 352
Suguta	296	CE 116
Suguti	300	BV 110
Sukses	241	DK 76
Sukwane	244	DJ 91
Suleja	381	OD 326
Sulima	377	OF 307
Sultulta	324	AY 120
Sulu	291	CB 91
Suluq	335	NF 339
Sumbawanga	294	CH 105
Sumbe	274	CP 70
Sumbi	286	CB 69
Sumbu	281	CK 103
Sumbuya	377	OE 307
Summerdown	242	DK 80
Summerstrand	211	EK 94
Summit	361	NT 356
Sun City / Lost City	227	DS 97
Suna	300	BU 111
Sunate	273	CT 123
Sundra	228	DU 100
Sunga	296	CB 119
Sungawula	294	CF 107
Sunginge	276	CK 76
Sungo	259	DA 111
Sungue	248	DK 108
Sunland	211	EK 94
Sunnyside	211	EK 93
Suntai	382	OE 329
Suntu	323	BA 116
Sunyani	379	OF 317
Suqa el Gamal	371	NZ 346
Sura	324	BC 124
Surman	333	NE 332
Surt	334	NG 336
Susijinda	295	CB 110
Sussendenga	248	DF 109
Suswe	258	DB 107
Sutherland	209	EG 84
Sutti	366	NZ 324
Sutton	225	DW 88
Sutukoba	362	NZ 305
Suurberg	211	EJ 94
Suurbraak	209	EL 84
Suurlaer	220	DZ 101
Suwala	295	CF 113
Swaershoek	211	EG 94
Swakopmund	230	DN 71
Swana-Mume	279	CP 95
Swart uMfolozi	229	DX 105
Swartberg	220	EC 101
Swartbooisdrift	251	DB 70
Swartkops	211	EK 94
Swartmodder	216	DY 83
Swartplaas	227	DU 96
Swartruggens	227	DT 96
Swartwater	236	DN 99
Swawel	216	EE 83
Sweetfontein	218	ED 90
Swellendam	209	EL 83
Swempoort	219	EE 97
Swinburne	220	DY 101
Sybrandskraal	228	DS 100
Sydney-on-Vaal	218	DY 91
Syfergat	219	EE 95
Syferkuil	227	DW 99
T. Bakare	366	OB 323
Taabo	379	OG 314
Taba	348	NJ 354
Tabarka	333	NA 328
Tabelbala	341	NJ 316
Tabelot	355	NU 328
Taberdga	332	NC 326
Tabligbo	380	OF 320
Tabora	294	CC 108
Tabou	378	OJ 312
Tabur	370	OB 343
Taca	251	CZ 70
Tacuane	260	CZ 116
Tadcaster	226	DX 92
Taddert	329	NG 312
Tadjemout	331	ND 322
Tadjmout	342	NM 323
Tadjoura	374	OA 362
Tadjrouna	331	NE 321
Tafelberg	211	EF 93
Tafnidilt	339	NJ 308
Tafraoute	339	NH 310
Tagab	359	NS 349
Tagau	368	NZ 331
Taghaoumit	352	NV 311
Taghit	330	NG 317
Tagounit	340	NH 314
Taguelmit	333	NE 330
Taharsouk	330	NC 315
Tahomi	378	OG 311
Tahoua	366	NX 324
Tahta	347	NL 350
Taï	378	OG 312
Taiama	377	OE 307
Taidalt	339	NJ 309
Taimana	364	NY 312
Tainton	212	EH 99
Taiyara	371	NZ 350
Taizz	374	NY 363
Tajarhi	344	NO 333
Tajura	333	NE 332
Takabba	316	BL 123
Takai	367	OA 328
Takalama	370	OC 341
Takara	384	OE 340
Takatokwane	234	DQ 91
Takatshwane	233	DN 87
Takiéta	367	NY 328
Takobanda	384	OF 339
Takochi	366	NX 325
Takorka	366	NY 325
Takpamba	365	OC 320
Takpolma	378	OF 308
Takum	382	OF 328
Takundi	288	CB 75
Tala	301	BU 117
Talata Mafara	366	NZ 325
Talcho	366	NX 322
Taleni	212	EG 99
Talguharai	360	NU 355
Tali Post	312	BF 104
Taliouine	329	NG 311
Talismanis	243	DL 84
Talmest	329	NF 310
Talodi	371	OB 349
Talras	367	NX 329
Tama	367	NZ 327
Tamale	380	OD 318
Tamanar	329	NG 309
Tamanhint	344	NL 334
Tamani	364	NZ 312
Tamanrasset	354	NP 325
Tamarou	366	OC 322
Tamayye	338	NO 303
Tamba	247	DK 102
Tambach	306	BQ 114
Tambacounda	362	NY 305
Tambakara	363	NX 308
Tambarga	365	OB 320
Tambo	250	CZ 67
Tamboura	385	OH 344
Tambura	385	OG 347
Tamchaket	351	NV 309
Tamelelt	329	NF 312
Tamezret	333	ND 329
Tamota	296	CD 118
Tamou	366	NZ 321
Tampa	250	CX 69
Tamri	329	NG 309
Tamsu	243	DE 83
Tan Emellel	343	NK 329
Tan Tan	339	NK 308
Tan Tan Plage	339	NJ 307
Tanal	365	NX 316
Tanantou	378	OD 311
Tanda	379	OE 316
Tandali	283	CL 111
Tandjouaré	365	OB 319
Tanene	362	OB 305
Tanga	297	CC 121
Tanganda	248	DH 108
Tangier (Tanger)	330	NB 313
Tanguiéta	365	OB 320
Tangulbei	307	BQ 115
Taninga	238	DS 108
Tânout	367	NX 328
Tanta	337	NG 350
Taoudenni	352	NP 315
Taounate	330	ND 314
Taourirt	330	ND 316
Taourirt	341	NL 319
Tapeta	378	OF 310
Tapili	385	OK 347
Tapol	383	OE 336
Taqatu Hayya	360	NU 355
Tara	256	DA 96
Taraghin	344	NM 334
Tarat	343	NM 328
Taratara	253	DD 83
Tarbaj	308	BN 123
Tarfaya	339	NK 306
Targuist	330	NC 315
Tarhacha	369	NY 340
Tarhunah	334	NF 333
Tarime	300	BU 111
Tarkastad	212	EG 95
Tarkwa	379	OH 317
Taroudant	339	NH 310
Tarteri	368	OA 332
Taru	295	CC 113
Tarube	244	DF 87
Tasawah	344	NM 333
Tasker	367	NX 330
Tassara	354	NV 325
Tata	340	NH 311
Tataguine	362	NY 302
Tatakpani	384	OG 338
Tataouine	333	NE 330
Tatokou	367	NX 328
Taufikia	321	AY 106
Taula	247	DK 102
Taung	226	DX 92
Taveta (Ken.)	301	BY 118
Taveta (Tan.)	283	CL 114
Taweisha	371	OA 346
Tawilah	370	NY 344
Tawurgha	334	NF 334
Tayeeglow	318	BJ 131
Taza	330	ND 315
Tazenakht	329	NG 312
Tazirbu	345	NM 340
Tazrouk	354	NP 325
Tazzarine	330	NG 313
Tchafchou	380	OD 322
Tchamba (Ben.)	380	OD 321
Tchamba (Cam.)	382	OD 332
Tchangsou	383	OD 334
Tchaourou	380	OD 322
Tchatchako	380	OD 319
Tcheriba	365	OA 316
Tchérré	387	ON 334
Tchetti	380	OE 321
Tchibanga	386	OQ 330
Tchifito	251	CZ 71
Tchighozerine	355	NV 327
Tchilounga	386	OR 330
Tchin-Tabaradene	366	NW 325
Tchipelongo	251	DA 72
Tcholliré	383	OE 333
Tebarat	366	NX 324
Tébé	387	OM 333
Tebessa	332	NC 327
Tebourba	333	NA 329
Tebour-souk	333	NB 328
Techaza	251	CY 73
Techiman	379	OE 317
Techine	333	NE 329
Techinoca	264	CW 78
Techipa	251	DA 71
Techirimba	263	CQ 73
Techissanha	264	CV 78
Techla	350	NQ 304
Techongolola	276	CN 76
Ted	318	BJ 130
Teebus	218	EE 94
Tegina	366	OC 325
Teguidda-n-Tessoumt	355	NV 326
Teheyzegorou	366	NX 322
Téhini	364	OC 315
Teiskot	355	NV 320
Teiti	359	NT 349
Tejira	367	NX 329
Tela	268	CR 100
Telagh	331	NC 319
Telde	338	NK 304
Telimele	363	OB 306
Teltele	315	BG 117
Tema	380	OG 319
Temba	227	DS 99
Tembisa	227	DU 99
Tembo	288	CH 77
Tembo Aluma	288	CH 77
Tembwe	282	CP 108
Temelon	386	OL 330
Temera	353	NV 318
Temki	369	OA 337
Tenado	365	OA 316
Tendaho	373	OA 360
Tendelti	372	NZ 351
Tendrara	330	NE 317
Tenes	331	NB 320
Tengue	252	CX 78
Te-n-Guembou	363	NW 309
Tenkodogo	365	OA 319
Tenta	373	OB 358
Tepa	379	OF 317
Tepere	272	CU 120
Tepi	322	BC 113
Téra	365	NY 320
Terakeka	313	BF 106
Termesse	363	OA 306
Termit	367	NW 330
Terra Firma	225	DT 89
Terrace Bay	240	DG 69
Teselima	379	OE 317
Tesenane	238	DN 110
Tessalit	353	NS 320
Tessaoua	367	NY 327
Tessenei	373	NX 356
Tessit	365	NX 319
Tessolo	248	DL 111
Testour (Tun.)	333	NB 328
Testour (Tun.)	333	NB 329
Tete	259	CZ 110
Tetouan	330	NC 314
Teturi	304	BP 101
Teufelsbach	231	DM 77
Teviot	211	EF 94
Tewana	235	DN 97
Teyateyaneng	219	EA 98
Teza	221	DZ 107
Thaba Bosiu	219	EA 98
Thaba Chitja	219	EC 99
Thaba Nchu	219	EA 96
Thaba Phatshwa	219	EA 97
Thaba-Tseka	220	EB 100
Thabatshukudu	245	DJ 94
Thabazimbi	227	DR 97
Thabong	227	DX 96
Thakadu	245	DK 96
Thala	333	NB 328
Thale	244	DF 87
Thamaga	226	DR 93
Tharaka	307	BS 118
Thavu	301	BW 118
Thazima	282	CO 110
The Baths	209	EH 81
The Crags	210	EK 89
The Downs	237	DQ 103
The Haven	213	EG 101
The Heads	210	EL 89
The Ranch	220	DZ 104
Thelepte	332	NC 328
Thenia	332	NA 323
Thenlet el Had	331	NB 321
Theron	219	DY 96
Theunissen	219	DY 96
Thies	362	NX 302
Thika	301	BU 116
Thilogne	362	NW 305
Thio	373	NX 360
Thiou	365	NY 316
Thitani	301	BU 118
Thohoyandou	237	DN 104
Thokazi	229	DX 106
Thomas River	212	EG 97
Thorndale	236	DP 102
Thornhill	211	EK 93
Thornville	220	EB 103
Three Sisters	210	EF 89
Thyolo	259	CZ 113
Thyou	365	OA 317
Tiama	287	CE 74

PLACE NAME	PG	GRID
Tianguel-Bori	363	OA 306
Tiankoura	365	OB 316
Tiaret	331	NC 320
Tiassale	379	OG 314
Tibati	382	OE 331
Tiberghamine	341	NJ 320
Tibo	385	OK 347
Tica	248	DF 111
Tichît	351	NT 310
Tidjikdja	351	NT 308
Tie Ndiekro	379	OF 314
Tiebila	364	OC 313
Tiebissou	379	OF 314
Tiebl	365	OB 318
Tiefora	364	OB 315
Tiegba	379	OF 314
Tiel	362	NX 304
Tieme	364	OC 312
Tieningboue	379	OE 313
Tienko	364	OC 311
Tierfontein	227	DX 95
Tierkloof	226	DO 92
Tierpoort	219	EA 95
Tietta Sidi Bouguedra	329	NF 310
Tiflet	330	ND 313
Tignère	382	OF 332
Tiguent	350	NV 303
Tiguezefene	366	NX 323
Tiji	333	NF 330
Tikem	368	OC 334
Tiko	376	OJ 328
Tilemses	366	NW 324
Tillabéri	365	NY 320
Tillia	366	NW 324
Tilrhemt	331	NE 322
Timau	307	BR 117
Timbe	379	OE 314
Timbédra	364	NW 311
Timbo	363	OB 307
Timbuktu (Tombouctou)	353	NV 316
Timgad	332	NB 326
Timia	355	NJ 328
Timimoun	351	NJ 319
Timmoudi	341	NJ 318
Tin Fouye	343	NK 326
Tina Bridge	220	EE 100
Ti-n-Aguelhaj (Tangoutranat)	353	NV 317
Ti-n-Akof	365	NW 320
Ti-n-Azabo	365	NW 320
Tindangou	365	OB 320
Tinde	256	DD 97
Tindlla	364	OC 311
Tindouf	340	NK 311
Tinè	370	NX 342
Tinerhin	330	NF 313
Tinfouchy	340	NJ 313
Tinga Tinga	301	BX 116
Tingréla	364	OC 312
Tingwe	250	CY 69
Tingya	372	OB 352
Tintane	363	NW 309
Tintioulen	363	OC 310
Tioribougou	364	NZ 311
Tioroniaradougou	379	OD 314
Tiouilit	350	NT 303
Tipaza	331	NA 322
Tiri	384	OD 339
Tiriri	305	BO 109
Tiriro	363	OC 310
Tirmini	367	NY 328
Tiro	363	OC 308
Tiroungoulou	370	OC 341
Tissa	331	ND 314
Tissemsilt	331	NB 321
Tit	354	NP 324
Titao	365	NY 317
Tite	362	OA 304
Titule	385	OK 345
Tivaouane	362	NX 302
Tiwi	302	CA 122
Tizgui Remt	339	NK 310
Tizi	384	OG 341
Tizi Ouzou	332	NA 323
Tiznit	339	NH 309
Tjera	364	OB 314
Tlalamabele	245	DK 95
Tlemcen	331	NC 318
Tlhakgameng	226	DU 91
Tmassah	344	NM 335
To	365	OB 317
Tobago Hills	370	NX 345
Tobli	362	OC 305
Tobre	366	OC 321
Tobruk (Tubruq)	314	BH 114
Todenyang	305	BL 112
Todin	365	NZ 316
Toeguin	365	NZ 317
Toeslaan	216	DY 83
Toesse	365	OA 318
Tog Wajaale	374	OC 362
Tognuf	373	NW 357
Togo (DRC)	312	BK 100
Togo (CAR)	384	OG 339
Togobala	378	OD 311
Togou	364	NY 313
Tokar	361	NU 357
Tokounou	363	OC 309
Tole	383	OF 335
Toleni	212	EG 99
Tolga	332	NC 324
Tolo	388	OQ 338
Tolode	378	OG 311
Tolwe	236	DO 100
Tom Burke	236	DN 98
Toma	365	NZ 316
Tombe	264	CS 78
Tombel	376	OH 329
Tombo	213	EF 101
Tomboco	286	CF 69
Tombua	250	CY 66
Tominian	364	NZ 315
Tompi Seleka	228	DR 102
Tonash	268	CU 100
Tonde	268	CU 100
Tondi Kwindi	365	NY 321
Tondidji	363	NZ 309
Tondon	365	OC 306
Tondoro	253	DC 80
Tonga (Sud.)	321	AY 105
Tonga (Cam.)	382	OH 330
Tongaat	221	EE 105
Tongamayel	365	NY 318
Tongwe	297	CD 125
Tonj	320	BC 100
Tonka	364	NW 315
Tonota	246	DL 98
Tontelbos	216	ED 83
Topping	210	EK 87
Torit	313	BJ 108
Toro	304	BP 104
Toro Kinkane	379	OD 315
Torodi	363	NZ 321
Toromoja	245	DK 92
Tororo	306	BQ 111
Torra Bay	240	DH 69
Torrock	368	OC 334
Tosamaganga	295	CH 113
Tosca	226	DT 90
Toscanini	240	DJ 69
Tosi	371	OB 350
Tosing	219	EC 98
Tot	306	BP 114
Toteng	244	DH 88
Toto	381	OE 326
Totota	378	OD 309
Tou	365	NY 316
Touajil	351	NQ 306
Touba (Sen.)	362	NX 303
Touba (Lib.)	378	OE 311
Toubacouta	362	NY 303
Toubere Bafal	362	NY 305
Touboro	383	OE 334
Toukoto	363	NZ 309
Toukountouna	365	OC 320
Toulépleu	378	OF 310
Toummo	356	NP 333
Toumodi	379	OG 314
Toumoundjila	364	OC 311
Toungo	382	OE 331
Tour de Merkala	340	NK 311
Tourba	368	NZ 334
Tourni	364	OB 314
Touroua	382	OD 332
Tourougoumbe	363	NX 310
Toussiana	364	OB 315
Townlands	223	DU 79
Toworth	322	BE 111
Tozeur	332	NB 327
Trawal	209	EF 82
Trekkopje	231	DM 73
Trena	373	OB 360
Triangle	247	DK 105
Trichardt	228	DU 101
Trichardtsdal	237	DQ 103
Trinkitat	361	NT 357
Tripoli (Tarabulus)	333	NE 332
Trole	253	CX 83
Trompsburg	218	EC 94
Trooilapspan	217	DZ 85
Troutbeck	258	DD 108
Tsama	387	OO 334
Tsandi	251	DC 72
Tsangano	259	CX 111
Tsaraxaibis	224	DW 81
Tsatsu	226	DS 93
Tsau	244	DH 87
Tsaukaib	222	DV 74
Tsavo	301	BY 119
Tsawisis	223	DU 79
Tsazo	212	EF 98
Tseikuru	307	BS 119
Tsembou	386	OR 331
Tses	223	DT 79
Tsesame	234	DP 92
Tsetsebjwe	236	DM 99
Tsetseng	234	DP 91
Tsetsserra	248	DF 108
Tsévié	380	OG 320
Tshabong	225	DU 87
Tshakhuma	237	DO 103
Tshako	278	CM 89
Tshala	278	CK 88
Tshane	233	DO 86
Tshaneni	229	DU 106
Tshani	213	EF 101
Tshauxaba	245	DK 93
Tshela	228	CB 68
Tshenge-Oshwe	388	OP 342
Tshesebe	246	DJ 98
Tshibamba	290	CF 87
Tshibambula	290	CC 87
Tshibeke	298	BX 100
Tshibuka	289	CE 83
Tshibwika	278	CK 86
Tshidilamolomo	226	DT 92
Tshidiwe	289	CE 80
Tshie	278	CJ 90
Tshikapa	289	CE 84
Tshikula	290	CE 88
Tshilenge	291	CE 90
Tshimbalanga	278	CM 89
Tshimboko	291	CE 92
Tshimbulu	290	CE 88
Tshimbungu	278	CL 88
Tshinsenda	268	CR 99
Tshintshanku	290	CE 89
Tshipise	237	DN 103
Tshisenge (DRC)	290	CF 86
Tshisenge (DRC)	290	CF 86
Tshisonge	278	CJ 87
Tshitadi	290	CF 86
Tshitanzu	278	CJ 87
Tshiturapadsi	237	DM 104
Tshofa	291	CC 93
Tshokwane	229	DR 106
Tsholotsho	246	DF 101
Tshongwe (DRC)	291	CH 91
Tshongwe (KZN)	229	DR 106
Tshootsha (Kalkfontein)	233	DM 84
Tshwagong	245	DJ 94
Tsia	234	DP 92
Tsiaki	387	OR 333
Tsigara	245	DH 94
Tsineng	225	DW 89
Tsintsabis	242	DE 78
Tsitsa Bridge	220	EE 100
Tsobis	242	DF 77
Tsoe	244	DJ 91
Tsoelike	220	EC 100
Tsolo	220	EE 100
Tsomo	212	EG 98
Tsuli	245	DG 96
Tsumbiri	387	OQ 335
Tsumeb	242	DF 78
Tsumis Park	231	DP 77
Tsumkwe	243	DG 83
Tswaane	233	DM 86
Tswaing	227	DS 99
Tswaraganang	218	DZ 92
Tubeya	290	CH 89
Tubmanburg	378	OF 308
Tudun Wada	367	OB 328
Tugela	221	EA 105
Tugela Ferry	220	DZ 103
Tugela Mouth	221	EA 106
Tuinplaas	228	DR 100
Tuisbly	228	DS 103
Tukuyu	282	CL 110
Tula	308	BT 122
Tula Yiri	367	OC 330
Tulbagh	209	EJ 81
Tuli	246	DL 101
Tulia	300	CA 111
Tullus	370	OB 344
Tulu Bolo	323	AZ 119
Tulume	307	BN 116
Tum	307	BN 116
Tumba (DRC)	290	CG 88
Tumba (DRC)	389	OO 343
Tumbili	294	CD 108
Tumbwe	280	CP 97
Tumu	365	OB 317
Tumungu	298	BZ 100
Tuna	365	OC 317
Tunaydah	347	NM 349
Tunda	251	DA 70
Tundulu	281	CL 102
Tunduma	282	CL 108
Tunduru	284	CP 117
Tunga	252	DA 78
Tunga	382	OE 328
Tunguru	371	OC 350
Tunguu	299	BZ 109
Tunguu	299	CG 105
Tunis	333	NA 329
Tunnel	209	EJ 82
Turda	371	OC 348
Turbfult	228	DR 101
Turiani	296	CE 118
Turki	315	BF 116
Turton	220	ED 104
Turton	306	BN 111
Tussenin	227	DR 97
Tutkpene	380	OE 319
Tutume	246	DH 97
Tuzule	290	CF 89
Twee Rivier	224	DS 82
Tweefontein (E.C.)	218	DZ 92
Tweefontein (N.C.)	209	EG 82
Tweeling	247	DK 105
Tweeputte	243	DG 83
Tweespruit	219	EA 96
Twilight	232	DQ 78
Twinbrook	227	DT 96
Twingi	269	CQ 102
Tylden	212	EG 97
Tzaneen	237	DP 103
Uaco Cungo	275	CP 73
Uamhomba	253	CZ 83
Uape	260	CZ 119
Ubenazomozi	296	CF 119
Ubombo	229	DX 107
Ubundu	389	ON 344
Ubungo	297	CF 121
Uchab	242	DG 78
Udegi	381	OE 327
Udi	381	OE 326
Ududu	367	OA 330
Ufana	300	CA 113
Ugab	382	OF 328
Ugbenu	381	OG 325
Ugep	381	OG 325
Ughelli	376	OH 327
Ugie	219	EE 99
Ugine	381	OE 326
Uhen	381	OE 325
Uhi	381	OF 325
Uhlenhorst	232	DP 78
Uige	241	DG 76
Uitenhage	211	EG 90
Uitdraai	218	EA 93
Uithoek	220	DY 103
Uitkomst	242	DK 79
Uitkyk (E.C.)	211	EG 90
Uitkyk (N.C.)	216	EB 80
Uitsig (F.S.)	218	EB 92
Uitsig (F.S.)	219	EC 95
Uitspanberg	217	EB 87
Uitspankraal	209	EG 81
Uitvlug	217	EA 87
Uitzicht	236	DP 100
Ujali	381	OG 326
Ujiji	293	CB 102
Ukata	366	OB 325
Ukimbo	295	CD 111
Uku	275	CP 71
Ukune	299	CA 107
Ukwatutu	365	OH 346
Ulaya	296	CG 116
Ulco	218	DY 91
Uledi	282	CN 110
Uletelwa	283	CJ 114
uLoliwe	221	DY 105
uLundi	221	DY 105
Ulu	372	OB 352
Ulungwe (Mal.)	271	CW 113
Ulungwe (Zim.)	271	CW 111
Ulva	219	EE 99
Ulyankulu	294	CB 107
Uma	389	OM 345
Umaisha	381	OE 326
uMbumbulu	220	EB 104
uMdloti	221	EB 105
uMgababa	220	EC 104
uMfolozi	221	DY 105
uMhlali	221	EA 105
uMhlanga	221	EB 105
uMhlongonek	221	EB 103
uMlazi	220	EC 104
Umm al Rizam	335	NF 342
Umm Aranib	344	NM 334
Umm Badr	371	NX 347
Umm Bel	371	NY 347
Umm Busha	371	NZ 346
Umm Dafag	370	OB 343
Umm Dam	371	NY 350
Umm Digulgulaya	370	OC 344
Umm Dubban	371	NY 349
Umm Keddada	371	NY 346
Umm Marahik	370	NY 344
Umm Qozein	371	NY 346
Umm Rahau	360	NT 351
Umm Rumetia	360	NV 351
Umm Ruwaba	371	NZ 350
Umm Sagura	371	OC 349
Umm Saiyala	371	NY 348
Umm Shugeira	371	NY 349
Umpuhua	272	CV 119
Umtentu	220	EE 103
uMtentweni	220	ED 104
Umuahia	381	OG 326
uMunywana	221	DY 106
Umutu	381	OG 325
Umzimkulu	220	EC 102
uMzimvubu	220	ED 104
uMzumbe	220	ED 104
Unango	271	CS 113
Uncondo	251	CZ 71
Underberg	220	EB 101
Unguana	239	DO 113
Unhe	254	DA 86
Uniondale	210	EK 89
Union's End	224	DR 83
Uno	362	OB 303
Uoteche	238	DM 111
Upington	217	DY 85
Urambo	294	CC 107
Urbi	359	NT 349
Urionskraal	209	EF 80
Uromi	381	OF 325
Uruwira	294	CE 105
Usa River	301	BY 116
Usagara	299	BX 109
Usakos	241	DL 74
Usango	283	CK 112
Usarangei	301	BY 118
Usengi	306	BS 111
Usevia	294	CG 105
Ushaa	266	CW 89
Ushetu	294	CA 107
Ushirombo	299	BY 106
Usiya	283	CP 111
Usoke	294	CC 107
Usuhilo	295	CE 111
Usure	295	CB 111
Usulu	236	DN 100
Utegi	306	BN 111
Utengule	282	CL 108
Utete	297	CH 120
Utinta	293	CG 104
Utokoto	253	DC 83
Utrecht	228	DX 103
Ututwa	300	BX 110
Uvinza	293	CC 103
Uvira	298	BY 101
uVongo	220	ED 103
Uvungo	389	OR 343
Uwemba	283	CL 112
Uwindi	295	CH 114
Uyo	376	OH 327
Uyole	282	CL 109
Uyowa	299	CA 106
Uyuklip	219	EA 96
Vaalbol	208	EF 79
Vaalplaas	228	DV 100
Vaalwater	236	DO 99
Vacha	260	CX 118
Vaga	387	OO 334
Vahiua	272	CU 117
Vakaranga	246	DJ 98
Vaku	286	CC 69
Val	228	DV 100
Valletta	334	NB 333
Valspan (N.C.)	217	EA 89
Valspan (N.C.)	218	EB 92
Valsrivier	219	DY 99
Van Amstel	217	EE 88
Van Reenen	220	DY 101
Van Rooyen	220	DY 103
Van Stadensrus	219	EB 97
Van Wyksdorp	210	EK 86
Van Wyksvlei (N.C.)	217	EG 82
Van Wyksvlei (N.C.)	217	EC 82
Van Zylsrus	225	DV 87
Vanalphensvlei	236	DQ 100
Vanderbijlpark	227	DW 98
Vanderkloof	218	EB 92
Vanduzi	259	DD 111
Vandyksdrif	228	DV 101
Vanrhynsdorp	209	EF 80
Vant's Drift	220	DY 103
Varalé	365	OC 316
Varela	362	OA 302
Vavoua	378	OF 312
Veertien Strome	218	DY 92
Velddrif	208	EH 79
Veldslag	236	DP 99
Velingara (Sen.)	362	NX 304
Velingara (Sen.)	362	NZ 305
Ventersburg	219	DY 97
Ventersdorp	227	DU 96
Venterskroon	227	DV 97
Venterstad	218	ED 94
Vereeniging	227	DV 99
Verena	228	DS 101
Vergeleë	228	DT 91
Verkeerdevlei	219	DZ 96
Verkykerskop	228	DX 101
Vermaaklikheid	210	EL 85
Vermaas	226	DV 94
Verster	210	EF 89
Verulam	221	EB 105
Viafé	386	ON 330
Vialadougou	378	OD 312
Viana	274	CK 69
Vibura	297	CG 121
Vickers	219	ED 97
Victoria	246	DF 101
Victoria Falls	255	DC 94
Victoria West	217	EE 88
Viedgesville	213	EF 100
Vier-en-Twintig Riviere	236	DQ 99
Vierfontein	227	DW 96
Vila Nova de Fronteira	259	DB 113
Vilanculos	249	DL 113
Viljoensdrif	227	DV 99
Viljoenskroon	227	DW 97
Villa Coutinho	271	CW 111
Villa de Senna	248	DE 108
Villa Nora	236	DP 99
Villiers	228	DV 100
Villiers (F.S.)	218	EA 94
Villiers (F.S.)	228	DW 100
Villiersdorp	209	EK 81
Vimioso	237	DN 107
Vineta	219	DV 96
Vineyard	219	ED 96
Violainville	386	ON 330
Vioolsdrif	215	DZ 78
Virei	250	CY 68
Virginia	219	DY 96
Visrivier	211	EF 93
Vista Alegre	275	CJ 72
Vitshumbi	304	BT 101
Vivo	236	DO 101
Vleesbaai	210	EL 87
Vleifontein (Lim.)	236	DO 103
Vleifontein (W.C.)	210	EJ 85
Vleiland	210	EJ 85
Viermuisvlakte	225	DW 88
Viergeraas	217	EC 89
Vogan	380	OG 321
Voëlweide	232	DQ 81
Voi	302	BY 120
Volksrust	228	DW 102
Volop	217	DZ 87
Volstruisleegte	210	EJ 89
Vom	367	OC 328
Vondeling	210	EF 89
Voo	301	BV 119
Voorspoed (F.S.)	218	EC 93
Voorspoed (N.W.)	226	DU 91
Vorstershoop	225	DT 89
Vosburg	217	ED 88
Vouga	237	DM 106
Vouka	387	OQ 333
Vouzela	237	DM 106
Vrede	228	DW 101
Vredefort	227	DV 97
Vredenburg	208	EH 78
Vredendal	209	EF 80
Vredeshoop	224	DW 82
Vriendskap	241	DH 75
Vrouggedeel	217	EB 87
Vrouenspan	224	DX 83
Vryburg	226	DU 94
Vryheid	228	DX 104
Vryhof	226	DU 94
Vuma	385	OK 347
Vumba	248	DF 108
Vundica	229	DV 106
Vuvulane	229	DU 106
Vwawa	282	CL 108
Waaipunt	217	ED 88
Waat	321	BA 107
Wabusana	365	OB 318
Wachile	316	BJ 121
Wad an Nail	372	NZ 353
Wad Banda	372	NZ 347
Wad Ben Naqa	360	NV 352
Wad Hassib	371	OA 346
Wad Medani	372	NY 353
Wad Rawa	372	NX 352
Waddah	371	NZ 352
Waddilove	258	DD 105
Waddan	344	NJ 335
Wadi Halfa	359	NQ 350
Wagenaarskraal	210	EF 88
Wahala	365	OC 317
Waine-Rukula	389	ON 345
Wairytwika	282	CL 108
Wajir	308	BO 123
Waka (Eth.)	323	BD 117
Waka (DRC)	388	OO 339
Wakayato	305	BQ 107
Wakkerstroom	228	DW 103
Wakwa	305	BP 107
Wal Athiang	320	BB 102
Walambele	365	OB 317
Waldau	241	DL 76
Walewale	365	OC 318
Walikale	389	OM 347
Walkerville	227	DW 98
Walkraal	211	EE 85
Wallis	223	DU 78
Walungu	298	BX 100
Walvis Bay	230	DO 71
Wamba (Ken.)	307	BQ 117
Wamba (Nig.)	382	OD 328
Wamba (DRC)	389	OL 347
Wamba-Luadi	288	CC 77
Wanche	373	OA 357
Wanda	218	EB 91
Wanga	312	BL 101
Wangasi-Turu	380	OD 319
Wangingombe	283	CK 112
Wankama	366	NY 322
Wanlaweyn	374	OD 361
Wapuli	365	OC 319
Waqu	212	EG 97
Warandab	326	BC 131
Warburton	228	DU 103
Warde	364	NY 312
Warden	228	DW 101
Warder	326	BD 133
Warmbad	216	DY 80
Warmfontein	224	DW 81
Warri	376	OH 325
Wartburg	221	EA 104
Wasagu	366	OB 325
Wasbank	220	DY 103
Wase	382	OE 328
Wasimi	380	NZ 322
Wassadou	362	NZ 305
Wasser	223	DU 79
Wassou	362	OC 305
Watata	246	DF 101
Watsi	388	ON 340
Watsi Kengo	388	OO 340
Watsomba	248	DE 108
Wau	385	OE 347
Wavecrest	213	EH 100
Waya	242	DJ 77
Waza	368	OA 333
Wazin	333	NF 330
We	382	OG 329
Weasua	378	OF 309
Webuye	306	BQ 113
Wedilelo	373	NW 358
Weenen	220	DZ 103
Wegdraai (N.C.)	217	DZ 86
Wegdraai (Nam.)	224	DT 81
Weila	379	OE 317
Weissbrünn	241	DG 72
Weldiya	373	OA 358
Welenchiti	324	AZ 121
Welgeleë	219	DY 96
Welkite	323	BA 118
Welkom (F.S.)	226	DX 94
Welkom (F.S.)	227	DX 96
Welkom (F.S.)	228	DX 100
Wellington	209	EK 81
Welvanpas	217	EE 89
Welverdiend (Gau.)	227	DU 97
Welverdiend (Nam.)	228	DX 100
Welwel	326	BC 133
Wema	380	ON 341
Wembley (KZN)	220	DZ 103
Wembley (KZN)	221	DY 104
Wenchi	379	OE 317
Wenchiki	365	OC 319
Wendo	323	BD 119
Wendou Mborou	362	OB 305
Wenge Bas	389	ON 343
Wepener	219	EB 97
Wer Ping	320	AY 101
Wera	306	BO 110
Werda (Bot.)	225	DS 89
Werda (N.W.)	227	DV 95
Werota	373	OA 357
Wesley	212	EJ 97
Wesselsbron	227	DX 95
Wesselton	228	DU 102
Wesseluwe	379	OE 317
West Nicholson	246	DK 101
Westerberg	217	DY 87
Westleigh	227	DX 97
Westminster	219	EA 97
Westonaria	227	DU 98
Westwood	256	CX 99
Wete	297	CC 122
Weto	381	OE 327
Weza	220	ED 102
White River	229	DS 105
Whites	219	DY 96
Whitmore	212	EG 98
Whittlesea	212	EG 96
Wiawer	379	OG 317
Wiegnaarspoort	211	EJ 89
Wikro	373	NY 359
Wildebeeste	217	EE 89
Wilderness	210	EL 88
Wildhoen	226	DX 93
Wildrand	228	DV 104
Wilhelmstal	241	DL 75
Willem	227	DW 99
Ware Lao	362	NW 304
Williston	216	EE 84
Willowmore	211	EJ 90
Willowvale	212	EG 99
Winburg	219	DZ 97
Wincanton	225	DX 88
Windhoek	231	DN 76
Windmill	209	EK 80
Windsorton	218	DY 92
Windsorton Road	218	DY 92
Winneba	380	OH 319
Winter's Rush	218	DY 91
Winterton	220	DY 102
Winterveld	227	DS 98
Wirsing	226	DU 93
Witbank	228	DS 101
Witbooisvlei	223	DS 79
Witdraai	224	DV 84
Witdrift	211	EH 93
Witkop	219	EE 96
Witloop	225	DW 88
Witmos	211	EH 94
Witpan	217	DY 87
Witpoort	227	DW 95
Witput	218	EB 91
Witpütz	223	DW 76
Witrand	228	DU 103
Witsand	209	EL 84
Wittedrift	210	EL 89
Witteklip	211	EK 93
Wittenberg	228	DW 104
Wittewater	209	EH 80
Witwater	215	DT 79
Wlotzkasbaken	230	DM 71
Wobulenzi	305	BQ 108
Woe	380	OG 320
Wofikehn	378	OH 311
Wolfhuis	208	EG 79
Wolmaransstad	226	DW 94
Wolplaas	216	DW 80
Wolseley	209	EK 81
Wolwefontein	211	EJ 92
Wolwehoek	227	DV 98
Wolwespruit	218	DZ 94
Wonderhoek	228	DT 101
Wonderkop	227	DV 95
Wondermere	227	DT 95
Woodbine	227	DW 97
Woodford	220	EB 102
Woodlands	211	EL 91
Wooldridge	212	EJ 97
Worcester	209	EK 82
Worofla	378	OE 312
Wortel	231	DO 77
Woudi	368	NZ 332
Woudkop	388	OD 333
Woumbou	383	OH 333
Wuchale	373	OA 357
Wudil	367	OA 328
Wukari	382	OE 329
Wun Shwai	320	AY 107
Wunagük	321	AY 107
Wundanyi	301	BY 119
Wuppertal	209	EG 81
Wurno	366	NZ 325
Wuyo	368	OC 331
Wydgeleë	209	EL 83
Wyford	226	CV 90
Wyllie's Poort	236	DN 102
Xhumaga	244	DH 91
Xigalo	237	DN 104
Xinavane	238	DS 108
Xinge	277	CM 81
Xitole	362	OA 304
Xobe	212	EG 98
Xuddur	318	BJ 130
Xudun	327	AY 137
Yabassi	376	OJ 329
Yabayo	378	OG 312
Yabelo	315	BH 119
Yabo	366	NZ 324
Yafran	333	NF 332
Yagoua	368	OC 334
Yahila	389	ON 344
Yahisuli	389	OL 343
Yajiwa	368	OO 333
Yakossi	379	OG 316
Yako	365	NZ 317
Yaloke	383	OH 336
Yalufi	389	OM 343
Yaluwe	389	OM 343
Yamba	365	OA 319
Yamba Yamba	389	OM 346
Yambio	385	OH 347
Yambo	363	OA 307
Yamoussoukro	379	OF 314
Yamuna	384	OK 341
Yana	363	OC 307
Yana	380	OE 320
Yandev	382	OF 328
Yanfolila	364	OB 311
Yanga	369	OC 338
Yangalia	389	OM 344
Yangambi	389	ON 344
Yangamo	383	OH 333
Yang-Yang	362	NW 304
Yankoman	379	OG 316
Yanonge	389	OM 344
Yao	365	NY 319
Yapei (Tamale Port)	380	OD 318
Yara	365	NY 318
Yarra	380	OD 321
Yashi	365	OA 327
Yatakala	365	NX 319
Yatako	365	NY 319
Yatolema	389	ON 343
Yatta	381	BU 118
Yebbi Bou	357	NR 337
Yeed	317	BH 129
Yegou	380	OE 320
Yei	312	BJ 102
Yeji	380	OE 318
Yekaba	388	OM 342
Yekepa	378	OF 307
Yele	377	OE 307
Yelimane	363	NX 309
Yelou	366	OA 323
Yelwa	382	OE 329
Yelwa	386	OC 323
Yen	386	ON 331
Yende Milimou	378	OO 309
Yendéré	364	OC 314
Yendi	380	OD 319
Yénéganou	378	OF 311
Yeno	378	OE 308
Yengema	378	OE 308
Yeo	306	BP 109
Yirba Muda	324	BE 120
Yirga Alem	323	BD 119
Yirgaf Chefe	323	BE 119
Yirol	320	BD 104
Yoboki	374	OA 363
Yohnnybli	378	OG 309
Yokadouma	383	OJ 334
Yoko	382	OG 331
Yokoboue	379	OG 314
Yola (Nig.)	382	OD 332
Yola (Cam.)	383	OJ 334
Yolombo	388	OP 342
Yombi	386	OO 331
Yomou	378	OG 309
Yongofondo	384	OH 342
Yonibana	377	OE 307
Yonofere	362	NX 305
Yontoy	309	BS 128
York	220	EA 103
Yorobougoula	364	OB 311
Yorosso	364	OA 314
Yoseki	388	OM 342
Youbandji	363	NZ 306
Youkounkoun	363	NZ 305
Youvarou	364	NX 315
Yubdo	322	AZ 113
Yubo	367	OC 329
Yuki	388	OP 339
Yuli	367	OC 329
Yumbe	313	BL 105
Yumbi (DRC)	387	OP 336
Yumbi (DRC)	389	OO 345
Yzerfontein	208	EJ 79
Zaaimansdal	210	EK 89
Zabe	384	OG 341
Zabori	366	NZ 323
Zabre	365	OB 318
Zafarana	348	NJ 352
Zagazig	337	NG 351
Zaghouan	333	NB 329
Zagora	340	NH 313
Zagrata	365	OA 319
Zaila	373	OC 360
Zakara	369	OC 338
Zaki Biam	382	OE 328
Zala	323	BE 117
Zalanga	367	OC 329
Zalingei	370	NZ 343
Zaliouan	379	OF 313
Zama	366	NY 322
Zamay	368	OB 333
Zamba-Kangaka	387	OM 333
Zambezi	266	CU 89
Zambezi Deka	256	DD 96
Zambué	257	CX 104
Zamoi	385	OJ 343
Zanaga	387	OQ 333
Zandamela	238	DR 111
Zangba	384	OJ 340
Zango	367	NZ 328
Zanre	365	OA 319
Zantie-bougou	364	OB 312
Zanzibar (Stone Town)	297	CE 121
Zanzra	379	OF 313
Zaoro-Songou	383	OH 335
Zaouatallaz	343	NN 328
Zara	228	DW 100
Zaranou	379	OG 315
Zari	368	NZ 332
Zaria	367	OB 327
Zaris	223	DS 75
Zarzaitine	343	NK 329
Zarzis	333	NE 330
Zastron	219	EC 97
Zave	257	DB 103
Zawilah	344	NM 334
Zawiyat al Mukhayla	335	NF 341
Zawiyat Masus	335	NF 340
Zebediela	236	DQ 101
Zeekoegat	236	DQ 102
Zeerust	227	DT 95
Zegbeli	365	OC 319
Zelfana	332	NC 323
Zelouane	330	NC 316
Zemio	385	OH 344
Zemmora	331	NB 320
Zenza do Itombe	275	CL 71
Zéralda	331	NA 322
Zeribet el Oued	332	NC 326
Zerouilet	330	ND 316
Zhombe	246	DE 101
Zia Town	378	OG 311
Ziba	299	CA 109
Zifta	337	NG 350
Ziguinchor	362	NY 303
Zihlakengele	229	DX 106
Zilitenfe	255	DC 91
Zillah	345	NJ 337
Zimba	256	DB 95
Zimmi	378	OF 308
Zina	368	OB 334
Zinder	367	NY 328
Zinga	297	CF 120
Zinga Mulika	284	CL 120
Ziniare	365	NZ 318
Zinkwazi Beach	221	EA 106
Zinna	382	OD 331
Zinzana	364	NZ 313
Zio	378	OG 311
Ziope	380	OG 320
Zirobwe	305	BQ 108
Zitouna	332	NA 325
Zitundo	229	DV 108
Ziwani	285	CN 123
Ziway	324	BA 120
Zlitan	334	NF 334
Zoar	210	EK 85
Zobia	385	OK 345
Zòbué	259	CY 111
Zoebefang	382	OK 331
Zogo	365	OA 318
Zogore	377	OE 307
Zoissa	296	CD 115
Zongia	259	CX 113
Zongo	389	OL 344
Zongwe	292	CC 98
Zonkwa	367	OC 327
Zoroga	245	DH 94
Zorzor	378	OE 309
Zotto	274	CJ 69
Zouan-Hounien	378	OF 311
Zouar	356	NS 335
Zouirat	351	NP 307
Zouirag	331	ND 320
Zoukouzou	384	OG 341
Zoulabot I	383	OK 333
Zoulabot II	383	OK 333
Zoupleu	378	OE 311
Zuburo	295	CD 113
Zuenoula	379	OF 313
Zugu	366	OA 324
Zumbo	257	CX 104
Zunckels	220	DZ 101
Zungeru	366	OA 326
Zurak	382	OD 330
Zuru	366	OA 324
Zvishavane	247	DH 103
Zwartkop	212	EC 95
Zwarts	210	EH 86
Zwedru	378	OG 311
Zwelitsha	212	EH 97
Zwingli	227	DR 95
Zyamatobwe	247	DE 106

ABBREVIATIONS

For provinces in South Africa

E.C. - Eastern Cape
F.S. - Free State
Gau. - Gauteng
KZN - KwaZulu-Natal
Lim. - Limpopo
Mpum. - Mpumalanga
N.C. - Northern Cape
N.W. - North West
W.C. - Western Cape

The first 3 letters of the country name (eg, below)

Ang. - Angola
Bot. - Botswana
Bur. - Burundi
CAR - Central African Republic
DRC - Democratic Republic of the Congo
Ken. - Kenya
Ct'l. - Côte d'Ivoire
Moz. - Mozambique
Nam. - Namibia

OTHER NAMES IN BRACKETS

Alternative spellings for placenames, and in South Africa they indicate name changes.